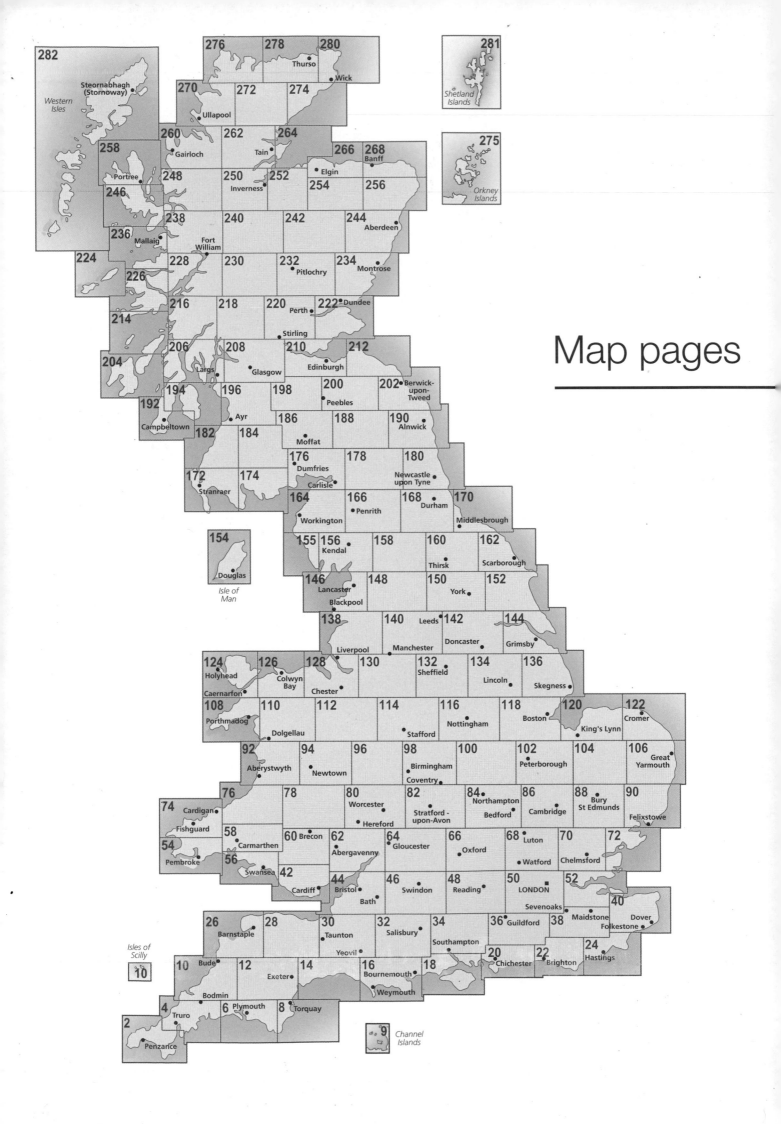

Map pages

Reprinted May 2004
4th edition August 2003

© Automobile Association Developments Limited 2004
This Edition published 2004 for Index Books Ltd.
Original edition printed 2000.

Ordnance Survey® This product includes mapping data licensed from Ordnance Survey® with the permission of the Controller of Her Majesty's Stationery Office. © Crown copyright 2004. All rights reserved. Licence number 399221.

Published by AA Publishing (a trading name of Automobile Association Developments Limited, whose registered office is Millstream, Maidenhead Road, Windsor, Berkshire SL4 5GD, UK. Registered number 1878835).

Mapping produced by the Cartography Department of The Automobile Association. This atlas has been compiled and produced from the Automaps database utilising electronic and computer technology (A02148).

A CIP catalogue record for this book is available from The British Library.

Printed in the U.A.E. by Oriental Press, Dubai.

The contents of this atlas are believed to be correct at the time of the latest revision. However, the publishers cannot be held responsible for loss occasioned to any person acting or refraining from action as a result of any material in this atlas, nor for any errors, omissions or changes in such material. This does not affect your statutory rights. The publishers would welcome information to correct any errors or omissions and to keep this atlas up to date. Please write to the Cartographic Editor, Publishing Division, The Automobile Association, Fanum House, Basing View, Basingstoke, Hampshire RG21 4EA, UK.

Information on National Parks and National Nature Reserves in England provided by The Countryside Agency. David Mcglade, North East Region, kindly provided information on Hadrian's Wall National Trail.

Information on National Parks, National Scenic Areas and National Nature Reserves in Scotland provided by Scottish Natural Heritage.

Information on National Parks and National Nature Reserves in Wales provided by The Countryside Council for Wales.

Information on Forest Parks provided by the Forestry Commission.

The RSPB sites shown are a selection chosen by the Royal Society for the Protection of Birds.

National Trust properties shown are a selection of those open to the public as indicated in the handbooks of the National Trust and the National Trust for Scotland.

EASY READ BRITAIN

Scale 1: 148,000 or 2.34 miles to 1 inch (1.5 km to 1 cm)

Atlas contents

Map pages	inside front cover
Route planner	II–VII
Road map symbols	VIII–1
Road maps 1:148,000 scale	2–283
Channel Islands 1:100,000 scale	9
Isle of Man 1:200,000 scale	154
Orkney Islands 1:450,000 scale	275
Shetland Islands 1:450,000 scale	281
Western Isles 1:480,000 scale	282–283
Index to place names	284–369
County, administrative area map	284–285

Route planner

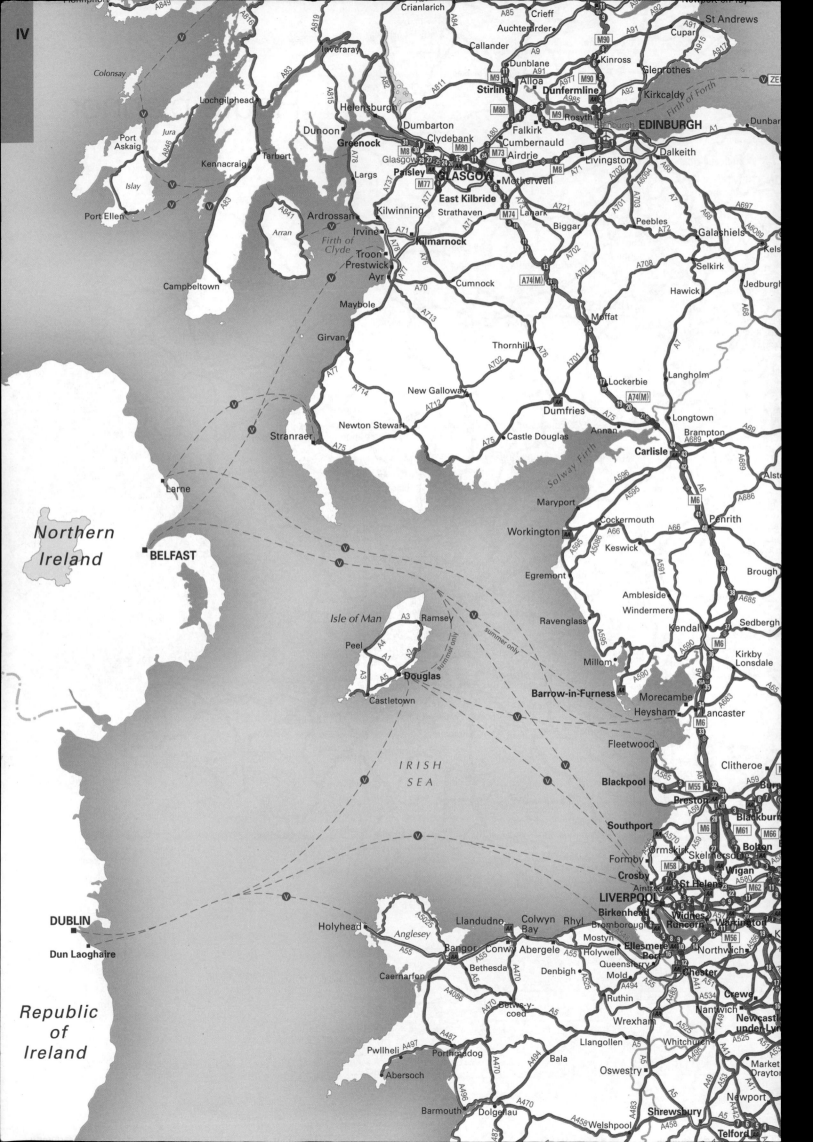

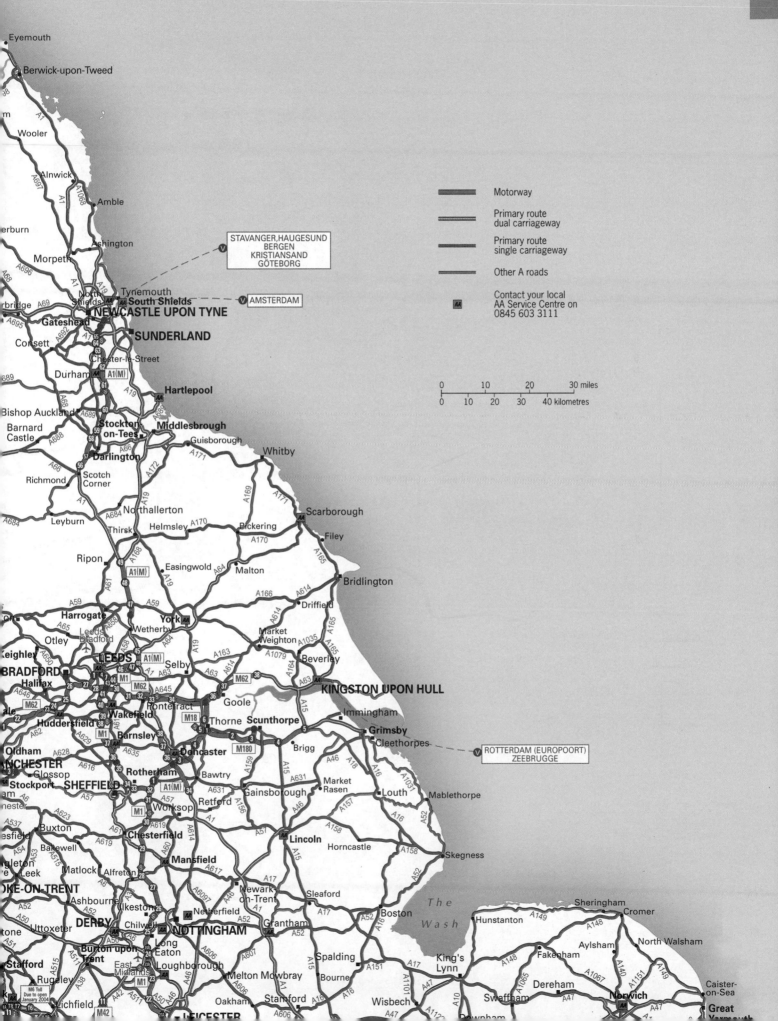

NORTH SEA

Motorway

Primary route
dual carriageway

Primary route
single carriageway

Other A roads

Contact your local
AA Service Centre on
0845 603 3111

| 0 | 10 | 20 | 30 miles |
| 0 | 10 | 20 | 30 | 40 kilometres |

STAVANGER, HAUGESUND
BERGEN
KRISTIANSAND
GÖTEBORG

AMSTERDAM

ROTTERDAM (EUROPOORT)
ZEEBRUGGE

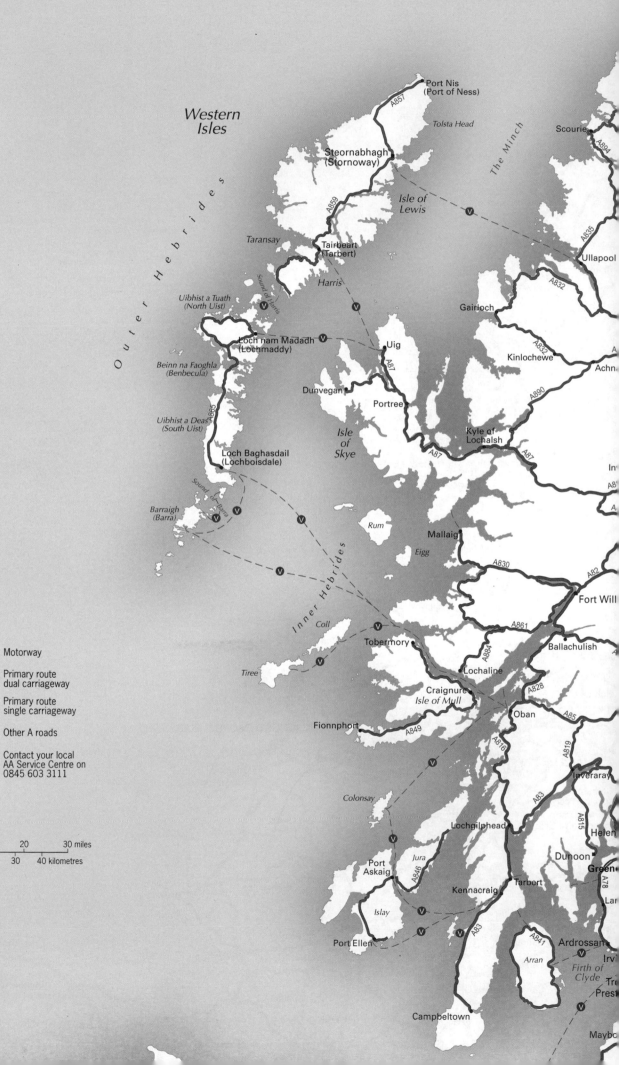

Western
Isles

Port Nis
(Port of Ness)

Tolsta Head

Scourie

A857

The Minch

A894

A835

Steornabhagh
(Stornoway)

*Isle of
Lewis*

Ullapool

A859

Taransay

Tairbeart
(Tarbert)

Harris

Gairloch

A832

Outer Hebrides

Uibhist a Tuath
(North Uist)

Sound of Harris

A832

Kinlochewe

Achn

Loch nam Madadh
(Lochmaddy)

Uig

A87

*Beinn na Faoghla
(Benbecula)*

Dunvegan

Portree

A890

A865

Kyle of
Lochalsh

In

Uibhist a Deas
(South Uist)

*Isle
of
Skye*

A87

A87

Loch Baghasdail
(Lochboisdale)

Sound of Barra

Rum

Mallaig

A

*Barraigh
(Barra)*

Eigg

A830

A82

Fort Will

Inner Hebrides

Coll

A861

Tobermory

Ballachulish

A864

Lochaline

A828

Tiree

Craignure
Isle of Mull

Oban

A85

Fionnphort

A849

A816

A819

Inveraray

Colonsay

A83

Lochgilphead

A815

Helen

Port
Askaig

Jura

Dunoon

A846

Tarbert

Green

Kennacraig

A78

A83

Islay

Lar

Port Ellen

Arran

A841

Ardrossam

Irv

*Firth of
Clyde*

Tre

Pres

Campbeltown

Maybo

——— Motorway

═══ Primary route
dual carriageway

Primary route
single carriageway

——— Other A roads

AA Contact your local
AA Service Centre on
0845 603 3111

0   10   20   30 miles
0   10   20   30   40 kilometres

Road map symbols

Motoring information

M4 Motorway with number

Toll T4 Toll motorway with toll station

11 Motorway junction with and without number

3 Restricted motorway junctions

S Fleet Motorway service area

Motorway and junction under construction

A3 Primary route single/dual carriageway

Primary route junction with and without number

3 Restricted primary route junctions

Grantham North Primary route service area

BATH Primary route destination

A1123 Other A road single/dual carriageway

B2070 B road single/dual carriageway

Unclassified road single/dual carriageway

Roundabout

Interchange/junction

Narrow primary/other A/B road with passing places (Scotland)

Road under construction

Road tunnel

Steep gradient (arrows point downhill)

Toll Road toll

5 Distance in miles between symbols

V St Malo Vehicle ferry

Railway line/in tunnel

Railway station and level crossing

Tourist railway

Airport

H Heliport

F International freight terminal

★ Major shopping centre

P+R Park and Ride location (at least 6 days)

AA AA Service Centre

City, town, village or other built-up area

628 ▲ Spot height in metres

348 Rannoch Moor Pass

River, canal, lake

Sandy beach

National boundary

County, administrative boundary

23 Page continuation number

Tourist information

i	Tourist Information Centre	RSPB	RSPB site		Show jumping/equestrian circuit
i	Tourist Information Centre (seasonal)		National Nature Reserve (England, Scotland, Wales)		Motor-racing circuit
V	Visitor or heritage centre		Local nature reserve		Air show venue
	Abbey, cathedral or priory	············	Forest drive		Ski slope – natural
	Ruined abbey, cathedral or priory	– – – – –	National trail		Ski slope – artificial
	Castle		Viewpoint	NT	National Trust property
	Historic house or building		Picnic site	NTS	National Trust for Scotland property
M	Museum or art gallery		Hill-fort	★	Other place of interest
	Industrial interest		Roman antiquity		Boxed symbols indicate attractions within urban areas
	Aqueduct or viaduct		Prehistoric monument		National Park
	Garden	1066	Battle site with year		National Scenic Area (Scotland)
	Arboretum		Steam centre (railway)		Forest Park
	Vineyard		Cave		Heritage coast
	Country park		Windmill	Travelodge	Travelodge
	Agricultural showground		Monument		Welcome Lodge
	Theme park		Golf course	DAYS INN	Days Inn Hotel
	Farm or animal centre		County cricket ground		Welcome Break or Moto Burger King
	Zoological or wildlife collection		Rugby Union national stadium	KFC	Kentucky Fried Chicken
	Bird collection		International athletics stadium		
	Aquarium		Horse racing		

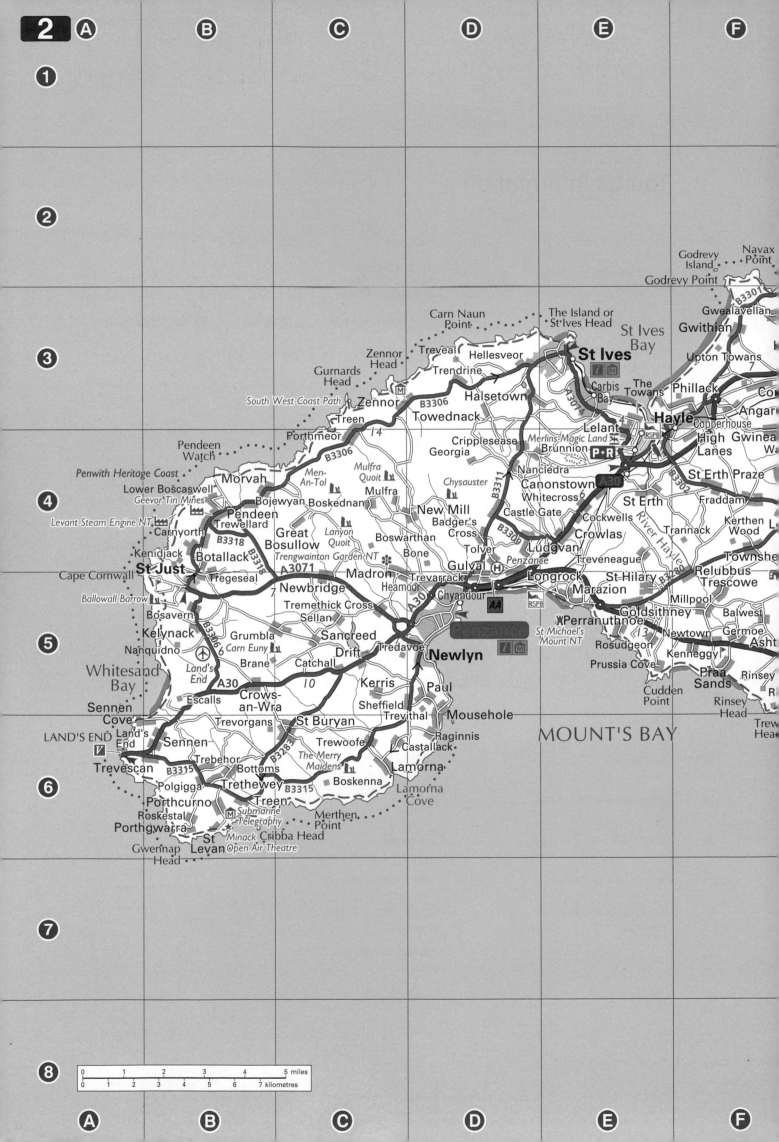

G   H   J   K   L   M

1   **2**   **3**   **4**   **5**   **6**   **7**   **8**

Cligga Point
Goonhavern
Carland Cross
Brighton
New Mills
Ladock
Trendeal
Treveale
Trispen
Pengelly
Treverbyn
Probus
St Agnes Heritage Coast
ST AGNES HEAD
Trevellas Downs
Jolingey
Cocks
Perranwell
Perranzabuloe
Zelah
St Allen
Treworgan
Killivose
Allet Common
St Erme
Bodrean
Tresillian
Penair
Tresawle
Trewirgie
Pencalenick
Merther
Trewarth
St Agnes
Cross Coombe
Penhallow
Callestick
Marazanvose
Idless
Buckshead
Kenwyn
Wheal Coates
Goonvrea
Mithian
Barkla Shop
Goonbell
Coldharbour
Silverwell
Shortlanesend
Treheveras
Three Mile Stone
Calenick
Kea
Malpas
St Michael Penkevil
Tregenna
St Clement
Ruan Lanihorne
Porthtowan
Mount Hawke
Three Burrows
R Kenwyn
Higher Town
Baldhu
Porthkea
Old Kea
Lamorran
Trelonk
Veryan Green
South West Coast Path
Portreath
Cambrose
Mawla
Blackwater
Chacewater
Saveock Water
Newbridge
Killiow
Chyeowling
Playing Place
Coombe
Trelissick Garden NT
Ruan High Lanes
Philleigh
Treworthal
Veryan
Portreath Coast
Bridge
Wheal Rose
North Country
Scorrier
Cross Lanes
Penelewey
Devoran
Trelissick
Trewithian
Cargurrel
Gerrans Bay
Nare Head
Illogan
Poynter's Lane End
Cornish Engines NT
Mount Ambrose
St Day
Twelveheads
Carnon Downs
Trevilla
St Just-in-Roseland
Rosevine
Portscatho
Tehidy Park Bottom
Roscroggan
Carharrack
Trevarth
Frogpool
Bissoe
Perran Wharf
Feock
Penpol
St Just Lane
Gerrans
Trewince
Greeb Point
eskadinnick
Tuckingmill
Pool
Carn Brea
Gwennap
Perranwell
Perranarworthal
Perran Wharf
Carclew
Angarrick
Mylor Bridge
Restronguet
St Mawes
Camborne
Carnkie
Lanner A393
Penhalurick
Stockdale
Enys
Lower Treluswell
Trelew
Mylor
Bohortha
Penponds
Bolenowe
Four Lanes
Penhalvean
Hendra
Ponsanooth
Burnthouse
Roskrow
St Gluvia's
Flushing
ZONE POINT
Troon
Croft Michael
Stithians
Tregolls
Tregew
Penryn
Praze-an-Beeble
Burras
Carnkie
Longdowns
Mabe Burnthouse
Kergilliack
Budock Water
Pendennis
South West Coast Path
Blackrock
Farms Common
Lezerea
Rame
Edgcombe
Trenoweth
Argal & College Water Park
Treverva
Lamanva
Penjerrick
Penjerrick
Pendennis Point
Crowan
Releath
Porkellis
Crelly
Sithney Green
Trevarno
Lower Town Bridges
Manhay
Seworgan
Tresahor
High Cross
Bareppa
Carlidnack
Maenporth
Mawnan Smith
Falmouth Bay
Prospidnick
Wendron
Trebarvah
Brill
Constantine
Trebah
Carwinion
Glendurgan NT
ROSEMULLION HEAD
Sithney
Antron
Trewennack
Tolvan
Porth Navas
Helford Passage
Durgan
Mawnan
Toll Point
Gweek
Mellangoose
Flambards
Seal Sanctuary
Helford River
Helford
St Anthony
Nare Point
Higher Pentire
Mawgan Cross
Gear
Manaccan
Gillan
Lestowder
Carminowe
Tregiddle
Berepper
Tregoose
Garras
Trelowarren
Halliggye Fogou
Newtown
St Martin
Tregidden
Carne
Fregarne
Roskorwell
Porthallow
Chyvarloe
Gunwalloe
Gwealeath
Tregowris
Lanarth
Treleague
Trenance
Porthoustock
White Cross
Wheel Inn
Cross Lanes
Goonhilly Satellite Earth Station
Traboe
St Keverne
Manacle Point
Rosenithon
Cury
Bochym
GOONHILLY DOWNS
Trelan
Zoar
Lowland Point
Angrouse
Poldhu Point
Marconi Memorial
Trewoon
Penhale
Gwenter
Ponsongath
North Corner
Mullion
Mullion Cove
Trenance
Erisey
Gwendreath
Coverack
Mullion Island
Mullion Cove
Ruan Major
Kuggar
Gwendreath
Trewillis
Predannack Head
Mount Hermon
Predannack Wollas
St Ruan
Poltescoe
Treleaver
Black Head
Vellan Head
Ruan Minor
Grade
Cadgwith
Lizard Heritage Coast
South West Coast Path
Devil's Frying Pan
Lizard Head
Kynance Cove
Lizard
Church Cove
LIZARD POINT
Bass Point

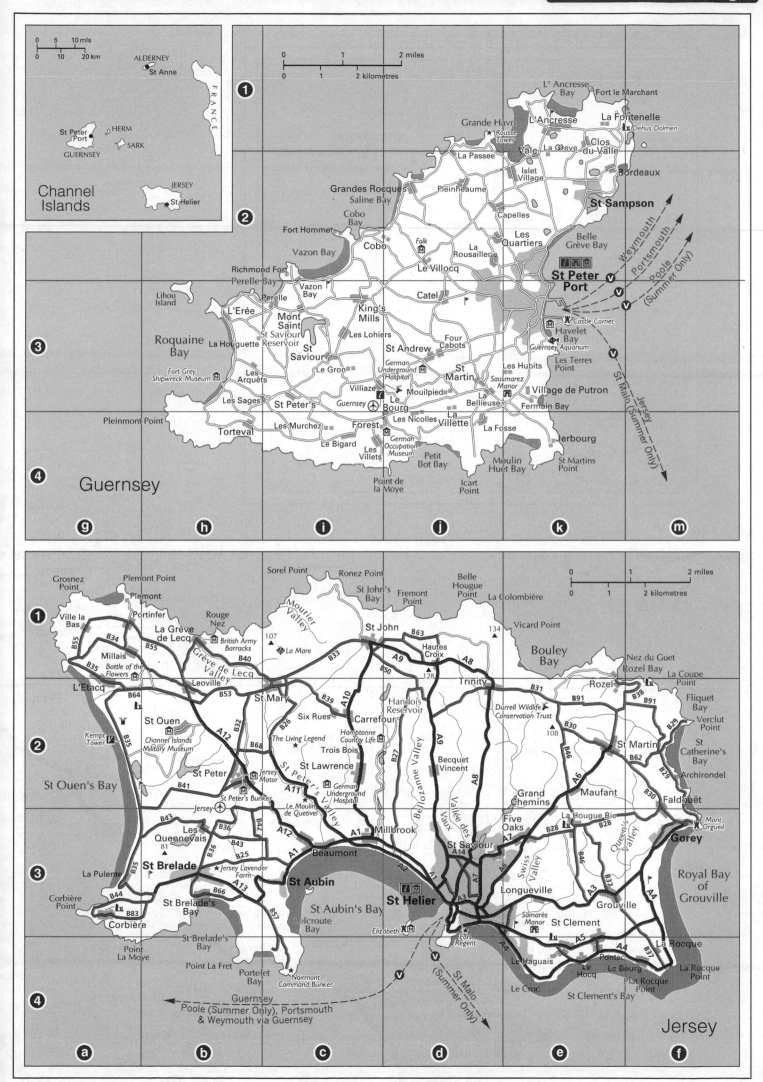

Channel Islands

ALDERNEY
• St Anne

FRANCE

St Peter Port • HERM
GUERNSEY • SARK

JERSEY
• St Helier

Guernsey

0 5 10 mls
0 10 20 km

0 1 2 miles
0 1 2 kilomètres

L' Ancresse Bay
Fort le Marchant
La Fontenelle
Grande Havre
L'Ancresse
Dehus Dolmen
Rousse Tower
Vale
La Grève
Clos du Valle
La Passee
Islet Village
Bordeaux
Pleinheaume
St-Sampson
Grandes Rocques
Saline Bay
Capelles
Cobo Bay
Les Quartiers
Belle Grève Bay
Fort Hommet
Folk
La Rousaillerie
Vazon Bay
Cobo
Le Villocq
St Peter Port
Richmond Fort
Perelle Bay
Vazon Bay
Catel
Castle Cornet
Lihou Island
Perelle
King's Mills
Havelet Bay
Guernsey Aquarium
L'Erée
Mont Saint
Les Lohiers
Four Cabots
Les Terres Point
Roquaine Bay
St Saviour Reservoir
St Saviour
St Andrew
La Houguette
Le Gron
German Underground Hospital
St Martin
Les Hubits
Fort Grey Shipwreck Museum
Les Arquêts
Villiaze
Mouilpied
Sausmarez Manor
Village de Putron
Les Sages
St Peter's
Guernsey
Le Bourg
La Bellieuse
Fermain Bay
Pleinmont Point
Torteval
Les Murchez
Forest
Les Nicolles
La Villette
La Fosse
Jerbourg
Le Bigard
German Occupation Museum
Les Villets
Petit Bot Bay
Moulin Huet Bay
St Martins Point
Point de la Moye
Icart Point

Weymouth
Portsmouth
Poole (Summer Only)
St Malo / Jersey (Summer Only)

Jersey

0 1 2 miles
0 1 2 kilomètres

Grosnez Point
Plemont Point
Sorel Point
Ronez Point
Belle Hougue Point
Plemont
Mourier Valley
St John's Bay
La Colombière
Ville la Bas
Portinfer
Rouge Nez
107
St John
B63
134
Vicard Point
La Grève de Lecq
B55
British Army Barracks
La Mare
Hautes Croix
A9
A8
Bouley Bay
Millais
B34
B55
Grève de Lecq Valley
B40
B33
B50
Nez du Guet
Rozel Bay
La Coupe Point
Battle of the Flowers
B35
Leoville
128
Trinity
B31
Rozel
L'Etacq
B64
B53
St Mary
B39
A10
Handois Reservoir
Durrell Wildlife Conservation Trust
B38
B91
Fliquet Bay
St Ouen
Six Rues
Carrefour
B91
Verclut Point
Kempt Tower
Channel Islands Military Museum
B26
B27
A9
108
B46
St Martin
St Catherine's Bay
B35
The Living Legend
Hamptonne Country Life
Becquet Vincent
B62
B29
Archirondel
St Peter
B68
Trois Bois
A8
B30
Faldouët
St Ouen's Bay
B41
St Lawrence
Grand Chemins
Maufant
Mont Orgueil
B43
Jersey Motor
A11
German Underground Hospital
Vallée des Vaux
La Hougue Bie
B28
Jersey
St Peter's Bunker
Le Moulin de Quetivel
Five Oaks
B28
Gorey
B36
B42
A12
A1
Millbrook
A9
A1
St Saviour
B37
Queen's Valley
B46
Les Quennevais
B43
B25
Beaumont
A14
A6
A3
Royal Bay of Grouville
81
St Brelade
Jersey Lavender Farm
A1
St Aubin
A2
A1
Swiss Valley
Longueville
A3
A4
La Pulente
B35
St Aubin's Bay
St Helier
A7
Grouville
Corbière Point
B44
B66
A13
Belcroute Bay
Elizabeth
A3
Samarès Manor
St Clement
A5
Corbière
B83
St Brelade's Bay
B57
Fort Régent
A4
La Rocque
Point La Moye
St Brelade's Bay
St Malo (Summer Only)
Le Haguais
Pontac
La Rocque Point
Point La Fret
Portelet Bay
Le Hocq
Plat Rocque Point
Noirmont Command Bunker
Le Bourg
Le Croc
St Clement's Bay
Guernsey
Poole (Summer Only), Portsmouth & Weymouth via Guernsey

(1)

Isles of Scilly

➊

White Island

King
Charles's
BRYHER   Old
          Grimsby   **ST.MARTIN'S**
Cromwell's   Old Blockhouse   38   49 St Martin's Head
Old Blockhouse   Higher
42   **New**   Lizard Point   **Town**
Grimsby
Isles of Scilly
Heritage Coast   Pool   Tresco   Crow Bar   Great Ganilly

          Tresco   Innisidgen   Great Arthur
          Abbey   Tomb   Crow
          TRESCO   Sound
Samson   Bant's Carn
          Burial   A3110   **ST MARY'S**

➋   North West Channel

          Harry's Walls   Longstone
          Deep Point
Hugh Town   Porth Hellick Downs Tombs
Garrison Walls   Isles of Scilly (St Mary's)
          Old Town

➌   Annet   St Mary's Sound   Peninnis Head

Broad Sound   Gugh
**Middle
Town**   **ST.AGNES**
          Horse Point

          Smith Sound
➍   Western Rocks

          0   1   2 miles
          0   1   2 kilometres

(a)   (b)   (c)   (d)

Witchcr
          Pentire Point - Widemouth
          Heritage Coast   **Boscastle**
          Trevalga
          Tintagel   B3263
TINTAGEL HEAD Tintagel   Tretheve
          Tintagel   Bossiney   Trefor
          Old Post Office NT
          Penhallic Point   Tregatta

(5)   Treknow   Trewarmett   Penpet
          Trebarwith
          Treligga   Rockhead   Gaia
          Energy
          Delabole   Centre
          South West Coast Path   Trevia
          Westdowns   Pengelly
          Port Isaac   Valley Truckl
          Bay   **Lanteglos**
          Varley   Kelland   Trewalder
          Head   Head   **Helstone**
          Rumps   Port Quin   Port Gaverne   B3314
(6)   Point   Bay   **Port Isaac**   **St Teath**
          Port   Trewetha   Knightsmill
          Pentire Point   New   Quin   Treburgett   **Treveigh**
Padstow Bay   Polzeath   Long   B3267
          Cross   **Trelights**   Pendoggett   **Michae**
          Hayle Bay   Porteath   Plain   Treharrock
          Street   **St Endellion**   Trelill   **Trenewth**
Stepper Point   **Polzeath**   B3314   Tregellist
          Trebetherick   Trequite   Trewen
          Trevanger   **St Minver**   **St Kew**
Trevose Head   Pityme   Tredrizzick   Trewethern   **St Kew**   **St**
Heritage Coast   Mother   Splatt   Trewethern   **Highway**   Lank
TREVOSE HEAD Ivey's   Crugmeer   Prideaux Place   Stoptide   **St Tudy**
          Bay   Harlyn   **Rock**   Hendra   Wenfordbridge
Dinas   Trevose   Bay   Pen
Head   Harlyn   **Chapel**   **St Mabyn**   Blislan
Constantine   Treator   Tregonce   **Amble**
(7)   Bay   **Trevone**   Bodieve   Wate
          Harlyn   **Padstow**   Tregunna   Trevanson
Constantine Bay   Windmill   Dinas   Edmonton   **Egloshayle**   Tredethy
          Treyarnon   Towan   Tregonce   Croanford   Hellandbridge
Trehemborne   Shop   Trevorrick   Bodieve   Pencarrow   Helland
          St Merryn   St Issey   **St Breock**   Treneague   Colquite
Trevorrick   Whitecross   Sladesbridge
Porthcothan   Treburick   Trenance   Royal   **Burlawn**   Washaway
          Little   Trewint   Cornwall   Hay   Lane   **Helland**
Park Head   Treburrick   **Petherick**   No Man's   End   Norton
(8)   Penrose   Rumford   Tredinnick   Land   Polbrock
Bedruthan Steps   St   **4**   **5**   Brocton   Dunmere
          Downhill   Ervan   Trelow   Shires Family   St Breock   **E**
          0   5 miles   Adve   Park   Downs
          0   7 kilometres   (C)   Monolith   (D)   (F)

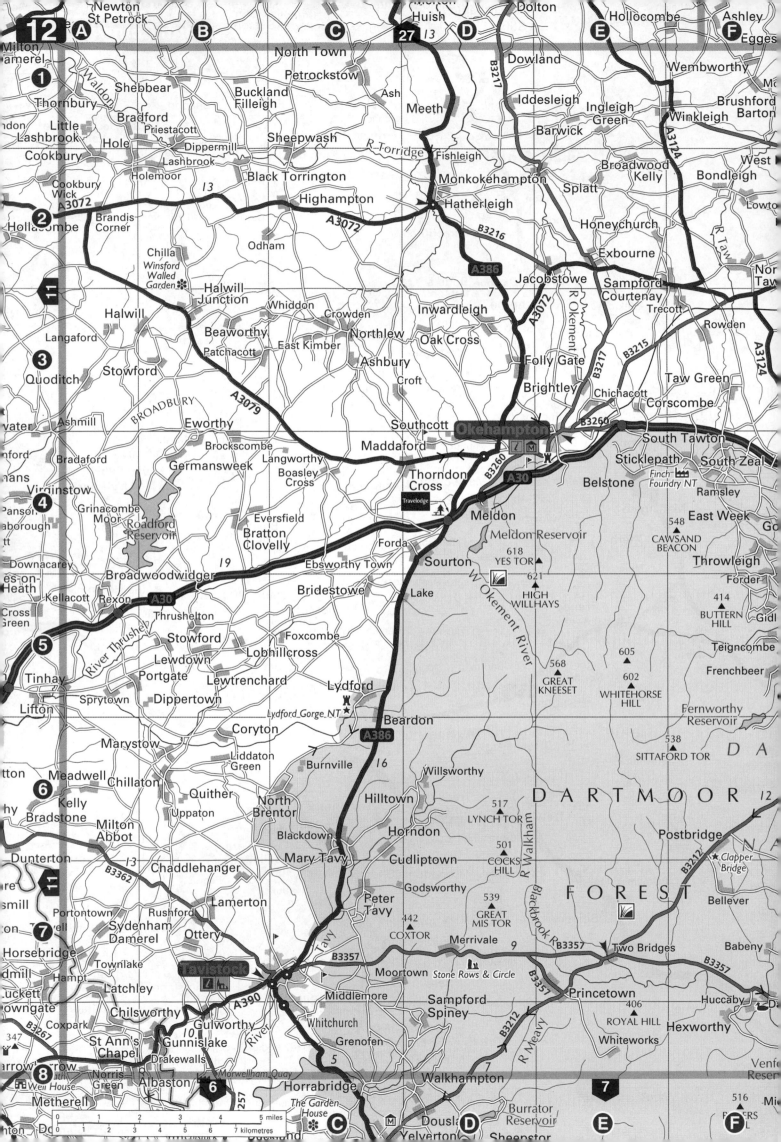

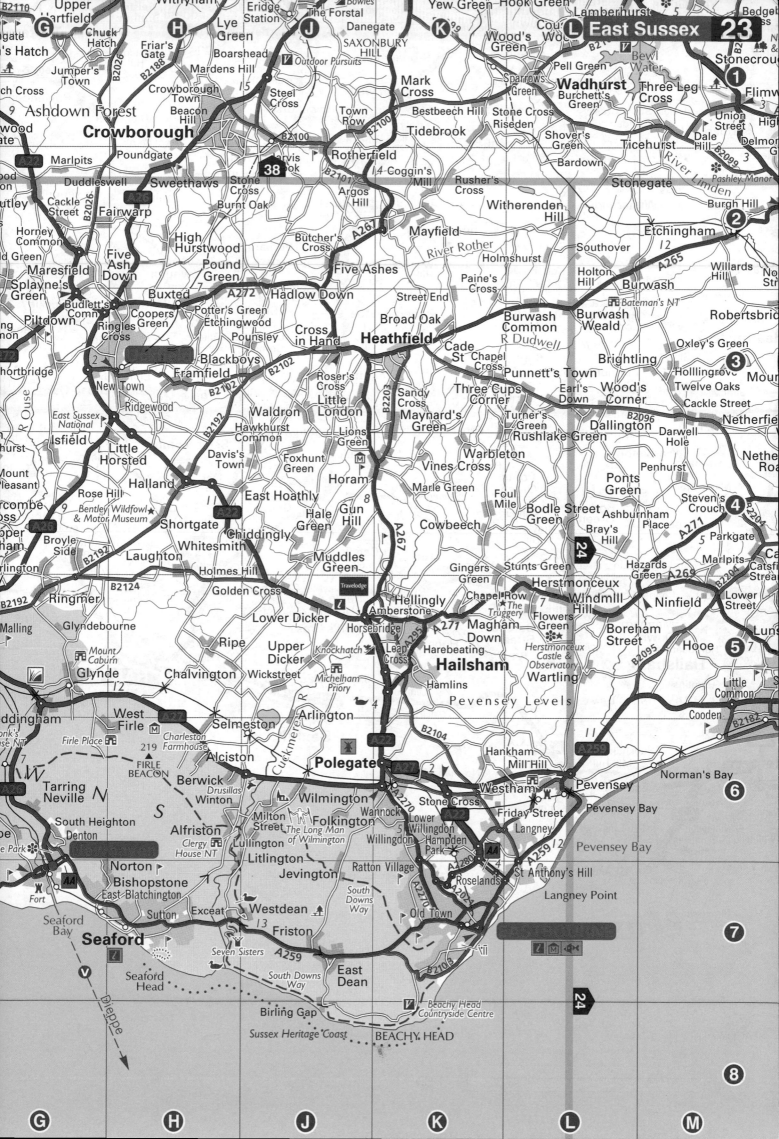

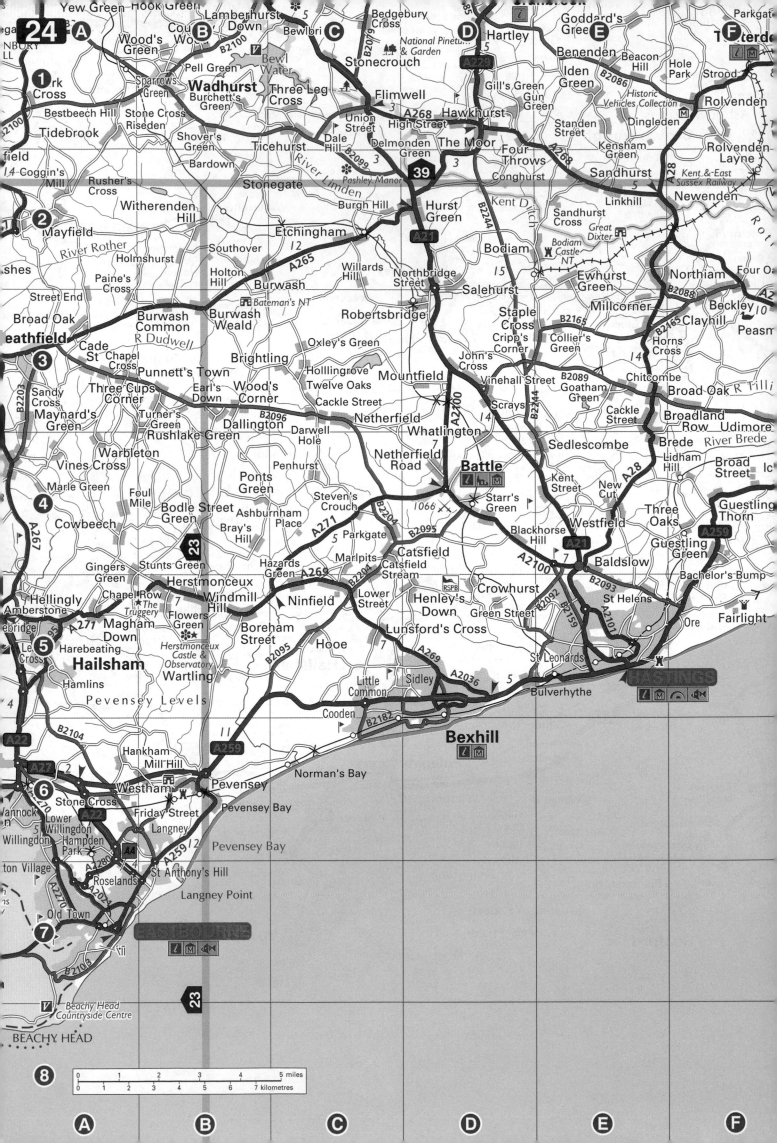

A   B   C   D   E   F

1

North West
Point
*Lundy
Heritage Coast*   LUNDY

2   △142
Marisco
♜ *Surf Point*
Shutter Point

3

4   B A R N S T A P L

                                                                O R

5   B I D E F O R D   B A

                                           Shipload
HARTLAND POINT   Bay

Damehole   Titchberry   Brownsham   *Hartl*
Point   *Hartland Abbey*   *Heritage*
Stoke   *& Garden*   Clovelly
Hartland Quay ⚓ Ⓜ   🏛   B3248   Velly   Buck's
Spekes Mill   Hartland   ▲   Higher   Mills
Mouth   ▲ Philham   4   B3237 Clovelly
6   Milford   *Milky Way*   Buck's ⚓   A39
Elmscott   Cross
Woolfardisworthy
Hardisworthy   Cranford   Pa
South
Hole   Parkha
Ash
Welcombe   Ashmanswor
Mead   Darracott   Meddon   East
7   Woolley   Putford
Gooseham   Eastcott   16   East   Wes
Morwenstow   Youlstone   Dinworthy   Putf
Higher Sharpnose Point   Shop   Colscott
South West   Woodford *Killarney* West Youlstone Bradworthy
Coast Path   *Springs*
Lower Sharpnose Point   *Tamar*   Kimworthy
Kilkhampton   Darracott *Lakes*   Sutcombe
Steeple Point   Stibb   Sutcombemill
8   *Brocklands*   Thurdon   Soldon   *River*

0   1   2   3   5 miles   Soldon
0 1 2 3 4 5 6 7 kilometres   C   A39 D **11**   E Cross F
Sandy
Mouth

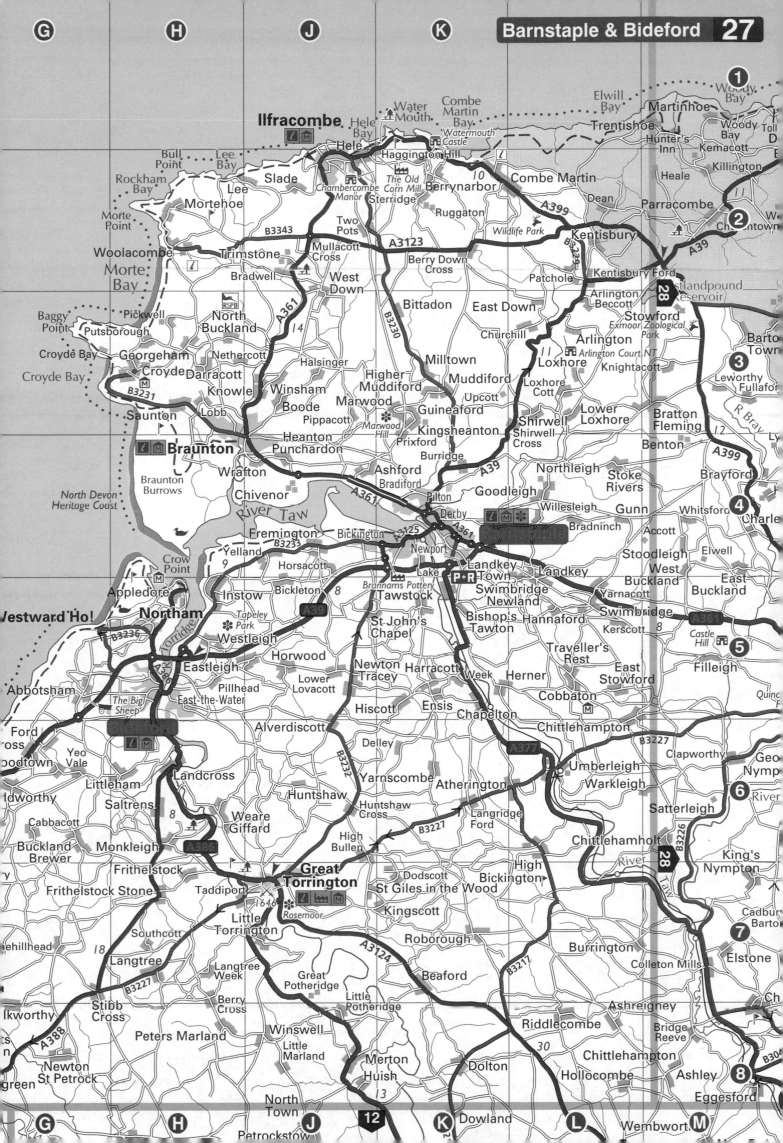

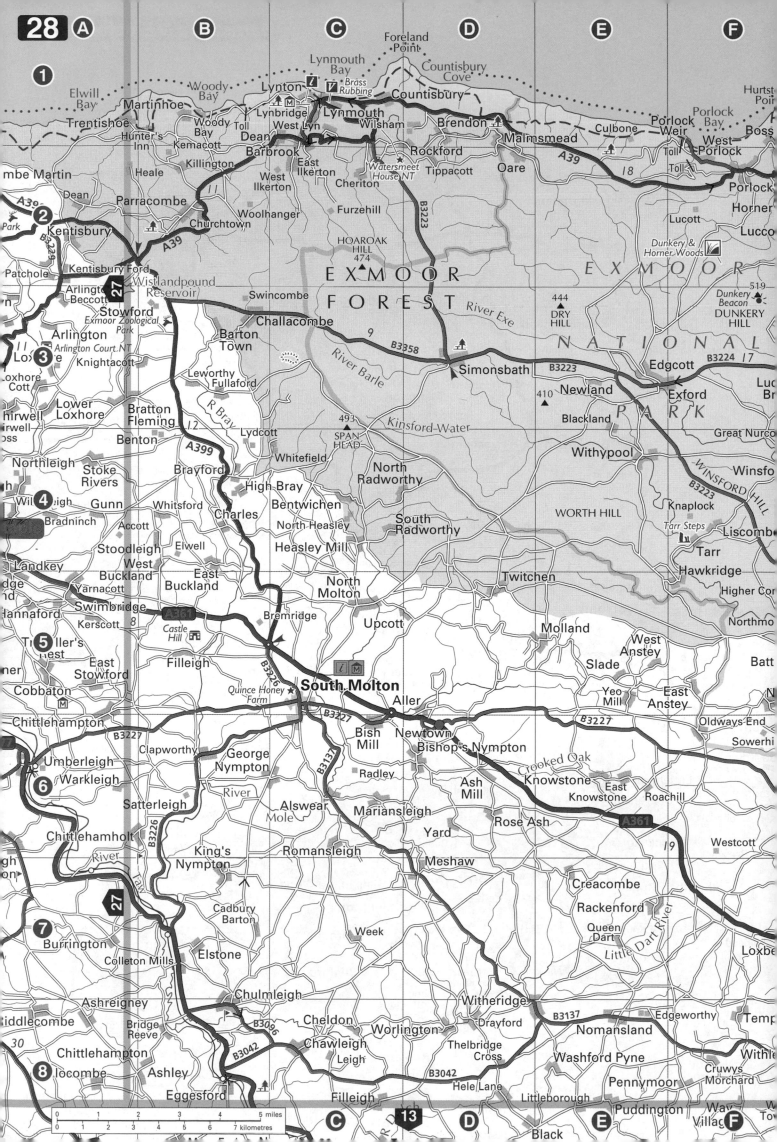

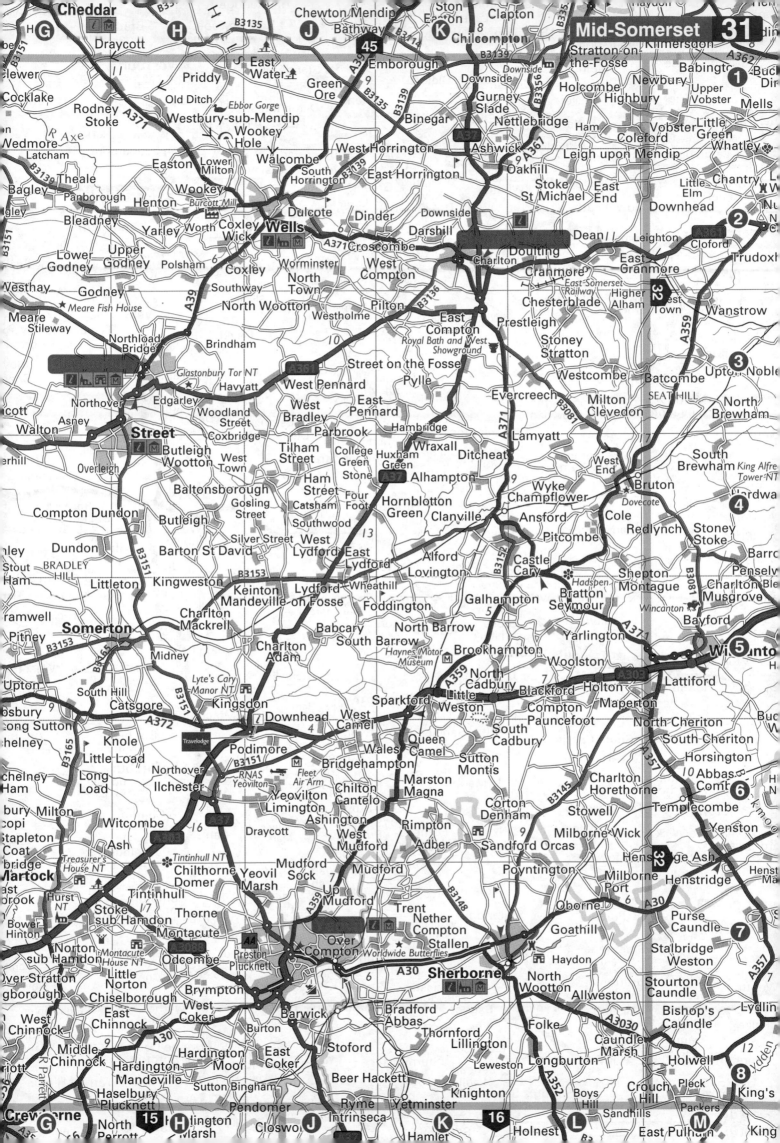

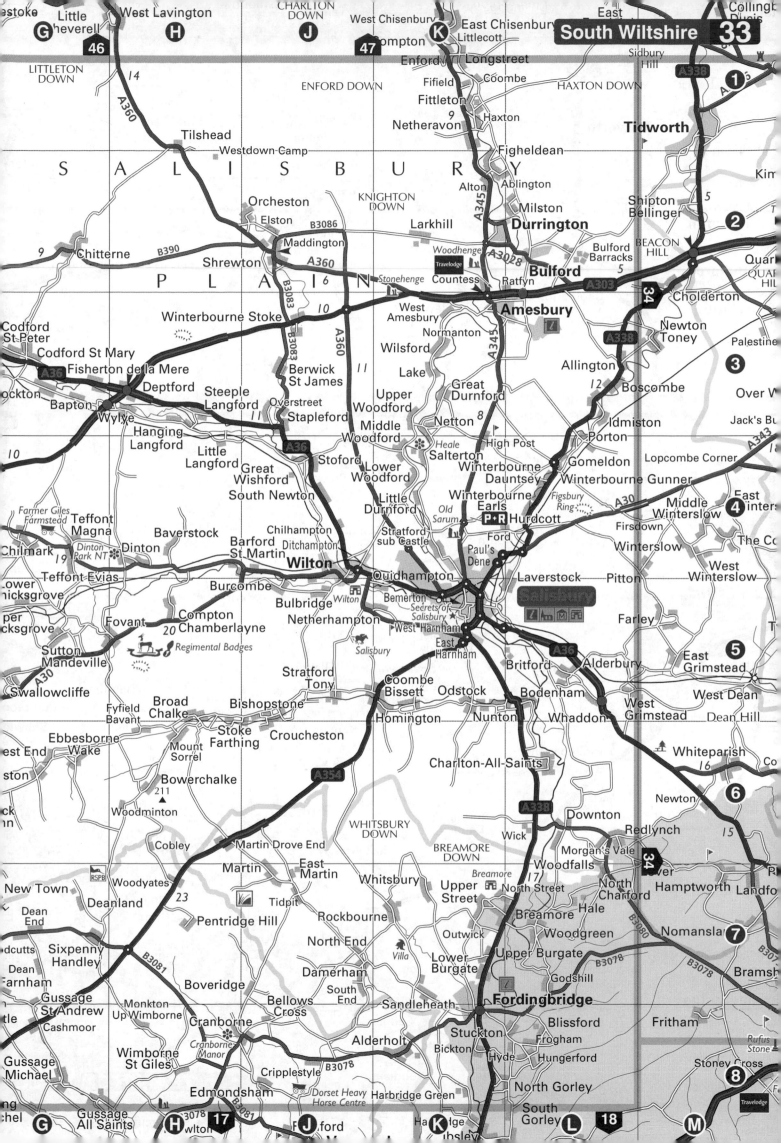

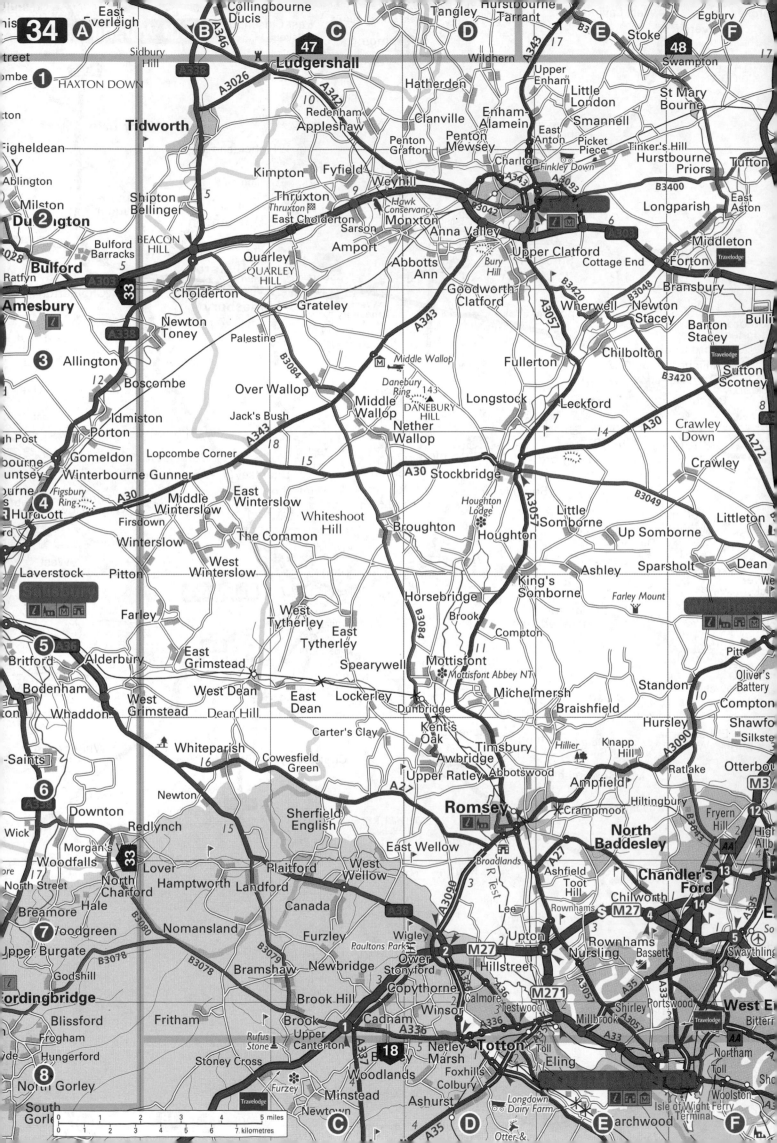

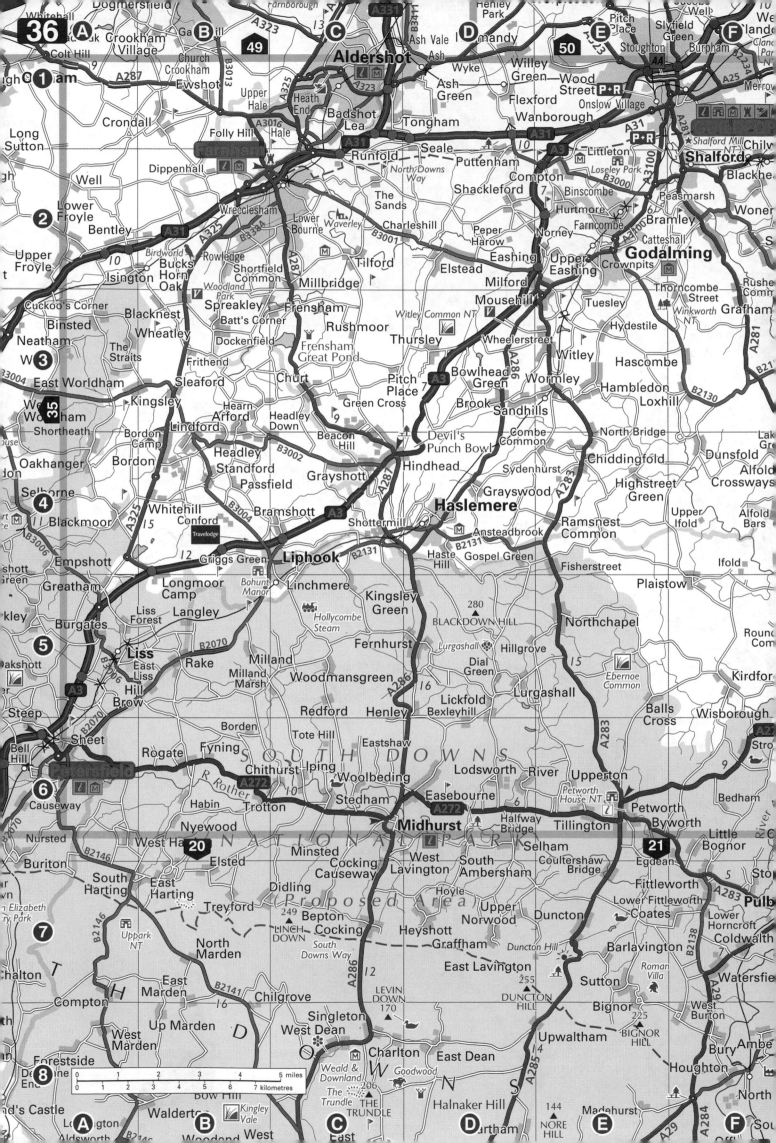

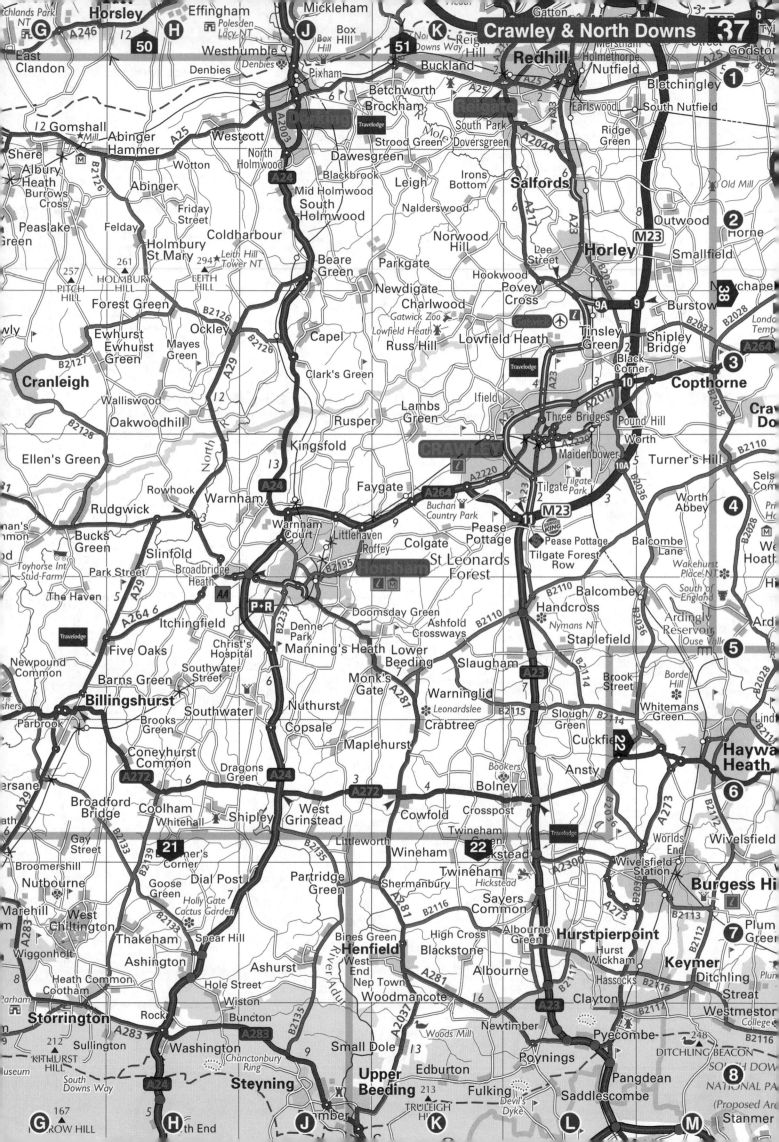

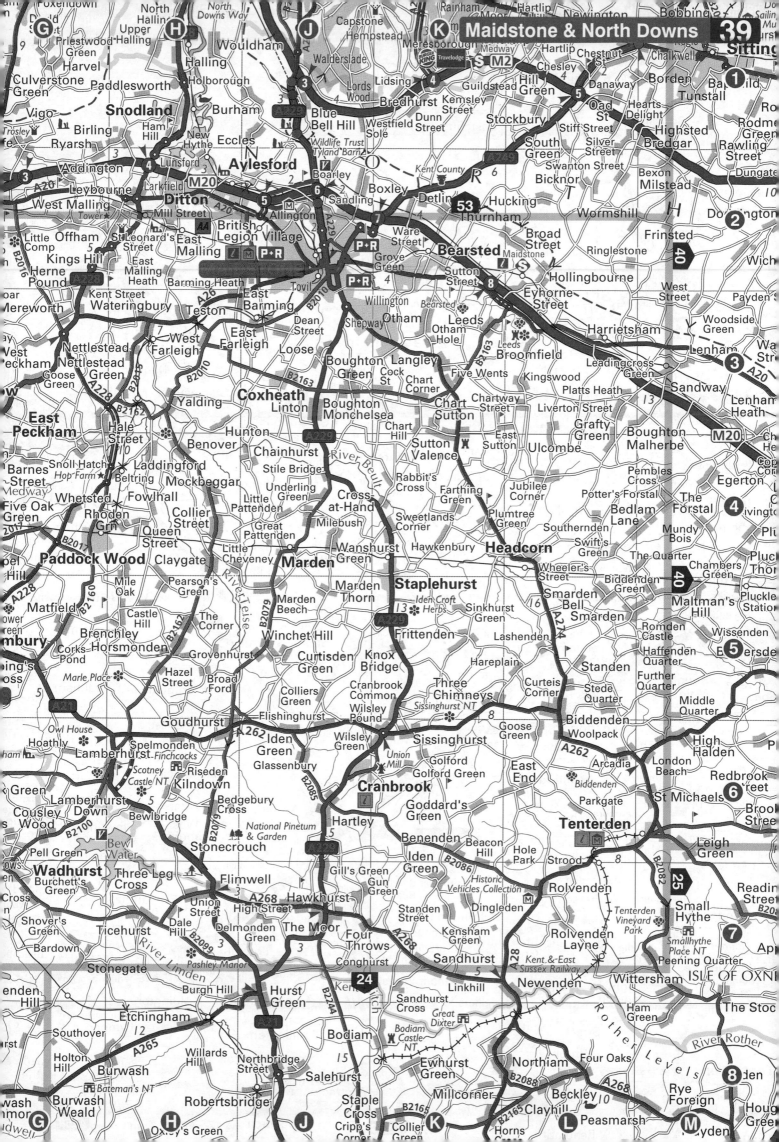

G   H   J   K   L

1

MARGATE   Foreness Point

B2051

Westgate on Sea   Cliftonville   Kingsgate
Minnis Bay   Westbrook   Northdown   B2052   NORTH FORELAND
Minnis Bay   Birchington   Garlinge   B2052
Herne Bay   Reculver   Brooks End   Salmestone Grange   A255   Reading Street   B2052
Bishopstone   Hillborough   Potten Street   B2048   Lydden   Westwood   St Peter's   Broadstairs
Beltinge   St Nicholas   A28   Acol   ISLE OF THANET   Haine   A254   Dumpton
Eddington   at Wade   B2190   Manston   Hereson
Broomfield   Boyden Gate   Sarre   Monkton way   A259   Manston   St Lawrence   Ramsgate
Herne   Highstead   Chislet   Gore Street   Hoo   Durlock   Cliffsend   Viking Ship 'Hugin'   Pegwell
Maypole   Hoath   A253   17   Plucks Gutter   Minster   St Augustine's Cross   Pegwell Bay
Hicks   Upstreet   10   West Stourmouth   R Stour   A256   Richborough   Sandwich Bay
Forstal   Hersden   A28   Grove   East Stourmouth   Westmarsh   Paramour Street   Prince's
Westbere   Preston Street   Goldstone   Great Stonar   Sandwich
Stodmarsh   Preston   Elmstone   Cop Street   Cooper Street   Royal St George's
ordwich   Wickhambreaux   Walmestone   Hoaden   Weddington
Littlebourne   Shatterling   Ash   A257   Sandwich
rbury   A257   Seaton   Ickham   Durlock   Guilton   Marshborough   Stone Cross   Woodnesborough   Toll
kesbourne   Bramling   Wingham   Twitham   Staple   Barnsole   Worth
Hill   Bekesbourne   Goodnestone   Eastry   Statenborough
Patrixbourne   B2046   Heronden   Ham   Hacklinge
Adisham   Ratling   Chillenden   Knowlton   West Street   Finglesham   The Downs
dres   Higham Park   Nonington   Marley   A258   Sholden   Deal
psbourne   Aylesham   Easole Street   Betteshanger   Northbourne   Upper Deal   Walmer
Kingston   Elmstead   Womenswold   Holt St   Tilmanstone   Great Mongeham   Ripple
Marley   Barham   Frogham   Elvington   13   Little Mongeham   Ringwould   Kingsdown
erringstone   Woolage Village   Barfreston   Lower Eythorne   Sutton   Sutton Downs
Breach   Woolage Green   Eythorne   East Studdal   Martin   A258
adbean   East Kent Railway   Shepherdswell   Ashley   West Langdon   East Langdon
Denton   Coldred   North Downs Way
more   Wootton   A2   9   Whitfield   A256   Guston   St Margaret's at Cliffe
Geddinge   Lydden   Temple Ewell   St Margaret's Bay
North Elham   Selsted   Ewell Minnis   Kearsney   River   West Cliffe   SOUTH FORELAND
Swingfield Minnis   Chilton   A2   Lighthouse NT   South Foreland Heritage Coast
Ridge Row   Swingfield Street   Wolverton   Buckland   Langdon Cliffs NT
Hawkinge   Densole   Alkham   St Radigund's   DOVER   Dunkerque Calais
Upper Standen   South Alkham   Maxton   Zeebrugge
Capel le Ferne   Lower Standen   West Hougham   Farthingloe   Oostende
Satmar   A20   Samphire Hoe   Dover - Folkestone Heritage Coast   Calais
Cheriton   Morehall   East Wear Bay   Channel Tunnel
FOLKESTONE

0   1   2   3   4   5 miles
0   1   2   3   4   5   6   7 kilometres

2

3

4

5

6

7

8

G   H   J   K   L   M

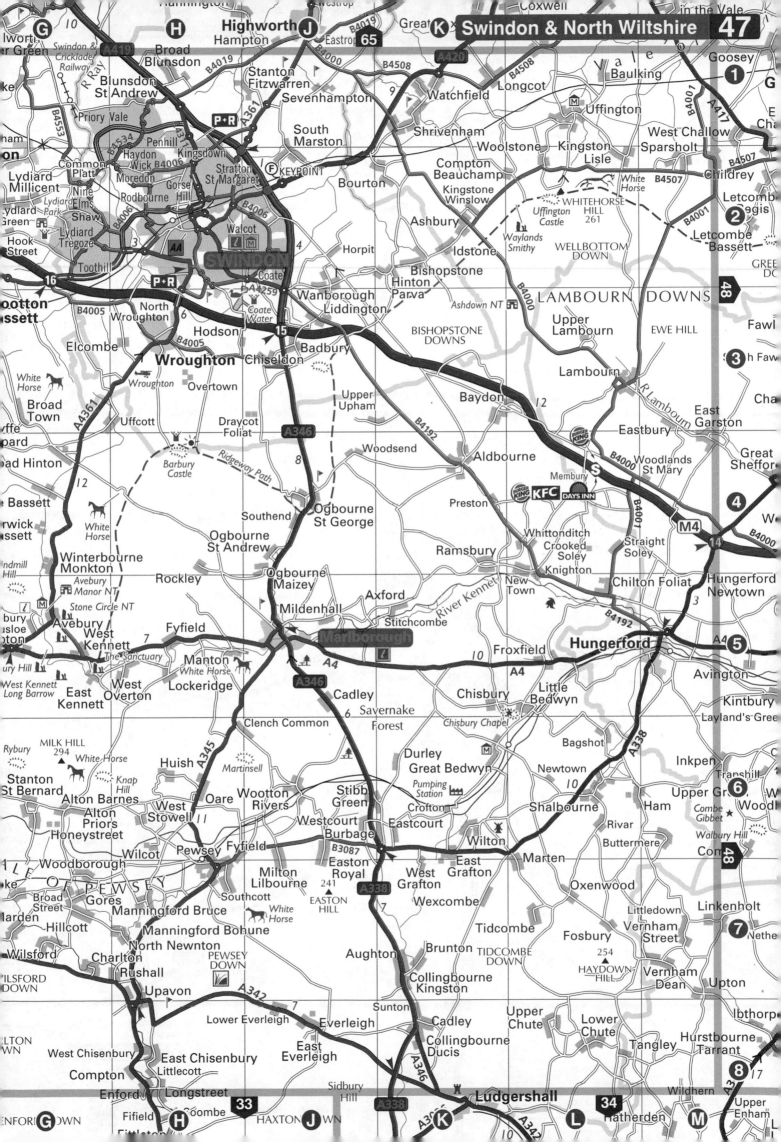

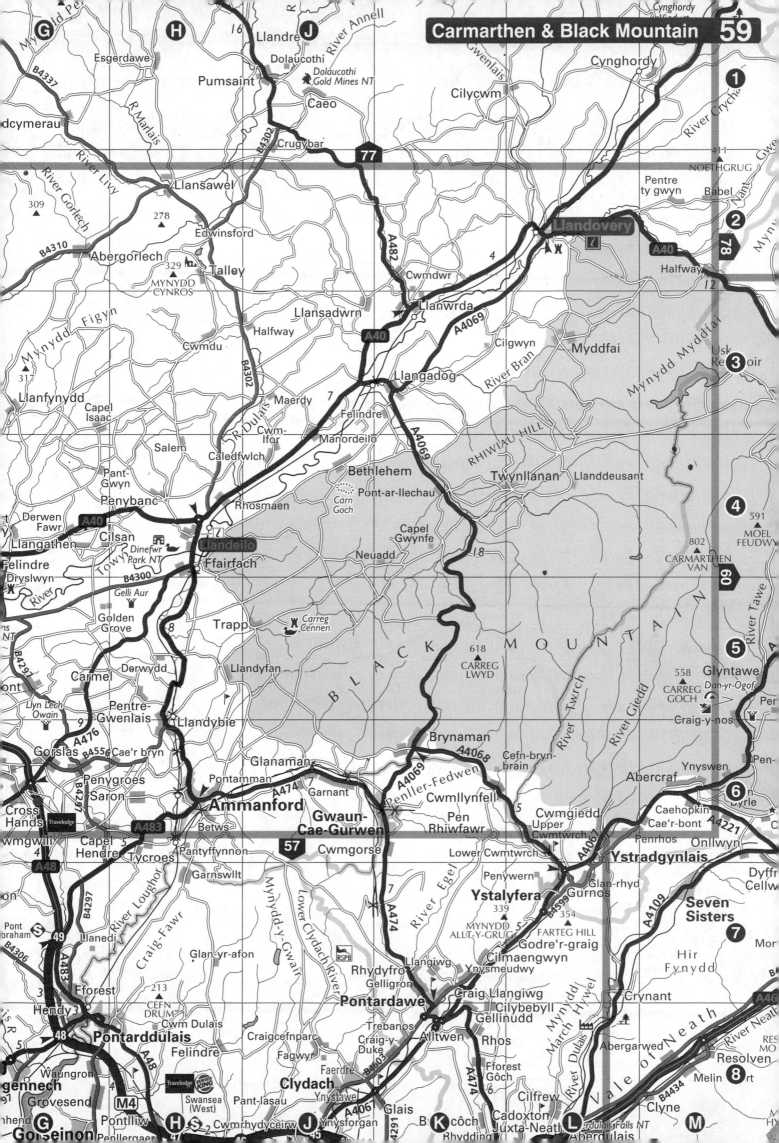

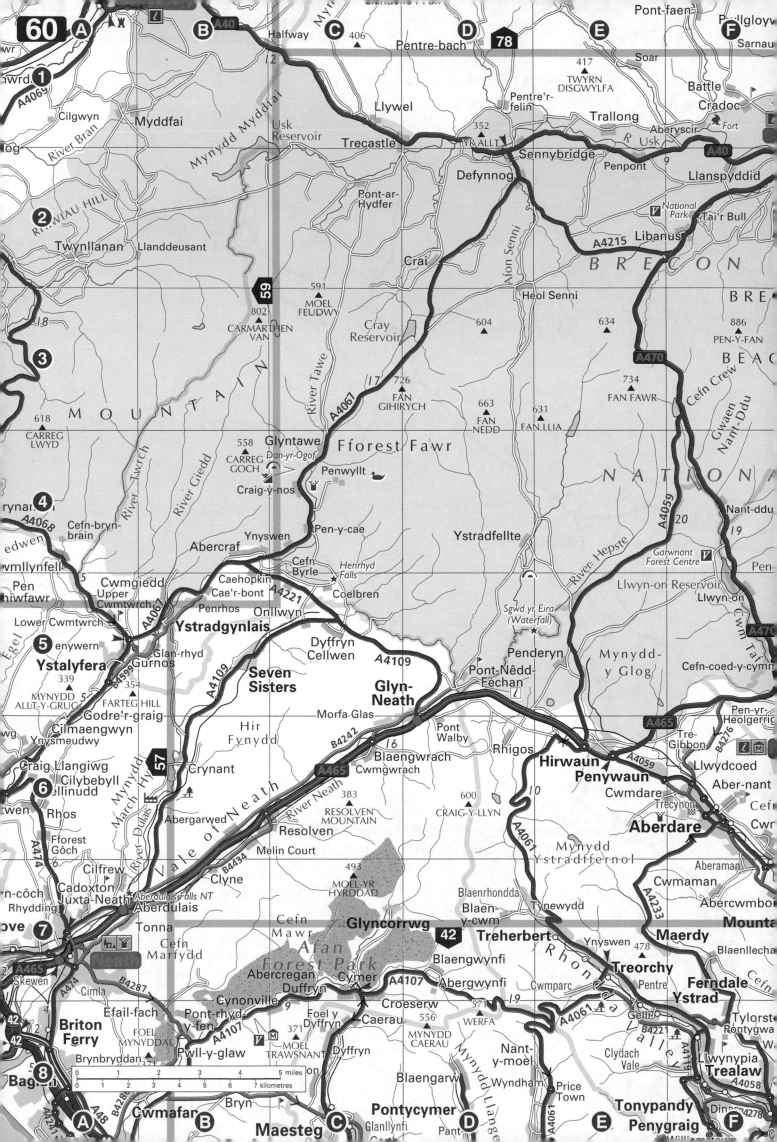

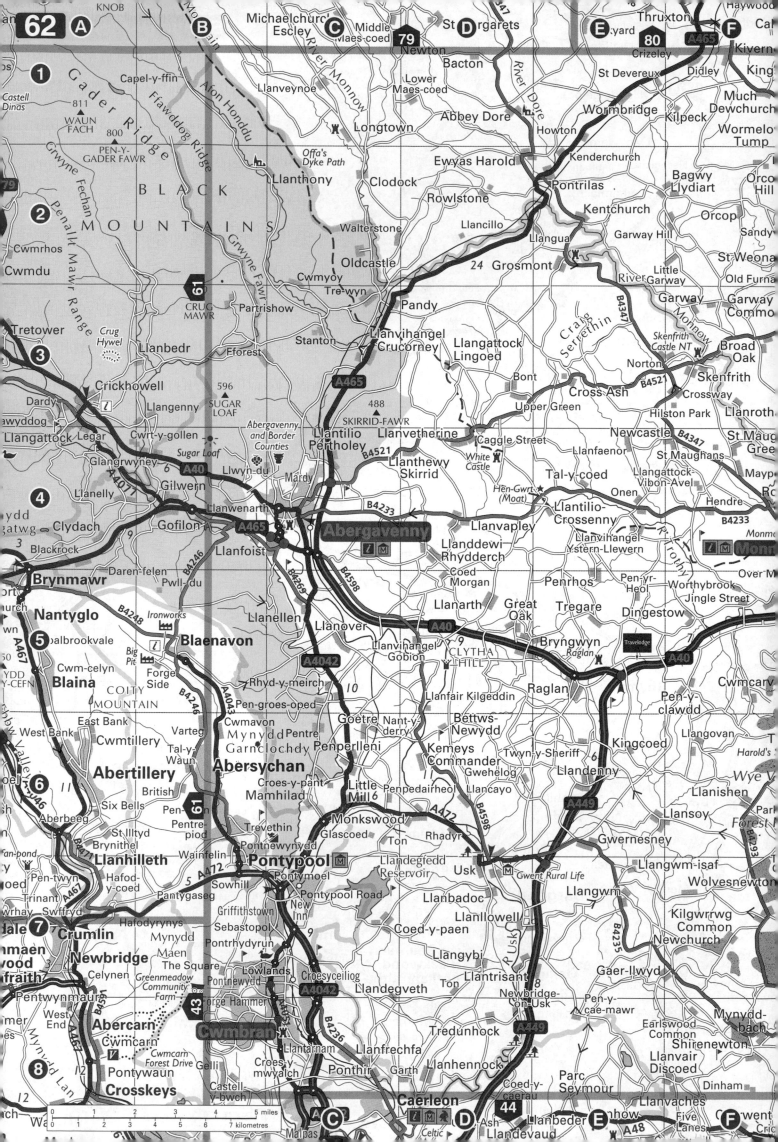

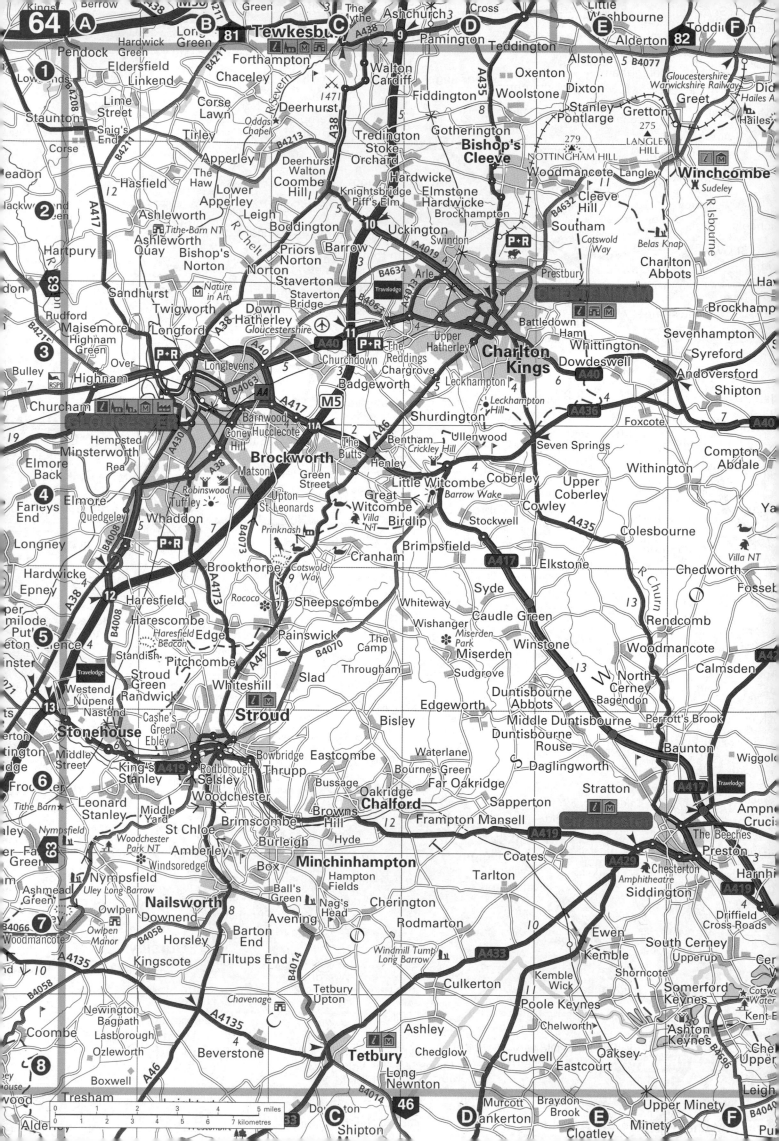

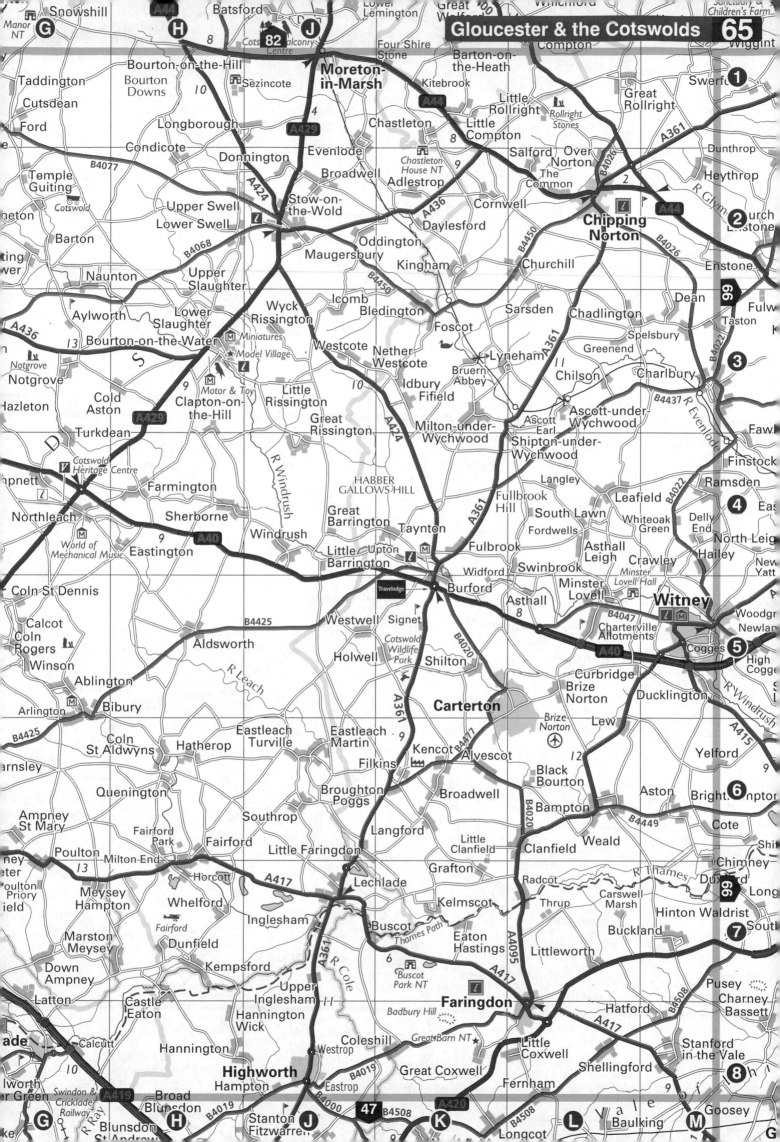

A   B   C   D   E   F

1

2

3

◄ Rosslare Harbour   V

STRUMBLE HEAD

Carregwas

4

Pen Brush

Llanwnda

Pwllderi

Ocean

Goodwick

Trefasser

Pembrokeshire
Coast Path

Manorowen

St Nicholas

Panteg

Scledd

5

Ynys
Daullyn

Granston

Carreg Sampson

Abercastle

Llangloffan

Jordanston

A40

Porthgain

Trefin

Mathry

Castle
Morris

B4331

Abereiddy

Llanrhian

16

A487

Newbrid

Berea

Square &
Compass

Letterston

6

Tretio

Croes-goch

Treffynnon

Welsh
Hook

ST DAVID'S HEAD

Treleddyd-fawr

Carnhedryn

Treglemais

Cerbyd

B4330

15

Rhodiad-
y-brenin

Caer
Farchell

River   Solva

Llandeloy

Whitesand
Bay

B4583

Tancredston

Pont-yr-hafod

Wolf's
Castle

Bishops
Palace

Whitchurch

Middle Mill

Treffgarne
Owen

Hayscastle

Hayscastle
Cross

St David's

RAMSEY
ISLAND

Nine
Wells

Solva

A487

Brawdy

Treffgarne

7

RSPB

54

Pen-y-cwn

178

Leweston

DUDWELL
MT

St David's Peninsula
Heritage Coast

Newgale

16

Roch

Wolfsdale

A40

PEMBROKESHIRE
COAST
NATIONAL PARK

Roch Gate

Simpson
Cross

Camrose

Pembrokeshire
County

Rickets Head

A487

Keeston

Tangiers

8

0   1   2   3   4   5 miles
0   1   2   3   4   5   6   7 kilometres

Nolton Haven

Nolton

Pelcomb Cross

Pelcomb

St Brides Bay
Heritage Coast

Lambston

Pelcomb
Bridge

Glanafon

St Brides Bay

Druidston

Sutton

A   B   C   D   E   F

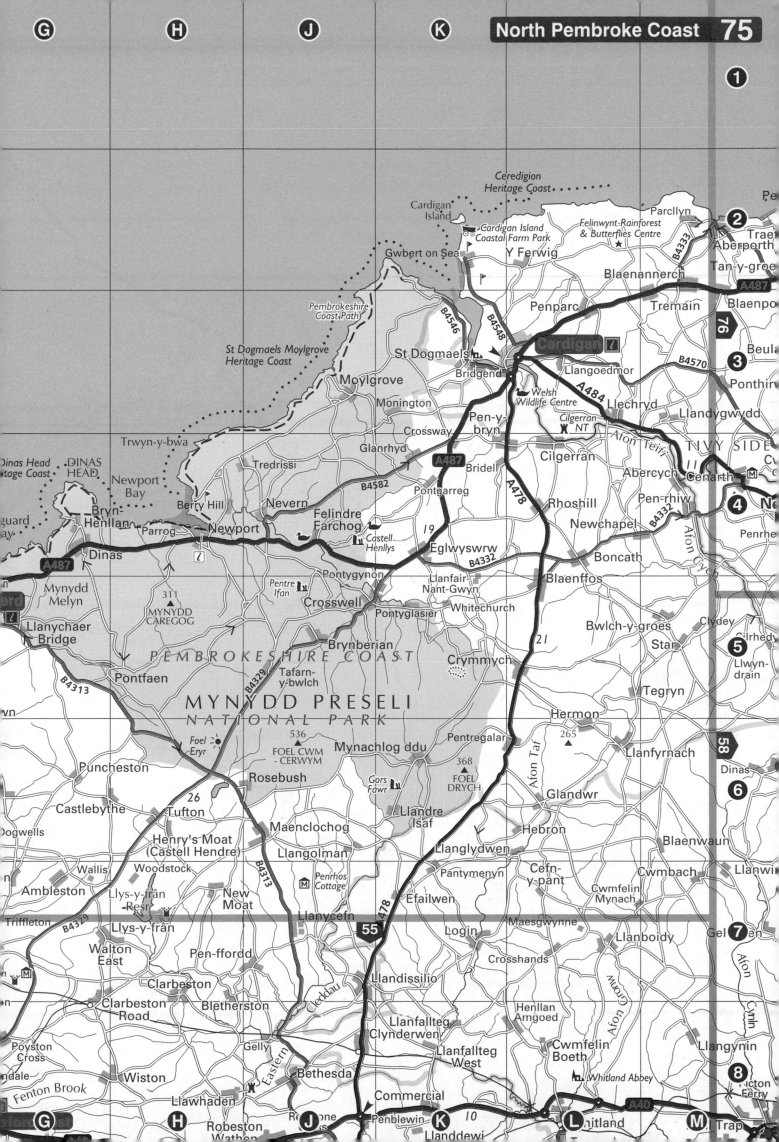

G   H   J   K

1

Ceredigion
Heritage Coast · · · · · · · ·

2

Cardigan
Island
Cardigan Island
Coastal Farm Park
Gwbert on Sea

Parcllyn

Felinwynt Rainforest
& Butterflies Centre

Trae
Aberporth
Tan-y-groe

Y Ferwig

A487

Blaenannerch

Blaenpo

Penparc

Tremáin

76

Pembrokeshire
Coast Path

B4546

B4548

Cardigan i

B4333

Beula

B4570

Ponthir

Llangoedmor

Llandygwydd

St Dogmaels Moylgrove
Heritage Coast

St Dogmaels

Bridgend

A487

Welsh
Wildlife Centre

Pen-y-
bryn

Cilgerran
NT

A484

Llechryd

Afon Teifi

TIVY SIDE

3

Moylgrove

Monington

Crossway

Glanrhyd

Bridell

Cilgerran

Abercych

Cenarth M

Dinas Head
tage Coast

DINAS
HEAD

Trwyn-y-bwa

Tredrissi

B4582

Pontgarreg

A478

Rhoshill

Pen-rhiw

4

N

Newport
Bay

Berry Hill

Nevern

Felindre
Farchog

19

Eglwyswrw

B4332

Newchapel

B4332

Penrhe

Bryn-
Henllan

Parrog

Newport

Castell
Henllys

Boncath

Blaenffos

Dinas

A487

i

Pontygynon

Llanfair
Nant-Gwyn

Blaenwaun

Mynydd
Melyn

Pentre
Ifan

Crosswell

Pontyglasier

Whitechurch

Bwlch-y-groes

Clydey

Cilrhedi

Llanychaer
Bridge

i

311

MYNYDD
CAREGOG

Brynberian

21

Star

5

Llwyn-
drain

ard

B4313

Pontfaen

PEMBROKESHIRE COAST

B4329

Tafarn-
y-bwlch

Crymmych

Tegryn

MYNYDD PRESELI

Hermon

265

58

NATIONAL PARK

Foel
Eryr

536

FOEL CWM
- CERWYM

Mynachlog ddu

Pentregalar

Llanfyrnach

Dinas

6

Puncheston

Rosebush

Gors
Fawr

368
FOEL
DRYCH

Afon Taf

Glandwr

Castlebythe

Tufton

26

Llandre
Isaf

Hebron

Blaenwaun

Llanwi

Dogwells

Henry's Moat
(Castell Hendre)

Maenclochog

Llangolman

Llanglydwen

Cefn-
y-pant

Cwmbach

Ambleston

Woodstock

B4313

New
Moat

Penrhos
Cottage

Pantymenyn

Cwmfelin
Mynach

Wallis

Llys-y-frân
Resr

Efailwen

Trffleton

B4329

Llys-y-frân

Llanycefn

478

Maesgwynne

Gel

7

en

Walton
East

Pen-ffordd

55

Login

Llanboidy

Afon

Clarbeston

Crosshands

Cleddau

Llandissilio

Henllan
Amgoed

Poyston
Cross

Clarbeston
Road

Bletherston

Afon
Cyff

Llangynin

ndale

Gelly

Eastern

Llanfallteg
Clynderwen

Llanfallteg
West

Cwmfelin
Boeth

Fenton Brook

Wiston

Bethesda

Llanfallteg

8

rfor est

Poyston
Cross

Llawhaden

Robeston
Wathen

Commercial

Whitland Abbey

cton
Ferry

A40

G   H   J   K   L   M   Trap

Penblewin

10

Llanddewi

hitland

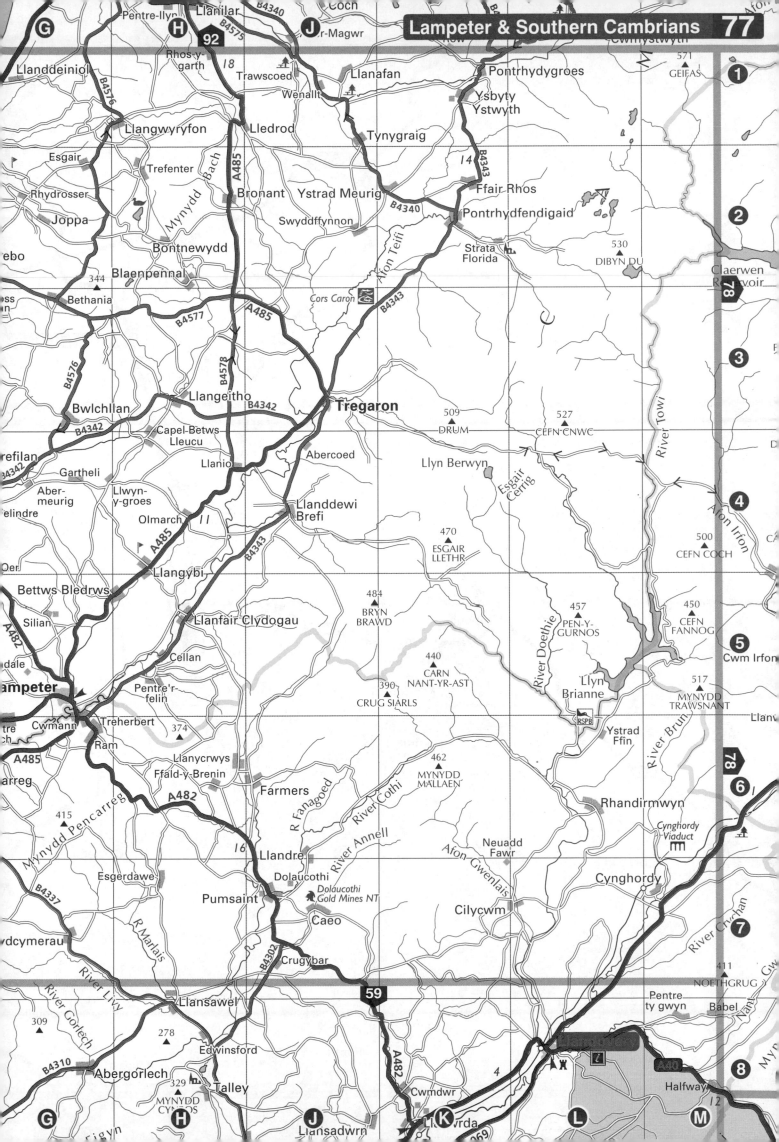

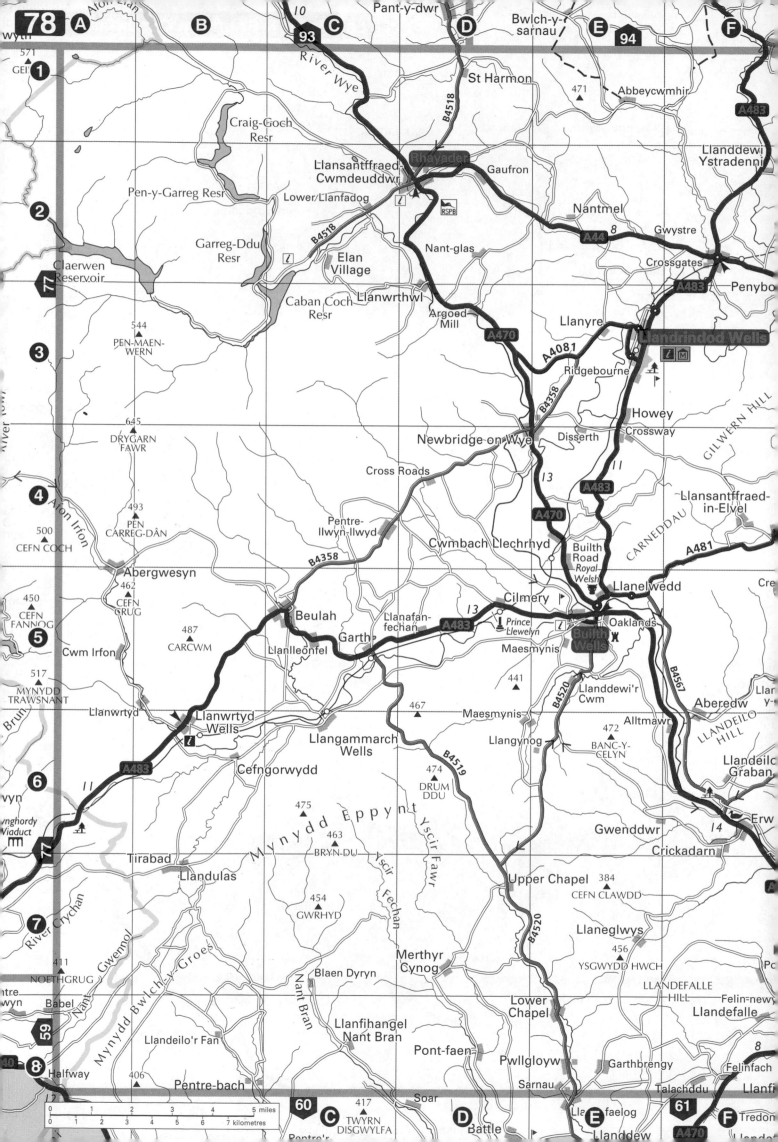

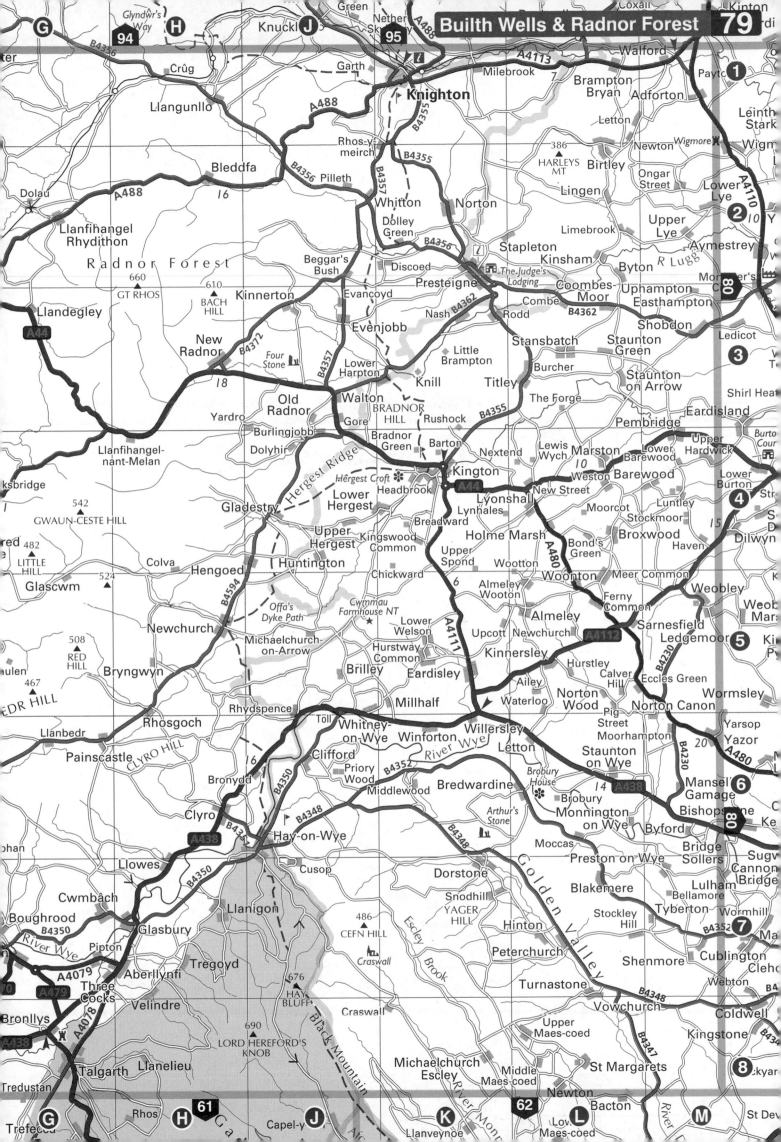

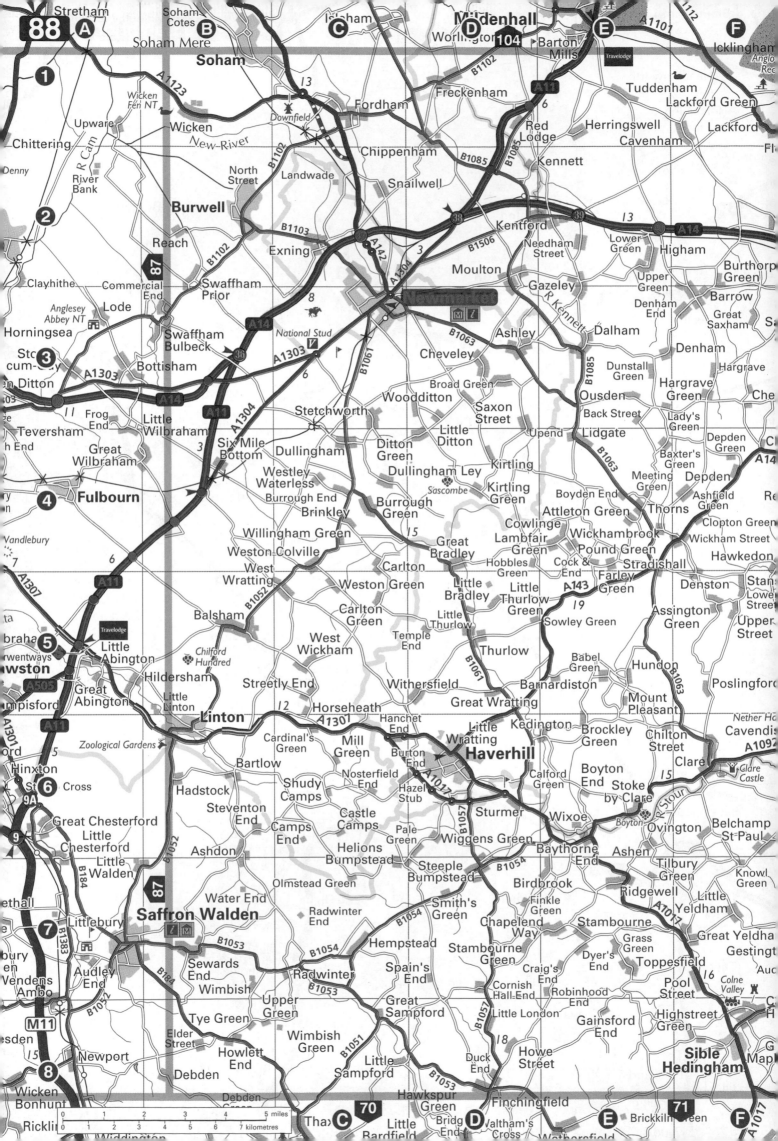

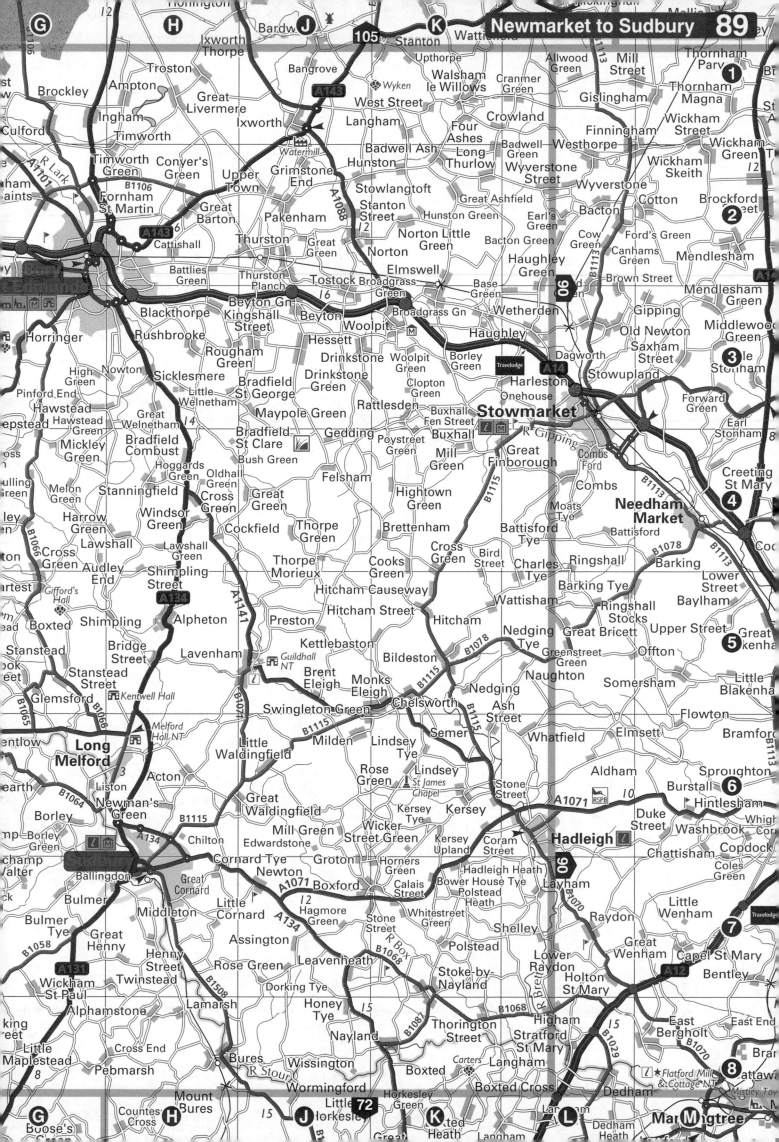

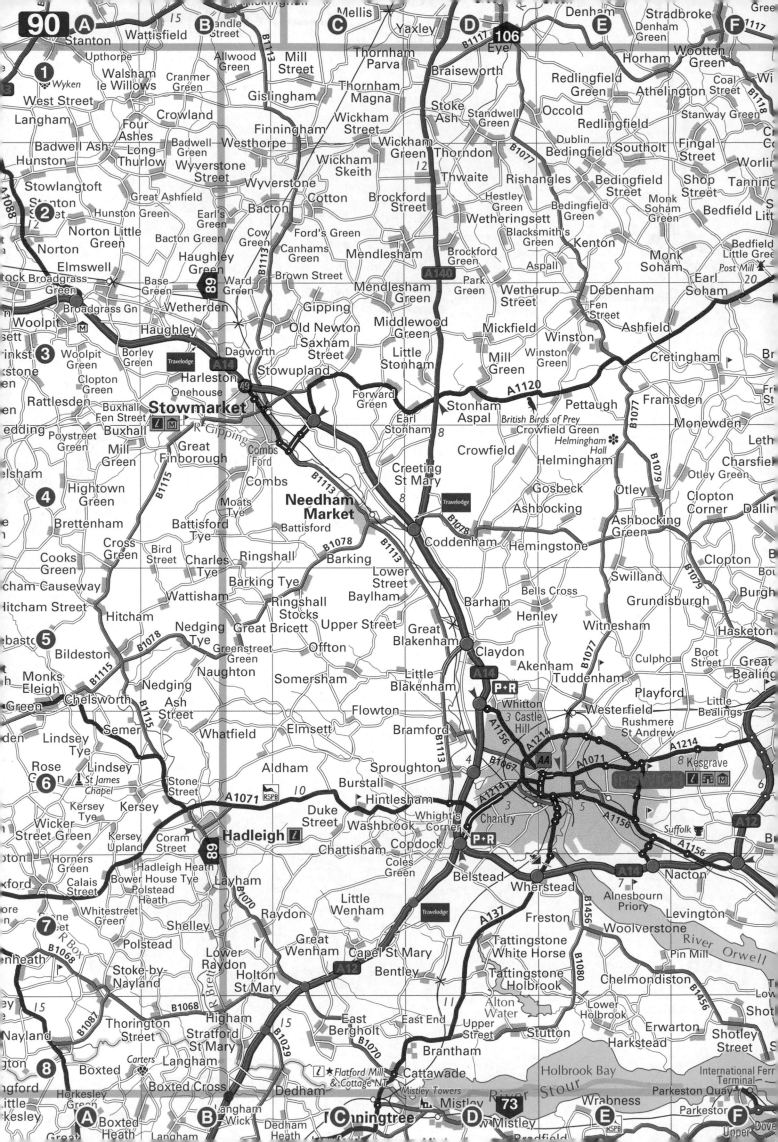

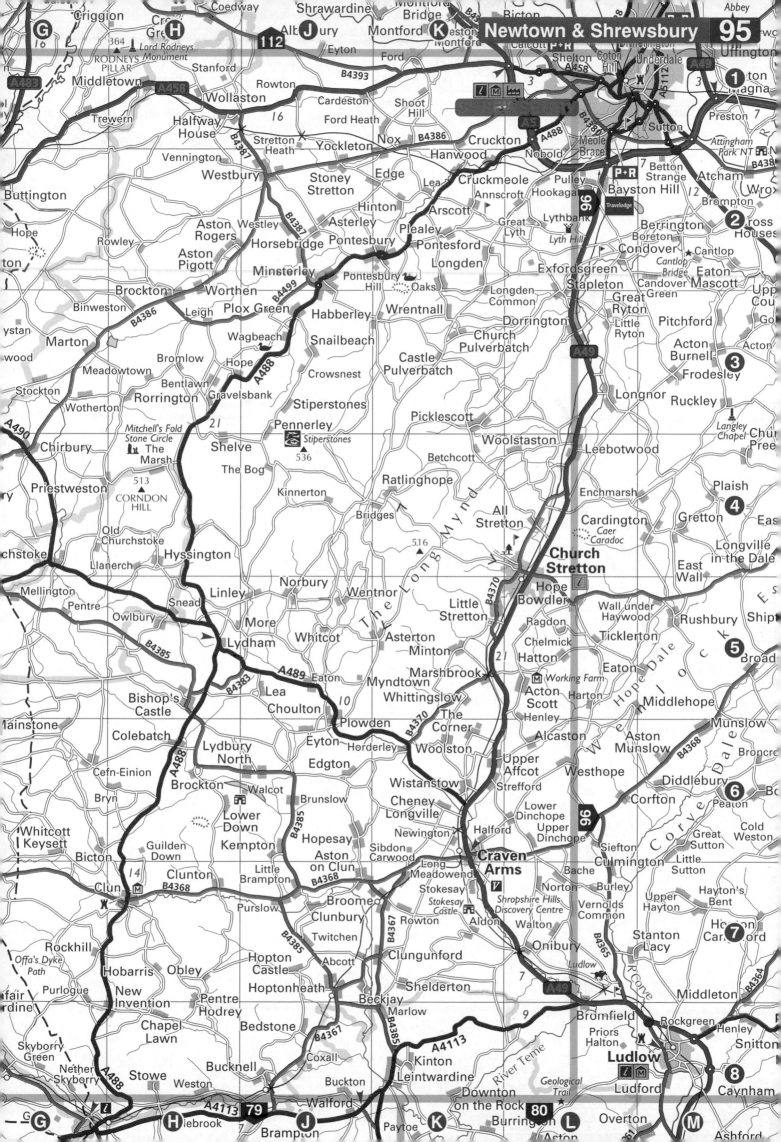

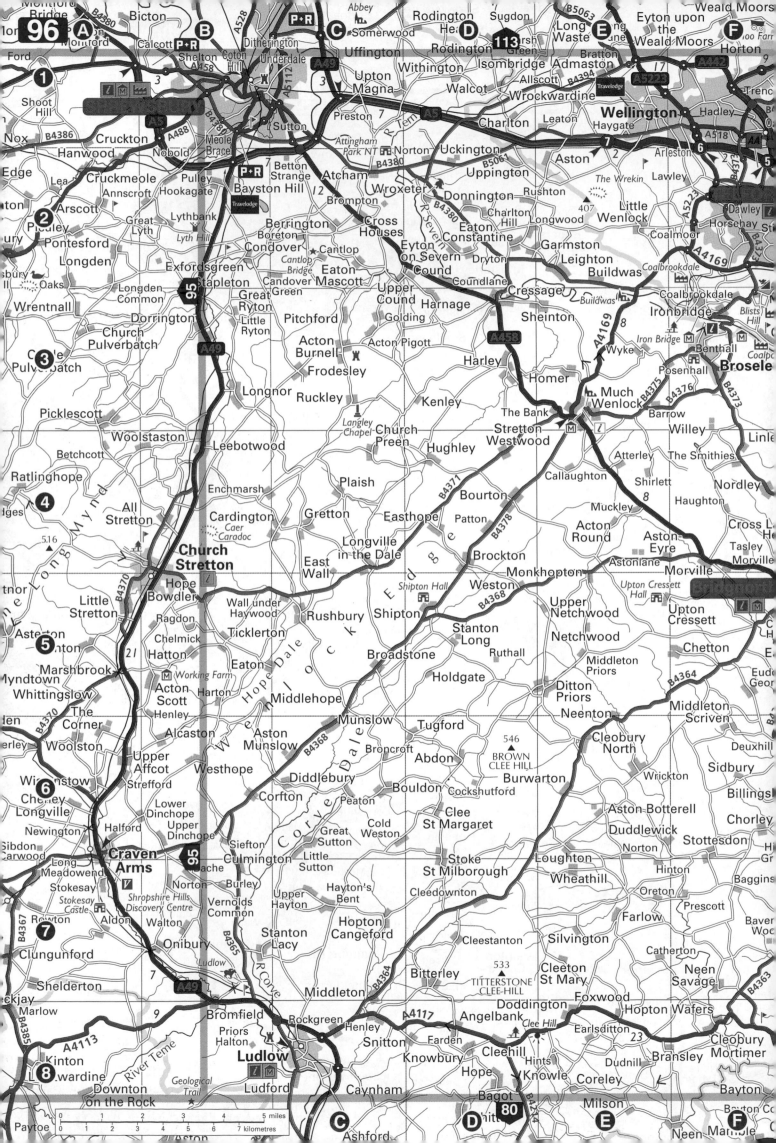

G **119** B116
H
J
West **120** Rattan Row
K
St Germa

St Giles 8
Ingleborough
River
Lawrence
St Germa

Sutton St Edmund
Holbeach Drove
Gedney Hill
Broadgate
Throckenhalt
Guanockgate
Parson Drove
Murrow
Gorefield
Fitton End
Leverington
Wisbech St Mary
Tholomas Drove
West Walton Highway
West Walton
Walsoken
New Walsoken
Emneth
Walpole Highway
Terrington St John
Lordsbridge
St John's Fen End
Marshland St James
Chequers Corner
Emneth Hungate
Gaultree
Holly End
Wiggenhall St Mary th rgin
Watling
Wiggenhall St Mary Magdalen
Runcton Holme
Thorpland
Stowbridge
West Head
Wimbotsham

B1166
B1187
B1166
A47
A47
A1101
A47

Thorney Toll
Guyhirn Gull
Guyhirn
Ring's End
Chainbridge
West Fen
Westry
Norwoodside
Little London
Coldham
Begdale
Elm
Friday Bridge
Laddus Fen
Outwell
Upwell
Three-Holes
Euximoor Fen
Euximoor Drove
Iron Bridge
Christchurch
Stow Bardolph Fen
Nordelph
Upwell Fen
Denv
Fordham
Ten Mile Bank
Hilgay Fen
Southery

River Nene
Moreton Leam
A605
A141
R. Nene (Old Course)
B1101
B1412
B1098
B1094
B1094
B1100
Old Bedford River
New Bedford River
River Great Ouse
104
A1122
B198

March
Badgeney
B1099
Town End
Hook
Stonea
Eastwood End
Wimblington
Benwick
Primrose Hill
Doddington
Tipp's End
Lakesend
Welney
Gold Hill
Wildfowl & Wetlands Trust
Brand Cree

Turves
White Fen
B1093
B1093
B1101
B1098
Sixteen Foot Drain
B1098
B1093
A141
A1101
B1411

Chatteris
Tick Fen
sey Foot
Horseley Fen
Langwood Fen
Purls Bridge
Welches Dam
Pymoor
Oxlode
Little Downham
Littleport Bridge
Littleport
Burnt
A141
A142
B1050
A10
104
River Ouse
B13

Somersham
Chatteris Fen
America
Mepal
Wardy Hill
Witcham
Sutton
Wentworth
Witchford
Coveney
Chettisham
Queen Adelaide
Prickwillow
Middle Fen
Great Fen
Broad Hill
Isle
B1096
Travelodge
A142
B1411
B1382
River Lark

l End
Fenton
Church End
Pidley
Colne Wood End
Bluntisham
Earith
Haddenham
Aldreth
Wilburton
Little Thetford
Stretham
Barway
Soham Cotes
Stuntney
B1040
B1086
B1050
B1381
A1421
A1123
A10
A142
7
8

Ouse Fen
Needingworth
Ouse or Ol West River
87
Soham Mere
Soham
G
H
J
K
L A1123
M
13

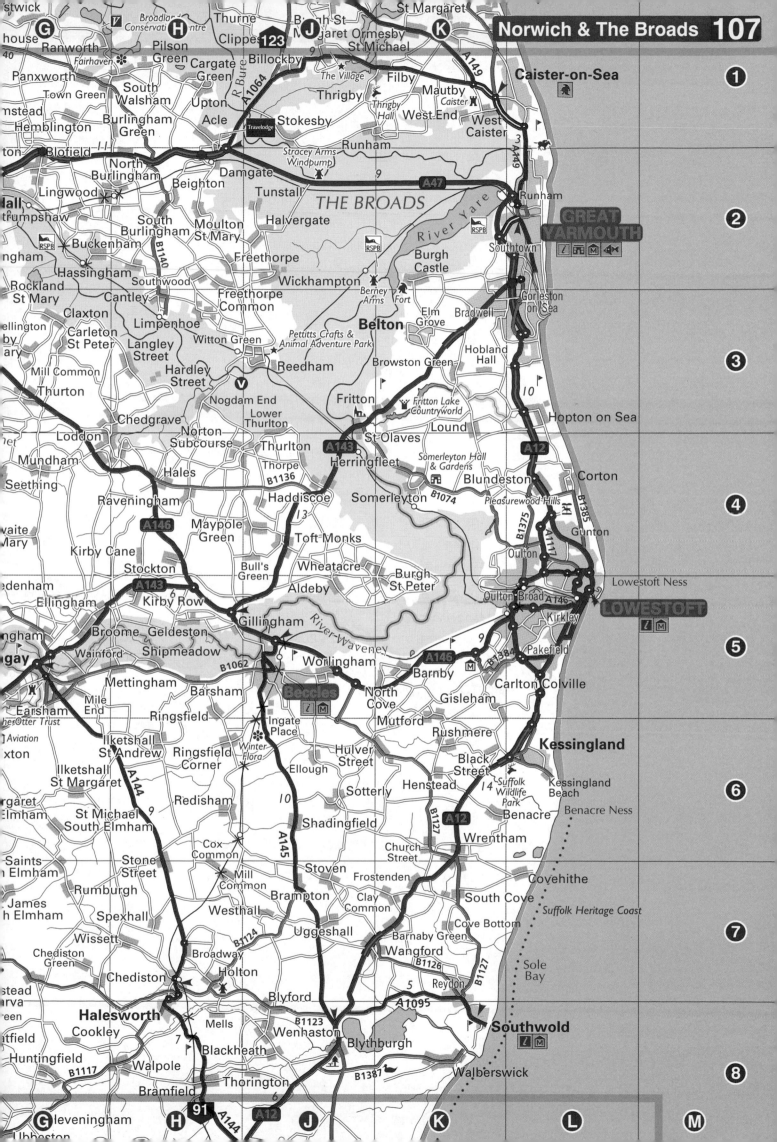

CAERNARFON

BAY

Lleyn Heritage Coast

Trefo

Trwyn y Grolech

564 ▲ YR EIFL

B4417

Llithfa

Carreg Ddu

Porth Nefyn

Pistyll

Llwy

Morfa Nefyn

Nefyn

Porth Dinllaen

Fron B43

Groesffordd

Edern

Bodfuan

Porth Ysgaden

LLEYN

Rhos-y-llan

Llandudwen

Llanne

A497

Tudweiliog

Efailnev

Porth Colman

Dinas

371

B4415

Denio

Carn Fadrum

Garn

Rhyd-y-clafdy

Bryn-mawr

Llaniestyn

A499

Pen-y-graig

B4417

14

7 Penrhos

Llangwnnadl

Meyllteyrn

Llanbedrog

Sarn

Botwnnog

Mynytho

B4413

B4413

Bryncroes

17

Nanhoron

Trwyn Llanbedro

Llandegwning

St Tudwal's Road

Rhydlios

Rhoshirwaun

Plas-Yn-Rhiw-NT

Llangian

B4413

Anelog

Penycaerau

Y Rhiw

Llanengan

Abersoch

Uwchmynydd

Llanfaelrhys

Porth Ysgo

Porth Neigwl

Bwlchtocyn

Sarn-bach

Marchros

St Tudwal's Island East

Aberdaron

Aberdaron Bay

St Tudwal's Island West

Bardsey Sound

Lleyn Heritage Coast

Porth Geiriad

St Mary's

BARDSEY ISLAND

| 0 | 1 | 2 | 3 | 4 | 5 miles |
| 0 | 1 | 2 | 3 | 4 | 5 | 6 | 7 kilometres |

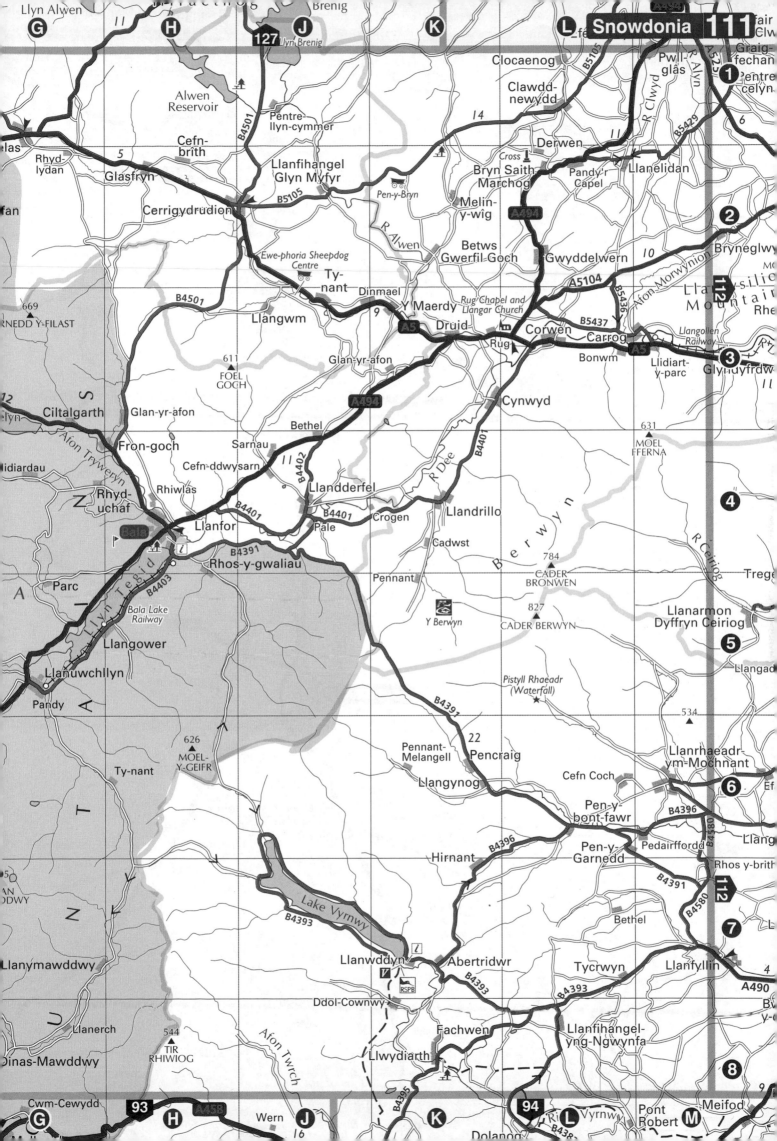

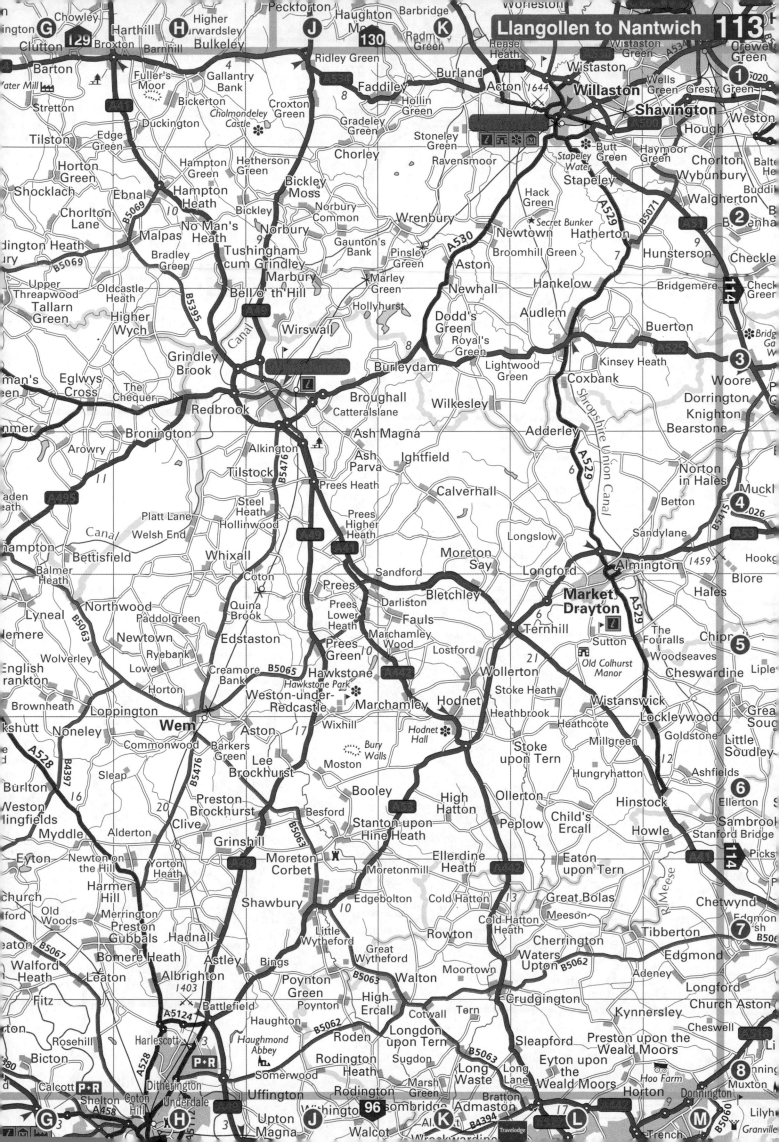

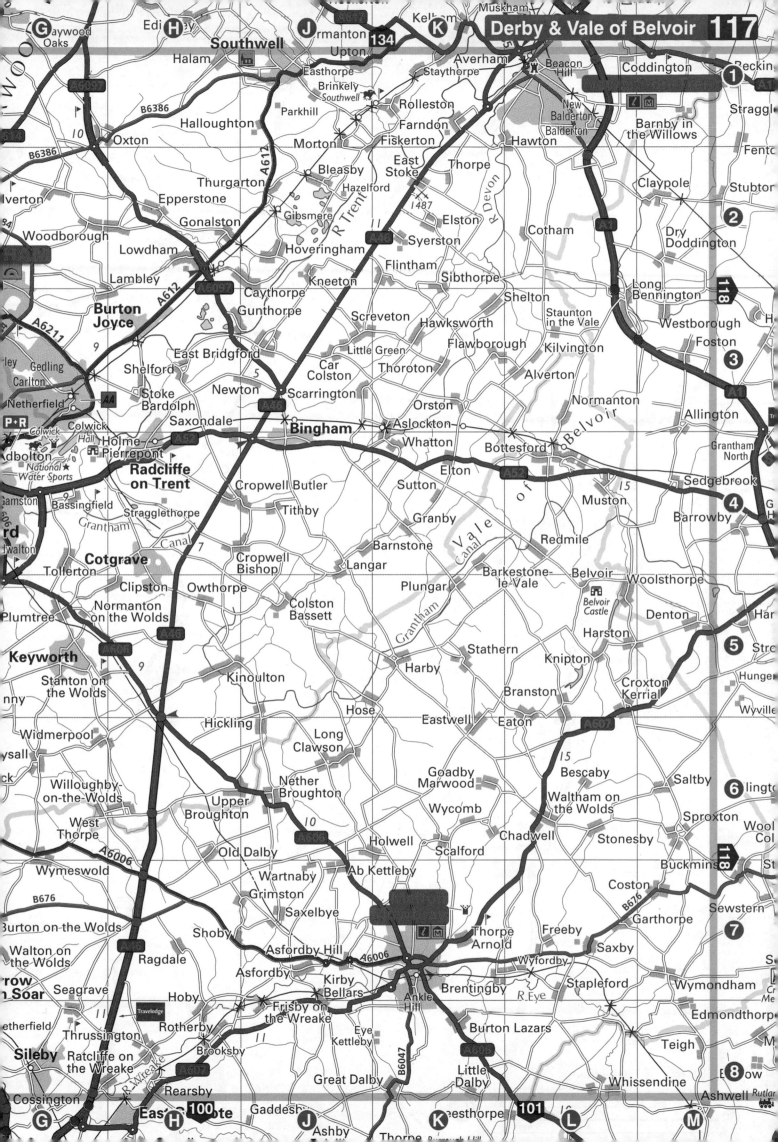

Friskney

Friskney Eaudike

Wrangle
Common ①

23

Wrangle
Lowgate

Wrangle

Hurn's End ②

asgate
gton
End

◀ 119

③

THE WASH

④

⑤

Dawsmere

Gedney
Drove End

B1359

⑥ utton

119

apelgate

Little London
★ Butterfly & Falconry Park

Long Sutton

Sutton
Bridge ▶

⑦ Travelodge

sses

Tydd
Gote

Tydd
St Mary

Walpole
Cross Keys

Walpole
St Andrew

Hay Green

Four
Gotes

Walpole
St Peter

Tydd
St Giles

8

⑧ wton

Ingleborough

River Nene

West
Walton

Rattan Row

**Terrington
St Clement**

Little
London

Clenchwarton
African Violet Centre

137
11

Tilney
All Saints

Tilney High End

12

St John's
Highway

Tilney St
Lawrence

West
Lynn

Saddle
Bow

Wiggenhall
St Germans

Wiggenhall
St Mary

Great Ouse

North
Wootton

South Wootton

Gaywood

West
Winch

A1078

A148

North
Runcton

Setchey

Old
Hunstanton

Holme ne
the Sea

🛈 📣
Hunstanton

Ringstead

A149

Norfolk
Lavender

Heacham

Sedgeford

Snettisham

Park Farm
Southgate

Shernb

RSPB

Ingoldisthorpe

12

B1440

Dersingham

Doddshill

Wolferton

Babingley River

A149

B1439

Sandringha
West New

B1440

Castle Rising

Congham

A148

Roydon

A149

B1145

Bawsey

Gayton

🛈 Ⓜ

Brow-of-
the-Hill

Ashwicke

East
Winch

Middleton

Blackborough
End

West
Bilne

Pott
Row

B1153

Na

Pentne

0   1   2   3   4   5 miles
0   1   2   3   4   5   6   7 kilometres

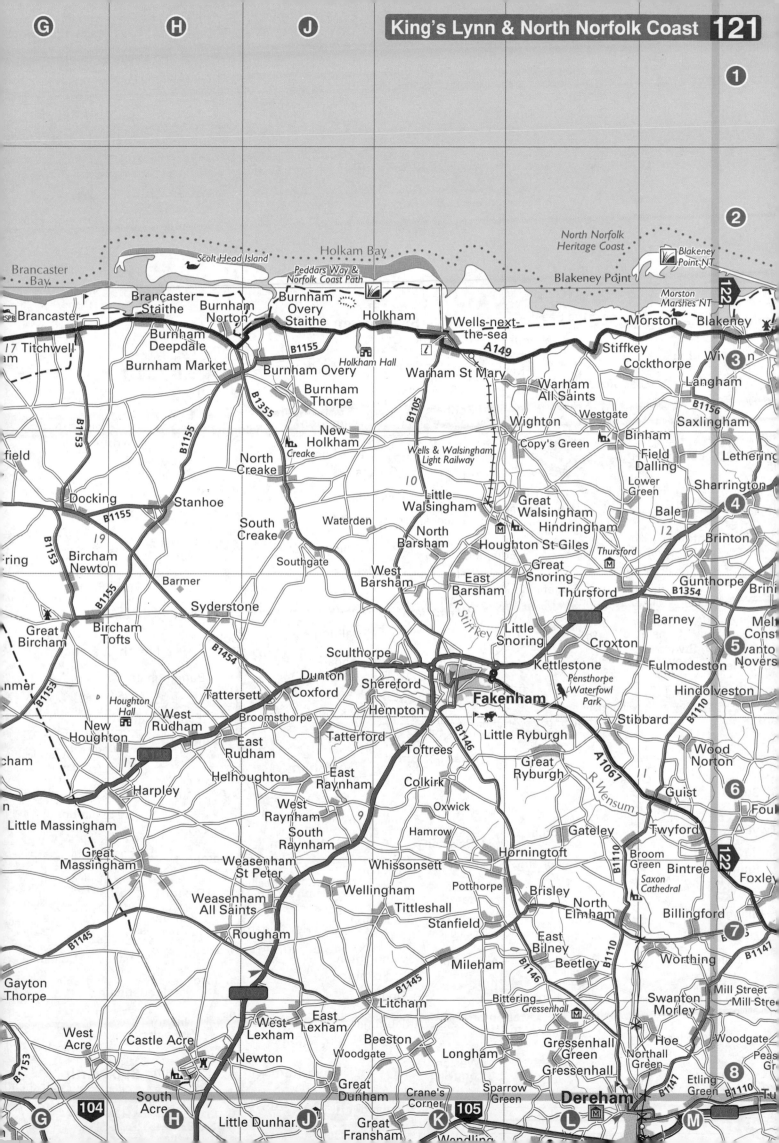

1

2

3

4

5

6

7

8

Mundesley

tow Mill

Paston
B1159

thorpe

Bacton

Walcott

Pollard
Street

Ridlington

rpe

Witton

Ridlington
Street

Happisburgh

Crostwight

Whimpwell Green

Happisburgh
Common

Eccles on Sea

oning

Hempstead

Lessingham

Ingham
Corner

Sea Palling

riggate

East
Ruston

B1159

Ingham

Waxham

tead

Stalham

Calthorpe
Street

Dilham

Stalham
Green

Hickling

Horsey Corner

Low
Street

A149

Sutton

Hickling Green

Horsey

burgh

Pennygate

Barton
Turf

Wood
Street

Hickling
Heath

Hill Common

Horsey Windpump NT

B1159

Barton
Broad

Catfield

Hickling
Broad

gate
eet

Neatishead

Irstead

R Ant

Catfield
Common

7

Potter
Heigham

West
Somerton

East
Somerton

Threehammer
Common

Sharp
Green

B1152

Winterton-on-Sea

oveton

Ludham

Martham

B1159

Johnson's
Street

Bastwick

Cess

Hemsby
Hole

A1062

pper
treet

R Thurne

Hemsby

Horning

Upper Street

Repps

9

Ormesby
Broad

Newport

Scratby

stwick

Rollesby

Ormesby
St Margaret

house

Broadland
Conservation Centre

Thurne

Burgh St
Margaret Ormesby
St Michael

California

Ranworth

40

Fairhaven

Pilson
Green

Clippesby

Billockby

9

A149

Pan orth

South

B1064

Mautby

The Skerries

CARMEL HEAD

*Dun Laoghaire
Dublin*

North Anglesey Heritage
Wylfa
Head Cemae
Bay

Cemlyn
Bay

Hen
Borth

Cemaes

Tregele

Llanfairynghornwy

Llanfechell

17

Llanfflewyn

Llanrhyddlad

Church
Bay

**Holyhead
Bay**

Porth
Tywynmawr

Llanb

Llanfaethlu

North Stack
**Gogarth
Bay**

Breakwater
Quarry

Llanfwrog

Llanddeusant

Stryd-y-
Facsen

Elim

Llaingoch

Llantrisant

Llanfigael

Pen-llyn

Llyn
Llywena

South Stack

*Holyhead
Mountain
Hut Group*

Llanfachraeth

Holyhead Mountain Heritage Coast

RSPB

South
Stack

Kingsland

Penrhos

Llanynghenedl

Penrhyn Mawr

Penrhos-
Feilw

A5

A5025

Valley

Bodedern

B5109

Trefignath

Caergeiliog

B454

Trearddur Bay

B454

Bryngw

HOLY ISLAND

Four Mile
Bridge

Llanfihangel
yn Nhowyn

Llanfair-yn-Neubwll

Llechylched

RSPB

Capel Gwyn

10

A4080

Rhoscolyn

Plas-
Cymyran

Ty Newydd

Pencar

Rhoscolyn
Head

Cymyran
Bay

Rhosneigr

Llanfaelog
Bryn Du

A4080

*Barclodiad
y Gawres*

Porth Trecastell

Llang

Aberffraw

**Aberffraw
Bay**

*Aberffraw Bay
Heritage Coast*

Malltrae

Llanddywn

C A E R N A R F O N

| 0 | 1 | 2 | 3 | 4 | 5 miles |
| 0 | 1 | 2 | 3 | 4 | 5 | 6 | 7 kilometres |

B A Y

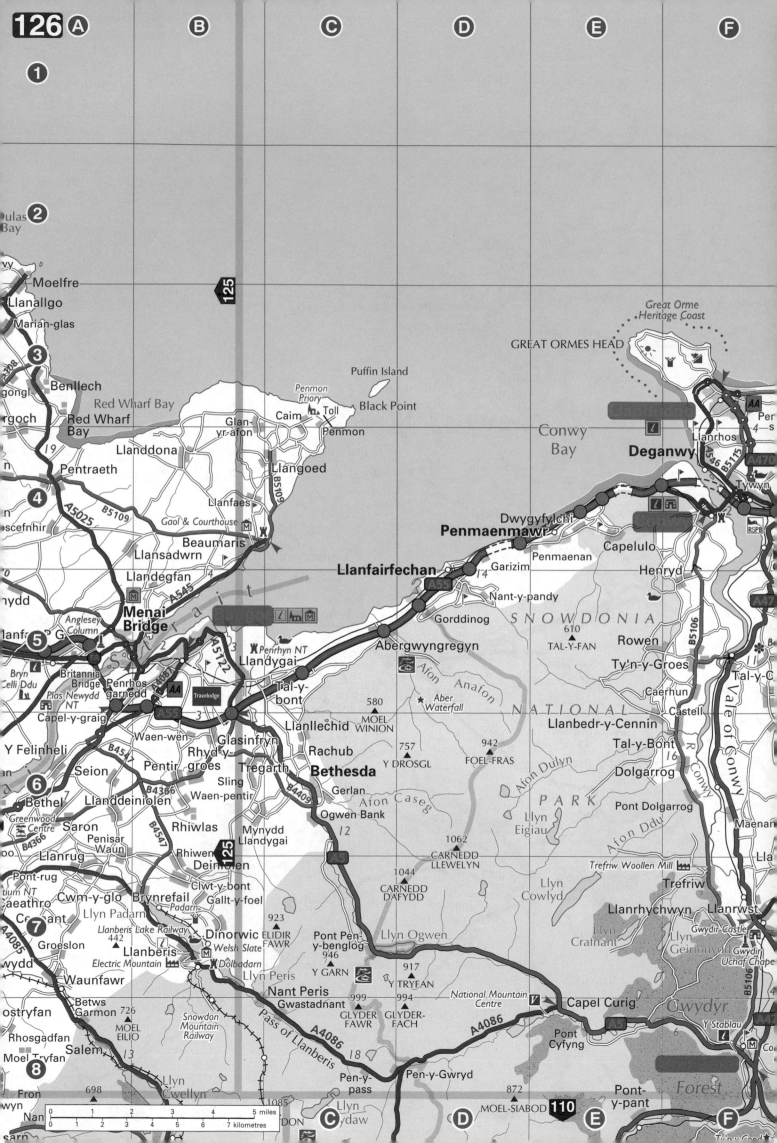

G   H   J

1

2

← Dublin

128

e Ormes Head

Penrhyn Bay

Rhos-on-Sea

Abergele-Roads

Kinmel Bay

Kinmel Bay

Rhyl

Prestatyn

RSPB   Tal
A548

Gronant
Llanasa   Picton
Gwaenysgor   Treloga

Meliden   Axton   Berthe
B5119   Wälwen

Colwyn Bay

ndrillo-yn-Rhos

7   A55

Mochdre   Old   Colwyn

udno   tion

Llanelian-yn-Rhos   B5383

Llysfaen   Rhyd-y-foel

Llanddulas   A547

Pensarn

5   Towyn

A547

Rhuddlan

Trelawnyd   A51
Dyserth   4   12 W
Cwm

B5429   Rhuallt   ll   Pen-

Pengwern

Bodelwyddan   3

A525   St Asaph

Offa's Dyke

Trelawnyd

Bryn-y-Maen

ffraid   nwy

B5381

Dolwen

Betws-yn-Rhos   B5381

A548

St George   6   25   A55

Bodelwyddan

Glascoed

Groesffordd   Marli

B5381

St Asaph

Tremeirchion

Graig   Caerwys   5
Sodom

A525

Trofarth   Dawn

Llanfair Talhaiarn

Pentre Isaf

A525

Trefnant   A541   Bodfari   Afon-w

River Elwy

17

A544

Llannefydd

B5428   5   River Clwyd   B5429   Clwy

Hafodunos

Llangernyw   B5382

Cefn Berain

Henllan   Green   Fron

B5382   Kilford   Waen   langw   6

Brook House   Llandyrnog

Llansannan

Tan-y-fron

Rhydgaled

6

A543

Denbigh

Llwyn   Llanynys

ren-y-fedw   lind   mon   A548

Pandy Tudur   B5384

Gwytherin

Afon Derfyn

Afon Aled

Bylchau   A544   B5435   Waen

Nantglyn

Groes   Peniel   Prion   Pentre   A525

Pant-pastynog   128

Pentre Llanrhaeadr   Pentre

B5113

Llyn Aled   A543   B4501

Archaeological Trail   Llyn Brenig

Pentre Saron

467   MOEL SEISIOG   448   MOEL LLYN

Mynydd Hiraethog

Llanfwrog

Y Gyffylliog   Bontuchel

Nebo   Llyn Alwen   Llyn Brenig

pel   mon   B5113

V   Llyn Brenig

Clocaenog   Pv   Clawdd-

Rhe

7

8   Efenecht

G   H   111   J   K   L   M

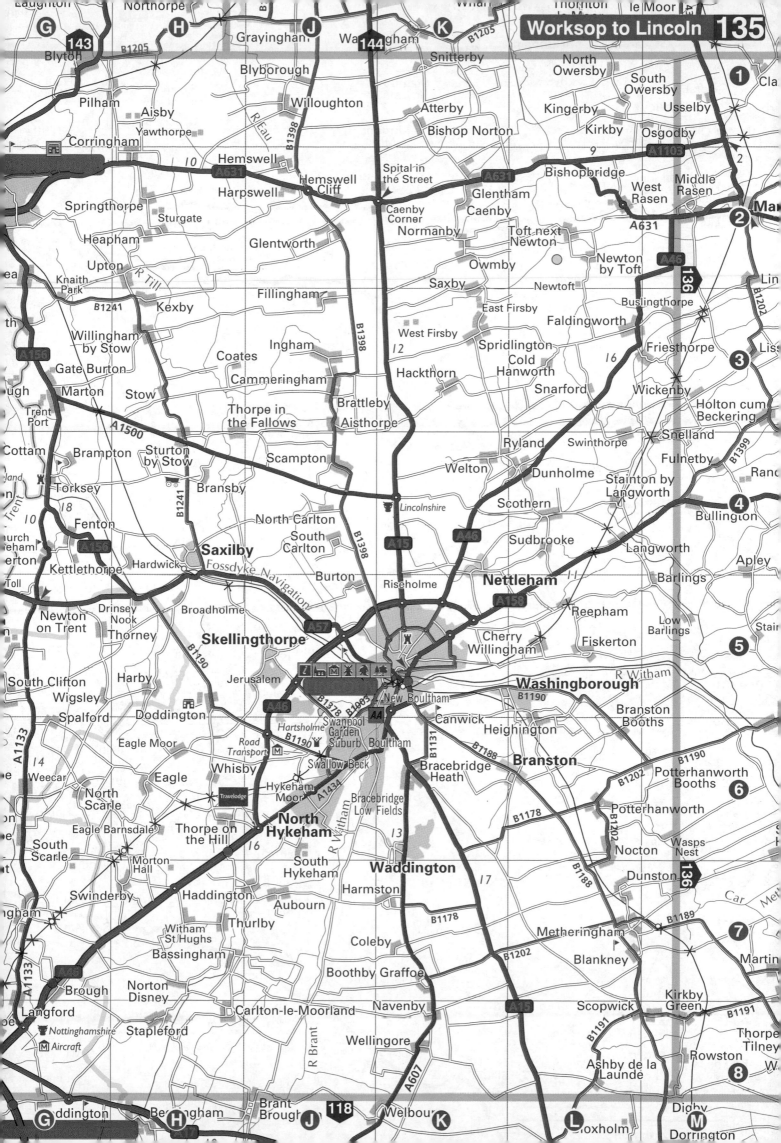

1

2

3

4

5

6

7

8

G H J K L M

Somercotes

C G ...holme
Church End
Skidbrooke North End
Saltfleet
A15

...omew
...urgh
...vingham
South Somercotes
North Cockerington
North End
South Cockerington
Grimoldby
Stewton
Manby
Little Carlton
Great Carlton
B1200
Saltfleetby St Clement
Saltfleetby All Saints
Saltfleetby St Peter
Theddlethorpe St Helen
Theddlethorpe All Saints
A1031

Skidbrooke

Mablethorpe

Great Eau
Legbourne
A157
North Reston
South Reston
Gayton le Marsh
Strubby
Withern
A1104
Thorpe
Maltby le Marsh
A52
Trusthorpe
Sutton on Sea
Sandilands

Tothill
Authorpe
B1373
Woodthorpe
Claythorpe
Belleau
Watermill & Wildfowl Gardens
Aby
Thoresthorpe
South Thoresby
Ailby
Hagnaby
Beesby
Saleby
Asserby Turn
Markby
Asserby
Hannah
A1111
A52
Anderby Creek

White Pit
Swaby
Calceby
Haugh
Rigsby
Bilsby
Thurlby
Huttoft
Anderby
B1449
18

Brinkhill
Driby
Ulceby Cross
A1104
Well
Mawthorpe
Ulceby
B1196
Farlesthorpe
Cumberworth
Bonthorpe
Helsey
Mumby
Authorpe Row
Chapel Point
Chapel St Leonards

...rrington
Sutterby
Langton
A1028
Claxby
Willoughby
Hogsthorpe
Slackholme End
Fantasy Island

...wardby
Dalby
Skendleby
Hasthorpe
Sloothby
Habertoft
Addlethorpe
Ingoldmells
Ingoldmells Point

Sausthorpe
Grebby
Partney
Scremby
Welton le Marsh
Candlesby
Orby
A52

R
Lymm
Raithby
A16
Ashby by Partney
Gunby
Winthorpe

Hundleby
Spilsby
New Spilsby
Halton Holegate
Monksthorpe
7
Burgh le Marsh
A158
SKEGNESS

Toynton All Saints
Northcote
Halton Fenside
B1195
Great Steeping
Bratoft
Seacroft

East Keal
Keal Cotes
Toynton St Peter
Toynton Fen Side
Little Steeping
Firsby
Irby in the Marsh
Croft
Wainfleet Haven
Gibraltar

...West ...eal
Fendike Corner
Thorpe St Peter
Wainfleet Bank
Wainfleet All Saints
Gibraltar Point

New Leake
Midville
East Fen
Eastville
Friskney
Key's Toft
A52
Friskney Eaudike

A15
119
Lade Bank
...rangle ...mmon
120

G H J

1

2

3

4

5

6

7

8

Etherdwick
Newton
G
B1238 B1242 H
Garton
153
atley
Humbleton
Fitling
Grimston
Hilston
Owstwick
North
End
Danthorpe
Tunstall
Elstronwick
End
on
Burton
Pidsea
Roos
Waxholme
B1242
Ry
ope
B1362
Rimswell
Owthorne
Burstwick
West
End
M **Withersea**
Thorngumbald
Halsham
East End
B1362
i
Keyingham
A1033
Hollym
Ryehill
16
Winestead
4
Holmpton
Ottringham
A1033
Patrington
Out
Newton
Welwick
Sunk
Island
Weeton
Easington
Skeffling
B1445
South End
Kilnsea

HUMBER

ingham
k

Spurn Heritage Coast

SPURN HEAD

Travelodge
M
GRIMSBY
A180
A180
i
West Marsh
Cleethorpes
A1210
Great
Coates
A1136
Little
Coates
Old
Clee
Thrunscoe
V
esby
6
Nunsthorpe
A46
Pleasure Island
A46
A46
A1098
Bradley
Scartho
Humberston
Rotterdam (Europoort)
Zeebrugge
Laceby
B1203
B1219
y upon
mber
Waltham
New Waltham
Barnoldby
le Beck
Holton
le Clay
A1031
Beelsby
Brigsley
North
End
RSPB
Tetney Lock
A18
Ashby-cum
Fenby
Hatcliffe
Waithe
Tetney
North Cotes
West
Ravendale
Grainsby
Marsh-Chapel
East
Ravendale
North
Thoresby
17
Eskham
West
End
29
Grainthorpe
Wold
Newton
B1201
Churchthorpe
North
Somercotes
15
A16
Fulstow
Conisholme
A1031
B1203
Ludborough
Covenham
St Bartholomew
Church
End
Skidbrooke North End
Binbrook
136
North
Ormsby
Covenha
St Mary
South
Somercotes
Saltf
G H J K L M

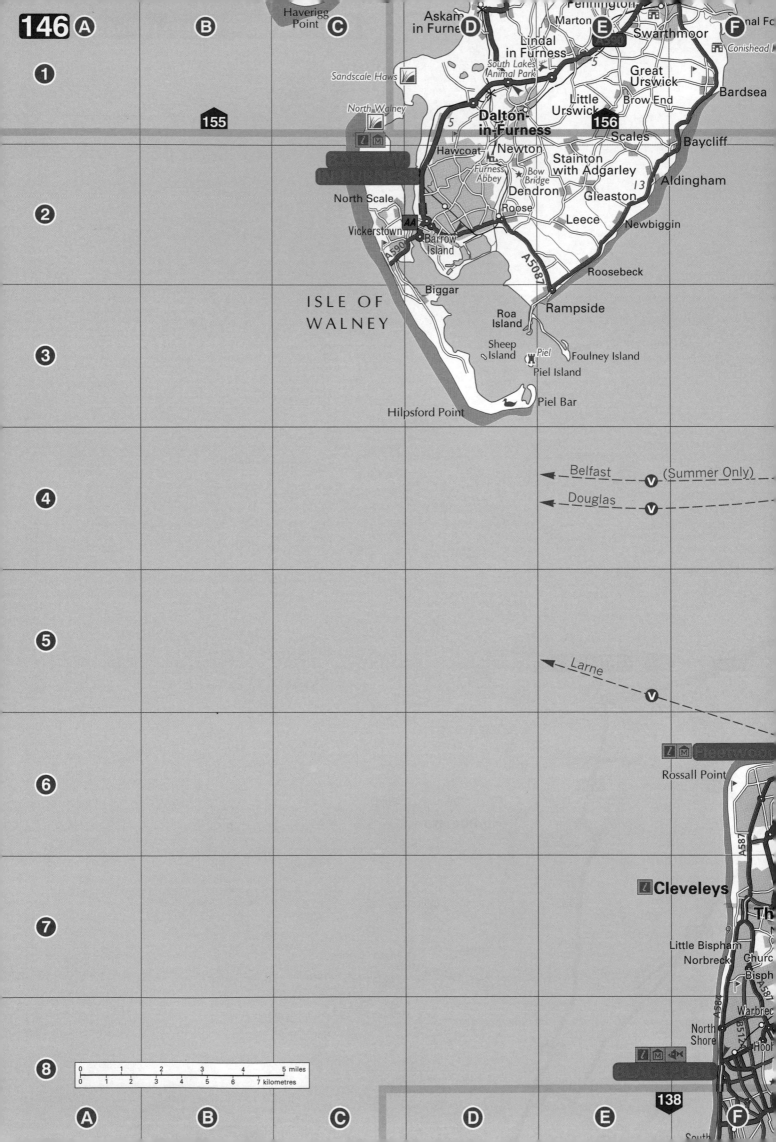

Haverigg
Point Ⓒ

Askam
in Furne Ⓓ

Pennington

Marton
Swarthmoor Ⓔ

nal Fo Ⓕ

Conishead

Sandscale Haws

South Lakes
Animal Park

Lindal
in Furness

5

Great
Urswick

Bardsea

North Walney

Brow End
Little
Urswick

5

Dalton-
in-Furness

156

Scales

Baycliff

Hawcoat

Newton

Stainton
with Adgarley

Aldingham

Furness
Abbey

Bow
Bridge

Dendron

13

Gleaston

North Scale

AA

Roose

Leece

Newbiggin

Vickerstown

Barrow
Island

A590

A5087

Roosebeck

Biggar

ISLE OF
WALNEY

Roa
Island

Rampside

Sheep
Island

Piel

Foulney Island

Piel Island

Piel Bar

Hilpsford Point

Belfast ◄ Ⓥ (Summer Only)

Douglas ◄ Ⓥ

Larne ◄

Ⓥ

Fleetwood

Rossall Point

Cleveleys

Th

Little Bispham

Norbreck
Churc

Bisph

A587

North
Shore

Warbrec

A584
B512

Hoo

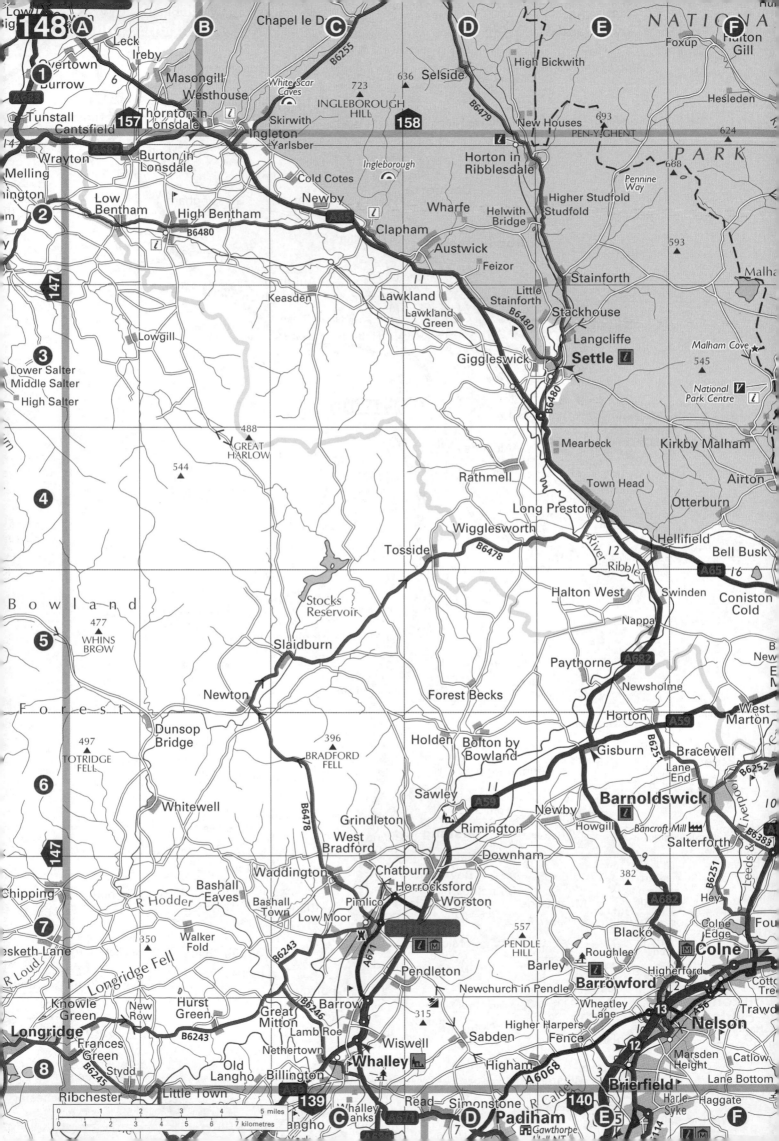

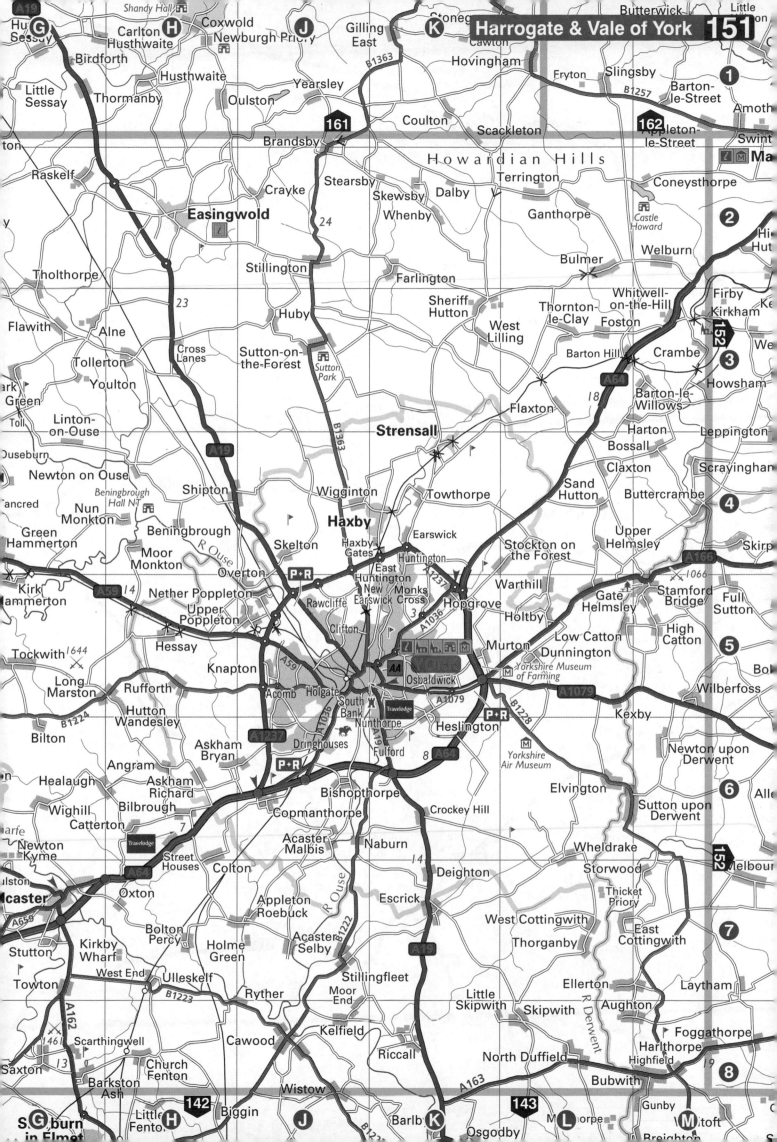

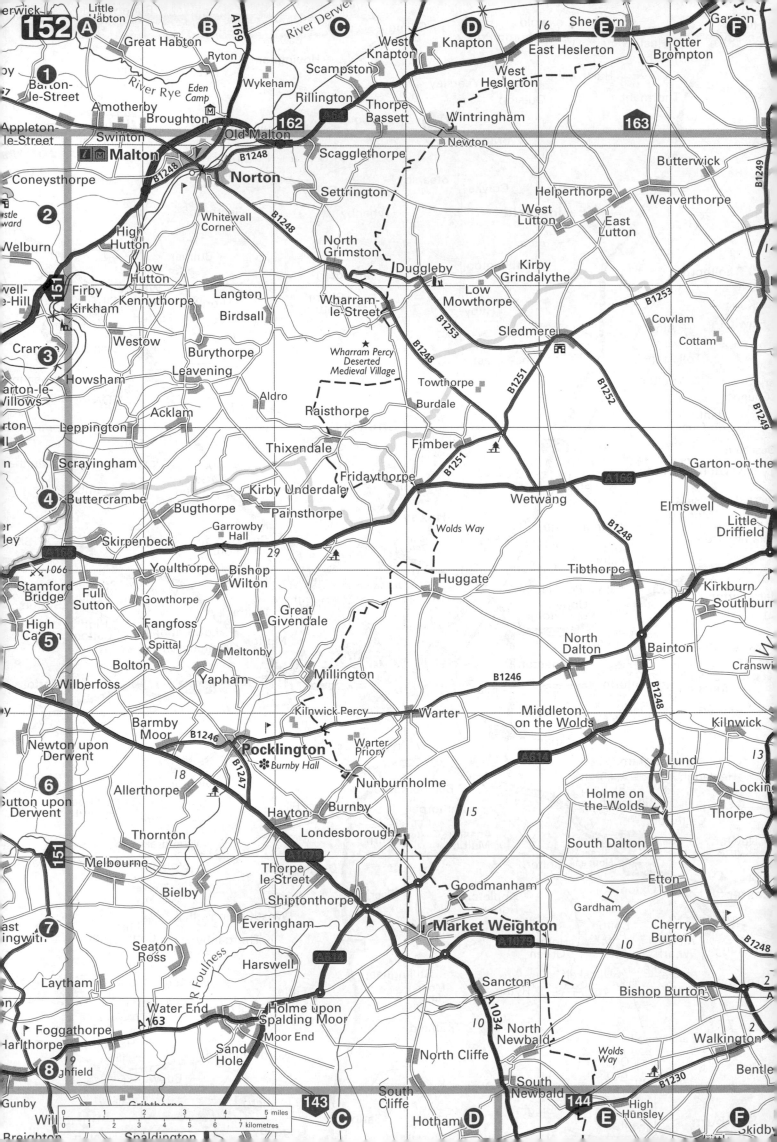

G **Hunmanby** H J

① ② ③ ④ ⑤ ⑥ ⑦ ⑧

Fordon

Wold Newton

Burton Fleming

Reighton

Speeton

B1229

163

A165

Grindale

Flamborough Head Heritage Coast
Thornwick Bay

RSPB

Buckton

Bempton

B1229

North Landing

Selwicks Bay

FLAMBOROUGH HEAD

Marton

B1259

B1255

Flamborough

Monolith

Rudston

B1253

Boynton

Sewerby

A1038

Bondville Miniature Village

BRIDLINGTON BAY

Bessingby

Carnaby

Hilderthorpe

i M

Haisthorpe

Thornholme

Kilham

Burton Agnes

12

Norman Manor House

S

A165

Harpham

ston Parva

Lowthorpe

D

Fraisthorpe

Nafferton

A614

Little Kelk

Gransmoor

Great Kelk

Lissett

Barmston

ield

L

Wansford

R Hull

Skerne

B1249

Gembling

15

B1242

Cruckley Animal Farm

Foston on the Wolds

Dringhoe

Ulrome

Skipsea

16

Beeford

Brigham

Upton

Skipsea Brough

North Frodingham

Rotsea

Dunnington

A165

Hempholme

Atwick

Nunkeeling

Bewholme

B1242

Burshill

Hornsea Mere

i M

Hornsea

Brandesburton

Seaton

6

B1244

Sigglesthorne

Rolston

Aike

gh

Leven

Catwick

Goxhill

Mappleton

Mappleton Sands

Great Cowden

rley

7

A1035

Routh

H

Little Catwick

B1243

Little Hatfield

Rise

Great Hatfield

B1242

i M

Tickton

Arnold

New Ellerby

North End

Withernwick

Meaux

O

Skirlaugh

Marton

Weel

Long Riston

West Newton

Aldbrough

A1174

Woodmansey

L

Old Ellerby

D

Etherdwick

17

East Newton

R Hull

Wawne

A165

Burton Constable Hall

Flinton

B1238

B1242

Garton

Thearne

8

079

13

Grimston

144

Dunswell

Swine

Coniston

Thirtleby

145

Humbleto

Hilston

G H J K L M

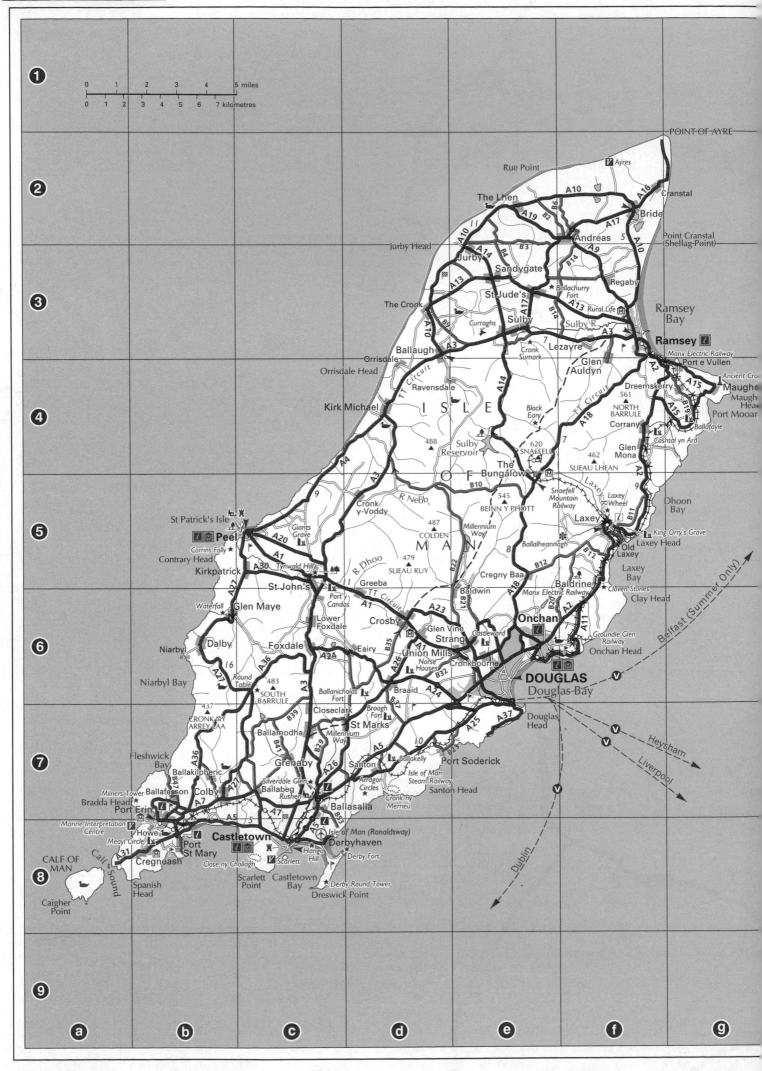

POINT OF AYRE

Rue Point
Ayres
The Lhen
A10
A16
Cranstal
A19
B2
B6
A17
Bride
Jurby Head
A14
B4
B3
Andreas
Point Cranstal (Shellag Point)
Jurby
A13
Sandygate
B14
A9
A10
St Jude's
Ballachurry Fort
Regaby
The Cronk
A17
Ramsey Bay
A10
Sulby
B14
Rural Life
Ramsey
Ballaugh
A3
Curraghs
Sulby R.
Cronk Sumark
Lezayre
Glen Auldyn
A2
Manx Electric Railway
Orrisdale
A3
Port e Vullen
Orrisdale Head
Ravensdale
A14
TT Circuit
561
Dreemskerry
A15
Ancient Cro
ISLE
Block Eary
NORTH BARRULE
Maugh
Kirk Michael
A18
Corrany
Maugh Hea
620
SNAEFELL
7
462
Glen Mona
Port Mooar
A4
488
Sulby Reservoir
SLIEAU LHEAN
Cashtal yn Ard
Ballafayle
A3
The Bungalow
Snaefell Mountain Railway
A2
OF
B10
Laxey Wheel
Dhoon Bay
St Patrick's Isle
R. Nebb
545
BEINN Y PHOTT
9
Corrins Folly
Peel
A20
Giants Grave
487
Millennium Way
Laxey
King Orry's Grave
Laxey Head
Contrary Head
A1
COLDEN
MAN
Ballalheannagh
Old Laxey
Laxey Bay
Kirkpatrick
A30
Tynwald Hill
479
SLIEAU RUY
B22
Cregny Baa
B12
Cloven Stones
St John's
R. Dhoo
8
B11
Clay Head
Glen Maye
Greeba
Baldwin
A18
Baldrine
Waterfall
Port y Candas
TT Circuit
A23
B20
Manx Electric Railway
Lower Foxdale
A1
Crosby
B21
Castleward
Groudle Glen Railway
Niarbyl
Dalby
Foxdale
Eairy
B35
Glen Vine
Onchan
A11
Onchan Head
Niarbyl Bay
A24
Union Mills
Strang
16
483
A26
Norse Houses
B32
DOUGLAS
Round Table
SOUTH BARRULE
Ballanicholas Fort
Cronkbourne
Douglas Bay
437
A3
Braaid
B37
A25
A37
Douglas Head
CRONK NY ARREY LAA
B39
Closeclark
Brooh Fort
Fleshwick Bay
A36
St Marks
Ballamodha
B30
Millennium Way
A5
10
Ballakilpheric
A27
Grenaby
A26
Santon
Isle of Man Steam Railway
Santon Head
Milners Tower
Ballafesson
Colby
Silverdale Glen
Ballakelly
Bradda Head
A7
Ballabeg Rushen
Arragon Circles
Port Soderick
Port Erin
A5
A7
Cronk ny Merreu
Marine Interpretation Centre
Ballasalla
Howe
Meayl Circle
Port St Mary
Isle of Man (Ronaldsway)
CALF OF MAN
A31
Castletown
Derbyhaven
Cregneash
Close ny Chollagh
Scarlett
Hango Hill
Derby Fort
Spanish Head
Scarlett Point
Castletown Bay
Derby Round Tower
Caigher Point
Dreswick Point

Belfast (Summer Only)

Heysham

Liverpool

Dublin

Scale: 0 1 2 3 4 5 miles
0 1 2 3 4 5 6 7 kilometres

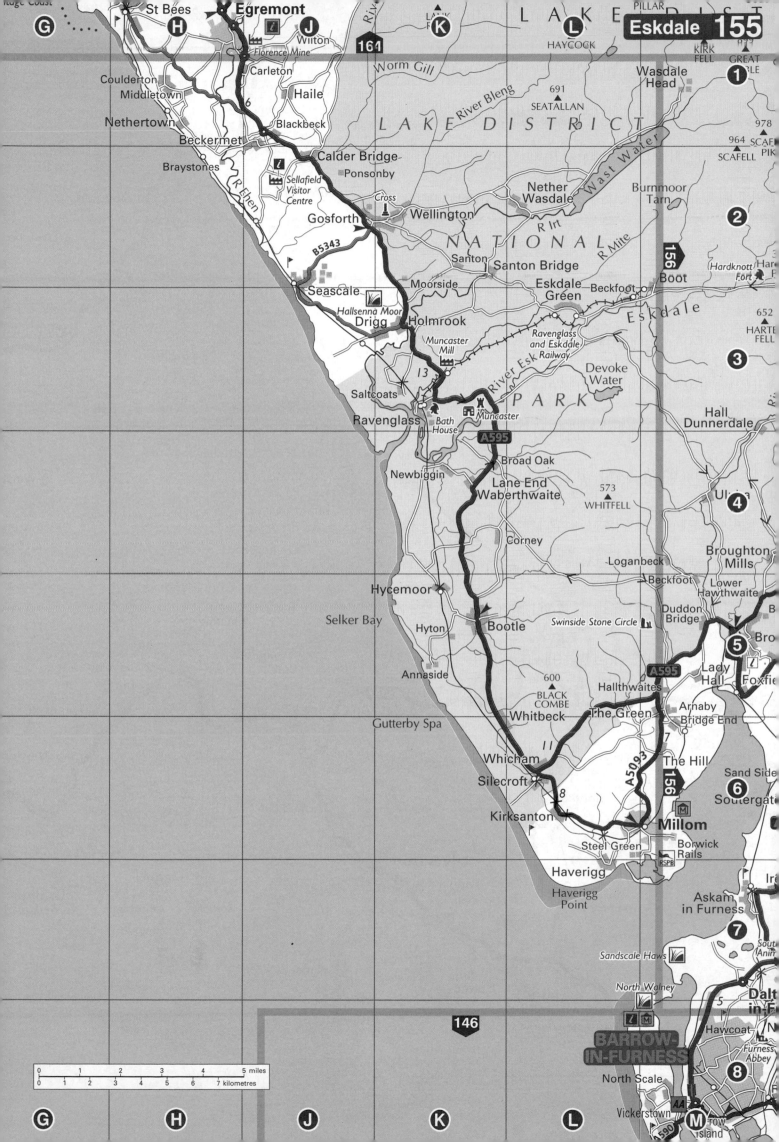

G · · · · · · **St Bees** **H** **Egremont** **J**

K

L **HAYCOCK** **LAKE DISTRICT**

PILLAR

KIRK FELL

GREAT ABLE **1**

Wilton

Florence Mine

Carleton

161

Worm Gill

Wasdale Head

2

Coulderton
Middletown

Haile

River Bleng

691
SEATALLAN

978

Nethertown

Blackbeck

LAKE DISTRICT

964 SCAFELL PIKE
SCAFELL

Beckermet

Braystones

Calder Bridge

Ponsonby

Nether Wasdale

Wast Water

R Irt

Burnmoor Tarn

R Ehen

Sellafield Visitor Centre

Cross

Wellington

Santon

NATIONAL

R Mite

156

Boot

Hardknott Fort

Hare

Gosforth

B5343

Moorside

Santon Bridge

Eskdale Green

Beckfoot

652
HARTE FELL

Seascale

Hallsenna Moor

Holmrook

Muncaster Mill

Ravenglass and Eskdale Railway

Eskdale

3

Drigg

13

PARK

River Esk

Devoke Water

Hall Dunnerdale

Saltcoats

Ravenglass

Bath House

Muncaster

A595

Broad Oak

Newbiggin

Lane End
Waberthwaite

573
WHITFELL

Ulpha **4**

Corney

Loganbeck

Broughton Mills

Beckfoot

Lower Hawthwaite

Hycemoor

Duddon Bridge

5 Bro

Selker Bay

Hyton

Bootle

Swinside Stone Circle

A595

Lady Hall

Foxfie

Annaside

600
BLACK COMBE

Hallthwaites

The Green

Arnaby
Bridge End

7

Gutterby Spa

Whitbeck

11

The Hill

Sand Side

Whicham

A5093

156

6 Soutergate

Silecroft

8

Kirksanton

Millom

Steel Green

Borwick Rails

RSPB

Haverigg

Askam in Furness

7

Haverigg Point

Sandscale Haws

North Walney

Dalt in F

146

BARROW-IN-FURNESS

Hawcoat

Furness Abbey

8

North Scale

Vickerstown

AA

M

row sland

A590

| 0 | 1 | 2 | 3 | 4 | 5 miles |
| 0 | 1 | 2 | 3 | 4 | 5 | 6 | 7 kilometres |

G **H** **J** **K** **L**

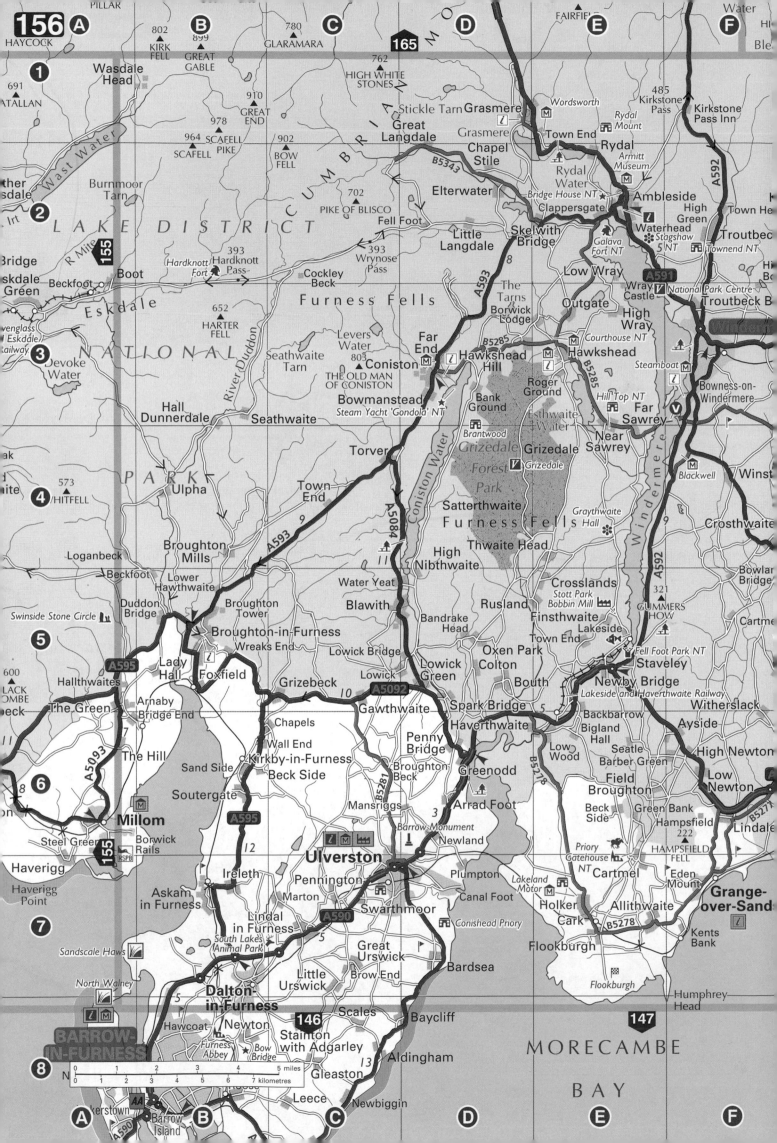

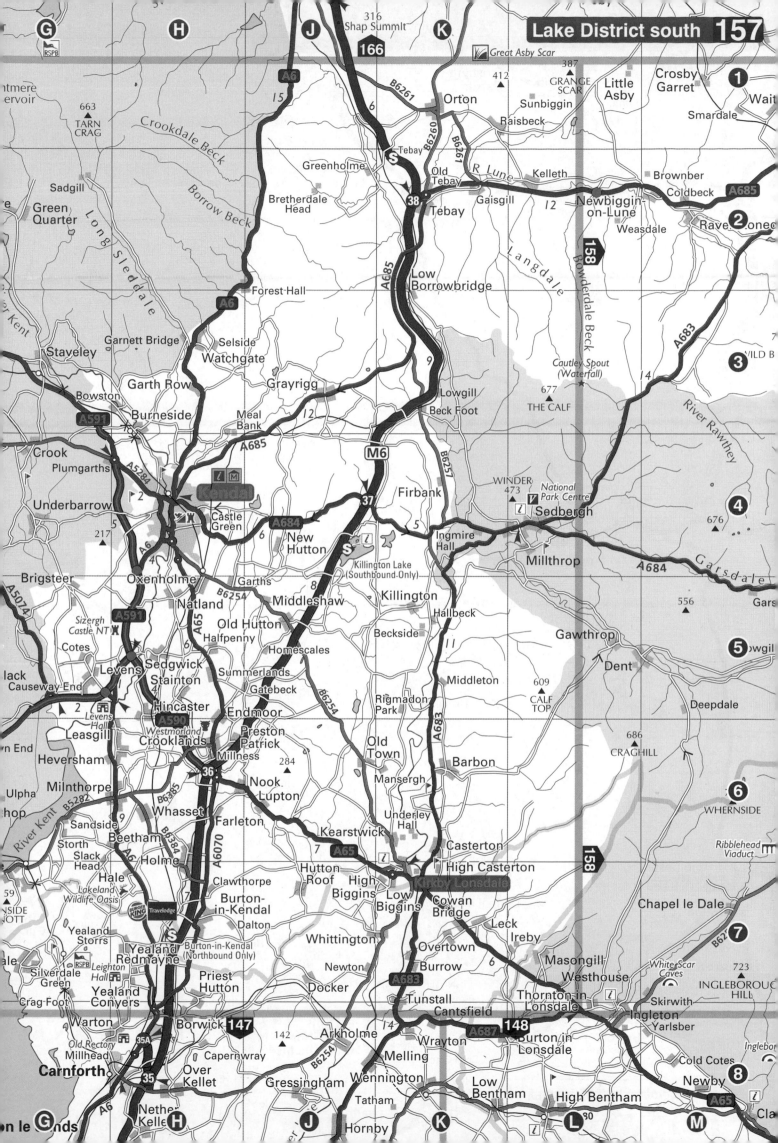

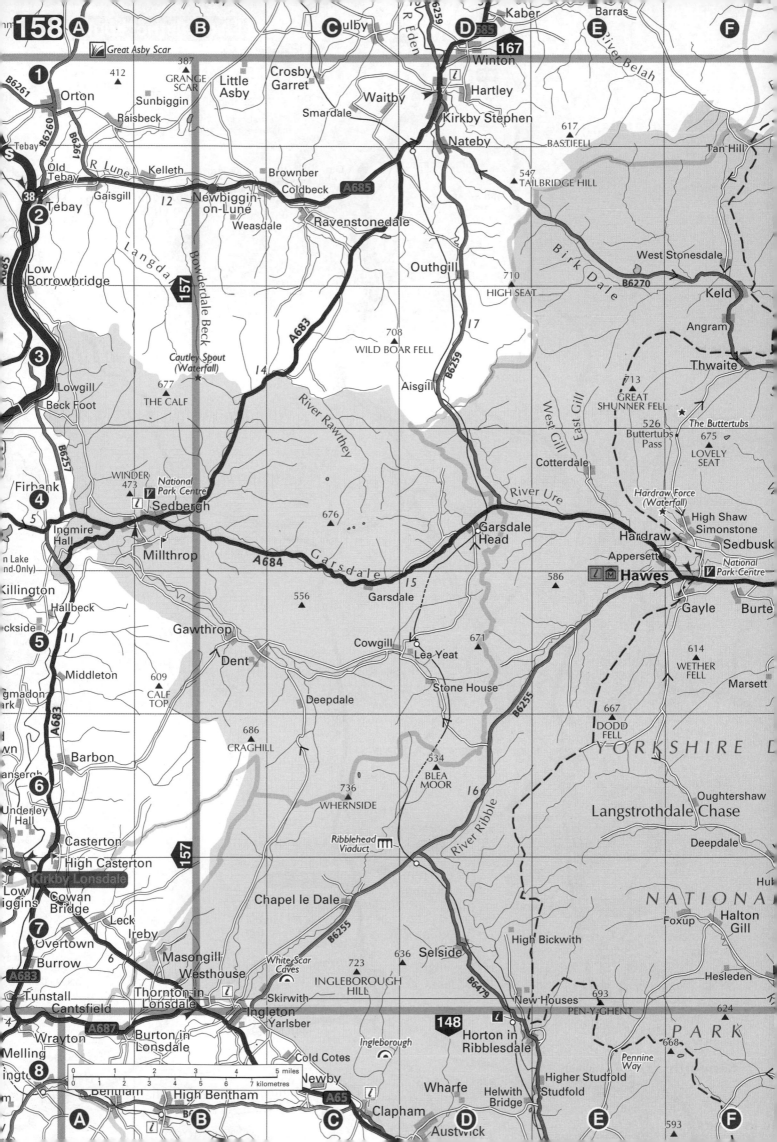

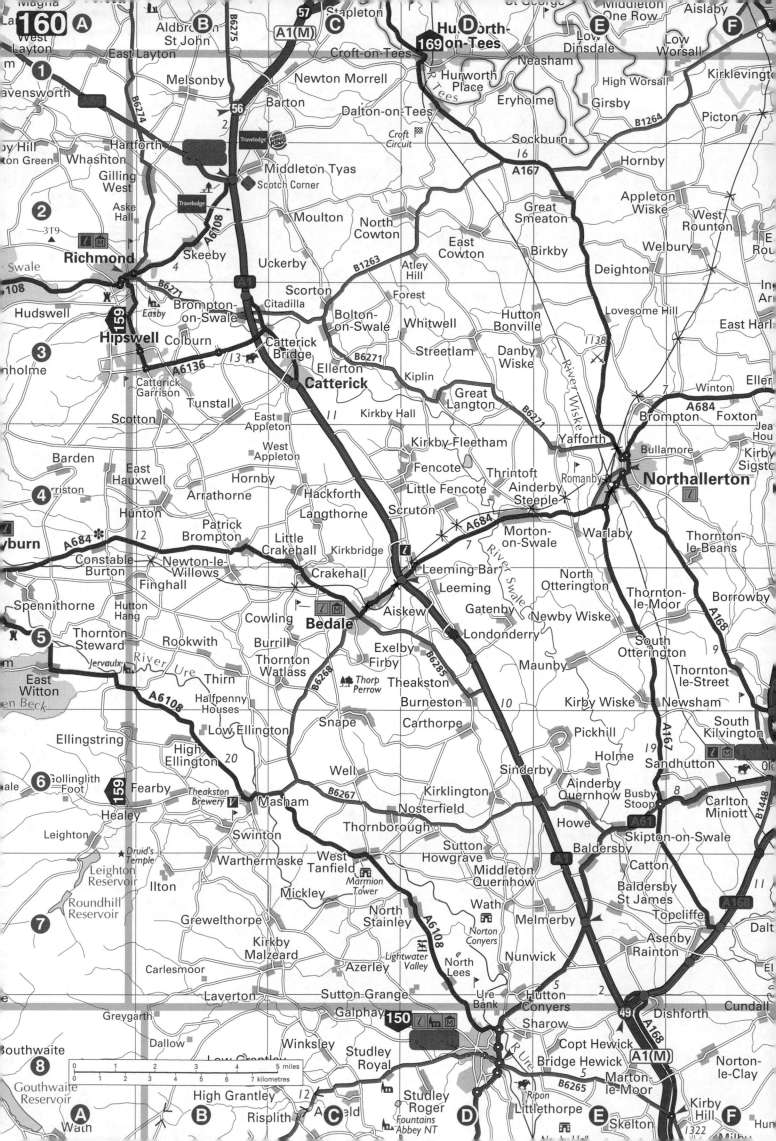

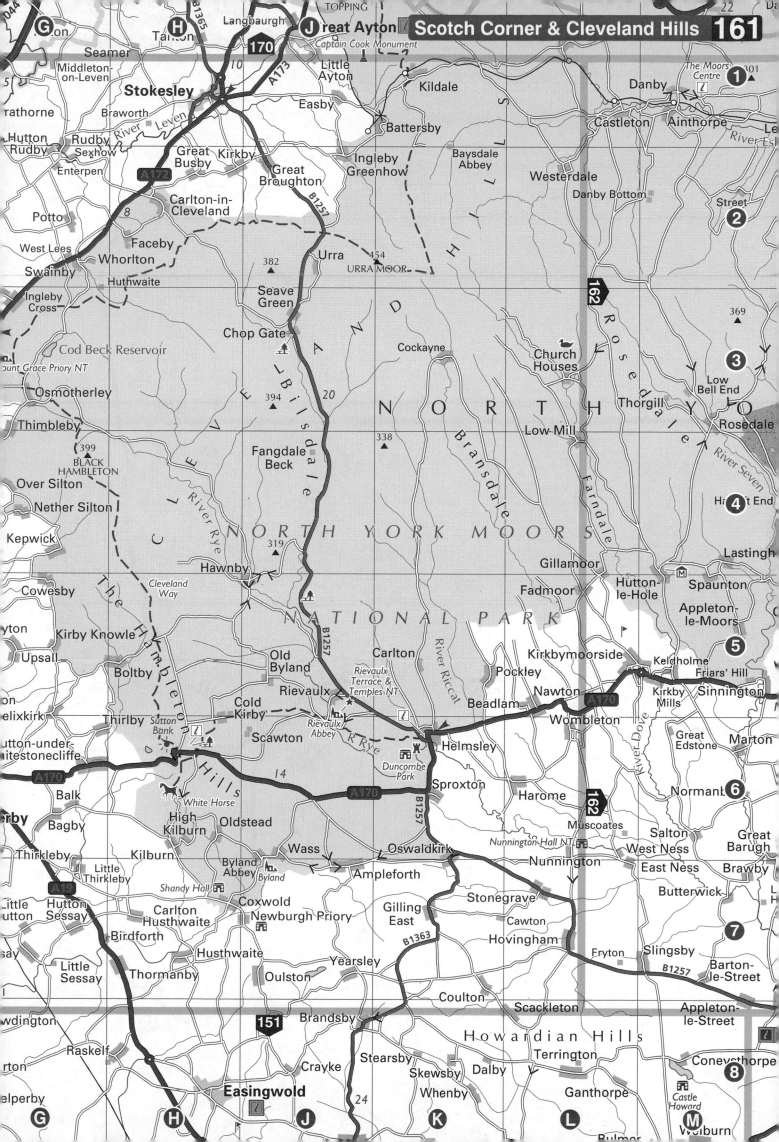

G · on

H Tanton
Langbaurgh

J reat Ayton
Captain Cook Monument

TOPPING

170

A173

Little Ayton

Easby

Kildale

1 The Moors Centre
301

Danby

Castleton · Ainthorpe · Le
River Es

B1365

Seamer
10

Middleton-on-Leven

Stokesley

rathorne

Braworth

River Leven

Hutton
Rudby

Rudby · Sexhow
Enterpen

Great Busby · Kirkby

Great Broughton

Battersby

Ingleby Greenhow

Baysdale Abbey

Westerdale

Danby Bottom

Street **2**

A172

8

Carlton-in-Cleveland

B1257

West Lees

Faceby

Whorlton

Huthwaite

Seave Green

Urra
454
URRA MOOR

382

162

369
3

Swainby

Ingleby Cross

Chop Gate

Cockayne

Church Houses

Low Bell End

Cod Beck Reservoir

ount Grace Priory NT

Osmotherley

N O R T H

Low Mill

Thorgill

Rosedale

River Seven

Thimbleby

394

20

Bransdale

Farndale

Ha t End **4**

399
BLACK HAMBLETON

Fangdale Beck

338

N O R T H   Y O R K   M O O R S

Over Silton

Nether Silton

Kepwick

River Rye

319

Hawnby

Gillamoor

Fadmoor

Hutton-le-Hole

Spaunton

Lastingh

Cowesby

Cleveland Way

Appleton-le-Moors

5

yton

Kirby Knowle

N A T I O N A L   P A R K

B1257

Old Byland

Carlton

River Riccal

Kirkbymoorside

Keldholme

Friars' Hill

Upsall

Boltby

Rievaulx Terrace & Temples NT

Pockley

Nawton

A170

Kirkby Mills

Sinnington

on
elixkirk

Thirlby

Sutton Bank

Cold Kirby

Rievaulx

Rievaulx Abbey

R Rye

Beadlam

Wombleton

Great Edstone

Marton

utton-under-
itestonecliffe

Scawton

Duncombe Park

Helmsley

Sproxton

Harome

162

Normanl **6**

A170

A170

Balk

Bagby

White Horse

High Kilburn

Oldstead

Wass

Oswaldkirk

Nunnington

Muscoates

Nunnington Hall NT

Salton

West Ness

East Ness

Great Barugh

Brawby

rby

Thirkleby

Little Thirkleby

Kilburn

Byland Abbey · Byland

Shandy Hall

Ampleforth

Gilling East

Stonegrave

Butterwick

7

A19

Little
utton

Hutton Sessay

Carlton Husthwaite

Coxwold
Newburgh Priory

Cawton

Hovingham

East Ness

say

Birdforth

B1363

Fryton

Slingsby

Barton-le-Street

Little Sessay

Thormanby

Husthwaite

Yearsley

Oulston

B1257

wdington

Raskelf

151

Brandsby

Coulton

Scackleton

H o w a r d i a n   H i l l s

Appleton-le-Street

8

rton

Easingwold

Crayke

Stearsby

Skewsby · Dalby

Terrington

Ganthorpe

Conevsthorpe

elperby

24

Whenby

Castle Howard

G　　**H**　　**J**　　**K**　　**L**　　**M**

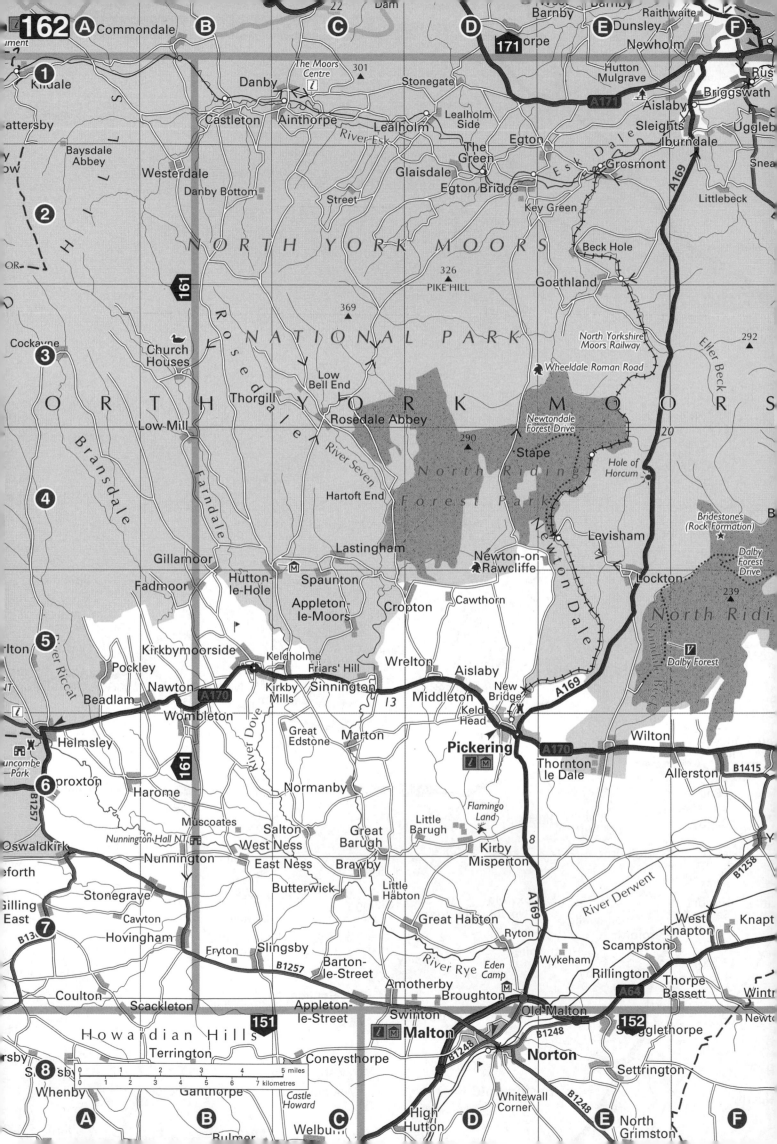

G
H
J

1
2
3
4
5
6
7
8

High Hawsker
Ness-Point or North-Cheek
Robin Hood's Bay
Raw
Fylingthorpe
Robin Hood's Bay
Old Peak or South Cheek
Ravenscar
20
Staintondale
Hayburn Wyke
Cloughton Newlands
Harwood Dale
Cloughton Wyke
Cloughton
Cromer Point
Burniston
Cleveland Way
Broxa
Silpho
Suffield
Newby
angdale End
Hackness
Scalby
Scarborough
Wrench Green
Everley
Sea Cut
Falsgrave
Hatherleigh Deep Sea Trawler
orest Park
River Derwent
A171
P+R
A170
AA
Oliver's Mount
Bee Dale
A165
West Ayton
East Ayton
Eastfield
Osgodby
Cayton Bay
Sawdon
Irton
Hutton Buscel
Seamer
Crossgates
B1261
High Killerby
The Wyke
Ruston
Wykeham
Cayton
7
7
Filey Brigg
snainton
17
Brompton
Lebberston
Gristhorpe
Filey
e
C
a
A64
R. Hertford
Muston
Willerby
Folkton
A1039
Flixton
West Flotmanby
Staxton
Filey Bay
16
Sherburn
Ganton
Wolds Way
Hunmanby
ast Heslerton
Potter Brompton
Fordon
Reighton
Speeton
Flambor
Foxholes
Wold Newton
RSPB
153
Burton Fleming
Buckton
Bempton
Butterwick
B1249
Grindale
A165
B1229
Helperthorpe
Weaverthorpe
Thwing
11
est
East Lutton
Octon
Ser...erby
Bondville
14

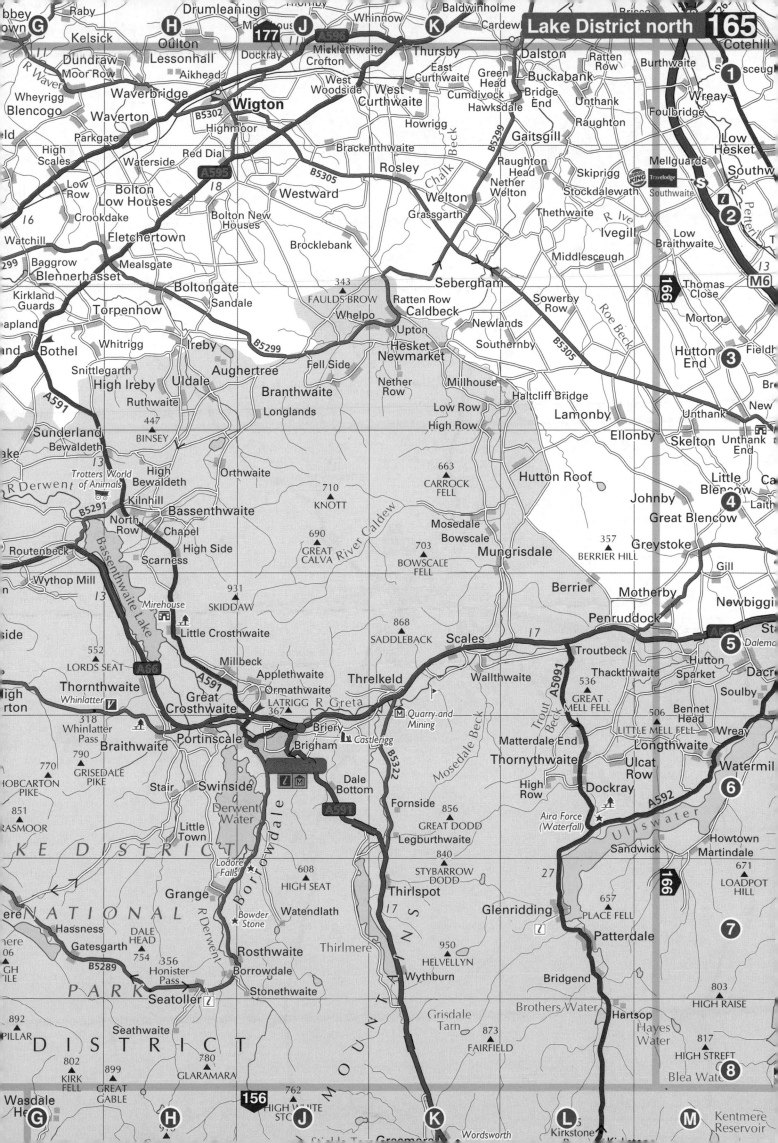

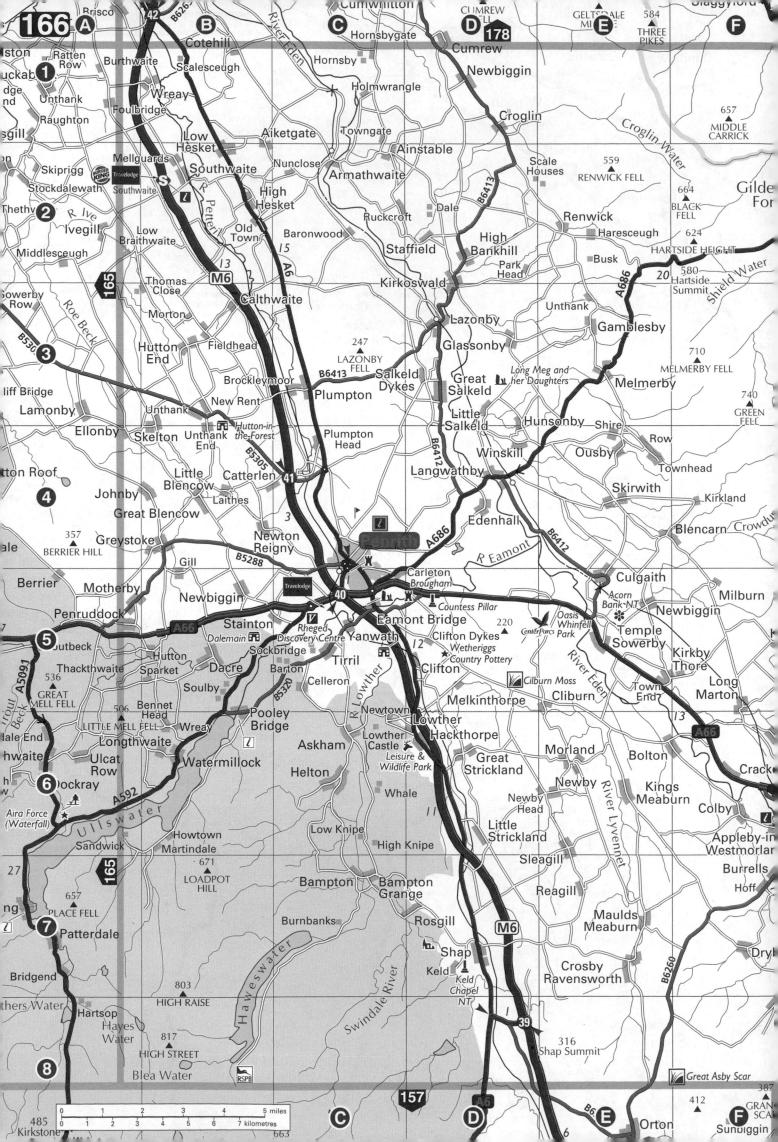

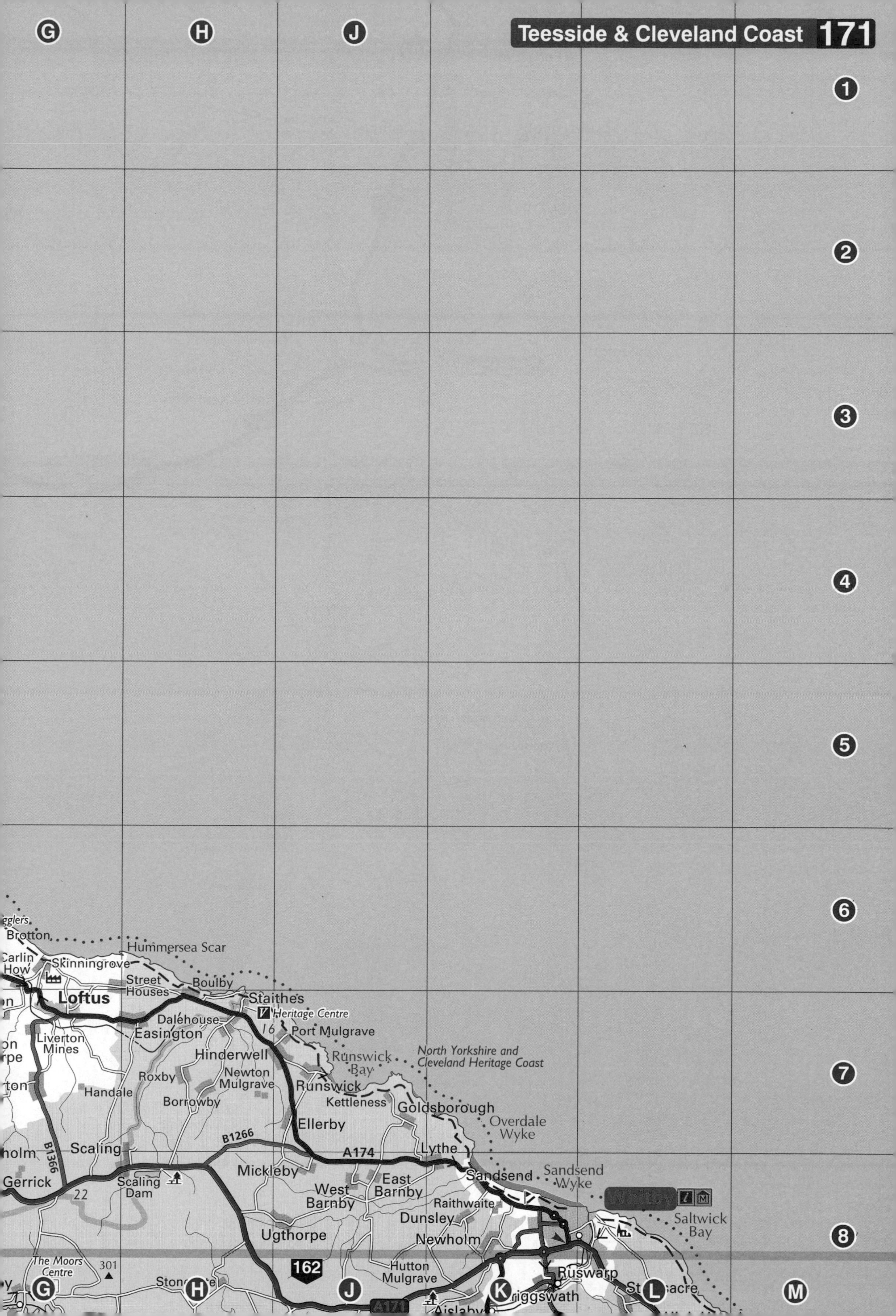

G H J

1

2

3

4

5

6

7

8

M

 gglers
Brotton
Carlin
How
Skinningrove
Hummersea Scar
Street
Houses
Boulby
Loftus
Staithes
Heritage Centre
Dalehouse
Easington
16
Port Mulgrave
Liverton
Mines
Hinderwell
North Yorkshire and
Cleveland Heritage Coast
Roxby
Newton
Mulgrave
Runswick
Bay
Handale
Borrowby
Runswick
Goldsborough
Kettleness
Overdale
Wyke
Scaling
B1266
Ellerby
Lythe
Gerrick
B1366
Scaling
Dam
Mickleby
A174
Sandsend
Sandsend
Wyke
22
West
Barnby
East
Barnby
Whitby
Raithwaite
Ugthorpe
Dunsley
Newholm
Saltwick
Bay
The Moors
Centre
301
162
Hutton
Mulgrave
Ruswarp
Stonegate
Aislaby
A171
riggswath
St Hacre

Corsewall Point
Barnhills
Portencalzie
182
Glenwhilly
Laggan Standing

Kirkcolm
Penwhirn Reservoir
Braid Fell
New Luce

B738
Loch Connell
Ervie
B798
Low Barbeth
Low Salchrie
Beoch Burn

Knocknain
Leswalt
B7043
Loch Ryan
Innermessan
Black Loch
Castle Kennedy

Balgracie
Castle of St John
A751
White Loch
Chlenry
164 CRAIG FELL

Auchnotteroch
Stranraer
Aird
Castle Kennedy
A75
10
Glenluce Abb

Portslogan
B738
Lochans
Kildrochet House
Glenwhan
Dunragit
Glenlu

Broadsea Bay
181
CAIRN PAT
8
14
B7077
Piltanton Burn
B7084
Whitecrook

Black Head
A77
A716
19
Ringdoo Point
Mil

Portpatrick
Stoneykirk
18
North Milmain
Stair Haw
A

B7042
Mull o

Sandhead
Cairngarroch
Money Head
Kirkmadrine

High Ardwell
Ardwell Bay
Ardwell House
Ardwell
Chapel Rossan

Drumbreddon
Logan
Balgowan
L U C E

Port Logan Bay
Port Logan
Garrochtrie
B7065
A716
Kilstay

Clanyard Bay
Kirkmaiden
Drummore

Laggantalluch Head
Barncorkrie
High Drummore
Killiness Point

Cardryne
B7041
Maryport

Cardrain
West Cairngaan
RSPB
MULL OF GALLOWA

A · B · C · D · E · F

1 · 2 · 3 · 4 · 5 · 6 · 7 · 8

GALLOWAY

Kh...
Carseriggan
Barfad
...NAN
Shennanton
B735
...33
Kirkcowan
B733
Clugston
B7052
Malzie
THE
MACHARS
B7005
...ter of
Malzie
B7005
...in
Barrachan
5
Elrig
Mochrum
B7085
rt William
6
Barsalloch Fort
Barsalloch Point
Point of Leg

Challoch
R Cree
Minnigaff
Newton Stewart
Creebridge
A714
173
Causeway End
Torhouse Stone Circle
B733
Bladnoch
Kirwaugh
B7005
Druchtag Motte
Drumtrodden Cup & Ring
Drumtrodden Standing Stones
Big Balcraig
'Wren's Egg' Standing Stones
B7021
Monreith
A747
10

RSPB

GARLICK HILL
Penkill Burn
Kirroughtree
Palnure
A75
Baltersan
7
Wigtown
Braehead
Kirkinner
B7052
B7085
Whauphill
11
12
Little Airies
A746
Sorbie
B7052
Drummoddie
Broughton Mains
B7004
Priory
B7063
173
Whithorn Cradle of Christianity
Rispain Camp
A746
Glasserton
St Ninian's Cave
Kidsdale
B7004
Whithorn
Portyerrock
Isle of Whithorn
St Ninian's Chapel (ruin)
Cutcloy
BURROW HEAD

Galloway Deer Range
184
Round Fell 402
Fell of Fleet 471
Auchencloy Hi... 208
L... Ske...
Loch Grannoch
Loch Fleet
Cairnsmore of Fleet 710
Gem Rock
Creetown
Kirkmabreck 18
Cairnharrow 455
Carsluith
Carsluith
Cairnholy Chambered Cairns
Ravenshall Point
Mossyard
Orchardton Bay
Culscadden
Garlieston
Pouton
Crugleton Bay

Big Water of Fleet
Little Water of Fleet
White Top of Culreach 335
Upper Ruscoe
B796
Fleet Valley
Skyre Burn
Anwoth
Cardoness
Gate
B7...
Girthon
Lennox Plunton
Margrie
Islands of Fleet
Kirkandrews
Borness
Ringdoo Point

Wigtown Bay

Fleet Bay

0   1   2   3   4   5 miles
0   1   2   3   4   5   6   7 kilometres

G   H   J   K

① ② ③ ④ ⑤ ⑥ ⑦ ⑧

Galloway Coast

Mossdale
Airds of Kells
Slogarie
Loch Ken
Woodhall Loch
Laurieston
Loch Anyeon
Kirkconnell
RAY
Longwood
Bridge of Dee
Rhonehouse
Ringford
f Fleet
Twynholm
A75
Compstonend
Kirkchrist
edpark
MacLellan's
Kirkcudbright
Mutehill
orgue
Ross
Little Ross
Balmae
Netherlaw
Abbey Head

Knockven Smithy
Loch Roan
Walbutt
Crossmichael
Crofts
Clarebrand
Glenlochar
Townhead of Greenlaw
Threave NTS
Threave Garden NTS
Carlingwark Loch
Castle Douglas
Hillowton
A745
Gelston
Craigley
Airieland
Tongland
Little Sypland
Whinnie Liggate
Dundrennan
Orroland
B727
B795
A762
A713
16
19
A762
B795
River Dee
10
15
A711
B727
Wildlife Park
Hydros Visitor Centre
Culnaightrie
A711

Kirkpatrick Durham
Old Bridge of Urr
Haugh of Urr
Redcastle
Hardgate
Milton
Springholm
Stonehouse
Kirkgunzeon
Edingham
Little Knox
Barlochan
Dalbeattie
Palnackie
Barnbarroch
Kippford or Scaur
Orchardton Tower
Mote of Mark
Rockcliffe
East Stewartry Coast
Castlehill Point
Auchencairn
Auchencairn Bay
Balcary
Heston Island
Balcary Point
Rascarrel
343 SCREEL HILL
390 BENGAIRN
Urr Water
A711
A710
B794
B793
B736
6
8
10
18

Auche Loch
Crocketf
Mill Loch
Drumcoltran Tower
A711
334 LOTUS HILL
Glensone Burn
Glaisters Burn
Beeswing
Kinha
Lochobe Loch
430 CUIL HILL
176
14
Caulkerbush
Fairgirth
Drumburn
Sandyhills
Colvend
Portling
Castlehill Point
RSPB

G   H   J   K   L   M

ROAN FELL
HILL

G H J K

Boreland
Castle O'er
Effgill
Georgefield
Arkleton
1

187

Bentpath
Kirkstile
13

331
HART FELL
Burnfoot
B709
188

Corrie
450
CAULDKINERIG
Craigcleuch
404
TINNIS HILL
2

Water of Milk
New Langholm
Langholm
Malcolm Memorial
Under Burnmouth

18
B7068
319
GRANGE FELL
B7068
Skipper's Bridge
B6318
178

Bankshill
Bigholms
A7
Tarras Water
Caulside
B6357

Tundergarth
252
COLLIN HAGS
R Esk
Claygate
3

Roman Camp
Waterbeck
Solwaybank
Hollows
Harelaw
Warwicksland

B725
Kirtle Water
Evertown
B720
Rowanburn
Pentonbridge

Middlebie
B722
B6357
Canonbie
Riddings

19
2
B7076
Milltown
Woodhouselees
Scuggate
4

A74(M)
Eaglesfield
Timpanheck
B72 5
Carwinley

Thomas Carlyle's Birthplace NTS
20
4
Merkland Cross
Chapelknowe
R Sark
Scotsdike
Netherby

Kirtlebridget
Bonshaw Tower
B6357
Prior
River Lyne
5

Brydekirk
Robgill Tower
Kirkpatrick-Fleming
21
Longtown
Kirklinton

Creca
B7076 Gretna
Springfield
A6071
4
Hetherside

Warmanbie
Hollee
B6357
4
Sandysike
Skitby

Annan
Gretna Green
Rigg
Gretna
River Esk
A7
Smithfield
A6071

Howes
A75
Dornock
Eastriggs
B721
Westlinton
Scalebyhill
Scaleby
6

Redkirk Point
A74
Travelodge
Newtown

Torduff Point
Rockcliffe Cross
Todhills
178

Bowness-on-Solway
Port Carlisle
R Eden
Rockcliffe
Harker
Blackford
Longpark
Wallhead
Walby

RSPB
Glasson
Hadrian's Wall Path
Beaumont
44
3
Houghton
Low Crosby
7

Drumburgh
Easton
Boustead Hill
Burgh by Sands
North End
Cargo
Kingstown
Grinsdale
Knowlefield
Linstock

Longcroft
Whitrigg
Angerton
Longburgh
West End
Monkhill
Kirkandrews upon Eden
Stainton
Stanwix
Warwick

Anthorn
Kirkbride
Whitrigglees
Fingland
Thurstonfield
Moorhouse
Belle Vue
43
Scotby

Finglandrigg Woods
Bow B5307
Wetheral

Kirkbride
Powhill
Laythes
Little Bampton
Kirkbampton
Oughterby
Little Orton
Morton
Harraby
M6

Newton Arlosh
Wampool
Great Orton
Newby
West Cummersdale
Upperby
3
8

Salt Cotes
Biglands
Aikton
Wiggonby
Newby Cross
Blackwell
Carleton

Moss Side
Raby
Gamelsby
Woodhouses
Orton Rigg
A595
Baldwinholme
Durdar
Brisco
B6263

Drumleaning
Moorhouse
Thornby
Whinnow
Cardewlees

G H J K L M

Dundraw
Oulton
Lessonhall
Dockray
Micklethwaite
Crofton
Thursby
165
Green Head
Buckabank
Durdar
Ratten Row
Burthw
Scalesceugh

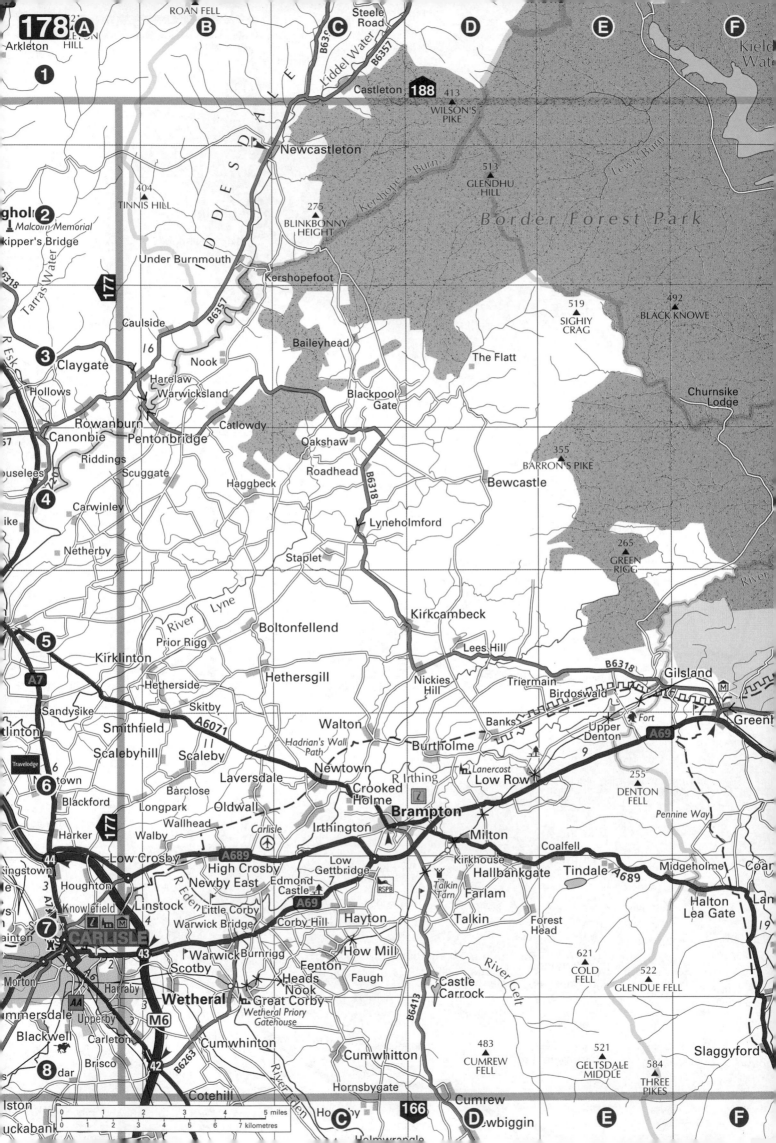

G Ellington
Lynemouth
191 Beacon Point
Woodhorn
Woodhorn Demesne
A197
Newbiggin-by-the-Sea
Wansbeck
Riverside
epwash
Stakeford
North Seaton Colliery
uide Post
West Sleekburn
Scotland
Gate
Bomarsund
Cambois
North Blyth
East
Sleekburn
llington
Blyth
Cowpen
Bebside
Newsham
East
Hartford
New
Delaval
A192
Shankhouse
New
Hartley
Seaton
Sluice
New
Seaton
Hartley
ngton
Cramlington
St Mary's Lighthouse
Seaton
Delaval
Seghill
Holywell
Annitsford
Dudley
Burradon
Earsdon
Whitley
Bay
Camperdown
Backworth
Monkseaton
Killingworth
Shiremoor
Murton
Cullercoats
Forest Hall
New
York
Rising
Sun
North
Shields
Longbenton
Willington
Quay
Wallsend
Heaton
Int. Ferry
Terminal
Jarrow
Walker
Westoe
Harton
Byker
Hebburn
Monkton
Marsden
Marsden
Bay
Felling
Wardley
Souter Lighthouse NT
West
Boldon
Cleadon
Souter Point
Boldon
Colliery
Whitburn
East
Boldon
Whitburn
Bay
Springwell
Usworth
Wildfowl &
Wetlands Trust
Southwick
Castletown
Seaburn
Birtley
Portobello
South
Hylton
Roker
Monkwearmouth
WASHINGTON
Grindon
Hendon
Ouston
Offerton
Penshaw
High Newport
Grangetown
Fatfield
Herrington
New
Silksworth
Tunstall
Pelton
Shiney Row
Silksworth
Ryhope
Fell
Houghton
Gate
Philadelphia
New
Herrington
Newbottle
hester-
Burnmoor
Houghton le Spring
e-Street
169
Seaham

Stavanger — Haugesund
Bergen
Kristiansand
Göteborg
Amsterdam

G H J K L M

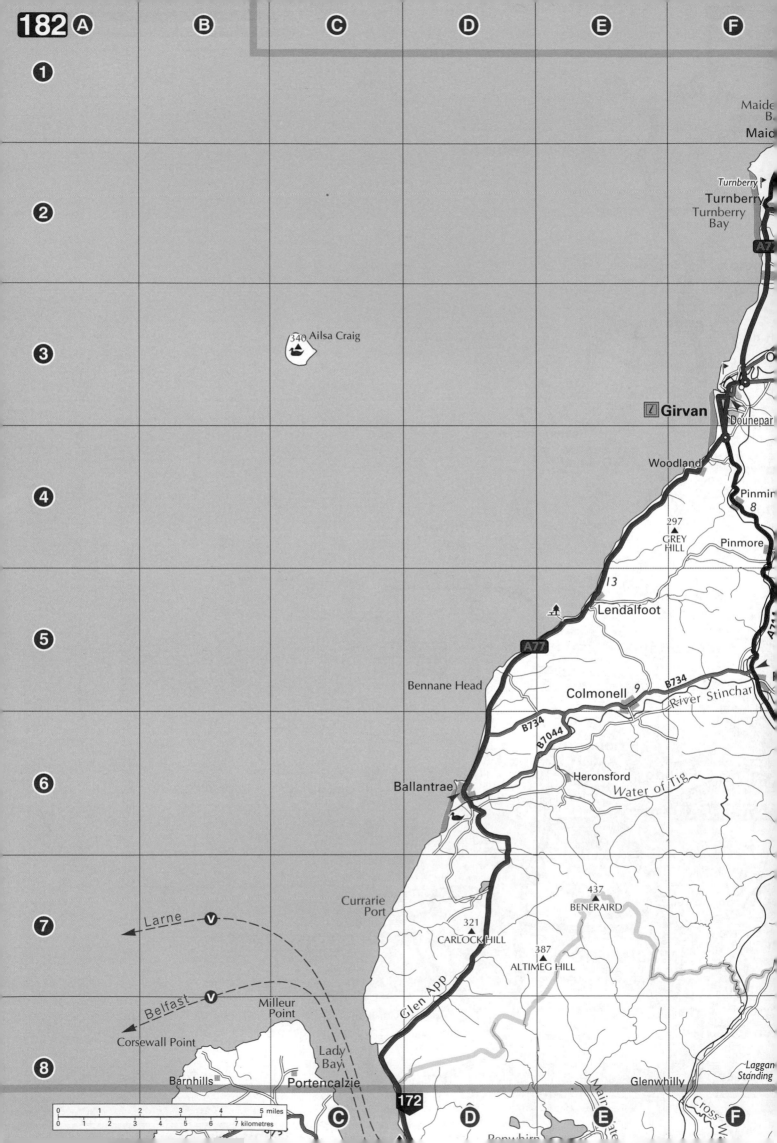

340 Ailsa Craig

Girvan
Dounepar
Woodland
Pinmi
8
297
GREY
HILL
Pinmore
13
Lendalfoot
A77
Bennane Head
Colmonell 9 B734
River Stinchar
B734
B7044
Ballantrae
Heronsford
Water of Tig

Currarie
Port
437
BENERAIRD
321
CARLOCK HILL
387
ALTIMEG HILL

Larne
Belfast
Milleur
Point
Corsewall Point
Lady
Bay
Barnhills
Portencalzie
Glenwhilly
Laggan
Standing

172

Maide
B.
Maid
Turnberry
Turnberry
Turnberry
Bay
A7

Glen App

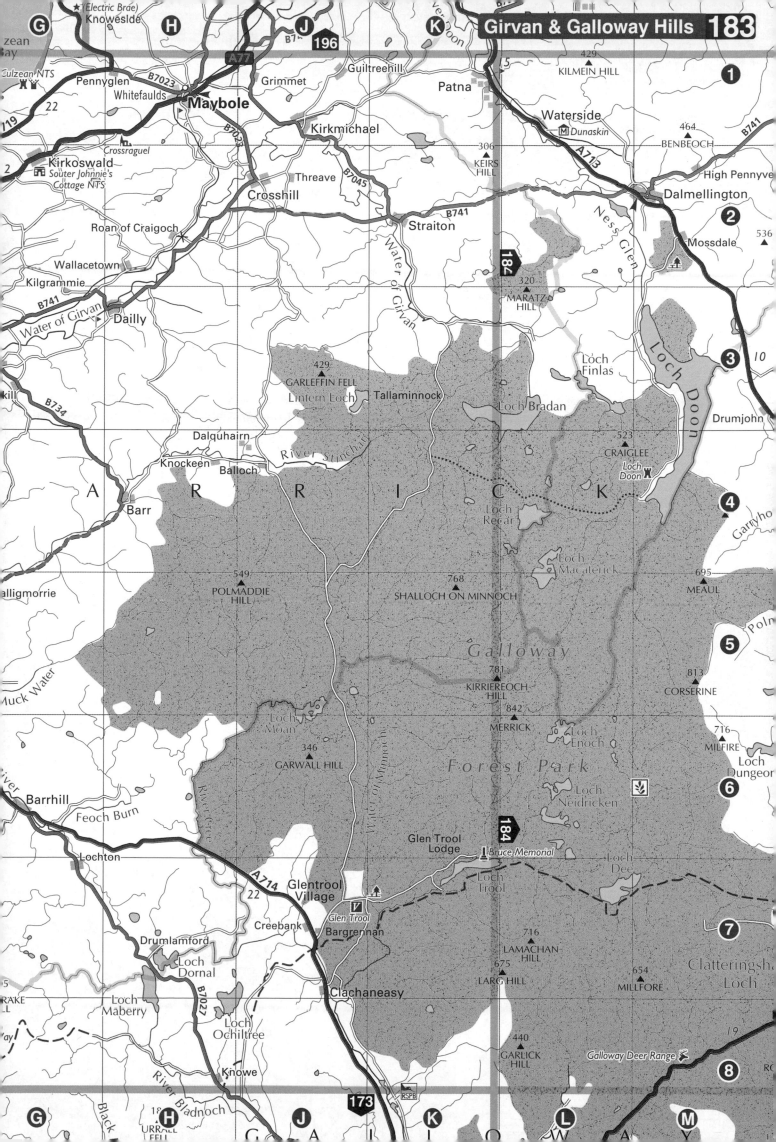

G   H   J   K   1

★(Electric Brae)
Knoweslde

B7023

196

A77

zean ay

Culzean NTS

Pennyglen

Whitefaulds

Maybole

Crossraguel

Kirkoswald

Souter Johnnie's
Cottage NTS

22

719

2

Grimmet

Guiltreehill

Kirkmichael

Threave

Crosshill

B7045

B7023

B7023

Patna

Waterside

Dunaskin

Kilmein Hill

429

M

306
KEIRS
HILL

464
BENBEOCH

High Pennyve

B741

Dalmellington

A713

2

536

Mossdale

Roan of Craigoch

Wallacetown

Kilgrammie

B741

B734

Dailly

Water of Girvan

Water of Girvan

Straiton

B741

184

320
MARATZ
HILL

Ness Glen

Loch Doon

Loch
Finlas

3

10

Drumjohn

429
GARLEFFIN FELL

Lintern Loch

Tallaminnock

Loch Bradan

523
CRAIGLEE

Loch
Doon

Dalquhairn

River Stinchar

Knockeen

Balloch

A

R

R

R

I

C

K

Loch
Recar

4

Garryho

Barr

549
POLMADDIE
HILL

768
SHALLOCH ON MINNOCH

Loch
Macaterick

695
MEAUL

alligmorrie

Muck Water

Galloway

781
KIRRIEREOCH
HILL

813
CORSERINE

5

Poln

Loch
Moan

346
GARWALL HILL

842
MERRICK

Loch
Enoch

716
MILFIRE

Forest Park

Loch
Neidricken

6

Loch
Dungeor

River Cree

Barrhill

Feoch Burn

Water of Minnoch

Glen Trool
Lodge

Bruce Memorial

184

Loch
Dee

Lochton

A714

22

Glentrool
Village

Loch
Trool

7

Clatteringsha
Loch

Creebank

Glen Trool

Bargrennan

716
LAMACHAN
HILL

654
MILLFORE

Drumlamford

Clachaneasy

675
LARG HILL

Loch
Dornal

RAKE

Loch
Maberry

Loch
Ochiltree

B7027

440
GARLICK
HILL

Galloway Deer Range

8

Knowe

173

RSPB

19

RO

River Bladnoch

Black

G   H   J   K   L   M

URRALL FELL

G

A

L

O

W

A

Y

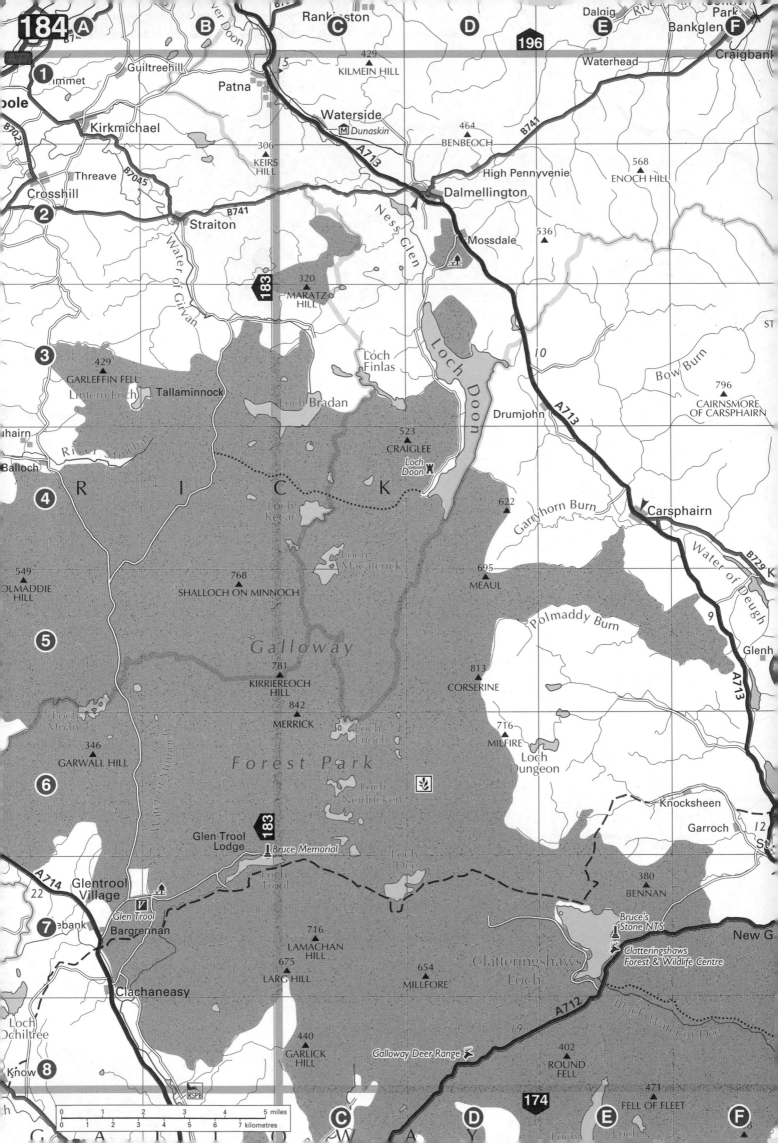

G **H** **J**

Wanlockhead

197

Kirkconnel

Kelloholm

GREEN LOWTHER

B797

1
725
LOWTHER
HILL
N...ther
Fi...nd

Crawick

Newtown

Sanquhar

594
HARE
HILL

Kello Water

Mennock

River Nith

23

Enterkin Burn

Dalveen

17

2
691
BALLENCL...
LAW

Durisdeermill

Euchan Water

700
BLACKCRAIG

ackcraig

450
CLOUD
HILL

Polgown

478

Enterkinfoot

186

A76

A702

Durisdeer

Gateslack

East
Morton

6...

475
COUNTAM

554
CAIRNKINNA
HILL

Cleuch-
head

Drumlanrig

Morton Loc...
Morton

3

598
COLT HILL

Big
Carlae

Old Auchenbrack

Auchenhessnane

Scaur Water

Carronbridge

Tibbers

N

Burnhead

Thornhill

Closeburnmill

Southern
Upland Way

Benbuie

Shinnel Water

Penpont

Keir
Mill

Cample

4

L...
Ett...

of Ken

532
CORNHARROW HILL

337
BENNAN

9

Closeburn

G...

Stenhouse

Tynron

15

B729

Moniaive

Kirkland

Maxwelton

A702

Keir Hills

Park

Kirkpatrick

Glencrosh

Breckonside

...ligh
...dgirth

5

Black Water

385
WETHER HILL

Craigneston

A702

13

431
BOGRIE
HILL

Skelston

Snade

Blackwood

Lag

Auldgirth

Dalsw...

15

...uhairn

Loch
Urr

Sundaywell

Dunscore

Throughgate

B729

17

A...

Loch Howie

Upper Stepford

6

Bogue

B7075

176

Holyw...

...n

A713

392
SKEOCH
HILL

Drumpark

Twelve Apos...

Newbri...

A712

281
LARGLEAR
HILL

Corsock

Crochmore
House

Te...les

7

Shawhead

Cargen ...

Ironmacannie

Lochfoot

Cargenb...

A711

25

Mo...le

Airds
of Kells

G **H** **J**

Knockvennie
Smithy

B794

Eastlands

Crocketford

Auchenreoch
Loch

Milton
Loch

Lochrutton
Loch

8

175

16

Loch...

Kirkpatrick
Durham

K

Springholm

Milton

18

L

M

Beeswing

Lochober
Loch

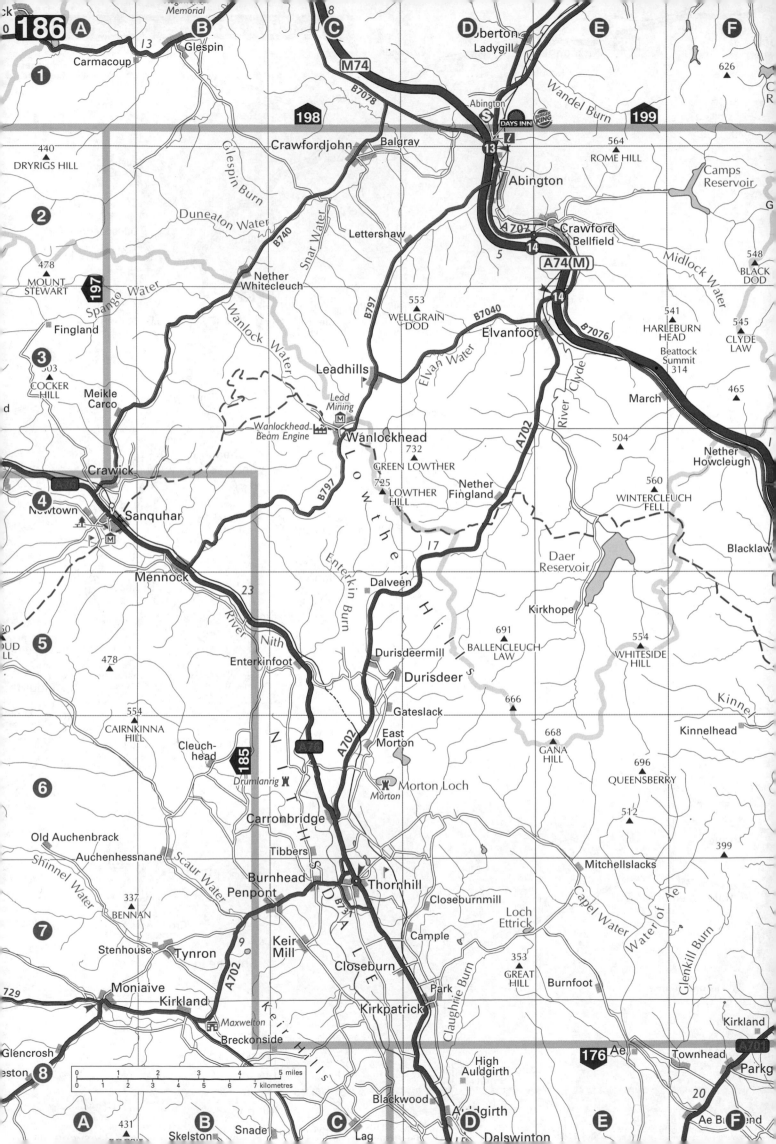

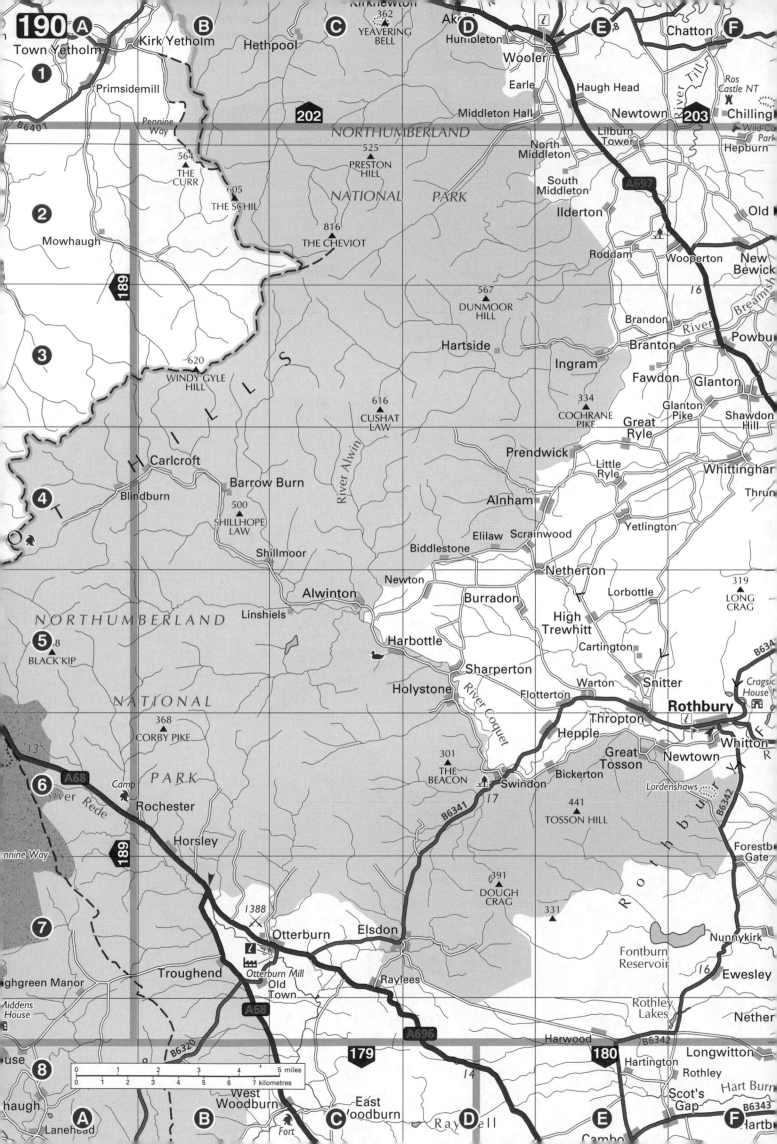

Imachar

G Carradale
B879
Carradale House
Carradale Point
Carradale Bay

H Balliekine

J

792
BEINN NUIS

K

Glen Rosa

Merkland Point

Brodick NTS

Brodick Bay

1

Iorsa Water

A R R A N

Brodick

Strathwhillan

Corriegills

Machrie Bay

Auchagallon Stone Circle
Machrie

512
A'CHRUACH

A841

4

Clauchlands Point

2

Machrie Moor Stone Circles

B880

Tormore

Lamlash

Margnaheglish

Balmichael

503
BEINN BHREAC

Lamlash Bay

Holy Island

Moss Farm Road Stone Circle

Balmichael

Cordon

Torbeg

Shiskine

Blackwaterfoot

Auchencairn

Kingscross

Knockenkelly

3

Drumadoon Bay

Kilpatrick

Glen Scorrodale

Carn Ban

Whiting Bay

Whiting Bay

Kilpatrick Dun

194 Brown Head

A841

Glen Ashdale

Largymore

Corriecravie

Kilmory Water

Largybeg

Torr a' Chaisteal Fort
Sliddery

Dippen

Dippen Head

16

Kilmory

Bennan

Lagg
Torrylin Cairn

Kildonan

4

Bennan Head

Pladda

195

5

6

7

340 Ailsa Craig

8

K I L B R A N
Carradale Point

G **H** **J** **K** **L** **M**

206

Cock Of Arran

Loch Ciàran
Loch Garasdale

Crossaig

247 CRUACH MHIC GOUGAIN

264 CNOC-AN T-SAMHLAIDH

Cour Bay

Cour

Rhunahaorine

38

205

354 CRUACH NAN GABHAR

dale

Clan

319

Carradale Water

B842

39

B879

Carradale

Dippen

Carradale House

Torrisdale

454 BEINN-AN TUIRC

Carradale Bay

Carradale Point

408 BORD MOR

Saddell

Saddell Bay

396 SGREADAN HILL

Ugadale

192

Glen Lussa

Peninver

Ardnacross Bay

Kilm el

Campbeltown

B842

Campbeltown Loch

Island Davarr

Kilkerran

Kildalloig

352 NN GHUILEAN

Achinhoan

Ru Stafnish

Grogport

Barmollack

K I L B R A N N A N   S O U N D

193

Lochranza

Catacol

Glen Catacol

Glen Chalmadale 8

Pirnmill

Penrioch

A841

17

North Arran

834 CAISTEAL ABHAIL

Loch Tanna

Whitefarland

715 BEINN BHARRAIN

874 GOATFEL

Imachar

Balliekine

Iorsa Water

Glen Iorsa

792 BEINN NUIS

Glen Rosa

A R R A N

Machrie Bay

Auchagallon Stone Circle

Machrie

512 A'CHRUACH

Tormore

Machrie Moor Stone Circles

B880

Moss Farm Road Stone Circle

Balmichel

503 BEINN BHREAC

Balmichael

BEINN BHREAC

Torbeg

Shiskine

Drumadoon Bay

Blackwaterfoot

Kilpatrick

Kilpatrick Dun

Carn Ban

Brown Head

A841

Glen Scorrodale

Corriecravie

Sliddery

Torr a' Chaisteal Fort

16

Kilmory Water

Kilmory

Lagg

Torrylin Cairn

Benna

Polliwilline Bay

Bennan Head

Ru Stafnish

0 1 2 3 4 5 miles
0 1 2 3 4 5 6 7 kilometres

G
H
J
K

Gar...nty

Garroch Head

207

Little
Cumbrae
Island

Fairlie Road

Hunsterston
Power Station

12

Crosbie

Blackshaw

Portencross
Farland Head

B7048

B7047

**West
Kilbride**

Seamill

Munnoch

Drakemyre

Hig

Dalry

B780

B780

C...

Dalgarven
Mill

A737

Dalgarven

U

N

7

2

B778

A78

B781

B780

Kilwinning

A738

B78

Ardrossan

Horse Isle

A738

A78

A738

Stevenston

Ardeer

3

M

Saltcoats

196

Maritime

The Big Idea

V

Fulla

Corrie

A841

6 Merkland Point

Brodick
Bay

Strathwhillan

Corriegills

Clauchlands Point

Margnaheglish

Lamlash
Bay
Cordon

Holy Island

4

...hencairn

Kingscross

Knockenkelly

Whiting
Bay

...iting Bay

Ashdale

Largymore

Largybeg

Dippen   Dippen Head

Kildonan

...da

**FIRTH

OF

CLYDE**

Irvine
Bay

4

Baras

Belfast

V

Troon

5   Royal

Pr

Ne

6 Ayr
Bay

i M

196

Heads
of Ayr

Doonfoo

Heads of Ayr

Burns Cottg

Fisherton

A719

7 Allo

Dunure

Culroy

Drumshang

Croy Brae
(Electric Brae)

Knoweside

Culzean
Bay

8

A

Culzea...

Pennyglen

Whitefaulas

...ybel

G H Jackton J

The Murray
Calderglen

209

Eaglesham

A726

Larkhall
Quarter

Auldhouse
Leigh
Knoweglass 8

330 8 Limekilnburn
Millheugh
AGIOCH HILL
Shawsburn
164 Heads Ashgill
Roseba

Chapelton A72

Strutherhill
Netherburn
Crossford

Lochgoin
Reservoir 8 Craignetha

A M E Glassford Stonehouse 2 lietlude

361 Carnduff Strathaven 6 A71 Draffan B7086

LAIRDS 8 Blackwood Auchen
SEAT

Sandford Kirkmuirhill

Caldermill 198 Boghead 9

B7086 10

Avon Water

Drumclog B743 Lesmahagow 3

15 Dungavel New Trows

A71 Auchlochan

Newmilns Darvel B745 Logan Water Stockbriggs

Greenholm Priestland 13 461 Coalbu 4

AUCHINGILLOCH River Nethan Be

335 522

MILL RIG NUTBERRY
HILL

383 492 Douglas West

dleyard DISTINKHORN B743 PRIESTHILL St Bride's Church
HEIGHT Cameronians

B7037 408 466 Regimental
Memorial

MID HILL MIDDLEFIELD
LAW Glenbuck

chmillan A70 5

arswood B743 Muirkirk 13 Glespi

Sorn Limmerhaugh Carmacoup

B713 Kames

atrine 593 440

River Ayr CAIRN TABLE DRYRIGS HILL 6

10 497

Cronberry A70 WARDLAW
HILL 186

B7036 Gass 562

Lugar

uchinleck Holmhead Water

B7083 Logan Laigh Glenmuir

Cumnock 478

Garrallan MOUNT
STEWART

res Glenmuir Water

Roadside 6 450

HALFMERK HILL Fingland

363 503

CARSGAILOCH HILL Mansfield COCKER Meikle
HILL Carco

Dalgig River Nith Connel Kirkland Spango Water

Park Kirkconnel 8

Bankglen New

Craigbank Cumnock

Waterhead 184 185 Kelloholm A76 Crawick

G H J K L Newtown M Sanquhar

594

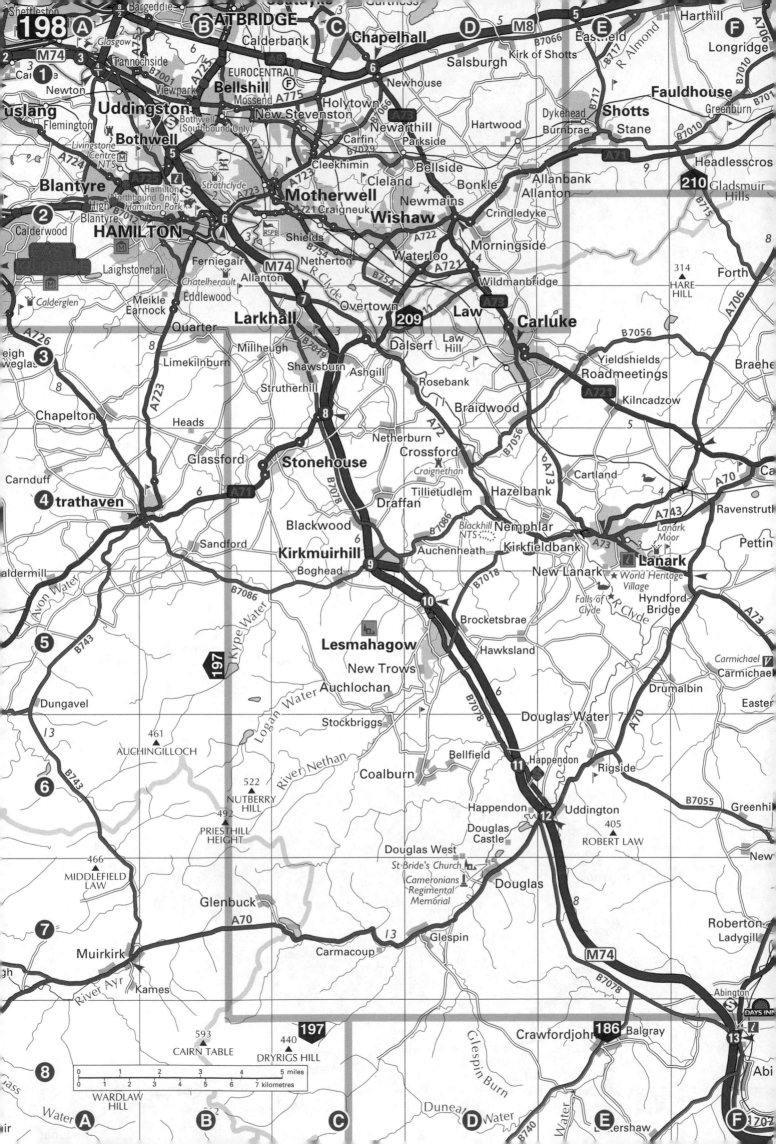

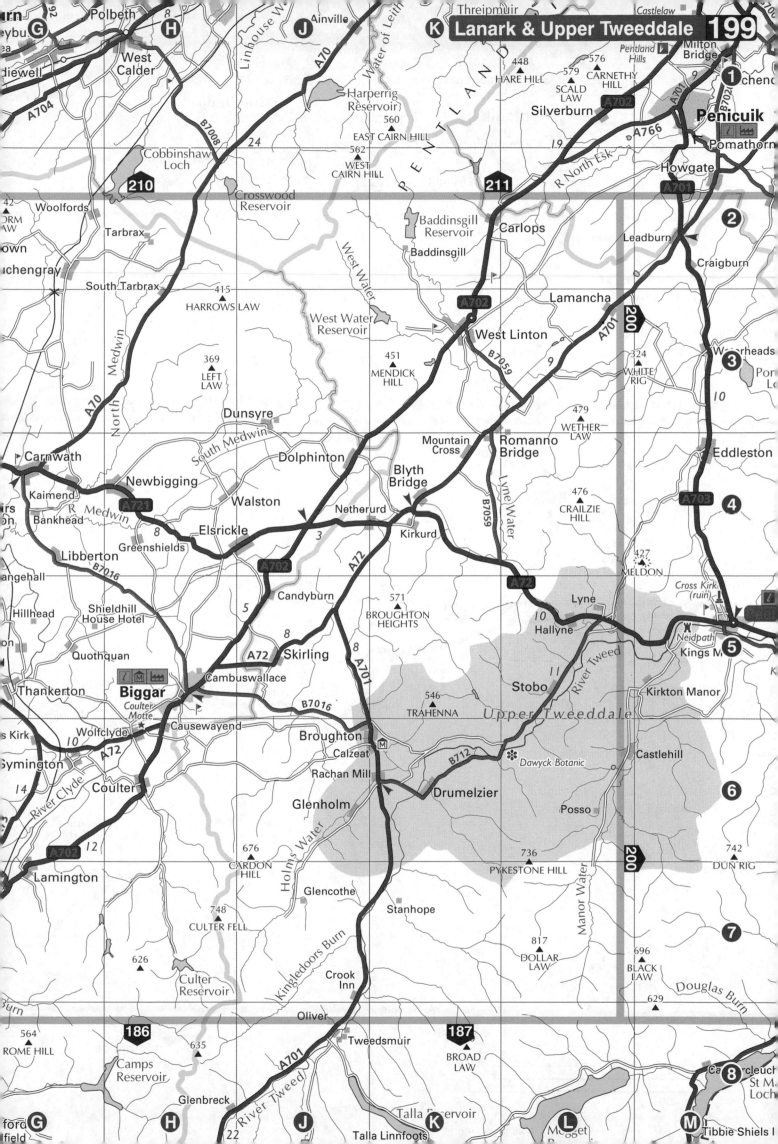

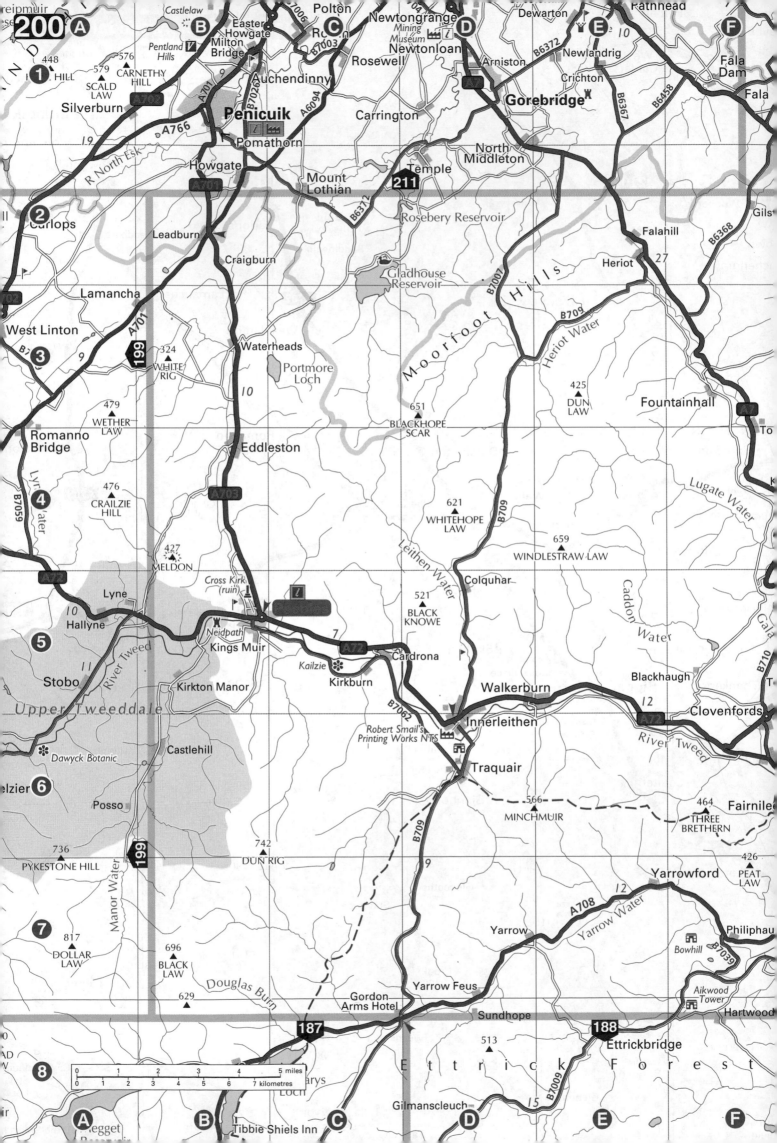

G   H   J   K

Blegbie

Cranshaws

Whiteadder
Reservoir

St A

Abbey St Bathan

Ellemford

Quix

Edin'
Hall Br

1

528
LAMMER
LAW

533

MEIKLE
SAYS LAW

Whitchester

325
COCKBURN
LAW

nmit

509
CRIB
LAW

513
SEENES
LAW

467
MEIKLE LAW

Longformacus

B6355

Primroseh

495
HUNT
LAW

212

Southern
Upland Way

2

Oxton

448
HOGS
LAW

Wedderlie
Burn

399
DIRRINGTON
GREAT LAW

Carfraemill

14

B6456

202

Gavinton

383
COLLIE
LAW

17

Blythe

Spottiswoode

Westruther

Polwarth

7

Fogo

3

A6105

Lauder

Thirlestane

Thornydykes

Houndslow

A697   8

Blackadder Water

Char

B6362

B6362

Boon

A6089

5

Bassendean

Greenlaw

B6460

4

Leader Water

Nether
Blainslie

Greenknowe
Tower

Middlethird

10

Threepwood

Legerwood

6

Gordon

Byrewalls

Hume

B6364

Lambden

Eccles

A68

A6105

West
Morriston

Fans

Mellerstain

6

Stichill

B6461

5

Bi

A698

Galashiels

B6397

9

Nenthorn

Ednam

9

Earlston

B6356

Eden Water

Smailholm

A6089

Kelso
Hendersyde
Park

Sprous

Priorwood
Garden NTS

3

Redpath

Smailholm
Tower

B6397

Floors

6

Langlee

Gattonside

B6360

Scott's View

B6404

Border
Union

Kelso

A6091

Darnick

B6361

Newstead

Eildon
and
Leaderfoot

Wallace
Monument

Manorhill

202

Easter Sof

Melrose

Trimontium

6

Dryburgh

Mertoun

River Tweed

A699

Heiton

B6352

Abbotsford

422

EILDON HILLS

Newtown
St Boswells

2

Clintmains

10

Roxburgh

A698

9

B6436

Selkirk

B6359

St Boswells

Maxton

Rutherford

Pirnie

7

Frogde

A699

9

Bowden

Camieston

Waterloo
Monument

Teviot
Water
Gardens

Caverton
Mill

Midlem

B6453

Longnewton

Ale Water

7

Nisbet

Eckford

B6401

Linton

Lilliesleaf

188

Belses

B6400

189

Crailing

Morebattle

Riddell

Greenhouse

Bloomfield

Chesters

Ancrum

A698

Lanton

2

Bonjedward

8

B6400

Harelaw

B6359

Minto

276

N

Buccastle

Gateshaw

12

G   H   J   K   L   M

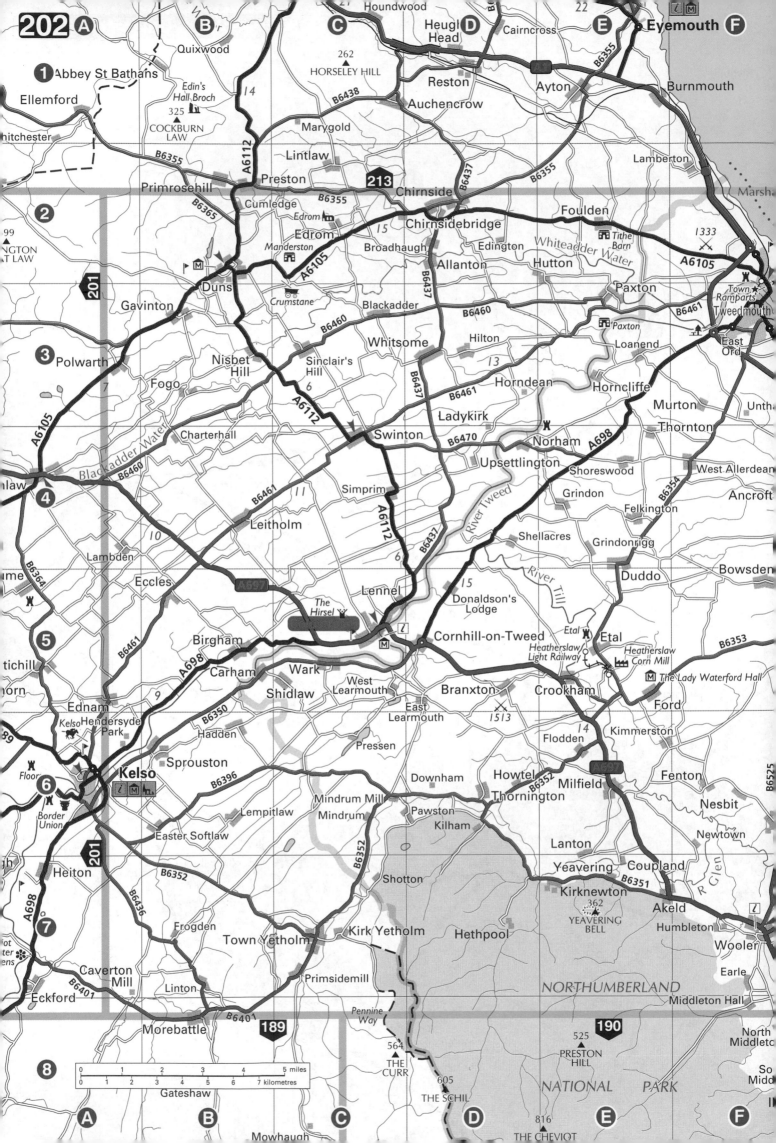

G   H   J

① ② ③ ④ ⑤ ⑥ ⑦ ⑧

ws Bay

Northumberland Heritage Coast

🛈 Ⓜ

Huds
Head
merston

Cheswick

Goswick

CAUSEWAY
FLOODED
AT HIGH TIDE

HOLY ISLAND

Haggerston

15

Beal

Holy
Island

Fenham

Lindisfarne
Priory

Lindisfarne NT
Castle Point

6353

Kyloe

Guile Point

owick

East
Kyloe

Fenwick

FARNE
ISLANDS

Buckton

Staple
Sound

Detchant

Smeafield

Elwick

Ross

*North Northumberland
Heritage Coast*

Holburn

Low
Middleton

Budle
Bay

Inner
Sound

St Cuthbert's
Cave NT

Middleton

Easington

Bamburgh

B1342

Hetton
Steads

North
Hazelrigg

Belford

Waren
Mill

Budle

Bamburgh

B1340

Ouchester

Spindlestone

Glororum

New
Shoreston

B6349

Burton

South
Hazelrigg

Bradford

Seahouses

East
Horton

Bellshill

🛈

Elford

North Sunderland

Warenton

Lucker

B1341

Chatton

Adderstone

Beadnell

B6348

Warenford

Newham

Swinhoe

B1340

Ros
Castle NT

Chathill

Tughall

Beadnell
Bay

Chillingham

Newstead

River Till

Wild Cattle
Park

Ellingham

Preston

Newton-by-the-Sea

190

Hepburn

Preston
Pele Tower

191

Brunton

267
CATERAN
HILL

Brownieside

Doxford

Christon
Bank

Embleton

Embleton
Bay

Old Bewick

North
Charlton

Falloden

B1339

Dunstan
Steads

Dunstanburgh
NT

A697

Ditchbur

South
Charlton

B347

Dunstan

B6346 Harehope

G   H   J   K   L   M

A B C D **214** E F

1

ISLAY

Rudha
Bholsa

363
SGARE
BREA

Nave Island
Ardnave
Point

Gortantaoid
Point

Bunnahabhai

316
GUIR-
BHEINN

2

Ton Mhòr

Eilean Mòr

Sanaigmore

Kilnave

Loch Gruinart

Loch
Gòrr

Finlaggan

Loch
Finlaggan

Kiells

Rudha Lamanais

Lecht Gruinart

RSPB

B8018

B8017

Gruinart

Gleann Mòr

Ballygrant

8

A846

3

Saligo Bay

Loch
Gorm

Coul Point

Sunderland

B8018

Kilchoman

A847

Brìdgend

Gartachossan

4

Machir
Bay

Bruichladdich

ISLAY

Loch
Indaal

Bowmore

Kilennan Burn

Kilchiaran Bay

15

M

Port
Charlotte

i

Lossit Bay

231
BEINN TART A'MHILL

RHINNS

Nereabolls

River Laggan

Duich R.

A846

B8016

454
BEINN URARA
Loch

5

Rudha na
Faing

OF

A847

Laggan

Glenegedale

6

Portnahaven

Port Wemyss

Orsay

RHINNS
POINT

Bay

Islay

Rudha Mòr

346
BEINN SHOLUM

7

165
MAOL BUIDHE

T H E   O A

Port
Ellen

A846

Ard

Lagav

Laphroaig

Texa

Lower
Killeyan

Risabus

Kilnaughton Bay

RSPB

Kinnabus

American
Monument

Loch
Kinnabus

MULL
OF OA

Rudha nan Leacan

8

| 0 | 1 | 2 | 3 | 4 | 5 miles |
| 0 | 1 | 2 | 3 | 4 | 5 | 6 | 7 kilometres |

A B C D E F

G **H** **J** **K** 215

Danna Island

Loch na

Ellary

206

1

St Cormacs Chapel

Kilmory Knap Chapel

Kilmory

Lo Caolisn

Kilmory Bay

Point of Knap

2

506 SCRINADLE

214

398 BEINN TARSUINN

Jura Forest

C henga

Coulaghai

3

Kilberry Sculptured Stones ★

Kilberry

Loch a' Chnuic Bhric

784 BEINN AN OIR

Paps of Jura

24

Kilberry Head

Keppoch Point

Tiretigan

213 CRUACH A

734

560 GLASS BHEINN

Jura

A846

Keils

Small Isles

4

Loch Stornoway

V Feolin Ferry

529 DUBHA BHEINN

Craighouse

342 BRAT BHEINN

Rudha na Gaillich

Cabrach

Am Fraoch Eilean

Rudha na Tràille

Brosdale Island

9

Ar

McArthur's Head

NAM ANN

V Port Askaig - Kennacraig

Rona n Poi

5

IGEIR

Rudha Liath

Ardtalla

Claggain Bay

Kinerarach

Tarbert

Kintour

Kildalton Cross

Ardmore Point

V

GIGHA

Rhunahaorine Point

Rhunahaorine

6

194

Eilean a' Chuirn

Port Ellen - Kennacraig

Ardminish

Achamore

W

V

Sound of Gigha

38

Rudha na Gainmhich

Cara

Tayinloan

7

Muasdale

8

Glenacardoch Point

Belloch

Barr Water

G 192 **H** **J** **K** **L** arr **M**

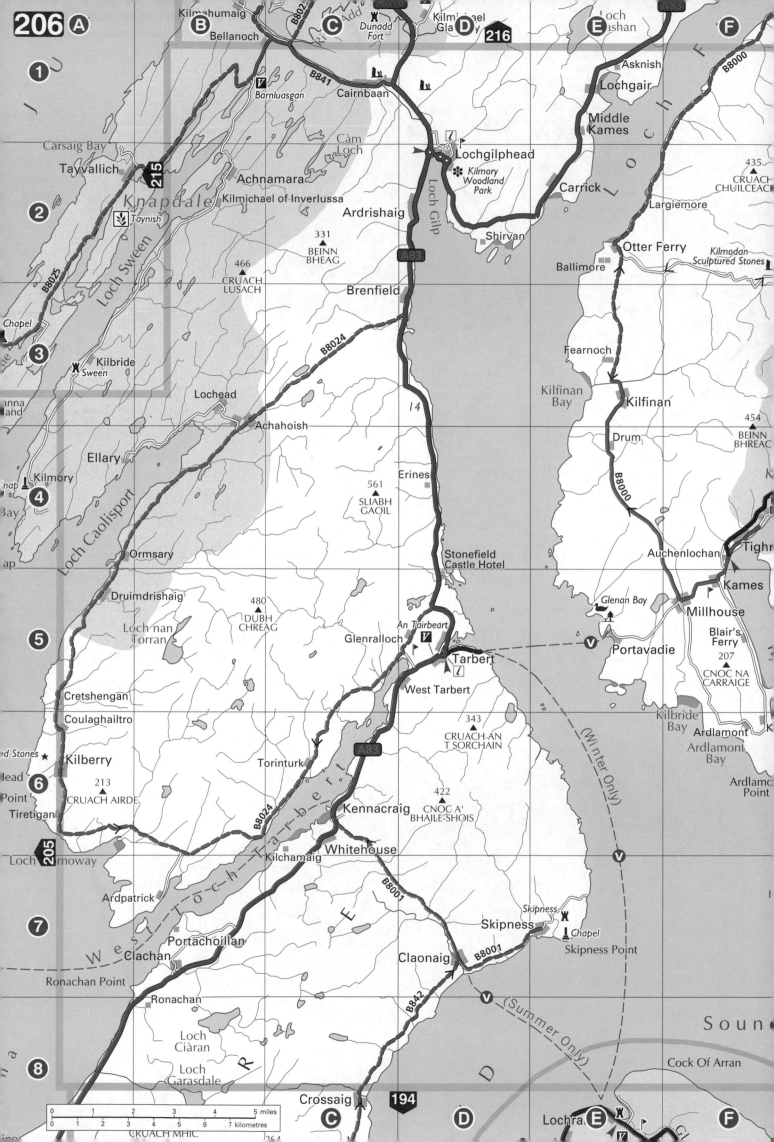

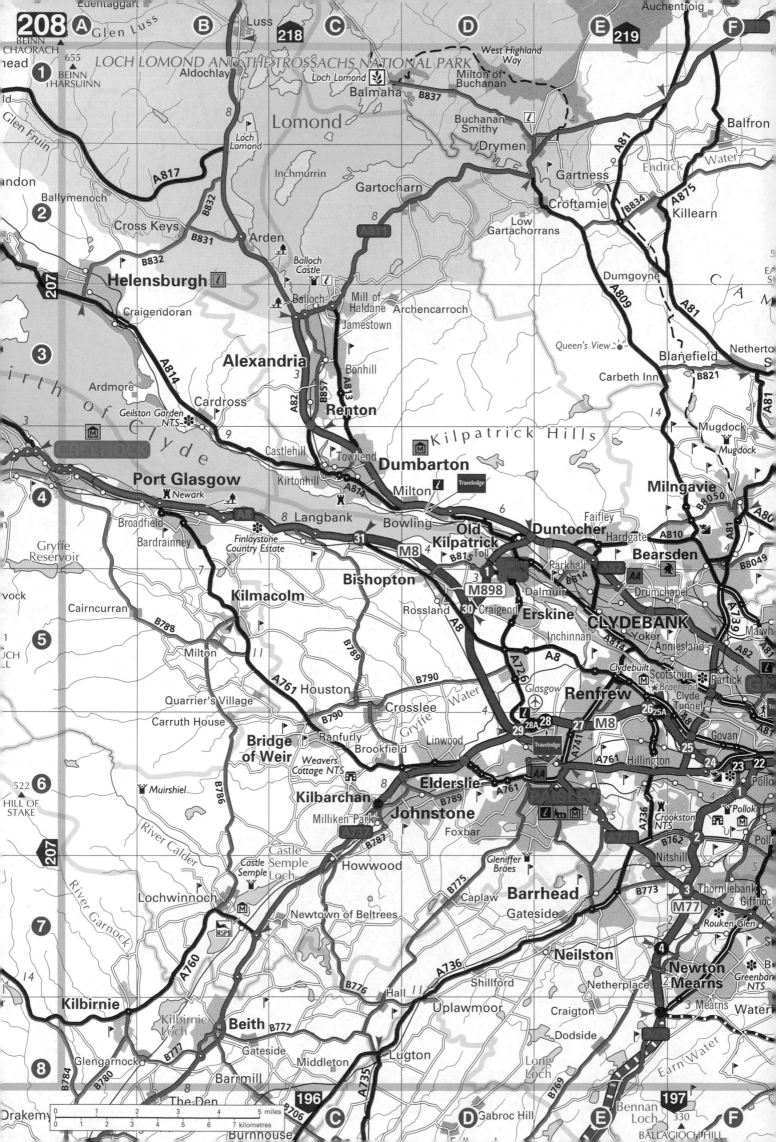

Cowdenbeath

ngelly
G **H** 222 **J** Dysant
B''ly Chapel Pathhead
Lumphinnans Loch Gelly A910
Auchtertool B925 Linktown
B9157 6
Donibristle B923
Balmule B921
B925 A909 Kinghorn
Aberdour A921 Pettycur
8 Pettycur
St Bridget's **Burntisland**
Kirk Silversands Bay
Dalgety Inchcolm Abbey Inchkeith
Bay Cramond
Island Dalmeny
sferry Eagle Cramond
Rock

1

Zeebrugge

2

Gullane B
Gullane Point

212

Aberlady Bay

Craigelaw Point **3**
Aberlady

Gosford
Bay

F I R T H   O F   F O R T H

Granton A901 Britannia
Newhaven
Lauriston Castle Leith
Barnton Davidson's Warriston St Triduana's Chapel
Blackhall B900 AA
Mains A902 A199
Dovecot A8 Portobello **Musselburgh**
Corstorphine ARTHUR'S SEAT Joppa
South Gyle A71 251 Duddingston Newcraighall Fisherrow
Craiglockhart Royal Duddingston Craigmillar Inveresk
Morningside Observatory Hilltown Lodge NTS Inveresk
Water Newton Wallyford
of Leith Blackford Danderhall A720
Juniper Green Hill Liberton Millerhill Elphinstone
Currie A720 Gilmerton Dalkeith Whitecraig
Bonaly Hillend Park Crossgatehall
Kinleith Straiton Butterfly **Dalkeith** Cousland
Malleny Bonaly Farm Eskbank
NTS Loanhead Lasswade Newbattle
Malleny Mills Boghall Bilston Bonnyrigg Mayfield
Woodhouselee Polton Chesterhill Pathhead
Castlelaw Roslin Newtongrange Dewarton
Easter Mining Vogrie
Pentland Howgate Museum Newlandrig
Hills Milton Newtonloan Arniston
Bridge Rosewell Crichton
Carnethy Auchendinny North **Gorebridge**
Scald Penicuik Carrington Middleton
Law Pomathorn Temple
Silverburn Mount
Howgate Lothian
199 Leadburn **200** Falahill
Heriot
Lamancha Craigburn Gladhouse Heriot
Linton Reservoir Rosebery Reservoir

Cockenzie and
Port Seton
Market Collegiate
Cross Church Seton
Prestonpans Mains
Heritage Museum 1745 8
Tranent A199
A1 Macmerry
New
Winton
Market Boggs
Cross Holding
Ormiston **5**
A6093 Pencaitland

4

Longnidd
vings

6
212
Fala
Dam
Fala

7 394
DUN
LAW
Gilston

8

G **H** 324 **J** **K** **L** **M**
Waterheads
WHITE
RIG Portmore
Moorfoot Hills
Heriot Water

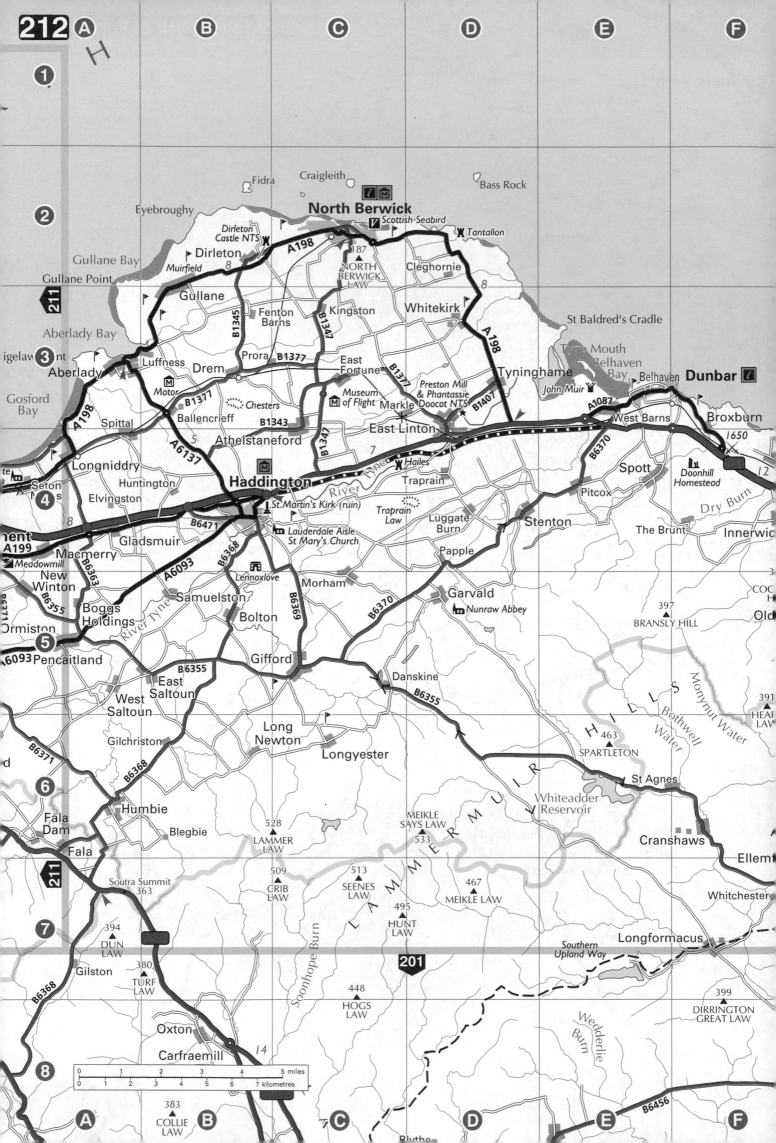

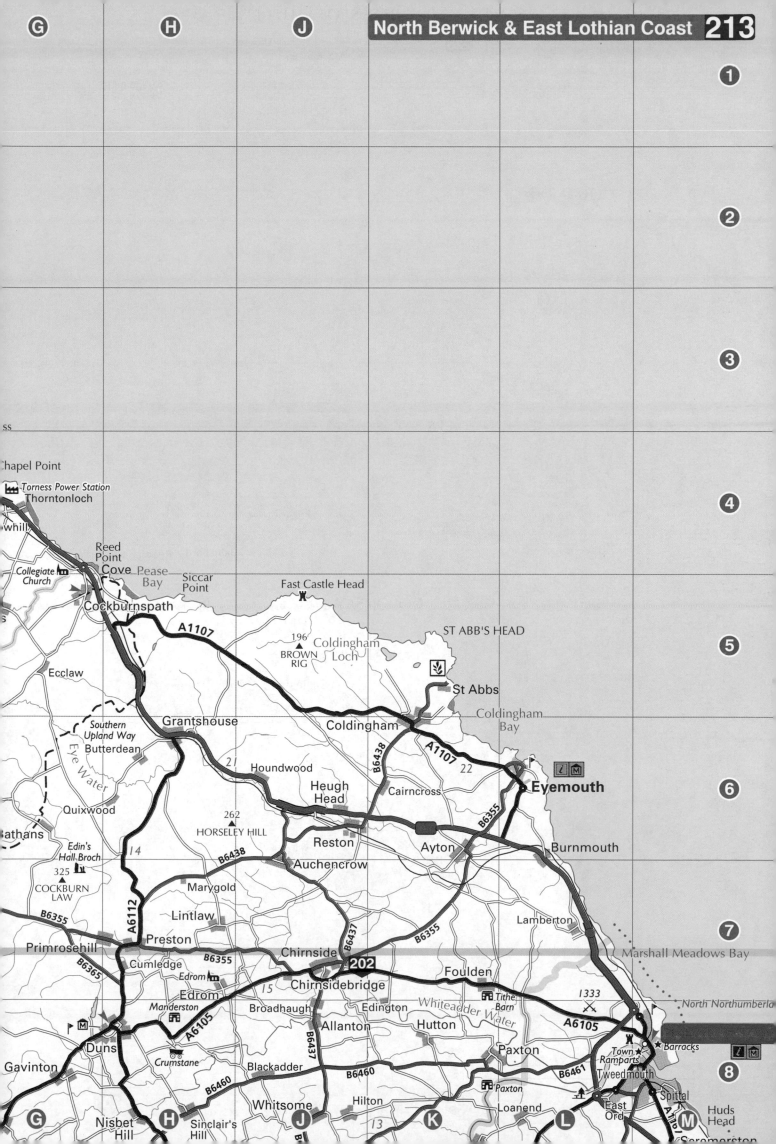

Chapel Point
Torness Power Station
Thorntonloch
whill
Reed Point
Collegiate Church
Cove
Pease Bay
Siccar Point
Cockburnspath
A1107
Ecclaw
196
BROWN RIG
Coldingham Loch
Fast Castle Head
ST ABB'S HEAD
St Abbs
Coldingham Bay
Grantshouse
Southern Upland Way
Butterdean
Eye Water
21
Houndwood
Heugh Head
B6438
A1107
22
Eyemouth
Coldingham
Cairncross
Quixwood
athans
262
HORSELEY HILL
Reston
Ayton
B6355
Burnmouth
Edin's Hall Broch
14
B6438
Auchencrow
325
COCKBURN LAW
Marygold
B6437
B6355
Lamberton
B6355
Lintlaw
A6112
Primrosehill
Preston
Chirnside
Marshall Meadows Bay
Cumledge
B6365
Edrom
202
Foulden
North Northumberla
Edrom
15
Chirnsidebridge
Tithe Barn
1333
A6105
Manderston
Broadhaugh
Edington
Whiteadder Water
Hutton
A6105
Barracks
Duns
A6105
Allanton
B6437
Paxton
Town Ramparts
Gavinton
Crumstane
Blackadder
B6460
B6461
Tweedmouth
Paxton
B6460
Hilton
Loanend
East Ord
Spittal
Nisbet Hill
Sinclair's Hill
Whitsome
13
Huds Head
Scremerston

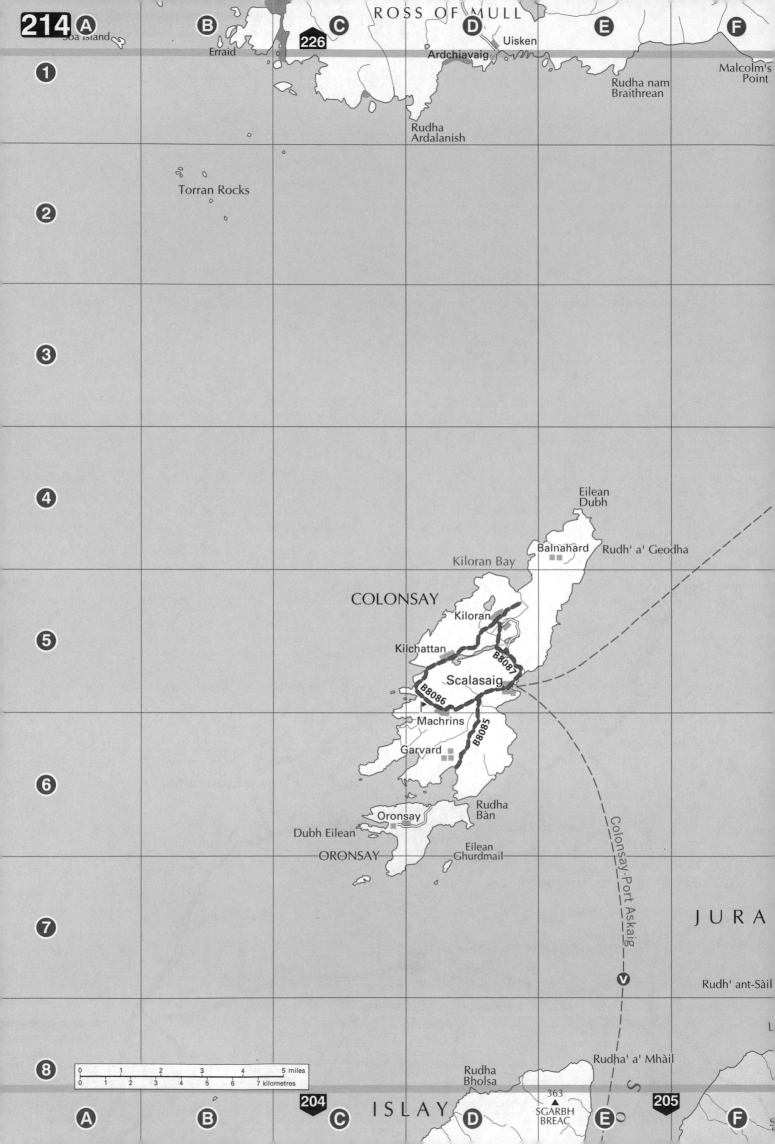

A **B** **C** **D** **E** **F**

ROSS OF MULL

Soa Island

Erraid

226

Uisken

Ardchiavaig

Malcolm's
Point

Rudha nam
Braithrean

1

Rudha
Ardalanish

Torran Rocks

2

3

Eilean
Dubh

4

Balnahard   Rudh' a' Geodha

Kiloran Bay

COLONSAY

Kiloran

5

Kilchattan

B8087

Scalasaig

B8086

Machrins

B8085

Garvard

6

Rudha
Bàn

Oronsay

Dubh Eilean

ORONSAY

Eilean
Ghurdmail

Colonsay-Port Askaig

J U R A

7

V

Rudh' ant-Sàil

Rudha' a' Mhàil

0   1   2   3   4   5 miles

0   1   2   3   4   5   6   7 kilometres

Rudha
Bholsa

363
▲
SGARBH
BREAC

8

204   ISLAY   205

A **B** **C** **D** **E** **F**

G H J K

227

G H J K L M

1
2
3
4
5
6
7
8

FIRTH

Colonsay - Oban

Dubh

Inish
Island
Clachan-Seil
SEIL
Easdale
Ellanbeich
Easdale
B844
Balvicar
B8003

Cuan Ferry Village

V

Cullipool
House
Torsay
Island

LUING

Seil Sound

Degnish

Loch Melfort

Garbh Eileach

Eilean
Dubh Mòr

GARVELLACHS
★ *Monastery & Beehive Cells*

Eileach
an Naoimh

LUNGA

Toberonochy

Scarba, Lunga
and the
Garvellachs

Sound of Luing

Shuna Sound

SHUNA

Arduaine
Garden NTS
Arduaine

Cr
Hav

12

A

SCARBA

448
▲
CRUACH SCARBA

Shuna
Point

Craigdhu

Ardfern
Kint

B8002

En Mhic

En Rig

Gulf of Corryvreckan

Aird

Loch Craignish

Ca

Glengarrisdale
Bay

295
▲
CRUACH NA
SEILCHEIG

Craignish Point

Island
Macaskin

Slockavulli
Temple Wood
Stone Circle

Glendebadel Bay

Ri Cruin C
Poltalloc

5

Loch Crinan

Glendebadel Bay

364
▲
BEN
GARRISDALE

Lealt Burn

Crinan

Kilmahumaig

B8025

River

Corpach Bay

Lussa River

466
▲
BEINN
BHREAC

Glen Grundale

Bellanoch

B841

Barnlu

V

6

Carsaig Bay

453
▲
RAINBERG MÒR

Ardlussa

Taynish

Tayvallich

Knapdale

Achnamara
Kilmichael of Inverluss

A846

Lussa
Point

206

7

331
▲
BEINN
BHEAC

och
h Mòr

N D O F J U R A

Loch Sween

B8025

466
▲
CRUACH
LUSACH

arbert

Keills Chapel

Loch na Cille

Danna
Island

Kilbride
Sween

Lochead

M
hahoish

8

G H J L M

205

398

A   B   C   D   E   F

1
2
3
4
5
6
7
8

Lochdon
Loch Don
Gorten
Grass Point

247 ▲
CARN BAN

Crobhan

Rudha Seanach

KERRERA

Altnacraig

Sound of Kerrera

Caithness
Glass

Ariogan

Kilbride

Gallanach

Ardentallen

Kilmore

Loch Feochan

Dunstaffnage
Chapel
(ruin)
228

Ganavan Bay

McCaig's
Tower ★

Rare Breeds
Farm Park

Dunbeg

Connel

Ac. even

Airds
Bay

Taynui

Clenamacrie

River Lonan

Glen Lonan

Loch
Nell

515 ▲
BEINN GHLAS

227

OF LORNE

Barrnacarry Bay

Kilninver
A816
15

356 ▲
AN
CREACHAN

Loch
Scamadale

482 ▲
BEINN
DEARG

Loch
Nant

Insh
Island

Clachan

Clachan-Seil

B844

SEIL

Ellanbeich
Easdale

Easdale

B844

Balvicar

B8003

Seil Sound

Loch
Tralaig

Inverinan

Lochavich

Loch Avich

Cuan Ferry Village

Cullipool
House

Torsay
Island

Degnish

Melfort

Loch Melfort

Kilmelford

Barnline Stables
V

Dalavich

Ardcho

LUING

Shuna Sound

SHUNA

Arduaine
Garden NTS

Arduaine

Gleann Domhain

Newyork

Portinnishe

Toberonochy

Sound of Luing

Shuna
Point

A816
12

Craobh
Haven

Inverliever Lodge

Glen Liever

B840

Durran

Braevallich

BEINN

Lunga
the
lachs

Craigdhu

Ardfern

Kintraw

En Mhic Chrion

Ford

Fincharn

458 ▲
CRUACH MHIC
FHIONNLAIRDH

433 ▲
BEINN
LAOIGH

ARBA

B8002

215

En Righ

B840

Loch
Gaineamhach

Sandho

Aird

Loch Craignish

Carnassarie

Kilmartin House M

Kilmartin

Loch
Leathan

Crarae

24

Crarae Glen

Craignish Point

Island
Macaskin

Slockavullin

Temple Wood
Stone Circle

Glebe
Cairn

The Nether Largie Cairns

Duncharagaig
Cairn

Minard

Ri Cruin Cairn

Poltalloch

Gleann Airidh

Tullochgorm

10

orryvreckan

Loch Crinan

Crinan

Kilmahumaig

B8025

Moine
Mhor

River Add

Kilmichael Glassary
Inscribed Stone

Dunadd Fort

Kilmichael
Glassary

Loch
Glashan

URA

Bellanoch

B841

206

esknish

Lochgair

B8000

E   F

OF FYNE

0   1   2   3   4   5 miles
0   1   2   3   4   5   6   7 kilometres

C   D

G H J **229** 988 K 771 **1**

River Noe

River Noe

BEINN EUNAICH

BEINN UDLAIDH

we Ironworks
Inverawe

648
BEINN
DONACHAN

Tyndru

River Orchy

River Lochy

River Lochy

12

1124
BEN
CRUACHAN

B8077

B8074

Glen Lochy

2

1130
BEN LUI

Cruachan
Reservoir

Kilchurn

Stronmilchan

1028
BEN OSS

977
BEINN
DUBHCHR

Pass of Brander

Lochawe

Inverlochy

Cruachan
Power Station

Upper
Kinchrackine

Dalmally

A85

River Awe

A819

6

636

A82
218

739

LOCH·LOMOND·AND

ant B845
B840

renan

W e

Ardanaiseig
Ardanaiseig Hotel

Hayfield

NATIONAL

Taychreggan
Hotel

Cladich

Lochan
Shira

3

Portsonachan
Hotel

947
BEINN
BHUIDHE

645
MAOL BREAC

A·llui
4

Glenfyne
Lodge

589
CRUACH
MHOR

ghour

Glen Aray

Glen Shira

658

CLACHAN
HILL

942
BEN
VORLICH

A819

9

Glen Fyne

Loch
Sloy

11

Cairndow

5

Inver nglas

Bell Tower

Ardkinglas
Woodland
Garden

Glen Kinglas

1011
BEN IME

Inveraray Castle

Loch Shira

Loch Fyne

Ardno

912
BEINN AN
LOCHAIN

Rest and be thankful

925
BEINN NARNAIN

416
CRUACH
TAIRBEIRT

Inveraray

Inveraray Jail

Argyll
Wildlife Park

10

St Catherines

A815

B839

B828

881
THE
COBBLER

Succoth

6

A83

Douglas Water

565
CRUACH
NAN CAPULL

Glen
Croe

A83

Arrochar

845
BEN
DONICH

Ardgartan

Glen Dou

Auchindrain
Township

Strachur

River Cur

River Goil

218

Argyll Forest Park

661
BEN
REACH

7

Furnace

A886

Corrow

Lochgoilhead

Loch Long

Glen Dou

Newton

Balliemore

Douglas Pier

A814

10

Glenbranter

Invernoaden

779
BEINN
BHEULA

Loch Goil

734
DOUNE
HILL

480
CRUACH
NAN CAPULL

A815

Arddarroch

702
BEINN EICH
Edentaggart

8

505
CRUACH AN
LOCHAIN

Loch
Eck

Carrick Castle

Portincaple

Whistlefield

713
BEINN
CHAORACH

A886

15

618
BEINN
BHEAG

Whistlefield
Inn

657

A814

A814

55

Dunans Castle

G H **207** J *est Park* K L *arelochhead* M

742

Argyll F *est Park*

Sligrachan

CREA N

L

Glen Lu

BEINN
THARSUINN

218 A B 229 C D E 230 F

988 BEINN EUNAICH
1 648 BEINN DONACHAN
771 BEINN UDLAIDH
818 BEINN CHAORACH

B8077
Stronmilchan
Inverlochy
A85
Glen Lochy
River Orchy B8074
River Lochy
12
Tyndrum
A82
5
Strath Fillan
Loch Lubhair

Upper Kinchrackine
Dalmally
A919
6
2
Glen

1130
BEN LUI
1028 BEN OSS
977 BEINN DUBHCHRAIG
Inverherive Hotel
Crianlarich
Glen

636
217
739
LOCH LOMOND AND THE TROSSACHS
NATIONAL PARK
Glen Falloch

3
Lochan Shira
West Highland Way
★ Falls of Falloch

947 BEINN BHUIDHE
Inverarnan
A82
17
946 BEINN A' CHROIN
LOCH LOMOND A

Glenfyne Lodge
645 MAOL BREAC
Ardlui
865 STOB A' CH
747 MEALL MÒR

4
Glen Shira
658 CLACHAN HILL
Glen Fyne

942 BEN VORLICH
Loch Sloy

11
Cairndow
Stronachlachar

5
Ardkinglas Woodland Garden
Glen Kinglas
Inveruglas
Inversnaid Hotel
Loch Arklet

Loch Fyne
Ardno
912 BEINN AN LOCHAIN
1011 BEN IME
Rest and be thankful
RSPB
Loch Lomond
B843

St Catherines
B839
11
Glen Croe
925 BEINN NARNAIN
416 CRUACH TAIRBEIRT
633 CRUINN A' BHEINN
Loch Chon

565 CRUACH NAN CAPULL
B828
881 THE COBBLER
Succoth
Arrochar
Tarbet
2
Queen Elizabeth Forest Park

6
845 BEN DONICH
A83
Ardgartan
973 BEN LOMOND

217
661 BEN REACH

Lochgoilhead
Corrow
Argyll Forest Park
Glen Douglas
Rowardennan Lodge
596 BEINN UIRD

7
Invernoaden
779 BEINN BHEULA
Douglas Pier
Loch Goil
A814
10
734 DOUNE HILL
Inverbeg
Rowardennan Hotel
Queen Elizabeth Forest Park
BEN VRAC

Loch Eck
A815
Arddarroch
702 BEINN EICH
Edentaggart
A82
Loch

8
618 BEINN BHEAG
Whistlefield Inn
Carrick Castle
Portincaple
Whistlefield
713 BEINN CHAORACH
Inchlonaig
Luss

Bernice
657
A814
207 C lochhead
655 BEINN THARSUINN
D
Aldoch E
208
F

0   1   2   3   4   5 miles
0   1 2 3 4 5 6 7 kilometres

Map labels:

Finlarig
Killin
Falls of Dochart ★
Breadalbane Folklore Centre
Bovain
Auchlyne
River Dochart
Dochart
Loch Lednock
879 CREAG UCHDAG
682 RUADH MHEALL
MEALL AN FHIODHAIN 778
A85
Glen Beich
SRON MHOR 671
Dalveich
Lochearnhead
Loch Earn
St Fillans
River Earn
A85
Balquhidder
Auchtubh
Ardvorlich
Glen Vorlich
Craigruie
Tulloch
Loch Voil
Loch Doine
Kingshouse Hotel
BEN VORLICH 985
STUC A' CHROIN 975
Dalchruin
Ballimore
Strathyre
THE TROSSACHS NATIONAL PARK
Ardchullarie More
MEALL ODHAR 630
BENVANE 818
MEALL CALA 671
Queen Elizabeth Forest Park
Loch Lubnaig
Katrine
BEN LEDI 876
Kilmahog Woollen Mill
Falls of Leny ★
Kilmahog
Callander
Upper Drumbane
Loch Katrine Pier
The Trossachs
Brig o'Turk
Coilantogle
A821
Rob Roy and Trossachs
BEN VENUE 729
BEINN BHREAC 700
Loch Achray
Lendrick
Loch Venachar
A84
Drumvaich
Burn of Cambus
Buchany
Queen Elizabeth Forest Park
A821
Loch Drunkie
Menteith Hills
BEINN DEARG 427
A81
Altskeith Hotel
Loch Ard
Queen Elizabeth Forest Park
Milton
Aberfoyle
Port of Menteith
Farmlife Centre
Ruskie
Goodie Water
Thornhill
Deanston
Doune
Meldrum
Duchray Water
Inchmahome
Lake of Menteith
B826
ELRIG 208
Cunninghame Graham Memorial NTS
Gartmore
Dykehead
River Forth
Arnprior
Kippen
Cauldhame
Gargunnock
Dalmary
B835
Auchentroig
A811
Buchlyvie
West Highland Way
Milton
Buchanan

Road numbers / grid: G 230 H J 231 D A85 5 A84 220 14 10 A821 7 6 B822 8 B8032 220 A81 4 13 A873 B8031 B8075 B834 B8037 B822 19 209 K L M A811 1 2 3 4 5 6 7 8

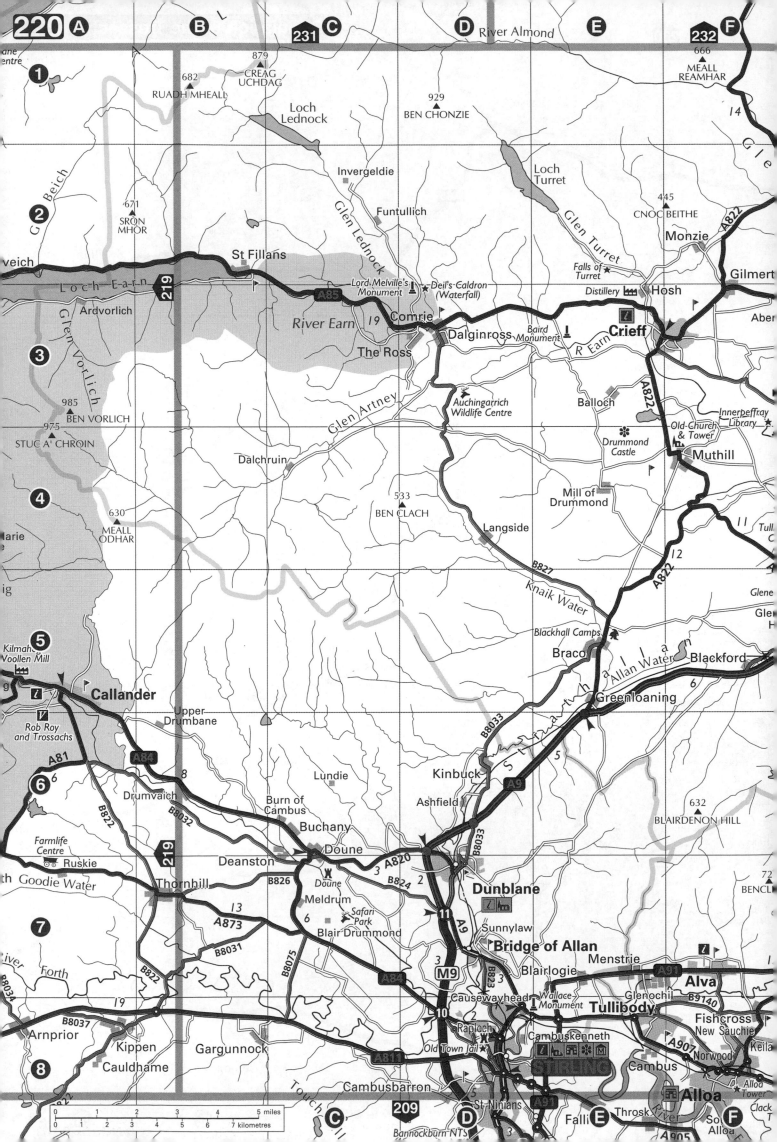

Grish
Clabhach
Hogh Bay Ballyh
Totrona
Ach
Feall
Bay Arileod
Uig
RSPB
Calgary Point
Crossapol
Bay
Gunna
Rudh
Fàsach
Loch Breachacha
Caoles
Rudha Dubh
B8069
Rudha Port
Bhiosd Clachan
Mor Balephetrish
Bay Ruaig
B8068
Loch
Bhasapoll
Haugh
Bay Ballevullin Cornoigmore
Kenovay
Gott
Bay
Kilkenneth
B8068
Tiree
Scarinish
Moss
Heylipoll
Middleton
B8065
Crossapoll
TIREE
Barrapoll
B8065
Hynish Bay
Loch a'
Phuill B8067 Balemartine
Mannel
Rinn
Thorbhais
Hynish
Balephuil Bay

0   1   2   3   4   5 miles
0 1 2 3 4 5 6 7 kilometres

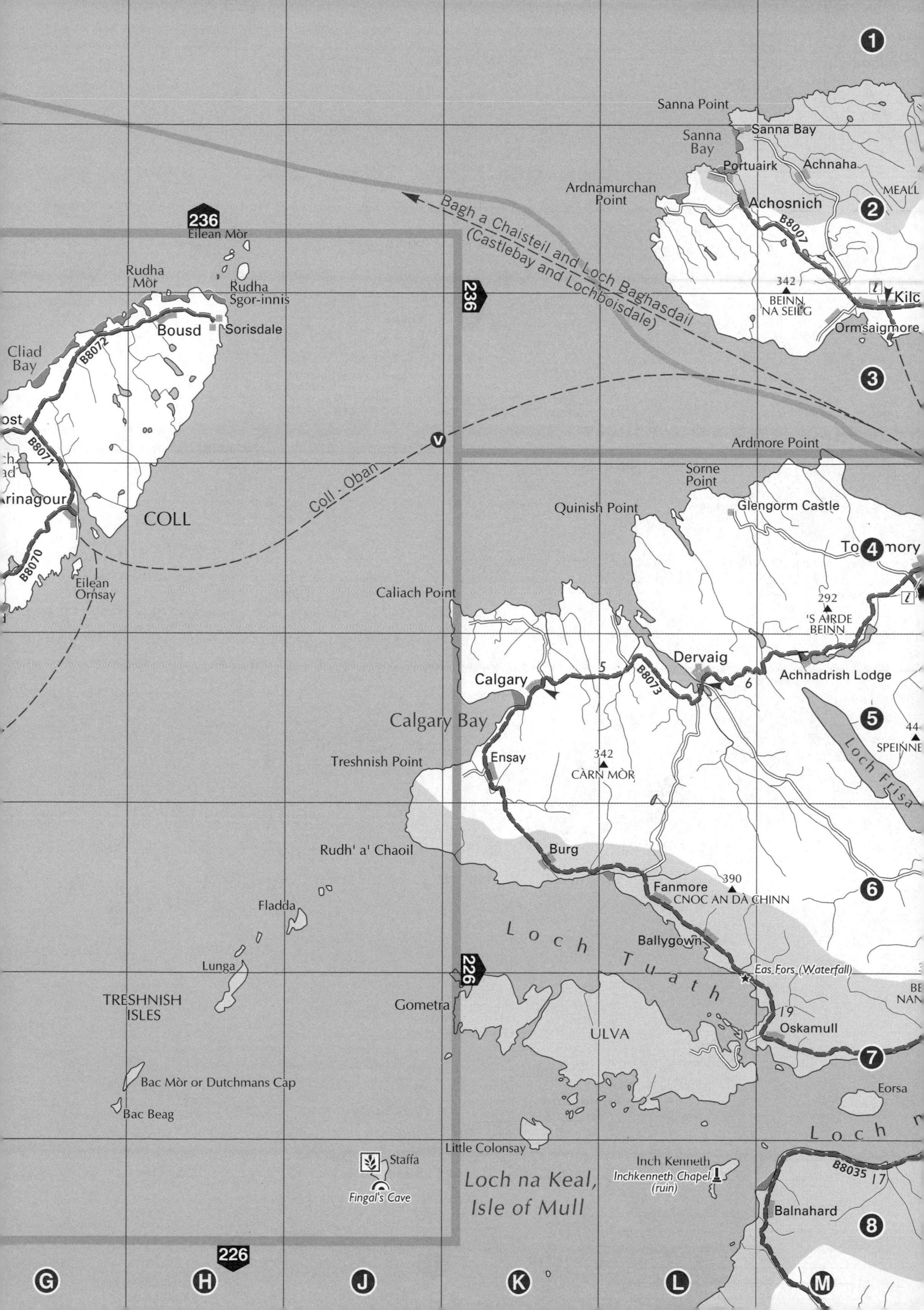

G   H   J   K   L

1

Sanna Point

Sanna Bay

Sanna Bay

Portuairk   Achnaha

2

Ardnamurchan Point

Achosnich

B8007

MEALL

236

Eilean Mòr

Rudha Mòr

Rudha Sgor-innis

Sorisdale

342

BEINN NA SEILG

Kilc

Ormsaigmore

3

Bousd

Cliad Bay

B8072

236

Bagh a Chaisteil and Loch Baghasdail
(Castlebay and Lochboisdale)

Ardmore Point

ost

B8071

Sorne Point

Glengòrm Castle

4

ch ad'

V

Coll - Oban

Quinish Point

292

'S AIRDE BEINN

To more

arinagour

COLL

5

Caliach Point

Dervaig

Achnadrish Lodge

SPEINNE

44

B8070

Eilean Ornsay

5

B8073

6

Loch Frisa

Calgary

Calgary Bay

Treshnish Point

Ensay

342

CÀRN MÒR

6

Rudh' a' Chaoil

Burg

390

CNOC AN DÀ CHINN

Fladda

Fanmore

Loch Tuath

Ballygown

Eas Fors (Waterfall)

BE NAN

Lunga

TRESHNISH ISLES

226

Gometra

ULVA

19

Oskamull

7

Bac Mòr or Dutchmans Cap

Eorsa

Bac Beag

Little Colonsay

Loch

Staffa

Inch Kenneth

B8035 17

Fingal's Cave

Loch na Keal, Isle of Mull

Inchkenneth Chapel (ruin)

Balnahard

8

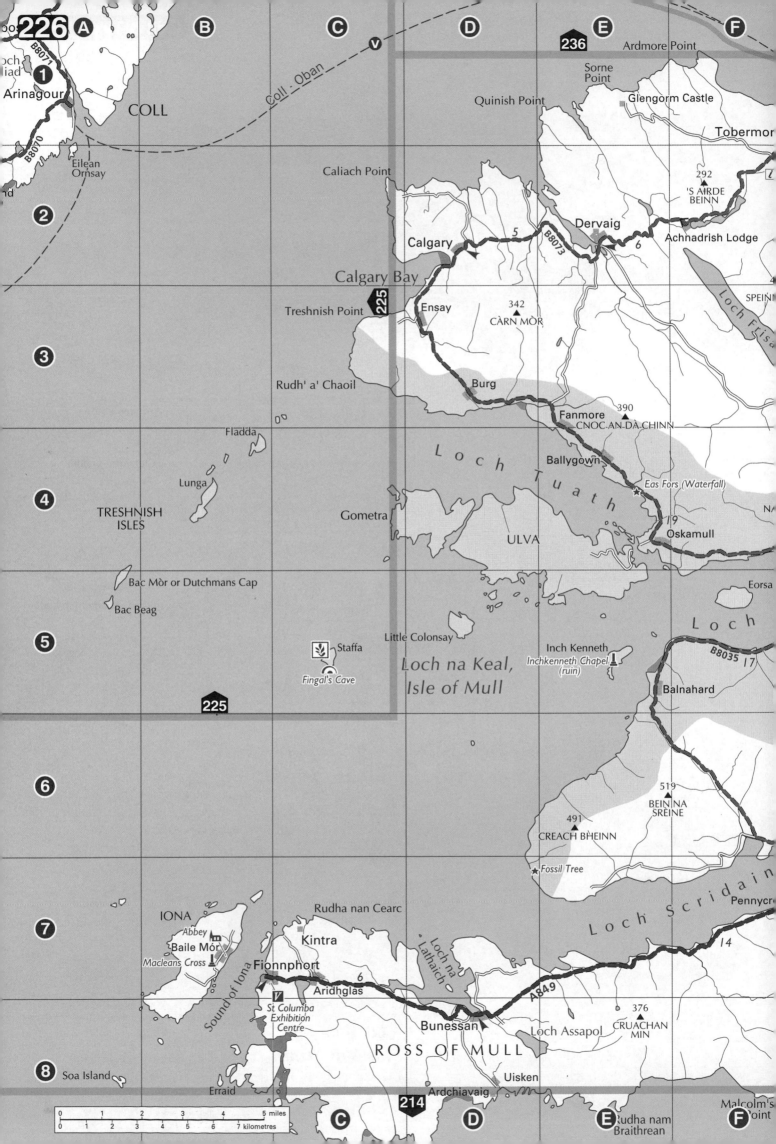

A B C V D E **236** F

1
Loch
Liad
B8071
Arinagour
B8070
Eilean
Ornsay

COLL

Coll - Oban

Ardmore Point

Quinish Point

Sorne
Point

Glengorm Castle

Tobermor

2

Caliach Point

292
'S AIRDE
BEINN

Dervaig

5
B8073

Calgary

6

Achnadrish Lodge

Calgary Bay

225

Treshnish Point

Ensay

342
CÀRN MÒR

Loch Frisa

SPEIN

3

Rudh' a' Chaoil

Burg

Fanmore

390
CNOC AN DÀ CHINN

Fladda

L o c h   T u a t h

Ballygown

Eas Fors (Waterfall)

4

Lunga

TRESHNISH
ISLES

Gometra

ULVA

19

Oskamull

NA

Bac Mòr or Dutchmans Cap

Eorsa

Bac Beag

L o c h

5

Staffa

Little Colonsay

Inch Kenneth
Inchkenneth Chapel
(ruin)

B8035 17

Fingal's Cave

**Loch na Keal,
Isle of Mull**

Balnahard

225

6

519
BEIN NA
SREINE

491
CREACH B'HEINN

Fossil Tree

Rudha nan Cearc

7

IONA

Abbey
Baile Mór
Macleans Cross

Kintra

Loch na
Lathaich

Pennycr

Loch Scridain

14

Fionnphort

6

A849

Sound of Iona

Aridhglas

376
CRUACHAN
MIN

St Columba
Exhibition
Centre

Bunessan

Loch Assapol

ROSS OF MULL

8

Soa Island

Erraid

Uisken

Ardchiavaig

214

Malcolm's
Point

0	1	2	3	4	5 miles
0	1	2	3	4	5	6	7 kilometres

C D E Rudha nam
Braithrean F

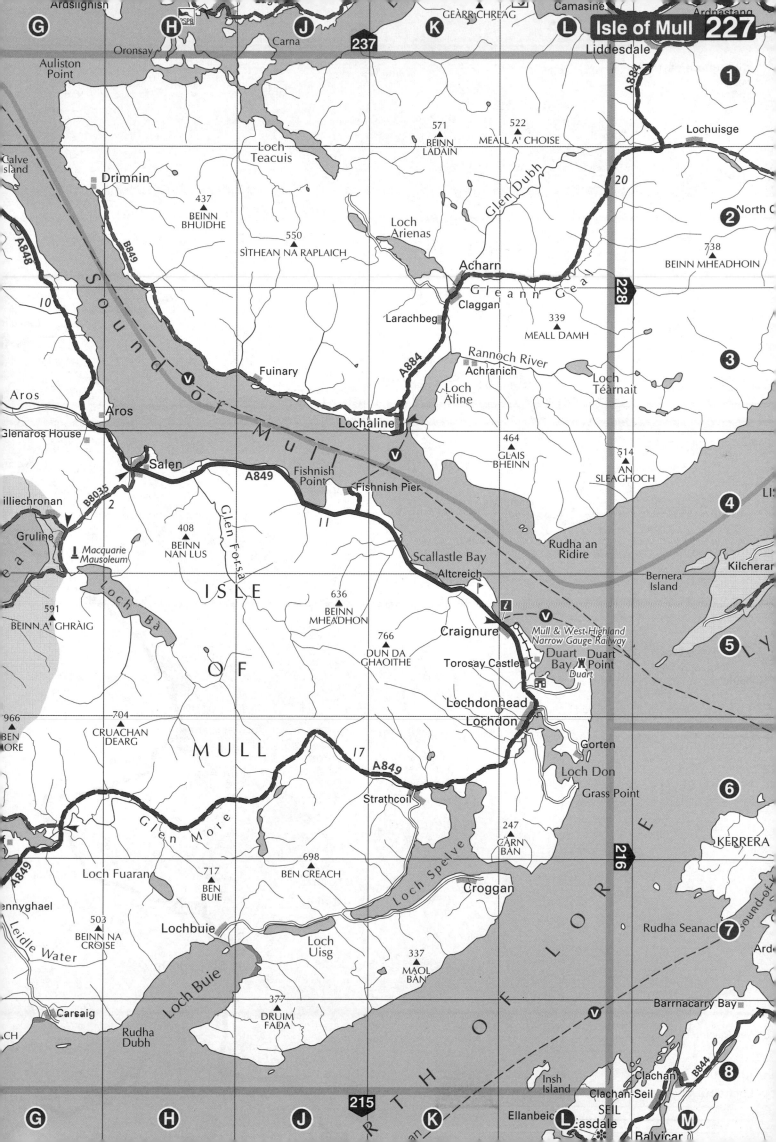

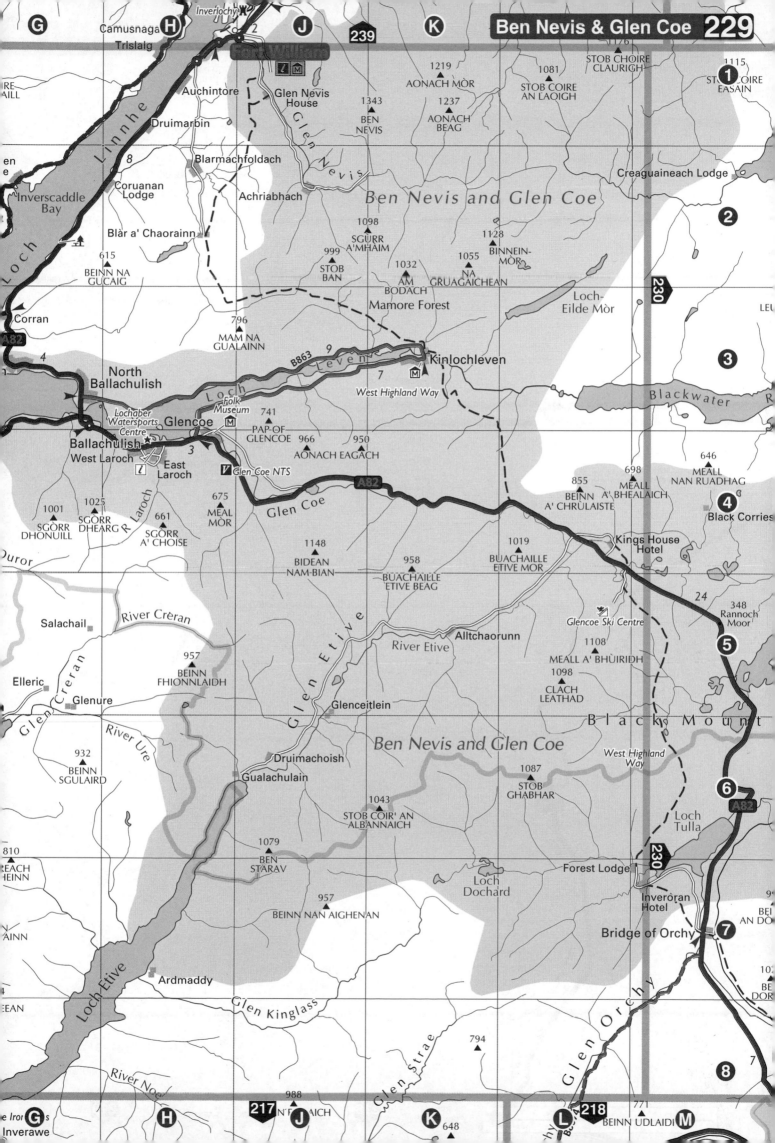

G
H
J
239
K

Camusnaga
Trìslaig
Inverlochy
Fort William
2

STOB CHOIRE
CLAURIGH
1176

1115
ST CHOIRE
EASAIN
1

1219
AONACH MÒR

1081

STOB COIRE
AN LAOIGH

Auchintore
Glen Nevis
House

Druimarbin

1343
BEN
NEVIS

1237
AONACH
BEAG

Blarmachfoldach

Achriabhach

Ben Nevis and Glen Coe

Creaguaineach Lodge

Linnhe
8
Coruanan
Lodge

1098
SGÙRR
A'MHAIM

1128
BINNEIN-
MÒR

230

Inverscaddle
Bay

Blàr a' Chaorainn

615
BEINN NA
GUCAIG

999
STOB
BAN

1032
AM
BODACH

1055
NA
GRUAGAICHEAN

Loch-
Eilde Mòr

2

Corran

796
MAM NA
GUALAINN

Mamore Forest

3

A82
4

North
Ballachulish

B863
9
Leven
Kinlochleven

Blackwater R

Loch
Lochaber
Watersports
Centre

Folk
Museum

7
M

West Highland Way

Glencoe

Ballachulish

741
PAP OF
GLENCOE

966
AONACH EAGACH

950

646
MEALL
NAN RUADHAG

West Laroch

3

East
Laroch

Glen Coe NTS

855
BEINN
A' CHRÙLAISTE

698
MEALL
A' BHEALAICH

4
Black Corries

1001
SGÒRR
DHONUILL

1025
SGÒRR
DHEARG

675
MEALL
MÒR

Glen Coe

A82

1019
BUACHAILLE
ETIVE MÒR

Kings House
Hotel

Duror

661
SGÒRR
A' CHOISE

1148
BIDEAN
NAM-BIAN

958
BUACHAILLE
ETIVE BEAG

Glencoe Ski Centre

24

348
Rannoch
Moor

Salachail

River Crèran

Glen Etive

Alltchaorunn

1108

5

Elleric

957
BEINN
FHIONNLAIDH

River Etive

River Ure

MEALL A' BHÙIRIDH

1098
CLACH
LEATHAD

Glenure

Glen Creran

Glenceitlein

Black Mount

932
BEINN
SGULAIRD

Druimachoish

Ben Nevis and Glen Coe

West Highland
Way

Gualachulain

1087
STOB
GHABHAR

6
A82

810
REACH
HEINN

1043
STOB COIR' AN
ALBANNAICH

Loch Tulla

Forest Lodge

230

1079
BEN
STARAV

Loch
Dochard

Inveròran
Hotel

9
BEI
AN DO

957
BEINN NAN AIGHENAN

Bridge of Orchy

7

Ardmaddy

Glen Kinglass

Loch Etive

794

Glen Orchy

EAN
AINN

River Noe

8
7

G
Iron s
Inverawe

H

217

988
N F AICH

J

K

648

218
L

771
BEINN ÙDLAIDH

10
BE
DOR

M

Ⓐ   Ⓑ   Ⓒ **240**   Ⓓ   Ⓔ   Ⓕ

1176
STOB CHOIRE
CLAURIGH
1081
STOB COIRE
AN LAOIGH

1046
CHNO
DEARG

Loch
Gulbin

1101
BEINN
EIBHINN

1145
BEN
ALDER

Creaguaineach Lodge

Glen Ossian

Loch Ossian

844
MEALL A'BHEALAICH

Loch Treig

1115
STOB COIRE
EASAIN

952
SGOR
GAIBHRE

626
SRON A
CHLAONAID

Loch
Eilde Mòr

229

906
LEUM UILLEIM

864
BEINN PHARIAGAIN

Blackwater   Reservoir

R Ericht

Bridge
of Erich

Rannoch
Station

855
BEINN A'
CHRULAISTE

698
MEALL
A' BHEALAICH

646
MEALL
NAN RUADHAG

Black Corries

738
A' CHRUACH

Loch
Laidon

Dunan
B846
Finna

Loch
Eigheach

Bridge
of Gaur

AILLE
MOR

Kings House
Hotel

Glencoe Ski Centre

24

348
Rannoch
Moor

R a n n o c h

M o o r

1108
MEALL A' BHÙIRIDH

1098
CLACH
LEATHAD

Loch Bà

931
MEALL
BUIDHE

B l a c k   M o u n t

Water of Tulla

Loch an
Daimh

West Highland
Way

1087
STOB
ABHAR

A82

Loch
Tulla

1079
BEINN
A' CHREACHAIN

Loch
Lyon

229

Forest Lodge

Inveroran
Hotel

953
BEINN
MHANACH

1038
MEALL
GHAORDIE

Bridge of Orchy

996
BEINN
AN DOTHAIDH

1076
BEINN HEASGARNICH

G l e n   O r c h y

1074
BEN
DORAIN

7

River Lochay

Glen Lochay

Falls

771

B80?

0   1   2   3   4   5 miles
0   1   2   3   4   5   6   7 kilometres

818
BEINN
CHA[C]CH

218

937
BEINN CHEATHAIC

219

Ⓒ   Ⓓ   Ⓔ   Ⓕ

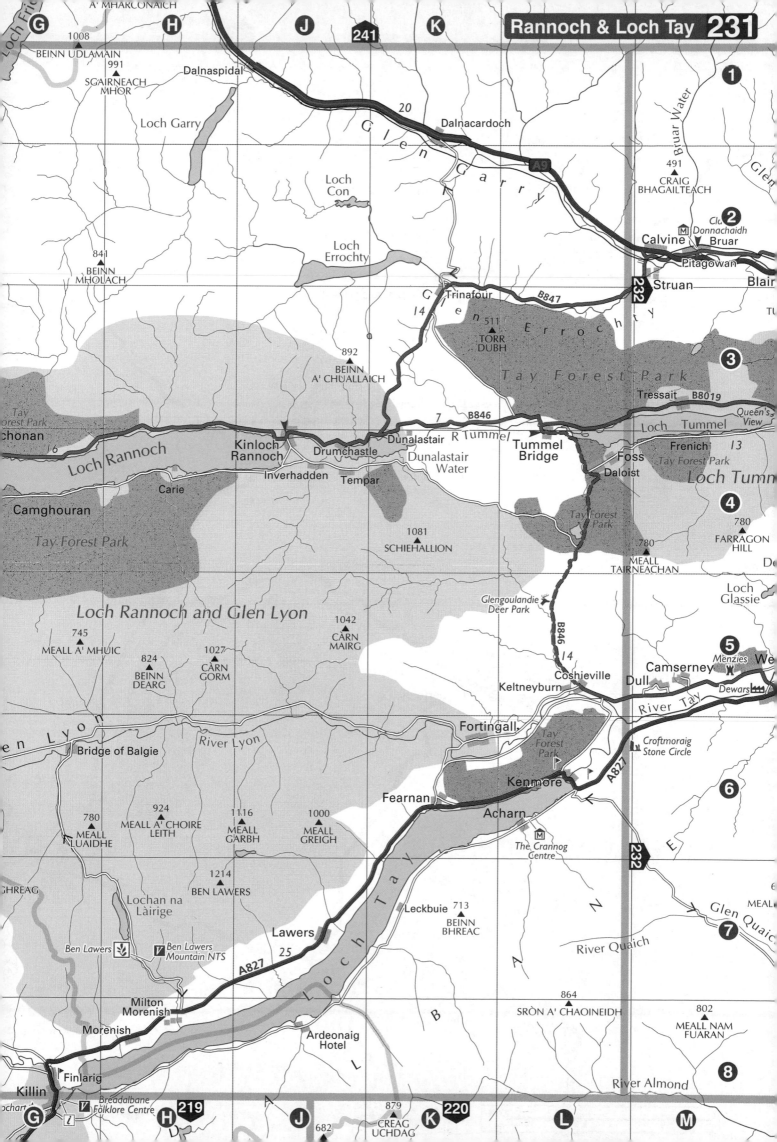

A' MHARCONAICH

G 1008 **H** Dalnaspidal **J** 241 **K**

BEINN UDLAMAIN

991
SGÀIRNEACH
MHOR

1

Loch Garry

20 Dalnacardoch

Loch
Con A9

841
BEINN
MHOLACH

Loch
Errochty

Glen Garry

Craig
Bhagailteach 491

Bruar Water

2

Clc
Donnachaidh

Calvine Bruar

Pitagowan

232 Struan

Blair

Trinafour B847

14

Glen Errochty

511
TORR
DUBH

Tay Forest Park

3

Tressait B8019

Queen's
View

892
BEINN
A' CHUALLAICH

7 B846

R Tummel Loch Tummel

chonan

16

Loch Rannoch

Kinloch
Rannoch

Drumchastle

Dunalastair

Dunalastair
Water

Tummel
Bridge

Foss
Daloist

Frenich 13

Tay Forest Park

Loch Tumm

Camghouran

Carie

Inverhadden Tempar

Tay Forest
Park

780
FARRAGON
HILL

4

Tay Forest Park

1081
SCHIEHALLION

Glengoulandie
Deer Park

780
MEALL
TAIRNEACHAN

Loch
Glassie

Loch Rannoch and Glen Lyon

745
MEALL A' MHUIC

824
BEINN
DEARG

1027
CÀRN
GORM

1042
CÀRN
MAIRG

B846

14

Coshieville

Keltneyburn

Camserney

Menzies

We

Dull

Dewars

5

Glen Lyon

Bridge of Balgie

River Lyon

Fortingall

Tay
Forest
Park

Croftmoraig
Stone Circle

A827

River Tay

6

232

E

780
MEALL
LUAIDHE

924
MEALL A' CHOIRE
LEITH

1116
MEALL
GARBH

1000
MEALL
GREIGH

Fearnan

Acharn

Kenmore

N

Glen Quaic

7

1214
BEN LAWERS

Leckbuie 713
BEINN
BHREAC

The Crannog
Centre

864
SRÒN A' CHAOINEIDH

A

B

802
MEALL NAM
FUARAN

GHREAG

Lochan na
Làirige

Lawers

25 A827

Loch Tay

Ben Lawers
Mountain NTS

Ben Lawers

Milton
Morenish

Morenish

Ardeonaig
Hotel

L

River Almond

8

Finlarig

Killin

Brèadalbane
Folklore Centre

G ochart **H** 219 **J** A **K** 220 **L** **M**

682

879
CREAG
UCHDAG

D

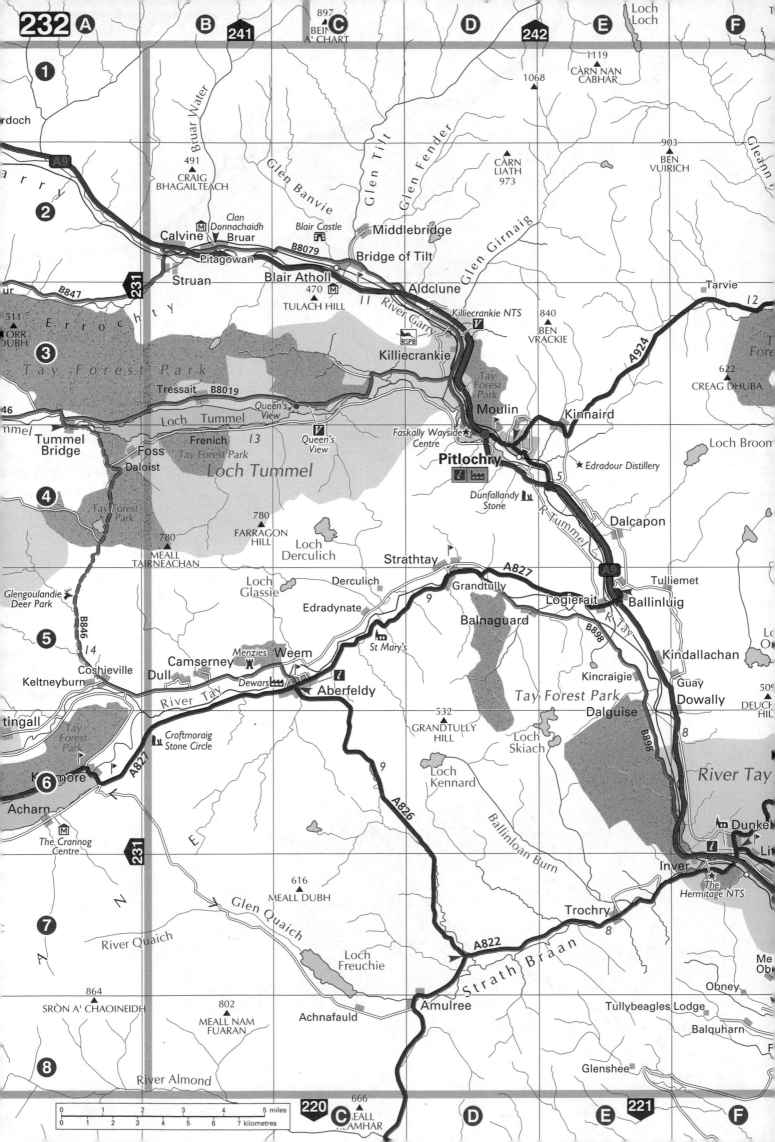

G H **242** J **243** K

34

861
CARN
AIT

928
MAYAR

946
DRIESH

Clova

1

Glen Clova

Glen Lochsie

805
BEN GULABIN

649
CAIRN
OF BAMS

2

LL A'
BHUIDHE

Spittal of
Glenshee

807
MONAMEANOCH

603
CAIRN
DAUNIE

Runtaleave

508

Pitcarity

Cormuir

234

Enochdhu

Glen Shee

792
MEALL
UAINE

700
DUCHRAY
HILL

740
BADENDUN
HILL

Presnerb

Glen Damff

Glen Finlet

Glen Prosen

3

Balvarran

Clackavoid

744
MOUNT BLAIR

Folda

Bridge of
Brewlands

Backwater
Reservoir

Balintore

michael

Upper Ardle

B951

Blacklunans

550
MEALL MOR

Glenisla

Bellaty

Dykends

Braes
of Coul

4

B950

Milton

Scruschloch

River Isla

Lintrathen
Reservoir

B951

Bridgend of
Lintrathen

Kingoldrun

Strath Ardle

13

Ballintuim

Forest of Alyth

Alyth Burn

Dykehead

Bridge of
Craigisla

Kirkton of
Airlie
Littleton

Westmui

A926

M

479

425
BALDUFF
HILL

Airlie

5

A924

A93

Netherton

Gauldswell

Bamff

B954

Craigton
of Airlie

Roun

Loch
Benachally

Bridge
of Cally

River Ericht

294
HILL OF
ALYTH

River Isla

15

H

Dean Water

Eassie

7

Ruthven

B952

Alyth

Ruthven
House

e

11

Achalader

New-Alyth

Balhary

B954

A94

7

Eassie
and Nevay

6

Lornty

Westfields of Rattray

A926

Balkeerie
Kirkinch

Concraigie

Blairgowrie

Kinloch *i* *V*

Rattray

Balharry

Leitfie

Kinloch

M

Sculptured
Stone Museum

h of
owes

Clunie

Craigie

Muirton of
Ardblair

Rosemount

A923

Meigle
Longleys

Newbigging

234

d

Lethendy

B947

5

A94

6

Ardler

Newtyle

B954

Spittalfield

A984

Delvine

A93

A984

R

Coupar
Angus

Bonnyton

Kirkton
Auchterho

Caputh
Gellyburn

Meikleour

Kinclaven

Meikleour
Beech
Hedge

Keithick

A94

Kettins

Leys

Sidlaw Hills

Auchterhouse

Murthly

Cargill

Woodside

Campmuir

13

Lundie

Dronley

Muir of Thorn

Balholmie

Strelitz

Burrelton

15

Muirhea

A923

15

River Tay

B9099

Gallowhill

376

Fowlis

8 Birkh

Airntully

V
Macbeth
Experience

A9

Redstone

Wolfhill

13

Saucher

Liff Gourdie
Denhead
of Gray

Camperdown

G **221** Stanley H Guildtown J Kinrossie Collace KING'S
SE **222** K
B953 L M

Abernyte

Kirkton
of Colla

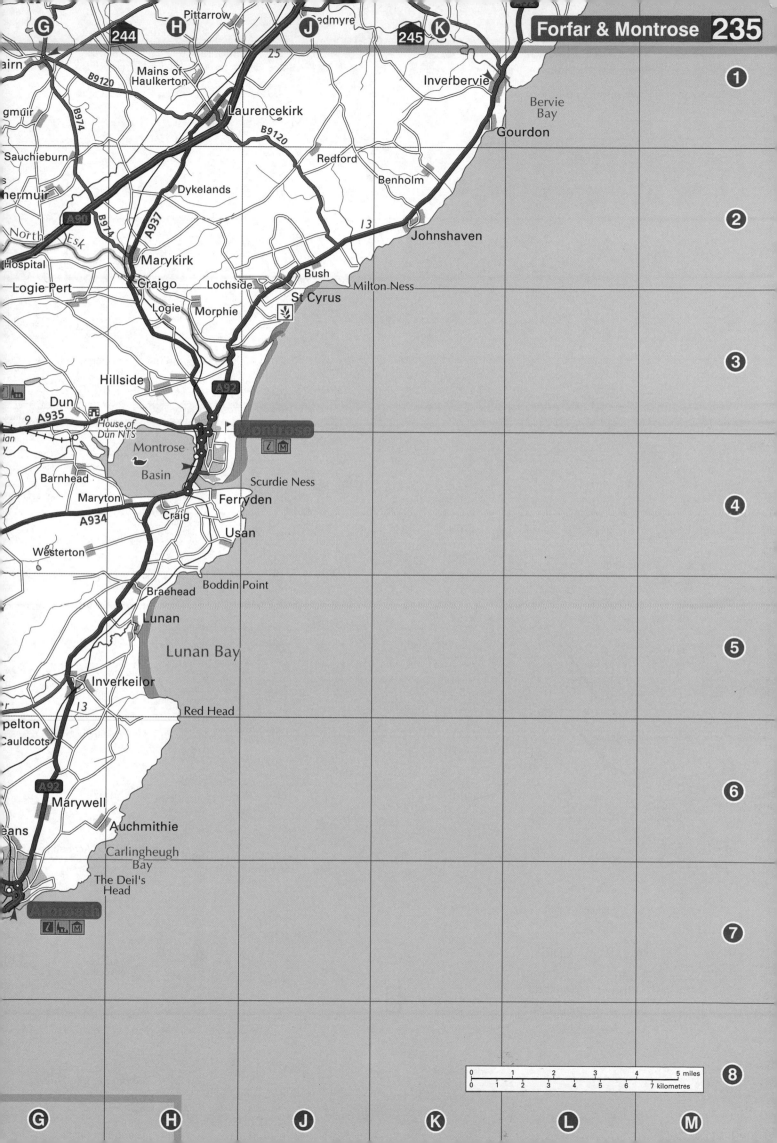

G   H   Pittarrow   J   edmyre   K

244   245

1

2

3

4

5

6

7

8

1

Mains of
Haulkerton

Inverbervie

Bervie
Bay

Laurencekirk   Gourdon

B9120

Redford

Dykelands   Benholm

A90   B974

North   13   Johnshaven

Esk

Hospital   Marykirk

Logie Pert   Craigo   Bush

Lochside   Milton Ness

Logie   Morphie   St Cyrus

Hillside

A92

Dun

9 A935   Montrose

House of
Dun NTS   Montrose   Scurdie Ness

Barnhead   Basin   Ferryden

Maryton   Usan

A934   Craig

Westerton

Boddin Point

Braehead

Lunan

Lunan Bay

Inverkeilor

13   Red Head

pelton

Cauldcots

A92

Marywell

eans   Auchmithie

Carlingheugh
Bay

The Deil's
Head

Arbroath

Ⓐ　Ⓑ　Ⓒ　Ⓓ　Ⓔ　Ⓕ

1

A Bhrideanach

570 ▲
ORVAL

246

MULLACH MÓR

Kinloch

Loch Scresort

Ru na Roinne

Ⓔ

RÙM

810 ▲
ASKIVAL

2

763 ▲
SGÙRR NAN GILLEAN

The Small Isles

Rudha nam Meirleach

Sound of Rum

Bay of Laig

Cleadale

299 ▲
AN CRUACHAN

3

Rudha an Fhasaidh

Laig

EIGG

Kildo

393 ▲
AN SGÙRR

Sandavo

Sound of Eigg

Eilean Chathastail

4

Eilean nan Each

MUCK

Port Mor

5

6

Sanna Point

Sanna Bay

Sanna Bay

Portuairk

Achnaha

MEAL

Ardnamurchan Point

Achosnich

B8007

Bagh a Chaisteil and Loch Baghasdail
(Castlebay and Lochboisdale)

7

Eilean Mòr

Rudha Mòr

Rudha Sgor-innis

225

342 ▲
BEINN NA SEILG

Ⓘ Ki

Bousd

Sorisdale

Ormsaigmor

Cliad Bay

B8072

8

bost

B8071

och liad

| 0 | 1 | 2 | 3 | 4 | 5 miles |
| 0 | 1 | 2 | 3 | 4 | 5 | 6 | 7 kilometres |

Arinagour

Ⓐ　Ⓑ

Coll · Oban

V

Ⓒ

Quinish Point

Ⓓ

Sorne P

226

Ⓔ

Glengorm Castle

Ardmore Point

Ⓕ

G H J K

KNOYD

1

2

3

4

5

6

7

8

Ard of
Sleat

Ard
Thurinish

247

Point
of Sleat

v

Inverie
Bay

Du

Courteachan

Mallaigvaig

Rudha
Raonuill

85

BEINN B

v

Marine
World

i

547

CÀRN A'GHOBHAIR

Glasnacardoch Bay

Loch an
Nostaire

437

SGÙRR BHUIDHE

Stoul

Beoraidbeg

Morar

Bracora

Bracorina

Tarbet

238

Swordland

Glenancross

Lettermorar

Loch

Morar

B8008

Bunacaimb

503

CÀRN A'
MHÀDAIDH-RUAIDH

Meoble

7

Eilean Ighe

MEITH

River Meoble

Back of
Keppoch

600

SIDHEAN
MÒR

Luinga Mhòr

Arisaig

Loch nan Ceall

Rudh' Arisaig

103

CRUACH
DOIRE

Druimindarroch

10

Arisaig
House

Prince Charlie's
Cairn

Kinlochnanuagh

Loch nan Uamh

Polnish

Lochailort

Loch
Eilt

Ardnish

Inverailort

Sound of Arisaig

Rudha
Choalais

Peanmeanach

Loch Ailort

A861

877

ROIS-BHEINN

Smearisary

Glenuig

712

Eilean
Shona

21

664

BEINN GAIRE

Rudha Aird
Druimnich

Loch Moidart

Tioram

Kinlochmoidart

Glen Forsian

Loch

Ockle
Point

Morar, Moidart and
Ardnamurchan

239

Ardmolich

Glen Moidart

MOIDART

Loch S

Imory

Ockle

356

BEINN
BHREAC

Ardtoe

Shielfoot

BEINN
BHREAC

Dalnabreck

228

Loch
Doil

Branault

B8044

Kentra

Blain

Mingarrypark

Polloch

Arevegaig

ARDNAMURCHAN

Acharacle

Claish Moss

A861

SUNAR

Loch
Mudle

437

846

BEINN
RESIPOL

7

527

BEN
HIANT

19

Glenbeg

512

BEN
LAGA

B8007

Salen

Resipole

12

Loch

Sunart

i

Ardslignish

Glenborrodale

Laga

Glencripesdale

Woodend

339

GEÀRR CHREAG

Camasine

Ardnastang

RSPB

Oronsay

Carna

Camasachoirce

Auliston
Point

227

Liddesdale

A884

G H J K L M

248

247

248

237

228

A830

A861

A B C D E F

1
2
3
4
5
6
7
8

BEINN NA H-RAIG

SOUND OF SLEAT

Loch na Dal

Ornsay

lemc

nsay

Sandaig Island

Rudha Buidhe

Rudh' Ard Slisneach

Inverguseran

Airor

518
DRUIM NA CLUAIN-AIRIDHE

Sandaig

Sandaig Bay

Rudha Raonuill

M igvaig

Marine World

547
CÀRN A'GHOBHAIR

Loch an Nostaire

437
SGÙRR BHUIDHE

raidbeg

orar

Bracora

Bracorina

ross

503
CÀRN A' MHÀDAIDH-RUAIDH

Lettermorar

600
SIDHEAN MÒR

10
Prince Charlie's Cairn

Arisaig House

Kinlochnanuag

Loch nan Uamh

Polnish

Ardnish

Peanmeanach

ha lais

Loch Ailort

ig

877
ROIS-BHEINN

712

664
BEINN GAIRE

Glen Guseran

Loch Nevis

Stoul

Tarbet

Swordland

Meoble

River Meoble

710
MEITH BHEINN

Loch Morar

Kylesmorar

Inverie

Inverie Bay

Knoydart
KNOYDART

Loch-an Dubh-Lochain

854
BEINN BHUIDHE

784
BEINN NA CAILLICH

Loch Hourn

974
BEINN SGRITHEAL

Gleneig Brochs

Glen Beag

Dalwaid

Arnisdale

Corran

Glen Arnisdale

773
BEINN NAN CAORACH

614

709
DRUM FADA

Barrisdale Bay

1019
LADHAR BHEINN

940
LUINNE BHEINN

Carnoch

1039
SGURR NA CICHE

859
SGURR NAH-AIDE

723
SGARR BREAC

716
AN STAC

Glen Dessarry

Glen Pean

1003
SGURR MÒR

949
SGURR NAN COIREACHAN

964
SGURR THUILM

Lochailort

Inverailort

Loch Eilt

633

796
SGÙRR AN UTHA

A830

14

Glen Finnan

M

Glenfinnan

Glenfinnan NTS

Glenfinnan Monument NTS

Glenfinnan

Drimsallie

Kinlocheil

Garvan

882
BEINN ODHAR BHEAG

Loch Shiel

Scamodale

718
MEALL NAM DAMH

758

Glen Garvan

Cona C

Gleann Dubhlighe

Gleann Fionnligh

Glen Shiel

SISTERS

SGURR FHUARA

1011
THE SADDLE

945
SGURR NA SGINE

Kinloch Hourn

102
SGUR MHAO

Loch Beoriad

THE SADDLE

G | H | J | K | 1 | 2 | 3 | 4 | 5 | 6 | 7 | 8

FRAOCH-CHOIRE
CISTE DHUBH
249

33 SQÙRR A'BHEALAICH
1030
1120 A'CHRALAIG
1108 SGURR NAN CONBHAIREAN
Dalchreichart
Tomchrasky
River Doe
Glen M
Ceannacroc Lodge
Glen M
Dun

A87
Cluanie Inn
Cluanie Lodge
Loch Cluanie
1019 AONACH AIR CHRITH
947 CREAG A'MHAIM
671 CEANN A'MHAIN
787 MEALL DUBH

1035 GLEOURAICH
996 SPIDEAN MIALACH
Glenquoich Forest
Loch Loyne
Glen Loyne
A87
240
13
3

h D Quoich
Glen Garry
Glen Garry
Ardochy House
Inchlaggan
Loch Garry
Inver
River Garry
Tomdoun
Greenfield
Mandally

919 GAIRICH
Glen Kingie
River Kingie
556 GLAS BHEINN
901 BEN TEE
Glengarry Forest
A
4
Lagg

879 SGURR HURLAGAIN
656 MEALL BLAIR
Loch Blair
Caonich
821 MEALL COIRE NAN-SAOBHAIDH
935 SRON A'CHOIRE GHAIRBH
Kilfinnan
803 BEINNIARUI
5

Loch Arkaig
Ardechive
Gleann Cia-aig
Corriegour Lodge Hotel
Letterfinlay Lodge Hotel
15
N

723
Glen Mallie
Clunes
Loch Lochy
L E

772 MEALL A' PHÙBUILL
Achnacarry
Bunarkaig
Invergloy
Glen Gloy
6
240
Glen Roy

796 BEINN BHAN
Great Glen Way
B8005
Glenfintaig Lodge
654 COIRE CEIRSLE
G L

Gairlochy
A82
Stronenaba
Bohuntine

Glen Loy
738 STOB A' GHRIANAIN
B8004
Brackletter
B8004
Spean Bridge
Inverroy

DRUIM FADA
Strone
Muirshearlich
228
Commando Memorial
i
River Spean
Roy Bridge
7
Mone Fa

Fassfern 11
Neptune's Staircase (Locks)
River Lochy
Torcastle
A82
8 Nevis Range
The Cour
714 BEINN CHLIANAIG

och Eil
A830
Corpach
Banavie
River Lundy
662 SGÙRR-FINNISG-AIG

Blaich
A861
Caol
B8006
Inverlochy
8

Camusnagaul
Trislaig

G | H | J | K | L | M
229
7 STOB COIRE
1219 AONACH MÒR
1081 STOB COIRE
1176 STOB CHOIRE CLAURIG

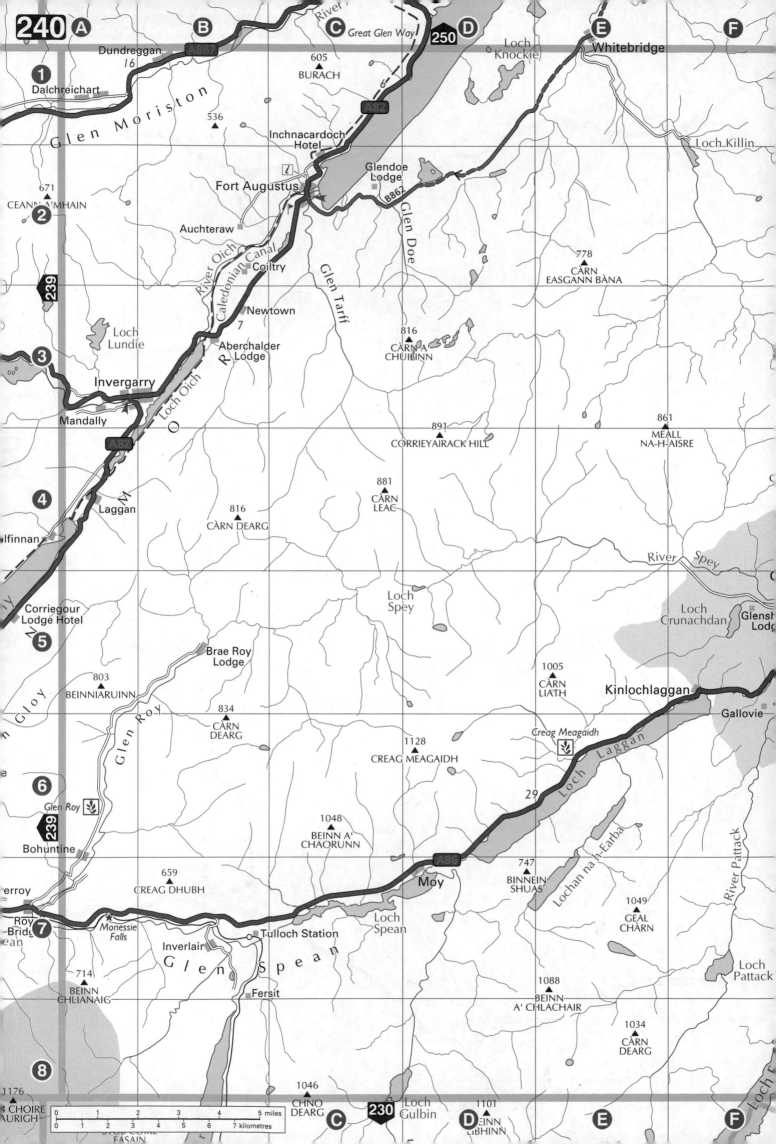

1 Dalchreichart

Dundreggan   A887   16

River

Great Glen Way

Loch Knockie

Whitebridge

Loch Killin

Glen Moriston

605 ▲ BURACH

536 ▲

Inchnacardoch Hotel

A82

671 ▲ CEANN A'MHAIN

2

Fort Augustus

Glendoe Lodge

B862

778 ▲ CÀRN EASGANN BÀNA

Auchteraw

River Oich

Caledonian Canal

Coiltry

Glen Doe

239

Loch Lundie

Newtown   7

Aberchalder Lodge

Glen Tarff

816 ▲ CÀRN A' CHUILINN

861 ▲ MEALL NA-H-AISRE

3 Invergarry

Loch Oich

891 ▲ CORRIEYAIRACK HILL

Mandally

A82

881 ▲ CÀRN LEAC

4

Laggan

816 ▲ CÀRN DEARG

Ilfinnan

River Spey

Loch Crunachdan

Glensh Lodge

Corriegour Lodge Hotel

Loch Spey

5

Brae Roy Lodge

1005 ▲ CÀRN LIATH

Kinlochlaggan

Gallovie

803 ▲ BEINN IARUINN

Glen Gloy

Glen Roy

834 ▲ CÀRN DEARG

1128 ▲ CREAG MEAGAIDH

Creag Meagaidh 🌿

Loch Laggan

6

Glen Roy 🌿

239

1048 ▲ BEINN A' CHAORUNN

29

Lochan na h-Earba

Bohuntine

River Pattack

erroy

659 ▲ CREAG DHUBH

A86

747 ▲ BINNEIN SHUAS

1049 ▲ GEAL CHÀRN

Roy Bridge ean

7

Monessie Falls

Inverlair

Tulloch Station

Glen Spean

Loch Spean

Moy

1088 ▲ BEINN A' CHLACHAIR

Fersit

1034 ▲ CÀRN DEARG

714 ▲ BEINN CHLIANAIG

Loch Pattack

8

1176 ▲ CHOIRE AURIGH

0   1   2   3   4   5 miles
0   1   2   3   4   5   6   7 kilometres

STOB COIRE EASAIN

1046 ▲ CHNO DEARG

C   **230**

Loch Gulbin

1101 ▲ BEINN LIBHINN

D   E   F

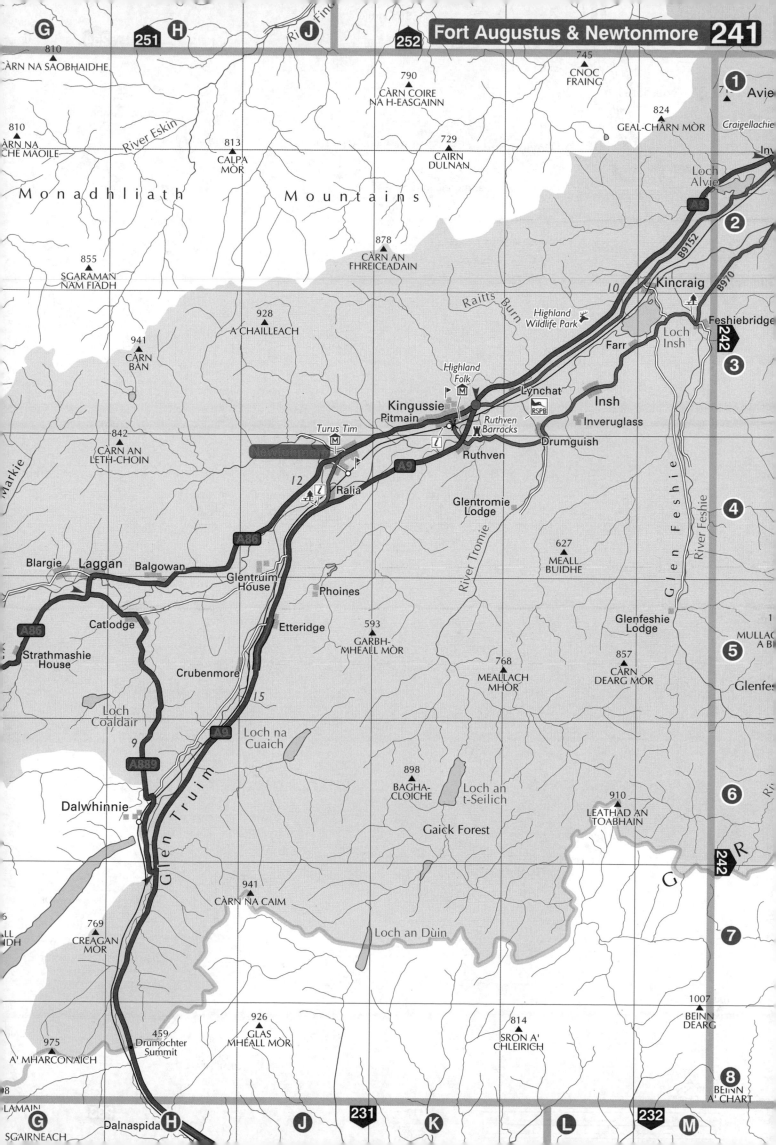

G | H 251 | J | 252

810
CÀRN NA SAOBHAIDHE

745
CNOC FRAING

1 Avie

790
CÀRN COIRE NA H-EASGAINN

810
ÀRN NA CHE MAOILE

River Eskin

813
CALPA MÒR

729
CAIRN DULNAN

824
GEAL-CHÀRN MÒR

Craigellachie

Inv

Loch Alvie

A9

B9152

M o n a d h l i a t h   M o u n t a i n s

878
CÀRN AN FHREICEADAIN

2

Raitts Burn

Highland Wildlife Park

10

Kincraig

B9970

855
SGARAMAN NAM FIADH

Farr

Loch Insh

242

Feshiebridge

3

928
A' CHAILLEACH

Highland Folk M

Lynchat

Insh

941
CÀRN BÀN

Kingussie
Pitmain

RSPB

Inveruglass

Markie

842
CÀRN AN LETH-CHOIN

Turus Tim M

Newtonmore

Ruthven Barracks

Drumguish

Ruthven

Glentromie Lodge

Glen Feshie

River Feshie

4

12 ℹ Ralia

A9

River Tromie

627
MEALL BUIDHE

Blargie | Laggan | Balgowan

A86

Glentruim House

Phoines

Glenfeshie Lodge

MULLAC A B

Catlodge

Etteridge

593
GARBH-MHEALL MÒR

857
CÀRN DEARG MÒR

5

Glenfes

Strathmashie House

A86

Crubenmore

768
MEALLACH MHÒR

Loch Coaldair

15

Loch na Cuaich

A9

A889

9

898
BAGHA-CLOICHE

Loch an t-Seilich

910
LEATHAD AN TOABHAIN

6

R

Dalwhinnie

Glen Truim

Gaick Forest

242

G

941
CÀRN NA CAIM

Loch an Dùin

7

769
CREAGAN MÒR

LL IDH

1007
BEINN DEARG

975
A' MHARCONAICH

459
Drumochter Summit

926
GLAS MHEALL MÒR

814
SRON A' CHLEIRICH

8
BEINN A' CHART

LAMAIN

SGAIRNEACH

G | H Dalnaspida | J | 231 | K | L | 232 | M

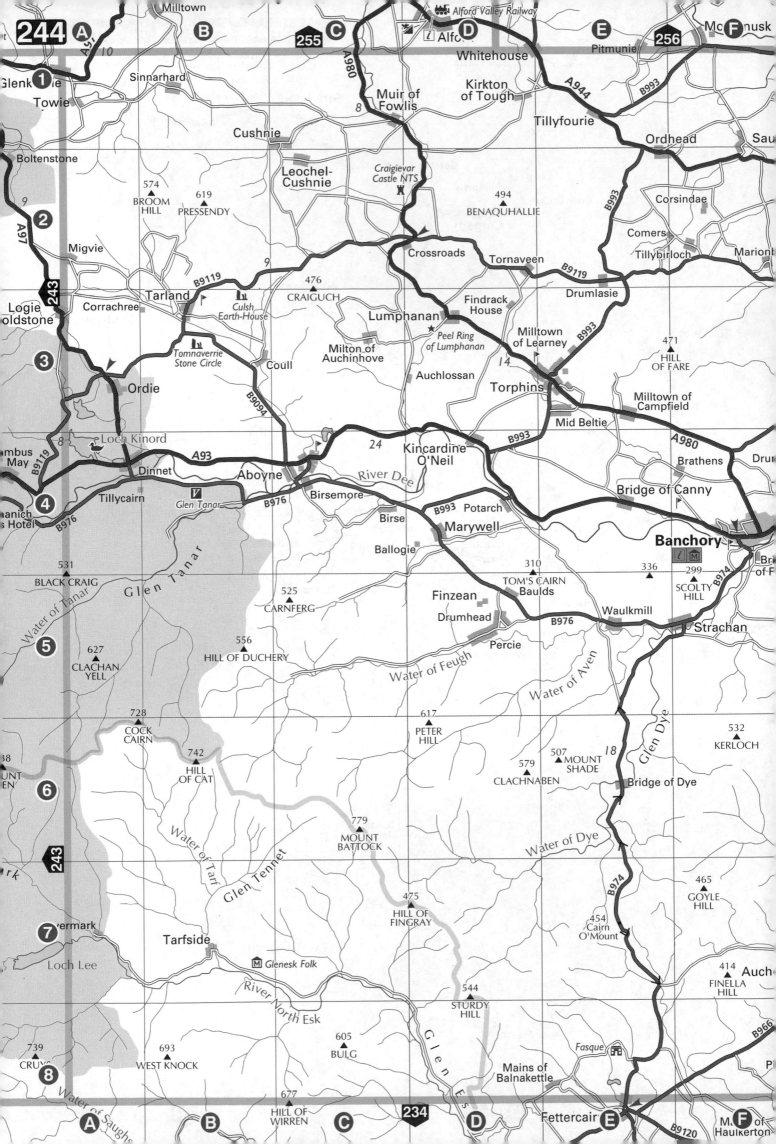

HEALAVAL
BHEAG (B)

Harlosh (C)

Loch

Os (D)

(E) LEE

(F) Gle

258

Colbost
Point

368
BEINN NA
BOINEID

Harlosh
Island

Bracadale

Loch
Duagrich

Mu

(1)

Tarner
Island

Struan

Coillore

Loch Bracadale

Ullinish
Lodge Hotel

23

OF

Wiay

Oronsay

439
ROINEVAL

Idrigill
Point

Portnalong

(2)

Fiskavaig

Loch Harport

B8009

Fernilea

S

Rudha nan Clach

369
ARNAVAL

Carbost

Drynoch

A86

Merkadale

Glen Dry

Talisker
Bay

Talisker

Glen Eynort

369
BEINN BH

(3)

447
BEINN
BHREAC

Grula

Loch Eynort

(4)

434
AN CRUACHIN

SG
A' GH

Cu

Glenbrittle House

Bualintur

S
AL

Loch Brittle

225
CEANN NA BEINNE

(5)

Rudh' an Dùnain

Soay Soun

(6)

R
Aor

CUILLI

CANNA

210
CÀRN A' GHAILL

Rudha
Shamhnan Insir

(7)

Garrisdale Point

A'Chill

Canna
Harbour

Sanday

Sound of Canna

302
MULLACH
MÒR

Rudha na

(8)

| 0 | 1 | 2 | 3 | 4 | 5 miles |
| 0 | 1 | 2 | 3 | 4 | 5 | 6 | 7 kilometres |

A Bhrideanach

236

570
ORVAL

Kinloch Loch
Scresort

(A)

(B)

(C)

(D)

(E)

(F)

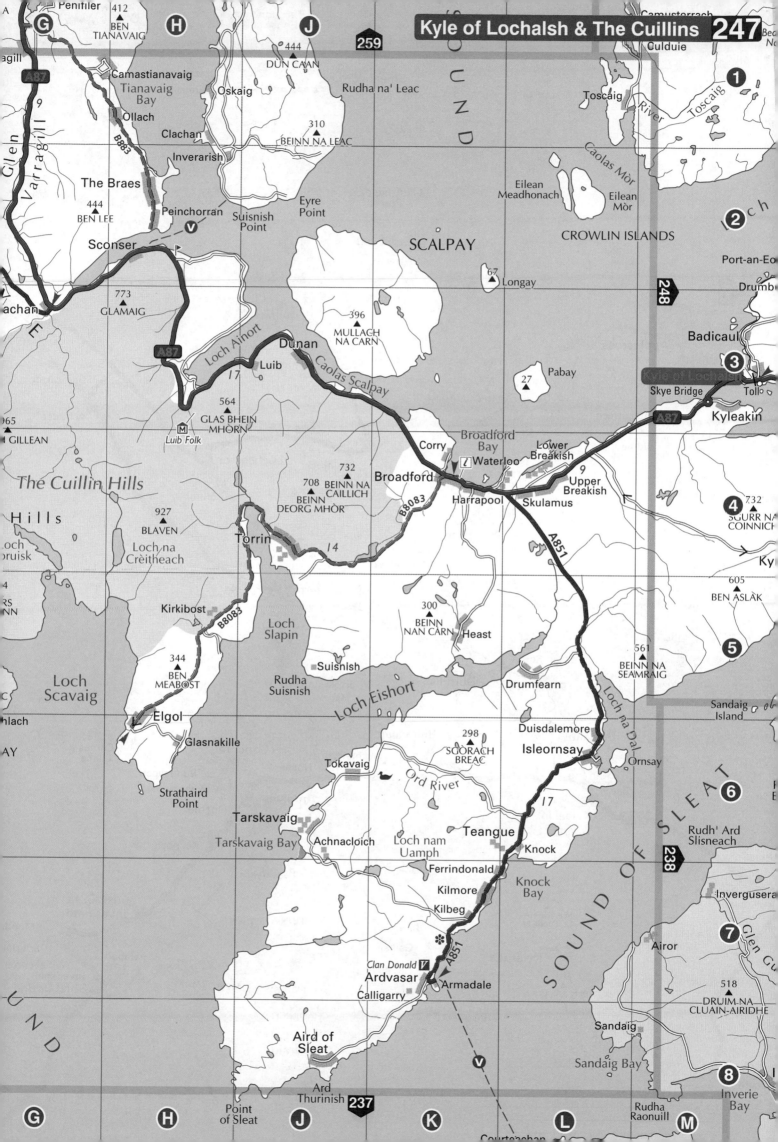

259

G
H
J

412
BEN
TIANAVAIG

Penifiler

Camustorrach

Culduie

444
DÙN CAAN

Camustianavaig
Tianavaig
Bay

Ollach

Oskaig

Rudha na' Leac

Toscaig
River

Toscaig

Clachan

Inverarish

310
BEINN NA LEAC

Caolas Mòr

1

The Braes

Eyre
Point

Eilean
Meadhonach

Eilean
Mòr

CROWLIN ISLANDS

2

444
BEN LEE

Peinchorran

Suisnish
Point

SCALPAY

Port-an-Eo

Drumb

Sconser

67
Longay

248

965
GILLEAN

773
GLAMAIG

Loch Ainort

Dunan

396
MULLACH
NA CARN

27
Pabay

Badicaul

Luib

564
GLAS BHEIN
MHORN

Caolas Scalpay

3
Kyle of Lochal

Skye Bridge

Toll

17

M
Luib Folk

Corry

Broadford
Bay

Lower
Breakish

A87

Kyleakin

The Cuillin Hills

732
BEINN NA
CAILLICH

Waterloo

9

Broadford

708
BEINN
DEORG MHÒR

Harrapool

Upper
Breakish

Hills

Skulamus

4
732
SGURR NA
COINNICH

927
BLAVEN

B8083

Torrin

14

605
BEN ASLÀK

Loch na
Crèitheach

Kirkibost

B8083

Loch
Slapin

300
BEINN
NAN CARN

Heast

A851

561
BEINN NA
SEAMRAIG

5

344
BEN
MEABOST

Suisnish

Drumfearn

*Loch
Scavaig*

Loch Eishort

Sandaig
Island

Elgol

Rudha
Suisnish

Duisdalemore

Loch na Dal

6

Glasnakille

298
SGORACH
BREAC

Isleornsay

Ornsay

Rudh' Ard
Slisneach

Strathaird
Point

Tokavaig

Ord River

Teangue

17

238

Tarskavaig

Achnacloich

Loch nam
Uamph

Knock

Knock
Bay

Invergusera

Tarskavaig Bay

Ferrindonald

7

Airor

Kilmore

A851

Kilbeg

518
DRUM NA
CLUAIN-AIRIDHE

Clan Donald

Aird of
Sleat

Ardvasar

Armadale

Calligarry

Sandaig

Sandaig Bay

8

237

Ard
Thurinish

Point
of Sleat

Inverie
Bay

G
H
J
K
L
M

SOUND OF SLEAT

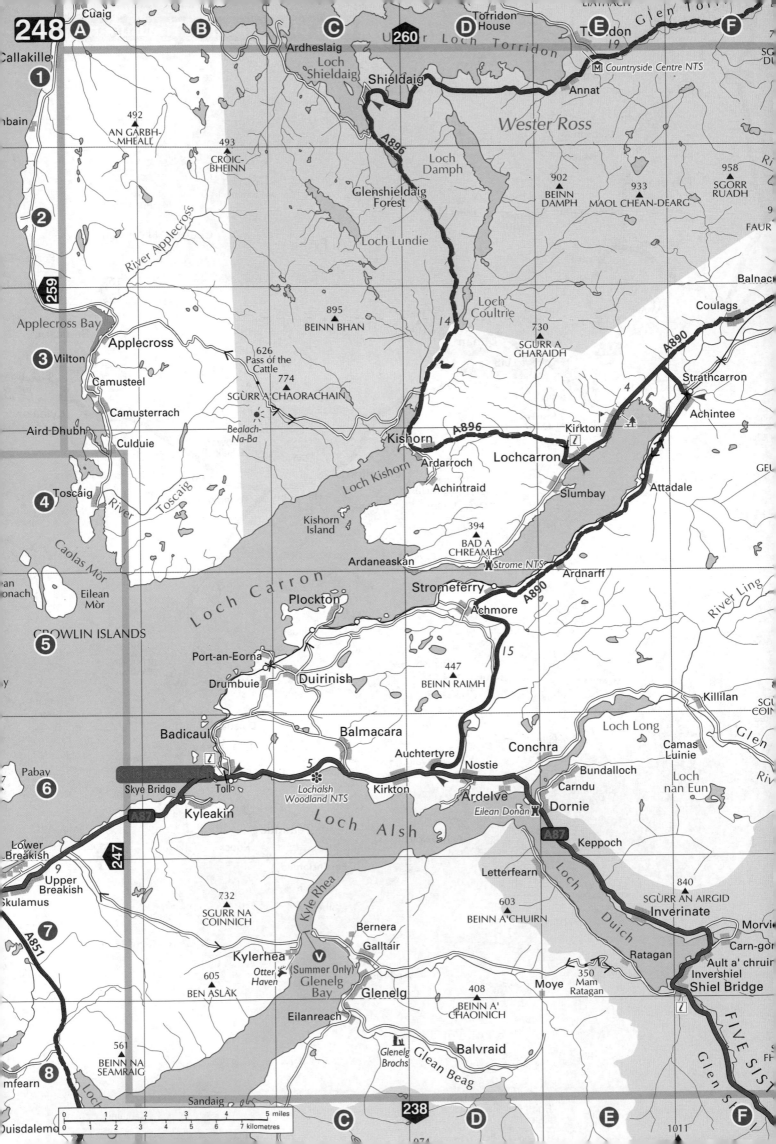

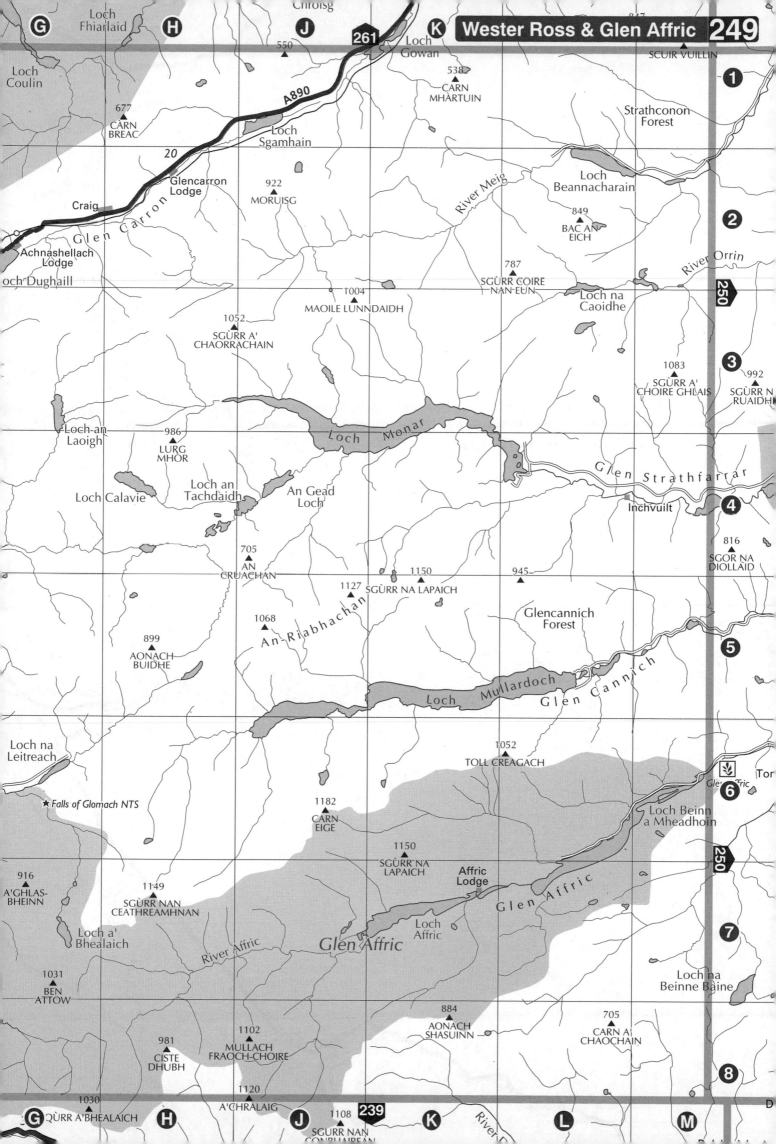

Chroisg

G Loch Fhiarlaid H J 550 261 Loch Gowan K SCUIR VUILLIN 1

Loch
Coulin

677
▲
CARN
BREAC

A890

Loch
Sgamhain

538
▲
CARN
MHÀRTUIN

Strathconon
Forest

20

Glencarron
Lodge

922
▲
MORUISG

River Meig

Loch
Beannacharain

849
▲
BAC AN
EICH

2

Craig

Glen Carron

2

Achnashellach
Lodge

787
▲
SGÙRR COIRE
NAN-EUN

Loch na
Caoidhe

River Orrin

250

och Dughaill

1004
▲
MAOILE LUNNDAIDH

1083
▲
SGÙRR A'
CHOIRE GHLAIS

992
▲
SGÙRR N
RUAIDH

3

1052
▲
SGÙRR A'
CHAORRACHAIN

Loch-an
Laoigh

986
▲
LURG
MHOR

Loch Monar

Glen Strathfarrar

Inchvuilt

4

Loch Calavie

Loch an
Tachdaidh

An Gead
Loch

816
▲
SGOR NA
DIOLLAID

705
▲
AN
CRUACHAN

1150
▲

945
▲

1127
▲
SGÙRR NA LAPAICH

1068
▲

An Riabhachan

Glencannich
Forest

899
▲
AONACH
BUIDHE

Loch Mullardoch

Glen Cannich

5

Loch na
Leitreach

1052
▲
TOLL CREAGACH

Glen Affric

Tor

6

★ Falls of Glomach NTS

1182
▲
CARN
EIGE

Loch Beinn
a Mheadhoin

916
▲
A'GHLAS-
BHEINN

1149
▲
SGÙRR NAN
CEATHREAMHNAN

1150
▲
SGÙRR NA
LAPAICH

Affric
Lodge

Glen Affric

250

Loch a'
Bhealaich

River Affric

Glen Affric

Loch
Affric

7

Loch na
Beinne Bàine

1031
▲
BEN
ATTOW

884
▲
AONACH
SHASUINN

705
▲
CARN A'
CHAOCHAIN

981
▲
CISTE
DHUBH

1102
▲
MULLACH
FRAOCH-CHOIRE

1120
▲
A'CHRALAIG

1030
▲
SGÙRR A'BHEALAICH

G H J 1108
▲
SGURR NAN
CONBHAIREAN 239 K River L M

8

D

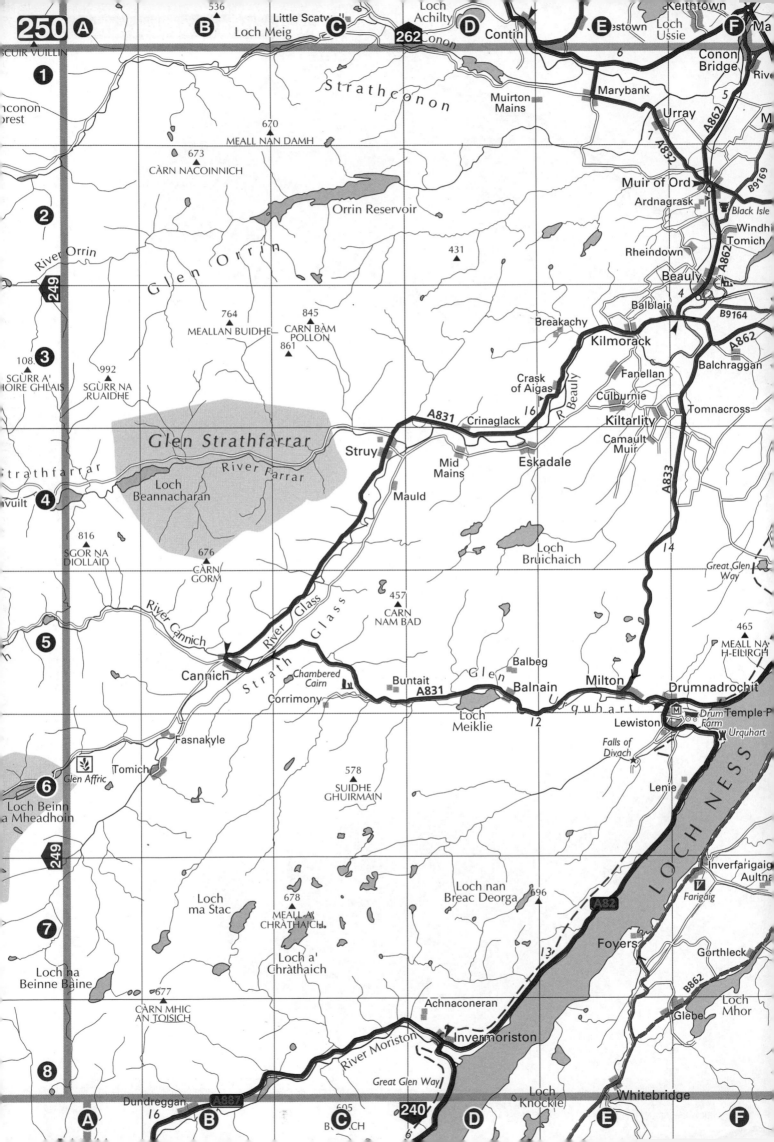

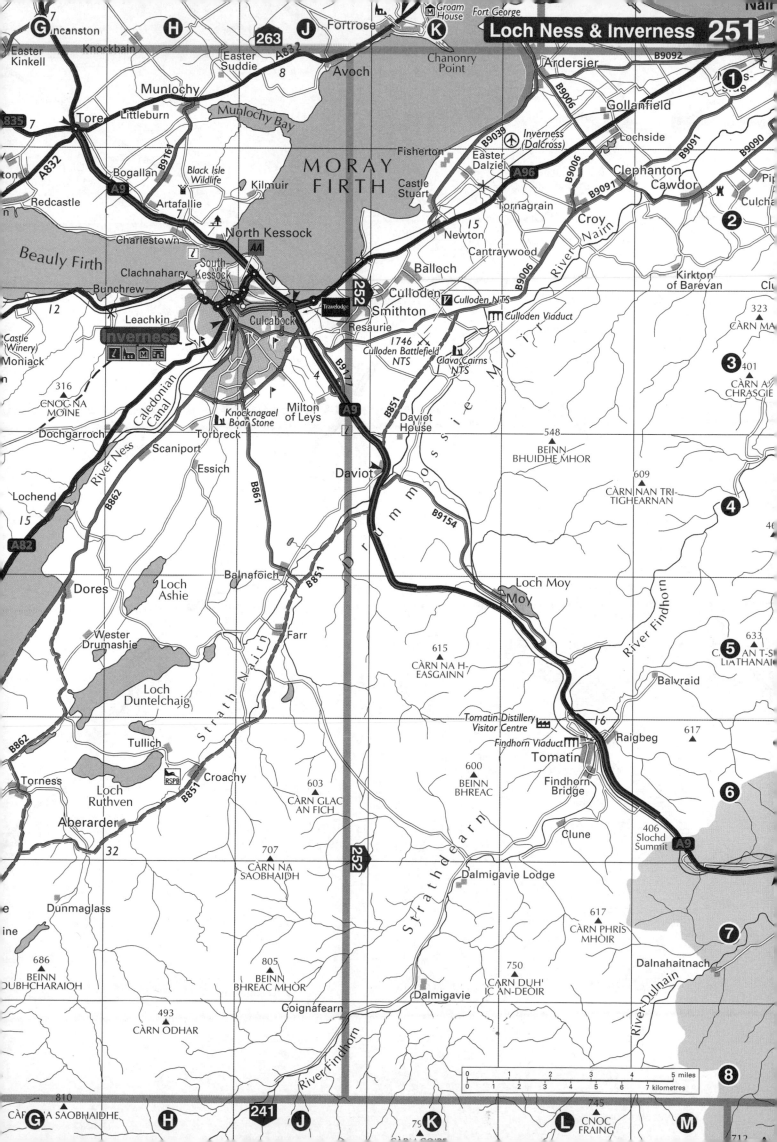

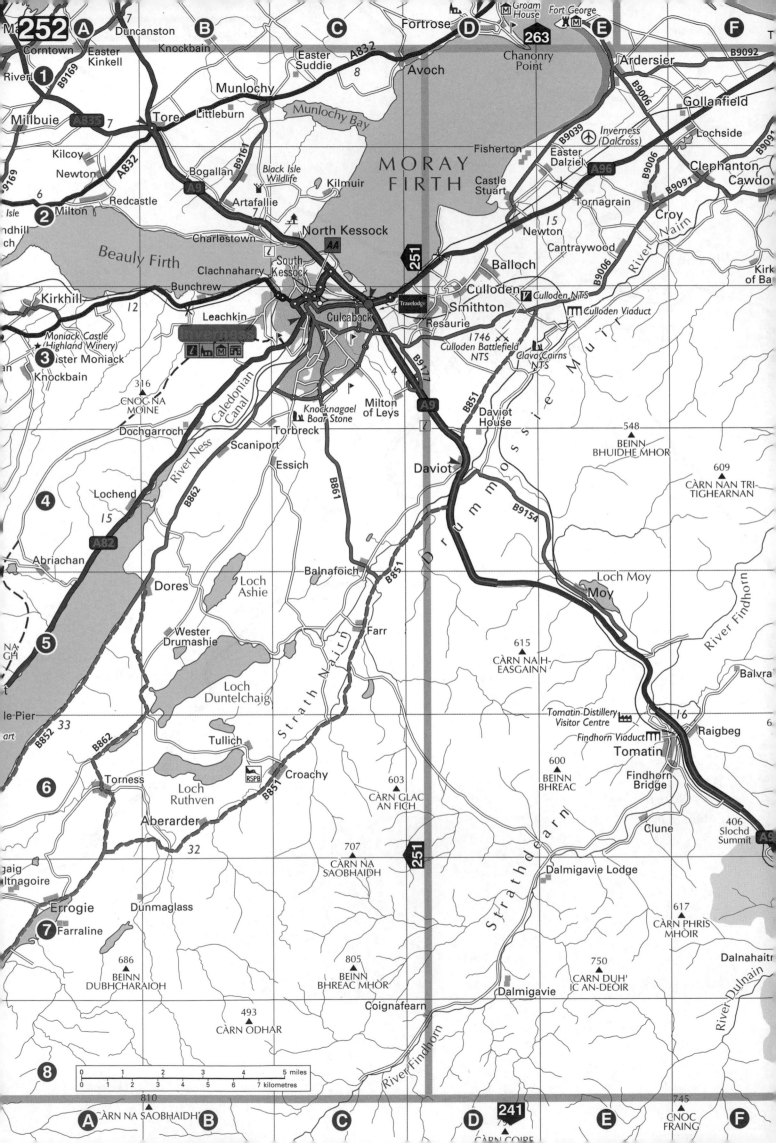

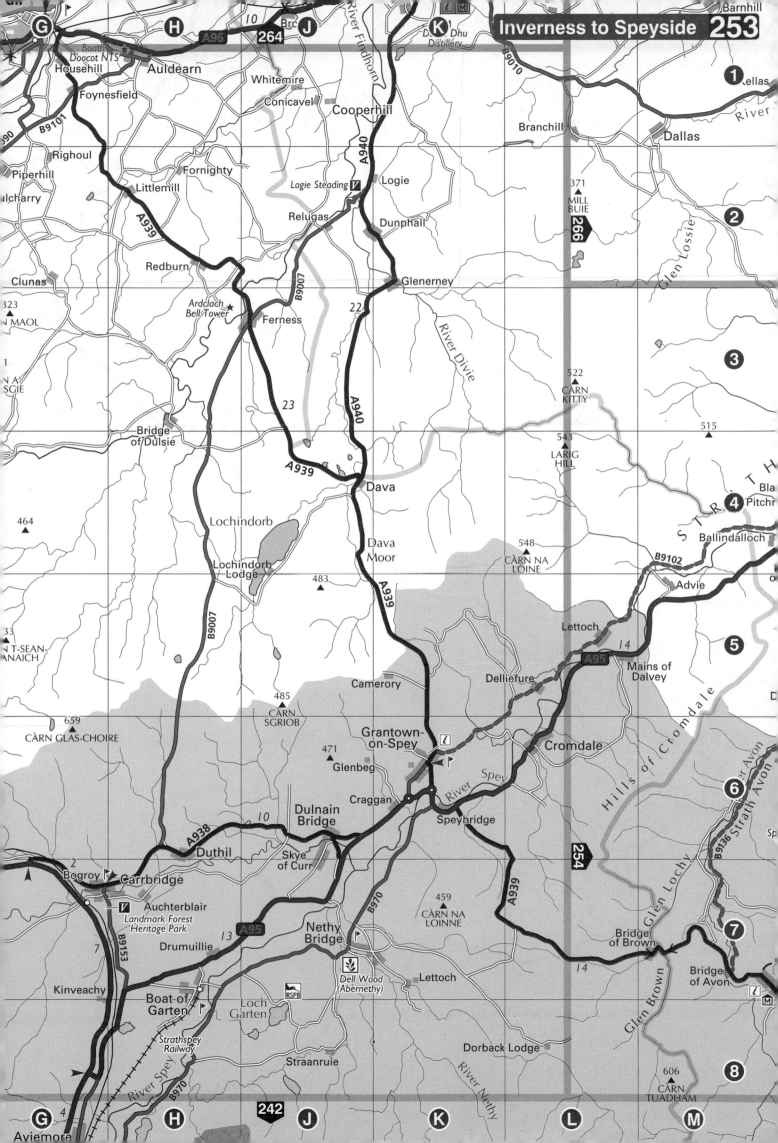

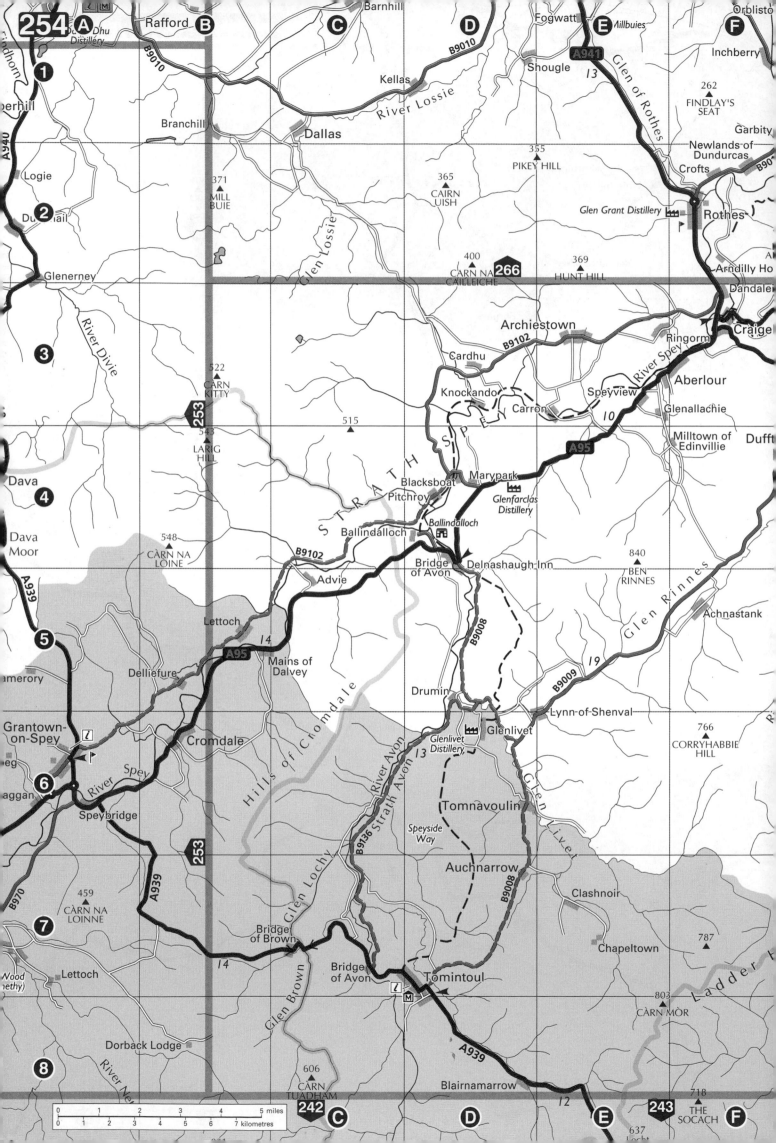

G   equish
Craiglug
WHITEASH HILL   H
MILLSTONE HILL
J
K   LURG HILL
A96
429
250
THIEF'S HILL
Forgie
8
KNOCK HILL 20
Glenbarry
271
WETHER HILL
Lootcherbrae
1
Sound Muir
Aultmore Forgieside
Grange Crossroads
Berryhillock
Knock
Bridge of Marnoch
Cairnty
hroisk
Newmill
Bracobrae
Davoch of Grange
Drumnagorrach
Upper Mulben
Rumbach
B9017
Strath Isla
A95
Farmtown
B9022
103
Mulben
Strathisla Distillery
Fife Keith
Keith
River Isla
Rothiemay
B9117
2
Deanshaugh
Tauchers
Rosarie
365
MEIKLE BALLOCH
Inverkeith
A95
2
338
HILL OF TOWIE
Keith and Dufftown Railway
A96
267
Newtack
Ruthven
Bogniebrae
Forgue
12
372
KNOCKAN
11
11
Cairnie
A97
256
3
B9 01
gieknockater
B9115
Drummuir
River Deveron
B9022
enfiddich istillery
B9014
Balvenie
A920
14
Invermarkie
Affleck
Drumblade
Huntly
Haugh of Glass
Brideswell
A96
4
5
Bridgend
Thomastown
A941
Kirkstile
Newtongarry Croft
Bainsho
503
Glens of Foudlan
525
Culdrain
419 WICHACH HILL
466 HILL OF FOUDLAN
5
440 CRANSMILL HILL
Kirkney
Gartly
Largie
Picardy Symbol Stone
564
Leith Hall NTS
TAP O' NOTH
18
A941
Kennethmont
B9002
Dunnideer
Insch
571 ROUND HILL
Cabrach
Belhinnie
Rhynie
Cottown
Clatt
Duncanstone
6
Aldivalloch
Aldunie
A97
B9002
Leslie
256
722 THE BUCK
St Mary's Kirk (Ruin)
484 MIRE OF MIDGATES
B992
629 HILL OF THREE STONES
5
Lumsden
475
CORREEN HILLS
7
BRUX HILL
Lethenty
nyon
632 CREAG AN EUNAN
Mossat
A944
Tullynessle
Keig
6
Scotsmill
Kildrummy
Bridge of Alford
Montgarrie
Haughton House
Belnacraig
Kildrummy
Milltown
Alford Valley Railway
8
Kirkton of Glenbuchat
A97
Glenbuchat
Alford
243
G   H
J
K   244
L
M
Bellabeg
Glenkindie
Sinnarhard
Whitehouse
Muir of
Kirkton
10

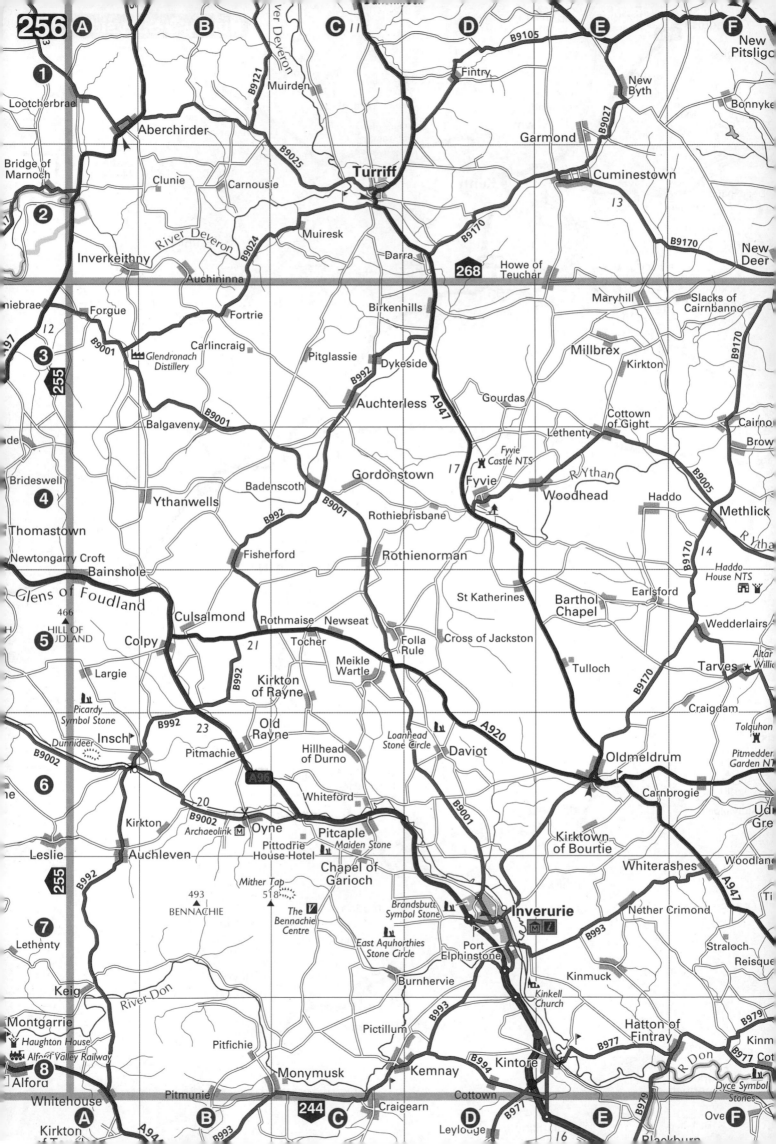

Ⓐ Ⓑ Ⓒ Ⓓ Ⓔ Ⓕ

① ② ③ ④ ⑤ ⑥ ⑦ ⑧

Fladda-chùain

Rudha Hun

Dù

Lùb Score

Borneskitaig

Kilmuir
Kilva

Balgown
Lin

Totscore

Tairbeart
(Tarbert)

Ⓥ

Loch nam Madadh
(Lochmaddy)

Idrigill

ⓘ

Uig Bay

Ⓥ

Waternish Point

Ascrib
Islands

Loch Snizort

Ea

283
BEN
GEARY

Geary

16

A87

Trumpan

Gillen

Ardmore
Point

Hallin

DUNVEGAN
HEAD

Isay Mingay

Stein Lusta

214
BEN
DIUBAIG

Greshornish
House
Hotel

Loch
Bay

Loch Greshornish

Loch Snizor

K

Claigan

Boreraig

Bay

22
Treaslane

Uig

327
BEINN
BHREAC

B886

Flashader

A850

Loch
Pooltiel

Loch Dunvegan

Upperglen

Edinbane

Bernisdale

Feriniquarrie

Totaig

Oisgill Bay Milovaig

Glendale

Colbost

Dunvegan

A850

Waterstein

Lephin

B884

Colbost Croft

ⓘ Dunvegan

ⓜ

265
BEN
AKETIL

271
CRUACHAN BEINN
A' CHEARCAILL

Toy

ⓜ Giant Angus MacAskill

Skinidin

Kilmuir

Caroy River

Neist
Point

Lonmore

ⓘ

Moonen Bay

469
HEALAVAL
MORE

Roskhill

Roag

Loch Caroy

Ramasaig

Orbost

Vatten

A863

Glen Ose

Hoe Rape

488
HEALAVAL
BHEAG

Harlosh

I S L E

Hoe Point

Ose

368
BEINN NA
COINEID

246

Harlosh
Island

Colbost
Point

Bracadale

Coillore

Ⓒ Ⓓ Tarner Island Ⓔ Ⓕ

G · H · J · K · L

1
2
260 Sout
3
Red
Poir
4
Rudha
na Fearn
Òb
Chuaig
5 Jaig
Callakille
Lonbain
6
248
7
Applecross Bay
Ap
Milton
Camus
Aird Dhu' 8
Car
Cu
Toscaig
M

an Trodday

North
Duntùlm
Kilmaluag
useum
d Life
Flodigarry
Eilean Flodigarry
Poldorais
17
542
MEAL NA
SUIREAMACH
Digg
Staffin
Bay
Staffin Island
Brogaig
464
BIODA
BUIDHE
Stenscholl
Staffin
Trotternish
Kilt Rock Waterfall
Ellishader
River Conon
Marishader
Valtos
611
BEINN
EDRA
Garros
Rudha nam Brathairean
Culnaknock
Lealt
Tote
A855
einlich
608
CREAG A' LAIN
nisdal
Loch a' Bhràige
RONA
451
BEINN
A' SGÀ
esdal
River Romesdal
Old Man
719 of Storr
THE
STORR
Eilean
Tigh
Kensaleyre
River Haulton
Loch
Leathan
16
SOUND OF RAASAY
Eilean Fladday
Umachan
Loch
Fada
Manish
Point
Loch
Arnish
Torran
Carbost
Borve
Arnish
Drumuie
A855
312
Brochel
INNER SO
Glengrasco
RAASAY
Torvaig
Portree
Seafield
444
417
BEINN NA
GRÉINE
Penifiler
412
BEN
TIANAVAIG
247 DÙN CAAN
Glenmore
Glenvarragill
G Mugeary
A87 H
Camastianav
Tianavaig
Bay
J
Oskaig
K Rudha na' Leac
L
M

G
Scoraig

H Annat 270
Bay

Rhireavach

635
BEINN GHOBHLACH

Little Loch Broom

Badcaul

Ardessie

Camusnagaul

32

764
SÀIL
MHOR

Dundonnell

Lochan
Gaineamhaich

Strathnasheallag Forest

1062
AN TEALLACH

Loch na
Sealga

906
BEINN DEARG MHOR

S

974
SGÙRRBÀN

1019
MULLACH COIRE
MHIC FHEARCHAIR

Lochan
Fada

981
SLIOCH

680
BEINN A' MHÙINIDH

Kinlochewe
Forest

Beinn Eighe

Kinlochewe

Glen Docharty

Loch
Fhiarlaid

Loch
Coulin

G

H

J Ardmair

Morefield

Ullapool

A835

Ardindrean

Letters

Loch Achall

558
BEINN
EILIDEACH

Leckmelm

Ardcharnich

Inverlael

Loch Broom

507
CARN
BHIORAIN

Inverbroom

R Broom

Auchindrean

387
CARN
BREAC BEAG

Braemore

*Corrieshalloch
Gorge*

Falls of
Measach

A832

601
MEALL AN
T-SITHE

Loch a'
Bhraoin

999
A' CHAILLEACH

Cabvie
Lodge

711
BEINN NAN RAMH

933
FIONN
BHEINN

A832

10

Loch a'
Chroisg

550

249

Loch
Gowan

Achnasheen

Glen Achall

K 271

K

538
CARN

J

Loch an
Daimh

1

677
MEALL NAM
BRADHAN

2

Loch a'
Choire Mho

642
MEALL
DUBH

647
CÀRN MÒR

262

3

1081
BEINN
DEARG

4

Loch
Coire Làir

618
MEALL
LEACACHAIN

662
BEINN
LIATH BHEAG

Loch
Droma

5

1109
SGÙRR
MÒR

680
BEINN
DEARG

6

Fannich Lodge

Loch Fannich

262

558
AN CABAR

Achanalt

7 **A832**

Loch
Achanalt

Strath Bran

847

867
SGUIR VUILLIN

8

L

M

A B 271 C D E 272 F

1

Loch an
Daimh

412
CREAG
LOISGTE

BEINN
ULBHAIDH

506
MEALL
DHEIRGIDH

463
BREAC BHEINN

Brealangwell
Lodge

677
ME... IAM
BRA... HAN

2

Loch a'
Choire Mhòir

Strath Mulzie

Giasha Burn

701
CARN A'
CHOIN DEIRG

Croik

Strathcarron

River Carron

261

842
CARN
BAN

Glencalvie Forest

634
CÀRN BHREN

3

Gleann Beag

Crom Loch

710
BEINN
THARSUINN

838
CÀRN
CHUINNEAG

628

1081
BEINN
DEARG

602
CÀRN CAS NAN GABHAR

4

Loch
Coire Làir

771
MEALL A'
GHRIANAIN

Loch a'
Chaorunn

E A

Loch
Morie

...AIN

Loch
Vaich

742
BEINN
NAN EUN

Loch
Droma

742
TOM
BÀN MÒR

Strathkvaich Forest

Loch
Glascarnoch

737
MEALL
MÒR

5

...EAG

Aultguish
Inn

20

A835

Loch Glass

Glen Gla...

600

Inchbae
Lodge Hotel

680
BEINN
DEARG

1045
BEN WYVIS

6

479

261

Corriemoille Forest

Strath Garve

Ben Wyvis

558
N CABAR

439
CÀRN NA
DUBH CHOILLE

Corriemoille

761
LITTLE
WYVIS

484
CLOCH MHÒR

Lochluichart

Gorstan

7

Ach...lt

A832

16

Loch Luichart

Garve

Loch
Garve

Auchterneed

7

A834

Gower

Dingwall

Loch
Achanalt

579
SGÙRR MARCASAIDH

Rogie
Falls

Strathpeffer

Highland Museum
of Childhood

Keithtown

8

536

Little Scatwell

Loch
Achilty

Jamestown

Loch
Ussie

Ma...

867
SCUIR VUILLIN

Loch Meig

R Conon

Contin

Conon
Brid...

Riv...

G   **272**   H   349   J   **273**   K

1

2

3

4

5

6

7

8

Sleasdairidh

BEINN
DONUILL

Cambusavie
Platform

Loch
Fleet

A836

River Evelix

Badninish

Skelbo

Skelbo Street

Fourpenny

Achvaich

7

Embo

Kyle of
Sutherland

Rearquhar

Birichin

B9168

Embo Street

Lower
ledfield

Astle

Pitgrudy

Bonar
Bridge

Evelix

A949

Dornoch

Ardgay

Loch
Migdale

Spinningdale

Clashmore

A9

3
Camore

Kincardine

A949

10

Whiteface

6

Cuthill

264

Upper Ardchronie

A836

Dornoch Firth

Innis Mhor

15

Ferrytown

Cambuscurrie
Bay

Dornoch

Struie Hill

Ardmore

Ferry Point

Firth

Edderton

3

Inver

477
BEINN CLACH
AN FHEADAIN

19

A836

Morangie

Aultnamain Inn

284

Tain

Toulv

ROSS

692
BEINN
THARSUINN

Loch
Eye

379
CNOC AN
T-SABHAIL

B9176

Newfield

B9165

Fearn

Rh ie

4

Hill of
Fearn

Bal

Ardross

Ballchraggan

Arabella

B9166

Tullich

Rusdale

Kildary

Shandwick

Bal

River Alness

Achandunie

Milton

Ankerville

Shan

Rhicullen

Delny

Kilmuir

B9175

Pitcalnie

5

523
CNOC
CEISLEIN

Millcraig

A9

Barbaraville

Nigg

Moultavie

Tomich

8

Balintraid

Nigg Bay

Alness

Achnagarron

Saltburn

B817

Balnapaling

Dalmore

Invergordon

Cromarty

6

2

Balblair

Hugh Miller's Cottage NTS

Evanton

B817

Resolis

Cromarty
Bay

Newton

Teanord

5

Cromarty Firth

Udale
Bay

B9163

Allerton

B9163

264

Navity

Clanland
& Seapoint

Jemimaville

Upper Eathie

Cullicudden

Brae

BLACK ISLE

B9169

A832

10

Findon
Mains

B9160

Culbokie

255
MOUNT
EAGLE

Raddery

Whiteness Head

7

A9

B9163

Killen

RSPB

Knockbain

Rosemarkie

Nair

7

Duncanston

Groam
House

Fort George

8

Easter
Kinkell

Fortrose

Tradespark

251   G   H   Easter
Suddie   A832   J   8   Avoch   Chanonry
  int   K   **252**   L   Ardersier   M   Moss-
side

B9092

1

Cambusavie Platform
Loch Fleet

Badninish
Achvaich
Skelbo
7
Skelbo Street
Fourpenny
Rearquhar
Birichin
Embo
Astle
Embo Street
Pitgrudy
2 Evelix
A949
ngda
Clashmore
A9
Camore
Dornoch
Whiteface
6
Cuthill
263
Tarbat Ness
noch Firth
Ferrytown
Innis Mhor
Brucefield
Wilkhaven
Ardmore
Cambuscurrie
Bay
Ferry Point
Dornoch Firth
Portmahomack
3 A836
Morangie
Inver
Rockfield
B9165
Arboll
284 ▲
Tain
Toulvaddie
Loch Eye
Rhynie
4
379
Fearn
Balmuchy
OC AN
BHAIL
Newfield
B9165
Hill of Fearn
Hilton of Cadboll Chapel (ruin)
6
Tullich
Arabella
Hilton
Ballchraggan
B9166
Balintore
Kildary
Shandwick
Shandwick Bay
Milton
Ankerville
5
B9175
Delny
Kilmuir
Pitcalnie
A9
Barbaraville
Nigg
8
Nigg Bay
hagarron
Balintraid
Saltburn
B817
Balnapaling
Invergordon
6
Cromarty
Cromarty Bay
Hugh Miller's Cottage NTS
air
Udale Bay
Newton
B9163
RSPB
Allerton
263
Navity
Jemimaville
Upper Eathie
7
A832
Culbin
Forest
B9160
Kintessa
E
Raddery
RSPB
Whiteness Head
Brodie
Castle NTS
Rosemarkie
Groam
House
Nairn
8 Fo se
Fort George
Brodie
Chanonry
Tradespark
A96
Avo
B9092
252
Moss-
side
Boath
Doocot NTS
253
Household
earn
Whitemire
Ⓒ Ⓓ Ⓔ Ⓕ

0 1 2 3 4 5 miles
0 1 2 3 4 5 6 7 kilometres

1

2

3

4

5

266

Branderburgh

B9040   Stotfield
Lossiemouth

Burghead
Well   Hopeman   Burnside
Burghead

B9012   Duffus   Kinneddar
Cummingston   St Peter's Kirk   6
& Parish Cross

B9013   Roseisle   B9012   Duffus   B9135   Loch
Spynie

Burghead Bay   College of   6
Roseisle   A941
Spynie   B9103
Palace   Stonewells   King
Findhorn   B9089   Quarrywood   Lochill   on-S
Hempriggs   Viewfield
Calcots   Binns
Kinloss   Newton   Bishopmill   Innesmill   Farm
Findhorn   Coltfield
Bay   Urquhart   7
ncorth   Alves   12   New Elgin   Lhanbryde   The
ouse   Grange Hall   Lochs
266   Linkwood   9
eno's Stone   Kilbuiack
Muir of   Mosstodlo
Miltonduff   Crofts
of Dippl
Forres   Pluscarden   Clackmarras
B9103
Califer   Longmorn
Barnhill   Orbliston   8
Dallas Dhu   Rafford   Fogwatt   Millbuies
Distillery
B9010   Inchberry   B9015
253
G   **H**   B9010   **J**   **K**   Shougle   **L** Glen   **M**
Kellas

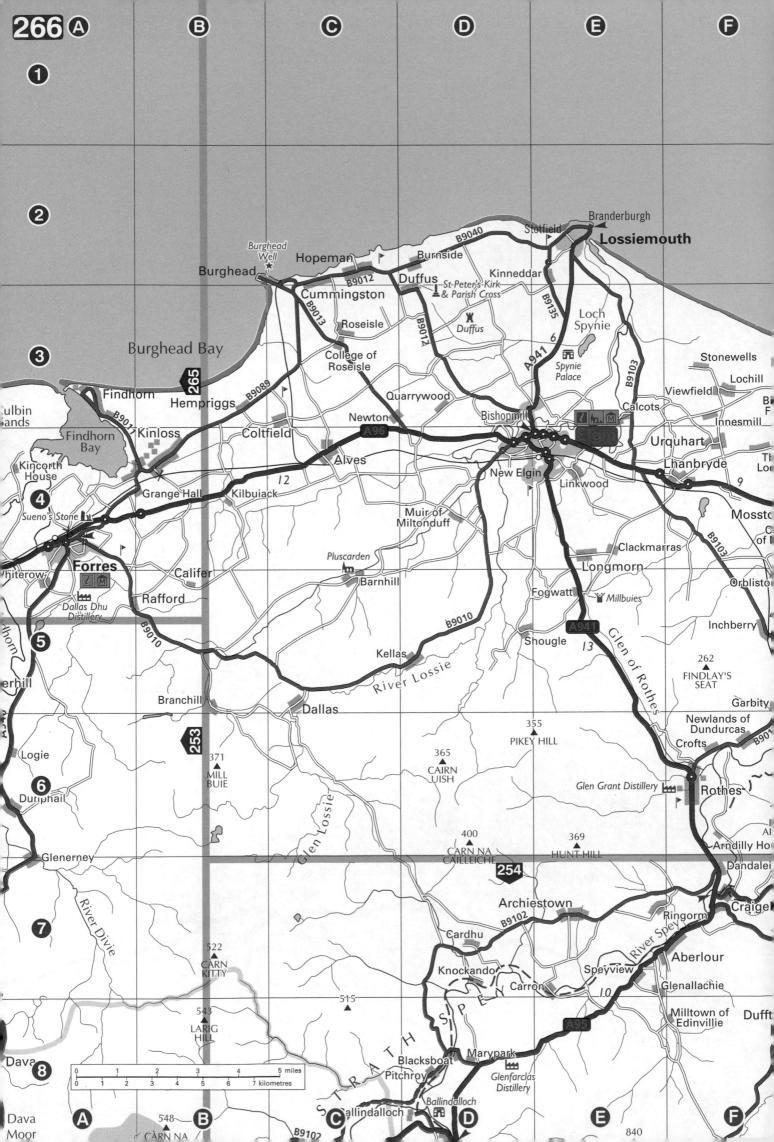

A   B   C   D   E   F

1

2

Burghead
Well

Burghead   Hopeman   Burnside   Stotfield   Branderburgh
B9040

Lossiemouth

Cummingston   Duffus   Kinneddar
B9012   St-Peter's-Kirk
& Parish Cross

3   Burghead Bay   Roseisle   Duffus   Loch
B9013   Spynie
B9012   Stonewells
Lochill

College of
Roseisle   Spynie   Calcots   Viewfield
265   Palace   A941   Innesmill

Findhorn
Hempriggs   B9089   Quarrywood   Bishopmill   Urquhart
Newton   A96   Lhanbryde   9
ulbin
ands   Kinloss   Coltfield   Alves   New Elgin
Findhorn
Bay   Linkwood   Mossto
Kincorth
House   Grange Hall   Kilbuiack   12   Muir of
Miltonduff   Clackmarras

4   Sueno's Stone   Longmorn   Orblisto
Pluscarden   Fogwatt   Millbuies
Barnhill   Inchberry
hiterow   **Forres**   Califer
Dallas Dhu Distillery   B9010   A941   13
Rafford   Shougle   262
B9010   FINDLAY'S
5   Kellas   River Lossie   SEAT
Garbity
Newlands of
Branchill   Dundurcas
Dallas   Crofts
253   355
PIKEY HILL
6   371   365   B901
Logie   MILL   CAIRN   Glen Grant Distillery   Rothes
BUIE   UISH
Dunphail   Arndilly Ho

Glenerney   400   369   Dandale
CARN NA   HUNT-HILL
CAILLEICHE   254
River Divie
7   Archiestown   Craige
B9102   Ringorm
Cardhu   River Spey   Aberlour
522   Knockando   Speyview
CARN   Carron   Glenallachie
KITTY   10
543   515   Milltown of
LARIG   A95   Edinvillie   Dufft
8   HILL   Marypark
Blacksboat
Dava   Pitchroy   Glenfarclas
Distillery
Dava   A   548   B   allindalloch   D   E   840   F
Moor   CÀRN NA   B9102

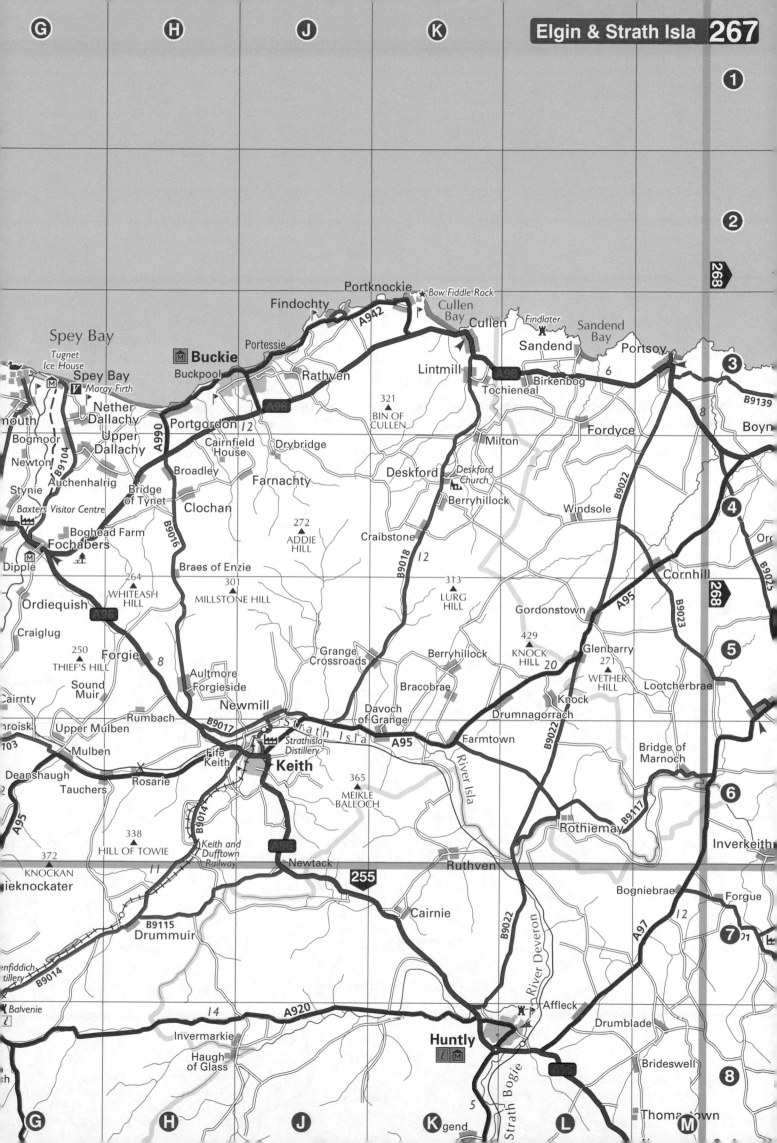

G H J K

1

2

Rosehearty
Sandhaven
Lighthouse · M · Kinnaird Head
Fraserburgh · i
Pittulie
Peathill
aigiefold
Kirktown
Fraserburgh Bay
Cairnbulg
Inverallochy
Percyhorner
Pitblae
Maggie's Hoosie
Whitelinks Bay
B9031
Coburby
Mid Ardlaw
A90
B9033
ndlie
10
B9032
Memsie
St Combs
A98
Memsie Cairn
Rathen
Crofts of Savoch

3

12
A981
Newburgh
Lonmay
Rattray Head
B9093
234
WAUGHTON HILL
RSPB
Loch of Strathbeg
A952
Crimond
Blackhill
Strichen
12
18

4

B9093
New Leeds
Leys
Kirktown
St Fergus
Denhead
Backfolds
Fetterangus
Rora
A981
A950
River Ugie
A90

5

6
Deer Abbey
Dunshillock
Mintlaw
Longside
Inverugie
Maud
B9106
Aden
Buchanhaven
Peterhead · M
B9029
Old Deer
B9029
A950
Peterhead Bay
Blackhill of Clackriach
Stuartfield
257
Inverquhomery
9
A982
Burnhaven
B9028
Drymuir
Bulwark
Millbreck
Nether Kinmundy
Hillhead of Cocklaw
Buchan Ness

6

7
Nethermuir
Clola
Little Dens
Blackhill
Stirling
Boddam
B9030
Kinnadie
Lendrum Terrace
uchnagatt
12
Kinknockie
Blackhill
Longhaven
Inkhorn
Coldwells
A948
A952
A90
Bullers of Buchan

8
Arthrath
Muirtack
14
Hatton
17
Auchiries
North Haven
Slains
Cruden Bay

G H J K L M

A B C D E F

1

2

3

4

5

6

7

8

Point of Stoer

Old Man
of Stoer

OLDANY
ISLAND

Eddrach
Bay

Culkein
Drumbeg

Culkein

Clashnessie
Bay

Oldany

Drumbeg

Achnacarnin

Nedd

Clashmore

Loch
Poll

Clashnessie

Stoer

Clachtoll

B869

Loch
Beanna

Bay of Clachtoll

Rhicarn

Achmelvich
Bay

A837

Achmelvich

Baddidarrach

Assy

Soyea Island

Loch Inver

Lochinver

Strathan

Inverkirkaig

River Kirkaig

Fionn
Loch

Eilean Mòr

Rhu
Coigach

Enard Bay

Loch
Sionaso

Rubha Mòr

Reiff

Achnahaird

Altandhu

Eilean Mullagrach

Loch
Osgaig

612
STAC POLLAIDH

Isle Ristol

Polbain

Glas-leac Mòr

SUMMER ISLES

769
CUL BE

Achiltibuie

Loch
Lurgainn

Badentarbat
Bay

Polglass

Tanera
Beg

Steornabhagh (Stornoway)

C O I G A C H

Tanera
Mòr

Glas-leac Beag

Horse
Island

Horse
Sound

652
BEN MORE
COIGACH

Achduart

Eilean Dubh

Culnacraig

Strathcana

Priest
Island

A835

Greenstone
Point

Leac Dhonn

Isle
Martin

Cailleach Head

Ardmair

Rudha Beag

Scoraig

Annat
Bay

Mo

ld

261

Rhireavach

635

Strath

0 1 2 3 4 5 miles
0 1 2 3 4 5 6 7 kilometres

C D E F

G
H
276
J
K

BEN SCREAVIE
A838
Loch More
Loch idhe
1

419
BEN STROME
Loch an Leathaid Bhuain
Kinloch
CARN AN...
873
BEN HEE

Locha' Chàirn Bhàin
Kylestrome
Kylesku
Glen Dhu
680
MEALL AN LIATH MOR
Loch Ghorm-ch
2

Loch Glendhu
Unapool
525
BEINN AIRD DA LOCH
613
MEALL AN FHEUR LOCH
272
Loch Fiag
Fiag Lodg

Loch Glencoul
792
BEINN LEOID
Loch Merkland

Loch an Leothaid
776
SAIL GHORM
809
QUINAG

Leirg
Eas Coul Aulin (Waterfall)
372
CNOC A' GHRIAMA
3

A894
774
GLAS BHEINN
37
Overscaig Hotel

Loch Assynt
Ardvreck
A838
4

Coigach
539
BEINN GHARBH
Inchnadamph
510
MAOVALLY

Loch na Gainimh
847
CANISP
Stronchrubie
Loanan
998
BEN MORE ASSYNT

River
8
713
BREABAG
Duchally
435
BEN SCREAV
5

814

Loch Awe
Loch Veyatie
Càm Loch
Benmore Forest
Glen Muic
476
BEINN SGEIREACH

MÒR
Ledmore Junction
A837
Loch Ailsh
6

Knockan
Elphin
Loch Urigill
364
AN STICHD
544
BEINN AN EOIN
River Cassley

Knockan Cliff
V
Knockan Crag
307
CNOC NA GLAS CHOILLE
272
Loch na Claise Mòire

Cromalt Hills
Glen Cassley
7

Drumrunie Lodge
Loch a' Chroisg
Rappach
River Oykel
Oykel Bridge Hotel
Roseha
A837

408
NA DROMANNAN
Doune
Strat

Rappich Water
Glen Einig
493
BEINN ULBHAIDH
8

G
261
H
J
K
262
412
CREAG LOISGTE
L
M

A **B** **C** **277** **D** **E** **F**

1
Kinloch

CÀRN ARG
CARN AN TIONAIL

Loch Coire na Saidhe Duibhe

230
MEALL A' BHROLLAICH

Strath Naver
Loch Naver

873
BEN HEE

Altnaharra

680
MEALL AN LIATH MOR

Loch a' Ghorm-choire

2
MEALL FHEUR LOCH
613

472
MEALL AN FHUARAIN

959
BEN KLIBRECK

Loch Choire Fore

Loch Merkland

Loch Fiag

Fiag Lodge

Strath Bagastie

A836

Loch a' Bhealaich

Loch Choire

271

372
CNOC A' GHRIAMA

3
37
Overscaig Hotel

Crask Inn

346
CNOC A' GHIUBHAIS

21

Glen Fiag

A838

510
MAOVALLY

4
Loch
Shin

Duchally

Strath Tirry

435
BEN SCREAVIL

Shinness

317
SITHEAN ACHADH NAN

5
Glen Muic
orest

Achnairn

Loch Beannach

A836

Glen Cassley

476
BEINN SGEIREACH

Colaboll

ICHD 6

River Cassley

544
BEINN AN EÒIN

Ferrycroft Countryside Centre
i

323
BEN DOULA

Loch Craggie

271

Loch na Claise Mòire

402
CNOC A' CHOIRE

Lairg

Tomich

River Oy

7

Torrobull

A4839

Rosehall
A837
27

Achany

B864

A836

333
MEALL EACHAINN

Oykel Bridge Hotel

Doune
31
Altass

Linsidemore
A837

Falls of Shin

Glen Einig

Strath Oykel

8

493
BEINN

Inveran

Invershin

Sleasdairidh

0 1 2 3 4 5 miles
0 1 2 3 4 5 6 7 kilometres

C **262** **D** **E** **263** **F**

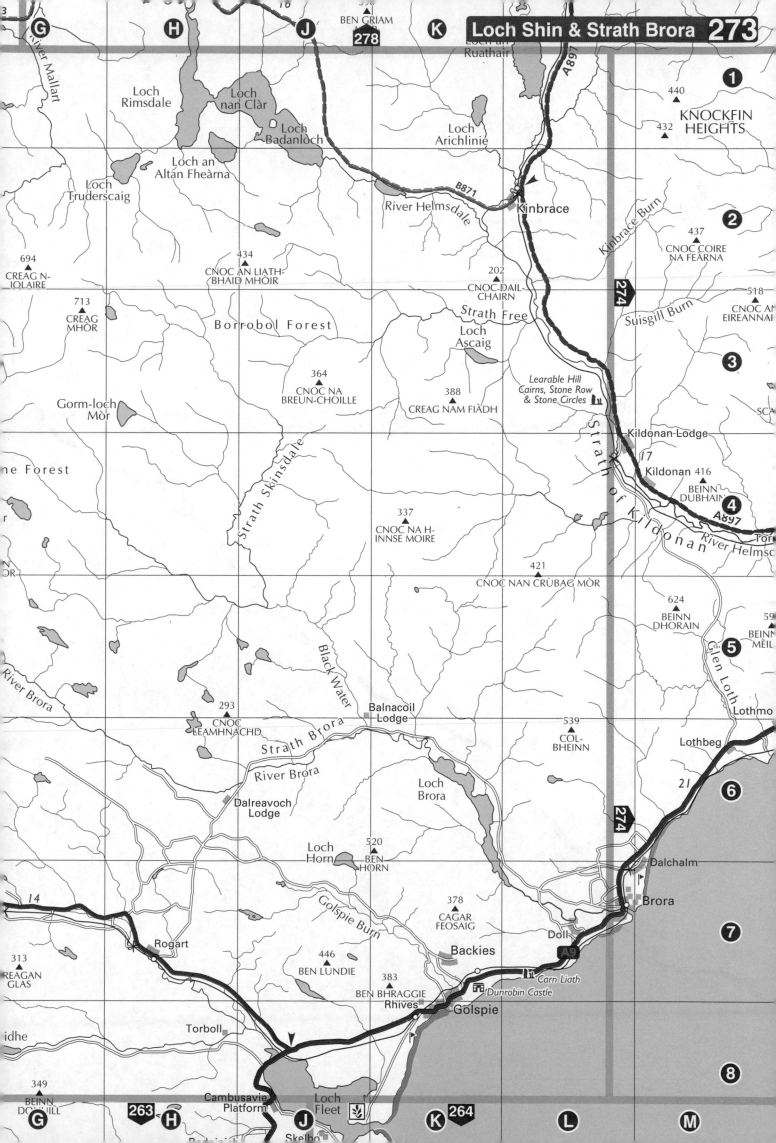

G   H   J   278   K   1

BEN GRIAM
Loch an
Ruathair
A897

Loch Rimsdale
Loch nan Clàr
KNOCKFIN
HEIGHTS
440
432

Loch
Badanloch
Loch
Arichlinie
2

Loch an
Altán Fheàrna
River Helmsdale
B871
Kinbrace
437
CNOC COIRE
NA FEARNA
Kinbrace Burn

Loch
Truderscaig
694
CREAG N-
IOLAIRE
434
CNOC AN LIATH-
BHAID MHÒIR
202
CNOC DAIL-
CHAIRN
Strath Free
274
518
CNOC AN
EIREANNAI
Suisgill Burn

713
CREAG
MHÒR
Borrobol Forest
Loch
Ascaig
3

364
CNOC NA
BREUN-CHOILLE
388
CREAG NAM FIÀDH
Learable Hill
Cairns, Stone Row
& Stone Circles
Kildonan Lodge

Gorm-loch
Mòr
Strath of Kildonan
17
Kildonan 416
BEINN
DUBHAIN
4
A897

ne Forest
Strath Skinsdale
337
CNOC NA H-
INNSE MOIRE
River Helmsd
Tor

421
CNOC NAN CRÙBAG MÒR
624
BEINN
DHORAIN
59
BEINN
MÈIL

River Brora
Black Water
5
Glen Loth
Lothmo

293
CNOC
LEAMHNACHD
Balnacoil
Lodge
539
COL-
BHEINN
Lothbeg

Strath Brora
River Brora
Loch
Brora
21
6

Dalreavoch
Lodge
Loch
Horn
520
BEN
HORN
274
Dalchalm
Brora

14
378
CAGAR
FEOSAIG
Doll
7

313
REAGAN
GLAS
Rogart
446
BEN LUNDIE
Golspie Burn
Backies
A9
Carn Liath

idhe
Torboll
383
BEN BHRAGGIE
Rhives
Dunrobin Castle
Golspie

349
BEINN
DO HILL
Cambusavie
Platform
Loch
Fleet
263   H   J   264   K   L   M   8

Skelbo

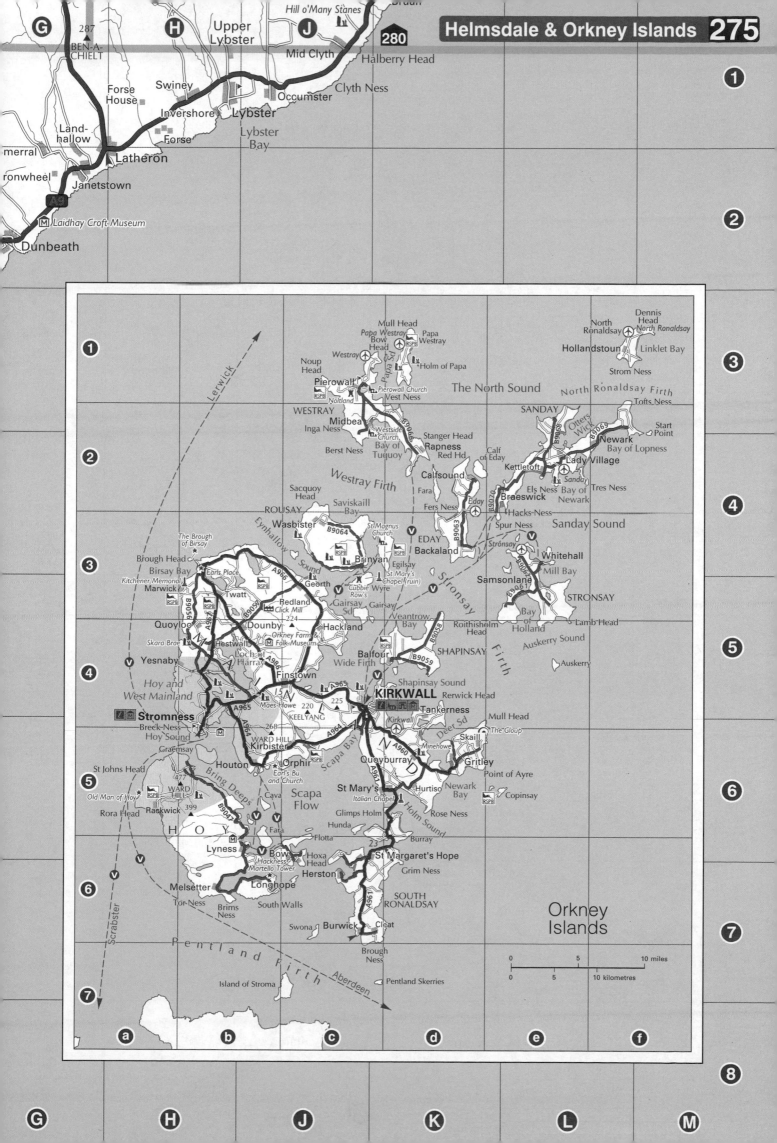

G
BEN-A-CHIELT
287
H
Upper Lybster
J
Hill o'Many Stanes
Braun
280
Mid Clyth
Halberry Head
Forse House
Swiney
Clyth Ness
Invershore
Occumster
Lybster
Landhallow
Forse
Lybster Bay
merral
Latheron
Lybster Bay
ronwheel
Janetstown
A9
Laidhay Croft Museum
Dunbeath

Orkney Islands

Lerwick

Mull Head
Papa Westray
Bow Head
Papa Westray
Noup Head
Westray
Holm of Papa
Pierowall
Pierowall Church
The North Sound
North Ronaldsay
Dennis Head
North Ronaldsay
North Ronaldsay
Hollandstoun
Linklet Bay
Strom Ness
North Ronaldsay Firth
Tofts Ness
Noltland
Vest Ness
WESTRAY
Midbea
SANDAY
Otters Wick
Start Point
Inga Ness
Westside Church
Stanger Head
Newark
Bay of Lopness
Berst Ness
Bay of Tuquoy
Rapness
Red Hd
Kettletoft
Lady Village
Westray Firth
Calfsound
Calf of Eday
Sanday
Tres Ness
Sacquoy Head
Fara
Els Ness
Bay of Newark
Saviskaill Bay
Fers Ness
Eday
Braeswick
ROUSAY
St Magnus Church
Hacks-Ness
Sanday Sound
Wasbister
B9064
Brinyan
EDAY
Spur Ness
Egilsay
Backaland
Strönsay
Whitehall
The Brough of Birsay
Eynhallow Sound
St Mary's Chapel (ruin)
B9063
Mill Bay
Brough Head
Earls Place
Georth
Cubbie Row's
Samsonlane
Birsay Bay
Kitchener Memorial
Twatt
Gairsay Sd
Gairsay
STRONSAY
Marwick
A966
Veantrow Bay
Roithisholm Head
Bay of Holland
Lamb Head
Quoyloo
B9056
Redland Click Mill
Hackland
B9058
Auskerry Sound
Skara Brae
Dounby
224
Balfour
SHAPINSAY
Auskerry
Hestwall
Orkney Farm & Folk Museum
Wide Firth
B9059
Yesnaby
Loch of Harray
Finstown
A965
Shapinsay Sound
Hoy and West Mainland
A986
KIRKWALL
Rerwick Head
Maes Howe
225
Tankerness
Mull Head
Stromness
A965
220
KEELYANG
Kirkwall
Deer Sd
The Gloup
Breck-Ness
A964
268
Skaill
Hoy Sound
Kirbister
Minehowe
Graemsay
Houton
Orphir
A960
Gritley
St Johns Head
477
Earl's Bu and Church
Quoyburray
Point of Ayre
WARD HILL
Bring Deeps
Cava
Scapa Bay
St Mary's
Hurtiso
Newark Bay
Copinsay
Old Man of Hoy
Rackwick
399
Fara
Italian Chapel
Rose Ness
Rora Head
B9047
Scapa Flow
Glimps Holm
Holm Sound
HOY
Hunda
Lyness
Flotta
23
Burray
Hackness
Martello Tower
Bow
Hoxa Head
St Margaret's Hope
Melsetter
Longhope
Herston
Grim Ness
Tor Ness
Brims Ness
South Walls
SOUTH RONALDSAY
Swona
Burwick
Cleat
Orkney Islands
Pentland Firth
Island of Stroma
Brough Ness
Aberdeen
Pentland Skerries

Scrabster

0   5   10 miles
0   5   10 kilometres

a   b   c   d   e   f

G   H   J   K   L   M

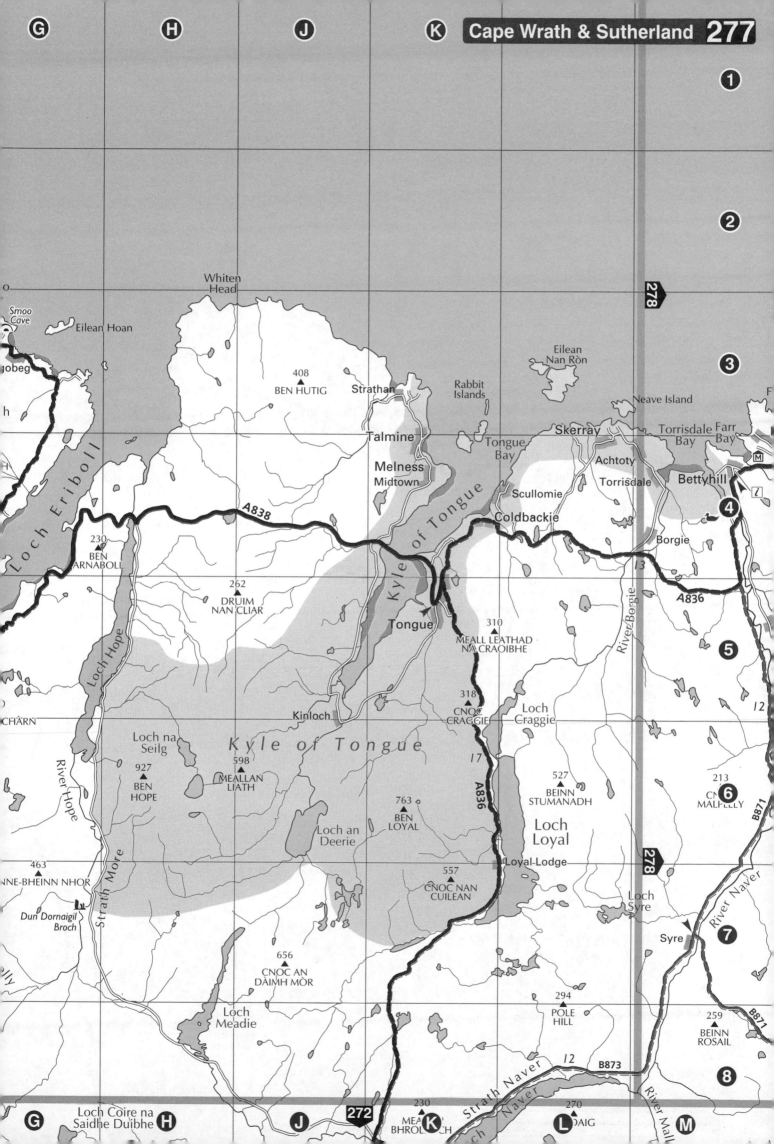

G H J K

1
2
3

Smoo
Cave
Eilean Hoan
Whiten
Head
jobeg
h

Loch Eriboll

408
BEN HUTIG
Strathan
Talmine
Melness
Midtown

Eilean
Nan Ròn
Rabbit
Islands
Neave Island
Tongue
Bay
Skerray
Torrisdale
Bay
Farr
Bay
Achtoty
Torrisdale
Bettyhill
Scullomie
Coldbackie

278

A838

230
BEN
ARNABOLL
Borgie
13
A836

262
DRUIM
NAN CLIAR

Kyle of Tongue

Tongue

310
MEALL LEATHAD
NA CRAOIBHE

River Borgie

4
5

Loch Hope

CHÀRN

Kinloch

318
CNOC
CRAGGIE

Loch
Craggie

17

A836

12

Loch na
Seilg
Kyle of Tongue

927
BEN
HOPE
598
MEALLAN
LIATH

527
BEINN
STUMANADH

213
CN
MALPELLY

6

278

B871

763
BEN
LOYAL
Loch an
Deerie
Loch
Loyal

463
NNE-BHEINN NHOR
Strath More
Loyal-Lodge

557
CNOC NAN
CUILEAN
Loch
Syre
Syre
River Naver

7

Dun Dornaigil
Broch
River Hope

656
CNOC AN
DÀIMH MÒR

294
POLE
HILL

259
BEINN
ROSAIL

B871

Loch
Meadie

12
B873

Strath Naver

272

230
MEA
BHROL CH
270
AIG

River Mall

8

Loch Coire na
Saidhe Duibhe

G H J K L M

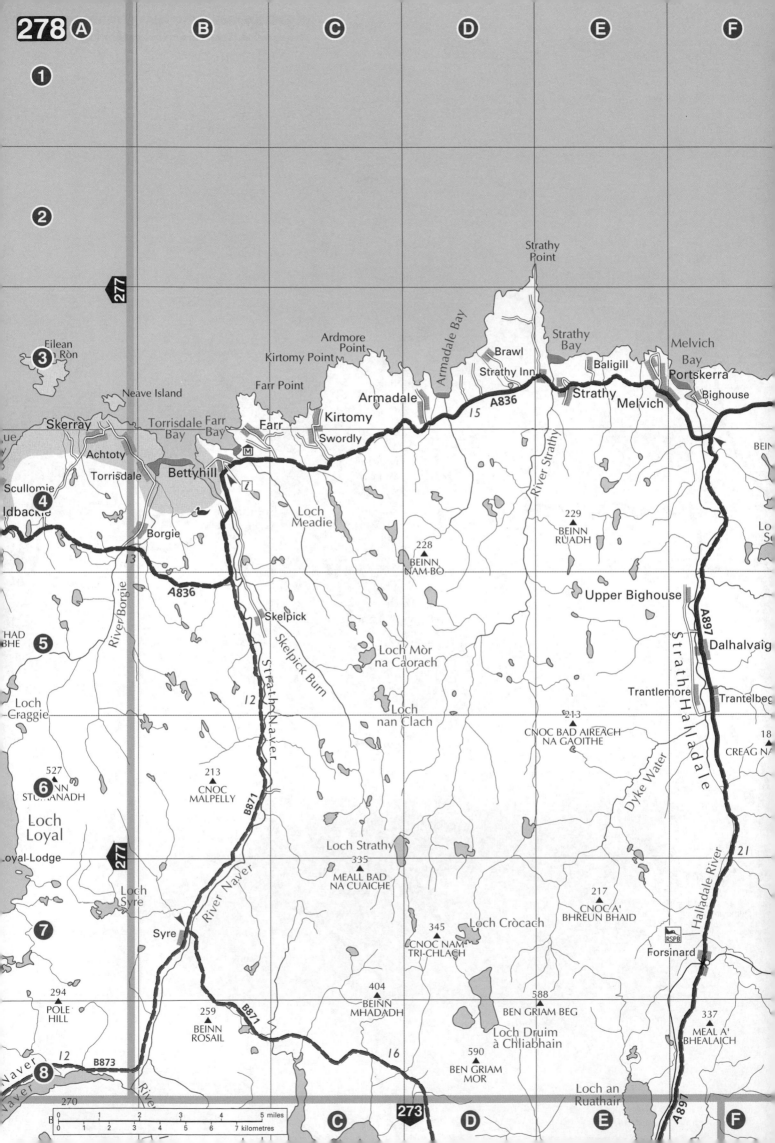

1

DUNNET HEAD   127

Briga Head

121
DUNNET
HILL

Brough

B855

St John's
Loch

2

West Dunnet

Dunnet

Dunnet
Bay

Brims Ness

Holborn
Head

Stromness

St Mary's
Chapel (ruin)

Scrabster

Thurso Bay

A9

280

Castlehill

Castletown

Crosskirk

A836

Murkle

A836

5

Gre

Buldoo

Dounreay
Visitor Centre

Skiall

Bridge of Forss

Lythmore

Glengolly

B874

Olrig
House

Tai

3

B876

Sandside
Bay

16

Achreamie

Cnoc Freiceadain
Long Cairns

Forss Water

Weydale

Hilliclay

B

Isauld

Upper
Dounreay

Shebster

Westfield

A9

Bower

Reay

Sordale

242
BEINN
RATHA

Loch
Calder

Knockdee

Roadside

B874

4   Halcro

Clayock

Gillock

Broubster

Loch
Scarmclate

243
NOC AN
RAIN BHÀIN

Shurrery

Halkirk

B870

21

Loch Watten

Shurrery
Lodge

Scotscalder
Station

Harpsdale

176
SPITTAL
HILL

B870

5

290
BEIN NAM
BAD MHOR

Loch
Scye

Dorrery

Watten

Loch
Shurrery

Spittal

Backlass

160
BRAIGH FÉITH HEMIGAL

132
DRUIM A'
CHRACAIRNIE

River Thurso

Mybster

Loch-of-
Toftingall

203
CNOC PREAS
A'MHADAIDH

Loch Tuim
Ghlais

Loch
Caluim

Westerdale

23

6

200
CNOC BEUL
NA FAIRE

136
BEINN CHÀITEAG

Strath Beg

280

Altnabreac Station

A9

7   BALLHA
HILL

145

Loch
More

Loch
Ruard

Achavanich

Loch
Stemster

Loch
Sand

248
STEMSTER HILL

Rumsdale Water

Strathmore Water

Loch an
Thulachan

Loch
Rangag

226
COIRE
NA BEINN

Clutt Water

Dalnawillan Lodge

348
BEN
ALISKY

287
BEN-A-
CHIELT

8

Up
Lyl

Gl Lodge

CNOCAN

Swiney

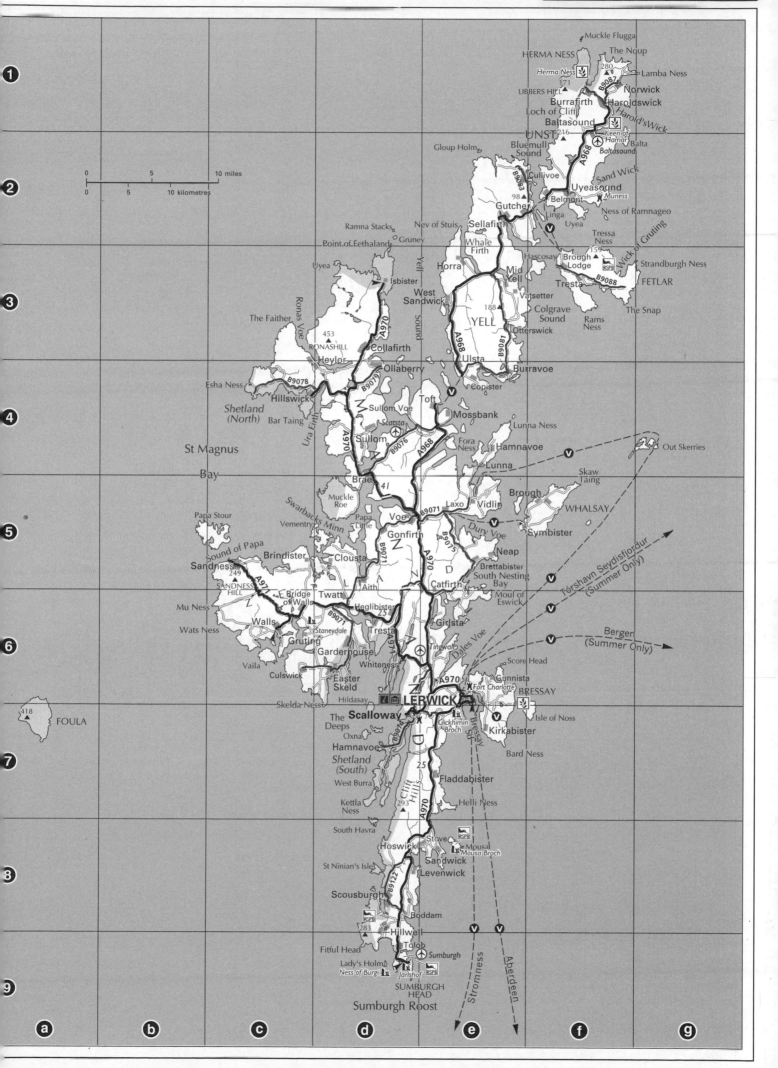

Muckle Flugga
HERMA NESS
The Noup
Herma Ness 280
171 B9087 Lamba Ness
LIBBERS HILL
Norwick
Burrafirth Haroldswick
Loch of Cliff Harold'sWick
Baltasound
UNST
Keen of
Gloup Holm Bluemull Hamar
Sound 216 Balta
B9083 Cullivoe Baltasound
Sand Wick
Uyeasound
98 Belmont Ness of Ramnageo
Gutcher Linga Muness
Ramna Stacks Nev of Stuis Uyea
Point of Eethaland Gruney Sellafirth Tressa
Whale Ness
Firth Hascosay Brough 159
Uyea Lodge RSPB Strandburgh Ness
Isbister Horra B9088 Wick of Gruting
West Mid Tresta FETLAR
Sandwick Yell Vatsetter
The Faither YELL Colgrave The Snap
453 188 Sound
RONASHILL Collafirth A968 Otterswick Rams
Heylor B9081 Ness
Ollaberry Ulsta
Esha Ness B9078 Toft Burravoe
Hillswick B9079 Copister
Shetland Sullom Voe Mossbank
(North) Bar Taing Scatsta Fora Lunna Ness
St Magnus Sullom Ness Hamnavoe
Bay B9076 A968 Lunna Out Skerries
Brae 41 Skaw
Muckle Taing
Roe Laxo Brough WHALSAY
Swarbacks B9071 Vidlin
Papa Stour Minn Papa Voe Symbister
Vementry Little Dury Voe
Sandness Brindister Gonfirth Neap
249 Clousta B9071 Brettabister Tórshavn Seydisfjördur
SANDNESS Aith South Nesting (Summer Only)
HILL Bridge A971 Catfirth Bay
Mu Ness of Walls Twatt B9075 Moul of Bergen
Wats Ness Heglibister Eswick (Summer Only)
Walls B9071 23 Tresta Girlsta
Staneydale A970 Score Head
Gruting Tingwall Gunnista
Vaila Gardenhouse Dales Voe
Whiteness Fort Charlotte BRESSAY
Culswick A970
418 Easter LERWICK Isle of Noss
FOULA Skeld Clickhimin
Hildasay Broch Kirkabister
Skelda Ness
The Scalloway Bard Ness
Deeps Oxna
Hamnavoe Fladdabister
Shetland B9074
(South) 25 Helli Ness
West Burra Clift Hills
Kettla A970
Ness 293
South Havra Stove
Hoswick Mousal RSPB
St Ninian's Isle Mousa Broch
Sandwick
Levenwick
Scousburgh B9122 Boddam
RSPB
283 Hillwell
Fitful Head Tolob
Lady's Holm Sumburgh
Ness of Burgi Jarlshof RSPB
SUMBURGH Stromness Aberdeen
HEAD
Sumburgh Roost

0   5   10 miles
0   5   10 kilometres

1 2 3 4 5 6 7 8 9
a b c d e f g

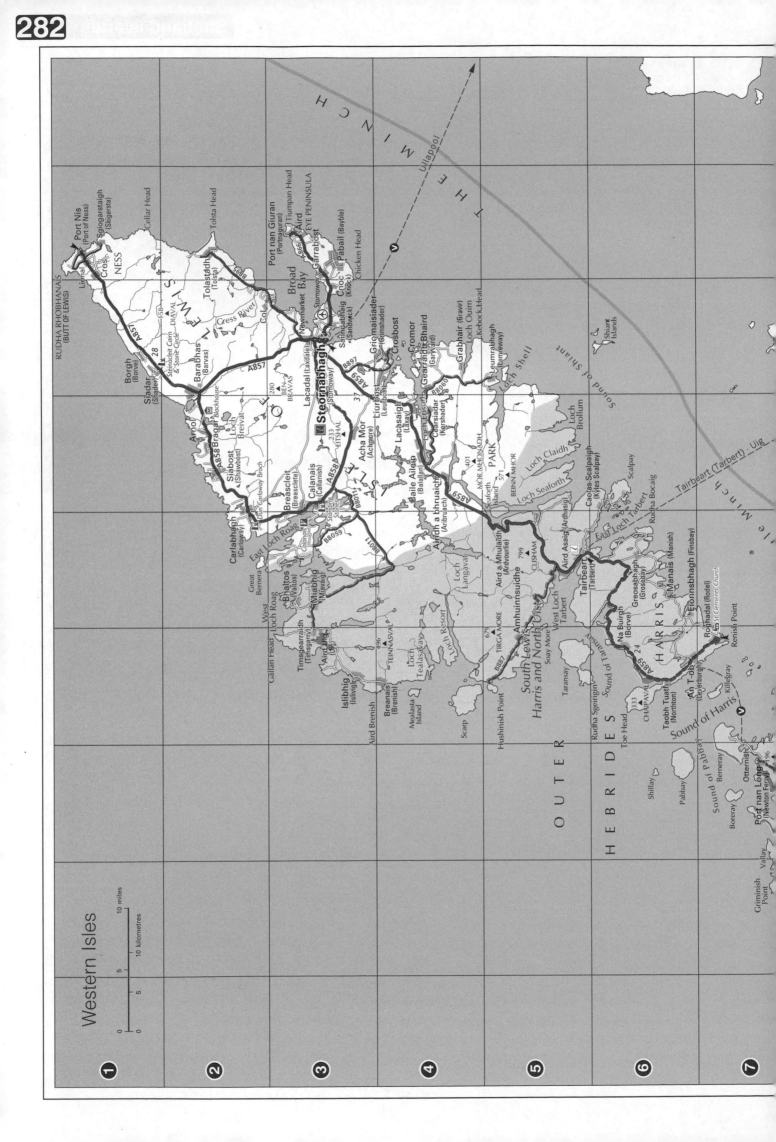

Western Isles

10 miles

10 kilometres

THE MINCH

Ullapool

RUDHA RHOBHANAIS
(BUTT OF LEWIS)

Port Nis
(Port of Ness)
Sgiogarstaigh
(Skigersta)

Lional

Cros
(Cross)

NESS

Cellar Head

Tolsta Head

Tolastadh
(Tolsta)

B895

Borgh
(Borve)

Siadar
(Shader)

A857

28

Barabhas
(Barvas)

Steinacleit Cairn
& Stone Circle

DIABAL

658

Gress River

Col

Port nan Giuran
(Portnaguran)

Tiumpan Head

EYE PENINSULA

Aird

B866

Garrabost

Pabail (Bayble)

Stornoway

Newmarket

Broad
Bay

Cnoc
(Knock)

Chicken Head

Sandabhaig
(Sandwick)

Griomaisiadar
(Grimshader)

Crosbost

Grabhair (Gravir)

Loch Ouirn

Kebock Head

Arnol

Blackhouse

A858 Bragar

Loch
Breivat

Siabost
(Shawbost)

Dùn Carloway Broch

A857

BEN
BRAVAS

280

Lacadal (Laxdale)

Steòrnabhagh
Stornoway

A859

B897

Leurbost
(Leurbost)

Liùrbost

Cromor

Gearraidh Bhaird
(Garyvard)

Leumrabhagh
(Lemreway)

Loch Shell

A859

37

Liùrbost
(Leurbost)

Cearsiadar
(Kershader)

Loch Seaforth

Loch Shell

Loch
Brollum

Loch Claidh

Shiant
Islands

Sound of Shiant

Calanais
(Callanish)

Breascleit
(Breasclete)

EITSHAL

233

A858

Standing
Stones

B8011

Acha Mòr
(Achmore)

Lacasaigh
(Laxay)

401

MOR MHONADH

BEINN MHOR

571

PARK

Carlabhagh
(Carloway)

Calanais

B8059

East Loch Roag

Baile Ailein
(Balallan)

Seaforth
Island

Great
Bernera

West Loch Roag

Bhaltos
(Valtos)

Miabhig
(Miavaig)

B8011

Airdh a bhruaich
(Aribruach)

Loch
Langavat

Aird a Mhulaidh
(Ardvourlie)

CLISHAM

799

Caolas Scalpaigh
(Kyles Scalpay)

Scalpay

Scalpay

Callan Head

Timsgearraidh
(Timsgarry)

Aird Uig
(Uig)

Loch Resort

TIRGA MORE

679

Aird Asaig
(Ardhasig)

East Loch Tarbert

Rudha Bocaig

Islibhig
(Islivig)

496

TEINNASVAL

Loch
Tealasbhay

Amhuinnsuidhe

West Loch
Tarbert

Tairbeart
(Tarbert)

Greosabhagh
(Grosebay)

Manais (Manish)

Fionnsbhagh (Finsbay)

Aird Brenish

Breanais
(Brenish)

Mealasta
Island

Scarp

Hushinish Point

Soay More

Soay
Beg

Na Buirgh
(Borve)

HARRIS

Roghadal (Rodel)

St Clements Church

Renish Point

Taransay

Rudha Sgeirigin

Sound of Taransay

A859

24

An T-òb
(Leverburgh)

Roghadal

Killegray

Toe Head

Taobh Tuath
(Northton)

CHAIPAVAL

333

Sound of Harris

Shillay

Pabbay

Bernera

Sound of Pabbay

Boreray

Port nan Long
(Newton Ferry)

Otternish

A865
196

Griminish
Point

Vallay

South Lewis,
Harris and North Uist

OUTER

HEBRIDES

THE MINCH

Tairbeart (Tarbert) - Uig

An Caolas Scalpaigh

Le Minch

①
②
③
④
⑤
⑥
⑦

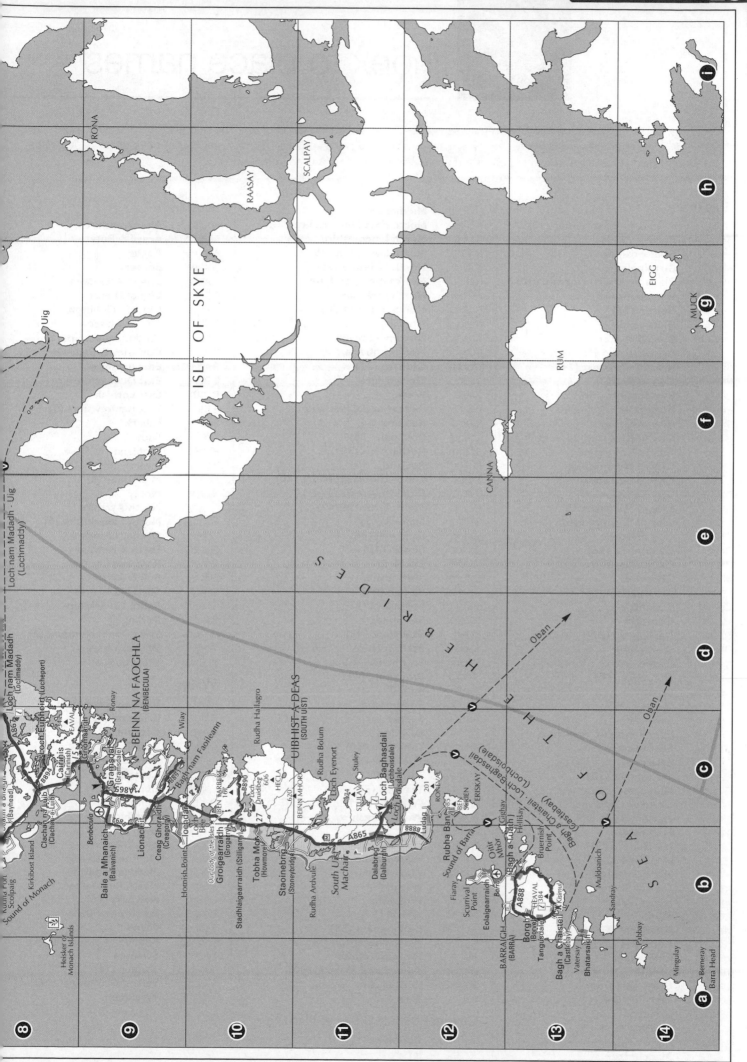

ISLE OF SKYE

Uig

RONA

RAASAY

SCALPAY

EIGG

MUCK

RUM

CANNA

THE HEBRIDES

SEA OF THE HEBRIDES

Oban

Oban

Loch nam Madadh · Uig
(Lochmaddy)

Loch nam Madadh
(Lochmaddy)

BEINN NA FAOGHLA
(BENBECULA)

UIBHIST A DEAS
(SOUTH UIST)

Loch Baghasdail
(Lochboisdale)

Bàgh a Chaisteil · Loch Baghasdail
(Lochboisdale)

Heisker of
Monach Islands

Rubha Port
Scolpaig

Sound of Monach

Clachan na Luib
(Clachan-a-Luib)

Càirinis
(Carinish)

Baile a Mhanaich
(Balivanich)

Berneray

Benbecula

Grimsaigh
(Gramsdale)

Lionacleit

Creag Ghoraidh
(Creagorry)

Iochdar

Loch a
Bee

Hornish Point

Stadhlaigearraidh (Stilligarry)

Groigearraidh
(Grogarry)

Our Lady of the Isles

Tobha Mòr
(Howmore)

27

Staoinebrig
(Stoneybridge)

South Uist
Machair

Rubha Ardvule

Dalabrog
(Daliburgh)

Ludag

A865

Loch Boisdale

Rubha Bàn

Sound of Barra

Oitir
Mhòr

Eolaigearraidh

Fiaray

Scurrival
Point

BARRAIGH
(BARRA)

Borgh
(Borve)

Tangusdale

THEAVAL
384

Bàgh a Chaisteil
(Castlebay)

Vatersay

Bhatarsaigh

Pabbay

Mingulay

Bernaray

Barra Head

Muldoanich

Sandray

ERISKAY

RONEVAL
201

Loch Eynenort

Rudha Bolum

Rudha Hallagro

HECLA

BEINN MHOR

Stuley

Loch Druidbeg
Druidbeg
606

620

Bàgh nam Faoileann

Wiay

Ronay

A887

A865

A867

A888

A888

Helisay

Gighay

Bruernish
Point

Bàgh a' Tuath

8

9

10

11

12

13

14

a

b

c

d

e

f

g

h

i

Index to place names

This index lists places appearing in the main-map section of the atlas in alphabetical order. The reference before each name gives the atlas page number and grid reference of the square in which the place appears. The map shows counties, unitary authorities and administrative areas, together with a list of the abbreviated name forms used in the index.

England

BaNES	**Bath & N E Somerset (18)**
Barns	**Barnsley (19)**
Beds	**Bedfordshire**
Birm	**Birmingham**
Bl w D	**Blackburn with Darwen (20)**
Bmouth	**Bournemouth**
Bolton	**Bolton (21)**
Bpool	**Blackpool**
Brad	**Bradford (22)**
Br & H	**Brighton and Hove (23)**
Br For	**Bracknell Forest (24)**
Bristl	**City of Bristol**
Bucks	**Buckinghamshire**
Bury	**Bury (25)**
C Derb	**City of Derby**
C KuH	**City of Kingston upon Hull**
C Leic	**City of Leicester**
C Nott	**City of Nottingham**
C Pete	**City of Peterborough**
C Plym	**City of Plymouth**
C Port	**City of Portsmouth**
C Sotn	**City of Southampton**
C Stke	**City of Stoke**
Calder	**Calderdale (26)**
Cambs	**Cambridgeshire**
Ches	**Cheshire**
Cnwll	**Cornwall**
Covtry	**Coventry**
Cumb	**Cumbria**
Darltn	**Darlington (27)**
Derbys	**Derbyshire**
Devon	**Devon**
Donc	**Doncaster (28)**
Dorset	**Dorset**
Dudley	**Dudley (29)**
Dur	**Durham**
E R Yk	**East Riding of Yorkshire**
E Susx	**East Sussex**
Essex	**Essex**
Gatesd	**Gateshead (30)**
Gloucs	**Gloucestershire**
Gt Lon	**Greater London**
Halton	**Halton (31)**
Hants	**Hampshire**
Hartpl	**Hartlepool (32)**
Herefs	**Herefordshire**
Herts	**Hertfordshire**
IoS	**Isles of Scilly**
IoW	**Isle of Wight**
Kent	**Kent**
Kirk	**Kirklees (33)**
Knows	**Knowsley (34)**
Lancs	**Lancashire**
Leeds	**Leeds**
Leics	**Leicestershire**
Lincs	**Lincolnshire**
Lpool	**Liverpool**
Luton	**Luton**
M Keyn	**Milton Keynes**
Manch	**Manchester**
Medway	**Medway**

Middsb	**Middlesbrough**
NE Lin	**North East Lincolnshire**
N Linc	**North Lincolnshire**
N Som	**North Somerset (35)**
N Tyne	**North Tyneside (36)**
N u Ty	**Newcastle upon Tyne**
N York	**North Yorkshire**
Nhants	**Northamptonshire**
Norfk	**Norfolk**
Notts	**Nottinghamshire**
Nthumb	**Northumberland**
Oldham	**Oldham (37)**
Oxon	**Oxfordshire**
Poole	**Poole**
R & Cl	**Redcar and Cleveland**
Readg	**Reading**
Rochdl	**Rochdale (38)**
Rothm	**Rotherham (39)**
Rutlnd	**Rutland**
S Glos	**South Gloucestershire (40)**
S on T	**Stockton-on-Tees (41)**
S Tyne	**South Tyneside (42)**
Salfd	**Salford (43)**
Sandw	**Sandwell (44)**
Sefton	**Sefton (45)**
Sheff	**Sheffield**
Shrops	**Shropshire**
Slough	**Slough (46)**
Solhll	**Solihull (47)**
Somset	**Somerset**
St Hel	**St Helens (48)**
Staffs	**Staffordshire**
Sthend	**Southend-on-Sea**
Stockp	**Stockport (49)**
Suffk	**Suffolk**
Sundld	**Sunderland**
Surrey	**Surrey**
Swindn	**Swindon**
Tamesd	**Tameside (50)**
Thurr	**Thurrock (51)**
Torbay	**Torbay**
Traffd	**Trafford (52)**
W & M	**Windsor & Maidenhead (53)**
W Berk	**West Berkshire**
W Susx	**West Sussex**
Wakefd	**Wakefield (54)**
Warrtn	**Warrington (55)**
Warwks	**Warwickshire**
Wigan	**Wigan (56)**
Wilts	**Wiltshire**
Wirral	**Wirral (57)**
Wokham	**Wokingham (58)**
Wolves	**Wolverhampton (59)**
Worcs	**Worcestershire**
Wrekin	**Telford and Wrekin (60)**
Wsall	**Walsall (61)**
York	**York**

Channel Islands & Isle of Man

Guern	**Guernsey**
Jersey	**Jersey**
IoM	**Isle of Man**

Scotland

Abers	**Aberdeenshire**
Ag & B	**Argyll & Bute**
Angus	**Angus**
Border	**Borders**
C Aber	**City of Aberdeen**
C Dund	**City of Dundee**
C Edin	**City of Edinburgh**
C Glas	**City of Glasgow**
Clacks	**Clackmannanshire (1)**
D & G	**Dumfries & Galloway**
E Ayrs	**East Ayrshire**
E Duns	**East Dunbartonshire (2)**
E Loth	**East Lothian**
E Rens	**East Renfrewshire (3)**
Falk	**Falkirk**
Fife	**Fife**
Highld	**Highland**
Inver	**Inverclyde (4)**
Mdloth	**Midlothian (5)**
Moray	**Moray**
N Ayrs	**North Ayrshire**
N Lans	**North Lanarkshire (6)**
Ork	**Orkney Islands**
P & K	**Perth & Kinross**
Rens	**Renfrewshire (7)**
S Ayrs	**South Ayrshire**
Shet	**Shetland Islands**
S Lans	**South Lanarkshire**
Stirlg	**Stirling**
W Duns	**West Dunbartonshire (8)**
W Isls	**Western Isles**
W Loth	**West Lothian**

Wales

Blae G	**Blaenau Gwent (9)**
Brdgnd	**Bridgend (10)**
Caerph	**Caerphilly (11)**
Cardif	**Cardiff**
Carmth	**Carmarthenshire**
Cerdgn	**Ceredigion**
Conwy	**Conwy**
Denbgs	**Denbighshire**
Flints	**Flintshire**
Gwynd	**Gwynedd**
IoA	**Isle of Anglesey**
Mons	**Monmouthshire**
Myr Td	**Merthyr Tydfil (12)**
Neath	**Neath Port Talbot (13)**
Newpt	**Newport (14)**
Pembks	**Pembrokeshire**
Powys	**Powys**
Rhondd	**Rhondda Cynon Taff (15)**
Swans	**Swansea**
Torfn	**Torfaen (16)**
V Glam	**Vale of Glamorgan (17)**
Wrexhm	**Wrexham**

ORKNEY ISLANDS

SHETLAND ISLANDS

WESTERN ISLES

HIGHLAND

MORAY

ABERDEENSHIRE

Aberdeen

ANGUS

PERTH & KINROSS

Dundee

ARGYLL & BUTE

STIRLING

FIFE

1

8

2

FALK

Edinburgh

E LOTH

4 Glasgow

W LOTH

7

6

5

3

NORTH AYRSHIRE

S LANS

BORDERS

E AYRS

S AYRS

DUMFRIES & GALLOWAY

NORTHUMBERLAND

Newcastle upon Tyne

36

30

42

Sunderland

CUMBRIA

DURHAM

32

R & CL

27 41

Middlesbrough

IoM

NORTH YORKSHIRE

Blackpool

LANCASTER

York

EAST RIDING OF YORKSHIRE

22

Leeds

Kingston upon Hull

20

26

54

33

28

N LINCS

N E LINCS

21 25 38

56

37

43 60

45 48 55 52 49

Liverpool 34 31

57

Manchester

39

Sheffield

IoA

CONWY

FLINTS

DENBGS

CHESHIRE

DERBYS

NOTTS

LINCOLNSHIRE

WREXHAM

Stoke-on-Trent

Derby

Nottingham

GWYNEDD

STAFFS

60

LEICS

RUTLAND

NORFOLK

SHROPSHIRE

59 61

29 44

Birmingham

47

Coventry

Leicester

Peterborough

CAMBS

POWYS

WORCS

WARWKS

NHANTS

SUFFOLK

CERDGN

Milton Keynes

BEDS

PEMBKS

HEREFS

Luton

ESSEX

CARMTH

9

MONS

GLOUCS

HERTS

12

16

OXON

BUCKS

GREATER LONDON

Southend-on-Sea

13

15 11

BUCKS

51

Swansea

10

Cardiff

14

40

Swindon

Reading

53 46

MEDWAY

17

35

18

W BERKS

58 24

KENT

WILTSHIRE

SURREY

SOMERSET

HAMPSHIRE

W SUSX

E SUSX

DEVON

DORSET

Southampton

Portsmouth

23

Bournemouth

Poole

IoW

Guernsey

CORNWALL

Plymouth

Torbay

CHANNEL ISLANDS

Jersey

IoS

A

246 C7 **A'Chill** Highld
117 J7 **Ab Kettleby** Leics
82 B5 **Ab Lench** Worcs
32 B6 **Abbas Combe** Somset
81 H2 **Abberley** Worcs
81 G2 **Abberley Common** Worcs
72 E3 **Abberton** Essex
82 A4 **Abberton** Worcs
191 G3 **Abberwick** Nthumb
70 E5 **Abbess Roding** Essex
29 L8 **Abbey** Devon
62 D1 **Abbey Dore** Herefs
131 J8 **Abbey Green** Staffs
30 D7 **Abbey Hill** Somset
213 G6 **Abbey St Bathans** Border
177 G8 **Abbey Town** Cumb
139 J3 **Abbey Village** Lancs
52 A3 **Abbey Wood** Gt Lon
78 E1 **Abbeycwmhir** Powys
132 F3 **Abbeydale** Sheff
147 L5 **Abbeystead** Lancs
131 K2 **Abbot's Chair** Derbys
82 C5 **Abbot's Salford** Warwks
189 G4 **Abbotrule** Border
27 G8 **Abbots Bickington** Devon
115 H6 **Abbots Bromley** Staffs
221 K5 **Abbots Deuglie** P & K
68 E6 **Abbots Langley** Herts
45 G4 **Abbots Leigh** N Som
82 B4 **Abbots Morton** Worcs
102 E7 **Abbots Ripton** Cambs
35 G4 **Abbots Worthy** Hants
16 A5 **Abbotsbury** Dorset
27 G5 **Abbotsham** Devon
8 C1 **Abbotskerswell** Devon
8 B5 **Abbotsleigh** Devon
86 E4 **Abbotsley** Cambs
35 H4 **Abbotstone** Hants
34 D6 **Abbotswood** Hants
17 J2 **Abbott Street** Dorset
34 D2 **Abbotts Ann** Hants
95 J7 **Abcott** Shrops
96 D6 **Abdon** Shrops
63 K4 **Abenhall** Gloucs
61 H3 **Aber Clydach** Powys
76 B7 **Aber-arad** Carmth
76 C7 **Aber-banc** Cerdgn
76 F7 **Aber-giar** Carmth
92 E8 **Aber-Magwr** Cerdgn
77 G4 **Aber-meurig** Cerdgn
60 F6 **Aber-nant** Rhondd
76 E3 **Aberaeron** Cerdgn
60 F7 **Aberaman** Rhondd
93 J2 **Aberangell** Gwynd
251 H6 **Aberarder** Highld
222 B4 **Aberargie** P & K
76 E3 **Aberarth** Cerdgn
57 K7 **Aberavon** Neath
61 J7 **Aberbargoed** Caerph
61 K6 **Aberbeeg** Blae G
221 G3 **Abercairny** P & K
61 G6 **Abercanaid** Myr Td
43 K3 **Abercarn** Caerph
74 D5 **Abercastle** Pembks
93 H3 **Abercegir** Powys
240 B3 **Aberchalder Lodge** Highld
268 A5 **Aberchirder** Abers
77 J4 **Abercoed** Cerdgn
59 M6 **Abercraf** Powys
42 C2 **Abercregan** Neath
60 F7 **Abercwmboi** Rhondd
75 M4 **Abercych** Pembks
43 G3 **Abercynon** Rhondd
221 K3 **Aberdalgie** P & K
60 F6 **Aberdare** Rhondd
108 C6 **Aberdaron** Gwynd
245 L2 **Aberdeen** C Aber
109 G1 **Aberdesach** Gwynd
211 G2 **Aberdour** Fife
57 L5 **Aberdulais** Neath
92 D4 **Aberdyfi** Gwynd
78 F6 **Aberedw** Powys
74 C6 **Abereiddy** Pembks
109 G4 **Abererch** Gwynd
61 G7 **Aberfan** Myr Td
232 C5 **Aberfeldy** P & K
124 F6 **Aberffraw** IOA
92 E7 **Aberffrwd** Cerdgn
150 F8 **Aberford** Leeds
219 H7 **Aberfoyle** Stirlg
42 D5 **Abergarw** Brdgnd
60 B6 **Abergarwed** Neath

62 C4 **Abergavenny** Mons
127 J4 **Abergele** Conwy
59 G2 **Abergorlech** Carmth
78 A4 **Abergwesyn** Powys
58 D5 **Abergwili** Carmth
93 G3 **Abergwydol** Powys
42 D3 **Abergwynfi** Neath
126 C5 **Abergwyngregyn** Gwynd
92 E2 **Abergynolwyn** Gwynd
94 C5 **Aberhafesp** Powys
93 H4 **Aberhosan** Powys
42 D5 **Aberkenfig** Brdgnd
212 A3 **Aberlady** E Loth
234 E4 **Aberlemno** Angus
93 G2 **Aberllefenni** Powys
79 H7 **Aberllynfi** Powys
254 E3 **Aberlour** Moray
129 G8 **Abermorddu** Flints
94 E4 **Abermule** Powys
58 E4 **Abernant** Carmth
222 C4 **Abernethy** P & K
222 D1 **Abernyte** P & K
76 A5 **Aberporth** Cerdgn
108 E6 **Abersoch** Gwynd
62 B6 **Abersychan** Torfn
42 F6 **Aberthin** V Glam
61 K6 **Abertillery** Blae G
43 H4 **Abertridwr** Caerph
111 K7 **Abertridwr** Powys
61 H6 **Abertysswg** Caerph
221 H4 **Aberuthven** P & K
60 F1 **Aberyscir** Powys
92 C7 **Aberystwyth** Cerdgn
66 C7 **Abingdon** Oxon
37 H2 **Abinger** Surrey
37 G2 **Abinger Hammer** Surrey
84 F3 **Abington** Nhants
186 D2 **Abington** S Lans
86 F6 **Abington Pigotts** Cambs
65 G5 **Ablington** Gloucs
33 K2 **Ablington** Wilts
132 D4 **Abney** Derbys
115 G2 **Above Church** Staffs
244 C4 **Aboyne** Abers
139 J7 **Abram** Wigan
250 F4 **Abriachan** Highld
70 C7 **Abridge** Essex
45 L4 **Abson** S Glos
84 C6 **Abthorpe** Nhants
137 H4 **Aby** Lincs
151 J6 **Acaster Malbis** York
151 J7 **Acaster Selby** N York
27 M4 **Accott** Devon
139 M2 **Accrington** Lancs
224 F4 **Acha** Ag & B
282 f3 **Acha Mor** W Isls
206 B3 **Achahoish** Ag & B
233 H6 **Achalader** P & K
228 E8 **Achaleven** Ag & B
261 M7 **Achanalt** Highld
263 H5 **Achandunie** Highld
272 E7 **Achany** Highld
237 K7 **Acharacle** Highld
227 K2 **Acharn** Highld
231 L6 **Acharn** P & K
279 L7 **Achavanich** Highld
270 D7 **Achduart** Highld
276 D8 **Achfary** Highld
270 D6 **Achiltibuie** Highld
192 F5 **Achinhoan** Ag & B
248 F3 **Achintee** Highld
248 D4 **Achintraid** Highld
270 E3 **Achmelvich** Highld
248 D5 **Achmore** Highld
282 f3 **Achmore** W Isls
270 D2 **Achnacarnin** Highld
239 K6 **Achnacarry** Highld
247 J6 **Achnacloich** Highld
250 D8 **Achnaconeran** Highld
228 C7 **Achnacroish** Ag & B
226 F2 **Achnadrish Lodge** Ag & B
232 C8 **Achnafauld** P & K
263 J6 **Achnagarron** Highld
236 F6 **Achnaha** Highld
270 D5 **Achnahaird** Highld
272 E5 **Achnairn** Highld
228 C3 **Achnalea** Highld
206 B2 **Achnamara** Ag & B
261 K8 **Achnasheen** Highld
249 G2 **Achnashellach Lodge** Highld
254 F5 **Achnastank** Moray
236 E7 **Achosnich** Highld
227 K3 **Achranich** Highld
279 H3 **Achreamie** Highld
229 J2 **Achriabhach** Highld

276 D5 **Achriesgill** Highld
277 M4 **Achtoty** Highld
102 A6 **Achurch** Nhants
263 J1 **Achvaich** Highld
280 E5 **Ackergill** Highld
170 C7 **Acklam** Middsb
152 B3 **Acklam** N York
97 H4 **Ackleton** Shrops
191 J6 **Acklington** Nthumb
142 C3 **Ackton** Wakefd
142 C4 **Ackworth Moor Top** Wakefd
107 H1 **Acle** Norfk
98 E6 **Acock's Green** Birm
41 J2 **Acol** Kent
179 L5 **Acomb** Nthumb
151 J5 **Acomb** York
30 B8 **Acombe** Somset
80 C8 **Aconbury** Herefs
140 B3 **Acre** Lancs
112 D3 **Acrefair** Wrexhm
99 J1 **Acresford** Derbys
113 K1 **Acton** Ches
17 J6 **Acton** Dorset
51 G3 **Acton** Gt Lon
114 C3 **Acton** Staffs
89 H6 **Acton** Suffk
81 J2 **Acton** Worcs
80 F5 **Acton Beauchamp** Herefs
130 B4 **Acton Bridge** Ches
96 C3 **Acton Burnell** Shrops
81 G5 **Acton Green** Herefs
112 E1 **Acton Park** Wrexhm
96 C3 **Acton Pigott** Shrops
96 E4 **Acton Round** Shrops
95 L5 **Acton Scott** Shrops
114 E7 **Acton Trussell** Staffs
46 A3 **Acton Turville** S Glos
114 B6 **Adbaston** Staffs
31 K6 **Adber** Dorset
113 L3 **Adderley** Shrops
203 J7 **Adderstone** Nthumb
210 C6 **Addiewell** W Loth
149 K6 **Addingham** Brad
67 H2 **Addington** Bucks
51 K6 **Addington** Gt Lon
52 E7 **Addington** Kent
51 J5 **Addiscombe** Gt Lon
50 D6 **Addlestone** Surrey
50 D6 **Addlestonemoor** Surrey
137 K6 **Addlethorpe** Lincs
113 M7 **Adeney** Wrekin
68 D5 **Adeyfield** Herts
94 C3 **Adfa** Powys
79 M1 **Adforton** Herefs
41 H4 **Adisham** Kent
65 K2 **Adlestrop** Gloucs
143 L3 **Adlingfleet** E R Yk
131 H4 **Adlington** Ches
139 J5 **Adlington** Lancs
115 G7 **Admaston** Staffs
96 E1 **Admaston** Wrekin
82 E6 **Admington** Warwks
30 D5 **Adsborough** Somset
30 B3 **Adscombe** Somset
67 H1 **Adstock** Bucks
84 B5 **Adstone** Nhants
131 H2 **Adswood** Stockp
37 G6 **Adversane** W Susx
254 C5 **Advie** Highld
141 K2 **Adwalton** Leeds
67 G7 **Adwell** Oxon
142 E6 **Adwick Le Street** Donc
142 D7 **Adwick upon Dearne** Donc
176 C1 **Ae** D & G
176 D2 **Ae Bridgend** D & G
139 M5 **Affetside** Bury
255 L4 **Affleck** Abers
16 F4 **Affpuddle** Dorset
249 K7 **Affric Lodge** Highld
128 D5 **Afon-wen** Flints
8 C2 **Afton** Devon
159 K5 **Agglethorpe** N York
129 J2 **Aigburth** Lpool
153 G6 **Aike** E R Yk
166 B1 **Aiketgate** Cumb
165 H1 **Aikhead** Cumb
177 J8 **Aikton** Cumb
137 H4 **Ailby** Lincs
79 L5 **Ailey** Herefs
102 C4 **Ailsworth** C Pete
160 E6 **Ainderby Quernhow** N York
160 E4 **Ainderby Steeple** N York
73 G3 **Aingers Green** Essex

138 C5 **Ainsdale** Sefton
138 C5 **Ainsdale-on-Sea** Sefton
166 C2 **Ainstable** Cumb
139 M5 **Ainsworth** Bury
162 C1 **Ainthorpe** N York
138 D8 **Aintree** Sefton
210 F6 **Ainville** W Loth
216 B7 **Aird** Ag & B
172 D3 **Aird** D & G
282 h3 **Aird** W Isls
282 e5 **Aird a Mhulaidh** W Isls
282 e5 **Aird Asaig** W Isls
248 A4 **Aird Dhubh** Highld
227 G6 **Aird of Kinloch** Ag & B
247 J8 **Aird of Sleat** Highld
282 d3 **Aird Uig** W Isls
216 F1 **Airdeny** Ag & B
209 K6 **Airdrie** N Lans
209 K5 **Airdriehill** N Lans
216 F1 **Airds Bay** Ag & B
175 G1 **Airds of Kells** D & G
282 f4 **Airidh a bhruaich** W Isls
175 J3 **Airieland** D & G
233 M5 **Airlie** Angus
143 J3 **Airmyn** E R Yk
233 G8 **Airntully** P & K
247 M7 **Airor** Highld
210 B2 **Airth** Falk
148 F4 **Airton** N York
135 H1 **Aisby** Lincs
118 D4 **Aisby** Lincs
158 D3 **Aisgill** Cumb
7 K3 **Aish** Devon
8 C3 **Aish** Devon
30 B4 **Aisholt** Somset
160 C5 **Aiskew** N York
162 F1 **Aislaby** N York
162 D5 **Aislaby** N York
169 L8 **Aislaby** S on T
135 J3 **Aisthorpe** Lincs
281 d5 **Aith** Shet
202 E7 **Akeld** Nthumb
84 D7 **Akeley** Bucks
90 D5 **Akenham** Suffk
6 E1 **Albaston** Devon
112 E8 **Alberbury** Shrops
22 C4 **Albourne** W Susx
22 C4 **Albourne Green** W Susx
113 H7 **Albrighton** Shrops
97 H3 **Albrighton** Shrops
106 F6 **Alburgh** Norfk
70 B2 **Albury** Herts
67 G6 **Albury** Oxon
37 G2 **Albury** Surrey
70 B2 **Albury End** Herts
37 G2 **Albury Heath** Surrey
122 D5 **Alby Hill** Norfk
263 G8 **Alcaig** Highld
95 L6 **Alcaston** Shrops
82 C4 **Alcester** Warwks
98 D7 **Alcester Lane End** Birm
23 H6 **Alciston** E Susx
46 A5 **Alcombe** Wilts
102 D8 **Alconbury** Cambs
102 D7 **Alconbury Weston** Cambs
150 F3 **Aldborough** N York
122 D5 **Aldborough** Norfk
47 K4 **Aldbourne** Wilts
153 L8 **Aldbrough** E R Yk
169 L8 **Aldbrough St John** N York
68 B4 **Aldbury** Herts
147 J4 **Aldcliffe** Lancs
232 D3 **Aldclune** P & K
91 K4 **Aldeburgh** Suffk
107 J5 **Aldeby** Norfk
68 F7 **Aldenham** Herts
115 L6 **Alder Moor** Staffs
33 L5 **Alderbury** Wilts
116 D2 **Aldercar** Derbys
33 K8 **Alderholt** Dorset
45 M1 **Alderley** Gloucs
131 G4 **Alderley Edge** Ches
99 K6 **Aldermans Green** Covtry
48 E6 **Aldermaston** W Berk
82 F5 **Alderminster** Warwks
129 K8 **Aldersey Green** Ches
36 C1 **Aldershot** Hants
82 B8 **Alderton** Gloucs
84 E6 **Alderton** Nhants
113 H6 **Alderton** Shrops
91 H7 **Alderton** Suffk
46 B2 **Alderton** Wilts
116 A1 **Alderwasley** Derbys
150 C2 **Aldfield** N York

129 K7 **Aldford** Ches
101 L3 **Aldgate** Rutlnd
72 D2 **Aldham** Essex
90 B6 **Aldham** Suffk
20 F5 **Aldingbourne** W Susx
146 E2 **Aldingham** Cumb
40 E8 **Aldington** Kent
82 C6 **Aldington** Worcs
40 E7 **Aldington Corner** Kent
255 G6 **Aldivalloch** Moray
208 B1 **Aldochlay** Ag & B
95 K7 **Aldon** Shrops
164 F1 **Aldoth** Cumb
103 J8 **Aldreth** Cambs
98 D3 **Aldridge** Wsall
91 K3 **Aldringham** Suffk
152 B3 **Aldro** N York
65 H5 **Aldsworth** Gloucs
20 C5 **Aldsworth** W Susx
255 G6 **Aldunie** Moray
132 E8 **Aldwark** Derbys
151 G3 **Aldwark** N York
20 E7 **Aldwick** W Susx
101 M7 **Aldwincle** Nhants
48 E3 **Aldworth** W Berk
208 C3 **Alexandria** W Duns
30 B3 **Aley** Somset
26 E8 **Alfardisworthy** Devon
14 D3 **Alfington** Devon
36 F4 **Alfold** Surrey
36 F4 **Alfold Bars** W Susx
36 F4 **Alfold Crossways** Surrey
255 M8 **Alford** Abers
137 H4 **Alford** Lincs
31 K4 **Alford** Somset
133 H8 **Alfreton** Derbys
81 H4 **Alfrick** Worcs
81 G5 **Alfrick Pound** Worcs
23 H6 **Alfriston** E Susx
119 J4 **Algarkirk** Lincs
31 K4 **Alhampton** Somset
143 M3 **Alkborough** N Linc
63 M6 **Alkerton** Gloucs
83 J6 **Alkerton** Oxon
41 H6 **Alkham** Kent
113 H4 **Alkington** Shrops
115 K4 **Alkmonton** Derbys
46 F6 **All Cannings** Wilts
107 G7 **All Saints South Elmham** Suffk
95 L4 **All Stretton** Shrops
8 B4 **Allaleigh** Devon
242 F5 **Allanaquoich** Abers
209 M7 **Allanbank** N Lans
202 D2 **Allanton** Border
209 M7 **Allanton** N Lans
209 K8 **Allanton** S Lans
63 J6 **Allaston** Gloucs
34 F6 **Allbrook** Hants
98 F4 **Allen End** Warwks
70 C4 **Allen's Green** Herts
179 J7 **Allendale** Nthumb
167 K2 **Allenheads** Nthumb
168 D1 **Allensford** Dur
80 B8 **Allensmore** Herefs
116 B5 **Allenton** C Derb
28 D5 **Aller** Devon
30 F5 **Aller** Somset
164 E3 **Allerby** Cumb
14 B4 **Allercombe** Devon
28 F2 **Allerford** Somset
162 F6 **Allerston** N York
152 B6 **Allerthorpe** E R Yk
141 H1 **Allerton** Brad
263 K6 **Allerton** Highld
129 J2 **Allerton** Lpool
142 C2 **Allerton Bywater** Leeds
150 F4 **Allerton Mauleverer** N York
99 J7 **Allesley** Covtry
116 B4 **Allestree** C Derb
4 C5 **Allet Common** Cnwll
101 H3 **Allexton** Leics
131 J6 **Allgreave** Ches
53 H3 **Allhallows** Medway
53 H3 **Allhallows-on-Sea** Medway
260 D8 **Alligin Shuas** Highld
114 D7 **Allimore Green** Staffs
15 K4 **Allington** Dorset
53 G7 **Allington** Kent
117 M3 **Allington** Lincs
46 C4 **Allington** Wilts
46 F6 **Allington** Wilts
33 L3 **Allington** Wilts
156 E7 **Allithwaite** Cumb
220 F8 **Alloa** Clacks

164 E2 **Allonby** Cumb
130 E5 **Allostock** Ches
196 C7 **Alloway** S Ayrs
30 F8 **Allowenshay** Somset
97 G4 **Allscott** Shrops
96 E1 **Allscott** Wrekin
129 G6 **Alltami** Flints
229 K5 **Alltchaorunn** Highld
78 F6 **Alltmawr** Powys
58 E3 **Alltwalis** Carmth
57 K4 **Alltwen** Neath
76 F6 **Alltyblaca** Cerdgn
31 L8 **Allweston** Dorset
90 B1 **Allwood Green** Suffk
79 L5 **Almeley** Herefs
79 L5 **Almeley Wooton** Herefs
17 H3 **Almer** Dorset
142 F6 **Almholme** Donc
113 M4 **Almington** Staffs
20 D7 **Almodington** W Susx
221 J2 **Almondbank** P & K
141 J5 **Almondbury** Kirk
45 J2 **Almondsbury** S Glos
151 G3 **Alne** N York
90 E7 **Alnesbourn Priory** Suffk
263 H6 **Alness** Highld
190 E4 **Alnham** Nthumb
191 J4 **Alnmouth** Nthumb
191 H3 **Alnwick** Nthumb
50 F2 **Alperton** Gt Lon
89 H8 **Alphamstone** Essex
89 H5 **Alpheton** Suffk
13 L4 **Alphington** Devon
106 F3 **Alpington** Norfk
132 D6 **Alport** Derbys
130 B7 **Alpraham** Ches
72 F3 **Alresford** Essex
115 K8 **Alrewas** Staffs
130 F8 **Alsager** Ches
114 C2 **Alsagers Bank** Staffs
132 C8 **Alsop en le Dale** Derbys
167 G2 **Alston** Cumb
15 G2 **Alston** Devon
44 E8 **Alston Sutton** Somset
82 A8 **Alstone** Gloucs
30 D2 **Alstone** Somset
114 D7 **Alstone Green** Staffs
132 C8 **Alstonefield** Staffs
28 C6 **Alswear** Devon
140 E7 **Alt** Oldham
270 C5 **Altandhu** Highld
11 J6 **Altarnun** Cnwll
272 D8 **Altass** Highld
227 K5 **Altcreich** Ag & B
207 G4 **Altgaltraig** Ag & B
140 A1 **Altham** Lancs
72 D7 **Althorne** Essex
143 L6 **Althorpe** N Linc
279 H7 **Altnabreac Station** Highld
216 C2 **Altnacraig** Ag & B
272 E1 **Altnaharra** Highld
142 B3 **Altofts** Wakefd
133 G6 **Alton** Derbys
35 L3 **Alton** Hants
115 H3 **Alton** Staffs
33 K2 **Alton** Wilts
47 G6 **Alton Barnes** Wilts
16 D2 **Alton Pancras** Dorset
47 G6 **Alton Priors** Wilts
130 E2 **Altrincham** Traffd
219 G6 **Altskeith Hotel** Stirlg
220 F7 **Alva** Clacks
268 B4 **Alvah** Abers
129 L5 **Alvanley** Ches
116 C5 **Alvaston** C Derb
82 B1 **Alvechurch** Worcs
99 H3 **Alvecote** Warwks
33 G6 **Alvediston** Wilts
97 G6 **Alveley** Shrops
27 J6 **Alverdiscott** Devon
19 K4 **Alverstoke** Hants
19 K6 **Alverstone** IOW
141 M3 **Alverthorpe** Wakefd
117 L3 **Alverton** Notts
266 C4 **Alves** Moray
65 K6 **Alvescot** Oxon
45 J1 **Alveston** Gloucs
82 F4 **Alveston** Warwks
137 G2 **Alvingham** Lincs
63 J7 **Alvington** Gloucs
102 C4 **Alwalton** Cambs
190 C5 **Alwinton** Nthumb
150 C7 **Alwoodley** Leeds
150 D7 **Alwoodley Gates** Leeds
233 K5 **Alyth** P & K

119 H2 **Amber Hill** Lincs
133 G8 **Amber Row** Derbys
116 B1 **Ambergate** Derbys
64 B6 **Amberley** Gloucs
21 H4 **Amberley** W Susx
23 K5 **Amberstone** E Susx
191 K5 **Amble** Nthumb
97 K6 **Amblecote** Dudley
141 H2 **Ambler Thorn** Brad
156 E2 **Ambleside** Cumb
75 G7 **Ambleston** Pembks
66 F3 **Ambrosden** Oxon
143 L5 **Amcotts** N Linc
103 J7 **America** Cambs
68 B7 **Amersham** Bucks
68 B7 **Amersham on the Hill** Bucks
114 F6 **Amerton** Staffs
33 K3 **Amesbury** Wilts
282 d5 **Amhuinnsuidhe** W Isls
99 G3 **Amington** Staffs
176 D2 **Amisfield Town** D & G
125 H1 **Amlwch** IOA
59 H6 **Ammanford** Carmth
162 C7 **Amotherby** N York
34 E6 **Ampfield** Hants
161 J7 **Ampleforth** N York
64 F6 **Ampney Crucis** Gloucs
65 G6 **Ampney St Mary** Gloucs
65 G6 **Ampney St Peter** Gloucs
34 C2 **Amport** Hants
85 K7 **Ampthill** Beds
89 H1 **Ampton** Suffk
55 K5 **Amroth** Pembks
232 D8 **Amulree** P & K
68 F4 **Amwell** Herts
282 d6 **An t-Ob** W Isls
228 C3 **Anaheilt** Highld
118 C3 **Ancaster** Lincs
94 E6 **Anchor** Shrops
202 F4 **Ancroft** Nthumb
189 H1 **Ancrum** Border
21 G2 **Ancton** W Susx
137 K4 **Anderby** Lincs
30 E4 **Andersea** Somset
30 C4 **Andersfield** Somset
17 G3 **Anderson** Dorset
130 C4 **Anderton** Ches
6 E4 **Anderton** Cnwll
34 D2 **Andover** Hants
64 F3 **Andoversford** Gloucs
154 f2 **Andreas** IOM
108 B6 **Anelog** Gwynd
51 J5 **Anerley** Gt Lon
129 J1 **Anfield** Lpool
2 F3 **Angarrack** Cnwll
3 K4 **Angarrick** Cnwll
96 D8 **Angelbank** Shrops
30 B7 **Angersleigh** Somset
177 H7 **Angerton** Cumb
54 D6 **Angle** Pembks
21 H6 **Angmering** W Susx
158 F3 **Angram** N York
151 H6 **Angram** N York
3 H7 **Angrouse** Cnwll
179 L5 **Anick** Nthumb
264 C5 **Ankerville** Highld
117 K7 **Ankle Hill** Leics
144 C2 **Anlaby** E R Yk
121 G5 **Anmer** Norfk
19 L1 **Anmore** Hants
34 D2 **Anna Valley** Hants
177 G5 **Annan** D & G
155 K5 **Annaside** Cumb
248 E1 **Annat** Highld
209 J3 **Annathill** N Lans
196 E6 **Annbank** S Ayrs
116 E1 **Annesley** Notts
116 E1 **Annesley Woodhouse** Notts
180 E8 **Annfield Plain** Dur
208 F5 **Anniesland** C Glas
181 G4 **Annitsford** N Tyne
95 L2 **Annscroft** Shrops
138 D2 **Ansdell** Lancs
31 L4 **Ansford** Somset
99 J5 **Ansley** Warwks
115 L6 **Anslow** Staffs
115 K6 **Anslow Gate** Staffs
115 K6 **Anslow Lees** Staffs
36 D4 **Ansteadbrook** Surrey
35 L3 **Anstey** Hants
87 H8 **Anstey** Herts
100 C2 **Anstey** Leics
223 K6 **Anstruther** Fife
37 L6 **Ansty** W Susx
99 L6 **Ansty** Warwks

33 G5 **Ansty** Wilts
16 E2 **Ansty Cross** Dorset
19 L1 **Anthill Common** Hants
50 C6 **Anthonys** Surrey
177 G7 **Anthorn** Cumb
122 E5 **Antingham** Norfk
119 J2 **Anton's Gowt** Lincs
6 D4 **Antony** Cnwll
130 C3 **Antrobus** Ches
3 G5 **Antron** Cnwll
11 M2 **Anvil Corner** Devon
40 E5 **Anvil Green** Kent
118 F2 **Anwick** Lincs
174 F4 **Anwoth** D & G
51 L7 **Aperfield** Gt Lon
82 A1 **Apes Dale** Worcs
102 A4 **Apethorpe** Nhants
114 D7 **Apeton** Staffs
136 B5 **Apley** Lincs
133 H4 **Apperknowle** Derbys
64 B2 **Apperley** Gloucs
150 B8 **Apperley Bridge** Brad
180 C7 **Apperley Dene** Nthumb
158 E4 **Appersett** N York
228 E6 **Appin** Ag & B
144 B5 **Appleby** N Linc
99 J2 **Appleby Magna** Leics
99 J2 **Appleby Parva** Leics
69 J6 **Appleby Street** Herts
166 F6 **Appleby-in-Westmorland** Cumb
248 A3 **Applecross** Highld
27 H5 **Appledore** Devon
29 K7 **Appledore** Devon
25 H2 **Appledore** Kent
25 H1 **Appledore Heath** Kent
66 D8 **Appleford** Oxon
176 F2 **Applegarth Town** D & G
142 A5 **Applehaigh** Wakefd
34 C1 **Appleshaw** Hants
165 J5 **Applethwaite** Cumb
129 M2 **Appleton** Halton
66 C6 **Appleton** Oxon
130 B3 **Appleton** Warrtn
151 J7 **Appleton Roebuck** N York
130 C3 **Appleton Thorn** Warrtn
160 F2 **Appleton Wiske** N York
162 C5 **Appleton-le-Moors** N York
162 C7 **Appleton-le-Street** N York
188 F3 **Appletreehall** Border
149 J4 **Appletreewick** N York
29 K6 **Appley** Somset
139 G6 **Appley Bridge** Lancs
19 J7 **Apse Heath** IOW
86 C8 **Apsley End** Beds
20 D6 **Apuldram** W Susx
264 C5 **Arabella** Highld
234 F7 **Arbirlot** Angus
264 D3 **Arboll** Highld
49 H5 **Arborfield** Wokham
49 J5 **Arborfield Cross** Wokham
133 G3 **Arbourthorne** Sheff
235 G7 **Arbroath** Angus
245 H8 **Arbuthnott** Abers
39 L6 **Arcadia** Kent
56 E4 **Archddu** Carmth
169 H7 **Archdeacon Newton** Darltn
208 C3 **Archencarroch** W Duns
254 E3 **Archiestown** Moray
9 f2 **Archirondel** Jersey
130 F7 **Arclid Green** Ches
217 H2 **Ardanaiseig Hotel** Ag & B
248 D4 **Ardaneaskan** Highld
248 D4 **Ardarroch** Highld
204 F7 **Ardbeg** Ag & B
207 H5 **Ardbeg** Ag & B
207 K2 **Ardbeg** Ag & B
261 K2 **Ardcharnich** Highld
214 D1 **Ardchiavaig** Ag & B
216 F5 **Ardchonnel** Ag & B
219 K4 **Ardchullarie More** Stirlg
218 C8 **Arddarroch** Ag & B
112 C8 **Arddleen** Powys
239 J5 **Ardechive** Highld
196 B3 **Ardeer** N Ayrs
69 J2 **Ardeley** Herts
248 D6 **Ardelve** Highld
208 B2 **Arden** Ag & B
82 D4 **Ardens Grafton** Warwks
216 C2 **Ardentallen** Ag & B
207 K2 **Ardentinny** Ag & B
207 G4 **Ardentraive** Ag & B
231 J8 **Ardeonaig Hotel** Stirlg
252 E1 **Ardersier** Highld
261 H2 **Ardessie** Highld

216 C6 **Ardfern** Ag & B
263 G2 **Ardgay** Highld
229 G3 **Ardgour** Highld
207 L4 **Ardgowan** Inver
207 K4 **Ardhallow** Ag & B
282 e5 **Ardhasig** W Isls
260 C8 **Ardheslaig** Highld
261 K2 **Ardindrean** Highld
38 A7 **Ardingly** W Susx
48 B1 **Ardington** Oxon
48 B1 **Ardington Wick** Oxon
206 F6 **Ardlamont** Ag & B
72 F1 **Ardleigh** Essex
72 F1 **Ardleigh Heath** Essex
233 L7 **Ardler** P & K
66 D2 **Ardley** Oxon
70 D4 **Ardley End** Essex
218 D4 **Ardlui** Ag & B
215 J6 **Ardlussa** Ag & B
229 H7 **Ardmaddy** Ag & B
270 F8 **Ardmair** Highld
207 H5 **Ardmaleish** Ag & B
205 L6 **Ardminish** Ag & B
237 K6 **Ardmolich** Highld
208 A3 **Ardmore** Ag & B
263 J3 **Ardmore** Highld
207 K3 **Ardnadam** Ag & B
250 F2 **Ardnagrask** Highld
248 E4 **Ardnarff** Highld
228 B3 **Ardnastang** Highld
217 J5 **Ardno** Ag & B
239 L3 **Ardochy House** Highld
206 B7 **Ardpatrick** Ag & B
206 D2 **Ardrishaig** Ag & B
263 H5 **Ardross** Highld
195 L3 **Ardrossan** N Ayrs
142 B6 **Ardsley** Barns
141 M3 **Ardsley East** Leeds
237 H8 **Ardslignish** Highld
205 G5 **Ardtalla** Ag & B
237 J6 **Ardtoe** Highld
216 B5 **Arduaine** Ag & B
263 G7 **Ardullie** Highld
247 K7 **Ardvasar** Highld
219 K3 **Ardvorlich** P & K
282 e5 **Ardvourlie** W Isls
172 D5 **Ardwell** D & G
140 C8 **Ardwick** Manch
81 H1 **Areley Kings** Worcs
237 J7 **Arevegaig** Highld
36 B3 **Arford** Hants
61 J7 **Argoed** Caerph
112 E7 **Argoed** Shrops
78 D3 **Argoed Mill** Powys
23 J2 **Argos Hill** E Susx
282 f4 **Aribruach** W Isls
226 C7 **Aridhglas** Ag & B
224 F4 **Arileod** Ag & B
225 G4 **Arinagour** Ag & B
216 D2 **Ariogan** Ag & B
237 J3 **Arisaig** Highld
237 K4 **Arisaig House** Highld
150 E4 **Arkendale** N York
87 K8 **Arkesden** Essex
147 L2 **Arkholme** Lancs
159 H2 **Arkle Town** N York
164 F3 **Arkleby** Cumb
188 C7 **Arkleton** D & G
69 G7 **Arkley** Gt Lon
142 F6 **Arksey** Donc
133 H5 **Arkwright Town** Derbys
64 D2 **Arle** Gloucs
164 D7 **Arlecdon** Cumb
83 J5 **Arlescote** Warwks
86 D7 **Arlesey** Beds
96 F1 **Arleston** Wrekin
130 C3 **Arley** Ches
99 H5 **Arley** Warwks
63 L5 **Arlingham** Gloucs
27 L3 **Arlington** Devon
23 J5 **Arlington** E Susx
65 G5 **Arlington** Gloucs
27 L3 **Arlington Beccott** Devon
278 D3 **Armadale** Highld
247 K7 **Armadale** Highld
210 B5 **Armadale** W Loth
164 F5 **Armaside** Cumb
166 C2 **Armathwaite** Cumb
106 E3 **Arminghall** Norfk
115 H8 **Armitage** Staffs
141 H5 **Armitage Bridge** Kirk
141 L1 **Armley** Leeds
82 F6 **Armscote** Warwks
114 E2 **Armshead** Staffs
102 B6 **Armston** Nhants

143 G6 **Armthorpe** Donc
225 G3 **Arnabost** Ag & B
156 A5 **Arnaby** Cumb
149 G2 **Arncliffe** N York
149 G2 **Arncliffe Cote** N York
223 J6 **Arncroach** Fife
266 F6 **Arndilly House** Moray
17 J5 **Arne** Dorset
100 D5 **Arnesby** Leics
140 F8 **Arnfield** Derbys
221 L5 **Arngask** P & K
238 D2 **Arnisdale** Highld
259 K7 **Arnish** Highld
211 K6 **Arniston** Mdloth
282 f2 **Arnol** W Isls
153 H7 **Arnold** E R Yk
117 G2 **Arnold** Notts
219 K8 **Arnprior** Stirlg
157 G7 **Arnside** Cumb
227 G3 **Aros** Ag & B
113 G4 **Arowry** Wrexhm
156 D6 **Arrad Foot** Cumb
153 G7 **Arram** E R Yk
160 B4 **Arrathorne** N York
19 J6 **Arreton** IOW
260 B8 **Arrina** Highld
87 G5 **Arrington** Cambs
218 D6 **Arrochar** Ag & B
82 C4 **Arrow** Warwks
98 C8 **Arrowfield Top** Worcs
95 K2 **Arscott** Shrops
251 H2 **Artafallie** Highld
150 C6 **Arthington** Leeds
101 G7 **Arthingworth** Nhants
110 C8 **Arthog** Gwynd
257 H4 **Arthrath** Abers
150 E8 **Arthursdale** Leeds
257 J5 **Artrochie** Abers
21 G5 **Arundel** W Susx
164 E6 **Asby** Cumb
207 J6 **Ascog** Ag & B
50 A5 **Ascot** W & M
83 H8 **Ascott** Warwks
65 L3 **Ascott Earl** Oxon
65 L3 **Ascott-under-Wychwood**
 Oxon
160 F7 **Asenby** N York
117 J7 **Asfordby** Leics
117 J7 **Asfordby Hill** Leics
118 F3 **Asgarby** Lincs
136 F6 **Asgarby** Lincs
12 C1 **Ash** Devon
8 C5 **Ash** Devon
32 E8 **Ash** Dorset
52 D6 **Ash** Kent
41 J4 **Ash** Kent
30 D6 **Ash** Somset
31 G6 **Ash** Somset
36 D1 **Ash** Surrey
36 D1 **Ash Green** Surrey
99 J6 **Ash Green** Warwks
113 J4 **Ash Magna** Shrops
28 D6 **Ash Mill** Devon
113 J4 **Ash Parva** Shrops
29 L5 **Ash Priors** Somset
89 K6 **Ash Street** Suffk
29 H8 **Ash Thomas** Devon
49 L8 **Ash Vale** Surrey
48 E4 **Ashampstead** W Berk
48 E3 **Ashampstead Green** W Berk
90 E4 **Ashbocking** Suffk
90 E4 **Ashbocking Green** Suffk
115 K2 **Ashbourne** Derbys
115 K2 **Ashbourne Green** Derbys
29 J6 **Ashbrittle** Somset
24 C4 **Ashburnham Place** E Susx
7 L1 **Ashburton** Devon
12 C3 **Ashbury** Devon
47 K2 **Ashbury** Oxon
143 M6 **Ashby** N Linc
137 H6 **Ashby by Partney** Lincs
145 H7 **Ashby cum Fenby** NE Lin
135 L8 **Ashby de la Launde** Lincs
100 F1 **Ashby Folville** Leics
100 C5 **Ashby Magna** Leics
100 C5 **Ashby Parva** Leics
136 F5 **Ashby Puerorum** Lincs
84 B2 **Ashby St Ledgers** Nhants
107 G3 **Ashby St Mary** Norfk
116 B8 **Ashby-de-la-Zouch** Leics
81 L8 **Ashchurch** Gloucs
13 L6 **Ashcombe** Devon
44 C6 **Ashcombe** N Som
31 G3 **Ashcott** Somset
88 B6 **Ashdon** Essex

35 H1 **Ashe** Hants
72 E6 **Asheldham** Essex
88 E6 **Ashen** Essex
67 H4 **Ashendon** Bucks
68 B6 **Asheridge** Bucks
34 E7 **Ashfield** Hants
63 H2 **Ashfield** Herefs
220 D6 **Ashfield** Stirlg
90 F3 **Ashfield** Suffk
88 F4 **Ashfield Green** Suffk
106 F8 **Ashfield Green** Suffk
113 M6 **Ashfields** Shrops
37 K5 **Ashfold Crossways** W Susx
27 J4 **Ashford** Devon
7 K5 **Ashford** Devon
40 D6 **Ashford** Kent
50 D4 **Ashford** Surrey
80 C1 **Ashford Bowdler** Shrops
80 C1 **Ashford Carbonel** Shrops
48 E6 **Ashford Hill** Hants
132 D5 **Ashford in the Water** Derbys
198 C3 **Ashgill** S Lans
29 K8 **Ashill** Devon
105 H3 **Ashill** Norfk
30 D7 **Ashill** Somset
72 C8 **Ashingdon** Essex
181 G1 **Ashington** Nthumb
17 K3 **Ashington** Poole
31 J6 **Ashington** Somset
21 K4 **Ashington** W Susx
188 E2 **Ashkirk** Border
19 J3 **Ashlett** Hants
64 A2 **Ashleworth** Gloucs
64 B2 **Ashleworth Quay** Gloucs
88 D3 **Ashley** Cambs
130 F3 **Ashley** Ches
28 B8 **Ashley** Devon
18 A3 **Ashley** Dorset
64 D8 **Ashley** Gloucs
34 E4 **Ashley** Hants
18 C4 **Ashley** Hants
41 J5 **Ashley** Kent
101 H5 **Ashley** Nhants
114 B4 **Ashley** Staffs
46 B5 **Ashley** Wilts
68 B6 **Ashley Green** Bucks
17 M2 **Ashley Heath** Dorset
80 B2 **Ashley Moor** Herefs
48 B7 **Ashmansworth** Hants
26 F7 **Ashmansworthy** Devon
63 M7 **Ashmead Green** Gloucs
11 M3 **Ashmill** Devon
32 F7 **Ashmore** Dorset
48 D5 **Ashmore Green** W Berk
83 G4 **Ashorne** Warwks
133 G7 **Ashover** Derbys
133 G7 **Ashover Hay** Derbys
83 H1 **Ashow** Warwks
80 E7 **Ashperton** Herefs
8 B3 **Ashprington** Devon
27 L8 **Ashreigney** Devon
68 C4 **Ashridge Park** Herts
50 F7 **Ashtead** Surrey
102 B2 **Ashton** C Pete
129 L6 **Ashton** Ches
2 F5 **Ashton** Cnwll
6 D1 **Ashton** Cnwll
13 K5 **Ashton** Devon
35 H7 **Ashton** Hants
80 C2 **Ashton** Herefs
207 L4 **Ashton** Inver
84 E5 **Ashton** Nhants
102 B5 **Ashton** Nhants
30 F1 **Ashton** Somset
46 C7 **Ashton Common** Wilts
46 C7 **Ashton Hill** Wilts
64 F8 **Ashton Keynes** Wilts
82 A7 **Ashton under Hill** Worcs
130 F1 **Ashton upon Mersey** Traffd
45 G5 **Ashton Watering** N Som
139 H7 **Ashton-in-Makerfield** Wigan
140 E7 **Ashton-under-Lyne** Tamesd
18 E2 **Ashurst** Hants
38 D5 **Ashurst** Kent
21 L4 **Ashurst** W Susx
38 B6 **Ashurstwood** W Susx
11 M3 **Ashwater** Devon
86 F7 **Ashwell** Herts
101 J1 **Ashwell** Rutlnd
30 E7 **Ashwell** Somset
86 E7 **Ashwell End** Herts
106 C4 **Ashwellthorpe** Norfk
31 K1 **Ashwick** Somset
120 F7 **Ashwicken** Norfk
97 K5 **Ashwood** Staffs

156 B7 **Askam in Furness** Cumb
160 B2 **Aske Hall** N York
142 F5 **Askern** Donc
15 M4 **Askerswell** Dorset
67 K6 **Askett** Bucks
166 C6 **Askham** Cumb
134 E5 **Askham** Notts
151 H6 **Askham Bryan** York
151 H6 **Askham Richard** York
206 E1 **Asknish** Ag & B
159 G4 **Askrigg** N York
149 L6 **Askwith** N York
118 E5 **Aslackby** Lincs
106 D5 **Aslacton** Norfk
117 K3 **Aslockton** Notts
31 G3 **Asney** Somset
90 E2 **Aspall** Suffk
164 F2 **Aspatria** Cumb
69 K2 **Aspenden** Herts
131 K2 **Aspenshaw** Derbys
119 J4 **Asperton** Lincs
114 C5 **Aspley** Staffs
85 J8 **Aspley Guise** Beds
85 H8 **Aspley Heath** Beds
82 C1 **Aspley Heath** Warwks
139 J6 **Aspull** Wigan
139 J8 **Aspull Common** Wigan
143 H2 **Asselby** E R Yk
137 J4 **Asserby** Lincs
137 J4 **Asserby Turn** Lincs
89 J7 **Assington** Suffk
88 F5 **Assington Green** Suffk
131 G7 **Astbury** Ches
84 D4 **Astcote** Nhants
136 E4 **Asterby** Lincs
95 J2 **Asterley** Shrops
95 K5 **Asterton** Shrops
65 L5 **Asthall** Oxon
65 L4 **Asthall Leigh** Oxon
263 K2 **Astle** Highld
142 B2 **Astley** Leeds
113 H7 **Astley** Shrops
99 J5 **Astley** Warwks
139 L7 **Astley** Wigan
81 H2 **Astley** Worcs
96 F4 **Astley Abbots** Shrops
139 L5 **Astley Bridge** Bolton
81 J1 **Astley Cross** Worcs
139 L7 **Astley Green** Wigan
81 H2 **Astley Town** Worcs
98 D5 **Aston** Birm
130 A4 **Aston** Ches
113 K2 **Aston** Ches
132 D3 **Aston** Derbys
129 G6 **Aston** Flints
80 B3 **Aston** Herefs
80 B1 **Aston** Herefs
69 H3 **Aston** Herts
65 M6 **Aston** Oxon
133 J3 **Aston** Rothm
113 H6 **Aston** Shrops
97 H5 **Aston** Shrops
114 B3 **Aston** Staffs
114 D6 **Aston** Staffs
114 E5 **Aston** Staffs
49 J2 **Aston** Wokham
96 E2 **Aston** Wrekin
67 K3 **Aston Abbotts** Bucks
96 E6 **Aston Botterell** Shrops
82 D3 **Aston Cantlow** Warwks
67 L4 **Aston Clinton** Bucks
63 K3 **Aston Crews** Herefs
81 L8 **Aston Cross** Gloucs
69 H2 **Aston End** Herts
81 M2 **Aston Fields** Worcs
100 A5 **Aston Flamville** Leics
130 A4 **Aston Heath** Ches
63 K3 **Aston Ingham** Herefs
130 C8 **Aston juxta Mondrum** Ches
83 L5 **Aston le Walls** Nhants
82 E8 **Aston Magna** Gloucs
96 C6 **Aston Munslow** Shrops
95 J7 **Aston on Clun** Shrops
95 H2 **Aston Pigott** Shrops
95 H2 **Aston Rogers** Shrops
67 H7 **Aston Rowant** Oxon
67 J5 **Aston Sandford** Bucks
82 B7 **Aston Somerville** Worcs
82 D7 **Aston Subedge** Gloucs
48 E2 **Aston Tirrold** Oxon
48 E2 **Aston Upthorpe** Oxon
96 E4 **Aston-Eyre** Shrops
116 C5 **Aston-upon-Trent** Derbys
96 E4 **Astonlane** Shrops
83 L7 **Astrop** Nhants

67 L4 **Astrope** Herts
86 E7 **Astwick** Beds
133 J6 **Astwith** Derbys
85 J5 **Astwood** M Keyn
81 L2 **Astwood** Worcs
82 B3 **Astwood Bank** Worcs
118 E4 **Aswarby** Lincs
137 G5 **Aswardby** Lincs
82 B5 **Atch Lench** Worcs
96 C2 **Atcham** Shrops
16 E4 **Athelhampton** Dorset
90 F1 **Athelington** Suffk
30 E5 **Athelney** Somset
212 C4 **Athelstaneford** E Loth
19 G7 **Atherfield Green** IOW
27 L6 **Atherington** Devon
21 G6 **Atherington** W Susx
30 F7 **Atherstone** Somset
99 J4 **Atherstone** Warwks
82 F5 **Atherstone on Stour** Warwks
139 K7 **Atherton** Wigan
160 D2 **Atley Hill** N York
115 L2 **Atlow** Derbys
248 E4 **Attadale** Highld
116 E5 **Attenborough** Notts
135 K1 **Atterby** Lincs
133 G2 **Attercliffe** Sheff
96 E4 **Atterley** Shrops
99 K4 **Atterton** Leics
105 L4 **Attleborough** Norfk
99 K5 **Attleborough** Warwks
122 E4 **Attlebridge** Norfk
88 E4 **Attleton Green** Suffk
153 K5 **Atwick** E R Yk
46 B6 **Atworth** Wilts
80 C6 **Auberrow** Herefs
135 J7 **Aubourn** Lincs
257 G5 **Auchedly** Abers
244 F7 **Auchenblae** Abers
209 L2 **Auchenbowie** Stirlg
175 K4 **Auchencairn** D & G
176 C2 **Auchencairn** D & G
195 G5 **Auchencairn** N Ayrs
213 J7 **Auchencrow** Border
211 H6 **Auchendinny** Mdloth
199 G2 **Auchengray** S Lans
267 H4 **Auchenhalrig** Moray
198 D4 **Auchenheath** S Lans
185 K4 **Auchenhessnane** D & G
206 F4 **Auchenlochan** Ag & B
196 C2 **Auchenmade** N Ayrs
173 G4 **Auchenmalg** D & G
196 D2 **Auchentiber** N Ayrs
219 J8 **Auchentroig** Stirlg
261 K4 **Auchindrean** Highld
268 B6 **Auchininna** Abers
197 G6 **Auchinleck** E Ayrs
209 H5 **Auchinloch** N Lans
209 J4 **Auchinstarry** N Lans
229 H1 **Auchintore** Highld
257 K4 **Auchiries** Abers
245 K4 **Auchlee** Abers
256 A6 **Auchleven** Abers
198 C5 **Auchlochan** S Lans
244 D3 **Auchlossan** Abers
219 H1 **Auchlyne** Stirlg
197 G5 **Auchmillan** E Ayrs
235 G6 **Auchmithie** Angus
222 C7 **Auchmuirbridge** Fife
234 C3 **Auchnacree** Angus
257 G3 **Auchnagatt** Abers
254 D7 **Auchnarrow** Moray
272 B3 **Auchnotteroch** D & G
267 G6 **Auchroisk** Moray
221 G4 **Auchterarder** P & K
240 B2 **Auchteraw** Highld
253 H7 **Auchterblair** Highld
260 C4 **Auchtercairn** Highld
222 C8 **Auchterderran** Fife
233 M7 **Auchterhouse** Angus
256 C3 **Auchterless** Abers
222 D5 **Auchtermuchty** Fife
262 E7 **Auchterneed** Highld
211 H1 **Auchtertool** Fife
248 D6 **Auchtertyre** Highld
219 J3 **Auchtubh** Stirlg
280 E3 **Auckengill** Highld
143 G7 **Auckley** Donc
140 D8 **Audenshaw** Tamesd
113 L3 **Audlem** Ches
114 C2 **Audley** Staffs
87 L7 **Audley End** Essex
89 G7 **Audley End** Essex
89 G4 **Audley End** Suffk
114 C7 **Audmore** Staffs

97 K6 **Audnam** Dudley
165 H3 **Aughertree** Cumb
151 L8 **Aughton** E R Yk
138 E6 **Aughton** Lancs
147 L2 **Aughton** Lancs
133 J2 **Aughton** Rothm
47 K7 **Aughton** Wilts
138 E6 **Aughton Park** Lancs
253 H1 **Auldearn** Highld
80 B4 **Aulden** Herefs
176 B2 **Auldgirth** D & G
197 J1 **Auldhouse** S Lans
248 F7 **Ault a' chruinn** Highld
133 J6 **Ault Hucknall** Derbys
260 D2 **Aultbea** Highld
260 B3 **Aultgrishin** Highld
262 B6 **Aultguish Inn** Highld
267 H5 **Aultmore** Moray
250 F7 **Aultnagoire** Highld
263 J4 **Aultnamain Inn** Highld
118 D8 **Aunby** Lincs
14 B3 **Aunk** Devon
118 D4 **Aunsby** Lincs
45 H1 **Aust** S Glos
119 J7 **Austendike** Lincs
134 D1 **Austerfield** Donc
140 E6 **Austerlands** Oldham
142 B1 **Austhorpe** Leeds
141 H6 **Austonley** Kirk
99 J2 **Austrey** Warwks
148 D2 **Austwick** N York
137 G3 **Authorpe** Lincs
137 K5 **Authorpe Row** Lincs
47 G5 **Avebury** Wilts
47 G5 **Avebury Trusloe** Wilts
52 C3 **Aveley** Thurr
64 C7 **Avening** Gloucs
117 K1 **Averham** Notts
7 K5 **Aveton Gifford** Devon
242 B1 **Aviemore** Highld
48 A5 **Avington** W Berk
251 J1 **Avoch** Highld
18 A4 **Avon** Dorset
83 K5 **Avon Dassett** Warwks
210 B4 **Avonbridge** Falk
45 G3 **Avonmouth** Bristl
7 K3 **Avonwick** Devon
34 D6 **Awbridge** Hants
45 H2 **Awkley** S Glos
14 D2 **Awliscombe** Devon
63 L5 **Awre** Gloucs
116 E3 **Awsworth** Notts
97 J7 **Axborough** Worcs
44 E8 **Axbridge** Somset
35 J2 **Axford** Hants
47 K5 **Axford** Wilts
15 G3 **Axminster** Devon
14 F4 **Axmouth** Devon
128 D4 **Axton** Flints
169 H6 **Aycliffe** Dur
180 B5 **Aydon** Nthumb
63 J6 **Aylburton** Gloucs
167 G1 **Ayle** Cumb
14 B4 **Aylesbeare** Devon
67 K4 **Aylesbury** Bucks
145 G6 **Aylesby** NE Lin
52 F7 **Aylesford** Kent
41 H5 **Aylesham** Kent
100 C3 **Aylestone** C Leic
100 D3 **Aylestone Park** C Leic
122 D4 **Aylmerton** Norfk
122 D6 **Aylsham** Norfk
80 F7 **Aylton** Gloucs
65 G3 **Aylworth** Gloucs
80 A2 **Aymestrey** Herefs
83 L8 **Aynho** Nhants
69 L4 **Ayot Green** Herts
69 G4 **Ayot St Lawrence** Herts
69 G4 **Ayot St Peter** Herts
196 C6 **Ayr** S Ayrs
159 H5 **Aysgarth** N York
29 J7 **Ayshford** Devon
156 F6 **Ayside** Cumb
101 J3 **Ayston** Rutlnd
70 E4 **Aythorpe Roding** Essex
213 K6 **Ayton** Border
160 C7 **Azerley** N York

B

8 D2 **Babbacombe** Torbay
116 E3 **Babbington** Notts
112 E5 **Babbinswood** Shrops

69 K4 **Babbs Green** Herts
31 J5 **Babcary** Somset
59 M2 **Babel** Carmth
88 E5 **Babel Green** Suffk
128 E5 **Babell** Flints
12 F7 **Babeny** Devon
32 B1 **Babington** Somset
66 B6 **Bablock Hythe** Oxon
87 K5 **Babraham** Cambs
134 D3 **Babworth** Notts
125 H3 **Bachau** IOA
95 L7 **Bache** Shrops
94 F5 **Bacheldre** Powys
24 F5 **Bachelor's Bump** E Susx
115 H1 **Back o' th' Brook** Staffs
237 J3 **Back of Keppoch** Highld
88 E3 **Back Street** Suffk
275 d3 **Backaland** Ork
156 E5 **Backbarrow** Cumb
58 A5 **Backe** Carmth
269 J5 **Backfolds** Abers
129 J5 **Backford** Ches
129 J5 **Backford Cross** Ches
273 K7 **Backies** Highld
280 B5 **Backlass** Highld
44 F5 **Backwell** N Som
181 H4 **Backworth** N Tyne
98 F6 **Bacon's End** Solhll
122 C4 **Baconsthorpe** Norfk
62 D1 **Bacton** Herefs
123 G5 **Bacton** Norfk
90 C2 **Bacton** Suffk
90 B2 **Bacton Green** Suffk
140 C3 **Bacup** Lancs
260 C5 **Badachro** Highld
47 J3 **Badbury** Swindn
84 A3 **Badby** Nhants
276 B7 **Badcall** Highld
276 C5 **Badcall** Highld
261 G2 **Badcaul** Highld
114 E1 **Baddeley Edge** C Stke
114 E1 **Baddeley Green** C Stke
82 F1 **Baddesley Clinton** Warwks
99 H4 **Baddesley Ensor** Warwks
270 E3 **Baddidarrach** Highld
199 K2 **Baddinsgill** Border
256 C4 **Badenscoth** Abers
255 G7 **Badenyon** Abers
11 J5 **Badgall** Cnwll
103 J4 **Badgeney** Cambs
97 H3 **Badger** Shrops
2 D4 **Badger's Cross** Cnwll
52 B6 **Badgers Mount** Kent
64 C3 **Badgeworth** Gloucs
44 E8 **Badgworth** Somset
11 J5 **Badharlick** Cnwll
248 B6 **Badicaul** Highld
91 G2 **Badingham** Suffk
40 D4 **Badlesmere** Kent
187 G2 **Badlieu** Border
280 B6 **Badlipster** Highld
261 G1 **Badluachrach** Highld
263 K1 **Badninish** Highld
261 H2 **Badrallach** Highld
82 C6 **Badsey** Worcs
36 C1 **Badshot Lea** Surrey
142 D5 **Badsworth** Wakefd
89 K2 **Badwell Ash** Suffk
89 K2 **Badwell Green** Suffk
136 F5 **Bag Enderby** Lincs
32 C8 **Bagber** Dorset
161 G6 **Bagby** N York
64 E5 **Bagendon** Gloucs
96 F7 **Bagginswood** Shrops
165 G2 **Baggrow** Cumb
283 b13 **Bagh a Chaisteil** W Isls
283 b13 **Bagh a Tuath** W Isls
40 E4 **Bagham** Kent
128 F4 **Bagillt** Flints
99 K8 **Baginton** Warwks
57 K6 **Baglan** Neath
141 K1 **Bagley** Leeds
112 F6 **Bagley** Shrops
31 G2 **Bagley** Somset
35 K2 **Bagmore** Hants
114 E1 **Bagnall** Staffs
48 C5 **Bagnor** W Berk
96 D8 **Bagot** Shrops
49 M6 **Bagshot** Surrey
47 L6 **Bagshot** Wilts
45 K2 **Bagstone** S Glos
116 D1 **Bagthorpe** Notts
99 M2 **Bagworth** Leics
62 F2 **Bagwy Llydiart** Herefs
149 L7 **Baildon** Brad

149 L7 **Baildon Green** Brad
283 c9 **Baile a Mhanaich** W Isls
282 f4 **Baile Ailein** W Isls
226 B7 **Baile Mor** Ag & B
35 K5 **Bailey Green** Hants
178 C3 **Baileyhead** Cumb
141 J3 **Bailiff Bridge** Calder
209 H6 **Baillieston** C Glas
147 J4 **Bailrigg** Lancs
159 G4 **Bainbridge** N York
256 A5 **Bainshole** Abers
102 B2 **Bainton** C Pete
152 E5 **Bainton** E R Yk
66 E2 **Bainton** Oxon
222 F6 **Baintown** Fife
189 H3 **Bairnkine** Border
52 D3 **Baker Street** Thurr
69 L4 **Baker's End** Herts
132 D6 **Bakewell** Derbys
111 H4 **Bala** Gwynd
282 f4 **Balallan** W Isls
250 D5 **Balbeg** Highld
222 B1 **Balbeggie** P & K
250 E3 **Balblair** Highld
263 J6 **Balblair** Highld
142 E7 **Balby** Donc
175 K5 **Balcary** D & G
250 F3 **Balchraggan** Highld
276 B4 **Balchreick** Highld
37 M5 **Balcombe** W Susx
37 M4 **Balcombe Lane** W Susx
223 L5 **Balcomie Links** Fife
160 E7 **Baldersby** N York
160 E7 **Baldersby St James** N York
139 J1 **Balderstone** Lancs
140 D5 **Balderstone** Rochdl
117 L1 **Balderton** Notts
4 C6 **Baldhu** Cnwll
223 G5 **Baldinnie** Fife
221 J4 **Baldinnies** P & K
86 E8 **Baldock** Herts
234 C8 **Baldovie** C Dund
154 f5 **Baldrine** IOM
24 E4 **Baldslow** E Susx
154 e6 **Baldwin** IOM
114 B3 **Baldwin's Gate** Staffs
38 B5 **Baldwin's Hill** Surrey
177 K8 **Baldwinholme** Cumb
121 M4 **Bale** Norfk
222 D1 **Baledgarno** P & K
224 C7 **Balemartine** Ag & B
211 G5 **Balerno** C Edin
222 D6 **Balfarg** Fife
234 E2 **Balfield** Angus
275 d4 **Balfour** Ork
208 F1 **Balfron** Stirlg
256 B4 **Balgaveny** Abers
234 E5 **Balgavies** Angus
221 J8 **Balgonar** Fife
172 E6 **Balgowan** D & G
241 H4 **Balgowan** Highld
258 F3 **Balgown** Highld
172 B3 **Balgracie** D & G
234 B7 **Balgray** Angus
186 C2 **Balgray** S Lans
51 H4 **Balham** Gt Lon
233 L6 **Balhary** P & K
233 H8 **Balholmie** P & K
278 E3 **Baligill** Highld
233 L4 **Balintore** Angus
264 D5 **Balintore** Highld
263 K5 **Balintraid** Highld
283 c9 **Balivanich** W Isls
161 G6 **Balk** N York
233 M6 **Balkeerie** Angus
143 K2 **Balkholme** E R Yk
114 D1 **Ball Green** C Stke
131 K8 **Ball Haye Green** Staffs
48 B6 **Ball Hill** Hants
64 B7 **Ball's Green** Gloucs
154 c7 **Ballabeg** IOM
229 H4 **Ballachulish** Highld
154 b7 **Ballafesson** IOM
154 b7 **Ballakilpheric** IOM
154 c7 **Ballamodha** IOM
207 G6 **Ballanlay** Ag & B
182 D6 **Ballantrae** S Ayrs
72 C8 **Ballards Gore** Essex
99 H5 **Ballards Green** Warwks
154 c7 **Ballasalla** IOM
243 L4 **Ballater** Abers
154 d3 **Ballaugh** IOM
263 K5 **Ballchraggan** Highld
212 B3 **Ballencrieff** E Loth
224 B6 **Ballevullin** Ag & B

115 K1 **Ballidon** Derbys
194 D3 **Balliekine** N Ayrs
217 H7 **Balliemore** Ag & B
183 G5 **Balligmorrie** S Ayrs
206 E2 **Ballimore** Ag & B
219 H4 **Ballimore** Stirlg
254 D4 **Ballindalloch** Moray
222 D2 **Ballindean** P & K
89 H7 **Ballingdon** Essex
67 M6 **Ballinger Common** Bucks
63 H1 **Ballingham** Herefs
222 B7 **Ballingry** Fife
232 E5 **Ballinluig** P & K
234 B5 **Ballinshoe** Angus
233 G4 **Ballintuim** P & K
252 D2 **Balloch** Highld
209 K4 **Balloch** N Lans
220 E3 **Balloch** P & K
183 J4 **Balloch** S Ayrs
208 C3 **Balloch** W Duns
244 D4 **Ballogie** Abers
36 E5 **Balls Cross** W Susx
38 D6 **Balls Green** E Susx
226 E4 **Ballygown** Ag & B
204 F3 **Ballygrant** Ag & B
224 F4 **Ballyhaugh** Ag & B
208 A2 **Ballymenoch** Ag & B
248 C6 **Balmacara** Highld
185 G7 **Balmaclellan** D & G
175 H6 **Balmae** D & G
208 C1 **Balmaha** Stirlg
222 E5 **Balmalcolm** Fife
175 G5 **Balmangan** D & G
257 H8 **Balmedie** Abers
113 G4 **Balmer Heath** Shrops
222 F2 **Balmerino** Fife
18 D3 **Balmerlawn** Hants
194 E5 **Balmichael** N Ayrs
209 G4 **Balmore** E Duns
264 D4 **Balmuchy** Highld
234 E5 **Balmuir** Angus
211 H2 **Balmule** Fife
223 G3 **Balmullo** Fife
273 J5 **Balnacoil Lodge** Highld
248 F3 **Balnacra** Highld
243 J5 **Balnacroft** Abers
251 J4 **Balnafoich** Highld
232 D5 **Balnaguard** P & K
226 E5 **Balnahard** Ag & B
214 E4 **Balnahard** Ag & B
250 D5 **Balnain** Highld
276 F3 **Balnakeil** Highld
264 B6 **Balnapaling** Highld
142 F4 **Balne** N York
232 F8 **Balquharn** P & K
219 H3 **Balquhidder** Stirlg
99 G8 **Balsall Common** Solhll
98 D6 **Balsall Heath** Birm
99 G8 **Balsall Street** Solhll
83 J6 **Balscote** Oxon
88 B5 **Balsham** Cambs
281 f1 **Baltasound** Shet
114 B2 **Balterley** Staffs
114 B2 **Balterley Green** Staffs
114 A2 **Balterley Heath** Staffs
174 C3 **Baltersan** D & G
31 J4 **Baltonsborough** Somset
233 G3 **Balvarran** P & K
216 B4 **Balvicar** Ag & B
248 D8 **Balvraid** Highld
252 F5 **Balvraid** Highld
2 F5 **Balwest** Cnwll
139 H3 **Bamber Bridge** Lancs
70 E3 **Bamber's Green** Essex
203 K6 **Bamburgh** Nthumb
233 K5 **Bamff** P & K
132 D3 **Bamford** Derbys
140 C5 **Bamford** Rochdl
166 C7 **Bampton** Cumb
29 G6 **Bampton** Devon
65 L6 **Bampton** Oxon
166 C7 **Bampton Grange** Cumb
239 J8 **Banavie** Highld
83 K7 **Banbury** Oxon
76 D7 **Banc-y-ffordd** Carmth
58 E6 **Bancffosfelen** Carmth
244 F4 **Banchory** Abers
245 K3 **Banchory-Devenick** Abers
58 D6 **Bancycapel** Carmth
58 B5 **Bancyfelin** Carmth
222 C1 **Bandirran** P & K
156 D5 **Bandrake Head** Cumb
268 C3 **Banff** Abers
125 K5 **Bangor** Gwynd
138 D6 **Bangor's Green** Lancs

112 F2 **Bangor-is-y-coed** Wrexhm
11 H3 **Bangors** Cnwll
89 J1 **Bangrove** Suffk
106 B6 **Banham** Norfk
18 D2 **Bank** Hants
156 D3 **Bank Ground** Cumb
148 F5 **Bank Newton** N York
80 E3 **Bank Street** Worcs
141 H3 **Bank Top** Calder
139 G6 **Bank Top** Lancs
176 D5 **Bankend** D & G
233 G8 **Bankfoot** P & K
197 H8 **Bankglen** E Ayrs
245 K2 **Bankhead** C Aber
199 G4 **Bankhead** S Lans
209 K3 **Banknock** Falk
178 D6 **Banks** Cumb
138 E4 **Banks** Lancs
82 A2 **Banks Green** Worcs
177 G3 **Bankshill** D & G
122 E5 **Banningham** Norfk
71 G3 **Bannister Green** Essex
209 L1 **Bannockburn** Stirlg
51 H7 **Banstead** Surrey
7 K6 **Bantham** Devon
209 K3 **Banton** N Lans
44 E7 **Banwell** N Som
40 B3 **Bapchild** Kent
33 G3 **Bapton** Wilts
87 H3 **Bar Hill** Cambs
282 g2 **Barabhas** W Isls
196 C4 **Barassie** S Ayrs
263 K5 **Barbaraville** Highld
132 B3 **Barber Booth** Derbys
156 F6 **Barber Green** Cumb
196 E7 **Barbieston** S Ayrs
157 K6 **Barbon** Cumb
130 B8 **Barbridge** Ches
28 C2 **Barbrook** Devon
84 A1 **Barby** Nhants
228 F7 **Barcaldine** Ag & B
83 G7 **Barcheston** Warwks
178 B6 **Barclose** Cumb
22 F4 **Barcombe** E Susx
23 G4 **Barcombe Cross** E Susx
149 J8 **Barcroft** Brad
159 L4 **Barden** N York
38 F4 **Barden Park** Kent
70 F1 **Bardfield End Green** Essex
71 G2 **Bardfield Saling** Essex
136 B6 **Bardney** Lincs
99 M1 **Bardon** Leics
179 H6 **Bardon Mill** Nthumb
209 G4 **Bardowie** E Duns
39 G7 **Bardown** E Susx
208 B4 **Bardrainney** Inver
156 D7 **Bardsea** Cumb
150 E7 **Bardsey** Leeds
140 D7 **Bardsley** Oldham
105 J8 **Bardwell** Suffk
147 J3 **Bare** Lancs
3 K5 **Bareppa** Cnwll
79 M4 **Barewood** Herefs
173 J2 **Barfad** D & G
106 C2 **Barford** Norfk
83 G3 **Barford** Warwks
83 K8 **Barford St John** Oxon
33 J4 **Barford St Martin** Wilts
83 K8 **Barford St Michael** Oxon
41 H5 **Barfrestone** Kent
116 B2 **Bargate** Derbys
209 J6 **Bargeddie** N Lans
61 J7 **Bargoed** Caerph
183 J7 **Bargrennan** D & G
102 C8 **Barham** Cambs
41 G5 **Barham** Kent
90 D5 **Barham** Suffk
102 B1 **Barholm** Lincs
100 E2 **Barkby** Leics
100 E2 **Barkby Thorpe** Leics
113 H6 **Barkers Green** Shrops
117 K4 **Barkestone-le-Vale** Leics
49 J5 **Barkham** Wokham
51 L2 **Barking** Gt Lon
90 C4 **Barking** Suffk
90 C5 **Barking Tye** Suffk
51 L1 **Barkingside** Gt Lon
141 G4 **Barkisland** Calder
4 B5 **Barkla Shop** Cnwll
118 B3 **Barkston** Lincs
151 G8 **Barkston Ash** N York
87 H8 **Barkway** Herts
209 H6 **Barlanark** C Glas
114 D4 **Barlaston** Staffs
21 G4 **Barlavington** W Susx

133 J4 **Barlborough** Derbys
143 G1 **Barlby** N York
99 L2 **Barlestone** Leics
87 H7 **Barley** Herts
148 E7 **Barley** Lancs
142 B8 **Barley Hole** Rothm
70 B2 **Barleycroft End** Herts
101 J2 **Barleythorpe** Rutlnd
53 K1 **Barling** Essex
135 M5 **Barlings** Lincs
175 K3 **Barlochan** D & G
133 G5 **Barlow** Derbys
180 E6 **Barlow** Gatesd
143 G2 **Barlow** N York
152 B6 **Barmby Moor** E R Yk
143 H2 **Barmby on the Marsh** E R Yk
121 H5 **Barmer** Norfk
39 J2 **Barming Heath** Kent
194 C2 **Barmollack** Ag & B
109 L8 **Barmouth** Gwynd
169 J7 **Barmpton** Darltn
153 J4 **Barmston** E R Yk
107 K7 **Barnaby Green** Suffk
216 F8 **Barnacarry** Ag & B
102 B2 **Barnack** C Pete
99 K6 **Barnacle** Warwks
168 D7 **Barnard Castle** Dur
66 B5 **Barnard Gate** Oxon
88 E5 **Barnardiston** Suffk
175 L3 **Barnbarroch** D & G
142 D7 **Barnburgh** Donc
107 K5 **Barnby** Suffk
142 F6 **Barnby Dun** Donc
117 M1 **Barnby in the Willows** Notts
134 D3 **Barnby Moor** Notts
172 D7 **Barncorkrie** D & G
52 B4 **Barnehurst** Gt Lon
51 G4 **Barnes** Gt Lon
39 G4 **Barnes Street** Kent
69 H7 **Barnet** Gt Lon
69 G8 **Barnet Gate** Gt Lon
144 D6 **Barnetby le Wold** N Linc
121 M5 **Barney** Norfk
105 H7 **Barnham** Suffk
20 F6 **Barnham** W Susx
106 B2 **Barnham Broom** Norfk
235 G4 **Barnhead** Angus
223 H1 **Barnhill** C Dund
113 H1 **Barnhill** Ches
266 C5 **Barnhill** Moray
182 B8 **Barnhills** D & G
168 D8 **Barningham** Dur
105 K8 **Barningham** Suffk
145 G7 **Barnoldby le Beck** NE Lin
148 F6 **Barnoldswick** Lancs
37 H5 **Barns Green** W Susx
142 D5 **Barnsdale Bar** Donc
142 A6 **Barnsley** Barns
65 G6 **Barnsley** Gloucs
97 G5 **Barnsley** Shrops
41 J4 **Barnsole** Kent
27 K4 **Barnstaple** Devon
70 F3 **Barnston** Essex
129 G3 **Barnston** Wirral
117 J4 **Barnstone** Notts
98 C8 **Barnt Green** Worcs
211 G4 **Barnton** C Edin
130 C5 **Barnton** Ches
102 A6 **Barnwell All Saints** Nhants
102 A6 **Barnwell St Andrew** Nhants
64 B3 **Barnwood** Gloucs
80 B4 **Baron's Cross** Herefs
13 G2 **Barons Wood** Devon
166 C2 **Baronwood** Cumb
183 H4 **Barr** S Ayrs
173 J5 **Barrachan** D & G
224 B6 **Barrapoll** Ag & B
167 J8 **Barras** Cumb
179 L4 **Barrasford** Nthumb
130 B7 **Barrets Green** Ches
208 E7 **Barrhead** E Rens
183 G6 **Barrhill** S Ayrs
87 H5 **Barrington** Cambs
30 F7 **Barrington** Somset
3 G3 **Barripper** Cnwll
196 D1 **Barrmill** N Ayrs
216 C3 **Barrnacarry Bay** Ag & B
280 C2 **Barrock** Highld
64 C2 **Barrow** Gloucs
148 C8 **Barrow** Lancs
118 A8 **Barrow** Rutlnd
96 E3 **Barrow** Shrops
32 B4 **Barrow** Somset
88 F3 **Barrow** Suffk
139 K5 **Barrow Bridge** Bolton

190 B4 **Barrow Burn** Nthumb
45 G5 **Barrow Gurney** N Som
144 D3 **Barrow Haven** N Linc
133 H4 **Barrow Hill** Derbys
146 D2 **Barrow Island** Cumb
138 F7 **Barrow Nook** Lancs
32 D5 **Barrow Street** Wilts
116 F8 **Barrow upon Soar** Leics
116 B6 **Barrow upon Trent** Derbys
45 J7 **Barrow Vale** BaNES
130 D8 **Barrow's Green** Ches
129 M2 **Barrow's Green** Halton
146 D2 **Barrow-in-Furness** Cumb
144 D4 **Barrow-upon-Humber** N Linc
104 B3 **Barroway Drove** Norfk
118 A4 **Barrowby** Lincs
101 L3 **Barrowden** Rutlnd
148 E7 **Barrowford** Lancs
234 E8 **Barry** Angus
43 H7 **Barry** V Glam
43 H8 **Barry Island** V Glam
100 F1 **Barsby** Leics
107 H5 **Barsham** Suffk
99 G7 **Barston** Solhll
80 D7 **Bartestree** Herefs
256 E5 **Barthol Chapel** Abers
71 H3 **Bartholomew Green** Essex
114 B1 **Barthomley** Ches
18 D1 **Bartley** Hants
98 C7 **Bartley Green** Birm
88 B6 **Bartlow** Cambs
87 H4 **Barton** Cambs
113 G1 **Barton** Ches
166 C5 **Barton** Cumb
65 G2 **Barton** Gloucs
79 K4 **Barton** Herefs
138 D6 **Barton** Lancs
147 K8 **Barton** Lancs
160 C1 **Barton** N York
66 E5 **Barton** Oxon
8 D2 **Barton** Torbay
82 D5 **Barton** Warwks
104 E2 **Barton Bendish** Norfk
64 B7 **Barton End** Gloucs
115 K7 **Barton Green** Staffs
66 F1 **Barton Hartshorn** Bucks
151 L3 **Barton Hill** N York
116 E5 **Barton in Fabis** Notts
99 L2 **Barton in the Beans** Leics
104 E8 **Barton Mills** Suffk
101 J7 **Barton Seagrave** Nhants
31 J4 **Barton St David** Somset
34 F3 **Barton Stacey** Hants
28 B3 **Barton Town** Devon
123 G7 **Barton Turf** Norfk
140 A8 **Barton upon Irwell** Salfd
144 C3 **Barton Waterside** N Linc
68 D1 **Barton-le-Clay** Beds
162 C7 **Barton-le-Street** N York
151 M3 **Barton-le-Willows** N York
18 C5 **Barton-on-Sea** Hants
83 G8 **Barton-on-the-Heath** Warwk
115 K7 **Barton-under-Needwood** Staffs
144 C3 **Barton-upon-Humber** N Linc
141 M6 **Barugh** Barns
141 M6 **Barugh Green** Barns
282 g2 **Barvas** W Isls
103 L8 **Barway** Cambs
99 L4 **Barwell** Leics
12 E1 **Barwick** Devon
69 K3 **Barwick** Herts
31 J8 **Barwick** Somset
150 F8 **Barwick in Elmet** Leeds
112 F7 **Baschurch** Shrops
83 J3 **Bascote** Warwks
83 J3 **Bascote Heath** Warwks
89 L3 **Base Green** Suffk
114 F1 **Basford Green** Staffs
148 B7 **Bashall Eaves** Lancs
148 C7 **Bashall Town** Lancs
18 C4 **Bashley** Hants
52 F1 **Basildon** Essex
48 F8 **Basingstoke** Hants
132 E5 **Baslow** Derbys
30 E2 **Bason Bridge** Somset
44 B2 **Bassaleg** Newpt
201 K4 **Bassendean** Border
165 H4 **Bassenthwaite** Cumb
34 F7 **Bassett** C Sotn
87 G6 **Bassingbourn** Cambs
117 G4 **Bassingfield** Notts
135 H7 **Bassingham** Lincs
118 C6 **Bassingthorpe** Lincs
69 J2 **Bassus Green** Herts

38 F2 **Basted** Kent	203 L7 **Beadnell** Nthumb	39 M4 **Bedlam Lane** Kent	38 F6 **Bells Yew Green** E Susx
102 C1 **Baston** Lincs	27 K7 **Beaford** Devon	181 G3 **Bedlington** Nthumb	209 J7 **Bellshill** N Lans
123 J8 **Bastwick** Norfk	142 E3 **Beal** N York	61 H6 **Bedlinog** Myr Td	203 J7 **Bellshill** Nthumb
44 C7 **Batch** Somset	203 H4 **Beal** Nthumb	45 H5 **Bedminster** Bristl	209 L7 **Bellside** N Lans
68 D8 **Batchworth** Herts	6 D2 **Bealbury** Cnwll	45 H5 **Bedminster Down** Bristl	210 D6 **Bellsquarry** W Loth
68 D8 **Batchworth Heath** Herts	11 L7 **Bealsmill** Cnwll	68 E6 **Bedmond** Herts	45 J6 **Belluton** BaNES
16 B2 **Batcombe** Dorset	115 L6 **Beam Hill** Staffs	114 F7 **Bednall** Staffs	102 A2 **Belmesthorpe** Rutlnd
31 M3 **Batcombe** Somset	115 H4 **Beamhurst** Staffs	189 G3 **Bedrule** Border	139 K4 **Belmont** Bl w D
130 D4 **Bate Heath** Ches	15 L2 **Beaminster** Dorset	95 J8 **Bedstone** Shrops	51 H6 **Belmont** Gt Lon
68 F4 **Batford** Herts	180 F8 **Beamish** Dur	43 J4 **Bedwas** Caerph	196 C7 **Belmont** S Ayrs
45 L6 **Bath** BaNES	149 K5 **Beamsley** N York	61 J7 **Bedwellty** Caerph	281 f2 **Belmont** Shet
73 K1 **Bath Side** Essex	52 C4 **Bean** Kent	99 K6 **Bedworth** Warwks	255 H8 **Belnacraig** Abers
45 M5 **Bathampton** BaNES	46 C5 **Beanacre** Wilts	99 K6 **Bedworth Woodlands** Warwks	4 F3 **Belowda** Cnwll
29 K6 **Bathealton** Somset	190 F3 **Beanley** Nthumb	100 E2 **Beeby** Leics	116 B2 **Belper** Derbys
45 M5 **Batheaston** BaNES	12 C5 **Beardon** Devon	35 L3 **Beech** Hants	116 B2 **Belper Lane End** Derbys
46 A5 **Bathford** BaNES	139 K2 **Beardwood** Bl w D	114 D4 **Beech** Staffs	133 L4 **Belph** Derbys
210 C5 **Bathgate** W Loth	14 A2 **Beare** Devon	49 G6 **Beech Hill** W Berk	180 D3 **Belsay** Nthumb
134 F7 **Bathley** Notts	37 J2 **Beare Green** Surrey	47 G7 **Beechingstoke** Wilts	201 J8 **Belses** Border
11 K7 **Bathpool** Cnwll	82 E3 **Bearley** Warwks	48 C3 **Beedon** W Berk	7 L3 **Belsford** Devon
30 C5 **Bathpool** Somset	82 E3 **Bearley Cross** Warwks	48 C3 **Beedon Hill** W Berk	68 D7 **Belsize** Herts
210 B5 **Bathville** W Loth	169 G2 **Bearpark** Dur	153 H5 **Beeford** E R Yk	90 D7 **Belstead** Suffk
45 H8 **Bathway** Somset	208 F4 **Bearsden** E Duns	132 E6 **Beeley** Derbys	12 E4 **Belstone** Devon
141 K3 **Batley** Kirk	39 K2 **Bearsted** Kent	145 G7 **Beelsby** NE Lin	139 L3 **Belthorn** Lancs
82 E8 **Batsford** Gloucs	114 A4 **Bearstone** Shrops	48 E5 **Beenham** W Berk	41 G2 **Beltinge** Kent
7 L7 **Batson** Devon	98 C6 **Bearwood** Birm	49 K4 **Beenham's Heath** W & M	179 H6 **Beltingham** Nthumb
36 B3 **Batt's Corner** Surrey	17 L3 **Bearwood** Poole	11 G4 **Beeny** Cnwll	143 K6 **Beltoft** N Linc
161 K1 **Battersby** N York	187 G6 **Beattock** D & G	14 F5 **Beer** Devon	116 D7 **Belton** Leics
51 H4 **Battersea** Gt Lon	70 E5 **Beauchamp Roding** Essex	30 F4 **Beer** Somset	118 B3 **Belton** Lincs
7 H5 **Battisborough Cross** Devon	132 F3 **Beauchief** Sheff	31 K8 **Beer Hackett** Dorset	143 K6 **Belton** N Linc
90 C4 **Battisford** Suffk	82 E2 **Beaudesert** Warwks	30 D6 **Beercrocombe** Somset	107 K3 **Belton** Norfk
89 L4 **Battisford Tye** Suffk	61 J5 **Beaufort** Blae G	8 B6 **Beesands** Devon	101 H3 **Belton** Rutlnd
24 D4 **Battle** E Susx	18 F3 **Beaulieu** Hants	137 J4 **Beesby** Lincs	39 H4 **Beltring** Kent
60 F1 **Battle** Powys	18 E2 **Beaulieu Road Station** Hants	8 B6 **Beeson** Devon	52 B3 **Belvedere** Gt Lon
30 E1 **Battleborough** Somset	250 F2 **Beauly** Highld	86 D5 **Beeston** Beds	117 L5 **Belvoir** Leics
64 D3 **Battledown** Gloucs	126 B4 **Beaumaris** IOA	129 M7 **Beeston** Ches	19 L6 **Bembridge** IOW
234 C4 **Battledykes** Angus	177 K7 **Beaumont** Cumb	141 L2 **Beeston** Leeds	114 D1 **Bemersley Green** C Stke
113 H8 **Battlefield** Shrops	73 H2 **Beaumont** Essex	121 K8 **Beeston** Norfk	33 K5 **Bemerton** Wilts
71 J8 **Battlesbridge** Essex	9 c3 **Beaumont** Jersey	116 E4 **Beeston** Notts	153 K2 **Bempton** E R Yk
68 B2 **Battlesden** Beds	169 J7 **Beaumont Hill** Darltn	122 D3 **Beeston Regis** Norfk	149 L6 **Ben Rhydding** Brad
29 G5 **Battleton** Somset	82 F1 **Beausale** Warwks	176 A5 **Beeswing** D & G	107 K6 **Benacre** Suffk
89 H2 **Battlies Green** Suffk	35 J5 **Beauworth** Hants	157 H6 **Beetham** Cumb	185 H4 **Benbuie** D & G
18 E4 **Battramsley Cross** Hants	40 C7 **Beaver** Kent	30 D8 **Beetham** Somset	228 D7 **Benderloch** Ag & B
141 J4 **Battyeford** Kirk	40 C7 **Beaver Green** Kent	121 L7 **Beetley** Norfk	39 K6 **Benenden** Kent
81 K6 **Baughton** Worcs	12 B3 **Beaworthy** Devon	43 K5 **Began** Cardif	180 D8 **Benfieldside** Dur
48 E7 **Baughurst** Hants	71 H1 **Beazley End** Essex	66 C4 **Begbroke** Oxon	122 F6 **Bengates** Norfk
244 D5 **Baulds** Abers	129 H3 **Bebington** Wirral	103 J2 **Begdale** Cambs	82 B6 **Bengeworth** Worcs
47 L1 **Baulking** Oxon	181 G3 **Bebside** Nthumb	55 J5 **Begelly** Pembks	91 J3 **Benhall Green** Suffk
136 D5 **Baumber** Lincs	107 J5 **Beccles** Suffk	79 J2 **Beggar's Bush** Powys	91 H3 **Benhall Street** Suffk
64 E6 **Baunton** Gloucs	138 F3 **Becconsall** Lancs	141 L4 **Beggarington Hill** Leeds	235 K2 **Benholm** Abers
96 F7 **Baveney Wood** Shrops	157 K3 **Beck Foot** Cumb	94 F7 **Beguildy** Powys	151 H4 **Beningbrough** N York
33 H4 **Baverstock** Wilts	162 E2 **Beck Hole** N York	107 H2 **Beighton** Norfk	69 J2 **Benington** Herts
106 D2 **Bawburgh** Norfk	104 D7 **Beck Row** Suffk	133 J3 **Beighton** Sheff	119 L2 **Benington** Lincs
122 A7 **Bawdeswell** Norfk	156 B6 **Beck Side** Cumb	115 M1 **Beighton Hill** Derbys	119 L2 **Benington Sea End** Lincs
30 E3 **Bawdrip** Somset	156 E6 **Beck Side** Cumb	222 B4 **Bein Inn** P & K	125 J3 **Benllech** IOA
91 H7 **Bawdsey** Suffk	97 H3 **Beckbury** Shrops	208 B8 **Beith** N Ayrs	207 J2 **Benmore** Ag & B
120 E7 **Bawsey** Norfk	51 K5 **Beckenham** Gt Lon	41 G4 **Bekesbourne** Kent	11 K4 **Bennacott** Cnwll
134 C1 **Bawtry** Donc	136 B3 **Beckering** Lincs	41 G4 **Bekesbourne Hill** Kent	193 K4 **Bennan** N Ayrs
140 A2 **Baxenden** Lancs	155 J1 **Beckermet** Cumb	122 F7 **Belaugh** Norfk	166 B6 **Bennet Head** Cumb
88 E4 **Baxter's Green** Suffk	104 F4 **Beckett End** Norfk	97 L7 **Belbroughton** Worcs	143 L2 **Bennetland** E R Yk
99 H4 **Baxterley** Warwks	164 E1 **Beckfoot** Cumb	16 F1 **Belchalwell** Dorset	67 J7 **Bennett End** Bucks
258 D6 **Bay** Highld	155 L3 **Beckfoot** Cumb	16 F1 **Belchalwell Street** Dorset	136 D3 **Benniworth** Lincs
147 K5 **Bay Horse** Lancs	156 B5 **Beckfoot** Cumb	88 F6 **Belchamp Otten** Essex	39 H4 **Benover** Kent
282 h3 **Bayble** W Isls	82 A8 **Beckford** Worcs	88 F6 **Belchamp St Paul** Essex	66 F8 **Benson** Oxon
35 H6 **Baybridge** Hants	47 G5 **Beckhampton** Wilts	89 G7 **Belchamp Walter** Essex	70 D2 **Bentfield Green** Essex
168 B1 **Baybridge** Nthumb	118 A1 **Beckingham** Lincs	136 E4 **Belchford** Lincs	96 F3 **Benthall** Shrops
146 F2 **Baycliff** Cumb	134 F2 **Beckingham** Notts	203 H6 **Belford** Nthumb	64 C4 **Bentham** Gloucs
47 L3 **Baydon** Wilts	46 A8 **Beckington** Somset	100 D2 **Belgrave** C Leic	245 H3 **Benthoul** C Aber
69 J5 **Bayford** Herts	95 J7 **Beckjay** Shrops	212 E3 **Belhaven** E Loth	95 H3 **Bentlawnt** Shrops
32 B5 **Bayford** Somset	24 F3 **Beckley** E Susx	257 H8 **Belhelvie** Abers	142 E6 **Bentley** Donc
283 b8 **Bayhead** W Isls	18 C4 **Beckley** Hants	255 J6 **Belhinnie** Abers	152 F8 **Bentley** E R Yk
38 D3 **Bayley's Hill** Kent	66 E5 **Beckley** Oxon	69 H6 **Bell Bar** Herts	36 A2 **Bentley** Hants
90 C5 **Baylham** Suffk	149 J6 **Becks** Brad	148 F4 **Bell Busk** N York	90 D7 **Bentley** Suffk
66 E1 **Baynard's Green** Oxon	157 K5 **Beckside** Cumb	97 L7 **Bell End** Worcs	99 H4 **Bentley** Warwks
61 K1 **Baysdale Abbey** N York	51 L3 **Beckton** Gt Lon	97 L7 **Bell Heath** Worcs	69 H7 **Bentley Heath** Herts
63 H2 **Baysham** Herefs	150 C5 **Beckwithshaw** N York	35 M6 **Bell Hill** Hants	98 F8 **Bentley Heath** Solhll
96 B2 **Bayston Hill** Shrops	52 A2 **Becontree** Gt Lon	113 H2 **Bell o' th' Hill** Ches	28 B4 **Benton** Devon
88 E6 **Baythorne End** Essex	9 d2 **Becquet Vincent** Jersey	243 K1 **Bellabeg** Abers	188 B8 **Bentpath** D & G
96 F8 **Bayton** Worcs	160 C5 **Bedale** N York	79 M7 **Bellamore** Herefs	28 C4 **Bentwichen** Devon
81 G1 **Bayton Common** Worcs	168 E4 **Bedburn** Dur	216 B8 **Bellanoch** Ag & B	35 K3 **Bentworth** Hants
66 D6 **Bayworth** Oxon	32 E7 **Bedchester** Dorset	143 K2 **Bellasize** E R Yk	222 E1 **Benvie** Angus
45 L5 **Beach** BaNES	43 G4 **Beddau** Rhondd	233 K3 **Bellaty** Angus	15 M2 **Benville** Dorset
84 E7 **Beachampton** Bucks	109 L2 **Beddgelert** Gwynd	177 L7 **Belle Vue** Cumb	103 G5 **Benwick** Cambs
104 E2 **Beachamwell** Norfk	23 G5 **Beddingham** E Susx	142 A4 **Belle Vue** Wakefd	82 C1 **Beoley** Worcs
41 G7 **Beachborough** Kent	51 J6 **Beddington** Gt Lon	137 G4 **Belleau** Lincs	237 K2 **Beoraidbeg** Highld
45 H1 **Beachley** Gloucs	51 H5 **Beddington Corner** Gt Lon	159 K4 **Bellerby** N York	20 D3 **Bepton** W Susx
14 E2 **Beacon** Devon	90 F2 **Bedfield** Suffk	12 F7 **Bellever** Devon	70 C1 **Berden** Essex
72 D2 **Beacon End** Essex	90 F2 **Bedfield Little Green** Suffk	198 D6 **Bellfield** S Lans	6 E2 **Bere Alston** Devon
38 D7 **Beacon Hill** E Susx	85 L5 **Bedford** Beds	186 E2 **Bellfield** S Lans	6 E2 **Bere Ferrers** Devon
39 K6 **Beacon Hill** Kent	39 H6 **Bedgebury Cross** Kent	68 B6 **Bellingdon** Bucks	17 G3 **Bere Regis** Dorset
17 L1 **Beacon Hill** Notts	36 F6 **Bedham** W Susx	179 J2 **Bellingham** Nthumb	74 C6 **Berea** Pembks
36 C3 **Beacon Hill** Surrey	20 A5 **Bedhampton** Hants	192 D1 **Belloch** Ag & B	3 G6 **Berepper** Cnwll
67 J8 **Beacon's Bottom** Bucks	90 E2 **Bedingfield** Suffk	192 D2 **Bellochantuy** Ag & B	106 F3 **Bergh Apton** Norfk
50 B1 **Beaconsfield** Bucks	90 E2 **Bedingfield Green** Suffk	33 J8 **Bellows Cross** Dorset	31 G4 **Berhill** Somset
61 L5 **Beadlam** N York	90 E2 **Bedingfield Street** Suffk	90 D5 **Bells Cross** Suffk	66 E7 **Berinsfield** Oxon
86 C7 **Beadlow** Beds	150 C3 **Bedlam** N York		63 K7 **Berkeley** Gloucs

63 K7 Berkeley Heath Gloucs
63 L7 Berkeley Road Gloucs
68 C5 Berkhamsted Herts
32 D1 Berkley Somset
99 H7 Berkswell Solhll
51 J3 Bermondsey Gt Lon
248 C7 Bernera Highld
207 J1 Bernice Ag & B
258 F6 Bernisdale Highld
66 F8 Berrick Prior Oxon
66 F8 Berrick Salome Oxon
274 F3 Berriedale Highld
165 L5 Berrier Cumb
94 E3 Berriew Powys
202 F4 Berrington Nthumb
96 C2 Berrington Shrops
80 D2 Berrington Worcs
80 D2 Berrington Green Worcs
44 C8 Berrow Somset
81 H8 Berrow Worcs
81 H3 Berrow Green Worcs
141 H5 Berry Brow Kirk
27 H7 Berry Cross Devon
27 K2 Berry Down Cross Devon
63 H4 Berry Hill Gloucs
75 H4 Berry Hill Pembks
8 B3 Berry Pomeroy Devon
51 L7 Berry's Green Gt Lon
267 K5 Berryhillock Moray
267 K4 Berryhillock Moray
27 K2 Berrynarbor Devon
112 D2 Bersham Wrexhm
128 D4 Berthengam Flints
23 H6 Berwick E Susx
47 G4 Berwick Bassett Wilts
180 E4 Berwick Hill Nthumb
33 J3 Berwick St James Wilts
32 F6 Berwick St John Wilts
32 F4 Berwick St Leonard Wilts
202 F3 Berwick-upon-Tweed Nthumb
117 L6 Bescaby Leics
138 E5 Bescar Lancs
113 J6 Besford Shrops
81 L6 Besford Worcs
140 E6 Besom Hill Oldham
142 F7 Bessacarr Donc
66 C6 Bessels Leigh Oxon
140 B6 Besses o' th' Barn Bury
153 J3 Bessingby E R Yk
122 D4 Bessingham Norfk
38 F7 Bestbeech Hill E Susx
106 B4 Besthorpe Norfk
135 G6 Besthorpe Notts
116 F2 Bestwood Village Notts
152 F6 Beswick E R Yk
95 K4 Betchcott Shrops
37 K1 Betchworth Surrey
77 G3 Bethania Cerdgn
110 D3 Bethania Gwynd
125 J6 Bethel Gwynd
111 J4 Bethel Gwynd
125 G5 Bethel IOA
111 L7 Bethel Powys
40 B7 Bethersden Kent
126 C6 Bethesda Gwynd
55 J3 Bethesda Pembks
59 J4 Bethlehem Carmth
51 K2 Bethnal Green Gt Lon
114 B2 Betley Staffs
52 D4 Betsham Kent
41 J5 Betteshanger Kent
15 J3 Bettiscombe Dorset
113 G4 Bettisfield Wrexhm
113 M4 Betton Shrops
96 C2 Betton Strange Shrops
44 C1 Bettws Newpt
77 H5 Bettws Bledrws Cerdgn
94 D4 Bettws Cedewain Powys
76 B5 Bettws Evan Cerdgn
62 D6 Bettws-Newydd Mons
278 B4 Bettyhill Highld
42 D4 Betws Brdgnd
59 H6 Betws Carmth
125 K8 Betws Garmon Gwynd
111 K2 Betws Gwerfil Goch Denbgs
126 F8 Betws-y-coed Conwy
127 H5 Betws-yn-Rhos Conwy
76 B6 Beulah Cerdgn
78 C5 Beulah Powys
22 E6 Bevendean Br & H
134 D5 Bevercotes Notts
153 G7 Beverley E R Yk
64 B8 Beverstone Gloucs
63 K7 Bevington Gloucs

165 H4 Bewaldeth Cumb
178 D4 Bewcastle Cumb
97 H8 Bewdley Worcs
149 L3 Bewerley N York
153 J6 Bewholme E R Yk
39 H6 Bewlbridge Kent
24 D5 Bexhill E Susx
52 B4 Bexley Gt Lon
52 A4 Bexleyheath Gt Lon
36 D6 Bexleyhill W Susx
53 J7 Bexon Kent
104 C3 Bexwell Norfk
89 J3 Beyton Suffk
89 J3 Beyton Green Suffk
282 e3 Bhaltos W Isls
283 b13 Bhatarsaigh W Isls
45 K1 Bibstone S Glos
65 G5 Bibury Gloucs
66 E3 Bicester Oxon
99 G7 Bickenhill Solhll
119 H4 Bicker Lincs
119 H4 Bicker Bar Lincs
119 H4 Bicker Gauntlet Lincs
139 J7 Bickershaw Wigan
138 F7 Bickerstaffe Lancs
113 H1 Bickerton Ches
8 B7 Bickerton Devon
151 G5 Bickerton N York
190 E6 Bickerton Nthumb
114 D8 Bickford Staffs
27 J4 Bickington Devon
13 J8 Bickington Devon
13 M1 Bickleigh Devon
7 G2 Bickleigh Devon
27 J5 Bickleton Devon
113 J2 Bickley Ches
51 L5 Bickley Gt Lon
163 G4 Bickley N York
80 E1 Bickley Worcs
113 J2 Bickley Moss Ches
71 J6 Bicknacre Essex
29 K3 Bicknoller Somset
53 J7 Bicknor Kent
33 K8 Bickton Hants
80 B2 Bicton Herefs
113 G8 Bicton Shrops
95 G6 Bicton Shrops
38 E5 Bidborough Kent
35 L1 Bidden Hants
39 L5 Biddenden Kent
39 M5 Biddenden Green Kent
85 K5 Biddenham Beds
46 B4 Biddestone Wilts
44 D8 Biddisham Somset
84 C7 Biddlesden Bucks
190 D4 Biddlestone Nthumb
131 H7 Biddulph Staffs
131 H8 Biddulph Moor Staffs
27 H5 Bideford Devon
82 D5 Bidford-on-Avon Warwks
129 G2 Bidston Wirral
152 B7 Bielby E R Yk
245 K3 Bieldside C Aber
19 H8 Bierley IOW
67 K4 Bierton Bucks
173 K6 Big Balcraig D & G
185 G3 Big Carlae D & G
260 B4 Big Sand Highld
7 K5 Bigbury Devon
7 J6 Bigbury-on-Sea Devon
144 D6 Bigby Lincs
146 D3 Biggar Cumb
199 H5 Biggar S Lans
115 L2 Biggin Derbys
132 C7 Biggin Derbys
142 E1 Biggin N York
51 L7 Biggin Hill Gt Lon
86 D6 Biggleswade Beds
177 K3 Bigholms D & G
278 F3 Bighouse Highld
35 J4 Bighton Hants
156 E6 Bigland Hall Cumb
177 H8 Biglands Cumb
21 G4 Bignor W Susx
164 D8 Bigrigg Cumb
116 E3 Bilborough C Nott
29 J3 Bilbrook Somset
97 K3 Bilbrook Staffs
151 H6 Bilbrough N York
280 C5 Bilbster Highld
169 G6 Bildershaw Dur
89 K5 Bildeston Suffk
11 J4 Billacott Cnwll
71 G8 Billericay Essex
100 F3 Billesdon Leics

82 D4 Billesley Warwks
118 F5 Billingborough Lincs
139 G7 Billinge St Hel
121 M7 Billingford Norfk
106 D7 Billingford Norfk
170 B6 Billingham S on T
136 C8 Billinghay Lincs
142 C6 Billingley Barns
37 G5 Billingshurst W Susx
96 F6 Billingsley Shrops
68 B3 Billington Beds
148 C8 Billington Lancs
114 D7 Billington Staffs
107 J1 Billockby Norfk
168 F3 Billy Row Dur
147 K7 Bilsborrow Lancs
137 J4 Bilsby Lincs
21 G6 Bilsham W Susx
40 D8 Bilsington Kent
134 C7 Bilsthorpe Notts
134 C7 Bilsthorpe Moor Notts
211 J6 Bilston Mdloth
98 B4 Bilston Wolves
99 K2 Bilstone Leics
40 D5 Bilting Kent
144 F1 Bilton E R Yk
151 G6 Bilton N York
150 D4 Bilton N York
191 J4 Bilton Nthumb
100 B8 Bilton Warwks
191 J4 Bilton Banks Nthumb
136 D1 Binbrook Lincs
169 G4 Binchester Blocks Dur
16 D5 Bincombe Dorset
31 K1 Binegar Somset
21 L3 Bines Green W Susx
49 K4 Binfield Br For
49 H3 Binfield Heath Oxon
180 A4 Bingfield Nthumb
117 J3 Bingham Notts
16 E2 Bingham's Melcombe Dorset
149 K7 Bingley Brad
113 J7 Bings Shrops
121 L4 Binham Norfk
99 K7 Binley Covtry
48 B8 Binley Hants
17 G5 Binnegar Dorset
209 M4 Binniehill Falk
266 F3 Binns Farm Moray
36 E2 Binscombe Surrey
66 C5 Binsey Oxon
19 K5 Binstead IOW
36 A3 Binsted Hants
21 G5 Binsted W Susx
82 D4 Binton Warwks
121 M7 Bintree Norfk
95 H3 Binweston Shrops
72 D3 Birch Essex
140 C6 Birch Rochdl
17 G2 Birch Close Dorset
115 J5 Birch Cross Staffs
72 D3 Birch Green Essex
69 J5 Birch Green Herts
81 K6 Birch Green Worcs
130 A7 Birch Heath Ches
129 M5 Birch Hill Ches
131 K2 Birch Vale Derbys
30 C8 Birch Wood Somset
121 G5 Bircham Newton Norfk
121 G5 Bircham Tofts Norfk
70 D3 Birchanger Essex
141 H4 Birchencliffe Kirk
80 B2 Bircher Herefs
98 D5 Birchfield Birm
43 J5 Birchgrove Cardif
38 B7 Birchgrove E Susx
57 K5 Birchgrove Swans
41 J2 Birchington Kent
99 H4 Birchley Heath Warwks
99 H3 Birchmoor Warwks
85 J8 Birchmoor Green Beds
132 E7 Birchover Derbys
130 C2 Birchwood Warrtn
80 E4 Birchyfield Herefs
134 C2 Bircotes Notts
89 K5 Bird Street Suffk
88 E7 Birdbrook Essex
161 G7 Birdforth N York
20 D6 Birdham W Susx
83 K2 Birdingbury Warwks
64 D4 Birdlip Gloucs
178 E5 Birdoswald Cumb
141 K6 Birds Edge Kirk
70 E5 Birds Green Essex

152 B3 Birdsall N York
97 H6 Birdsgreen Shrops
15 G2 Birdsmoorgate Dorset
142 A7 Birdwell Barns
63 L3 Birdwood Gloucs
202 B5 Birgham Border
263 K2 Birichin Highld
139 H5 Birkacre Lancs
160 D2 Birkby N York
138 C5 Birkdale Sefton
267 L3 Birkenbog Abers
129 H2 Birkenhead Wirral
256 D3 Birkenhills Abers
141 K2 Birkenshaw Kirk
243 K5 Birkhall Abers
234 A8 Birkhill Angus
187 J3 Birkhill D & G
118 C6 Birkholme Lincs
142 E2 Birkin N York
141 L2 Birks Leeds
179 H5 Birkshaw Nthumb
80 B4 Birley Herefs
133 G1 Birley Carr Sheff
52 E6 Birling Kent
191 K5 Birling Nthumb
23 J8 Birling Gap E Susx
81 L6 Birlingham Worcs
98 D6 Birmingham Birm
232 F7 Birnam P & K
257 H5 Birness Abers
244 C4 Birse Abers
244 C4 Birsemore Abers
141 K3 Birstall Kirk
100 D2 Birstall Leics
150 B4 Birstwith N York
118 E5 Birthorpe Lincs
181 G7 Birtley Gatesd
79 L2 Birtley Herefs
179 K3 Birtley Nthumb
81 H7 Birts Street Worcs
101 J3 Bisbrooke Rutlnd
136 D3 Biscathorpe Lincs
5 H4 Biscovey Cnwll
28 C6 Bish Mill Devon
49 K2 Bisham W & M
82 A5 Bishampton Worcs
169 G5 Bishop Auckland Dur
152 F7 Bishop Burton E R Yk
169 J4 Bishop Middleham Dur
150 D3 Bishop Monkton N York
135 K1 Bishop Norton Lincs
45 H7 Bishop Sutton BaNES
150 C3 Bishop Thornton N York
152 B5 Bishop Wilton E R Yk
95 H5 Bishop's Castle Shrops
32 B8 Bishop's Caundle Dorset
64 D2 Bishop's Cleeve Gloucs
80 F5 Bishop's Frome Herefs
70 F3 Bishop's Green Essex
48 D6 Bishop's Green W Berk
83 J4 Bishop's Itchington Warwks
64 B2 Bishop's Norton Gloucs
28 D6 Bishop's Nympton Devon
114 B5 Bishop's Offley Staffs
70 C3 Bishop's Stortford Herts
35 J4 Bishop's Sutton Hants
83 H3 Bishop's Tachbrook Warwks
27 K5 Bishop's Tawton Devon
35 H7 Bishop's Waltham Hants
97 J2 Bishop's Wood Staffs
135 L2 Bishopbridge Lincs
209 G5 Bishopbriggs E Duns
266 E3 Bishopmill Moray
46 F6 Bishops Cannings Wilts
50 B5 Bishops Gate Surrey
30 B6 Bishops Hull Somset
29 M5 Bishops Lydeard Somset
41 G5 Bishopsbourne Kent
13 L7 Bishopsteignton Devon
34 F7 Bishopstoke Hants
57 G7 Bishopston Swans
67 J5 Bishopstone Bucks
23 G7 Bishopstone E Susx
80 A6 Bishopstone Herefs
41 G2 Bishopstone Kent
47 K2 Bishopstone Swindn
33 J5 Bishopstone Wilts
32 E2 Bishopstrow Wilts
30 C8 Bishopswood Somset
45 H5 Bishopsworth Bristl
151 J6 Bishopthorpe York
169 K6 Bishopton Darltn
208 D5 Bishopton Rens
82 E4 Bishopton Warwks
44 D2 Bishton Newpt

115 G7 **Bishton** Staffs
64 C6 **Bisley** Gloucs
50 B7 **Bisley** Surrey
50 B7 **Bisley Camp** Surrey
146 F7 **Bispham** Bpool
138 F5 **Bispham Green** Lancs
3 K3 **Bissoe** Cnwll
18 A3 **Bisterne** Hants
38 E3 **Bitchet Green** Kent
118 C6 **Bitchfield** Lincs
27 K3 **Bittadon** Devon
7 K3 **Bittaford** Devon
121 K8 **Bittering** Norfk
96 D7 **Bitterley** Shrops
34 F8 **Bitterne** C Sotn
100 C6 **Bitteswell** Leics
45 K5 **Bitton** S Glos
49 H2 **Bix** Oxon
100 C4 **Blaby** Leics
65 L6 **Black Bourton** Oxon
180 E5 **Black Callerton** N u Ty
106 B4 **Black Car** Norfk
37 L3 **Black Corner** W Susx
230 B4 **Black Corries** Highld
228 E8 **Black Crofts** Ag & B
4 E3 **Black Cross** Cnwll
13 J1 **Black Dog** Devon
180 C4 **Black Heddon** Nthumb
140 A6 **Black Lane** Bury
149 G7 **Black Lane Ends** Lancs
150 D7 **Black Moor** Leeds
71 J3 **Black Notley** Essex
57 H6 **Black Pill** Swans
107 K6 **Black Street** Suffk
55 G5 **Black Tar** Pembks
12 B2 **Black Torrington** Devon
202 C3 **Blackadder** Border
8 B4 **Blackawton** Devon
99 K6 **Blackbank** Warwks
155 J1 **Blackbeck** Cumb
14 C1 **Blackborough** Devon
120 E8 **Blackborough End** Norfk
23 J3 **Blackboys** E Susx
116 B2 **Blackbrook** Derbys
114 B4 **Blackbrook** Staffs
37 J2 **Blackbrook** Surrey
45 J1 **Blackburn** Abers
139 K2 **Blackburn** Bl w D
133 H1 **Blackburn** Rothm
10 C6 **Blackburn** W Loth
185 G1 **Blackcraig** E Ayrs
30 F5 **Blackden Heath** Ches
245 L1 **Blackdog** Abers
12 C6 **Blackdown** Devon
15 J2 **Blackdown** Dorset
76 F8 **Blackdyke** Cumb
142 A5 **Blacker** Barns
142 B7 **Blacker Hill** Barns
51 M4 **Blackfen** Gt Lon
19 G3 **Blackfield** Hants
77 L6 **Blackford** Cumb
20 F5 **Blackford** P & K
30 F2 **Blackford** Somset
31 L5 **Blackford** Somset
140 B6 **Blackford Bridge** Bury
116 B7 **Blackfordby** Leics
19 H8 **Blackgang** IOW
11 G4 **Blackhall** C Edin
70 B3 **Blackhall** Dur
70 B3 **Blackhall Colliery** Dur
200 F5 **Blackhaugh** Border
72 E3 **Blackheath** Essex
51 K4 **Blackheath** Gt Lon
98 B6 **Blackheath** Sandw
107 J8 **Blackheath** Suffk
36 F2 **Blackheath** Surrey
57 J4 **Blackhill** Abers
69 K5 **Blackhill** Abers
57 K3 **Blackhill** Abers
80 D8 **Blackhill** Dur
69 G7 **Blackhill of Clackriach** Abers
14 A4 **Blackhorse** Devon
24 D4 **Blackhorse Hill** E Susx
118 E3 **Blackjack** Lincs
28 E3 **Blackland** Somset
46 E5 **Blackland** Wilts
86 F4 **Blacklaw** D & G
140 C7 **Blackley** Manch
193 H3 **Blacklunans** P & K
80 C7 **Blackmarstone** Herefs
42 E4 **Blackmill** Brdgnd
36 A4 **Blackmoor** Hants
14 F6 **Blackmoor** N Som
141 H5 **Blackmoorfoot** Kirk
70 F6 **Blackmore** Essex

71 H1 **Blackmore End** Essex
68 F4 **Blackmore End** Herts
210 E3 **Blackness** Falk
36 B3 **Blacknest** Hants
50 B5 **Blacknest** W & M
148 E7 **Blacko** Lancs
146 F8 **Blackpool** Bpool
8 C5 **Blackpool** Devon
13 J7 **Blackpool** Devon
178 C3 **Blackpool Gate** Cumb
210 A5 **Blackridge** W Loth
3 G4 **Blackrock** Cnwll
61 K4 **Blackrock** Mons
45 G1 **Blackrock** Mons
139 J5 **Blackrod** Bolton
254 D4 **Blacksboat** Moray
176 D5 **Blackshaw** D & G
140 E2 **Blackshaw Head** Calder
90 D2 **Blacksmith's Green** Suffk
139 L3 **Blacksnape** Bl w D
22 C4 **Blackstone** W Susx
66 F3 **Blackthorn** Oxon
89 H3 **Blackthorpe** Suffk
143 L3 **Blacktoft** E R Yk
245 J3 **Blacktop** C Aber
115 L2 **Blackwall** Derbys
4 B5 **Blackwater** Cnwll
49 K7 **Blackwater** Hants
19 H6 **Blackwater** IOW
30 C7 **Blackwater** Somset
194 D5 **Blackwaterfoot** N Ayrs
177 L8 **Blackwell** Cumb
169 H8 **Blackwell** Darltn
132 C5 **Blackwell** Derbys
133 J7 **Blackwell** Derbys
82 F6 **Blackwell** Warwks
82 A1 **Blackwell** Worcs
63 M2 **Blackwellsend Green** Gloucs
43 J2 **Blackwood** Caerph
176 B2 **Blackwood** D & G
198 C4 **Blackwood** S Lans
131 H8 **Blackwood Hill** Staffs
129 J6 **Blacon** Ches
41 G6 **Bladbean** Kent
174 C4 **Bladnoch** D & G
66 C4 **Bladon** Oxon
30 F6 **Bladon** Somset
78 C7 **Blaen Dyryn** Powys
58 C3 **Blaen-y-Coed** Carmth
61 H5 **Blaen-y-cwm** Blae G
60 D7 **Blaen-y-cwm** Rhondd
75 M2 **Blaenannerch** Cerdgn
110 D2 **Blaenau Ffestiniog** Gwynd
61 L5 **Blaenavon** Torfn
75 L5 **Blaenffos** Pembks
42 D3 **Blaengarw** Brdgnd
92 E7 **Blaengeuffordd** Cerdgn
60 C6 **Blaengwrach** Neath
42 D2 **Blaengwynfi** Neath
42 F2 **Blaenllechau** Rhondd
77 H2 **Blaenpennal** Cerdgn
92 C8 **Blaenplwyf** Cerdgn
76 A5 **Blaenporth** Cerdgn
60 D7 **Blaenrhondda** Rhondd
75 M6 **Blaenwaun** Carmth
93 H8 **Blaenycwm** Cerdgn
45 G7 **Blagdon** N Som
30 B7 **Blagdon** Somset
8 C3 **Blagdon** Torbay
30 B7 **Blagdon Hill** Somset
167 G1 **Blagill** Cumb
138 F6 **Blaguegate** Lancs
239 G8 **Blaich** Highld
237 K6 **Blain** Highld
61 K5 **Blaina** Blae G
232 C2 **Blair Atholl** P & K
220 C7 **Blair Drummond** Stirlg
206 F5 **Blair's Ferry** Ag & B
233 J6 **Blairgowrie** P & K
221 H7 **Blairingone** P & K
220 E7 **Blairlogie** Stirlg
207 K2 **Blairmore** Ag & B
276 B4 **Blairmore** Highld
254 D8 **Blairnamarrow** Moray
63 K4 **Blaisdon** Gloucs
71 H3 **Blake End** Essex
97 J8 **Blakebrook** Worcs
97 K7 **Blakedown** Worcs
114 F2 **Blakeley Lane** Staffs
130 A5 **Blakemere** Ches
79 L7 **Blakemere** Herefs
7 M3 **Blakemore** Devon
98 C3 **Blakenall Heath** Wsall
63 K5 **Blakeney** Gloucs
122 A3 **Blakeney** Norfk

114 A2 **Blakenhall** Ches
97 K4 **Blakenhall** Wolves
97 J7 **Blakeshall** Worcs
84 C5 **Blakesley** Nhants
168 B1 **Blanchland** Nthumb
150 B5 **Bland Hill** N York
17 H1 **Blandford Camp** Dorset
17 G1 **Blandford Forum** Dorset
17 G2 **Blandford St Mary** Dorset
208 F3 **Blanefield** Stirlg
135 L7 **Blankney** Lincs
209 J7 **Blantyre** S Lans
229 H2 **Blar a' Chaorainn** Highld
241 G4 **Blargie** Highld
229 H2 **Blarmachfoldach** Highld
18 A2 **Blashford** Hants
101 H4 **Blaston** Leics
101 L4 **Blatherwycke** Nhants
156 C5 **Blawith** Cumb
184 F6 **Blawquhairn** D & G
91 J4 **Blaxhall** Suffk
143 H7 **Blaxton** Donc
180 F6 **Blaydon** Gatesd
31 H2 **Bleadney** Somset
44 C7 **Bleadon** N Som
32 C4 **Bleak Street** Somset
40 F3 **Blean** Kent
136 B3 **Bleasby** Lincs
117 J2 **Bleasby** Notts
147 L6 **Bleasdale** Lancs
167 G7 **Bleatarn** Cumb
80 D1 **Bleathwood** Herefs
223 G4 **Blebocraigs** Fife
79 H2 **Bleddfa** Powys
65 K3 **Bledington** Gloucs
67 J6 **Bledlow** Bucks
67 J7 **Bledlow Ridge** Bucks
46 C7 **Bleet** Wilts
212 B6 **Blegbie** E Loth
166 E4 **Blencarn** Cumb
165 G1 **Blencogo** Cumb
35 L8 **Blendworth** Hants
165 G2 **Blennerhasset** Cumb
66 D3 **Bletchingdon** Oxon
37 M1 **Bletchingley** Surrey
85 G8 **Bletchley** M Keyn
113 K5 **Bletchley** Shrops
55 H3 **Bletherston** Pembks
85 K4 **Bletsoe** Beds
48 D2 **Blewbury** Oxon
122 D6 **Blickling** Norfk
134 B8 **Blidworth** Notts
117 G1 **Blidworth Bottoms** Notts
189 L4 **Blindburn** Nthumb
164 F4 **Blindcrake** Cumb
38 A4 **Blindley Heath** Surrey
10 F7 **Blisland** Cnwll
81 G1 **Bliss Gate** Worcs
33 L8 **Blissford** Hants
84 D4 **Blisworth** Nhants
115 H7 **Blithbury** Staffs
176 F8 **Blitterlees** Cumb
105 K7 **Blo Norton** Norfk
82 E8 **Blockley** Gloucs
107 G2 **Blofield** Norfk
189 G2 **Bloomfield** Border
114 A4 **Blore** Staffs
115 J2 **Blore** Staffs
35 L2 **Blounce** Hants
115 H5 **Blounts Green** Staffs
138 D4 **Blowick** Sefton
83 K8 **Bloxham** Oxon
118 E1 **Bloxholm** Lincs
98 C3 **Bloxwich** Wsall
17 G4 **Bloxworth** Dorset
149 L5 **Blubberhouses** N York
4 E3 **Blue Anchor** Cnwll
29 J7 **Blue Anchor** Somset
52 F6 **Blue Bell Hill** Kent
138 C7 **Blundellsands** Sefton
107 L4 **Blundeston** Suffk
86 C5 **Blunham** Beds
47 H1 **Blunsdon St Andrew** Swindn
97 K8 **Bluntington** Worcs
103 H8 **Bluntisham** Cambs
6 C2 **Blunts** Cnwll
82 D2 **Blunts Green** Warwks
114 D3 **Blurton** C Stke
135 J1 **Blyborough** Lincs
107 J8 **Blyford** Suffk
97 H1 **Blymhill** Staffs
97 J1 **Blymhill Lawn** Staffs
134 C2 **Blyth** Notts
181 H3 **Blyth** Nthumb
199 K4 **Blyth Bridge** Border

107 J8 **Blythburgh** Suffk
201 J3 **Blythe** Border
114 F3 **Blythe Bridge** Staffs
99 G5 **Blythe End** Warwks
114 F3 **Blythe Marsh** Staffs
135 G1 **Blyton** Lincs
210 D3 **Bo'ness** Falk
139 H6 **Boar's Head** Wigan
223 K4 **Boarhills** Fife
19 K2 **Boarhunt** Hants
53 G7 **Boarley** Kent
66 D6 **Boars Hill** Oxon
140 C4 **Boarsgreave** Lancs
38 E6 **Boarshead** E Susx
66 F4 **Boarstall** Bucks
12 C4 **Boasley Cross** Devon
253 H7 **Boat of Garten** Highld
265 G5 **Boath** Highld
53 J6 **Bobbing** Kent
97 H5 **Bobbington** Staffs
70 D6 **Bobbingworth** Essex
5 L3 **Bocaddon** Cnwll
3 H7 **Bochym** Cnwll
71 J2 **Bocking** Essex
71 J2 **Bocking Churchstreet** Essex
80 D3 **Bockleton** Worcs
5 K3 **Boconnoc** Cnwll
257 L3 **Boddam** Abers
281 d8 **Boddam** Shet
64 C2 **Boddington** Gloucs
124 F4 **Bodedern** IOA
127 K4 **Bodelwyddan** Denbgs
80 C5 **Bodenham** Herefs
33 L5 **Bodenham** Wilts
80 D5 **Bodenham Moor** Herefs
125 G2 **Bodewryd** IOA
128 C5 **Bodfari** Denbgs
125 G4 **Bodffordd** IOA
108 E4 **Bodfuan** Gwynd
122 C3 **Bodham** Norfk
24 E2 **Bodiam** E Susx
83 K7 **Bodicote** Oxon
10 D7 **Bodieve** Cnwll
5 K4 **Bodinnick** Cnwll
23 L4 **Bodle Street Green** E Susx
5 H2 **Bodmin** Cnwll
105 G4 **Bodney** Norfk
125 G6 **Bodorgan** IOA
4 D5 **Bodrean** Cnwll
40 E6 **Bodsham Green** Kent
5 H3 **Bodwen** Cnwll
99 G4 **Bodymoor Heath** Warwks
251 H2 **Bogallan** Highld
257 J4 **Bogbrae** Abers
212 A5 **Boggs Holdings** E Loth
211 H6 **Boghall** Mdloth
210 C5 **Boghall** W Loth
198 C5 **Boghead** S Lans
267 G4 **Boghead Farm** Moray
267 G4 **Bogmoor** Moray
235 G1 **Bogmuir** Abers
255 M3 **Bogniebrae** Abers
20 F7 **Bognor Regis** W Susx
253 G7 **Bogroy** Highld
185 G6 **Bogue** D & G
6 E1 **Bohetherick** Devon
3 L4 **Bohortha** Cnwll
240 A6 **Bohuntine** Highld
2 B4 **Bojewyan** Cnwll
5 H2 **Bokiddick** Cnwll
169 G6 **Bolam** Dur
180 D2 **Bolam** Nthumb
7 K7 **Bolberry** Devon
129 M2 **Bold Heath** St Hel
98 E4 **Boldmere** Birm
181 J6 **Boldon Colliery** S Tyne
18 E4 **Boldre** Hants
168 C7 **Boldron** Dur
134 F2 **Bole** Notts
133 G5 **Bole Hill** Derbys
132 F8 **Bolehill** Derbys
3 H3 **Bolenowe** Cnwll
29 G7 **Bolham** Devon
29 L8 **Bolham Water** Devon
4 C4 **Bolingey** Cnwll
131 J4 **Bollington** Ches
131 H4 **Bollington Cross** Ches
63 L4 **Bollow** Gloucs
37 L6 **Bolney** W Susx
86 B3 **Bolnhurst** Beds
234 F5 **Bolshan** Angus
133 J5 **Bolsover** Derbys
141 G5 **Bolster Moor** Kirk
141 L8 **Bolsterstone** Sheff
161 H5 **Boltby** N York

243 M2 **Boltenstone** Abers
67 J8 **Bolter End** Bucks
139 L6 **Bolton** Bolton
166 E6 **Bolton** Cumb
212 B5 **Bolton** E Loth
152 B5 **Bolton** E R Yk
191 G3 **Bolton** Nthumb
149 K5 **Bolton Abbey** N York
149 K5 **Bolton Bridge** N York
148 D6 **Bolton by Bowland** Lancs
159 K5 **Bolton Hall** N York
147 J2 **Bolton le Sands** Lancs
165 H2 **Bolton Low Houses** Cumb
165 H2 **Bolton New Houses** Cumb
151 H7 **Bolton Percy** N York
147 J2 **Bolton Town End** Lancs
142 C7 **Bolton Upon Dearne** Barns
160 C3 **Bolton-on-Swale** N York
178 B5 **Boltonfellend** Cumb
165 H3 **Boltongate** Cumb
11 H7 **Bolventor** Cnwll
181 G2 **Bomarsund** Nthumb
113 G7 **Bomere Heath** Shrops
263 G2 **Bonar Bridge** Highld
228 F8 **Bonawe** Ag & B
144 C5 **Bonby** N Linc
75 L4 **Boncath** Pembks
189 G4 **Bonchester Bridge** Border
19 K8 **Bonchurch** IOW
79 L4 **Bond's Green** Herefs
12 F2 **Bondleigh** Devon
147 J6 **Bonds** Lancs
2 D4 **Bone** Cnwll
13 G7 **Bonehill** Devon
99 G3 **Bonehill** Staffs
98 D2 **Boney Hay** Staffs
208 C3 **Bonhill** W Duns
97 J3 **Boningale** Shrops
189 H2 **Bonjedward** Border
209 M7 **Bonkle** N Lans
234 F7 **Bonnington** Angus
40 D8 **Bonnington** Kent
222 F6 **Bonnybank** Fife
209 L3 **Bonnybridge** Falk
268 F5 **Bonnykelly** Abers
211 J6 **Bonnyrigg** Mdloth
233 M7 **Bonnyton** Angus
132 E8 **Bonsall** Derbys
177 H4 **Bonshaw Tower** D & G
62 D3 **Bont** Mons
93 J3 **Bont-Dolgadfan** Powys
110 C7 **Bontddu** Gwynd
137 J5 **Bonthorpe** Lincs
77 H2 **Bontnewydd** Cerdgn
125 J7 **Bontnewydd** Gwynd
128 C8 **Bontuchel** Denbgs
43 G7 **Bonvilston** V Glam
111 L3 **Bonwm** Denbgs
57 J6 **Bonymaen** Swans
27 J3 **Boode** Devon
8 D4 **Boohay** Devon
49 K1 **Booker** Bucks
113 J6 **Booley** Shrops
201 J4 **Boon** Border
114 C2 **Boon Hill** Staffs
35 G8 **Boorley Green** Hants
170 F7 **Boosbeck** R & Cl
71 K1 **Boose's Green** Essex
11 K3 **Boot** Cnwll
155 M3 **Boot** Cumb
90 F5 **Boot Street** Suffk
141 G2 **Booth** Calder
143 J3 **Booth** E R Yk
131 H3 **Booth Green** Ches
141 G2 **Booth Town** Calder
135 K7 **Boothby Graffoe** Lincs
118 C5 **Boothby Pagnell** Lincs
139 L7 **Boothstown** Salfd
84 F2 **Boothville** Nhants
155 K5 **Bootle** Cumb
138 D8 **Bootle** Sefton
130 E5 **Boots Green** Ches
159 H2 **Booze** N York
80 E1 **Boraston** Shrops
9 k2 **Bordeaux** Guern
53 J6 **Borden** Kent
36 B6 **Borden** W Susx
177 G8 **Border** Cumb
149 G3 **Bordley** N York
36 B4 **Bordon** Hants
36 B4 **Bordon Camp** Hants
71 J5 **Boreham** Essex
32 E2 **Boreham** Wilts
24 B5 **Boreham Street** E Susx
69 G7 **Borehamwood** Herts

187 J8 **Boreland** D & G
258 B6 **Boreraig** Highld
7 M4 **Boreston** Devon
96 C2 **Boreton** Ches
282 g1 **Borgh** W Isls
283 b13 **Borgh** W Isls
278 B4 **Borgie** Highld
175 G5 **Borgue** D & G
274 F3 **Borgue** Highld
89 G6 **Borley** Essex
89 G6 **Borley Green** Essex
89 K3 **Borley Green** Suffk
258 F2 **Borneskitaig** Highld
174 F5 **Borness** D & G
38 F2 **Borough Green** Kent
150 E3 **Boroughbridge** N York
112 E1 **Borras Head** Wrexhm
116 C4 **Borrowash** Derbys
171 H7 **Borrowby** N York
160 F5 **Borrowby** N York
165 H7 **Borrowdale** Cumb
210 D3 **Borrowstoun** Falk
52 F5 **Borstal** Medway
92 D5 **Borth** Cerdgn
109 K4 **Borth-y-Gest** Gwynd
188 C3 **Borthwickbrae** Border
188 D3 **Borthwickshiels** Border
259 G7 **Borve** Highld
282 g1 **Borve** W Isls
283 b13 **Borve** W Isls
282 d6 **Borve** W Isls
147 K1 **Borwick** Lancs
156 E3 **Borwick Lodge** Cumb
156 A6 **Borwick Rails** Cumb
2 B5 **Bosavern** Cnwll
80 F6 **Bosbury** Herefs
5 H1 **Boscarne** Cnwll
10 F4 **Boscastle** Cnwll
17 M4 **Boscombe** Bmouth
33 L3 **Boscombe** Wilts
5 H4 **Boscoppa** Cnwll
20 C6 **Bosham** W Susx
20 D6 **Bosham Hoe** W Susx
54 F7 **Bosherston** Pembks
2 C4 **Boskednan** Cnwll
2 C6 **Boskenna** Cnwll
131 H6 **Bosley** Ches
4 E3 **Bosoughan** Cnwll
151 M4 **Bossall** N York
10 F5 **Bossiney** Cnwll
40 F5 **Bossingham** Kent
28 F1 **Bossington** Somset
130 C6 **Bostock Green** Ches
119 K3 **Boston** Lincs
150 F6 **Boston Spa** Leeds
2 C4 **Boswarthan** Cnwll
5 G6 **Boswinger** Cnwll
2 B4 **Botallack** Cnwll
69 J7 **Botany Bay** Gt Lon
100 B2 **Botcheston** Leics
105 L8 **Botesdale** Suffk
180 F2 **Bothal** Nthumb
48 D4 **Bothampstead** W Berk
134 D5 **Bothamsall** Notts
165 G3 **Bothel** Cumb
15 L4 **Bothenhampton** Dorset
209 J7 **Bothwell** S Lans
68 B6 **Botley** Bucks
35 G8 **Botley** Hants
66 C6 **Botley** Oxon
67 H2 **Botolph Claydon** Bucks
40 F8 **Botolph's Bridge** Kent
21 L5 **Botolphs** W Susx
117 L4 **Bottesford** Leics
143 M6 **Bottesford** N Linc
87 L3 **Bottisham** Cambs
139 K5 **Bottom o' th' Moor** Bolton
138 F2 **Bottom of Hutton** Lancs
222 F2 **Bottomcraig** Fife
140 D3 **Bottoms** Calder
2 B6 **Bottoms** Cnwll
99 H5 **Botts Green** Warwks
6 E3 **Botusfleming** Cnwll
108 D5 **Botwnnog** Gwynd
38 D4 **Bough Beech** Kent
79 G7 **Boughrood** Powys
63 H7 **Boughspring** Gloucs
86 D2 **Boughton** Cambs
84 E2 **Boughton** Nhants
104 D3 **Boughton** Norfk
134 D6 **Boughton** Notts
40 D6 **Boughton Aluph** Kent
85 J7 **Boughton End** Beds
39 J3 **Boughton Green** Kent
39 M3 **Boughton Malherbe** Kent

39 J3 **Boughton Monchelsea** Kent
40 D3 **Boughton Street** Kent
171 H7 **Boulby** R & Cl
140 F3 **Boulder Clough** Calder
18 F5 **Bouldnor** IOW
96 C6 **Bouldon** Shrops
90 F5 **Boulge** Suffk
191 K3 **Boulmer** Nthumb
55 G4 **Boulston** Pembks
135 J6 **Boultham** Lincs
87 G4 **Bourn** Cambs
118 E7 **Bourne** Lincs
85 J6 **Bourne End** Beds
85 K3 **Bourne End** Beds
49 L2 **Bourne End** Bucks
68 C6 **Bourne End** Herts
70 D8 **Bournebridge** Essex
98 D6 **Bournebrook** Birm
17 L4 **Bournemouth** Bmouth
64 C6 **Bournes Green** Gloucs
53 K2 **Bournes Green** Sthend
98 B8 **Bournheath** Worcs
63 L8 **Bournstream** Gloucs
98 D7 **Bournville** Birm
32 C5 **Bourton** Dorset
44 D6 **Bourton** N Som
47 K2 **Bourton** Oxon
96 D4 **Bourton** Shrops
46 F6 **Bourton** Wilts
83 K1 **Bourton on Dunsmore** Warwks
65 J1 **Bourton-on-the-Hill** Gloucs
65 H3 **Bourton-on-the-Water** Gloucs
225 H3 **Bousd** Ag & B
177 J7 **Boustead Hill** Cumb
156 D5 **Bouth** Cumb
149 L2 **Bouthwaite** N York
82 B3 **Bouts** Worcs
219 J1 **Bovain** Stirlg
50 B3 **Boveney** Bucks
33 J7 **Boveridge** Dorset
13 J6 **Bovey Tracey** Devon
68 C6 **Bovingdon** Herts
49 K2 **Bovingdon Green** Bucks
70 D6 **Bovinger** Essex
16 F5 **Bovington** Dorset
16 F5 **Bovington Camp** Dorset
177 K7 **Bow** Cumb
13 G2 **Bow** Devon
8 B3 **Bow** Devon
51 K2 **Bow** Gt Lon
275 c6 **Bow** Ork
85 H8 **Bow Brickhill** M Keyn
222 E4 **Bow of Fife** Fife
92 D6 **Bow Street** Cerdgn
105 L4 **Bow Street** Norfk
168 B6 **Bowbank** Dur
64 B6 **Bowbridge** Gloucs
169 J3 **Bowburn** Dur
19 H6 **Bowcombe** IOW
14 D4 **Bowd** Devon
201 H7 **Bowden** Border
8 C5 **Bowden** Devon
46 D5 **Bowden Hill** Wilts
130 E2 **Bowdon** Traffd
280 B4 **Bower** Highld
45 H4 **Bower Ashton** Bristl
31 G7 **Bower Hinton** Somset
89 K7 **Bower House Tye** Suffk
142 B2 **Bower's Row** Leeds
33 H6 **Bowerchalke** Wilts
46 C6 **Bowerhill** Wilts
280 B3 **Bowermadden** Highld
114 C4 **Bowers** Staffs
53 G1 **Bowers Gifford** Essex
210 E1 **Bowershall** Fife
168 C7 **Bowes** Dur
147 K7 **Bowgreave** Lancs
176 D5 **Bowhouse** D & G
11 H6 **Bowithick** Cnwll
138 E6 **Bowker's Green** Lancs
200 F5 **Bowland** Border
156 F5 **Bowland Bridge** Cumb
140 C6 **Bowlee** Rochdl
80 C5 **Bowley** Herefs
80 C5 **Bowley Town** Herefs
36 D3 **Bowlhead Green** Surrey
141 J2 **Bowling** Brad
208 D4 **Bowling** W Duns
112 F2 **Bowling Bank** Wrexhm
81 J5 **Bowling Green** Worcs
156 D3 **Bowmanstead** Cumb
204 D4 **Bowmore** Ag & B
177 H6 **Bowness-on-Solway** Cumb

156 F3 **Bowness-on-Windermere** Cumb
234 D5 **Bowriefauld** Angus
165 K4 **Bowscale** Cumb
202 F5 **Bowsden** Nthumb
157 H3 **Bowston** Cumb
106 D2 **Bowthorpe** Norfk
64 B7 **Box** Gloucs
46 B5 **Box** Wilts
85 K5 **Box End** Beds
51 G8 **Box Hill** Surrey
11 H2 **Box's Shop** Cnwll
63 K3 **Boxbush** Gloucs
63 L4 **Boxbush** Gloucs
89 K7 **Boxford** Suffk
48 B4 **Boxford** W Berk
20 E5 **Boxgrove** W Susx
53 G7 **Boxley** Kent
68 D6 **Boxmoor** Herts
89 K8 **Boxted** Essex
89 G5 **Boxted** Suffk
72 E1 **Boxted Cross** Essex
72 E1 **Boxted Heath** Essex
A A8 **Boxwell** Gloucs
87 G2 **Boxworth** Cambs
87 G2 **Boxworth End** Cambs
88 E4 **Boyden End** Suffk
41 H2 **Boyden Gate** Kent
115 K4 **Boylestone** Derbys
268 B3 **Boyndie** Abers
269 G4 **Boyndlie** Abers
153 J2 **Boynton** E R Yk
16 C1 **Boys Hill** Dorset
234 F5 **Boysack** Angus
133 G5 **Boythorpe** Derbys
11 L4 **Boyton** Cnwll
91 J6 **Boyton** Suffk
32 F3 **Boyton** Wilts
70 F5 **Boyton Cross** Essex
88 E6 **Boyton End** Suffk
85 H3 **Bozeat** Nhants
154 d6 **Braaid** IOM
91 G2 **Brabling Green** Suffk
40 E7 **Brabourne** Kent
40 E7 **Brabourne Lees** Kent
280 D2 **Brabstermire** Highld
246 E1 **Bracadale** Highld
102 B1 **Braceborough** Lincs
135 K6 **Bracebridge Heath** Lincs
135 J6 **Bracebridge Low Fields** Lincs
118 D4 **Braceby** Lincs
148 F6 **Bracewell** Lancs
133 G7 **Brackenfield** Derbys
209 K5 **Brackenhirst** N Lans
165 J1 **Brackenthwaite** Cumb
150 C5 **Brackenthwaite** N York
20 C7 **Bracklesham** W Susx
239 K7 **Brackletter** Highld
84 B7 **Brackley** Nhants
84 C7 **Brackley Hatch** Nhants
49 L5 **Bracknell** Br For
220 E5 **Braco** P & K
267 K5 **Bracobrae** Moray
106 D3 **Bracon Ash** Norfk
237 L2 **Bracora** Highld
237 L2 **Bracorina** Highld
11 M4 **Bradaford** Devon
115 K1 **Bradbourne** Derbys
169 J5 **Bradbury** Dur
84 C5 **Bradden** Nhants
5 K2 **Braddock** Cnwll
114 D1 **Bradeley** C Stke
67 K7 **Bradenham** Bucks
46 E3 **Bradenstoke** Wilts
14 B1 **Bradfield** Devon
73 H1 **Bradfield** Essex
122 F5 **Bradfield** Norfk
132 E1 **Bradfield** Sheff
48 F4 **Bradfield** W Berk
89 H4 **Bradfield Combust** Suffk
130 D7 **Bradfield Green** Ches
73 H1 **Bradfield Heath** Essex
89 H4 **Bradfield St Clare** Suffk
89 H3 **Bradfield St George** Suffk
141 J1 **Bradford** Brad
11 G7 **Bradford** Cnwll
12 A1 **Bradford** Devon
203 J6 **Bradford** Nthumb
180 C3 **Bradford** Nthumb
31 K8 **Bradford Abbas** Dorset
46 B6 **Bradford Leigh** Wilts
16 C4 **Bradford Peverell** Dorset
46 B6 **Bradford-on-Avon** Wilts
30 B6 **Bradford-on-Tone** Somset
27 K4 **Bradiford** Devon

19 K6 **Brading** IOW
129 M4 **Bradley** Ches
115 L2 **Bradley** Derbys
35 K3 **Bradley** Hants
141 J4 **Bradley** Kirk
159 J6 **Bradley** N York
145 G6 **Bradley** NE Lin
114 D7 **Bradley** Staffs
98 B4 **Bradley** Wolves
82 A3 **Bradley** Worcs
112 E1 **Bradley** Wrexhm
113 H2 **Bradley Green** Ches
30 C3 **Bradley Green** Somset
99 H3 **Bradley Green** Warwks
82 A3 **Bradley Green** Worcs
115 H3 **Bradley in the Moors** Staffs
45 J3 **Bradley Stoke** S Glos
117 G5 **Bradmore** Notts
30 E3 **Bradney** Somset
27 L4 **Bradninch** Devon
14 A2 **Bradninch** Devon
131 K8 **Bradnop** Staffs
79 K4 **Bradnor Green** Herefs
15 L4 **Bradpole** Dorset
139 L5 **Bradshaw** Bolton
141 G2 **Bradshaw** Calder
141 G5 **Bradshaw** Kirk
11 M6 **Bradstone** Devon
130 E7 **Bradwall Green** Ches
132 C3 **Bradwell** Derbys
27 J2 **Bradwell** Devon
71 K3 **Bradwell** Essex
85 G7 **Bradwell** M Keyn
107 K3 **Bradwell** Norfk
72 E5 **Bradwell Waterside** Essex
72 E5 **Bradwell-on-Sea** Essex
26 E8 **Bradworthy** Devon
163 H7 **Brae** Highld
281 d4 **Brae** Shet
140 B5 **Brae Roy Lodge** Highld
209 K3 **Braeface** Falk
235 H5 **Braehead** Angus
173 K4 **Braehead** D & G
98 F3 **Braehead** S Lans
243 G5 **Braemar** Abers
74 E2 **Braemore** Highld
161 L4 **Braemore** Highld
233 L4 **Braes of Coul** Angus
267 H4 **Braes of Enzie** Moray
207 L4 **Braeside** Inver
275 e2 **Braeswick** Ork
216 E5 **Braevallich** Ag & B
169 H6 **Brafferton** Darltn
150 F2 **Brafferton** N York
84 F3 **Brafield-on-the-Green** Nhants
282 f2 **Bragar** W Isls
69 H3 **Bragbury End** Herts
98 D3 **Braidwood** S Lans
115 L3 **Brailsford** Derbys
115 L3 **Brailsford Green** Derbys
63 K5 **Brain's Green** Gloucs
71 J2 **Braintree** Essex
90 D1 **Braiseworth** Suffk
34 E6 **Braishfield** Hants
149 J7 **Braithwaite** Brad
155 H6 **Braithwaite** Cumb
143 K1 **Braithwell** Donc
142 C4 **Braken Hill** Wakefd
21 L5 **Bramber** W Susx
35 G6 **Brambridge** Hants
116 E4 **Bramcote** Notts
99 L5 **Bramcote** Warwks
35 J5 **Bramdean** Hants
106 F2 **Bramerton** Norfk
69 H4 **Bramfield** Herts
107 H8 **Bramfield** Suffk
90 D6 **Bramford** Suffk
131 H3 **Bramhall** Stockp
150 F7 **Bramham** Leeds
150 C7 **Bramhope** Leeds
133 H4 **Bramley** Derbys
49 G7 **Bramley** Hants
41 K1 **Bramley** Leeds
143 K1 **Bramley** Rothm
36 F2 **Bramley** Surrey
48 F7 **Bramley Corner** Hants
49 G5 **Bramley Green** Hants
49 L4 **Bramley Head** N York
41 H4 **Bramling** Kent
3 L3 **Brampford Speke** Devon
6 E1 **Brampton** Cambs
6 C6 **Brampton** Cumb
6 F6 **Brampton** Cumb
5 G4 **Brampton** Lincs

122 E6 **Brampton** Norfk
142 C7 **Brampton** Rothm
107 J7 **Brampton** Suffk
63 J2 **Brampton Abbotts** Herefs
101 H6 **Brampton Ash** Nhants
79 L1 **Brampton Bryan** Herefs
133 J2 **Brampton-en-le-Morthen** Rothm
115 H5 **Bramshall** Staffs
34 C7 **Bramshaw** Hants
49 H6 **Bramshill** Hants
36 C4 **Bramshott** Hants
31 G5 **Bramwell** Somset
71 G2 **Bran End** Essex
237 G6 **Branault** Highld
121 G3 **Brancaster** Norfk
121 H3 **Brancaster Staithe** Norfk
169 G3 **Brancepeth** Dur
266 B5 **Branchill** Moray
119 L3 **Brand End** Lincs
63 L2 **Brand Green** Gloucs
266 E2 **Branderburgh** Moray
153 H6 **Brandesburton** E R Yk
90 F3 **Brandeston** Suffk
12 A2 **Brandis Corner** Devon
122 C7 **Brandiston** Norfk
169 G3 **Brandon** Dur
118 B2 **Brandon** Lincs
190 F3 **Brandon** Nthumb
104 F6 **Brandon** Suffk
99 L8 **Brandon** Warwks
104 C5 **Brandon Bank** Norfk
104 C5 **Brandon Creek** Norfk
106 B2 **Brandon Parva** Norfk
151 J1 **Brandsby** N York
144 C8 **Brandy Wharf** Lincs
2 B5 **Brane** Cnwll
17 L4 **Branksome** Poole
17 L4 **Branksome Park** Poole
34 F2 **Bransbury** Hants
135 H4 **Bransby** Lincs
14 E5 **Branscombe** Devon
81 H5 **Bransford** Worcs
18 B4 **Bransgore** Hants
144 E1 **Bransholme** C KuH
96 E8 **Bransley** Shrops
82 C1 **Branson's Cross** Worcs
117 L5 **Branston** Leics
135 K6 **Branston** Lincs
115 L7 **Branston** Staffs
135 L6 **Branston Booths** Lincs
19 J7 **Branstone** IOW
118 B1 **Brant Broughton** Lincs
90 D8 **Brantham** Suffk
164 E5 **Branthwaite** Cumb
165 J3 **Branthwaite** Cumb
144 B2 **Brantingham** E R Yk
143 G7 **Branton** Donc
190 F3 **Branton** Nthumb
150 F3 **Branton Green** N York
202 D5 **Branxton** Nthumb
129 M7 **Brassey Green** Ches
115 L1 **Brassington** Derbys
38 D2 **Brasted** Kent
51 M8 **Brasted Chart** Kent
244 F4 **Brathens** Abers
137 J6 **Bratoft** Lincs
135 J3 **Brattleby** Lincs
29 G2 **Bratton** Somset
46 C8 **Bratton** Wilts
96 E1 **Bratton** Wrekin
12 B4 **Bratton Clovelly** Devon
27 M3 **Bratton Fleming** Devon
31 L5 **Bratton Seymour** Somset
69 K2 **Braughing** Herts
70 B2 **Braughing Friars** Herts
83 M2 **Braunston** Nhants
101 H2 **Braunston** Rutlnd
100 C3 **Braunstone** Leics
27 J4 **Braunton** Devon
162 C7 **Brawby** N York
54 D2 **Brawdy** Pembks
278 D3 **Brawl** Highld
161 H1 **Braworth** N York
49 L3 **Bray** W & M
11 L7 **Bray Shop** Cnwll
24 B4 **Bray's Hill** E Susx
101 G6 **Braybrooke** Nhants
46 F1 **Braydon** Wilts
64 E8 **Braydon Brook** Wilts
46 E2 **Braydon Side** Wilts
28 B4 **Brayford** Devon
155 H2 **Braystones** Cumb
150 C6 **Braythorn** N York
142 F2 **Brayton** N York

49 L3 **Braywick** W & M
49 L4 **Braywoodside** W & M
11 K4 **Brazacott** Cnwll
53 H6 **Breach** Kent
41 G6 **Breach** Kent
68 F3 **Breachwood Green** Herts
113 G4 **Breaden Heath** Shrops
116 B4 **Breadsall** Derbys
63 L7 **Breadstone** Gloucs
79 K4 **Breadward** Herefs
3 G5 **Breage** Cnwll
250 E3 **Breakachy** Highld
262 F1 **Brealangwell Lodge** Highld
63 J6 **Bream** Gloucs
33 L7 **Breamore** Hants
44 C7 **Brean** Somset
282 d4 **Breanais** W Isls
140 F3 **Brearley** Calder
150 D4 **Brearton** N York
282 f3 **Breascleit** W Isls
282 f3 **Breasclete** W Isls
116 D5 **Breaston** Derbys
58 F3 **Brechfa** Carmth
234 F3 **Brechin** Angus
105 J4 **Breckles** Norfk
185 L5 **Breckonside** D & G
61 G2 **Brecon** Powys
131 H2 **Bredbury** Stockp
24 E4 **Brede** E Susx
80 E4 **Bredenbury** Herefs
91 G4 **Bredfield** Suffk
53 J7 **Bredgar** Kent
53 G6 **Bredhurst** Kent
81 L7 **Bredon** Worcs
81 L8 **Bredon's Hardwick** Worcs
81 L7 **Bredon's Norton** Worcs
79 L6 **Bredwardine** Herefs
116 C7 **Breedon on the Hill** Leics
210 C7 **Breich** W Loth
139 L6 **Breightmet** Bolton
143 H1 **Breighton** E R Yk
80 B7 **Breinton** Herefs
46 E4 **Bremhill** Wilts
28 B5 **Bremridge** Devon
39 H5 **Brenchley** Kent
11 L1 **Brendon** Devon
28 D1 **Brendon** Devon
29 J4 **Brendon Hill** Somset
206 D3 **Brenfield** Ag & B
282 d4 **Brenish** W Isls
180 F4 **Brenkley** N u Ty
89 J5 **Brent Eleigh** Suffk
30 E1 **Brent Knoll** Somset
7 K3 **Brent Mill** Devon
70 B1 **Brent Pelham** Herts
50 F3 **Brentford** Gt Lon
117 K7 **Brentingby** Leics
70 E8 **Brentwood** Essex
25 J2 **Brenzett** Kent
25 J2 **Brenzett Green** Kent
115 G8 **Brereton** Staffs
130 F6 **Brereton Green** Ches
130 F6 **Brereton Heath** Ches
115 G8 **Brereton Hill** Staffs
106 B7 **Bressingham** Norfk
106 B7 **Bressingham Common** Norfk
116 A7 **Bretby** Derbys
99 L7 **Bretford** Warwks
82 C6 **Bretforton** Worcs
157 J2 **Bretherdale Head** Cumb
138 F4 **Bretherton** Lancs
281 e5 **Brettabister** Shet
105 J6 **Brettenham** Norfk
89 K4 **Brettenham** Suffk
132 D4 **Bretton** Derbys
129 H7 **Bretton** Flints
51 J8 **Brewer Street** Surrey
70 E3 **Brewers End** Essex
97 K2 **Brewood** Staffs
16 F4 **Briantspuddle** Dorset
70 E2 **Brick End** Essex
132 F3 **Brick Houses** Sheff
69 J5 **Brickendon** Herts
68 E6 **Bricket Wood** Herts
71 H1 **Brickkiln Green** Essex
82 A6 **Bricklehampton** Worcs
154 f2 **Bride** IOM
164 F4 **Bridekirk** Cumb
75 L4 **Bridell** Pembks
12 C4 **Bridestowe** Devon
255 M4 **Brideswell** Abers
13 J5 **Bridford** Devon
3 H2 **Bridge** Cnwll
41 G4 **Bridge** Kent
85 K5 **Bridge End** Beds

165 L1 **Bridge End** Cumb
156 A6 **Bridge End** Cumb
7 K5 **Bridge End** Devon
168 C3 **Bridge End** Dur
71 G1 **Bridge End** Essex
118 F4 **Bridge End** Lincs
179 L5 **Bridge End** Nthumb
50 D7 **Bridge End** Surrey
87 K7 **Bridge Green** Essex
150 D2 **Bridge Hewick** N York
255 L8 **Bridge of Alford** Abers
220 D7 **Bridge of Allan** Stirlg
254 D4 **Bridge of Avon** Moray
254 C7 **Bridge of Avon** Moray
231 G6 **Bridge of Balgie** P & K
233 J3 **Bridge of Brewlands** Angus
254 C7 **Bridge of Brown** Highld
255 H5 **Bridge of Cally** P & K
244 E4 **Bridge of Canny** Abers
233 K4 **Bridge of Craigisla** Angus
175 J3 **Bridge of Dee** D & G
245 L2 **Bridge of Don** C Aber
253 H3 **Bridge of Dulsie** Highld
244 E6 **Bridge of Dye** Abers
221 L3 **Bridge of Earn** P & K
230 F4 **Bridge of Ericht** P & K
244 F4 **Bridge of Feugh** Abers
279 J3 **Bridge of Forss** Highld
243 K4 **Bridge of Gairn** Abers
230 F4 **Bridge of Gaur** P & K
267 M6 **Bridge of Marnoch** Abers
230 B7 **Bridge of Orchy** Ag & B
232 C2 **Bridge of Tilt** P & K
267 H4 **Bridge of Tynet** Moray
281 c6 **Bridge of Walls** Shet
208 C6 **Bridge of Weir** Rens
28 B8 **Bridge Reeve** Devon
80 A6 **Bridge Sollers** Herefs
89 H5 **Bridge Street** Suffk
129 K5 **Bridge Trafford** Ches
45 K4 **Bridge Yate** S Glos
164 E5 **Bridgefoot** Cumb
31 J6 **Bridgehampton** Somset
180 D8 **Bridgehill** Dur
149 L3 **Bridgehouse Gate** N York
19 K3 **Bridgemary** Hants
113 M2 **Bridgemere** Ches
255 K4 **Bridgend** Abers
204 E4 **Bridgend** Ag & B
234 E2 **Bridgend** Angus
42 D5 **Bridgend** Brdgnd
75 L3 **Bridgend** Cerdgn
165 L7 **Bridgend** Cumb
187 G4 **Bridgend** D & G
7 G5 **Bridgend** Devon
223 G5 **Bridgend** Fife
255 H5 **Bridgend** Moray
221 L2 **Bridgend** P & K
210 D4 **Bridgend** W Loth
233 L4 **Bridgend of Lintrathen** Angus
11 K2 **Bridgerule** Devon
95 J4 **Bridges** Shrops
11 L4 **Bridgetown** Devon
29 G4 **Bridgetown** Somset
105 J6 **Bridgham** Norfk
97 G5 **Bridgnorth** Shrops
98 B2 **Bridgtown** Staffs
30 D3 **Bridgwater** Somset
153 K3 **Bridlington** E R Yk
15 K4 **Bridport** Dorset
63 H2 **Bridstow** Herefs
148 E8 **Brierfield** Lancs
142 B5 **Brierley** Barns
63 J4 **Brierley** Gloucs
80 C4 **Brierley** Herefs
97 L6 **Brierley Hill** Dudley
170 B5 **Brierton** Hartpl
165 J6 **Briery** Cumb
219 J6 **Brig o'Turk** Stirlg
144 C6 **Brigg** N Linc
123 G6 **Briggate** Norfk
162 F1 **Briggswath** N York
164 E4 **Brigham** Cumb
165 J6 **Brigham** Cumb
153 H5 **Brigham** E R Yk
141 J3 **Brighouse** Calder
19 G7 **Brighstone** IOW
132 E7 **Brightgate** Derbys
66 A6 **Brighthampton** Oxon
132 F1 **Brightholmlee** Sheff
12 E3 **Brightley** Devon
24 C3 **Brightling** E Susx
73 G4 **Brightlingsea** Essex
22 D6 **Brighton** Br & H

4 E4	**Brighton** Cnwll
138 C7	**Brighton le Sands** Sefton
210 B3	**Brightons** Falk
6 D3	**Brightor** Cnwll
48 B3	**Brightwalton** W Berk
48 B3	**Brightwalton Green** W Berk
48 B3	**Brightwalton Holt** W Berk
90 F6	**Brightwell** Suffk
67 G8	**Brightwell Baldwin** Oxon
67 G8	**Brightwell Upperton** Oxon
48 E1	**Brightwell-cum-Sotwell** Oxon
168 D8	**Brignall** Dur
145 H7	**Brigsley** NE Lin
157 G5	**Brigsteer** Cumb
101 L6	**Brigstock** Nhants
67 G4	**Brill** Bucks
3 J5	**Brill** Cnwll
79 J5	**Brilley** Herefs
80 C2	**Brimfield** Herefs
80 C2	**Brimfield Cross** Herefs
133 H5	**Brimington** Derbys
13 J7	**Brimley** Devon
64 D4	**Brimpsfield** Gloucs
48 E6	**Brimpton** W Berk
48 E6	**Brimpton Common** W Berk
64 C6	**Brimscombe** Gloucs
129 G3	**Brimstage** Wirral
132 F3	**Brincliffe** Sheff
143 J2	**Brind** E R Yk
31 H3	**Brindham** Somset
281 C5	**Brindister** Shet
139 J3	**Brindle** Lancs
97 H1	**Brineton** Staffs
101 J5	**Bringhurst** Leics
102 B8	**Brington** Cambs
122 A5	**Briningham** Norfk
117 J1	**Brinkely** Notts
137 G5	**Brinkhill** Lincs
88 C4	**Brinkley** Cambs
99 L7	**Brinklow** Warwks
46 E2	**Brinkworth** Wilts
139 J3	**Brinscall** Lancs
44 E8	**Brinscombe** Somset
44 F6	**Brinsea** N Som
116 D2	**Brinsley** Notts
80 B6	**Brinsop** Herefs
133 H2	**Brinsworth** Rothm
122 A4	**Brinton** Norfk
275 C3	**Brinyan** Ork
178 A8	**Brisco** Cumb
121 L7	**Brisley** Norfk
45 J5	**Brislington** Bristl
40 B7	**Brissenden Green** Kent
45 H4	**Bristol** Bristl
122 B5	**Briston** Norfk
7 G2	**Brisworthy** Devon
140 C3	**Britannia** Lancs
33 L5	**Britford** Wilts
61 J6	**Brithdir** Caerph
110 E7	**Brithdir** Gwynd
61 L6	**British** Torfn
52 F7	**British Legion Village** Kent
57 K6	**Briton Ferry** Neath
67 G8	**Britwell Salome** Oxon
8 D4	**Brixham** Torbay
7 G4	**Brixton** Devon
51 J4	**Brixton** Gt Lon
32 E3	**Brixton Deverill** Wilts
84 E1	**Brixworth** Nhants
65 L5	**Brize Norton** Oxon
81 K2	**Broad Alley** Worcs
47 H1	**Broad Blunsdon** Swindn
82 E7	**Broad Campden** Gloucs
141 H4	**Broad Carr** Calder
33 H5	**Broad Chalke** Wilts
140 C3	**Broad Clough** Lancs
39 H5	**Broad Ford** Kent
72 C2	**Broad Green** Essex
81 H4	**Broad Green** Worcs
82 A1	**Broad Green** Worcs
54 D4	**Broad Haven** Pembks
104 B8	**Broad Hill** Cambs
47 G4	**Broad Hinton** Wilts
48 B6	**Broad Laying** Hants
82 D6	**Broad Marston** Worcs
114 C2	**Broad Meadow** Staffs
155 K4	**Broad Oak** Cumb
24 E3	**Broad Oak** E Susx
23 K3	**Broad Oak** E Susx
49 H8	**Broad Oak** Hants
62 F3	**Broad Oak** Herefs
41 G3	**Broad Oak** Kent
139 G8	**Broad Oak** St Hel
106 F8	**Broad Road** Suffk

24 F4	**Broad Street** E Susx
70 E4	**Broad Street** Essex
39 L2	**Broad Street** Kent
53 G4	**Broad Street** Medway
47 G7	**Broad Street** Wilts
72 B5	**Broad Street Green** Essex
47 G3	**Broad Town** Wilts
71 G4	**Broad's Green** Essex
131 K1	**Broadbottom** Tamesd
20 D6	**Broadbridge** W Susx
37 H4	**Broadbridge Heath** W Susx
14 A3	**Broadclyst** Devon
208 B4	**Broadfield** Inver
55 K6	**Broadfield** Pembks
247 K4	**Broadford** Highld
37 G6	**Broadford Bridge** W Susx
187 K4	**Broadgairhill** Border
103 H2	**Broadgate** Lincs
89 K3	**Broadgrass Green** Suffk
202 D2	**Broadhaugh** Border
130 E2	**Broadheath** Traffd
80 F2	**Broadheath** Worcs
14 C2	**Broadhembury** Devon
8 B2	**Broadhempston** Devon
135 H5	**Broadholme** Notts
24 F3	**Broadland Row** E Susx·
56 C3	**Broadlay** Carmth
70 B5	**Broadley** Essex
140 C4	**Broadley** Lancs
267 H4	**Broadley** Moray
70 B5	**Broadley Common** Essex
16 D5	**Broadmayne** Dorset
35 J2	**Broadmere** Hants
63 J4	**Broadmoor** Gloucs
55 J5	**Broadmoor** Pembks
13 G2	**Broadnymett** Devon
15 K3	**Broadoak** Dorset
63 K4	**Broadoak** Gloucs
129 J7	**Broadoak** Wrexhm
41 L2	**Broadstairs** Kent
63 G6	**Broadstone** Mons
17 K3	**Broadstone** Poole
96 C5	**Broadstone** Shrops
81 H4	**Broadwas** Worcs
69 H3	**Broadwater** Herts
21 K6	**Broadwater** W Susx
97 J7	**Broadwaters** Worcs
56 B3	**Broadway** Carmth
56 C3	**Broadway** Carmth
54 E4	**Broadway** Pembks
30 D7	**Broadway** Somset
107 H7	**Broadway** Suffk
82 C7	**Broadway** Worcs
63 H5	**Broadwell** Gloucs
65 J2	**Broadwell** Gloucs
65 K6	**Broadwell** Oxon
83 K2	**Broadwell** Warwks
16 C6	**Broadwey** Dorset
15 K2	**Broadwindsor** Dorset
12 E1	**Broadwood Kelly** Devon
12 A5	**Broadwoodwidger** Devon
79 L6	**Brobury** Herefs
259 K7	**Brochel** Highld
147 K7	**Brock** Lancs
48 D6	**Brock's Green** Hants
81 H4	**Brockamin** Worcs
35 J7	**Brockbridge** Hants
106 E7	**Brockdish** Norfk
97 K8	**Brockencote** Worcs
18 D3	**Brockenhurst** Hants
198 D5	**Brocketsbrae** S Lans
90 D2	**Brockford Green** Suffk
90 D2	**Brockford Street** Suffk
84 C3	**Brockhall** Nhants
37 J1	**Brockham** Surrey
64 D2	**Brockhampton** Gloucs
64 F3	**Brockhampton** Gloucs
20 B5	**Brockhampton** Hants
63 H1	**Brockhampton** Herefs
16 D1	**Brockhampton Green** Dorset
141 J5	**Brockholes** Kirk
133 G6	**Brockhurst** Derbys
100 A6	**Brockhurst** Warwks
165 J2	**Brocklebank** Cumb
144 E5	**Brocklesby** Lincs
44 F5	**Brockley** N Som
89 G1	**Brockley** Suffk
88 E6	**Brockley Green** Suffk
89 G4	**Brockley Green** Suffk
166 C3	**Brockleymoor** Cumb
97 K5	**Brockmoor** Dudley
12 B3	**Brockscombe** Devon
95 H3	**Brockton** Shrops
97 G3	**Brockton** Shrops
95 H6	**Brockton** Shrops

96 D4	**Brockton** Shrops
114 C5	**Brockton** Staffs
63 G6	**Brockweir** Gloucs
35 K5	**Brockwood Park** Hants
64 C4	**Brockworth** Gloucs
5 G1	**Brocton** Cnwll
114 F7	**Brocton** Staffs
195 G4	**Brodick** N Ayrs
264 F8	**Brodie** Moray
142 D6	**Brodsworth** Donc
259 H3	**Brogaig** Highld
85 J7	**Brogborough** Beds
130 D5	**Broken Cross** Ches
131 H5	**Broken Cross** Ches
46 D1	**Brokenborough** Wilts
46 B8	**Brokerswood** Wilts
129 H3	**Bromborough** Wirral
106 C8	**Brome** Suffk
106 C8	**Brome Street** Suffk
91 G5	**Bromeswell** Suffk
165 G1	**Bromfield** Cumb
96 B8	**Bromfield** Shrops
85 K5	**Bromham** Beds
46 D6	**Bromham** Wilts
141 M7	**Bromley** Barns
97 K5	**Bromley** Dudley
51 L5	**Bromley** Gt Lon
97 G4	**Bromley** Shrops
51 L5	**Bromley Common** Gt Lon
72 F2	**Bromley Cross** Essex
95 H3	**Bromlow** Shrops
53 G5	**Brompton** Medway
160 E3	**Brompton** N York
163 G6	**Brompton** N York
96 C2	**Brompton** Shrops
29 K4	**Brompton Ralph** Somset
29 G4	**Brompton Regis** Somset
160 B3	**Brompton-on-Swale** N York
63 J2	**Bromsash** Herefs
81 G8	**Bromsberrow** Gloucs
81 G8	**Bromsberrow Heath** Gloucs
81 M1	**Bromsgrove** Worcs
114 B8	**Bromstead Heath** Staffs
80 F4	**Bromyard** Herefs
80 F4	**Bromyard Downs** Herefs
110 D5	**Bronaber** Gwynd
77 H2	**Bronant** Cerdgn
96 C6	**Broncroft** Shrops
76 B6	**Brongest** Cerdgn
113 H3	**Bronington** Wrexhm
79 G8	**Bronllys** Powys
58 D4	**Bronwydd** Carmth
79 J6	**Bronydd** Powys
112 C4	**Bronygarth** Shrops
56 A3	**Brook** Carmth
34 C8	**Brook** Hants
34 D5	**Brook** Hants
18 F6	**Brook** IOW
40 E6	**Brook** Kent
36 D3	**Brook** Surrey
37 G2	**Brook** Surrey
86 B3	**Brook End** Beds
86 D5	**Brook End** Beds
86 B1	**Brook End** Cambs
85 H6	**Brook End** M Keyn
34 C7	**Brook Hill** Hants
128 C6	**Brook House** Denbgs
70 E8	**Brook Street** Essex
40 B8	**Brook Street** Kent
89 G5	**Brook Street** Suffk
22 D2	**Brook Street** W Susx
106 F3	**Brooke** Norfk
101 J2	**Brooke** Rutlnd
145 G8	**Brookenby** Lincs
208 C6	**Brookfield** Rens
66 F7	**Brookhampton** Oxon
31 K5	**Brookhampton** Somset
147 K3	**Brookhouse** Lancs
133 K2	**Brookhouse** Rothm
130 F7	**Brookhouse Green** Ches
131 K2	**Brookhouses** Derbys
25 J2	**Brookland** Kent
130 F2	**Brooklands** Traffd
69 H6	**Brookmans Park** Herts
94 E3	**Brooks** Powys
41 J2	**Brooks End** Kent
37 H6	**Brooks Green** W Susx
117 H8	**Brooksby** Leics
64 B4	**Brookthorpe** Gloucs
104 E4	**Brookville** Norfk
50 B7	**Brookwood** Surrey
86 D6	**Broom** Beds
169 H2	**Broom** Dur
133 J1	**Broom** Rothm
82 C4	**Broom** Warwks

121 L6	**Broom Green** Norfk
142 C7	**Broom Hill** Barns
17 K2	**Broom Hill** Dorset
116 F2	**Broom Hill** Notts
97 L8	**Broom Hill** Worcs
40 D3	**Broom Street** Kent
81 G8	**Broom's Green** Gloucs
107 G5	**Broome** Norfk
95 K7	**Broome** Shrops
97 K7	**Broome** Worcs
191 G4	**Broome Park** Nthumb
130 D3	**Broomedge** Warrtn
21 K3	**Broomer's Corner** W Susx
21 H3	**Broomershill** W Susx
71 H5	**Broomfield** Essex
39 L3	**Broomfield** Kent
41 G2	**Broomfield** Kent
30 B4	**Broomfield** Somset
112 F7	**Broomfields** Shrops
143 M2	**Broomfleet** E R Yk
50 B5	**Broomhall** W & M
180 B6	**Broomhaugh** Nthumb
191 J6	**Broomhill** Nthumb
113 K2	**Broomhill Green** Ches
180 C6	**Broomley** Nthumb
121 J6	**Broomsthorpe** Norfk
274 B7	**Brora** Highld
96 F3	**Broseley** Shrops
119 J8	**Brotherhouse Bar** Lincs
167 L3	**Brotherlee** Dur
119 J2	**Brothertoft** Lincs
142 D3	**Brotherton** N York
170 F6	**Brotton** R & Cl
279 J4	**Broubster** Highld
167 J7	**Brough** Cumb
132 D3	**Brough** Derbys
144 B2	**Brough** E R Yk
280 B2	**Brough** Highld
135 G7	**Brough** Notts
281 f5	**Brough** Shet
281 f3	**Brough Lodge** Shet
167 J8	**Brough Sowerby** Cumb
113 J3	**Broughall** Shrops
199 K6	**Broughton** Border
67 K4	**Broughton** Bucks
102 F7	**Broughton** Cambs
129 H7	**Broughton** Flints
34 C4	**Broughton** Hants
139 G1	**Broughton** Lancs
85 H7	**Broughton** M Keyn
144 B6	**Broughton** N Linc
149 G5	**Broughton** N York
162 D8	**Broughton** N York
101 H8	**Broughton** Nhants
83 K7	**Broughton** Oxon
140 B7	**Broughton** Salfd
114 B5	**Broughton** Staffs
42 D7	**Broughton** V Glam
100 C5	**Broughton Astley** Leics
156 C6	**Broughton Beck** Cumb
46 C6	**Broughton Gifford** Wilts
81 M3	**Broughton Green** Worcs
81 L4	**Broughton Hackett** Worcs
174 C6	**Broughton Mains** D & G
156 B4	**Broughton Mills** Cumb
164 E4	**Broughton Moor** Cumb
65 K6	**Broughton Poggs** Oxon
156 B5	**Broughton Tower** Cumb
156 B5	**Broughton-in-Furness** Cumb
223 H1	**Broughty Ferry** C Dund
156 C7	**Brow End** Cumb
120 E7	**Brow-of-the-Hill** Norfk
35 J3	**Brown Candover** Hants
138 D5	**Brown Edge** Lancs
114 E1	**Brown Edge** Staffs
129 K6	**Brown Heath** Ches
131 G8	**Brown Lees** Staffs
90 C3	**Brown Street** Suffk
98 D5	**Brown's Green** Birm
158 B2	**Brownber** Cumb
113 G5	**Brownheath** Shrops
256 F4	**Brownhill** Abers
223 J4	**Brownhills** Fife
98 D2	**Brownhills** Wsall
191 H2	**Brownieside** Nthumb
48 E7	**Browninghill Green** Hants
131 G7	**Brownlow Heath** Ches
164 D6	**Brownrigg** Cumb
177 G8	**Brownrigg** Cumb
64 C6	**Browns Hill** Gloucs
26 E5	**Brownsham** Devon
100 B7	**Brownsover** Warwks
7 K4	**Brownston** Devon
107 K3	**Browston Green** Norfk
163 G4	**Broxa** N York

69 K5 **Broxbourne** Herts
212 F3 **Broxburn** E Loth
210 E4 **Broxburn** W Loth
191 J3 **Broxfield** Nthumb
70 E2 **Broxted** Essex
113 H1 **Broxton** Ches
79 L4 **Broxwood** Herefs
23 G4 **Broyle Side** E Susx
280 D8 **Bruan** Highld
232 B2 **Bruar** P & K
264 E3 **Brucefield** Highld
207 J7 **Bruchag** Ag & B
129 K7 **Bruera** Ches
65 K3 **Bruern Abbey** Oxon
204 C4 **Bruichladdich** Ag & B
91 H2 **Bruisyard** Suffk
91 H2 **Bruisyard Street** Suffk
143 M6 **Brumby** N Linc
132 B7 **Brund** Staffs
107 G2 **Brundall** Norfk
91 G1 **Brundish** Suffk
91 G1 **Brundish Street** Suffk
2 D4 **Brunnion** Cnwll
95 J6 **Brunslow** Shrops
141 L2 **Bruntcliffe** Leeds
149 J6 **Brunthwaite** Brad
100 D5 **Bruntingthorpe** Leics
222 E3 **Brunton** Fife
191 J1 **Brunton** Nthumb
47 K7 **Brunton** Wilts
29 G5 **Brushford** Somset
12 F1 **Brushford Barton** Devon
31 L4 **Bruton** Somset
81 K2 **Bryan's Green** Worcs
17 G1 **Bryanston** Dorset
67 L7 **Bryant's Bottom** Bucks
77 G5 **Brydekirk** D & G
12 D1 **Brymbo** Wrexhm
31 H7 **Brympton** Somset
130 B5 **Bryn** Ches
42 B3 **Bryn** Neath
95 H6 **Bryn** Shrops
39 H7 **Bryn** Wigan
24 F5 **Bryn Du** IOA
39 J7 **Bryn Gates** Wigan
42 F4 **Bryn Golau** Rhondd
11 L2 **Bryn Saith Marchog** Denbgs
10 B4 **Bryn-bwbach** Gwynd
57 K5 **Bryn-coch** Neath
10 D5 **Bryn-Eden** Gwynd
75 G4 **Bryn-Henllan** Pembks
108 D5 **Bryn-mawr** Gwynd
12 B3 **Bryn-newydd** Denbgs
94 D3 **Bryn-penarth** Powys
28 F6 **Bryn-y-bal** Flints
27 G4 **Bryn-y-Maen** Conwy
12 D3 **Bryn-yr-Eos** Wrexhm
59 K6 **Brynaman** Carmth
75 J5 **Brynberian** Pembks
57 L6 **Brynbryddan** Neath
42 F5 **Bryncae** Rhondd
42 D5 **Bryncethin** Brdgnd
109 H3 **Bryncir** Gwynd
108 C5 **Bryncroes** Gwynd
92 D3 **Bryncrug** Gwynd
12 A2 **Bryneglwys** Denbgs
12 D3 **Brynfields** Wrexhm
28 E5 **Brynford** Flints
24 F4 **Bryngwran** IOA
62 D5 **Bryngwyn** Mons
79 H5 **Bryngwyn** Powys
76 B5 **Brynhoffnant** Cerdgn
38 E2 **Bryning** Lancs
61 K6 **Brynithel** Blae G
61 J5 **Brynmawr** Blae G
42 D5 **Brynmenyn** Brdgnd
57 H6 **Brynmill** Swans
42 F5 **Brynna** Rhondd
25 K7 **Brynrefail** Gwynd
25 H2 **Brynrefail** IOA
42 F5 **Brynsadler** Rhondd
25 H6 **Brynsiencyn** IOA
25 J3 **Brynteg** IOA
46 F4 **Bualintur** Highld
28 E4 **Buarth-draw** Flints
83 J1 **Bubbenhall** Warwks
151 M8 **Bubwith** E R Yk
208 D1 **Buchanan Smithy** Stirlg
259 L6 **Buchanhaven** Abers
221 G2 **Buchanty** P & K
220 C6 **Buchany** Stirlg
219 J8 **Buchlyvie** Stirlg
26 F6 **Buck's Cross** Devon
26 F6 **Buck's Mills** Devon
155 L1 **Buckabank** Cumb

86 D2 **Buckden** Cambs
159 G7 **Buckden** N York
107 G2 **Buckenham** Norfk
14 D2 **Buckerell** Devon
7 L2 **Buckfast** Devon
7 L2 **Buckfastleigh** Devon
222 F7 **Buckhaven** Fife
63 G4 **Buckholt** Mons
32 C6 **Buckhorn Weston** Dorset
69 L8 **Buckhurst Hill** Essex
267 J3 **Buckie** Moray
84 D8 **Buckingham** Bucks
67 L4 **Buckland** Bucks
7 K6 **Buckland** Devon
82 C8 **Buckland** Gloucs
18 E4 **Buckland** Hants
87 G8 **Buckland** Herts
41 J6 **Buckland** Kent
65 M7 **Buckland** Oxon
37 K1 **Buckland** Surrey
27 G6 **Buckland Brewer** Devon
68 A5 **Buckland Common** Bucks
32 C1 **Buckland Dinham** Somset
12 B1 **Buckland Filleigh** Devon
13 G7 **Buckland in the Moor** Devon
6 F1 **Buckland Monachorum** Devon
16 D2 **Buckland Newton** Dorset
16 C6 **Buckland Ripers** Dorset
30 C8 **Buckland St Mary** Somset
7 L5 **Buckland-Tout-Saints** Devon
48 E5 **Bucklebury** W Berk
18 F4 **Bucklers Hard** Hants
90 F6 **Bucklesham** Suffk
129 G7 **Buckley** Flints
82 E2 **Buckley Green** Warwks
129 G6 **Buckley Mountain** Flints
130 E3 **Bucklow Hill** Ches
118 A7 **Buckminster** Leics
114 E2 **Bucknall** C Stke
136 C6 **Bucknall** Lincs
66 E2 **Bucknell** Oxon
95 J8 **Bucknell** Shrops
267 H3 **Buckpool** Moray
37 G4 **Bucks Green** W Susx
68 D7 **Bucks Hill** Herts
36 B3 **Bucks Horn Oak** Hants
245 K2 **Bucksburn** C Aber
4 D5 **Buckshead** Cnwll
153 K1 **Buckton** E R Yk
95 J8 **Buckton** Herefs
203 H5 **Buckton** Nthumb
102 C8 **Buckworth** Cambs
11 J2 **Budd's Titson** Cnwll
114 B2 **Buddileigh** Staffs
223 J1 **Buddon** Angus
11 H2 **Bude** Cnwll
6 C3 **Budge's Shop** Cnwll
14 A3 **Budlake** Devon
203 J6 **Budle** Nthumb
14 C6 **Budleigh Salterton** Devon
23 H3 **Budlett's Common** E Susx
3 K5 **Budock Water** Cnwll
113 L3 **Buerton** Ches
84 D4 **Bugbrooke** Nhants
8 B5 **Bugford** Devon
131 G7 **Buglawton** Ches
5 G3 **Bugle** Cnwll
32 C6 **Bugley** Dorset
152 B4 **Bugthorpe** E R Yk
96 E2 **Buildwas** Shrops
78 E4 **Builth Road** Powys
78 E5 **Builth Wells** Powys
68 B4 **Bulbourne** Herts
33 J5 **Bulbridge** Wilts
118 D6 **Bulby** Lincs
279 H3 **Buldoo** Highld
33 L2 **Bulford** Wilts
33 L2 **Bulford Barracks** Wilts
113 J1 **Bulkeley** Ches
99 K6 **Bulkington** Warwks
46 D7 **Bulkington** Wilts
27 G8 **Bulkworthy** Devon
125 G1 **Bull Bay** IOA
69 H4 **Bull's Green** Herts
107 J4 **Bull's Green** Norfk
160 F4 **Bullamore** N York
116 B1 **Bullbridge** Derbys
49 L5 **Bullbrook** Br For
69 G6 **Bullen's Green** Herts
63 M3 **Bulley** Gloucs
164 E3 **Bullgill** Cumb
80 C7 **Bullinghope** Herefs
34 F3 **Bullington** Hants

136 A4 **Bullington** Lincs
84 F6 **Bullington End** M Keyn
41 G2 **Bullockstone** Kent
89 G7 **Bulmer** Essex
151 L2 **Bulmer** N York
89 G7 **Bulmer Tye** Essex
52 D2 **Bulphan** Thurr
14 E4 **Bulstone** Devon
68 C6 **Bulstrode** Herts
50 C1 **Bulstrode Park** Bucks
24 D5 **Bulverhythe** E Susx
257 G3 **Bulwark** Abers
116 F3 **Bulwell** C Nott
101 L4 **Bulwick** Nhants
69 L6 **Bumble's Green** Essex
237 J3 **Bunacaimb** Highld
239 K6 **Bunarkaig** Highld
130 A8 **Bunbury** Ches
130 A8 **Bunbury Heath** Ches
251 H3 **Bunchrew** Highld
21 K4 **Buncton** W Susx
248 E6 **Bundalloch** Highld
226 D8 **Bunessan** Ag & B
107 G5 **Bungay** Suffk
119 J1 **Bunker's Hill** Lincs
204 F2 **Bunnahabhain** Ag & B
117 G5 **Bunny** Notts
250 C5 **Buntait** Highld
69 K1 **Buntingford** Herts
106 C5 **Bunwell** Norfk
106 C4 **Bunwell Street** Norfk
115 L4 **Bupton** Derbys
131 L5 **Burbage** Derbys
99 L5 **Burbage** Leics
47 K6 **Burbage** Wilts
79 L3 **Burcher** Herefs
39 G7 **Burchett's Green** E Susx
49 K3 **Burchett's Green** W & M
33 J5 **Burcombe** Wilts
66 E7 **Burcot** Oxon
82 A1 **Burcot** Worcs
97 G4 **Burcote** Shrops
67 K4 **Burcott** Bucks
67 L2 **Burcott** Bucks
152 D3 **Burdale** N York
89 H8 **Bures** Essex
65 K5 **Burford** Oxon
80 D2 **Burford** Shrops
226 D3 **Burg** Ag & B
106 B8 **Burgate** Suffk
36 A5 **Burgates** Hants
68 F1 **Burge End** Herts
22 E3 **Burgess Hill** W Susx
90 F5 **Burgh** Suffk
177 K7 **Burgh by Sands** Cumb
107 K2 **Burgh Castle** Norfk
51 H7 **Burgh Heath** Surrey
24 C2 **Burgh Hill** E Susx
137 J6 **Burgh le Marsh** Lincs
122 E6 **Burgh next Aylsham** Norfk
136 D2 **Burgh on Bain** Lincs
123 J8 **Burgh St Margaret** Norfk
107 K5 **Burgh St Peter** Norfk
48 C6 **Burghclere** Hants
266 C2 **Burghead** Moray
49 G5 **Burghfield** W Berk
49 G5 **Burghfield Common** W Berk
80 B6 **Burghill** Herefs
142 E5 **Burghwallis** Donc
52 F6 **Burham** Kent
20 B3 **Buriton** Hants
113 K1 **Burland** Ches
5 G1 **Burlawn** Cnwll
64 C6 **Burleigh** Gloucs
29 K7 **Burlescombe** Devon
16 E4 **Burleston** Dorset
8 B5 **Burlestone** Devon
18 C3 **Burley** Hants
101 J1 **Burley** Rutlnd
96 B7 **Burley** Shrops
80 E6 **Burley Gate** Herefs
149 L6 **Burley in Wharfedale** Brad
18 C3 **Burley Lawn** Hants
18 B3 **Burley Street** Hants
149 L7 **Burley Wood Head** Brad
113 K3 **Burleydam** Ches
107 H1 **Burlingham Green** Norfk
79 J3 **Burlingjobb** Powys
97 H1 **Burlington** Shrops
113 G6 **Burlton** Shrops
25 L1 **Burmarsh** Kent
83 G7 **Burmington** Warwks
142 F2 **Burn** N York
142 A8 **Burn Cross** Sheff
147 G7 **Burn Naze** Lancs

220 C6 **Burn of Cambus** Stirlg
131 G1 **Burnage** Manch
115 M5 **Burnaston** Derbys
166 C7 **Burnbanks** Cumb
210 A7 **Burnbrae** N Lans
152 C6 **Burnby** E R Yk
21 G6 **Burndell** W Susx
139 L6 **Burnden** Bolton
140 D5 **Burnedge** Rochdl
157 H3 **Burneside** Cumb
160 D5 **Burneston** N York
45 K6 **Burnett** BaNES
188 C4 **Burnfoot** Border
188 F3 **Burnfoot** Border
186 E7 **Burnfoot** D & G
177 K1 **Burnfoot** D & G
188 C6 **Burnfoot** D & G
221 H6 **Burnfoot** P & K
50 A3 **Burnham** Bucks
144 D4 **Burnham** N Linc
121 H3 **Burnham Deepdale** Norfk
69 H4 **Burnham Green** Herts
121 H3 **Burnham Market** Norfk
121 H3 **Burnham Norton** Norfk
121 J3 **Burnham Overy** Norfk
121 J3 **Burnham Overy Staithe** Norfk
121 J3 **Burnham Thorpe** Norfk
72 D7 **Burnham-on-Crouch** Essex
30 D1 **Burnham-on-Sea** Somset
257 L3 **Burnhaven** Abers
186 C7 **Burnhead** D & G
256 C7 **Burnhervie** Abers
97 H3 **Burnhill Green** Staffs
169 G1 **Burnhope** Dur
196 D1 **Burnhouse** N Ayrs
163 H4 **Burniston** N York
140 C1 **Burnley** Lancs
181 H8 **Burnmoor** Dur
213 L6 **Burnmouth** Border
180 E7 **Burnopfield** Dur
178 C7 **Burnrigg** Cumb
149 J3 **Burnsall** N York
234 D5 **Burnside** Angus
234 C3 **Burnside** Angus
222 B5 **Burnside** Fife
266 D2 **Burnside** Moray
210 E4 **Burnside** W Loth
234 C8 **Burnside of Duntrune** Angus
72 F2 **Burnt Heath** Essex
48 E4 **Burnt Hill** W Berk
168 E6 **Burnt Houses** Dur
23 H2 **Burnt Oak** E Susx
150 C4 **Burnt Yates** N York
50 D8 **Burntcommon** Surrey
115 L5 **Burntheath** Derbys
3 K4 **Burnthouse** Cnwll
211 H2 **Burntisland** Fife
98 D2 **Burntwood** Staffs
98 D2 **Burntwood Green** Staffs
12 C6 **Burnville** Devon
30 B7 **Burnworthy** Somset
50 C8 **Burpham** Surrey
21 H5 **Burpham** W Susx
181 G4 **Burradon** N Tyne
190 D5 **Burradon** Nthumb
281 f1 **Burrafirth** Shet
3 H4 **Burras** Cnwll
6 E2 **Burraton** Cnwll
7 H4 **Burraton** Devon
281 e4 **Burravoe** Shet
166 F7 **Burrells** Cumb
233 J7 **Burrelton** P & K
27 K4 **Burridge** Devon
15 H1 **Burridge** Devon
19 J2 **Burridge** Hants
160 C5 **Burrill** N York
143 L6 **Burringham** N Linc
27 L7 **Burrington** Devon
80 B1 **Burrington** Herefs
44 F7 **Burrington** N Som
88 C4 **Burrough End** Cambs
88 C4 **Burrough Green** Cambs
101 G1 **Burrough on the Hill** Leics
157 K7 **Burrow** Lancs
29 G2 **Burrow** Somset
30 E5 **Burrow Bridge** Somset
50 B6 **Burrowhill** Surrey
37 G2 **Burrows Cross** Surrey
56 E6 **Burry** Swans
56 E6 **Burry Green** Swans
56 E5 **Burry Port** Carmth
138 E5 **Burscough** Lancs
138 F5 **Burscough Bridge** Lancs
143 K1 **Bursea** E R Yk

153 H6 **Burshill** E R Yk
19 H2 **Bursledon** Hants
114 D2 **Burslem** C Stke
90 C6 **Burstall** Suffk
15 K2 **Burstock** Dorset
106 C6 **Burston** Norfk
114 E5 **Burston** Staffs
37 M3 **Burstow** Surrey
145 G2 **Burstwick** E R Yk
158 F5 **Burtersett** N York
178 D6 **Burtholme** Cumb
88 F2 **Burthorpe Green** Suffk
165 M1 **Burthwaite** Cumb
4 E4 **Burthy** Cnwll
30 F2 **Burtle Hill** Somset
119 J4 **Burtoft** Lincs
129 H5 **Burton** Ches
129 L7 **Burton** Ches
16 D4 **Burton** Dorset
18 B5 **Burton** Dorset
135 J5 **Burton** Lincs
203 K6 **Burton** Nthumb
55 G5 **Burton** Pembks
30 B2 **Burton** Somset
31 H8 **Burton** Somset
46 B3 **Burton** Wilts
32 D4 **Burton** Wilts
153 H3 **Burton Agnes** E R Yk
15 L4 **Burton Bradstock** Dorset
118 C6 **Burton Coggles** Lincs
83 J5 **Burton Dassett** Warwks
70 D2 **Burton End** Essex
88 D6 **Burton End** Suffk
153 H2 **Burton Fleming** E R Yk
99 H8 **Burton Green** Warwks
129 H7 **Burton Green** Wrexhm
99 L5 **Burton Hastings** Warwks
148 A2 **Burton in Lonsdale** N York
117 H3 **Burton Joyce** Notts
101 K8 **Burton Latimer** Nhants
117 K8 **Burton Lazars** Leics
150 D3 **Burton Leonard** N York
117 G7 **Burton on the Wolds** Leics
100 E4 **Burton Overy** Leics
118 F3 **Burton Pedwardine** Lincs
145 H2 **Burton Pidsea** E R Yk
142 D2 **Burton Salmon** N York
143 L4 **Burton upon Stather** N Linc
115 L6 **Burton upon Trent** Staffs
71 K2 **Burton's Green** Essex
157 H7 **Burton-in-Kendal** Cumb
130 A1 **Burtonwood** Warrtn
129 L8 **Burwardsley** Ches
96 E6 **Burwarton** Shrops
24 B2 **Burwash** E Susx
23 L3 **Burwash Common** E Susx
23 L3 **Burwash Weald** E Susx
88 B2 **Burwell** Cambs
137 G4 **Burwell** Lincs
125 G1 **Burwen** IOA
275 C6 **Burwick** Ork
140 B5 **Bury** Bury
102 F6 **Bury** Cambs
29 G5 **Bury** Somset
21 G4 **Bury** W Susx
86 C8 **Bury End** Beds
68 B7 **Bury End** Bucks
70 C3 **Bury Green** Herts
89 G2 **Bury St Edmunds** Suffk
152 B3 **Burythorpe** N York
208 F7 **Busby** E Rens
160 E6 **Busby Stoop** N York
65 J7 **Buscot** Wilts
235 J2 **Bush** Abers
11 J1 **Bush** Cnwll
80 B5 **Bush Bank** Herefs
106 E6 **Bush Green** Norfk
89 H4 **Bush Green** Suffk
69 J7 **Bush Hill Park** Gt Lon
97 L3 **Bushbury** Wolves
100 E3 **Bushby** Leics
68 E8 **Bushey** Herts
68 F8 **Bushey Heath** Herts
81 K8 **Bushley** Worcs
81 K8 **Bushley Green** Worcs
86 C3 **Bushmead** Beds
46 F3 **Bushton** Wilts
166 E2 **Busk** Cumb
135 M3 **Buslingthorpe** Lincs
64 C6 **Bussage** Gloucs
30 E4 **Bussex** Somset
140 D3 **Butcher Hill** Calder
23 J2 **Butcher's Cross** E Susx
45 G6 **Butcombe** N Som
31 H4 **Butleigh** Somset

31 H4 **Butleigh Wootton** Somset
67 K5 **Butler's Cross** Bucks
116 F2 **Butler's Hill** Notts
83 H5 **Butlers Marston** Warwks
91 J5 **Butley** Suffk
91 J5 **Butley High Corner** Suffk
113 L1 **Butt Green** Ches
114 C1 **Butt Lane** Staffs
71 J6 **Butt's Green** Essex
151 M4 **Buttercrambe** N York
213 H6 **Butterdean** Border
168 E5 **Butterknowle** Dur
14 A1 **Butterleigh** Devon
116 C1 **Butterley** Derbys
165 G7 **Buttermere** Cumb
47 M6 **Buttermere** Wilts
114 C2 **Butters Green** Staffs
141 H2 **Buttershaw** Brad
233 G6 **Butterstone** P & K
114 C3 **Butterton** Staffs
131 L8 **Butterton** Staffs
169 K5 **Butterwick** Dur
119 L3 **Butterwick** Lincs
162 C7 **Butterwick** N York
152 F2 **Butterwick** N York
95 G2 **Buttington** Powys
97 G7 **Buttonbridge** Shrops
97 G7 **Buttonoak** Shrops
19 G2 **Butts Ash** Hants
11 K2 **Buttsbear Cross** Cnwll
89 K4 **Buxhall** Suffk
89 K3 **Buxhall Fen Street** Suffk
23 H3 **Buxted** E Susx
131 L5 **Buxton** Derbys
122 E7 **Buxton** Norfk
122 D7 **Buxton Heath** Norfk
61 J3 **Bwlch** Powys
112 B8 **Bwlch-y-cibau** Powys
112 B7 **Bwlch-y-Ddar** Powys
94 C4 **Bwlch-y-ffridd** Powys
75 M5 **Bwlch-y-groes** Pembks
94 B8 **Bwlch-y-sarnau** Powys
112 C1 **Bwlchgwyn** Wrexhm
77 G3 **Bwlchllan** Cerdgn
58 C4 **Bwlchnewydd** Carmth
108 E6 **Bwlchtocyn** Gwynd
76 D5 **Bwlchyfadfa** Cerdgn
57 G5 **Bwlchymyrdd** Swans
180 F7 **Byermoor** Gatesd
169 J3 **Byers Garth** Dur
169 G4 **Byers Green** Dur
83 M4 **Byfield** Nhants
50 D6 **Byfleet** Surrey
79 M6 **Byford** Herefs
86 F7 **Bygrave** Herts
181 G6 **Byker** N u Ty
161 J6 **Byland Abbey** N York
127 K7 **Bylchau** Conwy
130 E6 **Byley** Ches
57 G5 **Bynea** Carmth
201 K4 **Byrewalls** Border
189 K5 **Byrness** Nthumb
14 B6 **Bystock** Devon
102 B8 **Bythorn** Cambs
79 L2 **Byton** Herefs
180 C6 **Bywell** Nthumb
36 E6 **Byworth** W Susx

C

27 G6 **Cabbacott** Devon
144 F7 **Cabourne** Lincs
205 H3 **Cabrach** Ag & B
255 H6 **Cabrach** Moray
147 J6 **Cabus** Lancs
261 K6 **Cabvie Lodge** Highld
23 G2 **Cackle Street** E Susx
24 C3 **Cackle Street** E Susx
24 E3 **Cackle Street** E Susx
13 L2 **Cadbury** Devon
28 B7 **Cadbury Barton** Devon
209 G4 **Cadder** E Duns
68 D3 **Caddington** Beds
200 F6 **Caddonfoot** Border
23 K3 **Cade Street** E Susx
142 E7 **Cadeby** Donc
99 L3 **Cadeby** Leics
13 L1 **Cadeleigh** Devon
3 J8 **Cadgwith** Cnwll
222 D6 **Cadham** Fife
130 D1 **Cadishead** Salfd
57 H5 **Cadle** Swans
139 G2 **Cadley** Lancs

47 J5 **Cadley** Wilts
47 K8 **Cadley** Wilts
67 J8 **Cadmore End** Bucks
34 C8 **Cadnam** Hants
144 C7 **Cadney** N Linc
128 E7 **Cadole** Flints
43 H7 **Cadoxton** V Glam
57 L5 **Cadoxton Juxta-Neath** Neath
67 K6 **Cadsden** Bucks
111 K4 **Cadwst** Denbgs
59 H6 **Cae'r bryn** Carmth
59 M6 **Cae'r-bont** Powys
125 J7 **Caeathro** Gwynd
59 M6 **Caehopkin** Powys
135 K2 **Caenby** Lincs
135 K2 **Caenby Corner** Lincs
77 J7 **Caeo** Carmth
74 C6 **Caer Farchell** Pembks
42 C3 **Caerau** Brdgnd
43 H6 **Caerau** Cardif
110 C7 **Caerdeon** Gwynd
124 E4 **Caergeiliog** IOA
129 G8 **Caergwrle** Flints
126 F5 **Caerhun** Conwy
188 C5 **Caerlanrig** Border
44 D1 **Caerleon** Newpt
125 H7 **Caernarfon** Gwynd
43 J4 **Caerphilly** Caerph
94 B5 **Caersws** Powys
76 C4 **Caerwedros** Cerdgn
44 F1 **Caerwent** Mons
128 D5 **Caerwys** Flints
110 E8 **Caerynwch** Gwynd
62 D4 **Caggle Street** Mons
126 C3 **Caim** IOA
283 C8 **Cairinis** W Isls
206 C1 **Cairnbaan** Ag & B
269 J3 **Cairnbulg** Abers
213 K6 **Cairncross** Border
208 A5 **Cairncurran** Inver
217 K5 **Cairndow** Ag & B
210 D2 **Cairneyhill** Fife
267 H4 **Cairnfield House** Moray
172 C5 **Cairngarroch** D & G
245 K4 **Cairngrassie** Abers
255 K3 **Cairnie** Abers
256 F3 **Cairnorrie** Abers
172 D1 **Cairnryan** D & G
267 G5 **Cairnty** Moray
107 L1 **Caister-on-Sea** Norfk
144 E7 **Caistor** Lincs
106 E3 **Caistor St Edmund** Norfk
106 B5 **Cake Street** Norfk
81 K1 **Cakebole** Worcs
89 K7 **Calais Street** Suffk
282 f3 **Calanais** W Isls
19 G6 **Calbourne** IOW
137 G4 **Calceby** Lincs
128 E5 **Calcot** Flints
65 G5 **Calcot** Gloucs
49 G4 **Calcot** W Berk
49 G4 **Calcot Row** W Berk
266 E3 **Calcots** Moray
41 G3 **Calcott** Kent
95 K1 **Calcott** Shrops
150 E4 **Calcutt** N York
65 G8 **Calcutt** Wilts
165 K3 **Caldbeck** Cumb
159 K5 **Caldbergh** N York
102 C5 **Caldecote** Cambs
87 G4 **Caldecote** Cambs
86 E7 **Caldecote** Herts
84 D5 **Caldecote** Nhants
87 G3 **Caldecote Highfields** Cambs
85 K2 **Caldecott** Nhants
66 D7 **Caldecott** Oxon
101 J4 **Caldecott** Rutlnd
85 H8 **Caldecotte** M Keyn
155 J2 **Calder Bridge** Cumb
141 M4 **Calder Grove** Wakefd
147 K6 **Calder Vale** Lancs
209 K6 **Calderbank** N Lans
140 E4 **Calderbrook** Rochdl
209 L5 **Caldercruix** N Lans
197 J3 **Caldermill** S Lans
140 D4 **Caldermore** Rochdl
209 H7 **Calderwood** S Lans
44 F1 **Caldicot** Mons
98 C4 **Caldmore** W Mids
168 F8 **Caldwell** N York
128 F3 **Caldy** Wirral
59 J4 **Caledfwlch** Carmth
4 F6 **Calendra** Cnwll
4 D6 **Calenick** Cnwll
88 D6 **Calford Green** Suffk

275 d2 **Calfsound** Ork
226 D2 **Calgary** Ag & B
265 H8 **Califer** Moray
210 B4 **California** Falk
123 K8 **California** Norfk
7 K4 **California Cross** Devon
116 B7 **Calke** Derbys
259 M5 **Callakille** Highld
219 K5 **Callander** Stirlg
282 f3 **Callanish** W Isls
96 E4 **Callaughton** Shrops
4 C5 **Callestick** Cnwll
247 K7 **Calligarry** Highld
6 D1 **Callington** Cnwll
115 K6 **Callingwood** Staffs
80 C8 **Callow** Herefs
81 J5 **Callow End** Worcs
46 F2 **Callow Hill** Wilts
97 G8 **Callow Hill** Worcs
82 B2 **Callow Hill** Worcs
80 D2 **Callows Grave** Worcs
34 D7 **Calmore** Hants
64 F5 **Calmsden** Gloucs
46 E5 **Calne** Wilts
133 H5 **Calow** Derbys
19 H3 **Calshot** Hants
6 E1 **Calstock** Cnwll
46 F5 **Calstone Wellington** Wilts
122 D5 **Calthorpe** Norfk
123 H6 **Calthorpe Street** Norfk
166 B3 **Calthwaite** Cumb
148 F4 **Calton** N York
115 H2 **Calton** Staffs
115 J2 **Calton Green** Staffs
130 B7 **Calveley** Ches
132 E5 **Calver** Derbys
79 L5 **Calver Hill** Herefs
132 E5 **Calver Sough** Derbys
113 K4 **Calverhall** Shrops
29 G8 **Calverleigh** Devon
150 B8 **Calverley** Leeds
67 G2 **Calvert** Bucks
84 F7 **Calverton** M Keyn
117 G2 **Calverton** Notts
232 B2 **Calvine** P & K
176 F8 **Calvo** Cumb
199 K6 **Calzeat** Border
63 M7 **Cam** Gloucs
248 F6 **Camas Luinie** Highld
228 B3 **Camasachoirce** Highld
237 L8 **Camasine** Highld
247 G1 **Camastianavaig** Highld
250 E4 **Camault Muir** Highld
25 H3 **Camber** E Susx
49 L6 **Camberley** Surrey
51 J4 **Camberwell** Gt Lon
143 G3 **Camblesforth** N York
180 B2 **Cambo** Nthumb
181 H2 **Cambois** Nthumb
3 G3 **Camborne** Cnwll
87 G3 **Cambourne** Cambs
87 J3 **Cambridge** Cambs
63 L6 **Cambridge** Gloucs
4 A5 **Cambrose** Cnwll
220 E8 **Cambus** Clacks
243 M4 **Cambus o' May** Abers
263 L1 **Cambusavie Platform** Highl
220 D8 **Cambusbarron** Stirlg
220 D8 **Cambuskenneth** Stirlg
209 H7 **Cambuslang** S Lans
199 H5 **Cambuswallace** S Lans
51 H2 **Camden Town** Gt Lon
45 J7 **Cameley** BaNES
10 F6 **Camelford** Cnwll
209 M3 **Camelon** Falk
81 H8 **Camer's Green** Worcs
253 K5 **Camerory** Highld
45 K7 **Camerton** BaNES
164 D4 **Camerton** Cumb
231 G4 **Camghouran** P & K
201 J7 **Camieston** Border
245 K4 **Cammachmore** Abers
135 J3 **Cammeringham** Lincs
263 L2 **Camore** Highld
192 E4 **Campbeltown** Ag & B
181 G4 **Camperdown** N Tyne
186 D7 **Cample** D & G
233 K7 **Campmuir** Angus
210 E5 **Camps** W Loth
88 C6 **Camps End** Cambs
142 E5 **Campsall** Donc
91 H4 **Campsea Ash** Suffk
86 C7 **Campton** Beds
189 J4 **Camptown** Border
54 F3 **Camrose** Pembks

232 B5 **Camserney** P & K
261 H2 **Camusnagaul** Highld
239 H8 **Camusnagaul** Highld
248 A3 **Camusteel** Highld
248 A3 **Camusterrach** Highld
34 C7 **Canada** Hants
156 D7 **Canal Foot** Cumb
55 H4 **Canaston Bridge** Pembks
243 K4 **Candacraig** Abers
105 L8 **Candle Street** Suffk
137 H6 **Candlesby** Lincs
96 C2 **Candover Green** Shrops
199 J5 **Candyburn** Border
49 G3 **Cane End** Oxon
72 C8 **Canewdon** Essex
17 K2 **Canford Bottom** Dorset
17 L5 **Canford Cliffs** Poole
17 K4 **Canford Heath** Poole
17 K3 **Canford Magna** Poole
90 C2 **Canhams Green** Suffk
280 D2 **Canisbay** Highld
133 H2 **Canklow** Rothm
99 J7 **Canley** Covtry
32 E6 **Cann** Dorset
250 B5 **Cannich** Highld
51 L3 **Canning Town** Gt Lon
30 C3 **Cannington** Somset
98 B2 **Cannock** Staffs
98 D1 **Cannock Wood** Staffs
80 A7 **Cannon Bridge** Herefs
80 F6 **Canon Frome** Herefs
80 B5 **Canon Pyon** Herefs
177 L4 **Canonbie** D & G
84 B5 **Canons Ashby** Nhants
2 E4 **Canonstown** Cnwll
40 F4 **Canterbury** Kent
107 H3 **Cantley** Norfk
96 C2 **Cantlop** Shrops
43 J6 **Canton** Cardif
252 E2 **Cantraywood** Highld
147 M1 **Cantsfield** Lancs
53 G2 **Canvey Island** Essex
135 K6 **Canwick** Lincs
11 J4 **Canworthy Water** Cnwll
239 J8 **Caol** Highld
282 f6 **Caolas Scalpaigh** W Isls
224 D5 **Caoles** Ag & B
239 H5 **Caonich** Highld
39 G4 **Capel** Kent
37 J3 **Capel** Surrey
92 E7 **Capel Bangor** Cerdgn
77 H4 **Capel Betws Lleucu** Cerdgn
125 H3 **Capel Coch** IOA
126 E8 **Capel Curig** Conwy
76 C5 **Capel Cynon** Cerdgn
58 E5 **Capel Dewi** Carmth
76 E6 **Capel Dewi** Cerdgn
127 G8 **Capel Garmon** Conwy
91 J5 **Capel Green** Suffk
58 E4 **Capel Gwyn** Carmth
124 F4 **Capel Gwyn** IOA
59 K4 **Capel Gwynfe** Carmth
59 G6 **Capel Hendre** Carmth
59 G3 **Capel Isaac** Carmth
58 B2 **Capel Iwan** Carmth
41 H7 **Capel le Ferne** Kent
43 H5 **Capel Llanilltern** Cardif
125 G5 **Capel Mawr** IOA
92 D7 **Capel Seion** Cerdgn
91 J5 **Capel St Andrew** Suffk
90 C7 **Capel St Mary** Suffk
92 F8 **Capel Trisant** Cerdgn
92 D7 **Capel-Dewi** Cerdgn
61 L1 **Capel-y-ffin** Powys
125 K6 **Capel-y-graig** Gwynd
9 j2 **Capelles** Guern
109 H2 **Capeluchaf** Gwynd
126 E4 **Capelulo** Conwy
129 J5 **Capenhurst** Ches
147 K2 **Capernwray** Lancs
180 C3 **Capheaton** Nthumb
208 D7 **Caplaw** E Rens
91 G2 **Capon's Green** Suffk
187 K2 **Cappercleuch** Border
39 G6 **Capstone** Medway
8 C4 **Capton** Devon
29 K3 **Capton** Somset
233 G7 **Caputh** P & K
17 J3 **Car Colston** Notts
11 K8 **Caradon Town** Cnwll
208 E3 **Carbeth Inn** Stirlg
5 G3 **Carbis** Cnwll
2 E3 **Carbis Bay** Cnwll
246 E2 **Carbost** Highld
259 G7 **Carbost** Highld

133 G2 **Carbrook** Sheff
105 J3 **Carbrooke** Norfk
134 C5 **Carburton** Notts
5 H4 **Carclaze** Cnwll
3 K3 **Carclew** Cnwll
142 E6 **Carcroft** Donc
222 C8 **Cardenden** Fife
95 J1 **Cardeston** Shrops
177 K8 **Cardewlees** Cumb
254 D3 **Cardhu** Moray
43 J6 **Cardiff** Cardif
75 L3 **Cardigan** Cerdgn
88 C6 **Cardinal's Green** Cambs
86 B5 **Cardington** Beds
96 C4 **Cardington** Shrops
5 J1 **Cardinham** Cnwll
172 E8 **Cardrain** D & G
200 C5 **Cardrona** Border
208 B3 **Cardross** Ag & B
172 E8 **Cardryne** D & G
177 G7 **Cardurnock** Cumb
118 D8 **Careby** Lincs
234 E3 **Careston** Angus
55 H6 **Carew** Pembks
55 H6 **Carew Cheriton** Pembks
55 H6 **Carew Newton** Pembks
63 H1 **Carey** Herefs
209 K7 **Carfin** N Lans
201 G2 **Carfraemill** Border
107 H1 **Cargate Green** Norfk
176 C4 **Cargen** D & G
176 C4 **Cargenbridge** D & G
233 H8 **Cargill** P & K
177 L7 **Cargo** Cumb
6 E2 **Cargreen** Cnwll
3 M4 **Cargurrel** Cnwll
202 B5 **Carham** Nthumb
29 H2 **Carhampton** Somset
3 J3 **Carharrack** Cnwll
231 H4 **Carie** P & K
283 c8 **Carinish** W Isls
19 H6 **Carisbrooke** IOW
156 E7 **Cark** Cumb
6 E3 **Carkeel** Cnwll
282 e2 **Carlabhagh** W Isls
4 D4 **Carland Cross** Cnwll
169 G7 **Carlbury** Darltn
102 A1 **Carlby** Lincs
190 B4 **Carlcroft** Nthumb
141 J7 **Carlecotes** Barns
3 G5 **Carleen** Cnwll
160 B7 **Carlesmoor** N York
178 A8 **Carleton** Cumb
166 C5 **Carleton** Cumb
155 J1 **Carleton** Cumb
146 F7 **Carleton** Lancs
149 H6 **Carleton** N York
142 D4 **Carleton** Wakefd
106 B2 **Carleton Forehoe** Norfk
106 C5 **Carleton Rode** Norfk
107 G3 **Carleton St Peter** Norfk
3 K5 **Carlidnack** Cnwll
171 G6 **Carlin How** R & Cl
256 B3 **Carlincraig** Abers
45 K7 **Carlingcott** BaNES
177 L7 **Carlisle** Cumb
4 E2 **Carloggas** Cnwll
199 K2 **Carlops** Border
282 e2 **Carloway** W Isls
142 B5 **Carlton** Barns
85 J4 **Carlton** Beds
88 C4 **Carlton** Cambs
142 A2 **Carlton** Leeds
99 L2 **Carlton** Leics
159 J5 **Carlton** N York
161 K5 **Carlton** N York
143 G3 **Carlton** N York
117 G3 **Carlton** Notts
169 K6 **Carlton** S on T
91 J2 **Carlton** Suffk
107 K5 **Carlton Colville** Suffk
100 F4 **Carlton Curlieu** Leics
88 C5 **Carlton Green** Cambs
161 H7 **Carlton Husthwaite** N York
134 B3 **Carlton in Lindrick** Notts
160 F6 **Carlton Miniott** N York
118 B3 **Carlton Scroop** Lincs
161 H2 **Carlton-in-Cleveland** N York
135 H8 **Carlton-le-Moorland** Lincs
134 F7 **Carlton-on-Trent** Notts
5 H4 **Carluddon** Cnwll
198 D3 **Carluke** S Lans
5 H4 **Carlyon Bay** Cnwll
198 C7 **Carmacoup** S Lans
58 D5 **Carmarthen** Carmth

59 G5 **Carmel** Carmth
128 E4 **Carmel** Flints
125 J8 **Carmel** Gwynd
198 F5 **Carmichael** S Lans
3 H6 **Carminowe** Cnwll
209 G7 **Carmunnock** C Glas
209 H6 **Carmyle** C Glas
234 E6 **Carmyllie** Angus
3 H3 **Carn Brea** Cnwll
248 F7 **Carn-gorm** Highld
153 J3 **Carnaby** E R Yk
223 J6 **Carnbee** Fife
221 J6 **Carnbo** P & K
256 F6 **Carnbrogie** Abers
248 E6 **Carndu** Highld
197 J2 **Carnduff** S Lans
3 K6 **Carne** Cnwll
4 E7 **Carne** Cnwll
4 F3 **Carne** Cnwll
196 F4 **Carnell** E Ayrs
4 D1 **Carnewas** Cnwll
147 K2 **Carnforth** Lancs
74 C6 **Carnhedryn** Pembks
3 G4 **Carnhell Green** Cnwll
245 H2 **Carnie** Abers
3 H4 **Carnkie** Cnwll
3 H3 **Carnkie** Cnwll
4 C4 **Carnkiet** Cnwll
93 L4 **Carno** Powys
238 D4 **Carnoch** Highld
210 D1 **Carnock** Fife
3 K3 **Carnon Downs** Cnwll
268 B6 **Carnousie** Abers
234 E8 **Carnoustie** Angus
199 G4 **Carnwath** S Lans
2 B4 **Carnyorth** Cnwll
99 H7 **Carol Green** Solhll
4 F4 **Carpalla** Cnwll
159 H5 **Carperby** N York
140 B4 **Carr** Bury
133 K2 **Carr** Rothm
141 M3 **Carr Gate** Wakefd
167 J1 **Carr Shield** Nthumb
133 J5 **Carr Vale** Derbys
194 C3 **Carradale** Ag & B
253 G7 **Carrbridge** Highld
140 E7 **Carrbrook** Tamesd
9 c2 **Carrefour** Jersey
125 G2 **Carreglefn** IOA
143 K6 **Carrhouse** N Linc
206 E2 **Carrick** Ag & B
217 K8 **Carrick Castle** Ag & B
210 D3 **Carriden** Falk
136 F8 **Carrington** Lincs
211 K7 **Carrington** Mdloth
130 E1 **Carrington** Traffd
5 G3 **Carrismerry** Cnwll
110 E2 **Carrog** Conwy
111 L3 **Carrog** Denbgs
210 A3 **Carron** Falk
254 E3 **Carron** Moray
209 K2 **Carron Bridge** Stirlg
186 C6 **Carronbridge** D & G
210 A2 **Carronshore** Falk
44 E1 **Carrow Hill** Mons
208 B6 **Carruth House** Inver
176 E4 **Carrutherstown** D & G
169 J2 **Carrville** Dur
179 L3 **Carrycoats Hall** Nthumb
227 G8 **Carsaig** Ag & B
234 C4 **Carse Gray** Angus
173 H1 **Carseriggan** D & G
176 C7 **Carsethorn** D & G
51 H6 **Carshalton** Gt Lon
115 L1 **Carsington** Derbys
192 D6 **Carskey** Ag & B
174 D4 **Carsluith** D & G
184 E4 **Carsphairn** D & G
198 F4 **Carstairs** S Lans
198 F4 **Carstairs Junction** S Lans
65 L7 **Carswell Marsh** Oxon
34 C6 **Carter's Clay** Hants
70 D5 **Carters Green** Essex
65 L5 **Carterton** Oxon
180 E8 **Carterway Heads** Dur
5 G4 **Carthew** Cnwll
160 D6 **Carthorpe** N York
190 E5 **Cartington** Nthumb
198 E4 **Cartland** S Lans
132 F4 **Cartledge** Derbys
156 E7 **Cartmel** Cumb
156 F5 **Cartmel Fell** Cumb
56 E3 **Carway** Carmth
177 L4 **Carwinley** Cumb
64 B6 **Cashe's Green** Gloucs

33 G8 **Cashmoor** Dorset
66 C5 **Cassington** Oxon
169 K3 **Cassop Colliery** Dur
2 C6 **Castallack** Cnwll
126 F6 **Castell** Conwy
62 B8 **Castell-y-bwch** Torfn
157 K6 **Casterton** Lancs
5 J3 **Castle** Cnwll
121 H8 **Castle Acre** Norfk
85 G3 **Castle Ashby** Nhants
159 J4 **Castle Bolton** N York
98 F5 **Castle Bromwich** Solhll
118 C7 **Castle Bytham** Lincs
94 E2 **Castle Caereinion** Powys
88 C6 **Castle Camps** Cambs
178 D7 **Castle Carrock** Cumb
31 L4 **Castle Cary** Somset
46 B3 **Castle Combe** Wilts
116 D6 **Castle Donington** Leics
175 J2 **Castle Douglas** D & G
65 H7 **Castle Eaton** Swindn
169 L3 **Castle Eden** Dur
102 C2 **Castle End** C Pete
80 F6 **Castle Frome** Herefs
2 D4 **Castle Gate** Cnwll
157 H4 **Castle Green** Cumb
50 B6 **Castle Green** Surrey
115 M7 **Castle Gresley** Derbys
88 F8 **Castle Hedingham** Essex
39 H5 **Castle Hill** Kent
90 D6 **Castle Hill** Suffk
172 D3 **Castle Kennedy** D & G
217 G8 **Castle Lachlan** Ag & B
74 E6 **Castle Morris** Pembks
187 K7 **Castle O'er** D & G
95 K3 **Castle Pulverbatch** Shrops
120 E6 **Castle Rising** Norfk
140 E3 **Castle Street** Calder
252 D2 **Castle Stuart** Highld
283 b13 **Castlebay** W Isls
75 H6 **Castlebythe** Pembks
209 L3 **Castlecary** Falk
142 C3 **Castleford** Wakefd
200 B6 **Castlehill** Border
280 B3 **Castlehill** Highld
208 C4 **Castlehill** W Duns
54 E7 **Castlemartin** Pembks
209 G7 **Castlemilk** C Glas
81 H7 **Castlemorton** Worcs
168 D1 **Castleside** Dur
84 F6 **Castlethorpe** M Keyn
144 B6 **Castlethorpe** N Linc
188 E8 **Castleton** Border
132 C3 **Castleton** Derbys
162 B1 **Castleton** N York
43 L5 **Castleton** Newpt
140 C5 **Castleton** Rochdl
16 D7 **Castletown** Dorset
280 A3 **Castletown** Highld
154 c8 **Castletown** IOM
181 J7 **Castletown** Sundld
150 C6 **Castley** N York
105 J4 **Caston** Norfk
102 C4 **Castor** C Pete
57 G7 **Caswell Bay** Swans
131 K5 **Cat and Fiddle** Ches
44 D1 **Cat's Ash** Newpt
194 E1 **Catacol** N Ayrs
63 G6 **Catbrook** Mons
128 F5 **Catch** Flints
2 C5 **Catchall** Cnwll
99 H8 **Catchem's Corner** Solhll
180 E8 **Catchgate** Dur
133 H2 **Catcliffe** Rothm
46 E4 **Catcomb** Wilts
30 F3 **Catcott** Somset
30 F2 **Catcott Burtle** Somset
9 j3 **Catel** Guern
51 J7 **Caterham** Surrey
123 H7 **Catfield** Norfk
123 H7 **Catfield Common** Norfk
281 e6 **Catfirth** Shet
51 K4 **Catford** Gt Lon
138 F1 **Catforth** Lancs
209 G2 **Cathcart** C Glas
61 J2 **Cathedine** Powys
141 G2 **Catherine Slack** Brad
98 F7 **Catherine-de-Barnes** Solhll
35 L8 **Catherington** Hants
15 J4 **Catherston Leweston** Dorset
96 E7 **Catherton** Shrops
19 J2 **Catisfield** Hants
80 F6 **Catley** Herefs
140 C4 **Catley Lane Head** Rochdl
241 H5 **Catlodge** Highld

148 F8 **Catlow** Lancs
178 B3 **Catlowdy** Cumb
87 K7 **Catmere End** Essex
48 C3 **Catmore** W Berk
13 H8 **Caton** Devon
147 K3 **Caton** Lancs
147 L3 **Caton Green** Lancs
13 G7 **Cator Court** Devon
197 G6 **Catrine** E Ayrs
24 C4 **Catsfield** E Susx
24 C4 **Catsfield Stream** E Susx
31 H5 **Catsgore** Somset
31 J4 **Catsham** Somset
98 B8 **Catshill** Worcs
97 G4 **Catstree** Shrops
192 D6 **Cattadale** Ag & B
150 F5 **Cattal** N York
90 C8 **Cattawade** Suffk
147 K7 **Catterall** Lancs
113 J3 **Catteralslane** Shrops
160 C3 **Catterick** N York
160 B3 **Catterick Bridge** N York
160 B3 **Catterick Garrison** N York
166 B4 **Catterlen** Cumb
245 J7 **Catterline** Abers
151 H6 **Catterton** N York
36 E2 **Catteshall** Surrey
100 C7 **Catthorpe** Leics
89 H2 **Cattishall** Suffk
16 B3 **Cattistock** Dorset
179 J7 **Catton** Cumb
160 E7 **Catton** N York
106 E1 **Catton** Norfk
153 J6 **Catwick** E R Yk
86 B1 **Catworth** Cambs
64 D5 **Caudle Green** Gloucs
85 K6 **Caulcott** Beds
66 D2 **Caulcott** Oxon
235 G6 **Cauldcots** Angus
219 L8 **Cauldhame** Stirlg
188 F3 **Cauldmill** Border
115 H2 **Cauldon** Staffs
115 H2 **Cauldon Lowe** Staffs
115 L8 **Cauldwell** Derbys
176 B7 **Caulkerbush** D & G
178 B3 **Caulside** D & G
31 L8 **Caundle Marsh** Dorset
97 J7 **Caunsall** Worcs
134 E7 **Caunton** Notts
35 M6 **Causeway** Hants
157 G5 **Causeway End** Cumb
173 K3 **Causeway End** D & G
71 G3 **Causeway End** Essex
199 H6 **Causewayend** S Lans
176 F8 **Causewayhead** Cumb
220 D8 **Causewayhead** Stirlg
191 H7 **Causey Park** Nthumb
191 H7 **Causey Park Bridge** Nthumb
257 H7 **Causeyend** Abers
88 F6 **Cavendish** Suffk
88 F1 **Cavenham** Suffk
66 E2 **Caversfield** Oxon
49 H4 **Caversham** Readg
114 F3 **Caverswall** Staffs
202 A7 **Caverton Mill** Border
143 J2 **Cavil** E R Yk
252 F2 **Cawdor** Highld
136 E4 **Cawkwell** Lincs
151 J8 **Cawood** N York
6 E5 **Cawsand** Cnwll
122 C6 **Cawston** Norfk
100 A8 **Cawston** Warwks
162 D5 **Cawthorn** N York
141 L6 **Cawthorne** Barns
161 K7 **Cawton** N York
86 F3 **Caxton** Cambs
87 G4 **Caxton End** Cambs
86 F3 **Caxton Gibbet** Cambs
80 D1 **Caynham** Shrops
118 B2 **Caythorpe** Lincs
117 J2 **Caythorpe** Notts
163 J6 **Cayton** N York
283 b8 **Ceann a Bhaigh** W Isls
239 L1 **Ceannacroc Lodge** Highld
282 f4 **Cearsiadar** W Isls
63 G6 **Ceciliford** Mons
44 B1 **Cefn** Newpt
127 K6 **Cefn Berain** Conwy
60 C5 **Cefn Byrle** Powys
112 C6 **Cefn Canel** Powys
111 L6 **Cefn Coch** Powys
42 C5 **Cefn Cribwr** Brdgnd
42 C5 **Cefn Cross** Brdgnd
43 K5 **Cefn Mably** Caerph
111 H2 **Cefn-brith** Conwy

59 K6 **Cefn-bryn-brain** Carmth
60 F5 **Cefn-coed-y-cymmer** Myr Td
111 J4 **Cefn-ddwysarn** Gwynd
95 G6 **Cefn-Einion** Shrops
112 D3 **Cefn-mawr** Wrexhm
129 H8 **Cefn-y-bedd** Wrexhm
75 L7 **Cefn-y-pant** Carmth
59 G6 **Cefneithin** Carmth
78 B6 **Cefngorwydd** Powys
61 G7 **Cefnpennar** Rhondd
125 J4 **Ceint** IOA
77 H5 **Cellan** Cerdgn
223 K6 **Cellardyke** Fife
114 F2 **Cellarhead** Staffs
166 C5 **Celleron** Cumb
43 K3 **Celynen** Caerph
124 F1 **Cemaes** IOA
93 H2 **Cemmaes** Powys
93 H3 **Cemmaes Road** Powys
76 A7 **Cenarth** Cerdgn
74 D6 **Cerbyd** Pembks
223 G5 **Ceres** Fife
16 C2 **Cerne Abbas** Dorset
65 G7 **Cerney Wick** Gloucs
125 G5 **Cerrigceinwen** IOA
111 J2 **Cerrigydrudion** Conwy
123 J7 **Cess** Norfk
125 J7 **Ceunant** Gwynd
64 B1 **Chaceley** Gloucs
4 B6 **Chacewater** Cnwll
84 D8 **Chackmore** Bucks
83 L6 **Chacombe** Nhants
82 B6 **Chadbury** Worcs
140 D6 **Chadderton** Oldham
140 D6 **Chadderton Fold** Oldham
116 C4 **Chaddesden** C Derb
97 K8 **Chaddesley Corbett** Worcs
12 B7 **Chaddlehanger** Devon
48 B3 **Chaddleworth** W Berk
65 M3 **Chadlington** Oxon
83 H4 **Chadshunt** Warwks
117 K6 **Chadwell** Leics
114 B8 **Chadwell** Shrops
86 B2 **Chadwell End** Beds
52 A1 **Chadwell Heath** Gt Lon
52 E3 **Chadwell St Mary** Thurr
81 J2 **Chadwick** Worcs
82 F1 **Chadwick End** Solhll
139 G7 **Chadwick Green** St Hel
15 H1 **Chaffcombe** Somset
52 D3 **Chafford Hundred** Thurr
13 G5 **Chagford** Devon
22 F3 **Chailey** E Susx
103 J3 **Chainbridge** Cambs
39 J4 **Chainhurst** Kent
17 K1 **Chalbury** Dorset
17 K1 **Chalbury Common** Dorset
51 J7 **Chaldon** Surrey
19 H8 **Chale** IOW
19 H7 **Chale Green** IOW
68 C8 **Chalfont Common** Bucks
68 C8 **Chalfont St Giles** Bucks
50 C1 **Chalfont St Peter** Bucks
64 C6 **Chalford** Gloucs
67 H7 **Chalford** Oxon
32 E1 **Chalford** Wilts
68 C2 **Chalgrave** Beds
66 F7 **Chalgrove** Oxon
52 E4 **Chalk** Kent
70 F5 **Chalk End** Essex
49 H3 **Chalkhouse Green** Oxon
15 J1 **Chalkway** Somset
53 J6 **Chalkwell** Kent
7 J6 **Challaborough** Devon
28 B3 **Challacombe** Devon
173 K2 **Challoch** D & G
40 C5 **Challock** Kent
16 B2 **Chalmington** Dorset
68 C2 **Chalton** Beds
86 C5 **Chalton** Beds
20 B4 **Chalton** Hants
50 B3 **Chalvey** Slough
23 H5 **Chalvington** E Susx
40 B6 **Chambers Green** Kent
68 D7 **Chandler's Cross** Herts
34 F7 **Chandler's Ford** Hants
81 H7 **Chandlers Cross** Worcs
86 C4 **Channel's End** Beds
32 B2 **Chantry** Somset
90 D6 **Chantry** Suffk
165 H4 **Chapel** Cumb
222 D8 **Chapel** Fife
150 D8 **Chapel Allerton** Leeds
30 F1 **Chapel Allerton** Somset
10 D7 **Chapel Amble** Cnwll

84 E2 **Chapel Brampton** Nhants
114 C4 **Chapel Chorlton** Staffs
23 K3 **Chapel Cross** E Susx
85 L6 **Chapel End** Beds
86 B4 **Chapel End** Beds
102 C6 **Chapel End** Cambs
99 J5 **Chapel End** Warwks
140 B6 **Chapel Field** Bury
99 H6 **Chapel Green** Warwks
83 L3 **Chapel Green** Warwks
142 F3 **Chapel Haddlesey** N York
257 K4 **Chapel Hill** Abers
119 G1 **Chapel Hill** Lincs
63 G7 **Chapel Hill** Mons
150 D6 **Chapel Hill** N York
95 H8 **Chapel Lawn** Shrops
158 C7 **Chapel le Dale** N York
29 L5 **Chapel Leigh** Somset
131 L3 **Chapel Milton** Derbys
256 C7 **Chapel of Garioch** Abers
172 D6 **Chapel Rossan** D & G
23 L5 **Chapel Row** E Susx
71 J7 **Chapel Row** Essex
48 E5 **Chapel Row** W Berk
137 K5 **Chapel St Leonards** Lincs
156 D2 **Chapel Stile** Cumb
4 E4 **Chapel Town** Cnwll
131 L3 **Chapel-en-le-Frith** Derbys
102 F4 **Chapelbridge** Cambs
88 E7 **Chapelend Way** Essex
119 L6 **Chapelgate** Lincs
209 K6 **Chapelhall** N Lans
187 K2 **Chapelhope** Border
177 K4 **Chapelknowe** D & G
156 B6 **Chapels** Cumb
234 F6 **Chapelton** Angus
27 K5 **Chapelton** Devon
197 K1 **Chapelton** S Lans
139 L4 **Chapeltown** Bl w D
254 E7 **Chapeltown** Moray
142 A8 **Chapeltown** Sheff
11 L4 **Chapmans Well** Devon
32 D1 **Chapmanslade** Wilts
69 J4 **Chapmore End** Herts
72 C2 **Chappel** Essex
6 B1 **Charaton** Cnwll
15 H1 **Chard** Somset
15 H2 **Chard Junction** Somset
30 D8 **Chardleigh Green** Somset
15 G2 **Chardstock** Devon
63 L8 **Charfield** S Glos
64 D3 **Chargrove** Gloucs
40 B5 **Charing** Kent
40 B5 **Charing Heath** Kent
40 B5 **Charing Hill** Kent
82 E7 **Charingworth** Gloucs
65 M3 **Charlbury** Oxon
45 L5 **Charlcombe** BaNES
46 E4 **Charlcutt** Wilts
83 G4 **Charlecote** Warwks
98 C4 **Charlemont** W Mids
28 B4 **Charles** Devon
89 L5 **Charles Tye** Suffk
36 D2 **Charleshill** Surrey
234 B6 **Charleston** Angus
149 L8 **Charlestown** Brad
245 L3 **Charlestown** C Aber
140 E2 **Charlestown** Calder
5 H4 **Charlestown** Cnwll
131 L1 **Charlestown** Derbys
16 C6 **Charlestown** Dorset
210 E2 **Charlestown** Fife
260 C5 **Charlestown** Highld
251 H2 **Charlestown** Highld
140 B7 **Charlestown** Salfd
131 K1 **Charlesworth** Derbys
30 C3 **Charlinch** Somset
222 E5 **Charlottetown** Fife
51 L3 **Charlton** Gt Lon
34 D2 **Charlton** Hants
68 F2 **Charlton** Herts
83 M8 **Charlton** Nhants
179 J2 **Charlton** Nthumb
48 B1 **Charlton** Oxon
30 D5 **Charlton** Somset
31 K2 **Charlton** Somset
45 K8 **Charlton** Somset
50 D5 **Charlton** Surrey
20 E4 **Charlton** W Susx
32 F6 **Charlton** Wilts
46 D1 **Charlton** Wilts
47 G7 **Charlton** Wilts
81 J1 **Charlton** Worcs
82 B6 **Charlton** Worcs
96 D1 **Charlton** Wrekin

64 F2 **Charlton Abbots** Gloucs
31 J5 **Charlton Adam** Somset
96 D2 **Charlton Hill** Shrops
31 L6 **Charlton Horethorne** Somset
64 D3 **Charlton Kings** Gloucs
31 H5 **Charlton Mackrell** Somset
17 H2 **Charlton Marshall** Dorset
32 B5 **Charlton Musgrove** Somset
17 H2 **Charlton on the Hill** Dorset
33 L6 **Charlton-all-Saints** Wilts
66 E4 **Charlton-on-Otmoor** Oxon
35 K4 **Charlwood** Hants
37 K3 **Charlwood** Surrey
16 C4 **Charminster** Dorset
15 H4 **Charmouth** Dorset
67 G2 **Charndon** Bucks
66 A8 **Charney Bassett** Oxon
139 H4 **Charnock Green** Lancs
139 H4 **Charnock Richard** Lancs
90 F4 **Charsfield** Suffk
39 K3 **Chart Corner** Kent
39 K3 **Chart Hill** Kent
39 K3 **Chart Sutton** Kent
48 E7 **Charter Alley** Hants
202 B4 **Charterhall** Border
45 G7 **Charterhouse** Somset
209 L1 **Chartershall** Stirlg
65 L5 **Charterville Allotments** Oxon
40 E4 **Chartham** Kent
40 E4 **Chartham Hatch** Kent
68 B6 **Chartridge** Bucks
39 L3 **Chartway Street** Kent
49 J4 **Charvil** Wokham
83 M4 **Charwelton** Nhants
98 D2 **Chase Terrace** Staffs
98 D2 **Chasetown** Staffs
65 K1 **Chastleton** Oxon
11 L2 **Chasty** Devon
148 D7 **Chatburn** Lancs
114 B4 **Chatcull** Staffs
43 K4 **Chatham** Caerph
53 G5 **Chatham** Medway
71 H4 **Chatham Green** Essex
203 K7 **Chathill** Nthumb
81 J3 **Chatley** Worcs
53 G4 **Chattenden** Medway
70 C2 **Chatter End** Essex
103 H6 **Chatteris** Cambs
140 B4 **Chatterton** Lancs
90 C6 **Chattisham** Suffk
189 K3 **Chatto** Border
203 G7 **Chatton** Nthumb
68 D3 **Chaul End** Beds
28 C8 **Chawleigh** Devon
66 C6 **Chawley** Oxon
86 C4 **Chawston** Beds
35 L3 **Chawton** Hants
63 L4 **Chaxhill** Gloucs
49 G3 **Chazey Heath** Oxon
115 G3 **Cheadle** Staffs
131 G2 **Cheadle** Stockp
131 G2 **Cheadle Heath** Stockp
131 G2 **Cheadle Hulme** Stockp
51 H6 **Cheam** Gt Lon
50 B5 **Cheapside** W & M
67 H5 **Chearsley** Bucks
114 D6 **Chebsey** Staffs
49 G2 **Checkendon** Oxon
114 A2 **Checkley** Ches
115 G4 **Checkley** Staffs
114 A2 **Checkley Green** Ches
88 F4 **Chedburgh** Suffk
44 F8 **Cheddar** Somset
68 A4 **Cheddington** Bucks
114 F1 **Cheddleton** Staffs
114 F1 **Cheddleton Heath** Staffs
30 C5 **Cheddon Fitzpaine** Somset
64 D8 **Chedglow** Wilts
107 H3 **Chedgrave** Norfk
15 L2 **Chedington** Dorset
107 G7 **Chediston** Suffk
107 G7 **Chediston Green** Suffk
64 F5 **Chedworth** Gloucs
30 E3 **Chedzoy** Somset
140 B4 **Cheesden** Rochdl
40 D7 **Cheeseman's Green** Kent
140 C7 **Cheetham Hill** Manch
28 C8 **Cheldon** Devon
130 F5 **Chelford** Ches
116 C5 **Chellaston** C Derb
85 J4 **Chellington** Beds
97 G5 **Chelmarsh** Shrops
95 L5 **Chelmick** Shrops
90 E7 **Chelmondiston** Suffk
132 B5 **Chelmorton** Derbys

71 H5 **Chelmsford** Essex
98 F6 **Chelmsley Wood** Solhll
51 H3 **Chelsea** Gt Lon
52 A6 **Chelsfield** Gt Lon
51 K7 **Chelsham** Surrey
29 L6 **Chelston** Somset
89 K5 **Chelsworth** Suffk
64 D3 **Cheltenham** Gloucs
85 K1 **Chelveston** Nhants
44 F5 **Chelvey** N Som
45 J6 **Chelwood** BaNES
38 B7 **Chelwood Common** E Susx
38 B7 **Chelwood Gate** E Susx
64 E8 **Chelworth** Wilts
65 G8 **Chelworth Lower Green** Wilts
65 G8 **Chelworth Upper Green** Wilts
95 K6 **Cheney Longville** Shrops
68 C7 **Chenies** Bucks
63 G8 **Chepstow** Mons
139 K6 **Chequerbent** Bolton
103 K2 **Chequers Corner** Norfk
46 F5 **Cherhill** Wilts
64 C7 **Cherington** Gloucs
83 G7 **Cherington** Warwks
28 C2 **Cheriton** Devon
35 J5 **Cheriton** Hants
41 G7 **Cheriton** Kent
56 E6 **Cheriton** Swans
13 H4 **Cheriton Bishop** Devon
13 K1 **Cheriton Fitzpaine** Devon
55 G7 **Cheriton or Stackpole Elidor** Pembks
113 L7 **Cherrington** Wrekin
152 F7 **Cherry Burton** E R Yk
87 K4 **Cherry Hinton** Cambs
81 K4 **Cherry Orchard** Worcs
135 L5 **Cherry Willingham** Lincs
50 D5 **Chertsey** Surrey
16 E3 **Cheselbourne** Dorset
68 B6 **Chesham** Bucks
140 B5 **Chesham** Bury
68 B7 **Chesham Bois** Bucks
69 K6 **Cheshunt** Herts
53 J6 **Chesley** Kent
98 B2 **Cheslyn Hay** Staffs
99 G8 **Chessetts Wood** Warwks
50 F6 **Chessington** Surrey
129 J6 **Chester** Ches
169 H1 **Chester Moor** Dur
181 G8 **Chester-le-Street** Dur
31 L3 **Chesterblade** Somset
133 G5 **Chesterfield** Derbys
98 E2 **Chesterfield** Staffs
211 L6 **Chesterhill** Mdloth
189 G2 **Chesters** Border
189 H4 **Chesters** Border
102 C4 **Chesterton** Cambs
87 K3 **Chesterton** Cambs
64 E7 **Chesterton** Gloucs
66 E3 **Chesterton** Oxon
97 H4 **Chesterton** Shrops
114 C2 **Chesterton** Staffs
83 H4 **Chesterton Green** Warwks
179 J6 **Chesterwood** Nthumb
40 F2 **Chestfield** Kent
53 J6 **Chestnut Street** Kent
7 K3 **Cheston** Devon
114 A5 **Cheswardine** Shrops
113 M8 **Cheswell** Wrekin
203 G4 **Cheswick** Nthumb
98 E8 **Cheswick Green** Solhll
16 B1 **Chetnole** Dorset
29 H7 **Chettiscombe** Devon
103 L6 **Chettisham** Cambs
32 F8 **Chettle** Dorset
96 F5 **Chetton** Shrops
66 F1 **Chetwode** Bucks
114 A7 **Chetwynd** Wrekin
114 B8 **Chetwynd Aston** Wrekin
88 D3 **Cheveley** Cambs
52 A7 **Chevening** Kent
19 G6 **Cheverton** IOW
88 F3 **Chevington** Suffk
91 K6 **Chevington Drift** Nthumb
29 H7 **Chevithorne** Devon
45 H6 **Chew Magna** BaNES
39 K6 **Chew Moor** Bolton
45 H5 **Chew Stoke** BaNES
45 K5 **Chewton Keynsham** BaNES
45 H8 **Chewton Mendip** Somset
12 E3 **Chichacott** Devon
35 H6 **Chicheley** M Keyn
20 E6 **Chichester** W Susx
16 C6 **Chickerell** Dorset
106 E8 **Chickering** Suffk

32 F4 **Chicklade** Wilts
79 K4 **Chickward** Herefs
35 K7 **Chidden** Hants
36 E4 **Chiddingfold** Surrey
23 J4 **Chiddingly** E Susx
38 D4 **Chiddingstone** Kent
38 E4 **Chiddingstone Causeway** Kent
15 K4 **Chideock** Dorset
20 C6 **Chidham** W Susx
141 L3 **Chidswell** Kirk
48 C4 **Chieveley** W Berk
71 G5 **Chignall Smealy** Essex
71 G5 **Chignall St James** Essex
70 B8 **Chigwell** Essex
70 C8 **Chigwell Row** Essex
34 E3 **Chilbolton** Hants
35 G5 **Chilcomb** Hants
15 M4 **Chilcombe** Dorset
45 J8 **Chilcompton** Somset
99 H1 **Chilcote** Leics
32 D8 **Child Okeford** Dorset
113 L6 **Child's Ercall** Shrops
129 J4 **Childer Thornton** Ches
48 A2 **Childrey** Oxon
82 C7 **Childswickham** Worcs
129 K2 **Childwall** Lpool
68 F5 **Childwick Bury** Herts
68 F5 **Childwick Green** Herts
16 B3 **Chilfrome** Dorset
20 D4 **Chilgrove** W Susx
40 E4 **Chilham** Kent
33 J4 **Chilhampton** Wilts
12 B2 **Chilla** Devon
12 B6 **Chillaton** Devon
41 J4 **Chillenden** Kent
19 H6 **Chillerton** IOW
91 J5 **Chillesford** Suffk
203 G8 **Chillingham** Nthumb
8 B6 **Chillington** Devon
30 F8 **Chillington** Somset
33 G4 **Chilmark** Wilts
40 C7 **Chilmington Green** Kent
65 L3 **Chilson** Oxon
12 A8 **Chilsworthy** Cnwll
11 L1 **Chilsworthy** Devon
68 E3 **Chiltern Green** Beds
31 H7 **Chilthorne Domer** Somset
67 G5 **Chilton** Bucks
13 K2 **Chilton** Devon
169 H5 **Chilton** Dur
41 J6 **Chilton** Kent
48 C2 **Chilton** Oxon
89 H6 **Chilton** Suffk
35 J3 **Chilton Candover** Hants
31 J6 **Chilton Cantelo** Somset
47 L5 **Chilton Foliat** Wilts
30 E3 **Chilton Polden** Somset
88 E6 **Chilton Street** Suffk
30 D3 **Chilton Trinity** Somset
116 E4 **Chilwell** Notts
34 E7 **Chilworth** Hants
36 F2 **Chilworth** Surrey
65 M7 **Chimney** Oxon
49 G7 **Chineham** Hants
69 K8 **Chingford** Gt Lon
131 L3 **Chinley** Derbys
67 J6 **Chinnor** Oxon
179 K4 **Chipchase Castle** Nthumb
114 A5 **Chipnall** Shrops
88 D1 **Chippenham** Cambs
46 D4 **Chippenham** Wilts
68 D6 **Chipperfield** Herts
69 K1 **Chipping** Herts
147 M7 **Chipping** Lancs
82 E7 **Chipping Campden** Gloucs
71 K4 **Chipping Hill** Essex
65 L2 **Chipping Norton** Oxon
70 E6 **Chipping Ongar** Essex
45 J3 **Chipping Sodbury** S Glos
83 L5 **Chipping Warden** Nhants
29 J5 **Chipstable** Somset
38 D2 **Chipstead** Kent
51 H7 **Chipstead** Surrey
95 G4 **Chirbury** Shrops
112 D4 **Chirk** Wrexhm
202 D2 **Chirnside** Border
202 C2 **Chirnsidebridge** Border
47 G7 **Chirton** Wilts
47 K5 **Chisbury** Wilts
31 G7 **Chiselborough** Somset
47 J3 **Chiseldon** Swindn
66 E7 **Chiselhampton** Oxon
188 D4 **Chisholme** Border
51 L5 **Chislehurst** Gt Lon

41 H2 **Chislet** Kent
140 F2 **Chisley** Calder
68 E6 **Chiswell Green** Herts
51 G3 **Chiswick** Gt Lon
87 H6 **Chiswick End** Cambs
131 K2 **Chisworth** Derbys
24 E3 **Chitcombe** E Susx
36 C6 **Chithurst** W Susx
87 K1 **Chittering** Cambs
33 G2 **Chitterne** Wilts
28 B6 **Chittlehamholt** Devon
27 L5 **Chittlehampton** Devon
28 B8 **Chittlehampton** Devon
46 D5 **Chittoe** Wilts
8 A7 **Chivelstone** Devon
27 J4 **Chivenor** Devon
172 E3 **Chlenry** D & G
50 B6 **Chobham** Surrey
34 B2 **Cholderton** Wilts
68 B5 **Cholesbury** Bucks
179 L5 **Chollerford** Nthumb
179 L4 **Chollerton** Nthumb
130 C7 **Cholmondeston** Ches
48 E2 **Cholsey** Oxon
80 B3 **Cholstrey** Herefs
161 J3 **Chop Gate** N York
181 G2 **Choppington** Nthumb
180 D7 **Chopwell** Gatesd
113 J1 **Chorley** Ches
139 H4 **Chorley** Lancs
96 F6 **Chorley** Shrops
98 D1 **Chorley** Staffs
68 D7 **Chorleywood** Herts
68 C7 **Chorleywood West** Herts
114 A2 **Chorlton** Ches
113 G2 **Chorlton Lane** Ches
130 F1 **Chorlton-cum-Hardy** Manch
95 J3 **Choulton** Shrops
129 L8 **Chowley** Ches
87 J7 **Chrishall** Essex
207 L4 **Chrisswell** Inver
37 H5 **Christ's Hospital** W Susx
103 K4 **Christchurch** Cambs
18 B5 **Christchurch** Dorset
63 H4 **Christchurch** Gloucs
44 D1 **Christchurch** Mons
46 D3 **Christian Malford** Wilts
129 K6 **Christleton** Ches
67 H8 **Christmas Common** Oxon
44 D7 **Christon** N Som
191 J2 **Christon Bank** Nthumb
13 J5 **Christow** Devon
38 D6 **Chuck Hatch** E Susx
13 K6 **Chudleigh** Devon
13 K7 **Chudleigh Knighton** Devon
28 B8 **Chulmleigh** Devon
131 L2 **Chunal** Derbys
139 L2 **Church** Lancs
114 A8 **Church Aston** Wrekin
84 D2 **Church Brampton** Nhants
167 J7 **Church Brough** Cumb
115 K5 **Church Broughton** Derbys
3 H8 **Church Cove** Cnwll
49 K8 **Church Crookham** Hants
114 C8 **Church Eaton** Staffs
85 J8 **Church End** Beds
68 C3 **Church End** Beds
85 K8 **Church End** Beds
85 L3 **Church End** Beds
86 C3 **Church End** Beds
86 D7 **Church End** Beds
102 B8 **Church End** Cambs
102 E6 **Church End** Cambs
103 G7 **Church End** Cambs
87 K4 **Church End** Cambs
70 F3 **Church End** Essex
71 H2 **Church End** Essex
71 H4 **Church End** Essex
51 H1 **Church End** Gt Lon
49 G7 **Church End** Hants
68 E5 **Church End** Herts
69 H1 **Church End** Herts
70 C3 **Church End** Herts
119 H5 **Church End** Lincs
145 L8 **Church End** Lincs
99 H5 **Church End** Warwks
99 H5 **Church End** Warwks
66 A2 **Church Enstone** Oxon
151 H6 **Church Fenton** N York
14 E3 **Church Green** Devon
115 M7 **Church Gresley** Derbys
66 B4 **Church Hanborough** Oxon
130 C6 **Church Hill** Ches
98 C1 **Church Hill** Staffs
161 L3 **Church Houses** N York

17 H6 **Church Knowle** Dorset
135 G4 **Church Laneham** Notts
100 F5 **Church Langton** Leics
99 M8 **Church Lawford** Warwks
130 F8 **Church Lawton** Ches
115 G4 **Church Leigh** Staffs
82 B5 **Church Lench** Worcs
115 J3 **Church Mayfield** Staffs
130 C7 **Church Minshull** Ches
20 E7 **Church Norton** W Susx
96 C4 **Church Preen** Shrops
95 K3 **Church Pulverbatch** Shrops
84 C4 **Church Stowe** Nhants
88 F6 **Church Street** Essex
52 F4 **Church Street** Kent
107 K6 **Church Street** Suffk
95 L4 **Church Stretton** Shrops
143 K6 **Church Town** N Linc
43 G4 **Church Village** Rhondd
133 L6 **Church Warsop** Notts
116 D5 **Church Wilne** Derbys
63 M3 **Churcham** Gloucs
98 C2 **Churchbridge** Staffs
64 C3 **Churchdown** Gloucs
72 E8 **Churchend** Essex
98 C5 **Churchfield** Birm
69 K6 **Churchgate** Herts
70 C5 **Churchgate Street** Essex
27 L3 **Churchill** Devon
15 G2 **Churchill** Devon
44 E7 **Churchill** N Som
65 L2 **Churchill** Oxon
97 K7 **Churchill** Worcs
81 L4 **Churchill** Worcs
30 B8 **Churchinford** Somset
100 B7 **Churchover** Warwks
30 B7 **Churchstanton** Somset
95 G4 **Churchstoke** Powys
7 K5 **Churchstow** Devon
145 J8 **Churchthorpe** Lincs
146 F7 **Churchtown** Bpool
10 F7 **Churchtown** Cnwll
132 E7 **Churchtown** Derbys
28 B2 **Churchtown** Devon
147 J7 **Churchtown** Lancs
138 D4 **Churchtown** Sefton
178 F3 **Churnsike Lodge** Nthumb
8 D4 **Churston Ferrers** Torbay
36 C3 **Churt** Surrey
129 K8 **Churton** Ches
141 L2 **Churwell** Leeds
109 H4 **Chwilog** Gwynd
2 D5 **Chyandour** Cnwll
3 G6 **Chyanvounder** Cnwll
3 K3 **Chyeowling** Cnwll
3 G6 **Chyvarloe** Cnwll
94 E3 **Cil** Powys
128 E6 **Cilcain** Flints
76 F3 **Cilcennin** Cerdgn
94 F3 **Cilcewydd** Powys
57 L5 **Cilfrew** Neath
43 H3 **Cilfynydd** Rhondd
75 L4 **Cilgerran** Pembks
59 K3 **Cilgwyn** Carmth
109 J1 **Cilgwyn** Gwynd
76 F4 **Ciliau-Aeron** Cerdgn
57 K4 **Cilmaengwyn** Neath
78 D5 **Cilmery** Powys
58 A2 **Cilrhedyn** Pembks
59 H4 **Cilsan** Carmth
111 G3 **Ciltalgarth** Gwynd
57 K4 **Cilybebyll** Neath
77 L7 **Cilycwm** Carmth
57 L5 **Cimla** Neath
97 L4 **Cinder Hill** Wolves
63 K4 **Cinderford** Gloucs
50 B3 **Cippenham** Slough
64 F6 **Cirencester** Gloucs
160 B3 **Citadilla** N York
51 J3 **City** Gt Lon
42 F6 **City** V Glam
125 H2 **City Dulas** IOA
224 F3 **Clabhach** Ag & B
207 J3 **Clachaig** Ag & B
216 B3 **Clachan** Ag & B
228 D6 **Clachan** Ag & B
206 B7 **Clachan** Ag & B
247 H1 **Clachan** Highld
224 C5 **Clachan Mor** Ag & B
283 c8 **Clachan na Luib** W Isls
209 G3 **Clachan of Campsie** E Duns
283 c8 **Clachan-a-Luib** W Isls
216 B3 **Clachan-Seil** Ag & B
183 J7 **Clachaneasy** D & G
251 H2 **Clachnaharry** Highld

270 D3 **Clachtoll** Highld
233 H3 **Clackavoid** P & K
210 B1 **Clackmannan** Clacks
266 E4 **Clackmarras** Moray
73 J4 **Clacton-on-Sea** Essex
217 H3 **Cladich** Ag & B
82 C3 **Cladswell** Worcs
227 K3 **Claggan** Highld
258 C6 **Claigan** Highld
45 K7 **Clandown** BaNES
35 L7 **Clanfield** Hants
65 L6 **Clanfield** Oxon
13 H2 **Clannaborough** Devon
34 D1 **Clanville** Hants
31 K4 **Clanville** Somset
206 D7 **Claonaig** Ag & B
40 D7 **Clap Hill** Kent
17 K2 **Clapgate** Dorset
70 C2 **Clapgate** Herts
85 K5 **Clapham** Beds
13 L5 **Clapham** Devon
51 H4 **Clapham** Gt Lon
148 C2 **Clapham** N York
21 J5 **Clapham** W Susx
85 K5 **Clapham Folly** Beds
156 E2 **Clappersgate** Cumb
15 J1 **Clapton** Somset
45 J8 **Clapton** Somset
44 F4 **Clapton-in-Gordano** N Som
65 H3 **Clapton-on-the-Hill** Gloucs
28 B6 **Clapworthy** Devon
92 D6 **Clarach** Cerdgn
180 E6 **Claravale** Gatesd
55 H3 **Clarbeston** Pembks
55 G3 **Clarbeston Road** Pembks
134 E3 **Clarborough** Notts
88 F6 **Clare** Suffk
175 J2 **Clarebrand** D & G
176 E5 **Clarencefield** D & G
150 E4 **Clareton** N York
180 B5 **Clarewood** Nthumb
188 F3 **Clarilaw** Border
37 J3 **Clark's Green** Surrey
35 H1 **Clarken Green** Hants
208 F7 **Clarkston** E Rens
270 D2 **Clashmore** Highld
263 K2 **Clashmore** Highld
270 E2 **Clashnessie** Highld
254 E7 **Clashnoir** Moray
221 H3 **Clathy** P & K
221 H3 **Clathymore** P & K
255 L6 **Clatt** Abers
94 B4 **Clatter** Powys
70 F4 **Clatterford End** Essex
29 J4 **Clatworthy** Somset
147 K7 **Claughton** Lancs
147 L3 **Claughton** Lancs
129 G2 **Claughton** Wirral
30 C4 **Clavelshay** Somset
82 E2 **Claverdon** Warwks
44 F5 **Claverham** N Som
70 C1 **Clavering** Essex
97 H5 **Claverley** Shrops
46 A6 **Claverton** BaNES
45 M6 **Claverton Down** BaNES
43 G6 **Clawdd-coch** V Glam
111 L1 **Clawdd-newydd** Denbgs
157 H7 **Clawthorpe** Cumb
11 L3 **Clawton** Devon
136 B1 **Claxby** Lincs
137 H5 **Claxby** Lincs
151 L4 **Claxton** N York
107 G3 **Claxton** Norfk
107 K7 **Clay Common** Suffk
100 D8 **Clay Coton** Nhants
133 H7 **Clay Cross** Derbys
69 J2 **Clay End** Herts
100 B5 **Claybrooke Magna** Leics
83 K5 **Claydon** Oxon
90 D5 **Claydon** Suffk
177 L3 **Claygate** D & G
39 H4 **Claygate** Kent
50 F6 **Claygate** Surrey
38 F2 **Claygate Cross** Kent
51 L1 **Clayhall** Gt Lon
29 J6 **Clayhanger** Devon
98 D3 **Clayhanger** Wsall
29 L7 **Clayhidon** Devon
24 F3 **Clayhill** E Susx
18 D2 **Clayhill** Hants
87 K2 **Clayhithe** Cambs
279 L4 **Clayock** Highld
87 G4 **Claypit Hill** Cambs
63 M6 **Claypits** Gloucs
117 M2 **Claypole** Lincs

137 H4 **Claythorpe** Lincs
141 H2 **Clayton** Brad
142 C6 **Clayton** Donc
22 D3 **Clayton** W Susx
139 H3 **Clayton Green** Lancs
141 L5 **Clayton West** Kirk
139 M2 **Clayton-le-Moors** Lancs
139 H3 **Clayton-le-Woods** Lancs
134 E2 **Clayworth** Notts
236 F3 **Cleadale** Highld
181 J6 **Cleadon** S Tyne
7 G2 **Clearbrook** Devon
63 H5 **Clearwell** Gloucs
63 H5 **Clearwell Meend** Gloucs
169 H8 **Cleasby** N York
275 c6 **Cleat** Ork
168 E7 **Cleatlam** Dur
164 D7 **Cleator** Cumb
164 D7 **Cleator Moor** Cumb
141 J3 **Cleckheaton** Kirk
96 D6 **Clee St Margaret** Shrops
96 D7 **Cleedownton** Shrops
96 D8 **Cleehill** Shrops
209 K7 **Cleekhimin** N Lans
96 D7 **Cleestanton** Shrops
145 J6 **Cleethorpes** NE Lin
96 F7 **Cleeton St Mary** Shrops
44 F5 **Cleeve** N Som
48 F3 **Cleeve** Oxon
64 E2 **Cleeve Hill** Gloucs
82 C5 **Cleeve Prior** Worcs
212 D2 **Cleghornie** E Loth
80 B7 **Clehonger** Herefs
221 K7 **Cleish** P & K
209 L7 **Cleland** N Lans
52 B5 **Clement Street** Kent
68 C4 **Clement's End** Beds
216 E2 **Clenamacrie** Ag & B
47 H6 **Clench Common** Wilts
120 D7 **Clenchwarton** Norfk
268 D4 **Clenerty** Abers
97 L7 **Clent** Worcs
96 F8 **Cleobury Mortimer** Shrops
96 E6 **Cleobury North** Shrops
192 D2 **Cleongart** Ag & B
252 F2 **Clephanton** Highld
187 L6 **Clerkhill** D & G
185 K3 **Cleuch-head** D & G
46 F4 **Clevancy** Wilts
44 E5 **Clevedon** N Som
66 B2 **Cleveley** Oxon
146 F7 **Cleveleys** Lancs
81 J6 **Clevelode** Worcs
46 E2 **Cleverton** Wilts
31 G1 **Clewer** Somset
122 A3 **Cley next the Sea** Norfk
166 E5 **Cliburn** Cumb
35 K1 **Cliddesden** Hants
99 G4 **Cliff** Warwks
25 G4 **Cliff End** E Susx
139 L1 **Cliffe** Lancs
52 F4 **Cliffe** Medway
169 G7 **Cliffe** N York
143 G2 **Cliffe** N York
52 F4 **Cliffe Woods** Medway
79 J6 **Clifford** Herefs
150 F7 **Clifford** Leeds
82 E5 **Clifford Chambers** Warwks
63 K2 **Clifford's Mesne** Gloucs
41 K2 **Cliffsend** Kent
86 D7 **Clifton** Beds
45 H4 **Clifton** Bristl
116 F4 **Clifton** C Nott
141 J3 **Clifton** Calder
166 C5 **Clifton** Cumb
115 K3 **Clifton** Derbys
142 E8 **Clifton** Donc
138 F2 **Clifton** Lancs
150 B6 **Clifton** N York
180 F2 **Clifton** Nthumb
66 C1 **Clifton** Oxon
140 A7 **Clifton** Salfd
81 J6 **Clifton** Worcs
151 J5 **Clifton** York
99 H1 **Clifton Campville** Staffs
166 D5 **Clifton Dykes** Cumb
66 D7 **Clifton Hampden** Oxon
85 H5 **Clifton Reynes** M Keyn
100 C8 **Clifton upon Dunsmore** Warwks
81 G3 **Clifton upon Teme** Worcs
41 L1 **Cliftonville** Kent
21 G6 **Climping** W Susx
32 C1 **Clink** Somset
150 C4 **Clint** N York

105 L1 **Clint Green** Norfk
245 J1 **Clinterty** C Aber
201 J6 **Clintmains** Border
93 H1 **Clipiau** Gwynd
123 J8 **Clippesby** Norfk
118 C8 **Clipsham** Rutlnd
100 F7 **Clipston** Nhants
117 H5 **Clipston** Notts
68 B2 **Clipstone** Beds
134 B7 **Clipstone** Notts
148 C7 **Clitheroe** Lancs
113 H6 **Clive** Shrops
144 E7 **Clixby** Lincs
46 E1 **Cloatley** Wilts
111 L1 **Clocaenog** Denbgs
267 H4 **Clochan** Moray
234 D5 **Clochtow** Angus
129 M2 **Clock Face** St Hel
94 F2 **Cloddiau** Powys
62 C2 **Clodock** Herefs
32 B2 **Cloford** Somset
257 J3 **Clola** Abers
86 B7 **Clophill** Beds
102 B7 **Clopton** Nhants
90 F4 **Clopton** Suffk
90 F4 **Clopton Corner** Suffk
88 F4 **Clopton Green** Suffk
89 K3 **Clopton Green** Suffk
9 k1 **Clos du Valle** Guern
186 D7 **Closeburn** D & G
186 D7 **Closeburnmill** D & G
154 c7 **Closeclark** IOM
16 A1 **Closworth** Somset
69 H1 **Clothall** Herts
129 M6 **Clotton** Ches
100 A6 **Cloudesley Bush** Warwks
140 E6 **Clough** Oldham
140 D3 **Clough Foot** Calder
141 H4 **Clough Head** Calder
163 H4 **Cloughton** N York
163 H3 **Cloughton Newlands** N York
281 d5 **Clousta** Shet
233 M1 **Clova** Angus
26 E6 **Clovelly** Devon
200 F6 **Clovenfords** Border
228 F3 **Clovulin** Highld
140 B2 **Clow Bridge** Lancs
133 K4 **Clowne** Derbys
81 G1 **Clows Top** Worcs
112 F3 **Cloy** Wrexhm
239 H1 **Cluanie Inn** Highld
239 H2 **Cluanie Lodge** Highld
11 K4 **Clubworthy** Cnwll
173 J3 **Clugston** D & G
95 H7 **Clun** Shrops
253 G2 **Clunas** Highld
95 J7 **Clunbury** Shrops
252 E6 **Clune** Highld
239 K6 **Clunes** Highld
95 K7 **Clungunford** Shrops
268 B6 **Clunie** Abers
233 H6 **Clunie** P & K
95 H7 **Clunton** Shrops
222 D8 **Cluny** Fife
45 J7 **Clutton** BaNES
113 G1 **Clutton** Ches
45 J7 **Clutton Hill** BaNES
125 K7 **Clwt-y-bont** Gwynd
61 K4 **Clydach** Mons
57 J4 **Clydach** Swans
42 E3 **Clydach Vale** Rhondd
208 E5 **Clydebank** W Duns
75 M5 **Clydey** Pembks
47 G3 **Clyffe Pypard** Wilts
207 L2 **Clynder** Ag & B
55 J3 **Clynderwen** Carmth
60 B7 **Clyne** Neath
109 G2 **Clynnog-fawr** Gwynd
79 H6 **Clyro** Powys
14 A4 **Clyst Honiton** Devon
14 B2 **Clyst Hydon** Devon
14 A5 **Clyst St George** Devon
14 B3 **Clyst St Lawrence** Devon
14 A4 **Clyst St Mary** Devon
282 g3 **Cnoc** W Isls
92 E8 **Cnwch Coch** Cerdgn
11 K7 **Coad's Green** Cnwll
133 G4 **Coal Aston** Derbys
98 C3 **Coal Pool** Wsall
90 F1 **Coal Street** Suffk
96 F3 **Coalbrookdale** Wrekin
61 K5 **Coalbrookvale** Blae G
198 D6 **Coalburn** S Lans
180 D6 **Coalburns** Gatesd
167 J2 **Coalcleugh** Nthumb

63 M6 **Coaley** Gloucs
178 E7 **Coalfell** Cumb
71 J7 **Coalhill** Essex
96 F2 **Coalmoor** Wrekin
45 K3 **Coalpit Heath** S Glos
114 C1 **Coalport** Wrekin
96 F3 **Coalpit Hill** Staffs
221 G8 **Coalsnaughton** Clacks
222 E7 **Coaltown of Balgonie** Fife
222 E8 **Coaltown of Wemyss** Fife
116 D8 **Coalville** Leics
178 F7 **Coanwood** Nthumb
31 G6 **Coat** Somset
209 J6 **Coatbridge** N Lans
209 K6 **Coatdyke** N Lans
47 J2 **Coate** Swindn
46 F6 **Coate** Wilts
102 F4 **Coates** Cambs
64 E7 **Coates** Gloucs
135 G3 **Coates** Lincs
135 H3 **Coates** Lincs
21 G3 **Coates** W Susx
170 E5 **Coatham** R & Cl
169 H6 **Coatham Mundeville** Darltn
27 L5 **Cobbaton** Devon
64 D4 **Coberley** Gloucs
80 B8 **Cobhall Common** Herefs
52 E5 **Cobham** Kent
50 E7 **Cobham** Surrey
71 G3 **Coblers Green** Essex
33 H6 **Cobley** Dorset
80 B3 **Cobnash** Herefs
9 j2 **Cobo** Guern
114 D2 **Cobridge** C Stke
269 G3 **Coburby** Abers
88 E4 **Cock & End** Suffk
133 H5 **Cock Alley** Derbys
112 E2 **Cock Bank** Wrexhm
82 C5 **Cock Bevington** Warwks
243 J2 **Cock Bridge** Abers
71 K6 **Cock Clarks** Essex
71 G3 **Cock Green** Essex
24 F3 **Cock Marling** E Susx
39 K3 **Cock Street** Kent
161 K3 **Cockayne** N York
86 F5 **Cockayne Hatley** Beds
213 G5 **Cockburnspath** Border
211 L4 **Cockenzie and Port Seton** E Loth
139 G3 **Cocker Bar** Lancs
139 L3 **Cocker Brook** Lancs
147 J5 **Cockerham** Lancs
164 F4 **Cockermouth** Cumb
68 E2 **Cockernhoe Green** Herts
141 K2 **Cockersdale** Leeds
57 H6 **Cockett** Swans
168 E5 **Cockfield** Dur
89 H4 **Cockfield** Suffk
69 H7 **Cockfosters** Gt Lon
20 E3 **Cocking** W Susx
20 E3 **Cocking Causeway** W Susx
8 D2 **Cockington** Torbay
31 G1 **Cocklake** Somset
191 J7 **Cockle Park** Nthumb
156 C2 **Cockley Beck** Cumb
104 F3 **Cockley Cley** Norfk
49 J3 **Cockpole Green** Wokham
4 C4 **Cocks** Cnwll
96 D6 **Cockshutford** Shrops
113 G5 **Cockshutt** Shrops
121 L3 **Cockthorpe** Norfk
2 E4 **Cockwells** Cnwll
14 A6 **Cockwood** Devon
30 B2 **Cockwood** Somset
131 L4 **Cockyard** Derbys
80 A8 **Cockyard** Herefs
90 D4 **Coddenham** Suffk
129 K8 **Coddington** Ches
81 G6 **Coddington** Herefs
117 L1 **Coddington** Notts
33 G3 **Codford St Mary** Wilts
33 G3 **Codford St Peter** Wilts
69 G3 **Codicote** Herts
21 H3 **Codmore Hill** W Susx
116 C2 **Codnor** Derbys
45 L3 **Codrington** S Glos
97 K3 **Codsall** Staffs
97 J2 **Codsall Wood** Staffs
62 D5 **Coed Morgan** Mons
129 G7 **Coed Talon** Flints
109 K6 **Coed Ystumgwern** Gwynd
76 C6 **Coed-y-Bryn** Cerdgn
44 D1 **Coed-y-caerau** Newpt
62 C7 **Coed-y-paen** Mons
61 J3 **Coed-yr-ynys** Powys

Coedana - Copsale 303

125 H3 **Coedana** IOA
42 F4 **Coedely** Rhondd
44 B2 **Coedkernew** Newpt
112 D1 **Coedpoeth** Wrexhm
112 E8 **Coedway** Powys
60 C5 **Coelbren** Powys
8 D1 **Coffinswell** Devon
85 K3 **Coffle End** Beds
13 M6 **Cofton** Devon
98 C8 **Cofton Hackett** Worcs
43 J7 **Cogan** V Glam
84 F3 **Cogenhoe** Nhants
65 M5 **Cogges** Oxon
71 K3 **Coggeshall** Essex
23 K2 **Coggin's Mill** E Susx
251 J8 **Coignafearn** Highld
243 K4 **Coilacriech** Abers
219 K5 **Coilantogle** Stirlg
246 E1 **Coillore** Highld
240 B2 **Coiltry** Highld
42 D5 **Coity** Brdgnd
282 g3 **Col** W Isls
272 E6 **Colaboll** Highld
4 E3 **Colan** Cnwll
14 C5 **Colaton Raleigh** Devon
258 C7 **Colbost** Highld
160 B3 **Colburn** N York
18 E2 **Colbury** Hants
166 F6 **Colby** Cumb
154 b7 **Colby** IOM
122 E5 **Colby** Norfk
72 E2 **Colchester** Essex
48 D5 **Cold Ash** W Berk
100 E8 **Cold Ashby** Nhants
45 L4 **Cold Ashton** S Glos
65 H3 **Cold Aston** Gloucs
55 J4 **Cold Blow** Pembks
85 H5 **Cold Brayfield** M Keyn
148 C2 **Cold Cotes** N York
80 F6 **Cold Green** Herefs
135 L3 **Cold Hanworth** Lincs
68 F4 **Cold Harbour** Herts
48 F3 **Cold Harbour** Oxon
32 E2 **Cold Harbour** Wilts
113 K7 **Cold Hatton** Wrekin
113 K7 **Cold Hatton Heath** Wrekin
169 L2 **Cold Hesledon** Dur
142 B5 **Cold Hiendley** Wakefd
84 C4 **Cold Higham** Nhants
161 H6 **Cold Kirby** N York
100 F2 **Cold Newton** Leics
11 H5 **Cold Northcott** Cnwll
71 K7 **Cold Norton** Essex
101 H2 **Cold Overton** Leics
96 C6 **Cold Weston** Shrops
277 K4 **Coldbackie** Highld
158 C2 **Coldbeck** Cumb
22 E5 **Coldean** Br & H
13 J7 **Coldeast** Devon
140 E2 **Colden** Calder
35 G6 **Colden Common** Hants
91 K3 **Coldfair Green** Suffk
103 J3 **Coldham** Cambs
4 B5 **Coldharbour** Cnwll
29 J8 **Coldharbour** Devon
63 H6 **Coldharbour** Gloucs
37 H2 **Coldharbour** Surrey
213 K6 **Coldingham** Border
114 D5 **Coldmeece** Staffs
41 J6 **Coldred** Kent
13 G1 **Coldridge** Devon
202 C5 **Coldstream** Border
21 H3 **Coldwaltham** W Susx
80 A8 **Coldwell** Herefs
257 H4 **Coldwells** Abers
31 L4 **Cole** Somset
99 G5 **Cole End** Warwks
69 H5 **Cole Green** Herts
70 B1 **Cole Green** Herts
34 F1 **Cole Henley** Hants
8 A5 **Cole's Cross** Devon
95 H6 **Colebatch** Shrops
7 G3 **Colebrook** C Plym
14 B1 **Colebrook** Devon
13 H3 **Colebrooke** Devon
35 K7 **Coleby** Lincs
43 M4 **Coleby** N Linc
13 H2 **Coleford** Devon
63 H5 **Coleford** Gloucs
31 L1 **Coleford** Somset
29 L4 **Coleford Water** Somset
106 D6 **Colegate End** Norfk
17 K2 **Colehill** Dorset
69 G4 **Coleman Green** Herts
38 C6 **Coleman's Hatch** E Susx
113 G5 **Colemere** Shrops
35 L5 **Colemore** Hants
97 G4 **Colemore Green** Shrops
221 K1 **Colenden** P & K
116 C8 **Coleorton** Leics
46 B5 **Colerne** Wilts
15 J2 **Coles Cross** Dorset
90 C7 **Coles Green** Suffk
64 E4 **Colesbourne** Gloucs
86 C4 **Colesden** Beds
68 B8 **Coleshill** Bucks
65 K8 **Coleshill** Oxon
99 G5 **Coleshill** Warwks
14 C2 **Colestocks** Devon
45 H7 **Coley** BaNES
37 K4 **Colgate** W Susx
223 H6 **Colinsburgh** Fife
211 H5 **Colinton** C Edin
207 G4 **Colintraive** Ag & B
121 K6 **Colkirk** Norfk
222 C1 **Collace** P & K
281 d3 **Collafirth** Shet
7 L7 **Collaton** Devon
8 B4 **Collaton** Devon
8 C3 **Collaton St Mary** Torbay
31 J4 **College Green** Somset
266 C3 **College of Roseisle** Moray
49 K6 **College Town** Br For
222 D4 **Collessie** Fife
28 B7 **Colleton Mills** Devon
52 B1 **Collier Row** Gt Lon
39 H4 **Collier Street** Kent
69 K3 **Collier's End** Herts
24 E3 **Collier's Green** Kent
39 J5 **Colliers Green** Kent
169 J1 **Colliery Row** Sundld
257 J6 **Collieston** Abers
176 D4 **Collin** D & G
47 K8 **Collingbourne Ducis** Wilts
47 K7 **Collingbourne Kingston** Wilts
150 E6 **Collingham** Leeds
135 G7 **Collingham** Notts
80 F3 **Collington** Herefs
84 E4 **Collingtree** Nhants
130 A1 **Collins Green** Warrtn
81 G4 **Collins Green** Worcs
234 F6 **Colliston** Angus
14 C2 **Colliton** Devon
101 M3 **Collyweston** Nhants
182 E5 **Colmonell** S Ayrs
86 C4 **Colmworth** Beds
65 G5 **Coln Rogers** Gloucs
65 H5 **Coln St Aldwyns** Gloucs
65 G5 **Coln St Dennis** Gloucs
50 C3 **Colnbrook** Slough
103 H8 **Colne** Cambs
148 F7 **Colne** Lancs
141 J4 **Colne Bridge** Kirk
148 F7 **Colne Edge** Lancs
71 K1 **Colne Engaine** Essex
106 D2 **Colney** Norfk
69 G6 **Colney Heath** Herts
68 F6 **Colney Street** Herts
256 B5 **Colpy** Abers
200 D5 **Colquhar** Border
10 E8 **Colquite** Cnwll
26 F7 **Colscott** Devon
159 L6 **Colsterdale** N York
118 B6 **Colsterworth** Lincs
117 J5 **Colston Bassett** Notts
49 H8 **Colt Hill** Hants
39 G4 **Colt's Hill** Kent
266 C3 **Coltfield** Moray
122 F7 **Coltishall** Norfk
156 D5 **Colton** Cumb
142 B1 **Colton** Leeds
151 H6 **Colton** N York
106 C2 **Colton** Norfk
115 G7 **Colton** Staffs
13 M3 **Columbjohn** Devon
79 H4 **Colva** Powys
175 L4 **Colvend** D & G
81 H6 **Colwall** Herefs
179 M4 **Colwell** Nthumb
115 G7 **Colwich** Staffs
117 G3 **Colwick** Notts
42 E6 **Colwinston** V Glam
20 F6 **Colworth** W Susx
127 G4 **Colwyn Bay** Conwy
14 F4 **Colyford** Devon
14 F4 **Colyton** Devon
7 L7 **Combe** Devon
8 C5 **Combe** Devon
79 L3 **Combe** Herefs
66 B4 **Combe** Oxon
48 A6 **Combe** W Berk
17 J3 **Combe Almer** Dorset
36 E4 **Combe Common** Surrey
45 M6 **Combe Down** BaNES
8 C2 **Combe Fishacre** Devon
29 L4 **Combe Florey** Somset
45 L7 **Combe Hay** BaNES
27 K2 **Combe Martin** Devon
14 E2 **Combe Raleigh** Devon
30 D8 **Combe St Nicholas** Somset
13 L8 **Combeinteignhead** Devon
130 C4 **Comberbach** Ches
99 G2 **Comberford** Staffs
87 H4 **Comberton** Cambs
80 C2 **Comberton** Herefs
15 G4 **Combpyne** Devon
115 H4 **Combridge** Staffs
83 H5 **Combrook** Warwks
131 L4 **Combs** Derbys
90 B4 **Combs** Suffk
90 B4 **Combs Ford** Suffk
30 C2 **Combwich** Somset
244 F2 **Comers** Abers
81 J2 **Comhampton** Worcs
55 K3 **Commercial** Pembks
87 L3 **Commercial End** Cambs
93 H3 **Commins Coch** Powys
138 C1 **Common Edge** Bpool
164 D6 **Common End** Cumb
6 A1 **Common Moor** Cnwll
47 G2 **Common Platt** Wilts
133 G4 **Common Side** Derbys
170 F8 **Commondale** N York
130 A5 **Commonside** Ches
115 L3 **Commonside** Derbys
113 H6 **Commonwood** Shrops
112 F1 **Commonwood** Wrexhm
30 D4 **Compass** Somset
131 J2 **Compstall** Stockp
175 G4 **Compstonend** D & G
8 C2 **Compton** Devon
34 D5 **Compton** Hants
34 F5 **Compton** Hants
97 J6 **Compton** Staffs
36 E2 **Compton** Surrey
48 D3 **Compton** W Berk
20 C4 **Compton** W Susx
47 H8 **Compton** Wilts
32 E7 **Compton Abbas** Dorset
64 F4 **Compton Abdale** Gloucs
46 F4 **Compton Bassett** Wilts
47 K2 **Compton Beauchamp** Oxon
44 E7 **Compton Bishop** Somset
33 H5 **Compton Chamberlayne** Wilts
45 J6 **Compton Dando** BaNES
31 H4 **Compton Dundon** Somset
30 F7 **Compton Durville** Somset
45 H3 **Compton Greenfield** S Glos
45 G7 **Compton Martin** BaNES
31 L5 **Compton Pauncefoot** Somset
16 B4 **Compton Valence** Dorset
83 H5 **Compton Verney** Warwks
210 D1 **Comrie** Fife
220 D3 **Comrie** P & K
229 G2 **Conaglen House** Highld
248 E6 **Conchra** Highld
233 G6 **Concraigie** P & K
147 J4 **Conder Green** Lancs
81 M7 **Conderton** Worcs
65 H2 **Condicote** Gloucs
209 K4 **Condorrat** N Lans
96 B2 **Condover** Shrops
64 B3 **Coney Hill** Gloucs
105 J7 **Coney Weston** Suffk
37 H6 **Coneyhurst Common** W Susx
151 M2 **Coneysthorpe** N York
150 E4 **Coneythorpe** N York
36 B4 **Conford** Hants
11 K6 **Congdon's Shop** Cnwll
99 K2 **Congerstone** Leics
120 F6 **Congham** Norfk
24 D2 **Conghurst** Kent
110 D3 **Congl-y-wal** Gwynd
131 G7 **Congleton** Ches
44 E6 **Congresbury** N Som
97 K1 **Congreve** Staffs
176 C5 **Conheath** D & G
253 J1 **Conicavel** Moray
136 D8 **Coningsby** Lincs
102 D6 **Conington** Cambs
87 G2 **Conington** Cambs
142 D8 **Conisbrough** Donc
145 L8 **Conisholme** Lincs
156 D3 **Coniston** Cumb
144 F1 **Coniston** E R Yk
148 F5 **Coniston Cold** N York
149 H2 **Conistone** N York
129 G6 **Connah's Quay** Flints
228 E8 **Connel** Ag & B
197 H8 **Connel Park** E Ayrs
2 F3 **Connor Downs** Cnwll
250 F1 **Conon Bridge** Highld
149 H6 **Cononley** N York
114 F2 **Consall** Staffs
180 D8 **Consett** Dur
159 L4 **Constable Burton** N York
140 B3 **Constable Lee** Lancs
3 J5 **Constantine** Cnwll
10 B7 **Constantine Bay** Cnwll
262 D8 **Contin** Highld
126 F4 **Conwy** Conwy
40 C2 **Conyer** Kent
89 H2 **Conyer's Green** Suffk
24 C6 **Cooden** E Susx
73 J3 **Cook's Green** Essex
12 A1 **Cookbury** Devon
11 M2 **Cookbury Wick** Devon
49 L2 **Cookham** W & M
49 L2 **Cookham Dean** W & M
49 L2 **Cookham Rise** W & M
82 C3 **Cookhill** Warwks
107 G8 **Cookley** Suffk
97 J7 **Cookley** Worcs
49 G1 **Cookley Green** Oxon
245 J5 **Cookney** Abers
89 K4 **Cooks Green** Suffk
22 F4 **Cooksbridge** E Susx
81 L1 **Cooksey Green** Worcs
114 E3 **Cookshill** Staffs
5 J1 **Cooksland** Cnwll
70 F6 **Cooksmill Green** Essex
130 B5 **Cookson Green** Ches
169 H4 **Cookson's Green** Dur
37 H6 **Coolham** W Susx
53 G4 **Cooling** Medway
52 F4 **Cooling Street** Medway
3 G3 **Coombe** Cnwll
3 L3 **Coombe** Cnwll
13 J5 **Coombe** Devon
13 L7 **Coombe** Devon
14 C4 **Coombe** Devon
63 M8 **Coombe** Gloucs
35 K6 **Coombe** Hants
33 K1 **Coombe** Wilts
33 K5 **Coombe Bissett** Wilts
13 L8 **Coombe Cellars** Devon
35 K6 **Coombe Cross** Hants
29 J5 **Coombe End** Somset
64 C2 **Coombe Hill** Gloucs
17 G5 **Coombe Keynes** Dorset
8 D2 **Coombe Pafford** Torbay
32 C4 **Coombe Street** Somset
21 L5 **Coombes** W Susx
79 L3 **Coombes-Moor** Herefs
98 B6 **Coombeswood** Dudley
41 J3 **Cooper Street** Kent
139 J6 **Cooper Turning** Bolton
38 D3 **Cooper's Corner** Kent
253 J1 **Cooperhill** Moray
23 H3 **Coopers Green** E Susx
69 G5 **Coopers Green** Herts
70 C6 **Coopersale Common** Essex
70 C6 **Coopersale Street** Essex
21 J4 **Cootham** W Susx
41 J3 **Cop Street** Kent
90 D6 **Copdock** Suffk
72 D3 **Copford Green** Essex
150 D3 **Copgrove** N York
281 e4 **Copister** Shet
86 C5 **Cople** Beds
141 G3 **Copley** Calder
168 D5 **Copley** Dur
140 E8 **Copley** Tamesd
132 C4 **Coplow Dale** Derbys
151 J6 **Copmanthorpe** York
114 C5 **Copmere End** Staffs
147 H7 **Copp** Lancs
11 H2 **Coppathorne** Cnwll
114 E7 **Coppenhall** Staffs
130 D8 **Coppenhall Moss** Ches
2 F3 **Copperhouse** Cnwll
97 G7 **Coppicegate** Shrops
102 D7 **Coppingford** Cambs
40 B5 **Coppins Corner** Kent
13 H2 **Copplestone** Devon
139 H5 **Coppull** Lancs
139 H5 **Coppull Moor** Lancs
37 J6 **Copsale** W Susx

139 K1	**Copster Green** Lancs
99 M5	**Copston Magna** Warwks
98 F7	**Copt Heath** Solhll
150 D2	**Copt Hewick** N York
100 B1	**Copt Oak** Leics
70 B7	**Copthall Green** Essex
11 K4	**Copthorne** Cnwll
37 M3	**Copthorne** W Susx
121 L4	**Copy's Green** Norfk
34 C8	**Copythorne** Hants
89 K6	**Coram Street** Suffk
52 C2	**Corbets Tey** Gt Lon
9 a3	**Corbiere** Jersey
180 B6	**Corbridge** Nthumb
101 K5	**Corby** Nhants
118 C6	**Corby Glen** Lincs
178 B7	**Corby Hill** Cumb
195 G5	**Cordon** N Ayrs
132 F4	**Cordwell** Derbys
96 E8	**Coreley** Shrops
49 L2	**Cores End** Bucks
30 C7	**Corfe** Somset
17 J6	**Corfe Castle** Dorset
17 J3	**Corfe Mullen** Dorset
96 B6	**Corfton** Shrops
243 J2	**Corgarff** Abers
35 J6	**Corhampton** Hants
39 G5	**Corks Pond** Kent
99 J6	**Corley** Warwks
99 J6	**Corley Ash** Warwks
99 H6	**Corley Moor** Warwks
233 L2	**Cormuir** Angus
89 H7	**Cornard Tye** Suffk
13 G5	**Corndon** Devon
138 E1	**Corner Row** Lancs
155 K4	**Corney** Cumb
169 J4	**Cornforth** Dur
267 M4	**Cornhill** Abers
202 D5	**Cornhill-on-Tweed** Nthumb
140 D3	**Cornholme** Calder
88 D7	**Cornish Hall End** Essex
224 C6	**Cornoigmore** Ag & B
167 K2	**Cornriggs** Dur
168 F2	**Cornsay** Dur
168 F2	**Cornsay Colliery** Dur
262 F8	**Corntown** Highld
42 D6	**Corntown** V Glam
65 K2	**Cornwell** Oxon
7 H3	**Cornwood** Devon
8 B4	**Cornworthy** Devon
239 H8	**Corpach** Highld
122 C5	**Corpusty** Norfk
244 B3	**Corrachree** Abers
5 G5	**Corran** Cnwll
238 D2	**Corran** Highld
229 G3	**Corran** Highld
154 f4	**Corrany** IOM
177 G2	**Corrie** D & G
195 G2	**Corrie** N Ayrs
193 J4	**Corriecravie** N Ayrs
195 G4	**Corriegills** N Ayrs
239 M5	**Corriegour Lodge Hotel** Highld
262 C7	**Corriemoille** Highld
250 C5	**Corrimony** Highld
135 H2	**Corringham** Lincs
52 F2	**Corringham** Thurr
93 G2	**Corris** Gwynd
92 F2	**Corris Uchaf** Gwynd
217 K7	**Corrow** Ag & B
247 K4	**Corry** Highld
109 L7	**Cors-y-Gedol** Gwynd
12 E3	**Corscombe** Devon
15 L2	**Corscombe** Dorset
64 A2	**Corse** Gloucs
64 B1	**Corse Lawn** Gloucs
46 C5	**Corsham** Wilts
244 F2	**Corsindae** Abers
32 D2	**Corsley** Wilts
32 D2	**Corsley Heath** Wilts
185 J7	**Corsock** D & G
45 K6	**Corston** BaNES
46 D2	**Corston** Wilts
211 G4	**Corstorphine** C Edin
234 B3	**Cortachy** Angus
107 L4	**Corton** Suffk
32 F3	**Corton** Wilts
31 K6	**Corton Denham** Somset
229 H2	**Coruanan Lodge** Highld
111 L3	**Corwen** Denbgs
16 B5	**Coryates** Dorset
12 B6	**Coryton** Devon
52 F2	**Coryton** Thurr
100 C4	**Cosby** Leics
97 L4	**Coseley** Dudley
97 H2	**Cosford** Shrops
84 F6	**Cosgrove** Nhants
19 L3	**Cosham** C Port
55 G6	**Cosheston** Pembks
231 L5	**Coshieville** P & K
116 E3	**Cossall** Notts
116 E3	**Cossall Marsh** Notts
100 D1	**Cossington** Leics
30 E3	**Cossington** Somset
106 D1	**Costessey** Norfk
116 F6	**Costock** Notts
117 M7	**Coston** Leics
106 B2	**Coston** Norfk
65 M6	**Cote** Oxon
30 E2	**Cote** Somset
130 B6	**Cotebrook** Ches
166 B1	**Cotehill** Cumb
157 G5	**Cotes** Cumb
116 F7	**Cotes** Leics
114 C4	**Cotes** Staffs
114 C4	**Cotes Heath** Staffs
100 C7	**Cotesbach** Leics
117 H4	**Cotgrave** Notts
256 F8	**Cothal** Abers
117 L2	**Cotham** Notts
30 B4	**Cothelstone** Somset
168 C6	**Cotherstone** Dur
66 C7	**Cothill** Oxon
14 E2	**Cotleigh** Devon
116 D3	**Cotmanhay** Derbys
87 H3	**Coton** Cambs
84 D1	**Coton** Nhants
113 J4	**Coton** Shrops
114 C7	**Coton** Staffs
114 F5	**Coton** Staffs
98 F2	**Coton** Staffs
114 D7	**Coton Clanford** Staffs
114 F5	**Coton Hayes** Staffs
96 B1	**Coton Hill** Shrops
115 K5	**Coton in the Clay** Staffs
115 L8	**Coton in the Elms** Derbys
115 M7	**Coton Park** Derbys
8 B3	**Cott** Devon
34 E2	**Cottage End** Hants
152 F3	**Cottam** E R Yk
139 G1	**Cottam** Lancs
135 G4	**Cottam** Notts
87 J2	**Cottenham** Cambs
158 E4	**Cotterdale** N York
69 J1	**Cottered** Herts
98 D7	**Cotteridge** Birm
102 A5	**Cotterstock** Nhants
100 F8	**Cottesbrooke** Nhants
101 K1	**Cottesmore** Rutlnd
144 D1	**Cottingham** E R Yk
101 J5	**Cottingham** Nhants
149 K8	**Cottingley** Brad
66 E1	**Cottisford** Oxon
90 C2	**Cotton** Suffk
86 B6	**Cotton End** Beds
148 F7	**Cotton Tree** Lancs
255 K6	**Cottown** Abers
256 D8	**Cottown** Abers
256 E4	**Cottown of Gight** Abers
43 G6	**Cottrell** V Glam
6 E2	**Cotts** Devon
113 K8	**Cotwall** Wrekin
114 E4	**Cotwalton** Staffs
5 K3	**Couch's Mill** Cnwll
63 H3	**Coughton** Herefs
82 C3	**Coughton** Warwks
206 A6	**Coulaghailtro** Ag & B
248 F3	**Coulags** Highld
155 H1	**Coulderton** Cumb
244 B3	**Coull** Abers
207 L2	**Coulport** Ag & B
51 J7	**Coulsdon** Gt Lon
46 D8	**Coulston** Wilts
199 H6	**Coulter** S Lans
21 L3	**Coultershaw Bridge** W Susx
30 C3	**Coultings** Somset
161 K7	**Coulton** N York
222 F3	**Coultra** Fife
96 D2	**Cound** Shrops
96 D2	**Coundlane** Shrops
169 G5	**Coundon** Dur
169 G5	**Coundon Grange** Dur
159 G5	**Countersett** N York
33 K2	**Countess** Wilts
72 C1	**Countess Cross** Essex
13 M4	**Countess Wear** Devon
100 D4	**Countesthorpe** Leics
28 C1	**Countisbury** Devon
139 H2	**Coup Green** Lancs
233 K7	**Coupar Angus** P & K
167 G7	**Coupland** Cumb
202 E7	**Coupland** Nthumb
194 C2	**Cour** Ag & B
187 G8	**Courance** D & G
59 G4	**Court Henry** Carmth
40 E8	**Court-at-Street** Kent
237 K1	**Courteachan** Highld
84 E4	**Courteenhall** Nhants
72 F8	**Courtsend** Essex
30 B4	**Courtway** Somset
211 L5	**Cousland** Mdloth
39 G6	**Cousley Wood** E Susx
207 L3	**Cove** Ag & B
213 G4	**Cove** Border
29 G7	**Cove** Devon
49 L7	**Cove** Hants
260 C2	**Cove** Highld
245 L3	**Cove Bay** C Aber
107 K7	**Cove Bottom** Suffk
107 L7	**Covehithe** Suffk
97 K2	**Coven** Staffs
97 K2	**Coven Lawn** Staffs
103 K7	**Coveney** Cambs
136 F1	**Covenham St Bartholomew** Lincs
136 F1	**Covenham St Mary** Lincs
99 J7	**Coventry** Covtry
3 K7	**Coverack** Cnwll
3 H5	**Coverack Bridges** Cnwll
159 K5	**Coverham** N York
85 L1	**Covington** Cambs
199 G5	**Covington** S Lans
90 C2	**Cow Green** Suffk
82 D6	**Cow Honeybourne** Worcs
157 K7	**Cowan Bridge** Lancs
23 K4	**Cowbeech** E Susx
119 H7	**Cowbit** Lincs
42 F6	**Cowbridge** V Glam
132 B5	**Cowdale** Derbys
38 C5	**Cowden** Kent
38 C5	**Cowden Pound** Kent
38 D5	**Cowden Station** Kent
211 G1	**Cowdenbeath** Fife
116 A2	**Cowers Lane** Derbys
19 H4	**Cowes** IOW
161 G5	**Cowesby** N York
34 B6	**Cowesfield Green** Wilts
37 K6	**Cowfold** W Susx
158 C5	**Cowgill** Cumb
45 J1	**Cowhill** S Glos
209 M1	**Cowie** Stirlg
152 E3	**Cowlam** E R Yk
133 G4	**Cowley** Derbys
13 L3	**Cowley** Devon
64 D4	**Cowley** Gloucs
50 D3	**Cowley** Gt Lon
66 D6	**Cowley** Oxon
67 G2	**Cowley** Oxon
139 J4	**Cowling** Lancs
149 H7	**Cowling** N York
160 C5	**Cowling** N York
88 E4	**Cowlinge** Suffk
141 J4	**Cowmes** Kirk
140 C4	**Cowpe** Lancs
181 H3	**Cowpen** Nthumb
170 B5	**Cowpen Bewley** S on T
19 M2	**Cowplain** Hants
167 K3	**Cowshill** Dur
44 F6	**Cowslip Green** N Som
150 F5	**Cowthorpe** N York
107 H7	**Cox Common** Suffk
95 J8	**Coxall** Shrops
113 L3	**Coxbank** Ches
116 C3	**Coxbench** Derbys
31 J3	**Coxbridge** Somset
11 H3	**Coxford** Cnwll
121 J5	**Coxford** Norfk
97 H6	**Coxgreen** Staffs
39 J3	**Coxheath** Kent
169 J3	**Coxhoe** Dur
31 H2	**Coxley** Somset
141 L4	**Coxley** Wakefd
31 H2	**Coxley Wick** Somset
12 A8	**Coxpark** Cnwll
70 E7	**Coxtie Green** Essex
161 H7	**Coxwold** N York
42 E6	**Coychurch** Brdgnd
196 E7	**Coylton** S Ayrs
242 B1	**Coylumbridge** Highld
42 D4	**Coytrahen** Brdgnd
17 L1	**Crab Orchard** Dorset
82 B2	**Crabbs Cross** Worcs
37 K6	**Crabtree** W Susx
112 E3	**Crabtree Green** Wrexhm
166 F6	**Crackenthorpe** Cumb
11 G3	**Crackington Haven** Cnwll
114 C2	**Crackley** Staffs
99 J8	**Crackley** Warwks
97 G1	**Crackleybank** Shrops
159 H3	**Crackpot** N York
149 H4	**Cracoe** N York
29 K8	**Craddock** Devon
70 C3	**Cradle End** Herts
97 L6	**Cradley** Dudley
81 G6	**Cradley** Herefs
97 L6	**Cradley Heath** Sandw
60 F1	**Cradoc** Powys
6 D4	**Crafthole** Cnwll
67 L3	**Crafton** Bucks
157 G7	**Crag Foot** Lancs
150 B8	**Cragg Hill** Leeds
140 F3	**Cragg Vale** Calder
253 K6	**Craggan** Highld
180 F8	**Craghead** Dur
60 D2	**Crai** Powys
267 K4	**Craibstone** Moray
234 D6	**Craichie** Angus
235 H4	**Craig** Angus
249 H2	**Craig** Highld
57 K4	**Craig Llangiwg** Neath
42 E6	**Craig Penllyn** V Glam
88 E7	**Craig's End** Essex
57 K4	**Craig-y-Duke** Neath
60 C4	**Craig-y-nos** Powys
197 H8	**Craigbank** E Ayrs
200 B2	**Craigburn** Border
57 J4	**Craigcefnparc** Swans
177 K2	**Craigcleuch** D & G
256 F5	**Craigdam** Abers
216 C6	**Craigdhu** Ag & B
245 G1	**Craigearn** Abers
254 F3	**Craigellachie** Moray
221 K3	**Craigend** P & K
208 D5	**Craigend** Rens
208 A3	**Craigendoran** Ag & B
173 H3	**Craighlaw** D & G
205 H3	**Craighouse** Ag & B
233 H6	**Craigie** P & K
196 E4	**Craigie** S Ayrs
269 G3	**Craigiefold** Abers
175 J3	**Craigley** D & G
211 H5	**Craiglockhart** C Edin
267 G5	**Craiglug** Moray
211 J4	**Craigmillar** C Edin
112 C4	**Craignant** Shrops
185 J5	**Craigneston** D & G
209 K6	**Craigneuk** N Lans
209 K7	**Craigneuk** N Lans
227 L5	**Craignure** Ag & B
235 H3	**Craigo** Angus
222 F5	**Craigrothie** Fife
219 H3	**Craigruie** Stirlg
234 D7	**Craigton** Angus
245 J3	**Craigton** C Aber
208 E8	**Craigton** E Rens
233 M5	**Craigton of Airlie** Angus
223 L5	**Crail** Fife
189 J1	**Crailing** Border
143 J8	**Craiselound** N Linc
160 C5	**Crakehall** N York
160 F7	**Crakehill** N York
115 H4	**Crakemarsh** Staffs
151 M3	**Crambe** N York
181 G3	**Cramlington** Nthumb
211 G4	**Cramond** C Edin
211 G4	**Cramond Bridge** C Edin
34 E6	**Crampmoor** Hants
130 E6	**Cranage** Ches
114 C4	**Cranberry** Staffs
33 H8	**Cranborne** Dorset
39 J6	**Cranbrook** Kent
39 K5	**Cranbrook Common** Kent
141 M7	**Crane Moor** Barns
105 L1	**Crane's Corner** Norfk
85 J6	**Cranfield** Beds
26 F6	**Cranford** Devon
50 E4	**Cranford** Gt Lon
101 K7	**Cranford St Andrew** Nhants
101 K8	**Cranford St John** Nhants
64 C4	**Cranham** Gloucs
52 C2	**Cranham** Gt Lon
82 D4	**Cranhill** Warwks
139 G7	**Crank** St Hel
37 G3	**Cranleigh** Surrey
89 L1	**Cranmer Green** Suffk
18 F5	**Cranmore** IOW
31 L2	**Cranmore** Somset
101 G4	**Cranoe** Leics
91 H2	**Cransford** Suffk
212 F6	**Cranshaws** Border

154 f2 **Cranstal** IOM
152 F5 **Cranswick** E R Yk
4 C3 **Crantock** Cnwll
118 D2 **Cranwell** Lincs
104 F4 **Cranwich** Norfk
105 K3 **Cranworth** Norfk
216 B5 **Craobh Haven** Ag & B
6 F1 **Crapstone** Devon
216 F7 **Crarae** Ag & B
272 D3 **Crask Inn** Highld
250 E3 **Crask of Aigas** Highld
191 K2 **Craster** Nthumb
79 K8 **Craswall** Herefs
97 K2 **Crateford** Staffs
107 G8 **Cratfield** Suffk
245 G4 **Crathes** Abers
243 J4 **Crathie** Abers
241 G5 **Crathie** Highld
161 G1 **Crathorne** N York
95 K6 **Craven Arms** Shrops
180 D6 **Crawcrook** Gatesd
139 G7 **Crawford** Lancs
186 E2 **Crawford** S Lans
186 C2 **Crawfordjohn** S Lans
185 K1 **Crawick** D & G
34 F4 **Crawley** Hants
65 M4 **Crawley** Oxon
37 L4 **Crawley** W Susx
38 A6 **Crawley Down** W Susx
168 C3 **Crawleyside** Dur
140 B3 **Crawshawbooth** Lancs
245 J7 **Crawton** Abers
72 D3 **Craxe's Green** Essex
159 G6 **Cray** N York
48 F3 **Cray's Pond** Oxon
52 B4 **Crayford** Gt Lon
151 J2 **Crayke** N York
122 B5 **Craymere Beck** Norfk
71 H8 **Crays Hill** Essex
115 L6 **Craythorne** Staffs
29 H8 **Craze Lowman** Devon
49 J3 **Crazies Hill** Wokham
28 E7 **Creacombe** Devon
283 c9 **Creag Ghoraidh** W Isls
228 F6 **Creagan Inn** Ag & B
283 c9 **Creagorry** W Isls
230 B2 **Creaguaineach Lodge** Highld
113 H5 **Creamore Bank** Shrops
84 D1 **Creaton** Nhants
177 H5 **Creca** D & G
80 B6 **Credenhill** Herefs
13 J3 **Crediton** Devon
183 J7 **Creebank** D & G
173 K2 **Creebridge** D & G
30 D5 **Creech Heathfield** Somset
30 C6 **Creech St Michael** Somset
4 F5 **Creed** Cnwll
13 J2 **Creedy Park** Devon
51 M3 **Creekmouth** Gt Lon
90 C4 **Creeting St Mary** Suffk
118 D7 **Creeton** Lincs
174 D3 **Creetown** D & G
154 b8 **Cregneash** IOM
154 e5 **Cregny Baa** IOM
79 G5 **Cregrina** Powys
222 E3 **Creich** Fife
43 G5 **Creigiau** Cardif
3 H4 **Crelly** Cnwll
6 E4 **Cremyll** Cnwll
96 D3 **Cressage** Shrops
132 C5 **Cressbrook** Derbys
55 H5 **Cresselly** Pembks
67 K8 **Cressex** Bucks
71 J3 **Cressing** Essex
191 K7 **Cresswell** Nthumb
55 H5 **Cresswell** Pembks
114 F4 **Cresswell** Staffs
133 K5 **Creswell** Derbys
98 D1 **Creswell Green** Staffs
90 F3 **Cretingham** Suffk
206 A5 **Cretshengan** Ag & B
112 D8 **Crew Green** Powys
112 F1 **Crewe** Ches
130 D8 **Crewe** Ches
130 E8 **Crewe Green** Ches
15 K1 **Crewkerne** Somset
63 K3 **Crews Hill** Herefs
69 J7 **Crews Hill Station** Herts
116 C5 **Crewton** C Derb
218 F2 **Crianlarich** Stirlg
45 H3 **Cribbs Causeway** S Glos
76 F5 **Cribyn** Cerdgn
109 J4 **Criccieth** Gwynd
116 B1 **Crich** Derbys
116 B1 **Crich Carr** Derbys

116 B1 **Crich Common** Derbys
211 L6 **Crichton** Mdloth
44 F1 **Crick** Mons
84 B1 **Crick** Nhants
78 F6 **Crickadarn** Powys
15 J1 **Cricket St Thomas** Somset
112 D7 **Crickheath** Shrops
61 K3 **Crickhowell** Powys
65 G8 **Cricklade** Wilts
51 G2 **Cricklewood** Gt Lon
142 E3 **Cridling Stubbs** N York
220 F3 **Crieff** P & K
5 G3 **Criggan** Cnwll
112 D8 **Criggion** Powys
141 M4 **Crigglestone** Wakefd
140 C5 **Crimble** Rochdl
269 K5 **Crimond** Abers
104 C3 **Crimplesham** Norfk
82 F5 **Crimscote** Warwks
250 D4 **Crinaglack** Highld
216 B8 **Crinan** Ag & B
209 L7 **Crindledyke** N Lans
106 D2 **Cringleford** Norfk
149 J6 **Cringles** Brad
55 K4 **Crinow** Pembks
24 D3 **Cripp's Corner** E Susx
2 D4 **Cripplesease** Cnwll
33 J8 **Cripplestyle** Dorset
62 F1 **Crizeley** Herefs
251 H6 **Croachy** Highld
10 E8 **Croanford** Cnwll
176 A3 **Crochmore House** D & G
30 D8 **Crock Street** Somset
52 B5 **Crockenhill** Kent
49 H2 **Crocker End** Oxon
63 G4 **Crocker's Ash** Herefs
20 F5 **Crockerhill** W Susx
13 H4 **Crockernwell** Devon
32 E2 **Crockerton** Wilts
185 K8 **Crocketford** D & G
151 K6 **Crockey Hill** York
38 C3 **Crockham Hill** Kent
39 G4 **Crockhurst Street** Kent
72 F2 **Crockleford Heath** Essex
74 D6 **Croes-goch** Pembks
76 C6 **Croes-lan** Cerdgn
62 C8 **Croes-y-mwyalch** Torfn
62 C6 **Croes-y-pant** Mons
42 C3 **Croeserw** Neath
110 B3 **Croesor** Gwynd
58 D5 **Croesyceiliog** Carmth
62 C7 **Croesyceiliog** Torfn
12 C3 **Croft** Devon
100 B4 **Croft** Leics
137 J7 **Croft** Lincs
130 C1 **Croft** Warrtn
3 H4 **Croft Michael** Cnwll
160 D1 **Croft-on-Tees** N York
208 E2 **Croftamie** Stirlg
165 J1 **Crofton** Cumb
142 B4 **Crofton** Wakefd
47 K6 **Crofton** Wilts
175 J2 **Crofts** D & G
266 F6 **Crofts** Moray
139 M8 **Crofts Bank** Traffd
267 G4 **Crofts of Dipple** Moray
269 J4 **Crofts of Savoch** Abers
56 F6 **Crofty** Swans
111 K4 **Crogen** Gwynd
227 K7 **Croggan** Ag & B
166 D1 **Croglin** Cumb
262 D2 **Croik** Highld
264 B6 **Cromarty** Highld
210 E2 **Crombie** Fife
253 L6 **Cromdale** Highld
69 J2 **Cromer** Herts
122 E3 **Cromer** Norfk
132 F8 **Cromford** Derbys
45 K1 **Cromhall** S Glos
45 K1 **Cromhall Common** S Glos
282 g4 **Cromor** W Isls
140 E6 **Crompton Fold** Oldham
134 F7 **Cromwell** Notts
197 H6 **Cronberry** E Ayrs
36 B1 **Crondall** Hants
154 d5 **Cronk-y-Voddy** IOM
154 e6 **Cronkbourne** IOM
129 L2 **Cronton** Knows
157 G4 **Crook** Cumb
168 F4 **Crook** Dur
199 J7 **Crook Inn** Border
221 J7 **Crook of Devon** P & K
165 G2 **Crookdake** Cumb
139 H6 **Crooke** Wigan
63 J3 **Crooked End** Gloucs

178 C6 **Crooked Holme** Cumb
47 L4 **Crooked Soley** Wilts
196 E3 **Crookedholm** E Ayrs
132 F2 **Crookes** Sheff
180 D8 **Crookhall** Dur
202 E5 **Crookham** Nthumb
48 D6 **Crookham** W Berk
49 J8 **Crookham Village** Hants
157 H6 **Crooklands** Cumb
115 L4 **Crppper** Derbys
83 L6 **Cropredy** Oxon
100 C1 **Cropston** Leics
82 B6 **Cropthorne** Worcs
162 D5 **Cropton** N York
117 H4 **Cropwell Bishop** Notts
117 J4 **Cropwell Butler** Notts
282 h1 **Cros** W Isls
195 K1 **Crosbie** N Ayrs
282 g4 **Crosbost** W Isls
164 E3 **Crosby** Cumb
154 d6 **Crosby** IOM
143 M5 **Crosby** N Linc
138 C8 **Crosby** Sefton
158 C1 **Crosby Garret** Cumb
166 E7 **Crosby Ravensworth** Cumb
164 E3 **Crosby Villa** Cumb
31 K2 **Croscombe** Somset
113 G5 **Crosemere** Shrops
141 H5 **Crosland Edge** Kirk
141 H5 **Crosland Hill** Kirk
44 E8 **Cross** Somset
62 E3 **Cross Ash** Mons
4 B4 **Cross Coombe** Cnwll
85 L4 **Cross End** Beds
89 G8 **Cross End** Essex
149 K7 **Cross Flatts** Brad
142 B1 **Cross Gates** Leeds
11 M5 **Cross Green** Devon
141 M2 **Cross Green** Leeds
97 K2 **Cross Green** Staffs
89 G4 **Cross Green** Suffk
89 H4 **Cross Green** Suffk
89 K4 **Cross Green** Suffk
59 G6 **Cross Hands** Carmth
55 H4 **Cross Hands** Pembks
116 C2 **Cross Hill** Derbys
149 H6 **Cross Hills** N York
96 C2 **Cross Houses** Shrops
96 F5 **Cross Houses** Shrops
23 J3 **Cross in Hand** E Susx
76 D4 **Cross Inn** Cerdgn
77 G2 **Cross Inn** Cerdgn
55 J5 **Cross Inn** Pembks
43 G5 **Cross Inn** Rhondd
208 B2 **Cross Keys** Ag & B
46 C5 **Cross Keys** Wilts
19 H5 **Cross Lane** IOW
97 G4 **Cross Lane Head** Shrops
3 H6 **Cross Lanes** Cnwll
4 C6 **Cross Lanes** Cnwll
151 H3 **Cross Lanes** N York
112 E2 **Cross Lanes** Wrexhm
115 M2 **Cross o' th' hands** Derbys
61 H2 **Cross Oak** Powys
256 D5 **Cross of Jackston** Abers
78 D4 **Cross Roads** Powys
106 D8 **Cross Street** Suffk
130 E4 **Cross Town** Ches
39 K4 **Cross-at-Hand** Kent
194 C1 **Crossaig** Ag & B
224 C6 **Crossapoll** Ag & B
21 H5 **Crossbush** W Susx
164 E3 **Crosscanonby** Cumb
122 E4 **Crossdale Street** Norfk
138 D4 **Crossens** Sefton
210 E2 **Crossford** Fife
198 D4 **Crossford** S Lans
11 L5 **Crossgate** Cnwll
119 H6 **Crossgate** Lincs
114 E4 **Crossgate** Staffs
211 L5 **Crossgatehall** E Loth
196 D2 **Crossgates** E Ayrs
210 F1 **Crossgates** Fife
163 J6 **Crossgates** N York
78 F2 **Crossgates** Powys
147 L3 **Crossgill** Lancs
55 L2 **Crosshands** Carmth
196 F5 **Crosshands** E Ayrs
222 B7 **Crosshill** Fife
183 J2 **Crosshill** S Ayrs
196 D3 **Crosshouse** E Ayrs
43 K3 **Crosskeys** Caerph
279 H2 **Crosskirk** Highld
156 E5 **Crosslands** Cumb
112 E7 **Crosslanes** Shrops

208 C6 **Crosslee** Rens
141 K3 **Crossley** Kirk
175 J2 **Crossmichael** D & G
37 L6 **Crosspost** W Susx
244 D2 **Crossroads** Abers
245 G5 **Crossroads** Abers
234 E4 **Crosston** Angus
62 F3 **Crossway** Mons
75 K4 **Crossway** Pembks
78 E4 **Crossway** Powys
63 G8 **Crossway Green** Mons
81 J2 **Crossway Green** Worcs
16 E5 **Crossways** Dorset
75 J5 **Crosswell** Pembks
156 F4 **Crosthwaite** Cumb
138 F4 **Croston** Lancs
122 E8 **Crostwick** Norfk
123 G5 **Crostwight** Norfk
40 D4 **Crouch** Kent
38 F2 **Crouch** Kent
51 J1 **Crouch End** Gt Lon
32 B8 **Crouch Hill** Dorset
33 J6 **Croucheston** Wilts
38 C4 **Crough House Green** Kent
84 A8 **Croughton** Nhants
268 E3 **Crovie** Abers
18 B3 **Crow** Hants
141 J6 **Crow Edge** Barns
87 G4 **Crow End** Cambs
70 E7 **Crow Green** Essex
63 J2 **Crow Hill** Herefs
71 G2 **Crow's Green** Essex
6 B1 **Crow's Nest** Cnwll
3 G4 **Crowan** Cnwll
38 D7 **Crowborough** E Susx
38 D7 **Crowborough Town** E Susx
29 L3 **Crowcombe** Somset
132 B6 **Crowdecote** Derbys
141 G7 **Crowden** Derbys
12 C3 **Crowden** Devon
35 G6 **Crowdhill** Hants
52 C7 **Crowdleham** Kent
67 H7 **Crowell** Oxon
84 B7 **Crowfield** Nhants
90 D4 **Crowfield** Suffk
90 D4 **Crowfield Green** Suffk
123 G7 **Crowgate Street** Norfk
213 G4 **Crowhill** E Loth
133 G4 **Crowhole** Derbys
24 D5 **Crowhurst** E Susx
38 B4 **Crowhurst** Surrey
38 B4 **Crowhurst Lane End** Surrey
102 E2 **Crowland** Lincs
89 K1 **Crowland** Suffk
2 E4 **Crowlas** Cnwll
143 K5 **Crowle** N Linc
81 L4 **Crowle** Worcs
81 L4 **Crowle Green** Worcs
48 F1 **Crowmarsh Gifford** Oxon
90 F1 **Crown Corner** Suffk
6 F3 **Crownhill** C Plym
36 E2 **Crownpits** Surrey
106 B3 **Crownthorpe** Norfk
3 G5 **Crowntown** Cnwll
2 B5 **Crows-an-Wra** Cnwll
105 J2 **Crowshill** Norfk
95 J3 **Crowsnest** Shrops
49 K6 **Crowthorne** Wokham
130 B5 **Crowton** Ches
99 G1 **Croxall** Staffs
144 F8 **Croxby** NE Lin
169 H3 **Croxdale** Dur
115 H4 **Croxden** Staffs
68 D7 **Croxley Green** Herts
86 E3 **Croxton** Cambs
144 E5 **Croxton** N Linc
121 L5 **Croxton** Norfk
105 H6 **Croxton** Norfk
114 B5 **Croxton** Staffs
113 J1 **Croxton Green** Ches
117 L5 **Croxton Kerrial** Leics
114 B5 **Croxtonbank** Staffs
252 E2 **Croy** Highld
209 J4 **Croy** N Lans
27 H3 **Croyde** Devon
27 G3 **Croyde Bay** Devon
87 G5 **Croydon** Cambs
51 J6 **Croydon** Gt Lon
241 J5 **Crubenmore** Highld
95 K2 **Cruckmeole** Shrops
95 K1 **Cruckton** Shrops
257 K4 **Cruden Bay** Abers
113 K7 **Crudgington** Wrekin
64 D8 **Crudwell** Wilts
79 H1 **Crug** Powys

94 E7 **Crug-y-byddar** Powys
10 C7 **Crugmeer** Cnwll
77 J7 **Crugybar** Carmth
43 K2 **Crumlin** Caerph
5 L4 **Crumplehorn** Cnwll
140 C7 **Crumpsall** Manch
40 E5 **Crundale** Kent
54 F3 **Crundale** Pembks
55 L5 **Crunwear** Pembks
28 F8 **Cruwys Morchard** Devon
48 B7 **Crux Easton** Hants
16 B3 **Cruxton** Dorset
58 E6 **Crwbin** Carmth
67 L7 **Cryers Hill** Bucks
75 L5 **Crymmych** Pembks
60 B6 **Crynant** Neath
51 J5 **Crystal Palace** Gt Lon
260 A8 **Cuaig** Highld
215 L2 **Cuan Ferry Village** Ag & B
83 H2 **Cubbington** Warwks
4 C3 **Cubert** Cnwll
141 K7 **Cubley** Barns
67 K3 **Cublington** Bucks
79 M7 **Cublington** Herefs
22 D2 **Cuckfield** W Susx
32 C5 **Cucklington** Somset
133 L5 **Cuckney** Notts
53 H4 **Cuckold's Green** Medway
119 G7 **Cuckoo Bridge** Lincs
35 M3 **Cuckoo's Corner** Hants
129 J7 **Cuckoo's Nest** Ches
66 F6 **Cuddesdon** Oxon
67 H5 **Cuddington** Bucks
130 B5 **Cuddington** Ches
113 G2 **Cuddington Heath** Ches
147 J8 **Cuddy Hill** Lancs
51 L7 **Cudham** Gt Lon
12 C6 **Cudliptown** Devon
17 L3 **Cudnell** Bmouth
142 B6 **Cudworth** Barns
30 F8 **Cudworth** Somset
142 B6 **Cudworth Common** Barns
139 H3 **Cuerden Green** Lancs
130 A2 **Cuerdley Cross** Warrtn
49 G7 **Cufaude** Hants
69 J6 **Cuffley** Herts
228 F4 **Cuil** Highld
263 G7 **Culbokie** Highld
28 E1 **Culbone** Somset
250 E3 **Culburnie** Highld
251 J3 **Culcabock** Highld
253 G2 **Culcharry** Highld
130 C1 **Culcheth** Warrtn
255 K5 **Culdrain** Abers
248 A4 **Culduie** Highld
89 G1 **Culford** Suffk
166 E5 **Culgaith** Cumb
66 D8 **Culham** Oxon
270 D2 **Culkein** Highld
270 F1 **Culkein Drumbeg** Highld
64 D7 **Culkerton** Gloucs
267 K3 **Cullen** Moray
181 J4 **Cullercoats** N Tyne
245 G3 **Cullerlie** Abers
263 H7 **Cullicudden** Highld
149 J8 **Cullingworth** Brad
215 L2 **Cullipool House** Ag & B
281 e2 **Cullivoe** Shet
252 D3 **Culloden** Highld
14 B1 **Cullompton** Devon
29 L7 **Culm Davy** Devon
96 B7 **Culmington** Shrops
29 K8 **Culmstock** Devon
270 E7 **Culnacraig** Highld
175 J5 **Culnaightrie** D & G
259 J4 **Culnaknock** Highld
90 F5 **Culpho** Suffk
263 G1 **Culrain** Highld
210 C2 **Culross** Fife
196 C8 **Culroy** S Ayrs
256 B5 **Culsalmond** Abers
174 D5 **Culscadden** D & G
173 H4 **Culshabbin** D & G
281 c6 **Culswick** Shet
257 G7 **Cultercullen** Abers
245 K3 **Cults** C Aber
52 D6 **Culverstone Green** Kent
118 D3 **Culverthorpe** Lincs
84 A6 **Culworth** Nhants
209 K4 **Cumbernauld** N Lans
209 K4 **Cumbernauld Village** N Lans
137 J5 **Cumberworth** Lincs
165 K1 **Cumdivock** Cumb
268 E6 **Cuminestown** Abers
202 B2 **Cumledge** Border

177 L8 **Cummersdale** Cumb
176 F5 **Cummertrees** D & G
266 C2 **Cummingston** Moray
197 H7 **Cumnock** E Ayrs
66 C6 **Cumnor** Oxon
178 D8 **Cumrew** Cumb
176 E2 **Cumrue** D & G
178 B8 **Cumwhinton** Cumb
178 C8 **Cumwhitton** Cumb
150 F1 **Cundall** N York
196 D3 **Cunninghamhead** N Ayrs
222 F4 **Cupar** Fife
222 F4 **Cupar Muir** Fife
132 E5 **Curbar** Derbys
19 J1 **Curbridge** Hants
65 M5 **Curbridge** Oxon
35 H8 **Curdridge** Hants
98 F5 **Curdworth** Warwks
30 C7 **Curland** Somset
48 C4 **Curridge** W Berk
211 G5 **Currie** C Edin
30 E6 **Curry Mallet** Somset
30 F6 **Curry Rivel** Somset
39 L5 **Curteis Corner** Kent
39 J5 **Curtisden Green** Kent
7 L4 **Curtisknowle** Devon
3 H6 **Cury** Cnwll
244 C1 **Cushnie** Abers
30 B5 **Cushuish** Somset
79 J7 **Cusop** Herefs
174 C7 **Cutcloy** D & G
29 G3 **Cutcombe** Somset
140 C5 **Cutgate** Rochdl
263 K2 **Cuthill** Highld
110 B8 **Cutiau** Gwynd
70 E1 **Cutler's Green** Essex
5 J2 **Cutmadoc** Cnwll
6 C3 **Cutmere** Cnwll
81 K2 **Cutnall Green** Worcs
65 G1 **Cutsdean** Gloucs
142 C3 **Cutsyke** Wakefd
133 G5 **Cutthorpe** Derbys
6 D2 **Cuttivett** Cnwll
67 G8 **Cuxham** Oxon
52 F5 **Cuxton** Medway
144 F7 **Cuxwold** Lincs
61 J6 **Cwm** Blae G
128 C4 **Cwm** Denbgs
56 E4 **Cwm Capel** Carmth
61 J3 **Cwm Crawnon** Powys
57 H4 **Cwm Dulais** Swans
78 A5 **Cwm Irfon** Powys
93 J2 **Cwm Llinau** Powys
58 B2 **Cwm Morgan** Carmth
110 E2 **Cwm Penmachno** Conwy
56 E4 **Cwm-bach** Carmth
61 K5 **Cwm-celyn** Blae G
93 J1 **Cwm-Cewydd** Gwynd
76 B6 **Cwm-cou** Cerdgn
59 J4 **Cwm-Ifor** Carmth
59 G6 **Cwm-y-glo** Carmth
125 K7 **Cwm-y-glo** Gwynd
57 L6 **Cwmafan** Neath
60 F7 **Cwmaman** Rhondd
77 G6 **Cwmann** Carmth
62 B6 **Cwmavon** Torfn
75 M7 **Cwmbach** Carmth
79 G7 **Cwmbach** Powys
60 F6 **Cwmbach** Rhondd
78 E4 **Cwmbach Llechrhyd** Powys
93 K7 **Cwmbelan** Powys
62 C8 **Cwmbran** Torfn
92 F7 **Cwmbrwyno** Cerdgn
43 K3 **Cwmcarn** Caerph
62 F5 **Cwmcarvan** Mons
60 F6 **Cwmdare** Rhondd
59 H3 **Cwmdu** Carmth
61 J2 **Cwmdu** Powys
57 H6 **Cwmdu** Swans
58 C3 **Cwmduad** Carmth
59 K2 **Cwmdwr** Carmth
93 G6 **Cwmergyr** Cerdgn
42 C4 **Cwmfelin** Brdgnd
61 H6 **Cwmfelin** Myr Td
55 L3 **Cwmfelin Boeth** Carmth
75 L7 **Cwmfelin Mynach** Carmth
43 J3 **Cwmfelinfach** Caerph
58 D5 **Cwmffrwd** Carmth
59 L6 **Cwmgiedd** Powys
57 K3 **Cwmgorse** Carmth
57 G3 **Cwmgwili** Carmth
60 C6 **Cwmgwrach** Neath
76 C7 **Cwmhiraeth** Carmth
58 F5 **Cwmisfael** Carmth
59 K6 **Cwmllynfell** Neath

58 F6 **Cwmmawr** Carmth
42 E3 **Cwmparc** Rhondd
58 C2 **Cwmpengraig** Carmth
61 G7 **Cwmpennar** Rhondd
61 J2 **Cwmrhos** Powys
57 J5 **Cwmrhydyceirw** Swans
76 E6 **Cwmsychbant** Cerdgn
61 K6 **Cwmtillery** Blae G
62 C3 **Cwmyoy** Mons
93 G8 **Cwmystwyth** Cerdgn
92 E3 **Cwrt** Gwynd
76 E5 **Cwrt-newydd** Cerdgn
61 K4 **Cwrt-y-gollen** Powys
94 E2 **Cyfronydd** Powys
42 C3 **Cymer** Neath
42 F3 **Cymmer** Rhondd
77 M7 **Cynghordy** Carmth
56 E3 **Cynheidre** Carmth
42 C3 **Cynonville** Neath
111 K3 **Cynwyd** Denbgs
58 C3 **Cynwyl Elfed** Carmth

D

8 D1 **Daccombe** Devon
166 B5 **Dacre** Cumb
150 B4 **Dacre** N York
150 B3 **Dacre Banks** N York
167 K3 **Daddry Shield** Dur
84 C7 **Dadford** Bucks
99 L4 **Dadlington** Leics
56 F4 **Dafen** Carmth
105 J2 **Daffy Green** Norfk
52 B2 **Dagenham** Gt Lon
64 E6 **Daglingworth** Gloucs
68 C4 **Dagnall** Bucks
89 L3 **Dagworth** Suffk
183 H3 **Dailly** S Ayrs
8 C2 **Dainton** Devon
223 G4 **Dairsie** Fife
139 K6 **Daisy Hill** Bolton
141 L2 **Daisy Hill** Leeds
283 b11 **Dalabrog** W Isls
216 F5 **Dalavich** Ag & B
175 L3 **Dalbeattie** D & G
115 M5 **Dalbury** Derbys
154 b6 **Dalby** IOM
137 H5 **Dalby** Lincs
151 K2 **Dalby** N York
232 E4 **Dalcapon** P & K
274 B6 **Dalchalm** Highld
240 A1 **Dalchreichart** Highld
220 C4 **Dalchruin** P & K
221 J2 **Dalcrue** P & K
136 E6 **Dalderby** Lincs
14 B6 **Dalditch** Devon
166 D2 **Dale** Cumb
116 D4 **Dale** Derbys
54 C5 **Dale** Pembks
165 J6 **Dale Bottom** Cumb
132 D7 **Dale End** Derbys
149 G6 **Dale End** N York
39 H7 **Dale Hill** E Susx
171 H7 **Dalehouse** N York
196 B2 **Dalgarven** N Ayrs
211 G2 **Dalgety Bay** Fife
197 G8 **Dalgig** E Ayrs
220 D3 **Dalginross** P & K
232 E6 **Dalguise** P & K
278 F5 **Dalhalvaig** Highld
88 E3 **Dalham** Suffk
283 b11 **Daliburgh** W Isls
211 K5 **Dalkeith** Mdloth
266 C5 **Dallas** Moray
91 G4 **Dallinghoo** Suffk
24 B3 **Dallington** E Susx
84 E3 **Dallington** Nhants
150 B2 **Dallow** N York
217 K2 **Dalmally** Ag & B
219 H8 **Dalmary** Stirlg
184 D2 **Dalmellington** E Ayrs
210 F3 **Dalmeny** C Edin
252 D7 **Dalmigavie** Highld
252 E7 **Dalmigavie Lodge** Highld
263 H6 **Dalmore** Highld
208 E5 **Dalmuir** W Duns
237 K6 **Dalnabreck** Highld
231 K1 **Dalnacardoch** P & K
252 F7 **Dalnahaitnach** Highld
231 J1 **Dalnaspidal** P & K
279 H8 **Dalnawillan Lodge** Highld
231 L4 **Daloist** P & K
221 K6 **Dalqueich** P & K

183 J4 **Dalquhairn** S Ayrs
273 H6 **Dalreavoch Lodge** Highld
196 B1 **Dalry** N Ayrs
196 D8 **Dalrymple** E Ayrs
198 C3 **Dalserf** S Lans
192 D5 **Dalsmeran** Ag & B
165 L1 **Dalston** Cumb
51 J2 **Dalston** Gt Lon
176 B2 **Dalswinton** D & G
157 H7 **Dalton** Cumb
176 F4 **Dalton** D & G
139 G6 **Dalton** Lancs
159 K1 **Dalton** N York
160 F7 **Dalton** N York
180 D4 **Dalton** Nthumb
133 J1 **Dalton** Rothm
133 J1 **Dalton Magna** Rothm
133 J1 **Dalton Parva** Rothm
170 B4 **Dalton Piercy** Hartpl
156 B7 **Dalton-in-Furness** Cumb
169 L1 **Dalton-le-Dale** Dur
160 D1 **Dalton-on-Tees** N York
186 C5 **Dalveen** D & G
219 K2 **Dalveich** Stirlg
241 H6 **Dalwhinnie** Highld
14 F2 **Dalwood** Devon
105 L6 **Dam Green** Norfk
69 H1 **Damask Green** Herts
33 J7 **Damerham** Hants
107 H2 **Damgate** Norfk
53 J6 **Danaway** Kent
71 J6 **Danbury** Essex
162 C1 **Danby** N York
162 B2 **Danby Bottom** N York
160 E3 **Danby Wiske** N York
254 F3 **Dandaleith** Moray
211 J5 **Danderhall** Mdloth
69 J3 **Dane End** Herts
100 C3 **Dane Hills** C Leic
40 D5 **Dane Street** Kent
131 J6 **Danebridge** Ches
38 E6 **Danegate** E Susx
22 F2 **Danehill** E Susx
105 L2 **Danemoor Green** Norfk
97 G5 **Danesford** Shrops
133 H7 **Danesmoor** Derbys
40 C7 **Daniel's Water** Kent
268 C5 **Danshillock** Abers
212 C5 **Danskine** E Loth
145 H1 **Danthorpe** E R Yk
82 D2 **Danzey Green** Warwks
115 G6 **Dapple Heath** Staffs
49 K7 **Darby Green** Hants
139 L6 **Darcy Lever** Bolton
61 K3 **Dardy** Powys
61 K4 **Daren-felen** Mons
52 C5 **Darenth** Kent
130 B3 **Daresbury** Halton
142 C6 **Darfield** Barns
133 L4 **Darfoulds** Notts
40 E3 **Dargate** Kent
6 B1 **Darite** Cnwll
53 G6 **Darland** Medway
129 J8 **Darland** Wrexhm
114 D4 **Darlaston** Staffs
98 B4 **Darlaston** Wsall
98 B4 **Darlaston Green** Wsall
150 B4 **Darley** N York
116 B4 **Darley Abbey** C Derb
132 E7 **Darley Bridge** Derbys
132 E7 **Darley Dale** Derbys
98 F8 **Darley Green** Solhll
150 B4 **Darley Head** N York
68 F3 **Darleyhall** Herts
82 F6 **Darlingscott** Warwks
169 H7 **Darlington** Darltn
113 J5 **Darliston** Shrops
134 F5 **Darlton** Notts
98 E2 **Darnford** Staffs
201 H6 **Darnick** Border
93 H3 **Darowen** Powys
268 D6 **Darra** Abers
26 D8 **Darracott** Cnwll
26 D7 **Darracott** Devon
27 H3 **Darracott** Devon
180 E5 **Darras Hall** Nthumb
142 D4 **Darrington** Wakefd
91 K1 **Darsham** Suffk
31 K2 **Darshill** Somset
52 B4 **Dartford** Kent
8 B2 **Dartington** Devon
12 F7 **Dartmeet** Devon
8 C4 **Dartmouth** Devon
141 M5 **Darton** Barns
197 H3 **Darvel** E Ayrs

24 C3 **Darwell Hole** E Susx
139 K3 **Darwen** Bl w D
50 C2 **Datchet** W & M
69 H3 **Datchworth** Herts
69 H3 **Datchworth Green** Herts
139 L6 **Daubhill** Bolton
46 E3 **Dauntsey** Wilts
253 J4 **Dava** Highld
130 C5 **Davenham** Ches
131 H2 **Davenport** Stockp
131 G4 **Davenport Green** Ches
130 F2 **Davenport Green** Traffd
84 B3 **Daventry** Nhants
52 E6 **David Street** Kent
211 H4 **Davidson's Mains** C Edin
11 G5 **Davidstow** Cnwll
187 K5 **Davington** D & G
40 D3 **Davington Hill** Kent
256 D6 **Daviot** Abers
252 D4 **Daviot** Highld
252 D4 **Daviot House** Highld
23 J4 **Davis's Town** E Susx
267 K6 **Davoch of Grange** Moray
139 M8 **Davyhulme** Traffd
98 C3 **Daw End** Wsall
11 K6 **Daw's House** Cnwll
37 K2 **Dawesgreen** Surrey
96 F2 **Dawley** Wrekin
13 M7 **Dawlish** Devon
14 A6 **Dawlish Warren** Devon
127 G5 **Dawn** Conwy
30 B6 **Daws Green** Somset
53 H1 **Daws Heath** Essex
120 A5 **Dawsmere** Lincs
130 F8 **Day Green** Ches
116 F3 **Daybrook** Notts
114 F5 **Dayhills** Staffs
98 B7 **Dayhouse Bank** Worcs
65 K2 **Daylesford** Gloucs
128 D5 **Ddol** Flints
111 K8 **Ddol-Cownwy** Powys
41 L5 **Deal** Kent
164 E5 **Dean** Cumb
27 L2 **Dean** Devon
28 C1 **Dean** Devon
7 L2 **Dean** Devon
33 G7 **Dean** Dorset
34 F4 **Dean** Hants
35 H7 **Dean** Hants
140 C3 **Dean** Lancs
65 M3 **Dean** Oxon
31 L2 **Dean** Somset
52 C5 **Dean Bottom** Kent
66 C6 **Dean Court** Oxon
33 G7 **Dean End** Dorset
141 L7 **Dean Head** Barns
7 L2 **Dean Prior** Devon
131 G4 **Dean Row** Ches
39 J3 **Dean Street** Kent
188 C4 **Deanburnhaugh** Border
7 L2 **Deancombe** Devon
139 K6 **Deane** Bolton
35 H1 **Deane** Hants
141 G4 **Deanhead** Kirk
33 G7 **Deanland** Dorset
20 B4 **Deanlane End** W Susx
179 J6 **Deanraw** Nthumb
210 D5 **Deans** W Loth
164 E5 **Deanscales** Cumb
84 E7 **Deanshanger** Nhants
267 G6 **Deanshaugh** Moray
220 C6 **Deanston** Stirlg
164 E3 **Dearham** Cumb
140 D4 **Dearnley** Rochdl
90 F4 **Debach** Suffk
87 L8 **Debden** Essex
70 C7 **Debden** Essex
70 E1 **Debden Green** Essex
90 E3 **Debenham** Suffk
81 J5 **Deblin's Green** Worcs
210 D5 **Dechmont** W Loth
210 D5 **Dechmont Road** W Loth
66 C1 **Deddington** Oxon
90 C8 **Dedham** Essex
72 F1 **Dedham Heath** Essex
50 B4 **Dedworth** W & M
101 L5 **Deene** Nhants
101 L5 **Deenethorpe** Nhants
141 L8 **Deepcar** Sheff
49 L7 **Deepcut** Surrey
158 C5 **Deepdale** Cumb
158 F6 **Deepdale** N York
02 C2 **Deeping Gate** C Pete
02 D2 **Deeping St James** Lincs
19 H8 **Deeping St Nicholas** Lincs

64 C1 **Deerhurst** Gloucs
64 C2 **Deerhurst Walton** Gloucs
40 C3 **Deerton Street** Kent
81 L6 **Defford** Worcs
60 D2 **Defynnog** Powys
126 F4 **Deganwy** Conwy
216 B5 **Degnish** Ag & B
160 E2 **Deighton** N York
151 K7 **Deighton** York
125 K7 **Deiniolen** Gwynd
10 F5 **Delabole** Cnwll
130 A6 **Delamere** Ches
257 H7 **Delfrigs** Abers
20 D6 **Dell Quay** W Susx
27 K6 **Delley** Devon
253 L5 **Delliefure** Highld
65 M4 **Delly End** Oxon
39 J7 **Delmonden Green** Kent
254 D4 **Delnashaugh Inn** Moray
263 K5 **Delny** Highld
140 E6 **Delph** Oldham
168 E1 **Delves** Dur
233 H7 **Delvine** P & K
118 D4 **Dembleby** Lincs
5 G2 **Demelza** Cnwll
222 D4 **Den of Lindores** Fife
142 D7 **Denaby** Donc
142 D7 **Denaby Main** Donc
37 H1 **Denbies** Surrey
128 C6 **Denbigh** Denbgs
222 F3 **Denbrae** Fife
8 B1 **Denbury** Devon
116 C2 **Denby** Derbys
116 C2 **Denby Bottles** Derbys
141 K6 **Denby Dale** Kirk
48 A1 **Denchworth** Oxon
146 E2 **Dendron** Cumb
85 K8 **Denel End** Beds
221 G4 **Denfield** P & K
101 L8 **Denford** Nhants
72 E6 **Dengie** Essex
50 D2 **Denham** Bucks
88 E3 **Denham** Suffk
106 D8 **Denham** Suffk
88 F3 **Denham End** Suffk
50 D1 **Denham Green** Bucks
106 D8 **Denham Green** Suffk
269 J5 **Denhead** Abers
223 H4 **Denhead** Fife
222 F1 **Denhead of Gray** C Dund
189 G3 **Denholm** Border
141 G1 **Denholme** Brad
141 G1 **Denholme Clough** Brad
108 F4 **Denio** Gwynd
19 L1 **Denmead** Hants
245 L1 **Denmore** C Aber
37 J5 **Denne Park** W Susx
91 G2 **Dennington** Suffk
209 L3 **Denny** Falk
209 L3 **Dennyloanhead** Falk
140 E5 **Denshaw** Oldham
245 H4 **Denside** Abers
41 G7 **Densole** Kent
88 F5 **Denston** Suffk
115 H3 **Denstone** Staffs
40 E3 **Denstroude** Kent
158 B5 **Dent** Cumb
102 C6 **Denton** Cambs
169 G7 **Denton** Darltn
23 G6 **Denton** E Susx
52 E4 **Denton** Kent
41 G6 **Denton** Kent
117 M5 **Denton** Lincs
149 L6 **Denton** N York
85 G4 **Denton** Nhants
106 F5 **Denton** Norfk
66 E6 **Denton** Oxon
131 H1 **Denton** Tamesd
104 C3 **Denver** Norfk
191 J3 **Denwick** Nthumb
105 L3 **Deopham** Norfk
105 L4 **Deopham Green** Norfk
88 F4 **Depden** Suffk
88 F4 **Depden Green** Suffk
51 K3 **Deptford** Gt Lon
33 H3 **Deptford** Wilts
116 B4 **Derby** C Derb
27 K4 **Derby** Devon
154 C8 **Derbyhaven** IOM
232 C5 **Derculich** P & K
105 K1 **Dereham** Norfk
61 H6 **Deri** Caerph
11 K2 **Derril** Devon
41 G5 **Derringstone** Kent
114 D7 **Derrington** Staffs

11 L2 **Derriton** Devon
46 D5 **Derry Hill** Wilts
143 L6 **Derrythorpe** N Linc
120 F5 **Dersingham** Norfk
226 E2 **Dervaig** Ag & B
111 L2 **Derwen** Denbgs
59 G4 **Derwen Fawr** Carmth
92 F4 **Derwenlas** Powys
59 H5 **Derwydd** Carmth
101 H6 **Desborough** Nhants
100 B3 **Desford** Leics
267 K4 **Deskford** Moray
203 H6 **Detchant** Nthumb
53 G7 **Detling** Kent
96 F6 **Deuxhill** Shrops
62 F7 **Devauden** Mons
92 F8 **Devil's Bridge** Cerdgn
6 C4 **Deviock** Cnwll
99 H5 **Devitts Green** Warwks
46 E6 **Devizes** Wilts
6 E4 **Devonport** C Plym
221 G7 **Devonside** Clacks
3 K3 **Devoran** Cnwll
211 L6 **Dewarton** Mdloth
16 E3 **Dewlish** Dorset
141 K3 **Dewsbury** Kirk
141 K3 **Dewsbury Moor** Kirk
112 C8 **Deytheur** Powys
45 G5 **Dial** N Som
36 D5 **Dial Green** W Susx
139 M2 **Dial Hall** Lancs
21 K3 **Dial Post** W Susx
15 K2 **Dibberford** Dorset
18 F2 **Dibden** Hants
18 F2 **Dibden Purlieu** Hants
98 E8 **Dickens Heath** Solhll
106 D7 **Dickleburgh** Norfk
64 F1 **Didbrook** Gloucs
48 D1 **Didcot** Oxon
86 D2 **Diddington** Cambs
96 C6 **Diddlebury** Shrops
62 F1 **Didley** Herefs
20 D3 **Didling** W Susx
46 B2 **Didmarton** Gloucs
131 G1 **Didsbury** Manch
7 K2 **Didworthy** Devon
135 M8 **Digby** Lincs
259 H3 **Digg** Highld
140 F6 **Diggle** Oldham
139 G6 **Digmoor** Lancs
69 H4 **Digswell** Herts
69 H4 **Digswell Water** Herts
76 E4 **Dihewyd** Cerdgn
123 G6 **Dilham** Norfk
114 F3 **Dilhorne** Staffs
86 C2 **Dillington** Cambs
180 A6 **Dilston** Nthumb
32 E1 **Dilton** Wilts
32 D1 **Dilton Marsh** Wilts
80 A4 **Dilwyn** Herefs
139 L4 **Dimple** Bolton
132 F7 **Dimple** Derbys
58 A3 **Dinas** Carmth
10 C7 **Dinas** Cnwll
108 D4 **Dinas** Gwynd
75 G4 **Dinas** Pembks
42 F3 **Dinas** Rhondd
125 H8 **Dinas Dinlle** Gwynd
43 J7 **Dinas Powys** V Glam
111 G8 **Dinas-Mawddwy** Gwynd
31 J2 **Dinder** Somset
80 C7 **Dinedor** Herefs
62 F5 **Dingestow** Mons
129 J2 **Dingle** Lpool
39 K7 **Dingleden** Kent
101 G6 **Dingley** Nhants
262 F8 **Dingwall** Highld
62 F8 **Dinham** Mons
111 J3 **Dinmael** Conwy
244 A4 **Dinnet** Abers
180 F4 **Dinnington** N u Ty
133 K3 **Dinnington** Rothm
30 F8 **Dinnington** Somset
125 L7 **Dinorwic** Gwynd
67 J5 **Dinton** Bucks
33 H4 **Dinton** Wilts
187 H8 **Dinwoodie** D & G
26 E7 **Dinworthy** Devon
30 B6 **Dipford** Somset
49 H7 **Dipley** Hants
194 B3 **Dippen** Ag & B
195 G6 **Dippen** N Ayrs
36 B2 **Dippenhall** Surrey
12 B1 **Dippermill** Devon
12 B5 **Dippertown** Devon

267 G4 **Dipple** Moray
182 F2 **Dipple** S Ayrs
7 L3 **Diptford** Devon
180 E8 **Dipton** Dur
179 L6 **Diptonmill** Nthumb
212 B2 **Dirleton** E Loth
167 K2 **Dirt Pot** Nthumb
79 K2 **Discoed** Powys
116 D6 **Diseworth** Leics
160 E8 **Dishforth** N York
131 J3 **Disley** Ches
106 C7 **Diss** Norfk
78 E4 **Disserth** Powys
164 D6 **Distington** Cumb
33 J4 **Ditchampton** Wilts
191 G2 **Ditchburn** Nthumb
31 K4 **Ditcheat** Somset
107 G5 **Ditchingham** Norfk
66 A3 **Ditchley** Oxon
22 E4 **Ditchling** E Susx
113 H8 **Ditherington** Shrops
46 B5 **Ditteridge** Wilts
8 C4 **Dittisham** Devon
129 L2 **Ditton** Halton
52 F7 **Ditton** Kent
88 D4 **Ditton Green** Cambs
96 E5 **Ditton Priors** Shrops
64 E1 **Dixton** Gloucs
63 G4 **Dixton** Mons
11 H3 **Dizzard** Cnwll
140 F6 **Dobcross** Oldham
140 D3 **Dobroyd Castle** Calder
5 L2 **Dobwalls** Cnwll
13 H5 **Doccombe** Devon
251 H3 **Dochgarroch** Highld
36 B3 **Dockenfield** Surrey
157 J7 **Docker** Lancs
121 G4 **Docking** Norfk
80 D4 **Docklow** Herefs
165 J1 **Dockray** Cumb
165 L6 **Dockray** Cumb
115 G4 **Dod's Leigh** Staffs
7 L6 **Dodbrooke** Devon
113 K3 **Dodd's Green** Ches
70 E7 **Doddinghurst** Essex
103 H5 **Doddington** Cambs
40 B4 **Doddington** Kent
135 H5 **Doddington** Lincs
202 F6 **Doddington** Nthumb
96 E8 **Doddington** Shrops
13 K5 **Doddiscombsleigh** Devon
120 F5 **Doddshill** Norfk
6 C2 **Doddy Cross** Cnwll
84 B3 **Dodford** Nhants
97 L8 **Dodford** Worcs
45 L3 **Dodington** S Glos
30 A3 **Dodington** Somset
129 J7 **Dodleston** Ches
27 K7 **Dodscott** Devon
208 E8 **Dodside** E Rens
141 M6 **Dodworth** Barns
141 M7 **Dodworth Bottom** Barns
141 M6 **Dodworth Green** Barns
98 E4 **Doe Bank** Birm
133 J6 **Doe Lea** Derbys
14 A3 **Dog Village** Devon
136 D8 **Dogdyke** Lincs
141 J5 **Dogley Lane** Kirk
49 J8 **Dogmersfield** Hants
47 G2 **Dogridge** Wilts
102 D3 **Dogsthorpe** C Pete
93 H2 **Dol-for** Powys
58 D2 **Dol-gran** Carmth
94 C1 **Dolanog** Powys
79 G2 **Dolau** Powys
77 J7 **Dolaucothi** Carmth
109 J3 **Dolbenmaen** Gwynd
114 A5 **Doley** Shrops
93 K3 **Dolfach** Powys
94 D6 **Dolfor** Powys
126 F6 **Dolgarrog** Conwy
110 D7 **Dolgellau** Gwynd
92 E3 **Dolgoch** Gwynd
273 L7 **Doll** Highld
221 G7 **Dollar** Clacks
221 G7 **Dollarfield** Clacks
79 K2 **Dolley Green** Powys
92 E7 **Dollwen** Cerdgn
128 E5 **Dolphin** Flints
147 K5 **Dolphinholme** Lancs
199 J4 **Dolphinton** S Lans
27 K8 **Dolton** Devon
127 H5 **Dolwen** Conwy
110 D1 **Dolwyddelan** Conwy
92 D5 **Dolybont** Cerdgn

79 J4 **Dolyhir** Powys
112 D7 **Domgay** Powys
202 D5 **Donaldson's Lodge** Nthumb
142 F7 **Doncaster** Donc
142 F7 **Doncaster Carr** Donc
32 F6 **Donhead St Andrew** Wilts
32 F6 **Donhead St Mary** Wilts
211 G1 **Donibristle** Fife
29 K2 **Doniford** Somset
119 H4 **Donington** Lincs
136 D3 **Donington on Bain** Lincs
119 G5 **Donington Southing** Lincs
99 J1 **Donisthorpe** Leics
25 L1 **Donkey Street** Kent
50 B6 **Donkey Town** Surrey
65 J2 **Donnington** Gloucs
81 G8 **Donnington** Herefs
96 D2 **Donnington** Shrops
48 C5 **Donnington** W Berk
20 D6 **Donnington** W Susx
113 M8 **Donnington** Wrekin
97 G1 **Donnington Wood** Wrekin
30 E8 **Donyatt** Somset
37 J5 **Doomsday Green** W Susx
196 C7 **Doonfoot** S Ayrs
196 C7 **Doonholm** S Ayrs
253 L8 **Dorback Lodge** Highld
16 D4 **Dorchester** Dorset
66 E8 **Dorchester** Oxon
99 H3 **Dordon** Warwks
132 F3 **Dore** Sheff
251 G5 **Dores** Highld
37 J1 **Dorking** Surrey
89 J7 **Dorking Tye** Suffk
38 B5 **Dormans Land** Surrey
38 B5 **Dormans Park** Surrey
80 D7 **Dormington** Herefs
82 A4 **Dormston** Worcs
82 F8 **Dorn** Gloucs
50 B3 **Dorney** Bucks
248 D6 **Dornie** Highld
264 B2 **Dornoch** Highld
177 H5 **Dornock** D & G
279 J5 **Dorrery** Highld
98 F8 **Dorridge** Solhll
118 E1 **Dorrington** Lincs
96 B3 **Dorrington** Shrops
114 A3 **Dorrington** Shrops
82 D5 **Dorsington** Warwks
79 K7 **Dorstone** Herefs
67 G4 **Dorton** Bucks
99 G3 **Dosthill** Staffs
15 K3 **Dottery** Dorset
5 L2 **Doublebois** Cnwll
46 C1 **Doughton** Gloucs
154 e6 **Douglas** IOM
198 D7 **Douglas** S Lans
234 C8 **Douglas and Angus** C Dund
198 D6 **Douglas Castle** S Lans
217 K7 **Douglas Pier** Ag & B
198 E6 **Douglas Water** S Lans
198 D6 **Douglas West** S Lans
234 B6 **Douglastown** Angus
31 L2 **Doulting** Somset
275 b4 **Dounby** Ork
272 B7 **Doune** Highld
220 C6 **Doune** Stirlg
182 F3 **Dounepark** S Ayrs
263 G2 **Dounie** Highld
7 G1 **Dousland** Devon
112 E7 **Dovaston** Shrops
116 D1 **Dove Green** Notts
131 L4 **Dove Holes** Derbys
164 E4 **Dovenby** Cumb
41 K7 **Dover** Kent
139 J7 **Dover** Wigan
73 K1 **Dovercourt** Essex
81 K2 **Doverdale** Worcs
115 J5 **Doveridge** Derbys
37 L1 **Doversgreen** Surrey
232 F5 **Dowally** P & K
138 E2 **Dowbridge** Lancs
64 E3 **Dowdeswell** Gloucs
61 G5 **Dowlais** Myr Td
12 D1 **Dowland** Devon
30 E8 **Dowlish Ford** Somset
30 E8 **Dowlish Wake** Somset
65 G5 **Down Ampney** Gloucs
64 C3 **Down Hatherley** Gloucs
13 H2 **Down St Mary** Devon
6 F5 **Down Thomas** Devon
11 M4 **Downacarey** Devon
6 C4 **Downderry** Cnwll
51 L6 **Downe** Gt Lon
64 B7 **Downend** Gloucs

19 J6 **Downend** IOW
45 K3 **Downend** S Glos
48 C4 **Downend** W Berk
223 G1 **Downfield** C Dund
11 K8 **Downgate** Cnwll
11 L7 **Downgate** Cnwll
71 H7 **Downham** Essex
51 K4 **Downham** Gt Lon
148 D7 **Downham** Lancs
202 D6 **Downham** Nthumb
104 C3 **Downham Market** Norfk
31 J6 **Downhead** Somset
32 A2 **Downhead** Somset
4 D1 **Downhill** Cnwll
221 K1 **Downhill** P & K
138 D6 **Downholland Cross** Lancs
159 K3 **Downholme** N York
245 K4 **Downies** Abers
128 D4 **Downing** Flints
67 K8 **Downley** Bucks
31 K2 **Downside** Somset
31 L1 **Downside** Somset
50 E7 **Downside** Surrey
18 D5 **Downton** Hants
33 L6 **Downton** Wilts
95 K8 **Downton on the Rock** Herefs
118 F5 **Dowsby** Lincs
102 F2 **Dowsdale** Lincs
72 C2 **Dowsland Green** Essex
114 D6 **Doxey** Staffs
191 H2 **Doxford** Nthumb
45 L4 **Doynton** S Glos
43 K4 **Draethen** Caerph
198 C4 **Draffan** S Lans
143 M5 **Dragonby** N Linc
37 H6 **Dragons Green** W Susx
134 E2 **Drakeholes** Notts
97 J7 **Drakelow** Worcs
196 B1 **Drakemyre** N Ayrs
81 L5 **Drakes Broughton** Worcs
12 B8 **Drakewalls** Cnwll
149 J5 **Draughton** N York
101 G8 **Draughton** Nhants
143 H3 **Drax** N York
143 H3 **Drax Hales** N York
47 J3 **Draycot Foliat** Swindn
83 K1 **Draycote** Warwks
116 D5 **Draycott** Derbys
82 E8 **Draycott** Gloucs
97 H5 **Draycott** Shrops
31 G1 **Draycott** Somset
31 J6 **Draycott** Somset
81 K5 **Draycott** Worcs
115 J6 **Draycott in the Clay** Staffs
114 F3 **Draycott in the Moors** Staffs
28 D8 **Drayford** Devon
5 L1 **Draynes** Cnwll
19 L3 **Drayton** C Port
101 H5 **Drayton** Leics
119 H4 **Drayton** Lincs
106 D1 **Drayton** Norfk
83 K7 **Drayton** Oxon
66 C8 **Drayton** Oxon
30 F6 **Drayton** Somset
97 K8 **Drayton** Worcs
99 G3 **Drayton Bassett** Staffs
67 L5 **Drayton Beauchamp** Bucks
67 K2 **Drayton Parslow** Bucks
66 E7 **Drayton St Leonard** Oxon
149 J4 **Drebley** N York
154 g4 **Dreemskerry** IOM
54 F4 **Dreen Hill** Pembks
76 C7 **Drefach** Carmth
58 F6 **Drefach** Carmth
76 F6 **Drefach** Cerdgn
76 C7 **Drefelin** Carmth
196 C3 **Dreghorn** N Ayrs
41 H7 **Drellingore** Kent
212 B3 **Drem** E Loth
114 E3 **Dresden** C Stke
13 H4 **Drewsteignton** Devon
137 G5 **Driby** Lincs
152 F4 **Driffield** E R Yk
65 G7 **Driffield** Gloucs
64 F7 **Driffield Cross Roads** Gloucs
2 C5 **Drift** Cnwll
155 K3 **Drigg** Cumb
141 K2 **Drighlington** Leeds
227 G2 **Drimnin** Highld
15 K2 **Drimpton** Dorset
238 F7 **Drimsallie** Highld
153 J5 **Dringhoe** E R Yk
151 J6 **Dringhouses** York
89 J3 **Drinkstone** Suffk

89 J3 **Drinkstone Green** Suffk
135 H5 **Drinsey Nook** Notts
16 B1 **Drive End** Dorset
69 G3 **Driver's End** Herts
115 G6 **Drointon** Staffs
81 K3 **Droitwich** Worcs
221 L4 **Dron** P & K
133 G4 **Dronfield** Derbys
133 G4 **Dronfield Woodhouse** Derbys
196 E7 **Drongan** E Ayrs
234 A8 **Dronley** Angus
16 E1 **Droop** Dorset
133 H1 **Dropping Well** Rothm
35 J7 **Droxford** Hants
140 D8 **Droylsden** Tamesd
111 K3 **Druid** Denbgs
54 E3 **Druidston** Pembks
229 J6 **Druimachoish** Highld
229 H1 **Druimarbin** Highld
206 A5 **Druimdrishaig** Ag & B
237 K4 **Druimindarroch** Highld
206 E4 **Drum** Ag & B
221 J7 **Drum** P & K
198 F5 **Drumalbin** S Lans
270 F2 **Drumbeg** Highld
255 M4 **Drumblade** Abers
172 D6 **Drumbreddon** D & G
248 B5 **Drumbuie** Highld
177 J7 **Drumburgh** Cumb
175 L4 **Drumburn** D & G
208 E5 **Drumchapel** C Glas
231 J4 **Drumchastle** P & K
197 J3 **Drumclog** S Lans
223 G6 **Drumeldrie** Fife
199 K6 **Drumelzier** Border
247 L5 **Drumfearn** Highld
244 F4 **Drumfrennie** Abers
241 L3 **Drumguish** Highld
244 D5 **Drumhead** Abers
254 D5 **Drumin** Moray
184 E3 **Drumjohn** D & G
183 H7 **Drumlamford** S Ayrs
244 E2 **Drumlasie** Abers
177 J8 **Drumleaning** Cumb
192 D4 **Drumlemble** Ag & B
245 H7 **Drumlithie** Abers
173 K6 **Drummoddie** D & G
172 E7 **Drummore** D & G
255 H3 **Drummuir** Moray
250 E5 **Drumnadrochit** Highld
267 L5 **Drumnagorrach** Moray
185 L7 **Drumpark** D & G
271 G7 **Drumrunie Lodge** Highld
195 L8 **Drumshang** S Ayrs
259 G7 **Drumuie** Highld
253 H7 **Drumuillie** Highld
220 B6 **Drumvaich** Stirlg
221 L5 **Drunzie** P & K
191 K7 **Druridge** Nthumb
129 G6 **Drury** Flints
117 M2 **Dry Doddington** Lincs
87 H3 **Dry Drayton** Cambs
66 C7 **Dry Sandford** Oxon
52 E2 **Dry Street** Essex
166 F7 **Drybeck** Cumb
267 J4 **Drybridge** Moray
196 D4 **Drybridge** N Ayrs
63 J4 **Drybrook** Gloucs
201 J6 **Dryburgh** Border
3 G4 **Drym** Cnwll
208 E1 **Drymen** Stirlg
257 G3 **Drymuir** Abers
246 F2 **Drynoch** Highld
59 G5 **Dryslwyn** Carmth
96 D2 **Dryton** Shrops
268 E3 **Dubford** Abers
90 E1 **Dublin** Suffk
271 L4 **Duchally** Highld
85 L6 **Duck End** Beds
86 E2 **Duck End** Cambs
71 G2 **Duck End** Essex
88 D8 **Duck End** Essex
86 C4 **Duck's Cross** Beds
71 H3 **Duckend Green** Essex
113 H1 **Duckington** Ches
65 M5 **Ducklington** Oxon
87 J7 **Duddenhoe End** Essex
211 J4 **Duddingston** C Edin
101 L3 **Duddington** Nhants
30 C6 **Duddlestone** Somset
38 C7 **Duddleswell** E Susx
96 F6 **Duddlewick** Shrops
202 E4 **Duddo** Nthumb
129 L6 **Duddon** Ches

156 B5 **Duddon Bridge** Cumb
112 E4 **Dudleston** Shrops
112 E4 **Dudleston Heath** Shrops
97 L5 **Dudley** Dudley
181 G4 **Dudley** N Tyne
141 J2 **Dudley Hill** Brad
98 B5 **Dudley Port** Sandw
96 E8 **Dudnill** Shrops
17 L3 **Dudsbury** Dorset
68 B5 **Dudswell** Herts
116 B3 **Duffield** Derbys
42 C3 **Duffryn** Neath
255 G4 **Dufftown** Moray
266 D3 **Duffus** Moray
166 F5 **Dufton** Cumb
152 D2 **Duggleby** N York
248 C5 **Duirinish** Highld
247 L6 **Duisdalemore** Highld
239 G8 **Duisky** Highld
90 C6 **Duke Street** Suffk
61 J5 **Dukestown** Blae G
140 E8 **Dukinfield** Tamesd
125 H2 **Dulas** IOA
31 J2 **Dulcote** Somset
14 C1 **Dulford** Devon
232 B5 **Dull** P & K
209 K4 **Dullatur** N Lans
88 C4 **Dullingham** Cambs
88 C4 **Dullingham Ley** Cambs
253 J6 **Dulnain Bridge** Highld
86 D3 **Duloe** Beds
5 M3 **Duloe** Cnwll
29 G5 **Dulverton** Somset
51 J4 **Dulwich** Gt Lon
208 C4 **Dumbarton** W Duns
82 B8 **Dumbleton** Gloucs
176 C4 **Dumfries** D & G
208 E2 **Dumgoyne** Stirlg
35 J2 **Dummer** Hants
41 L2 **Dumpton** Kent
235 G3 **Dun** Angus
231 K4 **Dunalastair** P & K
207 J5 **Dunan** Ag & B
247 J3 **Dunan** Highld
230 E4 **Dunan** P & K
192 E6 **Dunaverty** Ag & B
30 D3 **Dunball** Somset
212 E3 **Dunbar** E Loth
275 G2 **Dunbeath** Highld
228 D8 **Dunbeg** Ag & B
220 D7 **Dunblane** Stirlg
222 D4 **Dunbog** Fife
34 D5 **Dunbridge** Hants
263 G8 **Duncanston** Highld
255 M6 **Duncanstone** Abers
13 K5 **Dunchideock** Devon
83 L1 **Dunchurch** Warwks
84 C5 **Duncote** Nhants
176 C2 **Duncow** D & G
221 L5 **Duncrievie** P & K
20 F3 **Duncton** W Susx
223 G1 **Dundee** C Dund
31 G4 **Dundon** Somset
196 D4 **Dundonald** S Ayrs
261 J2 **Dundonnell** Highld
165 H1 **Dundraw** Cumb
240 B1 **Dundreggan** Highld
175 J5 **Dundrennan** D & G
45 H5 **Dundry** N Som
245 G2 **Dunecht** Abers
210 E2 **Dunfermline** Fife
65 H7 **Dunfield** Gloucs
141 J7 **Dunford Bridge** Barns
40 B3 **Dungate** Kent
197 J3 **Dungavel** S Lans
46 C8 **Dunge** Wilts
132 E2 **Dungworth** Sheff
135 G5 **Dunham** Notts
130 E2 **Dunham Town** Traffd
130 E2 **Dunham Woodhouses** Traffd
129 L5 **Dunham-on-the-Hill** Ches
81 L3 **Dunhampstead** Worcs
81 J2 **Dunhampton** Worcs
135 L4 **Dunholme** Lincs
223 J5 **Dunino** Fife
209 L2 **Dunipace** Falk
38 F3 **Dunk's Green** Kent
232 F6 **Dunkeld** P & K
45 L7 **Dunkerton** BaNES
14 D1 **Dunkeswell** Devon
150 D6 **Dunkeswick** N York
129 J5 **Dunkirk** Ches
40 E3 **Dunkirk** Kent
46 A2 **Dunkirk** S Glos

Dunkirk - East Lexham 309

114 C1 **Dunkirk** Staffs
46 E6 **Dunkirk** Wilts
234 F2 **Dunlappie** Angus
48 C8 **Dunley** Hants
81 H2 **Dunley** Worcs
196 E1 **Dunlop** E Ayrs
251 G7 **Dunmaglass** Highld
5 H1 **Dunmere** Cnwll
210 A1 **Dunmore** Falk
53 G6 **Dunn Street** Kent
280 B2 **Dunnet** Highld
234 D5 **Dunnichen** Angus
221 J4 **Dunning** P & K
153 J5 **Dunnington** E R Yk
82 C4 **Dunnington** Warwks
151 L5 **Dunnington** York
140 B2 **Dunnockshaw** Lancs
207 K4 **Dunoon** Ag & B
253 J2 **Dunphail** Moray
172 E3 **Dunragit** D & G
202 B2 **Duns** Border
66 C2 **Duns Tew** Oxon
132 E5 **Dunsa** Derbys
118 E6 **Dunsby** Lincs
139 L5 **Dunscar** Bolton
185 L6 **Dunscore** D & G
143 G6 **Dunscroft** Donc
170 E6 **Dunsdale** R & Cl
49 H3 **Dunsden Green** Oxon
11 K1 **Dunsdon** Devon
36 F4 **Dunsfold** Surrey
13 J4 **Dunsford** Devon
222 D5 **Dunshalt** Fife
269 H6 **Dunshillock** Abers
133 J7 **Dunsill** Notts
171 K8 **Dunsley** N York
97 J6 **Dunsley** Staffs
67 L6 **Dunsmore** Bucks
148 B6 **Dunsop Bridge** Lancs
68 C3 **Dunstable** Beds
115 K7 **Dunstall** Staffs
81 K6 **Dunstall Common** Worcs
88 E3 **Dunstall Green** Suffk
191 K2 **Dunstan** Nthumb
191 J2 **Dunstan Steads** Nthumb
29 H2 **Dunster** Somset
180 F6 **Dunston** Gatesd
135 L7 **Dunston** Lincs
106 E3 **Dunston** Norfk
114 E8 **Dunston** Staffs
114 E8 **Dunston Heath** Staffs
7 H4 **Dunstone** Devon
13 G7 **Dunstone** Devon
143 G6 **Dunsville** Donc
144 D1 **Dunswell** E R Yk
199 J3 **Dunsyre** S Lans
11 M6 **Dunterton** Devon
65 M2 **Dunthrop** Oxon
64 E5 **Duntisbourne Abbots** Gloucs
64 E6 **Duntisbourne Rouse** Gloucs
16 D1 **Duntish** Dorset
208 E4 **Duntocher** W Duns
86 E6 **Dunton** Beds
67 K2 **Dunton** Bucks
121 J5 **Dunton** Norfk
100 C5 **Dunton Bassett** Leics
38 D2 **Dunton Green** Kent
52 E1 **Dunton Wayletts** Essex
259 G2 **Duntulm** Highld
195 L7 **Dunure** S Ayrs
57 G6 **Dunvant** Swans
258 C7 **Dunvegan** Highld
91 L1 **Dunwich** Suffk
131 J8 **Dunwood** Staffs
177 L8 **Durdar** Cumb
3 K5 **Durgan** Cnwll
169 H2 **Durham** Dur
186 C5 **Durisdeer** D & G
186 C5 **Durisdeermill** D & G
141 M4 **Durkar** Wakefd
30 C4 **Durleigh** Somset
35 G7 **Durley** Hants
47 K6 **Durley** Wilts
35 H7 **Durley Street** Hants
41 J4 **Durlock** Kent
41 J2 **Durlock** Kent
80 E7 **Durlow Common** Gloucs
234 C5 **Durmgley** Angus
140 E4 **Durn** Rochdl
276 F3 **Durness** Highld
228 F4 **Duror** Highld
216 F5 **Durran** Ag & B
21 J6 **Durrington** W Susx
33 K2 **Durrington** Wilts
245 G4 **Durris** Abers
63 M7 **Dursley** Gloucs
63 K3 **Dursley Cross** Gloucs
30 D5 **Durston** Somset
17 G1 **Durweston** Dorset
84 D3 **Duston** Nhants
253 H6 **Duthil** Highld
94 F7 **Dutlas** Powys
70 F2 **Duton Hill** Essex
11 L5 **Dutson** Cnwll
130 B4 **Dutton** Ches
87 K6 **Duxford** Cambs
66 A7 **Duxford** Oxon
126 E4 **Dwygyfylchi** Conwy
125 H6 **Dwyran** IOA
245 K1 **Dyce** C Aber
88 E7 **Dyer's End** Essex
56 E5 **Dyfatty** Carmth
110 D8 **Dyffrydan** Gwynd
42 C3 **Dyffryn** Brdgnd
61 G6 **Dyffryn** Myr Td
43 H7 **Dyffryn** V Glam
109 K7 **Dyffryn Ardudwy** Gwynd
93 G7 **Dyffryn Castell** Cerdgn
60 C5 **Dyffryn Cellwen** Neath
118 E7 **Dyke** Lincs
264 F8 **Dyke** Moray
233 K4 **Dykehead** Angus
234 B3 **Dykehead** Angus
210 A7 **Dykehead** N Lans
219 K7 **Dykehead** Stirlg
235 H2 **Dykelands** Abers
233 K4 **Dykends** Angus
256 C3 **Dykeside** Abers
93 J4 **Dylife** Powys
25 L1 **Dymchurch** Kent
63 K1 **Dymock** Gloucs
45 L4 **Dyrham** S Glos
222 E8 **Dysart** Fife
128 C4 **Dyserth** Denbgs

E

98 C8 **Eachway** Worcs
180 D4 **Eachwick** Nthumb
147 H6 **Eagland Hill** Lancs
135 H6 **Eagle** Lincs
135 H6 **Eagle Barnsdale** Lincs
135 H6 **Eagle Moor** Lincs
169 L7 **Eaglescliffe** S on T
164 E5 **Eaglesfield** Cumb
177 H4 **Eaglesfield** D & G
208 F8 **Eaglesham** E Rens
139 L5 **Eagley** Bolton
154 d6 **Eairy** IOM
84 F5 **Eakley Lanes** M Keyn
134 D7 **Eakring** Notts
143 K5 **Ealand** N Linc
50 F3 **Ealing** Gt Lon
178 F7 **Eals** Nthumb
166 C5 **Eamont Bridge** Cumb
148 F6 **Earby** Lancs
139 K3 **Earcroft** Bl w D
97 G5 **Eardington** Shrops
80 A4 **Eardisland** Herefs
79 K5 **Eardisley** Herefs
112 E6 **Eardiston** Shrops
80 F2 **Eardiston** Worcs
103 H8 **Earith** Cambs
100 A4 **Earl Shilton** Leics
90 F3 **Earl Soham** Suffk
132 B6 **Earl Sterndale** Derbys
90 D3 **Earl Stonham** Suffk
81 K6 **Earl's Croome** Worcs
23 L3 **Earl's Down** E Susx
90 B2 **Earl's Green** Suffk
202 F7 **Earle** Nthumb
130 B1 **Earlestown** St Hel
49 H4 **Earley** Wokham
106 D2 **Earlham** Norfk
258 F4 **Earlish** Highld
85 G3 **Earls Barton** Nhants
71 L1 **Earls Colne** Essex
81 M3 **Earls Common** Worcs
96 E8 **Earlsditton** Shrops
99 J7 **Earlsdon** Covtry
223 H7 **Earlsferry** Fife
51 H4 **Earlsfield** Gt Lon
256 E5 **Earlsford** Abers
141 L3 **Earlsheaton** Kirk
201 J5 **Earlston** Border
196 D4 **Earlston** E Ayrs
37 L1 **Earlswood** Surrey
98 E8 **Earlswood** Warwks
62 F8 **Earlswood Common** Mons
20 D7 **Earnley** W Susx
139 G3 **Earnshaw Bridge** Lancs
181 H4 **Earsdon** N Tyne
191 J7 **Earsdon** Nthumb
107 G5 **Earsham** Norfk
151 K4 **Earswick** York
20 F5 **Eartham** W Susx
45 K2 **Earthcott** S Glos
161 J1 **Easby** N York
215 L1 **Easdale** Ag & B
36 D6 **Easebourne** W Susx
100 A7 **Easenhall** Warwks
36 E2 **Eashing** Surrey
67 G5 **Easington** Bucks
169 L2 **Easington** Dur
145 K4 **Easington** E R Yk
203 J6 **Easington** Nthumb
67 G7 **Easington** Oxon
171 H7 **Easington** R & Cl
169 L2 **Easington Colliery** Dur
169 K2 **Easington Lane** Sundld
151 H2 **Easingwold** N York
41 H5 **Easole Street** Kent
233 M6 **Eassie and Nevay** Angus
42 F8 **East Aberthaw** V Glam
7 M5 **East Allington** Devon
28 F5 **East Anstey** Devon
34 E1 **East Anton** Hants
160 C3 **East Appleton** N York
19 K6 **East Ashey** IOW
20 D5 **East Ashling** W Susx
34 F2 **East Aston** Hants
163 H5 **East Ayton** N York
11 K3 **East Balsdon** Cnwll
61 K6 **East Bank** Blae G
136 C3 **East Barkwith** Lincs
39 H3 **East Barming** Kent
171 J8 **East Barnby** N York
69 H8 **East Barnet** Gt Lon
212 F4 **East Barns** E Loth
121 K5 **East Barsham** Norfk
122 D4 **East Beckham** Norfk
50 D4 **East Bedfont** Gt Lon
90 C8 **East Bergholt** Suffk
141 J2 **East Bierley** Kirk
121 L7 **East Bilney** Norfk
23 H7 **East Blatchington** E Susx
17 H4 **East Bloxworth** Dorset
181 J6 **East Boldon** S Tyne
18 F4 **East Boldre** Hants
191 G3 **East Bolton** Nthumb
30 D3 **East Bower** Somset
105 J2 **East Bradenham** Norfk
44 D8 **East Brent** Somset
117 J3 **East Bridgford** Notts
168 B6 **East Briscoe** Dur
28 B4 **East Buckland** Devon
14 C5 **East Budleigh** Devon
50 B2 **East Burnham** Bucks
16 F5 **East Burton** Dorset
168 E2 **East Butsfield** Dur
143 L6 **East Butterwick** N Linc
210 E5 **East Calder** W Loth
106 D3 **East Carleton** Norfk
150 B7 **East Carlton** Leeds
101 H5 **East Carlton** Nhants
16 F6 **East Chaldon (Chaldon Herring)** Dorset
48 A1 **East Challow** Oxon
7 L6 **East Charleton** Devon
16 A2 **East Chelborough** Dorset
191 K6 **East Chevington** Nthumb
22 F4 **East Chiltington** E Susx
31 H8 **East Chinnock** Somset
47 H8 **East Chisenbury** Wilts
34 C2 **East Cholderton** Hants
50 D8 **East Clandon** Surrey
67 H2 **East Claydon** Bucks
44 E5 **East Clevedon** N Som
31 J8 **East Coker** Somset
29 L4 **East Combe** Somset
31 K3 **East Compton** Somset
8 C4 **East Cornworthy** Devon
176 F7 **East Cote** Cumb
151 L7 **East Cottingwith** E R Yk
19 H4 **East Cowes** IOW
143 G4 **East Cowick** E R Yk
160 D2 **East Cowton** N York
181 G4 **East Cramlington** Nthumb
31 L2 **East Cranmore** Somset
17 H6 **East Creech** Dorset
165 K1 **East Curthwaite** Cumb
23 J7 **East Dean** E Susx
63 K3 **East Dean** Gloucs
34 C5 **East Dean** Hants
20 E4 **East Dean** W Susx
27 L3 **East Down** Devon
134 F4 **East Drayton** Notts
51 J4 **East Dulwich** Gt Lon
45 H5 **East Dundry** N Som
144 D2 **East Ella** C KuH
85 J6 **East End** Beds
86 C4 **East End** Beds
145 G2 **East End** E R Yk
145 H2 **East End** E R Yk
70 B5 **East End** Essex
48 B6 **East End** Hants
18 E4 **East End** Hants
70 C2 **East End** Herts
39 L6 **East End** Kent
53 L4 **East End** Kent
85 J6 **East End** M Keyn
44 F5 **East End** N Som
66 B4 **East End** Oxon
31 L2 **East End** Somset
90 C8 **East End** Suffk
47 J8 **East Everleigh** Wilts
39 J3 **East Farleigh** Kent
100 F6 **East Farndon** Nhants
143 K7 **East Ferry** Lincs
135 K3 **East Firsby** Lincs
212 C3 **East Fortune** E Loth
142 C1 **East Garforth** Leeds
47 M4 **East Garston** W Berk
48 C2 **East Ginge** Oxon
100 E1 **East Goscote** Leics
47 K6 **East Grafton** Wilts
91 J2 **East Green** Suffk
34 B5 **East Grimstead** Wilts
38 B5 **East Grinstead** W Susx
25 H3 **East Guldeford** E Susx
84 C2 **East Haddon** Nhants
48 D1 **East Hagbourne** Oxon
144 E4 **East Halton** N Linc
51 L2 **East Ham** Gt Lon
66 B8 **East Hanney** Oxon
71 J6 **East Hanningfield** Essex
142 D4 **East Hardwick** Wakefd
105 K6 **East Harling** Norfk
160 F3 **East Harlsey** N York
33 K5 **East Harnham** Wilts
45 H7 **East Harptree** BaNES
169 L7 **East Hartburn** S on T
181 G3 **East Hartford** Nthumb
20 C3 **East Harting** W Susx
32 F5 **East Hatch** Wilts
86 F5 **East Hatley** Cambs
159 L4 **East Hauxwell** N York
234 F8 **East Haven** Angus
119 G3 **East Heckington** Lincs
168 F3 **East Hedleyhope** Dur
274 D5 **East Helmsdale** Highld
48 C1 **East Hendred** Oxon
163 G7 **East Heslerton** N York
44 E6 **East Hewish** N Som
23 H4 **East Hoathly** E Susx
17 H5 **East Holme** Dorset
31 J2 **East Horrington** Somset
50 E8 **East Horsley** Surrey
203 G7 **East Horton** Nthumb
17 L3 **East Howe** Bmouth
151 K5 **East Huntington** York
30 E2 **East Huntspill** Somset
68 E4 **East Hyde** Beds
28 C2 **East Ilkerton** Devon
48 C3 **East Ilsley** W Berk
137 G7 **East Keal** Lincs
47 G5 **East Kennett** Wilts
150 E7 **East Keswick** Leeds
209 H8 **East Kilbride** S Lans
12 C3 **East Kimber** Devon
136 F7 **East Kirkby** Lincs
16 F5 **East Knighton** Dorset
28 E6 **East Knowstone** Devon
32 E5 **East Knoyle** Wilts
203 G5 **East Kyloe** Nthumb
31 G7 **East Lambrook** Somset
41 K6 **East Langdon** Kent
100 F5 **East Langton** Leics
229 H4 **East Laroch** Highld
20 D5 **East Lavant** W Susx
20 F4 **East Lavington** W Susx
159 L1 **East Layton** N York
116 F6 **East Leake** Notts
202 D5 **East Learmouth** Nthumb
13 G2 **East Leigh** Devon
7 K4 **East Leigh** Devon
7 L3 **East Leigh** Devon
121 J8 **East Lexham** Norfk

212 D3 **East Linton** E Loth
36 A5 **East Liss** Hants
48 B2 **East Lockinge** Oxon
143 K7 **East Lound** N Linc
17 G6 **East Lulworth** Dorset
152 E2 **East Lutton** N York
30 B5 **East Lydeard** Somset
31 J4 **East Lydford** Somset
39 H2 **East Malling** Kent
39 H2 **East Malling Heath** Kent
20 C4 **East Marden** W Susx
134 E5 **East Markham** Notts
33 J7 **East Martin** Hants
148 F5 **East Marton** N York
35 L6 **East Meon** Hants
29 H7 **East Mere** Devon
72 F4 **East Mersea** Essex
50 F5 **East Molesey** Surrey
17 H3 **East Morden** Dorset
149 K7 **East Morton** Brad
186 C6 **East Morton** D & G
162 B7 **East Ness** N York
153 L8 **East Newton** E R Yk
101 G3 **East Norton** Leics
8 C1 **East Ogwell** Devon
32 D7 **East Orchard** Dorset
202 F3 **East Ord** Nthumb
11 L4 **East Panson** Devon
17 M3 **East Parley** Dorset
39 G4 **East Peckham** Kent
54 F6 **East Pennar** Pembks
31 K3 **East Pennard** Somset
86 C2 **East Perry** Cambs
7 L7 **East Portlemouth** Devon
8 A7 **East Prawle** Devon
21 J6 **East Preston** W Susx
16 D1 **East Pulham** Dorset
26 F7 **East Putford** Devon
29 L2 **East Quantoxhead** Somset
53 H5 **East Rainham** Medway
169 J1 **East Rainton** Sundld
145 G7 **East Ravendale** NE Lin
121 J6 **East Raynham** Norfk
150 E7 **East Rigton** Leeds
44 E6 **East Rolstone** N Som
160 F2 **East Rounton** N York
121 H6 **East Rudham** Norfk
122 D3 **East Runton** Norfk
123 G6 **East Ruston** Norfk
212 B5 **East Saltoun** E Loth
159 K5 **East Scrafton** N York
51 G4 **East Sheen** Gt Lon
48 A4 **East Shefford** W Berk
181 G2 **East Sleekburn** Nthumb
123 K7 **East Somerton** Norfk
134 F1 **East Stockwith** Lincs
17 G5 **East Stoke** Dorset
117 K2 **East Stoke** Notts
32 D6 **East Stour** Dorset
41 H3 **East Stourmouth** Kent
27 L5 **East Stowford** Devon
35 H3 **East Stratton** Hants
41 J5 **East Studdal** Kent
39 L3 **East Sutton** Kent
5 L2 **East Taphouse** Cnwll
191 J6 **East Thirston** Nthumb
52 E3 **East Tilbury** Thurr
35 L4 **East Tisted** Hants
136 B3 **East Torrington** Lincs
106 B1 **East Tuddenham** Norfk
34 C5 **East Tytherley** Hants
46 D4 **East Tytherton** Wilts
13 K2 **East Village** Devon
96 C4 **East Wall** Shrops
121 G8 **East Walton** Norfk
31 J1 **East Water** Somset
12 F4 **East Week** Devon
34 C6 **East Wellow** Hants
222 F7 **East Wemyss** Fife
210 C6 **East Whitburn** W Loth
51 M3 **East Wickham** Gt Lon
55 J6 **East Williamston** Pembks
120 F8 **East Winch** Norfk
34 B4 **East Winterslow** Wilts
20 C7 **East Wittering** W Susx
159 L5 **East Witton** N York
179 L2 **East Woodburn** Nthumb
48 B6 **East Woodhay** Hants
32 C2 **East Woodlands** Somset
35 M3 **East Worldham** Hants
105 J5 **East Wretham** Norfk
26 D7 **East Youlstone** Devon
27 H5 **East-the-Water** Devon
169 J7 **Eastbourne** Darltn
23 K7 **Eastbourne** E Susx

91 K2 **Eastbridge** Suffk
43 J7 **Eastbrook** V Glam
149 J7 **Eastburn** Brad
68 E8 **Eastbury** Herts
47 M3 **Eastbury** W Berk
149 J5 **Eastby** N York
53 L5 **Eastchurch** Kent
64 C6 **Eastcombe** Gloucs
50 E1 **Eastcote** Gt Lon
84 D4 **Eastcote** Nhants
99 G7 **Eastcote** Solhll
26 D7 **Eastcott** Cnwll
46 F7 **Eastcott** Wilts
64 E8 **Eastcourt** Wilts
47 K6 **Eastcourt** Wilts
8 B5 **Eastdown** Devon
72 D8 **Eastend** Essex
198 F5 **Eastend** S Lans
243 J5 **Easter Balmoral** Abers
45 H2 **Easter Compton** S Glos
252 E2 **Easter Dalziel** Highld
211 H6 **Easter Howgate** Mdloth
263 G8 **Easter Kinkell** Highld
250 F3 **Easter Moniack** Highld
245 J3 **Easter Ord** Abers
223 K6 **Easter Pitkierie** Fife
281 d6 **Easter Skeld** Shet
202 B6 **Easter Softlaw** Border
251 H1 **Easter Suddie** Highld
20 F7 **Eastergate** W Susx
209 J6 **Easterhouse** C Glas
99 H7 **Eastern Green** Covtry
46 F8 **Easterton** Wilts
44 D8 **Eastertown** Somset
210 A6 **Eastfield** N Lans
163 J6 **Eastfield** N York
168 B3 **Eastgate** Dur
118 F7 **Eastgate** Lincs
122 C7 **Eastgate** Norfk
129 H4 **Eastham** Wirral
129 J3 **Eastham Ferry** Wirral
49 L5 **Easthampstead** Br For
80 A3 **Easthampton** Herefs
49 J5 **Eastheath** Wokham
96 D4 **Easthope** Shrops
72 C3 **Easthorpe** Essex
117 J1 **Easthorpe** Notts
13 H1 **Eastington** Devon
65 H4 **Eastington** Gloucs
63 M6 **Eastington** Gloucs
185 K8 **Eastlands** D & G
65 J6 **Eastleach Martin** Gloucs
65 J6 **Eastleach Turville** Gloucs
27 J5 **Eastleigh** Devon
34 F7 **Eastleigh** Hants
40 C4 **Eastling** Kent
104 E3 **Eastmoor** Norfk
19 L4 **Eastney** C Port
81 G7 **Eastnor** Herefs
143 K4 **Eastoft** N Linc
86 C1 **Easton** Cambs
177 J7 **Easton** Cumb
13 G5 **Easton** Devon
16 D8 **Easton** Dorset
35 G4 **Easton** Hants
118 B6 **Easton** Lincs
106 C1 **Easton** Norfk
31 H2 **Easton** Somset
91 G3 **Easton** Suffk
48 B4 **Easton** W Berk
46 C5 **Easton** Wilts
46 C2 **Easton Grey** Wilts
85 H3 **Easton Maudit** Nhants
101 M3 **Easton on the Hill** Nhants
47 J7 **Easton Royal** Wilts
45 G4 **Easton-in-Gordano** N Som
11 L4 **Eastpeek** Devon
102 F4 **Eastrea** Cambs
177 H5 **Eastriggs** D & G
143 K2 **Eastrington** E R Yk
65 J8 **Eastrop** Swindn
41 J4 **Eastry** Kent
36 C6 **Eastshaw** W Susx
45 J4 **Eastville** Bristl
137 H8 **Eastville** Lincs
117 K6 **Eastwell** Leics
70 B5 **Eastwick** Herts
140 E3 **Eastwood** Calder
116 D2 **Eastwood** Notts
53 H1 **Eastwood** Sthend
103 J5 **Eastwood End** Cambs
83 J2 **Eathorpe** Warwks
130 B7 **Eaton** Ches
131 G6 **Eaton** Ches
117 L5 **Eaton** Leics

106 D2 **Eaton** Norfk
134 E4 **Eaton** Notts
66 C6 **Eaton** Oxon
95 J5 **Eaton** Shrops
96 B5 **Eaton** Shrops
80 B7 **Eaton Bishop** Herefs
68 B3 **Eaton Bray** Beds
96 D2 **Eaton Constantine** Shrops
86 D3 **Eaton Ford** Beds
68 B3 **Eaton Green** Beds
65 K7 **Eaton Hastings** Oxon
96 C2 **Eaton Mascott** Shrops
86 D3 **Eaton Socon** Cambs
113 L7 **Eaton upon Tern** Shrops
130 C1 **Eaves Brow** Warrtn
99 H6 **Eaves Green** Solhll
162 F6 **Ebberston** N York
33 G6 **Ebbesborne Wake** Wilts
61 J5 **Ebbw Vale** Blae G
180 D7 **Ebchester** Dur
44 D6 **Ebdon** N Som
14 A5 **Ebford** Devon
64 B6 **Ebley** Gloucs
113 H2 **Ebnal** Ches
80 B3 **Ebnall** Herefs
82 E7 **Ebrington** Gloucs
12 C4 **Ebsworthy Town** Devon
48 D7 **Ecchinswell** Hants
213 G5 **Ecclaw** Border
177 G4 **Ecclefechan** D & G
202 B5 **Eccles** Border
52 F6 **Eccles** Kent
140 A8 **Eccles** Salfd
79 L5 **Eccles Green** Herefs
123 H5 **Eccles on Sea** Norfk
105 L5 **Eccles Road** Norfk
132 F3 **Ecclesall** Sheff
133 G1 **Ecclesfield** Sheff
114 C5 **Eccleshall** Staffs
149 M8 **Eccleshill** Brad
210 E4 **Ecclesmachan** W Loth
129 J7 **Eccleston** Ches
139 G4 **Eccleston** Lancs
138 F8 **Eccleston** St Hel
139 G4 **Eccleston Green** Lancs
245 G2 **Echt** Abers
201 L7 **Eckford** Border
133 H4 **Eckington** Derbys
81 L7 **Eckington** Worcs
84 F3 **Ecton** Nhants
132 B8 **Ecton** Staffs
132 B3 **Edale** Derbys
22 C5 **Edburton** W Susx
164 E2 **Edderside** Cumb
263 J3 **Edderton** Highld
41 G2 **Eddington** Kent
200 B4 **Eddleston** Border
209 J8 **Eddlewood** S Lans
156 F7 **Eden Mount** Cumb
51 K5 **Eden Park** Gt Lon
38 C4 **Edenbridge** Kent
140 B4 **Edenfield** Lancs
166 D4 **Edenhall** Cumb
118 E7 **Edenham** Lincs
132 E5 **Edensor** Derbys
218 D8 **Edentaggart** Ag & B
143 G6 **Edenthorpe** Donc
108 E4 **Edern** Gwynd
31 H3 **Edgarley** Somset
98 D6 **Edgbaston** Birm
3 J4 **Edgcombe** Cnwll
67 G3 **Edgcott** Bucks
28 E3 **Edgcott** Somset
64 B5 **Edge** Gloucs
95 K2 **Edge** Shrops
63 H4 **Edge End** Gloucs
113 H1 **Edge Green** Ches
113 J7 **Edgebolton** Shrops
122 B5 **Edgefield** Norfk
122 B4 **Edgefield Green** Norfk
139 L6 **Edgefold** Bolton
83 J5 **Edgehill** Warwks
112 E7 **Edgerley** Shrops
141 H4 **Edgerton** Kirk
140 C3 **Edgeside** Lancs
64 D6 **Edgeworth** Gloucs
28 E8 **Edgeworthy** Devon
8 C2 **Edginswell** Torbay
82 B3 **Edgiock** Worcs
114 A7 **Edgmond** Wrekin
114 A7 **Edgmond Marsh** Wrekin
95 J6 **Edgton** Shrops
51 G1 **Edgware** Gt Lon
139 L4 **Edgworth** Bl w D
258 E6 **Edinbane** Highld

211 J4 **Edinburgh** C Edin
99 G1 **Edingale** Staffs
175 L2 **Edingham** D & G
134 D8 **Edingley** Notts
123 G5 **Edingthorpe** Norfk
122 F5 **Edingthorpe Green** Norfk
202 D2 **Edington** Border
180 E2 **Edington** Nthumb
30 F3 **Edington** Somset
46 D8 **Edington** Wilts
30 F2 **Edington Burtle** Somset
44 D8 **Edingworth** Somset
101 K2 **Edith Weston** Rutlnd
30 E1 **Edithmead** Somset
68 B3 **Edlesborough** Bucks
191 G4 **Edlingham** Nthumb
136 D5 **Edlington** Lincs
178 C7 **Edmond Castle** Cumb
33 J8 **Edmondsham** Dorset
169 G1 **Edmondsley** Dur
117 M8 **Edmondthorpe** Leics
10 D7 **Edmonton** Cnwll
69 J8 **Edmonton** Gt Lon
168 C1 **Edmundbyers** Dur
202 A5 **Ednam** Border
115 L3 **Ednaston** Derbys
232 C5 **Edradynate** P & K
202 C2 **Edrom** Border
113 H5 **Edstaston** Shrops
82 E3 **Edstone** Warwks
80 F3 **Edvin Loach** Herefs
117 G4 **Edwalton** Notts
89 J6 **Edwardstone** Suffk
43 G2 **Edwardsville** Myr Td
59 H2 **Edwinsford** Carmth
134 C6 **Edwinstowe** Notts
86 E7 **Edworth** Beds
80 F4 **Edwyn Ralph** Herefs
234 F2 **Edzell** Angus
234 F2 **Edzell Woods** Angus
43 H5 **Efail Isaf** Rhondd
57 L6 **Efail-fach** Neath
112 A6 **Efail-Rhyd** Powys
108 F4 **Efailnewydd** Gwynd
75 K7 **Efailwen** Carmth
128 D8 **Efenechtyd** Denbgs
187 L7 **Effgill** D & G
50 E8 **Effingham** Surrey
115 K8 **Efflinch** Staffs
13 K2 **Efford** Devon
48 B8 **Egbury** Hants
21 G3 **Egdean** W Susx
139 L5 **Egerton** Bolton
40 B6 **Egerton** Kent
6 F3 **Eggbuckland** C Plym
28 B8 **Eggesford** Devon
68 B2 **Eggington** Beds
115 M6 **Egginton** Derbys
169 L7 **Egglescliffe** S on T
168 C6 **Eggleston** Dur
50 C5 **Egham** Surrey
50 B5 **Egham Wick** Surrey
101 J2 **Egleton** Rutlnd
191 G2 **Eglingham** Nthumb
10 D8 **Egloshayle** Cnwll
11 K5 **Egloskerry** Cnwll
113 G3 **Eglwys Cross** Wrexhm
92 F4 **Eglwys Fach** Cerdgn
42 F7 **Eglwys-Brewis** V Glam
126 F5 **Eglwysbach** Conwy
75 K4 **Eglwyswrw** Pembks
134 E6 **Egmanton** Notts
164 D8 **Egremont** Cumb
129 H1 **Egremont** Wirral
162 E2 **Egton** N York
162 D2 **Egton Bridge** N York
143 L2 **Eight and Forty** E R Yk
72 D2 **Eight Ash Green** Essex
248 C8 **Eilanreach** Highld
78 C2 **Elan Village** Powys
45 J1 **Elberton** S Glos
20 F6 **Elbridge** W Susx
7 G4 **Elburton** C Plym
47 H3 **Elcombe** Swindn
48 B5 **Elcot** W Berk
88 B8 **Elder Street** Essex
103 G4 **Eldernell** Cambs
64 A1 **Eldersfield** Worcs
208 D6 **Elderslie** Rens
160 F7 **Eldmire** N York
169 G5 **Eldon** Dur
149 L7 **Eldwick** Brad
245 H6 **Elfhill** Abers
203 K7 **Elford** Nthumb
98 F1 **Elford** Staffs

Elgin - Eyton upon the Weald Moors 311

266 E4 Elgin Moray
247 H6 Elgol Highld
41 G6 Elham Kent
223 J7 Elie Fife
190 D4 Elilaw Nthumb
124 F3 Elim IOA
18 F1 Eling Hants
134 D4 Elkesley Notts
64 D4 Elkstone Gloucs
268 B4 Ella Abers
8 D2 Ellacombe Torbay
215 L1 Ellanbeich Ag & B
141 H4 Elland Calder
141 H3 Elland Lower Edge Calder
206 A4 Ellary Ag & B
115 J3 Ellastone Staffs
147 J4 Ellel Lancs
212 F7 Ellemford Border
37 G4 Ellen's Green Surrey
164 D3 Ellenborough Cumb
139 L7 Ellenbrook Salfd
114 C6 Ellenhall Staffs
160 F3 Ellerbeck N York
171 J7 Ellerby N York
113 K7 Ellerdine Heath Wrekin
14 A2 Ellerhayes Devon
229 G5 Elleric Ag & B
144 A2 Ellerker E R Yk
149 H7 Ellers N York
151 L7 Ellerton E R Yk
160 C3 Ellerton N York
113 M6 Ellerton Shrops
67 K6 Ellesborough Bucks
112 F4 Ellesmere Shrops
129 J4 Ellesmere Port Ches
29 H2 Ellicombe Somset
18 A2 Ellingham Hants
107 G5 Ellingham Norfk
203 K8 Ellingham Nthumb
159 M6 Ellingstring N York
86 D1 Ellington Cambs
191 K7 Ellington Nthumb
86 D1 Ellington Thorpe Cambs
32 D2 Elliots Green Somset
35 K2 Ellisfield Hants
259 H3 Ellishader Highld
99 L1 Ellistown Leics
257 H5 Ellon Abers
166 A4 Ellonby Cumb
107 J6 Ellough Suffk
144 B2 Elloughton E R Yk
63 H5 Ellwood Gloucs
103 K2 Elm Cambs
71 J6 Elm Green Essex
107 K3 Elm Grove Norfk
52 B2 Elm Park Gt Lon
81 K2 Elmbridge Worcs
87 J7 Elmdon Essex
98 F6 Elmdon Solhll
98 F7 Elmdon Heath Solhll
21 G6 Elmer W Susx
139 G6 Elmer's Green Lancs
51 K5 Elmers End Gt Lon
100 A4 Elmesthorpe Leics
98 E1 Elmhurst Staffs
82 A7 Elmley Castle Worcs
81 K1 Elmley Lovett Worcs
64 A4 Elmore Gloucs
63 M4 Elmore Back Gloucs
81 G2 Elms Green Worcs
26 D6 Elmscott Devon
90 C6 Elmsett Suffk
72 F3 Elmstead Heath Essex
72 F2 Elmstead Market Essex
72 F3 Elmstead Row Essex
40 F6 Elmsted Court Kent
41 H3 Elmstone Kent
64 D2 Elmstone Hardwicke Gloucs
152 F4 Elmswell E R Yk
89 K2 Elmswell Suffk
133 K5 Elmton Derbys
271 H6 Elphin Highld
211 L5 Elphinstone E Loth
245 H2 Elrick Abers
173 J5 Elrig D & G
179 K6 Elrington Nthumb
190 C7 Elsdon Nthumb
142 B7 Elsecar Barns
70 D2 Elsenham Essex
66 D5 Elsfield Oxon
144 C5 Elsham N Linc
245 K4 Elsick House Abers
122 B8 Elsing Norfk
149 G6 Elslack N York
19 K3 Elson Hants
112 F4 Elson Shrops
199 J4 Elsrickle S Lans
36 D2 Elstead Surrey
20 D3 Elsted W Susx
118 E6 Elsthorpe Lincs
169 J6 Elstob Dur
139 J1 Elston Lancs
117 K2 Elston Notts
33 J2 Elston Wilts
28 B7 Elstone Devon
85 L6 Elstow Beds
68 F8 Elstree Herts
145 G1 Elstronwick E R Yk
147 H8 Elswick Lancs
180 F6 Elswick N u Ty
87 G3 Elsworth Cambs
156 D2 Elterwater Cumb
51 L4 Eltham Gt Lon
86 F3 Eltisley Cambs
140 B5 Elton Bury
102 B4 Elton Cambs
129 K4 Elton Ches
132 D7 Elton Derbys
63 K4 Elton Gloucs
80 B1 Elton Herefs
117 K4 Elton Notts
169 L7 Elton S on T
129 K5 Elton Green Ches
180 C6 Eltringham Nthumb
186 E3 Elvanfoot S Lans
116 C5 Elvaston Derbys
105 G7 Elveden Suffk
49 J7 Elvetham Heath Hants
212 A4 Elvingston E Loth
41 J5 Elvington Kent
151 L6 Elvington York
28 B4 Elwell Devon
170 B4 Elwick Hartpl
203 J5 Elwick Nthumb
130 E7 Elworth Ches
29 K4 Elworthy Somset
103 L7 Ely Cambs
43 J6 Ely Cardif
85 H5 Emberton M Keyn
165 G5 Embleton Cumb
169 L5 Embleton Dur
191 J2 Embleton Nthumb
264 C1 Embo Highld
264 C2 Embo Street Highld
31 K1 Emborough Somset
149 H5 Embsay N York
18 D2 Emery Down Hants
141 K5 Emley Kirk
141 K5 Emley Moor Kirk
49 J5 Emmbrook Wokham
49 H4 Emmer Green Readg
133 J4 Emmett Carr Derbys
67 H6 Emmington Oxon
103 K2 Emneth Cambs
103 K2 Emneth Hungate Norfk
101 L2 Empingham Rutlnd
35 M4 Empshott Hants
35 M5 Empshott Green Hants
20 B5 Emsworth Hants
48 B6 Enborne W Berk
48 C6 Enborne Row W Berk
96 B4 Enchmarsh Shrops
100 C3 Enderby Leics
157 H5 Endmoor Cumb
114 E1 Endon Staffs
114 E1 Endon Bank Staffs
69 K7 Enfield Gt Lon
69 K7 Enfield Lock Gt Lon
69 K7 Enfield Wash Gt Lon
47 H8 Enford Wilts
45 K2 Engine Common S Glos
80 D5 England's Gate Herefs
48 F4 Englefield W Berk
50 C4 Englefield Green Surrey
114 B1 Engleseabrook Ches
63 H4 English Bicknor Gloucs
113 G5 English Frankton Shrops
45 L6 Englishcombe BaNES
4 E1 Engollan Cnwll
34 E1 Enham-Alamein Hants
30 C4 Enmore Somset
32 E6 Enmore Green Dorset
164 E7 Ennerdale Bridge Cumb
4 F3 Enniscaven Cnwll
233 G3 Enochdhu P & K
226 D3 Ensay Ag & B
17 L3 Ensbury Bmouth
112 F8 Ensdon Shrops
27 K5 Ensis Devon
114 E6 Enson Staffs
66 A2 Enstone Oxon
186 C5 Enterkinfoot D & G
161 G2 Enterpen N York
97 J6 Enville Staffs
3 K4 Enys Cnwll
283 b12 Eolaigearraidh W Isls
63 M5 Epney Gloucs
117 H2 Epperstone Notts
70 C6 Epping Essex
70 B6 Epping Green Essex
69 J5 Epping Green Herts
70 C6 Epping Upland Essex
168 F8 Eppleby N York
144 C2 Eppleworth E R Yk
51 G6 Epsom Surrey
83 H7 Epwell Oxon
143 K7 Epworth N Linc
143 J7 Epworth Turbary N Linc
112 E3 Erbistock Wrexhm
98 E5 Erdington Birm
38 E6 Eridge Green E Susx
38 E6 Eridge Station E Susx
206 D4 Erines Ag & B
3 H7 Erisey Cnwll
228 D6 Eriska Ag & B
104 E7 Eriswell Suffk
52 B3 Erith Gt Lon
46 D8 Erlestoke Wilts
7 J4 Ermington Devon
122 D5 Erpingham Norfk
40 B3 Erriottwood Kent
250 F7 Errogie Highld
222 D3 Errol P & K
208 D5 Erskine Rens
172 B1 Ervie D & G
90 F8 Erwarton Suffk
78 F6 Erwood Powys
160 D1 Eryholme N York
128 E8 Eryrys Denbgs
2 B5 Escalls Cnwll
168 F4 Escomb Dur
29 K3 Escott Somset
151 K7 Escrick York
58 C3 Esgair Carmth
77 G2 Esgair Cerdgn
93 G2 Esgairgeiliog Powys
77 H7 Esgerdawe Carmth
126 F4 Esgyryn Conwy
169 G2 Esh Dur
169 G2 Esh Winning Dur
50 F6 Esher Surrey
150 A7 Esholt Brad
191 J6 Eshott Nthumb
149 G4 Eshton N York
250 D4 Eskadale Highld
211 K5 Eskbank Mdloth
155 L3 Eskdale Green Cumb
187 K6 Eskdalemuir D & G
164 E7 Eskett Cumb
145 K8 Eskham Lincs
143 G4 Eskholme Donc
168 E6 Esperley Lane Ends Dur
147 H8 Esprick Lancs
102 A1 Essendine Rutlnd
69 H5 Essendon Herts
251 H4 Essich Highld
98 B3 Essington Staffs
257 G6 Esslemont Abers
170 D7 Eston R & Cl
202 E5 Etal Nthumb
46 F7 Etchilhampton Wilts
24 C2 Etchingham E Susx
41 G7 Etchinghill Kent
115 G7 Etchinghill Staffs
23 H3 Etchingwood E Susx
153 L8 Etherdwick E R Yk
105 K1 Etling Green Norfk
63 K6 Etloe Gloucs
50 B3 Eton W & M
50 B3 Eton Wick W & M
114 D2 Etruria C Stke
241 J5 Etteridge Highld
167 K5 Ettersgill Dur
130 E7 Ettiley Heath Ches
97 L4 Ettingshall Wolves
83 G5 Ettington Warwks
102 C2 Etton C Pete
152 F7 Etton E R Yk
187 L3 Ettrick Border
188 C1 Ettrickbridge Border
187 L3 Ettrickhill Border
115 M5 Etwall Derbys
96 F5 Eudon George Shrops
105 H7 Euston Suffk
103 K4 Euximoor Drove Cambs
139 H4 Euxton Lancs
79 J3 Evancoyd Powys
263 G6 Evanton Highld
118 E2 Evedon Lincs
97 G2 Evelith Shrops
263 L2 Evelix Highld
79 J3 Evenjobb Powys
84 B8 Evenley Oxon
65 J1 Evenlode Gloucs
168 F5 Evenwood Dur
168 F6 Evenwood Gate Dur
31 L3 Evercreech Somset
152 B7 Everingham E R Yk
47 J8 Everleigh Wilts
163 H5 Everley N York
12 B4 Eversfield Devon
85 K8 Eversholt Beds
16 A2 Evershot Dorset
49 J6 Eversley Hants
49 J6 Eversley Cross Hants
144 A2 Everthorpe E R Yk
86 D5 Everton Beds
18 D5 Everton Hants
129 H1 Everton Lpool
134 D2 Everton Notts
177 K4 Evertown D & G
80 F5 Evesbatch Herefs
82 B6 Evesham Worcs
100 D3 Evington C Leic
141 L8 Ewden Village Sheff
97 G4 Ewdness Shrops
51 G6 Ewell Surrey
41 H6 Ewell Minnis Kent
48 F1 Ewelme Oxon
64 E7 Ewen Gloucs
42 D6 Ewenny V Glam
118 F2 Ewerby Lincs
118 F2 Ewerby Thorpe Lincs
190 F7 Ewesley Nthumb
37 G3 Ewhurst Surrey
24 E2 Ewhurst Green E Susx
37 G3 Ewhurst Green Surrey
129 G6 Ewloe Flints
129 G6 Ewloe Green Flints
139 K3 Ewood Bl w D
140 B4 Ewood Bridge Lancs
12 B3 Eworthy Devon
36 B1 Ewshot Hants
62 D2 Ewyas Harold Herefs
12 E2 Exbourne Devon
19 G4 Exbury Hants
23 H7 Exceat E Susx
29 G6 Exebridge Somset
160 D5 Exelby N York
13 L4 Exeter Devon
28 E3 Exford Somset
95 L2 Exfordsgreen Shrops
82 D4 Exhall Warwks
99 J6 Exhall Warwks
49 G3 Exlade Street Oxon
149 J7 Exley Head Brad
13 M5 Exminster Devon
14 A6 Exmouth Devon
88 C2 Exning Suffk
41 G6 Exted Kent
14 A5 Exton Devon
35 J6 Exton Hants
101 K1 Exton Rutlnd
29 G4 Exton Somset
13 L4 Exwick Devon
132 D4 Eyam Derbys
83 M5 Eydon Nhants
102 E3 Eye C Pete
80 C2 Eye Herefs
106 C8 Eye Suffk
102 E3 Eye Green C Pete
117 K8 Eye Kettleby Leics
213 L6 Eyemouth Border
86 E6 Eyeworth Beds
39 L2 Eyhorne Street Kent
91 H5 Eyke Suffk
86 D3 Eynesbury Cambs
52 C6 Eynsford Kent
66 B5 Eynsham Oxon
15 K4 Eype Dorset
259 G6 Eyre Highld
41 J5 Eythorne Kent
80 B3 Eyton Herefs
112 F8 Eyton Shrops
113 G7 Eyton Shrops
95 J6 Eyton Shrops
112 E3 Eyton Wrexhm
96 D2 Eyton on Severn Shrops
113 L8 Eyton upon the Weald Moors Wrekin

F

48 A7 Faccombe Hants
161 H2 Faceby N York
111 K8 Fachwen Powys
140 D4 Facit Lancs
133 J7 Fackley Notts
113 K1 Faddiley Ches
161 L5 Fadmoor N York
57 J4 Faerdre Swans
57 J4 Fagwyr Swans
208 E4 Faifley W Duns
45 G4 Failand N Som
196 F5 Failford S Ayrs
140 D7 Failsworth Oldham
35 G7 Fair Oak Hants
49 G6 Fair Oak Green Hants
92 D1 Fairbourne Gwynd
142 D2 Fairburn N York
131 L5 Fairfield Derbys
25 H2 Fairfield Kent
97 L8 Fairfield Worcs
65 H6 Fairford Gloucs
65 H6 Fairford Park Gloucs
175 L3 Fairgirth D & G
138 C2 Fairhaven Lancs
207 L8 Fairlie N Ayrs
24 F5 Fairlight E Susx
14 C3 Fairmile Devon
50 E6 Fairmile Surrey
200 F6 Fairnilee Border
114 B5 Fairoak Staffs
52 D6 Fairseat Kent
71 J4 Fairstead Essex
122 F6 Fairstead Norfk
23 G2 Fairwarp E Susx
43 J6 Fairwater Cardif
27 G6 Fairy Cross Devon
121 K5 Fakenham Norfk
105 H8 Fakenham Magna Suffk
211 M6 Fala Mdloth
211 M6 Fala Dam Mdloth
211 L7 Falahill Border
77 G5 Falcondale Cerdgn
84 B6 Falcut Nhants
135 L3 Faldingworth Lincs
9 f2 Faldouet Jersey
63 K8 Falfield S Glos
91 G7 Falkenham Suffk
210 A3 Falkirk Falk
222 D5 Falkland Fife
133 G7 Fallgate Derbys
209 L1 Fallin Stirlg
191 H2 Falloden Nthumb
131 G1 Fallowfield Manch
179 L5 Fallowfield Nthumb
216 F4 Falls of Blarghour Ag & B
22 E5 Falmer E Susx
3 K4 Falmouth Cnwll
188 C5 Falnash Border
163 J5 Falsgrave N York
179 G2 Falstone Nthumb
276 B6 Fanagmore Highld
68 C2 Fancott Beds
250 E3 Fanellan Highld
161 J4 Fangdale Beck N York
152 A5 Fangfoss E R Yk
226 E3 Fanmore Ag & B
261 L6 Fannich Lodge Highld
201 J5 Fans Border
85 G8 Far Bletchley M Keyn
84 E3 Far Cotton Nhants
156 D3 Far End Cumb
97 G8 Far Forest Worcs
63 M7 Far Green Gloucs
139 G7 Far Moor Wigan
64 D6 Far Oakridge Gloucs
156 E4 Far Sawrey Cumb
136 E5 Far Thorpe Lincs
102 D4 Farcet Cambs
96 D8 Farden Shrops
19 K2 Fareham Hants
98 D1 Farewell Staffs
136 F4 Farforth Lincs
65 L8 Faringdon Oxon
139 G3 Farington Lancs
232 F8 Farkhill P & K
178 D7 Farlam Cumb
7 L4 Farleigh Devon
45 G5 Farleigh N Som
51 K7 Farleigh Surrey
46 A7 Farleigh Hungerford Somset
35 J2 Farleigh Wallop Hants
137 J5 Farlesthorpe Lincs

157 H6 Farleton Cumb
147 L2 Farleton Lancs
132 F7 Farley Derbys
115 H3 Farley Staffs
34 B5 Farley Wilts
88 E4 Farley Green Suffk
37 G2 Farley Green Surrey
49 H6 Farley Hill Wokham
63 M4 Farleys End Gloucs
19 M3 Farlington C Port
151 K2 Farlington N York
96 E7 Farlow Shrops
116 C8 Farm Town Leics
45 K7 Farmborough BaNES
70 F5 Farmbridge End Essex
64 F1 Farmcote Gloucs
97 H5 Farmcote Shrops
77 J6 Farmers Carmth
65 H4 Farmington Gloucs
66 C5 Farmoor Oxon
3 H4 Farms Common Cnwll
267 K6 Farmtown Moray
267 J4 Farnachty Moray
116 B2 Farnah Green Derbys
51 L6 Farnborough Gt Lon
49 L8 Farnborough Hants
48 B3 Farnborough W Berk
83 K5 Farnborough Warwks
49 L7 Farnborough Park Hants
49 L7 Farnborough Street Hants
36 E2 Farncombe Surrey
85 H3 Farndish Beds
112 F1 Farndon Ches
117 K1 Farndon Notts
235 G4 Farnell Angus
33 G7 Farnham Dorset
70 C2 Farnham Essex
150 E4 Farnham N York
91 H3 Farnham Suffk
36 C2 Farnham Surrey
50 B2 Farnham Common Bucks
70 C2 Farnham Green Essex
50 B2 Farnham Royal Bucks
52 C5 Farningham Kent
150 B6 Farnley Leeds
141 L1 Farnley Leeds
141 J5 Farnley Tyas Kirk
134 C8 Farnsfield Notts
139 L6 Farnworth Bolton
129 L2 Farnworth Halton
278 B4 Farr Highld
251 J5 Farr Highld
241 L3 Farr Highld
251 G7 Farraline Highld
14 B4 Farringdon Devon
45 J7 Farrington Gurney BaNES
141 K1 Farsley Leeds
71 K6 Farther Howegreen Essex
39 K4 Farthing Green Kent
51 L6 Farthing Street Gt Lon
83 M7 Farthinghoe Nhants
41 J7 Farthingloe Kent
84 B4 Farthingstone Nhants
141 J4 Fartown Kirk
141 K1 Fartown Leeds
14 E3 Farway Street Devon
229 G6 Fasnacloich Ag & B
250 B6 Fasnakyle Highld
239 G7 Fassfern Highld
181 H8 Fatfield Sundld
178 C7 Faugh Cumb
115 K6 Fauld Staffs
210 B4 Fauldhouse W Loth
71 J4 Faulkbourne Essex
45 L8 Faulkland Somset
113 K5 Fauls Shrops
40 D3 Faversham Kent
150 F1 Fawdington N York
180 F5 Fawdon N u Ty
190 E3 Fawdon Nthumb
131 L7 Fawfieldhead Staffs
52 C6 Fawkham Green Kent
66 A4 Fawler Oxon
49 J2 Fawley Bucks
19 G3 Fawley Hants
48 B3 Fawley W Berk
63 H1 Fawley Chapel Herefs
128 F6 Fawnog Flints
84 A4 Fawsley Nhants
143 L3 Faxfleet E R Yk
37 K4 Faygate W Susx
138 D8 Fazakerley Lpool
99 G3 Fazeley Staffs
160 B6 Fearby N York
264 C4 Fearn Highld

231 K6 Fearnan P & K
260 B7 Fearnbeg Highld
130 C2 Fearnhead Warrtn
260 A7 Fearnmore Highld
206 E3 Fearnoch Ag & B
97 L2 Featherstone Staffs
142 C3 Featherstone Wakefd
82 B3 Feckenham Worcs
72 C3 Feering Essex
159 H3 Feetham N York
148 D2 Feizor N York
38 B5 Felbridge Surrey
122 E4 Felbrigg Norfk
38 B5 Felcourt Surrey
37 H2 Felday Surrey
68 D6 Felden Herts
76 F4 Felin Fach Cerdgn
58 F4 Felin gwm Isaf Carmth
58 F4 Felin gwm Uchaf Carmth
78 F6 Felin-newydd Powys
59 G4 Felindre Carmth
59 K3 Felindre Carmth
76 C7 Felindre Carmth
77 G4 Felindre Cerdgn
94 E7 Felindre Powys
61 J2 Felindre Powys
57 H4 Felindre Swans
75 J4 Felindre Farchog Pembks
78 F3 Felinfach Powys
56 F4 Felinfoel Carmth
161 G5 Felixkirk N York
91 G8 Felixstowe Suffk
91 H7 Felixstowe Ferry Suffk
202 E4 Felkington Nthumb
142 B5 Felkirk Wakefd
156 D2 Fell Foot Cumb
149 J7 Fell Lane Brad
165 J3 Fell Side Cumb
181 G6 Felling Gatesd
85 K4 Felmersham Beds
122 E5 Felmingham Norfk
20 F7 Felpham W Susx
89 J4 Felsham Suffk
71 G3 Felsted Essex
50 E4 Feltham Gt Lon
50 E5 Felthamhill Gt Lon
122 D7 Felthorpe Norfk
80 D5 Felton Herefs
45 G6 Felton N Som
191 H6 Felton Nthumb
112 F8 Felton Butler Shrops
104 E5 Feltwell Norfk
87 K3 Fen Ditton Cambs
87 G2 Fen Drayton Cambs
119 H7 Fen End Lincs
99 G8 Fen End Solhll
105 K4 Fen Street Norfk
90 E3 Fen Street Suffk
141 J4 Fenay Bridge Kirk
148 E8 Fence Lancs
133 J3 Fence Rothm
169 J1 Fence Houses Sundld
160 D4 Fencote N York
66 E4 Fencott Oxon
137 H7 Fendike Corner Lincs
203 H5 Fenham Nthumb
139 K2 Feniscliffe Bl w D
139 K3 Feniscowles Bl w D
14 D3 Feniton Devon
97 H6 Fenn Green Shrops
53 G4 Fenn Street Medway
115 K2 Fenny Bentley Derbys
14 D3 Fenny Bridges Devon
83 K5 Fenny Compton Warwks
99 K4 Fenny Drayton Leics
85 G8 Fenny Stratford M Keyn
191 H7 Fenrother Nthumb
87 G2 Fenstanton Cambs
88 F5 Fenstead End Suffk
114 D3 Fenton C Stke
103 G7 Fenton Cambs
178 C7 Fenton Cumb
135 G4 Fenton Lincs
118 A1 Fenton Lincs
134 F3 Fenton Notts
202 F6 Fenton Nthumb
212 B3 Fenton Barns E Loth
142 F4 Fenwick Donc
196 F2 Fenwick E Ayrs
203 H5 Fenwick Nthumb
180 C4 Fenwick Nthumb
3 L3 Feock Cnwll
205 G3 Feolin Ferry Ag & B
196 C2 Fergushill N Ayrs
258 B6 Feriniquarrie Highld

9 k3 Fermain Bay Guern
234 D3 Fern Angus
42 F2 Ferndale Rhondd
17 L2 Ferndown Dorset
253 J3 Ferness Moray
65 L8 Fernham Oxon
81 K3 Fernhill Heath Worcs
36 D5 Fernhurst W Susx
222 E4 Fernie Fife
209 K8 Ferniegair S Lans
246 E2 Fernilea Highld
131 K4 Fernilee Derbys
79 L5 Ferny Common Herefs
150 E4 Ferrensby N York
144 B4 Ferriby Sluice N Linc
247 L7 Ferrindonald Highld
21 J6 Ferring W Susx
263 K3 Ferry Point Highld
142 D3 Ferrybridge Wakefd
235 H4 Ferryden Angus
169 H4 Ferryhill Dur
56 C3 Ferryside Carmth
263 K2 Ferrytown Highld
106 B6 Fersfield Norfk
240 B7 Fersit Highld
241 M3 Feshiebridge Highld
50 F7 Fetcham Surrey
269 H6 Fetterangus Abers
235 G1 Fettercairn Abers
66 D2 Fewcott Oxon
150 B5 Fewston N York
77 K2 Ffair Rhos Cerdgn
59 H4 Ffairfach Carmth
77 H6 Ffald-y-Brenin Carmth
61 K3 Ffawyddog Powys
110 D3 Ffestiniog Gwynd
128 D6 Ffordd-las Denbgs
57 G4 Fforest Carmth
62 B3 Fforest Mons
57 H5 Fforest Fach Swans
57 K4 Fforest Goch Neath
76 C5 Ffostrasol Cerdgn
129 G8 Ffrith Flints
76 F4 Ffynnon-Oer Cerdgn
76 C4 Ffynnonddewi Cerdgn
128 D3 Ffynnongroyw Flints
272 C2 Fiag Lodge Highld
51 K6 Fickleshole Surrey
64 D1 Fiddington Gloucs
30 B3 Fiddington Somset
32 D8 Fiddleford Dorset
4 D4 Fiddlers Green Cnwll
70 C6 Fiddlers Hamlet Essex
115 G5 Field Staffs
156 E6 Field Broughton Cumb
121 M4 Field Dalling Norfk
100 B2 Field Head Leics
166 B3 Fieldhead Cumb
267 H6 Fife Keith Moray
32 C6 Fifehead Magdalen Dorset
32 C8 Fifehead Neville Dorset
16 E1 Fifehead St Quintin Dorset
65 K3 Fifield Oxon
49 L4 Fifield W & M
33 K1 Fifield Wilts
33 K2 Figheldean Wilts
46 D1 Filands Wilts
107 K1 Filby Norfk
163 L6 Filey N York
85 G5 Filgrave M Keyn
65 K6 Filkins Oxon
28 B5 Filleigh Devon
28 C8 Filleigh Devon
135 J3 Fillingham Lincs
99 H6 Fillongley Warwks
35 K5 Filmore Hill Hants
45 J3 Filton S Glos
152 D4 Fimber E R Yk
234 D4 Finavon Angus
104 D2 Fincham Norfk
49 J6 Finchampstead Wokham
216 D6 Fincharn Ag & B
20 B4 Finchdean Hants
88 D8 Finchingfield Essex
51 H1 Finchley Gt Lon
116 A5 Findern Derbys
265 G7 Findhorn Moray
252 E6 Findhorn Bridge Highld
221 H3 Findo Gask P & K
267 J3 Findochty Moray
245 L4 Findon Abers
21 J5 Findon W Susx
263 G7 Findon Mains Highld
244 D3 Findrack House Abers
85 H1 Finedon Nhants

101 L4 Fineshade Nhants	131 K6 Flash Staffs	52 A5 Foots Cray Gt Lon	34 F2 Forton Hants
90 F1 Fingal Street Suffk	258 E6 Flashader Highld	243 L1 Forbestown Abers	147 J5 Forton Lancs
222 B3 Fingask P & K	68 C7 Flaunden Herts	168 F8 Forcett N York	113 G8 Forton Shrops
49 J1 Fingest Bucks	117 K3 Flawborough Notts	216 D6 Ford Ag & B	15 H1 Forton Somset
160 B5 Finghall N York	151 G3 Flawith N York	67 J5 Ford Bucks	114 B7 Forton Staffs
177 H7 Fingland Cumb	45 G5 Flax Bourton N Som	133 H4 Ford Derbys	256 B3 Fortrie Abers
197 L7 Fingland D & G	150 E4 Flaxby N York	27 G6 Ford Devon	263 K8 Fortrose Highld
41 K4 Finglesham Kent	63 K4 Flaxley Gloucs	7 J5 Ford Devon	16 D7 Fortuneswell Dorset
72 F3 Fingringhoe Essex	130 A5 Flaxmere Ches	8 B6 Ford Devon	50 A1 Forty Green Bucks
88 D7 Finkle Green Essex	29 L4 Flaxpool Somset	65 G1 Ford Gloucs	69 J7 Forty Hill Gt Lon
141 M7 Finkle Street Barns	151 L3 Flaxton N York	202 E5 Ford Nthumb	90 C3 Forward Green Suffk
231 G8 Finlarig Stirlg	100 E5 Fleckney Leics	95 K1 Ford Shrops	47 L7 Fosbury Wilts
84 C8 Finmere Oxon	83 M3 Flecknoe Warwks	29 K5 Ford Somset	65 K3 Foscot Oxon
230 F4 Finnart P & K	134 F5 Fledborough Notts	45 H8 Ford Somset	84 C6 Foscote Nhants
90 C2 Finningham Suffk	16 C6 Fleet Dorset	115 H1 Ford Staffs	119 K5 Fosdyke Lincs
143 H7 Finningley Donc	20 B6 Fleet Hants	21 G6 Ford W Susx	119 K5 Fosdyke Bridge Lincs
282 e6 Finsbay W Isls	49 K8 Fleet Hants	46 B4 Ford Wilts	231 L4 Foss P & K
82 A1 Finstall Worcs	119 L6 Fleet Lincs	33 L4 Ford Wilts	76 E3 Foss-y-ffin Cerdgn
156 E5 Finsthwaite Cumb	119 L6 Fleet Hargate Lincs	71 G4 Ford End Essex	65 G5 Fossebridge Gloucs
66 A4 Finstock Oxon	19 H3 Fleetend Hants	147 J6 Ford Green Lancs	70 C5 Foster Street Essex
275 C4 Finstown Ork	146 F6 Fleetwood Lancs	95 K1 Ford Heath Shrops	143 G5 Fosterhouses Donc
268 D5 Fintry Abers	42 F7 Flemingston V Glam	29 L7 Ford Street Somset	115 K5 Foston Derbys
209 G2 Fintry Stirlg	209 H7 Flemington S Lans	90 C2 Ford's Green Suffk	100 D4 Foston Leics
244 D5 Finzean Abers	89 G1 Flempton Suffk	12 D4 Forda Devon	117 M3 Foston Lincs
226 B7 Fionnphort Ag & B	38 E3 Fletcher Green Kent	38 E5 Fordcombe Kent	151 L3 Foston N York
282 e6 Fionnsbhagh W Isls	5 J2 Fletchersbridge Cnwll	211 G1 Fordell Fife	153 H4 Foston on the Wolds E R Yk
168 F4 Fir Tree Dur	165 G2 Fletchertown Cumb	94 F3 Forden Powys	136 F2 Fotherby Lincs
157 K4 Firbank Cumb	23 G3 Fletching E Susx	12 F4 Forder Devon	164 D4 Fothergill Cumb
133 L2 Firbeck Rothm	43 J3 Fleur-de-lis Caerph	8 B2 Forder Green Devon	102 B5 Fotheringhay Nhants
160 C5 Firby N York	11 J1 Flexbury Cnwll	88 C1 Fordham Cambs	99 H4 Foul End Warwks
152 A3 Firby N York	36 D1 Flexford Surrey	72 D2 Fordham Essex	23 K4 Foul Mile E Susx
140 D5 Firgrove Rochdl	164 D4 Flimby Cumb	104 C3 Fordham Norfk	165 M1 Foulbridge Cumb
137 H7 Firsby Lincs	39 H7 Flimwell E Susx	72 D2 Fordham Heath Essex	142 B4 Foulby Wakefd
34 B4 Firsdown Dorset	128 F5 Flint Flints	33 K8 Fordingbridge Hants	202 E2 Foulden Border
19 J5 Fishbourne IOW	128 F5 Flint Mountain Flints	163 J7 Fordon E R Yk	104 F4 Foulden Norfk
20 D6 Fishbourne W Susx	99 H7 Flint's Green Solhll	245 G8 Fordoun Abers	148 F7 Foulridge Lancs
169 K4 Fishburn Dur	117 K2 Flintham Notts	72 D2 Fordstreet Essex	122 A6 Foulsham Norfk
220 F8 Fishcross Clacks	153 K8 Flinton E R Yk	13 J3 Fordton Devon	200 F3 Fountainhall Border
20 E6 Fisher W Susx	39 J6 Flishinghurst Kent	65 L4 Fordwells Oxon	98 F8 Four Ashes Solhll
35 G6 Fisher's Pond Hants	120 F6 Flitcham Norfk	41 G3 Fordwich Kent	97 L2 Four Ashes Staffs
147 H6 Fisher's Row Lancs	85 L8 Flitton Beds	267 L3 Fordyce Abers	97 H6 Four Ashes Staffs
256 B4 Fisherford Abers	85 K8 Flitwick Beds	114 E7 Forebridge Staffs	89 K1 Four Ashes Suffk
211 K4 Fisherrow E Loth	143 L5 Flixborough N Linc	116 B6 Foremark Derbys	9 j3 Four Cabots Guern
36 E4 Fisherstreet W Susx	143 L5 Flixborough Stather N Linc	9 j4 Forest Guern	112 C7 Four Crosses Powys
252 D2 Fisherton Highld	163 J6 Flixton N York	160 C3 Forest N York	98 B2 Four Crosses Staffs
196 B7 Fisherton S Ayrs	107 G6 Flixton Suffk	148 D5 Forest Becks Lancs	38 C4 Four Elms Kent
33 G3 Fisherton de la Mere Wilts	130 E1 Flixton Traffd	131 J5 Forest Chapel Ches	31 J4 Four Foot Somset
98 F2 Fisherwick Staffs	141 K5 Flockton Kirk	51 L2 Forest Gate Gt Lon	30 C3 Four Forks Somset
49 L3 Fishery Estate W & M	141 L5 Flockton Green Kirk	37 H3 Forest Green Surrey	139 J6 Four Gates Bolton
74 F5 Fishguard Pembks	202 E6 Flodden Nthumb	157 J2 Forest Hall Cumb	120 A8 Four Gotes Cambs
143 G5 Fishlake Donc	259 H2 Flodigarry Highld	181 G5 Forest Hall N Tyne	141 L7 Four Lane End Barns
12 D2 Fishleigh Devon	156 E7 Flookburgh Cumb	178 D7 Forest Head Cumb	130 A7 Four Lane Ends Ches
119 J4 Fishmere End Lincs	106 D4 Flordon Norfk	51 K4 Forest Hill Gt Lon	3 H3 Four Lanes Cnwll
227 J4 Fishnish Pier Ag & B	84 C3 Flore Nhants	66 E5 Forest Hill Oxon	35 K4 Four Marks Hants
15 J3 Fishpond Bottom Dorset	190 E5 Flotterton Nthumb	150 D4 Forest Lane Head N York	124 E4 Four Mile Bridge IOA
45 J4 Fishponds Bristl	23 L5 Flowers Green E Susx	229 M7 Forest Lodge Ag & B	98 E4 Four Oaks Birm
140 B6 Fishpool Bury	90 C6 Flowton Suffk	221 G8 Forest Mill Clacks	24 F2 Four Oaks E Susx
119 K3 Fishtoft Lincs	141 L3 Flushdyke Wakefd	38 C6 Forest Row E Susx	63 K2 Four Oaks Gloucs
119 K2 Fishtoft Drove Lincs	3 K4 Flushing Cnwll	19 H5 Forest Side IOW	99 H7 Four Oaks Solhll
139 H2 Fishwick Lancs	14 C4 Fluxton Devon	133 L7 Forest Town Notts	48 E3 Four Points W Berk
246 D2 Fiskavaig Highld	82 A4 Flyford Flavell Worcs	167 K4 Forest-in-Teesdale Dur	56 E3 Four Roads Carmth
135 L5 Fiskerton Lincs	52 F2 Fobbing Thurr	190 F7 Forestburn Gate Nthumb	65 K1 Four Shire Stone Warwks
117 K4 Fiskerton Notts	267 G4 Fochabers Moray	20 C4 Forestside W Susx	39 J7 Four Throws Kent
145 H1 Fitling E R Yk	61 H6 Fochriw Caerph	234 C5 Forfar Angus	38 F3 Four Wents Kent
33 K1 Fittleton Wilts	143 L4 Fockerby N Linc	221 K3 Forgandenny P & K	130 F7 Fourlanes End Ches
21 G3 Fittleworth W Susx	31 J5 Foddington Somset	93 G3 Forge Powys	264 C1 Fourpenny Highld
103 J1 Fitton End Cambs	94 B1 Foel Powys	62 B7 Forge Hammer Torfn	179 K5 Fourstones Nthumb
113 G7 Fitz Shrops	42 C3 Foel y Dyffryn Brdgnd	61 L5 Forge Side Torfn	33 H5 Fovant Wilts
29 L5 Fitzhead Somset	59 G6 Foelgastell Carmth	267 H5 Forgie Moray	257 H7 Foveran Abers
30 B5 Fitzroy Somset	152 A8 Foggathorpe E R Yk	267 H5 Forgieside Moray	5 K4 Fowey Cnwll
142 C5 Fitzwilliam Wakefd	202 B3 Fogo Border	256 A3 Forgue Abers	139 K8 Fowley Common Warrtn
23 H3 Five Ash Down E Susx	266 E5 Fogwatt Moray	98 D8 Forhill Worcs	39 H4 Fowlhall Kent
23 J2 Five Ashes E Susx	276 B6 Foindle Highld	138 C6 Formby Sefton	233 M8 Fowlis Angus
29 K2 Five Bells Somset	233 J3 Folda Angus	106 C4 Forncett End Norfk	221 G2 Fowlis Wester P & K
80 F6 Five Bridges Herefs	115 G4 Fole Staffs	106 D4 Forncett St Mary Norfk	87 J6 Fowlmere Cambs
5 Five Lanes Mons	99 K7 Foleshill Covtry	106 D5 Forncett St Peter Norfk	80 D8 Fownhope Herefs
39 G4 Five Oak Green Kent	49 L4 Foliejon Park Br For	89 G2 Fornham All Saints Suffk	50 B7 Fox Corner Surrey
9 e3 Five Oaks Jersey	31 L8 Folke Dorset	89 G2 Fornham St Martin Suffk	70 E7 Fox Hatch Essex
37 G5 Five Oaks W Susx	41 H8 Folkestone Kent	253 H2 Fornighty Highld	72 F2 Fox Street Essex
56 E4 Five Roads Carmth	118 E5 Folkingham Lincs	165 K6 Fornside Cumb	208 D6 Foxbar Rens
39 K3 Five Wents Kent	23 J6 Folkington E Susx	265 G8 Forres Moray	12 C5 Foxcombe Devon
29 M4 Fivecrosses Ches	102 C5 Folksworth Cambs	114 F3 Forsbrook Staffs	64 E3 Foxcote Gloucs
30 E6 Fivehead Somset	163 J6 Folkton N York	275 H1 Forse Highld	45 L7 Foxcote Somset
11 J6 Fivelanes Cnwll	256 C5 Folla Rule Abers	275 H1 Forse House Highld	154 C6 Foxdale IOM
71 J4 Flack's Green Essex	150 D5 Follifoot N York	98 E8 Forshaw Heath Warwks	89 G6 Foxearth Essex
49 L1 Flackwell Heath Bucks	12 D3 Folly Gate Devon	278 F7 Forsinard Highld	52 E5 Foxendown Kent
82 A6 Fladbury Worcs	36 B1 Folly Hill Surrey	16 C3 Forston Dorset	156 B5 Foxfield Cumb
81 e7 Fladdabister Shet	43 G8 Fonmon V Glam	240 C2 Fort Augustus Highld	46 E3 Foxham Wilts
32 C6 Flagg Derbys	43 G8 Font-y-gary V Glam	9 i2 Fort Hommet Guern	18 E1 Foxhills Hants
53 K2 Flamborough E R Yk	32 F4 Fonthill Bishop Wilts	9 k1 Fort le Marchant Guern	4 F4 Foxhole Cnwll
68 D4 Flamstead Herts	32 F4 Fonthill Gifford Wilts	239 J8 Fort William Highld	57 J6 Foxhole Swans
20 F6 Flansham W Susx	32 E7 Fontmell Magna Dorset	221 J4 Forteviot P & K	163 H8 Foxholes N York
41 M4 Flanshaw Wakefd	32 D7 Fontmell Parva Dorset	198 F2 Forth S Lans	23 J4 Foxhunt Green E Susx
49 J8 Flappit Spring Brad	20 F5 Fontwell W Susx	64 B1 Forthampton Gloucs	84 C5 Foxley Nhants
49 G4 Flasby N York	132 D4 Foolow Derbys	231 K6 Fortingall P & K	122 A7 Foxley Norfk

46 C2	**Foxley** Wilts
46 C2	**Foxley Green** Wilts
82 B2	**Foxlydiate** Worcs
115 G2	**Foxt** Staffs
87 H5	**Foxton** Cambs
169 K5	**Foxton** Dur
100 F5	**Foxton** Leics
160 F3	**Foxton** N York
158 F7	**Foxup** N York
130 C6	**Foxwist Green** Ches
96 E8	**Foxwood** Shrops
63 H2	**Foy** Herefs
250 E7	**Foyers** Highld
253 G1	**Foynesfield** Highld
2 F4	**Fraddam** Cnwll
4 E3	**Fraddon** Cnwll
98 F1	**Fradley** Staffs
114 F5	**Fradswell** Staffs
153 J3	**Fraisthorpe** E R Yk
23 H3	**Framfield** E Susx
106 F3	**Framingham Earl** Norfk
106 F3	**Framingham Pigot** Norfk
91 G3	**Framlingham** Suffk
16 B3	**Frampton** Dorset
119 K4	**Frampton** Lincs
45 K3	**Frampton Cotterell** S Glos
64 D6	**Frampton Mansell** Gloucs
63 L5	**Frampton on Severn** Gloucs
119 J3	**Frampton West End** Lincs
90 E3	**Framsden** Suffk
169 H2	**Framwellgate Moor** Dur
148 A8	**Frances Green** Lancs
97 J7	**Franche** Worcs
130 C4	**Frandley** Ches
11 M4	**Frankaborough** Devon
128 F2	**Frankby** Wirral
122 F6	**Frankfort** Norfk
80 C6	**Franklands Gate** Herefs
98 C7	**Frankley** Worcs
78 F4	**Franksbridge** Powys
83 K1	**Frankton** Warwks
38 F6	**Frant** E Susx
269 J3	**Fraserburgh** Abers
73 G3	**Frating** Essex
73 G2	**Frating Green** Essex
19 L4	**Fratton** C Port
6 D4	**Freathy** Cnwll
88 D1	**Freckenham** Suffk
138 E2	**Freckleton** Lancs
132 F5	**Freebirch** Derbys
117 L7	**Freeby** Leics
35 G1	**Freefolk** Hants
115 G3	**Freehay** Staffs
66 B4	**Freeland** Oxon
107 H2	**Freethorpe** Norfk
107 H2	**Freethorpe Common** Norfk
119 L3	**Freiston** Lincs
27 J4	**Fremington** Devon
159 J3	**Fremington** N York
51 M8	**French Street** Kent
45 J3	**Frenchay** S Glos
12 F5	**Frenchbeer** Devon
232 B4	**Frenich** P & K
36 C3	**Frensham** Surrey
138 C6	**Freshfield** Sefton
46 A7	**Freshford** Wilts
18 E6	**Freshwater** IOW
18 E6	**Freshwater Bay** IOW
55 G7	**Freshwater East** Pembks
106 F7	**Fressingfield** Suffk
90 E7	**Freston** Suffk
280 E3	**Freswick** Highld
63 L5	**Fretherne** Gloucs
122 E8	**Frettenham** Norfk
222 E6	**Freuchie** Fife
54 F4	**Freystrop** Pembks
98 C4	**Friar Park** W Mids
16 C5	**Friar Waddon** Dorset
38 D6	**Friar's Gate** E Susx
162 C5	**Friars' Hill** N York
103 K2	**Friday Bridge** Cambs
23 K6	**Friday Street** E Susx
90 F3	**Friday Street** Suffk
91 H5	**Friday Street** Suffk
91 J3	**Friday Street** Suffk
37 H2	**Friday Street** Surrey
152 D4	**Fridaythorpe** E R Yk
132 C7	**Friden** Derbys
141 G3	**Friendly** Calder
69 H8	**Friern Barnet** Gt Lon
225 G4	**Friesland Bay** Ag & B
135 M3	**Friesthorpe** Lincs
118 B2	**Frieston** Lincs
49 J1	**Frieth** Bucks
116 D2	**Friezeland** Notts

66 B7	**Frilford** Oxon
48 E4	**Frilsham** W Berk
49 L7	**Frimley** Surrey
49 L7	**Frimley Green** Surrey
52 F5	**Frindsbury** Medway
121 G4	**Fring** Norfk
66 F1	**Fringford** Oxon
40 A4	**Frinsted** Kent
73 K3	**Frinton-on-Sea** Essex
234 F5	**Friockheim** Angus
92 D1	**Friog** Gwynd
117 J8	**Frisby on the Wreake** Leics
137 J8	**Friskney** Lincs
137 J8	**Friskney Eaudike** Lincs
23 J7	**Friston** E Susx
91 J3	**Friston** Suffk
116 B1	**Fritchley** Derbys
119 K2	**Frith Bank** Lincs
80 F1	**Frith Common** Worcs
34 B8	**Fritham** Hants
27 H7	**Frithelstock** Devon
27 H7	**Frithelstock Stone** Devon
36 B3	**Frithend** Hants
68 C5	**Frithsden** Herts
119 K2	**Frithville** Lincs
39 K5	**Frittenden** Kent
8 B6	**Frittiscombe** Devon
107 K3	**Fritton** Norfk
106 E5	**Fritton** Norfk
66 D1	**Fritwell** Oxon
149 L8	**Frizinghall** Brad
164 D7	**Frizington** Cumb
63 M6	**Frocester** Gloucs
96 C3	**Frodesley** Shrops
129 M4	**Frodsham** Ches
87 H6	**Frog End** Cambs
87 L3	**Frog End** Cambs
81 J2	**Frog Pool** Worcs
202 B7	**Frogden** Border
132 E4	**Froggatt** Derbys
115 G2	**Froghall** Staffs
33 L8	**Frogham** Hants
41 H5	**Frogham** Kent
7 M6	**Frogmore** Devon
102 D2	**Frognall** Lincs
3 J3	**Frogpool** Cnwll
6 C1	**Frogwell** Cnwll
100 B5	**Frolesworth** Leics
32 C1	**Frome** Somset
16 B2	**Frome St Quintin** Dorset
16 D4	**Frome Whitfield** Dorset
80 F6	**Fromes Hill** Herefs
128 C6	**Fron** Denbgs
108 F4	**Fron** Gwynd
109 J1	**Fron** Gwynd
94 F3	**Fron** Powys
94 E4	**Fron** Powys
112 C3	**Fron Isaf** Wrexhm
111 H4	**Fron-goch** Gwynd
112 C3	**Froncysyllte** Denbgs
107 K7	**Frostenden** Suffk
168 C3	**Frosterley** Dur
85 J8	**Froxfield** Beds
47 L5	**Froxfield** Wilts
35 L5	**Froxfield Green** Hants
34 F6	**Fryern Hill** Hants
70 F7	**Fryerning** Essex
162 B7	**Fryton** N York
227 J3	**Fuinary** Highld
118 B2	**Fulbeck** Lincs
87 L4	**Fulbourn** Cambs
65 K4	**Fulbrook** Oxon
35 G5	**Fulflood** Hants
30 B5	**Fulford** Somset
114 F4	**Fulford** Staffs
151 K6	**Fulford** York
51 H4	**Fulham** Gt Lon
22 C5	**Fulking** W Susx
152 A5	**Full Sutton** E R Yk
28 B3	**Fullaford** Devon
196 C3	**Fullarton** N Ayrs
71 H4	**Fuller Street** Essex
38 E2	**Fuller Street** Kent
70 D2	**Fuller's End** Essex
113 H1	**Fuller's Moor** Ches
34 E3	**Fullerton** Hants
136 E5	**Fulletby** Lincs
83 G6	**Fullready** Warwks
196 E1	**Fullwood** E Ayrs
50 C2	**Fulmer** Bucks
121 M5	**Fulmodeston** Norfk
136 B4	**Fulnetby** Lincs
119 J6	**Fulney** Lincs
141 J6	**Fulstone** Kirk
145 J8	**Fulstow** Lincs

66 A3	**Fulwell** Oxon
181 J7	**Fulwell** Sundld
139 H2	**Fulwood** Lancs
133 J8	**Fulwood** Notts
132 F3	**Fulwood** Sheff
30 B6	**Fulwood** Somset
106 C4	**Fundenhall** Norfk
20 C5	**Funtington** W Susx
19 J2	**Funtley** Hants
220 C2	**Funtullich** P & K
15 G2	**Furley** Devon
217 G7	**Furnace** Ag & B
56 F4	**Furnace** Carmth
92 E4	**Furnace** Cerdgn
99 H5	**Furnace End** Warwks
22 F2	**Furner's Green** E Susx
131 K3	**Furness Vale** Derbys
70 B2	**Furneux Pelham** Herts
39 M5	**Further Quarter** Kent
84 E6	**Furtho** Nhants
49 L3	**Furze Platt** W & M
28 C2	**Furzehill** Devon
17 K2	**Furzehill** Dorset
136 E5	**Furzehills** Lincs
19 L2	**Furzeley Corner** Hants
34 C7	**Furzley** Hants
30 C7	**Fyfett** Somset
70 E5	**Fyfield** Essex
34 C2	**Fyfield** Hants
66 B7	**Fyfield** Oxon
47 H5	**Fyfield** Wilts
47 H6	**Fyfield** Wilts
33 H6	**Fyfield Bavant** Wilts
66 B7	**Fyfield Wick** Oxon
163 G2	**Fylingthorpe** N York
36 B6	**Fyning** W Susx
256 D4	**Fyvie** Abers

G

196 E1	**Gabroc Hill** E Ayrs
100 F1	**Gaddesby** Leics
68 D4	**Gaddesden Row** Herts
125 H2	**Gadfa** IOA
196 E6	**Gadgirth** S Ayrs
112 E4	**Gadlas** Shrops
61 J3	**Gaer** Powys
62 F7	**Gaer-llwyd** Mons
125 H5	**Gaerwen** IOA
66 B2	**Gagingwell** Oxon
196 C4	**Gailes** N Ayrs
97 K1	**Gailey** Staffs
168 F7	**Gainford** Dur
135 G2	**Gainsborough** Lincs
88 E8	**Gainsford End** Essex
260 C4	**Gairloch** Highld
239 K6	**Gairlochy** Highld
221 L7	**Gairneybridge** P & K
149 L8	**Gaisby** Brad
157 K2	**Gaisgill** Cumb
165 L1	**Gaitsgill** Cumb
201 G6	**Galashiels** Border
147 J5	**Galgate** Lancs
31 K5	**Galhampton** Somset
216 C2	**Gallanach** Ag & B
113 H1	**Gallantry Bank** Ches
222 E8	**Gallatown** Fife
99 J5	**Galley Common** Warwks
71 H6	**Galleywood** Essex
240 F5	**Gallovie** Highld
234 C7	**Gallowfauld** Angus
233 J8	**Gallowhill** P & K
72 D2	**Gallows Green** Essex
81 L3	**Gallows Green** Worcs
49 G3	**Gallowstree Common** Oxon
125 K7	**Gallt-y-foel** Gwynd
248 C7	**Galltair** Highld
49 K8	**Gally Hill** Hants
38 D6	**Gallypot Street** E Susx
7 K6	**Galmpton** Devon
8 D4	**Galmpton** Torbay
150 C1	**Galphay** N York
196 F4	**Galston** E Ayrs
16 E5	**Galton** Dorset
131 L6	**Gamballs Green** Staffs
71 J4	**Gambles Green** Essex
166 E3	**Gamblesby** Cumb
177 H8	**Gamelsby** Cumb
131 K1	**Gamesley** Derbys
86 E5	**Gamlingay** Cambs
86 E5	**Gamlingay Cinques** Cambs
86 E5	**Gamlingay Great Heath** Beds
159 J6	**Gammersgill** N York

268 E4	**Gamrie** Abers
134 E4	**Gamston** Notts
117 G4	**Gamston** Notts
63 G4	**Ganarew** Herefs
216 D1	**Ganavan Bay** Ag & B
6 C1	**Gang** Cnwll
110 D6	**Ganllwyd** Gwynd
234 F1	**Gannachy** Angus
144 F1	**Ganstead** E R Yk
151 L2	**Ganthorpe** N York
163 H7	**Ganton** N York
69 H7	**Ganwick Corner** Herts
13 K7	**Gappah** Devon
266 F5	**Garbity** Moray
105 K7	**Garboldisham** Norfk
243 J2	**Garchory** Abers
129 H6	**Garden City** Flints
141 L8	**Garden Village** Sheff
49 K5	**Gardeners Green** Wokham
268 E3	**Gardenstown** Abers
281 d6	**Garderhouse** Shet
152 E7	**Gardham** E R Yk
32 C3	**Gare Hill** Somset
207 L1	**Garelochhead** Ag & B
66 B7	**Garford** Oxon
142 B1	**Garforth** Leeds
142 B1	**Garforth Bridge** Leeds
149 G5	**Gargrave** N York
220 B8	**Gargunnock** Stirlg
126 D4	**Garizim** Conwy
106 E6	**Garlic Street** Norfk
174 D5	**Garlieston** D & G
41 K2	**Garlinge** Kent
40 F5	**Garlinge Green** Kent
245 H2	**Garlogie** Abers
268 E5	**Garmond** Abers
169 J4	**Garmondsway** Dur
267 G3	**Garmouth** Moray
96 E2	**Garmston** Shrops
108 E5	**Garn** Gwynd
109 J3	**Garn-Dolbenmaen** Gwynd
59 J6	**Garnant** Carmth
157 H3	**Garnett Bridge** Cumb
209 H5	**Garnkirk** N Lans
57 H3	**Garnswllt** Swans
282 h3	**Garrabost** W Isls
197 G7	**Garrallan** E Ayrs
3 H6	**Garras** Cnwll
109 L3	**Garreg** Gwynd
167 H2	**Garrigill** Cumb
159 L4	**Garriston** N York
184 F6	**Garroch** D & G
172 D7	**Garrochtrie** D & G
207 H8	**Garrochty** Ag & B
259 H4	**Garros** Highld
152 B4	**Garrowby Hall** E R Yk
158 C5	**Garsdale** Cumb
158 D4	**Garsdale Head** Cumb
46 D2	**Garsdon** Wilts
114 F5	**Garshall Green** Staffs
66 E6	**Garsington** Oxon
147 J6	**Garstang** Lancs
68 E7	**Garston** Herts
129 J3	**Garston** Lpool
204 E4	**Gartachossan** Ag & B
209 J5	**Gartcosh** N Lans
42 C4	**Garth** Brdgnd
112 C3	**Garth** Denbgs
62 D8	**Garth** Mons
78 C5	**Garth** Powys
79 K1	**Garth** Powys
92 E6	**Garth Penrhyncoch** Cerdgn
157 H3	**Garth Row** Cumb
209 H5	**Garthamlock** C Glas
78 E8	**Garthbrengy** Powys
77 G4	**Gartheli** Cerdgn
94 F3	**Garthmyl** Powys
117 L7	**Garthorpe** Leics
143 L4	**Garthorpe** N Linc
157 H5	**Garths** Cumb
255 K5	**Gartly** Abers
219 H7	**Gartmore** Stirlg
209 K6	**Gartness** N Lans
208 E2	**Gartness** Stirlg
208 D2	**Gartocharn** W Duns
145 H1	**Garton** E R Yk
152 F4	**Garton-on-the-Wolds** E R Yk
274 D5	**Gartymore** Highld
212 D5	**Garvald** E Loth
238 F8	**Garvan** Highld
214 D6	**Garvard** Ag & B
262 C7	**Garve** Highld
105 L2	**Garvestone** Norfk
207 L5	**Garvock** Inver
62 F3	**Garway** Herefs

62 F3	**Garway Common** Herefs
62 F2	**Garway Hill** Herefs
282 g4	**Garyvard** W Isls
32 C4	**Gasper** Wilts
46 C5	**Gastard** Wilts
105 K7	**Gasthorpe** Norfk
70 D4	**Gaston Green** Essex
19 H6	**Gatcombe** IOW
135 G3	**Gate Burton** Lincs
151 L5	**Gate Helmsley** N York
157 J5	**Gatebeck** Cumb
134 B3	**Gateford** Notts
142 E2	**Gateforth** N York
196 D4	**Gatehead** E Ayrs
179 H1	**Gatehouse** Nthumb
174 F4	**Gatehouse of Fleet** D & G
121 L6	**Gateley** Norfk
160 D5	**Gatenby** N York
129 L7	**Gates Heath** Ches
165 G7	**Gatesgarth** Cumb
189 L2	**Gateshaw** Border
181 G6	**Gateshead** Gatesd
234 C6	**Gateside** Angus
208 E7	**Gateside** E Rens
222 B5	**Gateside** Fife
208 B8	**Gateside** N Ayrs
186 C5	**Gateslack** D & G
139 G6	**Gathurst** Wigan
131 G2	**Gatley** Stockp
51 H8	**Gatton** Surrey
201 H6	**Gattonside** Border
78 D2	**Gaufron** Powys
100 F3	**Gaulby** Leics
222 F2	**Gauldry** Fife
233 K5	**Gauldswell** P & K
139 M3	**Gaulkthorn** Lancs
103 K2	**Gaultree** Norfk
17 K2	**Gaunt's Common** Dorset
70 E2	**Gaunt's End** Essex
113 J2	**Gaunton's Bank** Ches
136 C5	**Gautby** Lincs
202 B3	**Gavinton** Border
141 M6	**Gawber** Barns
67 G1	**Gawcott** Bucks
131 H5	**Gawsworth** Ches
141 L3	**Gawthorpe** Wakefd
158 B5	**Gawthrop** Cumb
156 C5	**Gawthwaite** Cumb
71 J6	**Gay Bowers** Essex
21 J3	**Gay Street** W Susx
83 J4	**Gaydon** Warwks
85 G6	**Gayhurst** M Keyn
158 F5	**Gayle** N York
159 L1	**Gayles** N York
84 D4	**Gayton** Nhants
120 F7	**Gayton** Norfk
114 F6	**Gayton** Staffs
129 G4	**Gayton** Wirral
137 H3	**Gayton le Marsh** Lincs
121 G7	**Gayton Thorpe** Norfk
120 E7	**Gaywood** Norfk
88 E2	**Gazeley** Suffk
3 J6	**Gear** Cnwll
282 g4	**Gearraidh Bhaird** W Isls
258 D4	**Geary** Highld
89 J4	**Gedding** Suffk
41 H6	**Geddinge** Kent
101 K6	**Geddington** Nhants
117 G3	**Gedling** Notts
119 L6	**Gedney** Lincs
119 L7	**Gedney Broadgate** Lincs
120 A5	**Gedney Drove End** Lincs
119 L6	**Gedney Dyke** Lincs
103 G1	**Gedney Hill** Lincs
131 J1	**Gee Cross** Tamesd
101 L3	**Geeston** Rutlnd
107 H5	**Geldeston** Norfk
42 E3	**Gelli** Rhondd
62 B8	**Gelli** Torfn
128 D7	**Gellifor** Denbgs
43 H2	**Gelligaer** Caerph
43 J3	**Gelligroes** Caerph
57 K4	**Gelligron** Neath
110 C4	**Gellilydan** Gwynd
57 K4	**Gellinudd** Neath
55 J3	**Gelly** Carmth
233 G7	**Gellyburn** P & K
58 A4	**Gellywen** Carmth
175 J3	**Gelston** D & G
118 B3	**Gelston** Lincs
153 H4	**Gembling** E R Yk
98 D1	**Gentleshaw** Staffs
50 C3	**George Green** Bucks
28 B6	**George Nympton** Devon
187 L7	**Georgefield** D & G
27 H3	**Georgeham** Devon
61 J5	**Georgetown** Blae G
2 D4	**Georgia** Cnwll
275 C3	**Georth** Ork
126 C6	**Gerlan** Gwynd
12 B4	**Germansweek** Devon
2 F5	**Germoe** Cnwll
3 M4	**Gerrans** Cnwll
50 C1	**Gerrards Cross** Bucks
171 G8	**Gerrick** R & Cl
89 G7	**Gestingthorpe** Essex
112 B8	**Geuffordd** Powys
130 C4	**Gib Hill** Ches
137 K7	**Gibraltar** Lincs
117 J2	**Gibsmere** Notts
46 B4	**Giddeahall** Wilts
16 F5	**Giddy Green** Dorset
52 B1	**Gidea Park** Gt Lon
12 F5	**Gidleigh** Devon
208 F7	**Giffnock** E Rens
212 C5	**Gifford** E Loth
222 E5	**Giffordtown** Fife
148 D3	**Giggleswick** N York
143 L2	**Gilberdyke** E R Yk
35 K4	**Gilbert Street** Hants
97 J6	**Gilbert's Cross** Staffs
81 J6	**Gilbert's End** Worcs
212 B6	**Gilchriston** E Loth
164 F3	**Gilcrux** Cumb
141 K2	**Gildersome** Leeds
133 L3	**Gildingwells** Rothm
169 J2	**Gilesgate Moor** Dur
42 F8	**Gileston** V Glam
43 J2	**Gilfach** Caerph
42 E4	**Gilfach Goch** Brdgnd
76 D3	**Gilfachrheda** Cerdgn
164 D6	**Gilgarran** Cumb
166 B5	**Gill** Cumb
39 J7	**Gill's Green** Kent
162 B4	**Gillamoor** N York
3 K6	**Gillan** Cnwll
258 D5	**Gillen** Highld
187 J7	**Gillesbie** D & G
161 K7	**Gilling East** N York
160 B2	**Gilling West** N York
32 D5	**Gillingham** Dorset
53 G5	**Gillingham** Medway
107 H5	**Gillingham** Norfk
280 B4	**Gillock** Highld
131 H7	**Gillow Heath** Staffs
280 D2	**Gills** Highld
188 B2	**Gilmanscleuch** Border
211 J5	**Gilmerton** C Edin
220 F2	**Gilmerton** P & K
168 C8	**Gilmonby** Dur
100 C6	**Gilmorton** Leics
178 E5	**Gilsland** Nthumb
99 G5	**Gilson** Warwks
149 L7	**Gilstead** Brad
70 B4	**Gilston** Herts
200 F2	**Gilston** Mdloth
116 E2	**Giltbrook** Notts
61 L4	**Gilwern** Mons
122 F4	**Gimingham** Norfk
131 J4	**Ginclough** Ches
23 K5	**Gingers Green** E Susx
90 C3	**Gipping** Suffk
119 J2	**Gipsey Bridge** Lincs
196 C3	**Girdle Toll** N Ayrs
141 H1	**Girlington** Brad
281 e6	**Girlsta** Shet
160 E1	**Girsby** N York
86 D5	**Girtford** Beds
174 F4	**Girthon** D & G
87 J3	**Girton** Cambs
135 G6	**Girton** Notts
182 F3	**Girvan** S Ayrs
148 E6	**Gisburn** Lancs
107 K5	**Gisleham** Suffk
90 C1	**Gislingham** Suffk
106 C6	**Gissing** Norfk
14 D3	**Gittisham** Devon
79 J4	**Gladestry** Powys
212 A4	**Gladsmuir** E Loth
57 K5	**Glais** Swans
162 D2	**Glaisdale** N York
234 B6	**Glamis** Angus
76 F6	**Glan-Duar** Carmth
109 J3	**Glan-Dwyfach** Gwynd
57 L3	**Glan-rhyd** Powys
128 E4	**Glan-y-don** Flints
43 H5	**Glan-y-llyn** Rhondd
93 K6	**Glan-y-nant** Powys
111 H3	**Glan-yr-afon** Gwynd
111 K3	**Glan-yr-afon** Gwynd
126 B4	**Glan-yr-afon** IOA
57 H4	**Glan-yr-afon** Swans
110 B1	**Glanaber** Gwynd
54 F3	**Glanafon** Pembks
59 J6	**Glanaman** Carmth
122 A3	**Glandford** Norfk
75 L6	**Glandwr** Pembks
92 F4	**Glandyfi** Cerdgn
61 K4	**Glangrwyney** Powys
42 C3	**Glanllynfi** Brdgnd
94 E5	**Glanmule** Powys
75 K4	**Glanrhyd** Pembks
190 F3	**Glanton** Nthumb
190 F3	**Glanton Pike** Nthumb
16 C1	**Glanvilles Wootton** Dorset
101 M5	**Glapthorn** Nhants
133 J6	**Glapwell** Derbys
79 H7	**Glasbury** Powys
127 K5	**Glascoed** Denbgs
62 C6	**Glascoed** Mons
99 C3	**Glascote** Staffs
79 G5	**Glascwm** Powys
111 H2	**Glasfryn** Conwy
209 G6	**Glasgow** C Glas
125 K6	**Glasinfryn** Gwynd
237 K2	**Glasnacardoch Bay** Highld
247 H6	**Glasnakille** Highld
92 F4	**Glaspwll** Powys
142 C3	**Glass Houghton** Wakefd
39 J6	**Glassenbury** Kent
174 C7	**Glasserton** D & G
197 L2	**Glassford** S Lans
63 L3	**Glasshouse** Gloucs
63 L3	**Glasshouse Hill** Gloucs
149 L3	**Glasshouses** N York
177 H6	**Glasson** Cumb
147 J4	**Glasson** Lancs
166 D3	**Glassonby** Cumb
234 F5	**Glasterlaw** Angus
101 K3	**Glaston** Rutlnd
31 H3	**Glastonbury** Somset
102 C6	**Glatton** Cambs
130 D1	**Glazebrook** Warrtn
139 K8	**Glazebury** Warrtn
96 F5	**Glazeley** Shrops
130 F6	**Gleadsmoss** Ches
146 E2	**Gleaston** Cumb
250 F8	**Glebe** Highld
150 D8	**Gledhow** Leeds
175 G5	**Gledpark** D & G
112 D4	**Gledrid** Shrops
89 G5	**Glemsford** Suffk
154 f4	**Glen Auldyn** IOM
242 F7	**Glen Clunie Lodge** Abers
154 b6	**Glen Maye** IOM
154 f4	**Glen Mona** IOM
229 J1	**Glen Nevis House** Highld
100 C4	**Glen Parva** Leics
183 K7	**Glen Trool Lodge** D & G
154 d6	**Glen Vine** IOM
254 E3	**Glenallachie** Highld
237 K2	**Glenancross** Highld
227 G4	**Glenaros House** Ag & B
192 D1	**Glenbarr** Ag & B
267 L5	**Glenbarry** Abers
237 H8	**Glenbeg** Highld
253 J6	**Glenbeg** Highld
245 G7	**Glenbervie** Abers
209 J3	**Glenboig** N Lans
237 H8	**Glenborrodale** Highld
217 J7	**Glenbranter** Ag & B
187 G2	**Glenbreck** Border
246 F4	**Glenbrittle House** Highld
198 B7	**Glenbuck** E Ayrs
234 A3	**Glencally** Angus
176 C5	**Glencaple** D & G
249 H2	**Glencarron Lodge** Highld
222 C3	**Glencarse** P & K
229 J5	**Glenceitlein** Highld
229 H4	**Glencoe** Highld
199 J7	**Glencothe** Border
222 B8	**Glencraig** Fife
185 J5	**Glencrosh** D & G
258 B6	**Glendale** Highld
206 F2	**Glendaruel** Ag & B
221 H6	**Glendevon** P & K
240 C2	**Glendoe Lodge** Highld
222 C3	**Glendoick** P & K
222 D3	**Glenduckie** Fife
221 G5	**Gleneagles** P & K
221 G5	**Gleneagles Hotel** P & K
204 E6	**Glenegedale** Ag & B
248 C7	**Glenelg** Highld
253 K2	**Glenerney** Moray
221 L5	**Glenfarg** P & K
241 M5	**Glenfeshie Lodge** Highld
100 C2	**Glenfield** Leics
238 E7	**Glenfinnan** Highld
239 L6	**Glenfintaig Lodge** Highld
222 B4	**Glenfoot** P & K
218 B4	**Glenfyne Lodge** Ag & B
208 B8	**Glengarnock** N Ayrs
279 K3	**Glengolly** Highld
226 E1	**Glengorm Castle** Ag & B
259 G7	**Glengrasco** Highld
199 J6	**Glenholm** Border
184 F5	**Glenhoul** D & G
233 K3	**Glenisla** Angus
207 J3	**Glenkin** Ag & B
243 M1	**Glenkindie** Abers
254 D6	**Glenlivet** Moray
175 J2	**Glenlochar** D & G
222 B6	**Glenlomond** P & K
172 F3	**Glenluce** D & G
207 H2	**Glenmassen** Ag & B
209 K5	**Glenmavis** N Lans
259 G8	**Glenmore** Highld
242 C2	**Glenmore Lodge** Highld
234 C3	**Glenquiech** Angus
206 D5	**Glenralloch** Ag & B
165 L7	**Glenridding** Cumb
222 D7	**Glenrothes** Fife
232 E8	**Glenshee** P & K
240 F5	**Glenshera Lodge** Highld
207 H3	**Glenstriven** Ag & B
135 K2	**Glentham** Lincs
241 L4	**Glentromie Lodge** Highld
183 J7	**Glentrool Village** D & G
241 J4	**Glentruim House** Highld
135 J2	**Glentworth** Lincs
237 K5	**Glenuig** Highld
229 G5	**Glenure** Ag & B
259 H8	**Glenvarragill** Highld
182 F8	**Glenwhilly** D & G
198 D7	**Glespin** S Lans
63 H3	**Glewstone** Herefs
102 C2	**Glinton** C Pete
101 G4	**Glooston** Leics
203 K6	**Glororum** Nthumb
131 L1	**Glossop** Derbys
191 K5	**Gloster Hill** Nthumb
64 B3	**Gloucester** Gloucs
149 H6	**Glusburn** N York
274 D1	**Glutt Lodge** Highld
4 F2	**Gluvian** Cnwll
66 B3	**Glympton** Oxon
112 B4	**Glyn Ceiriog** Wrexhm
60 D5	**Glyn-Neath** Neath
76 B5	**Glynarthen** Cerdgn
60 C7	**Glyncorrwg** Neath
23 G5	**Glynde** E Susx
23 G5	**Glyndebourne** E Susx
112 A3	**Glyndyfrdwy** Denbgs
43 H4	**Glyntaff** Rhondd
60 C4	**Glyntawe** Powys
76 C7	**Glynteg** Carmth
114 C7	**Gnosall** Staffs
114 C7	**Gnosall Heath** Staffs
101 G4	**Goadby** Leics
117 K6	**Goadby Marwood** Leics
40 D6	**Goat Lees** Kent
46 F4	**Goatacre** Wilts
217 G7	**Goatfield** Ag & B
24 E3	**Goatham Green** E Susx
31 L7	**Goathill** Dorset
162 E2	**Goathland** N York
30 C4	**Goathurst** Somset
38 D3	**Goathurst Common** Kent
112 D5	**Gobowen** Shrops
36 E2	**Godalming** Surrey
91 G2	**Goddard's Corner** Suffk
39 K6	**Goddard's Green** Kent
14 D2	**Godford Cross** Devon
66 F2	**Godington** Bucks
140 E8	**Godley** Tamesd
86 E1	**Godmanchester** Cambs
16 C3	**Godmanstone** Dorset
40 D5	**Godmersham** Kent
31 H2	**Godney** Somset
2 F5	**Godolphin Cross** Cnwll
57 L3	**Godre'r-graig** Neath
33 L7	**Godshill** Hants
19 J7	**Godshill** IOW
115 G5	**Godstone** Staffs
51 K8	**Godstone** Surrey
12 C7	**Godsworthy** Devon
18 B4	**Godwinscroft** Hants
62 C6	**Goetre** Mons
69 J6	**Goff's Oak** Herts
61 L4	**Gofilon** Mons

211 G4 **Gogar** C Edin
92 E7 **Goginan** Cerdgn
109 J3 **Golan** Gwynd
5 K4 **Golant** Cnwll
11 L8 **Golberdon** Cnwll
139 J8 **Golborne** Wigan
141 H4 **Golcar** Kirk
103 L5 **Gold Hill** Cambs
32 D8 **Gold Hill** Dorset
44 D2 **Goldcliff** Newpt
23 J5 **Golden Cross** E Susx
39 G4 **Golden Green** Kent
59 G5 **Golden Grove** Carmth
55 G6 **Golden Hill** Pembks
35 L2 **Golden Pot** Hants
116 C1 **Golden Valley** Derbys
114 D1 **Goldenhill** C Stke
51 H2 **Golders Green** Gt Lon
48 D6 **Goldfinch Bottom** W Berk
72 C5 **Goldhanger** Essex
96 C3 **Golding** Shrops
86 B5 **Goldington** Beds
98 C5 **Golds Green** Sandw
171 J7 **Goldsborough** N York
150 E4 **Goldsborough** N York
2 E5 **Goldsithney** Cnwll
41 J3 **Goldstone** Kent
113 M6 **Goldstone** Shrops
50 C7 **Goldsworth Park** Surrey
142 C7 **Goldthorpe** Barns
27 G6 **Goldworthy** Devon
39 K6 **Golford** Kent
39 K6 **Golford Green** Kent
252 F1 **Gollanfield** Highld
159 L6 **Gollinglith Foot** N York
129 H7 **Golly** Wrexhm
29 J3 **Golsoncott** Somset
273 K8 **Golspie** Highld
33 L4 **Gomeldon** Wilts
141 K3 **Gomersal** Kirk
37 G1 **Gomshall** Surrey
117 H2 **Gonalston** Notts
118 B4 **Gonerby Hill Foot** Lincs
281 d5 **Gonfirth** Shet
70 F5 **Good Easter** Essex
7 G2 **Goodameavy** Devon
104 F3 **Gooderstone** Norfk
27 L4 **Goodleigh** Devon
152 D7 **Goodmanham** E R Yk
51 M2 **Goodmayes** Gt Lon
40 D3 **Goodnestone** Kent
41 H4 **Goodnestone** Kent
63 H3 **Goodrich** Herefs
8 D3 **Goodrington** Torbay
140 B3 **Goodshaw** Lancs
140 B2 **Goodshaw Fold** Lancs
13 H8 **Goodstone** Devon
74 F4 **Goodwick** Pembks
34 D2 **Goodworth Clatford** Hants
99 J6 **Goodyers End** Warwks
143 J3 **Goole** E R Yk
143 J4 **Goole Fields** E R Yk
82 B4 **Goom's Hill** Worcs
4 B5 **Goonbell** Cnwll
4 C4 **Goonhavern** Cnwll
4 B5 **Goonvrea** Cnwll
73 H2 **Goose Green** Essex
73 H2 **Goose Green** Essex
39 G3 **Goose Green** Kent
39 L6 **Goose Green** Kent
45 K4 **Goose Green** S Glos
21 J3 **Goose Green** W Susx
139 H7 **Goose Green** Wigan
80 B7 **Goose Pool** Herefs
245 G7 **Goosecruives** Abers
12 F4 **Gooseford** Devon
26 D7 **Gooseham** Cnwll
81 L3 **Goosehill Green** Worcs
29 G4 **Goosemoor** Somset
47 M1 **Goosey** Oxon
147 L8 **Goosnargh** Lancs
130 F5 **Goostrey** Ches
126 D5 **Gorddinog** Conwy
201 K4 **Gordon** Border
200 C8 **Gordon Arms Hotel** Border
267 L5 **Gordonstown** Abers
256 C4 **Gordonstown** Abers
79 J3 **Gore** Powys
72 C3 **Gore Pit** Essex
41 J2 **Gore Street** Kent
211 K6 **Gorebridge** Mdloth
103 J1 **Gorefield** Cambs
47 G7 **Gores** Wilts
9 f3 **Gorey** Jersey
48 F3 **Goring** Oxon

49 G3 **Goring Heath** Oxon
21 J6 **Goring-by-Sea** W Susx
107 L3 **Gorleston on Sea** Norfk
268 D4 **Gorrachie** Abers
5 G6 **Gorran** Cnwll
5 G6 **Gorran Haven** Cnwll
5 G6 **Gorran High Lanes** Cnwll
76 D6 **Gorrig** Cerdgn
92 D7 **Gors** Cerdgn
47 H2 **Gorse Hill** Swindn
128 E4 **Gorsedd** Flints
57 G5 **Gorseinon** Swans
115 M1 **Gorseybank** Derbys
76 E5 **Gorsgoch** Cerdgn
59 G6 **Gorslas** Carmth
63 K2 **Gorsley** Gloucs
63 K2 **Gorsley Common** Herefs
97 G8 **Gorst Hill** Worcs
130 B5 **Gorstage** Ches
262 C7 **Gorstan** Highld
129 H7 **Gorstello** Ches
115 H6 **Gorsty Hill** Staffs
227 L6 **Gorten** Ag & B
250 F7 **Gorthleck** Highld
140 C8 **Gorton** Manch
90 D4 **Gosbeck** Suffk
119 H5 **Gosberton** Lincs
119 G5 **Gosberton Clough** Lincs
71 J1 **Gosfield** Essex
14 C3 **Gosford** Devon
155 J2 **Gosforth** Cumb
180 F5 **Gosforth** N u Ty
130 B8 **Gosland Green** Ches
31 J4 **Gosling Street** Somset
68 F2 **Gosmore** Herts
97 K4 **Gospel End** Staffs
36 D4 **Gospel Green** W Susx
19 K4 **Gosport** Hants
85 J6 **Gossard's Green** Beds
63 L6 **Gossington** Gloucs
203 G4 **Goswick** Nthumb
116 F5 **Gotham** Notts
64 D1 **Gotherington** Gloucs
30 C5 **Gotton** Somset
39 H6 **Goudhurst** Kent
136 E4 **Goulceby** Lincs
256 D3 **Gourdas** Abers
222 F1 **Gourdie** Angus
235 K1 **Gourdon** Abers
207 L3 **Gourock** Inver
208 F6 **Govan** C Glas
7 L5 **Goveton** Devon
143 G3 **Gowdall** E R Yk
262 E4 **Gower** Highld
57 G5 **Gowerton** Swans
210 E1 **Gowkhall** Fife
152 A5 **Gowthorpe** E R Yk
153 K6 **Goxhill** E R Yk
144 E3 **Goxhill** N Linc
282 g4 **Grabhair** W Isls
118 E5 **Graby** Lincs
3 H8 **Grade** Cnwll
113 K1 **Gradeley Green** Ches
20 F3 **Graffham** W Susx
86 D2 **Grafham** Cambs
36 F3 **Grafham** Surrey
80 C7 **Grafton** Herefs
150 F3 **Grafton** N York
65 K7 **Grafton** Oxon
113 G7 **Grafton** Shrops
80 D3 **Grafton** Worcs
82 A7 **Grafton** Worcs
81 M4 **Grafton Flyford** Worcs
84 E6 **Grafton Regis** Nhants
101 K7 **Grafton Underwood** Nhants
39 L4 **Grafty Green** Kent
128 F8 **Graianrhyd** Denbgs
126 F5 **Graig** Conwy
128 C5 **Graig** Denbgs
112 A1 **Graig-fechan** Denbgs
53 J4 **Grain** Medway
140 E6 **Grains Bar** Oldham
145 H7 **Grainsby** Lincs
145 K8 **Grainthorpe** Lincs
4 F5 **Grampound** Cnwll
4 E5 **Grampound Road** Cnwll
283 c9 **Gramsdal** W Isls
283 c9 **Gramsdale** W Isls
67 J2 **Granborough** Bucks
117 K4 **Granby** Notts
9 e3 **Grand Chemins** Jersey
83 L2 **Grandborough** Warwks
9 j2 **Grandes Rocques** Guern
232 D5 **Grandtully** P & K
165 H7 **Grange** Cumb

53 G5 **Grange** Medway
222 D2 **Grange** P & K
128 F2 **Grange** Wirral
267 K5 **Grange Crossroads** Moray
17 H6 **Grange Gate** Dorset
265 H7 **Grange Hall** Moray
70 C8 **Grange Hill** Gt Lon
141 K4 **Grange Moor** Kirk
222 D4 **Grange of Lindores** Fife
180 F8 **Grange Villa** Dur
156 F7 **Grange-over-Sands** Cumb
199 G4 **Grangehall** S Lans
132 E8 **Grangemill** Derbys
210 B3 **Grangemouth** Falk
210 D3 **Grangepans** Falk
170 D6 **Grangetown** R & Cl
181 K8 **Grangetown** Sundld
153 H4 **Gransmoor** E R Yk
71 G3 **Gransmore Green** Essex
74 E5 **Granston** Pembks
87 J4 **Grantchester** Cambs
118 B4 **Grantham** Lincs
211 H4 **Granton** C Edin
253 K6 **Grantown-on-Spey** Highld
80 C3 **Grantsfield** Herefs
213 H6 **Grantshouse** Border
130 C2 **Grappenhall** Warrtn
144 D6 **Grasby** Lincs
156 D1 **Grasmere** Cumb
88 E7 **Grass Green** Essex
140 E6 **Grasscroft** Oldham
129 J3 **Grassendale** Lpool
165 K2 **Grassgarth** Cumb
149 H3 **Grassington** N York
133 H6 **Grassmoor** Derbys
134 F6 **Grassthorpe** Notts
34 C3 **Grateley** Hants
115 G5 **Gratwich** Staffs
86 E3 **Graveley** Cambs
69 G2 **Graveley** Herts
98 E5 **Gravelly Hill** Birm
95 H3 **Gravelsbank** Shrops
40 D3 **Graveney** Kent
52 E4 **Gravesend** Kent
282 g4 **Gravir** W Isls
144 A8 **Grayingham** Lincs
157 J3 **Grayrigg** Cumb
52 D3 **Grays** Thurr
36 C4 **Grayshott** Hants
164 C5 **Grayson Green** Cumb
36 D4 **Grayswood** Surrey
170 C5 **Graythorpe** Hartpl
49 G5 **Grazeley** Wokham
142 C8 **Greasbrough** Rothm
128 F2 **Greasby** Wirral
116 E2 **Greasley** Notts
87 L5 **Great Abington** Cambs
101 L8 **Great Addington** Nhants
82 D3 **Great Alne** Warwks
138 C6 **Great Altcar** Lancs
69 K4 **Great Amwell** Herts
166 F8 **Great Asby** Cumb
89 K2 **Great Ashfield** Suffk
170 D8 **Great Ayton** N York
71 H6 **Great Baddow** Essex
46 A2 **Great Badminton** S Glos
71 G1 **Great Bardfield** Essex
86 C5 **Great Barford** Beds
98 D4 **Great Barr** Sandw
65 J4 **Great Barrington** Gloucs
129 L6 **Great Barrow** Ches
89 H2 **Great Barton** Suffk
162 C6 **Great Barugh** N York
180 B3 **Great Bavington** Nthumb
90 F5 **Great Bealings** Suffk
47 K6 **Great Bedwyn** Wilts
73 G3 **Great Bentley** Essex
84 F3 **Great Billing** Nhants
121 G5 **Great Bircham** Norfk
90 D5 **Great Blakenham** Suffk
166 B4 **Great Blencow** Cumb
113 L7 **Great Bolas** Wrekin
50 E8 **Great Bookham** Surrey
2 C4 **Great Bosullow** Cnwll
83 K6 **Great Bourton** Oxon
101 G5 **Great Bowden** Leics
88 D4 **Great Bradley** Suffk
72 B4 **Great Braxted** Essex
90 B5 **Great Bricett** Suffk
67 L1 **Great Brickhill** Bucks
114 D6 **Great Bridgeford** Staffs
84 C2 **Great Brington** Nhants
73 G2 **Great Bromley** Essex
164 E4 **Great Broughton** Cumb
161 J2 **Great Broughton** N York

130 C4 **Great Budworth** Ches
169 J7 **Great Burdon** Darltn
71 G8 **Great Burstead** Essex
161 H2 **Great Busby** N York
70 E3 **Great Canfield** Essex
137 H3 **Great Carlton** Lincs
101 M2 **Great Casterton** Rutlnd
46 B6 **Great Chalfield** Wilts
40 C7 **Great Chart** Kent
114 B8 **Great Chatwell** Staffs
114 D1 **Great Chell** C Stke
87 K6 **Great Chesterford** Essex
46 E8 **Great Cheverell** Wilts
87 J7 **Great Chishill** Cambs
73 J4 **Great Clacton** Essex
141 M4 **Great Cliffe** Wakefd
164 D5 **Great Clifton** Cumb
145 G6 **Great Coates** NE Lin
81 L6 **Great Comberton** Worcs
39 G2 **Great Comp** Kent
178 B7 **Great Corby** Cumb
89 H7 **Great Cornard** Suffk
153 L4 **Great Cowden** E R Yk
65 K8 **Great Coxwell** Oxon
101 H8 **Great Cransley** Nhants
105 G3 **Great Cressingham** Norfk
165 J6 **Great Crosthwaite** Cumb
115 K4 **Great Cubley** Derbys
117 K8 **Great Dalby** Leics
85 H2 **Great Doddington** Nhants
63 G4 **Great Doward** Herefs
121 J8 **Great Dunham** Norfk
70 F3 **Great Dunmow** Essex
33 K3 **Great Durnford** Wilts
70 F2 **Great Easton** Essex
101 J5 **Great Easton** Leics
147 H7 **Great Eccleston** Lancs
162 C6 **Great Edstone** N York
105 L4 **Great Ellingham** Norfk
32 C1 **Great Elm** Somset
8 A3 **Great Englebourne** Devon
84 B4 **Great Everdon** Nhants
87 H4 **Great Eversden** Cambs
89 K4 **Great Finborough** Suffk
105 H1 **Great Fransham** Norfk
68 C5 **Great Gaddesden** Herts
102 C6 **Great Gidding** Cambs
152 B5 **Great Givendale** E R Yk
91 H3 **Great Glemham** Suffk
100 E4 **Great Glen** Leics
118 B4 **Great Gonerby** Lincs
86 F4 **Great Gransden** Cambs
86 F6 **Great Green** Cambs
106 F5 **Great Green** Norfk
89 J4 **Great Green** Suffk
89 J2 **Great Green** Suffk
162 D7 **Great Habton** N York
118 F3 **Great Hale** Lincs
70 D3 **Great Hallingbury** Essex
85 G1 **Great Harrowden** Nhants
139 L1 **Great Harwood** Lancs
66 F6 **Great Haseley** Oxon
153 K7 **Great Hatfield** E R Yk
114 F7 **Great Haywood** Staffs
142 F3 **Great Heck** N York
89 H7 **Great Henny** Essex
46 C7 **Great Hinton** Wilts
105 J5 **Great Hockham** Norfk
73 J3 **Great Holland** Essex
72 E1 **Great Horkesley** Essex
69 L1 **Great Hormead** Herts
141 J2 **Great Horton** Brad
67 J1 **Great Horwood** Bucks
142 C6 **Great Houghton** Barns
84 F3 **Great Houghton** Nhants
132 D4 **Great Hucklow** Derbys
153 H4 **Great Kelk** E R Yk
67 K6 **Great Kimble** Bucks
67 L7 **Great Kingshill** Bucks
156 D2 **Great Langdale** Cumb
160 D3 **Great Langton** N York
71 H4 **Great Leighs** Essex
144 E6 **Great Limber** Lincs
85 G6 **Great Linford** M Keyn
89 H1 **Great Livermere** Suffk
132 D5 **Great Longstone** Derbys
169 H1 **Great Lumley** Dur
95 L2 **Great Lyth** Shrops
81 H6 **Great Malvern** Worcs
89 G8 **Great Maplestead** Essex
138 C1 **Great Marton** Bpool
121 H7 **Great Massingham** Norfk
106 C2 **Great Melton** Norfk
128 F2 **Great Meols** Wirral
66 F6 **Great Milton** Oxon

67 L6 **Great Missenden** Bucks
148 C8 **Great Mitton** Lancs
41 K5 **Great Mongeham** Kent
106 D5 **Great Moulton** Norfk
69 K2 **Great Munden** Herts
167 H7 **Great Musgrave** Cumb
112 F7 **Great Ness** Shrops
71 H3 **Great Notley** Essex
28 F4 **Great Nurcott** Somset
62 D5 **Great Oak** Mons
73 J2 **Great Oakley** Essex
101 J6 **Great Oakley** Nhants
68 F2 **Great Offley** Herts
167 G7 **Great Ormside** Cumb
177 K7 **Great Orton** Cumb
150 F3 **Great Ouseburn** N York
100 F6 **Great Oxendon** Nhants
71 G6 **Great Oxney Green** Essex
39 J4 **Great Pattenden** Kent
86 E2 **Great Paxton** Cambs
138 D1 **Great Plumpton** Lancs
106 F2 **Great Plumstead** Norfk
118 B5 **Great Ponton** Lincs
27 J7 **Great Potheridge** Devon
142 B2 **Great Preston** Leeds
83 M7 **Great Purston** Nhants
102 E7 **Great Raveley** Cambs
65 J4 **Great Rissington** Gloucs
65 L1 **Great Rollright** Oxon
54 F3 **Great Rudbaxton** Pembks
121 L6 **Great Ryburgh** Norfk
190 E4 **Great Ryle** Nthumb
96 B3 **Great Ryton** Shrops
71 G2 **Great Saling** Essex
166 D3 **Great Salkeld** Cumb
88 C8 **Great Sampford** Essex
130 B2 **Great Sankey** Warrtn
98 B2 **Great Saredon** Staffs
129 H5 **Great Saughall** Ches
88 F3 **Great Saxham** Suffk
48 A4 **Great Shefford** W Berk
87 J5 **Great Shelford** Cambs
160 E2 **Great Smeaton** N York
121 L4 **Great Snoring** Norfk
46 D2 **Great Somerford** Wilts
114 A5 **Great Soudley** Shrops
169 J6 **Great Stainton** Darltn
53 J1 **Great Stambridge** Essex
86 C2 **Great Staughton** Cambs
137 H6 **Great Steeping** Lincs
45 J3 **Great Stoke** S Glos
41 K3 **Great Stonar** Kent
166 D6 **Great Strickland** Cumb
102 E8 **Great Stukeley** Cambs
136 D4 **Great Sturton** Lincs
129 J4 **Great Sutton** Ches
96 C6 **Great Sutton** Shrops
179 L4 **Great Swinburne** Nthumb
66 B1 **Great Tew** Oxon
72 C2 **Great Tey** Essex
27 J7 **Great Torrington** Devon
190 E6 **Great Tosson** Nthumb
72 B5 **Great Totham** Essex
72 C4 **Great Totham** Essex
136 D2 **Great Tows** Lincs
156 C7 **Great Urswick** Cumb
53 K2 **Great Wakering** Essex
89 J6 **Great Waldingfield** Suffk
121 L4 **Great Walsingham** Norfk
71 G4 **Great Waltham** Essex
130 F4 **Great Warford** Ches
52 C1 **Great Warley** Essex
82 A8 **Great Washbourne** Gloucs
13 G5 **Great Weeke** Devon
101 K5 **Great Weldon** Nhants
89 H3 **Great Welnetham** Suffk
90 C7 **Great Wenham** Suffk
180 B5 **Great Whittington** Nthumb
72 D4 **Great Wigborough** Essex
87 L4 **Great Wilbraham** Cambs
33 J4 **Great Wishford** Wilts
122 C7 **Great Witchingham** Norfk
64 D4 **Great Witcombe** Gloucs
81 H2 **Great Witley** Worcs
82 F8 **Great Wolford** Warwks
88 D5 **Great Wratting** Essex
69 G2 **Great Wymondley** Herts
98 C2 **Great Wyrley** Staffs
113 J7 **Great Wytheford** Shrops
107 L2 **Great Yarmouth** Norfk
88 F7 **Great Yeldham** Essex
47 G2 **Greatfield** Wilts
102 B1 **Greatford** Lincs
115 G3 **Greatgate** Staffs
36 A5 **Greatham** Hants

170 C5 **Greatham** Hartpl
21 H4 **Greatham** W Susx
25 K3 **Greatstone-on-Sea** Kent
84 A6 **Greatworth** Nhants
137 H6 **Grebby** Lincs
154 d6 **Greeba** IOM
128 C6 **Green** Denbgs
156 E6 **Green Bank** Cumb
36 C3 **Green Cross** Surrey
45 H8 **Green Down** Somset
85 K5 **Green End** Beds
86 B2 **Green End** Beds
86 B3 **Green End** Beds
86 C5 **Green End** Beds
102 E8 **Green End** Cambs
87 H4 **Green End** Cambs
87 K2 **Green End** Cambs
87 K3 **Green End** Cambs
102 D6 **Green End** Cambs
69 H1 **Green End** Herts
69 J3 **Green End** Herts
87 G8 **Green End** Herts
99 H6 **Green End** Warwks
151 G4 **Green Hammerton** N York
165 L1 **Green Head** Cumb
98 C1 **Green Heath** Staffs
46 F2 **Green Hill** Wilts
13 H7 **Green Lane** Devon
82 C2 **Green Lane** Warwks
141 L7 **Green Moor** Barns
143 K2 **Green Oak** E R Yk
31 J1 **Green Ore** Somset
157 G2 **Green Quarter** Cumb
24 D5 **Green Street** E Susx
64 C4 **Green Street** Gloucs
70 C3 **Green Street** Herts
69 G7 **Green Street** Herts
81 K5 **Green Street** Worcs
51 M6 **Green Street Green** Gt Lon
52 C5 **Green Street Green** Kent
70 C3 **Green Tye** Herts
210 B7 **Greenburn** W Loth
168 F1 **Greencroft Hall** Dur
65 L3 **Greenend** Oxon
207 L1 **Greenfield** Ag & B
85 L8 **Greenfield** Beds
128 E4 **Greenfield** Flints
239 L3 **Greenfield** Highld
140 F7 **Greenfield** Oldham
49 H1 **Greenfield** Oxon
50 F3 **Greenford** Gt Lon
209 L5 **Greengairs** N Lans
150 B8 **Greengates** Brad
164 F3 **Greengill** Cumb
147 H8 **Greenhalgh** Lancs
29 K6 **Greenham** Somset
48 C6 **Greenham** W Berk
179 J2 **Greenhaugh** Nthumb
178 F6 **Greenhead** Nthumb
139 L7 **Greenheys** Salfd
176 F3 **Greenhill** D & G
209 L3 **Greenhill** Falk
81 G5 **Greenhill** Herefs
40 F2 **Greenhill** Kent
198 F6 **Greenhill** S Lans
116 C2 **Greenhillocks** Derbys
52 C4 **Greenhithe** Kent
197 G3 **Greenholm** E Ayrs
157 J2 **Greenholme** Cumb
188 F2 **Greenhouse** Border
149 K3 **Greenhow Hill** N York
280 B3 **Greenland** Highld
133 H2 **Greenland** Sheff
49 J2 **Greenlands** Bucks
201 L4 **Greenlaw** Border
176 D4 **Greenlea** D & G
220 E5 **Greenloaning** P & K
49 G3 **Greenmoor Hill** Oxon
140 A5 **Greenmount** Bury
207 M4 **Greenock** Inver
156 D6 **Greenodd** Cumb
84 C5 **Greens Norton** Nhants
122 B8 **Greensgate** Norfk
199 H4 **Greenshields** S Lans
180 E6 **Greenside** Gatesd
141 J4 **Greenside** Kirk
72 E2 **Greenstead** Essex
71 K2 **Greenstead Green** Essex
70 D6 **Greensted** Essex
90 B5 **Greenstreet Green** Suffk
81 G8 **Greenway** Gloucs
30 D6 **Greenway** Somset
43 G7 **Greenway** V Glam
81 G1 **Greenway** Worcs
51 K3 **Greenwich** Gt Lon

64 F1 **Greet** Gloucs
80 D1 **Greete** Shrops
136 F5 **Greetham** Lincs
118 B8 **Greetham** Rutlnd
141 G3 **Greetland** Calder
139 J2 **Gregson Lane** Lancs
30 F4 **Greinton** Somset
154 c7 **Grenaby** IOM
85 G3 **Grendon** Nhants
99 H3 **Grendon** Warwks
80 E4 **Grendon Green** Herefs
67 G3 **Grendon Underwood** Bucks
12 C8 **Grenofen** Devon
133 G1 **Grenoside** Sheff
282 e6 **Greosabhagh** W Isls
112 E1 **Gresford** Wrexhm
122 D4 **Gresham** Norfk
258 E6 **Greshornish House Hotel** Highld
121 L8 **Gressenhall** Norfk
121 L8 **Gressenhall Green** Norfk
147 L2 **Gressingham** Lancs
113 M1 **Gresty Green** Ches
168 D8 **Greta Bridge** Dur
177 K5 **Gretna** D & G
177 K5 **Gretna Green** D & G
64 E1 **Gretton** Gloucs
101 K4 **Gretton** Nhants
96 C4 **Gretton** Shrops
160 C7 **Grewelthorpe** N York
91 L1 **Grey Friars** Suffk
143 K6 **Grey Green** N Linc
150 A1 **Greygarth** N York
30 F4 **Greylake** Somset
176 E1 **Greyrigg** D & G
49 H2 **Greys Green** Oxon
164 E5 **Greysouthen** Cumb
166 B4 **Greystoke** Cumb
234 E6 **Greystone** Angus
35 L1 **Greywell** Hants
15 J2 **Gribb** Dorset
143 J1 **Gribthorpe** E R Yk
99 K5 **Griff** Warwks
62 C7 **Griffithstown** Torfn
116 C7 **Griffydam** Leics
36 B4 **Griggs Green** Hants
139 J5 **Grimeford Village** Lancs
133 G2 **Grimesthorpe** Sheff
142 C6 **Grimethorpe** Barns
81 J3 **Grimley** Worcs
183 J1 **Grimmet** S Ayrs
137 G2 **Grimoldby** Lincs
112 E6 **Grimpo** Shrops
139 H1 **Grimsargh** Lancs
145 H5 **Grimsby** NE Lin
84 C4 **Grimscote** Nhants
11 J1 **Grimscott** Cnwll
282 g4 **Grimshader** W Isls
139 L3 **Grimshaw** Bl w D
139 G5 **Grimshaw Green** Lancs
118 D7 **Grimsthorpe** Lincs
145 H1 **Grimston** E R Yk
117 J7 **Grimston** Leics
120 F7 **Grimston** Norfk
134 D6 **Grimston Hill** Notts
16 C4 **Grimstone** Dorset
89 J2 **Grimstone End** Suffk
12 A4 **Grinacombe Moor** Devon
153 J2 **Grindale** E R Yk
97 G3 **Grindle** Shrops
132 E4 **Grindleford** Derbys
148 D6 **Grindleton** Lancs
113 H3 **Grindley Brook** Shrops
132 D4 **Grindlow** Derbys
202 E4 **Grindon** Nthumb
169 K5 **Grindon** S on T
115 H1 **Grindon** Staffs
181 J7 **Grindon** Sundld
179 J5 **Grindon Hill** Nthumb
202 E4 **Grindonrigg** Nthumb
134 E2 **Gringley on the Hill** Notts
177 L7 **Grinsdale** Cumb
113 H6 **Grinshill** Shrops
159 J3 **Grinton** N York
282 g4 **Griomaisiader** W Isls
283 c9 **Griomsaigh** W Isls
224 F3 **Grishipoll** Ag & B
23 G3 **Grisling Common** E Susx
163 K6 **Gristhorpe** N York
105 J4 **Griston** Norfk
275 d5 **Gritley** Ork
46 F2 **Grittenham** Wilts
46 B3 **Grittleton** Wilts
156 C5 **Grizebeck** Cumb
156 D4 **Grizedale** Cumb

100 B2 **Groby** Leics
127 K6 **Groes** Conwy
43 G5 **Groes-faen** Rhondd
43 H4 **Groes-Wen** Caerph
108 D4 **Groesffordd** Gwynd
127 K5 **Groesffordd Marli** Denbgs
94 F1 **Groeslwyd** Powys
125 H8 **Groeslon** Gwynd
125 J7 **Groeslon** Gwynd
91 J3 **Gromford** Suffk
128 C3 **Gronant** Flints
38 E6 **Groombridge** E Susx
282 e6 **Grosebay** W Isls
62 E2 **Grosmont** Mons
162 E2 **Grosmont** N York
89 J7 **Groton** Suffk
140 E6 **Grotton** Oldham
9 e3 **Grouville** Jersey
67 M3 **Grove** Bucks
16 D7 **Grove** Dorset
41 H3 **Grove** Kent
134 E4 **Grove** Notts
48 B1 **Grove** Oxon
55 G6 **Grove** Pembks
39 K2 **Grove Green** Kent
51 L4 **Grove Park** Gt Lon
39 H5 **Grovenhurst** Kent
45 K1 **Grovesend** S Glos
57 G5 **Grovesend** Swans
52 C5 **Grubb Street** Kent
260 F2 **Gruinard** Highld
204 D3 **Gruinart** Ag & B
246 E3 **Grula** Highld
227 G4 **Gruline** Ag & B
2 C5 **Grumbla** Cnwll
90 F5 **Grundisburgh** Suffk
281 c6 **Gruting** Shet
229 J6 **Gualachulain** Highld
103 H2 **Guanockgate** Lincs
223 H3 **Guardbridge** Fife
81 J6 **Guarlford** Worcs
232 F5 **Guay** P & K
24 F4 **Guestling Green** E Susx
24 F4 **Guestling Thorn** E Susx
122 B6 **Guestwick** Norfk
139 L3 **Guide** Bl w D
140 D8 **Guide Bridge** Tamesd
181 G2 **Guide Post** Nthumb
95 H6 **Guilden Down** Shrops
86 F6 **Guilden Morden** Cambs
129 K6 **Guilden Sutton** Ches
36 F1 **Guildford** Surrey
53 H6 **Guildstead** Kent
221 L1 **Guildtown** P & K
84 D1 **Guilsborough** Nhants
94 F1 **Guilsfield** Powys
41 J4 **Guilton** Kent
183 J1 **Guiltreehill** S Ayrs
27 K3 **Guineaford** Devon
170 E7 **Guisborough** R & Cl
150 B7 **Guiseley** Leeds
121 M6 **Guist** Norfk
65 G2 **Guiting Power** Gloucs
212 B2 **Gullane** E Loth
89 G4 **Gulling Green** Suffk
2 D5 **Gulval** Cnwll
12 B8 **Gulworthy** Devon
55 J6 **Gumfreston** Pembks
100 F5 **Gumley** Leics
4 E3 **Gummow's Shop** Cnwll
39 J7 **Gun Green** Kent
23 J4 **Gun Hill** E Susx
99 H5 **Gun Hill** Warwks
143 H1 **Gunby** E R Yk
118 B7 **Gunby** Lincs
137 J6 **Gunby** Lincs
35 J4 **Gundleton** Hants
27 L4 **Gunn** Devon
159 G3 **Gunnerside** N York
179 L4 **Gunnerton** Nthumb
143 L5 **Gunness** N Linc
12 B8 **Gunnislake** Cnwll
281 e6 **Gunnista** Shet
102 D3 **Gunthorpe** C Pete
143 K8 **Gunthorpe** N Linc
121 M4 **Gunthorpe** Norfk
117 H3 **Gunthorpe** Notts
107 L4 **Gunton** Suffk
3 G6 **Gunwalloe** Cnwll
29 H4 **Gupworthy** Somset
19 H4 **Gurnard** IOW
131 H5 **Gurnett** Ches

31 K1 **Gurney Slade** Somset
57 L3 **Gurnos** Powys
40 D4 **Gushmere** Kent
33 G8 **Gussage All Saints** Dorset
33 G8 **Gussage St Andrew** Dorset
33 G8 **Gussage St Michael** Dorset
41 K6 **Guston** Kent
281 f2 **Gutcher** Shet
234 E5 **Guthrie** Angus
32 D6 **Guy's Marsh** Dorset
103 H3 **Guyhirn** Cambs
103 H3 **Guyhirn Gull** Cambs
191 J5 **Guyzance** Nthumb
128 C3 **Gwaenysgor** Flints
125 G4 **Gwalchmai** IOA
126 C8 **Gwastadnant** Gwynd
59 J6 **Gwaun-Cae-Gurwen** Carmth
75 K2 **Gwbert on Sea** Cerdgn
2 F3 **Gwealavellan** Cnwll
3 H6 **Gwealeath** Cnwll
3 H5 **Gweek** Cnwll
62 D6 **Gwehelog** Mons
78 E6 **Gwenddwr** Powys
3 J7 **Gwendreath** Cnwll
3 J3 **Gwennap** Cnwll
3 J7 **Gwenter** Cnwll
128 F6 **Gwernaffield** Flints
62 E6 **Gwernesney** Mons
58 F2 **Gwernogle** Carmth
128 F7 **Gwernymynydd** Flints
112 D1 **Gwersyllt** Wrexhm
128 D3 **Gwespyr** Flints
4 F4 **Gwindra** Cnwll
2 F4 **Gwinear** Cnwll
2 F3 **Gwithian** Cnwll
125 G3 **Gwredog** IOA
61 J7 **Gwrhay** Caerph
111 L2 **Gwyddelwern** Denbgs
58 E2 **Gwyddgrug** Carmth
112 C1 **Gwynfryn** Wrexhm
78 E2 **Gwystre** Powys
127 H7 **Gwytherin** Conwy
112 E3 **Gyfelia** Wrexhm
109 G2 **Gyrn-goch** Gwynd

H

95 K3 **Habberley** Shrops
97 H7 **Habberley** Worcs
140 B1 **Habergham** Lancs
137 J6 **Habertoft** Lincs
36 B6 **Habin** W Susx
144 F5 **Habrough** NE Lin
118 E6 **Hacconby** Lincs
118 D4 **Haceby** Lincs
91 G3 **Hacheston** Suffk
113 L2 **Hack Green** Ches
51 H5 **Hackbridge** Gt Lon
133 H3 **Hackenthorpe** Sheff
106 B3 **Hackford** Norfk
160 C4 **Hackforth** N York
275 C4 **Hackland** Ork
84 F4 **Hackleton** Nhants
41 K4 **Hacklinge** Kent
97 K7 **Hackman's Gate** Worcs
163 H4 **Hackness** N York
30 E2 **Hackness** Somset
51 K2 **Hackney** Gt Lon
135 K3 **Hackthorn** Lincs
166 D6 **Hackthorpe** Cumb
52 C2 **Hacton** Gt Lon
202 B6 **Hadden** Border
67 H5 **Haddenham** Bucks
103 J8 **Haddenham** Cambs
212 B4 **Haddington** E Loth
135 H7 **Haddington** Lincs
107 J4 **Haddiscoe** Norfk
256 E4 **Haddo** Abers
102 C5 **Haddon** Cambs
141 J6 **Hade Edge** Kirk
140 F8 **Hadfield** Derbys
70 B3 **Hadham Cross** Herts
70 B3 **Hadham Ford** Herts
53 H2 **Hadleigh** Essex
89 L6 **Hadleigh** Suffk
89 K7 **Hadleigh Heath** Suffk
81 K2 **Hadley** Worcs
96 F1 **Hadley** Wrekin
115 J7 **Hadley End** Staffs
69 H7 **Hadley Wood** Gt Lon
39 G3 **Hadlow** Kent
23 J2 **Hadlow Down** E Susx
113 H7 **Hadnall** Shrops

88 B6 **Hadstock** Essex
81 L3 **Hadzor** Worcs
39 M5 **Haffenden Quarter** Kent
112 D2 **Hafod-y-bwch** Wrexhm
61 K7 **Hafod-y-coed** Blae G
127 H6 **Hafodunos** Conwy
61 K7 **Hafodyrynys** Caerph
140 C1 **Haggate** Lancs
178 B4 **Haggbeck** Cumb
203 G4 **Haggerston** Nthumb
27 K2 **Haggington Hill** Devon
209 L3 **Haggs** Falk
80 D7 **Hagley** Herefs
97 K7 **Hagley** Worcs
89 J7 **Hagmore Green** Suffk
136 F7 **Hagnaby** Lincs
137 J4 **Hagnaby** Lincs
136 F6 **Hagworthingham** Lincs
139 J6 **Haigh** Wigan
139 H1 **Haighton Green** Lancs
86 D3 **Hail Weston** Cambs
155 J1 **Haile** Cumb
64 F1 **Hailes** Gloucs
69 K5 **Hailey** Herts
48 F2 **Hailey** Oxon
65 M4 **Hailey** Oxon
23 K5 **Hailsham** E Susx
70 C8 **Hainault** Gt Lon
41 K2 **Haine** Kent
122 E7 **Hainford** Norfk
136 C3 **Hainton** Lincs
149 J8 **Hainworth** Brad
153 H3 **Haisthorpe** E R Yk
54 E5 **Hakin** Pembks
117 H1 **Halam** Notts
210 F1 **Halbeath** Fife
29 H8 **Halberton** Devon
280 B4 **Halcro** Highld
157 H7 **Hale** Cumb
129 L3 **Hale** Halton
33 L7 **Hale** Hants
32 C5 **Hale** Somset
36 C1 **Hale** Surrey
130 F2 **Hale** Traffd
129 L3 **Hale Bank** Halton
23 J4 **Hale Green** E Susx
147 G7 **Hale Nook** Lancs
39 G3 **Hale Street** Kent
130 F3 **Halebarns** Traffd
107 H4 **Hales** Norfk
113 M5 **Hales** Staffs
115 K3 **Hales Green** Derbys
40 F3 **Hales Place** Kent
119 K6 **Halesgate** Lincs
98 B6 **Halesowen** Dudley
72 C8 **Halesville** Essex
107 H7 **Halesworth** Suffk
129 K3 **Halewood** Knows
13 J7 **Halford** Devon
95 K6 **Halford** Shrops
83 G6 **Halford** Warwks
157 H5 **Halfpenny** Cumb
97 J5 **Halfpenny Green** Staffs
160 B5 **Halfpenny Houses** N York
59 J3 **Halfway** Carmth
59 M2 **Halfway** Carmth
133 J3 **Halfway** Sheff
48 B5 **Halfway** W Berk
36 D6 **Halfway Bridge** W Susx
95 H1 **Halfway House** Shrops
53 K4 **Halfway Houses** Kent
141 H3 **Halifax** Calder
279 K4 **Halkirk** Highld
128 F5 **Halkyn** Flints
208 C8 **Hall** E Rens
141 L4 **Hall Cliffe** Wakefd
138 E2 **Hall Cross** Lancs
156 B3 **Hall Dunnerdale** Cumb
85 K6 **Hall End** Beds
86 B7 **Hall End** Beds
210 A3 **Hall Glen** Falk
98 E7 **Hall Green** Birm
69 L5 **Hall's Green** Essex
69 H2 **Hall's Green** Herts
116 D4 **Hallam Fields** Derbys
23 H4 **Halland** E Susx
101 H4 **Hallaton** Leics
45 J7 **Hallatrow** BaNES
178 D7 **Hallbankgate** Cumb
157 K5 **Hallbeck** Cumb
45 H3 **Hallen** S Glos
133 H8 **Hallfield Gate** Derbys
169 J2 **Hallgarth** Dur
258 C5 **Hallin** Highld
52 F6 **Halling** Medway

136 F3 **Hallington** Lincs
180 B4 **Hallington** Nthumb
139 L5 **Halliwell** Bolton
117 J1 **Halloughton** Notts
81 J3 **Hallow** Worcs
81 J3 **Hallow Heath** Worcs
8 B7 **Hallsands** Devon
156 A5 **Hallthwaites** Cumb
119 L3 **Halltoft End** Lincs
11 H5 **Hallworthy** Cnwll
199 L5 **Hallyne** Border
114 B2 **Halmer End** Staffs
80 F5 **Halmond's Frome** Herefs
63 K6 **Halmore** Gloucs
20 E5 **Halnaker** W Susx
138 D5 **Halsall** Lancs
84 A7 **Halse** Nhants
29 L5 **Halse** Somset
2 D3 **Halsetown** Cnwll
145 H2 **Halsham** E R Yk
27 J3 **Halsinger** Devon
71 K1 **Halstead** Essex
52 A6 **Halstead** Kent
101 G2 **Halstead** Leics
15 M1 **Halstock** Dorset
29 L3 **Halsway** Somset
165 L3 **Haltcliff Bridge** Cumb
136 D7 **Haltham** Lincs
67 L5 **Halton** Bucks
129 M3 **Halton** Halton
147 K3 **Halton** Lancs
142 A1 **Halton** Leeds
180 B5 **Halton** Nthumb
112 D3 **Halton** Wrexhm
149 J5 **Halton East** N York
137 H7 **Halton Fenside** Lincs
158 F7 **Halton Gill** N York
147 K3 **Halton Green** Lancs
137 H6 **Halton Holegate** Lincs
178 F7 **Halton Lea Gate** Nthumb
6 E2 **Halton Quay** Cnwll
180 B5 **Halton Shields** Nthumb
148 E5 **Halton West** N York
179 G6 **Haltwhistle** Nthumb
107 J2 **Halvergate** Norfk
8 A4 **Halwell** Devon
12 B3 **Halwill** Devon
12 B3 **Halwill Junction** Devon
14 F2 **Ham** Devon
64 E3 **Ham** Gloucs
63 K7 **Ham** Gloucs
50 F4 **Ham** Gt Lon
41 K4 **Ham** Kent
30 D6 **Ham** Somset
31 L1 **Ham** Somset
47 L6 **Ham** Wilts
32 D5 **Ham Common** Dorset
81 H6 **Ham Green** Herefs
53 H5 **Ham Green** Kent
25 G2 **Ham Green** Kent
45 G4 **Ham Green** N Som
82 B3 **Ham Green** Worcs
52 F6 **Ham Hill** Kent
31 J4 **Ham Street** Somset
19 H2 **Hamble-le-Rice** Hants
49 J2 **Hambleden** Bucks
35 K7 **Hambledon** Hants
36 E3 **Hambledon** Surrey
147 G7 **Hambleton** Lancs
142 E2 **Hambleton** N York
147 G7 **Hambleton Moss Side** Lancs
30 F6 **Hambridge** Somset
31 K3 **Hambridge** Somset
45 J3 **Hambrook** S Glos
20 C5 **Hambrook** W Susx
136 F6 **Hameringham** Lincs
102 C7 **Hamerton** Cambs
209 J7 **Hamilton** S Lans
16 B1 **Hamlet** Dorset
23 K5 **Hamlins** E Susx
21 H5 **Hammerpot** W Susx
51 G3 **Hammersmith** Gt Lon
98 D2 **Hammerwich** Staffs
38 C5 **Hammerwood** E Susx
69 J6 **Hammond Street** Herts
32 D7 **Hammoon** Dorset
281 d1 **Hamnavoe** Shet
281 e4 **Hamnavoe** Shet
23 K6 **Hampden Park** E Susx
67 K6 **Hampden Row** Bucks
70 E1 **Hamperden End** Essex
65 G4 **Hampnett** Gloucs
142 D5 **Hampole** Donc
17 L3 **Hampreston** Dorset
156 F6 **Hampsfield** Cumb

147 J5 **Hampson Green** Lancs
51 H2 **Hampstead** Gt Lon
48 D4 **Hampstead Norrey's** W Berk
150 C4 **Hampsthwaite** N York
11 M7 **Hampt** Cnwll
15 G3 **Hampton** Devon
50 F5 **Hampton** Gt Lon
40 F2 **Hampton** Kent
97 G6 **Hampton** Shrops
65 J8 **Hampton** Swindn
82 B6 **Hampton** Worcs
80 D7 **Hampton Bishop** Herefs
64 C7 **Hampton Fields** Gloucs
113 H2 **Hampton Green** Ches
113 H2 **Hampton Heath** Ches
99 G7 **Hampton in Arden** Solhll
97 G6 **Hampton Loade** Shrops
81 K2 **Hampton Lovett** Worcs
82 F4 **Hampton Lucy** Warwks
83 G2 **Hampton Magna** Warwks
82 F2 **Hampton on the Hill** Warwks
66 D4 **Hampton Poyle** Oxon
50 F5 **Hampton Wick** Gt Lon
34 B7 **Hamptworth** Wilts
121 K6 **Hamrow** Norfk
22 F5 **Hamsey** E Susx
51 K7 **Hamsey Green** Gt Lon
115 H7 **Hamstall Ridware** Staffs
98 D5 **Hamstead** Birm
18 F5 **Hamstead** IOW
48 B6 **Hamstead Marshall** W Berk
180 D7 **Hamsterley** Dur
168 E4 **Hamsterley** Dur
40 C8 **Hamstreet** Kent
44 D7 **Hamwood** N Som
17 K4 **Hamworthy** Poole
115 K6 **Hanbury** Staffs
81 M2 **Hanbury** Worcs
118 D5 **Hanby** Lincs
88 C6 **Hanchet End** Suffk
114 C3 **Hanchurch** Staffs
14 B3 **Hand and Pen** Devon
130 A7 **Hand Green** Ches
171 G7 **Handale** R & Cl
129 J6 **Handbridge** Ches
37 L5 **Handcross** W Susx
131 G3 **Handforth** Ches
129 L8 **Handley** Ches
133 G7 **Handley** Derbys
71 G6 **Handley Green** Essex
115 H8 **Handsacre** Staffs
98 D5 **Handsworth** Birm
133 H2 **Handsworth** Sheff
49 K1 **Handy Cross** Bucks
114 D3 **Hanford** C Stke
32 D8 **Hanford** Dorset
101 G8 **Hanging Houghton** Nhants
33 H3 **Hanging Langford** Wilts
22 D6 **Hangleton** Br & H
21 J6 **Hangleton** W Susx
45 J4 **Hanham** S Glos
113 L2 **Hankelow** Ches
46 E1 **Hankerton** Wilts
23 K6 **Hankham** E Susx
114 D2 **Hanley** C Stke
81 J6 **Hanley Castle** Worcs
80 F2 **Hanley Child** Worcs
81 J6 **Hanley Swan** Worcs
80 F2 **Hanley William** Worcs
148 F3 **Hanlith** N York
113 G3 **Hanmer** Wrexhm
27 L5 **Hannaford** Devon
137 J4 **Hannah** Lincs
48 D7 **Hannington** Hants
84 F1 **Hannington** Nhants
65 H8 **Hannington** Swindn
65 H8 **Hannington Wick** Swindn
86 C8 **Hanscombe End** Beds
84 F6 **Hanslope** M Keyn
118 E6 **Hanthorpe** Lincs
50 F3 **Hanwell** Gt Lon
83 K6 **Hanwell** Oxon
95 K2 **Hanwood** Shrops
50 E5 **Hanworth** Gt Lon
122 D4 **Hanworth** Norfk
198 E6 **Happendon** S Lans
123 H5 **Happisburgh** Norfk
123 H5 **Happisburgh Common** Norfk
129 L5 **Hapsford** Ches
140 B2 **Hapton** Lancs
106 D4 **Hapton** Norfk
8 A3 **Harberton** Devon
8 A4 **Harbertonford** Devon
40 F4 **Harbledown** Kent
98 C6 **Harborne** Birm

100 B7 **Harborough Magna** Warwks
190 C5 **Harbottle** Nthumb
7 K2 **Harbourneford** Devon
81 M2 **Harbours Hill** Worcs
18 A2 **Harbridge** Hants
33 K8 **Harbridge Green** Hants
83 J3 **Harbury** Warwks
117 K5 **Harby** Leics
135 H5 **Harby** Notts
13 K6 **Harcombe** Devon
14 D4 **Harcombe** Devon
15 H3 **Harcombe Bottom** Devon
149 K8 **Harden** Brad
98 C3 **Harden** Wsall
46 C4 **Hardenhuish** Wilts
245 H3 **Hardgate** Abers
175 K2 **Hardgate** D & G
150 C3 **Hardgate** N York
208 E4 **Hardgate** W Duns
21 H3 **Hardham** W Susx
147 G8 **Hardhorn** Lancs
105 L3 **Hardingham** Norfk
84 E4 **Hardingstone** Nhants
45 L8 **Hardington** Somset
31 H8 **Hardington Mandeville** Somset
15 L1 **Hardington Marsh** Somset
31 H8 **Hardington Moor** Somset
26 D6 **Hardisworthy** Devon
19 G3 **Hardley** Hants
107 H3 **Hardley Street** Norfk
85 J5 **Hardmead** M Keyn
158 F4 **Hardraw** N York
140 B4 **Hardsough** Lancs
133 J7 **Hardstoft** Derbys
19 K3 **Hardway** Hants
32 B4 **Hardway** Somset
67 K3 **Hardwick** Bucks
87 H3 **Hardwick** Cambs
135 H4 **Hardwick** Lincs
85 G1 **Hardwick** Nhants
106 E5 **Hardwick** Norfk
66 A6 **Hardwick** Oxon
66 E1 **Hardwick** Oxon
133 K3 **Hardwick** Rothm
98 D4 **Hardwick** Wsall
81 J8 **Hardwick Green** Worcs
64 A4 **Hardwicke** Gloucs
64 C2 **Hardwicke** Gloucs
72 D3 **Hardy's Green** Essex
149 K8 **Hare Croft** Brad
73 G2 **Hare Green** Essex
49 J3 **Hare Hatch** Wokham
70 B5 **Hare Street** Essex
70 D7 **Hare Street** Essex
69 K1 **Hare Street** Herts
23 K5 **Harebeating** E Susx
136 F6 **Hareby** Lincs
50 D1 **Harefield** Gt Lon
115 K4 **Harehill** Derbys
141 M1 **Harehills** Leeds
191 G2 **Harehope** Nthumb
188 F2 **Harelaw** Border
178 B3 **Harelaw** D & G
180 E8 **Harelaw** Dur
39 L5 **Hareplain** Kent
166 E2 **Haresceugh** Cumb
64 B5 **Harescombe** Gloucs
64 A5 **Haresfield** Gloucs
34 F4 **Harestock** Hants
150 D6 **Harewood** Leeds
63 G2 **Harewood End** Herefs
7 J3 **Harford** Devon
106 C5 **Hargate** Norfk
132 B4 **Hargatewall** Derbys
129 L7 **Hargrave** Ches
85 K1 **Hargrave** Nhants
88 F3 **Hargrave** Suffk
88 F3 **Hargrave Green** Suffk
177 L6 **Harker** Cumb
90 E8 **Harkstead** Suffk
99 G1 **Harlaston** Staffs
118 A5 **Harlaxton** Lincs
140 C1 **Harle Syke** Lancs
109 K5 **Harlech** Gwynd
113 H8 **Harlescott** Shrops
51 G2 **Harlesden** Gt Lon
133 K4 **Harlesthorpe** Derbys
8 B6 **Harleston** Devon
106 E6 **Harleston** Norfk
89 L3 **Harleston** Suffk
84 D2 **Harlestone** Nhants
142 B8 **Harley** Rothm
96 D3 **Harley** Shrops
68 D1 **Harlington** Beds

142 D7 **Harlington** Donc
50 E3 **Harlington** Gt Lon
258 D8 **Harlosh** Highld
70 C5 **Harlow** Essex
180 C5 **Harlow Hill** Nthumb
152 A8 **Harlthorpe** E R Yk
87 H5 **Harlton** Cambs
10 B7 **Harlyn** Cnwll
17 J6 **Harman's Cross** Dorset
159 L5 **Harmby** N York
69 H4 **Harmer Green** Herts
113 H7 **Harmer Hill** Shrops
50 D3 **Harmondsworth** Gt Lon
135 K7 **Harmston** Lincs
96 D3 **Harnage** Shrops
180 C3 **Harnham** Nthumb
64 F7 **Harnhill** Gloucs
70 D8 **Harold Hill** Gt Lon
52 C1 **Harold Wood** Gt Lon
54 D4 **Haroldston West** Pembks
281 f1 **Haroldswick** Shet
161 L6 **Harome** N York
68 E4 **Harpenden** Herts
14 C4 **Harpford** Devon
153 H3 **Harpham** E R Yk
121 H6 **Harpley** Norfk
80 F3 **Harpley** Worcs
84 D3 **Harpole** Nhants
279 K5 **Harpsdale** Highld
49 J3 **Harpsden** Oxon
135 J2 **Harpswell** Lincs
131 L5 **Harpur Hill** Derbys
140 C7 **Harpurhey** Manch
177 M7 **Harraby** Cumb
27 K5 **Harracott** Devon
247 K4 **Harrapool** Highld
221 H1 **Harrietfield** P & K
39 L3 **Harrietsham** Kent
51 J1 **Harringay** Gt Lon
164 C5 **Harrington** Cumb
137 G5 **Harrington** Lincs
101 G7 **Harrington** Nhants
101 K4 **Harringworth** Nhants
131 G8 **Harriseahead** Staffs
165 G2 **Harriston** Cumb
150 D5 **Harrogate** N York
85 J4 **Harrold** Beds
140 F6 **Harrop Dale** Oldham
50 F1 **Harrow** Gt Lon
89 H4 **Harrow Green** Suffk
50 F2 **Harrow on the Hill** Gt Lon
50 F1 **Harrow Weald** Gt Lon
6 D1 **Harrowbarrow** Cnwll
85 L6 **Harrowden** Beds
169 H7 **Harrowgate Village** Darltn
87 J5 **Harston** Cambs
117 L5 **Harston** Leics
152 C7 **Harswell** E R Yk
170 B4 **Hart** Hartpl
170 B3 **Hart Station** Hartpl
180 D2 **Hartburn** Nthumb
89 G5 **Hartest** Suffk
38 D6 **Hartfield** E Susx
86 E1 **Hartford** Cambs
130 C5 **Hartford** Ches
29 G5 **Hartford** Somset
71 G3 **Hartford End** Essex
49 J7 **Hartfordbridge** Hants
159 L2 **Hartforth** N York
32 D7 **Hartgrove** Dorset
129 L8 **Harthill** Ches
210 B6 **Harthill** N Lans
133 K3 **Harthill** Rothm
132 C7 **Hartington** Derbys
180 B1 **Hartington** Nthumb
26 D6 **Hartland** Devon
26 C6 **Hartland Quay** Devon
81 J1 **Hartlebury** Worcs
170 C4 **Hartlepool** Hartpl
158 D1 **Hartley** Cumb
52 D5 **Hartley** Kent
39 J6 **Hartley** Kent
181 H4 **Hartley** Nthumb
52 D5 **Hartley Green** Kent
114 F5 **Hartley Green** Staffs
49 G7 **Hartley Wespall** Hants
49 J7 **Hartley Wintney** Hants
53 H6 **Hartlip** Kent
53 H6 **Hartlip Hill** Kent
162 C4 **Hartoft End** N York
151 L3 **Harton** N York
181 J6 **Harton** S Tyne
96 B5 **Harton** Shrops
64 A2 **Hartpury** Gloucs
141 J3 **Hartshead** Kirk

114 D2 **Hartshill** C Stke
99 J4 **Hartshill** Warwks
116 B7 **Hartshorne** Derbys
190 D3 **Hartside** Nthumb
165 L8 **Hartsop** Cumb
29 K5 **Hartswell** Somset
84 F5 **Hartwell** Nhants
150 B3 **Hartwith** N York
209 M7 **Hartwood** N Lans
188 D1 **Hartwoodmyres** Border
52 E6 **Harvel** Kent
97 K8 **Harvington** Worcs
82 C5 **Harvington** Worcs
134 D2 **Harwell** Notts
48 C1 **Harwell** Oxon
73 K1 **Harwich** Essex
139 L5 **Harwood** Bolton
167 J4 **Harwood** Dur
190 E8 **Harwood** Nthumb
163 H3 **Harwood Dale** N York
139 L5 **Harwood Lee** Bolton
134 C2 **Harworth** Notts
98 B6 **Hasbury** Dudley
36 F3 **Hascombe** Surrey
100 F7 **Haselbech** Nhants
31 G8 **Haselbury Plucknett** Somset
82 F2 **Haseley** Warwks
82 F1 **Haseley Green** Warwks
82 F1 **Haseley Knob** Warwks
82 D4 **Haselor** Warwks
64 B2 **Hasfield** Gloucs
54 D5 **Hasguard** Pembks
138 D6 **Haskayne** Lancs
90 F5 **Hasketon** Suffk
133 H5 **Hasland** Derbys
133 H6 **Hasland Green** Derbys
36 D4 **Haslemere** Surrey
140 B3 **Haslingden** Lancs
139 M3 **Haslingden Grane** Lancs
87 H5 **Haslingfield** Cambs
130 E8 **Haslington** Ches
130 E5 **Hassall** Ches
130 F7 **Hassall Green** Ches
40 E6 **Hassell Street** Kent
107 H2 **Hassingham** Norfk
165 G7 **Hassness** Cumb
22 D4 **Hassocks** W Susx
132 D5 **Hassop** Derbys
36 D4 **Haste Hill** Surrey
280 D6 **Haster** Highld
137 J5 **Hasthorpe** Lincs
40 E6 **Hastingleigh** Kent
24 E5 **Hastings** E Susx
30 D7 **Hastings** Somset
70 C5 **Hastingwood** Essex
68 A5 **Hastoe** Herts
169 K2 **Haswell** Dur
169 K2 **Haswell Plough** Dur
86 D5 **Hatch** Beds
30 D6 **Hatch Beauchamp** Somset
86 B3 **Hatch End** Beds
50 E1 **Hatch End** Gt Lon
18 F3 **Hatch Gate** Hants
68 E4 **Hatching Green** Herts
130 A5 **Hatchmere** Ches
145 G7 **Hatcliffe** NE Lin
143 H6 **Hatfield** Donc
80 E3 **Hatfield** Herefs
69 G5 **Hatfield** Herts
81 K5 **Hatfield** Worcs
70 E4 **Hatfield Broad Oak** Essex
70 D4 **Hatfield Heath** Essex
71 J5 **Hatfield Peverel** Essex
143 H6 **Hatfield Woodhouse** Donc
65 M8 **Hatford** Oxon
34 D1 **Hatherden** Hants
12 D2 **Hatherleigh** Devon
116 E7 **Hathern** Leics
65 H6 **Hatherop** Gloucs
132 E3 **Hathersage** Derbys
132 E3 **Hathersage Booths** Derbys
113 L2 **Hatherton** Ches
98 B1 **Hatherton** Staffs
86 F5 **Hatley St George** Cambs
6 D2 **Hatt** Cnwll
131 K1 **Hattersley** Tamesd
35 K3 **Hattingley** Hants
257 K4 **Hatton** Abers
234 C6 **Hatton** Angus
115 L5 **Hatton** Derbys
50 E4 **Hatton** Gt Lon
136 C4 **Hatton** Lincs
95 L5 **Hatton** Shrops
130 B3 **Hatton** Warrtn
82 F2 **Hatton** Warwks

129 K7 **Hatton Heath** Ches
256 F8 **Hatton of Fintray** Abers
196 F6 **Haugh** E Ayrs
137 H4 **Haugh** Lincs
140 D5 **Haugh** Rochdl
202 F7 **Haugh Head** Nthumb
255 H4 **Haugh of Glass** Moray
175 K2 **Haugh of Urr** D & G
136 F3 **Haugham** Lincs
209 G3 **Haughhead Inn** E Duns
89 L3 **Haughley** Suffk
89 L2 **Haughley Green** Suffk
134 D5 **Haughton** Notts
112 D7 **Haughton** Powys
112 F6 **Haughton** Shrops
113 J8 **Haughton** Shrops
97 G2 **Haughton** Shrops
96 F4 **Haughton** Shrops
114 D7 **Haughton** Staffs
131 J1 **Haughton Green** Tamesd
169 J7 **Haughton le Skerne** Darltn
130 B8 **Haughton Moss** Ches
69 J3 **Haultwick** Herts
99 G1 **Haunton** Staffs
9 d1 **Hautes Croix** Jersey
191 K5 **Hauxley** Nthumb
87 J5 **Hauxton** Cambs
131 G6 **Havannah** Ches
20 B5 **Havant** Hants
79 M4 **Haven** Herefs
119 H1 **Haven Bank** Lincs
144 F2 **Haven Side** E R Yk
19 J5 **Havenstreet** IOW
142 B5 **Havercroft** Wakefd
54 F4 **Haverfordwest** Pembks
88 D6 **Haverhill** Suffk
155 L7 **Haverigg** Cumb
70 D8 **Havering-atte-Bower** Essex
84 F6 **Haversham** M Keyn
156 E6 **Haverthwaite** Cumb
170 C6 **Haverton Hill** S on T
44 F6 **Havyat** N Som
31 H3 **Havyatt** Somset
129 H6 **Hawarden** Flints
81 L5 **Hawbridge** Worcs
71 J3 **Hawbush Green** Essex
146 D2 **Hawcoat** Cumb
106 E4 **Hawe's Green** Norfk
76 C6 **Hawen** Cerdgn
158 F5 **Hawes** N York
81 J3 **Hawford** Worcs
188 E3 **Hawick** Border
131 J2 **Hawk Green** Stockp
15 H2 **Hawkchurch** Devon
88 F4 **Hawkedon** Suffk
39 K4 **Hawkenbury** Kent
46 B8 **Hawkeridge** Wilts
14 C5 **Hawkerland** Devon
99 J6 **Hawkes End** Covtry
45 M2 **Hawkesbury** S Glos
99 K6 **Hawkesbury** Warwks
45 M2 **Hawkesbury Upton** S Glos
191 J4 **Hawkhill** Nthumb
39 J7 **Hawkhurst** Kent
23 J4 **Hawkhurst Common** E Susx
41 H7 **Hawkinge** Kent
35 M5 **Hawkley** Hants
28 F5 **Hawkridge** Somset
165 L1 **Hawksdale** Cumb
139 M5 **Hawkshaw** Bury
156 E3 **Hawkshead** Cumb
156 D3 **Hawkshead Hill** Cumb
198 D5 **Hawksland** S Lans
71 G1 **Hawkspur Green** Essex
113 J5 **Hawkstone** Shrops
149 G2 **Hawkswick** N York
149 L7 **Hawksworth** Leeds
117 K3 **Hawksworth** Notts
53 J1 **Hawkwell** Essex
180 C4 **Hawkwell** Nthumb
49 L7 **Hawley** Hants
52 C4 **Hawley** Kent
64 F3 **Hawling** Gloucs
161 J5 **Hawnby** N York
149 J8 **Haworth** Brad
68 B6 **Hawridge** Bucks
89 G3 **Hawstead** Suffk
89 H3 **Hawstead Green** Suffk
169 L2 **Hawthorn** Dur
35 K4 **Hawthorn** Hants
43 H4 **Hawthorn** Rhondd
49 L4 **Hawthorn Hill** Br For
136 D8 **Hawthorn Hill** Lincs
118 D6 **Hawthorpe** Lincs
117 L1 **Hawton** Notts

151 K4 **Haxby** York
151 K4 **Haxby Gates** York
143 J7 **Haxey** N Linc
143 J7 **Haxey Turbary** N Linc
38 C4 **Haxted** Surrey
33 K1 **Haxton** Wilts
4 E4 **Hay** Cnwll
4 F6 **Hay** Cnwll
4 F4 **Hay** Cnwll
10 D8 **Hay** Cnwll
120 C7 **Hay Green** Norfk
69 K2 **Hay Street** Herts
79 J6 **Hay-on-Wye** Powys
139 H8 **Haydock** St Hel
45 K8 **Haydon** BaNES
31 L7 **Haydon** Dorset
30 C6 **Haydon** Somset
179 J6 **Haydon Bridge** Nthumb
47 H2 **Haydon Wick** Swindn
6 C1 **Haye** Cnwll
50 E3 **Hayes** Gt Lon
51 L5 **Hayes** Gt Lon
50 D3 **Hayes End** Gt Lon
217 H2 **Hayfield** Ag & B
131 L2 **Hayfield** Derbys
96 E1 **Haygate** Wrekin
234 E7 **Hayhillock** Angus
2 F4 **Hayle** Cnwll
98 B6 **Hayley Green** Dudley
113 L2 **Haymoor Green** Ches
29 G7 **Hayne** Devon
13 H5 **Hayne** Devon
86 B7 **Haynes (Church End)** Beds
86 B6 **Haynes (Northwood End)** Beds
86 B6 **Haynes (Silver End)** Beds
85 L7 **Haynes (West End)** Beds
74 E7 **Hayscastle** Pembks
74 E7 **Hayscastle Cross** Pembks
38 F4 **Haysden** Kent
164 F2 **Hayton** Cumb
178 C7 **Hayton** Cumb
152 C6 **Hayton** E R Yk
134 E3 **Hayton** Notts
96 C7 **Hayton's Bent** Shrops
13 H7 **Haytor Vale** Devon
26 F7 **Haytown** Devon
22 E2 **Haywards Heath** W Susx
142 F5 **Haywood** Donc
80 B8 **Haywood** Herefs
134 C8 **Haywood Oaks** Notts
24 C5 **Hazards Green** E Susx
131 H2 **Hazel Grove** Stockp
39 H5 **Hazel Street** Kent
88 D6 **Hazel Stub** Suffk
198 D4 **Hazelbank** S Lans
16 E1 **Hazelbury Bryan** Dorset
71 K6 **Hazeleigh** Essex
49 H7 **Hazeley** Hants
117 J2 **Hazelford** Notts
140 E7 **Hazelhurst** Tamesd
98 C1 **Hazelslade** Staffs
222 E3 **Hazelton Walls** Fife
116 B2 **Hazelwood** Derbys
67 L8 **Hazlemere** Bucks
180 F4 **Hazlerigg** N u Ty
114 F2 **Hazles** Staffs
65 G3 **Hazleton** Gloucs
120 E4 **Heacham** Norfk
35 G4 **Headbourne Worthy** Hants
79 K4 **Headbrook** Herefs
39 L4 **Headcorn** Kent
150 C8 **Headingley** Leeds
66 D5 **Headington** Oxon
168 F7 **Headlam** Dur
82 B2 **Headless Cross** Worcs
210 B7 **Headlesscross** N Lans
48 D6 **Headley** Hants
36 B4 **Headley** Hants
51 G8 **Headley** Surrey
36 B4 **Headley Down** Hants
98 D8 **Headley Heath** Worcs
134 E4 **Headon** Notts
197 L2 **Heads** S Lans
178 C7 **Heads Nook** Cumb
116 B2 **Heage** Derbys
159 H3 **Healaugh** N York
151 G6 **Healaugh** N York
131 G3 **Heald Green** Stockp
28 A2 **Heale** Devon
30 C6 **Heale** Somset
30 F5 **Heale** Somset
160 B6 **Healey** N York
180 B7 **Healey** Nthumb
140 C4 **Healey** Rochdl

141 L4 **Healey** Wakefd
168 D1 **Healeyfield** Dur
145 G5 **Healing** NE Lin
2 D5 **Heamoor** Cnwll
116 D2 **Heanor** Derbys
27 J4 **Heanton Punchardon** Devon
139 J4 **Heapey** Lancs
135 H2 **Heapham** Lincs
36 B3 **Hearn** Hants
53 J6 **Hearts Delight** Kent
28 C4 **Heasley Mill** Devon
247 K5 **Heast** Highld
133 J6 **Heath** Derbys
142 A4 **Heath** Wakefd
68 A2 **Heath and Reach** Beds
21 J4 **Heath Common** W Susx
67 L7 **Heath End** Bucks
48 B6 **Heath End** Hants
116 B7 **Heath End** Leics
36 C1 **Heath End** Surrey
82 F3 **Heath End** Warwks
82 C1 **Heath Green** Worcs
176 C3 **Heath Hall** D & G
98 C2 **Heath Hayes & Wimblebury** Staffs
97 H1 **Heath Hill** Shrops
30 F2 **Heath House** Somset
97 L3 **Heath Town** Wolves
113 K6 **Heathbrook** Shrops
132 C7 **Heathcote** Derbys
113 L6 **Heathcote** Shrops
84 D5 **Heathencote** Nhants
99 K1 **Heather** Leics
13 J7 **Heathfield** Devon
23 K3 **Heathfield** E Susx
149 L2 **Heathfield** N York
29 L5 **Heathfield** Somset
66 D4 **Heathfield Village** Oxon
14 F2 **Heathstock** Devon
97 H5 **Heathton** Shrops
115 H6 **Heatley** Staffs
130 D2 **Heatley** Warrtn
139 L6 **Heaton** Bolton
149 L8 **Heaton** Brad
147 J4 **Heaton** Lancs
181 G5 **Heaton** N u Ty
131 J7 **Heaton** Staffs
131 H1 **Heaton Chapel** Stockp
131 G2 **Heaton Mersey** Stockp
131 H2 **Heaton Norris** Stockp
138 E5 **Heaton's Bridge** Lancs
52 C7 **Heaverham** Kent
131 H2 **Heaviley** Stockp
13 L4 **Heavitree** Devon
181 H6 **Hebburn** S Tyne
149 J3 **Hebden** N York
140 F2 **Hebden Bridge** Calder
130 C6 **Hebden Green** Ches
69 J3 **Hebing End** Herts
75 L6 **Hebron** Carmth
125 H3 **Hebron** IOA
191 J8 **Hebron** Nthumb
49 H6 **Heckfield** Hants
106 D8 **Heckfield Green** Suffk
72 D3 **Heckfordbridge** Essex
118 F3 **Heckington** Lincs
141 K3 **Heckmondwike** Kirk
46 E5 **Heddington** Wilts
180 D5 **Heddon-on-the-Wall** Nthumb
107 G5 **Hedenham** Norfk
19 H1 **Hedge End** Hants
50 B2 **Hedgerley** Bucks
50 B2 **Hedgerley Green** Bucks
30 D5 **Hedging** Somset
180 C7 **Hedley on the Hill** Nthumb
98 C1 **Hednesford** Staffs
145 G2 **Hedon** E R Yk
49 L2 **Hedsor** Bucks
80 D4 **Hegdon Hill** Herefs
281 d6 **Heglibister** Shet
169 H6 **Heighington** Darltn
135 L6 **Heighington** Lincs
81 H1 **Heightington** Worcs
201 L7 **Heiton** Border
11 J3 **Hele** Cnwll
27 J2 **Hele** Devon
14 A2 **Hele** Devon
7 L1 **Hele** Devon
30 B6 **Hele** Somset
28 D8 **Hele Lane** Devon
11 J2 **Helebridge** Cnwll
208 A3 **Helensburgh** Ag & B
196 D5 **Helenton** S Ayrs
3 J6 **Helford** Cnwll
3 J5 **Helford Passage** Cnwll

121 J6 **Helhoughton** Norfk
88 C7 **Helions Bumpstead** Essex
48 A6 **Hell Corner** W Berk
133 K1 **Hellaby** Rothm
10 F8 **Helland** Cnwll
10 F8 **Hellandbridge** Cnwll
11 K5 **Hellescott** Cnwll
106 D1 **Hellesdon** Norfk
2 D3 **Hellesveor** Cnwll
83 M4 **Hellidon** Nhants
148 E4 **Hellifield** N York
23 K5 **Hellingly** E Susx
107 G3 **Hellington** Norfk
191 H7 **Helm** Nthumb
84 B6 **Helmdon** Nhants
141 H5 **Helme** Kirk
90 E4 **Helmingham** Suffk
168 F4 **Helmington Row** Dur
274 D5 **Helmsdale** Highld
140 B3 **Helmshore** Lancs
161 K6 **Helmsley** N York
150 F2 **Helperby** N York
152 E2 **Helperthorpe** N York
118 F3 **Helpringham** Lincs
102 C2 **Helpston** C Pete
129 L4 **Helsby** Ches
137 K5 **Helsey** Lincs
3 G5 **Helston** Cnwll
10 F6 **Helstone** Cnwll
166 C6 **Helton** Cumb
159 K2 **Helwith** N York
148 B3 **Helwith Bridge** N York
107 G1 **Hemblington** Norfk
68 D5 **Hemel Hempstead** Herts
7 H3 **Hemerdon** Devon
143 H2 **Hemingbrough** N York
136 D5 **Hemingby** Lincs
142 B7 **Hemingfield** Barns
86 F1 **Hemingford Abbots** Cambs
86 F1 **Hemingford Grey** Cambs
90 D4 **Hemingstone** Suffk
116 D6 **Hemington** Leics
102 B6 **Hemington** Nhants
45 L8 **Hemington** Somset
91 G6 **Hemley** Suffk
170 C7 **Hemlington** Middsb
153 H5 **Hempholme** E R Yk
106 E4 **Hempnall** Norfk
106 E5 **Hempnall Green** Norfk
266 B3 **Hempriggs** Moray
88 C7 **Hempstead** Essex
53 G6 **Hempstead** Medway
122 C4 **Hempstead** Norfk
123 H6 **Hempstead** Norfk
64 B4 **Hempsted** Gloucs
121 K5 **Hempton** Norfk
66 C1 **Hempton** Oxon
123 K8 **Hemsby** Norfk
135 J2 **Hemswell** Lincs
135 J2 **Hemswell Cliff** Lincs
142 C5 **Hemsworth** Wakefd
29 L8 **Hemyock** Devon
45 H3 **Henbury** Bristl
131 H5 **Henbury** Ches
202 A6 **Hendersyde Park** Border
7 L5 **Hendham** Devon
94 F4 **Hendomen** Powys
51 G1 **Hendon** Gt Lon
181 K7 **Hendon** Sundld
3 J4 **Hendra** Cnwll
10 E7 **Hendra** Cnwll
42 E5 **Hendre** Brdgnd
128 E6 **Hendre** Flints
62 F4 **Hendre** Mons
57 J4 **Hendy** Carmth
125 G4 **Heneglwys** IOA
22 C4 **Henfield** W Susx
11 M4 **Henford** Devon
40 B8 **Henghurst** Kent
43 J3 **Hengoed** Caerph
79 J4 **Hengoed** Powys
112 D5 **Hengoed** Shrops
89 G2 **Hengrave** Suffk
70 E2 **Henham** Essex
52 E5 **Henhurst** Kent
94 D2 **Heniarth** Powys
30 C6 **Henley** Somset
16 D2 **Henley** Dorset
64 C4 **Henley** Gloucs
95 L5 **Henley** Shrops
96 C8 **Henley** Shrops
30 F4 **Henley** Somset
90 E5 **Henley** Suffk
36 D5 **Henley** W Susx
99 K7 **Henley Green** Covtry

50 B8 **Henley Park** Surrey
52 E5 **Henley Street** Kent
24 D5 **Henley's Down** E Susx
82 E2 **Henley-in-Arden** Warwks
49 J2 **Henley-on-Thames** Oxon
76 C7 **Henllan** Cerdgn
127 L6 **Henllan** Denbgs
55 L3 **Henllan Amgoed** Carmth
44 B1 **Henllys** Torfn
86 D7 **Henlow** Beds
13 J6 **Hennock** Devon
89 H7 **Henny Street** Essex
75 H6 **Henry's Moat (Castell Hendre)** Pembks
126 F5 **Henryd** Conwy
142 F3 **Hensall** N York
179 H6 **Henshaw** Nthumb
164 C7 **Hensingham** Cumb
107 K6 **Henstead** Suffk
35 G6 **Hensting** Hants
32 B7 **Henstridge** Somset
32 B6 **Henstridge Ash** Somset
32 B6 **Henstridge Marsh** Somset
67 J6 **Henton** Oxon
31 H2 **Henton** Somset
81 J4 **Henwick** Worcs
11 K7 **Henwood** Cnwll
66 C6 **Henwood** Oxon
60 D2 **Heol Senni** Powys
57 J5 **Heol-las** Swans
42 E5 **Heol-y-Cyw** Brdgnd
190 F1 **Hepburn** Nthumb
190 E6 **Hepple** Nthumb
180 F2 **Hepscott** Nthumb
140 E2 **Heptonstall** Calder
141 J6 **Hepworth** Kirk
105 K8 **Hepworth** Suffk
54 E5 **Herbrandston** Pembks
80 C7 **Hereford** Herefs
41 L2 **Hereson** Kent
258 F3 **Heribusta** Highld
200 E2 **Heriot** Border
211 G5 **Hermiston** C Edin
141 M7 **Hermit Hill** Barns
188 E7 **Hermitage** Border
16 C1 **Hermitage** Dorset
20 C5 **Hermitage** Hants
48 D4 **Hermitage** W Berk
125 G6 **Hermon** IOA
75 L6 **Hermon** Pembks
41 G2 **Herne** Kent
41 G2 **Herne Bay** Kent
41 G2 **Herne Common** Kent
51 J4 **Herne Hill** Gt Lon
39 G2 **Herne Pound** Kent
27 K5 **Herner** Devon
40 E3 **Hernhill** Kent
5 L3 **Herodsfoot** Cnwll
41 J4 **Heronden** Kent
52 D1 **Herongate** Essex
182 E6 **Heronsford** S Ayrs
68 C8 **Heronsgate** Herts
35 K2 **Herriard** Hants
86 B6 **Herring's Green** Beds
107 K4 **Herringfleet** Suffk
88 E1 **Herringswell** Suffk
133 J1 **Herringthorpe** Rothm
181 J8 **Herrington** Sundld
41 G3 **Hersden** Kent
11 J1 **Hersham** Cnwll
50 E6 **Hersham** Surrey
23 L5 **Herstmonceux** E Susx
17 K6 **Herston** Dorset
275 c6 **Herston** Ork
69 J4 **Hertford** Herts
69 K5 **Hertford Heath** Herts
69 J5 **Hertingfordbury** Herts
165 K3 **Hesket Newmarket** Cumb
138 F3 **Hesketh Bank** Lancs
147 M7 **Hesketh Lane** Lancs
139 G4 **Heskin Green** Lancs
170 B3 **Hesleden** Dur
158 F7 **Hesleden** N York
134 C1 **Hesley** Donc
179 J2 **Hesleyside** Nthumb
151 K5 **Heslington** York
151 H5 **Hessay** York
6 C3 **Hessenford** Cnwll
89 J3 **Hessett** Suffk
144 C3 **Hessle** E R Yk
142 C4 **Hessle** Wakefd
147 J3 **Hest Bank** Lancs
90 D2 **Hestley Green** Suffk
50 E3 **Heston** Gt Lon
275 b4 **Hestwall** Ork

Heswall - Hilton 321

129 G3 **Heswall** Wirral
66 E1 **Hethe** Oxon
106 C2 **Hethersett** Norfk
178 B5 **Hethersgill** Cumb
178 B5 **Hetherside** Cumb
113 H2 **Hetherson Green** Ches
202 D7 **Hethpool** Nthumb
169 H3 **Hett** Dur
149 G4 **Hetton** N York
203 G6 **Hetton Steads** Nthumb
169 K1 **Hetton-le-Hole** Sundld
180 D4 **Heugh** Nthumb
213 J6 **Heugh Head** Border
243 L1 **Heughhead** Abers
91 H1 **Heveningham** Suffk
38 D4 **Hever** Kent
157 H6 **Heversham** Cumb
122 D7 **Hevingham** Norfk
4 F5 **Hewas Water** Cnwll
63 H6 **Hewelsfield** Gloucs
149 K8 **Hewenden** Brad
44 E6 **Hewish** N Som
15 K1 **Hewish** Somset
15 H2 **Hewood** Dorset
179 L6 **Hexham** Nthumb
52 B5 **Hextable** Kent
142 F7 **Hexthorpe** Donc
68 E1 **Hexton** Herts
11 L6 **Hexworthy** Cnwll
12 F8 **Hexworthy** Devon
148 F7 **Hey** Lancs
138 D2 **Hey Houses** Lancs
71 L5 **Heybridge** Essex
70 F7 **Heybridge** Essex
72 C5 **Heybridge Basin** Essex
6 F5 **Heybrook Bay** Devon
87 J7 **Heydon** Cambs
122 C6 **Heydon** Norfk
118 D4 **Heydour** Lincs
131 G3 **Heyhead** Manch
224 B6 **Heylipoll** Ag & B
281 d4 **Heylor** Shet
140 E7 **Heyrod** Tamesd
147 H4 **Heysham** Lancs
149 L3 **Heyshaw** N York
20 E3 **Heyshott** W Susx
140 D6 **Heyside** Oldham
32 F2 **Heytesbury** Wilts
65 M2 **Heythrop** Oxon
140 C5 **Heywood** Rochdl
46 C8 **Heywood** Wilts
144 B7 **Hibaldstow** N Linc
142 D6 **Hickleton** Donc
123 J6 **Hickling** Norfk
117 J6 **Hickling** Notts
123 H6 **Hickling Green** Norfk
123 H7 **Hickling Heath** Norfk
40 E4 **Hickmans Green** Kent
41 G3 **Hicks Forstal** Kent
22 D3 **Hickstead** W Susx
82 E6 **Hidcote Bartrim** Gloucs
82 E6 **Hidcote Boyce** Gloucs
142 C4 **High Ackworth** Wakefd
180 D2 **High Angerton** Nthumb
172 D5 **High Ardwell** D & G
176 B1 **High Auldgirth** D & G
166 D2 **High Bankhill** Cumb
69 L7 **High Beach** Essex
148 B2 **High Bentham** N York
165 H4 **High Bewaldeth** Cumb
27 L6 **High Bickington** Devon
158 D7 **High Bickwith** N York
157 K7 **High Biggins** Cumb
209 H7 **High Blantyre** S Lans
209 L3 **High Bonnybridge** Falk
56 F3 **High Borrans** Cumb
49 H6 **High Bradley** N York
28 B4 **High Bray** Devon
38 F5 **High Brooms** Kent
27 J6 **High Bullen** Devon
91 J4 **High Buston** Nthumb
80 E5 **High Callerton** Nthumb
57 K7 **High Casterton** Cumb
51 M5 **High Catton** E R Yk
68 F7 **High Close** N York
66 A5 **High Cogges** Oxon
05 K2 **High Common** Norfk
69 G7 **High Coniscliffe** Darltn
78 B6 **High Crosby** Cumb
3 J5 **High Cross** Cnwll
96 D2 **High Cross** E Ayrs
35 L5 **High Cross** Hants
69 K3 **High Cross** Herts
22 C4 **High Cross** W Susx
82 E2 **High Cross** Warwks
115 M8 **High Cross Bank** Derbys
172 E7 **High Drummore** D & G
169 J1 **High Dubmire** Sundld
70 F4 **High Easter** Essex
142 F3 **High Eggborough** N York
160 B6 **High Ellington** N York
113 K8 **High Ercall** Wrekin
168 F5 **High Etherley** Dur
119 K2 **High Ferry** Lincs
141 K6 **High Flats** Kirk
71 J2 **High Garrett** Essex
168 F4 **High Grange** Dur
150 B2 **High Grantley** N York
156 F2 **High Green** Cumb
141 K5 **High Green** Kirk
106 C2 **High Green** Norfk
106 D5 **High Green** Norfk
106 F4 **High Green** Norfk
142 A8 **High Green** Sheff
96 F6 **High Green** Shrops
89 G3 **High Green** Suffk
81 K6 **High Green** Worcs
40 A7 **High Halden** Kent
53 G4 **High Halstow** Medway
30 F4 **High Ham** Somset
164 D5 **High Harrington** Cumb
150 D5 **High Harrogate** N York
169 K2 **High Haswell** Dur
113 K6 **High Hatton** Shrops
163 G1 **High Hawsker** N York
166 B2 **High Hesket** Cumb
141 L5 **High Hoyland** Barns
144 B1 **High Hunsley** E R Yk
23 H2 **High Hurstwood** E Susx
152 A2 **High Hutton** N York
165 H3 **High Ireby** Cumb
122 C3 **High Kelling** Norfk
161 H6 **High Kilburn** N York
163 J6 **High Killerby** N York
166 C6 **High Knipe** Cumb
168 E5 **High Lands** Dur
131 J3 **High Lane** Stockp
2 F4 **High Lanes** Cnwll
70 D5 **High Laver** Essex
130 D3 **High Legh** Ches
170 B8 **High Leven** S on T
45 J7 **High Littleton** BaNES
165 G5 **High Lorton** Cumb
134 F5 **High Marnham** Notts
142 D7 **High Melton** Donc
180 C6 **High Mickley** Nthumb
169 J2 **High Moorsley** Sundld
181 J8 **High Newport** Sundld
156 F6 **High Newton** Cumb
156 D5 **High Nibthwaite** Cumb
114 B6 **High Offley** Staffs
70 E6 **High Ongar** Essex
114 C8 **High Onn** Staffs
72 F3 **High Park Corner** Essex
184 D2 **High Pennyvenie** E Ayrs
33 K4 **High Post** Wilts
70 F4 **High Roding** Essex
165 K3 **High Row** Cumb
165 L6 **High Row** Cumb
147 M3 **High Salter** Lancs
21 K5 **High Salvington** W Susx
165 G2 **High Scales** Cumb
164 D4 **High Seaton** Cumb
158 F4 **High Shaw** N York
165 H4 **High Side** Cumb
180 E7 **High Spen** Gatesd
168 E3 **High Stoop** Dur
5 G4 **High Street** Cnwll
39 J7 **High Street** Kent
91 J1 **High Street** Suffk
91 K4 **High Street** Suffk
170 C4 **High Throston** Hartpl
98 C1 **High Town** Staffs
136 E5 **High Toynton** Lincs
190 E5 **High Trewhitt** Nthumb
181 G8 **High Urpeth** Dur
210 D2 **High Valleyfield** Fife
179 L5 **High Warden** Nthumb
180 D7 **High Westwood** Dur
63 H7 **High Woolaston** Gloucs
160 F1 **High Worsall** N York
156 E3 **High Wray** Cumb
70 C4 **High Wych** Herts
67 L8 **High Wycombe** Bucks
141 M6 **Higham** Barns
133 H7 **Higham** Derbys
38 F4 **Higham** Kent
52 F5 **Higham** Kent
148 E8 **Higham** Lancs
88 E2 **Higham** Suffk
89 L8 **Higham** Suffk
180 D4 **Higham Dykes** Nthumb
85 J2 **Higham Ferrers** Nhants
86 C8 **Higham Gobion** Beds
51 K1 **Higham Hill** Gt Lon
99 K4 **Higham on the Hill** Leics
12 C2 **Highampton** Devon
69 K8 **Highams Park** Gt Lon
34 F6 **Highbridge** Hants
30 D2 **Highbridge** Somset
38 A7 **Highbrook** W Susx
141 J5 **Highburton** Kirk
51 J2 **Highbury** Gt Lon
31 M1 **Highbury** Somset
48 B7 **Highclere** Hants
18 C5 **Highcliffe** Dorset
147 G8 **Highcross** Lancs
31 L3 **Higher Alham** Somset
16 E2 **Higher Ansty** Dorset
138 D2 **Higher Ballam** Lancs
139 G1 **Higher Bartle** Lancs
85 J8 **Higher Berry End** Beds
16 D4 **Higher Bockhampton** Dorset
8 D4 **Higher Brixham** Torbay
14 B3 **Higher Burrowton** Devon
129 M8 **Higher Burwardsley** Ches
15 J1 **Higher Chillington** Somset
26 E6 **Higher Clovelly** Devon
28 F5 **Higher Combe** Somset
15 M4 **Higher Coombe** Dorset
131 J3 **Higher Disley** Ches
8 D1 **Higher Gabwell** Devon
15 L1 **Higher Halstock Leigh** Dorset
148 E8 **Higher Harpers** Lancs
147 H4 **Higher Heysham** Lancs
131 J5 **Higher Hurdsfield** Ches
130 E1 **Higher Irlam** Salfd
15 M3 **Higher Kingcombe** Dorset
129 H7 **Higher Kinnerton** Flints
16 E2 **Higher Melcombe** Dorset
27 K3 **Higher Muddiford** Devon
32 B6 **Higher Nyland** Dorset
140 E5 **Higher Ogden** Rochdl
3 G6 **Higher Pentire** Cnwll
139 G2 **Higher Penwortham** Lancs
148 E2 **Higher Studfold** N York
4 C6 **Higher Town** Cnwll
5 G3 **Higher Town** Cnwll
10 c2 **Higher Town** IOS
6 D4 **Higher Tregantle** Cnwll
139 H2 **Higher Walton** Lancs
130 B3 **Higher Walton** Warrtn
15 G1 **Higher Wambrook** Somset
16 D3 **Higher Waterston** Dorset
17 G2 **Higher Whatcombe** Dorset
139 J3 **Higher Wheelton** Lancs
11 J4 **Higher Whiteleigh** Cnwll
130 B4 **Higher Whitley** Ches
16 A2 **Higher Wraxhall** Dorset
113 H3 **Higher Wych** Ches
148 F7 **Higherford** Lancs
13 G3 **Highfield** Devon
151 M8 **Highfield** E R Yk
180 E7 **Highfield** Gatesd
196 C1 **Highfield** N Ayrs
142 E6 **Highfields** Donc
38 C6 **Highgate** E Susx
51 H2 **Highgate** Gt Lon
131 L2 **Highgate Head** Derbys
189 L7 **Highgreen Manor** Nthumb
131 H6 **Highlane** Ches
133 H3 **Highlane** Derbys
164 F1 **Highlaws** Cumb
63 M2 **Highleadon** Gloucs
20 D7 **Highleigh** W Susx
97 G6 **Highley** Shrops
165 J1 **Highmoor** Cumb
49 H2 **Highmoor** Oxon
49 H2 **Highmoor Cross** Oxon
44 F1 **Highmoor Hill** Mons
64 A3 **Highnam** Gloucs
64 A3 **Highnam Green** Gloucs
45 H5 **Highridge** N Som
41 G2 **Highstead** Kent
40 B3 **Highsted** Kent
40 E3 **Highstreet** Kent
88 F8 **Highstreet Green** Essex
36 E4 **Highstreet Green** Surrey
176 E3 **Hightae** D & G
98 E7 **Highter's Heath** Birm
131 G7 **Hightown** Ches
18 B3 **Hightown** Hants
138 C7 **Hightown** Sefton
89 K4 **Hightown Green** Suffk
80 B5 **Highway** Herefs
46 F4 **Highway** Wilts
13 K8 **Highweek** Devon
115 H5 **Highwood** Staffs
69 G8 **Highwood Hill** Gt Lon
65 J8 **Highworth** Swindn
105 E4 **Hilborough** Norfk
133 J8 **Hilcote** Derbys
38 F4 **Hilden Park** Kent
38 E4 **Hildenborough** Kent
87 L5 **Hildersham** Cambs
114 E4 **Hilderstone** Staffs
153 J3 **Hilderthorpe** E R Yk
16 C2 **Hilfield** Dorset
104 C4 **Hilgay** Norfk
63 J8 **Hill** S Glos
83 K2 **Hill** Warwks
36 B5 **Hill Brow** Hants
114 B4 **Hill Chorlton** Staffs
123 H7 **Hill Common** Norfk
29 L5 **Hill Common** Somset
32 E3 **Hill Deverill** Wilts
119 K2 **Hill Dyke** Lincs
168 C3 **Hill End** Dur
221 J8 **Hill End** Fife
81 K7 **Hill End** Gloucs
53 H6 **Hill Green** Kent
19 J3 **Hill Head** Hants
210 F1 **Hill of Beath** Fife
264 C4 **Hill of Fearn** Highld
115 H8 **Hill Ridware** Staffs
141 J4 **Hill Side** Kirk
81 H3 **Hill Side** Worcs
168 C6 **Hill Top** Dur
18 F3 **Hill Top** Hants
141 G5 **Hill Top** Kirk
133 H1 **Hill Top** Rothm
98 C5 **Hill Top** Sandw
142 A4 **Hill Top** Wakefd
142 D2 **Hillam** N York
167 H7 **Hillbeck** Dur
41 G2 **Hillborough** Kent
17 K2 **Hillbutts** Dorset
115 M2 **Hillcliffiane** Derbys
47 G7 **Hillcott** Wilts
210 F2 **Hillend** Fife
211 H5 **Hillend** Mdloth
209 L5 **Hillend** N Lans
56 D6 **Hillend** Swans
63 H4 **Hillersland** Gloucs
13 G3 **Hillerton** Devon
67 G1 **Hillesden** Bucks
45 M1 **Hillesley** Gloucs
29 L6 **Hillfarrance** Somset
36 D5 **Hillgrove** W Susx
80 D6 **Hillhampton** Herefs
8 D4 **Hillhead** Devon
199 G5 **Hillhead** S Lans
257 K3 **Hillhead of Cocklaw** Abers
256 C6 **Hillhead of Durno** Abers
98 F1 **Hilliard's Cross** Staffs
279 L3 **Hilliclay** Highld
50 D2 **Hillingdon** Gt Lon
208 E6 **Hillington** C Glas
120 F6 **Hillington** Norfk
19 H5 **Hillis Corner** IOW
100 C8 **Hillmorton** Warwks
140 A2 **Hillock Vale** Lancs
175 J2 **Hillowton** D & G
97 K8 **Hillpool** Worcs
35 J7 **Hillpound** Hants
133 J5 **Hills Town** Derbys
245 K4 **Hillside** Abers
235 H3 **Hillside** Angus
7 K3 **Hillside** Devon
34 D7 **Hillstreet** Hants
281 c4 **Hillswick** Shet
12 D6 **Hilltown** Devon
211 K5 **Hilltown** E Loth
281 d8 **Hillwell** Shet
46 E4 **Hilmarton** Wilts
46 C7 **Hilperton** Wilts
46 C7 **Hilperton Marsh** Wilts
19 L3 **Hilsea** C Port
145 H1 **Hilston** E R Yk
62 F3 **Hilston Park** Mons
34 F6 **Hiltingbury** Hants
202 D3 **Hilton** Border
86 F2 **Hilton** Cambs
167 G6 **Hilton** Cumb
115 L5 **Hilton** Derbys
16 E2 **Hilton** Dorset
168 F6 **Hilton** Dur
264 D4 **Hilton** Highld
170 B8 **Hilton** S on T
97 H4 **Hilton** Shrops

81 L3 **Himbleton** Worcs
97 K5 **Himley** Staffs
157 H5 **Hincaster** Cumb
50 F6 **Hinchley Wood** Surrey
99 L4 **Hinckley** Leics
105 L8 **Hinderclay** Suffk
171 J7 **Hinderwell** N York
112 E5 **Hindford** Shrops
36 C4 **Hindhead** Surrey
139 L1 **Hindle Fold** Lancs
180 C7 **Hindley** Nthumb
139 J6 **Hindley** Wigan
139 J7 **Hindley Green** Wigan
81 K3 **Hindlip** Worcs
122 A5 **Hindolveston** Norfk
32 F4 **Hindon** Wilts
121 L4 **Hindringham** Norfk
105 L3 **Hingham** Norfk
97 J5 **Hinksford** Staffs
97 G3 **Hinnington** Shrops
113 M6 **Hinstock** Shrops
90 C6 **Hintlesham** Suffk
63 K6 **Hinton** Gloucs
18 C4 **Hinton** Hants
79 L7 **Hinton** Herefs
45 L4 **Hinton** S Glos
95 K2 **Hinton** Shrops
96 E7 **Hinton** Shrops
18 C4 **Hinton Admiral** Hants
35 J5 **Hinton Ampner** Hants
45 H7 **Hinton Blewett** BaNES
45 M7 **Hinton Charterhouse** BaNES
82 B7 **Hinton Green** Worcs
35 J5 **Hinton Marsh** Hants
17 K1 **Hinton Martell** Dorset
82 B7 **Hinton on the Green** Worcs
47 K2 **Hinton Parva** Swindn
30 F8 **Hinton St George** Somset
32 C7 **Hinton St Mary** Dorset
66 A7 **Hinton Waldrist** Oxon
84 A7 **Hinton-in-the-Hedges** Nhants
96 E8 **Hints** Shrops
98 F3 **Hints** Staffs
85 J3 **Hinwick** Beds
40 D6 **Hinxhill** Kent
87 K6 **Hinxton** Cambs
86 E7 **Hinxworth** Herts
141 H3 **Hipperholme** Calder
191 J4 **Hipsburn** Nthumb
160 B3 **Hipswell** N York
245 G3 **Hirn** Abers
111 K7 **Hirnant** Powys
181 G2 **Hirst** Nthumb
142 F3 **Hirst Courtney** N York
128 D7 **Hirwaen** Denbgs
60 E6 **Hirwaun** Rhondd
27 K5 **Hiscott** Devon
87 J3 **Histon** Cambs
89 K5 **Hitcham** Suffk
89 K5 **Hitcham Causeway** Suffk
89 K5 **Hitcham Street** Suffk
68 F1 **Hitchin** Herts
51 K4 **Hither Green** Gt Lon
13 G3 **Hittisleigh** Devon
13 G3 **Hittisleigh Cross** Devon
143 K2 **Hive** E R Yk
114 F6 **Hixon** Staffs
41 J3 **Hoaden** Kent
115 J7 **Hoar Cross** Staffs
63 G1 **Hoarwithy** Herefs
41 G2 **Hoath** Kent
39 G6 **Hoathly** Kent
95 H7 **Hobarris** Shrops
88 D4 **Hobbles Green** Suffk
70 C7 **Hobbs Cross** Essex
70 D5 **Hobbs Cross** Essex
189 G4 **Hobkirk** Border
107 K3 **Hobland Hall** Norfk
116 D2 **Hobsick** Notts
180 E7 **Hobson** Dur
117 H8 **Hoby** Leics
29 K5 **Hoccombe** Somset
106 B1 **Hockering** Norfk
134 E8 **Hockerton** Notts
131 J3 **Hockley** Ches
99 H7 **Hockley** Covtry
71 K8 **Hockley** Essex
99 G3 **Hockley** Staffs
82 E1 **Hockley Heath** Solhll
68 B2 **Hockliffe** Beds
104 E6 **Hockwold cum Wilton** Norfk
29 J7 **Hockworthy** Devon
69 K5 **Hoddesdon** Herts
139 L3 **Hoddlesden** Bl w D
177 G4 **Hoddom Cross** D & G

177 G4 **Hoddom Mains** D & G
131 G5 **Hodgehill** Ches
55 H7 **Hodgeston** Pembks
113 K6 **Hodnet** Shrops
52 D6 **Hodsall Street** Kent
134 C3 **Hodsock** Notts
47 H3 **Hodson** Swindn
133 L4 **Hodthorpe** Derbys
35 H7 **Hoe** Hants
121 M8 **Hoe** Norfk
35 K8 **Hoe Gate** Hants
166 F7 **Hoff** Cumb
25 G4 **Hog Hill** E Susx
40 D4 **Hogben's Hill** Kent
89 H4 **Hoggards Green** Suffk
67 K2 **Hoggeston** Bucks
99 G5 **Hoggrill's End** Warwks
139 J2 **Hoghton** Lancs
139 J2 **Hoghton Bottoms** Lancs
115 L2 **Hognaston** Derbys
137 K5 **Hogsthorpe** Lincs
119 K6 **Holbeach** Lincs
119 K6 **Holbeach Bank** Lincs
119 K6 **Holbeach Clough** Lincs
103 G1 **Holbeach Drove** Lincs
119 L6 **Holbeach Hurn** Lincs
119 K7 **Holbeach St Johns** Lincs
119 L5 **Holbeach St Mark's** Lincs
119 L5 **Holbeach St Matthew** Lincs
133 L5 **Holbeck** Notts
133 L5 **Holbeck Woodhouse** Notts
82 B3 **Holberrow Green** Worcs
7 J5 **Holbeton** Devon
51 J3 **Holborn** Gt Lon
52 F6 **Holborough** Kent
116 B3 **Holbrook** Derbys
133 J3 **Holbrook** Sheff
90 E7 **Holbrook** Suffk
116 B3 **Holbrook Moor** Derbys
203 G6 **Holburn** Nthumb
19 G3 **Holbury** Hants
140 A4 **Holcombe** Bury
13 M7 **Holcombe** Devon
31 L1 **Holcombe** Somset
140 A5 **Holcombe Brook** Bury
29 J7 **Holcombe Rogus** Devon
84 F1 **Holcot** Nhants
148 D6 **Holden** Lancs
140 D3 **Holden Gate** Calder
84 D2 **Holdenby** Nhants
70 F1 **Holder's Green** Essex
96 D5 **Holdgate** Shrops
118 E2 **Holdingham** Lincs
15 H2 **Holditch** Dorset
141 G2 **Holdsworth** Calder
12 A1 **Hole** Devon
39 L6 **Hole Park** Kent
21 K4 **Hole Street** W Susx
63 J2 **Hole-in-the-Wall** Herefs
131 K1 **Holehouse** Derbys
12 A2 **Holemoor** Devon
29 L3 **Holford** Somset
151 J5 **Holgate** York
156 E7 **Holker** Cumb
121 K3 **Holkham** Norfk
11 M2 **Hollacombe** Devon
29 G4 **Hollam** Somset
119 H2 **Holland Fen** Lincs
139 G6 **Holland Lees** Lancs
73 J4 **Holland-on-Sea** Essex
275 f1 **Hollandstoun** Ork
177 J5 **Hollee** D & G
91 H6 **Hollesley** Suffk
8 D2 **Hollicombe** Torbay
97 L7 **Hollies Hill** Worcs
113 K1 **Hollin Green** Ches
39 L2 **Hollingbourne** Kent
22 D5 **Hollingbury** Br & H
67 L2 **Hollingdon** Bucks
142 B2 **Hollingthorpe** Leeds
115 L4 **Hollington** Derbys
115 G4 **Hollington** Staffs
140 F8 **Hollingworth** Tamesd
131 G3 **Hollinlane** Ches
140 B6 **Hollins** Bury
132 F5 **Hollins** Derbys
114 F2 **Hollins** Staffs
133 H3 **Hollins End** Sheff
130 D2 **Hollins Green** Warrtn
147 K5 **Hollins Lane** Lancs
131 L6 **Hollinsclough** Staffs
96 F2 **Hollinswood** Wrekin
113 H4 **Hollinwood** Shrops
24 C3 **Hollingrove** E Susx
27 L8 **Hollocombe** Devon

132 F8 **Holloway** Derbys
51 J2 **Holloway** Gt Lon
32 E5 **Holloway** Wilts
84 D1 **Hollowell** Nhants
129 L6 **Hollowmoor Heath** Ches
177 L3 **Hollows** D & G
103 K2 **Holly End** Norfk
81 K7 **Holly Green** Worcs
61 J6 **Hollybush** Caerph
196 D7 **Hollybush** E Ayrs
81 H7 **Hollybush** Herefs
113 J3 **Hollyhurst** Ches
145 J3 **Hollym** E R Yk
98 D7 **Hollywood** Worcs
141 H6 **Holmbridge** Kirk
37 H2 **Holmbury St Mary** Surrey
5 H4 **Holmbush** Cnwll
114 E6 **Holmcroft** Staffs
102 D6 **Holme** Cambs
157 H7 **Holme** Cumb
141 H6 **Holme** Kirk
144 A6 **Holme** N Linc
160 E6 **Holme** N York
134 F7 **Holme** Notts
140 C2 **Holme Chapel** Lancs
151 J7 **Holme Green** N York
105 H2 **Holme Hale** Norfk
80 D8 **Holme Lacy** Herefs
79 L4 **Holme Marsh** Herefs
120 F3 **Holme next the Sea** Norfk
152 E6 **Holme on the Wolds** E R Yk
117 G4 **Holme Pierrepont** Notts
164 F1 **Holme St Cuthbert** Cumb
152 B8 **Holme upon Spalding Moor** E R Yk
80 C6 **Holmer** Herefs
67 L7 **Holmer Green** Bucks
130 E6 **Holmes Chapel** Ches
23 J4 **Holmes Hill** E Susx
132 F4 **Holmesfield** Derbys
138 E4 **Holmeswood** Lancs
51 H8 **Holmethorpe** Surrey
133 H6 **Holmewood** Derbys
141 G2 **Holmfield** Calder
141 H6 **Holmfirth** Kirk
133 G7 **Holmgate** Derbys
197 H7 **Holmhead** E Ayrs
145 K3 **Holmpton** E R Yk
155 K3 **Holmrook** Cumb
104 D7 **Holmsey Green** Suffk
23 L2 **Holmshurst** E Susx
169 G1 **Holmside** Dur
166 C1 **Holmwrangle** Cumb
7 K1 **Holne** Devon
16 C1 **Holnest** Dorset
29 G2 **Holnicote** Somset
11 L2 **Holsworthy** Devon
11 L1 **Holsworthy Beacon** Devon
17 K2 **Holt** Dorset
122 B4 **Holt** Norfk
46 B6 **Holt** Wilts
81 J3 **Holt** Worcs
112 F1 **Holt** Wrexhm
82 C1 **Holt End** Worcs
81 J3 **Holt Fleet** Worcs
138 E6 **Holt Green** Lancs
17 L2 **Holt Heath** Dorset
81 J3 **Holt Heath** Worcs
41 H5 **Holt Street** Kent
151 L5 **Holtby** York
66 F5 **Holton** Oxon
31 L5 **Holton** Somset
107 H7 **Holton** Suffk
136 B3 **Holton cum Beckering** Lincs
17 J4 **Holton Heath** Dorset
24 B2 **Holton Hill** E Susx
145 H7 **Holton le Clay** Lincs
144 D8 **Holton le Moor** Lincs
90 C7 **Holton St Mary** Suffk
38 C5 **Holtye** E Susx
128 E4 **Holway** Flints
32 B8 **Holwell** Dorset
86 D8 **Holwell** Herts
117 J6 **Holwell** Leics
65 K5 **Holwell** Oxon
167 L5 **Holwick** Dur
16 E6 **Holworth** Dorset
97 L7 **Holy Cross** Worcs
203 J5 **Holy Island** Nthumb
35 M3 **Holybourne** Hants
69 K6 **Holyfield** Essex
124 D3 **Holyhead** IOA
133 G6 **Holymoorside** Derbys
49 L3 **Holyport** W & M
190 D5 **Holystone** Nthumb

209 K6 **Holytown** N Lans
87 G1 **Holywell** Cambs
4 C3 **Holywell** Cnwll
16 B2 **Holywell** Dorset
128 E4 **Holywell** Flints
181 H4 **Holywell** Nthumb
82 E2 **Holywell** Warwks
141 G4 **Holywell Green** Calder
29 K6 **Holywell Lake** Somset
104 E7 **Holywell Row** Suffk
176 B3 **Holywood** D & G
176 C3 **Holywood Village** D & G
63 H3 **Hom Green** Herefs
96 E3 **Homer** Shrops
138 D7 **Homer Green** Sefton
106 F6 **Homersfield** Suffk
157 J5 **Homescales** Cumb
33 K5 **Homington** Wilts
40 F3 **Honey Hill** Kent
89 J8 **Honey Tye** Suffk
54 F5 **Honeyborough** Pembks
82 D6 **Honeybourne** Worcs
12 E2 **Honeychurch** Devon
47 G6 **Honeystreet** Wilts
82 F1 **Honiley** Warwks
123 G6 **Honing** Norfk
106 C1 **Honingham** Norfk
118 B3 **Honington** Lincs
105 H8 **Honington** Suffk
83 G6 **Honington** Warwks
14 E2 **Honiton** Devon
141 H5 **Honley** Kirk
114 A8 **Honnington** Wrekin
41 J2 **Hoo** Kent
68 F3 **Hoo End** Herts
130 D3 **Hoo Green** Ches
7 G2 **Hoo Meavy** Devon
53 G4 **Hoo St Werburgh** Medway
97 J8 **Hoobrook** Worcs
141 M7 **Hood Green** Barns
142 B8 **Hood Hill** Rothm
6 F4 **Hooe** C Plym
24 C5 **Hooe** E Susx
146 F8 **Hoohill** Bpool
103 J5 **Hook** Cambs
15 G2 **Hook** Devon
143 J3 **Hook** E R Yk
19 H3 **Hook** Hants
49 H8 **Hook** Hants
52 D5 **Hook** Kent
55 G4 **Hook** Pembks
50 F6 **Hook** Surrey
47 G2 **Hook** Wilts
81 J7 **Hook Bank** Worcs
70 E7 **Hook End** Essex
39 G6 **Hook Green** Kent
83 H8 **Hook Norton** Oxon
63 K7 **Hook Street** Gloucs
47 G2 **Hook Street** Wilts
95 L2 **Hookagate** Shrops
15 M3 **Hooke** Dorset
114 A4 **Hookgate** Staffs
13 K3 **Hookway** Devon
37 L2 **Hookwood** Surrey
51 H7 **Hooley** Surrey
140 C5 **Hooley Bridge** Rochdl
129 J4 **Hooton** Ches
133 K2 **Hooton Levitt** Rothm
142 D6 **Hooton Pagnell** Donc
142 D8 **Hooton Roberts** Rothm
102 D1 **Hop Pole** Lincs
66 C2 **Hopcrofts Holt** Oxon
132 C3 **Hope** Derbys
7 K6 **Hope** Devon
129 G7 **Hope** Flints
95 G2 **Hope** Powys
95 H3 **Hope** Shrops
96 D8 **Hope** Shrops
132 B8 **Hope** Staffs
.95 L5 **Hope Bowdler** Shrops
70 E3 **Hope End Green** Essex
63 J3 **Hope Mansell** Herefs
80 C5 **Hope under Dinmore** Herefs
187 L3 **Hopehouse** Border
266 C2 **Hopeman** Moray
95 J6 **Hopesay** Shrops
142 B3 **Hopetown** Wakefd
151 K5 **Hopgrove** York
150 F4 **Hopperton** N York
99 L6 **Hopsford** Warwks
97 H6 **Hopstone** Shrops
115 L1 **Hopton** Derbys
112 F7 **Hopton** Shrops
114 E6 **Hopton** Staffs
105 K7 **Hopton** Suffk

Hopton Cangeford - Husborne Crawley 323

96 C7 **Hopton Cangeford** Shrops
95 J7 **Hopton Castle** Shrops
107 L3 **Hopton on Sea** Norfk
96 E8 **Hopton Wafers** Shrops
95 J7 **Hoptonheath** Shrops
98 F3 **Hopwas** Staffs
140 C6 **Hopwood** Rochdl
98 C8 **Hopwood** Worcs
23 K4 **Horam** E Susx
118 F4 **Horbling** Lincs
141 L4 **Horbury** Wakefd
65 H7 **Horcott** Gloucs
170 B3 **Horden** Dur
95 K6 **Horderley** Shrops
18 D4 **Hordle** Hants
12 F5 **Hordley** Shrops
56 F4 **Horeb** Carmth
76 D6 **Horeb** Cerdgn
45 H4 **Horfield** Bristl
90 F1 **Horham** Suffk
72 E1 **Horkesley Green** Essex
72 E1 **Horkesley Heath** Essex
44 C4 **Horkstow** N Linc
83 K6 **Horley** Oxon
37 L2 **Horley** Surrey
68 C8 **Horn Hill** Bucks
41 G8 **Horn Street** Kent
31 K4 **Hornblotton Green** Somset
47 L2 **Hornby** Lancs
60 E2 **Hornby** N York
60 B4 **Hornby** N York
36 E6 **Horncastle** Lincs
52 B2 **Hornchurch** Gt Lon
02 E3 **Horncliffe** Nthumb
02 D3 **Horndean** Border
35 L8 **Horndean** Hants
12 C6 **Horndon** Devon
52 E2 **Horndon on the Hill** Thurr
38 A4 **Horne** Surrey
71 J6 **Horne Row** Essex
28 F2 **Horner** Somset
89 K7 **Horners Green** Suffk
23 G2 **Horney Common** E Susx
23 G8 **Horning** Norfk
01 H4 **Horninghold** Leics
15 L6 **Horninglow** Staffs
87 K3 **Horningsea** Cambs
32 D3 **Horningsham** Wilts
21 K6 **Horningtoft** Norfk
6 B3 **Horningtops** Cnwll
27 G6 **Horns Cross** Devon
24 E3 **Horns Cross** E Susx
30 E8 **Hornsbury** Somset
66 C1 **Hornsby** Cumb
66 C1 **Hornsbygate** Cumb
53 K6 **Hornsea** E R Yk
51 J1 **Hornsey** Gt Lon
83 J6 **Hornton** Oxon
47 J2 **Horpit** Swindn
81 e3 **Horra** Shet
7 G1 **Horrabridge** Devon
13 H7 **Horridge** Devon
89 G3 **Horringer** Suffk
19 J6 **Horringford** IOW
39 L5 **Horrocks Fold** Bolton
48 C7 **Horrocksford** Lancs
27 J4 **Horsacott** Devon
12 A7 **Horsebridge** Devon
23 K5 **Horsebridge** E Susx
34 D5 **Horsebridge** Hants
95 J2 **Horsebridge** Shrops
14 F1 **Horsebridge** Staffs
97 K1 **Horsebrook** Staffs
44 E5 **Horsecastle** N Som
3 G4 **Horsedown** Cnwll
02 C2 **Horsegate** Lincs
96 F2 **Horsehay** Wrekin
88 C5 **Horseheath** Cambs
59 J6 **Horsehouse** N York
50 C7 **Horsell** Surrey
13 G3 **Horseman's Green** Wrexhm
67 J6 **Horsenden** Bucks
23 J7 **Horsey** Norfk
30 D3 **Horsey** Somset
23 J6 **Horsey Corner** Norfk
22 D8 **Horsford** Norfk
50 B8 **Horsforth** Leeds
57 J5 **Horsham** W Susx
31 G4 **Horsham** Worcs
22 E8 **Horsham St Faith** Norfk
36 C6 **Horsington** Lincs
52 B6 **Horsington** Somset
16 C3 **Horsley** Derbys
54 B7 **Horsley** Gloucs
30 B6 **Horsley** Nthumb
180 D5 **Horsley** Nthumb
73 H2 **Horsley Cross** Essex
116 C3 **Horsley Woodhouse** Derbys
67 J8 **Horsley's Green** Bucks
132 F4 **Horsley-Gate** Derbys
73 G1 **Horsleycross Street** Essex
188 F2 **Horsleyhill** Border
39 H5 **Horsmonden** Kent
66 E6 **Horspath** Oxon
122 F7 **Horstead** Norfk
22 F2 **Horsted Keynes** W Susx
68 A3 **Horton** Bucks
17 K1 **Horton** Dorset
148 E6 **Horton** Lancs
84 F4 **Horton** Nhants
45 M2 **Horton** S Glos
113 H5 **Horton** Shrops
30 D7 **Horton** Somset
131 J8 **Horton** Staffs
51 G6 **Horton** Surrey
56 E7 **Horton** Swans
50 C4 **Horton** W & M
46 F6 **Horton** Wilts
113 L8 **Horton** Wrekin
30 E7 **Horton Cross** Somset
113 G2 **Horton Green** Ches
35 G7 **Horton Heath** Hants
148 D2 **Horton in Ribblesdale** N York
52 C5 **Horton Kirby** Kent
66 F4 **Horton-cum-Studley** Oxon
139 J5 **Horwich** Bolton
131 K3 **Horwich End** Derbys
27 J5 **Horwood** Devon
138 F5 **Hoscar** Lancs
188 C4 **Hoscote** Border
117 J5 **Hose** Leics
51 M8 **Hosey Hill** Kent
220 E3 **Hosh** P & K
281 e8 **Hoswick** Shet
143 M1 **Hotham** E R Yk
40 C6 **Hothfield** Kent
116 F7 **Hoton** Leics
179 H2 **Hott** Nthumb
113 M1 **Hough** Ches
131 G4 **Hough** Ches
141 K1 **Hough End** Leeds
129 L2 **Hough Green** Halton
118 B2 **Hough-on-the-Hill** Lincs
118 A3 **Hougham** Lincs
86 F1 **Houghton** Cambs
177 L7 **Houghton** Cumb
34 D4 **Houghton** Hants
180 D5 **Houghton** Nthumb
55 G5 **Houghton** Pembks
21 H4 **Houghton** W Susx
85 L7 **Houghton Conquest** Beds
181 H8 **Houghton Gate** Dur
25 G3 **Houghton Green** E Susx
130 C1 **Houghton Green** Warrtn
169 G6 **Houghton le Side** Darltn
169 J1 **Houghton le Spring** Sundld
100 E3 **Houghton on the Hill** Leics
68 C2 **Houghton Regis** Beds
121 K4 **Houghton St Giles** Norfk
49 H7 **Hound Green** Hants
201 K4 **Houndslow** Border
29 L5 **Houndsmoor** Somset
213 J6 **Houndwood** Border
50 F4 **Hounslow** Gt Lon
71 G3 **Hounslow Green** Essex
253 G1 **Househill** Highld
141 K4 **Houses Hill** Kirk
257 G6 **Housieside** Abers
208 C5 **Houston** Rens
275 G1 **Houstry** Highld
275 b5 **Houton** Ork
22 D6 **Hove** Br & H
141 H3 **Hove Edge** Calder
117 J2 **Hoveringham** Notts
122 F7 **Hoveton** Norfk
161 L7 **Hovingham** N York
63 J1 **How Caple** Herefs
85 K7 **How End** Beds
178 C7 **How Mill** Cumb
141 M8 **Howbrook** Barns
143 J2 **Howden** E R Yk
168 F4 **Howden-le-Wear** Dur
280 D4 **Howe** Highld
154 b8 **Howe** IOM
160 E6 **Howe** N York
106 F3 **Howe** Norfk
139 K7 **Howe Bridge** Wigan
71 H6 **Howe Green** Essex
268 E6 **Howe of Teuchar** Abers
71 G4 **Howe Street** Essex
88 D8 **Howe Street** Essex
71 K6 **Howegreen** Essex
118 F2 **Howell** Lincs
177 G5 **Howes** D & G
78 E3 **Howey** Powys
211 H7 **Howgate** Mdloth
148 E6 **Howgill** N York
191 K3 **Howick** Nthumb
168 E5 **Howle** Dur
113 M6 **Howle** Wrekin
63 J3 **Howle Hill** Herefs
88 B8 **Howlett End** Essex
15 G1 **Howley** Somset
283 b10 **Howmore** W Isls
189 L2 **Hownam** Border
165 K1 **Howrigg** Cumb
144 D6 **Howsham** N Linc
151 M3 **Howsham** N York
53 J6 **Howt Green** Kent
202 D6 **Howtel** Nthumb
13 H5 **Howton** Devon
62 E1 **Howton** Herefs
166 B6 **Howtown** Cumb
208 C7 **Howwood** Rens
106 D7 **Hoxne** Suffk
128 F2 **Hoylake** Wirral
142 B7 **Hoyland Common** Barns
142 B7 **Hoyland Nether** Barns
141 L6 **Hoyland Swaine** Barns
20 E3 **Hoyle** W Susx
142 A6 **Hoyle Mill** Barns
159 G7 **Hubberholme** N York
54 E5 **Hubberston** Pembks
119 J3 **Hubbert's Bridge** Lincs
150 C6 **Huby** N York
151 J3 **Huby** N York
12 F7 **Huccaby** Devon
64 C4 **Hucclecote** Gloucs
53 H7 **Hucking** Kent
116 F2 **Hucknall** Notts
141 H4 **Huddersfield** Kirk
81 L4 **Huddington** Worcs
159 L3 **Hudswell** N York
152 D5 **Huggate** E R Yk
99 L1 **Hugglescote** Leics
10 c3 **Hugh Town** IOS
67 L7 **Hughenden Valley** Bucks
96 D4 **Hughley** Shrops
27 J8 **Huish** Devon
47 H6 **Huish** Wilts
29 J5 **Huish Champflower** Somset
31 G5 **Huish Episcopi** Somset
52 B6 **Hulberry** Kent
85 J7 **Hulcote** Beds
67 K4 **Hulcott** Bucks
14 B6 **Hulham** Devon
115 L2 **Hulland** Derbys
115 L2 **Hulland Ward** Derbys
46 C3 **Hullavington** Wilts
71 K8 **Hullbridge** Essex
140 C8 **Hulme** Manch
114 E2 **Hulme** Staffs
130 B2 **Hulme** Warrtn
132 B7 **Hulme End** Staffs
131 G6 **Hulme Walfield** Ches
130 E3 **Hulse Heath** Ches
139 K6 **Hulton Lane Ends** Bolton
105 J1 **Hulver Street** Norfk
107 K6 **Hulver Street** Suffk
18 F6 **Hulverstone** IOW
13 L7 **Humber** Devon
80 C4 **Humber** Herefs
145 J6 **Humberston** NE Lin
100 E2 **Humberstone** C Leic
150 F2 **Humberton** N York
212 A6 **Humbie** E Loth
145 G1 **Humbleton** E R Yk
202 F7 **Humbleton** Nthumb
118 D5 **Humby** Lincs
201 L5 **Hume** Border
179 L4 **Humshaugh** Nthumb
280 E2 **Huna** Highld
140 A2 **Huncoat** Lancs
100 B4 **Huncote** Leics
189 H3 **Hundalee** Border
133 H4 **Hundall** Derbys
168 C6 **Hunderthwaite** Dur
119 H1 **Hundle Houses** Lincs
137 G6 **Hundleby** Lincs
54 F6 **Hundleton** Pembks
88 E5 **Hundon** Suffk
19 K1 **Hundred Acres** Hants
138 E3 **Hundred End** Lancs
78 F4 **Hundred House** Powys
100 F2 **Hungarton** Leics
84 F6 **Hungate End** M Keyn
139 K6 **Hunger Hill** Bolton
139 G5 **Hunger Hill** Lancs
33 L8 **Hungerford** Hants
29 J3 **Hungerford** Somset
47 M5 **Hungerford** W Berk
47 M4 **Hungerford Newtown** W Berk
80 B8 **Hungerstone** Herefs
118 A5 **Hungerton** Lincs
113 L6 **Hungryhatton** Shrops
163 K7 **Hunmanby** N York
83 J2 **Hunningham** Warwks
98 B7 **Hunnington** Worcs
69 L4 **Hunsdon** Herts
150 F5 **Hunsingore** N York
141 M2 **Hunslet** Leeds
166 D4 **Hunsonby** Cumb
120 E3 **Hunstanton** Norfk
168 B1 **Hunstanworth** Dur
113 M2 **Hunsterson** Ches
89 K2 **Hunston** Suffk
20 D6 **Hunston** W Susx
89 K2 **Hunston Green** Suffk
45 J6 **Hunstrete** BaNES
141 J2 **Hunsworth** Kirk
82 B2 **Hunt End** Worcs
105 L5 **Hunt's Corner** Norfk
129 K3 **Hunt's Cross** Lpool
28 B1 **Hunter's Inn** Devon
207 K3 **Hunter's Quay** Ag & B
30 E5 **Huntham** Somset
234 D1 **Hunthill Lodge** Angus
86 E1 **Huntingdon** Cambs
107 G8 **Huntingfield** Suffk
32 D5 **Huntingford** Dorset
129 K6 **Huntington** Ches
212 B4 **Huntington** E Loth
79 J4 **Huntington** Herefs
80 B6 **Huntington** Herefs
98 B1 **Huntington** Staffs
151 K4 **Huntington** York
63 L3 **Huntley** Gloucs
255 L4 **Huntly** Abers
35 G3 **Hunton** Hants
39 H3 **Hunton** Kent
160 B4 **Hunton** N York
68 D7 **Hunton Bridge** Herts
67 L6 **Hunts Green** Bucks
98 F4 **Hunts Green** Warwks
29 G2 **Huntscott** Somset
29 H6 **Huntsham** Devon
27 J6 **Huntshaw** Devon
27 J6 **Huntshaw Cross** Devon
30 D2 **Huntspill** Somset
30 C4 **Huntstile** Somset
30 D4 **Huntworth** Somset
168 F4 **Hunwick** Dur
122 B4 **Hunworth** Norfk
30 F7 **Hurcott** Somset
33 L4 **Hurdcott** Wilts
131 H5 **Hurdsfield** Ches
49 K2 **Hurley** W & M
99 H4 **Hurley** Warwks
49 K2 **Hurley Bottom** W & M
99 H4 **Hurley Common** Warwks
196 E4 **Hurlford** E Ayrs
138 E5 **Hurlston Green** Lancs
18 A4 **Hurn** Dorset
119 M2 **Hurn's End** Lincs
34 F6 **Hursley** Hants
16 F4 **Hurst** Dorset
159 J2 **Hurst** N York
31 G7 **Hurst** Somset
49 J4 **Hurst** Wokham
24 D2 **Hurst Green** E Susx
73 G4 **Hurst Green** Essex
148 B8 **Hurst Green** Lancs
51 K8 **Hurst Green** Surrey
97 L4 **Hurst Hill** Dudley
22 D4 **Hurst Wickham** W Susx
34 F2 **Hurstbourne Priors** Hants
48 A8 **Hurstbourne Tarrant** Hants
79 L5 **Hurstley** Herefs
22 D4 **Hurstpierpoint** W Susx
79 K5 **Hurstway Common** Herefs
140 C2 **Hurstwood** Lancs
275 d5 **Hurtiso** Ork
36 E2 **Hurtmore** Surrey
169 L4 **Hurworth Burn** Dur
160 D1 **Hurworth Place** Darltn
169 J8 **Hurworth-on-Tees** Darltn
168 B6 **Hury** Dur
100 E6 **Husbands Bosworth** Leics
85 J8 **Husborne Crawley** Beds

324 Husthwaite - Jevington

161 H7 Husthwaite N York
142 F3 Hut Green N York
8 A5 Hutcherleigh Devon
161 G2 Huthwaite N York
133 J7 Huthwaite Notts
137 K4 Huttoft Lincs
202 E2 Hutton Border
166 B5 Hutton Cumb
152 F5 Hutton E R Yk
70 F8 Hutton Essex
139 G2 Hutton Lancs
44 D7 Hutton N Som
160 E3 Hutton Bonville N York
163 H6 Hutton Buscel N York
160 D7 Hutton Conyers N York
153 G5 Hutton Cranswick E R Yk
166 B3 Hutton End Cumb
170 E7 Hutton Hall R & Cl
159 L5 Hutton Hang N York
169 L3 Hutton Henry Dur
170 E7 Hutton Lowcross R & Cl
168 E8 Hutton Magna Dur
162 E1 Hutton Mulgrave N York
165 L4 Hutton Roof Cumb
157 J7 Hutton Roof Cumb
161 G2 Hutton Rudby N York
161 G7 Hutton Sessay N York
151 H5 Hutton Wandesley N York
162 B4 Hutton-le-Hole N York
13 M3 Huxham Devon
31 K4 Huxham Green Somset
129 L7 Huxley Ches
129 K2 Huyton Knows
155 K5 Hycemoor Cumb
64 C6 Hyde Gloucs
33 L8 Hyde Hants
131 J1 Hyde Tamesd
49 H5 Hyde End Wokham
68 B7 Hyde Heath Bucks
114 E7 Hyde Lea Staffs
30 D4 Hyde Park Corner Somset
36 E3 Hydestile Surrey
135 J6 Hykeham Moor Lincs
198 F5 Hyndford Bridge S Lans
224 C7 Hynish Ag & B
95 H4 Hyssington Powys
63 K7 Hystfield Gloucs
19 G2 Hythe Hants
41 G8 Hythe Kent
44 F8 Hythe Somset
50 C4 Hythe End W & M
155 K5 Hyton Cumb

I

16 F1 Ibberton Dorset
132 E8 Ible Derbys
18 A2 Ibsley Hants
99 L2 Ibstock Leics
67 J8 Ibstone Bucks
48 A8 Ibthorpe Hants
162 F1 Iburndale N York
48 E7 Ibworth Hants
44 D6 Icelton N Som
105 G4 Ickburgh Norfk
50 D2 Ickenham Gt Lon
66 F5 Ickford Bucks
41 H4 Ickham Kent
68 F1 Ickleford Herts
24 F4 Icklesham E Susx
87 K6 Ickleton Cambs
88 F1 Icklingham Suffk
149 G7 Ickornshaw N York
86 C6 Ickwell Green Beds
65 J3 Icomb Gloucs
65 K3 Idbury Oxon
12 D1 Iddesleigh Devon
13 L4 Ide Devon
38 D3 Ide Hill Kent
13 K7 Ideford Devon
25 G3 Iden E Susx
39 J6 Iden Green Kent
39 K7 Iden Green Kent
149 M8 Idle Brad
4 D5 Idless Cnwll
83 G6 Idlicote Warwks
33 L3 Idmiston Wilts
115 M2 Idridgehay Derbys
258 F4 Idrigill Highld
47 K2 Idstone Oxon
66 D6 Iffley Oxon
37 K3 Ifield W Susx
36 F4 Ifold W Susx
18 A5 Iford Bmouth
22 F5 Iford E Susx
44 F1 Ifton Mons
112 E4 Ifton Heath Shrops
113 K4 Ightfield Shrops
38 F2 Ightham Kent
91 J4 Iken Suffk
115 J2 Ilam Staffs
31 H6 Ilchester Somset
190 E2 Ilderton Nthumb
51 L2 Ilford Gt Lon
30 E7 Ilford Somset
27 J2 Ilfracombe Devon
116 D3 Ilkeston Derbys
107 H6 Ilketshall St Andrew Suffk
107 G6 Ilketshall St Margaret Suffk
149 K6 Ilkley Brad
11 K6 Illand Cnwll
98 B7 Illey Dudley
130 F7 Illidge Green Ches
141 G2 Illingworth Calder
3 H2 Illogan Cnwll
100 F3 Illston on the Hill Leics
67 J6 Ilmer Bucks
82 F6 Ilmington Warwks
30 E7 Ilminster Somset
13 H7 Ilsington Devon
16 E4 Ilsington Dorset
57 G6 Ilston Swans
160 B7 Ilton N York
30 E7 Ilton Somset
194 D3 Imachar N Ayrs
144 F5 Immingham NE Lin
145 G4 Immingham Dock NE Lin
87 J3 Impington Cambs
129 K4 Ince Ches
138 C7 Ince Blundell Sefton
139 J6 Ince-in-Makerfield Wigan
262 C6 Inchbae Lodge Hotel Highld
234 F2 Inchbare Angus
266 F5 Inchberry Moray
208 E5 Inchinnan Rens
239 K3 Inchlaggan Highld
222 D2 Inchmichael P & K
240 C2 Inchnacardoch Hotel Highld
271 H4 Inchnadamph Highld
222 D2 Inchture P & K
249 L4 Inchvuilt Highld
222 C3 Inchyra P & K
4 E3 Indian Queens Cnwll
107 J5 Ingate Place Suffk
70 F7 Ingatestone Essex
141 K6 Ingbirchworth Barns
150 C3 Ingerthorpe N York
114 F6 Ingestre Staffs
135 J3 Ingham Lincs
123 H6 Ingham Norfk
89 G1 Ingham Suffk
123 H6 Ingham Corner Norfk
120 B8 Ingleborough Norfk
116 B6 Ingleby Derbys
161 G3 Ingleby Arncliffe N York
170 B7 Ingleby Barwick S on T
161 G3 Ingleby Cross N York
161 J2 Ingleby Greenhow N York
12 E1 Ingleigh Green Devon
45 L6 Inglesbatch BaNES
65 J7 Inglesham Swindn
176 C6 Ingleston D & G
168 F6 Ingleton Dur
158 B8 Ingleton N York
147 L7 Inglewhite Lancs
157 K4 Ingmire Hall Cumb
180 C4 Ingoe Nthumb
139 G1 Ingol Lancs
120 F5 Ingoldisthorpe Norfk
137 K6 Ingoldmells Lincs
118 D5 Ingoldsby Lincs
190 E3 Ingram Nthumb
52 D1 Ingrave Essex
149 J7 Ingrow Brad
157 G3 Ings Cumb
45 H2 Ingst S Glos
101 M2 Ingthorpe Lincs
122 D5 Ingworth Norfk
82 B4 Inkberrow Worcs
168 E3 Inkerman Dur
257 G4 Inkhorn Abers
48 A6 Inkpen W Berk
280 C2 Inkstack Highld
46 D6 Inmarsh Wilts
207 J5 Innellan Ag & B
200 D6 Innerleithen Border
222 F7 Innerleven Fife
172 D2 Innermessan D & G
212 F4 Innerwick E Loth
266 F3 Innesmill Moray
256 A6 Insch Abers
241 L3 Insh Highld
147 J8 Inskip Lancs
147 J8 Inskip Moss Side Lancs
27 H5 Instow Devon
6 E4 Insworke Cnwll
133 H3 Intake Sheff
243 H5 Inver Abers
264 D3 Inver Highld
232 F7 Inver P & K
268 B3 Inver-boyndie Abers
238 B7 Inverailort Highld
260 D8 Inveralligin Highld
269 J3 Inverallochy Abers
272 E8 Inveran Highld
217 H5 Inveraray Ag & B
247 H2 Inverarish Highld
234 C6 Inverarity Angus
218 D3 Inverarnan Stirlg
260 C3 Inverasdale Highld
210 C3 Inveravon Falk
217 G1 Inverawe Ag & B
218 E7 Inverbeg Ag & B
235 K1 Inverbervie Abers
261 K3 Inverbroom Highld
229 G6 Invercreran House Hotel Ag & B
242 B1 Inverdruie Highld
211 K5 Inveresk E Loth
228 F8 Inveresragan Ag & B
242 E5 Inverey Abers
250 F7 Inverfarigaig Highld
228 E6 Inverfolla Ag & B
240 A3 Invergarry Highld
220 C2 Invergeldie P & K
239 L6 Invergloy Highld
263 J6 Invergordon Highld
222 F1 Invergowrie P & K
238 B2 Inverguseran Highld
231 J4 Inverhadden P & K
218 E2 Inverherive Hotel Stirlg
238 B3 Inverie Highld
216 F4 Inverinan Ag & B
248 E7 Inverinate Highld
235 G5 Inverkeilor Angus
210 F2 Inverkeithing Fife
268 A6 Inverkeithny Abers
207 K4 Inverkip Inver
270 E4 Inverkirkaig Highld
261 K3 Inverlael Highld
240 B7 Inverlair Highld
216 D6 Inverliever Lodge Ag & B
217 K2 Inverlochy Ag & B
244 A7 Invermark Angus
255 J4 Invermarkie Abers
250 D8 Invermoriston Highld
251 H3 Inverness Highld
217 J7 Invernoaden Ag & B
229 M7 Inveroran Hotel Ag & B
234 B4 Inverquharity Angus
257 J2 Inverquhomery Abers
239 M7 Inverroy Highld
228 E3 Inversanda Highld
248 F7 Invershiel Highld
272 E8 Invershin Highld
275 H1 Invershore Highld
218 E5 Inversnaid Hotel Stirlg
269 L6 Inverugie Abers
218 D5 Inveruglas Ag & B
241 L3 Inveruglass Highld
256 D7 Inverurie Abers
12 D3 Inwardleigh Devon
72 C3 Inworth Essex
283 b9 Iochdar W Isls
36 C6 Iping W Susx
8 B2 Ipplepen Devon
48 F2 Ipsden Oxon
115 G2 Ipstones Staffs
90 E6 Ipswich Suffk
128 F3 Irby Wirral
137 J7 Irby in the Marsh Lincs
145 G6 Irby upon Humber NE Lin
85 H2 Irchester Nhants
165 H3 Ireby Cumb
157 L7 Ireby Lancs
86 C7 Ireland Beds
156 B7 Ireleth Cumb
167 K3 Ireshopeburn Dur
115 M2 Ireton Wood Derbys
130 E1 Irlam Salfd
118 D6 Irnham Lincs
45 K2 Iron Acton S Glos
103 K4 Iron Bridge Cambs
82 C5 Iron Cross Warwks
96 F3 Ironbridge Wrekin
185 G7 Ironmacannie D & G
37 K2 Irons Bottom Surrey
116 D1 Ironville Derbys
123 H7 Irstead Norfk
178 C6 Irthington Cumb
85 J1 Irthlingborough Nhants
163 H6 Irton N York
196 C3 Irvine N Ayrs
279 G3 Isauld Highld
281 d3 Isbister Shet
23 G4 Isfield E Susx
101 J8 Isham Nhants
36 B2 Isington Hants
97 K7 Island Pool Worcs
30 E6 Isle Abbotts Somset
30 E6 Isle Brewers Somset
51 K3 Isle of Dogs Gt Lon
174 D7 Isle of Whithorn D & G
104 C8 Isleham Cambs
247 L6 Isleornsay Highld
176 C4 Islesteps D & G
9 k2 Islet Village Guern
50 F4 Isleworth Gt Lon
116 C6 Isley Walton Leics
282 d3 Islibhig W Isls
51 J2 Islington Gt Lon
101 L7 Islip Nhants
66 D4 Islip Oxon
282 d3 Islivig W Isls
96 E1 Isombridge Wrekin
52 D5 Istead Rise Kent
35 H4 Itchen Abbas Hants
35 H4 Itchen Stoke Hants
37 H5 Itchingfield W Susx
45 K2 Itchington S Glos
122 C5 Itteringham Norfk
12 F3 Itton Devon
62 F8 Itton Mons
165 M2 Ivegill Cumb
159 G3 Ivelet N York
50 D3 Iver Bucks
50 C2 Iver Heath Bucks
168 E1 Iveston Dur
68 B4 Ivinghoe Bucks
68 B3 Ivinghoe Aston Bucks
80 B4 Ivington Herefs
80 B4 Ivington Green Herefs
32 E6 Ivy Cross Dorset
38 F3 Ivy Hatch Kent
105 H2 Ivy Todd Norfk
7 J4 Ivybridge Devon
25 J2 Ivychurch Kent
40 A2 Iwade Kent
32 E8 Iwerne Courtney or Shroton Dorset
32 E8 Iwerne Minster Dorset
89 J1 Ixworth Suffk
89 J1 Ixworth Thorpe Suffk

J

139 J3 Jack Green Lancs
150 B5 Jack Hill N York
34 C3 Jack's Bush Hants
14 B3 Jack-in-the-Green Devon
116 D1 Jacksdale Notts
141 J6 Jackson Bridge Kirk
209 G8 Jackton S Lans
50 C8 Jacobs Well Surrey
11 H3 Jacobstow Cnwll
12 E2 Jacobstowe Devon
55 H7 Jameston Pembks
262 E8 Jamestown Highld
208 C3 Jamestown W Duns
280 D6 Janets-town Highld
275 G2 Janetstown Highld
176 E1 Jardine Hall D & G
181 H6 Jarrow S Tyne
38 E7 Jarvis Brook E Susx
71 H2 Jasper's Green Essex
209 M4 Jawcraig Falk
73 H4 Jaywick Essex
49 L4 Jealott's Hill Br For
160 F4 Jeater Houses N York
189 H2 Jedburgh Border
55 J5 Jeffreyston Pembks
263 K7 Jemimaville Highld
9 k4 Jerbourg Guern
135 J5 Jerusalem Lincs
181 G5 Jesmond N u Ty
23 J7 Jevington E Susx

62 F5 **Jingle Street** Mons
68 D4 **Jockey End** Herts
130 F5 **Jodrell Bank** Ches
280 E2 **John o' Groats** Highld
24 D3 **John's Cross** E Susx
166 B4 **Johnby** Cumb
235 K2 **Johnshaven** Abers
123 H8 **Johnson's Street** Norfk
54 F5 **Johnston** Pembks
187 K6 **Johnstone** D & G
208 D6 **Johnstone** Rens
187 G7 **Johnstonebridge** D & G
58 D5 **Johnstown** Carmth
112 D2 **Johnstown** Wrexhm
211 K4 **Joppa** C Edin
77 G2 **Joppa** Cerdgn
196 E7 **Joppa** S Ayrs
50 B1 **Jordans** Bucks
74 F5 **Jordanston** Pembks
133 G3 **Jordanthorpe** Sheff
52 B4 **Joyden's Wood** Kent
39 L4 **Jubilee Corner** Kent
142 B7 **Jump** Barns
38 C6 **Jumper's Town** E Susx
179 L7 **Juniper** Nthumb
211 G5 **Juniper Green** C Edin
154 e3 **Jurby** IOM
13 G5 **Jurston** Devon

K

167 J8 **Kaber** Cumb
199 G4 **Kaimend** S Lans
206 F5 **Kames** Ag & B
197 K5 **Kames** E Ayrs
4 C6 **Kea** Cnwll
143 L5 **Keadby** N Linc
137 G7 **Keal Cotes** Lincs
150 E6 **Kearby Town End** N York
139 M6 **Kearsley** Bolton
180 B4 **Kearsley** Nthumb
41 J6 **Kearsney** Kent
157 K6 **Kearstwick** Cumb
159 H3 **Kearton** N York
148 C3 **Keasden** N York
6 C1 **Keason** Cnwll
7 J4 **Keaton** Devon
130 B3 **Keckwick** Halton
36 F2 **Keddington** Lincs
37 G2 **Keddington Corner** Lincs
88 E6 **Kedington** Suffk
16 A3 **Kedleston** Derbys
44 F5 **Keelby** Lincs
14 C3 **Keele** Staffs
14 C3 **Keele University** Staffs
85 K6 **Keeley Green** Beds
41 G1 **Keelham** Brad
54 E3 **Keeston** Pembks
46 D7 **Keevil** Wilts
16 E6 **Kegworth** Leics
3 G3 **Kehelland** Cnwll
56 A7 **Keig** Abers
49 J7 **Keighley** Brad
20 F8 **Keilarsbrae** Clacks
21 H2 **Keillour** P & K
43 G5 **Keiloch** Abers
05 H3 **Keils** Ag & B
31 J5 **Keinton Mandeville** Somset
86 C7 **Keir Mill** D & G
79 H8 **Keirsleywell Row** Nthumb
18 D6 **Keisby** Lincs
67 G6 **Keisley** Cumb
80 D4 **Keiss** Highld
67 J6 **Keith** Moray
33 J7 **Keithick** P & K
34 F3 **Keithock** Angus
62 F8 **Keithtown** Highld
48 F7 **Kelbrook** Lancs
07 L7 **Kelburn** N Ayrs
18 D3 **Kelby** Lincs
66 D7 **Keld** Cumb
58 F3 **Keld** N York
62 D5 **Keld Head** N York
62 C5 **Keldholme** N York
43 L7 **Kelfield** N Linc
51 J8 **Kelfield** N York
34 F8 **Kelham** Notts
76 F5 **Kelhead** D & G
12 A5 **Kellacott** Devon
58 E2 **Kellamergh** Lancs
34 C8 **Kellas** Angus
66 D5 **Kellas** Moray
8 B7 **Kellaton** Devon

157 L2 **Kelleth** Cumb
122 B3 **Kelling** Norfk
142 E3 **Kellington** N York
169 K3 **Kelloe** Dur
185 J1 **Kelloholm** D & G
164 C7 **Kells** Cumb
11 M6 **Kelly** Devon
11 L8 **Kelly Bray** Cnwll
101 G7 **Kelmarsh** Nhants
65 K7 **Kelmscot** Oxon
91 J2 **Kelsale** Suffk
129 M6 **Kelsall** Ches
87 G7 **Kelshall** Herts
165 G1 **Kelsick** Cumb
201 M6 **Kelso** Border
133 G7 **Kelstedge** Derbys
136 D2 **Kelstern** Lincs
129 G5 **Kelsterton** Flints
45 K5 **Kelston** BaNES
231 L5 **Keltneyburn** P & K
176 C5 **Kelton** D & G
221 L8 **Kelty** Fife
72 C3 **Kelvedon** Essex
70 E7 **Kelvedon Hatch** Essex
2 B5 **Kelynack** Cnwll
28 B2 **Kemacott** Devon
223 G4 **Kemback** Fife
97 G3 **Kemberton** Shrops
64 E7 **Kemble** Gloucs
64 E7 **Kemble Wick** Gloucs
81 L7 **Kemerton** Worcs
62 D6 **Kemeys Commander** Mons
256 D8 **Kemnay** Abers
22 E6 **Kemp Town** Br & H
40 D6 **Kempe's Corner** Kent
63 K1 **Kempley** Gloucs
63 K1 **Kempley Green** Gloucs
82 D1 **Kemps Green** Warwks
81 J5 **Kempsey** Worcs
65 H7 **Kempsford** Gloucs
35 J1 **Kempshott** Hants
85 K5 **Kempston** Beds
85 K6 **Kempston Hardwick** Beds
95 J6 **Kempton** Shrops
52 C7 **Kemsing** Kent
40 B2 **Kemsley** Kent
53 H6 **Kemsley Street** Kent
25 H1 **Kenardington** Kent
80 B6 **Kenchester** Herefs
65 K6 **Kencot** Oxon
157 H4 **Kendal** Cumb
62 E2 **Kenderchurch** Herefs
45 K3 **Kendleshire** S Glos
42 B5 **Kenfig** Brdgnd
42 C5 **Kenfig Hill** Brdgnd
2 B4 **Kenidjack** Cnwll
83 G1 **Kenilworth** Warwks
51 J7 **Kenley** Gt Lon
96 D3 **Kenley** Shrops
260 B8 **Kenmore** Highld
231 L6 **Kenmore** P & K
13 L5 **Kenn** Devon
44 E5 **Kenn** N Som
206 C6 **Kennacraig** Ag & B
11 K6 **Kennards House** Cnwll
2 F5 **Kenneggy** Cnwll
13 J1 **Kennerleigh** Devon
138 D7 **Kennessee Green** Sefton
210 B1 **Kennet** Clacks
255 L6 **Kennethmont** Abers
88 D2 **Kennett** Cambs
13 L5 **Kennford** Devon
105 L6 **Kenninghall** Norfk
40 D6 **Kennington** Kent
66 D6 **Kennington** Oxon
222 F6 **Kennoway** Fife
30 D7 **Kenny** Somset
104 D7 **Kennyhill** Suffk
152 B3 **Kennythorpe** N York
224 C6 **Kenovay** Ag & B
259 G6 **Kensaleyre** Highld
39 K7 **Kensham Green** Kent
51 H3 **Kensington** Gt Lon
68 C3 **Kensworth** Beds
68 C3 **Kensworth Common** Beds
64 F8 **Kent End** Wilts
131 G8 **Kent Green** Ches
24 E4 **Kent Street** E Susx
39 G2 **Kent Street** Kent
63 L2 **Kent's Green** Gloucs
34 D6 **Kent's Oak** Hants
228 F4 **Kentallen** Highld
62 E2 **Kentchurch** Herefs
88 E2 **Kentford** Suffk
14 C1 **Kentisbeare** Devon

27 L2 **Kentisbury** Devon
27 L2 **Kentisbury Ford** Devon
51 H2 **Kentish Town** Gt Lon
157 G2 **Kentmere** Cumb
13 M6 **Kenton** Devon
50 F1 **Kenton** Gt Lon
180 F5 **Kenton** N u Ty
90 E2 **Kenton** Suffk
180 F5 **Kenton Bankfoot** N u Ty
237 J6 **Kentra** Highld
156 F7 **Kents Bank** Cumb
112 F5 **Kenwick** Shrops
4 D5 **Kenwyn** Cnwll
139 J8 **Kenyon** Ches
276 F3 **Keoldale** Highld
248 E6 **Keppoch** Highld
161 G4 **Kepwick** N York
99 J7 **Keresley** Covtry
99 J6 **Keresley Green** Covtry
3 K4 **Kergilliack** Cnwll
8 B6 **Kernborough** Devon
63 H3 **Kerne Bridge** Herefs
131 J4 **Kerridge** Ches
131 J4 **Kerridge-end** Ches
2 C5 **Kerris** Cnwll
94 E5 **Kerry** Powys
207 J6 **Kerrycroy** Ag & B
134 E7 **Kersall** Notts
14 C6 **Kersbrook** Devon
27 L5 **Kerscott** Devon
89 K6 **Kersey** Suffk
89 K6 **Kersey Tye** Suffk
89 K6 **Kersey Upland** Suffk
282 f4 **Kershader** W Isls
178 B2 **Kershopefoot** Cumb
82 A7 **Kersoe** Worcs
14 C1 **Kerswell** Devon
81 K6 **Kerswell Green** Worcs
2 F4 **Kerthen Wood** Cnwll
90 F6 **Kesgrave** Suffk
107 L6 **Kessingland** Suffk
107 L6 **Kessingland Beach** Suffk
5 G5 **Kestle** Cnwll
4 D3 **Kestle Mill** Cnwll
51 L6 **Keston** Gt Lon
165 J6 **Keswick** Cumb
106 E2 **Keswick** Norfk
137 G4 **Ketsby** Lincs
101 J7 **Kettering** Nhants
106 D3 **Ketteringham** Norfk
233 K7 **Kettins** Angus
69 L3 **Kettle Green** Herts
89 K5 **Kettlebaston** Suffk
222 E5 **Kettlebridge** Fife
99 G3 **Kettlebrook** Staffs
91 G3 **Kettleburgh** Suffk
176 F3 **Kettleholm** D & G
171 J7 **Kettleness** N York
131 K4 **Kettleshulme** Ches
150 B4 **Kettlesing** N York
150 B4 **Kettlesing Bottom** N York
121 L5 **Kettlestone** Norfk
135 G4 **Kettlethorpe** Lincs
275 e2 **Kettletoft** Ork
149 H2 **Kettlewell** N York
101 L3 **Ketton** Rutlnd
50 F4 **Kew** Gt Lon
44 C6 **Kewstoke** N Som
141 M6 **Kexbrough** Barns
135 H3 **Kexby** Lincs
151 L5 **Kexby** York
131 H7 **Key Green** Ches
162 D2 **Key Green** N York
53 J6 **Key Street** Kent
137 J8 **Key's Toft** Lincs
100 E2 **Keyham** Leics
18 D5 **Keyhaven** Hants
145 H3 **Keyingham** E R Yk
22 D4 **Keymer** W Susx
45 K5 **Keynsham** BaNES
86 B3 **Keysoe** Beds
86 B3 **Keysoe Row** Beds
102 A8 **Keyston** Cambs
117 G5 **Keyworth** Notts
30 B6 **Kibbear** Somset
181 G7 **Kibblesworth** Gatesd
100 F4 **Kibworth Beauchamp** Leics
100 F4 **Kibworth Harcourt** Leics
51 L4 **Kidbrooke** Gt Lon
164 E6 **Kidburngill** Cumb
106 C3 **Kidd's Moor** Norfk
97 J2 **Kiddemore Green** Staffs
97 H3 **Kidderminster** Worcs
66 B3 **Kiddington** Oxon
66 D4 **Kidlington** Oxon

49 G3 **Kidmore End** Oxon
174 C7 **Kidsdale** D & G
131 G8 **Kidsgrove** Staffs
159 G6 **Kidstones** N York
56 D3 **Kidwelly** Carmth
228 D7 **Kiel Crofts** Ag & B
189 H7 **Kielder** Nthumb
204 F3 **Kiells** Ag & B
208 C6 **Kilbarchan** Rens
247 K7 **Kilbeg** Highld
206 A6 **Kilberry** Ag & B
208 A8 **Kilbirnie** N Ayrs
216 C2 **Kilbride** Ag & B
215 L8 **Kilbride** Ag & B
207 G5 **Kilbride** Ag & B
266 B4 **Kilbuiack** Moray
116 C2 **Kilburn** Derbys
51 H2 **Kilburn** Gt Lon
161 H6 **Kilburn** N York
100 D4 **Kilby** Leics
206 C6 **Kilchamaig** Ag & B
214 D5 **Kilchattan** Ag & B
207 H8 **Kilchattan** Ag & B
228 C7 **Kilcheran** Ag & B
236 F7 **Kilchoan** Highld
204 B4 **Kilchoman** Ag & B
217 G3 **Kilchrenan** Ag & B
223 H6 **Kilconquhar** Fife
63 K2 **Kilcot** Gloucs
251 G2 **Kilcoy** Highld
207 L3 **Kilcreggan** Ag & B
161 K1 **Kildale** N York
192 F4 **Kildalloig** Ag & B
263 K5 **Kildary** Highld
206 F6 **Kildavaig** Ag & B
207 G5 **Kildavanan** Ag & B
274 B4 **Kildonan** Highld
195 G6 **Kildonan** N Ayrs
274 B4 **Kildonan Lodge** Highld
236 F3 **Kildonnan** Highld
172 D4 **Kildrochet House** D & G
255 J8 **Kildrummy** Abers
149 H6 **Kildwick** N York
206 E3 **Kilfinan** Ag & B
239 M4 **Kilfinnan** Highld
128 C6 **Kilford** Denbgs
55 K5 **Kilgetty** Pembks
183 G3 **Kilgrammie** S Ayrs
62 F7 **Kilgwrrwg Common** Mons
153 G3 **Kilham** E R Yk
202 D6 **Kilham** Nthumb
224 B6 **Kilkenneth** Ag & B
192 D3 **Kilkenzie** Ag & B
192 E4 **Kilkerran** Ag & B
26 D8 **Kilkhampton** Cnwll
133 J3 **Killamarsh** Derbys
57 H6 **Killay** Swans
208 E2 **Killearn** Stirlg
263 J8 **Killen** Highld
169 G6 **Killerby** Darltn
14 A3 **Killerton** Devon
231 G4 **Killichonan** P & K
227 G4 **Killiechronan** Ag & B
232 D3 **Killiecrankie** P & K
248 F5 **Killilan** Highld
231 G8 **Killin** Stirlg
150 C4 **Killinghall** N York
157 K5 **Killington** Cumb
28 B2 **Killington** Devon
181 G5 **Killingworth** N Tyne
4 C6 **Killiow** Cnwll
4 C5 **Killivose** Cnwll
200 F4 **Killochyett** Border
208 B5 **Kilmacolm** Inver
219 K5 **Kilmahog** Stirlg
216 B8 **Kilmahumaig** Ag & B
259 G2 **Kilmaluag** Highld
222 F3 **Kilmany** Fife
196 E3 **Kilmarnock** E Ayrs
216 C7 **Kilmartin** Ag & B
196 E3 **Kilmaurs** E Ayrs
216 C4 **Kilmelford** Ag & B
45 K8 **Kilmersdon** Somset
35 J5 **Kilmeston** Hants
192 E4 **Kilmichael** Ag & B
216 D8 **Kilmichael Glassary** Ag & B
206 B2 **Kilmichael of Inverlussa** Ag & B
15 G3 **Kilmington** Devon
32 C3 **Kilmington** Wilts
32 C4 **Kilmington Common** Wilts
32 C4 **Kilmington Street** Wilts
250 E3 **Kilmorack** Highld
216 D2 **Kilmore** Ag & B
247 K7 **Kilmore** Highld

205 M2	**Kilmory**	Ag & B
237 G6	**Kilmory**	Highld
193 K4	**Kilmory**	N Ayrs
258 D7	**Kilmuir**	Highld
258 F3	**Kilmuir**	Highld
251 J2	**Kilmuir**	Highld
263 K5	**Kilmuir**	Highld
207 K3	**Kilmun**	Ag & B
49 K3	**Kiln Green**	Wokham
180 C7	**Kiln Pit Hill**	Nthumb
204 D2	**Kilnave**	Ag & B
198 E3	**Kilncadzow**	S Lans
39 H6	**Kilndown**	Kent
165 H4	**Kilnhill**	Cumb
130 C6	**Kilnhouses**	Ches
142 C8	**Kilnhurst**	Rothm
216 C3	**Kilninver**	Ag & B
145 L4	**Kilnsea**	E R Yk
149 H2	**Kilnsey**	N York
152 F6	**Kilnwick**	E R Yk
152 C6	**Kilnwick Percy**	E R Yk
214 D5	**Kiloran**	Ag & B
194 D5	**Kilpatrick**	N Ayrs
62 F1	**Kilpeck**	Herefs
143 K2	**Kilpin**	E R Yk
143 J2	**Kilpin Pike**	E R Yk
223 K6	**Kilrenny**	Fife
84 A1	**Kilsby**	Nhants
222 C2	**Kilspindie**	P & K
172 E7	**Kilstay**	D & G
209 J3	**Kilsyth**	N Lans
250 E3	**Kiltarlity**	Highld
171 G7	**Kilton**	R & Cl
171 G7	**Kilton Thorpe**	R & Cl
258 F3	**Kilvaxter**	Highld
29 L2	**Kilve**	Somset
117 L3	**Kilvington**	Notts
196 B2	**Kilwinning**	N Ayrs
106 B3	**Kimberley**	Norfk
116 E3	**Kimberley**	Notts
133 H1	**Kimberworth**	Rothm
67 J5	**Kimble Wick**	Bucks
169 H1	**Kimblesworth**	Dur
86 B2	**Kimbolton**	Cambs
80 C3	**Kimbolton**	Herefs
100 D6	**Kimcote**	Leics
17 H6	**Kimmeridge**	Dorset
202 E6	**Kimmerston**	Nthumb
34 C2	**Kimpton**	Hants
68 F3	**Kimpton**	Herts
26 E8	**Kimworthy**	Devon
273 L2	**Kinbrace**	Highld
220 D6	**Kinbuck**	Stirlg
223 H3	**Kincaple**	Fife
210 B2	**Kincardine**	Fife
263 G2	**Kincardine**	Highld
244 D4	**Kincardine O'Neil**	Abers
233 H7	**Kinclaven**	P & K
245 L3	**Kincorth**	C Aber
265 G7	**Kincorth House**	Moray
241 M2	**Kincraig**	Highld
232 E5	**Kincraigie**	P & K
232 E5	**Kindallachan**	P & K
205 L5	**Kinerarach**	Ag & B
65 G2	**Kineton**	Gloucs
83 H5	**Kineton**	Warwks
222 B3	**Kinfauns**	P & K
196 D4	**Kinfold**	S Ayrs
132 B5	**King Sterndale**	Derbys
80 B7	**King's Acre**	Herefs
115 J8	**King's Bromley**	Staffs
101 M4	**King's Cliffe**	Nhants
82 C3	**King's Coughton**	Warwks
98 D7	**King's Heath**	Birm
99 J8	**King's Hill**	Warwks
98 C4	**King's Hill**	Wsall
120 D7	**King's Lynn**	Norfk
9 i3	**King's Mills**	Guern
139 G7	**King's Moss**	Lancs
116 C6	**King's Newton**	Derbys
98 D7	**King's Norton**	Birm
100 F3	**King's Norton**	Leics
28 B7	**King's Nympton**	Devon
80 B5	**King's Pyon**	Herefs
34 D4	**King's Somborne**	Hants
32 B8	**King's Stag**	Dorset
64 A6	**King's Stanley**	Gloucs
83 L8	**King's Sutton**	Oxon
68 F2	**King's Walden**	Herts
207 H7	**Kingarth**	Ag & B
245 J3	**Kingcausie**	Abers
62 E6	**Kingcoed**	Mons
135 L1	**Kingerby**	Lincs
11 K1	**Kingford**	Devon
65 K2	**Kingham**	Oxon
176 C4	**Kingholm Quay**	D & G
211 J2	**Kinghorn**	Fife
222 C7	**Kinglassie**	Fife
233 M4	**Kingoldrum**	Angus
222 F1	**Kingoodie**	P & K
57 G5	**Kings Bridge**	Swans
63 H2	**Kings Caple**	Herefs
81 H8	**Kings Green**	Gloucs
39 H2	**Kings Hill**	Kent
229 L4	**Kings House Hotel**	Highld
68 D6	**Kings Langley**	Herts
166 E6	**Kings Meaburn**	Cumb
200 B5	**Kings Muir**	Border
99 M7	**Kings Newnham**	Warwks
102 F8	**Kings Ripton**	Cambs
45 G3	**Kings Weston**	Bristl
35 G4	**Kings Worthy**	Hants
6 E5	**Kingsand**	Cnwll
67 L6	**Kingsash**	Bucks
223 K5	**Kingsbarns**	Fife
7 L6	**Kingsbridge**	Devon
29 H3	**Kingsbridge**	Somset
258 F5	**Kingsburgh**	Highld
51 G1	**Kingsbury**	Gt Lon
99 G4	**Kingsbury**	Warwks
31 G6	**Kingsbury Episcopi**	Somset
48 D7	**Kingsclere**	Hants
64 B7	**Kingscote**	Gloucs
27 K7	**Kingscott**	Devon
195 G5	**Kingscross**	N Ayrs
31 H5	**Kingsdon**	Somset
41 L5	**Kingsdown**	Kent
47 H1	**Kingsdown**	Swindn
46 A5	**Kingsdown**	Wilts
210 F1	**Kingseat**	Fife
67 H6	**Kingsey**	Bucks
37 J4	**Kingsfold**	W Susx
245 J2	**Kingsford**	C Aber
196 E2	**Kingsford**	E Ayrs
97 J7	**Kingsford**	Worcs
41 L1	**Kingsgate**	Kent
89 J3	**Kingshall Street**	Suffk
27 K3	**Kingsheanton**	Devon
219 J3	**Kingshouse Hotel**	Stirlg
98 F5	**Kingshurst**	Solhll
177 G8	**Kingside Hill**	Cumb
8 C1	**Kingskerswell**	Devon
222 E5	**Kingskettle**	Fife
15 K3	**Kingsland**	Dorset
80 B3	**Kingsland**	Herefs
124 D3	**Kingsland**	IOA
130 A5	**Kingsley**	Ches
36 B3	**Kingsley**	Hants
115 G2	**Kingsley**	Staffs
36 D5	**Kingsley Green**	W Susx
84 E3	**Kingsley Park**	Nhants
97 H4	**Kingslow**	Shrops
35 J8	**Kingsmead**	Hants
234 D5	**Kingsmuir**	Angus
223 J5	**Kingsmuir**	Fife
40 C7	**Kingsnorth**	Kent
98 D4	**Kingstanding**	Birm
13 K7	**Kingsteignton**	Devon
63 G1	**Kingsthorne**	Herefs
84 E3	**Kingsthorpe**	Nhants
87 G4	**Kingston**	Cambs
11 L7	**Kingston**	Cnwll
7 J5	**Kingston**	Devon
14 C5	**Kingston**	Devon
16 E1	**Kingston**	Dorset
17 J6	**Kingston**	Dorset
212 C3	**Kingston**	E Loth
21 J6	**Kingston**	E Susx
18 A3	**Kingston**	Hants
19 H7	**Kingston**	IOW
41 G5	**Kingston**	Kent
66 B7	**Kingston Bagpuize**	Oxon
67 H7	**Kingston Blount**	Oxon
32 D3	**Kingston Deverill**	Wilts
47 L2	**Kingston Lisle**	Oxon
22 F5	**Kingston near Lewes**	E Susx
116 E6	**Kingston on Soar**	Notts
267 G3	**Kingston on Spey**	Moray
16 A4	**Kingston Russell**	Dorset
44 E5	**Kingston Seymour**	N Som
30 B5	**Kingston St Mary**	Somset
67 H7	**Kingston Stert**	Oxon
144 E2	**Kingston upon Hull**	C KuH
50 F5	**Kingston upon Thames**	Gt Lon
80 A8	**Kingstone**	Herefs
30 E8	**Kingstone**	Somset
115 H5	**Kingstone**	Staffs
47 K2	**Kingstone Winslow**	Oxon
177 L7	**Kingstown**	Cumb
8 C4	**Kingswear**	Devon
245 J2	**Kingswells**	C Aber
97 K5	**Kingswinford**	Dudley
67 G3	**Kingswood**	Bucks
63 L8	**Kingswood**	Gloucs
39 L3	**Kingswood**	Kent
94 F3	**Kingswood**	Powys
45 J4	**Kingswood**	S Glos
29 K3	**Kingswood**	Somset
51 H7	**Kingswood**	Surrey
82 E1	**Kingswood**	Warwks
82 E1	**Kingswood Brook**	Warwks
79 K4	**Kingswood Common**	Herefs
97 J3	**Kingswood Common**	Staffs
136 B4	**Kingthorpe**	Lincs
79 K4	**Kington**	Herefs
45 J1	**Kington**	S Glos
82 A4	**Kington**	Worcs
46 D3	**Kington Langley**	Wilts
32 C6	**Kington Magna**	Dorset
46 C3	**Kington St Michael**	Wilts
241 K3	**Kingussie**	Highld
31 H5	**Kingweston**	Somset
257 G5	**Kinharrachie**	Abers
176 B5	**Kinharvie**	D & G
221 G4	**Kinkell Bridge**	P & K
257 J3	**Kinknockie**	Abers
211 G5	**Kinleith**	C Edin
97 G7	**Kinlet**	Shrops
271 K1	**Kinloch**	Highld
277 J5	**Kinloch**	Highld
246 E8	**Kinloch**	Highld
233 H6	**Kinloch**	P & K
233 L6	**Kinloch**	P & K
238 F2	**Kinloch Hourn**	Highld
231 J4	**Kinloch Rannoch**	P & K
219 G6	**Kinlochard**	Stirlg
276 C5	**Kinlochbervie**	Highld
238 F7	**Kinlocheil**	Highld
261 G7	**Kinlochewe**	Highld
240 F5	**Kinlochlaggan**	Highld
229 K3	**Kinlochleven**	Highld
237 K6	**Kinlochmoidart**	Highld
237 L4	**Kinlochnanuagh**	Highld
265 H7	**Kinloss**	Moray
127 K4	**Kinmel Bay**	Conwy
256 E7	**Kinmuck**	Abers
256 F8	**Kinmundy**	Abers
204 D7	**Kinnabus**	Ag & B
257 H3	**Kinnadie**	Abers
232 E4	**Kinnaird**	P & K
235 G4	**Kinnaird Castle**	Angus
266 E2	**Kinneddar**	Moray
245 J8	**Kinneff**	Abers
186 F6	**Kinnelhead**	D & G
234 F5	**Kinnell**	Angus
112 E7	**Kinnerley**	Shrops
79 L5	**Kinnersley**	Herefs
81 K6	**Kinnersley**	Worcs
79 J3	**Kinnerton**	Powys
95 J4	**Kinnerton**	Shrops
129 H7	**Kinnerton Green**	Flints
222 B6	**Kinnesswood**	P & K
168 D6	**Kinninvie**	Dur
234 B4	**Kinnordy**	Angus
117 H5	**Kinoulton**	Notts
221 K6	**Kinross**	P & K
222 C1	**Kinrossie**	P & K
68 E4	**Kinsbourne Green**	Herts
113 L3	**Kinsey Heath**	Ches
79 L2	**Kinsham**	Herefs
81 L8	**Kinsham**	Worcs
142 C5	**Kinsley**	Wakefd
17 L3	**Kinson**	Bmouth
48 A5	**Kintbury**	W Berk
264 F7	**Kintessack**	Moray
221 L4	**Kintillo**	P & K
95 K8	**Kinton**	Herefs
112 E7	**Kinton**	Shrops
256 E8	**Kintore**	Abers
205 G6	**Kintour**	Ag & B
226 C7	**Kintra**	Ag & B
216 C6	**Kintraw**	Ag & B
253 G7	**Kinveachy**	Highld
97 J6	**Kinver**	Staffs
160 C3	**Kiplin**	N York
142 C2	**Kippax**	Leeds
219 J3	**Kippen**	Stirlg
175 L4	**Kippford or Scaur**	D & G
39 G5	**Kipping's Cross**	Kent
275 c5	**Kirbister**	Ork
199 K4	**Kirburd**	Border
106 F2	**Kirby Bedon**	Norfk
117 J7	**Kirby Bellars**	Leics
107 H4	**Kirby Cane**	Norfk
99 J8	**Kirby Corner**	Covtry
73 J3	**Kirby Cross**	Essex
100 B3	**Kirby Fields**	Leics
152 D2	**Kirby Grindalythe**	N York
159 L2	**Kirby Hill**	N York
150 E2	**Kirby Hill**	N York
161 G5	**Kirby Knowle**	N York
73 J3	**Kirby le Soken**	Essex
162 D6	**Kirby Misperton**	N York
100 B3	**Kirby Muxloe**	Leics
107 H5	**Kirby Row**	Norfk
160 F4	**Kirby Sigston**	N York
152 B4	**Kirby Underdale**	E R Yk
160 E5	**Kirby Wiske**	N York
176 C5	**Kirconnel**	D & G
36 F5	**Kirdford**	W Susx
280 C4	**Kirk**	Highld
143 G5	**Kirk Bramwith**	Donc
150 F5	**Kirk Deighton**	N York
144 C2	**Kirk Ella**	E R Yk
116 D3	**Kirk Hallam**	Derbys
151 G5	**Kirk Hammerton**	N York
115 M2	**Kirk Ireton**	Derbys
115 M4	**Kirk Langley**	Derbys
169 H4	**Kirk Merrington**	Dur
154 d4	**Kirk Michael**	IOM
209 M6	**Kirk of Shotts**	N Lans
142 F6	**Kirk Sandall**	Donc
142 E4	**Kirk Smeaton**	N York
202 C7	**Kirk Yetholm**	Border
281 e7	**Kirkabister**	Shet
174 F5	**Kirkandrews**	D & G
177 K7	**Kirkandrews upon Eden**	Cumb
177 J7	**Kirkbampton**	Cumb
176 C7	**Kirkbean**	D & G
177 H7	**Kirkbride**	Cumb
160 C4	**Kirkbridge**	N York
234 D6	**Kirkbuddo**	Angus
200 C5	**Kirkburn**	Border
152 F5	**Kirkburn**	E R Yk
141 K5	**Kirkburton**	Kirk
138 E7	**Kirkby**	Knows
135 L1	**Kirkby**	Lincs
161 H2	**Kirkby**	N York
160 D4	**Kirkby Fleetham**	N York
136 A8	**Kirkby Green**	Lincs
160 C3	**Kirkby Hall**	N York
133 K8	**Kirkby in Ashfield**	Notts
118 E2	**Kirkby la Thorpe**	Lincs
157 K7	**Kirkby Lonsdale**	Cumb
148 F4	**Kirkby Malham**	N York
99 M3	**Kirkby Mallory**	Leics
160 C7	**Kirkby Malzeard**	N York
162 C5	**Kirkby Mills**	N York
136 D7	**Kirkby on Bain**	Lincs
150 D6	**Kirkby Overblow**	N York
158 D1	**Kirkby Stephen**	Cumb
166 E5	**Kirkby Thore**	Cumb
118 E6	**Kirkby Underwood**	Lincs
151 H7	**Kirkby Wharf**	N York
116 E1	**Kirkby Woodhouse**	Notts
156 B6	**Kirkby-in-Furness**	Cumb
162 B5	**Kirkbymoorside**	N York
211 J1	**Kirkcaldy**	Fife
178 C5	**Kirkcambeck**	Cumb
175 G4	**Kirkchrist**	D & G
172 C1	**Kirkcolm**	D & G
197 L8	**Kirkconnel**	D & G
175 G3	**Kirkconnell**	D & G
173 J3	**Kirkcowan**	D & G
175 H5	**Kirkcudbright**	D & G
129 H1	**Kirkdale**	Lpool
198 E4	**Kirkfieldbank**	S Lans
175 L2	**Kirkgunzeon**	D & G
138 E1	**Kirkham**	Lancs
151 M3	**Kirkham**	N York
141 L3	**Kirkhamgate**	Wakefd
180 B2	**Kirkharle**	Nthumb
167 G1	**Kirkhaugh**	Nthumb
141 J4	**Kirkheaton**	Kirk
180 B3	**Kirkheaton**	Nthumb
250 F3	**Kirkhill**	Highld
186 E5	**Kirkhope**	S Lans
178 D7	**Kirkhouse**	Cumb
143 G5	**Kirkhouse Green**	Donc
247 H5	**Kirkibost**	Highld
233 L6	**Kirkinch**	P & K
174 C4	**Kirkinner**	D & G
209 H4	**Kirkintilloch**	E Duns
164 E7	**Kirkland**	Cumb
166 F4	**Kirkland**	Cumb
197 L8	**Kirkland**	D & G
185 K5	**Kirkland**	D & G
186 F8	**Kirkland**	D & G

165 G3 **Kirkland Guards** Cumb
170 E6 **Kirkleatham** R & Cl
160 F1 **Kirklevington** S on T
107 L5 **Kirkley** Suffk
160 D6 **Kirklington** N York
134 D8 **Kirklington** Notts
178 B5 **Kirklinton** Cumb
210 F4 **Kirkliston** C Edin
174 D4 **Kirkmabreck** D & G
172 E7 **Kirkmaiden** D & G
233 G3 **Kirkmichael** P & K
183 J1 **Kirkmichael** S Ayrs
198 C4 **Kirkmuirhill** S Lans
202 E7 **Kirknewton** Nthumb
210 F5 **Kirknewton** W Loth
255 K5 **Kirkney** Abers
166 D3 **Kirkoswald** Cumb
183 G2 **Kirkoswald** S Ayrs
186 D8 **Kirkpatrick** D & G
154 C5 **Kirkpatrick** IOM
175 K1 **Kirkpatrick Durham** D & G
177 J5 **Kirkpatrick-Fleming** D & G
155 L6 **Kirksanton** Cumb
150 C8 **Kirkstall** Leeds
136 C7 **Kirkstead** Lincs
255 L5 **Kirkstile** Abers
188 C8 **Kirkstile** D & G
156 F1 **Kirkstone Pass Inn** Cumb
280 D2 **Kirkstyle** Highld
142 B3 **Kirkthorpe** Wakefd
256 B6 **Kirkton** Abers
256 E3 **Kirkton** Abers
176 C3 **Kirkton** D & G
222 F2 **Kirkton** Fife
248 C6 **Kirkton** Highld
248 E3 **Kirkton** Highld
221 G3 **Kirkton** P & K
200 B5 **Kirkton Manor** Border
233 M5 **Kirkton of Airlie** Angus
234 A7 **Kirkton of Auchterhouse** Angus
252 F2 **Kirkton of Barevan** Highld
222 C1 **Kirkton of Collace** P & K
255 H8 **Kirkton of Glenbuchat** Abers
257 H6 **Kirkton of Logie Buchan** Abers
234 E3 **Kirkton of Menmuir** Angus
234 D7 **Kirkton of Monikie** Angus
256 C5 **Kirkton of Rayne** Abers
245 H2 **Kirkton of Skene** Abers
234 B8 **Kirkton of Strathmartine** Angus
234 B7 **Kirkton of Tealing** Angus
244 D1 **Kirkton of Tough** Abers
269 J3 **Kirktown** Abers
269 K6 **Kirktown** Abers
256 E6 **Kirktown of Bourtie** Abers
245 J6 **Kirktown of Fetteresso** Abers
254 F4 **Kirktown of Mortlach** Moray
257 J6 **Kirktown of Slains** Abers
275 C4 **Kirkwall** Ork
180 B2 **Kirkwhelpington** Nthumb
130 F6 **Kirmincham** Ches
144 E5 **Kirmington** N Linc
136 C1 **Kirmond le Mire** Lincs
207 K3 **Kirn** Ag & B
234 B4 **Kirriemuir** Angus
106 F4 **Kirstead Green** Norfk
177 H4 **Kirtlebridge** D & G
88 D4 **Kirtling** Cambs
88 D4 **Kirtling Green** Suffk
66 D3 **Kirtlington** Oxon
278 C3 **Kirtomy** Highld
119 J4 **Kirton** Lincs
134 D6 **Kirton** Notts
91 G7 **Kirton** Suffk
119 J3 **Kirton End** Lincs
119 J3 **Kirton Holme** Lincs
144 B8 **Kirton in Lindsey** N Linc
208 C4 **Kirtonhill** W Duns
173 K4 **Kirwaugh** D & G
248 D4 **Kishorn** Highld
84 D3 **Kislingbury** Nhants
82 E2 **Kite Green** Warwks
65 K1 **Kitebrook** Warwks
83 L2 **Kites Hardwick** Warwks
11 J3 **Kitleigh** Cnwll
39 H6 **Kitt Green** Wigan
98 F6 **Kitt's Green** Birm
29 K6 **Kittisford** Somset
57 G7 **Kittle** Swans
245 K2 **Kittybrewster** C Aber
35 K4 **Kitwood** Hants
62 F1 **Kivernoll** Herefs

133 K3 **Kiveton Park** Rothm
135 G3 **Knaith** Lincs
135 G3 **Knaith Park** Lincs
32 D6 **Knap Corner** Dorset
50 B7 **Knaphill** Surrey
28 F4 **Knaplock** Somset
30 D5 **Knapp** Somset
34 E6 **Knapp Hill** Hants
134 E7 **Knapthorpe** Notts
162 F7 **Knapton** N York
122 F5 **Knapton** Norfk
151 J5 **Knapton** York
80 B5 **Knapton Green** Herefs
87 G3 **Knapwell** Cambs
150 E4 **Knaresborough** N York
178 F8 **Knarsdale** Nthumb
257 G3 **Knaven** Abers
160 F5 **Knayton** N York
69 H3 **Knebworth** Herts
143 J2 **Knedlington** E R Yk
134 D6 **Kneesall** Notts
87 G6 **Kneesworth** Cambs
117 J2 **Kneeton** Notts
56 E7 **Knelston** Swans
114 E4 **Knenhall** Staffs
105 K7 **Knettishall** Suffk
28 B3 **Knightacott** Devon
83 J4 **Knightcote** Warwks
114 C6 **Knightley** Staffs
114 C6 **Knightley Dale** Staffs
100 D3 **Knighton** C Leic
7 G5 **Knighton** Devon
31 K8 **Knighton** Dorset
17 L3 **Knighton** Poole
79 K1 **Knighton** Powys
30 B2 **Knighton** Somset
114 A3 **Knighton** Staffs
114 B6 **Knighton** Staffs
47 L4 **Knighton** Wilts
80 E1 **Knighton on Teme** Worcs
64 C2 **Knightsbridge** Gloucs
10 F6 **Knightsmill** Cnwll
81 G4 **Knightwick** Worcs
79 K3 **Knill** Herefs
117 L5 **Knipton** Leics
168 E1 **Knitsley** Dur
115 K2 **Kniveton** Derbys
166 F5 **Knock** Cumb
247 L6 **Knock** Highld
267 L5 **Knock** Moray
282 g3 **Knock** W Isls
207 K6 **Knock Castle** N Ayrs
274 F2 **Knockally** Highld
271 H6 **Knockan** Highld
254 D3 **Knockando** Moray
250 F3 **Knockbain** Highld
263 H8 **Knockbain** Highld
279 L4 **Knockdee** Highld
46 B1 **Knockdown** Wilts
183 H4 **Knockeen** S Ayrs
195 G5 **Knockenkelly** N Ayrs
196 D3 **Knockentiber** E Ayrs
52 C4 **Knockhall** Kent
51 M7 **Knockholt** Kent
52 A7 **Knockholt Pound** Kent
112 E7 **Knockin** Shrops
196 E3 **Knockinlaw** E Ayrs
52 C6 **Knockmill** Kent
172 B2 **Knocknain** D & G
184 F6 **Knocksheen** D & G
175 J1 **Knockvennie Smithy** D & G
91 K3 **Knodishall** Suffk
31 G6 **Knole** Somset
45 H2 **Knole Park** S Glos
130 F4 **Knolls Green** Ches
112 F4 **Knolton** Wrexhm
32 F3 **Knook** Wilts
101 H2 **Knossington** Leics
147 G6 **Knott End-on-Sea** Lancs
85 K3 **Knotting** Beds
85 K3 **Knotting Green** Beds
142 D3 **Knottingley** Wakefd
129 J1 **Knotty Ash** Lpool
68 B8 **Knotty Green** Bucks
96 D8 **Knowbury** Shrops
183 H8 **Knowe** D & G
184 F5 **Knowehead** D & G
195 L8 **Knoweside** S Ayrs
88 F7 **Knowl Green** Essex
49 K3 **Knowl Hill** W & M
45 J5 **Knowle** Bristl
27 J3 **Knowle** Devon
13 H2 **Knowle** Devon
14 B1 **Knowle** Devon
14 B6 **Knowle** Devon

96 D8 **Knowle** Shrops
98 F8 **Knowle** Solhll
29 H2 **Knowle** Somset
14 B3 **Knowle Cross** Devon
148 A8 **Knowle Green** Lancs
50 C5 **Knowle Hill** Surrey
30 E8 **Knowle St Giles** Somset
177 L7 **Knowlefield** Cumb
17 K1 **Knowlton** Dorset
41 J4 **Knowlton** Kent
138 E8 **Knowsley** Knows
28 E6 **Knowstone** Devon
150 C4 **Knox** N York
39 K5 **Knox Bridge** Kent
95 G8 **Knucklas** Powys
85 H2 **Knuston** Nhants
130 E4 **Knutsford** Ches
114 C2 **Knutton** Staffs
131 H8 **Knypersley** Staffs
141 G4 **Krumlin** Calder
3 J7 **Kuggar** Cnwll
248 B6 **Kyle of Lochalsh** Highld
248 B6 **Kyleakin** Highld
248 C7 **Kylerhea** Highld
282 f6 **Kyles Scalpay** W Isls
271 H1 **Kylesku** Highld
238 C5 **Kylesmorar** Highld
271 H1 **Kylestrome** Highld
203 G5 **Kyloe** Nthumb
80 E8 **Kynaston** Herefs
112 E7 **Kynaston** Shrops
113 L8 **Kynnersley** Wrekin
80 E3 **Kyre Green** Worcs
80 E3 **Kyre Park** Worcs
80 E2 **Kyrewood** Worcs
29 J6 **Kyrle** Somset

L

9 k1 **L'Ancresse** Guern
9 h3 **L'Eree** Guern
9 a2 **L'Etacq** Jersey
9 j3 **La Bellieuse** Guern
9 k1 **La Fontenelle** Guern
9 j4 **La Fosse** Guern
9 k2 **La Greve** Guern
9 b1 **La Greve de Lecq** Jersey
9 e3 **La Hougue Bie** Jersey
9 h3 **La Houguette** Guern
9 j2 **La Passee** Guern
9 a3 **La Pulente** Jersey
9 f4 **La Rocque** Jersey
9 j2 **La Rousaillerie** Guern
9 j3 **La Villette** Guern
282 g3 **Lacadal** W Isls
282 f4 **Lacasaigh** W Isls
145 G6 **Laceby** NE Lin
67 K7 **Lacey Green** Bucks
130 D5 **Lach Dennis** Ches
170 D6 **Lackenby** R & Cl
88 F1 **Lackford** Suffk
88 F1 **Lackford Green** Suffk
46 C5 **Lacock** Wilts
83 K3 **Ladbroke** Warwks
114 F1 **Ladderedge** Staffs
39 H4 **Laddingford** Kent
119 L1 **Lade Bank** Lincs
4 E5 **Ladock** Cnwll
156 B5 **Lady Hall** Cumb
275 e2 **Lady Village** Ork
88 E3 **Lady's Green** Suffk
222 E5 **Ladybank** Fife
11 L5 **Ladycross** Cnwll
198 F7 **Ladygill** S Lans
202 D3 **Ladykirk** Border
63 H1 **Ladyridge** Herefs
98 D6 **Ladywood** Birm
81 K3 **Ladywood** Worcs
185 L5 **Lag** D & G
237 J8 **Laga** Highld
204 F7 **Lagavulin** Ag & B
193 K4 **Lagg** N Ayrs
240 A4 **Laggan** Highld
241 G5 **Laggan** Highld
277 G4 **Laid** Highld
260 E2 **Laide** Highld
236 F3 **Laig** Highld
196 F2 **Laigh Clunch** E Ayrs
196 F3 **Laigh Fenwick** E Ayrs
197 J7 **Laigh Glenmuir** E Ayrs
209 J8 **Laighstonehall** S Lans
52 E1 **Laindon** Essex
272 E6 **Lairg** Highld

141 J1 **Laisterdyke** Brad
166 B4 **Laithes** Cumb
27 K4 **Lake** Devon
12 C5 **Lake** Devon
19 K7 **Lake** IOW
17 J4 **Lake** Poole
33 K3 **Lake** Wilts
104 E6 **Lakenheath** Suffk
36 F4 **Laker's Green** Surrey
103 L4 **Lakesend** Norfk
156 E5 **Lakeside** Cumb
50 D5 **Laleham** Surrey
42 C5 **Laleston** Brdgnd
199 L3 **Lamancha** Border
3 J5 **Lamanva** Cnwll
89 H8 **Lamarsh** Essex
122 E7 **Lamas** Norfk
148 C8 **Lamb Roe** Lancs
202 A4 **Lambden** Border
39 H6 **Lamberhurst** Kent
39 G6 **Lamberhurst Down** Kent
213 L7 **Lamberton** Border
51 J3 **Lambeth** Gt Lon
88 E4 **Lambfair Green** Suffk
117 H2 **Lambley** Notts
178 F7 **Lambley** Nthumb
47 L3 **Lambourn** W Berk
70 C8 **Lambourne End** Essex
37 K3 **Lambs Green** W Susx
54 E3 **Lambston** Pembks
6 A2 **Lamellion** Cnwll
12 B7 **Lamerton** Devon
181 G7 **Lamesley** Gatesd
199 G7 **Lamington** S Lans
195 G5 **Lamlash** N Ayrs
165 L3 **Lamonby** Cumb
5 H2 **Lamorick** Cnwll
2 C6 **Lamorna** Cnwll
4 E6 **Lamorran** Cnwll
5 L2 **Lampen** Cnwll
77 G5 **Lampeter** Cerdgn
55 K4 **Lampeter Velfrey** Pembks
55 G6 **Lamphey** Pembks
164 E6 **Lamplugh** Cumb
101 G8 **Lamport** Nhants
31 L4 **Lamyatt** Somset
11 K1 **Lana** Devon
11 L3 **Lana** Devon
198 E4 **Lanark** S Lans
3 K6 **Lanarth** Cnwll
147 J3 **Lancaster** Lancs
63 G7 **Lancaut** Gloucs
168 F1 **Lanchester** Dur
21 L6 **Lancing** W Susx
2 A6 **Land's End** Cnwll
275 G2 **Land-hallow** Highld
87 K2 **Landbeach** Cambs
27 H6 **Landcross** Devon
245 G3 **Landerberry** Abers
34 B7 **Landford** Wilts
56 E6 **Landimore** Swans
27 L4 **Landkey** Devon
27 L4 **Landkey Town** Devon
57 J5 **Landore** Swans
6 D3 **Landrake** Cnwll
7 M2 **Landscove** Devon
55 G4 **Landshipping** Pembks
11 L6 **Landue** Cnwll
6 E3 **Landulph** Cnwll
88 C2 **Landwade** Suffk
98 C2 **Landywood** Staffs
4 D3 **Lane** Cnwll
140 C1 **Lane Bottom** Lancs
49 K1 **Lane End** Bucks
5 H1 **Lane End** Cnwll
35 H5 **Lane End** Hants
52 C4 **Lane End** Kent
148 F6 **Lane End** Lancs
130 D2 **Lane End** Warrtn
32 D2 **Lane End** Wilts
155 K4 **Lane End Waberthwaite** Cumb
115 L4 **Lane Ends** Derbys
168 F4 **Lane Ends** Dur
140 B2 **Lane Ends** Lancs
149 H7 **Lane Ends** N York
97 K3 **Lane Green** Staffs
168 E8 **Lane Head** Dur
139 J8 **Lane Head** Wigan
98 B3 **Lane Head** Wsall
147 H7 **Lane Heads** Lancs
140 B3 **Lane Side** Lancs
11 J5 **Laneast** Cnwll
134 F4 **Laneham** Notts
167 J2 **Lanehead** Dur

328 Lanehead - Lennoxtown

179 H2 **Lanehead** Nthumb
149 G7 **Laneshaw Bridge** Lancs
12 A3 **Langaford** Devon
30 C5 **Langaller** Somset
117 J4 **Langar** Notts
208 C4 **Langbank** Rens
149 K5 **Langbar** N York
170 D8 **Langbaurgh** N York
148 E3 **Langcliffe** N York
163 G4 **Langdale End** N York
11 K4 **Langdon** Cnwll
167 K4 **Langdon Beck** Dur
19 G2 **Langdown** Hants
222 E6 **Langdyke** Fife
72 E3 **Langenhoe** Essex
86 D7 **Langford** Beds
14 B2 **Langford** Devon
71 K5 **Langford** Essex
44 F6 **Langford** N Som
135 G7 **Langford** Notts
65 K6 **Langford** Oxon
29 K6 **Langford Budville** Somset
32 C5 **Langham** Dorset
89 L8 **Langham** Essex
121 M3 **Langham** Norfk
101 J1 **Langham** Rutlnd
89 K1 **Langham** Suffk
72 E1 **Langham Moor** Essex
72 F1 **Langham Wick** Essex
139 L1 **Langho** Lancs
177 L2 **Langholm** D & G
57 H7 **Langland** Swans
201 G6 **Langlee** Border
131 J5 **Langley** Ches
116 D2 **Langley** Derbys
64 E2 **Langley** Gloucs
19 G3 **Langley** Hants
69 G3 **Langley** Herts
39 K3 **Langley** Kent
179 J6 **Langley** Nthumb
65 L4 **Langley** Oxon
140 C6 **Langley** Rochdl
50 C3 **Langley** Slough
29 K5 **Langley** Somset
36 B5 **Langley** W Susx
82 E3 **Langley** Warwks
46 D4 **Langley Burrell** Wilts
179 J6 **Langley Castle** Nthumb
115 M4 **Langley Common** Derbys
115 M4 **Langley Green** Derbys
72 C3 **Langley Green** Essex
82 E3 **Langley Green** Warwks
87 J8 **Langley Lower Green** Essex
29 K5 **Langley Marsh** Somset
116 D2 **Langley Mill** Derbys
169 H3 **Langley Moor** Dur
169 G2 **Langley Park** Dur
107 H3 **Langley Street** Norfk
87 J8 **Langley Upper Green** Essex
68 D7 **Langleybury** Herts
23 L6 **Langney** E Susx
134 B2 **Langold** Notts
11 K5 **Langore** Cnwll
30 F5 **Langport** Somset
119 J2 **Langrick** Lincs
45 L5 **Langridge** BaNES
27 K6 **Langridge Ford** Devon
165 G2 **Langrigg** Cumb
35 L6 **Langrish** Hants
141 K7 **Langsett** Barns
220 D4 **Langside** P & K
20 B6 **Langstone** Hants
44 D1 **Langstone** Newpt
160 C4 **Langthorne** N York
150 E2 **Langthorpe** N York
159 H2 **Langthwaite** N York
152 F3 **Langtoft** E R Yk
102 C1 **Langtoft** Lincs
168 F6 **Langton** Dur
136 D6 **Langton** Lincs
137 G5 **Langton** Lincs
152 B2 **Langton** N York
136 C4 **Langton by Wragby** Lincs
38 E5 **Langton Green** Kent
106 C8 **Langton Green** Suffk
16 B6 **Langton Herring** Dorset
17 K6 **Langton Matravers** Dorset
27 H7 **Langtree** Devon
27 H7 **Langtree Week** Devon
166 D4 **Langwathby** Cumb
274 F3 **Langwell House** Highld
135 L4 **Langworth** Lincs
12 C4 **Langworthy** Devon
5 H2 **Lanivet** Cnwll
5 G4 **Lanjeth** Cnwll
10 F7 **Lank** Cnwll
5 J3 **Lanlivery** Cnwll
3 J3 **Lanner** Cnwll
11 K7 **Lanoy** Cnwll
5 L3 **Lanreath** Cnwll
5 K4 **Lansallos** Cnwll
10 F6 **Lanteglos** Cnwll
5 K4 **Lanteglos Highway** Cnwll
189 G2 **Lanton** Border
202 E6 **Lanton** Nthumb
13 G1 **Lapford** Devon
204 F7 **Laphroaig** Ag & B
97 K1 **Lapley** Staffs
82 E1 **Lapworth** Warwks
227 K3 **Larachbeg** Highld
209 M3 **Larbert** Falk
147 H7 **Larbreck** Lancs
256 A5 **Largie** Abers
206 E2 **Largiemore** Ag & B
223 H5 **Largoward** Fife
207 K7 **Largs** N Ayrs
195 G6 **Largybeg** N Ayrs
195 G6 **Largymore** N Ayrs
14 C3 **Larkbeare** Devon
207 L4 **Larkfield** Inver
52 F7 **Larkfield** Kent
198 C3 **Larkhall** S Lans
33 K2 **Larkhill** Wilts
105 K5 **Larling** Norfk
168 C7 **Lartington** Dur
64 B8 **Lasborough** Gloucs
35 K2 **Lasham** Hants
12 B2 **Lashbrook** Devon
39 L5 **Lashenden** Kent
131 H8 **Lask Edge** Staffs
221 K8 **Lassodie** Fife
211 J6 **Lasswade** Mdloth
162 C4 **Lastingham** N York
31 G2 **Latcham** Somset
69 K3 **Latchford** Herts
67 G6 **Latchford** Oxon
72 C7 **Latchingdon** Essex
12 A7 **Latchley** Cnwll
139 K8 **Lately Common** Warrtn
85 G6 **Lathbury** M Keyn
275 G2 **Latheron** Highld
275 G2 **Latheronwheel** Highld
223 H5 **Lathones** Fife
68 C7 **Latimer** Bucks
45 K2 **Latteridge** S Glos
32 B5 **Lattiford** Somset
65 G7 **Latton** Wilts
201 H4 **Lauder** Border
56 B3 **Laugharne** Carmth
135 G4 **Laughterton** Lincs
23 H4 **Laughton** E Susx
100 E5 **Laughton** Leics
143 L8 **Laughton** Lincs
118 E5 **Laughton** Lincs
133 K2 **Laughton-en-le-Morthen** Rothm
11 J2 **Launcells** Cnwll
11 K2 **Launcells Cross** Cnwll
11 L5 **Launceston** Cnwll
66 F3 **Launton** Oxon
235 H1 **Laurencekirk** Abers
175 H2 **Laurieston** D & G
210 B3 **Laurieston** Falk
85 H4 **Lavendon** M Keyn
89 J5 **Lavenham** Suffk
43 J8 **Lavernock** V Glam
178 B6 **Laversdale** Cumb
33 L5 **Laverstock** Wilts
35 G1 **Laverstoke** Hants
82 C8 **Laverton** Gloucs
160 B7 **Laverton** N York
45 M8 **Laverton** Somset
129 J8 **Lavister** Wrexhm
209 L8 **Law** S Lans
209 L8 **Law Hill** S Lans
231 J7 **Lawers** P & K
73 G1 **Lawford** Essex
29 L4 **Lawford** Somset
221 K2 **Lawgrove** P & K
11 L6 **Lawhitton** Cnwll
148 D3 **Lawkland** N York
148 D3 **Lawkland Green** N York
96 F2 **Lawley** Wrekin
114 C6 **Lawnhead** Staffs
68 F3 **Lawrence End** Herts
55 G5 **Lawrenny** Pembks
89 H4 **Lawshall** Suffk
89 H4 **Lawshall Green** Suffk
80 B3 **Lawton** Herefs
282 f4 **Laxay** W Isls
282 g3 **Laxdale** W Isls
154 f5 **Laxey** IOM
91 G1 **Laxfield** Suffk
276 C7 **Laxford Bridge** Highld
281 e5 **Laxo** Shet
143 K3 **Laxton** E R Yk
101 L4 **Laxton** Nhants
134 E6 **Laxton** Notts
149 J7 **Laycock** Brad
72 D3 **Layer Breton** Essex
72 D4 **Layer Marney** Essex
72 D3 **Layer-de-la-Haye** Essex
89 L7 **Layham** Suffk
48 A5 **Layland's Green** W Berk
15 J2 **Laymore** Dorset
50 C1 **Layter's Green** Bucks
152 A7 **Laytham** E R Yk
177 H7 **Laythes** Cumb
170 D6 **Lazenby** R & Cl
166 D3 **Lazonby** Cumb
9 i4 **Le Bigard** Guern
9 j4 **Le Bourg** Guern
9 f4 **Le Bourg** Jersey
9 i3 **Le Gron** Guern
9 e4 **Le Haguais** Jersey
9 e4 **Le Hocq** Jersey
9 j2 **Le Villocq** Guern
132 F8 **Lea** Derbys
63 K3 **Lea** Herefs
135 G2 **Lea** Lincs
95 K2 **Lea** Shrops
95 J5 **Lea** Shrops
46 D2 **Lea** Wilts
132 F8 **Lea Bridge** Derbys
115 G6 **Lea Heath** Staffs
99 G5 **Lea Marston** Warwks
138 F2 **Lea Town** Lancs
158 D5 **Lea Yeat** Cumb
251 H3 **Leachkin** Highld
200 B2 **Leadburn** Mdloth
70 E4 **Leaden Roding** Essex
118 B1 **Leadenham** Lincs
180 D8 **Leadgate** Dur
180 D7 **Leadgate** Gatesd
186 C3 **Leadhills** S Lans
39 M3 **Leadingcross Green** Kent
132 E3 **Leadmill** Derbys
65 L4 **Leafield** Oxon
68 D2 **Leagrave** Luton
130 D6 **Leahead** Ches
160 F4 **Leake** N York
119 L1 **Leake Common Side** Lincs
162 D1 **Lealholm** N York
162 D1 **Lealholm Side** N York
259 H4 **Lealt** Highld
132 E4 **Leam** Derbys
83 K2 **Leamington Hastings** Warwks
83 H2 **Leamington Spa** Warwks
169 J1 **Leamside** Dur
23 K5 **Leap Cross** E Susx
157 H6 **Leasgill** Cumb
118 E2 **Leasingham** Lincs
169 H4 **Leasingthorne** Dur
50 F7 **Leatherhead** Surrey
150 B6 **Leathley** N York
113 G7 **Leaton** Shrops
96 E1 **Leaton** Wrekin
40 C4 **Leaveland** Kent
89 J7 **Leavenheath** Suffk
152 B3 **Leavening** N York
51 L6 **Leaves Green** Gt Lon
163 K6 **Lebberston** N York
65 J7 **Lechlade** Gloucs
204 D3 **Lecht Gruinart** Ag & B
157 K7 **Leck** Lancs
231 K7 **Leckbuie** P & K
34 E3 **Leckford** Hants
84 D7 **Leckhampstead** Bucks
48 B4 **Leckhampstead** W Berk
48 B4 **Leckhampstead Thicket** W Berk
64 D3 **Leckhampton** Gloucs
261 K2 **Leckmelm** Highld
43 J6 **Leckwith** V Glam
152 F7 **Leconfield** E R Yk
228 E7 **Ledaig** Ag & B
67 L3 **Ledburn** Bucks
81 G7 **Ledbury** Herefs
80 F8 **Leddington** Gloucs
80 A5 **Ledgemoor** Herefs
80 A3 **Ledicot** Herefs
271 H5 **Ledmore Junction** Highld
129 H5 **Ledsham** Ches
142 C2 **Ledsham** Leeds
142 C2 **Ledston** Leeds
142 C2 **Ledston Luck** Leeds
7 L5 **Ledstone** Devon
66 B2 **Ledwell** Oxon
27 H2 **Lee** Devon
51 K4 **Lee** Gt Lon
34 D7 **Lee** Hants
112 F5 **Lee** Shrops
113 J6 **Lee Brockhurst** Shrops
52 E2 **Lee Chapel** Essex
67 M6 **Lee Clump** Bucks
67 M6 **Lee Common** Bucks
130 C7 **Lee Green** Ches
7 H4 **Lee Mill** Devon
7 H3 **Lee Moor** Devon
37 L2 **Lee Street** Surrey
19 J3 **Lee-on-the-Solent** Hants
96 B4 **Leebotwood** Shrops
146 E2 **Leece** Cumb
68 B2 **Leedon** Beds
39 K3 **Leeds** Kent
141 L1 **Leeds** Leeds
2 F4 **Leedstown** Cnwll
131 K8 **Leek** Staffs
83 G2 **Leek Wootton** Warwks
141 G1 **Leeming** Brad
160 D5 **Leeming** N York
160 D4 **Leeming Bar** N York
149 J8 **Lees** Brad
115 L4 **Lees** Derbys
140 E6 **Lees** Oldham
115 L4 **Lees Green** Derbys
178 D5 **Lees Hill** Cumb
101 H1 **Leesthorpe** Leics
129 G7 **Leeswood** Flints
222 C3 **Leetown** P & K
130 C5 **Leftwich** Ches
61 K4 **Legar** Powys
137 G3 **Legbourne** Lincs
165 K6 **Legburthwaite** Cumb
201 J4 **Legerwood** Border
136 B3 **Legsby** Lincs
100 D3 **Leicester** C Leic
100 B3 **Leicester Forest East** Leics
28 C8 **Leigh** Devon
16 B1 **Leigh** Dorset
64 C2 **Leigh** Gloucs
38 E4 **Leigh** Kent
95 H3 **Leigh** Shrops
37 K2 **Leigh** Surrey
139 K7 **Leigh** Wigan
64 F8 **Leigh** Wilts
81 H4 **Leigh** Worcs
53 H2 **Leigh Beck** Essex
46 C3 **Leigh Delamere** Wilts
40 A8 **Leigh Green** Kent
197 J1 **Leigh Knoweglass** S Lans
17 K3 **Leigh Park** Dorset
81 H5 **Leigh Sinton** Worcs
31 M2 **Leigh upon Mendip** Somset
45 H4 **Leigh Woods** N Som
53 H2 **Leigh-on-Sea** Sthend
29 J4 **Leighland Chapel** Somset
98 D3 **Leighswood** W Mids
46 B1 **Leighterton** Gloucs
159 L6 **Leighton** N York
94 F2 **Leighton** Powys
96 E2 **Leighton** Shrops
32 B2 **Leighton** Somset
102 C8 **Leighton Bromswold** Cambs
68 A2 **Leighton Buzzard** Beds
80 B2 **Leinthall Earls** Herefs
80 A1 **Leinthall Starkes** Herefs
95 K8 **Leintwardine** Herefs
100 B5 **Leire** Leics
91 K3 **Leiston** Suffk
233 L6 **Leitfie** P & K
211 J4 **Leith** C Edin
202 B4 **Leitholm** Border
2 E4 **Lelant** Cnwll
145 G1 **Lelley** E R Yk
97 G8 **Lem Hill** Worcs
191 G4 **Lemmington Hall** Nthumb
202 B6 **Lempitlaw** Border
282 g5 **Lemreway** W Isls
69 G4 **Lemsford** Herts
82 B6 **Lenchwick** Worcs
182 E5 **Lendalfoot** S Ayrs
219 J6 **Lendrick** Stirlg
257 L3 **Lendrum Terrace** Abers
40 A5 **Lenham** Kent
40 B5 **Lenham Heath** Kent
250 F6 **Lenie** Highld
202 C5 **Lennel** Border
174 F4 **Lennox Plunton** D & G
209 G3 **Lennoxtown** E Duns

50 A3	**Lent** Bucks	
116 F4	**Lenton** C Nott	
118 D5	**Lenton** Lincs	
122 B7	**Lenwade** Norfk	
209 H4	**Lenzie** E Duns	
244 C2	**Leochel-Cushnie** Abers	
98 E2	**Leomansley** Staffs	
80 C3	**Leominster** Herefs	
64 A6	**Leonard Stanley** Gloucs	
9 b2	**Leoville** Jersey	
19 G4	**Lepe** Hants	
258 B6	**Lephin** Highld	
152 A4	**Leppington** N York	
141 K5	**Lepton** Kirk	
5 K3	**Lerryn** Cnwll	
281 e6	**Lerwick** Shet	
9 h3	**Les Arquets** Guern	
9 k3	**Les Hubits** Guern	
9 i3	**Les Lohiers** Guern	
9 i4	**Les Murchez** Guern	
9 j4	**Les Nicolles** Guern	
9 j2	**Les Quartiers** Guern	
9 b3	**Les Quennevais** Jersey	
9 i3	**Les Sages** Guern	
9 i4	**Les Villets** Guern	
191 J4	**Lesbury** Nthumb	
255 M6	**Leslie** Abers	
222 D6	**Leslie** Fife	
198 D5	**Lesmahagow** S Lans	
11 G4	**Lesnewth** Cnwll	
123 H6	**Lessingham** Norfk	
165 H1	**Lessonhall** Cumb	
3 K6	**Lestowder** Cnwll	
172 C2	**Leswalt** D & G	
68 F7	**Letchmore Heath** Herts	
86 E8	**Letchworth** Herts	
48 A2	**Letcombe Bassett** Oxon	
48 A2	**Letcombe Regis** Oxon	
234 E5	**Letham** Angus	
189 J4	**Letham** Border	
210 B2	**Letham** Falk	
222 E4	**Letham** Fife	
235 G6	**Letham Grange** Angus	
233 H7	**Lethendy** P & K	
255 M7	**Lethenty** Abers	
256 E4	**Lethenty** Abers	
91 G4	**Letheringham** Suffk	
122 B4	**Letheringsett** Norfk	
51 M7	**Lett's Green** Kent	
13 G5	**Lettaford** Devon	
260 F5	**Letterewe** Highld	
248 D7	**Letterfearn** Highld	
239 L5	**Letterfinlay Lodge Hotel** Highld	
237 L3	**Lettermorar** Highld	
261 K2	**Letters** Highld	
186 D2	**Lettershaw** S Lans	
74 F6	**Letterston** Pembks	
253 K7	**Lettoch** Highld	
254 B5	**Lettoch** Highld	
79 L6	**Letton** Herefs	
79 L1	**Letton** Herefs	
69 H5	**Letty Green** Herts	
133 L2	**Letwell** Rothm	
223 H3	**Leuchars** Fife	
282 g5	**Leumrabhagh** W Isls	
282 g4	**Leurbost** W Isls	
5 G5	**Levalsa Meor** Cnwll	
114 D8	**Levedale** Staffs	
70 C2	**Level's Green** Essex	
53 H6	**Leven** E R Yk	
222 F7	**Leven** Fife	
57 G5	**Levens** Cumb	
69 K3	**Levens Green** Herts	
31 G1	**Levenshulme** Manch	
281 d8	**Levenwick** Shet	
282 d6	**Leverburgh** W Isls	
103 J1	**Leverington** Cambs	
68 D5	**Leverstock Green** Herts	
119 L2	**Leverton** Lincs	
90 F7	**Levington** Suffk	
162 E4	**Levisham** N York	
65 L6	**Lew** Oxon	
11 K6	**Lewannick** Cnwll	
12 B5	**Lewdown** Devon	
22 F5	**Lewes** E Susx	
31 K8	**Leweston** Dorset	
54 F2	**Leweston** Pembks	
79 L4	**Lewis Wych** Herefs	
51 K4	**Lewisham** Gt Lon	
250 F6	**Lewiston** Highld	
67 H7	**Lewknor** Oxon	
11 L2	**Leworthy** Devon	
28 B3	**Leworthy** Devon	
40 C3	**Lewson Street** Kent	
147 J8	**Lewth** Lancs	
12 B5	**Lewtrenchard** Devon	
72 D2	**Lexden** Essex	
30 C4	**Lexworthy** Somset	
5 K2	**Ley** Cnwll	
68 C6	**Ley Hill** Bucks	
52 E7	**Leybourne** Kent	
159 K4	**Leyburn** N York	
114 B2	**Leycett** Staffs	
68 F2	**Leygreen** Herts	
139 H3	**Leyland** Lancs	
139 H7	**Leyland Green** St Hel	
245 G1	**Leylodge** Abers	
269 J5	**Leys** Abers	
233 K7	**Leys** Angus	
234 B5	**Leys of Cossans** Angus	
53 M5	**Leysdown-on-Sea** Kent	
234 F6	**Leysmill** Angus	
80 D2	**Leysters** Herefs	
51 K2	**Leyton** Gt Lon	
51 K2	**Leytonstone** Gt Lon	
11 L6	**Lezant** Cnwll	
154 f3	**Lezayre** IOM	
3 H4	**Lezerea** Cnwll	
266 F4	**Lhanbryde** Moray	
60 F2	**Libanus** Powys	
199 G4	**Libberton** S Lans	
211 J5	**Liberton** C Edin	
98 E2	**Lichfield** Staffs	
98 C8	**Lickey** Worcs	
81 M1	**Lickey End** Worcs	
98 B8	**Lickey Rock** Worcs	
36 D5	**Lickfold** W Susx	
12 B6	**Liddaton Green** Devon	
228 B3	**Liddesdale** Highld	
47 J3	**Liddington** Swindn	
132 F4	**Lidgate** Derbys	
88 E4	**Lidgate** Suffk	
143 G7	**Lidget** Donc	
134 C6	**Lidgett** Notts	
24 F4	**Lidham Hill** E Susx	
85 K7	**Lidlington** Beds	
53 G6	**Lidsing** Kent	
222 E1	**Liff** Angus	
98 D7	**Lifford** Birm	
11 M5	**Lifton** Devon	
11 M5	**Liftondown** Devon	
140 F4	**Lighthazles** Calder	
83 H4	**Lighthorne** Warwks	
83 H4	**Lighthorne Heath** Warwks	
50 B6	**Lightwater** Surrey	
114 E3	**Lightwood** C Stke	
113 L3	**Lightwood Green** Ches	
112 F3	**Lightwood Green** Wrexhm	
100 C8	**Lilbourne** Nhants	
190 E1	**Lilburn Tower** Nthumb	
114 A8	**Lilleshall** Wrekin	
68 E2	**Lilley** Herts	
48 C3	**Lilley** W Berk	
201 H8	**Lilliesleaf** Border	
84 D7	**Lillingstone Dayrell** Bucks	
84 D7	**Lillingstone Lovell** Bucks	
31 K8	**Lillington** Dorset	
17 K4	**Lilliput** Poole	
29 L2	**Lilstock** Somset	
97 G1	**Lilyhurst** Shrops	
139 J4	**Limbrick** Lancs	
68 D2	**Limbury** Luton	
64 A1	**Lime Street** Worcs	
79 L2	**Limebrook** Herefs	
140 B5	**Limefield** Bury	
197 K1	**Limekilnburn** S Lans	
210 E2	**Limekilns** Fife	
209 M5	**Limerigg** Falk	
19 G7	**Limerstone** IOW	
167 J1	**Limestone Brae** Nthumb	
31 J6	**Limington** Somset	
197 J5	**Limmerhaugh** E Ayrs	
107 H3	**Limpenhoe** Norfk	
45 M6	**Limpley Stoke** Wilts	
51 L8	**Limpsfield** Surrey	
51 L8	**Limpsfield Chart** Surrey	
116 F1	**Linby** Notts	
36 C5	**Linchmere** W Susx	
176 C3	**Lincluden** D & G	
135 K5	**Lincoln** Lincs	
81 J2	**Lincomb** Worcs	
7 L6	**Lincombe** Devon	
156 C7	**Lindal in Furness** Cumb	
156 F6	**Lindale** Cumb	
22 E2	**Lindfield** W Susx	
36 B4	**Lindford** Hants	
141 H4	**Lindley** Kirk	
150 B6	**Lindley Green** N York	
130 F4	**Lindow End** Ches	
80 F2	**Lindridge** Worcs	
70 F2	**Lindsell** Essex	
89 K6	**Lindsey** Suffk	
89 K6	**Lindsey Tye** Suffk	
30 E4	**Liney** Somset	
18 B2	**Linford** Hants	
52 E3	**Linford** Thurr	
149 K8	**Lingbob** Brad	
79 L2	**Lingen** Herefs	
38 B4	**Lingfield** Surrey	
130 A2	**Lingley Green** Warrtn	
107 G2	**Lingwood** Norfk	
258 F3	**Linicro** Highld	
64 B1	**Linkend** Worcs	
48 A7	**Linkenholt** Hants	
24 E2	**Linkhill** Kent	
11 L7	**Linkinhorne** Cnwll	
211 J1	**Linktown** Fife	
266 E4	**Linksness** Moray	
95 J5	**Linley** Shrops	
80 F4	**Linley Green** Herefs	
96 F4	**Linleygreen** Shrops	
210 C4	**Linlithgow** W Loth	
190 C5	**Linshiels** Nthumb	
272 D8	**Linsidemore** Highld	
67 M2	**Linslade** Beds	
107 G7	**Linstead Parva** Suffk	
178 A7	**Linstock** Cumb	
82 B1	**Linthurst** Worcs	
141 H5	**Linthwaite** Kirk	
213 H7	**Lintlaw** Border	
267 K3	**Lintmill** Moray	
202 B7	**Linton** Border	
88 B6	**Linton** Cambs	
115 M8	**Linton** Derbys	
63 K2	**Linton** Herefs	
39 J3	**Linton** Kent	
150 E6	**Linton** Leeds	
149 H3	**Linton** N York	
191 K7	**Linton** Nthumb	
115 M8	**Linton Heath** Derbys	
63 K2	**Linton Hill** Gloucs	
151 G4	**Linton-on-Ouse** N York	
18 B2	**Linwood** Hants	
136 B2	**Linwood** Lincs	
208 D6	**Linwood** Rens	
283 c9	**Lionacleit** W Isls	
282 h1	**Lional** W Isls	
23 J4	**Lions Green** E Susx	
36 C4	**Liphook** Hants	
114 A5	**Lipley** Shrops	
129 G1	**Liscard** Wirral	
28 F4	**Liscombe** Somset	
6 B2	**Liskeard** Cnwll	
36 A5	**Liss** Hants	
36 A5	**Liss Forest** Hants	
153 J4	**Lissett** E R Yk	
136 B3	**Lissington** Lincs	
89 G6	**Liston** Essex	
43 J5	**Lisvane** Cardif	
44 D2	**Liswerry** Newpt	
121 J8	**Litcham** Norfk	
42 D5	**Litchard** Brdgnd	
84 C4	**Litchborough** Nhants	
48 C8	**Litchfield** Hants	
138 D8	**Litherland** Sefton	
87 G6	**Litlington** Cambs	
23 J7	**Litlington** E Susx	
87 L5	**Little Abington** Cambs	
101 L8	**Little Addington** Nhants	
173 K5	**Little Airies** D & G	
69 G2	**Little Almshoe** Herts	
82 D3	**Little Alne** Warwks	
138 C6	**Little Altcar** Sefton	
69 K5	**Little Amwell** Herts	
158 B1	**Little Asby** Cumb	
98 E3	**Little Aston** Staffs	
19 G7	**Little Atherfield** IOW	
170 D8	**Little Ayton** N York	
71 J5	**Little Baddow** Essex	
46 A2	**Little Badminton** S Glos	
177 J7	**Little Bampton** Cumb	
71 G1	**Little Bardfield** Essex	
86 D4	**Little Barford** Beds	
122 C5	**Little Barningham** Norfk	
65 J4	**Little Barrington** Gloucs	
129 L5	**Little Barrow** Ches	
162 D6	**Little Barugh** N York	
180 B3	**Little Bavington** Nthumb	
99 K6	**Little Bayton** Warwks	
90 F5	**Little Bealings** Suffk	
47 L5	**Little Bedwyn** Wilts	
73 G2	**Little Bentley** Essex	
69 H5	**Little Berkhamsted** Herts	
84 F3	**Little Billing** Nhants	
68 B3	**Little Billington** Beds	
63 G1	**Little Birch** Herefs	
146 F7	**Little Bispham** Bpool	
90 C5	**Little Blakenham** Suffk	
166 B4	**Little Blencow** Cumb	
98 C3	**Little Bloxwich** Wsall	
21 G3	**Little Bognor** W Susx	
116 A1	**Little Bolehill** Derbys	
130 E2	**Little Bollington** Ches	
50 E8	**Little Bookham** Surrey	
83 K6	**Little Bourton** Oxon	
101 G6	**Little Bowden** Leics	
88 D5	**Little Bradley** Suffk	
79 K3	**Little Brampton** Herefs	
95 J7	**Little Brampton** Shrops	
71 K4	**Little Braxted** Essex	
234 F3	**Little Brechin** Angus	
85 H8	**Little Brickhill** M Keyn	
114 D6	**Little Bridgeford** Staffs	
84 C3	**Little Brington** Nhants	
73 G2	**Little Bromley** Essex	
164 E4	**Little Broughton** Cumb	
130 B6	**Little Budworth** Ches	
71 G8	**Little Burstead** Essex	
118 D7	**Little Bytham** Lincs	
70 E3	**Little Canfield** Essex	
137 G3	**Little Carlton** Lincs	
134 F8	**Little Carlton** Notts	
101 M2	**Little Casterton** Rutlnd	
153 H6	**Little Catwick** E R Yk	
86 B1	**Little Catworth** Cambs	
137 G3	**Little Cawthorpe** Lincs	
46 B6	**Little Chalfield** Wilts	
68 C7	**Little Chalfont** Bucks	
30 C3	**Little Charlinch** Somset	
40 B6	**Little Chart** Kent	
87 L7	**Little Chesterford** Essex	
39 H4	**Little Cheveney** Kent	
46 E8	**Little Cheverell** Wilts	
87 J7	**Little Chishill** Cambs	
73 H3	**Little Clacton** Essex	
65 K6	**Little Clanfield** Oxon	
164 E5	**Little Clifton** Cumb	
145 H6	**Little Coates** NE Lin	
81 M6	**Little Comberton** Worcs	
24 C5	**Little Common** E Susx	
39 G2	**Little Comp** Kent	
65 K1	**Little Compton** Warwks	
178 B7	**Little Corby** Cumb	
89 H7	**Little Cornard** Suffk	
80 E5	**Little Cowarne** Herefs	
65 L8	**Little Coxwell** Oxon	
160 C4	**Little Crakehall** N York	
101 H8	**Little Cransley** Nhants	
105 H3	**Little Cressingham** Norfk	
138 C7	**Little Crosby** Sefton	
165 H5	**Little Crosthwaite** Cumb	
115 J4	**Little Cubley** Derbys	
117 K8	**Little Dalby** Leics	
257 K3	**Little Dens** Abers	
63 G1	**Little Dewchurch** Herefs	
88 D3	**Little Ditton** Cambs	
63 G4	**Little Doward** Herefs	
103 L6	**Little Downham** Cambs	
152 F4	**Little Driffield** E R Yk	
105 H1	**Little Dunham** Norfk	
232 F7	**Little Dunkeld** P & K	
71 G3	**Little Dunmow** Essex	
33 K4	**Little Durnford** Wilts	
70 F2	**Little Easton** Essex	
116 B3	**Little Eaton** Derbys	
105 K3	**Little Ellingham** Norfk	
32 B2	**Little Elm** Somset	
84 B4	**Little Everdon** Nhants	
87 H4	**Little Eversden** Cambs	
65 J6	**Little Faringdon** Oxon	
160 D4	**Little Fencote** N York	
142 E1	**Little Fenton** N York	
105 H1	**Little Fransham** Norfk	
68 C4	**Little Gaddesden** Herts	
62 F2	**Little Garway** Herefs	
102 C7	**Little Gidding** Cambs	
91 H4	**Little Glemham** Suffk	
63 K2	**Little Gorsley** Herefs	
86 F4	**Little Gransden** Cambs	
117 J3	**Little Green** Notts	
32 B1	**Little Green** Somset	
136 F2	**Little Grimsby** Lincs	
134 E3	**Little Gringley** Notts	
162 C7	**Little Habton** N York	
70 B3	**Little Hadham** Herts	
118 F3	**Little Hale** Lincs	
116 D3	**Little Hallam** Derbys	
70 D4	**Little Hallingbury** Essex	

330 Little Hanford - Llanedi

32 D8 **Little Hanford** Dorset
85 G1 **Little Harrowden** Nhants
66 F7 **Little Haseley** Oxon
153 J7 **Little Hatfield** E R Yk
122 E7 **Little Hautbois** Norfk
54 D4 **Little Haven** Pembks
98 E3 **Little Hay** Staffs
131 K2 **Little Hayfield** Derbys
115 G7 **Little Haywood** Staffs
99 K7 **Little Heath** Covtry
114 D8 **Little Heath** Staffs
49 G4 **Little Heath** W Berk
80 D2 **Little Hereford** Herefs
52 F5 **Little Hermitage** Kent
72 D1 **Little Horkesley** Essex
69 L1 **Little Hormead** Herts
23 H4 **Little Horsted** E Susx
141 J2 **Little Horton** Brad
46 F6 **Little Horton** Wilts
67 J1 **Little Horwood** Bucks
142 C6 **Little Houghton** Barns
84 F3 **Little Houghton** Nhants
132 C4 **Little Hucklow** Derbys
139 L7 **Little Hulton** Salfd
48 D4 **Little Hungerford** W Berk
161 G7 **Little Hutton** N York
114 F6 **Little Ingestre** Staffs
85 H2 **Little Irchester** Nhants
153 H4 **Little Kelk** E R Yk
32 C2 **Little Keyford** Somset
67 K5 **Little Kimble** Bucks
83 H5 **Little Kineton** Warwks
67 L7 **Little Kingshill** Bucks
175 K3 **Little Knox** D & G
156 D2 **Little Langdale** Cumb
33 H4 **Little Langford** Wilts
12 A1 **Little Lashbrook** Devon
70 E5 **Little Laver** Essex
130 B4 **Little Leigh** Ches
71 H4 **Little Leighs** Essex
139 M6 **Little Lever** Bolton
85 G6 **Little Linford** M Keyn
87 L5 **Little Linton** Cambs
31 G6 **Little Load** Somset
150 B7 **Little London** Brad
66 F4 **Little London** Bucks
103 J4 **Little London** Cambs
23 J3 **Little London** E Susx
70 C1 **Little London** Essex
88 D8 **Little London** Essex
63 L3 **Little London** Gloucs
34 E1 **Little London** Hants
48 F7 **Little London** Hants
119 H7 **Little London** Lincs
136 F5 **Little London** Lincs
119 M6 **Little London** Lincs
120 C7 **Little London** Norfk
94 C5 **Little London** Powys
132 D5 **Little Longstone** Derbys
114 B3 **Little Madeley** Staffs
81 H7 **Little Malvern** Worcs
129 H6 **Little Mancot** Flints
89 G8 **Little Maplestead** Essex
80 F7 **Little Marcle** Herefs
27 J8 **Little Marland** Devon
49 L2 **Little Marlow** Bucks
121 H6 **Little Massingham** Norfk
106 D2 **Little Melton** Norfk
62 C6 **Little Mill** Mons
66 F7 **Little Milton** Oxon
68 A7 **Little Missenden** Bucks
41 K5 **Little Mongeham** Kent
30 D4 **Little Moor** Somset
167 H8 **Little Musgrave** Cumb
112 F7 **Little Ness** Shrops
129 G4 **Little Neston** Ches
75 G6 **Little Newcastle** Pembks
168 E7 **Little Newsham** Dur
31 G7 **Little Norton** Somset
73 J1 **Little Oakley** Essex
101 K6 **Little Oakley** Nhants
85 J4 **Little Odell** Beds
68 E2 **Little Offley** Herts
114 C8 **Little Onn** Staffs
167 G7 **Little Ormside** Cumb
177 K7 **Little Orton** Cumb
104 C5 **Little Ouse** Cambs
150 F4 **Little Ouseburn** N York
100 F6 **Little Oxendon** Nhants
99 G6 **Little Packington** Warwks
39 J4 **Little Pattenden** Kent
86 D3 **Little Paxton** Cambs
10 C8 **Little Petherick** Cnwll
138 D1 **Little Plumpton** Lancs
107 G1 **Little Plumstead** Norfk
118 B5 **Little Ponton** Lincs
19 J3 **Little Posbrook** Hants
27 J8 **Little Potheridge** Devon
142 B2 **Little Preston** Leeds
84 B4 **Little Preston** Nhants
102 E7 **Little Raveley** Cambs
143 K3 **Little Reedness** E R Yk
150 E5 **Little Ribston** N York
65 J3 **Little Rissington** Gloucs
65 L1 **Little Rollright** Oxon
132 E6 **Little Rowsley** Derbys
121 L6 **Little Ryburgh** Norfk
190 E4 **Little Ryle** Nthumb
96 B3 **Little Ryton** Shrops
166 D3 **Little Salkeld** Cumb
88 C8 **Little Sampford** Essex
49 K6 **Little Sandhurst** Br For
97 L2 **Little Saredon** Staffs
129 J6 **Little Saughall** Ches
88 F3 **Little Saxham** Suffk
262 C8 **Little Scatwell** Highld
161 G7 **Little Sessay** N York
87 J5 **Little Shelford** Cambs
13 K2 **Little Silver** Devon
13 L1 **Little Silver** Devon
147 G7 **Little Singleton** Lancs
151 K8 **Little Skipwith** N York
142 E4 **Little Smeaton** N York
121 L5 **Little Snoring** Norfk
45 M2 **Little Sodbury** S Glos
45 L2 **Little Sodbury End** S Glos
34 E4 **Little Somborne** Hants
46 D2 **Little Somerford** Wilts
114 A6 **Little Soudley** Shrops
148 E2 **Little Stainforth** N York
169 K6 **Little Stainton** Darltn
129 J5 **Little Stanney** Ches
86 B3 **Little Staughton** Beds
137 H7 **Little Steeping** Lincs
90 D3 **Little Stonham** Suffk
100 E3 **Little Stretton** Leics
95 K5 **Little Stretton** Shrops
166 D6 **Little Strickland** Cumb
102 E8 **Little Stukeley** Cambs
114 C5 **Little Sugnall** Staffs
129 J4 **Little Sutton** Ches
96 C6 **Little Sutton** Shrops
179 M3 **Little Swinburne** Nthumb
175 H4 **Little Sypland** D & G
66 A2 **Little Tew** Oxon
72 C2 **Little Tey** Essex
103 L8 **Little Thetford** Cambs
161 G7 **Little Thirkleby** N York
122 B4 **Little Thornage** Norfk
147 G7 **Little Thornton** Lancs
169 L2 **Little Thorpe** Dur
88 D5 **Little Thurlow** Suffk
88 D5 **Little Thurlow Green** Suffk
52 D3 **Little Thurrock** Thurr
27 J7 **Little Torrington** Devon
72 C5 **Little Totham** Essex
165 H6 **Little Town** Cumb
148 B8 **Little Town** Lancs
130 C1 **Little Town** Warrtn
99 J2 **Little Twycross** Leics
156 C7 **Little Urswick** Cumb
53 K1 **Little Wakering** Essex
87 L7 **Little Walden** Essex
89 J6 **Little Waldingfield** Suffk
121 K4 **Little Walsingham** Norfk
71 H4 **Little Waltham** Essex
52 D1 **Little Warley** Essex
82 A8 **Little Washbourne** Gloucs
144 B1 **Little Weighton** E R Yk
101 K5 **Little Weldon** Nhants
89 H3 **Little Welnetham** Suffk
136 F2 **Little Welton** Lincs
90 C7 **Little Wenham** Suffk
96 E2 **Little Wenlock** Wrekin
31 K5 **Little Weston** Somset
19 K5 **Little Whitefield** IOW
180 B5 **Little Whittington** Nthumb
87 L3 **Little Wilbraham** Cambs
64 C4 **Little Witcombe** Gloucs
81 H3 **Little Witley** Worcs
66 E8 **Little Wittenham** Oxon
83 G8 **Little Wolford** Warwks
51 H6 **Little Woodcote** Surrey
88 D6 **Little Wratting** Suffk
85 J2 **Little Wymington** Beds
69 G2 **Little Wymondley** Herts
98 C2 **Little Wyrley** Staffs
113 J7 **Little Wytheford** Shrops
88 F7 **Little Yeldham** Essex
162 F2 **Littlebeck** N York
28 E8 **Littleborough** Devon
135 G3 **Littleborough** Notts
140 E4 **Littleborough** Rochdl
41 G4 **Littlebourne** Kent
16 B5 **Littlebredy** Dorset
251 H1 **Littleburn** Highld
87 L7 **Littlebury** Essex
87 K7 **Littlebury Green** Essex
47 H8 **Littlecott** Wilts
63 K4 **Littledean** Gloucs
47 M7 **Littledown** Hants
27 H6 **Littleham** Devon
14 B6 **Littleham** Devon
21 H6 **Littlehampton** W Susx
180 B2 **Littleharle Tower** Nthumb
37 J4 **Littlehaven** W Susx
8 B2 **Littlehempston** Devon
191 J3 **Littlehoughton** Nthumb
243 K4 **Littlemill** Abers
253 H2 **Littlemill** Highld
133 G7 **Littlemoor** Derbys
66 D6 **Littlemore** Oxon
116 B5 **Littleover** C Derb
104 B6 **Littleport** Cambs
104 B6 **Littleport Bridge** Cambs
130 C6 **Littler** Ches
25 K2 **Littlestone-on-Sea** Kent
100 C4 **Littlethorpe** Leics
150 D2 **Littlethorpe** N York
233 M5 **Littleton** Angus
45 H6 **Littleton** BaNES
129 K6 **Littleton** Ches
175 G4 **Littleton** D & G
17 H2 **Littleton** Dorset
34 F4 **Littleton** Hants
31 H5 **Littleton** Somset
36 E2 **Littleton** Surrey
50 D5 **Littleton** Surrey
46 B3 **Littleton Drew** Wilts
46 E8 **Littleton Pannell** Wilts
45 H1 **Littleton-on-Severn** S Glos
169 J2 **Littletown** Dur
19 J5 **Littletown** IOW
49 K3 **Littlewick Green** W & M
15 K2 **Littlewindsor** Dorset
98 C2 **Littlewood** Staffs
67 L3 **Littleworth** Bucks
65 L7 **Littleworth** Oxon
114 E7 **Littleworth** Staffs
98 C1 **Littleworth** Staffs
21 L3 **Littleworth** W Susx
81 K5 **Littleworth** Worcs
82 B3 **Littleworth** Worcs
50 B2 **Littleworth Common** Bucks
86 E2 **Littleworth End** Cambs
71 G4 **Littley Green** Essex
45 H8 **Litton** BaNES
132 C4 **Litton** Derbys
158 F7 **Litton** N York
16 A4 **Litton Cheney** Dorset
282 g4 **Liurbost** W Isls
129 H2 **Liverpool** Lpool
141 J3 **Liversedge** Kirk
13 J7 **Liverton** Devon
171 G7 **Liverton** R & Cl
171 G7 **Liverton Mines** R & Cl
39 L3 **Liverton Street** Kent
210 E5 **Livingston** W Loth
210 D5 **Livingston Village** W Loth
7 K5 **Lixton** Devon
128 E5 **Lixwm** Flints
3 H8 **Lizard** Cnwll
124 D3 **Llaingoch** IOA
94 C7 **Llaithddu** Powys
93 J3 **Llan** Powys
112 F1 **Llan-y-pwll** Wrexhm
109 L7 **Llanaber** Gwynd
109 G3 **Llanaelhaearn** Gwynd
77 J1 **Llanafan** Cerdgn
78 D5 **Llanafan-fechan** Powys
125 J3 **Llanallgo** IOA
109 G4 **Llanarmon** Gwynd
112 A5 **Llanarmon Dyffryn Ceiriog** Wrexhm
128 E8 **Llanarmon-yn-Ial** Denbgs
76 D4 **Llanarth** Cerdgn
62 D5 **Llanarth** Mons
58 F5 **Llanarthne** Carmth
128 D3 **Llanasa** Flints
124 F2 **Llanbabo** IOA
92 D7 **Llanbadarn Fawr** Cerdgn
94 D7 **Llanbadarn Fynydd** Powys
78 F5 **Llanbadarn-y-garreg** Powys
62 D7 **Llanbadoc** Mons
124 F1 **Llanbadrig** IOA
44 D1 **Llanbeder** Newpt
109 K6 **Llanbedr** Gwynd
79 G6 **Llanbedr** Powys
61 K3 **Llanbedr** Powys
128 D7 **Llanbedr-Dyffryn-Clwyd** Denbgs
126 E6 **Llanbedr-y-Cennin** Conwy
125 J4 **Llanbedrgoch** IOA
108 F5 **Llanbedrog** Gwynd
125 K7 **Llanberis** Gwynd
43 G7 **Llanbethery** V Glam
94 D8 **Llanbister** Powys
42 F7 **Llanblethian** V Glam
55 L2 **Llanboidy** Carmth
43 J4 **Llanbradach** Caerph
93 K3 **Llanbrynmair** Powys
42 F8 **Llancadle** V Glam
43 G7 **Llancarfan** V Glam
62 D6 **Llancayo** Mons
62 D2 **Llancillo** Herefs
63 G3 **Llancloudy** Herefs
92 E5 **Llancynfelyn** Cerdgn
43 J6 **Llandaff** Cardif
109 K6 **Llandanwg** Gwynd
58 A6 **Llandawke** Carmth
125 J5 **Llanddanielfab** IOA
58 F5 **Llanddarog** Carmth
77 G1 **Llanddeiniol** Cerdgn
125 K6 **Llanddeiniolen** Gwynd
111 J4 **Llandderfel** Gwynd
59 L4 **Llanddeusant** Carmth
124 F3 **Llanddeusant** IOA
61 G1 **Llanddew** Powys
56 E7 **Llanddewi** Swans
77 J4 **Llanddewi Brefi** Cerdgn
62 D4 **Llanddewi Rhydderch** Mons
55 K4 **Llanddewi Velfrey** Pembks
78 F2 **Llanddewi Ystradenni** Powys
78 E5 **Llanddewi'r Cwm** Powys
126 F7 **Llanddoget** Conwy
125 K4 **Llanddona** IOA
55 M4 **Llanddowror** Carmth
127 H4 **Llanddulas** Conwy
109 K7 **Llanddwywe** Gwynd
125 J4 **Llanddyfnan** IOA
110 B4 **Llandecwyn** Gwynd
60 F1 **Llandefaelog** Powys
61 H1 **Llandefaelog-Trer-Graig** Powys
78 F8 **Llandefalle** Powys
125 K5 **Llandegfan** IOA
112 B1 **Llandegla** Denbgs
79 G3 **Llandegley** Powys
62 C8 **Llandegveth** Mons
108 D5 **Llandegwning** Gwynd
59 H4 **Llandeilo** Carmth
78 F6 **Llandeilo Graban** Powys
78 B8 **Llandeilo'r Fan** Powys
74 D6 **Llandeloy** Pembks
62 E6 **Llandenny** Mons
44 E1 **Llandevaud** Newpt
44 E2 **Llandevenny** Mons
63 G2 **Llandinabo** Herefs
94 B5 **Llandinam** Powys
55 J3 **Llandissilio** Pembks
63 G6 **Llandogo** Mons
42 F7 **Llandough** V Glam
43 J7 **Llandough** V Glam
59 L2 **Llandovery** Carmth
42 E7 **Llandow** V Glam
77 J6 **Llandre** Carmth
92 D6 **Llandre** Cerdgn
75 K6 **Llandre Isaf** Pembks
111 K4 **Llandrillo** Denbgs
127 G4 **Llandrillo-yn-Rhos** Conwy
78 E3 **Llandrindod Wells** Powys
112 D8 **Llandrinio** Powys
126 F3 **Llandudno** Conwy
126 F4 **Llandudno Junction** Conwy
108 D4 **Llandudwen** Gwynd
78 B7 **Llandulas** Powys
125 H8 **Llandwrog** Gwynd
59 H6 **Llandybie** Carmth
58 D6 **Llandyfaelog** Carmth
59 H5 **Llandyfan** Carmth
76 B7 **Llandyfriog** Cerdgn
125 H3 **Llandyfrydog** IOA
126 B5 **Llandygai** Gwynd
75 M3 **Llandygwydd** Cerdgn
112 B3 **Llandynan** Denbgs
128 D6 **Llandyrnog** Denbgs
94 F4 **Llandyssil** Powys
76 D7 **Llandysul** Cerdgn
43 K5 **Llanedeyrn** Cardif
57 G3 **Llanedi** Carmth

78 E7 **Llaneglwys** Powys
92 D2 **Llanegryn** Gwynd
58 F4 **Llanegwad** Carmth
125 H1 **Llaneilian** IOA
127 G4 **Llanelian-yn-Rhos** Conwy
111 L2 **Llanelidan** Denbgs
79 H8 **Llanelieu** Powys
62 C5 **Llanellen** Mons
56 F5 **Llanelli** Carmth
110 D7 **Llanelltyd** Gwynd
61 K4 **Llanelly** Mons
78 E5 **Llanelwedd** Powys
109 L6 **Llanenddwyn** Gwynd
108 E6 **Llanengan** Gwynd
111 G8 **Llanerch** Gwynd
95 H4 **Llanerch** Powys
125 G3 **Llanerchymedd** IOA
94 B2 **Llanerfyl** Powys
124 E3 **Llanfachraeth** IOA
110 E7 **Llanfachreth** Gwynd
124 F5 **Llanfaelog** IOA
108 C6 **Llanfaelrhys** Gwynd
62 E4 **Llanfaenor** Mons
126 B4 **Llanfaes** IOA
61 G2 **Llanfaes** Powys
124 E2 **Llanfaethlu** IOA
109 K5 **Llanfair** Gwynd
94 D2 **Llanfair Caereinion** Powys
77 H5 **Llanfair Clydogau** Cerdgn
128 D8 **Llanfair Dyffryn Clwyd** Denbgs
62 D5 **Llanfair Kilgeddin** Mons
125 J5 **Llanfair P G** IOA
127 J5 **Llanfair Talhaiarn** Conwy
94 F8 **Llanfair Waterdine** Shrops
125 J6 **Llanfair-is-gaer** Gwynd
75 K5 **Llanfair-Nant-Gwyn** Pembks
125 H6 **Llanfair-y-Cwmwd** IOA
124 E4 **Llanfair-yn-Neubwll** IOA
126 D5 **Llanfairfechan** Conwy
124 E2 **Llanfairynghornwy** IOA
55 K3 **Llanfallteg** Carmth
55 K3 **Llanfallteg West** Carmth
92 D7 **Llanfarian** Cerdgn
112 B7 **Llanfechain** Powys
124 F2 **Llanfechell** IOA
128 E7 **Llanferres** Denbgs
124 F2 **Llanfflewyn** IOA
124 F3 **Llanfigael** IOA
111 J2 **Llanfihangel Glyn Myfyr** Conwy
78 C8 **Llanfihangel Nant Bran** Powys
79 G2 **Llanfihangel Rhydithon** Powys
44 F2 **Llanfihangel Rogiet** Mons
61 H2 **Llanfihangel Tal-y-llyn** Powys
124 E4 **Llanfihangel yn Nhowyn** IOA
76 E7 **Llanfihangel-ar-Arth** Carmth
79 H4 **Llanfihangel-nant-Melan** Powys
58 E4 **Llanfihangel-uwch-Gwili** Carmth
92 E8 **Llanfihangel-y-Creuddyn** Cerdgn
109 J3 **Llanfihangel-y-pennant** Gwynd
92 E2 **Llanfihangel-y-pennant** Gwynd
109 L4 **Llanfihangel-y-traethau** Gwynd
111 L8 **Llanfihangel-yng-Ngwynfa** Powys
78 F8 **Llanfilo** Powys
62 B4 **Llanfoist** Mons
111 H4 **Llanfor** Gwynd
62 C8 **Llanfrechfa** Torfn
110 B3 **Llanfrothen** Gwynd
61 G2 **Llanfrynach** Powys
128 D8 **Llanfwrog** Denbgs
124 E3 **Llanfwrog** IOA
112 A7 **Llanfyllin** Powys
59 G3 **Llanfynydd** Carmth
129 G8 **Llanfynydd** Flints
75 L6 **Llanfyrnach** Pembks
94 B1 **Llangadfan** Powys
56 D3 **Llangadog** Carmth
59 K3 **Llangadog** Carmth
125 G6 **Llangadwaladr** IOA
112 B5 **Llangadwaladr** Powys
125 H6 **Llangaffo** IOA
58 C5 **Llangain** Carmth

78 C6 **Llangammarch Wells** Powys
42 E6 **Llangan** V Glam
63 G3 **Llangarron** Herefs
61 H2 **Llangasty-Talyllyn** Powys
59 G4 **Llangathen** Carmth
61 K3 **Llangattock** Powys
62 D3 **Llangattock Lingoed** Mons
62 F4 **Llangattock-Vibon-Avel** Mons
112 B6 **Llangedwyn** Powys
125 H4 **Llangefni** IOA
42 D4 **Llangeinor** Brdgnd
125 H6 **Llangeinwen** IOA
77 H3 **Llangeitho** Cerdgn
76 C7 **Llangeler** Carmth
92 C2 **Llangelynin** Gwynd
58 E6 **Llangendeirne** Carmth
57 G4 **Llangennech** Carmth
56 D6 **Llangennith** Swans
61 K3 **Llangenny** Powys
127 H6 **Llangernyw** Conwy
108 E5 **Llangian** Gwynd
57 K4 **Llangiwg** Neath
74 E5 **Llangloffan** Pembks
75 L6 **Llanglydwen** Carmth
126 C4 **Llangoed** IOA
75 L3 **Llangoedmor** Cerdgn
112 B3 **Llangollen** Denbgs
75 J6 **Llangolman** Pembks
61 H2 **Llangors** Powys
62 F6 **Llangovan** Mons
111 G5 **Llangower** Gwynd
76 B4 **Llangranog** Cerdgn
125 H5 **Llangristiolus** IOA
63 G3 **Llangrove** Herefs
62 E2 **Llangua** Mons
79 H1 **Llangunllo** Powys
58 D5 **Llangunnor** Carmth
93 K7 **Llangurig** Powys
111 J3 **Llangwm** Conwy
62 E7 **Llangwm** Mons
55 G5 **Llangwm** Pembks
62 E7 **Llangwm-isaf** Mons
108 C5 **Llangwnnadl** Gwynd
128 D6 **Llangwyfan** Denbgs
125 H4 **Llangwyllog** IOA
77 H1 **Llangwyryfon** Cerdgn
77 H4 **Llangybi** Cerdgn
109 G3 **Llangybi** Gwynd
62 D7 **Llangybi** Mons
57 H5 **Llangyfelach** Swans
128 D7 **Llangynhafal** Denbgs
61 J3 **Llangynidr** Powys
55 M3 **Llangynin** Carmth
76 C6 **Llangynllo** Cerdgn
58 C6 **Llangynog** Carmth
111 K6 **Llangynog** Powys
78 E6 **Llangynog** Powys
42 C4 **Llangynwyd** Brdgnd
61 H2 **Llanhamlach** Powys
42 F5 **Llanharan** Rhondd
42 F5 **Llanharry** Rhondd
62 D8 **Llanhennock** Mons
61 K7 **Llanhilleth** Blae G
125 J6 **Llanidan** IOA
93 L6 **Llanidloes** Powys
108 D5 **Llaniestyn** Gwynd
79 H7 **Llanigon** Powys
92 D8 **Llanilar** Cerdgn
42 E5 **Llanilid** Rhondd
76 D3 **Llanina** Cerdgn
77 H4 **Llanio** Cerdgn
43 J5 **Llanishen** Cardif
62 F6 **Llanishen** Mons
126 C6 **Llanllechid** Gwynd
78 C5 **Llanlleonfel** Powys
62 D7 **Llanllowell** Mons
94 C3 **Llanllugan** Powys
58 C5 **Llanllwch** Carmth
94 D5 **Llanllwchaiarn** Powys
76 E7 **Llanllwni** Carmth
109 H1 **Llanllyfni** Gwynd
56 D6 **Llanmadoc** Swans
42 E7 **Llanmaes** V Glam
44 E1 **Llanmartin** Newpt
94 E5 **Llanmerewig** Powys
42 E7 **Llanmihangel** V Glam
55 M5 **Llanmiloe** Carmth
56 F6 **Llanmorlais** Swans
127 K5 **Llannefydd** Conwy
56 F3 **Llannon** Carmth
108 F4 **Llannor** Gwynd
76 F2 **Llanon** Cerdgn
62 C5 **Llanover** Mons
58 D3 **Llanpumsaint** Carmth

111 M6 **Llanrhaeadr-ym-Mochnant** Powys
74 D6 **Llanrhian** Pembks
56 F6 **Llanrhidian** Swans
126 F4 **Llanrhos** Conwy
126 F7 **Llanrhychwyn** Conwy
124 F2 **Llanrhyddlad** IOA
76 F1 **Llanrhystud** Cerdgn
62 F3 **Llanrothal** Herefs
125 J7 **Llanrug** Gwynd
43 K5 **Llanrumney** Cardif
126 F7 **Llanrwst** Conwy
56 A3 **Llansadurnen** Carmth
59 J3 **Llansadwrn** Carmth
125 K4 **Llansadwrn** IOA
56 C3 **Llansaint** Carmth
57 J5 **Llansamlet** Swans
126 F4 **Llansanffraid Glan Conwy** Conwy
127 J6 **Llansannan** Conwy
42 F6 **Llansannor** V Glam
61 H2 **Llansantffraed** Powys
78 D2 **Llansantffraed-Cwmdeuddwr** Powys
78 F4 **Llansantffraed-in-Elvel** Powys
76 F2 **Llansantffraid** Cerdgn
112 C7 **Llansantffraid-ym-Mechain** Powys
59 H2 **Llansawel** Carmth
112 B6 **Llansilin** Powys
62 E6 **Llansoy** Mons
60 F2 **Llanspyddid** Powys
54 F6 **Llanstadwell** Pembks
56 C3 **Llansteffan** Carmth
78 F6 **Llanstephan** Powys
62 C8 **Llantarnam** Torfn
55 L5 **Llanteg** Pembks
62 D4 **Llanthewy Skirrid** Mons
62 B2 **Llanthony** Mons
62 C4 **Llantilio Pertholey** Mons
62 E4 **Llantilio-Crossenny** Mons
124 F3 **Llantrisant** IOA
62 D7 **Llantrisant** Mons
43 G5 **Llantrisant** Rhondd
43 G7 **Llantrithyd** V Glam
43 G4 **Llantwit Fardre** Rhondd
42 E7 **Llantwit Major** V Glam
112 B3 **Llantysilio** Denbgs
111 G5 **Llanuwchllyn** Gwynd
44 E1 **Llanvaches** Newpt
62 F8 **Llanvair Discoed** Mons
62 D4 **Llanvapley** Mons
62 D4 **Llanvetherine** Mons
62 C1 **Llanveynoe** Herefs
62 C3 **Llanvihangel Crucorney** Mons
62 D5 **Llanvihangel Gobion** Mons
62 E4 **Llanvihangel-Ystern-Llewern** Mons
63 G2 **Llanwarne** Herefs
111 K7 **Llanwddyn** Powys
62 B4 **Llanwenarth** Mons
76 F6 **Llanwenog** Cerdgn
44 D2 **Llanwern** Newpt
58 A4 **Llanwinio** Carmth
125 H8 **Llanwnda** Gwynd
74 F4 **Llanwnda** Pembks
76 F6 **Llanwnnen** Cerdgn
94 B4 **Llanwnog** Powys
42 F3 **Llanwonno** Rhondd
59 K3 **Llanwrda** Carmth
93 G3 **Llanwrin** Powys
78 D3 **Llanwrthwl** Powys
78 B5 **Llanwrtyd** Powys
78 B6 **Llanwrtyd Wells** Powys
94 C3 **Llanwyddelan** Powys
112 C7 **Llanyblodwel** Shrops
58 B6 **Llanybri** Carmth
76 F6 **Llanybydder** Carmth
55 J2 **Llanycefn** Pembks
75 G5 **Llanychaer Bridge** Pembks
77 H6 **Llanycrwys** Carmth
111 G7 **Llanymawddwy** Gwynd
112 C7 **Llanymynech** Powys
124 E3 **Llanynghenedl** IOA
128 C7 **Llanynys** Denbgs
78 E3 **Llanyre** Powys
109 H4 **Llanystumdwy** Gwynd
61 H2 **Llanywern** Powys
55 H3 **Llawhaden** Pembks
112 C5 **Llawnt** Shrops
93 K5 **Llawryglyn** Powys
129 H8 **Llay** Wrexhm
125 G3 **Llechcynfarwy** IOA

61 G2 **Llechfaen** Powys
61 H5 **Llechrhyd** Caerph
75 L3 **Llechryd** Cerdgn
124 F4 **Llechylched** IOA
77 H1 **Lledrod** Cerdgn
111 G4 **Llidiardau** Gwynd
111 M3 **Llidiart-y-parc** Denbgs
77 G7 **Llidiartnenog** Carmth
108 F3 **Llithfaen** Gwynd
128 D4 **Lloc** Flints
129 G7 **Llong** Flints
79 H7 **Llowes** Powys
60 F6 **Llwydcoed** Rhondd
111 K8 **Llwydiarth** Powys
128 C6 **Llwyn** Denbgs
58 A2 **Llwyn-drain** Pembks
62 C4 **Llwyn-du** Mons
60 F5 **Llwyn-on** Myr Td
55 L4 **Llwyn-y-brain** Carmth
77 G4 **Llwyn-y-groes** Cerdgn
76 E3 **Llwyncelyn** Cerdgn
76 C4 **Llwyndafydd** Cerdgn
94 F3 **Llwynderw** Powys
108 F3 **Llwyndyrys** Gwynd
92 D2 **Llwyngwril** Gwynd
56 F5 **Llwynhendy** Carmth
112 C4 **Llwynmawr** Wrexhm
42 F3 **Llwynypia** Rhondd
128 E6 **Llyn-y-pandy** Flints
112 D6 **Llynclys** Shrops
125 G4 **Llynfaes** IOA
55 H2 **Llys-y-fran** Pembks
127 H4 **Llysfaen** Conwy
76 E3 **Llyswen** Cerdgn
79 G7 **Llyswen** Powys
42 E6 **Llysworney** V Glam
60 C1 **Llywel** Powys
132 E2 **Load Brook** Sheff
210 C4 **Loan** Falk
202 E3 **Loanend** Nthumb
211 J6 **Loanhead** Mdloth
176 C7 **Loaningfoot** D & G
196 C4 **Loans** S Ayrs
27 H3 **Lobb** Devon
12 B5 **Lobhillcross** Devon
283 c11 **Loch Baghasdail** W Isls
283 c8 **Loch Euphoirt** W Isls
219 H5 **Loch Katrine Pier** Stirlg
260 E6 **Loch Maree Hotel** Highld
283 d8 **Loch nam Madadh** W Isls
238 B7 **Lochailort** Highld
227 K3 **Lochaline** Highld
172 D3 **Lochans** D & G
176 C3 **Locharbriggs** D & G
216 E4 **Lochavich** Ag & B
217 J2 **Lochawe** Ag & B
283 c11 **Lochboisdale** W Isls
227 H7 **Lochbuie** Ag & B
248 E4 **Lochcarron** Highld
227 L6 **Lochdon** Ag & B
227 L5 **Lochdonhead** Ag & B
206 B3 **Lochead** Ag & B
219 K2 **Lochearnhead** Stirlg
222 F1 **Lochee** C Dund
239 G7 **Locheilside Station** Highld
251 G4 **Lochend** Highld
283 c8 **Locheport** W Isls
176 B4 **Lochfoot** D & G
206 E1 **Lochgair** Ag & B
222 C8 **Lochgelly** Fife
206 D2 **Lochgilphead** Ag & B
217 K7 **Lochgoilhead** Ag & B
222 D4 **Lochieheads** Fife
266 F3 **Lochill** Moray
253 J4 **Lochindorb Lodge** Highld
270 E4 **Lochinver** Highld
262 B7 **Lochluichart** Highld
176 E2 **Lochmaben** D & G
283 d8 **Lochmaddy** W Isls
222 B7 **Lochore** Fife
194 E1 **Lochranza** N Ayrs
235 J3 **Lochside** Abers
176 C3 **Lochside** D & G
252 F1 **Lochside** Highld
183 G7 **Lochton** S Ayrs
234 E3 **Lochty** Angus
223 J5 **Lochty** Fife
228 B4 **Lochuisge** Highld
208 B7 **Lochwinnoch** Rens
187 G6 **Lochwood** D & G
5 H3 **Lockengate** Cnwll
176 F3 **Lockerbie** D & G
47 H5 **Lockeridge** Wilts
34 C5 **Lockerley** Hants
44 D7 **Locking** N Som

130 C1 **Locking Stumps** Warrtn
152 F6 **Lockington** E R Yk
116 D6 **Lockington** Leics
113 M6 **Lockleywood** Shrops
19 H2 **Locks Heath** Hants
51 L6 **Locksbottom** Gt Lon
19 G5 **Locksgreen** IOW
162 E5 **Lockton** N York
101 H3 **Loddington** Leics
101 H7 **Loddington** Nhants
7 L5 **Loddiswell** Devon
107 G4 **Loddon** Norfk
87 L3 **Lode** Cambs
98 F7 **Lode Heath** Solhll
15 L4 **Loders** Dorset
99 H6 **Lodge Green** Solhll
36 D6 **Lodsworth** W Susx
142 A3 **Lofthouse** Leeds
159 K8 **Lofthouse** N York
142 A3 **Lofthouse Gate** Wakefd
171 G7 **Loftus** R & Cl
197 H6 **Logan** E Ayrs
156 A4 **Loganbeck** Cumb
210 C6 **Loganlea** W Loth
114 A4 **Loggerheads** Staffs
235 H3 **Logie** Angus
223 G3 **Logie** Fife
253 K2 **Logie** Moray
243 M3 **Logie Coldstone** Abers
235 G3 **Logie Pert** Angus
232 E5 **Logierait** P & K
257 G6 **Logierieve** Abers
55 K2 **Login** Carmth
87 H2 **Lolworth** Cambs
57 K5 **Lon-las** Swans
259 M6 **Lonbain** Highld
152 C6 **Londesborough** E R Yk
51 H3 **London** Gt Lon
5 G5 **London Apprentice** Cnwll
39 M6 **London Beach** Kent
68 F6 **London Colney** Herts
85 H2 **London End** Nhants
160 D5 **Londonderry** N York
118 C4 **Londonthorpe** Lincs
260 D4 **Londubh** Highld
260 C4 **Lonemore** Highld
45 H5 **Long Ashton** N Som
97 H8 **Long Bank** Worcs
117 L3 **Long Bennington** Lincs
16 A4 **Long Bredy** Dorset
84 C2 **Long Buckby** Nhants
8 B3 **Long Cause** Devon
117 J6 **Long Clawson** Leics
35 G7 **Long Common** Hants
114 D7 **Long Compton** Staffs
83 G8 **Long Compton** Warwks
67 G5 **Long Crendon** Bucks
17 J1 **Long Crichel** Dorset
50 F5 **Long Ditton** Surrey
143 H2 **Long Drax** N York
133 J5 **Long Duckmanton** Derbys
116 E5 **Long Eaton** Derbys
129 L5 **Long Green** Ches
81 J8 **Long Green** Worcs
66 B4 **Long Hanborough** Oxon
119 K2 **Long Hedges** Lincs
83 K2 **Long Itchington** Warwks
113 K8 **Long Lane** Wrekin
100 A8 **Long Lawford** Warwks
31 G6 **Long Load** Somset
67 L4 **Long Marston** Herts
151 H5 **Long Marston** N York
82 E5 **Long Marston** Warwks
166 F5 **Long Marton** Cumb
95 K7 **Long Meadow End** Shrops
89 H6 **Long Melford** Suffk
64 C8 **Long Newnton** Gloucs
212 B6 **Long Newton** E Loth
148 E4 **Long Preston** N York
153 H7 **Long Riston** E R Yk
140 D6 **Long Sight** Oldham
106 D5 **Long Stratton** Norfk
84 F5 **Long Street** M Keyn
35 M2 **Long Sutton** Hants
119 M7 **Long Sutton** Lincs
31 G6 **Long Sutton** Somset
89 K2 **Long Thurlow** Suffk
113 K8 **Long Waste** Wrekin
116 D6 **Long Whatton** Leics
66 E8 **Long Wittenham** Oxon
181 G5 **Longbenton** N Tyne
65 J1 **Longborough** Gloucs
98 C7 **Longbridge** Birm
83 G3 **Longbridge** Warwks
32 E3 **Longbridge Deverill** Wilts

177 J7 **Longburgh** Cumb
31 L8 **Longburton** Dorset
132 D8 **Longcliffe** Derbys
8 C3 **Longcombe** Devon
47 K1 **Longcot** Oxon
177 H7 **Longcroft** Cumb
50 C6 **Longcross** Surrey
95 K2 **Longden** Shrops
95 K2 **Longden Common** Shrops
115 H8 **Longdon** Staffs
81 J7 **Longdon** Worcs
98 D1 **Longdon Green** Staffs
81 J7 **Longdon Heath** Worcs
113 K8 **Longdon upon Tern** Wrekin
13 K4 **Longdown** Devon
3 J4 **Longdowns** Cnwll
52 D5 **Longfield** Kent
99 K6 **Longford** Covtry
115 L4 **Longford** Derbys
64 B3 **Longford** Gloucs
50 D4 **Longford** Gt Lon
38 D2 **Longford** Kent
113 L5 **Longford** Shrops
114 A7 **Longford** Wrekin
222 E1 **Longforgan** P & K
212 F7 **Longformacus** Border
191 G6 **Longframlington** Nthumb
17 L3 **Longham** Dorset
121 L8 **Longham** Norfk
257 L4 **Longhaven** Abers
191 J8 **Longhirst** Nthumb
63 K3 **Longhope** Gloucs
275 b6 **Longhope** Ork
191 H7 **Longhorsley** Nthumb
191 J3 **Longhoughton** Nthumb
165 J3 **Longlands** Cumb
115 L4 **Longlane** Derbys
64 B3 **Longlevens** Gloucs
141 G3 **Longley** Calder
141 J6 **Longley** Kirk
81 G5 **Longley Green** Worcs
233 L6 **Longleys** P & K
268 D4 **Longmanhill** Abers
36 B4 **Longmoor Camp** Hants
266 E4 **Longmorn** Moray
131 H5 **Longmoss** Ches
201 J7 **Longnewton** Border
169 K7 **Longnewton** S on T
63 M4 **Longney** Gloucs
212 A4 **Longniddry** E Loth
96 B3 **Longnor** Shrops
132 B6 **Longnor** Staffs
34 F2 **Longparish** Hants
178 A6 **Longpark** Cumb
147 M8 **Longridge** Lancs
114 E8 **Longridge** Staffs
210 C6 **Longridge** W Loth
209 L5 **Longriggend** N Lans
2 C6 **Longrock** Cnwll
114 E3 **Longton** C Stke
138 F3 **Longton** Lancs
177 L5 **Longtown** Cumb
62 C1 **Longtown** Herefs
9 e3 **Longueville** Jersey
96 C6 **Longville in the Dale** Shrops
67 J6 **Longwick** Bucks
180 C1 **Longwitton** Nthumb
175 H3 **Longwood** D & G
96 D2 **Longwood** Shrops
35 H6 **Longwood House** Hants
66 A7 **Longworth** Oxon
212 C6 **Longyester** E Loth
269 J4 **Lonmay** Abers
258 D7 **Lonmore** Highld
6 B4 **Looe** Cnwll
39 J3 **Loose** Kent
13 G2 **Loosebeare** Devon
119 K6 **Loosegate** Lincs
67 K7 **Loosley Row** Bucks
268 A5 **Lootcherbrae** Abers
34 B4 **Lopcombe Corner** Wilts
30 F8 **Lopen** Somset
113 C2 **Loppington** Shrops
190 E5 **Lorbottle** Nthumb

20 C5 **Lordington** W Susx
53 G6 **Lords Wood** Medway
104 B1 **Lordsbridge** Norfk
233 J6 **Lornty** P & K
116 C2 **Loscoe** Derbys
15 L3 **Loscombe** Dorset
266 E2 **Lossiemouth** Moray
113 K5 **Lostford** Shrops
130 D5 **Lostock Gralam** Ches
130 D5 **Lostock Green** Ches
139 H3 **Lostock Hall** Lancs
139 K6 **Lostock Hall Fold** Bolton
139 K6 **Lostock Junction** Bolton
5 J3 **Lostwithiel** Cnwll
274 C6 **Lothbeg** Highld
149 G6 **Lothersdale** N York
274 C6 **Lothmore** Highld
49 L1 **Loudwater** Bucks
116 F7 **Loughborough** Leics
57 G5 **Loughor** Swans
70 B7 **Loughton** Essex
85 G7 **Loughton** M Keyn
96 E6 **Loughton** Shrops
118 E7 **Lound** Lincs
134 D2 **Lound** Notts
107 K4 **Lound** Suffk
13 J7 **Lounston** Devon
116 C7 **Lount** Leics
136 F2 **Louth** Lincs
140 B2 **Love Clough** Lancs
19 M1 **Lovedean** Hants
34 B6 **Lover** Wilts
142 F8 **Loversall** Donc
70 F6 **Loves Green** Essex
160 E3 **Lovesome Hill** N York
55 J5 **Loveston** Pembks
31 K5 **Lovington** Somset
142 C4 **Low Ackworth** Wakefd
180 D2 **Low Angerton** Nthumb
172 C2 **Low Barbeth** D & G
136 A5 **Low Barlings** Lincs
162 C3 **Low Bell End** N York
148 A2 **Low Bentham** N York
157 K7 **Low Biggins** Cumb
157 K2 **Low Borrowbridge** Cumb
132 E2 **Low Bradfield** Sheff
149 H6 **Low Bradley** N York
166 A2 **Low Braithwaite** Cumb
143 K7 **Low Burnham** N Linc
191 J5 **Low Buston** Nthumb
151 L5 **Low Catton** E R Yk
169 H7 **Low Coniscliffe** Darltn
178 B7 **Low Crosby** Cumb
169 K8 **Low Dinsdale** Darltn
142 E3 **Low Eggborough** N York
160 B6 **Low Ellington** N York
181 G7 **Low Fell** Gatesd
208 D2 **Low Gartachorrans** Stirlg
179 L6 **Low Gate** Nthumb
178 C7 **Low Gettbridge** Cumb
150 B2 **Low Grantley** N York
150 B4 **Low Green** N York
97 H7 **Low Habberley** Worcs
30 F5 **Low Ham** Somset
150 C5 **Low Harrogate** N York
163 G1 **Low Hawsker** N York
166 B2 **Low Hesket** Cumb
97 J8 **Low Hill** Worcs
152 A2 **Low Hutton** N York
166 C6 **Low Knipe** Cumb
150 B3 **Low Laithe** N York
136 C4 **Low Langton** Lincs
131 K3 **Low Leighton** Derbys
164 F5 **Low Lorton** Cumb
134 F6 **Low Marnham** Notts
203 H6 **Low Middleton** Nthumb
161 L4 **Low Mill** N York
141 J2 **Low Moor** Brad
148 C7 **Low Moor** Lancs
169 J2 **Low Moorsley** Sundld
152 D2 **Low Mowthorpe** N York
156 F6 **Low Newton** Cumb
164 F5 **Low Rogerscales** Cumb
165 G2 **Low Row** Cumb
165 K3 **Low Row** Cumb
178 D6 **Low Row** Cumb
159 H3 **Low Row** N York
172 C2 **Low Salchrie** D & G
144 B5 **Low Santon** N Linc
123 G6 **Low Street** Norfk
52 E3 **Low Street** Thurr
106 D4 **Low Tharston** Norfk
210 D2 **Low Torry** Fife
136 E5 **Low Toynton** Lincs
142 B7 **Low Valley** Barns

169 G7 **Low Walworth** Darltn
156 E6 **Low Wood** Cumb
160 F1 **Low Worsall** N York
156 E2 **Low Wray** Cumb
63 M1 **Lowbands** Gloucs
164 C6 **Lowca** Cumb
117 H2 **Lowdham** Notts
113 H5 **Lowe** Shrops
131 K8 **Lowe Hill** Staffs
30 B4 **Lower Aisholt** Somset
16 E2 **Lower Ansty** Dorset
64 B2 **Lower Apperley** Gloucs
66 F3 **Lower Arncott** Oxon
13 K5 **Lower Ashton** Devon
49 H2 **Lower Assendon** Oxon
138 D2 **Lower Ballam** Lancs
79 M4 **Lower Barewood** Herefs
139 G1 **Lower Bartle** Lancs
48 F3 **Lower Basildon** W Berk
37 K5 **Lower Beeding** W Susx
101 L5 **Lower Benefield** Nhants
82 A2 **Lower Bentley** Worcs
97 H5 **Lower Beobridge** Shrops
116 D1 **Lower Birchwood** Derbys
83 L5 **Lower Boddington** Nhants
2 B4 **Lower Boscaswell** Cnwll
36 C2 **Lower Bourne** Surrey
83 H7 **Lower Brailes** Warwks
247 L4 **Lower Breakish** Highld
131 H2 **Lower Bredbury** Stockp
81 J4 **Lower Broadheath** Worcs
80 E8 **Lower Buckenhill** Herefs
80 C7 **Lower Bullingham** Herefs
33 K7 **Lower Burgate** Hants
14 B3 **Lower Burrowton** Devon
80 A4 **Lower Burton** Herefs
86 D6 **Lower Caldecote** Beds
63 L7 **Lower Cam** Gloucs
44 D7 **Lower Canada** N Som
83 M3 **Lower Catesby** Nhants
78 E8 **Lower Chapel** Powys
33 G5 **Lower Chicksgrove** Wilts
47 L8 **Lower Chute** Wilts
51 K2 **Lower Clapton** Gt Lon
97 L7 **Lower Clent** Worcs
82 E6 **Lower Clopton** Warwks
13 K2 **Lower Creedy** Devon
131 L4 **Lower Crossings** Derbys
141 K6 **Lower Cumberworth** Kirk
57 L3 **Lower Cwmtwrch** Powys
139 K3 **Lower Darwen** Bl w D
85 L2 **Lower Dean** Beds
141 K6 **Lower Denby** Kirk
260 C7 **Lower Diabaig** Highld
23 J5 **Lower Dicker** E Susx
95 L6 **Lower Dinchope** Shrops
95 H6 **Lower Down** Shrops
150 F3 **Lower Dunsforth** N York
80 E6 **Lower Egleton** Herefs
131 L8 **Lower Elkstone** Staffs
115 J3 **Lower Ellastone** Staffs
67 G5 **Lower End** Bucks
85 H7 **Lower End** M Keyn
85 H3 **Lower End** Nhants
47 J8 **Lower Everleigh** Wilts
19 G4 **Lower Exbury** Hants
41 J5 **Lower Eythorne** Kent
45 G4 **Lower Failand** N Som
35 L4 **Lower Farringdon** Hants
50 E4 **Lower Feltham** Gt Lon
21 G3 **Lower Fittleworth** W Susx
154 c6 **Lower Foxdale** IOM
112 E5 **Lower Frankton** Shrops
54 F4 **Lower Freystrop** Pembks
36 A2 **Lower Froyle** Hants
8 D1 **Lower Gabwell** Devon
263 G2 **Lower Gledfield** Highld
31 G2 **Lower Godney** Somset
86 C8 **Lower Gornal** Dudley
86 C8 **Lower Gravenhurst** Beds
86 D8 **Lower Green** Herts
87 J8 **Lower Green** Herts
38 E5 **Lower Green** Kent
39 G5 **Lower Green** Kent
84 F3 **Lower Green** Nhants
121 L4 **Lower Green** Norfk
97 K2 **Lower Green** Staffs
88 E2 **Lower Green** Suffk
139 L7 **Lower Green** Wigan
91 H4 **Lower Hacheston** Suffk
50 E5 **Lower Halliford** Surrey
15 M1 **Lower Halstock Leigh** Dorset
53 J5 **Lower Halstow** Kent
17 K4 **Lower Hamworthy** Poole
40 F5 **Lower Hardres** Kent

79 K3 **Lower Harpton** Herefs
53 H6 **Lower Hartlip** Kent
116 C1 **Lower Hartshay** Derbys
67 J4 **Lower Hartwell** Bucks
114 C4 **Lower Hatton** Staffs
156 B5 **Lower Hawthwaite** Cumb
79 K4 **Lower Hergest** Herefs
66 C2 **Lower Heyford** Oxon
147 H4 **Lower Heysham** Lancs
52 F4 **Lower Higham** Kent
90 E8 **Lower Holbrook** Suffk
112 F5 **Lower Hordley** Shrops
21 G3 **Lower Horncroft** W Susx
81 H5 **Lower Howsell** Worcs
130 D1 **Lower Irlam** Salfd
116 C3 **Lower Kilburn** Derbys
46 A1 **Lower Kilcott** Gloucs
204 D7 **Lower Killeyan** Ag & B
16 A3 **Lower Kingcombe** Dorset
51 H8 **Lower Kingswood** Surrey
129 H7 **Lower Kinnerton** Ches
44 F6 **Lower Langford** N Som
223 G6 **Lower Largo** Fife
115 G4 **Lower Leigh** Staffs
82 F8 **Lower Lemington** Gloucs
78 C2 **Lower Llanfadog** Powys
27 J5 **Lower Lovacott** Devon
27 L3 **Lower Loxhore** Devon
63 H4 **Lower Lydbrook** Gloucs
79 M2 **Lower Lye** Herefs
43 K4 **Lower Machen** Newpt
62 D1 **Lower Maes-coed** Herefs
17 L2 **Lower Mannington** Dorset
32 C2 **Lower Marston** Somset
63 H6 **Lower Meend** Gloucs
30 B4 **Lower Merridge** Somset
83 L7 **Lower Middleton Cheney** Nhants
31 J2 **Lower Milton** Somset
82 A6 **Lower Moor** Worcs
63 J8 **Lower Morton** S Glos
69 K6 **Lower Nazeing** Essex
82 F3 **Lower Norton** Warwks
32 C6 **Lower Nyland** Dorset
43 J7 **Lower Penarth** V Glam
97 K4 **Lower Penn** Staffs
18 E5 **Lower Pennington** Hants
139 G2 **Lower Penwortham** Lancs
130 E5 **Lower Peover** Ches
140 D5 **Lower Place** Rochdl
67 H4 **Lower Pollicott** Bucks
82 E6 **Lower Quinton** Warwks
53 H5 **Lower Rainham** Medway
90 B7 **Lower Raydon** Suffk
29 J3 **Lower Roadwater** Somset
147 M3 **Lower Salter** Lancs
46 D3 **Lower Seagry** Wilts
70 C4 **Lower Sheering** Essex
85 K6 **Lower Shelton** Beds
49 J3 **Lower Shiplake** Oxon
83 L3 **Lower Shuckburgh** Warwks
65 H3 **Lower Slaughter** Gloucs
141 L3 **Lower Soothill** Kirk
63 K5 **Lower Soudley** Gloucs
41 H7 **Lower Standen** Kent
46 D3 **Lower Stanton St Quintin** Wilts
53 H4 **Lower Stoke** Medway
63 K8 **Lower Stone** Gloucs
98 D3 **Lower Stonnall** Staffs
105 K4 **Lower Stow Bedon** Norfk
17 G3 **Lower Street** Dorset
24 C5 **Lower Street** E Susx
122 F4 **Lower Street** Norfk
88 F5 **Lower Street** Suffk
90 D5 **Lower Street** Suffk
130 C3 **Lower Stretton** Warrtn
15 K3 **Lower Stroud** Dorset
68 D2 **Lower Sundon** Beds
19 H2 **Lower Swanwick** Hants
65 H2 **Lower Swell** Gloucs
83 J7 **Lower Tadmarton** Oxon
14 C2 **Lower Tale** Devon
115 G4 **Lower Tean** Staffs
107 J3 **Lower Thurlton** Norfk
3 G5 **Lower Town** Cnwll
13 G7 **Lower Town** Devon
80 E6 **Lower Town** Herefs
74 F5 **Lower Town** Pembks
11 L7 **Lower Trebullett** Cnwll
6 D4 **Lower Tregantle** Cnwll
3 K4 **Lower Treluswell** Cnwll
83 H6 **Lower Tysoe** Warwks
91 G5 **Lower Ufford** Suffk
13 K6 **Lower Upcott** Devon

35 H7 **Lower Upham** Hants
53 G5 **Lower Upnor** Medway
29 L4 **Lower Vexford** Somset
130 B3 **Lower Walton** Warrtn
16 E3 **Lower Waterston** Dorset
44 E8 **Lower Weare** Somset
84 C3 **Lower Weedon** Nhants
79 K5 **Lower Welson** Herefs
81 L7 **Lower Westmancote** Worcs
17 G2 **Lower Whatcombe** Dorset
32 B2 **Lower Whatley** Somset
130 B4 **Lower Whitley** Ches
63 L7 **Lower Wick** Gloucs
81 J5 **Lower Wick** Worcs
35 K3 **Lower Wield** Hants
23 K6 **Lower Willingdon** E Susx
130 F5 **Lower Withington** Ches
49 K2 **Lower Woodend** Bucks
33 K4 **Lower Woodford** Wilts
16 A2 **Lower Wraxhall** Dorset
81 H6 **Lower Wyche** Worcs
141 J3 **Lower Wyke** Brad
140 B1 **Lowerhouse** Lancs
100 F2 **Lowesby** Leics
107 L5 **Lowestoft** Suffk
164 F6 **Loweswater** Cumb
37 L3 **Lowfield Heath** W Susx
157 K3 **Lowgill** Cumb
148 A3 **Lowgill** Lancs
156 D5 **Lowick** Cumb
101 L7 **Lowick** Nhants
203 G5 **Lowick** Nthumb
156 D5 **Lowick Bridge** Cumb
156 D5 **Lowick Green** Cumb
168 E5 **Lowlands** Dur
62 C7 **Lowlands** Torfn
82 E2 **Lowsonford** Warwks
166 D6 **Lowther** Cumb
166 C6 **Lowther Castle** Cumb
153 H4 **Lowthorpe** E R Yk
12 F2 **Lowton** Devon
30 B7 **Lowton** Somset
139 J8 **Lowton** Wigan
139 J8 **Lowton Common** Wigan
139 J8 **Lowton St Mary's** Wigan
29 G2 **Loxbeare** Devon
36 F3 **Loxhill** Surrey
27 L3 **Loxhore** Devon
27 L3 **Loxhore Cott** Devon
83 G4 **Loxley** Warwks
115 H5 **Loxley Green** Staffs
81 G7 **Loxter** Herefs
44 D7 **Loxton** N Som
36 F4 **Loxwood** W Susx
277 L7 **Loyal Lodge** Highld
100 F6 **Lubenham** Leics
50 B7 **Lucas Green** Surrey
119 M2 **Lucasgate** Lincs
29 G2 **Luccombe** Somset
19 K7 **Luccombe Village** IOW
203 J7 **Lucker** Nthumb
11 M7 **Luckett** Cnwll
89 G8 **Lucking Street** Essex
46 B2 **Luckington** Wilts
46 B4 **Lucknam** Wilts
28 F3 **Luckwell Bridge** Somset
28 F2 **Lucott** Somset
80 B2 **Lucton** Herefs
169 G8 **Lucy Cross** N York
283 c12 **Ludag** W Isls
145 H8 **Ludborough** Lincs
7 J4 **Ludbrook** Devon
55 K4 **Ludchurch** Pembks
141 G3 **Luddenden** Calder
140 F3 **Luddenden Foot** Calder
40 C3 **Luddenham Court** Kent
52 E5 **Luddesdown** Kent
143 L4 **Luddington** N Linc
82 E5 **Luddington** Warwks
102 C6 **Luddington in the Brook** Nhants
136 D2 **Ludford** Lincs
96 C8 **Ludford** Shrops
67 G4 **Ludgershall** Bucks
34 B1 **Ludgershall** Wilts
2 D4 **Ludgvan** Cnwll
123 H7 **Ludham** Norfk
96 C8 **Ludlow** Shrops
30 F8 **Ludney** Somset
32 F6 **Ludwell** Wilts
169 K2 **Ludworth** Dur
69 J1 **Luffenhall** Herts
11 L4 **Luffincott** Devon
212 B3 **Luffness** E Loth
197 H6 **Lugar** E Ayrs

80 B3 **Lugg Green** Herefs
212 D4 **Luggate Burn** E Loth
209 K4 **Luggiebank** N Lans
129 M3 **Lugsdale** Halton
80 D7 **Lugwardine** Herefs
247 J3 **Luib** Highld
80 A7 **Lulham** Herefs
99 H1 **Lullington** Derbys
23 J6 **Lullington** E Susx
45 M8 **Lullington** Somset
45 G6 **Lulsgate Bottom** N Som
81 G4 **Lulsley** Worcs
16 F6 **Lulworth Camp** Dorset
140 F3 **Lumb** Calder
140 C3 **Lumb** Lancs
140 E3 **Lumbutts** Calder
142 D2 **Lumby** N York
209 H5 **Lumloch** E Duns
244 D3 **Lumphanan** Abers
222 B8 **Lumphinnans** Fife
255 K7 **Lumsden** Abers
235 H5 **Lunan** Angus
234 D5 **Lunanhead** Angus
221 K1 **Luncarty** P & K
152 E6 **Lund** E R Yk
143 G1 **Lund** N York
233 L8 **Lundie** Angus
220 C6 **Lundin** Stirlg
223 G6 **Lundin Links** Fife
223 G6 **Lundin Mill** Fife
106 E5 **Lundy Green** Norfk
281 e4 **Lunna** Shet
52 F7 **Lunsford** Kent
24 C5 **Lunsford's Cross** E Susx
138 D7 **Lunt** Sefton
79 M4 **Luntley** Herefs
14 E1 **Luppitt** Devon
7 L4 **Lupridge** Devon
141 M4 **Lupset** Wakefd
157 J6 **Lupton** Cumb
36 D5 **Lurgashall** W Susx
29 G7 **Lurley** Devon
136 F6 **Lusby** Lincs
8 B3 **Luscombe** Devon
7 H5 **Luson** Devon
218 E8 **Luss** Ag & B
258 D5 **Lusta** Highld
13 H6 **Lustleigh** Devon
80 B3 **Luston** Herefs
235 G2 **Luthermuir** Abers
222 E3 **Luthrie** Fife
97 L6 **Lutley** Dudley
14 C2 **Luton** Devon
13 L7 **Luton** Devon
68 E3 **Luton** Luton
53 G5 **Luton** Medway
100 C6 **Lutterworth** Leics
7 H5 **Lutton** Devon
7 K3 **Lutton** Devon
119 M6 **Lutton** Lincs
102 C6 **Lutton** Nhants
29 H3 **Luxborough** Somset
5 H3 **Luxulyan** Cnwll
140 E7 **Luzley** Tamesd
275 H1 **Lybster** Highld
95 J6 **Lydbury North** Shrops
28 B4 **Lydcott** Devon
25 K3 **Lydd** Kent
41 H6 **Lydden** Kent
41 K2 **Lydden** Kent
101 J4 **Lyddington** Rutlnd
49 H7 **Lyde Green** Hants
29 L4 **Lydeard St Lawrence** Somset
46 F7 **Lydeway** Wilts
12 C5 **Lydford** Devon
31 J5 **Lydford on Fosse** Somset
140 D3 **Lydgate** Calder
140 E4 **Lydgate** Rochdl
95 H5 **Lydham** Shrops
47 G2 **Lydiard Green** Wilts
47 G2 **Lydiard Millicent** Wilts
47 G2 **Lydiard Tregoze** Swindn
138 D7 **Lydiate** Sefton
98 B8 **Lydiate Ash** Worcs
32 B8 **Lydlinch** Dorset
63 J6 **Lydney** Gloucs
55 J7 **Lydstep** Pembks
97 L6 **Lye** Dudley
44 F6 **Lye Cross** N Som
68 B6 **Lye Green** Bucks
38 D6 **Lye Green** E Susx
82 E2 **Lye Green** Warwks
97 G8 **Lye Head** Worcs
32 D2 **Lye's Green** Wilts

80 B3 **Lugg Green** Herefs
66 B8 **Lyford** Oxon
40 F6 **Lymbridge Green** Kent
15 H4 **Lyme Regis** Dorset
40 F7 **Lyminge** Kent
18 E4 **Lymington** Hants
21 H6 **Lyminster** W Susx
130 D2 **Lymm** Warrtn
40 F8 **Lympne** Kent
44 C8 **Lympsham** Somset
14 A5 **Lympstone** Devon
28 C1 **Lynbridge** Devon
28 F2 **Lynch** Somset
106 C2 **Lynch Green** Norfk
241 L3 **Lynchat** Highld
18 D2 **Lyndhurst** Hants
101 K3 **Lyndon** Rutlnd
98 F6 **Lyndon Green** Birm
199 L5 **Lyne** Border
50 C5 **Lyne** Surrey
63 J1 **Lyne Down** Herefs
245 G2 **Lyne of Skene** Abers
113 G5 **Lyneal** Shrops
13 K6 **Lyneham** Devon
65 K3 **Lyneham** Oxon
46 F3 **Lyneham** Wilts
178 C4 **Lyneholmford** Cumb
191 K7 **Lynemouth** Nthumb
275 b6 **Lyness** Ork
122 B7 **Lyng** Norfk
30 E5 **Lyng** Somset
79 K4 **Lynhales** Herefs
28 C1 **Lynmouth** Devon
98 D3 **Lynn** Staffs
114 B8 **Lynn** Wrekin
254 E6 **Lynn of Shenval** Moray
40 B3 **Lynsted** Kent
11 H2 **Lynstone** Cnwll
28 C1 **Lynton** Devon
16 C2 **Lyon's Gate** Dorset
79 L4 **Lyonshall** Herefs
17 J3 **Lytchett Matravers** Dorset
17 J4 **Lytchett Minster** Dorset
280 C4 **Lyth** Highld
138 D2 **Lytham** Lancs
138 D2 **Lytham St Anne's** Lancs
95 L2 **Lythbank** Shrops
171 K8 **Lythe** N York
279 J3 **Lythmore** Highld

M

3 J4 **Mabe Burnthouse** Cnwll
176 C5 **Mabie** D & G
137 J3 **Mablethorpe** Lincs
131 H5 **Macclesfield** Ches
268 C3 **Macduff** Abers
192 E6 **Macharioch** Ag & B
43 K4 **Machen** Caerph
194 D4 **Machrie** N Ayrs
192 D4 **Machrihanish** Ag & B
214 D5 **Machrins** Ag & B
93 G3 **Machynlleth** Powys
56 F5 **Machynys** Carmth
116 A4 **Mackworth** Derbys
211 M4 **Macmerry** E Loth
12 D4 **Maddaford** Devon
221 G3 **Madderty** P & K
33 J2 **Maddington** Wilts
210 B4 **Maddiston** Falk
21 G5 **Madehurst** W Susx
114 B3 **Madeley** Staffs
96 F3 **Madeley** Wrekin
114 B2 **Madeley Heath** Staffs
29 L8 **Madford** Devon
87 H3 **Madingley** Cambs
80 A7 **Madley** Herefs
81 J5 **Madresfield** Worcs
2 C5 **Madron** Cnwll
76 C3 **Maen-y-groes** Cerdgn
125 H3 **Maenaddwyn** IOA
126 F6 **Maenan** Conwy
75 J6 **Maenclochog** Pembks
42 F6 **Maendy** V Glam
3 K5 **Maenporth** Cnwll
110 C3 **Maentwrog** Gwynd
11 H1 **Maer** Cnwll
114 B4 **Maer** Staffs
59 J3 **Maerdy** Carmth
42 E2 **Maerdy** Rhondd
44 C2 **Maes-glas** Newpt
112 D7 **Maesbrook** Shrops
112 D6 **Maesbury** Shrops
112 D6 **Maesbury Marsh** Shrops

334 Maesgwynne - Mauchline

55 L2 **Maesgwynne** Carmth
128 E7 **Maeshafn** Denbgs
76 C6 **Maesllyn** Cerdgn
78 D6 **Maesmynis** Powys
78 E5 **Maesmynis** Powys
42 C3 **Maesteg** Brdgnd
59 G5 **Maesybont** Carmth
43 J3 **Maesycwmmer** Caerph
70 D5 **Magdalen Laver** Essex
254 F3 **Maggieknockater** Moray
70 C2 **Maggots End** Essex
23 K5 **Magham Down** E Susx
138 D7 **Maghull** Sefton
44 E2 **Magor** Mons
32 D3 **Maiden Bradley** Wilts
45 H5 **Maiden Head** N Som
168 F1 **Maiden Law** Dur
16 B3 **Maiden Newton** Dorset
55 G7 **Maiden Wells** Pembks
37 L4 **Maidenbower** W Susx
8 D1 **Maidencombe** Torbay
15 G3 **Maidenhayne** Devon
49 L3 **Maidenhead** W & M
182 F1 **Maidens** S Ayrs
49 L4 **Maidens Green** Br For
136 F4 **Maidenwell** Lincs
84 B5 **Maidford** Nhants
84 D8 **Maids Moreton** Bucks
39 J2 **Maidstone** Kent
101 G8 **Maidwell** Nhants
44 C1 **Maindee** Newpt
234 D3 **Mains of Balhall** Angus
244 E8 **Mains of Balnakettle** Abers
254 B5 **Mains of Dalvey** Highld
235 H1 **Mains of Haulkerton** Abers
169 J4 **Mainsforth** Dur
176 B7 **Mainsriddle** D & G
95 G6 **Mainstone** Shrops
64 A3 **Maisemore** Gloucs
98 E7 **Major's Green** Worcs
116 B3 **Makeney** Derbys
7 K7 **Malborough** Devon
131 L3 **Malcoff** Derbys
51 G5 **Malden** Surrey
50 F6 **Malden Rushett** Gt Lon
71 K5 **Maldon** Essex
148 F3 **Malham** N York
237 K1 **Mallaig** Highld
237 K1 **Mallaigvaig** Highld
211 G6 **Malleny Mills** C Edin
70 C2 **Mallows Green** Essex
125 G6 **Malltraeth** IOA
93 J1 **Mallwyd** Gwynd
46 D2 **Malmesbury** Wilts
28 D1 **Malmsmead** Somset
113 H2 **Malpas** Ches
4 D6 **Malpas** Cnwll
44 C1 **Malpas** Newpt
63 L2 **Malswick** Gloucs
136 F3 **Maltby** Lincs
133 K1 **Maltby** Rothm
170 B8 **Maltby** S on T
137 J3 **Maltby le Marsh** Lincs
72 E3 **Malting Green** Essex
40 B6 **Maltman's Hill** Kent
152 B2 **Malton** N York
81 H5 **Malvern Link** Worcs
81 H6 **Malvern Wells** Worcs
173 K4 **Malzie** D & G
80 F1 **Mamble** Worcs
62 C6 **Mamhilad** Mons
3 J6 **Manaccan** Cnwll
94 D3 **Manafon** Powys
282 e6 **Manais** W Isls
13 H6 **Manaton** Devon
137 G2 **Manby** Lincs
99 J4 **Mancetter** Warwks
140 C8 **Manchester** Manch
129 H6 **Mancot** Flints
240 A3 **Mandally** Highld
103 K5 **Manea** Cambs
98 E4 **Maney** Birm
169 G8 **Manfield** N York
15 L3 **Mangerton** Dorset
45 K4 **Mangotsfield** S Glos
68 E2 **Mangrove Green** Herts
3 H5 **Manhay** Cnwll
282 e6 **Manish** W Isls
140 E3 **Mankinholes** Calder
129 L5 **Manley** Ches
61 J6 **Manmoel** Caerph
224 C7 **Mannel** Ag & B
37 K5 **Manning's Heath** W Susx
47 H7 **Manningford Bohune** Wilts
47 H7 **Manningford Bruce** Wilts
141 J1 **Manningham** Brad
17 L2 **Mannington** Dorset
73 G1 **Manningtree** Essex
245 K3 **Mannofield** C Aber
51 L2 **Manor Park** Gt Lon
55 H7 **Manorbier** Pembks
55 H6 **Manorbier Newton** Pembks
59 J4 **Manordeilo** Carmth
201 K6 **Manorhill** Border
74 F5 **Manorowen** Pembks
79 M6 **Mansell Gamage** Herefs
80 A6 **Mansell Lacy** Herefs
157 K6 **Mansergh** Cumb
197 J8 **Mansfield** E Ayrs
133 K7 **Mansfield** Notts
133 L7 **Mansfield Woodhouse** Notts
156 D6 **Mansriggs** Cumb
32 D7 **Manston** Dorset
41 K2 **Manston** Kent
142 B1 **Manston** Leeds
17 J1 **Manswood** Dorset
118 B4 **Manthorpe** Lincs
118 E8 **Manthorpe** Lincs
144 A7 **Manton** N Linc
134 C4 **Manton** Notts
101 J3 **Manton** Rutlnd
47 H5 **Manton** Wilts
70 C2 **Manuden** Essex
70 E4 **Manwood Green** Essex
31 L5 **Maperton** Somset
68 C8 **Maple Cross** Herts
134 E7 **Maplebeck** Notts
49 G4 **Mapledurham** Oxon
49 G8 **Mapledurwell** Hants
37 J6 **Maplehurst** W Susx
52 C6 **Maplescombe** Kent
115 K2 **Mapleton** Derbys
38 C3 **Mapleton** Kent
116 D3 **Mapperley** Derbys
117 G3 **Mapperley Park** C Nott
15 L3 **Mapperton** Dorset
82 C2 **Mappleborough Green** Warwks
153 K7 **Mappleton** E R Yk
141 M5 **Mapplewell** Barns
16 E1 **Mappowder** Dorset
4 C5 **Marazanvose** Cnwll
2 E5 **Marazion** Cnwll
113 J2 **Marbury** Ches
103 J4 **March** Cambs
186 E3 **March** S Lans
66 C7 **Marcham** Oxon
113 K5 **Marchamley** Shrops
113 K5 **Marchamley Wood** Shrops
115 J5 **Marchington** Staffs
115 J6 **Marchington Woodlands** Staffs
108 E6 **Marchros** Gwynd
112 E2 **Marchwiel** Wrexhm
18 F2 **Marchwood** Hants
42 D7 **Marcross** V Glam
80 C6 **Marden** Herefs
39 J4 **Marden** Kent
47 G7 **Marden** Wilts
70 E6 **Marden Ash** Essex
39 J5 **Marden Beech** Kent
39 J5 **Marden Thorn** Kent
38 D7 **Mardens Hill** E Susx
69 H3 **Mardlebury** Herts
62 C4 **Mardy** Mons
101 J2 **Marefield** Leics
136 E7 **Mareham le Fen** Lincs
136 E6 **Mareham on the Hill** Lincs
116 C2 **Marehay** Derbys
21 H3 **Marehill** W Susx
23 G2 **Maresfield** E Susx
144 F2 **Marfleet** C KuH
129 H8 **Marford** Wrexhm
57 L7 **Margam** Neath
32 D7 **Margaret Marsh** Dorset
70 F5 **Margaret Roding** Essex
71 G6 **Margaretting** Essex
71 G7 **Margaretting Tye** Essex
41 K1 **Margate** Kent
195 G4 **Margnaheglish** N Ayrs
174 F5 **Margrie** D & G
170 F7 **Margrove Park** R & Cl
104 E2 **Marham** Norfk
11 J2 **Marhamchurch** Cnwll
102 C3 **Marholm** C Pete
125 J3 **Marian-glas** IOA
28 C6 **Mariansleigh** Devon
53 K4 **Marine Town** Kent
244 F2 **Marionburgh** Abers
259 H4 **Marishader** Highld
6 F2 **Maristow** Devon
176 E2 **Marjoriebanks** D & G
30 F1 **Mark** Somset
30 E2 **Mark Causeway** Somset
38 F7 **Mark Cross** E Susx
19 H5 **Mark's Corner** IOW
38 D5 **Markbeech** Kent
137 J4 **Markby** Lincs
116 B4 **Markeaton** C Derb
99 L3 **Market Bosworth** Leics
102 C2 **Market Deeping** Lincs
113 L5 **Market Drayton** Shrops
100 F6 **Market Harborough** Leics
46 E8 **Market Lavington** Wilts
118 A8 **Market Overton** Rutlnd
136 B2 **Market Rasen** Lincs
136 D4 **Market Stainton** Lincs
152 D7 **Market Weighton** E R Yk
105 K7 **Market Weston** Suffk
100 B2 **Markfield** Leics
61 J6 **Markham** Caerph
134 E5 **Markham Moor** Notts
222 E6 **Markinch** Fife
150 C3 **Markington** N York
212 C3 **Markle** E Loth
72 C2 **Marks Tey** Essex
45 K6 **Marksbury** BaNES
6 D3 **Markwell** Cnwll
68 D4 **Markyate** Herts
81 H7 **Marl Bank** Worcs
47 J5 **Marlborough** Wilts
80 C4 **Marlbrook** Herefs
98 B8 **Marlbrook** Worcs
82 C5 **Marlcliff** Warwks
8 C2 **Marldon** Devon
23 K4 **Marle Green** E Susx
91 H3 **Marlesford** Suffk
41 G5 **Marley** Kent
41 K4 **Marley** Kent
113 J2 **Marley Green** Ches
180 F7 **Marley Hill** Gatesd
106 C2 **Marlingford** Norfk
54 C5 **Marloes** Pembks
49 K2 **Marlow** Bucks
95 K8 **Marlow** Herefs
49 K1 **Marlow Bottom** Bucks
38 C4 **Marlpit Hill** Kent
38 C7 **Marlpits** E Susx
24 C4 **Marlpits** E Susx
116 D3 **Marlpool** Derbys
32 C7 **Marnhull** Dorset
131 J2 **Marple** Stockp
131 J2 **Marple Bridge** Stockp
142 E6 **Marr** Donc
159 K3 **Marrick** N York
55 L5 **Marros** Carmth
141 G5 **Marsden** Kirk
181 K6 **Marsden** S Tyne
148 F8 **Marsden Height** Lancs
158 F5 **Marsett** N York
149 J8 **Marsh** Brad
67 K5 **Marsh** Bucks
30 C8 **Marsh** Devon
66 E7 **Marsh Baldon** Oxon
48 B5 **Marsh Benham** W Berk
145 K7 **Marsh Chapel** Lincs
66 F3 **Marsh Gibbon** Bucks
14 B4 **Marsh Green** Devon
38 C4 **Marsh Green** Kent
131 H7 **Marsh Green** Staffs
113 K8 **Marsh Green** Wrekin
133 H4 **Marsh Lane** Derbys
63 H5 **Marsh Lane** Gloucs
29 H2 **Marsh Street** Somset
68 F4 **Marshall's Heath** Herts
68 F5 **Marshalswick** Herts
122 D6 **Marsham** Norfk
41 J4 **Marshborough** Kent
95 K5 **Marshbrook** Shrops
43 L5 **Marshfield** Newpt
45 M4 **Marshfield** S Glos
11 G4 **Marshgate** Cnwll
103 L2 **Marshland St James** Norfk
138 D4 **Marshside** Sefton
15 J3 **Marshwood** Dorset
159 K3 **Marske** N York
170 E6 **Marske-by-the-Sea** R & Cl
139 K7 **Marsland Green** Wigan
130 D5 **Marston** Ches
79 L4 **Marston** Herefs
118 A3 **Marston** Lincs
66 D5 **Marston** Oxon
97 J1 **Marston** Staffs
114 E6 **Marston** Staffs
99 G4 **Marston** Warwks
46 D7 **Marston** Wilts
98 F6 **Marston Green** Solhll
99 K5 **Marston Jabbet** Warwks
31 K6 **Marston Magna** Somset
65 H7 **Marston Meysey** Wilts
115 J4 **Marston Montgomery** Derbys
85 K7 **Marston Moretaine** Beds
115 L5 **Marston on Dove** Derbys
83 M6 **Marston St Lawrence** Nhants
80 D4 **Marston Stannett** Herefs
100 F6 **Marston Trussell** Nhants
63 H3 **Marstow** Herefs
68 A4 **Marsworth** Bucks
47 L7 **Marten** Wilts
130 F4 **Marthall** Ches
123 J7 **Martham** Norfk
33 J7 **Martin** Hants
41 K6 **Martin** Kent
136 B7 **Martin** Lincs
136 D6 **Martin** Lincs
136 C7 **Martin Dales** Lincs
33 H6 **Martin Drove End** Hants
81 K3 **Martin Hussingtree** Worcs
166 B6 **Martindale** Cumb
28 B1 **Martinhoe** Devon
130 C2 **Martinscroft** Warrtn
16 C5 **Martinstown** Dorset
90 F6 **Martlesham** Suffk
90 F6 **Martlesham Heath** Suffk
55 H5 **Martletwy** Pembks
81 H3 **Martley** Worcs
31 G7 **Martock** Somset
130 C6 **Marton** Ches
131 G6 **Marton** Ches
156 C7 **Marton** Cumb
153 J7 **Marton** E R Yk
153 K2 **Marton** E R Yk
135 G3 **Marton** Lincs
170 C7 **Marton** Middsb
150 F3 **Marton** N York
162 C6 **Marton** N York
95 G3 **Marton** Shrops
83 J2 **Marton** Warwks
150 E2 **Marton-le-Moor** N York
35 G4 **Martyr Worthy** Hants
50 E7 **Martyr's Green** Surrey
275 b3 **Marwick** Ork
27 K3 **Marwood** Devon
12 C6 **Mary Tavy** Devon
250 E1 **Marybank** Highld
262 F8 **Maryburgh** Highld
245 J4 **Maryculter** Abers
213 H7 **Marygold** Border
256 E3 **Maryhill** Abers
208 F5 **Maryhill** C Glas
235 H2 **Marykirk** Abers
63 G6 **Maryland** Mons
51 H3 **Marylebone** Gt Lon
139 H6 **Marylebone** Wigan
254 D4 **Marypark** Moray
164 D3 **Maryport** Cumb
172 E7 **Maryport** D & G
12 B6 **Marystow** Devon
235 H4 **Maryton** Angus
244 D4 **Marywell** Abers
245 L4 **Marywell** Abers
235 G6 **Marywell** Angus
160 B6 **Masham** N York
71 G5 **Mashbury** Essex
180 F4 **Mason** N u Ty
157 L7 **Masongill** N York
133 J4 **Mastin Moor** Derbys
70 D5 **Matching** Essex
70 D5 **Matching Green** Essex
70 D5 **Matching Tye** Essex
180 C4 **Matfen** Nthumb
39 G5 **Matfield** Kent
45 G1 **Mathern** Mons
81 G6 **Mathon** Herefs
74 E6 **Mathry** Pembks
122 C4 **Matlask** Norfk
132 F7 **Matlock** Derbys
132 F7 **Matlock Bank** Derbys
132 F8 **Matlock Bath** Derbys
132 F7 **Matlock Dale** Derbys
64 B4 **Matson** Gloucs
165 L6 **Matterdale End** Cumb
134 D2 **Mattersey** Notts
134 D2 **Mattersey Thorpe** Notts
49 H7 **Mattingley** Hants
105 L1 **Mattishall** Norfk
105 L1 **Mattishall Burgh** Norfk
196 F5 **Mauchline** E Ayrs

Maud - Middlewood 335

269 G6 **Maud** Abers
9 e2 **Maufant** Jersey
65 J2 **Maugersbury** Gloucs
154 g4 **Maughold** IOM
250 C4 **Mauld** Highld
85 L7 **Maulden** Beds
166 E7 **Maulds Meaburn** Cumb
160 E5 **Maunby** N York
80 D5 **Maund Bryan** Herefs
29 J5 **Maundown** Somset
107 K1 **Mautby** Norfk
115 H8 **Mavesyn Ridware** Staffs
137 G6 **Mavis Enderby** Lincs
130 D8 **Maw Green** Ches
164 E1 **Mawbray** Cumb
139 G5 **Mawdesley** Lancs
42 B5 **Mawdlam** Brdgnd
3 H6 **Mawgan** Cnwll
3 H6 **Mawgan Cross** Cnwll
4 D2 **Mawgan Porth** Cnwll
4 A5 **Mawla** Cnwll
3 K5 **Mawnan** Cnwll
3 K5 **Mawnan Smith** Cnwll
137 J5 **Mawthorpe** Lincs
102 C2 **Maxey** C Pete
99 G5 **Maxstoke** Warwks
40 F6 **Maxted Street** Kent
201 J7 **Maxton** Border
41 J7 **Maxton** Kent
176 C4 **Maxwell Town** D & G
11 J4 **Maxworthy** Cnwll
114 D2 **May Bank** Staffs
49 H3 **May's Green** Oxon
50 E7 **May's Green** Surrey
57 H6 **Mayals** Swans
183 H1 **Maybole** S Ayrs
50 C7 **Maybury** Surrey
37 H3 **Mayes Green** Surrey
23 K2 **Mayfield** E Susx
211 K6 **Mayfield** Mdloth
115 J2 **Mayfield** Staffs
50 C7 **Mayford** Surrey
72 D6 **Mayland** Essex
23 K3 **Maynard's Green** E Susx
98 D7 **Maypole** Birm
41 G2 **Maypole** Kent
62 F4 **Maypole** Mons
107 J4 **Maypole Green** Norfk
89 J3 **Maypole Green** Suffk
91 G2 **Maypole Green** Suffk
26 C7 **Mead** Devon
45 K7 **Meadgate** BaNES
67 K6 **Meadle** Bucks
169 H3 **Meadowfield** Dur
95 H3 **Meadowtown** Shrops
12 A6 **Meadwell** Devon
157 H4 **Meal Bank** Cumb
164 F2 **Mealrigg** Cumb
165 H2 **Mealsgate** Cumb
150 C8 **Meanwood** Leeds
148 E4 **Mearbeck** N York
31 G3 **Meare** Somset
30 E5 **Meare Green** Somset
30 D6 **Meare Green** Somset
208 F7 **Mearns** E Rens
85 G2 **Mears Ashby** Nhants
99 J1 **Measham** Leics
156 F6 **Meathop** Cumb
153 H7 **Meaux** E R Yk
7 G2 **Meavy** Devon
101 H5 **Medbourne** Leics
26 D7 **Meddon** Devon
134 B5 **Meden Vale** Notts
136 F8 **Medlam** Lincs
147 H8 **Medlar** Lancs
49 K2 **Medmenham** Bucks
180 D7 **Medomsley** Dur
35 K3 **Medstead** Hants
79 L5 **Meer Common** Herefs
131 K7 **Meerbrook** Staffs
70 B1 **Meesden** Herts
113 L7 **Meeson** Wrekin
12 D1 **Meeth** Devon
88 E4 **Meeting Green** Suffk
122 F6 **Meeting House Hill** Norfk
58 B5 **Meidrim** Carmth
94 E1 **Meifod** Powys
233 L6 **Meigle** P & K
186 A3 **Meikle Carco** D & G
209 J8 **Meikle Earnock** S Lans
207 G6 **Meikle Kilmory** Ag & B
232 F7 **Meikle Obney** P & K
256 C5 **Meikle Wartle** Abers
233 J7 **Meikleour** P & K
56 E3 **Meinciau** Carmth
114 E3 **Meir** C Stke
114 E3 **Meir Heath** Staffs
87 H6 **Melbourn** Cambs
116 C6 **Melbourne** Derbys
152 A7 **Melbourne** E R Yk
26 F7 **Melbury** Devon
32 E6 **Melbury Abbas** Dorset
16 B1 **Melbury Bubb** Dorset
16 A1 **Melbury Osmond** Dorset
16 A2 **Melbury Sampford** Dorset
85 K2 **Melchbourne** Beds
16 E2 **Melcombe Bingham** Dorset
12 D4 **Meldon** Devon
180 D2 **Meldon** Nthumb
180 D2 **Meldon Park** Nthumb
87 H6 **Meldreth** Cambs
220 C7 **Meldrum** Stirlg
4 F4 **Meledor** Cnwll
216 C4 **Melfort** Ag & B
234 E4 **Melgund Castle** Angus
128 C3 **Meliden** Denbgs
60 B6 **Melin Court** Neath
93 H4 **Melin-byrhedyn** Powys
127 G7 **Melin-y-coed** Conwy
94 D2 **Melin-y-ddol** Powys
111 K2 **Melin-y-wig** Denbgs
55 K4 **Melinau** Pembks
166 D5 **Melkinthorpe** Cumb
179 G6 **Melkridge** Nthumb
46 C6 **Melksham** Wilts
48 C3 **Mell Green** W Berk
3 H5 **Mellangoose** Cnwll
166 B2 **Mellguards** Cumb
147 M2 **Melling** Lancs
138 E7 **Melling** Sefton
138 E7 **Melling Mount** Sefton
95 G5 **Mellington** Powys
106 B8 **Mellis** Suffk
260 D2 **Mellon Charles** Highld
260 E1 **Mellon Udrigle** Highld
139 K2 **Mellor** Lancs
131 K2 **Mellor** Stockp
139 J2 **Mellor Brook** Lancs
32 B1 **Mells** Somset
107 H8 **Mells** Suffk
166 E3 **Melmerby** Cumb
159 K5 **Melmerby** N York
160 E7 **Melmerby** N York
277 K4 **Melness** Highld
89 G4 **Melon Green** Suffk
15 L3 **Melplash** Dorset
201 H6 **Melrose** Border
275 b6 **Melsetter** Ork
160 B1 **Melsonby** N York
141 H5 **Meltham** Kirk
141 H5 **Meltham Mills** Kirk
144 B3 **Melton** E R Yk
91 G5 **Melton** Suffk
122 A5 **Melton Constable** Norfk
117 K7 **Melton Mowbray** Leics
144 D5 **Melton Ross** N Linc
152 B5 **Meltonby** E R Yk
260 B3 **Melvaig** Highld
112 E8 **Melverley** Shrops
112 E7 **Melverley Green** Shrops
278 E3 **Melvich** Highld
15 G2 **Membury** Devon
269 H4 **Memsie** Abers
234 C4 **Memus** Angus
5 J4 **Menabilly** Cnwll
4 B5 **Menagissey** Cnwll
125 K5 **Menai Bridge** IOA
106 F6 **Mendham** Suffk
90 D2 **Mendlesham** Suffk
90 C3 **Mendlesham Green** Suffk
6 B2 **Menheniot** Cnwll
81 G2 **Menithwood** Worcs
185 K2 **Mennock** D & G
149 L7 **Menston** Brad
220 E7 **Menstrie** Clacks
143 H1 **Menthorpe** N York
67 M3 **Mentmore** Bucks
238 C6 **Meoble** Highld
96 B1 **Meole Brace** Shrops
35 J7 **Meonstoke** Hants
52 D5 **Meopham** Kent
52 D6 **Meopham Green** Kent
52 D5 **Meopham Station** Kent
103 J7 **Mepal** Cambs
86 C8 **Meppershall** Beds
130 E3 **Mere** Ches
32 D4 **Mere** Wilts
138 E4 **Mere Brow** Lancs
98 E4 **Mere Green** Birm
81 L3 **Mere Green** Worcs
130 C5 **Mere Heath** Ches
140 C2 **Mereclough** Lancs
53 H6 **Meresborough** Medway
39 G3 **Mereworth** Kent
99 G7 **Meriden** Solhll
246 E2 **Merkadale** Highld
17 K3 **Merley** Poole
54 F4 **Merlin's Bridge** Pembks
8 B5 **Merrifield** Devon
113 G7 **Merrington** Shrops
54 F7 **Merrion** Pembks
31 G8 **Merriott** Somset
12 D7 **Merrivale** Devon
36 F1 **Merrow** Surrey
17 K2 **Merry Field Hill** Dorset
68 E8 **Merry Hill** Herts
100 A2 **Merry Lees** Leics
97 K4 **Merryhill** Wolves
6 B2 **Merrymeet** Cnwll
40 D7 **Mersham** Kent
51 H8 **Merstham** Surrey
20 E6 **Merston** W Susx
19 J6 **Merstone** IOW
4 D6 **Merther** Cnwll
58 C5 **Merthyr** Carmth
78 D7 **Merthyr Cynog** Powys
43 H7 **Merthyr Dyfan** V Glam
42 D6 **Merthyr Mawr** Brdgnd
61 G6 **Merthyr Tydfil** Myr Td
61 G7 **Merthyr Vale** Myr Td
27 J8 **Merton** Devon
51 H5 **Merton** Gt Lon
105 H4 **Merton** Norfk
66 E3 **Merton** Oxon
28 D7 **Meshaw** Devon
72 C3 **Messing** Essex
143 M6 **Messingham** N Linc
106 F7 **Metfield** Suffk
6 E1 **Metherell** Cnwll
11 G7 **Metherin** Cnwll
135 L7 **Metheringham** Lincs
222 F7 **Methil** Fife
222 F7 **Methilhill** Fife
3 G5 **Methleigh** Cnwll
142 B2 **Methley** Leeds
142 B3 **Methley Junction** Leeds
256 F4 **Methlick** Abers
221 J2 **Methven** P & K
104 E4 **Methwold** Norfk
104 E4 **Methwold Hythe** Norfk
107 H5 **Mettingham** Suffk
122 D4 **Metton** Norfk
5 G6 **Mevagissey** Cnwll
142 D7 **Mexborough** Donc
280 C2 **Mey** Highld
108 D5 **Meyllteyrn** Gwynd
65 G7 **Meysey Hampton** Gloucs
282 e3 **Miabhig** W Isls
282 e3 **Miavaig** W Isls
63 G2 **Michaelchurch** Herefs
79 K8 **Michaelchurch Escley** Herefs
79 J5 **Michaelchurch-on-Arrow** Powys
43 J7 **Michaelston-le-Pit** V Glam
43 K5 **Michaelstone-y-Fedw** Newpt
10 F6 **Michaelstow** Cnwll
7 K1 **Michelcombe** Devon
35 G3 **Micheldever** Hants
35 G2 **Micheldever Station** Hants
34 D5 **Michelmersh** Hants
90 D3 **Mickfield** Suffk
129 K5 **Mickle Trafford** Ches
133 K1 **Micklebring** Donc
171 J8 **Mickleby** N York
142 C1 **Micklefield** Leeds
68 D7 **Micklefield Green** Herts
50 F8 **Mickleham** Surrey
116 A5 **Mickleover** C Derb
149 K7 **Micklethwaite** Brad
165 J1 **Micklethwaite** Cumb
168 B6 **Mickleton** Dur
82 E6 **Mickleton** Gloucs
142 B2 **Mickletown** Leeds
132 F4 **Mickley** Derbys
160 C7 **Mickley** N York
89 G4 **Mickley Green** Suffk
180 C6 **Mickley Square** Nthumb
269 H3 **Mid Ardlaw** Abers
244 E3 **Mid Beltie** Abers
18 B4 **Mid Bockhampton** Hants
210 E5 **Mid Calder** W Loth
280 C8 **Mid Clyth** Highld
37 J2 **Mid Holmwood** Surrey
20 D5 **Mid Lavant** W Susx
250 D4 **Mid Mains** Highld
136 E5 **Mid Thorpe** Lincs
281 e3 **Mid Yell** Shet
275 c2 **Midbea** Ork
49 H2 **Middle Assendon** Oxon
66 C2 **Middle Aston** Oxon
66 B2 **Middle Barton** Oxon
31 G8 **Middle Chinnock** Somset
67 H2 **Middle Claydon** Bucks
64 E6 **Middle Duntisbourne** Gloucs
133 H4 **Middle Handley** Derbys
105 K6 **Middle Harling** Norfk
206 E1 **Middle Kames** Ag & B
82 C6 **Middle Littleton** Worcs
114 B3 **Middle Madeley** Staffs
79 L8 **Middle Maes-coed** Herefs
115 J3 **Middle Mayfield** Staffs
74 C7 **Middle Mill** Pembks
40 A7 **Middle Quarter** Kent
136 A2 **Middle Rasen** Lincs
8 D1 **Middle Rocombe** Devon
147 M3 **Middle Salter** Lancs
30 B6 **Middle Stoford** Somset
53 H4 **Middle Stoke** Medway
30 F1 **Middle Stoughton** Somset
63 M6 **Middle Street** Gloucs
5 K2 **Middle Taphouse** Cnwll
10 b3 **Middle Town** IOS
83 H6 **Middle Tysoe** Warwks
34 C3 **Middle Wallop** Hants
34 B4 **Middle Winterslow** Wilts
33 K4 **Middle Woodford** Wilts
64 B6 **Middle Yard** Gloucs
177 H4 **Middlebie** D & G
232 C2 **Middlebridge** P & K
142 C6 **Middlecliffe** Barns
13 G5 **Middlecott** Devon
159 L5 **Middleham** N York
6 B1 **Middlehill** Cnwll
46 B5 **Middlehill** Wilts
96 B5 **Middlehope** Shrops
16 C1 **Middlemarsh** Dorset
12 C7 **Middlemore** Devon
170 C6 **Middlesbrough** Middsb
165 L2 **Middlesceugh** Cumb
157 J5 **Middleshaw** Cumb
159 K7 **Middlesmoor** N York
169 H4 **Middlestone** Dur
169 H4 **Middlestone Moor** Dur
141 L4 **Middlestown** Wakefd
201 L4 **Middlethird** Border
224 B6 **Middleton** Ag & B
157 K5 **Middleton** Cumb
132 D7 **Middleton** Derbys
132 E8 **Middleton** Derbys
89 H7 **Middleton** Essex
34 F2 **Middleton** Hants
80 D1 **Middleton** Herefs
147 H4 **Middleton** Lancs
141 M2 **Middleton** Leeds
208 C8 **Middleton** N Ayrs
149 L6 **Middleton** N York
162 D5 **Middleton** N York
101 J5 **Middleton** Nhants
120 E8 **Middleton** Norfk
203 H6 **Middleton** Nthumb
180 C2 **Middleton** Nthumb
221 L6 **Middleton** P & K
140 C6 **Middleton** Rochdl
112 D5 **Middleton** Shrops
96 C7 **Middleton** Shrops
91 K2 **Middleton** Suffk
56 D7 **Middleton** Swans
98 F4 **Middleton** Warwks
83 L7 **Middleton Cheney** Nhants
114 F4 **Middleton Green** Staffs
202 F8 **Middleton Hall** Nthumb
91 J2 **Middleton Moor** Suffk
80 C2 **Middleton on the Hill** Herefs
152 E6 **Middleton on the Wolds** E R Yk
169 K8 **Middleton One Row** Darltn
96 E5 **Middleton Priors** Shrops
160 E7 **Middleton Quernhow** N York
96 F6 **Middleton Scriven** Shrops
169 K8 **Middleton St George** Darltn
66 D2 **Middleton Stoney** Oxon
160 B2 **Middleton Tyas** N York
168 B5 **Middleton-in-Teesdale** Dur
161 G1 **Middleton-on-Leven** N York
20 F6 **Middleton-on-Sea** W Susx
155 H1 **Middletown** Cumb
44 F4 **Middletown** N Som
95 H1 **Middletown** Powys
130 D6 **Middlewich** Ches
11 K7 **Middlewood** Cnwll

79 K6 **Middlewood** Herefs
90 C3 **Middlewood Green** Suffk
197 G4 **Middleyard** E Ayrs
30 E4 **Middlezoy** Somset
169 H5 **Middridge** Dur
45 M6 **Midford** BaNES
139 G3 **Midge Hall** Lancs
178 E7 **Midgeholme** Cumb
48 E5 **Midgham** W Berk
140 F3 **Midgley** Calder
141 L5 **Midgley** Wakefd
141 K7 **Midhopestones** Sheff
36 C6 **Midhurst** W Susx
201 H7 **Midlem** Border
31 H5 **Midney** Somset
207 G7 **Midpark** Ag & B
45 K8 **Midsomer Norton** BaNES
277 K4 **Midtown** Highld
137 G8 **Midville** Lincs
131 H3 **Midway** Ches
244 A2 **Migvie** Abers
31 L7 **Milborne Port** Somset
16 F3 **Milborne St Andrew** Dorset
31 L6 **Milborne Wick** Somset
180 D4 **Milbourne** Nthumb
46 D2 **Milbourne** Wilts
166 F5 **Milburn** Cumb
45 K1 **Milbury Heath** S Glos
150 F2 **Milby** N York
83 K8 **Milcombe** Oxon
89 J6 **Milden** Suffk
104 E8 **Mildenhall** Suffk
47 J5 **Mildenhall** Wilts
46 E5 **Mile Elm** Wilts
72 E2 **Mile End** Essex
63 H5 **Mile End** Gloucs
107 G5 **Mile End** Suffk
22 C5 **Mile Oak** Br & H
39 H4 **Mile Oak** Kent
98 F3 **Mile Oak** Staffs
53 K4 **Mile Town** Kent
79 K1 **Milebrook** Powys
39 J4 **Milebush** Kent
121 K4 **Mileham** Norfk
80 D2 **Miles Hope** Herefs
140 C7 **Miles Platting** Manch
210 E1 **Milesmark** Fife
202 E6 **Milfield** Nthumb
116 B3 **Milford** Derbys
26 D6 **Milford** Devon
94 D5 **Milford** Powys
114 F7 **Milford** Staffs
36 E2 **Milford** Surrey
54 E5 **Milford Haven** Pembks
18 D5 **Milford on Sea** Hants
63 H5 **Milkwall** Gloucs
140 F3 **Mill Bank** Calder
131 J2 **Mill Brow** Stockp
107 G3 **Mill Common** Norfk
107 H7 **Mill Common** Suffk
7 L3 **Mill Cross** Devon
49 J2 **Mill End** Bucks
103 G7 **Mill End** Cambs
87 G8 **Mill End** Herts
88 C6 **Mill Green** Cambs
70 F6 **Mill Green** Essex
69 G5 **Mill Green** Herts
119 H6 **Mill Green** Lincs
106 C6 **Mill Green** Norfk
98 D3 **Mill Green** Staffs
115 H7 **Mill Green** Staffs
89 J6 **Mill Green** Suffk
89 K4 **Mill Green** Suffk
90 D3 **Mill Green** Suffk
91 H3 **Mill Green** Suffk
23 L6 **Mill Hill** E Susx
69 G8 **Mill Hill** Gt Lon
114 C5 **Mill Meece** Staffs
220 E4 **Mill of Drummond** P & K
208 C3 **Mill of Haldane** W Duns
157 G6 **Mill Side** Cumb
39 H2 **Mill Street** Kent
121 M7 **Mill Street** Norfk
122 B7 **Mill Street** Norfk
90 C1 **Mill Street** Suffk
9 a1 **Millais** Jersey
36 B5 **Milland** W Susx
36 C5 **Milland Marsh** W Susx
165 H5 **Millbeck** Cumb
257 J3 **Millbreck** Abers
256 E3 **Millbrex** Abers
36 C2 **Millbridge** Surrey
85 K7 **Millbrook** Beds
34 E8 **Millbrook** C Sotn
6 E4 **Millbrook** Cnwll

9 c3 **Millbrook** Jersey
140 E7 **Millbrook** Tamesd
245 H2 **Millbuie** Abers
250 F1 **Millbuie** Highld
196 E5 **Millburn** S Ayrs
8 B5 **Millcombe** Devon
24 E3 **Millcorner** E Susx
263 H5 **Millcraig** Highld
115 J1 **Milldale** Staffs
63 H5 **Millend** Gloucs
63 L7 **Millend** Gloucs
132 C5 **Miller's Dale** Derbys
70 E5 **Miller's Green** Essex
211 K5 **Millerhill** Mdloth
115 M1 **Millers Green** Derbys
209 H5 **Millerston** N Lans
140 D4 **Millgate** Lancs
113 L6 **Millgreen** Shrops
79 K5 **Millhalf** Herefs
14 F2 **Millhayes** Devon
147 K2 **Millhead** Lancs
198 B3 **Millheugh** S Lans
206 F5 **Millhouse** Ag & B
165 K3 **Millhouse** Cumb
141 K7 **Millhouse Green** Barns
176 F2 **Millhousebridge** D & G
142 C6 **Millhouses** Barns
133 G3 **Millhouses** Sheff
208 C6 **Milliken Park** Rens
55 G4 **Millin Cross** Pembks
152 C5 **Millington** E R Yk
152 C5 **Millness** Cumb
157 H6 **Millness** Cumb
155 M6 **Millom** Cumb
11 H3 **Millook** Cnwll
2 F5 **Millpool** Cnwll
11 G8 **Millpool** Cnwll
207 K8 **Millport** N Ayrs
132 F4 **Millthorpe** Derbys
157 L4 **Millthrop** Cumb
245 J3 **Milltimber** C Aber
243 J2 **Milltown** Abers
255 J8 **Milltown** Abers
5 J3 **Milltown** Cnwll
177 K4 **Milltown** D & G
133 G7 **Milltown** Derbys
27 K3 **Milltown** Devon
244 E3 **Milltown of Campfield** Abers
254 F4 **Milltown of Edinvillie** Moray
244 E3 **Milltown of Learney** Abers
221 L6 **Milnathort** P & K
208 F4 **Milngavie** W Duns
140 D5 **Milnrow** Rochdl
157 H6 **Milnthorpe** Cumb
142 A4 **Milnthorpe** Wakefd
258 B6 **Milovaig** Highld
80 E1 **Milson** Shrops
40 A3 **Milstead** Kent
33 L2 **Milston** Wilts
118 F5 **Milthorpe** Lincs
84 B6 **Milthorpe** Nhants
114 E2 **Milton** C Stke
87 K3 **Milton** Cambs
178 D6 **Milton** Cumb
172 F4 **Milton** D & G
175 L1 **Milton** D & G
116 A6 **Milton** Derbys
280 D6 **Milton** Highld
248 A3 **Milton** Highld
250 E5 **Milton** Highld
251 G2 **Milton** Highld
263 K5 **Milton** Highld
208 B5 **Milton** Inver
52 E4 **Milton** Kent
267 K3 **Milton** Moray
44 D6 **Milton** N Som
44 D1 **Milton** Newpt
134 E5 **Milton** Notts
83 K8 **Milton** Oxon
66 C8 **Milton** Oxon
233 H4 **Milton** P & K
55 H6 **Milton** Pembks
31 G6 **Milton** Somset
219 H7 **Milton** Stirlg
208 D4 **Milton** W Duns
16 F2 **Milton Abbas** Dorset
12 A6 **Milton Abbot** Devon
211 H6 **Milton Bridge** Mdloth
68 B1 **Milton Bryan** Beds
31 L3 **Milton Clevedon** Somset
6 F2 **Milton Combe** Devon
67 G6 **Milton Common** Oxon
27 G8 **Milton Damerel** Devon
63 L5 **Milton End** Gloucs
65 H7 **Milton End** Gloucs
85 K4 **Milton Ernest** Beds

129 K7 **Milton Green** Ches
48 C1 **Milton Hill** Oxon
85 G7 **Milton Keynes** M Keyn
47 J7 **Milton Lilbourne** Wilts
84 E4 **Milton Malsor** Nhants
231 H8 **Milton Morenish** P & K
244 C3 **Milton of Auchinhove** Abers
222 E7 **Milton of Balgonie** Fife
208 D1 **Milton of Buchanan** Stirlg
209 H4 **Milton of Campsie** E Duns
251 J3 **Milton of Leys** Highld
243 L4 **Milton of Tullich** Abers
32 D5 **Milton on Stour** Dorset
40 A2 **Milton Regis** Kent
23 J6 **Milton Street** E Susx
65 K3 **Milton-under-Wychwood** Oxon
29 L5 **Milverton** Somset
83 H2 **Milverton** Warwks
114 F5 **Milwich** Staffs
128 E5 **Milwr** Flints
216 F7 **Minard** Ag & B
33 G7 **Minchington** Dorset
64 D7 **Minchinhampton** Gloucs
202 C6 **Mindrum** Nthumb
202 C6 **Mindrum Mill** Nthumb
29 H2 **Minehead** Somset
112 C1 **Minera** Wrexhm
46 F1 **Minety** Wilts
109 L4 **Minffordd** Gwynd
237 K6 **Mingarrypark** Highld
136 F6 **Miningsby** Lincs
11 J8 **Minions** Cnwll
196 C8 **Minishant** S Ayrs
111 G8 **Minllyn** Gwynd
173 K2 **Minnigaff** D & G
41 J2 **Minnis Bay** Kent
268 D4 **Minnonie** Abers
130 D7 **Minshull Vernon** Ches
150 E3 **Minskip** N York
18 D2 **Minstead** Hants
20 D3 **Minsted** W Susx
53 L4 **Minster** Kent
41 J2 **Minster** Kent
65 L5 **Minster Lovell** Oxon
180 B7 **Minsteracres** Nthumb
95 J2 **Minsterley** Shrops
63 M4 **Minsterworth** Gloucs
16 C2 **Minterne Magna** Dorset
16 C2 **Minterne Parva** Dorset
136 C5 **Minting** Lincs
269 J6 **Mintlaw** Abers
188 F2 **Minto** Border
95 K5 **Minton** Shrops
55 H4 **Minwear** Pembks
98 F5 **Minworth** Birm
164 C7 **Mirehouse** Cumb
141 K4 **Mirfield** Kirk
64 D5 **Miserden** Gloucs
43 G5 **Miskin** Rhondd
43 G2 **Miskin** Rhondd
134 D1 **Misson** Notts
100 C6 **Misterton** Leics
134 F1 **Misterton** Notts
15 K1 **Misterton** Somset
73 G1 **Mistley** Essex
73 H1 **Mistley Heath** Essex
51 H5 **Mitcham** Gt Lon
62 F5 **Mitchel Troy** Mons
63 K3 **Mitcheldean** Gloucs
4 D4 **Mitchell** Cnwll
186 E7 **Mitchellslacks** D & G
180 E2 **Mitford** Nthumb
4 B5 **Mithian** Cnwll
114 D8 **Mitton** Staffs
84 B8 **Mixbury** Oxon
141 G2 **Mixenden** Calder
131 L8 **Mixon** Staffs
90 B4 **Moats Tye** Suffk
130 F4 **Mobberley** Ches
115 G3 **Mobberley** Staffs
79 L6 **Moccas** Herefs
127 G4 **Mochdre** Conwy
94 D7 **Mochdre** Powys
173 J5 **Mochrum** D & G
18 B2 **Mockbeggar** Hants
39 H4 **Mockbeggar** Kent
164 E6 **Mockerkin** Cumb
7 J4 **Modbury** Devon
114 E4 **Moddershall** Staffs
125 J8 **Moel Tryfan** Gwynd
125 J2 **Moelfre** IOA
112 B6 **Moelfre** Powys
187 G5 **Moffat** D & G
86 C5 **Mogerhanger** Beds

116 A8 **Moira** Leics
246 F6 **Mol-chlach** Highld
40 D5 **Molash** Kent
128 F7 **Mold** Flints
141 J4 **Moldgreen** Kirk
70 E2 **Molehill Green** Essex
71 H3 **Molehill Green** Essex
152 F7 **Molescroft** E R Yk
180 E2 **Molesden** Nthumb
102 B8 **Molesworth** Cambs
28 E5 **Molland** Devon
129 J5 **Mollington** Ches
83 K5 **Mollington** Oxon
209 J4 **Mollinsburn** N Lans
76 F3 **Monachty** Cerdgn
245 G7 **Mondynes** Abers
90 F3 **Monewden** Suffk
221 J1 **Moneydie** P & K
49 L3 **Moneyrow Green** W & M
185 J5 **Moniaive** D & G
223 J1 **Monifieth** Angus
234 D7 **Monikie** Angus
222 E4 **Monimail** Fife
75 K3 **Monington** Pembks
142 B6 **Monk Bretton** Barns
142 D2 **Monk Fryston** N York
48 F7 **Monk Sherborne** Hants
90 F2 **Monk Soham** Suffk
90 E2 **Monk Soham Green** Suffk
70 F1 **Monk Street** Essex
37 K5 **Monk's Gate** W Susx
69 H7 **Monken Hadley** Gt Lon
80 E6 **Monkhide** Herefs
177 K7 **Monkhill** Cumb
96 E5 **Monkhopton** Shrops
80 B4 **Monkland** Herefs
27 H6 **Monkleigh** Devon
42 D7 **Monknash** V Glam
12 E2 **Monkokehampton** Devon
151 K5 **Monks Cross** N York
89 K5 **Monks Eleigh** Suffk
131 G5 **Monks Heath** Ches
40 F7 **Monks Horton** Kent
100 A6 **Monks Kirby** Warwks
67 K6 **Monks Risborough** Bucks
181 J4 **Monkseaton** N Tyne
29 K3 **Monksilver** Somset
98 E8 **Monkspath** Solhll
137 H6 **Monksthorpe** Lincs
62 D6 **Monkswood** Mons
14 E2 **Monkton** Devon
41 J2 **Monkton** Kent
196 D5 **Monkton** S Ayrs
181 H6 **Monkton** S Tyne
42 D7 **Monkton** V Glam
45 M6 **Monkton Combe** BaNES
32 E3 **Monkton Deverill** Wilts
46 A6 **Monkton Farleigh** Wilts
30 C5 **Monkton Heathfield** Somset
33 H8 **Monkton Up Wimborne** Dorset
15 H3 **Monkton Wyld** Dorset
181 K7 **Monkwearmouth** Sundld
35 K5 **Monkwood** Hants
97 L4 **Monmore Green** Wolves
63 G4 **Monmouth** Mons
79 L6 **Monnington on Wye** Herefs
173 J6 **Monreith** D & G
9 i3 **Mont Saint** Guern
31 H7 **Montacute** Somset
139 K5 **Montcliffe** Bolton
112 F8 **Montford** Shrops
113 G8 **Montford Bridge** Shrops
255 L8 **Montgarrie** Abers
197 G5 **Montgarswood** E Ayrs
94 F4 **Montgomery** Powys
196 C2 **Montgreenan** N Ayrs
140 A7 **Monton** Salfd
235 H4 **Montrose** Angus
34 C2 **Monxton** Hants
132 C6 **Monyash** Derbys
256 C8 **Monymusk** Abers
220 F2 **Monzie** P & K
209 J5 **Moodiesburn** N Lans
222 F4 **Moonzie** Fife
150 D8 **Moor Allerton** Leeds
17 K1 **Moor Crichel** Dorset
68 B3 **Moor End** Beds
141 G2 **Moor End** Calder
12 F1 **Moor End** Devon
152 B8 **Moor End** E R Yk
147 G6 **Moor End** Lancs
151 J8 **Moor End** N York
69 J2 **Moor Green** Herts
141 K2 **Moor Head** Leeds

Moor Monkton - Nailsea 337

151 H4 **Moor Monkton** N York
164 D7 **Moor Row** Cumb
165 H1 **Moor Row** Cumb
168 F7 **Moor Row** Dur
147 K8 **Moor Side** Lancs
138 E1 **Moor Side** Lancs
136 E8 **Moor Side** Lincs
98 C6 **Moor Street** Birm
53 H6 **Moor Street** Medway
15 K3 **Moorbath** Dorset
136 E6 **Moorby** Lincs
79 L4 **Moorcot** Herefs
17 L4 **Moordown** Bmouth
130 B3 **Moore** Halton
63 L6 **Moorend** Gloucs
143 H4 **Moorends** Donc
35 G7 **Moorgreen** Hants
116 E2 **Moorgreen** Notts
132 F5 **Moorhall** Derbys
79 M6 **Moorhampton** Herefs
149 L8 **Moorhead** Brad
177 H8 **Moorhouse** Cumb
177 K7 **Moorhouse** Cumb
142 D5 **Moorhouse** Donc
134 E6 **Moorhouse** Notts
51 L8 **Moorhouse Bank** Surrey
30 E4 **Moorland** Somset
30 F3 **Moorlinch** Somset
170 F7 **Moorsholm** R & Cl
155 K2 **Moorside** Cumb
32 D7 **Moorside** Dorset
150 C8 **Moorside** Leeds
140 E6 **Moorside** Oldham
40 E7 **Moorstock** Kent
5 M2 **Moorswater** Cnwll
142 C5 **Moorthorpe** Wakefd
12 C7 **Moortown** Devon
18 A3 **Moortown** Hants
19 G7 **Moortown** IOW
150 D7 **Moortown** Leeds
144 D7 **Moortown** Lincs
113 K7 **Moortown** Wrekin
263 K3 **Morangie** Highld
237 K2 **Morar** Highld
102 C5 **Morborne** Cambs
13 H1 **Morchard Bishop** Devon
15 J4 **Morcombelake** Dorset
101 K3 **Morcott** Rutlnd
112 D6 **Morda** Shrops
17 H3 **Morden** Dorset
51 H5 **Morden** Gt Lon
80 D7 **Mordiford** Herefs
169 J5 **Mordon** Dur
95 H5 **More** Shrops
29 G6 **Morebath** Devon
189 K1 **Morebattle** Border
147 H3 **Morecambe** Lancs
47 H2 **Moredon** Swindn
261 J1 **Morefield** Highld
41 G7 **Morehall** Kent
7 L4 **Moreleigh** Devon
231 H8 **Morenish** P & K
164 C6 **Moresby** Cumb
164 C6 **Moresby Parks** Cumb
35 G6 **Morestead** Hants
16 F4 **Moreton** Dorset
70 D5 **Moreton** Essex
80 C2 **Moreton** Herefs
67 G6 **Moreton** Oxon
14 B8 **Moreton** Staffs
15 J5 **Moreton** Staffs
29 G2 **Moreton** Wirral
13 J6 **Moreton Corbet** Shrops
80 E5 **Moreton Jeffries** Herefs
83 H4 **Moreton Morrell** Warwks
80 C6 **Moreton on Lugg** Herefs
83 H4 **Moreton Paddox** Warwks
84 B5 **Moreton Pinkney** Nhants
13 K4 **Moreton Say** Shrops
63 M5 **Moreton Valence** Gloucs
65 J1 **Moreton-in-Marsh** Gloucs
13 H5 **Moretonhampstead** Devon
13 J7 **Moretonmill** Shrops
76 B4 **Morfa** Cerdgn
09 K4 **Morfa Bychan** Gwynd
25 H8 **Morfa Dinlle** Gwynd
60 C6 **Morfa Glas** Neath
08 E3 **Morfa Nefyn** Gwynd
33 L6 **Morgan's Vale** Wilts
43 H5 **Morganstown** Cardif
12 C5 **Morham** E Loth
92 D7 **Moriah** Cerdgn
66 E6 **Morland** Cumb
30 F3 **Morley** Ches
16 C3 **Morley** Derbys
168 E5 **Morley** Dur
141 L2 **Morley** Leeds
130 F3 **Morley Green** Ches
106 B3 **Morley St Botolph** Norfk
11 L8 **Mornick** Cnwll
211 H5 **Morningside** C Edin
209 L7 **Morningside** N Lans
106 E5 **Morningthorpe** Norfk
180 F2 **Morpeth** Nthumb
235 H3 **Morphie** Abers
115 J7 **Morrey** Staffs
115 G1 **Morridge Side** Staffs
131 K6 **Morridge Top** Staffs
57 J5 **Morriston** Swans
121 M3 **Morston** Norfk
27 H2 **Mortehoe** Devon
133 J2 **Morthen** Rothm
49 G6 **Mortimer** W Berk
49 G6 **Mortimer Common** W Berk
48 F6 **Mortimer West End** Hants
80 A3 **Mortimer's Cross** Herefs
51 G4 **Mortlake** Gt Lon
177 L7 **Morton** Cumb
166 B3 **Morton** Cumb
133 H7 **Morton** Derbys
19 K6 **Morton** IOW
134 F1 **Morton** Lincs
118 E6 **Morton** Lincs
117 J1 **Morton** Notts
112 D6 **Morton** Shrops
135 H7 **Morton Hall** Lincs
122 C8 **Morton on the Hill** Norfk
168 F6 **Morton Tinmouth** Dur
160 D4 **Morton-on-Swale** N York
2 B4 **Morvah** Cnwll
6 B3 **Morval** Cnwll
248 F7 **Morvich** Highld
96 F4 **Morville** Shrops
96 F4 **Morville Heath** Shrops
26 C7 **Morwenstow** Cnwll
133 H3 **Mosborough** Sheff
196 F3 **Moscow** E Ayrs
97 G5 **Mose** Shrops
165 K4 **Mosedale** Cumb
98 D6 **Moseley** Birm
97 L4 **Moseley** Wolves
81 J3 **Moseley** Worcs
139 L6 **Moses Gate** Bolton
224 B6 **Moss** Ag & B
142 F5 **Moss** Donc
112 D1 **Moss** Wrexhm
139 G8 **Moss Bank** St Hel
147 H7 **Moss Edge** Lancs
130 D4 **Moss End** Ches
177 G8 **Moss Side** Cumb
138 D2 **Moss Side** Lancs
138 D7 **Moss Side** Sefton
253 G1 **Moss-side** Highld
255 K7 **Mossat** Abers
281 e4 **Mossbank** Shet
164 C5 **Mossbay** Cumb
196 D6 **Mossblown** S Ayrs
130 D2 **Mossbrow** Traffd
189 H3 **Mossburnford** Border
175 G1 **Mossdale** D & G
184 D2 **Mossdale** E Ayrs
209 K7 **Mossend** N Lans
164 F5 **Mosser Mains** Cumb
131 H7 **Mossley** Ches
140 E7 **Mossley** Tamesd
188 C6 **Mosspaul Hotel** Border
267 G4 **Mosstodloch** Moray
139 G5 **Mossy Lea** Lancs
174 E4 **Mossyard** D & G
15 K2 **Mosterton** Dorset
140 C7 **Moston** Manch
113 J6 **Moston** Shrops
130 E7 **Moston Green** Ches
128 E4 **Mostyn** Flints
32 E6 **Motcombe** Dorset
7 H5 **Mothecombe** Devon
166 A5 **Motherby** Cumb
209 K7 **Motherwell** N Lans
51 G5 **Motspur Park** Gt Lon
51 L4 **Mottingham** Gt Lon
34 D5 **Mottisfont** Hants
18 F7 **Mottistone** IOW
140 F8 **Mottram in Longdendale** Tamesd
131 G4 **Mottram St Andrew** Ches
9 j3 **Mouilpied** Guern
129 L5 **Mouldsworth** Ches
232 D3 **Moulin** P & K
22 E6 **Moulsecoomb** Br & H
48 E2 **Moulsford** Oxon
85 H7 **Moulsoe** M Keyn
263 H5 **Moultavie** Highld
130 C5 **Moulton** Ches
119 J6 **Moulton** Lincs
160 C2 **Moulton** N York
84 F2 **Moulton** Nhants
88 D2 **Moulton** Suffk
43 G7 **Moulton** V Glam
119 J7 **Moulton Chapel** Lincs
119 K6 **Moulton Seas End** Lincs
107 H2 **Moulton St Mary** Norfk
4 C4 **Mount** Cnwll
5 K1 **Mount** Cnwll
141 H4 **Mount** Kirk
4 B6 **Mount Ambrose** Cnwll
89 H8 **Mount Bures** Essex
4 B5 **Mount Hawke** Cnwll
3 H7 **Mount Hermon** Cnwll
200 C2 **Mount Lothian** Mdloth
131 G8 **Mount Pleasant** Ches
116 B2 **Mount Pleasant** Derbys
169 H4 **Mount Pleasant** Dur
23 G4 **Mount Pleasant** E Susx
105 K4 **Mount Pleasant** Norfk
88 E5 **Mount Pleasant** Suffk
82 B2 **Mount Pleasant** Worcs
33 H6 **Mount Sorrel** Wilts
141 G2 **Mount Tabor** Calder
141 G2 **Mountain** Brad
61 G7 **Mountain Ash** Rhondd
199 K4 **Mountain Cross** Border
40 E5 **Mountain Street** Kent
24 D3 **Mountfield** E Susx
263 G7 **Mountgerald House** Highld
4 E3 **Mountjoy** Cnwll
70 F7 **Mountnessing** Essex
63 G8 **Mounton** Mons
116 F8 **Mountsorrel** Leics
36 E3 **Mousehill** Surrey
2 D5 **Mousehole** Cnwll
176 E4 **Mouswald** D & G
131 G8 **Mow Cop** Ches
189 L2 **Mowhaugh** Border
100 D2 **Mowmacre Hill** C Leic
100 E5 **Mowsley** Leics
245 J6 **Mowtie** Abers
252 E5 **Moy** Highld
240 D7 **Moy** Highld
248 D7 **Moye** Highld
18 B2 **Moyles Court** Hants
75 J3 **Moylgrove** Pembks
205 L8 **Muasdale** Ag & B
63 G1 **Much Birch** Herefs
80 E6 **Much Cowarne** Herefs
62 F1 **Much Dewchurch** Herefs
70 B3 **Much Hadham** Herts
138 F3 **Much Hoole** Lancs
138 F3 **Much Hoole Town** Lancs
80 F8 **Much Marcle** Herefs
96 E3 **Much Wenlock** Shrops
245 K5 **Muchalls** Abers
30 F6 **Muchelney** Somset
31 G6 **Muchelney Ham** Somset
5 L3 **Muchlarnick** Cnwll
52 E3 **Mucking** Thurr
52 E3 **Muckingford** Thurr
16 C4 **Muckleford** Dorset
114 A4 **Mucklestone** Staffs
96 E4 **Muckley** Shrops
137 G3 **Muckton** Lincs
53 M4 **Mud Row** Kent
27 K3 **Muddiford** Devon
23 J4 **Muddles Green** E Susx
18 B5 **Mudeford** Dorset
31 J7 **Mudford** Somset
31 J7 **Mudford Sock** Somset
31 G2 **Mudgley** Somset
208 F4 **Mugdock** Stirlg
246 F1 **Mugeary** Highld
115 M3 **Mugginton** Derbys
115 M3 **Muggintonlane End** Derbys
168 D1 **Muggleswick** Dur
244 C1 **Muir of Fowlis** Abers
266 D4 **Muir of Miltonduff** Moray
250 F2 **Muir of Ord** Highld
233 G7 **Muir of Thorn** P & K
268 C5 **Muirden** Abers
234 E7 **Muirdrum** Angus
268 C6 **Muiresk** Abers
233 M8 **Muirhead** Angus
222 D6 **Muirhead** Fife
209 J5 **Muirhead** N Lans
197 K5 **Muirkirk** E Ayrs
209 J2 **Muirmill** Stirlg
239 J7 **Muirshearlich** Highld
257 J4 **Muirtack** Abers
221 G5 **Muirton** P & K
250 E1 **Muirton Mains** Highld
233 J6 **Muirton of Ardblair** P & K
158 F3 **Muker** N York
106 D3 **Mulbarton** Norfk
267 G6 **Mulben** Moray
2 C4 **Mulfra** Cnwll
27 J2 **Mullacott Cross** Devon
3 H7 **Mullion** Cnwll
3 H7 **Mullion Cove** Cnwll
137 K5 **Mumby** Lincs
80 F5 **Munderfield Row** Herefs
80 F5 **Munderfield Stocks** Herefs
123 G4 **Mundesley** Norfk
104 F4 **Mundford** Norfk
107 G4 **Mundham** Norfk
72 C6 **Mundon Hill** Essex
40 B6 **Mundy Bois** Kent
165 L4 **Mungrisdale** Cumb
251 H1 **Munlochy** Highld
195 L1 **Munnoch** N Ayrs
80 F7 **Munsley** Herefs
96 C6 **Munslow** Shrops
13 G5 **Murchington** Devon
82 C7 **Murcot** Worcs
66 E4 **Murcott** Oxon
46 D1 **Murcott** Wilts
279 L3 **Murkle** Highld
239 G5 **Murlaggan** Highld
49 H7 **Murrell Green** Hants
234 C8 **Murroes** Angus
103 H2 **Murrow** Cambs
67 K2 **Mursley** Bucks
40 B2 **Murston** Kent
234 C4 **Murthill** Angus
233 G7 **Murthly** P & K
167 G6 **Murton** Cumb
169 K1 **Murton** Dur
181 H5 **Murton** N Tyne
202 F3 **Murton** Nthumb
151 K5 **Murton** York
15 G4 **Musbury** Devon
162 B6 **Muscoates** N York
211 K4 **Musselburgh** E Loth
117 L4 **Muston** Leics
163 K6 **Muston** N York
97 K8 **Mustow Green** Worcs
51 H1 **Muswell Hill** Gt Lon
175 H5 **Mutehill** D & G
107 K5 **Mutford** Suffk
220 F4 **Muthill** P & K
14 B2 **Mutterton** Devon
114 A8 **Muxton** Wrekin
279 L5 **Mybster** Highld
59 L3 **Myddfai** Carmth
113 G6 **Myddle** Shrops
76 E4 **Mydroilyn** Cerdgn
147 K7 **Myerscough** Lancs
3 L4 **Mylor** Cnwll
3 K4 **Mylor Bridge** Cnwll
75 K6 **Mynachlog ddu** Pembks
128 D5 **Myndd-llan** Flints
95 J5 **Myndtown** Shrops
92 F8 **Mynydd Buch** Cerdgn
128 F7 **Mynydd Isa** Flints
126 B6 **Mynydd Llandygai** Gwynd
62 F8 **Mynydd-bach** Mons
57 J5 **Mynydd-Bach** Swans
56 D3 **Mynyddgarreg** Carmth
108 E5 **Mynytho** Gwynd
245 G4 **Myrebird** Abers
189 G6 **Myredykes** Border
49 L7 **Mytchett** Surrey
140 E2 **Mytholm** Calder
140 F3 **Mytholmroyd** Calder
138 D1 **Mythop** Lancs
150 F3 **Myton-on-Swale** N York

N

282 d6 **Na Buirgh** W Isls
260 C3 **Naast** Highld
139 J2 **Nab's Head** Lancs
151 J6 **Naburn** York
40 D6 **Naccolt** Kent
40 F4 **Nackington** Kent
90 F7 **Nacton** Suffk
153 G4 **Nafferton** E R Yk
64 C7 **Nag's Head** Gloucs
63 J4 **Nailbridge** Gloucs
30 B5 **Nailsbourne** Somset
44 F5 **Nailsea** N Som

99 L2 **Nailstone** Leics
64 B7 **Nailsworth** Gloucs
264 D8 **Nairn** Highld
37 K2 **Nalderswood** Surrey
3 G4 **Nancegollan** Cnwll
2 D4 **Nancledra** Cnwll
108 E5 **Nanhoron** Gwynd
128 E5 **Nannerch** Flints
116 E8 **Nanpantan** Leics
4 F4 **Nanpean** Cnwll
2 B5 **Nanquidno** Cnwll
5 H2 **Nanstallon** Cnwll
110 B2 **Nant Gwynant** Gwynd
126 B7 **Nant Peris** Gwynd
60 F4 **Nant-ddu** Powys
78 D2 **Nant-glas** Powys
61 H5 **Nant-y-Bwch** Blae G
58 E5 **Nant-y-caws** Carmth
62 C6 **Nant-y-derry** Mons
112 C5 **Nant-y-gollen** Shrops
42 D3 **Nant-y-moel** Brdgnd
126 D5 **Nant-y-pandy** Conwy
76 C4 **Nanternis** Cerdgn
58 F4 **Nantgaredig** Carmth
43 H4 **Nantgarw** Rhondd
127 K7 **Nantglyn** Denbgs
93 L8 **Nantgwyn** Powys
109 J1 **Nantlle** Gwynd
112 C6 **Nantmawr** Shrops
78 E2 **Nantmel** Powys
109 L2 **Nantmor** Gwynd
113 L1 **Nantwich** Ches
42 C3 **Nantyffyllon** Brdgnd
61 K5 **Nantyglo** Blae G
67 K7 **Naphill** Bucks
81 K5 **Napleton** Worcs
148 E5 **Nappa** N York
83 L3 **Napton on the Hill** Warwks
55 J4 **Narberth** Pembks
100 C4 **Narborough** Leics
104 E1 **Narborough** Norfk
6 C4 **Narkurs** Cnwll
109 H2 **Nasareth** Gwynd
100 F7 **Naseby** Nhants
84 F8 **Nash** Bucks
51 L6 **Nash** Gt Lon
79 K3 **Nash** Herefs
44 D2 **Nash** Newpt
80 E1 **Nash** Shrops
97 H7 **Nash End** Worcs
67 K5 **Nash Lee** Bucks
52 D5 **Nash Street** Kent
35 K2 **Nash's Green** Hants
102 B4 **Nassington** Nhants
64 A6 **Nastend** Gloucs
69 K2 **Nasty** Herts
158 D1 **Nateby** Cumb
147 J7 **Nateby** Lancs
157 H5 **Natland** Cumb
89 L5 **Naughton** Suffk
65 G2 **Naunton** Gloucs
81 K7 **Naunton** Worcs
81 M5 **Naunton Beauchamp** Worcs
135 K8 **Navenby** Lincs
70 D7 **Navestock** Essex
70 E7 **Navestock Side** Essex
274 D5 **Navidale House Hotel** Highld
264 B7 **Navity** Highld
161 L5 **Nawton** N York
89 K8 **Nayland** Suffk
69 L6 **Nazeing** Essex
69 L6 **Nazeing Gate** Essex
18 B4 **Neacroft** Hants
99 J6 **Neal's Green** Warwks
281 e5 **Neap** Shet
115 H2 **Near Cotton** Staffs
156 E3 **Near Sawrey** Cumb
51 G2 **Neasden** Gt Lon
169 J8 **Neasham** Darltn
57 L5 **Neath** Neath
35 M3 **Neatham** Hants
123 G7 **Neatishead** Norfk
77 G2 **Nebo** Cerdgn
127 G8 **Nebo** Conwy
109 H2 **Nebo** Gwynd
125 H2 **Nebo** IOA
105 H2 **Necton** Norfk
270 F2 **Nedd** Highld
180 F2 **Nedderton** Nthumb
89 K5 **Nedging** Suffk
89 L5 **Nedging Tye** Suffk
106 E7 **Needham** Norfk
90 C4 **Needham Market** Suffk
88 E2 **Needham Street** Suffk
87 G1 **Needingworth** Cambs

96 F7 **Neen Savage** Shrops
80 F1 **Neen Sollars** Shrops
96 E6 **Neenton** Shrops
108 E3 **Nefyn** Gwynd
208 E7 **Neilston** E Rens
43 H3 **Nelson** Caerph
148 F8 **Nelson** Lancs
198 E4 **Nemphlar** S Lans
45 G7 **Nempnett Thrubwell** BaNES
167 H2 **Nenthall** Cumb
167 H2 **Nenthead** Cumb
201 L5 **Nenthorn** Border
13 J3 **Neopardy** Devon
22 B4 **Nep Town** W Susx
128 F7 **Nercwys** Flints
204 C5 **Nereabolls** Ag & B
209 H7 **Nerston** S Lans
202 F6 **Nesbit** Nthumb
149 K6 **Nesfield** N York
129 G4 **Ness** Ches
112 F7 **Nesscliffe** Shrops
129 G4 **Neston** Ches
46 B5 **Neston** Wilts
96 E5 **Netchwood** Shrops
131 G4 **Nether Alderley** Ches
201 H4 **Nether Blainslie** Border
117 J6 **Nether Broughton** Notts
16 C3 **Nether Cerne** Dorset
31 K7 **Nether Compton** Dorset
256 E7 **Nether Crimond** Abers
267 G3 **Nether Dallachy** Moray
13 L3 **Nether Exe** Devon
186 D4 **Nether Fingland** S Lans
133 H4 **Nether Handley** Derbys
234 B7 **Nether Handwick** Angus
142 C8 **Nether Haugh** Rothm
134 E4 **Nether Headon** Notts
116 B2 **Nether Heage** Derbys
84 C3 **Nether Heyford** Nhants
186 F4 **Nether Howcleugh** S Lans
147 K2 **Nether Kellet** Lancs
257 K3 **Nether Kinmundy** Abers
133 K5 **Nether Langwith** Notts
133 G6 **Nether Moor** Derbys
132 E4 **Nether Padley** Derbys
151 J5 **Nether Poppleton** York
165 K3 **Nether Row** Cumb
161 G4 **Nether Silton** N York
95 G8 **Nether Skyborry** Shrops
30 B3 **Nether Stowey** Somset
70 E5 **Nether Street** Essex
34 C4 **Nether Wallop** Hants
155 L2 **Nether Wasdale** Cumb
165 K2 **Nether Welton** Cumb
65 J3 **Nether Westcote** Gloucs
99 G5 **Nether Whitacre** Warwks
186 B2 **Nether Whitecleuch** S Lans
67 H4 **Nether Winchendon** Bucks
33 K1 **Netheravon** Wilts
268 E4 **Netherbrae** Abers
198 C4 **Netherburn** S Lans
15 L3 **Netherbury** Dorset
177 L4 **Netherby** Cumb
150 D6 **Netherby** N York
176 F2 **Nethercleuch** D & G
83 M2 **Nethercote** Warwks
27 H3 **Nethercott** Devon
11 L3 **Nethercott** Devon
63 H7 **Netherend** Gloucs
24 C3 **Netherfield** E Susx
117 G8 **Netherfield** Leics
117 G3 **Netherfield** Notts
24 D4 **Netherfield Road** E Susx
143 J7 **Nethergate** N Linc
122 B5 **Nethergate** Norfk
33 K5 **Netherhampton** Wilts
15 J2 **Netherhay** Dorset
115 H5 **Netherland Green** Staffs
175 J6 **Netherlaw** D & G
245 J5 **Netherley** Abers
176 D1 **Nethermill** D & G
257 G3 **Nethermuir** Abers
141 H4 **Netheroyd Hill** Kirk
208 E7 **Netherplace** E Rens
99 H1 **Netherseal** Derbys
46 E6 **Netherstreet** Wilts
141 H6 **Netherthong** Kirk
133 J5 **Netherthorpe** Derbys
234 E4 **Netherton** Angus
13 L8 **Netherton** Devon
97 L5 **Netherton** Dudley
48 A7 **Netherton** Hants
63 G2 **Netherton** Herefs
141 H5 **Netherton** Kirk
209 K8 **Netherton** N Lans

190 E4 **Netherton** Nthumb
66 B7 **Netherton** Oxon
233 H5 **Netherton** P & K
97 G6 **Netherton** Shrops
208 F3 **Netherton** Stirlg
141 L4 **Netherton** Wakefd
82 A7 **Netherton** Worcs
155 H1 **Nethertown** Cumb
280 E1 **Nethertown** Highld
148 C8 **Nethertown** Lancs
115 J8 **Nethertown** Staffs
199 K4 **Netherurd** Border
191 G8 **Netherwitton** Nthumb
253 J7 **Nethy Bridge** Highld
19 G2 **Netley** Hants
34 D8 **Netley Marsh** Hants
13 L3 **Nettacott** Devon
49 G2 **Nettlebed** Oxon
31 L1 **Nettlebridge** Somset
15 L3 **Nettlecombe** Dorset
19 J7 **Nettlecombe** IOW
68 C5 **Nettleden** Herts
135 K4 **Nettleham** Lincs
39 H3 **Nettlestead** Kent
39 H3 **Nettlestead Green** Kent
19 L5 **Nettlestone** IOW
169 H1 **Nettlesworth** Dur
144 E7 **Nettleton** Lincs
46 B3 **Nettleton** Wilts
46 B3 **Nettleton Shrub** Wilts
7 G5 **Netton** Devon
33 K3 **Netton** Wilts
59 K4 **Neuadd** Carmth
77 K7 **Neuadd Fawr** Carmth
93 K8 **Neuadd-ddu** Powys
55 G1 **Nevendon** Essex
75 J4 **Nevern** Pembks
101 H4 **Nevill Holt** Leics
176 C5 **New Abbey** D & G
268 F3 **New Aberdour** Abers
51 K6 **New Addington** Gt Lon
35 J4 **New Alresford** Hants
233 K6 **New Alyth** P & K
153 G7 **New Arram** E R Yk
52 D6 **New Ash Green** Kent
117 L1 **New Balderton** Notts
52 D5 **New Barn** Kent
69 H7 **New Barnet** Gt Lon
85 G2 **New Barton** Nhants
190 F2 **New Bewick** Nthumb
100 B8 **New Bilton** Warwks
136 F8 **New Bolingbroke** Lincs
135 K5 **New Boultham** Lincs
84 F7 **New Bradwell** M Keyn
133 G5 **New Brampton** Derbys
169 G2 **New Brancepeth** Dur
162 D5 **New Bridge** N York
128 F6 **New Brighton** Flints
129 G1 **New Brighton** Wirral
116 D2 **New Brinsley** Notts
171 G6 **New Brotton** R & Cl
112 D1 **New Broughton** Wrexhm
106 B5 **New Buckenham** Norfk
139 L6 **New Bury** Bolton
268 E5 **New Byth** Abers
106 D2 **New Costessey** Norfk
164 F2 **New Cowper** Cumb
142 B4 **New Crofton** Wakefd
92 D8 **New Cross** Cerdgn
51 K4 **New Cross** Gt Lon
30 F7 **New Cross** Somset
197 J8 **New Cumnock** E Ayrs
24 E4 **New Cut** E Susx
268 F6 **New Deer** Abers
181 H3 **New Delaval** Nthumb
140 F6 **New Delph** Oldham
50 D2 **New Denham** Bucks
84 D3 **New Duston** Nhants
151 K5 **New Earswick** York
116 D2 **New Eastwood** Notts
142 E7 **New Edlington** Donc
266 E4 **New Elgin** Moray
153 J7 **New Ellerby** E R Yk
51 L4 **New Eltham** Gt Lon
82 C3 **New End** Worcs
102 D3 **New England** C Pete
141 L2 **New Farnley** Leeds
129 H3 **New Ferry** Wirral
102 D4 **New Fletton** C Pete
142 C2 **New Fryston** Wakefd
185 G7 **New Galloway** D & G
223 G5 **New Gilston** Fife
10 b2 **New Grimsby** IOS
181 H3 **New Hartley** Nthumb
50 D6 **New Haw** Surrey

55 K6 **New Hedges** Pembks
181 H8 **New Herrington** Sundld
121 J4 **New Holkham** Norfk
144 D3 **New Holland** N Linc
133 K6 **New Houghton** Derbys
121 H6 **New Houghton** Norfk
158 D7 **New Houses** N York
139 H7 **New Houses** Wigan
157 J4 **New Hutton** Cumb
52 F7 **New Hythe** Kent
58 E2 **New Inn** Carmth
62 C7 **New Inn** Torfn
95 H8 **New Invention** Shrops
106 E2 **New Lakenham** Norfk
198 E4 **New Lanark** S Lans
138 E5 **New Lane** Lancs
130 C1 **New Lane End** Warrtn
177 K2 **New Langholm** D & G
137 G8 **New Leake** Lincs
269 H5 **New Leeds** Abers
142 A6 **New Lodge** Barns
139 G3 **New Longton** Lancs
172 F2 **New Luce** D & G
51 G5 **New Malden** Gt Lon
170 E6 **New Marske** R & Cl
66 D5 **New Marston** Oxon
112 E4 **New Marton** Shrops
245 H7 **New Mill** Abers
2 D4 **New Mill** Cnwll
68 A4 **New Mill** Herts
141 J6 **New Mill** Kirk
4 E4 **New Mills** Cnwll
131 K3 **New Mills** Derbys
94 D3 **New Mills** Powys
18 C4 **New Milton** Hants
73 H1 **New Mistley** Essex
75 H7 **New Moat** Pembks
134 D6 **New Ollerton** Notts
98 E4 **New Oscott** Birm
268 F5 **New Pitsligo** Abers
10 C6 **New Polzeath** Cnwll
196 C6 **New Prestwick** S Ayrs
76 D3 **New Quay** Cerdgn
72 F2 **New Quay** Essex
106 F1 **New Rackheath** Norfk
79 H3 **New Radnor** Powys
166 B3 **New Rent** Cumb
180 C7 **New Ridley** Nthumb
149 H7 **New Road Side** N York
25 K2 **New Romney** Kent
143 G8 **New Rossington** Donc
92 F8 **New Row** Cerdgn
148 A8 **New Row** Lancs
220 F8 **New Sauchie** Clacks
142 B4 **New Sharlston** Wakefd
203 K6 **New Shoreston** Nthumb
181 J8 **New Silksworth** Sundld
170 F7 **New Skelton** R & Cl
118 B4 **New Somerby** Lincs
137 H6 **New Spilsby** Lincs
139 J6 **New Springs** Wigan
209 K7 **New Stevenston** N Lans
79 L4 **New Street** Herefs
116 D8 **New Swannington** Leics
53 G1 **New Thundersley** Essex
86 D6 **New Town** Beds
32 F7 **New Town** Dorset
17 K1 **New Town** Dorset
33 G7 **New Town** Dorset
23 H3 **New Town** E Susx
101 L7 **New Town** Nhants
47 L4 **New Town** Wilts
61 J6 **New Tredegar** Caerph
198 D5 **New Trows** S Lans
133 H6 **New Tupton** Derbys
143 L2 **New Village** E R Yk
103 K2 **New Walsoken** Cambs
145 H6 **New Waltham** NE Lin
133 H4 **New Whittington** Derbys
211 M5 **New Winton** E Loth
66 A4 **New Yatt** Oxon
136 D8 **New York** Lincs
181 H5 **New York** N Tyne
150 B3 **New York** N York
150 B6 **Newall** Leeds
102 E3 **Newark** C Pete
275 f2 **Newark** Ork
117 L1 **Newark-on-Trent** Notts
209 L7 **Newarthill** N Lans
40 F7 **Newbarn** Kent
211 K6 **Newbattle** Mdloth
177 G6 **Newbie** D & G
166 B5 **Newbiggin** Cumb
166 D1 **Newbiggin** Cumb
166 E5 **Newbiggin** Cumb

155 K4 **Newbiggin** Cumb
146 E2 **Newbiggin** Cumb
167 L5 **Newbiggin** Dur
168 F1 **Newbiggin** Dur
159 G4 **Newbiggin** N York
159 H5 **Newbiggin** N York
181 H1 **Newbiggin-by-the-Sea** Nthumb
158 C2 **Newbiggin-on-Lune** Cumb
233 L7 **Newbigging** Angus
234 C7 **Newbigging** Angus
234 D8 **Newbigging** Angus
199 H4 **Newbigging** S Lans
133 G5 **Newbold** Derbys
116 C7 **Newbold** Leics
100 B7 **Newbold on Avon** Warks
82 F6 **Newbold on Stour** Warks
83 G4 **Newbold Pacey** Warks
99 M7 **Newbold Revel** Warks
99 L3 **Newbold Verdon** Leics
102 D2 **Newborough** C Pete
125 G6 **Newborough** IOA
115 J6 **Newborough** Staffs
83 M7 **Newbottle** Nhants
181 H8 **Newbottle** Sundld
91 G6 **Newbourne** Suffk
210 F4 **Newbridge** C Edin
43 K2 **Newbridge** Caerph
76 F3 **Newbridge** Cerdgn
2 C5 **Newbridge** Cnwll
4 C6 **Newbridge** Cnwll
176 C3 **Newbridge** D & G
34 C7 **Newbridge** Hants
18 F6 **Newbridge** IOW
66 B6 **Newbridge** Oxon
74 F6 **Newbridge** Pembks
112 D3 **Newbridge** Wrexhm
81 J7 **Newbridge Green** Worcs
78 E4 **Newbridge on Wye** Powys
62 D8 **Newbridge-on-Usk** Mons
179 K5 **Newbrough** Nthumb
13 J2 **Newbuildings** Devon
269 H4 **Newburgh** Abers
257 J6 **Newburgh** Abers
222 C3 **Newburgh** Fife
138 F5 **Newburgh** Lancs
161 J7 **Newburgh Priory** N York
80 E6 **Newburn** N u Ty
32 B1 **Newbury** Somset
48 C5 **Newbury** W Berk
32 D3 **Newbury** Wilts
51 L1 **Newbury Park** Gt Lon
66 E6 **Newby** Cumb
48 E6 **Newby** Lancs
70 C8 **Newby** N York
48 C2 **Newby** N York
63 J4 **Newby** N York
56 E5 **Newby Bridge** Cumb
77 L8 **Newby Cross** Cumb
78 B7 **Newby East** Cumb
66 E6 **Newby Head** Cumb
77 L8 **Newby West** Cumb
60 E5 **Newby Wiske** N York
62 F4 **Newcastle** Mons
95 G7 **Newcastle** Shrops
76 B7 **Newcastle Emlyn** Carmth
81 G6 **Newcastle upon Tyne** N u Ty
14 D2 **Newcastle-under-Lyme** Staffs
78 C2 **Newcastleton** Border
75 L4 **Newchapel** Pembks
131 G8 **Newchapel** Staffs
38 A5 **Newchapel** Surrey
61 J5 **Newchurch** Blae G
79 L5 **Newchurch** Herefs
19 J6 **Newchurch** IOW
25 K1 **Newchurch** Kent
62 F7 **Newchurch** Mons
79 H5 **Newchurch** Powys
115 J7 **Newchurch** Staffs
148 E7 **Newchurch in Pendle** Lancs
211 K4 **Newcraighall** C Edin
37 J3 **Newdigate** Surrey
49 L5 **Newell Green** Br For
24 F2 **Newenden** Kent
63 L2 **Newent** Gloucs
69 G4 **Newfield** Dur
81 G8 **Newfield** Dur
264 B4 **Newfield** Highld
48 E8 **Newfound** Hants
74 D2 **Newgale** Pembks
122 A3 **Newgate** Norfk
69 J6 **Newgate Street** Herts
3 K2 **Newhall** Ches

115 M7 **Newhall** Derbys
203 K7 **Newham** Nthumb
211 H4 **Newhaven** C Edin
132 C7 **Newhaven** Derbys
23 G7 **Newhaven** E Susx
140 E5 **Newhey** Rochdl
171 K8 **Newholm** N York
209 L6 **Newhouse** N Lans
22 F3 **Newick** E Susx
40 F8 **Newingreen** Kent
53 J6 **Newington** Kent
41 G7 **Newington** Kent
66 F7 **Newington** Oxon
95 K6 **Newington** Shrops
64 B8 **Newington Bagpath** Gloucs
144 D2 **Newland** C KuH
156 D6 **Newland** Cumb
143 K2 **Newland** E R Yk
63 H5 **Newland** Gloucs
143 H3 **Newland** N York
66 A5 **Newland** Oxon
28 E3 **Newland** Somset
81 H5 **Newland** Worcs
211 L6 **Newlandrig** Mdloth
188 E7 **Newlands** Border
165 K3 **Newlands** Cumb
180 D7 **Newlands** Nthumb
266 F6 **Newlands of Dundurcas** Moray
2 D5 **Newlyn** Cnwll
4 D3 **Newlyn East** Cnwll
256 F7 **Newmachar** Abers
209 L7 **Newmains** N Lans
70 D4 **Newman's End** Essex
89 H6 **Newman's Green** Suffk
88 C3 **Newmarket** Suffk
282 g3 **Newmarket** W Isls
188 D4 **Newmill** Border
267 J5 **Newmill** Moray
234 C3 **Newmill of Inshewan** Angus
141 M4 **Newmillerdam** Wakefd
211 G5 **Newmills** C Edin
210 D2 **Newmills** Fife
63 G5 **Newmills** Mons
221 L1 **Newmiln** P & K
197 G3 **Newmilns** E Ayrs
112 F5 **Newnes** Shrops
71 G5 **Newney Green** Essex
63 K5 **Newnham** Gloucs
49 H8 **Newnham** Hants
86 E7 **Newnham** Herts
40 B4 **Newnham** Kent
84 B3 **Newnham** Nhants
80 E2 **Newnham** Worcs
100 B6 **Newnham Paddox** Warks
11 L5 **Newport** Cnwll
27 K4 **Newport** Devon
17 G3 **Newport** Dorset
143 L2 **Newport** E R Yk
87 L8 **Newport** Essex
63 K7 **Newport** Gloucs
274 F3 **Newport** Highld
19 H6 **Newport** IOW
44 C1 **Newport** Newpt
123 K8 **Newport** Norfk
75 H4 **Newport** Pembks
114 A7 **Newport** Wrekin
85 G6 **Newport Pagnell** M Keyn
223 G2 **Newport-on-Tay** Fife
37 G5 **Newpound Common** W Susx
4 D3 **Newquay** Cnwll
142 B2 **Newsam Green** Leeds
131 G6 **Newsbank** Ches
256 C5 **Newseat** Abers
147 K8 **Newsham** Lancs
168 E8 **Newsham** N York
160 E5 **Newsham** N York
181 H3 **Newsham** Nthumb
143 H2 **Newsholme** E R Yk
148 E5 **Newsholme** Lancs
201 H6 **Newstead** Border
116 E1 **Newstead** Notts
203 J7 **Newstead** Nthumb
267 J7 **Newtack** Moray
142 D1 **Newthorpe** N York
116 E2 **Newthorpe** Notts
22 D4 **Newtimber** W Susx
135 L2 **Newtoft** Lincs
217 G7 **Newton** Ag & B
86 E6 **Newton** Beds
189 G2 **Newton** Border
42 C6 **Newton** Brdgnd
119 M8 **Newton** Cambs
87 J5 **Newton** Cambs
43 K6 **Newton** Cardif

129 J6 **Newton** Ches
129 L7 **Newton** Ches
129 M4 **Newton** Ches
146 D2 **Newton** Cumb
133 J7 **Newton** Derbys
79 L8 **Newton** Herefs
79 L1 **Newton** Herefs
80 C4 **Newton** Herefs
251 G2 **Newton** Highld
252 D2 **Newton** Highld
263 L6 **Newton** Highld
147 G8 **Newton** Lancs
157 J7 **Newton** Lancs
148 B5 **Newton** Lancs
142 C2 **Newton** Leeds
118 D4 **Newton** Lincs
211 K5 **Newton** Mdloth
266 C3 **Newton** Moray
267 G4 **Newton** Moray
152 D1 **Newton** N York
101 J6 **Newton** Nhants
121 H8 **Newton** Norfk
117 J3 **Newton** Notts
190 D5 **Newton** Nthumb
180 C6 **Newton** Nthumb
209 H6 **Newton** S Lans
198 F6 **Newton** S Lans
98 C4 **Newton** Sandw
112 F4 **Newton** Shrops
29 K3 **Newton** Somset
115 G6 **Newton** Staffs
89 J7 **Newton** Suffk
210 E3 **Newton** W Loth
100 C7 **Newton** Warks
34 B6 **Newton** Wilts
13 K8 **Newton Abbot** Devon
177 G7 **Newton Arlosh** Cumb
169 H5 **Newton Aycliffe** Dur
170 B5 **Newton Bewley** Hartpl
85 H5 **Newton Blossomville** M Keyn
85 K2 **Newton Bromswold** Beds
99 K2 **Newton Burgoland** Leics
135 L2 **Newton by Toft** Lincs
6 C2 **Newton Ferrers** Cnwll
7 G5 **Newton Ferrers** Devon
282 C7 **Newton Ferry** W Isls
106 E4 **Newton Flotman** Norfk
45 G1 **Newton Green** Mons
100 E4 **Newton Harcourt** Leics
140 C7 **Newton Heath** Manch
141 M3 **Newton Hill** Wakefd
151 G6 **Newton Kyme** N York
67 K1 **Newton Longville** Bucks
208 F7 **Newton Mearns** E Rens
160 C1 **Newton Morrell** N York
55 G5 **Newton Mountain** Pembks
171 H7 **Newton Mulgrave** N York
222 B5 **Newton of Balcanquhal** P & K
223 J6 **Newton of Balcormo** Fife
151 H4 **Newton on Ouse** N York
113 H7 **Newton on the Hill** Shrops
135 G5 **Newton on Trent** Lincs
14 C4 **Newton Poppleford** Devon
66 F1 **Newton Purcell** Oxon
99 H2 **Newton Regis** Warks
166 B4 **Newton Reigny** Cumb
280 D6 **Newton Row** Highld
115 M6 **Newton Solney** Derbys
13 K3 **Newton St Cyres** Devon
122 E8 **Newton St Faith** Norfk
45 L6 **Newton St Loe** BaNES
27 G8 **Newton St Petrock** Devon
34 E3 **Newton Stacey** Hants
173 K2 **Newton Stewart** D & G
34 B3 **Newton Toney** Wilts
27 J5 **Newton Tracey** Devon
170 D8 **Newton under Roseberry** R & Cl
180 E2 **Newton Underwood** Nthumb
151 M6 **Newton upon Derwent** E R Yk
35 L4 **Newton Valence** Hants
187 H7 **Newton Wamphray** D & G
138 F2 **Newton with Scales** Lancs
203 L8 **Newton-by-the-Sea** Nthumb
160 B5 **Newton-le-Willows** N York
139 H8 **Newton-le-Willows** St Hel
162 E4 **Newton-on-Rawcliffe** N York
191 H5 **Newton-on-the-Moor** Nthumb
255 M4 **Newtongarry Croft** Abers
211 K6 **Newtongrange** Mdloth
245 K5 **Newtonhill** Abers

211 K6 **Newtonloan** Mdloth
234 F3 **Newtonmill** Angus
241 J4 **Newtonmore** Highld
61 J5 **Newtown** Blae G
113 K2 **Newtown** Ches
131 H7 **Newtown** Ches
129 M4 **Newtown** Ches
2 F5 **Newtown** Cnwll
3 J6 **Newtown** Cnwll
5 J4 **Newtown** Cnwll
11 K6 **Newtown** Cnwll
164 E1 **Newtown** Cumb
178 C6 **Newtown** Cumb
166 C6 **Newtown** Cumb
177 L6 **Newtown** Cumb
185 J1 **Newtown** D & G
131 K3 **Newtown** Derbys
14 C3 **Newtown** Devon
28 D6 **Newtown** Devon
15 L2 **Newtown** Dorset
63 K6 **Newtown** Gloucs
18 D2 **Newtown** Hants
48 C6 **Newtown** Hants
35 J8 **Newtown** Hants
80 B4 **Newtown** Herefs
80 C8 **Newtown** Herefs
80 E6 **Newtown** Herefs
81 G7 **Newtown** Herefs
240 B3 **Newtown** Highld
19 G5 **Newtown** IOW
139 G4 **Newtown** Lancs
202 F6 **Newtown** Nthumb
190 E6 **Newtown** Nthumb
203 G8 **Newtown** Nthumb
17 K4 **Newtown** Poole
94 D5 **Newtown** Powys
61 G7 **Newtown** Rhondd
112 F7 **Newtown** Shrops
113 H5 **Newtown** Shrops
30 C8 **Newtown** Somset
98 C3 **Newtown** Staffs
139 H6 **Newtown** Wigan
32 F5 **Newtown** Wilts
47 L6 **Newtown** Wilts
81 K4 **Newtown** Worcs
98 B7 **Newtown** Worcs
100 B2 **Newtown Linford** Leics
208 C7 **Newtown of Beltrees** Rens
201 J6 **Newtown St Boswells** Border
100 B3 **Newtown Unthank** Leics
233 L7 **Newtyle** Angus
50 D1 **Newyears Green** Gt Lon
216 F5 **Newyork** Ag & B
79 L4 **Nextend** Herefs
54 F6 **Neyland** Pembks
154 b6 **Niarbyl** IOM
63 K5 **Nibley** Gloucs
45 K3 **Nibley** S Glos
63 L7 **Nibley Green** Gloucs
29 K7 **Nicholashayne** Devon
56 F7 **Nicholaston** Swans
178 D5 **Nickies Hill** Cumb
150 D4 **Nidd** N York
245 L3 **Nigg** C Aber
264 C5 **Nigg** Highld
28 F5 **Nightcott** Somset
45 L5 **Nimlet** BaNES
47 G2 **Nine Elms** Swindn
74 C7 **Nine Wells** Pembks
179 H8 **Ninebanks** Nthumb
80 E2 **Nineveh** Worcs
24 C5 **Ninfield** E Susx
18 F6 **Ningwood** IOW
201 L8 **Nisbet** Border
202 B3 **Nisbet Hill** Border
19 H8 **Niton** IOW
208 E7 **Nitshill** C Glas
113 H2 **No Man's Heath** Ches
99 H2 **No Man's Heath** Warks
4 F1 **No Man's Land** Cnwll
6 B3 **No Man's Land** Cnwll
52 C7 **Noah's Ark** Kent
52 E2 **Noak Bridge** Essex
70 D8 **Noak Hill** Essex
141 L6 **Noblethorpe** Barns
95 L2 **Nobold** Shrops
84 C3 **Nobottle** Nhants
135 L6 **Nocton** Lincs
107 H3 **Nogdam End** Norfk
66 E4 **Noke** Oxon
54 E3 **Nolton** Pembks
54 D3 **Nolton Haven** Pembks
28 E8 **Nomansland** Devon
34 B7 **Nomansland** Wilts

113 H6 **Noneley** Shrops
41 H5 **Nonington** Kent
178 B3 **Nook** Cumb
157 H6 **Nook** Cumb
51 G5 **Norbiton** Gt Lon
146 F7 **Norbreck** Bpool
81 G6 **Norbridge** Herefs
113 J2 **Norbury** Ches
115 J3 **Norbury** Derbys
51 J5 **Norbury** Gt Lon
95 J5 **Norbury** Shrops
114 B6 **Norbury** Staffs
113 J2 **Norbury Common** Ches
114 B7 **Norbury Junction** Staffs
81 J2 **Norchard** Worcs
130 B4 **Norcott Brook** Ches
146 F7 **Norcross** Lancs
103 L3 **Nordelph** Norfk
140 C5 **Norden** Rochdl
96 F4 **Nordley** Shrops
202 D4 **Norham** Nthumb
141 G3 **Norland Town** Calder
130 B5 **Norley** Ches
18 E4 **Norleywood** Hants
23 G4 **Norlington** E Susx
102 D5 **Norman Cross** Cambs
24 C6 **Norman's Bay** E Susx
14 C2 **Norman's Green** Devon
135 K2 **Normanby** Lincs
143 M4 **Normanby** N Linc
162 C6 **Normanby** N York
170 D7 **Normanby** R & Cl
136 B1 **Normanby le Wold** Lincs
50 B8 **Normandy** Surrey
116 B5 **Normanton** C Derb
117 L3 **Normanton** Leics
118 B2 **Normanton** Lincs
134 E8 **Normanton** Notts
101 K2 **Normanton** Rutlnd
142 B3 **Normanton** Wakefd
33 K3 **Normanton** Wilts
99 K1 **Normanton le Heath** Leics
116 E7 **Normanton on Soar** Notts
117 G5 **Normanton on the Wolds** Notts
134 F6 **Normanton on Trent** Notts
147 G8 **Normoss** Lancs
36 E2 **Norney** Surrey
46 C6 **Norrington Common** Wilts
6 E1 **Norris Green** Cnwll
141 K3 **Norristhorpe** Kirk
133 K3 **North Anston** Rothm
49 M5 **North Ascot** Br For
66 C1 **North Aston** Oxon
34 E6 **North Baddesley** Hants
229 G3 **North Ballachulish** Highld
31 K5 **North Barrow** Somset
121 K4 **North Barsham** Norfk
53 G1 **North Benfleet** Essex
20 F6 **North Bersted** W Susx
212 C2 **North Berwick** E Loth
168 F4 **North Bitchburn** Dur
181 H2 **North Blyth** Nthumb
19 K2 **North Boarhunt** Hants
18 B4 **North Bockhampton** Hants
13 H5 **North Bovey** Devon
46 B7 **North Bradley** Wilts
12 C6 **North Brentor** Devon
32 B3 **North Brewham** Somset
36 E3 **North Bridge** Surrey
86 F6 **North Brook End** Cambs
27 H3 **North Buckland** Devon
107 H2 **North Burlingham** Norfk
31 K5 **North Cadbury** Somset
135 J4 **North Carlton** Lincs
134 B3 **North Carlton** Notts
143 M1 **North Cave** E R Yk
64 E5 **North Cerney** Gloucs
22 F3 **North Chailey** E Susx
33 L7 **North Charford** Hants
191 H2 **North Charlton** Nthumb
51 G6 **North Cheam** Gt Lon
31 M5 **North Cheriton** Somset
15 K4 **North Chideock** Dorset
152 D8 **North Cliffe** E R Yk
135 G5 **North Clifton** Notts
169 H4 **North Close** Dur
137 G2 **North Cockerington** Lincs
228 E8 **North Connel** Ag & B
42 B5 **North Cornelly** Brdgnd
3 K7 **North Corner** Cnwll
228 C5 **North Corry** Highld
145 K7 **North Cotes** Lincs
4 A6 **North Country** Cnwll
107 K5 **North Cove** Suffk

160 D2 **North Cowton** N York
85 H6 **North Crawley** M Keyn
52 A4 **North Cray** Gt Lon
121 J4 **North Creake** Norfk
30 D6 **North Curry** Somset
152 E5 **North Dalton** E R Yk
150 E5 **North Deighton** N York
151 L8 **North Duffield** N York
259 G2 **North Duntulm** Highld
41 G6 **North Elham** Kent
136 E2 **North Elkington** Lincs
121 L7 **North Elmham** Norfk
142 D5 **North Elmsall** Wakefd
19 L3 **North End** C Port
177 K7 **North End** Cumb
32 D5 **North End** Dorset
153 K7 **North End** E R Yk
145 H2 **North End** E R Yk
71 G3 **North End** Essex
33 J7 **North End** Hants
35 J5 **North End** Hants
116 F8 **North End** Leics
145 J7 **North End** Lincs
144 D7 **North End** Lincs
119 H3 **North End** Lincs
137 H2 **North End** Lincs
144 E3 **North End** N Linc
44 E5 **North End** N Som
85 J2 **North End** Nhants
105 K5 **North End** Norfk
191 G6 **North End** Nthumb
138 C6 **North End** Sefton
21 G6 **North End** W Susx
21 J5 **North End** W Susx
260 B4 **North Erradale** Highld
100 D3 **North Evington** C Leic
71 K7 **North Fambridge** Essex
144 C3 **North Ferriby** E R Yk
153 H5 **North Frodingham** E R Yk
33 L8 **North Gorley** Hants
106 E5 **North Green** Norfk
91 G3 **North Green** Suffk
91 J2 **North Green** Suffk
152 C2 **North Grimston** N York
52 F6 **North Halling** Medway
20 B6 **North Hayling** Hants
203 G6 **North Hazelrigg** Nthumb
28 C4 **North Heasley** Devon
37 G6 **North Heath** W Susx
29 J6 **North Hele** Somset
11 K7 **North Hill** Cnwll
50 D2 **North Hillingdon** Gt Lon
66 C6 **North Hinksey** Oxon
37 J2 **North Holmwood** Surrey
7 K3 **North Huish** Devon
135 J6 **North Hykeham** Lincs
144 D7 **North Kelsey** Lincs
251 H2 **North Kessock** Highld
144 F4 **North Killingholme** N Linc
160 F5 **North Kilvington** N York
100 D6 **North Kilworth** Leics
18 B3 **North Kingston** Hants
118 F1 **North Kyme** Lincs
153 L2 **North Landing** E R Yk
67 K5 **North Lee** Bucks
160 D7 **North Lees** N York
40 F6 **North Leigh** Kent
66 A4 **North Leigh** Oxon
134 F3 **North Leverton with Habblesthorpe** Notts
82 C5 **North Littleton** Worcs
105 L6 **North Lopham** Norfk
101 K3 **North Luffenham** Rutlnd
20 C4 **North Marden** W Susx
67 J3 **North Marston** Bucks
211 K7 **North Middleton** Mdloth
190 E1 **North Middleton** Nthumb
172 D4 **North Milmain** D & G
28 C5 **North Molton** Devon
48 E1 **North Moreton** Oxon
20 E6 **North Mundham** W Susx
134 F7 **North Muskham** Notts
152 D8 **North Newbald** E R Yk
83 K7 **North Newington** Oxon
47 H7 **North Newnton** Wilts
30 D4 **North Newton** Somset
63 L7 **North Nibley** Gloucs
48 D8 **North Oakley** Hants
52 C2 **North Ockendon** Gt Lon
170 C6 **North Ormesby** Middsb
136 E1 **North Ormsby** Lincs
160 E5 **North Otterington** N York
135 L1 **North Owersby** Lincs
15 L1 **North Perrott** Somset
30 D4 **North Petherton** Somset

11 K4 **North Petherwin** Cnwll
105 H2 **North Pickenham** Norfk
81 M4 **North Piddle** Worcs
7 M6 **North Pool** Devon
15 M3 **North Poorton** Dorset
18 B2 **North Poulner** Hants
29 G3 **North Quarme** Somset
210 F3 **North Queensferry** C Edin
28 C4 **North Radworthy** Devon
118 D2 **North Rauceby** Lincs
137 G3 **North Reston** Lincs
150 C6 **North Rigton** N York
18 B4 **North Ripley** Hants
131 H6 **North Rode** Ches
165 H4 **North Row** Cumb
120 E8 **North Runcton** Norfk
146 C2 **North Scale** Cumb
135 G6 **North Scarle** Lincs
181 H2 **North Seaton** Nthumb
181 H2 **North Seaton Colliery** Nthumb
228 E6 **North Shian** Ag & B
181 J5 **North Shields** N Tyne
53 K2 **North Shoebury** Sthend
146 F8 **North Shore** Bpool
102 F3 **North Side** C Pete
164 C5 **North Side** Cumb
170 F7 **North Skelton** R & Cl
145 L8 **North Somercotes** Lincs
160 D7 **North Stainley** N York
167 J7 **North Stainmore** Cumb
52 D3 **North Stifford** Thurr
45 L5 **North Stoke** BaNES
48 F2 **North Stoke** Oxon
21 H5 **North Stoke** W Susx
88 B2 **North Street** Cambs
33 K7 **North Street** Hants
35 K4 **North Street** Hants
40 D4 **North Street** Kent
53 H4 **North Street** Medway
48 F4 **North Street** W Berk
203 K6 **North Sunderland** Nthumb
11 K3 **North Tamerton** Cnwll
12 F2 **North Tawton** Devon
209 K1 **North Third** Stirlg
145 H8 **North Thoresby** Lincs
34 B1 **North Tidworth** Wilts
12 C1 **North Town** Devon
31 J2 **North Town** Somset
49 L3 **North Town** W & M
122 A8 **North Tuddenham** Norfk
180 E5 **North Walbottle** N u Ty
122 F5 **North Walsham** Norfk
35 H2 **North Waltham** Hants
35 M8 **North Warnborough** Hants
70 D6 **North Weald Bassett** Essex
134 F3 **North Wheatley** Notts
8 C2 **North Whilborough** Devon
45 H6 **North Wick** BaNES
45 H7 **North Widcombe** BaNES
136 C2 **North Willingham** Lincs
133 H6 **North Wingfield** Derbys
118 B7 **North Witham** Lincs
31 L7 **North Wootton** Dorset
120 E6 **North Wootton** Norfk
31 J3 **North Wootton** Somset
46 B4 **North Wraxall** Wilts
47 H3 **North Wroughton** Swindn
105 J4 **Northacre** Norfk
68 B3 **Northall** Bucks
121 M8 **Northall Green** Norfk
160 E4 **Northallerton** N York
19 G1 **Northam** C Sotn
27 H5 **Northam** Devon
84 E3 **Northampton** Nhants
81 J2 **Northampton** Worcs
69 H6 **Northaw** Herts
30 D8 **Northay** Somset
102 C2 **Northborough** C Pete
41 K5 **Northbourne** Kent
24 D2 **Northbridge Street** E Susx
35 G3 **Northbrook** Hants
66 D3 **Northbrook** Oxon
36 E5 **Northchapel** W Susx
68 B5 **Northchurch** Herts
29 K8 **Northcott** Devon
14 D1 **Northcott** Devon
11 L4 **Northcott** Devon
66 D7 **Northcourt** Oxon
41 L1 **Northdown** Kent
133 G6 **Northedge** Derbys
67 H8 **Northend** Bucks
83 J5 **Northend** Warwks
49 L1 **Northend Woods** Bucks
131 G2 **Northenden** Manch

98 C7 **Northfield** Birm
245 K2 **Northfield** C Aber
144 C2 **Northfield** E R Yk
102 A2 **Northfields** Lincs
52 D4 **Northfleet** Kent
24 E2 **Northiam** E Susx
86 C6 **Northill** Beds
63 L5 **Northington** Gloucs
35 H3 **Northington** Hants
119 K1 **Northlands** Lincs
65 G4 **Northleach** Gloucs
27 L4 **Northleigh** Devon
14 E3 **Northleigh** Devon
12 C3 **Northlew** Devon
31 H3 **Northload Bridge** Somset
66 B6 **Northmoor** Oxon
28 F5 **Northmoor** Somset
234 B4 **Northmuir** Angus
20 B6 **Northney** Hants
50 E2 **Northolt** Gt Lon
128 F6 **Northop** Flints
129 G6 **Northop Hall** Flints
141 K3 **Northorpe** Kirk
143 M8 **Northorpe** Lincs
118 E8 **Northorpe** Lincs
119 G4 **Northorpe** Lincs
31 H3 **Northover** Somset
31 H6 **Northover** Somset
141 H2 **Northowram** Calder
17 H5 **Northport** Dorset
122 E4 **Northrepps** Norfk
282 d6 **Northton** W Isls
29 L5 **Northway** Somset
57 G7 **Northway** Swans
130 C5 **Northwich** Ches
45 H2 **Northwick** S Glos
30 E1 **Northwick** Somset
81 J4 **Northwick** Worcs
104 E4 **Northwold** Norfk
114 D2 **Northwood** C Stke
132 E6 **Northwood** Derbys
50 E1 **Northwood** Gt Lon
19 H5 **Northwood** IOW
113 G5 **Northwood** Shrops
63 L4 **Northwood Green** Gloucs
5 J1 **Norton** Cnwll
142 E5 **Norton** Donc
23 G7 **Norton** E Susx
64 B2 **Norton** Gloucs
130 A3 **Norton** Halton
86 E8 **Norton** Herts
18 E6 **Norton** IOW
62 F3 **Norton** Mons
44 D6 **Norton** N Som
152 B2 **Norton** N York
84 B3 **Norton** Nhants
133 L5 **Norton** Notts
79 K2 **Norton** Powys
170 B6 **Norton** S on T
133 G3 **Norton** Sheff
96 D2 **Norton** Shrops
97 G3 **Norton** Shrops
95 L7 **Norton** Shrops
96 E6 **Norton** Shrops
89 J2 **Norton** Suffk
57 H7 **Norton** Swans
20 F5 **Norton** W Susx
46 C2 **Norton** Wilts
81 K5 **Norton** Worcs
82 B5 **Norton** Worcs
32 F2 **Norton Bavant** Wilts
114 D5 **Norton Bridge** Staffs
98 C2 **Norton Canes** Staffs
79 M6 **Norton Canon** Herefs
122 B6 **Norton Corner** Norfk
135 H7 **Norton Disney** Lincs
32 C4 **Norton Ferris** Wilts
30 B5 **Norton Fitzwarren** Somset
18 E6 **Norton Green** IOW
45 H6 **Norton Hawkfield** BaNES
70 F6 **Norton Heath** Essex
113 M4 **Norton in Hales** Shrops
114 D1 **Norton in the Moors** C Stke
82 F3 **Norton Lindsey** Warwks
89 K2 **Norton Little Green** Suffk
45 J6 **Norton Malreward** BaNES
70 E6 **Norton Mandeville** Essex
45 M7 **Norton St Philip** Somset
31 G7 **Norton sub Hamdon** Somset
107 H4 **Norton Subcourse** Norfk
79 L5 **Norton Wood** Herefs
99 J2 **Norton-Juxta-Twycross** Leic
150 F2 **Norton-le-Clay** N York
134 F7 **Norwell** Notts
134 E7 **Norwell Woodhouse** Notts

Norwich - Orthwaite 341

106 E2 **Norwich** Norfk
281 f1 **Norwick** Shet
220 F8 **Norwood** Clacks
133 J3 **Norwood** Derbys
25 K1 **Norwood** Kent
70 E5 **Norwood End** Essex
141 H2 **Norwood Green** Calder
50 E3 **Norwood Green** Gt Lon
37 K2 **Norwood Hill** Surrey
103 H4 **Norwoodside** Cambs
101 G4 **Noseley** Leics
7 G5 **Noss Mayo** Devon
160 C6 **Nosterfield** N York
88 C6 **Nosterfield End** Cambs
248 D6 **Nostie** Highld
65 G3 **Notgrove** Gloucs
42 B6 **Nottage** Brdgnd
6 D3 **Notter** Cnwll
116 F4 **Nottingham** C Nott
16 C6 **Nottington** Dorset
142 A5 **Notton** Wakefd
46 C5 **Notton** Wilts
63 L3 **Nottswood Hill** Gloucs
71 J5 **Nounsley** Essex
81 J2 **Noutard's Green** Worcs
89 H3 **Nowton** Suffk
95 K1 **Nox** Shrops
49 G2 **Nuffield** Oxon
151 H4 **Nun Monkton** N York
152 C6 **Nunburnholme** E R Yk
116 E1 **Nuncargate** Notts
166 C2 **Nunclose** Cumb
99 K5 **Nuneaton** Warwks
66 E7 **Nuneham Courtenay** Oxon
51 K4 **Nunhead** Gt Lon
153 J6 **Nunkeeling** E R Yk
32 B2 **Nunney** Somset
32 B2 **Nunney Catch** Somset
80 D6 **Nunnington** Herefs
161 L6 **Nunnington** N York
190 F7 **Nunnykirk** Nthumb
145 H6 **Nunsthorpe** NE Lin
170 C7 **Nunthorpe** Middsb
151 J6 **Nunthorpe** York
170 D8 **Nunthorpe Village** Middsb
33 K5 **Nunton** Wilts
160 D7 **Nunwick** N York
179 K4 **Nunwick** Nthumb
67 L3 **Nup End** Bucks
63 J7 **Nupdown** S Glos
64 A5 **Nupend** Gloucs
49 L4 **Nuptow** Br For
34 E7 **Nursling** Hants
36 A6 **Nursted** Hants
46 F6 **Nursteed** Wilts
97 J3 **Nurton** Staffs
20 C6 **Nutbourne** W Susx
21 J3 **Nutbourne** W Susx
37 M1 **Nutfield** Surrey
16 E3 **Nuthall** Notts
87 H8 **Nuthampstead** Herts
37 J5 **Nuthurst** W Susx
23 G2 **Nutley** E Susx
35 J2 **Nutley** Hants
40 B4 **Nuttal Lane** Bury
43 G7 **Nutwell** Donc
80 E3 **Nybster** Highld
20 E7 **Nyetimber** W Susx
36 B6 **Nyewood** W Susx
13 G1 **Nymet Rowland** Devon
13 G2 **Nymet Tracey** Devon
64 A7 **Nympsfield** Gloucs
29 L6 **Nynehead** Somset
30 F4 **Nythe** Somset
20 F5 **Nyton** W Susx

O

53 J6 **Oad Street** Kent
00 D3 **Oadby** Leics
12 D3 **Oak Cross** Devon
69 K8 **Oak Tree** Darltn
81 J3 **Oakall Green** Worcs
15 G3 **Oakamoor** Staffs
10 E5 **Oakbank** W Loth
43 J2 **Oakdale** Caerph
29 L6 **Oake** Somset
97 J3 **Oaken** Staffs
47 K6 **Oakenclough** Lancs
96 F1 **Oakengates** Wrekin
29 G5 **Oakenholt** Flints
69 G3 **Oakenshaw** Dur
41 J2 **Oakenshaw** Kirk
132 E7 **Oaker Side** Derbys
133 H8 **Oakerthorpe** Derbys
76 E4 **Oakford** Cerdgn
29 G6 **Oakford** Devon
29 G6 **Oakfordbridge** Devon
131 H6 **Oakgrove** Ches
101 J2 **Oakham** Rutlnd
114 B1 **Oakhanger** Ches
36 A4 **Oakhanger** Hants
31 K2 **Oakhill** Somset
38 E3 **Oakhurst** Kent
87 H2 **Oakington** Cambs
78 E5 **Oaklands** Powys
63 M4 **Oakle Street** Gloucs
85 K4 **Oakley** Beds
66 F4 **Oakley** Bucks
210 D1 **Oakley** Fife
35 H1 **Oakley** Hants
67 H7 **Oakley** Oxon
17 K3 **Oakley** Poole
106 D7 **Oakley** Suffk
50 A4 **Oakley Green** W & M
93 L6 **Oakley Park** Powys
64 C6 **Oakridge** Gloucs
168 F5 **Oaks** Dur
139 K1 **Oaks** Lancs
95 K2 **Oaks** Shrops
115 J5 **Oaks Green** Derbys
64 E8 **Oaksey** Wilts
178 C4 **Oakshaw** Cumb
35 M5 **Oakshott** Hants
99 J1 **Oakthorpe** Leics
116 C4 **Oakwood** C Derb
179 L5 **Oakwood** Nthumb
37 H3 **Oakwoodhill** Surrey
149 J8 **Oakworth** Brad
40 C3 **Oare** Kent
28 D2 **Oare** Somset
47 H6 **Oare** Wilts
118 D4 **Oasby** Lincs
30 F5 **Oath** Somset
234 D4 **Oathlaw** Angus
50 E6 **Oatlands Park** Surrey
216 D1 **Oban** Ag & B
95 H7 **Obley** Shrops
232 F7 **Obney** P & K
31 L7 **Oborne** Dorset
118 E8 **Obthorpe** Lincs
90 D1 **Occold** Suffk
275 J1 **Occumster** Highld
196 F6 **Ochiltree** E Ayrs
116 C4 **Ockbrook** Derbys
98 B4 **Ocker Hill** Sandw
81 H3 **Ockeridge** Worcs
50 D7 **Ockham** Surrey
237 G6 **Ockle** Highld
37 H3 **Ockley** Surrey
80 E6 **Ocle Pychard** Herefs
153 G2 **Octon** E R Yk
31 H7 **Odcombe** Somset
45 L6 **Odd Down** BaNES
81 L3 **Oddingley** Worcs
65 J2 **Oddington** Gloucs
66 E4 **Oddington** Oxon
85 J4 **Odell** Beds
12 C2 **Odham** Devon
35 M1 **Odiham** Hants
141 J2 **Odsal** Brad
86 F7 **Odsey** Herts
33 K5 **Odstock** Wilts
99 K2 **Odstone** Leics
83 J2 **Offchurch** Warwks
82 C6 **Offenham** Worcs
131 H2 **Offerton** Gt Man
181 J7 **Offerton** Sundld
22 F5 **Offham** E Susx
39 G2 **Offham** Kent
21 H5 **Offham** W Susx
114 B5 **Offleymarsh** Shrops
86 E2 **Offord Cluny** Cambs
86 E2 **Offord Darcy** Cambs
90 C5 **Offton** Suffk
14 E3 **Offwell** Devon
47 J4 **Ogbourne Maizey** Wilts
47 J4 **Ogbourne St Andrew** Wilts
47 J4 **Ogbourne St George** Wilts
141 G2 **Ogden** Calder
180 E3 **Ogle** Nthumb
129 K3 **Oglet** Lpool
42 D6 **Ogmore** V Glam
42 E4 **Ogmore Vale** Brdgnd
42 C6 **Ogmore-by-Sea** V Glam
126 C6 **Ogwen Bank** Gwynd
32 D8 **Okeford Fitzpaine** Dorset
12 E3 **Okehampton** Devon
13 K7 **Olchard** Devon
84 F1 **Old** Nhants
245 L2 **Old Aberdeen** C Aber
35 J4 **Old Alresford** Hants
185 J3 **Old Auchenbrack** D & G
116 F3 **Old Basford** C Nott
49 G8 **Old Basing** Hants
190 F2 **Old Bewick** Nthumb
136 F6 **Old Bolingbroke** Lincs
49 L5 **Old Bracknell** Br For
150 B7 **Old Bramhope** Leeds
133 G5 **Old Brampton** Derbys
175 J1 **Old Bridge of Urr** D & G
106 B5 **Old Buckenham** Norfk
48 C7 **Old Burghclere** Hants
161 J5 **Old Byland** N York
143 G7 **Old Cantley** Donc
169 J3 **Old Cassop** Dur
42 D6 **Old Castle** Brdgnd
95 G4 **Old Churchstoke** Powys
145 H6 **Old Clee** NE Lin
29 J3 **Old Cleeve** Somset
134 C6 **Old Clipstone** Notts
127 G4 **Old Colwyn** Conwy
183 G3 **Old Dailly** S Ayrs
117 H6 **Old Dalby** Leics
132 B4 **Old Dam** Derbys
269 H6 **Old Deer** Abers
31 H1 **Old Ditch** Somset
142 E8 **Old Edlington** Donc
169 H5 **Old Eldon** Dur
153 J8 **Old Ellerby** E R Yk
91 H8 **Old Felixstowe** Suffk
102 D4 **Old Fletton** C Pete
63 H3 **Old Forge** Herefs
62 F2 **Old Furnace** Herefs
131 L1 **Old Glossop** Derbys
143 J3 **Old Goole** E R Yk
10 b2 **Old Grimsby** IOS
69 K3 **Old Hall Green** Herts
122 F5 **Old Hall Street** Norfk
70 C5 **Old Harlow** Essex
72 E3 **Old Heath** Essex
120 F3 **Old Hunstanton** Norfk
102 F7 **Old Hurst** Cambs
157 J5 **Old Hutton** Cumb
4 D6 **Old Kea** Cnwll
208 D4 **Old Kilpatrick** W Duns
69 G3 **Old Knebworth** Herts
106 E2 **Old Lakenham** Norfk
148 B8 **Old Langho** Lancs
154 f5 **Old Laxey** IOM
119 L2 **Old Leake** Lincs
152 B1 **Old Malton** N York
142 C1 **Old Micklefield** Leeds
83 G2 **Old Milverton** Warwks
90 B3 **Old Newton** Suffk
169 J3 **Old Quarrington** Dur
116 F3 **Old Radford** C Nott
79 J3 **Old Radnor** Powys
256 B6 **Old Rayne** Abers
25 J2 **Old Romney** Kent
22 B6 **Old Shoreham** W Susx
38 F3 **Old Soar** Kent
45 L3 **Old Sodbury** S Glos
118 C5 **Old Somerby** Lincs
84 E7 **Old Stratford** Nhants
97 K6 **Old Swinford** Dudley
157 K2 **Old Tebay** Cumb
160 F6 **Old Thirsk** N York
140 F2 **Old Town** Calder
166 B2 **Old Town** Cumb
157 J6 **Old Town** Cumb
23 K7 **Old Town** E Susx
10 c3 **Old Town** IOS
190 B7 **Old Town** Nthumb
140 B8 **Old Trafford** Traffd
133 H6 **Old Tupton** Derbys
86 C6 **Old Warden** Beds
102 B7 **Old Weston** Cambs
280 E6 **Old Wick** Highld
50 C4 **Old Windsor** W & M
40 E4 **Old Wives Lees** Kent
50 C7 **Old Woking** Surrey
84 F7 **Old Wolverton** M Keyn
113 G7 **Old Woods** Shrops
270 E2 **Oldany** Highld
82 D2 **Oldberrow** Warwks
38 F2 **Oldbury** Kent
98 C5 **Oldbury** Sandw
97 G5 **Oldbury** Shrops
99 J4 **Oldbury** Warwks
63 J8 **Oldbury Naite** S Glos
46 B1 **Oldbury on the Hill** Gloucs
63 J8 **Oldbury-on-Severn** S Glos
62 C2 **Oldcastle** Mons
113 G2 **Oldcastle Heath** Ches
134 B2 **Oldcotes** Notts
149 H8 **Oldfield** Brad
81 J2 **Oldfield** Worcs
32 C1 **Oldford** Somset
89 H4 **Oldhall Green** Suffk
140 D6 **Oldham** Oldham
213 G5 **Oldhamstocks** E Loth
45 K4 **Oldland** S Glos
256 E6 **Oldmeldrum** Abers
11 M7 **Oldmill** Cnwll
44 C7 **Oldmixon** N Som
13 J3 **Oldridge** Devon
276 C4 **Oldshoremore** Highld
161 H6 **Oldstead** N York
178 B6 **Oldwall** Cumb
56 E6 **Oldwalls** Swans
28 F6 **Oldways End** Somset
115 J7 **Olive Green** Staffs
187 G1 **Oliver** Border
34 F5 **Oliver's Battery** Hants
281 d4 **Ollaberry** Shet
247 H1 **Ollach** Highld
130 F4 **Ollerton** Ches
134 D6 **Ollerton** Notts
113 L6 **Ollerton** Shrops
77 H4 **Olmarch** Cerdgn
88 C7 **Olmstead Green** Cambs
85 H5 **Olney** M Keyn
279 L3 **Olrig House** Highld
98 E7 **Olton** Solhll
45 J2 **Olveston** S Glos
81 J3 **Ombersley** Worcs
134 D6 **Ompton** Notts
179 H5 **Once Brewed** Nthumb
154 e6 **Onchan** IOM
131 L8 **Onecote** Staffs
89 K3 **Onehouse** Suffk
62 E4 **Onen** Mons
79 M2 **Ongar Street** Herefs
95 L7 **Onibury** Shrops
229 G3 **Onich** Highld
60 C5 **Onllwyn** Neath
114 B3 **Onneley** Staffs
36 E1 **Onslow Village** Surrey
130 B5 **Onston** Ches
116 B2 **Openwoodgate** Derbys
260 B5 **Opinan** Highld
266 F5 **Orbliston** Moray
258 D7 **Orbost** Highld
137 J6 **Orby** Lincs
30 C6 **Orchard Portman** Somset
33 J2 **Orcheston** Wilts
62 F2 **Orcop** Herefs
62 F2 **Orcop Hill** Herefs
268 A4 **Ord** Abers
244 E2 **Ordhead** Abers
244 A3 **Ordie** Abers
267 G5 **Ordiequish** Moray
179 L7 **Ordley** Nthumb
134 D4 **Ordsall** Notts
24 F5 **Ore** E Susx
80 B2 **Oreleton Common** Herefs
96 E7 **Oreton** Shrops
91 K5 **Orford** Suffk
130 B2 **Orford** Warrtn
17 H4 **Organford** Dorset
115 J8 **Orgreave** Staffs
40 C8 **Orlestone** Kent
80 C2 **Orleton** Herefs
81 G2 **Orleton** Worcs
85 G1 **Orlingbury** Nhants
165 J5 **Ormathwaite** Cumb
170 C7 **Ormesby** R & Cl
123 K8 **Ormesby St Margaret** Norfk
123 K8 **Ormesby St Michael** Norfk
260 D2 **Ormiscaig** Highld
211 M5 **Ormiston** E Loth
236 F7 **Ormsaigmore** Highld
206 A4 **Ormsary** Ag & B
138 E6 **Ormskirk** Lancs
168 F1 **Ornsby Hill** Dur
214 C6 **Oronsay** Ag & B
275 b5 **Orphir** Ork
51 M5 **Orpington** Gt Lon
138 D8 **Orrell** Sefton
139 G7 **Orrell** Wigan
139 G6 **Orrell Post** Wigan
154 d4 **Orrisdale** IOM
175 J5 **Orroland** D & G
52 D3 **Orsett** Thurr
114 C8 **Orslow** Staffs
117 K3 **Orston** Notts
165 H4 **Orthwaite** Cumb

147 K5 **Ortner** Lancs
157 K1 **Orton** Cumb
101 H7 **Orton** Nhants
97 K4 **Orton** Staffs
102 D4 **Orton Longueville** C Pete
177 K8 **Orton Rigg** Cumb
102 C4 **Orton Waterville** C Pete
99 J3 **Orton-on-the-Hill** Leics
87 H5 **Orwell** Cambs
139 K2 **Osbaldeston** Lancs
139 K1 **Osbaldeston Green** Lancs
151 K5 **Osbaldwick** York
99 L3 **Osbaston** Leics
112 D7 **Osbaston** Shrops
19 H5 **Osborne** IOW
118 E4 **Osbournby** Lincs
129 L6 **Oscroft** Ches
258 E8 **Ose** Highld
116 D7 **Osgathorpe** Leics
135 M1 **Osgodby** Lincs
143 G1 **Osgodby** N York
163 J5 **Osgodby** N York
247 H1 **Oskaig** Highld
226 E4 **Oskamull** Ag & B
115 K3 **Osmaston** Derbys
16 D6 **Osmington** Dorset
16 D6 **Osmington Mills** Dorset
142 A1 **Osmondthorpe** Leeds
161 G3 **Osmotherley** N York
66 D6 **Osney** Oxon
40 C3 **Ospringe** Kent
141 L4 **Ossett** Wakefd
134 E6 **Ossington** Notts
72 D7 **Ostend** Essex
50 F3 **Osterley** Gt Lon
161 K6 **Oswaldkirk** N York
139 L2 **Oswaldtwistle** Lancs
112 D5 **Oswestry** Shrops
52 B7 **Otford** Kent
39 K3 **Otham** Kent
39 K3 **Otham Hole** Kent
30 F4 **Othery** Somset
150 B6 **Otley** Leeds
90 E4 **Otley** Suffk
90 F4 **Otley Green** Suffk
206 E2 **Otter Ferry** Ag & B
34 F6 **Otterbourne** Hants
148 F4 **Otterburn** N York
190 C7 **Otterburn** Nthumb
11 H4 **Otterham** Cnwll
53 H5 **Otterham Quay** Kent
30 C2 **Otterhampton** Somset
282 C7 **Otternish** W Isls
50 C6 **Ottershaw** Surrey
281 e3 **Otterswick** Shet
14 C5 **Otterton** Devon
18 F3 **Otterwood** Hants
12 B7 **Ottery** Devon
14 C3 **Ottery St Mary** Devon
41 G6 **Ottinge** Kent
145 H3 **Ottringham** E R Yk
177 J7 **Oughterby** Cumb
158 F6 **Oughtershaw** N York
164 F3 **Oughterside** Cumb
132 F1 **Oughtibridge** Sheff
130 D2 **Oughtrington** Warrtn
161 J7 **Oulston** N York
177 H8 **Oulton** Cumb
142 B2 **Oulton** Leeds
122 C6 **Oulton** Norfk
114 B7 **Oulton** Staffs
114 E4 **Oulton** Staffs
107 L4 **Oulton** Suffk
107 L5 **Oulton Broad** Suffk
122 C6 **Oulton Street** Norfk
102 A5 **Oundle** Nhants
97 K5 **Ounsdale** Staffs
166 E4 **Ousby** Cumb
88 E3 **Ousden** Suffk
143 L3 **Ousefleet** E R Yk
181 G8 **Ouston** Dur
41 G5 **Out Elmstead** Kent
145 K3 **Out Newton** E R Yk
147 H7 **Out Rawcliffe** Lancs
203 J6 **Outchester** Nthumb
156 E3 **Outgate** Cumb
158 D2 **Outhgill** Cumb
82 D2 **Outhill** Warwks
114 B5 **Outlands** Staffs
141 G4 **Outlane** Kirk
103 K3 **Outwell** Norfk
33 K7 **Outwick** Hants
37 M2 **Outwood** Surrey
142 A3 **Outwood** Wakefd
140 B6 **Outwood Gate** Bury

116 C7 **Outwoods** Leics
114 B7 **Outwoods** Staffs
99 H6 **Outwoods** Warwks
142 A3 **Ouzlewell Green** Leeds
141 G2 **Ovenden** Calder
87 H1 **Over** Cambs
130 C6 **Over** Ches
64 A3 **Over** Gloucs
45 H2 **Over** S Glos
115 L4 **Over Burrows** Derbys
31 K7 **Over Compton** Dorset
102 B5 **Over End** Cambs
98 F4 **Over Green** Warwks
132 D6 **Over Haddon** Derbys
147 K2 **Over Kellet** Lancs
66 B3 **Over Kiddington** Oxon
63 G4 **Over Monnow** Mons
65 L2 **Over Norton** Oxon
130 F5 **Over Peover** Ches
161 G4 **Over Silton** N York
30 B3 **Over Stowey** Somset
31 G7 **Over Stratton** Somset
130 E4 **Over Tabley** Ches
34 C3 **Over Wallop** Hants
99 H5 **Over Whitacre** Warwks
133 J5 **Over Woodhouse** Derbys
66 B1 **Over Worton** Oxon
81 M7 **Overbury** Worcs
16 D6 **Overcombe** Dorset
132 F5 **Overgreen** Derbys
31 G4 **Overleigh** Somset
115 J8 **Overley** Staffs
129 J4 **Overpool** Ches
272 B3 **Overscaig Hotel** Highld
116 A8 **Overseal** Derbys
40 D4 **Oversland** Kent
82 C4 **Oversley Green** Warwks
84 F2 **Overstone** Nhants
122 E3 **Overstrand** Norfk
33 J3 **Overstreet** Wilts
83 L7 **Overthorpe** Nhants
245 J1 **Overton** C Aber
129 M4 **Overton** Ches
35 G1 **Overton** Hants
147 H4 **Overton** Lancs
151 J5 **Overton** N York
80 C1 **Overton** Shrops
56 E7 **Overton** Swans
141 L4 **Overton** Wakefd
112 E3 **Overton** Wrexhm
112 E3 **Overton Bridge** Wrexhm
130 F7 **Overton Green** Ches
157 K7 **Overtown** Lancs
209 L8 **Overtown** N Lans
47 H3 **Overtown** Swindn
142 A4 **Overtown** Wakefd
66 E8 **Overy** Oxon
67 J3 **Oving** Bucks
20 E6 **Oving** W Susx
22 E6 **Ovingdean** Br & H
180 D6 **Ovingham** Nthumb
168 E7 **Ovington** Dur
88 F6 **Ovington** Essex
35 H4 **Ovington** Hants
105 J3 **Ovington** Norfk
180 C6 **Ovington** Nthumb
34 D7 **Ower** Hants
19 H3 **Ower** Hants
16 E5 **Owermoigne** Dorset
91 G1 **Owl's Green** Suffk
95 H5 **Owlbury** Shrops
133 G2 **Owlerton** Sheff
64 A7 **Owlpen** Gloucs
49 K6 **Owlsmoor** Br For
67 J6 **Owlswick** Bucks
144 D6 **Owmby** Lincs
135 K2 **Owmby** Lincs
35 G6 **Owslebury** Hants
142 E5 **Owston** Donc
101 G2 **Owston** Leics
143 K7 **Owston Ferry** N Linc
145 H1 **Owstwick** E R Yk
145 J2 **Owthorne** E R Yk
117 H5 **Owthorpe** Notts
104 E3 **Oxborough** Norfk
15 L3 **Oxbridge** Dorset
136 F4 **Oxcombe** Lincs
133 J5 **Oxcroft** Derbys
71 G1 **Oxen End** Essex
156 D5 **Oxen Park** Cumb
157 H5 **Oxenholme** Cumb
140 F1 **Oxenhope** Brad
31 G3 **Oxenpill** Somset
64 D1 **Oxenton** Gloucs
47 L7 **Oxenwood** Wilts

66 D6 **Oxford** Oxon
68 E8 **Oxhey** Herts
180 F8 **Oxhill** Dur
83 H6 **Oxhill** Warwks
97 K3 **Oxley** Wolves
72 C4 **Oxley Green** Essex
24 C3 **Oxley's Green** E Susx
103 K6 **Oxlode** Cambs
189 J3 **Oxnam** Border
122 E6 **Oxnead** Norfk
50 F6 **Oxshott** Surrey
50 E6 **Oxshott Heath** Surrey
141 L7 **Oxspring** Barns
51 K8 **Oxted** Surrey
201 G2 **Oxton** Border
151 H7 **Oxton** N York
117 G1 **Oxton** Notts
56 F7 **Oxwich** Swans
56 F7 **Oxwich Green** Swans
121 K6 **Oxwick** Norfk
271 L7 **Oykel Bridge Hotel** Highld
256 B6 **Oyne** Abers
57 H7 **Oystermouth** Swans
64 A8 **Ozleworth** Gloucs

P

282 h3 **Pabail** W Isls
16 D1 **Packers Hill** Dorset
116 B8 **Packington** Leics
114 D1 **Packmoor** C Stke
83 G2 **Packmores** Warwks
234 C5 **Padanaram** Angus
67 H1 **Padbury** Bucks
51 H3 **Paddington** Gt Lon
130 C2 **Paddington** Warrtn
52 E6 **Paddlesworth** Kent
41 G7 **Paddlesworth** Kent
39 G4 **Paddock Wood** Kent
113 H5 **Paddolgreen** Shrops
129 G7 **Padeswood** Flints
140 F8 **Padfield** Derbys
130 C2 **Padgate** Warrtn
70 F7 **Padhams Green** Essex
140 B1 **Padiham** Lancs
149 L4 **Padside** N York
10 C7 **Padstow** Cnwll
48 F5 **Padworth** W Berk
169 G4 **Page Bank** Dur
20 E7 **Pagham** W Susx
72 D8 **Paglesham** Essex
8 C3 **Paignton** Torbay
100 A7 **Pailton** Warwks
23 K3 **Paine's Cross** E Susx
115 G5 **Painleyhill** Staffs
79 G6 **Painscastle** Powys
180 C6 **Painshawfield** Nthumb
152 B4 **Painsthorpe** E R Yk
64 C5 **Painswick** Gloucs
40 C3 **Painter's Forstal** Kent
208 E6 **Paisley** Rens
107 L5 **Pakefield** Suffk
89 J2 **Pakenham** Suffk
111 J4 **Pale** Gwynd
88 D6 **Pale Green** Essex
34 B3 **Palestine** Hants
49 L4 **Paley Street** W & M
98 C4 **Palfrey** Wsall
106 C7 **Palgrave** Suffk
16 F4 **Pallington** Dorset
69 J8 **Palmers Green** Gt Lon
11 H7 **Palmersbridge** Cnwll
196 F2 **Palmerston** E Ayrs
43 H7 **Palmerstown** V Glam
175 K3 **Palnackie** D & G
174 C2 **Palnure** D & G
133 J6 **Palterton** Derbys
48 F7 **Pamber End** Hants
48 F7 **Pamber Green** Hants
48 F6 **Pamber Heath** Hants
81 L8 **Pamington** Gloucs
17 K3 **Pamphill** Dorset
87 K5 **Pampisford** Cambs
31 G2 **Panborough** Somset
234 E8 **Panbride** Angus
11 K2 **Pancrasweek** Devon
43 G7 **Pancross** V Glam
43 J4 **Pandy** Caerph
92 D3 **Pandy** Gwynd
111 G5 **Pandy** Gwynd
62 D2 **Pandy** Mons
93 K3 **Pandy** Powys
112 B4 **Pandy** Wrexhm

127 G6 **Pandy Tudur** Conwy
111 L2 **Pandy'r Capel** Denbgs
71 H2 **Panfield** Essex
48 F4 **Pangbourne** W Berk
22 D5 **Pangdean** W Susx
80 E5 **Panks Bridge** Herefs
150 D5 **Pannal** N York
150 C5 **Pannal Ash** N York
243 L4 **Pannanich Wells Hotel** Abers
112 D7 **Pant** Shrops
109 H2 **Pant Glas** Gwynd
93 J7 **Pant Mawr** Powys
42 E5 **Pant-ffrwyth** Brdgnd
59 G4 **Pant-Gwyn** Carmth
57 J5 **Pant-lasau** Swans
128 B7 **Pant-pastynog** Denbgs
93 L8 **Pant-y-dwr** Powys
94 E3 **Pant-y-ffridd** Powys
42 D3 **Pant-y-gog** Brdgnd
128 E6 **Pant-y-mwyn** Flints
128 E4 **Pantasaph** Flints
74 F5 **Panteg** Pembks
5 K1 **Pantersbridge** Cnwll
93 G4 **Pantglas** Powys
136 C4 **Panton** Lincs
93 G3 **Pantperthog** Gwynd
57 H3 **Pantyffynnon** Carmth
61 L7 **Pantygaseg** Torfn
75 K7 **Pantymenyn** Carmth
107 G1 **Panxworth** Norfk
164 F4 **Papcastle** Cumb
280 E6 **Papigoe** Highld
212 D4 **Papple** E Loth
116 F1 **Papplewick** Notts
86 F3 **Papworth Everard** Cambs
86 F2 **Papworth St Agnes** Cambs
5 H4 **Par** Cnwll
41 J3 **Paramour Street** Kent
139 G5 **Parbold** Lancs
31 J4 **Parbrook** Somset
37 G6 **Parbrook** W Susx
111 G5 **Parc** Gwynd
44 E1 **Parc Seymour** Newpt
75 M2 **Parcllyn** Cerdgn
164 E5 **Pardshaw** Cumb
91 G3 **Parham** Suffk
245 H4 **Park** Abers
186 D7 **Park** D & G
178 F6 **Park** Nthumb
3 H3 **Park Bottom** Cnwll
140 E7 **Park Bridge** Tamesd
38 E6 **Park Corner** E Susx
49 G1 **Park Corner** Oxon
49 K2 **Park Corner** W & M
85 K4 **Park End** Beds
179 K4 **Park End** Nthumb
114 B1 **Park End** Staffs
40 D7 **Park Farm** Kent
19 J2 **Park Gate** Hants
150 A7 **Park Gate** Leeds
81 L1 **Park Gate** Worcs
70 C2 **Park Green** Essex
90 D2 **Park Green** Suffk
166 D2 **Park Head** Cumb
116 B1 **Park Head** Derbys
63 H7 **Park Hill** Gloucs
51 G3 **Park Royal** Gt Lon
68 F6 **Park Street** Herts
37 H4 **Park Street** W Susx
63 J5 **Parkend** Gloucs
38 F4 **Parkers Green** Kent
73 K1 **Parkeston** Essex
90 F8 **Parkeston Quay** Essex
6 C2 **Parkfield** Cnwll
129 G4 **Parkgate** Ches
165 H1 **Parkgate** Cumb
176 D1 **Parkgate** D & G
24 C4 **Parkgate** E Susx
71 G1 **Parkgate** Essex
52 B6 **Parkgate** Kent
39 L6 **Parkgate** Kent
37 K2 **Parkgate** Surrey
208 E4 **Parkhall** W Duns
27 G6 **Parkham** Devon
26 F6 **Parkham Ash** Devon
117 J1 **Parkhill** Notts
245 K1 **Parkhill House** Abers
63 G6 **Parkhouse** Mons
57 G7 **Parkmill** Swans
169 L1 **Parkside** Dur
209 L7 **Parkside** N Lans
129 J8 **Parkside** Wrexhm
17 K4 **Parkstone** Poole
17 M3 **Parley Green** Dorset
150 F8 **Parlington** Leeds

49 J1	**Parmoor** Bucks	
70 B5	**Parndon** Essex	
28 B2	**Parracombe** Devon	
75 H4	**Parrog** Pembks	
103 H2	**Parson Drove** Cambs	
133 G1	**Parson's Cross** Sheff	
72 F2	**Parson's Heath** Essex	
116 A6	**Parson's Hill** Derbys	
164 F3	**Parsonby** Cumb	
208 F5	**Partick** C Glas	
130 D2	**Partington** Traffd	
137 H6	**Partney** Lincs	
164 C6	**Parton** Cumb	
22 B3	**Partridge Green** W Susx	
62 B3	**Partrishow** Powys	
115 K1	**Parwich** Derbys	
70 E6	**Paslow Wood Common** Essex	
84 F7	**Passenham** Nhants	
36 B4	**Passfield** Hants	
70 D7	**Passingford Bridge** Essex	
102 D3	**Paston** C Pete	
123 G4	**Paston** Norfk	
114 F6	**Pasturefields** Staffs	
12 B3	**Patchacott** Devon	
22 D5	**Patcham** Br & H	
68 F7	**Patchetts Green** Herts	
21 J5	**Patching** W Susx	
27 L2	**Patchole** Devon	
45 J3	**Patchway** S Glos	
149 L3	**Pateley Bridge** N York	
72 D4	**Paternoster Heath** Essex	
80 C3	**Pateshall** Herefs	
221 K5	**Path of Condie** P & K	
30 F5	**Pathe** Somset	
222 E8	**Pathhead** Fife	
211 L6	**Pathhead** Mdloth	
82 E3	**Pathlow** Warwks	
70 B2	**Patmore Heath** Herts	
183 K1	**Patna** E Ayrs	
47 G7	**Patney** Wilts	
160 B4	**Patrick Brompton** N York	
139 M8	**Patricroft** Salfd	
145 J3	**Patrington** E R Yk	
41 G4	**Patrixbourne** Kent	
165 L7	**Patterdale** Cumb	
97 J4	**Pattingham** Staffs	
84 C4	**Pattishall** Nhants	
71 K2	**Pattiswick Green** Essex	
96 D4	**Patton** Shrops	
2 D5	**Paul** Cnwll	
33 K4	**Paul's Dene** Wilts	
84 D6	**Paulerspury** Bucks	
144 F3	**Paull** E R Yk	
45 K7	**Paulton** BaNES	
80 F5	**Paunton** Herefs	
191 G6	**Pauperhaugh** Nthumb	
114 B8	**Pave Lane** Wrekin	
85 K4	**Pavenham** Beds	
30 D2	**Pawlett** Somset	
202 C6	**Pawston** Nthumb	
82 E7	**Paxford** Gloucs	
202 E3	**Paxton** Border	
40 B4	**Payden Street** Kent	
14 C2	**Payhembury** Devon	
148 E5	**Paythorne** Lancs	
80 A1	**Paytoe** Herefs	
22 F7	**Peacehaven** E Susx	
132 B4	**Peak Dale** Derbys	
132 B4	**Peak Forest** Derbys	
119 J8	**Peak Hill** Lincs	
102 D2	**Peakirk** C Pete	
237 K4	**Peanmeanach** Highld	
39 H4	**Pearson's Green** Kent	
80 E8	**Peartree Green** Herefs	
37 L4	**Pease Pottage** W Susx	
45 K7	**Peasedown St John** BaNES	
16 C2	**Peasehill** Derbys	
22 B8	**Peaseland Green** Norfk	
48 C3	**Peasemore** W Berk	
91 H2	**Peasenhall** Suffk	
37 G2	**Peaslake** Surrey	
29 M1	**Peasley Cross** St Hel	
25 G3	**Peasmarsh** E Susx	
30 E8	**Peasmarsh** Somset	
36 E2	**Peasmarsh** Surrey	
23 H5	**Peat Inn** Fife	
69 G3	**Peathill** Abers	
100 D5	**Peatling Magna** Leics	
100 D5	**Peatling Parva** Leics	
96 C6	**Peaton** Shrops	
89 G8	**Pebmarsh** Essex	
82 D6	**Pebworth** Worcs	
40 F2	**Pecket Well** Calder	
29 M8	**Peckforton** Ches	
51 J4	**Peckham** Gt Lon	
100 A3	**Peckleton** Leics	
111 M6	**Pedairffordd** Powys	
40 F8	**Pedlinge** Kent	
97 K7	**Pedmore** Dudley	
30 F4	**Pedwell** Somset	
200 B5	**Peebles** Border	
154 C5	**Peel** IOM	
138 D2	**Peel** Lancs	
19 K3	**Peel Common** Hants	
41 G7	**Peene** Kent	
39 M7	**Peening Quarter** Kent	
116 C7	**Peggs Green** Leics	
68 E1	**Pegsdon** Beds	
180 F2	**Pegswood** Nthumb	
41 K3	**Pegwell** Kent	
247 H2	**Peinchorran** Highld	
259 G5	**Peinlich** Highld	
54 F3	**Pelcomb** Pembks	
54 F3	**Pelcomb Bridge** Pembks	
54 F3	**Pelcomb Cross** Pembks	
72 E4	**Peldon** Essex	
39 G6	**Pell Green** E Susx	
98 C3	**Pelsall** Wsall	
98 C3	**Pelsall Wood** Wsall	
181 G8	**Pelton** Dur	
181 G8	**Pelton Fell** Dur	
164 F1	**Pelutho** Cumb	
5 L4	**Pelynt** Cnwll	
56 F5	**Pemberton** Carmth	
139 H7	**Pemberton** Wigan	
39 M4	**Pembles Cross** Kent	
56 D4	**Pembrey** Carmth	
79 M4	**Pembridge** Herefs	
55 G6	**Pembroke** Pembks	
54 F6	**Pembroke Dock** Pembks	
39 G5	**Pembury** Kent	
57 K3	**Pen Rhiwfawr** Neath	
92 E6	**Pen-bont Rhydybeddau** Cerdgn	
55 J2	**Pen-ffordd** Pembks	
62 C5	**Pen-groes-oped** Mons	
124 F3	**Pen-llyn** IOA	
125 G6	**Pen-lon** IOA	
75 M4	**Pen-rhiw** Pembks	
61 K7	**Pen-twyn** Caerph	
63 G5	**Pen-twyn** Mons	
61 L6	**Pen-twyn** Torfn	
112 B6	**Pen-y-bont** Powys	
111 L6	**Pen-y-bont-fawr** Powys	
42 C5	**Pen-y-bryn** Neath	
75 L4	**Pen-y-bryn** Pembks	
60 C4	**Pen-y-cae** Powys	
62 E8	**Pen-y-cae-mawr** Mons	
128 D4	**Pen-y-cefn** Flints	
62 F5	**Pen-y-clawdd** Mons	
43 G4	**Pen-y-coedcae** Rhondd	
54 D2	**Pen-y-cwn** Pembks	
61 G5	**Pen-y-darren** Myr Td	
42 D5	**Pen-y-fai** Brdgnd	
128 D5	**Pen-y-felin** Flints	
92 D6	**Pen-y-garn** Cerdgn	
111 L6	**Pen-y-Garnedd** Powys	
61 J1	**Pen-y-genffordd** Powys	
108 C5	**Pen-y-graig** Gwynd	
126 D8	**Pen-y-Gwryd** Gwynd	
42 F6	**Pen-y-lan** V Glam	
126 C8	**Pen-y-pass** Gwynd	
112 B1	**Pen-y-stryt** Denbgs	
62 E5	**Pen-yr-Heol** Mons	
60 F6	**Pen-yr-Heolgerrig** Myr Td	
4 D5	**Penair** Cnwll	
63 G5	**Penallt** Mons	
55 J7	**Penally** Pembks	
63 H1	**Penalt** Herefs	
5 G6	**Penare** Cnwll	
43 J7	**Penarth** V Glam	
55 J4	**Penblewin** Pembks	
76 B5	**Penbryn** Cerdgn	
58 E2	**Pencader** Carmth	
109 G3	**Pencaenewydd** Gwynd	
212 A5	**Pencaitland** E Loth	
4 D6	**Pencalenick** Cnwll	
124 F5	**Pencarnisiog** IOA	
76 F6	**Pencarreg** Carmth	
10 F6	**Pencarrow** Cnwll	
61 H2	**Pencelli** Powys	
57 G5	**Penclawdd** Swans	
42 E5	**Pencoed** Brdgnd	
80 E5	**Pencombe** Herefs	
63 G2	**Pencoyd** Herefs	
63 H3	**Pencraig** Herefs	
111 K6	**Pencraig** Powys	
2 B4	**Pendeen** Cnwll	
60 E5	**Penderyn** Rhondd	
55 L5	**Pendine** Carmth	
140 B7	**Pendlebury** Salfd	
148 D7	**Pendleton** Lancs	
81 H4	**Pendock** Worcs	
10 E6	**Pendoggett** Cnwll	
31 H8	**Pendomer** Somset	
43 G6	**Pendoylan** V Glam	
42 D5	**Pendre** Brdgnd	
93 G3	**Penegoes** Powys	
3 K3	**Penelewey** Cnwll	
43 J2	**Pengam** Caerph	
43 K6	**Pengam** Cardif	
51 K5	**Penge** Gt Lon	
4 D4	**Pengelly** Cnwll	
10 F6	**Pengelly** Cnwll	
125 H1	**Pengorffwysfa** IOA	
6 B2	**Pengover Green** Cnwll	
5 G5	**Pengrugla** Cnwll	
127 K4	**Pengwern** Denbgs	
3 H7	**Penhale** Cnwll	
4 E3	**Penhale** Cnwll	
5 J3	**Penhale** Cnwll	
6 E4	**Penhale** Cnwll	
4 C4	**Penhallow** Cnwll	
3 H3	**Penhalurick** Cnwll	
3 H3	**Penhalvean** Cnwll	
47 H1	**Penhill** Swindn	
44 E1	**Penhow** Newpt	
24 C4	**Penhurst** E Susx	
92 D2	**Peniarth** Gwynd	
211 H7	**Penicuik** Mdloth	
58 D4	**Peniel** Carmth	
127 L7	**Peniel** Denbgs	
259 H8	**Penifiler** Highld	
192 F3	**Peninver** Ag & B	
125 K7	**Penisar Waun** Gwynd	
141 K7	**Penistone** Barns	
3 K5	**Penjerrick** Cnwll	
5 L4	**Penkelly** Cnwll	
130 A2	**Penketh** Warrtn	
183 G3	**Penkill** S Ayrs	
97 L1	**Penkridge** Staffs	
11 H3	**Penlean** Cnwll	
112 F3	**Penley** Wrexhm	
57 H5	**Penllergaer** Swans	
42 E6	**Penllyn** V Glam	
110 E2	**Penmachno** Conwy	
43 J2	**Penmaen** Caerph	
56 F7	**Penmaen** Swans	
126 E4	**Penmaenan** Conwy	
126 E4	**Penmaenmawr** Conwy	
110 C7	**Penmaenpool** Gwynd	
43 G7	**Penmark** V Glam	
126 C3	**Penmon** IOA	
109 K3	**Penmorfa** Gwynd	
125 J5	**Penmynydd** IOA	
67 M8	**Penn** Bucks	
97 K4	**Penn** Wolves	
68 A7	**Penn Street** Bucks	
92 F3	**Pennal** Gwynd	
268 F3	**Pennan** Abers	
76 F3	**Pennant** Cerdgn	
111 K5	**Pennant** Denbgs	
93 M4	**Pennant** Powys	
111 K6	**Pennant-Melangell** Powys	
57 G7	**Pennard** Swans	
95 J3	**Pennerley** Shrops	
13 K2	**Pennicott** Devon	
156 C7	**Pennington** Cumb	
18 D4	**Pennington** Hants	
139 J6	**Pennington Green** Wigan	
61 H2	**Pennorth** Powys	
45 L4	**Pennsylvania** S Glos	
156 D6	**Penny Bridge** Cumb	
55 G6	**Penny Bridge** Pembks	
133 L4	**Penny Green** Notts	
119 K6	**Penny Hill** Lincs	
226 F7	**Pennycross** Ag & B	
123 G7	**Pennygate** Norfk	
227 G7	**Pennyghael** Ag & B	
183 H1	**Pennyglen** S Ayrs	
28 F8	**Pennymoor** Devon	
75 L3	**Penparc** Cerdgn	
92 D7	**Penparcau** Cerdgn	
43 J2	**Penpedairheol** Caerph	
62 C6	**Penpedairheol** Mons	
62 C6	**Penperlleni** Mons	
10 F5	**Penpethy** Cnwll	
5 J4	**Penpillick** Cnwll	
3 K3	**Penpol** Cnwll	
5 K4	**Penpoll** Cnwll	
3 G3	**Penponds** Cnwll	
10 F7	**Penpont** Cnwll	
186 C7	**Penpont** D & G	
60 E2	**Penpont** Powys	
7 J4	**Penquit** Devon	
11 L7	**Penrest** Cnwll	
76 B7	**Penrherber** Carmth	
76 C6	**Penrhiw-pal** Cerdgn	
43 G2	**Penrhiwceiber** Rhondd	
76 C6	**Penrhiwllan** Cerdgn	
108 F5	**Penrhos** Gwynd	
124 D3	**Penrhos** IOA	
62 E5	**Penrhos** Mons	
59 L6	**Penrhos** Powys	
125 K5	**Penrhos garnedd** Gwynd	
127 G3	**Penrhyn Bay** Conwy	
126 F3	**Penrhyn-side** Conwy	
92 D6	**Penrhyncoch** Cerdgn	
109 L4	**Penrhyndeudraeth** Gwynd	
56 F7	**Penrice** Swans	
194 D2	**Penrioch** N Ayrs	
166 C4	**Penrith** Cumb	
10 B8	**Penrose** Cnwll	
11 J5	**Penrose** Cnwll	
166 A5	**Penruddock** Cumb	
3 K4	**Penryn** Cnwll	
58 D5	**Pensarn** Carmth	
127 J4	**Pensarn** Conwy	
81 G2	**Pensax** Worcs	
129 G3	**Pensby** Wirral	
32 C4	**Penselwood** Somset	
45 J6	**Pensford** BaNES	
81 L6	**Pensham** Worcs	
181 H8	**Penshaw** Sundld	
38 E4	**Penshurst** Kent	
38 E4	**Penshurst Station** Kent	
6 B1	**Pensilva** Cnwll	
97 K5	**Pensnett** Dudley	
13 H3	**Penstone** Devon	
94 C5	**Penstrowed** Powys	
5 G5	**Pentewan** Cnwll	
125 K6	**Pentir** Gwynd	
4 C3	**Pentire** Cnwll	
55 J5	**Pentlepoir** Pembks	
89 G6	**Pentlow** Essex	
89 G6	**Pentlow Street** Essex	
120 F8	**Pentney** Norfk	
34 D2	**Penton Grafton** Hants	
34 D2	**Penton Mewsey** Hants	
178 B3	**Pentonbridge** Cumb	
125 J4	**Pentraeth** IOA	
128 C7	**Pentre** Denbgs	
129 H6	**Pentre** Flints	
62 C6	**Pentre** Mons	
94 C6	**Pentre** Powys	
94 E5	**Pentre** Powys	
95 G5	**Pentre** Powys	
42 E2	**Pentre** Rhondd	
112 E7	**Pentre** Shrops	
112 D3	**Pentre** Wrexhm	
77 G6	**Pentre Bach** Cerdgn	
128 F4	**Pentre Bach** Flints	
125 H5	**Pentre Berw** IOA	
128 F5	**Pentre Ffwrndan** Flints	
109 L6	**Pentre Gwynfryn** Gwynd	
128 E5	**Pentre Halkyn** Flints	
95 H7	**Pentre Hodrey** Shrops	
127 K5	**Pentre Isaf** Conwy	
128 C7	**Pentre Llanrhaeadr** Denbgs	
94 E4	**Pentre Llifior** Powys	
42 E6	**Pentre Meyrick** V Glam	
127 L7	**Pentre Saron** Denbgs	
59 M2	**Pentre ty gwyn** Carmth	
126 F6	**Pentre'r Felin** Conwy	
77 H5	**Pentre'r-felin** Cerdgn	
60 D1	**Pentre'r-felin** Powys	
76 D4	**Pentre'rbryn** Cerdgn	
78 B8	**Pentre-bach** Powys	
110 D1	**Pentre-bont** Conwy	
76 C7	**Pentre-cagel** Cerdgn	
112 A1	**Pentre-celyn** Denbgs	
93 J2	**Pentre-celyn** Powys	
57 J6	**Pentre-chwyth** Swans	
112 D5	**Pentre-clawdd** Shrops	
76 D7	**Pentre-cwrt** Carmth	
57 J5	**Pentre-dwr** Swans	
59 H5	**Pentre-Gwenlais** Carmth	
78 C4	**Pentre-llwyn-llwyd** Powys	
92 D8	**Pentre-llyn** Cerdgn	
111 J1	**Pentre-llyn-cymmer** Conwy	
93 J3	**Pentre-Maw** Powys	
62 B6	**Pentre-piod** Torfn	
44 B2	**Pentre-poeth** Newpt	
126 F7	**Pentre-tafarn-y-fedw** Conwy	
61 G6	**Pentrebach** Myr Td	
94 E1	**Pentrebeirdd** Powys	
112 B2	**Pentredwr** Denbgs	
109 J4	**Pentrefelin** Gwynd	
125 H1	**Pentrefelin** IOA	
111 G1	**Pentrefoelas** Conwy	

75 L6 **Pentregalar** Pembks
76 C5 **Pentregat** Cerdgn
116 C1 **Pentrich** Derbys
33 H7 **Pentridge Hill** Dorset
43 K2 **Pentwynmaur** Caerph
43 H5 **Pentyrch** Cardif
5 H4 **Penwithick** Cnwll
48 C6 **Penwood** Hants
60 C4 **Penwyllt** Powys
59 H4 **Penybanc** Carmth
78 F2 **Penybont** Powys
112 D3 **Penycae** Wrexhm
108 C6 **Penycaerau** Gwynd
129 G7 **Penyffordd** Flints
42 F3 **Penygraig** Rhondd
59 G6 **Penygroes** Carmth
109 H1 **Penygroes** Gwynd
125 H2 **Penysarn** IOA
60 E6 **Penywaun** Rhondd
57 L3 **Penywern** Neath
2 D5 **Penzance** Cnwll
81 L5 **Peopleton** Worcs
130 F5 **Peover Heath** Ches
36 D2 **Peper Harow** Surrey
113 K6 **Peplow** Shrops
70 F5 **Pepper's Green** Essex
67 G5 **Peppershill** Oxon
68 D3 **Pepperstock** Beds
196 C3 **Perceton** N Ayrs
244 D5 **Percie** Abers
269 H3 **Percyhorner** Abers
9 i3 **Perelle** Guern
29 G2 **Periton** Somset
50 F2 **Perivale** Gt Lon
14 B4 **Perkins Village** Devon
181 G8 **Perkinsville** Dur
134 C5 **Perlethorpe** Notts
3 K3 **Perran Wharf** Cnwll
3 K3 **Perranarworthal** Cnwll
4 B4 **Perranporth** Cnwll
2 E5 **Perranuthnoe** Cnwll
3 K3 **Perranwell** Cnwll
4 C4 **Perranwell** Cnwll
4 C4 **Perranzabuloe** Cnwll
64 E6 **Perrott's Brook** Gloucs
98 D5 **Perry** Birm
98 D5 **Perry Barr** Birm
71 K3 **Perry Green** Essex
70 B4 **Perry Green** Herts
46 E1 **Perry Green** Wilts
15 H2 **Perry Street** Somset
114 C5 **Pershall** Staffs
81 L6 **Pershore** Worcs
86 B2 **Pertenhall** Beds
221 K3 **Perth** P & K
112 E5 **Perthy** Shrops
80 E7 **Perton** Herefs
97 J3 **Perton** Staffs
32 E4 **Pertwood** Wilts
40 E6 **Pet Street** Kent
12 C7 **Peter Tavy** Devon
68 F3 **Peter's Green** Herts
102 D4 **Peterborough** C Pete
79 L7 **Peterchurch** Herefs
245 J3 **Peterculter** C Aber
257 L2 **Peterhead** Abers
169 L2 **Peterlee** Dur
27 H8 **Peters Marland** Devon
35 M6 **Petersfield** Hants
50 F4 **Petersham** Gt Lon
43 G6 **Peterston-super-Ely** V Glam
43 L5 **Peterstone Wentlooge** Newpt
63 H2 **Peterstow** Herefs
40 F5 **Petham** Kent
11 K5 **Petherwin Gate** Cnwll
12 C1 **Petrockstow** Devon
85 H5 **Petsoe End** M Keyn
24 F4 **Pett** E Susx
40 F5 **Pett Bottom** Kent
90 E3 **Pettaugh** Suffk
234 C7 **Petterden** Angus
198 F4 **Pettinain** S Lans
91 G4 **Pettistree** Suffk
29 H6 **Petton** Devon
113 G6 **Petton** Shrops
51 M5 **Petts Wood** Gt Lon
46 A2 **Petty France** S Glos
211 J2 **Pettycur** Fife
257 G7 **Pettymuk** Abers
36 E6 **Petworth** W Susx
23 L6 **Pevensey** E Susx
24 B6 **Pevensey Bay** E Susx
47 H7 **Pewsey** Wilts
49 J2 **Pheasant's Hill** Bucks

81 L3 **Phepson** Worcs
181 H8 **Philadelphia** Sundld
26 D6 **Philham** Devon
200 F7 **Philiphaugh** Border
2 F3 **Phillack** Cnwll
3 L3 **Philleigh** Cnwll
70 F3 **Philpot End** Essex
210 E4 **Philpstoun** W Loth
63 J2 **Phocle Green** Herefs
49 J7 **Phoenix Green** Hants
241 J5 **Phoines** Highld
31 G5 **Pibsbury** Somset
164 D6 **Pica** Cumb
99 G4 **Piccadilly** Warwks
68 D5 **Piccotts End** Herts
142 E6 **Pickburn** Donc
162 D6 **Pickering** N York
34 E2 **Picket Piece** Hants
18 B2 **Picket Post** Hants
99 H7 **Pickford** Covtry
99 H7 **Pickford Green** Covtry
160 E6 **Pickhill** N York
95 K5 **Picklescott** Shrops
130 D4 **Pickmere** Ches
30 B5 **Pickney** Somset
114 A6 **Pickstock** Wrekin
139 L3 **Pickup Bank** Bl w D
27 H3 **Pickwell** Devon
101 G1 **Pickwell** Leics
46 B5 **Pickwick** Wilts
101 L1 **Pickworth** Lincs
118 D5 **Pickworth** Lincs
63 H2 **Pict's Cross** Herefs
256 D8 **Pictillum** Abers
129 K5 **Picton** Ches
128 D3 **Picton** Flints
160 F1 **Picton** N York
58 A5 **Picton Ferry** Carmth
23 G6 **Piddinghoe** E Susx
67 K6 **Piddington** Bucks
84 F4 **Piddington** M Keyn
66 F4 **Piddington** Oxon
16 D3 **Piddlehinton** Dorset
16 D3 **Piddletrenthide** Dorset
103 G7 **Pidley** Cambs
80 F3 **Pie Corner** Herefs
169 G7 **Piercebridge** Darltn
275 C1 **Pierowall** Ork
64 C2 **Piff's Elm** Gloucs
17 K2 **Pig Oak** Dorset
79 L5 **Pig Street** Herefs
180 E1 **Pigdon** Nthumb
82 F3 **Pigeon Green** Warwks
132 D7 **Pikehall** Derbys
17 K2 **Pilford** Dorset
70 E7 **Pilgrims Hatch** Essex
135 H1 **Pilham** Lincs
45 G4 **Pill** N Som
6 D2 **Pillaton** Cnwll
6 D2 **Pillatonmill** Cnwll
83 G5 **Pillerton Hersey** Warwks
83 G5 **Pillerton Priors** Warwks
79 J2 **Pilleth** Powys
142 A7 **Pilley** Barns
18 E4 **Pilley** Hants
18 E4 **Pilley Bailey** Hants
44 C2 **Pillgwenlly** Newpt
27 H5 **Pillhead** Devon
147 H6 **Pilling** Lancs
147 G6 **Pilling Lane** Lancs
45 H2 **Pilning** S Glos
25 K4 **Pilot Inn** Kent
132 B7 **Pilsbury** Derbys
15 J3 **Pilsdon** Dorset
102 B2 **Pilsgate** C Pete
132 E5 **Pilsley** Derbys
133 H7 **Pilsley** Derbys
107 H1 **Pilson Green** Norfk
23 G3 **Piltdown** E Susx
27 K4 **Pilton** Devon
101 M6 **Pilton** Nhants
101 K3 **Pilton** Rutlnd
31 K3 **Pilton** Somset
56 E7 **Pilton Green** Swans
148 C7 **Pimlico** Lancs
84 B7 **Pimlico** Nhants
17 H1 **Pimperne** Dorset
69 H2 **Pin Green** Herts
90 E7 **Pin Mill** Suffk
119 H6 **Pinchbeck** Lincs
119 G6 **Pinchbeck Bars** Lincs
119 G6 **Pinchbeck West** Lincs
143 G4 **Pincheon Green** Donc
170 D7 **Pinchinthorpe** R & Cl
139 H4 **Pincock** Lancs

84 F5 **Pindon End** M Keyn
138 E5 **Pinfold** Lancs
89 G3 **Pinford End** Suffk
56 D4 **Pinged** Carmth
49 G5 **Pingewood** W Berk
13 M4 **Pinhoe** Devon
99 H7 **Pinkett's Booth** Covtry
46 B2 **Pinkney** Wilts
99 K7 **Pinley** Covtry
82 F2 **Pinley Green** Warwks
182 F4 **Pinminnoch** S Ayrs
182 F4 **Pinmore** S Ayrs
14 C5 **Pinn** Devon
50 E1 **Pinner** Gt Lon
50 E1 **Pinner Green** Gt Lon
113 K2 **Pinsley Green** Ches
81 M5 **Pinvin** Worcs
182 F5 **Pinwherry** S Ayrs
133 J8 **Pinxton** Derbys
80 C6 **Pipe and Lyde** Herefs
114 A3 **Pipe Gate** Shrops
98 E2 **Pipehill** Staffs
253 G2 **Piperhill** Highld
11 J5 **Pipers Pool** Cnwll
101 J6 **Pipewell** Nhants
27 J3 **Pippacott** Devon
139 H3 **Pippin Street** Lancs
79 G7 **Pipton** Powys
50 B7 **Pirbright** Surrey
50 B7 **Pirbright Camp** Surrey
201 K7 **Pirnie** Border
194 D2 **Pirnmill** N Ayrs
68 F1 **Pirton** Herts
81 K5 **Pirton** Worcs
92 E7 **Pisgah** Cerdgn
49 H1 **Pishill** Oxon
108 E3 **Pistyll** Gwynd
232 B2 **Pitagowan** P & K
269 H3 **Pitblae** Abers
221 J2 **Pitcairngreen** P & K
264 C5 **Pitcalnie** Highld
256 C6 **Pitcaple** Abers
233 M2 **Pitcarity** Angus
67 J6 **Pitch Green** Bucks
36 C3 **Pitch Place** Surrey
50 B8 **Pitch Place** Surrey
64 B5 **Pitchcombe** Gloucs
67 J3 **Pitchcott** Bucks
119 J5 **Pitcher Row** Lincs
96 C3 **Pitchford** Shrops
254 D4 **Pitchroy** Moray
31 L4 **Pitcombe** Somset
42 D6 **Pitcot** V Glam
212 E4 **Pitcox** E Loth
256 B8 **Pitfichie** Abers
256 C3 **Pitglassie** Abers
264 B2 **Pitgrudy** Highld
234 E4 **Pitkennedy** Angus
222 E5 **Pitlessie** Fife
232 D4 **Pitlochry** P & K
256 B6 **Pitmachie** Abers
241 K3 **Pitmain** Highld
256 F6 **Pitmedden** Abers
30 B7 **Pitminster** Somset
234 E5 **Pitmuies** Angus
256 B8 **Pitmunie** Abers
31 G5 **Pitney** Somset
222 C2 **Pitroddie** P & K
223 G4 **Pitscottie** Fife
52 F1 **Pitsea** Essex
140 E7 **Pitses** Oldham
84 E2 **Pitsford** Nhants
68 B4 **Pitstone** Bucks
29 J7 **Pitt** Devon
34 F5 **Pitt** Hants
63 L7 **Pitt Court** Gloucs
38 F3 **Pitt's Wood** Kent
245 G8 **Pittarrow** Abers
223 K6 **Pittenweem** Fife
222 D7 **Pitteuchar** Fife
169 J2 **Pittington** Dur
256 C6 **Pittodrie House Hotel** Abers
34 B4 **Pitton** Wilts
269 H3 **Pittulie** Abers
169 H2 **Pity Me** Dur
10 C7 **Pityme** Cnwll
40 B6 **Pivington** Kent
106 E8 **Pixey Green** Suffk
37 J1 **Pixham** Surrey
10 D6 **Plain Street** Cnwll
209 L5 **Plains** N Lans
96 C4 **Plaish** Shrops
133 G8 **Plaistow** Derbys
51 L2 **Plaistow** Gt Lon

80 F7 **Plaistow** Herefs
36 F5 **Plaistow** W Susx
34 C7 **Plaitford** Hants
139 J7 **Plank Lane** Wigan
124 E4 **Plas Cymyran** IOA
48 D6 **Plastow Green** Hants
39 G2 **Platt** Kent
139 J7 **Platt Bridge** Wigan
113 H4 **Platt Lane** Shrops
39 L3 **Platts Heath** Kent
169 H1 **Plawsworth** Dur
38 F3 **Plaxtol** Kent
49 H4 **Play Hatch** Oxon
25 G3 **Playden** E Susx
90 F5 **Playford** Suffk
4 C6 **Playing Place** Cnwll
63 M1 **Playley Green** Gloucs
95 K2 **Plealey** Shrops
209 M2 **Plean** Stirlg
222 C4 **Pleasance** Fife
139 J2 **Pleasington** Bl w D
133 K6 **Pleasley** Derbys
133 K6 **Pleasleyhill** Notts
32 B8 **Pleck** Dorset
70 E2 **Pledgdon Green** Essex
142 A4 **Pledwick** Wakefd
9 j2 **Pleinheaume** Guern
9 a1 **Plemont** Jersey
129 K5 **Plemstall** Ches
179 G6 **Plenmeller** Nthumb
71 G4 **Pleshey** Essex
248 C5 **Plockton** Highld
95 J6 **Plowden** Shrops
95 J3 **Plox Green** Shrops
40 B6 **Pluckley** Kent
40 B6 **Pluckley Station** Kent
40 B6 **Pluckley Thorne** Kent
41 J3 **Plucks Gutter** Kent
164 F3 **Plumbland** Cumb
157 G4 **Plumgarths** Cumb
130 E5 **Plumley** Ches
166 C3 **Plumpton** Cumb
156 D7 **Plumpton** Cumb
22 E4 **Plumpton** E Susx
84 B5 **Plumpton** Nhants
84 D6 **Plumpton End** Nhants
22 E4 **Plumpton Green** E Susx
166 C4 **Plumpton Head** Cumb
51 L3 **Plumstead** Gt Lon
122 C4 **Plumstead** Norfk
122 C4 **Plumstead Green** Norfk
117 G5 **Plumtree** Notts
39 K4 **Plumtree Green** Kent
117 K5 **Plungar** Leics
40 B7 **Plurenden** Kent
16 D2 **Plush** Dorset
11 J6 **Plusha** Cnwll
11 K8 **Plushabridge** Cnwll
76 C5 **Plwmp** Cerdgn
6 F4 **Plymouth** C Plym
7 G4 **Plympton** C Plym
7 G4 **Plymstock** C Plym
14 B2 **Plymtree** Devon
161 K5 **Pockley** N York
152 B6 **Pocklington** E R Yk
119 H7 **Pode Hole** Lincs
31 J6 **Podimore** Somset
85 J3 **Podington** Beds
114 B4 **Podmore** Staffs
73 G4 **Point Clear** Essex
118 F5 **Pointon** Lincs
18 A5 **Pokesdown** Bmouth
11 L4 **Polapit Tamar** Cnwll
270 C6 **Polbain** Highld
6 C3 **Polbathic** Cnwll
210 D6 **Polbeth** W Loth
5 G1 **Polbrock** Cnwll
81 J5 **Pole Elm** Worcs
141 G4 **Pole Moor** Kirk
102 B6 **Polebrook** Nhants
23 K6 **Polegate** E Susx
130 C4 **Polelane Ends** Ches
99 H3 **Polesworth** Warwks
2 B6 **Polgigga** Cnwll
270 D6 **Polglass** Highld
5 G5 **Polgooth** Cnwll
185 H2 **Polgown** D & G
21 H6 **Poling** W Susx
21 H5 **Poling Corner** W Susx
5 J4 **Polkerris** Cnwll
123 G5 **Pollard Street** Norfk
142 F4 **Pollington** E R Yk
228 B2 **Polloch** Highld
208 F6 **Pollokshaws** C Glas
208 F6 **Pollokshields** C Glas

5 G5 **Polmassick** Cnwll	3 H3 **Pool** Cnwll	58 F5 **Porthyrhyd** Carmth	7 M4 **Poulston** Devon
5 J4 **Polmear** Cnwll	10 b2 **Pool** IOS	218 C8 **Portincaple** Ag & B	65 G7 **Poulton** Gloucs
210 B3 **Polmont** Falk	150 C6 **Pool** Leeds	9 a1 **Portinfer** Jersey	129 G2 **Poulton** Wirral
237 L4 **Polnish** Highld	80 D5 **Pool Head** Herefs	143 K7 **Portington** E R Yk	65 G7 **Poulton Priory** Gloucs
5 L4 **Polperro** Cnwll	221 H7 **Pool of Muckhart** Clacks	216 F5 **Portinnisherrich** Ag & B	147 G7 **Poulton-le-Fylde** Lancs
5 K5 **Polruan** Cnwll	95 G1 **Pool Quay** Powys	165 H6 **Portinscale** Cumb	97 G8 **Pound Bank** Worcs
31 H2 **Polsham** Somset	88 F7 **Pool Street** Essex	44 F4 **Portishead** N Som	23 H3 **Pound Green** E Susx
89 K7 **Polstead** Suffk	17 K4 **Poole** Poole	267 K3 **Portknockie** Moray	88 E4 **Pound Green** Suffk
89 K7 **Polstead Heath** Suffk	64 E8 **Poole Keynes** Gloucs	16 D8 **Portland** Dorset	97 G7 **Pound Green** Worcs
216 C7 **Poltalloch** Ag & B	260 D4 **Poolewe** Highld	245 K4 **Portlethen** Abers	37 L3 **Pound Hill** W Susx
3 J7 **Poltescoe** Cnwll	166 B6 **Pooley Bridge** Cumb	175 L4 **Portling** D & G	48 C6 **Pound Street** Hants
13 M3 **Poltimore** Devon	105 L7 **Pooley Street** Norfk	4 F7 **Portloe** Cnwll	57 G6 **Poundffald** Swans
211 J6 **Polton** Mdloth	131 H7 **Poolfold** Staffs	6 A4 **Portlooe** Cnwll	38 D7 **Poundgate** E Susx
202 A3 **Polwarth** Border	63 L1 **Poolhill** Gloucs	264 E3 **Portmahomack** Highld	66 F2 **Poundon** Bucks
11 J6 **Polyphant** Cnwll	38 C3 **Pooting's** Kent	5 G6 **Portmellon** Cnwll	38 E5 **Poundsbridge** Kent
10 C6 **Polzeath** Cnwll	35 H2 **Popham** Hants	18 E4 **Portmore** Hants	13 G8 **Poundsgate** Devon
211 H7 **Pomathorn** Mdloth	51 K3 **Poplar** Gt Lon	228 E6 **Portnacroish** Ag & B	11 H3 **Poundstock** Cnwll
132 B6 **Pomeroy** Derbys	91 K2 **Poplar Street** Suffk	282 h3 **Portnaguran** W Isls	23 J3 **Pounsley** E Susx
78 F7 **Ponde** Powys	81 G1 **Porchbrook** Worcs	204 B6 **Portnahaven** Ag & B	174 C5 **Pouton** D & G
69 K7 **Ponders End** Gt Lon	19 G5 **Porchfield** IOW	246 D2 **Portnalong** Highld	91 H1 **Pouy Street** Suffk
102 F5 **Pondersbridge** Cambs	106 F3 **Poringland** Norfk	211 J4 **Portobello** C Edin	37 L3 **Povey Cross** Surrey
3 J3 **Ponsanooth** Cnwll	3 H4 **Porkellis** Cnwll	181 G7 **Portobello** Gatesd	81 G6 **Pow Green** Herefs
155 J2 **Ponsonby** Cumb	28 F2 **Porlock** Somset	98 B4 **Portobello** Wolves	190 F3 **Powburn** Nthumb
3 J7 **Ponsongath** Cnwll	28 F1 **Porlock Weir** Somset	33 L4 **Porton** Wilts	13 M5 **Powderham** Devon
13 G7 **Ponsworthy** Devon	228 D6 **Port Appin** Ag & B	12 A7 **Portonachan** Devon	15 L3 **Powerstock** Dorset
126 E8 **Pont Cyfyng** Conwy	205 G3 **Port Askaig** Ag & B	172 B4 **Portpatrick** D & G	176 F5 **Powfoot** D & G
126 F6 **Pont Dolgarrog** Conwy	207 H5 **Port Bannatyne** Ag & B	3 G2 **Portreath** Cnwll	177 H7 **Powhill** Cumb
56 F3 **Pont Morlais** Carmth	177 H6 **Port Carlisle** Cumb	259 H7 **Portree** Highld	81 J5 **Powick** Worcs
126 C7 **Pont Pen-y-benglog** Gwynd	204 C4 **Port Charlotte** Ag & B	3 M4 **Portscatho** Cnwll	221 J7 **Powmill** P & K
111 G6 **Pont Rhyd-sarn** Gwynd	170 C6 **Port Clarence** S on T	19 L4 **Portsea** C Port	16 E5 **Poxwell** Dorset
42 C4 **Pont Rhyd-y-cyff** Brdgnd	206 F4 **Port Driseach** Ag & B	278 E3 **Portskerra** Highld	50 C4 **Poyle** Slough
94 D1 **Pont Robert** Powys	154 g4 **Port e Vallen** IOM	45 G1 **Portskewett** Mons	22 C5 **Poynings** W Susx
60 D6 **Pont Walby** Neath	56 E7 **Port Einon** Swans	22 C6 **Portslade** Br & H	3 H2 **Poynter's Lane End** Cnwll
58 F4 **Pont-ar-gothi** Carmth	204 E7 **Port Ellen** Ag & B	22 C6 **Portslade-by-Sea** Br & H	31 L6 **Poyntington** Dorset
60 C2 **Pont-ar-Hydfer** Powys	256 D7 **Port Elphinstone** Abers	172 B3 **Portslogan** D & G	131 H3 **Poynton** Ches
59 K4 **Pont-ar-llechau** Carmth	154 b8 **Port Erin** IOM	19 L4 **Portsmouth** C Port	113 J8 **Poynton** Wrekin
44 C2 **Pont-Ebbw** Newpt	10 D6 **Port Gaverne** Cnwll	140 D3 **Portsmouth** Calder	113 J7 **Poynton Green** Wrekin
78 D8 **Pont-faen** Powys	208 B4 **Port Glasgow** Inver	217 G3 **Portsonachan Hotel** Ag & B	55 G3 **Poyston Cross** Pembks
60 D5 **Pont-Nedd-Fechan** Neath	260 B5 **Port Henderson** Highld	267 M3 **Portsoy** Abers	89 K4 **Poystreet Green** Suffk
42 B3 **Pont-rhyd-y-fen** Neath	10 D6 **Port Isaac** Cnwll	34 F8 **Portswood** C Sotn	2 F5 **Praa Sands** Cnwll
125 J7 **Pont-rug** Gwynd	172 D6 **Port Logan** D & G	236 E7 **Portuairk** Highld	52 A6 **Pratt's Bottom** Gt Lon
112 D4 **Pont-y-blew** Wrexhm	236 E4 **Port Mor** Highld	80 B6 **Portway** Herefs	3 G4 **Praze-an-Beeble** Cnwll
110 E1 **Pont-y-pant** Conwy	171 J7 **Port Mulgrave** N York	80 C8 **Portway** Herefs	3 H7 **Predannack Wollas** Cnwll
74 E7 **Pont-yr-hafod** Pembks	282 h3 **Port nan Giuran** W Isls	98 B6 **Portway** Sandw	113 J5 **Prees** Shrops
42 D4 **Pont-yr-Rhyl** Brdgnd	282 c7 **Port nan Long** W Isls	82 C1 **Portway** Worcs	113 J5 **Prees Green** Shrops
9 e4 **Pontac** Jersey	282 h1 **Port Nis** W Isls	6 D4 **Portwrinkle** Cnwll	113 J4 **Prees Heath** Shrops
59 H6 **Pontamman** Carmth	219 J7 **Port of Menteith** Stirlg	174 D7 **Portyerrock** D & G	113 J4 **Prees Higher Heath** Shrops
58 E6 **Pontantwn** Carmth	282 h1 **Port of Ness** W Isls	13 J3 **Posbury** Devon	113 J5 **Prees Lower Heath** Shrops
57 K4 **Pontardawe** Neath	10 D6 **Port Quin** Cnwll	96 E3 **Posenhall** Shrops	147 G6 **Preesall** Lancs
57 G4 **Pontarddulais** Swans	228 D6 **Port Ramsay** Ag & B	88 F5 **Poslingford** Suffk	112 D4 **Preesgweene** Shrops
58 E3 **Pontarsais** Carmth	154 d7 **Port Soderick** IOM	199 L6 **Posso** Border	76 D6 **Pren-gwyn** Cerdgn
129 G7 **Pontblyddyn** Flints	19 L3 **Port Solent** Hants	17 J4 **Post Green** Dorset	190 E4 **Prendwick** Nthumb
94 B5 **Pontdolgoch** Powys	154 b8 **Port St Mary** IOM	12 F6 **Postbridge** Devon	109 K3 **Prenteg** Gwynd
142 C3 **Pontefract** Wakefd	129 H3 **Port Sunlight** Wirral	67 H7 **Postcombe** Oxon	129 G2 **Prenton** Wirral
180 E4 **Ponteland** Nthumb	57 L7 **Port Talbot** Neath	40 F7 **Postling** Kent	129 L1 **Prescot** Knows
93 G7 **Ponterwyd** Cerdgn	57 J6 **Port Tennant** Swans	106 F2 **Postwick** Norfk	29 K8 **Prescott** Devon
95 K2 **Pontesbury** Shrops	204 B6 **Port Wemyss** Ag & B	244 D4 **Potarch** Abers	112 F7 **Prescott** Shrops
95 K2 **Pontesbury Hill** Shrops	173 J6 **Port William** D & G	5 G5 **Pothole** Cnwll	96 F7 **Prescott** Shrops
95 K2 **Pontesford** Shrops	248 B5 **Port-an-Eorna** Highld	68 B1 **Potsgrove** Beds	233 J2 **Presnerb** Angus
112 C4 **Pontfadog** Wrexhm	206 B7 **Portachoillan** Ag & B	120 F7 **Pott Row** Norfk	202 C6 **Pressen** Nthumb
75 H5 **Pontfaen** Pembks	206 E5 **Portavadie** Ag & B	131 J4 **Pott Shrigley** Ches	128 C3 **Prestatyn** Denbgs
76 B4 **Pontgarreg** Cerdgn	45 G4 **Portbury** N Som	72 C3 **Pott's Green** Essex	131 H4 **Prestbury** Ches
75 K4 **Pontgarreg** Pembks	19 K3 **Portchester** Hants	68 C5 **Potten End** Herts	64 E2 **Prestbury** Gloucs
56 E3 **Ponthenry** Carmth	10 D6 **Porteath** Cnwll	41 H2 **Potten Street** Kent	79 K2 **Presteigne** Powys
62 C8 **Ponthir** Torfn	182 C8 **Portencalzie** D & G	163 H7 **Potter Brompton** N York	31 K3 **Prestleigh** Somset
76 A6 **Ponthirwaun** Cerdgn	195 K1 **Portencross** N Ayrs	123 J7 **Potter Heigham** Norfk	139 M6 **Prestolee** Bolton
43 J3 **Pontllanfraith** Caerph	16 B5 **Portesham** Dorset	67 L6 **Potter Row** Bucks	213 H7 **Preston** Border
57 H5 **Pontlliw** Swans	267 J3 **Portessie** Moray	115 J4 **Potter Somersal** Derbys	22 D6 **Preston** Br & H
61 H6 **Pontlottyn** Caerph	54 F4 **Portfield Gate** Pembks	97 J6 **Potter's Cross** Staffs	7 L4 **Preston** Devon
109 H1 **Pontlyfni** Gwynd	12 A5 **Portgate** Devon	39 M4 **Potter's Forstal** Kent	13 K7 **Preston** Devon
62 B7 **Pontnewydd** Torfn	267 H3 **Portgordon** Moray	23 H3 **Potter's Green** E Susx	16 D6 **Preston** Dorset
62 B6 **Pontnewynydd** Torfn	274 D5 **Portgower** Highld	69 K3 **Potter's Green** Herts	212 D3 **Preston** E Loth
80 E8 **Pontop** Dur	4 D2 **Porth** Cnwll	106 D5 **Pottergate Street** Norfk	144 F2 **Preston** E R Yk
77 K2 **Pontrhydfendigaid** Cerdgn	42 F3 **Porth** Rhondd	135 L6 **Potterhanworth** Lincs	80 F8 **Preston** Gloucs
77 K1 **Pontrhydygroes** Cerdgn	108 D3 **Porth Dinllaen** Gwynd	135 M6 **Potterhanworth Booths** Lincs	64 F7 **Preston** Gloucs
62 C7 **Pontrhydyrun** Torfn	3 J5 **Porth Navas** Cnwll		68 F2 **Preston** Herts
62 E2 **Pontrilas** Herefs	112 C6 **Porth-y-Waen** Shrops	46 E7 **Potterne** Wilts	40 D3 **Preston** Kent
24 B4 **Ponts Green** E Susx	3 K6 **Porthallow** Cnwll	46 E7 **Potterne Wick** Wilts	41 H3 **Preston** Kent
76 D6 **Pontshaen** Cerdgn	5 L4 **Porthallow** Cnwll	69 H6 **Potters Bar** Herts	139 G2 **Preston** Lancs
63 J3 **Pontshill** Herefs	42 B6 **Porthcawl** Brdgnd	147 L6 **Potters Brook** Lancs	203 K8 **Preston** Nthumb
61 G5 **Pontsticill** Powys	10 B8 **Porthcothan** Cnwll	68 E6 **Potters Crouch** Herts	101 J3 **Preston** Rutlnd
76 D7 **Pontwelly** Carmth	2 B6 **Porthcurno** Cnwll	99 K7 **Potters Green** Covtry	96 C1 **Preston** Shrops
56 E3 **Pontyates** Carmth	74 D5 **Porthgain** Pembks	100 B4 **Potters Marston** Leics	29 K4 **Preston** Somset
58 F6 **Pontyberem** Carmth	2 B6 **Porthgwarra** Cnwll	69 G3 **Pottersheath** Herts	89 J5 **Preston** Suffk
29 G7 **Pontybodkin** Flints	114 D2 **Porthill** Staffs	84 E6 **Potterspury** Nhants	8 D3 **Preston** Torbay
42 F5 **Pontyclun** Rhondd	4 D6 **Porthkea** Cnwll	257 H8 **Potterton** Abers	46 F3 **Preston** Wilts
42 D3 **Pontycymer** Brdgnd	43 G8 **Porthkerry** V Glam	150 F8 **Potterton** Leeds	47 K4 **Preston** Wilts
75 K5 **Pontyglasier** Pembks	3 G6 **Porthleven** Cnwll	121 L7 **Potthorpe** Norfk	82 E2 **Preston Bagot** Warwks
42 F3 **Pontygwaith** Rhondd	109 K4 **Porthmadog** Gwynd	32 D3 **Pottle Street** Wilts	67 G1 **Preston Bissett** Bucks
75 K5 **Pontygynon** Pembks	2 C4 **Porthmeor** Cnwll	161 G2 **Potto** N York	29 L5 **Preston Bowyer** Somset
62 C7 **Pontymoel** Torfn	4 F6 **Portholland** Cnwll	86 E5 **Potton** Beds	113 J6 **Preston Brockhurst** Shrops
62 B7 **Pontypool** Torfn	3 K6 **Porthoustock** Cnwll	11 J1 **Poughill** Cnwll	130 B4 **Preston Brook** Halton
62 C7 **Pontypool Road** Torfn	5 H5 **Porthpean** Cnwll	13 K1 **Poughill** Devon	35 J3 **Preston Candover** Hants
43 G4 **Pontypridd** Rhondd	4 A5 **Porthtowan** Cnwll	18 B2 **Poulner** Hants	84 B4 **Preston Capes** Nhants
43 K3 **Pontywaun** Caerph	112 F2 **Porthwgan** Wrexhm	46 E7 **Poulshot** Wilts	48 F1 **Preston Crowmarsh** Oxon

84 F4 **Preston Deanery** Nhants
82 E2 **Preston Green** Warwks
113 H7 **Preston Gubbals** Shrops
113 G8 **Preston Montford** Shrops
82 F5 **Preston on Stour** Warwks
169 L7 **Preston on Tees** S on T
130 B3 **Preston on the Hill** Halton
79 M7 **Preston on Wye** Herefs
157 H6 **Preston Patrick** Cumb
31 H7 **Preston Plucknett** Somset
41 H3 **Preston Street** Kent
113 L8 **Preston upon the Weald Moors** Wrekin
80 D6 **Preston Wynne** Herefs
159 K4 **Preston-under-Scar** N York
211 L4 **Prestonpans** E Loth
140 B6 **Prestwich** Bury
180 E4 **Prestwick** Nthumb
196 C6 **Prestwick** S Ayrs
67 L7 **Prestwood** Bucks
97 K6 **Prestwood** Staffs
42 E3 **Price Town** Brdgnd
104 B7 **Prickwillow** Cambs
31 H1 **Priddy** Somset
157 H7 **Priest Hutton** Lancs
12 B1 **Priestacott** Devon
132 C5 **Priestcliffe** Derbys
132 C5 **Priestcliffe Ditch** Derbys
67 G6 **Priestend** Bucks
197 H3 **Priestland** E Ayrs
141 H3 **Priestley Green** Calder
95 H4 **Priestweston** Shrops
52 E6 **Priestwood Green** Kent
100 B5 **Primethorpe** Leics
122 B8 **Primrose Green** Norfk
103 H5 **Primrose Hill** Cambs
133 J8 **Primrose Hill** Derbys
97 L6 **Primrose Hill** Dudley
138 E6 **Primrose Hill** Lancs
213 H7 **Primrosehill** Border
202 C7 **Primsidemill** Border
55 K4 **Princes Gate** Pembks
67 K6 **Princes Risborough** Bucks
83 J1 **Princethorpe** Warwks
12 E7 **Princetown** Devon
20 C5 **Prinsted** W Susx
128 C7 **Prion** Denbgs
178 B5 **Prior Rigg** Cumb
96 B8 **Priors Halton** Shrops
83 L4 **Priors Hardwick** Warwks
83 L4 **Priors Marston** Warwks
64 C2 **Priors Norton** Gloucs
47 H1 **Priory Vale** Swindn
79 J6 **Priory Wood** Herefs
42 F6 **Prisk** V Glam
45 K7 **Priston** BaNES
106 C5 **Pristow Green** Norfk
53 J2 **Prittlewell** Sthend
35 L5 **Privett** Hants
27 K3 **Prixford** Devon
4 E5 **Probus** Cnwll
212 B3 **Prora** E Loth
164 F3 **Prospect** Cumb
3 G5 **Prospidnick** Cnwll
268 E3 **Protstonhill** Abers
45 G5 **Providence** N Som
180 D6 **Prudhoe** Nthumb
2 E5 **Prussia Cove** Cnwll
45 J6 **Publow** BaNES
69 K2 **Puckeridge** Herts
30 E7 **Puckington** Somset
45 K4 **Pucklechurch** S Glos
81 K7 **Puckrup** Gloucs
130 E5 **Puddinglake** Ches
129 H5 **Puddington** Ches
28 E8 **Puddington** Devon
105 L5 **Puddledock** Norfk
68 C2 **Puddlehill** Herts
16 E4 **Puddletown** Dorset
80 D3 **Pudleston** Herefs
141 K1 **Pudsey** Leeds
21 H3 **Pulborough** W Susx
114 A7 **Puleston** Wrekin
129 J7 **Pulford** Ches
16 D1 **Pulham** Dorset
106 D6 **Pulham Market** Norfk
106 E6 **Pulham St Mary** Norfk
63 J8 **Pullens Green** S Gloucs
96 B2 **Pulley** Shrops
85 L8 **Pulloxhill** Beds
210 E5 **Pumpherston** W Loth
77 J7 **Pumsaint** Carmth
75 G6 **Punchestown** Pembks
15 M5 **Puncknowle** Dorset
23 K3 **Punnett's Town** E Susx

19 M2 **Purbrook** Hants
52 C3 **Purfleet** Thurr
30 D3 **Puriton** Somset
71 K6 **Purleigh** Essex
51 J6 **Purley** Gt Lon
49 G4 **Purley** W Berk
95 G7 **Purlogue** Shrops
46 C5 **Purlpit** Wilts
103 K6 **Purls Bridge** Cambs
32 B7 **Purse Caundle** Dorset
81 K1 **Purshull Green** Worcs
95 J7 **Purslow** Shrops
142 C4 **Purston Jaglin** Wakefd
15 J1 **Purtington** Somset
63 K6 **Purton** Gloucs
63 K6 **Purton** Gloucs
47 G2 **Purton** Wilts
47 G1 **Purton Stoke** Wilts
84 D6 **Pury End** Nhants
65 M7 **Pusey** Oxon
80 E7 **Putley** Herefs
80 F7 **Putley Green** Herefs
63 M5 **Putloe** Gloucs
51 G4 **Putney** Gt Lon
9 k3 **Putron Village** Guern
27 H3 **Putsborough** Devon
67 L4 **Puttenham** Herts
36 D2 **Puttenham** Surrey
89 G7 **Puttock End** Essex
70 E3 **Puttock's End** Essex
16 C6 **Putton** Dorset
84 E6 **Puxley** Nhants
44 E6 **Puxton** N Som
56 E4 **Pwll** Carmth
58 A5 **Pwll Trap** Carmth
61 L5 **Pwll-du** Mons
111 M1 **Pwll-glas** Denbgs
42 B3 **Pwll-y-glaw** Neath
54 F6 **Pwllcrochan** Pembks
78 E8 **Pwllgloyw** Powys
108 F4 **Pwllheli** Gwynd
63 G8 **Pwllmeyric** Mons
126 F4 **Pydew** Conwy
116 D1 **Pye Bridge** Derbys
70 C4 **Pye Corner** Herts
44 D2 **Pye Corner** Newpt
114 F8 **Pye Green** Staffs
22 D4 **Pyecombe** W Susx
42 B5 **Pyle** Brdgnd
29 L5 **Pyleigh** Somset
31 K3 **Pylle** Somset
103 K6 **Pymoor** Cambs
15 L4 **Pymore** Dorset
50 D7 **Pyrford** Surrey
67 G7 **Pyrton** Oxon
101 J8 **Pytchley** Nhants
11 K2 **Pyworthy** Devon

Q

94 F7 **Quabbs** Shrops
119 H5 **Quadring** Lincs
119 H5 **Quadring Eaudike** Lincs
67 H3 **Quainton** Bucks
43 H3 **Quaker's Yard** Myr Td
180 F8 **Quaking Houses** Dur
34 C2 **Quarley** Hants
116 B3 **Quarndon** Derbys
19 K5 **Quarr Hill** IOW
208 B5 **Quarrier's Village** Inver
118 E3 **Quarrington** Lincs
169 J3 **Quarrington Hill** Dur
97 L6 **Quarry Bank** Dudley
130 A6 **Quarrybank** Ches
266 D3 **Quarrywood** Moray
207 K6 **Quarter** N Ayrs
197 L1 **Quarter** S Lans
97 G5 **Quatford** Shrops
97 G5 **Quatt** Shrops
168 F2 **Quebec** Dur
64 A4 **Quedgeley** Gloucs
104 B7 **Queen Adelaide** Cambs
31 K6 **Queen Camel** Somset
45 J5 **Queen Charlton** BaNES
28 E7 **Queen Dart** Devon
32 C4 **Queen Oak** Dorset
39 H4 **Queen Street** Kent
46 F2 **Queen Street** Wilts
19 J6 **Queen's Bower** IOW
112 E6 **Queen's Head** Shrops
85 L5 **Queen's Park** Beds
84 E3 **Queen's Park** Nhants
53 K4 **Queenborough** Kent

81 K7 **Queenhill** Worcs
141 H2 **Queensbury** Brad
129 H6 **Queensferry** Flints
209 H6 **Queenslie** C Glas
209 J3 **Queenzieburn** N Lans
70 D1 **Quendon** Essex
100 E1 **Queniborough** Leics
65 H6 **Quenington** Gloucs
147 K4 **Quernmore** Lancs
147 K3 **Quernmore Park Hall** Lancs
98 D4 **Queslett** Birm
6 C2 **Quethiock** Cnwll
48 E4 **Quick's Green** W Berk
105 L6 **Quidenham** Norfk
35 G1 **Quidhampton** Hants
33 K5 **Quidhampton** Wilts
113 H5 **Quina Brook** Shrops
84 B5 **Quinbury End** Nhants
98 C6 **Quinton** Dudley
84 E4 **Quinton** Nhants
84 F4 **Quinton Green** Nhants
4 D3 **Quintrell Downs** Cnwll
12 B6 **Quither** Devon
115 H3 **Quixhall** Staffs
213 H6 **Quixwood** Border
12 A3 **Quoditch** Devon
116 F8 **Quorn** Leics
199 G5 **Quothquan** S Lans
275 d5 **Quoyburray** Ork
275 b4 **Quoyloo** Ork

R

39 K4 **Rabbit's Cross** Kent
69 G3 **Rableyheath** Herts
177 G8 **Raby** Cumb
129 H4 **Raby** Wirral
199 K6 **Rachan Mill** Border
126 C6 **Rachub** Gwynd
28 E7 **Rackenford** Devon
21 H4 **Rackham** W Susx
122 F8 **Rackheath** Norfk
176 D4 **Racks** D & G
275 a5 **Rackwick** Ork
115 M4 **Radbourne** Derbys
140 B6 **Radcliffe** Bury
191 K5 **Radcliffe** Nthumb
117 H4 **Radcliffe on Trent** Notts
84 D8 **Radclive** Bucks
65 L7 **Radcot** Oxon
263 J7 **Raddery** Highld
29 J5 **Raddington** Somset
223 H5 **Radernie** Fife
83 H2 **Radford Semele** Warwks
30 B3 **Radlet** Somset
68 F7 **Radlett** Herts
28 C6 **Radley** Devon
66 D7 **Radley** Oxon
70 F6 **Radley Green** Essex
130 B8 **Radmore Green** Ches
67 J7 **Radnage** Bucks
45 K8 **Radstock** BaNES
84 B7 **Radstone** Nhants
83 J5 **Radway** Warwks
114 B1 **Radway Green** Ches
85 K4 **Radwell** Beds
86 E8 **Radwell** Herts
88 C7 **Radwinter** Essex
88 C7 **Radwinter End** Essex
43 H5 **Radyr** Cardif
118 D2 **RAF College (Cranwell)** Lincs
265 H8 **Rafford** Moray
117 H7 **Ragdale** Leics
95 L5 **Ragdon** Shrops
2 D6 **Raginnis** Cnwll
62 E5 **Raglan** Mons
134 F5 **Ragnall** Notts
252 F6 **Raigbeg** Highld
81 K4 **Rainbow Hill** Worcs
138 F7 **Rainford** St Hel
52 B3 **Rainham** Gt Lon
53 H6 **Rainham** Medway
129 L2 **Rainhill** St Hel
129 L2 **Rainhill Stoops** St Hel
131 J4 **Rainow** Ches
140 B7 **Rainsough** Bury
160 E7 **Rainton** N York
134 B8 **Rainworth** Notts
157 K1 **Raisbeck** Cumb
167 G2 **Raise** Cumb
152 C3 **Raisthorpe** N York
222 C2 **Rait** P & K
136 F3 **Raithby** Lincs

137 G6 **Raithby** Lincs
171 K8 **Raithwaite** N York
36 B5 **Rake** W Susx
140 E5 **Rakewood** Rochdl
241 J4 **Ralia** Highld
77 G6 **Ram** Carmth
45 K3 **Ram Hill** S Glos
40 C6 **Ram Lane** Kent
258 B7 **Ramasaig** Highld
3 J4 **Rame** Cnwll
6 E5 **Rame** Cnwll
16 A2 **Rampisham** Dorset
146 E3 **Rampside** Cumb
87 J2 **Rampton** Cambs
134 F4 **Rampton** Notts
140 B4 **Ramsbottom** Bury
47 K4 **Ramsbury** Wilts
274 F3 **Ramscraigs** Highld
35 L6 **Ramsdean** Hants
48 E7 **Ramsdell** Hants
65 M4 **Ramsden** Oxon
81 L6 **Ramsden** Worcs
71 H8 **Ramsden Bellhouse** Essex
71 H7 **Ramsden Heath** Essex
102 F6 **Ramsey** Cambs
73 J1 **Ramsey** Essex
154 f3 **Ramsey** IOM
102 F6 **Ramsey Forty Foot** Cambs
102 E6 **Ramsey Heights** Cambs
72 D6 **Ramsey Island** Essex
102 F5 **Ramsey Mereside** Cambs
102 E6 **Ramsey St Mary's** Cambs
41 L2 **Ramsgate** Kent
149 K2 **Ramsgill** N York
168 B1 **Ramshaw** Dur
91 H7 **Ramsholt** Suffk
189 K5 **Ramshope** Nthumb
115 H3 **Ramshorn** Staffs
12 F4 **Ramsley** Devon
36 E4 **Ramsnest Common** Surrey
136 D4 **Ranby** Lincs
134 C3 **Ranby** Notts
136 B4 **Rand** Lincs
64 B5 **Randwick** Gloucs
208 C6 **Ranfurly** Rens
115 K7 **Rangemore** Staffs
45 K2 **Rangeworthy** S Glos
71 H3 **Rank's Green** Essex
196 E8 **Rankinston** E Ayrs
101 H1 **Ranksborough** Rutlnd
139 L3 **Rann** Bl w D
230 D4 **Rannoch Station** P & K
29 G2 **Ranscombe** Somset
134 C2 **Ranskill** Notts
114 D6 **Ranton** Staffs
114 D7 **Ranton Green** Staffs
123 G8 **Ranworth** Norfk
220 D8 **Raploch** Stirlg
275 d2 **Rapness** Ork
30 E7 **Rapps** Somset
175 K5 **Rascarrel** D & G
207 J2 **Rashfield** Ag & B
81 L2 **Rashwood** Worcs
151 G2 **Raskelf** N York
61 J5 **Rassau** Blae G
141 H3 **Rastrick** Calder
248 E7 **Ratagan** Highld
100 B2 **Ratby** Leics
99 J3 **Ratcliffe Culey** Leics
116 E6 **Ratcliffe on Soar** Notts
117 G8 **Ratcliffe on the Wreake** Leic
33 L2 **Ratfyn** Wilts
269 J4 **Rathen** Abers
222 F3 **Rathillet** Fife
148 D4 **Rathmell** N York
210 F5 **Ratho** C Edin
267 J3 **Rathven** Moray
34 E6 **Ratlake** Hants
83 J5 **Ratley** Warwks
41 H4 **Ratling** Kent
95 K4 **Ratlinghope** Shrops
120 B8 **Rattan Row** Norfk
280 C2 **Rattar** Highld
165 K3 **Ratten Row** Cumb
165 L1 **Ratten Row** Cumb
147 H7 **Ratten Row** Lancs
7 L3 **Rattery** Devon
89 K3 **Rattlesden** Suffk
23 K7 **Ratton Village** E Susx
233 J6 **Rattray** P & K
165 L1 **Raughton** Cumb
165 L2 **Raughton Head** Cumb
85 K1 **Raunds** Nhants
138 C6 **Raven Meols** Sefton
133 J1 **Ravenfield** Rothm

155 K3 **Ravenglass** Cumb
81 G4 **Ravenhills Green** Worcs
107 H4 **Raveningham** Norfk
163 H2 **Ravenscar** N York
114 C1 **Ravenscliffe** C Stke
154 e4 **Ravensdale** IOM
86 B4 **Ravensden** Beds
133 L8 **Ravenshead** Notts
113 K2 **Ravensmoor** Ches
141 K4 **Ravensthorpe** Kirk
84 C1 **Ravensthorpe** Nhants
99 L1 **Ravenstone** Leics
85 G5 **Ravenstone** M Keyn
158 C2 **Ravenstonedale** Cumb
198 F4 **Ravenstruther** S Lans
159 L1 **Ravensworth** N York
163 G2 **Raw** N York
143 H3 **Rawcliffe** E R Yk
151 J5 **Rawcliffe** York
143 H3 **Rawcliffe Bridge** E R Yk
150 B7 **Rawdon** Leeds
40 B3 **Rawling Street** Kent
142 C8 **Rawmarsh** Rothm
98 C1 **Rawnsley** Staffs
71 J8 **Rawreth** Essex
14 E1 **Rawridge** Devon
140 B3 **Rawtenstall** Lancs
90 B7 **Raydon** Suffk
190 C7 **Raylees** Nthumb
53 H1 **Rayleigh** Essex
15 H3 **Raymond's Hill** Devon
71 H3 **Rayne** Essex
51 G5 **Raynes Park** Gt Lon
64 A4 **Rea** Gloucs
88 B2 **Reach** Cambs
140 A1 **Read** Lancs
49 H4 **Reading** Readg
25 G1 **Reading Street** Kent
41 L2 **Reading Street** Kent
166 E7 **Reagill** Cumb
263 K1 **Rearquhar** Highld
117 H8 **Rearsby** Leics
113 L1 **Rease Heath** Shrops
279 G3 **Reay** Highld
41 H2 **Reculver** Kent
29 K7 **Red Ball** Somset
131 G8 **Red Bull** Ches
87 K4 **Red Cross** Cambs
11 K2 **Red Cross** Cnwll
165 H2 **Red Dial** Cumb
17 L3 **Red Hill** Bmouth
82 D4 **Red Hill** Warwks
88 D1 **Red Lodge** Suffk
140 C4 **Red Lumb** Rochdl
139 H6 **Red Rock** Wigan
55 L4 **Red Roses** Carmth
191 K6 **Red Row** Nthumb
114 C1 **Red Street** Staffs
125 J3 **Red Wharf Bay** IOA
55 J6 **Redberth** Pembks
68 E4 **Redbourn** Herts
144 B7 **Redbourne** N Linc
63 G5 **Redbrook** Gloucs
113 H3 **Redbrook** Wrexhm
40 B8 **Redbrook Street** Kent
253 H2 **Redburn** Highld
179 H6 **Redburn** Nthumb
170 E6 **Redcar** R & Cl
175 K2 **Redcastle** D & G
251 G2 **Redcastle** Highld
210 B3 **Redding** Falk
210 B3 **Reddingmuirhead** Falk
131 H1 **Reddish** Stockp
82 B2 **Redditch** Worcs
88 F4 **Rede** Suffk
106 F6 **Redenhall** Norfk
34 C1 **Redenham** Hants
179 K3 **Redesmouth** Nthumb
235 J2 **Redford** Abers
234 E6 **Redford** Angus
36 C5 **Redford** W Susx
188 C3 **Redfordgreen** Border
42 F4 **Redgate** Rhondd
221 K2 **Redgorton** P & K
105 L7 **Redgrave** Suffk
45 H3 **Redhill** Abers
86 F8 **Redhill** Herts
45 G6 **Redhill** N Som
37 L1 **Redhill** Surrey
107 H6 **Redisham** Suffk
45 H4 **Redland** Bristl
75 c3 **Redland** Ork
90 E1 **Redlingfield** Suffk
90 E1 **Redlingfield Green** Suffk
32 B4 **Redlynch** Somset

33 L6 **Redlynch** Wilts
164 F4 **Redmain** Cumb
81 H2 **Redmarley** Worcs
63 L1 **Redmarley D'Abitot** Gloucs
169 K6 **Redmarshall** S on T
117 L4 **Redmile** Leics
159 J4 **Redmire** N York
245 G8 **Redmyre** Abers
98 C8 **Rednal** Birm
112 E6 **Rednal** Shrops
201 J6 **Redpath** Border
260 B6 **Redpoint** Highld
4 A6 **Redruth** Cnwll
46 D6 **Redstocks** Wilts
233 J8 **Redstone** P & K
55 J4 **Redstone Cross** Pembks
140 B6 **Redvales** Bury
44 E2 **Redwick** Newpt
45 H2 **Redwick** S Glos
169 G6 **Redworth** Darltn
87 H8 **Reed** Herts
107 J3 **Reedham** Norfk
143 K3 **Reedness** E R Yk
136 D6 **Reeds Beck** Lincs
140 B3 **Reeds Holme** Lancs
135 L5 **Reepham** Lincs
122 B7 **Reepham** Norfk
159 J3 **Reeth** N York
99 H7 **Reeves Green** Solhll
154 f3 **Regaby** IOM
270 C5 **Reiff** Highld
37 L1 **Reigate** Surrey
163 L7 **Reighton** N York
256 F7 **Reisque** Abers
280 D5 **Reiss** Highld
4 C4 **Rejerrah** Cnwll
3 G4 **Releath** Cnwll
2 F4 **Relubbus** Cnwll
253 J2 **Relugas** Moray
49 J2 **Remenham** Wokham
49 J2 **Remenham Hill** Wokham
116 F6 **Rempstone** Notts
64 E5 **Rendcomb** Gloucs
91 H2 **Rendham** Suffk
91 H4 **Rendlesham** Suffk
208 E5 **Renfrew** Rens
86 B5 **Renhold** Beds
133 J4 **Renishaw** Derbys
191 J3 **Rennington** Nthumb
208 C3 **Renton** W Duns
166 E2 **Renwick** Cumb
123 J8 **Repps** Norfk
116 A6 **Repton** Derbys
251 J3 **Resaurie** Highld
5 G6 **Rescassa** Cnwll
5 G5 **Rescorla** Cnwll
237 L7 **Resipole** Highld
3 G3 **Reskadinnick** Cnwll
263 J6 **Resolis** Highld
60 C6 **Resolven** Neath
218 C5 **Rest and be thankful** Ag & B
213 J6 **Reston** Border
3 K4 **Restronguet** Cnwll
234 D5 **Reswallie** Angus
4 F2 **Reterth** Cnwll
4 F3 **Retew** Cnwll
134 D3 **Retford** Notts
5 G2 **Retire** Cnwll
71 J7 **Rettendon** Essex
4 E3 **Retyn** Cnwll
136 E7 **Revesby** Lincs
13 H8 **Rew** Devon
7 K7 **Rew** Devon
19 H5 **Rew Street** IOW
13 M3 **Rewe** Devon
12 A5 **Rexon** Devon
107 K7 **Reydon** Suffk
105 L2 **Reymerston** Norfk
55 J5 **Reynalton** Pembks
56 E6 **Reynoldston** Swans
11 L7 **Rezare** Cnwll
62 D6 **Rhadyr** Mons
77 L6 **Rhandirmwyn** Carmth
78 D2 **Rhayader** Powys
250 F2 **Rheindown** Highld
128 E5 **Rhes-y-cae** Flints
128 D7 **Rhewl** Denbgs
112 B3 **Rhewl** Denbgs
128 D4 **Rhewl Mostyn** Flints
128 D3 **Rhewl-fawr** Flints
270 E3 **Rhicarn** Highld
276 D5 **Rhiconich** Highld
263 J5 **Rhicullen** Highld
60 D6 **Rhigos** Rhondd

261 G1 **Rhireavach** Highld
273 K7 **Rhives** Highld
43 J5 **Rhiwbina** Cardif
110 D2 **Rhiwbryfdir** Gwynd
43 L4 **Rhiwderyn** Newpt
125 K7 **Rhiwen** Gwynd
42 F4 **Rhiwinder** Rhondd
125 K6 **Rhiwlas** Gwynd
111 H4 **Rhiwlas** Gwynd
112 B5 **Rhiwlas** Powys
43 G5 **Rhiwsaeson** Cardif
30 C4 **Rhode** Somset
39 H4 **Rhoden Green** Kent
140 C6 **Rhodes** Bury
40 F6 **Rhodes Minnis** Kent
133 L4 **Rhodesia** Notts
74 C6 **Rhodiad-y-brenin** Pembks
175 J3 **Rhonehouse** D & G
43 G8 **Rhoose** V Glam
58 C2 **Rhos** Carmth
128 D7 **Rhos** Denbgs
57 K4 **Rhos** Neath
61 J1 **Rhos** Powys
76 F2 **Rhos Haminiog** Cerdgn
125 J2 **Rhos Lligwy** IOA
111 M7 **Rhos y-brithdir** Powys
109 G4 **Rhos-fawr** Gwynd
127 G3 **Rhos-on-Sea** Conwy
77 H1 **Rhos-y-garth** Cerdgn
111 H4 **Rhos-y-gwaliau** Gwynd
108 D4 **Rhos-y-llan** Gwynd
79 K1 **Rhos-y-meirch** Powys
125 G2 **Rhosbeirio** IOA
125 J4 **Rhoscefnhir** IOA
124 D4 **Rhoscolyn** IOA
54 E6 **Rhoscrowther** Pembks
128 F6 **Rhosesmor** Flints
125 J8 **Rhosgadfan** Gwynd
125 G2 **Rhosgoch** IOA
79 H5 **Rhosgoch** Powys
75 L4 **Rhoshill** Pembks
108 C5 **Rhoshirwaun** Gwynd
109 H3 **Rhoslan** Gwynd
92 C2 **Rhoslefain** Gwynd
112 D2 **Rhosllanerchrugog** Wrexhm
59 H4 **Rhosmaen** Carmth
125 H4 **Rhosmeirch** IOA
124 E5 **Rhosneigr** IOA
112 E2 **Rhosnesni** Wrexhm
112 E1 **Rhosrobin** Wrexhm
56 D7 **Rhossili** Swans
125 J8 **Rhostryfan** Gwynd
112 D2 **Rhostyllen** Wrexhm
125 G2 **Rhosybol** IOA
112 D2 **Rhosygadfa** Shrops
112 D3 **Rhosymedre** Wrexhm
207 M2 **Rhu** Ag & B
128 C5 **Rhuallt** Denbgs
207 G4 **Rhubodach** Ag & B
130 A7 **Rhuddall Heath** Ches
76 F6 **Rhuddlan** Cerdgn
127 L4 **Rhuddlan** Denbgs
79 G5 **Rhulen** Powys
205 M6 **Rhunahaorine** Ag & B
110 B3 **Rhyd** Gwynd
109 K1 **Rhyd-Ddu** Gwynd
111 G2 **Rhyd-lydan** Conwy
111 G4 **Rhyd-uchaf** Gwynd
92 D6 **Rhyd-y pennau** Cerdgn
108 E4 **Rhyd-y-clafdy** Gwynd
127 H4 **Rhyd-y-foel** Conwy
125 K6 **Rhyd-y-groes** Gwynd
62 C5 **Rhyd-y-meirch** Mons
110 C3 **Rhyd-y-sarn** Gwynd
92 D3 **Rhyd-yr-onnen** Gwynd
58 D4 **Rhydargaeau** Carmth
77 G7 **Rhydcymerau** Carmth
81 J6 **Rhydd** Worcs
57 K5 **Rhydding** Neath
127 K6 **Rhydgaled** Conwy
110 F1 **Rhydlanfair** Conwy
76 C5 **Rhydlewis** Cerdgn
108 C5 **Rhydlios** Gwynd
76 E6 **Rhydowen** Cerdgn
77 G2 **Rhydrosser** Cerdgn
79 J6 **Rhydspence** Herefs
128 F8 **Rhydtalog** Flints
112 C5 **Rhydycroesau** Shrops
92 D7 **Rhydyfelin** Cerdgn
43 H4 **Rhydyfelin** Rhondd
57 K4 **Rhydyfro** Neath
110 F7 **Rhydymain** Gwynd
128 E6 **Rhydymwyn** Flints
127 K3 **Rhyl** Denbgs

61 H5 **Rhymney** Caerph
222 B3 **Rhynd** P & K
255 K6 **Rhynie** Abers
264 C4 **Rhynie** Highld
97 H8 **Ribbesford** Worcs
139 H2 **Ribbleton** Lancs
138 E2 **Ribby** Lancs
139 K1 **Ribchester** Lancs
132 F7 **Riber** Derbys
144 F6 **Riby** Lincs
151 K8 **Riccall** N York
188 F7 **Riccarton** Border
196 E4 **Riccarton** E Ayrs
29 L4 **Rich's Holford** Somset
80 C1 **Richards Castle** Herefs
50 C3 **Richings Park** Bucks
50 F4 **Richmond** Gt Lon
159 M2 **Richmond** N York
133 H3 **Richmond** Sheff
9 i2 **Richmond Fort** Guern
114 E7 **Rickerscote** Staffs
44 F7 **Rickford** N Som
7 L7 **Rickham** Devon
105 L8 **Rickinghall** Suffk
70 D1 **Rickling** Essex
70 D1 **Rickling Green** Essex
68 D8 **Rickmansworth** Herts
188 E1 **Riddell** Border
177 L4 **Riddings** Cumb
116 C1 **Riddings** Derbys
27 L8 **Riddlecombe** Devon
149 K7 **Riddlesden** Brad
45 H7 **Ridge** BaNES
17 H5 **Ridge** Dorset
69 G7 **Ridge** Herts
33 G4 **Ridge** Wilts
37 L1 **Ridge Green** Surrey
99 J4 **Ridge Lane** Warwks
41 G6 **Ridge Row** Kent
78 E3 **Ridgebourne** Powys
45 G6 **Ridgehill** N Som
116 B1 **Ridgeway** Derbys
133 H3 **Ridgeway** Derbys
82 C3 **Ridgeway** Worcs
81 G5 **Ridgeway Cross** Herefs
88 E7 **Ridgewell** Essex
23 H3 **Ridgewood** E Susx
85 J8 **Ridgmont** Beds
180 B6 **Riding Mill** Nthumb
52 D6 **Ridley** Kent
179 H6 **Ridley** Nthumb
113 J1 **Ridley Green** Ches
123 G5 **Ridlington** Norfk
101 J3 **Ridlington** Rutlnd
123 G5 **Ridlington Street** Norfk
179 L2 **Ridsdale** Nthumb
161 J5 **Rievaulx** N York
177 J5 **Rigg** D & G
209 K5 **Riggend** N Lans
253 G2 **Righoul** Highld
157 K5 **Rigmadon Park** Cumb
137 H4 **Rigsby** Lincs
198 E6 **Rigside** S Lans
139 J3 **Riley Green** Lancs
115 J8 **Rileyhill** Staffs
11 K7 **Rilla Mill** Cnwll
11 K7 **Rillaton** Cnwll
162 E7 **Rillington** N York
148 D6 **Rimington** Lancs
31 K6 **Rimpton** Somset
145 J2 **Rimswell** E R Yk
75 G7 **Rinaston** Pembks
97 G4 **Rindleford** Shrops
138 F5 **Ring o'Bells** Lancs
103 H3 **Ring's End** Cambs
175 H3 **Ringford** D & G
132 F3 **Ringinglow** Sheff
106 C1 **Ringland** Norfk
23 H3 **Ringles Cross** E Susx
39 L2 **Ringlestone** Kent
139 M6 **Ringley** Bolton
23 G5 **Ringmer** E Susx
7 J5 **Ringmore** Devon
13 L8 **Ringmore** Devon
254 E3 **Ringorm** Moray
107 H5 **Ringsfield** Suffk
107 H6 **Ringsfield Corner** Suffk
68 C4 **Ringshall** Bucks
90 B4 **Ringshall** Suffk
90 B5 **Ringshall Stocks** Suffk
101 L8 **Ringstead** Nhants
120 F3 **Ringstead** Norfk
18 A3 **Ringwood** Hants
41 K5 **Ringwould** Kent
2 F5 **Rinsey** Cnwll

2 F5 **Rinsey Croft** Cnwll
23 H5 **Ripe** E Susx
116 C2 **Ripley** Derbys
18 B4 **Ripley** Hants
150 C4 **Ripley** N York
50 D7 **Ripley** Surrey
144 B2 **Riplingham** E R Yk
35 K6 **Riplington** Hants
150 D2 **Ripon** N York
118 E6 **Rippingale** Lincs
41 K5 **Ripple** Kent
81 K7 **Ripple** Worcs
140 F4 **Ripponden** Calder
204 D7 **Risabus** Ag & B
80 D4 **Risbury** Herefs
144 A5 **Risby** N Linc
88 F2 **Risby** Suffk
43 K3 **Risca** Caerph
153 J7 **Rise** E R Yk
38 F7 **Riseden** E Susx
39 H6 **Riseden** Kent
119 H5 **Risegate** Lincs
135 K5 **Riseholme** Lincs
164 D4 **Risehow** Cumb
85 L3 **Riseley** Beds
49 H6 **Riseley** Wokham
90 E2 **Rishangles** Suffk
139 L2 **Rishton** Lancs
140 F4 **Rishworth** Calder
140 A3 **Rising Bridge** Lancs
116 D4 **Risley** Derbys
130 C1 **Risley** Warrtn
150 B2 **Risplith** N York
47 L6 **Rivar** Wilts
71 K4 **Rivenhall End** Essex
41 J6 **River** Kent
36 D6 **River** W Susx
87 L2 **River Bank** Cambs
250 F1 **Riverford** Highld
38 D2 **Riverhead** Kent
32 C8 **Rivers Corner** Dorset
139 J5 **Rivington** Lancs
146 D3 **Roa Island** Cumb
28 E6 **Roachill** Devon
46 C7 **Road Ashton** Wilts
106 F4 **Road Green** Norfk
84 E5 **Roade** Nhants
178 C4 **Roadhead** Cumb
198 E3 **Roadmeetings** S Lans
197 H7 **Roadside** E Ayrs
279 L4 **Roadside** Highld
29 J3 **Roadwater** Somset
258 D7 **Roag** Highld
183 H2 **Roan of Craigoch** S Ayrs
87 J8 **Roast Green** Essex
43 K6 **Roath** Cardif
188 D3 **Roberton** Border
198 F7 **Roberton** S Lans
24 D3 **Robertsbridge** E Susx
141 J3 **Roberttown** Kirk
55 J4 **Robeston Wathen** Pembks
177 H4 **Robgill Tower** D & G
131 H8 **Robin Hill** Staffs
139 G5 **Robin Hood** Lancs
141 M2 **Robin Hood** Leeds
163 G2 **Robin Hood's Bay** N York
88 E7 **Robinhood End** Essex
27 K7 **Roborough** Devon
6 F2 **Roborough** Devon
129 K2 **Roby** Knows
139 G6 **Roby Mill** Lancs
115 J4 **Rocester** Staffs
54 E3 **Roch** Pembks
54 E3 **Roch Gate** Pembks
140 D5 **Rochdale** Rochdl
5 G3 **Roche** Cnwll
52 F5 **Rochester** Medway
189 M6 **Rochester** Nthumb
53 J1 **Rochford** Essex
80 E2 **Rochford** Worcs
10 C7 **Rock** Cnwll
57 L6 **Rock** Neath
191 J2 **Rock** Nthumb
21 K4 **Rock** W Susx
81 G1 **Rock** Worcs
129 H2 **Rock Ferry** Wirral
81 L1 **Rock Hill** Worcs
14 B3 **Rockbeare** Devon
33 K7 **Rockbourne** Hants
177 K6 **Rockcliffe** Cumb
175 L4 **Rockcliffe** D & G
177 K6 **Rockcliffe Cross** Cumb
8 D2 **Rockend** Torbay
2 B6 **Rockestal** Cnwll
264 E3 **Rockfield** Highld

62 F4 **Rockfield** Mons
28 D1 **Rockford** Devon
18 B2 **Rockford** Hants
96 C8 **Rockgreen** Shrops
63 K8 **Rockhampton** S Glos
10 F5 **Rockhead** Cnwll
95 G7 **Rockhill** Shrops
101 J5 **Rockingham** Nhants
105 H4 **Rockland All Saints** Norfk
107 G3 **Rockland St Mary** Norfk
105 K4 **Rockland St Peter** Norfk
134 E5 **Rockley** Notts
47 H4 **Rockley** Wilts
140 C3 **Rockliffe** Lancs
207 L1 **Rockville** Ag & B
49 J1 **Rockwell End** Bucks
29 L6 **Rockwell Green** Somset
64 B6 **Rodborough** Gloucs
47 H2 **Rodbourne** Swindn
46 D2 **Rodbourne** Wilts
79 K3 **Rodd** Herefs
190 E2 **Roddam** Nthumb
16 B5 **Rodden** Dorset
168 F3 **Roddymoor** Dur
46 A8 **Rode** Somset
130 F8 **Rode Heath** Ches
131 G6 **Rode Heath** Ches
282 d7 **Rodel** W Isls
113 J8 **Roden** Wrekin
29 J3 **Rodhuish** Somset
113 K8 **Rodington** Wrekin
113 K8 **Rodington Heath** Wrekin
63 L5 **Rodley** Gloucs
150 B8 **Rodley** Leeds
64 D7 **Rodmarton** Gloucs
22 F6 **Rodmell** E Susx
40 B3 **Rodmersham** Kent
40 B3 **Rodmersham Green** Kent
31 H1 **Rodney Stoke** Somset
115 K3 **Rodsley** Derbys
30 C3 **Rodway** Somset
140 E8 **Roe Cross** Tamesd
69 G3 **Roe Green** Herts
87 G8 **Roe Green** Herts
139 M7 **Roe Green** Salfd
150 E3 **Roecliffe** N York
51 G4 **Roehampton** Gt Lon
37 J4 **Roffey** W Susx
273 H7 **Rogart** Highld
36 B6 **Rogate** W Susx
156 E3 **Roger Ground** Cumb
44 B2 **Rogerstone** Newpt
282 d7 **Roghadal** W Isls
44 F2 **Rogiet** Mons
66 F8 **Roke** Oxon
181 K7 **Roker** Sundld
123 J8 **Rollesby** Norfk
100 F3 **Rolleston** Leics
117 K1 **Rolleston** Notts
115 L6 **Rolleston** Staffs
153 K6 **Rolston** E R Yk
44 D6 **Rolstone** N Som
39 L7 **Rolvenden** Kent
39 L7 **Rolvenden Layne** Kent
168 C6 **Romaldkirk** Dur
160 E4 **Romanby** N York
199 K3 **Romanno Bridge** Border
28 C6 **Romansleigh** Devon
40 A7 **Romden Castle** Kent
258 F6 **Romesdal** Highld
17 L1 **Romford** Dorset
52 B1 **Romford** Gt Lon
131 J2 **Romiley** Stockp
52 C6 **Romney Street** Kent
34 D6 **Romsey** Hants
97 H6 **Romsley** Shrops
98 B7 **Romsley** Worcs
206 B8 **Ronachan** Ag & B
167 L2 **Rookhope** Dur
19 H6 **Rookley** IOW
19 H7 **Rookley Green** IOW
44 D8 **Rooks Bridge** Somset
29 K4 **Rooks Nest** Somset
160 B5 **Rookwith** N York
145 H2 **Roos** E R Yk
146 D2 **Roose** Cumb
146 E2 **Roosebeck** Cumb
86 B4 **Roothams Green** Beds
35 K4 **Ropley** Hants
35 K4 **Ropley Dean** Hants
35 K4 **Ropley Soke** Hants
118 C5 **Ropsley** Lincs
269 K6 **Rora** Abers
95 H3 **Rorrington** Shrops
267 H6 **Rosarie** Moray

3 G3 **Roscroggan** Cnwll
4 C4 **Rose** Cnwll
28 D6 **Rose Ash** Devon
72 C2 **Rose Green** Essex
89 J7 **Rose Green** Suffk
89 K6 **Rose Green** Suffk
20 E7 **Rose Green** W Susx
23 G4 **Rose Hill** E Susx
140 B2 **Rose Hill** Lancs
147 H8 **Roseacre** Lancs
198 D3 **Rosebank** S Lans
75 J6 **Rosebush** Pembks
11 H3 **Rosecare** Cnwll
4 D3 **Rosecliston** Cnwll
162 C3 **Rosedale Abbey** N York
272 C7 **Rosehall** Highld
269 G2 **Rosehearty** Abers
113 G8 **Rosehill** Shrops
266 C3 **Roseisle** Moray
23 K7 **Roselands** E Susx
54 F5 **Rosemarket** Pembks
263 K8 **Rosemarkie** Highld
29 L7 **Rosemary Lane** Devon
233 J6 **Rosemount** P & K
4 F2 **Rosenannon** Cnwll
3 K6 **Rosenithon** Cnwll
5 H3 **Rosevean** Cnwll
3 M4 **Rosevine** Cnwll
2 F4 **Rosewarne** Cnwll
211 J6 **Rosewell** Mdloth
169 L6 **Roseworth** S on T
3 G3 **Roseworthy** Cnwll
166 D7 **Rosgill** Cumb
258 D7 **Roskhill** Highld
3 K6 **Roskorwell** Cnwll
3 J4 **Roskrow** Cnwll
165 K2 **Rosley** Cumb
211 J6 **Roslin** Mdloth
115 L8 **Rosliston** Derbys
207 L2 **Rosneath** Ag & B
175 G6 **Ross** D & G
203 J5 **Ross** Nthumb
63 J2 **Ross-on-Wye** Herefs
129 J8 **Rossett** Wrexhm
150 D5 **Rossett Green** N York
143 G8 **Rossington** Donc
208 D5 **Rossland** Rens
280 C8 **Roster** Highld
130 E3 **Rostherne** Ches
165 H7 **Rosthwaite** Cumb
115 J3 **Roston** Derbys
210 F2 **Rosyth** Fife
190 F6 **Rothbury** Nthumb
117 H8 **Rotherby** Leics
38 E7 **Rotherfield** E Susx
49 H3 **Rotherfield Greys** Oxon
49 H3 **Rotherfield Peppard** Oxon
133 H1 **Rotherham** Rothm
84 D4 **Rothersthorpe** Nhants
49 H7 **Rotherwick** Hants
266 F6 **Rothes** Moray
207 H6 **Rothesay** Ag & B
256 D4 **Rothiebrisbane** Abers
267 L6 **Rothiemay** Moray
242 C2 **Rothiemurchus Lodge** Highld
256 C4 **Rothienorman** Abers
100 D1 **Rothley** Leics
180 C1 **Rothley** Nthumb
256 B5 **Rothmaise** Abers
142 A2 **Rothwell** Leeds
144 F7 **Rothwell** Lincs
101 H7 **Rothwell** Nhants
142 A2 **Rothwell Haigh** Leeds
153 G5 **Rotsea** E R Yk
234 B2 **Rottal Lodge** Angus
22 F6 **Rottingdean** Br & H
164 C8 **Rottington** Cumb
176 D3 **Roucan** D & G
19 H7 **Roud** IOW
114 E4 **Rough Close** Staffs
40 F3 **Rough Common** Kent
121 H7 **Rougham** Norfk
89 H3 **Rougham Green** Suffk
148 E7 **Roughlee** Lancs
243 K1 **Roughpark** Abers
136 D6 **Roughton** Lincs
122 E4 **Roughton** Norfk
97 G4 **Roughton** Shrops
38 F3 **Roughway** Kent
68 F7 **Round Bush** Herts
68 E3 **Round Green** Luton
52 E5 **Round Street** Kent
72 B6 **Roundbush** Essex

70 E4 **Roundbush Green** Essex
15 K1 **Roundham** Somset
150 D8 **Roundhay** Leeds
98 C5 **Rounds Green** Sandw
37 G5 **Roundstreet Common** W Susx
46 E6 **Roundway** Wilts
234 B5 **Roundyhill** Angus
82 B4 **Rous Lench** Worcs
15 G4 **Rousdon** Devon
66 C2 **Rousham** Oxon
67 J7 **Rout's Green** Bucks
165 G4 **Routenbeck** Cumb
207 K6 **Routenburn** N Ayrs
153 H7 **Routh** E R Yk
10 F7 **Row** Cnwll
166 E4 **Row** Cumb
157 G5 **Row** Cumb
35 H8 **Row Ash** Hants
71 H3 **Row Green** Essex
50 D6 **Row Town** Surrey
177 L3 **Rowanburn** D & G
218 E7 **Rowardennan Hotel** Stirlg
218 E7 **Rowardennan Lodge** Stirlg
131 K2 **Rowarth** Derbys
44 F7 **Rowberrow** Somset
19 G6 **Rowborough** IOW
46 E6 **Rowde** Wilts
12 F3 **Rowden** Devon
126 E5 **Rowen** Conwy
115 K2 **Rowfield** Derbys
178 F6 **Rowfoot** Nthumb
30 C5 **Rowford** Somset
72 F3 **Rowhedge** Essex
37 H4 **Rowhook** W Susx
82 F2 **Rowington** Warwks
132 D5 **Rowland** Derbys
20 B5 **Rowland's Castle** Hants
180 E7 **Rowland's Gill** Gatesd
36 B2 **Rowledge** Surrey
168 E1 **Rowley** Dur
144 B1 **Rowley** E R Yk
95 H2 **Rowley** Shrops
99 K6 **Rowley Green** Covtry
141 J5 **Rowley Hill** Kirk
98 B6 **Rowley Regis** Sandw
62 D2 **Rowlstone** Herefs
37 G3 **Rowly** Surrey
19 K3 **Rowner** Hants
82 B1 **Rowney Green** Worcs
34 E7 **Rownhams** Hants
164 E7 **Rowrah** Cumb
131 G4 **Rows of Trees** Ches
67 K3 **Rowsham** Bucks
132 E6 **Rowsley** Derbys
48 C1 **Rowstock** Oxon
136 A8 **Rowston** Lincs
133 J6 **Rowthorne** Derbys
129 K6 **Rowton** Ches
95 J1 **Rowton** Shrops
95 K7 **Rowton** Shrops
113 K7 **Rowton** Wrekin
201 L7 **Roxburgh** Border
144 A4 **Roxby** N Linc
171 H7 **Roxby** N York
86 C4 **Roxton** Beds
70 F5 **Roxwell** Essex
239 M7 **Roy Bridge** Highld
169 G6 **Royal Oak** Dur
138 E7 **Royal Oak** Lancs
113 K3 **Royal's Green** Ches
141 K5 **Roydhouse** Kirk
69 L5 **Roydon** Essex
120 F7 **Roydon** Norfk
106 C7 **Roydon** Norfk
69 L5 **Roydon Hamlet** Essex
142 B5 **Royston** Barns
87 G7 **Royston** Herts
140 D6 **Royton** Oldham
9 e2 **Rozel** Jersey
112 D3 **Ruabon** Wrexhm
224 D5 **Ruaig** Ag & B
4 E6 **Ruan High Lanes** Cnwll
4 E6 **Ruan Lanihorne** Cnwll
3 H7 **Ruan Major** Cnwll
3 J8 **Ruan Minor** Cnwll
63 J3 **Ruardean** Gloucs
63 J4 **Ruardean Hill** Gloucs
63 J4 **Ruardean Woodside** Gloucs
98 C7 **Rubery** Birm
283 c12 **Rubha Ban** W Isls
166 C2 **Ruckcroft** Cumb
80 B7 **Ruckhall** Herefs
80 B7 **Ruckhall Common** Herefs
40 D8 **Ruckinge** Kent

136 F4	**Ruckland** Lincs
96 C3	**Ruckley** Shrops
161 G1	**Rudby** N York
180 D5	**Rudchester** Nthumb
116 F5	**Ruddington** Notts
63 K5	**Ruddle** Gloucs
5 G4	**Ruddlemoor** Cnwll
63 M3	**Rudford** Gloucs
46 B8	**Rudge** Somset
45 J2	**Rudgeway** S Glos
37 G4	**Rudgwick** W Susx
63 J2	**Rudhall** Herefs
130 D5	**Rudheath** Ches
71 K6	**Rudley Green** Essex
46 B5	**Rudloe** Wilts
43 K4	**Rudry** Caerph
153 H2	**Rudston** E R Yk
131 J8	**Rudyard** Staffs
189 G2	**Ruecastle** Border
138 F4	**Rufford** Lancs
151 H5	**Rufforth** York
111 K3	**Rug** Denbgs
100 B8	**Rugby** Warwks
115 G7	**Rugeley** Staffs
27 K2	**Ruggaton** Devon
30 C6	**Ruishton** Somset
50 E2	**Ruislip** Gt Lon
267 H5	**Rumbach** Moray
221 J7	**Rumbling Bridge** P & K
107 G7	**Rumburgh** Suffk
168 F4	**Rumby Hill** Dur
4 E1	**Rumford** Cnwll
210 B4	**Rumford** Falk
43 K6	**Rumney** Cardif
30 B6	**Rumwell** Somset
129 L3	**Runcorn** Halton
20 E6	**Runcton** W Susx
104 C2	**Runcton Holme** Norfk
36 C2	**Runfold** Surrey
105 L2	**Runhall** Norfk
107 J1	**Runham** Norfk
107 L2	**Runham** Norfk
29 L6	**Runnington** Somset
71 J6	**Runsell Green** Essex
139 G4	**Runshaw Moor** Lancs
171 J7	**Runswick** N York
233 L2	**Runtaleave** Angus
71 J8	**Runwell** Essex
49 J4	**Ruscombe** Wokham
73 H4	**Rush Green** Essex
52 B2	**Rush Green** Gt Lon
69 G2	**Rush Green** Herts
69 J2	**Rush Green** Herts
130 D2	**Rush Green** Warrtn
80 E8	**Rushall** Herefs
106 D6	**Rushall** Norfk
47 H7	**Rushall** Wilts
98 C3	**Rushall** Wsall
89 H3	**Rushbrooke** Suffk
96 C5	**Rushbury** Shrops
69 J1	**Rushden** Herts
85 J2	**Rushden** Nhants
53 K5	**Rushenden** Kent
38 F7	**Rusher's Cross** E Susx
36 F2	**Rushett Common** Surrey
12 B7	**Rushford** Devon
105 J7	**Rushford** Norfk
23 L3	**Rushlake Green** E Susx
107 K6	**Rushmere** Suffk
90 E6	**Rushmere St Andrew** Suffk
36 C3	**Rushmoor** Surrey
79 K3	**Rushock** Herefs
81 K1	**Rushock** Worcs
131 G1	**Rusholme** Manch
130 B7	**Rushton** Ches
101 J6	**Rushton** Nhants
96 D2	**Rushton** Shrops
131 J7	**Rushton Spencer** Staffs
81 J4	**Rushwick** Worcs
169 H5	**Rushyford** Dur
219 K7	**Ruskie** Stirlg
118 E1	**Ruskington** Lincs
156 E5	**Rusland** Cumb
37 K3	**Rusper** W Susx
63 K5	**Ruspidge** Gloucs
37 K3	**Russ Hill** Surrey
90 F1	**Russel's Green** Suffk
71 H4	**Russell Green** Essex
49 H1	**Russell's Water** Oxon
38 E5	**Rusthall** Kent
21 H6	**Rustington** W Susx
163 G6	**Ruston** N York
153 G3	**Ruston Parva** E R Yk
162 F1	**Ruswarp** N York
96 D5	**Ruthall** Shrops
201 K7	**Rutherford** Border
209 G6	**Rutherglen** S Lans
5 G2	**Ruthernbridge** Cnwll
128 D8	**Ruthin** Denbgs
245 K3	**Ruthrieston** C Aber
267 K6	**Ruthven** Abers
233 L5	**Ruthven** Angus
241 K4	**Ruthven** Highld
233 L6	**Ruthven House** Angus
4 F3	**Ruthvoes** Cnwll
165 H3	**Ruthwaite** Cumb
176 E5	**Ruthwell** D & G
52 A5	**Ruxley Corner** Gt Lon
63 G3	**Ruxton Green** Herefs
112 F7	**Ruyton-XI-Towns** Shrops
180 B4	**Ryal** Nthumb
15 J3	**Ryall** Dorset
81 K7	**Ryall** Worcs
52 E7	**Ryarsh** Kent
67 G6	**Rycote** Oxon
156 E2	**Rydal** Cumb
19 K5	**Ryde** IOW
25 G3	**Rye** E Susx
81 H8	**Rye Cross** Worcs
25 G3	**Rye Foreign** E Susx
25 H3	**Rye Harbour** E Susx
81 H8	**Rye Street** Worcs
113 H5	**Ryebank** Shrops
63 J3	**Ryeford** Herefs
145 G3	**Ryehill** E R Yk
49 H5	**Ryeish Green** Wokham
102 A1	**Ryhall** Rutlnd
142 B5	**Ryhill** Wakefd
181 K8	**Ryhope** Sundld
133 J6	**Rylah** Derbys
135 K4	**Ryland** Lincs
116 F4	**Rylands** Notts
149 H4	**Rylstone** N York
31 J8	**Ryme Intrinseca** Dorset
151 J7	**Ryther** N York
180 E6	**Ryton** Gatesd
162 D7	**Ryton** N York
97 G3	**Ryton** Shrops
99 L6	**Ryton** Warwks
180 E6	**Ryton Woodside** Gatesd
99 K8	**Ryton-on-Dunsmore** Warwks

S

148 D8	**Sabden** Lancs
70 E7	**Sabine's Green** Essex
69 J3	**Sacombe** Herts
69 J3	**Sacombe Green** Herts
169 G1	**Sacriston** Dur
169 J7	**Sadberge** Darltn
194 B4	**Saddell** Ag & B
100 E5	**Saddington** Leics
120 D8	**Saddle Bow** Norfk
22 D5	**Saddlescombe** W Susx
157 G2	**Sadgill** Cumb
87 L7	**Saffron Walden** Essex
55 H6	**Sageston** Pembks
105 H3	**Saham Hills** Norfk
105 H3	**Saham Toney** Norfk
129 K7	**Saighton** Ches
213 K5	**St Abbs** Border
212 F6	**St Agnes** Border
4 B5	**St Agnes** Cnwll
68 F5	**St Albans** Herts
4 D5	**St Allen** Cnwll
9 j3	**St Andrew** Guern
43 H7	**St Andrew's Major** V Glam
223 J4	**St Andrews** Fife
15 L4	**St Andrews Well** Dorset
187 G7	**St Ann's** D & G
12 A8	**St Ann's Chapel** Cnwll
7 J5	**St Ann's Chapel** Devon
138 C2	**St Anne's** Lancs
3 K6	**St Anthony** Cnwll
23 L7	**St Anthony's Hill** E Susx
63 G7	**St Arvans** Mons
128 B5	**St Asaph** Denbgs
42 F8	**St Athan** V Glam
9 c3	**St Aubin** Jersey
5 G4	**St Austell** Cnwll
164 C8	**St Bees** Cumb
5 H4	**St Blazey** Cnwll
5 H4	**St Blazey Gate** Cnwll
201 J7	**St Boswells** Border
9 b3	**St Brelade** Jersey
9 b3	**St Brelade's Bay** Jersey
10 D8	**St Breock** Cnwll
10 F7	**St Breward** Cnwll
63 H6	**St Briavels** Gloucs
42 D6	**St Bride's Major** V Glam
54 C5	**St Brides** Pembks
44 E1	**St Brides Netherwent** Mons
43 H6	**St Brides super-Ely** V Glam
44 C3	**St Brides Wentlooge** Newpt
6 E3	**St Budeaux** C Plym
2 C6	**St Buryan** Cnwll
45 M5	**St Catherine** BaNES
217 J5	**St Catherines** Ag & B
64 B6	**St Chloe** Gloucs
58 A5	**St Clears** Carmth
6 A1	**St Cleer** Cnwll
4 D6	**St Clement** Cnwll
9 e4	**St Clement** Jersey
11 H5	**St Clether** Cnwll
207 G5	**St Colmac** Ag & B
4 E2	**St Columb Major** Cnwll
4 D2	**St Columb Minor** Cnwll
4 E3	**St Columb Road** Cnwll
269 K4	**St Combs** Abers
106 F6	**St Cross South Elmham** Suffk
235 J2	**St Cyrus** Abers
221 G3	**St David's** P & K
74 B7	**St David's** Pembks
4 B6	**St Day** Cnwll
29 K2	**St Decumans** Somset
4 F3	**St Dennis** Cnwll
62 E1	**St Devereux** Herefs
75 K3	**St Dogmaels** Cerdgn
75 G6	**St Dogwells** Pembks
6 D1	**St Dominick** Cnwll
42 E8	**St Donats** V Glam
46 E6	**St Edith's Marsh** Wilts
10 D6	**St Endellion** Cnwll
4 E3	**St Enoder** Cnwll
4 D5	**St Erme** Cnwll
6 D3	**St Erney** Cnwll
2 E4	**St Erth** Cnwll
2 F4	**St Erth Praze** Cnwll
10 B8	**St Ervan** Cnwll
5 G5	**St Ewe** Cnwll
43 H6	**St Fagans** Cardif
269 K6	**St Fergus** Abers
220 B2	**St Fillans** P & K
55 J6	**St Florence** Pembks
11 G3	**St Gennys** Cnwll
127 K4	**St George** Conwy
43 H6	**St George's** V Glam
50 D6	**St George's Hill** Surrey
44 D6	**St Georges** N Som
6 D3	**St Germans** Cnwll
27 J7	**St Giles in the Wood** Devon
11 L4	**St Giles-on-the-Heath** Cnwll
3 K4	**St Gluvia's** Cnwll
78 D1	**St Harmon** Powys
168 F5	**St Helen Auckland** Dur
122 D8	**St Helena** Norfk
164 D4	**St Helens** Cumb
24 E5	**St Helens** E Susx
19 L6	**St Helens** IOW
139 G8	**St Helens** St Hel
51 H5	**St Helier** Gt Lon
9 d3	**St Helier** Jersey
2 E5	**St Hilary** Cnwll
42 F7	**St Hilary** V Glam
14 C1	**St Hill** Devon
38 B6	**St Hill** W Susx
61 K6	**St Illtyd** Blae G
69 G2	**St Ippollitts** Herts
54 D5	**St Ishmael's** Pembks
10 C8	**St Issey** Cnwll
6 C2	**St Ive** Cnwll
87 G1	**St Ives** Cambs
2 E3	**St Ives** Cnwll
17 M2	**St Ives** Dorset
122 F7	**St James** Norfk
107 G7	**St James South Elmham** Suffk
84 E3	**St James's End** Nhants
6 E4	**St John** Cnwll
9 c1	**St John** Jersey
154 C5	**St John's** IOM
27 J5	**St John's Chapel** Devon
167 K3	**St John's Chapel** Dur
103 L1	**St John's Fen End** Norfk
120 D8	**St John's Highway** Norfk
199 G6	**St John's Kirk** S Lans
184 F6	**St John's Town of Dalry** D & G
51 H2	**St John's Wood** Gt Lon
168 D4	**St Johns** Dur
38 E2	**St Johns** Kent
50 C7	**St Johns** Surrey
81 J4	**St Johns** Worcs
154 e3	**St Jude's** IOM
2 B5	**St Just** Cnwll
3 L4	**St Just Lane** Cnwll
3 L4	**St Just-in-Roseland** Cnwll
256 D5	**St Katherines** Abers
3 K6	**St Keverne** Cnwll
10 E7	**St Kew** Cnwll
10 E7	**St Kew Highway** Cnwll
6 A3	**St Keyne** Cnwll
5 H2	**St Lawrence** Cnwll
72 D6	**St Lawrence** Essex
19 J8	**St Lawrence** IOW
9 c2	**St Lawrence** Jersey
41 K2	**St Lawrence** Kent
39 H2	**St Leonard's Street** Kent
67 M5	**St Leonards** Bucks
17 M2	**St Leonards** Dorset
24 E5	**St Leonards** E Susx
2 B6	**St Levan** Cnwll
43 H7	**St Lythans** V Glam
10 E7	**St Mabyn** Cnwll
222 C3	**St Madoes** P & K
107 G6	**St Margaret South Elmham** Suffk
41 K6	**St Margaret's at Cliffe** Kent
275 c6	**St Margaret's Hope** Ork
79 L8	**St Margarets** Herefs
69 K5	**St Margarets** Herts
154 d7	**St Marks** IOM
6 B4	**St Martin** Cnwll
3 J6	**St Martin** Cnwll
9 j3	**St Martin** Guern
9 e2	**St Martin** Jersey
221 L1	**St Martin's** P & K
112 D4	**St Martin's Moor** Shrops
112 D4	**St Martins** Shrops
9 c2	**St Mary** Jersey
34 F1	**St Mary Bourne** Hants
42 F7	**St Mary Church** V Glam
52 A5	**St Mary Cray** Gt Lon
42 E6	**St Mary Hill** V Glam
25 K2	**St Mary in the Marsh** Kent
275 d5	**St Mary's** Ork
25 K2	**St Mary's Bay** Kent
44 F5	**St Mary's Grove** N Som
53 H4	**St Mary's Hoo** Medway
8 D2	**St Marychurch** Torbay
62 F4	**St Maughans** Mons
62 F4	**St Maughans Green** Mons
3 L4	**St Mawes** Cnwll
4 E2	**St Mawgan** Cnwll
6 D2	**St Mellion** Cnwll
43 K5	**St Mellons** Cardif
10 B7	**St Merryn** Cnwll
5 G4	**St Mewan** Cnwll
4 F6	**St Michael Caerhays** Cnwll
30 D5	**St Michael Church** Somset
4 D6	**St Michael Penkevil** Cnwll
107 G6	**St Michael South Elmham** Suffk
147 J7	**St Michael's on Wyre** Lancs
39 M6	**St Michaels** Kent
80 D2	**St Michaels** Worcs
10 D7	**St Minver** Cnwll
223 J6	**St Monans** Fife
5 L1	**St Neot** Cnwll
86 D3	**St Neots** Cambs
74 E5	**St Nicholas** Pembks
43 H6	**St Nicholas** V Glam
41 J2	**St Nicholas at Wade** Kent
209 L1	**St Ninians** Stirlg
107 J3	**St Olaves** Norfk
73 H4	**St Osyth** Essex
9 b2	**St Ouen** Jersey
63 G2	**St Owens Cross** Herefs
69 G3	**St Paul's Walden** Herts
52 A5	**St Pauls Cray** Gt Lon
9 b2	**St Peter** Jersey
9 k3	**St Peter Port** Guern
9 i3	**St Peter's** Guern
41 L2	**St Peter's** Kent
86 E1	**St Peter's Hill** Cambs
55 G7	**St Petrox** Pembks
5 L2	**St Pinnock** Cnwll
196 D6	**St Quivox** S Ayrs
3 J8	**St Ruan** Cnwll
9 k2	**St Sampson** Guern
9 i3	**St Saviour** Guern
9 d3	**St Saviour** Jersey
4 F4	**St Stephen** Cnwll
4 F4	**St Stephen's Coombe** Cnwll
11 L5	**St Stephens** Cnwll
6 E3	**St Stephens** Cnwll

10 F6 **St Teath** Cnwll
10 F7 **St Tudy** Cnwll
54 F7 **St Twynnells** Pembks
5 K4 **St Veep** Cnwll
235 G6 **St Vigeans** Angus
5 G2 **St Wenn** Cnwll
63 G2 **St Weonards** Herefs
43 H6 **St y-Nyll** V Glam
82 D7 **Saintbury** Gloucs
229 G5 **Salachail** Ag & B
7 L7 **Salcombe** Devon
14 D5 **Salcombe Regis** Devon
72 D4 **Salcott** Essex
130 F2 **Sale** Traffd
81 L4 **Sale Green** Worcs
137 J4 **Saleby** Lincs
24 D2 **Salehurst** E Susx
59 H4 **Salem** Carmth
92 E6 **Salem** Cerdgn
125 K8 **Salem** Gwynd
227 H4 **Salen** Ag & B
237 K7 **Salen** Highld
139 K1 **Salesbury** Lancs
85 J7 **Salford** Beds
65 L2 **Salford** Oxon
140 B8 **Salford** Salfd
82 C5 **Salford Priors** Warwks
37 L2 **Salfords** Surrey
123 G8 **Salhouse** Norfk
221 J8 **Saline** Fife
33 K5 **Salisbury** Wilts
166 D3 **Salkeld Dykes** Cumb
122 C6 **Salle** Norfk
136 F5 **Salmonby** Lincs
65 G3 **Salperton** Gloucs
86 B5 **Salph End** Beds
209 L6 **Salsburgh** N Lans
114 F6 **Salt** Staffs
177 G8 **Salt Cotes** Cumb
164 E2 **Salta** Cumb
149 L8 **Saltaire** Brad
6 E3 **Saltash** Cnwll
263 K6 **Saltburn** Highld
170 F6 **Saltburn-by-the-Sea** R & Cl
117 M6 **Saltby** Leics
155 K3 **Saltcoats** Cumb
195 L3 **Saltcoats** N Ayrs
138 D2 **Saltcotes** Lancs
22 F6 **Saltdean** Br & H
164 C5 **Salterbeck** Cumb
148 F6 **Salterforth** Lancs
130 C6 **Salterswall** Ches
33 K4 **Salterton** Wilts
137 H1 **Saltfleet** Lincs
137 H2 **Saltfleetby All Saints** Lincs
137 J1 **Saltfleetby St Clement** Lincs
137 H2 **Saltfleetby St Peter** Lincs
45 K5 **Saltford** BaNES
122 B3 **Salthouse** Norfk
98 E5 **Saltley** Birm
44 D2 **Saltmarsh** Newpt
143 K3 **Saltmarshe** E R Yk
129 J6 **Saltney** Flints
162 C6 **Salton** N York
27 H6 **Saltrens** Devon
180 E3 **Saltwick** Nthumb
40 F8 **Saltwood** Kent
21 K6 **Salvington** W Susx
81 K3 **Salwarpe** Worcs
15 K3 **Salwayash** Dorset
82 C3 **Sambourne** Warwks
113 M6 **Sambrook** Wrekin
139 H2 **Samlesbury** Lancs
139 J2 **Samlesbury Bottoms** Lancs
29 K7 **Sampford Arundel** Somset
29 K3 **Sampford Brett** Somset
12 F2 **Sampford Courtenay** Devon
29 K7 **Sampford Moor** Somset
29 J8 **Sampford Peverell** Devon
12 D8 **Sampford Spiney** Devon
73 G3 **Samson's Corner** Essex
275 e3 **Samsonlane** Ork
212 B5 **Samuelston** E Loth
204 C2 **Sanaigmore** Ag & B
2 C5 **Sancreed** Cnwll
152 D7 **Sancton** E R Yk
31 G2 **Sand** Somset
150 E7 **Sand Hills** Leeds
152 B8 **Sand Hole** E R Yk
151 L4 **Sand Hutton** N York
156 B6 **Sand Side** Cumb
247 M8 **Sandaig** Highld
142 A4 **Sandal Magna** Wakefd
165 H3 **Sandale** Cumb
236 F4 **Sandavore** Highld

130 E7 **Sandbach** Ches
207 K3 **Sandbank** Ag & B
17 K5 **Sandbanks** Poole
267 L3 **Sandend** Abers
51 J6 **Sanderstead** Gt Lon
167 G7 **Sandford** Cumb
13 J2 **Sandford** Devon
17 H5 **Sandford** Dorset
18 B3 **Sandford** Hants
19 J7 **Sandford** IOW
44 E7 **Sandford** N Som
197 L2 **Sandford** S Lans
112 E6 **Sandford** Shrops
113 J5 **Sandford** Shrops
31 K6 **Sandford Orcas** Dorset
66 B2 **Sandford St Martin** Oxon
66 D6 **Sandford-on-Thames** Oxon
41 G8 **Sandgate** Kent
269 H3 **Sandhaven** Abers
172 D5 **Sandhead** D & G
142 C8 **Sandhill** Rothm
16 B3 **Sandhills** Dorset
31 L8 **Sandhills** Dorset
66 E5 **Sandhills** Oxon
36 D3 **Sandhills** Surrey
180 A5 **Sandhoe** Nthumb
216 F7 **Sandhole** Ag & B
143 L2 **Sandholme** E R Yk
119 K4 **Sandholme** Lincs
49 K6 **Sandhurst** Br For
64 B2 **Sandhurst** Gloucs
39 K7 **Sandhurst** Kent
24 E2 **Sandhurst Cross** Kent
160 E6 **Sandhutton** N York
116 E4 **Sandiacre** Derbys
137 K3 **Sandilands** Lincs
130 B5 **Sandiway** Ches
33 K7 **Sandleheath** Hants
66 C6 **Sandleigh** Oxon
32 C6 **Sandley** Dorset
53 G7 **Sandling** Kent
130 F6 **Sandlow Green** Ches
281 C5 **Sandness** Shet
71 H6 **Sandon** Essex
87 G8 **Sandon** Herts
114 E5 **Sandon** Staffs
114 E6 **Sandon Bank** Staffs
19 K6 **Sandown** IOW
6 A3 **Sandplace** Cnwll
68 F5 **Sandridge** Herts
46 D6 **Sandridge** Wilts
120 F5 **Sandringham** Norfk
67 K8 **Sands** Bucks
171 K8 **Sandsend** N York
157 G6 **Sandside** Cumb
143 J6 **Sandtoft** N Linc
39 M3 **Sandway** Kent
41 K4 **Sandwich** Kent
166 A6 **Sandwick** Cumb
281 e8 **Sandwick** Shet
282 g3 **Sandwick** W Isls
164 C7 **Sandwith** Cumb
164 C7 **Sandwith Newtown** Cumb
86 D5 **Sandy** Beds
136 E8 **Sandy Bank** Lincs
23 K3 **Sandy Cross** E Susx
80 F4 **Sandy Cross** Herefs
54 D5 **Sandy Haven** Pembks
149 K8 **Sandy Lane** Brad
46 D5 **Sandy Lane** Wilts
112 F3 **Sandy Lane** Wrexhm
13 G4 **Sandy Park** Devon
129 H6 **Sandycroft** Flints
187 J7 **Sandyford** D & G
13 K7 **Sandygate** Devon
154 e3 **Sandygate** IOM
175 M4 **Sandyhills** D & G
147 H3 **Sandylands** Lancs
113 M4 **Sandylane** Staffs
57 G2 **Sandylane** Swans
177 L5 **Sandysike** Cumb
63 G2 **Sandyway** Herefs
277 G3 **Sangobeg** Highld
276 F3 **Sangomore** Highld
130 B2 **Sankey Bridges** Warrtn
81 H2 **Sankyn's Green** Worcs
236 E6 **Sanna Bay** Highld
282 g3 **Sanndabhaig** W Isls
195 G2 **Sannox** N Ayrs
185 K1 **Sanquhar** D & G
155 K2 **Santon** Cumb
154 d7 **Santon** IOM
155 K2 **Santon Bridge** Cumb
105 G6 **Santon Downham** Suffk
100 B5 **Sapcote** Leics

81 G2 **Sapey Common** Herefs
105 J8 **Sapiston** Suffk
102 E8 **Sapley** Cambs
115 K4 **Sapperton** Derbys
64 D6 **Sapperton** Gloucs
118 D5 **Sapperton** Lincs
119 K6 **Saracen's Head** Lincs
280 D7 **Sarclet** Highld
19 H2 **Sarisbury** Hants
42 D5 **Sarn** Brdgnd
108 D5 **Sarn** Gwynd
93 L4 **Sarn** Powys
94 F5 **Sarn** Powys
108 E6 **Sarn-bach** Gwynd
112 D7 **Sarn-wen** Powys
58 B5 **Sarnau** Carmth
76 B5 **Sarnau** Cerdgn
111 J4 **Sarnau** Gwynd
112 C8 **Sarnau** Powys
78 E8 **Sarnau** Powys
79 L5 **Sarnesfield** Herefs
76 C7 **Saron** Carmth
59 H6 **Saron** Carmth
125 J6 **Saron** Gwynd
125 H7 **Saron** Gwynd
68 D7 **Sarratt** Herts
41 H2 **Sarre** Kent
65 L3 **Sarsden** Oxon
34 C2 **Sarson** Hants
168 E2 **Satley** Dur
41 H7 **Satmar** Kent
159 G3 **Satron** N York
28 B6 **Satterleigh** Devon
156 D4 **Satterthwaite** Cumb
49 H2 **Satwell** Oxon
244 F1 **Sauchen** Abers
233 J8 **Saucher** P & K
235 G2 **Sauchieburn** Abers
63 L5 **Saul** Gloucs
134 F2 **Saundby** Notts
55 K6 **Saundersfoot** Pembks
67 J6 **Saunderton** Bucks
27 H3 **Saunton** Devon
137 G6 **Sausthorpe** Lincs
4 C6 **Saveock Water** Cnwll
114 F4 **Saverley Green** Staffs
141 K4 **Savile Town** Kirk
83 L2 **Sawbridge** Warwks
70 C4 **Sawbridgeworth** Herts
163 G5 **Sawdon** N York
116 D5 **Sawley** Derbys
148 D6 **Sawley** Lancs
150 C2 **Sawley** N York
87 K5 **Sawston** Cambs
102 D6 **Sawtry** Cambs
117 L7 **Saxby** Leics
135 K3 **Saxby** Lincs
144 C4 **Saxby All Saints** N Linc
117 J7 **Saxelbye** Leics
90 C3 **Saxham Street** Suffk
135 H4 **Saxilby** Lincs
122 A4 **Saxlingham** Norfk
106 E4 **Saxlingham Green** Norfk
106 E4 **Saxlingham Nethergate** Norfk
106 E4 **Saxlingham Thorpe** Norfk
91 J3 **Saxmundham** Suffk
88 D3 **Saxon Street** Cambs
117 H3 **Saxondale** Notts
91 G2 **Saxtead** Suffk
90 F2 **Saxtead Green** Suffk
90 F2 **Saxtead Little Green** Suffk
122 C5 **Saxthorpe** Norfk
151 G8 **Saxton** N York
22 D4 **Sayers Common** W Susx
161 L8 **Scackleton** N York
134 D2 **Scaftworth** Notts
152 C1 **Scagglethorpe** N York
214 D5 **Scalasaig** Ag & B
143 L2 **Scalby** E R Yk
163 H4 **Scalby** N York
85 L4 **Scald End** Beds
84 E1 **Scaldwell** Nhants
166 E2 **Scale Houses** Cumb
178 B6 **Scaleby** Cumb
178 B6 **Scalebyhill** Cumb
165 K5 **Scales** Cumb
146 E2 **Scales** Cumb
166 B1 **Scalesceugh** Cumb
117 K6 **Scalford** Leics
171 H7 **Scaling** N York
171 H8 **Scaling Dam** R & Cl
281 d7 **Scalloway** Shet
136 E4 **Scamblesby** Lincs
141 G4 **Scammonden** Kirk

228 C1 **Scamodale** Highld
162 F7 **Scampston** N York
135 J4 **Scampton** Lincs
251 H4 **Scaniport** Highld
141 G4 **Scapegoat Hill** Kirk
163 J5 **Scarborough** N York
4 F4 **Scarcewater** Cnwll
133 K6 **Scarcliffe** Derbys
150 E7 **Scarcroft** Leeds
150 E7 **Scarcroft Hill** Leeds
280 C2 **Scarfskerry** Highld
168 D8 **Scargill** Dur
224 D6 **Scarinish** Ag & B
138 D5 **Scarisbrick** Lancs
165 H4 **Scarness** Cumb
105 J1 **Scarning** Norfk
117 J3 **Scarrington** Notts
138 E6 **Scarth Hill** Lancs
151 G8 **Scarthingwell** N York
145 H6 **Scartho** Lincs
144 B6 **Scawby** N Linc
142 E6 **Scawsby** Donc
142 E6 **Scawthorpe** Donc
161 J6 **Scawton** N York
22 F3 **Scayne's Hill** W Susx
61 H2 **Scethrog** Powys
131 G8 **Scholar Green** Ches
141 J6 **Scholes** Kirk
141 J3 **Scholes** Kirk
150 E8 **Scholes** Leeds
142 B8 **Scholes** Rothm
139 J6 **Scholes** Wigan
142 B3 **Scholey Hill** Leeds
169 H6 **School Aycliffe** Dur
141 H1 **School Green** Brad
130 C6 **School Green** Ches
15 J2 **School House** Dorset
49 H5 **Schoolgreen** Wokham
141 L5 **Scissett** Kirk
74 F5 **Scleddau** Pembks
122 F7 **Sco Ruston** Norfk
134 C4 **Scofton** Notts
106 C7 **Scole** Norfk
221 L2 **Scone** P & K
247 H2 **Sconser** Highld
222 F6 **Scoonie** Fife
135 M8 **Scopwick** Lincs
261 G1 **Scoraig** Highld
152 F6 **Scorborough** E R Yk
4 B6 **Scorrier** Cnwll
7 K1 **Scorriton** Devon
147 K6 **Scorton** Lancs
160 C3 **Scorton** N York
114 C2 **Scot Hay** Staffs
139 J6 **Scot Lane End** Bolton
180 C2 **Scot's Gap** Nthumb
178 B7 **Scotby** Cumb
160 B2 **Scotch Corner** N York
147 J4 **Scotforth** Lancs
135 L4 **Scothern** Lincs
150 B7 **Scotland** Leeds
118 C5 **Scotland** Lincs
181 G2 **Scotland Gate** Nthumb
222 C7 **Scotlandwell** P & K
279 K5 **Scotscalder Station** Highld
177 L4 **Scotsdike** Cumb
255 L7 **Scotsmill** Abers
208 F5 **Scotstoun** C Glas
180 F6 **Scotswood** N u Ty
118 D4 **Scott Willoughby** Lincs
143 M7 **Scotter** Lincs
143 L7 **Scotterthorpe** Lincs
118 D7 **Scottlethorpe** Lincs
143 M7 **Scotton** Lincs
160 B3 **Scotton** N York
150 D4 **Scotton** N York
122 F6 **Scottow** Norfk
105 K3 **Scoulton** Norfk
115 H5 **Scounslow Green** Staffs
276 B7 **Scourie** Highld
276 A7 **Scourie More** Highld
281 d8 **Scousburgh** Shet
140 E6 **Scouthead** Oldham
279 K2 **Scrabster** Highld
189 J3 **Scraesburgh** Border
136 F6 **Scrafield** Lincs
190 D4 **Scrainwood** Nthumb
119 L3 **Scrane End** Lincs
100 E2 **Scraptoft** Leics
123 K8 **Scratby** Norfk
151 M4 **Scrayingham** N York
24 D3 **Scrays** E Susx
118 E3 **Scredington** Lincs
137 H6 **Scremby** Lincs
202 F3 **Scremerston** Nthumb

117 J3 **Screveton** Notts
136 E6 **Scrivelsby** Lincs
150 E4 **Scriven** N York
134 C2 **Scrooby** Notts
115 K5 **Scropton** Derbys
136 D8 **Scrub Hill** Lincs
233 K4 **Scruschloch** Angus
160 D4 **Scruton** N York
178 B4 **Scuggate** Cumb
277 L4 **Scullomie** Highld
121 K5 **Sculthorpe** Norfk
143 M5 **Scunthorpe** N Linc
56 E7 **Scurlage** Swans
30 E8 **Sea** Somset
123 J6 **Sea Palling** Norfk
15 K1 **Seaborough** Dorset
114 C3 **Seabridge** Staffs
41 G8 **Seabrook** Kent
181 K6 **Seaburn** Sundld
129 H2 **Seacombe** Wirral
150 E8 **Seacroft** Leeds
137 L7 **Seacroft** Lincs
119 K4 **Seadyke** Lincs
259 H8 **Seafield** Highld
210 D6 **Seafield** W Loth
23 H7 **Seaford** E Susx
138 C8 **Seaforth** Sefton
117 G8 **Seagrave** Leics
46 D3 **Seagry Heath** Wilts
169 L1 **Seaham** Dur
203 L6 **Seahouses** Nthumb
38 E2 **Seal** Kent
170 D6 **Seal Sands** S on T
36 D1 **Seale** Surrey
170 C8 **Seamer** N York
163 J6 **Seamer** N York
195 K2 **Seamill** N Ayrs
144 D6 **Searby** Lincs
40 E2 **Seasalter** Kent
155 J2 **Seascale** Cumb
165 H8 **Seathwaite** Cumb
156 B3 **Seathwaite** Cumb
156 E6 **Seatle** Cumb
165 H7 **Seatoller** Cumb
6 C4 **Seaton** Cnwll
164 D4 **Seaton** Cumb
14 F4 **Seaton** Devon
169 L1 **Seaton** Dur
153 J6 **Seaton** E R Yk
41 H4 **Seaton** Kent
181 H3 **Seaton** Nthumb
101 K4 **Seaton** Rutlnd
181 G4 **Seaton Burn** N Tyne
170 C5 **Seaton Carew** Hartpl
181 H4 **Seaton Delaval** Nthumb
152 B7 **Seaton Ross** E R Yk
181 H3 **Seaton Sluice** Nthumb
15 K4 **Seatown** Dorset
161 J3 **Seave Green** N York
19 L5 **Seaview** IOW
177 G8 **Seaville** Cumb
30 F7 **Seavington St Mary** Somset
30 F7 **Seavington St Michael** Somset
62 C7 **Sebastopol** Torfn
165 K2 **Sebergham** Cumb
99 H2 **Seckington** Warwks
157 L4 **Sedbergh** Cumb
63 H8 **Sedbury** Gloucs
158 F4 **Sedbusk** N York
104 D6 **Sedge Fen** Suffk
82 B7 **Sedgeberrow** Worcs
117 M4 **Sedgebrook** Lincs
169 K5 **Sedgefield** Dur
120 F4 **Sedgeford** Norfk
32 E5 **Sedgehill** Wilts
97 L4 **Sedgley** Dudley
140 B7 **Sedgley Park** Bury
157 H5 **Sedgwick** Cumb
24 E4 **Sedlescombe** E Susx
67 J5 **Sedrup** Bucks
40 B4 **Seed** Kent
46 D6 **Seend** Wilts
46 D6 **Seend Cleeve** Wilts
68 B8 **Seer Green** Bucks
107 G4 **Seething** Norfk
138 D7 **Sefton** Sefton
138 D7 **Sefton Town** Sefton
181 G4 **Seghill** Nthumb
114 D6 **Seighford** Staffs
125 K6 **Seion** Gwynd
97 J4 **Seisdon** Staffs
112 C5 **Selattyn** Shrops
35 M4 **Selborne** Hants
142 F1 **Selby** N York

20 F3 **Selham** W Susx
51 J5 **Selhurst** Gt Lon
201 G7 **Selkirk** Border
63 H2 **Sellack** Herefs
281 e2 **Sellafirth** Shet
2 C5 **Sellan** Cnwll
30 B7 **Sellick's Green** Somset
40 E7 **Sellindge** Kent
40 D4 **Selling** Kent
46 D6 **Sells Green** Wilts
98 D7 **Selly Oak** Birm
23 H6 **Selmeston** E Susx
51 K6 **Selsdon** Gt Lon
20 D8 **Selsey** W Susx
38 A6 **Selsfield Common** W Susx
157 H3 **Selside** Cumb
158 D7 **Selside** N York
64 B6 **Selsley** Gloucs
41 H6 **Selsted** Kent
116 D1 **Selston** Notts
29 G2 **Selworthy** Somset
89 K6 **Semer** Suffk
46 C6 **Semington** Wilts
32 E5 **Semley** Wilts
118 F5 **Sempringham** Lincs
50 C7 **Send** Surrey
50 D7 **Send Marsh** Surrey
43 H3 **Senghenydd** Caerph
2 B6 **Sennen** Cnwll
2 B6 **Sennen Cove** Cnwll
60 D2 **Sennybridge** Powys
134 C2 **Serlby** Notts
161 G7 **Sessay** N York
104 C1 **Setchey** Norfk
18 D3 **Setley** Hants
211 M4 **Seton Mains** E Loth
148 E3 **Settle** N York
179 K5 **Settlingstones** Nthumb
152 C2 **Settrington** N York
29 L4 **Seven Ash** Somset
51 M2 **Seven Kings** Gt Lon
60 B5 **Seven Sisters** Neath
64 D4 **Seven Springs** Gloucs
72 D2 **Seven Star Green** Essex
82 D8 **Seven Wells** Gloucs
64 F3 **Sevenhampton** Gloucs
47 J1 **Sevenhampton** Swindn
38 E2 **Sevenoaks** Kent
38 E3 **Sevenoaks Weald** Kent
45 G2 **Severn Beach** S Glos
81 K6 **Severn Stoke** Worcs
86 B4 **Sevick End** Beds
40 D7 **Sevington** Kent
88 B7 **Sewards End** Essex
69 K7 **Sewardstonebury** Gt Lon
68 C3 **Sewell** Beds
153 K2 **Sewerby** E R Yk
3 H5 **Seworgan** Cnwll
118 A7 **Sewstern** Leics
161 G2 **Sexhow** N York
65 H1 **Sezincote** Gloucs
282 h1 **Sgiogarstaigh** W Isls
67 G5 **Shabbington** Bucks
99 K2 **Shackerstone** Leics
116 C5 **Shacklecross** Derbys
36 D2 **Shackleford** Surrey
140 D3 **Shade** Calder
282 g1 **Shader** W Isls
169 J3 **Shadforth** Dur
107 J6 **Shadingfield** Suffk
40 C7 **Shadoxhurst** Kent
150 D7 **Shadwell** Leeds
105 J6 **Shadwell** Norfk
87 H7 **Shaftenhoe End** Herts
32 E6 **Shaftesbury** Dorset
142 F6 **Shaftholme** Donc
142 B5 **Shafton** Barns
142 B5 **Shafton Two Gates** Barns
47 L6 **Shalbourne** Wilts
18 F6 **Shalcombe** IOW
35 L3 **Shalden** Hants
35 L2 **Shalden Green** Hants
13 L8 **Shaldon** Devon
18 F6 **Shalfleet** IOW
71 H1 **Shalford** Essex
36 F2 **Shalford** Surrey
71 H2 **Shalford Green** Essex
114 D5 **Shallowford** Staffs
40 E4 **Shalmsford Street** Kent
84 C7 **Shalstone** Bucks
36 F2 **Shamley Green** Surrey
234 D3 **Shandford** Angus
207 L2 **Shandon** Ag & B
264 D5 **Shandwick** Highld
100 F4 **Shangton** Leics

181 G3 **Shankhouse** Nthumb
19 K7 **Shanklin** IOW
166 D7 **Shap** Cumb
17 H2 **Shapwick** Dorset
30 F3 **Shapwick** Somset
98 F5 **Shard End** Birm
116 D5 **Shardlow** Derbys
97 L2 **Shareshill** Staffs
142 B4 **Sharlston** Wakefd
142 B4 **Sharlston Common** Wakefd
98 E7 **Sharman's Cross** Solhll
53 G4 **Sharnal Street** Medway
85 K3 **Sharnbrook** Beds
140 C3 **Sharneyford** Lancs
100 B5 **Sharnford** Leics
16 D2 **Sharnhill Green** Dorset
139 G1 **Sharoe Green** Lancs
150 D2 **Sharow** N York
123 H7 **Sharp Green** Norfk
68 D7 **Sharpenhoe** Beds
190 D5 **Sharperton** Nthumb
63 K6 **Sharpness** Gloucs
38 B6 **Sharpthorne** W Susx
11 J7 **Sharptor** Cnwll
81 L2 **Sharpway Gate** Worcs
122 A4 **Sharrington** Norfk
97 H7 **Shatterford** Worcs
41 J4 **Shatterling** Kent
7 G2 **Shaugh Prior** Devon
15 J3 **Shave Cross** Dorset
113 M1 **Shavington** Ches
140 F1 **Shaw** Brad
140 D6 **Shaw** Oldham
47 G2 **Shaw** Swindn
48 C5 **Shaw** W Berk
46 C6 **Shaw** Wilts
63 K2 **Shaw Common** Gloucs
69 J1 **Shaw Green** Herts
139 G4 **Shaw Green** Lancs
150 C5 **Shaw Green** N York
139 H4 **Shaw Hill** Lancs
150 C3 **Shaw Mills** N York
282 f2 **Shawbost** W Isls
113 J7 **Shawbury** Shrops
140 D5 **Shawclough** Rochdl
190 F3 **Shawdon Hill** Nthumb
100 C7 **Shawell** Leics
34 F6 **Shawford** Hants
140 D4 **Shawforth** Lancs
185 L7 **Shawhead** D & G
198 C3 **Shawsburn** S Lans
32 E3 **Shear Cross** Wilts
176 D5 **Shearington** D & G
100 D5 **Shearsby** Leics
30 D5 **Shearston** Somset
12 B1 **Shebbear** Devon
114 B6 **Shebdon** Staffs
279 H3 **Shebster** Highld
208 F7 **Sheddens** E Rens
35 H8 **Shedfield** Hants
132 B7 **Sheen** Derbys
180 E7 **Sheep Hill** Dur
133 G5 **Sheepbridge** Derbys
141 J4 **Sheepridge** Kirk
141 M1 **Sheepscar** Leeds
64 C5 **Sheepscombe** Gloucs
7 G1 **Sheepstor** Devon
12 C1 **Sheepwash** Devon
181 G2 **Sheepwash** Nthumb
45 G4 **Sheepway** N Som
99 J3 **Sheepy Magna** Leics
99 J3 **Sheepy Parva** Leics
70 D4 **Sheering** Essex
53 K4 **Sheerness** Kent
50 D6 **Sheerwater** Surrey
36 A6 **Sheet** Hants
2 D5 **Sheffield** Cnwll
133 G2 **Sheffield** Sheff
49 G5 **Sheffield Bottom** W Berk
22 F2 **Sheffield Green** E Susx
86 C7 **Shefford** Beds
276 B4 **Sheigra** Highld
96 E3 **Sheinton** Shrops
95 K7 **Shelderton** Shrops
98 F6 **Sheldon** Birm
132 C6 **Sheldon** Derbys
14 D1 **Sheldon** Devon
40 D4 **Sheldwich** Kent
40 D4 **Sheldwich Lees** Kent
141 H2 **Shelf** Calder
106 C6 **Shelfanger** Norfk
82 D3 **Shelfield** Warwks
98 C3 **Shelfield** Wsall
82 D3 **Shelfield Green** Warwks
117 H3 **Shelford** Notts

99 L5 **Shelford** Warwks
202 D4 **Shellacres** Border
70 E6 **Shelley** Essex
141 K5 **Shelley** Kirk
89 L7 **Shelley** Suffk
141 K5 **Shelley Far Bank** Kirk
65 L8 **Shellingford** Oxon
70 F5 **Shellow Bowells** Essex
81 G3 **Shelsley Beauchamp** Worcs
81 G3 **Shelsley Walsh** Worcs
85 K2 **Shelton** Beds
106 E5 **Shelton** Norfk
117 K3 **Shelton** Notts
95 L1 **Shelton** Shrops
106 E5 **Shelton Green** Norfk
116 C5 **Shelton Lock** C Derb
114 C4 **Shelton Under Harley** Staffs
95 H4 **Shelve** Shrops
80 C6 **Shelwick** Herefs
70 F8 **Shenfield** Essex
83 J6 **Shenington** Oxon
68 F7 **Shenley** Herts
85 G8 **Shenley Brook End** M Keyn
85 G7 **Shenley Church End** M Keyn
68 F6 **Shenleybury** Herts
79 M7 **Shenmore** Herefs
173 J2 **Shennanton** D & G
98 E3 **Shenstone** Staffs
97 J8 **Shenstone** Worcs
98 E3 **Shenstone Woodend** Staffs
99 K3 **Shenton** Leics
102 F1 **Shepeau Stow** Lincs
69 H2 **Shephall** Herts
51 G3 **Shepherd's Bush** Gt Lon
49 H2 **Shepherd's Green** Oxon
4 D4 **Shepherds** Cnwll
63 L6 **Shepherds Patch** Gloucs
41 H5 **Shepherdswell** Kent
141 J6 **Shepley** Kirk
63 J8 **Shepperdine** S Glos
50 D5 **Shepperton** Surrey
50 D5 **Shepperton Green** Surrey
87 H5 **Shepreth** Cambs
116 E7 **Shepshed** Leics
30 F7 **Shepton Beauchamp** Somset
31 K2 **Shepton Mallet** Somset
31 L4 **Shepton Montague** Somset
39 J3 **Shepway** Kent
170 B4 **Sheraton** Dur
31 L7 **Sherborne** Dorset
65 H4 **Sherborne** Gloucs
45 H7 **Sherborne** Somset
32 D6 **Sherborne Causeway** Dorset
48 F7 **Sherborne St John** Hants
83 G3 **Sherbourne** Warwks
169 J2 **Sherburn** Dur
163 G7 **Sherburn** N York
169 J2 **Sherburn Hill** Dur
142 D1 **Sherburn in Elmet** N York
37 G1 **Shere** Surrey
121 K5 **Shereford** Norfk
34 C6 **Sherfield English** Hants
49 G7 **Sherfield on Loddon** Hants
140 B3 **Sherfin** Lancs
8 A6 **Sherford** Devon
17 H4 **Sherford** Dorset
151 K3 **Sheriff Hutton** N York
97 L5 **Sheriffhales** Shrops
122 D3 **Sheringham** Norfk
85 H6 **Sherington** M Keyn
22 B3 **Shermanbury** W Susx
120 F5 **Shernborne** Norfk
33 G3 **Sherrington** Wilts
46 B2 **Sherston** Wilts
116 F3 **Sherwood** C Nott
209 H6 **Shettleston** C Glas
139 H6 **Shevington** Wigan
139 H5 **Shevington Moor** Wigan
139 G6 **Shevington Vale** Wigan
6 D4 **Sheviock** Cnwll
141 H2 **Shibden Head** Brad
19 H6 **Shide** IOW
202 C5 **Shidlaw** Nthumb
248 F7 **Shiel Bridge** Highld
248 C1 **Shieldaig** Highld
176 D2 **Shieldhill** D & G
210 B4 **Shieldhill** Falk
199 G5 **Shieldhill House Hotel** S Lans
209 K7 **Shields** N Lans
237 J6 **Shielfoot** Highld
234 C4 **Shielhill** Angus
207 L4 **Shielhill** Inver
66 A6 **Shifford** Oxon
97 G2 **Shifnal** Shrops
191 J4 **Shilbottle** Nthumb

169 G5 Shildon Dur
208 D7 Shillford E Rens
29 H6 Shillingford Devon
66 E8 Shillingford Oxon
13 L5 Shillingford Abbot Devon
13 L5 Shillingford St George Devon
32 D8 Shillingstone Dorset
86 C8 Shillington Beds
190 B4 Shillmoor Nthumb
65 K5 Shilton Oxon
99 L6 Shilton Warwks
16 B5 Shilvinghampton Dorset
106 D6 Shimpling Norfk
89 H5 Shimpling Suffk
89 H4 Shimpling Street Suffk
169 H3 Shincliffe Dur
181 H8 Shiney Row Sundld
49 H5 Shinfield Wokham
86 F6 Shingay Cambs
91 J6 Shingle Street Suffk
8 B2 Shinnersbridge Devon
272 D5 Shinness Highld
38 F3 Shipbourne Kent
130 D5 Shipbrookhill Ches
105 J2 Shipdham Norfk
44 E7 Shipham Somset
8 D2 Shiphay Torbay
49 J3 Shiplake Oxon
49 H3 Shiplake Row Oxon
44 D7 Shiplate N Som
149 L8 Shipley Brad
116 D3 Shipley Derbys
97 H4 Shipley Shrops
37 H6 Shipley W Susx
37 M3 Shipley Bridge Surrey
40 C7 Shipley Hatch Kent
107 H5 Shipmeadow Suffk
104 C6 Shippea Hill Station Cambs
66 C7 Shippon Oxon
83 G7 Shipston on Stour Warwks
67 J2 Shipton Bucks
64 F3 Shipton Gloucs
151 H4 Shipton N York
96 D5 Shipton Shrops
34 B2 Shipton Bellinger Hants
15 L4 Shipton Gorge Dorset
20 C7 Shipton Green W Susx
46 C1 Shipton Moyne Gloucs
66 C4 Shipton-on-Cherwell Oxon
65 L3 Shipton-under-Wychwood Oxon
152 C7 Shiptonthorpe E R Yk
67 G7 Shirburn Oxon
138 D5 Shirdley Hill Lancs
166 E4 Shire Cumb
98 D3 Shire Oak Wsall
133 K6 Shirebrook Derbys
133 G1 Shiregreen Sheff
45 G4 Shirehampton Bristl
181 H4 Shiremoor N Tyne
62 F8 Shirenewton Mons
133 L3 Shireoaks Notts
40 B8 Shirkoak Kent
80 A3 Shirl Heath Herefs
133 H8 Shirland Derbys
96 E4 Shirlett Shrops
34 E8 Shirley C Sotn
115 L3 Shirley Derbys
51 K6 Shirley Gt Lon
98 E7 Shirley Solhll
35 H8 Shirrell Heath Hants
206 D2 Shirvan Ag & B
27 L3 Shirwell Devon
27 L3 Shirwell Cross Devon
194 E5 Shiskine N Ayrs
168 C3 Shittlehope Dur
79 M3 Shobdon Herefs
18 B2 Shobley Hants
13 K2 Shobrooke Devon
117 H7 Shoby Leics
113 G2 Shocklach Ches
113 G2 Shocklach Green Ches
53 K2 Shoeburyness Sthend
41 K5 Sholden Kent
19 L2 Sholing C Sotn
164 D5 Shoose Cumb
95 K1 Shoot Hill Shrops
26 D7 Shop Cnwll
10 B7 Shop Cnwll
90 F2 Shop Street Suffk
20 E6 Shopwyke W Susx
140 D4 Shore Rochdl
51 J2 Shoreditch Gt Lon
30 C6 Shoreditch Somset
52 B6 Shoreham Kent

22 C6 Shoreham-by-Sea W Susx
202 E4 Shoreswood Nthumb
35 J5 Shorley Hants
64 F7 Shorncote Gloucs
52 E5 Shorne Kent
52 E5 Shorne Ridgeway Kent
98 E5 Short Heath Birm
98 B3 Short Heath Wsall
6 B3 Shorta Cross Cnwll
23 G3 Shortbridge E Susx
36 C2 Shortfield Common Surrey
23 H4 Shortgate E Susx
36 A4 Shortheath Hants
4 C5 Shortlanesend Cnwll
86 B6 Shortstown Beds
19 G7 Shorwell IOW
45 L7 Shoscombe BaNES
106 E4 Shotesham Norfk
71 J8 Shotgate Essex
90 F8 Shotley Suffk
180 D8 Shotley Bridge Dur
90 F8 Shotley Gate Suffk
90 F8 Shotley Street Suffk
180 C8 Shotleyfield Nthumb
40 D4 Shottenden Kent
36 C4 Shottermill Surrey
82 E4 Shottery Warwks
83 K6 Shotteswell Warwks
91 H6 Shottisham Suffk
116 A2 Shottle Derbys
116 A2 Shottlegate Derbys
169 K5 Shotton Dur
169 L3 Shotton Dur
129 H6 Shotton Flints
202 C7 Shotton Nthumb
180 F3 Shotton Nthumb
169 K3 Shotton Colliery Dur
210 A7 Shotts N Lans
129 H5 Shotwick Ches
266 D5 Shougle Moray
104 D2 Shouldham Norfk
104 D2 Shouldham Thorpe Norfk
81 J3 Shoulton Worcs
39 G7 Shover's Green E Susx
114 B2 Shraleybrook Staffs
112 F8 Shrawardine Shrops
81 J2 Shrawley Worcs
50 C3 Shreding Green Bucks
82 F2 Shrewley Warwks
96 B1 Shrewsbury Shrops
33 J2 Shrewton Wilts
20 F6 Shripney W Susx
47 K1 Shrivenham Oxon
105 K5 Shropham Norfk
72 E2 Shrub End Essex
80 D6 Shucknall Herefs
88 C6 Shudy Camps Cambs
64 D3 Shurdington Gloucs
49 K4 Shurlock Row W & M
82 B3 Shurnock Worcs
279 J4 Shurrery Highld
279 J5 Shurrery Lodge Highld
30 B2 Shurton Somset
99 G5 Shustoke Warwks
114 D7 Shut Heath Staffs
13 L3 Shute Devon
14 F3 Shute Devon
83 J7 Shutford Oxon
81 K8 Shuthonger Gloucs
84 E5 Shutlanger Nhants
97 K2 Shutt Green Staffs
13 M6 Shutterton Devon
99 H2 Shuttington Warwks
133 J5 Shuttlewood Derbys
133 J5 Shuttlewood Common Derbys
140 B4 Shuttleworth Bury
282 f2 Siabost W Isls
282 g1 Siadar W Isls
100 E6 Sibbertoft Nhants
95 K6 Sibdon Carwood Shrops
83 H7 Sibford Ferris Oxon
83 H7 Sibford Gower Oxon
88 F8 Sible Hedingham Essex
70 F2 Sibley's Green Essex
11 J7 Siblyback Cnwll
119 K2 Sibsey Lincs
119 K1 Sibsey Fenside Lincs
102 B4 Sibson Cambs
99 K3 Sibson Leics
280 D5 Sibster Highld
134 E5 Sibthorpe Notts
117 K2 Sibthorpe Notts
91 J2 Sibton Suffk
89 H3 Sicklesmere Suffk

150 E6 Sicklinghall N York
142 B6 Sid Cop Barns
30 C5 Sidbrook Somset
14 D4 Sidbury Devon
96 F6 Sidbury Shrops
44 E7 Sidcot N Som
51 M4 Sidcup Gt Lon
164 D4 Siddick Cumb
131 G5 Siddington Ches
64 F7 Siddington Gloucs
81 L1 Sidemoor Worcs
122 F3 Sidestrand Norfk
14 D4 Sidford Devon
20 D7 Sidlesham W Susx
20 D6 Sidlesham Common W Susx
24 D5 Sidley E Susx
14 D5 Sidmouth Devon
96 B6 Siefton Shrops
13 H7 Sigford Devon
153 J6 Sigglesthorne E R Yk
42 E7 Sigingstone V Glam
65 K5 Signet Oxon
48 F6 Silchester Hants
117 G8 Sileby Leics
155 L6 Silecroft Cumb
106 C3 Silfield Norfk
77 G5 Silian Cerdgn
118 E3 Silk Willoughby Lincs
34 D4 Silkstead Hants
141 L6 Silkstone Barns
141 L6 Silkstone Common Barns
181 J8 Silksworth Sundld
176 F8 Silloth Cumb
163 H4 Silpho N York
149 J6 Silsden Brad
86 B8 Silsoe Beds
32 C5 Silton Dorset
71 K3 Silver End Essex
53 J7 Silver Street Kent
31 J4 Silver Street Somset
211 G7 Silverburn Mdloth
157 G7 Silverdale Lancs
114 C2 Silverdale Staffs
157 G7 Silverdale Green Lancs
268 D3 Silverford Abers
122 D6 Silvergate Norfk
91 H3 Silverlace Green Suffk
106 F8 Silverley's Green Suffk
84 C6 Silverstone Nhants
13 M2 Silverton Devon
96 E7 Silvington Shrops
131 K1 Simmondley Derbys
179 K4 Simonburn Nthumb
29 L7 Simons Burrow Devon
28 D3 Simonsbath Somset
140 A1 Simonstone Lancs
158 F4 Simonstone N York
202 C4 Simprim Border
85 H8 Simpson M Keyn
54 E3 Simpson Cross Pembks
202 C3 Sinclair's Hill Border
196 F7 Sinclairston E Ayrs
160 E6 Sinderby N York
179 K8 Sinderhope Nthumb
130 E2 Sinderland Green Traffd
49 J5 Sindlesham Wokham
116 B5 Sinfin C Derb
51 L7 Single Street Gt Lon
67 J1 Singleborough Bucks
147 G8 Singleton Lancs
20 E4 Singleton W Susx
52 E5 Singlewell Kent
39 K5 Sinkhurst Green Kent
244 B1 Sinnarhard Abers
162 C5 Sinnington N York
81 J3 Sinton Worcs
81 J3 Sinton Green Worcs
50 D3 Sipson Gt Lon
50 D3 Sirhowy Blae G
39 K6 Sissinghurst Kent
45 K4 Siston S Glos
11 L4 Sitcott Devon
3 G5 Sithney Cnwll
3 G5 Sithney Common Cnwll
3 G5 Sithney Green Cnwll
40 B3 Sittingbourne Kent
97 H5 Six Ashes Staffs
61 K6 Six Bells Blae G
88 B4 Six Mile Bottom Cambs
9 c2 Six Rues Jersey
136 C2 Sixhills Lincs
40 F6 Sixmile Cottages Kent
33 G7 Sixpenny Handley Dorset
91 L3 Sizewell Suffk

275 d5 Skaill Ork
197 G7 Skares E Ayrs
245 K5 Skateraw Abers
213 G4 Skateraw E Loth
259 G7 Skeabost Highld
160 B2 Skeeby N York
101 G3 Skeffington Leics
145 K4 Skeffling E R Yk
133 K7 Skegby Notts
134 F5 Skegby Notts
137 L7 Skegness Lincs
264 B1 Skelbo Highld
264 B1 Skelbo Street Highld
142 D5 Skelbrooke Donc
119 K4 Skeldyke Lincs
135 J5 Skellingthorpe Lincs
131 H3 Skellorm Green Ches
142 E5 Skellow Donc
141 K5 Skelmanthorpe Kirk
138 F6 Skelmersdale Lancs
207 K5 Skelmorlie N Ayrs
278 B5 Skelpick Highld
185 K5 Skelston D & G
166 B4 Skelton Cumb
143 J3 Skelton E R Yk
159 K3 Skelton N York
150 E2 Skelton N York
170 F7 Skelton R & Cl
151 J4 Skelton York
156 E2 Skelwith Bridge Cumb
137 H5 Skendleby Lincs
245 G2 Skene House Abers
62 F3 Skenfrith Mons
153 G5 Skerne E R Yk
277 L4 Skerray Highld
276 C6 Skerricha Highld
147 J3 Skerton Lancs
99 L5 Sketchley Leics
57 H6 Sketty Swans
57 K5 Skewen Neath
151 K2 Skewsby N York
122 E6 Skeyton Norfk
122 E6 Skeyton Corner Norfk
279 H3 Skiall Highld
137 H1 Skidbrooke Lincs
137 H1 Skidbrooke North End Lincs
144 C1 Skidby E R Yk
282 h1 Skigersta W Isls
29 H5 Skilgate Somset
118 A6 Skillington Lincs
176 F7 Skinburness Cumb
210 B2 Skinflats Falk
258 C7 Skinidin Highld
48 C6 Skinners Green W Berk
171 G6 Skinningrove R & Cl
206 E7 Skipness Ag & B
177 L2 Skipper's Bridge Cumb
165 L2 Skiprigg Cumb
153 J5 Skipsea E R Yk
153 J5 Skipsea Brough E R Yk
149 H5 Skipton N York
160 E6 Skipton-on-Swale N York
151 L8 Skipwith N York
153 J7 Skirlaugh E R Yk
199 J5 Skirling Border
49 J1 Skirmett Bucks
152 A4 Skirpenbeck E R Yk
166 E4 Skirwith Cumb
158 C7 Skirwith N York
280 E3 Skirza Highld
178 B5 Skitby Cumb
67 J6 Skittle Green Bucks
247 L4 Skulamus Highld
95 G8 Skyborry Green Shrops
72 C3 Skye Green Essex
253 J6 Skye of Curr Highld
149 J4 Skyreholme N York
140 E2 Slack Calder
133 G7 Slack Derbys
157 G6 Slack Head Cumb
140 E6 Slackcote Oldham
137 K5 Slackholme End Lincs
256 F3 Slacks of Cairnbanno Abers
64 C5 Slad Gloucs
27 J2 Slade Devon
14 D1 Slade Devon
28 E5 Slade Somset
48 E1 Slade End Oxon
52 B4 Slade Green Kent
97 L2 Slade Heath Staffs
133 K2 Slade Hooton Rothm
81 J8 Slades Green Worcs
10 E8 Sladesbridge Cnwll
178 F8 Slaggyford Nthumb
150 D7 Slaid Hill Leeds

148 C5 **Slaidburn** Lancs
141 G5 **Slaithwaite** Kirk
132 E8 **Slaley** Derbys
180 A7 **Slaley** Nthumb
209 M4 **Slamannan** Falk
68 B3 **Slapton** Bucks
8 B6 **Slapton** Devon
84 C6 **Slapton** Nhants
140 D6 **Slattocks** Rochdl
37 L5 **Slaugham** W Susx
46 B4 **Slaughterford** Wilts
101 G4 **Slawston** Leics
36 B3 **Sleaford** Hants
118 E2 **Sleaford** Lincs
166 E6 **Sleagill** Cumb
113 H6 **Sleap** Shrops
113 L8 **Sleapford** Wrekin
272 F8 **Sleasdairidh** Highld
81 J8 **Sledge Green** Worcs
152 E3 **Sledmere** E R Yk
17 J3 **Sleight** Dorset
168 B8 **Sleightholme** Dur
162 F1 **Sleights** N York
17 H4 **Slepe** Dorset
280 C3 **Slickly** Highld
193 J4 **Sliddery** N Ayrs
247 G3 **Sligachan** Highld
207 K1 **Sligrachan** Ag & B
63 L6 **Slimbridge** Gloucs
114 C5 **Slindon** Staffs
20 F5 **Slindon** W Susx
37 H4 **Slinfold** W Susx
126 B6 **Sling** Gwynd
162 B7 **Slingsby** N York
68 D3 **Slip End** Beds
86 F7 **Slip End** Herts
101 L7 **Slipton** Nhants
115 G8 **Slitting Mill** Staffs
216 C7 **Slockavullin** Ag & B
175 G1 **Slogarie** D & G
122 F6 **Sloley** Norfk
13 H5 **Sloncombe** Devon
137 J5 **Sloothby** Lincs
50 C3 **Slough** Slough
30 C7 **Slough Green** Somset
37 L5 **Slough Green** W Susx
248 E4 **Slumbay** Highld
50 C8 **Slyfield Green** Surrey
147 J3 **Slyne** Lancs
201 K6 **Smailholm** Border
22 C5 **Small Dole** W Susx
98 E6 **Small Heath** Birm
25 G1 **Small Hythe** Kent
147 H6 **Small Wood Hey** Lancs
140 D5 **Smallbridge** Rochdl
13 K3 **Smallbrook** Devon
63 H7 **Smallbrook** Gloucs
123 G6 **Smallburgh** Norfk
132 B4 **Smalldale** Derbys
132 C3 **Smalldale** Derbys
116 C3 **Smalley** Derbys
116 C3 **Smalley Common** Derbys
116 C3 **Smalley Green** Derbys
37 M2 **Smallfield** Surrey
15 G2 **Smallridge** Devon
114 D2 **Smallthorne** C Stke
168 E8 **Smallways** N York
130 F7 **Smallwood** Ches
105 K7 **Smallworth** Norfk
34 E1 **Smannell** Hants
158 C1 **Smardale** Cumb
39 L5 **Smarden** Kent
39 L5 **Smarden Bell** Kent
38 E5 **Smart's Hill** Kent
203 H5 **Smeafield** Nthumb
237 J5 **Smearisary** Highld
30 B8 **Smeatharpe** Devon
40 E7 **Smeeth** Kent
100 E5 **Smeeton Westerby** Leics
150 B3 **Smelthouses** N York
275 G2 **Smerral** Highld
97 J5 **Smestow** Staffs
98 C6 **Smethwick** Sandw
130 F7 **Smethwick Green** Ches
116 B7 **Smisby** Derbys
81 H5 **Smith End Green** Worcs
147 J5 **Smith Green** Lancs
87 H7 **Smith's End** Herts
70 E3 **Smith's Green** Essex
88 D7 **Smith's Green** Essex
19 J5 **Smithcclose** IOW
178 B6 **Smithfield** Cumb
142 A6 **Smithies** Barns
29 J8 **Smithincott** Devon
260 C4 **Smithstown** Highld

252 D3 **Smithton** Highld
140 D5 **Smithy Bridge** Rochdl
130 E5 **Smithy Green** Ches
131 G3 **Smithy Green** Stockp
116 C2 **Smithy Houses** Derbys
99 M5 **Smockington** Leics
277 G3 **Smoo** Highld
72 D3 **Smythe's Green** Essex
185 L5 **Snade** D & G
95 J3 **Snailbeach** Shrops
88 C2 **Snailwell** Cambs
163 G6 **Snainton** N York
143 G3 **Snaith** E R Yk
132 B2 **Snake Pass Inn** Derbys
160 C6 **Snape** N York
91 J3 **Snape** Suffk
138 D5 **Snape Green** Lancs
91 J4 **Snape Street** Suffk
51 L1 **Snaresbrook** Gt Lon
99 K2 **Snarestone** Leics
135 L3 **Snarford** Lincs
25 J2 **Snargate** Kent
25 J1 **Snave** Kent
81 L4 **Sneachill** Worcs
95 H5 **Snead** Powys
106 D5 **Sneath Common** Norfk
162 F1 **Sneaton** N York
162 F2 **Sneatonthorpe** N York
135 M4 **Snelland** Lincs
130 F5 **Snelson** Ches
115 J3 **Snelston** Derbys
105 K5 **Snetterton** Norfk
120 F4 **Snettisham** Norfk
116 C8 **Snibston** Leics
64 A1 **Snig's End** Gloucs
190 E5 **Snitter** Nthumb
135 K1 **Snitterby** Lincs
82 F3 **Snitterfield** Warwks
132 E7 **Snitterton** Derbys
165 H3 **Snittlegarth** Cumb
96 D8 **Snitton** Shrops
40 B6 **Snoadhill** Kent
79 K7 **Snodhill** Herefs
52 F6 **Snodland** Kent
39 G4 **Snoll Hatch** Kent
69 L1 **Snow End** Herts
106 B7 **Snow Street** Norfk
141 L7 **Snowden Hill** Barns
82 C8 **Snowshill** Gloucs
19 L2 **Soake** Hants
43 H5 **Soar** Cardif
7 K7 **Soar** Devon
60 E1 **Soar** Powys
35 J7 **Soberton** Hants
35 J8 **Soberton Heath** Hants
166 C5 **Sockbridge** Cumb
160 E1 **Sockburn** Darltn
128 C5 **Sodom** Denbgs
112 E3 **Sodylt Bank** Shrops
104 B8 **Soham** Cambs
104 B8 **Soham Cotes** Cambs
282 c7 **Solas** W Isls
54 E4 **Solbury** Pembks
26 E8 **Soldon** Devon
11 L1 **Soldon Cross** Devon
35 K4 **Soldridge** Hants
52 E5 **Sole Street** Kent
40 E5 **Sole Street** Kent
98 F7 **Solihull** Solhll
80 A4 **Sollers Dilwyn** Herefs
80 E8 **Sollers Hope** Herefs
138 F4 **Sollom** Lancs
74 C7 **Solva** Pembks
177 J3 **Solwaybank** D & G
101 G1 **Somerby** Leics
144 D6 **Somerby** Lincs
116 C1 **Somercotes** Derbys
18 B5 **Somerford** Dorset
64 E8 **Somerford Keynes** Gloucs
20 D7 **Somerley** W Susx
107 K4 **Somerleyton** Suffk
115 J4 **Somersal Herbert** Derbys
136 F5 **Somersby** Lincs
103 G7 **Somersham** Cambs
90 C5 **Somersham** Suffk
66 D2 **Somerton** Oxon
31 H5 **Somerton** Somset
89 G4 **Somerton** Suffk
113 J8 **Somerwood** Shrops
21 K6 **Sompting** W Susx
49 J4 **Sonning** Wokham
49 H3 **Sonning Common** Oxon
49 H4 **Sonning Eye** Oxon
112 E2 **Sontley** Wrexhm
18 B4 **Sopley** Hants

46 B2 **Sopworth** Wilts
174 C5 **Sorbie** D & G
279 L4 **Sordale** Highld
225 H3 **Sorisdale** Ag & B
197 G5 **Sorn** E Ayrs
280 C4 **Sortat** Highld
164 E6 **Sosgill** Cumb
136 D4 **Sotby** Lincs
136 B5 **Sots Hole** Lincs
107 J6 **Sotterly** Suffk
128 F6 **Soughton** Flints
67 L2 **Soulbury** Bucks
166 B5 **Soulby** Cumb
167 H8 **Soulby** Cumb
66 D1 **Souldern** Oxon
85 J3 **Souldrop** Beds
267 G5 **Sound Muir** Moray
45 J4 **Soundwell** S Glos
12 D4 **Sourton** Devon
156 B6 **Soutergate** Cumb
121 H8 **South Acre** Norfk
41 H7 **South Alkham** Kent
8 B7 **South Allington** Devon
210 A1 **South Alloa** Falk
20 F3 **South Ambersham** W Susx
133 K3 **South Anston** Rothm
50 A5 **South Ascot** W & M
40 C7 **South Ashford** Kent
18 E4 **South Baddesley** Hants
170 C6 **South Bank** R & Cl
151 J5 **South Bank** York
31 K5 **South Barrow** Somset
51 H6 **South Beddington** Gt Lon
11 K4 **South Beer** Cnwll
53 G2 **South Benfleet** Essex
20 F6 **South Bersted** W Susx
18 B4 **South Bockhampton** Dorset
15 K3 **South Bowood** Dorset
143 G5 **South Bramwith** Donc
7 K3 **South Brent** Devon
32 B4 **South Brewham** Somset
191 K6 **South Broomhill** Nthumb
107 H2 **South Burlingham** Norfk
31 K5 **South Cadbury** Somset
135 J4 **South Carlton** Lincs
134 B3 **South Carlton** Notts
144 A2 **South Cave** E R Yk
64 F7 **South Cerney** Gloucs
22 F4 **South Chailey** E Susx
15 H2 **South Chard** Somset
191 H2 **South Charlton** Nthumb
32 B6 **South Cheriton** Somset
169 G5 **South Church** Dur
168 E7 **South Cleatlam** Dur
152 B8 **South Cliffe** E R Yk
135 G5 **South Clifton** Notts
137 G2 **South Cockerington** Lincs
42 B5 **South Cornelly** Brdgnd
107 K7 **South Cove** Suffk
121 J4 **South Creake** Norfk
141 H5 **South Crosland** Kirk
100 F2 **South Croxton** Leics
152 E6 **South Dalton** E R Yk
52 C5 **South Darenth** Kent
143 H1 **South Duffield** N York
136 E2 **South Elkington** Lincs
142 D5 **South Elmsall** Wakefd
145 K4 **South End** E R Yk
33 J7 **South End** Hants
81 G6 **South End** Herefs
144 E4 **South End** N Linc
105 K5 **South End** Norfk
260 B5 **South Erradale** Highld
72 B8 **South Fambridge** Essex
48 A3 **South Fawley** W Berk
144 M4 **South Ferriby** N Linc
144 C3 **South Field** E R Yk
38 A4 **South Godstone** Surrey
18 B2 **South Gorley** Hants
181 G5 **South Gosforth** N u Ty
72 F3 **South Green** Essex
71 G8 **South Green** Essex
53 J7 **South Green** Kent
105 L1 **South Green** Norfk
106 D8 **South Green** Suffk
211 G4 **South Gyle** C Edin
71 H7 **South Hanningfield** Essex
20 C3 **South Harting** W Susx
20 B6 **South Hayling** Hants
203 G6 **South Hazelrigg** Nthumb
67 M6 **South Heath** Bucks
23 G6 **South Heighton** E Susx
169 K2 **South Hetton** Dur
142 B5 **South Hiendley** Wakefd
11 L7 **South Hill** Cnwll

31 G5 **South Hill** Somset
66 D6 **South Hinksey** Oxon
26 C6 **South Hole** Devon
37 J2 **South Holmwood** Surrey
52 B2 **South Hornchurch** Gt Lon
31 J2 **South Horrington** Somset
7 K6 **South Huish** Devon
135 J6 **South Hykeham** Lincs
181 J7 **South Hylton** Sundld
144 D8 **South Kelsey** Lincs
251 H2 **South Kessock** Highld
144 F4 **South Killingholme** N Linc
160 F6 **South Kilvington** N York
100 D7 **South Kilworth** Nhants
142 C5 **South Kirkby** Wakefd
13 J8 **South Knighton** Devon
119 G2 **South Kyme** Lincs
65 L4 **South Lawn** Oxon
66 B5 **South Leigh** Oxon
134 F3 **South Leverton** Notts
82 C6 **South Littleton** Worcs
105 L7 **South Lopham** Norfk
101 K3 **South Luffenham** Rutlnd
23 G5 **South Malling** E Susx
47 J2 **South Marston** Swindn
51 H8 **South Merstham** Surrey
190 E2 **South Middleton** Nthumb
142 D2 **South Milford** N York
7 K6 **South Milton** Devon
69 G6 **South Mimms** Herts
28 C5 **South Molton** Devon
180 F8 **South Moor** Dur
48 E1 **South Moreton** Oxon
20 E6 **South Mundham** W Susx
134 F8 **South Muskham** Notts
152 D8 **South Newbald** E R Yk
83 J8 **South Newington** Oxon
33 J4 **South Newton** Wilts
133 J8 **South Normanton** Derbys
51 J5 **South Norwood** Gt Lon
37 M1 **South Nutfield** Surrey
52 D2 **South Ockendon** Thurr
137 G4 **South Ormsby** Lincs
141 L4 **South Ossett** Wakefd
160 E5 **South Otterington** N York
135 L1 **South Owersby** Lincs
37 K1 **South Park** Surrey
15 L1 **South Perrott** Dorset
31 G7 **South Petherton** Somset
11 K6 **South Petherwin** Cnwll
105 G3 **South Pickenham** Norfk
6 E3 **South Pill** Cnwll
7 M6 **South Pool** Devon
15 M3 **South Poorton** Dorset
29 G4 **South Quarme** Somset
210 F3 **South Queensferry** C Edin
28 C4 **South Radworthy** Devon
118 D2 **South Rauceby** Lincs
121 J6 **South Raynham** Norfk
131 H1 **South Reddish** Stockp
137 G3 **South Reston** Lincs
104 C2 **South Runcton** Norfk
135 G7 **South Scarle** Notts
228 E7 **South Shian** Ag & B
181 J5 **South Shields** S Tyne
138 C1 **South Shore** Bpool
137 H1 **South Somercotes** Lincs
150 D3 **South Stainley** N York
52 D3 **South Stifford** Thurr
45 L6 **South Stoke** BaNES
118 B6 **South Stoke** Lincs
48 F2 **South Stoke** Oxon
21 H5 **South Stoke** W Susx
40 D7 **South Stour** Kent
52 D6 **South Street** Kent
40 D4 **South Street** Kent
40 F2 **South Street** Kent
199 H3 **South Tarbrax** S Lans
12 F4 **South Tawton** Devon
137 G4 **South Thoresby** Lincs
168 E7 **South Thorpe** Dur
35 K4 **South Town** Hants
107 H1 **South Walsham** Norfk
35 L2 **South Warnborough** Hants
70 E8 **South Weald** Essex
67 H7 **South Weston** Oxon
11 J4 **South Wheatley** Cnwll
45 H7 **South Widcombe** BaNES
100 D4 **South Wigston** Leics
40 D7 **South Willesborough** Kent
136 C3 **South Willingham** Lincs
169 L4 **South Wingate** Dur
133 G8 **South Wingfield** Derbys
118 B7 **South Witham** Lincs
34 F4 **South Wonston** Hants

71 K7 **South Woodham Ferrers** Essex
120 E7 **South Wootton** Norfk
46 B6 **South Wraxall** Wilts
12 F4 **South Zeal** Devon
50 E3 **Southall** Gt Lon
64 E2 **Southam** Gloucs
83 K3 **Southam** Warwks
19 G1 **Southampton** C Sotn
51 L5 **Southborough** Gt Lon
38 F5 **Southborough** Kent
18 A5 **Southbourne** Bmouth
20 C5 **Southbourne** W Susx
17 G4 **Southbrook** Dorset
105 K2 **Southburgh** Norfk
152 F5 **Southburn** E R Yk
53 J2 **Southchurch** Sthend
11 H3 **Southcott** Cnwll
27 H7 **Southcott** Devon
12 D3 **Southcott** Devon
13 H6 **Southcott** Devon
47 H7 **Southcott** Wilts
67 K5 **Southcourt** Bucks
23 G6 **Southease** E Susx
192 E6 **Southend** Ag & B
47 J4 **Southend** Wilts
53 J2 **Southend-on-Sea** Sthend
165 L3 **Southernby** Cumb
39 L4 **Southernden** Kent
42 D7 **Southerndown** V Glam
176 C7 **Southerness** D & G
14 C4 **Southerton** Devon
104 C4 **Southery** Norfk
209 M4 **Southfield** Falk
52 D5 **Southfleet** Kent
19 J7 **Southford** IOW
69 J8 **Southgate** Gt Lon
120 E5 **Southgate** Norfk
121 J4 **Southgate** Norfk
122 C6 **Southgate** Norfk
57 G7 **Southgate** Swans
86 C6 **Southill** Beds
35 G1 **Southington** Hants
14 E4 **Southleigh** Devon
72 D7 **Southminster** Essex
66 B7 **Southmoor** Oxon
234 B5 **Southmuir** Angus
86 D2 **Southoe** Cambs
90 E2 **Southolt** Suffk
102 B3 **Southorpe** C Pete
16 B4 **Southover** Dorset
24 B2 **Southover** E Susx
141 H3 **Southowram** Calder
138 D4 **Southport** Sefton
122 E4 **Southrepps** Norfk
136 B6 **Southrey** Lincs
65 J6 **Southrop** Gloucs
35 K2 **Southrope** Hants
19 L4 **Southsea** C Port
112 D1 **Southsea** Wrexhm
168 E5 **Southside** Dur
107 L2 **Southtown** Norfk
30 D7 **Southtown** Somset
166 B2 **Southwaite** Cumb
51 J3 **Southwark** Gt Lon
37 J5 **Southwater** W Susx
37 H5 **Southwater Street** W Susx
31 H2 **Southway** Somset
16 D8 **Southwell** Dorset
117 J1 **Southwell** Notts
19 L2 **Southwick** Hants
101 M5 **Southwick** Nhants
30 E2 **Southwick** Somset
181 J7 **Southwick** Sundld
22 C6 **Southwick** W Susx
46 B7 **Southwick** Wilts
107 K8 **Southwold** Suffk
107 H2 **Southwood** Norfk
31 J4 **Southwood** Somset
99 K6 **Sowe Common** Covtry
147 G7 **Sower Carr** Lancs
141 G3 **Sowerby** Kirk
160 F6 **Sowerby** N York
141 G3 **Sowerby Bridge** Calder
165 L3 **Sowerby Row** Cumb
28 F6 **Sowerhill** Somset
62 B7 **Sowhill** Torfn
88 D5 **Sowley Green** Suffk
141 G4 **Sowood** Calder
6 F2 **Sowton** Devon
14 A4 **Sowton** Devon
140 F4 **Soyland Town** Calder
122 F5 **Spa Common** Norfk
88 D7 **Spain's End** Essex
119 H7 **Spalding** Lincs

143 J1 **Spaldington** E R Yk
86 C1 **Spaldwick** Cambs
135 G6 **Spalford** Notts
118 E4 **Spanby** Lincs
49 G7 **Spanish Green** Hants
122 B7 **Sparham** Norfk
122 B7 **Sparhamill** Norfk
156 D5 **Spark Bridge** Cumb
166 B5 **Sparket** Cumb
31 K5 **Sparkford** Somset
98 E6 **Sparkhill** Birm
7 H3 **Sparkwell** Devon
121 L8 **Sparrow Green** Norfk
132 B4 **Sparrowpit** Derbys
39 G6 **Sparrows Green** E Susx
34 F4 **Sparsholt** Hants
47 M2 **Sparsholt** Oxon
167 K1 **Spartylea** Cumb
115 H4 **Spath** Staffs
162 C5 **Spaunton** N York
30 C3 **Spaxton** Somset
239 L7 **Spean Bridge** Highld
21 K3 **Spear Hill** W Susx
34 D5 **Spearywell** Hants
67 K7 **Speen** Bucks
48 C5 **Speen** W Berk
163 L7 **Speeton** N York
129 K3 **Speke** Lpool
38 E5 **Speldhurst** Kent
70 C4 **Spellbrook** Herts
39 H6 **Spelmonden** Kent
65 M3 **Spelsbury** Oxon
141 K3 **Spen** Kirk
130 F7 **Spen Green** Ches
49 H5 **Spencers Wood** Wokham
159 L5 **Spennithorne** N York
169 H4 **Spennymoor** Dur
82 C3 **Spernall** Warwks
13 G3 **Spestos** Devon
81 K4 **Spetchley** Worcs
17 H2 **Spetisbury** Dorset
107 H7 **Spexhall** Suffk
267 G3 **Spey Bay** Moray
253 K6 **Speybridge** Highld
254 E3 **Speyview** Moray
137 G6 **Spilsby** Lincs
203 J6 **Spindlestone** Nthumb
133 J4 **Spinkhill** Derbys
263 J2 **Spinningdale** Highld
133 L6 **Spion Kop** Notts
46 E4 **Spirthill** Wilts
129 H3 **Spital** Wirral
134 C1 **Spital Hill** Donc
135 K2 **Spital in the Street** Lincs
23 G4 **Spithurst** E Susx
212 A4 **Spittal** E Loth
152 B5 **Spittal** E R Yk
279 L5 **Spittal** Highld
202 F3 **Spittal** Nthumb
55 G2 **Spittal** Pembks
243 K6 **Spittal of Glenmuick** Abers
233 H2 **Spittal of Glenshee** P & K
189 G2 **Spittal-on-Rule** Border
233 H7 **Spittalfield** P & K
122 E8 **Spixworth** Norfk
10 C7 **Splatt** Cnwll
11 J5 **Splatt** Cnwll
12 E2 **Splatt** Devon
23 G2 **Splayne's Green** E Susx
43 K6 **Splottlands** Cardif
130 E3 **Spodegreen** Ches
150 E5 **Spofforth** N York
129 G7 **Spon Green** Flints
116 C4 **Spondon** C Derb
106 B4 **Spooner Row** Norfk
105 G1 **Sporle** Norfk
212 E4 **Spott** E Loth
201 J3 **Spottiswoode** Border
84 D1 **Spratton** Nhants
36 B3 **Spreakley** Surrey
13 G3 **Spreyton** Devon
7 G4 **Spriddlestone** Devon
135 K3 **Spridlington** Lincs
168 F5 **Spring Gardens** Dur
141 L7 **Spring Vale** Barns
209 G5 **Springburn** C Glas
177 K5 **Springfield** D & G
71 H5 **Springfield** Essex
222 F5 **Springfield** Fife
98 D2 **Springhill** Staffs
98 B3 **Springhill** Staffs
175 K1 **Springholm** D & G
196 D3 **Springside** N Ayrs
135 H2 **Springthorpe** Lincs
181 G7 **Springwell** Sundld

145 G1 **Sproatley** E R Yk
130 E6 **Sproston Green** Ches
142 E7 **Sprotbrough** Donc
90 D6 **Sproughton** Suffk
202 B6 **Sprouston** Border
106 E1 **Sprowston** Norfk
117 M6 **Sproxton** Leics
161 K6 **Sproxton** N York
12 A5 **Sprytown** Devon
112 F5 **Spunhill** Shrops
130 A8 **Spurstow** Ches
15 M4 **Spyway** Dorset
74 D6 **Square & Compass** Pembks
97 G4 **Stableford** Shrops
114 C4 **Stableford** Staffs
132 F2 **Stacey Bank** Sheff
148 E3 **Stackhouse** N York
55 G7 **Stackpole** Pembks
105 L5 **Stacksford** Norfk
140 C7 **Stacksteads** Lancs
7 G4 **Staddiscombe** C Plym
143 L2 **Staddlethorpe** E R Yk
131 L5 **Staden** Derbys
66 F7 **Stadhampton** Oxon
283 b10 **Stadhlaigearraidh** W Isls
166 D2 **Staffield** Cumb
259 H3 **Staffin** Highld
114 E7 **Stafford** Staffs
85 J5 **Stagsden** Beds
141 M7 **Stainborough** Barns
164 D5 **Stainburn** Cumb
150 C6 **Stainburn** N York
118 B7 **Stainby** Lincs
141 M5 **Staincross** Barns
168 E6 **Staindrop** Dur
50 D5 **Staines** Surrey
118 E6 **Stainfield** Lincs
136 B5 **Stainfield** Lincs
143 G5 **Stainforth** Donc
148 E2 **Stainforth** N York
147 G8 **Staining** Lancs
141 G4 **Stainland** Calder
163 G1 **Stainsacre** N York
133 J6 **Stainsby** Derbys
177 L7 **Stainton** Cumb
166 C5 **Stainton** Cumb
157 H5 **Stainton** Cumb
133 L1 **Stainton** Donc
168 D7 **Stainton** Dur
170 B7 **Stainton** Middsb
159 K3 **Stainton** N York
135 L4 **Stainton by Langworth** Lincs
136 C1 **Stainton le Vale** Lincs
146 E1 **Stainton with Adgarley** Cumb
163 H3 **Staintondale** N York
165 H6 **Stair** Cumb
196 E6 **Stair** E Ayrs
172 F4 **Stair Haven** D & G
142 B6 **Stairfoot** Barns
171 H7 **Staithes** N York
147 H6 **Stake Pool** Lancs
181 G2 **Stakeford** Nthumb
19 M2 **Stakes** Hants
32 B7 **Stalbridge** Dorset
32 B7 **Stalbridge Weston** Dorset
123 H6 **Stalham** Norfk
123 H6 **Stalham Green** Norfk
40 B5 **Stalisfield Green** Kent
31 K7 **Stallen** Dorset
159 G5 **Stalling Busk** N York
145 G5 **Stallingborough** NE Lin
114 E4 **Stallington** Staffs
147 G6 **Stalmine** Lancs
147 G6 **Stalmine Moss Side** Lancs
140 E8 **Stalybridge** Tamesd
88 E7 **Stambourne** Essex
88 D7 **Stambourne Green** Essex
102 A2 **Stamford** Lincs
191 J2 **Stamford** Nthumb
129 L6 **Stamford Bridge** Ches
151 M5 **Stamford Bridge** E R Yk
51 J2 **Stamford Hill** Gt Lon
180 C4 **Stamfordham** Nthumb
147 G7 **Stanah** Lancs
69 G5 **Stanborough** Herts
68 B2 **Stanbridge** Beds
17 K2 **Stanbridge** Dorset
149 H8 **Stanbury** Brad
140 B6 **Stand** Bury
209 K5 **Stand** N Lans
210 B4 **Standburn** Falk
97 K2 **Standeford** Staffs
39 L5 **Standen** Kent

39 K7 **Standen Street** Kent
32 D1 **Standerwick** Somset
36 B4 **Standford** Hants
164 D4 **Standingstone** Cumb
64 A5 **Standish** Gloucs
139 H5 **Standish** Wigan
139 H6 **Standish Lower Ground** Wigan
66 B6 **Standlake** Oxon
34 F5 **Standon** Hants
69 K3 **Standon** Herts
114 C4 **Standon** Staffs
69 K3 **Standon Green End** Herts
90 D1 **Standwell Green** Suffk
210 A7 **Stane** N Lans
121 K7 **Stanfield** Norfk
86 D7 **Stanford** Beds
40 F7 **Stanford** Kent
95 H1 **Stanford** Shrops
80 F5 **Stanford Bishop** Herefs
81 G2 **Stanford Bridge** Worcs
113 M6 **Stanford Bridge** Wrekin
48 E4 **Stanford Dingley** W Berk
65 M8 **Stanford in the Vale** Oxon
52 E3 **Stanford le Hope** Thurr
100 D7 **Stanford on Avon** Nhants
116 F7 **Stanford on Soar** Notts
81 G2 **Stanford on Teme** Worcs
70 D7 **Stanford Rivers** Essex
133 J5 **Stanfree** Derbys
170 F7 **Stanghow** R & Cl
102 D4 **Stanground** C Pete
139 L2 **Stanhill** Lancs
121 H4 **Stanhoe** Norfk
199 K7 **Stanhope** Border
168 C3 **Stanhope** Dur
115 M7 **Stanhope Bretby** Derbys
101 K6 **Stanion** Nhants
97 J8 **Stanklin** Worcs
116 C3 **Stanley** Derbys
180 F8 **Stanley** Dur
133 J7 **Stanley** Notts
221 K1 **Stanley** P & K
97 G6 **Stanley** Shrops
114 E1 **Stanley** Staffs
142 A3 **Stanley** Wakefd
116 C3 **Stanley Common** Derbys
168 F3 **Stanley Crook** Dur
142 A3 **Stanley Ferry** Wakefd
138 F6 **Stanley Gate** Lancs
114 E1 **Stanley Moor** Staffs
64 E1 **Stanley Pontlarge** Gloucs
22 E5 **Stanmer** Br & H
68 F8 **Stanmore** Gt Lon
34 F5 **Stanmore** Hants
48 C3 **Stanmore** W Berk
179 G2 **Stannersburn** Nthumb
89 H4 **Stanningfield** Suffk
141 K1 **Stanningley** Leeds
180 F3 **Stannington** Nthumb
132 F2 **Stannington** Sheff
180 F3 **Stannington Station** Nthumb
79 L3 **Stansbatch** Herefs
88 F5 **Stansfield** Suffk
115 J1 **Stanshope** Staffs
89 G5 **Stanstead** Suffk
69 K5 **Stanstead Abbotts** Herts
89 G5 **Stanstead Street** Suffk
52 D6 **Stansted** Kent
70 D2 **Stansted Mountfitchet** Essex
115 M7 **Stanton** Derbys
7 K5 **Stanton** Devon
82 C8 **Stanton** Gloucs
62 C3 **Stanton** Mons
191 G8 **Stanton** Nthumb
115 J2 **Stanton** Staffs
105 K8 **Stanton** Suffk
116 B6 **Stanton by Bridge** Derbys
116 D4 **Stanton by Dale** Derbys
45 H6 **Stanton Drew** BaNES
47 J1 **Stanton Fitzwarren** Swindn
66 B6 **Stanton Harcourt** Oxon
133 J7 **Stanton Hill** Notts
132 E6 **Stanton in Peak** Derbys
96 B7 **Stanton Lacy** Shrops
132 E7 **Stanton Lees** Derbys
96 D5 **Stanton Long** Shrops
117 G5 **Stanton on the Wolds** Notts
45 K6 **Stanton Prior** BaNES
47 G6 **Stanton St Bernard** Wilts
66 E5 **Stanton St John** Oxon
46 C3 **Stanton St Quintin** Wilts
89 J2 **Stanton Street** Suffk

100 A1 **Stanton under Bardon** Leics
113 J6 **Stanton upon Hine Heath** Shrops
45 J6 **Stanton Wick** BaNES
63 L4 **Stantway** Gloucs
112 F6 **Stanwardine in the Field** Shrops
113 G6 **Stanwardine in the Wood** Shrops
72 D2 **Stanway** Essex
64 F1 **Stanway** Gloucs
72 D2 **Stanway Green** Essex
90 F1 **Stanway Green** Suffk
50 D4 **Stanwell** Surrey
50 D4 **Stanwell Moor** Surrey
85 J1 **Stanwick** Nhants
177 L7 **Stanwix** Cumb
283 b10 **Staoinebrig** W Isls
162 D4 **Stape** N York
17 L2 **Stapehill** Dorset
113 L2 **Stapeley** Ches
115 L7 **Stapenhill** Staffs
41 J4 **Staple** Kent
29 K3 **Staple** Somset
29 J6 **Staple Cross** Devon
24 E3 **Staple Cross** E Susx
30 C7 **Staple Fitzpaine** Somset
98 B8 **Staple Hill** Worcs
37 L5 **Staplefield** W Susx
87 K5 **Stapleford** Cambs
69 J4 **Stapleford** Herts
117 L7 **Stapleford** Leics
135 H8 **Stapleford** Lincs
116 E4 **Stapleford** Notts
33 J3 **Stapleford** Wilts
70 D8 **Stapleford Abbotts** Essex
70 D7 **Stapleford Tawney** Essex
30 B5 **Staplegrove** Somset
30 B6 **Staplehay** Somset
39 K5 **Staplehurst** Kent
19 H6 **Staplers** IOW
40 D3 **Staplestreet** Kent
178 C4 **Staplet** Cumb
79 L2 **Stapleton** Herefs
99 L4 **Stapleton** Leics
169 H8 **Stapleton** N York
95 L3 **Stapleton** Shrops
31 G6 **Stapleton** Somset
30 B8 **Stapley** Somset
86 C3 **Staploe** Beds
80 F7 **Staplow** Herefs
222 E6 **Star** Fife
75 M5 **Star** Pembks
44 E7 **Star** Somset
150 D4 **Starbeck** N York
159 G7 **Starbotton** N York
14 A6 **Starcross** Devon
83 H1 **Stareton** Warwks
132 F7 **Starkholmes** Derbys
140 A5 **Starling** Bury
70 C1 **Starlings Green** Essex
24 D4 **Starr's Green** E Susx
106 E6 **Starston** Norfk
8 B6 **Start** Devon
168 D7 **Startforth** Dur
46 D3 **Startley** Wilts
41 J4 **Statenborough** Kent
130 D2 **Statham** Warrtn
30 E5 **Stathe** Somset
117 K5 **Stathern** Leics
169 L3 **Station Town** Dur
86 C2 **Staughton Green** Cambs
86 C2 **Staughton Highway** Cambs
63 H4 **Staunton** Gloucs
64 A1 **Staunton** Gloucs
79 L3 **Staunton Green** Herefs
117 L3 **Staunton in the Vale** Notts
79 L3 **Staunton on Arrow** Herefs
79 L6 **Staunton on Wye** Herefs
156 E5 **Staveley** Cumb
157 G3 **Staveley** Cumb
133 H5 **Staveley** Derbys
150 E3 **Staveley** N York
8 B2 **Staverton** Devon
64 C2 **Staverton** Gloucs
83 M3 **Staverton** Nhants
46 B6 **Staverton** Wilts
64 C3 **Staverton Bridge** Gloucs
30 E3 **Stawell** Somset
29 J6 **Stawley** Somset
280 E5 **Staxigoe** Highld
163 J6 **Staxton** N York
92 E5 **Staylittle** Cerdgn
93 J5 **Staylittle** Powys
147 G7 **Staynall** Lancs

117 K1 **Staythorpe** Notts
149 L6 **Stead** Brad
159 K8 **Stean** N York
84 A7 **Steane** Nhants
151 K2 **Stearsby** N York
30 C2 **Steart** Somset
71 G2 **Stebbing** Essex
71 G2 **Stebbing Green** Essex
71 G2 **Stebbing Park** Essex
98 E6 **Stechford** Birm
39 L5 **Stede Quarter** Kent
36 C6 **Stedham** W Susx
179 L7 **Steel** Nthumb
38 E7 **Steel Cross** E Susx
155 L6 **Steel Green** Cumb
113 J4 **Steel Heath** Shrops
188 F7 **Steele Road** Border
210 D1 **Steelend** Fife
80 C4 **Steen's Bridge** Herefs
35 M6 **Steep** Hants
140 F3 **Steep Lane** Calder
19 J8 **Steephill** IOW
17 H6 **Steeple** Dorset
72 D6 **Steeple** Essex
46 C7 **Steeple Ashton** Wilts
66 C2 **Steeple Aston** Oxon
66 C2 **Steeple Barton** Oxon
88 D7 **Steeple Bumpstead** Essex
67 H2 **Steeple Claydon** Bucks
102 C7 **Steeple Gidding** Cambs
33 H3 **Steeple Langford** Wilts
86 F6 **Steeple Morden** Cambs
149 J7 **Steeton** Brad
258 D5 **Stein** Highld
180 E6 **Stella** Gatesd
40 F6 **Stelling Minnis** Kent
30 F6 **Stembridge** Somset
5 G3 **Stenalees** Cnwll
185 K4 **Stenhouse** D & G
210 A2 **Stenhousemuir** Falk
136 D3 **Stenigot** Lincs
259 H3 **Stenscholl** Highld
212 D4 **Stenton** E Loth
282 g3 **Steornabhagh** W Isls
55 K5 **Stepaside** Pembks
51 K3 **Stepney** Gt Lon
131 H2 **Stepping Hill** Stockp
85 K8 **Steppingley** Beds
209 H5 **Stepps** N Lans
91 J3 **Sternfield** Suffk
27 K2 **Sterridge** Devon
46 F7 **Stert** Wilts
88 C3 **Stetchworth** Cambs
24 C4 **Steven's Crouch** E Susx
69 G2 **Stevenage** Herts
196 B3 **Stevenston** N Ayrs
35 H1 **Steventon** Hants
48 C1 **Steventon** Oxon
88 B6 **Steventon End** Essex
85 K4 **Stevington** Beds
85 K6 **Stewartby** Beds
209 G7 **Stewartfield** S Lans
196 E2 **Stewarton** E Ayrs
67 K2 **Stewkley** Bucks
30 D7 **Stewley** Somset
137 G2 **Stewton** Lincs
19 L6 **Steyne Cross** IOW
21 L4 **Steyning** W Susx
54 E5 **Steynton** Pembks
26 C8 **Stibb** Cnwll
27 G7 **Stibb Cross** Devon
47 J6 **Stibb Green** Wilts
121 L6 **Stibbard** Norfk
102 B4 **Stibbington** Cambs
201 L5 **Stichill** Border
5 G5 **Sticker** Cnwll
136 F7 **Stickford** Lincs
12 F4 **Sticklepath** Devon
29 J4 **Sticklepath** Somset
87 K8 **Stickling Green** Essex
136 F8 **Stickney** Lincs
53 J6 **Stiff Street** Kent
121 L3 **Stiffkey** Norfk
81 G5 **Stifford's Bridge** Herefs
39 J4 **Stile Bridge** Kent
31 G3 **Stileway** Somset
283 b10 **Stilligarry** W Isls
151 J7 **Stillingfleet** N York
151 J2 **Stillington** N York
169 K6 **Stillington** S on T
102 D5 **Stilton** Cambs
63 L7 **Stinchcombe** Gloucs
16 D4 **Stinsford** Dorset
95 J3 **Stiperstones** Shrops
98 D7 **Stirchley** Birm

96 F2 **Stirchley** Wrekin
257 L3 **Stirling** Abers
220 D8 **Stirling** Stirlg
86 D2 **Stirtloe** Cambs
149 H5 **Stirton** N York
71 J2 **Stisted** Essex
47 K5 **Stitchcombe** Wilts
3 J4 **Stithians** Cnwll
99 J8 **Stivichall** Covtry
136 C6 **Stixwould** Lincs
129 K5 **Stoak** Ches
199 L5 **Stobo** Border
17 H5 **Stoborough** Dorset
17 H5 **Stoborough Green** Dorset
188 E4 **Stobs Castle** Border
191 J7 **Stobswood** Nthumb
71 G7 **Stock** Essex
44 F6 **Stock** N Som
82 A3 **Stock Green** Worcs
82 B3 **Stock Wood** Worcs
34 D4 **Stockbridge** Hants
198 C6 **Stockbriggs** S Lans
53 H6 **Stockbury** Kent
48 B5 **Stockcross** W Berk
3 K4 **Stockdale** Cnwll
165 L2 **Stockdalewath** Cumb
40 C5 **Stocker's Hill** Kent
101 H4 **Stockerston** Leics
63 J1 **Stocking** Herefs
84 F5 **Stocking Green** M Keyn
70 C1 **Stocking Pelham** Herts
99 J5 **Stockingford** Warwks
14 F2 **Stockland** Devon
30 C2 **Stockland Bristol** Somset
38 E5 **Stockland Green** Kent
13 K1 **Stockleigh English** Devon
13 K2 **Stockleigh Pomeroy** Devon
46 E5 **Stockley** Wilts
79 L7 **Stockley Hill** Herefs
30 F7 **Stocklinch** Somset
79 M4 **Stockmoor** Herefs
131 H2 **Stockport** Stockp
141 L8 **Stocksbridge** Sheff
180 C6 **Stocksfield** Nthumb
71 K3 **Stockstreet** Essex
80 C3 **Stockton** Herefs
107 H4 **Stockton** Norfk
95 G3 **Stockton** Shrops
97 G3 **Stockton** Shrops
83 K3 **Stockton** Warwks
33 G3 **Stockton** Wilts
114 B8 **Stockton** Wrekin
114 E1 **Stockton Brook** Staffs
130 B3 **Stockton Heath** Warrtn
81 G2 **Stockton on Teme** Worcs
151 L4 **Stockton on the Forest** York
170 B6 **Stockton-on-Tees** S on T
64 D4 **Stockwell** Gloucs
97 K3 **Stockwell End** Wolves
115 G7 **Stockwell Heath** Staffs
45 J5 **Stockwood** Bristl
16 B1 **Stockwood** Dorset
147 J4 **Stodday** Lancs
41 H3 **Stodmarsh** Kent
122 B4 **Stody** Norfk
270 D2 **Stoer** Highld
31 J8 **Stoford** Somset
33 J4 **Stoford** Wilts
29 K3 **Stogumber** Somset
30 B2 **Stogursey** Somset
99 K7 **Stoke** Covtry
26 D6 **Stoke** Devon
48 B8 **Stoke** Hants
20 B6 **Stoke** Hants
53 H4 **Stoke** Medway
15 K2 **Stoke Abbott** Dorset
101 H5 **Stoke Albany** Nhants
90 D1 **Stoke Ash** Suffk
117 H3 **Stoke Bardolph** Notts
80 F3 **Stoke Bliss** Worcs
84 E5 **Stoke Bruerne** Nhants
88 E6 **Stoke by Clare** Suffk
13 L3 **Stoke Canon** Devon
35 G3 **Stoke Charity** Hants
11 L7 **Stoke Climsland** Cnwll
80 E5 **Stoke Cross** Herefs
50 E7 **Stoke D'Abernon** Surrey
102 A6 **Stoke Doyle** Nhants
101 J4 **Stoke Dry** Rutlnd
80 E7 **Stoke Edith** Herefs
98 F4 **Stoke End** Warwks
33 H5 **Stoke Farthing** Wilts
104 D3 **Stoke Ferry** Norfk
8 C5 **Stoke Fleming** Devon
8 C3 **Stoke Gabriel** Devon

45 J3 **Stoke Gifford** S Glos
99 L4 **Stoke Golding** Leics
85 G5 **Stoke Goldington** M Keyn
50 B3 **Stoke Green** Bucks
67 L1 **Stoke Hammond** Bucks
99 K7 **Stoke Heath** Covtry
113 L5 **Stoke Heath** Shrops
81 L2 **Stoke Heath** Worcs
106 E3 **Stoke Holy Cross** Norfk
80 E5 **Stoke Lacy** Herefs
66 E2 **Stoke Lyne** Oxon
67 K5 **Stoke Mandeville** Bucks
51 J2 **Stoke Newington** Gt Lon
64 D2 **Stoke Orchard** Gloucs
50 B2 **Stoke Poges** Bucks
81 M2 **Stoke Pound** Worcs
80 C4 **Stoke Prior** Herefs
81 L2 **Stoke Prior** Worcs
27 L4 **Stoke Rivers** Devon
49 G2 **Stoke Row** Oxon
30 E5 **Stoke St Gregory** Somset
30 C6 **Stoke St Mary** Somset
31 L2 **Stoke St Michael** Somset
96 D7 **Stoke St Milborough** Shrops
31 G7 **Stoke sub Hamdon** Somset
67 G7 **Stoke Talmage** Oxon
32 B5 **Stoke Trister** Somset
113 L6 **Stoke upon Tern** Shrops
16 E1 **Stoke Wake** Dorset
81 L2 **Stoke Wharf** Worcs
89 K7 **Stoke-by-Nayland** Suffk
114 D2 **Stoke-on-Trent** C Stke
114 D3 **Stoke-upon-Trent** C Stke
17 G5 **Stokeford** Dorset
134 F4 **Stokeham** Notts
13 L8 **Stokeinteignhead** Devon
67 J7 **Stokenchurch** Bucks
8 B6 **Stokenham** Devon
95 K7 **Stokesay** Shrops
107 J1 **Stokesby** Norfk
161 H1 **Stokesley** N York
30 C2 **Stolford** Somset
45 J8 **Ston Easton** Somset
70 E7 **Stondon Massey** Essex
67 J4 **Stone** Bucks
63 K8 **Stone** Gloucs
52 C4 **Stone** Kent
25 H2 **Stone** Kent
133 L2 **Stone** Rothm
31 J4 **Stone** Somset
114 E5 **Stone** Staffs
97 J8 **Stone** Worcs
30 F1 **Stone Allerton** Somset
102 F3 **Stone Bridge Corner** C Pete
141 H2 **Stone Chair** Calder
38 D7 **Stone Cross** E Susx
23 K6 **Stone Cross** E Susx
39 G7 **Stone Cross** E Susx
38 E5 **Stone Cross** Kent
40 D7 **Stone Cross** Kent
41 K4 **Stone Cross** Kent
143 H6 **Stone Hill** Donc
158 D5 **Stone House** Cumb
38 F2 **Stone Street** Kent
89 K7 **Stone Street** Suffk
89 K6 **Stone Street** Suffk
107 H6 **Stone Street** Suffk
44 F4 **Stone-edge-Batch** N Som
103 J5 **Stonea** Cambs
44 D7 **Stonebridge** N Som
105 J5 **Stonebridge** Norfk
99 G6 **Stonebridge** Solhll
133 H7 **Stonebroom** Derbys
89 G4 **Stonecross Green** Suffk
39 H6 **Stonecrouch** Kent
144 E2 **Stoneferry** C KuH
206 D5 **Stonefield Castle Hotel** Ag & B
39 G7 **Stonegate** E Susx
162 D1 **Stonegate** N York
161 L7 **Stonegrave** N York
81 K5 **Stonehall** Worcs
179 J4 **Stonehaugh** Nthumb
245 J6 **Stonehaven** Abers
52 B5 **Stonehill Green** Gt Lon
6 F4 **Stonehouse** C Plym
129 L5 **Stonehouse** Ches
175 K1 **Stonehouse** D & G
64 A6 **Stonehouse** Gloucs
179 G7 **Stonehouse** Nthumb
198 C4 **Stonehouse** S Lans
83 H1 **Stoneleigh** Warwks
113 K1 **Stoneley Green** Ches
86 C2 **Stonely** Cambs
35 M5 **Stoner Hill** Hants

73 H2 **Stones Green** Essex	88 E5 **Stradishall** Suffk	115 L6 **Stretton** Staffs	115 K5 **Sudbury** Derbys
117 L6 **Stonesby** Leics	104 D2 **Stradsett** Norfk	130 C3 **Stretton** Warrtn	50 F2 **Sudbury** Gt Lon
66 B4 **Stonesfield** Oxon	118 B1 **Stragglethorpe** Lincs	99 J1 **Stretton en le Field** Leics	89 H7 **Sudbury** Suffk
40 E7 **Stonestreet Green** Kent	117 H4 **Stragglethorpe** Notts	80 E6 **Stretton Grandison** Herefs	140 C5 **Sudden** Rochdl
165 J7 **Stonethwaite** Cumb	47 L4 **Straight Soley** Wilts	95 J1 **Stretton Heath** Shrops	81 J3 **Suddington** Worcs
266 F3 **Stonewells** Moray	211 J5 **Straiton** Mdloth	82 F7 **Stretton on Fosse** Warwks	64 D5 **Sudgrove** Gloucs
52 D4 **Stonewood** Kent	183 K2 **Straiton** S Ayrs	80 B6 **Stretton Sugwas** Herefs	163 H4 **Suffield** N York
18 D1 **Stoney Cross** Hants	256 F7 **Straloch** Abers	99 M7 **Stretton under Fosse** Warwks	122 E5 **Suffield** Norfk
132 E4 **Stoney Middleton** Derbys	232 F3 **Straloch** P & K	96 D4 **Stretton Westwood** Shrops	113 K8 **Sugdon** Wrekin
100 B4 **Stoney Stanton** Leics	115 H4 **Stramshall** Staffs	83 K1 **Stretton-on-Dunsmore** Warwks	114 B5 **Sugnall** Staffs
32 B4 **Stoney Stoke** Somset	154 e6 **Strang** IOM		80 B6 **Sugwas Pool** Herefs
31 L3 **Stoney Stratton** Somset	140 B7 **Strangeways** Salfd	269 H5 **Strichen** Abers	247 J5 **Suisnish** Highld
95 J2 **Stoney Stretton** Shrops	63 H2 **Strangford** Herefs	131 J3 **Strines** Stockp	154 e3 **Sulby** IOM
283 b10 **Stoneybridge** W Isls	172 C3 **Stranraer** D & G	30 B2 **Stringston** Somset	84 A6 **Sulgrave** Nhants
97 L8 **Stoneybridge** Worcs	77 K2 **Strata Florida** Cerdgn	85 H3 **Strixton** Nhants	48 F4 **Sulham** W Berk
210 C6 **Stoneyburn** W Loth	49 G6 **Stratfield Mortimer** W Berk	63 H7 **Stroat** Gloucs	48 F5 **Sulhamstead** W Berk
100 D3 **Stoneygate** C Leic	49 G6 **Stratfield Saye** Hants	248 D5 **Stromeferry** Highld	48 F5 **Sulhamstead Abbots** W Berk
72 D7 **Stoneyhills** Essex	49 G7 **Stratfield Turgis** Hants	275 b4 **Stromness** Ork	48 F5 **Sulhamstead Bannister** W Berk
172 D4 **Stoneykirk** D & G	86 D5 **Stratford** Beds	218 F5 **Stronachlachar** Stirlg	21 J4 **Sullington** W Susx
245 K1 **Stoneywood** C Aber	51 K2 **Stratford** Gt Lon	207 G3 **Stronafian** Ag & B	281 d4 **Sullom** Shet
209 L2 **Stoneywood** Falk	91 H3 **Stratford St Andrew** Suffk	271 H4 **Stronchrubie** Highld	281 d4 **Sullom Voe** Shet
90 D3 **Stonham Aspal** Suffk	90 B8 **Stratford St Mary** Suffk	207 K3 **Strone** Ag & B	43 J8 **Sully** V Glam
98 D3 **Stonnall** Staffs	33 K4 **Stratford sub Castle** Wilts	239 J7 **Strone** Highld	49 H1 **Summer Heath** Bucks
49 H1 **Stonor** Oxon	33 J5 **Stratford Tony** Wilts	239 L6 **Stronenaba** Highld	112 D1 **Summer Hill** Wrexhm
101 G4 **Stonton Wyville** Leics	82 F4 **Stratford-upon-Avon** Warwks	217 J2 **Stronmilchan** Ag & B	150 B3 **Summerbridge** N York
80 D2 **Stony Cross** Herefs		228 C3 **Strontian** Highld	4 E4 **Summercourt** Cnwll
81 G5 **Stony Cross** Herefs	260 C4 **Strath** Highld	39 L7 **Strood** Kent	121 G4 **Summerfield** Norfk
133 K6 **Stony Houghton** Derbys	270 E4 **Strathan** Highld	52 F5 **Strood** Medway	97 J8 **Summerfield** Worcs
84 F7 **Stony Stratford** M Keyn	277 K3 **Strathan** Highld	37 J1 **Strood Green** Surrey	98 D2 **Summerhill** Staffs
34 D7 **Stonyford** Hants	197 K2 **Strathaven** S Lans	36 F6 **Strood Green** W Susx	169 G6 **Summerhouse** Darltn
98 D1 **Stonywell** Staffs	208 F3 **Strathblane** Stirlg	64 B6 **Stroud** Gloucs	157 H5 **Summerlands** Cumb
28 B4 **Stoodleigh** Devon	270 F7 **Strathcanaird** Highld	35 L6 **Stroud** Hants	133 G4 **Summerley** Derbys
29 G7 **Stoodleigh** Devon	248 F3 **Strathcarron** Highld	53 J1 **Stroud Green** Essex	20 D5 **Summersdale** W Susx
21 H3 **Stopham** W Susx	227 K6 **Strathcoil** Ag & B	64 A5 **Stroud Green** Gloucs	140 B5 **Summerseat** Bury
68 E2 **Stopsley** Luton	243 K1 **Strathdon** Abers	50 C5 **Stroude** Surrey	66 D5 **Summertown** Oxon
10 C7 **Stoptide** Cnwll	223 H4 **Strathkinness** Fife	118 B5 **Stroxton** Lincs	140 D6 **Summit** Oldham
129 G3 **Storeton** Wirral	210 B4 **Strathloanhead** W Loth	246 D1 **Struan** Highld	140 E4 **Summit** Rochdl
81 G6 **Storeyard Green** Herefs	241 G5 **Strathmashie House** Highld	232 B2 **Struan** P & K	157 L1 **Sunbiggin** N York
138 F6 **Stormy Corner** Lancs	222 C5 **Strathmiglo** Fife	137 H3 **Strubby** Lincs	50 E5 **Sunbury** Surrey
282 g3 **Stornoway** W Isls	262 E8 **Strathpeffer** Highld	107 G2 **Strumpshaw** Norfk	185 K6 **Sundaywell** D & G
81 H5 **Storridge** Herefs	232 D4 **Strathtay** P & K	198 C3 **Strutherhill** S Lans	204 C3 **Sunderland** Ag & B
21 J4 **Storrington** W Susx	195 G4 **Strathwhillan** N Ayrs	222 F5 **Struthers** Fife	165 G4 **Sunderland** Cumb
157 G6 **Storth** Cumb	278 E3 **Strathy** Highld	250 C4 **Struy** Highld	147 H4 **Sunderland** Lancs
151 M7 **Storwood** E R Yk	278 E3 **Strathy Inn** Highld	124 F3 **Stryd-y-Facsen** IOA	181 K7 **Sunderland** Sundld
266 E2 **Stotfield** Moray	219 J4 **Strathyre** Stirlg	112 D2 **Stryt-issa** Wrexhm	169 H3 **Sunderland Bridge** Dur
86 E7 **Stotfold** Beds	11 J1 **Stratton** Cnwll	257 H3 **Stuartfield** Abers	200 D8 **Sundhope** Border
96 F6 **Stottesdon** Shrops	16 C4 **Stratton** Dorset	98 D3 **Stubbers Green** Wsall	68 D2 **Sundon Park** Luton
100 E3 **Stoughton** Leics	64 E6 **Stratton** Gloucs	19 J3 **Stubbington** Hants	38 D2 **Sundridge** Kent
50 C8 **Stoughton** Surrey	66 F2 **Stratton Audley** Oxon	140 B4 **Stubbins** N York	145 H4 **Sunk Island** E R Yk
20 C4 **Stoughton** W Susx	47 H2 **Stratton St Margaret** Swindn	106 E4 **Stubbs Green** Norfk	50 B5 **Sunningdale** W & M
238 B5 **Stoul** Highld	106 D4 **Stratton St Michael** Norfk	32 F8 **Stubhampton** Dorset	50 B5 **Sunninghill** W & M
81 L5 **Stoulton** Worcs	122 E7 **Stratton Strawless** Norfk	133 G4 **Stubley** Derbys	66 D7 **Sunningwell** Oxon
32 C6 **Stour Provost** Dorset	31 L1 **Stratton-on-the-Fosse** Somset	139 H7 **Stubshaw Cross** Wigan	168 F3 **Sunniside** Dur
32 D6 **Stour Row** Dorset	223 J4 **Stravithie** Fife	118 A2 **Stubton** Lincs	180 F7 **Sunniside** Gatesd
97 K6 **Stourbridge** Dudley	29 K3 **Stream** Somset	84 A6 **Stuchbury** Nhants	140 A4 **Sunny Bank** Lancs
17 G1 **Stourpaine** Dorset	22 E4 **Streat** E Susx	29 G6 **Stuckeridge** Devon	169 G4 **Sunny Brow** Dur
81 J1 **Stourport-on-Severn** Worcs	51 J4 **Streatham** Gt Lon	33 L8 **Stuckton** Hants	116 B5 **Sunnyhill** C Derb
141 M2 **Stourton** Leeds	68 D2 **Streatley** Beds	49 L3 **Stud Green** W & M	139 K3 **Sunnyhurst** Bl w D
97 K6 **Stourton** Staffs	48 E3 **Streatley** W Berk	148 E2 **Studfold** N York	220 D7 **Sunnylaw** Stirlg
83 G7 **Stourton** Warwks	14 E5 **Street** Devon	68 C4 **Studham** Beds	66 D5 **Sunnymead** Oxon
32 C4 **Stourton** Wilts	147 K5 **Street** Lancs	17 K6 **Studland** Dorset	47 K8 **Sunton** Wilts
32 B7 **Stourton Caundle** Dorset	162 C2 **Street** N York	82 C2 **Studley** Warwks	50 F5 **Surbiton** Gt Lon
31 G4 **Stout** Somset	31 H3 **Street** Somset	46 D4 **Studley** Wilts	119 H6 **Surfleet** Lincs
281 e8 **Stove** Shet	99 M7 **Street Ashton** Warwks	82 C2 **Studley Common** Warwks	119 J6 **Surfleet Seas End** Lincs
107 J7 **Stoven** Suffk	112 E4 **Street Dinas** Shrops	150 C2 **Studley Roger** N York	107 G2 **Surlingham** Norfk
200 F4 **Stow** Border	23 K3 **Street End** E Susx	150 C2 **Studley Royal** N York	72 C3 **Surrex** Essex
135 H3 **Stow** Lincs	40 F4 **Street End** Kent	87 K6 **Stump Cross** Cambs	122 D4 **Sustead** Norfk
104 C2 **Stow Bardolph** Norfk	20 D7 **Street End** W Susx	103 L7 **Stuntney** Cambs	143 L7 **Susworth** Lincs
105 J4 **Stow Bedon** Norfk	180 F7 **Street Gate** Gatesd	23 K4 **Stunts Green** E Susx	26 F8 **Sutcombe** Devon
86 C1 **Stow Longa** Cambs	171 G6 **Street Houses** N York	114 C5 **Sturbridge** Staffs	26 F8 **Sutcombemill** Devon
71 K7 **Stow Maries** Essex	151 H6 **Street Houses** N York	135 H2 **Sturgate** Lincs	106 B4 **Suton** Norfk
87 L3 **Stow-cum-Quy** Cambs	116 C2 **Street Lane** Derbys	88 D6 **Sturmer** Essex	137 G5 **Sutterby** Lincs
65 J2 **Stow-on-the-Wold** Gloucs	31 K3 **Street on the Fosse** Somset	32 C8 **Sturminster Common** Dorset	119 J4 **Sutterton** Lincs
104 B2 **Stowbridge** Norfk	98 F1 **Streethay** Staffs	17 J3 **Sturminster Marshall** Dorset	86 E5 **Sutton** Beds
63 H5 **Stowe** Gloucs	160 D3 **Streetlam** N York	32 C8 **Sturminster Newton** Dorset	102 B4 **Sutton** C Pete
95 H8 **Stowe** Shrops	98 D4 **Streetly** Wsall	41 G3 **Sturry** Kent	103 J7 **Sutton** Cambs
114 F6 **Stowe by Chartley** Staffs	88 C5 **Streetly End** Cambs	144 B7 **Sturton** N Linc	13 G2 **Sutton** Devon
84 C3 **Stowehill** Nhants	95 K6 **Strefford** Shrops	135 H4 **Sturton by Stow** Lincs	7 K6 **Sutton** Devon
31 L6 **Stowell** Somset	233 J8 **Strelitz** P & K	134 F3 **Sturton le Steeple** Notts	142 E5 **Sutton** Donc
45 H7 **Stowey** BaNES	116 E3 **Strelley** Notts	106 C7 **Stuston** Suffk	23 H7 **Sutton** E Susx
12 B3 **Stowford** Devon	151 K4 **Strensall** York	151 G7 **Stutton** N York	51 H6 **Sutton** Gt Lon
28 B3 **Stowford** Devon	81 L7 **Strensham** Worcs	90 D8 **Stutton** Suffk	41 K5 **Sutton** Kent
12 B5 **Stowford** Devon	30 D2 **Stretcholt** Somset	131 G3 **Styal** Ches	142 D3 **Sutton** N York
14 D4 **Stowford** Devon	8 C5 **Strete** Devon	148 A8 **Stydd** Lancs	123 H6 **Sutton** Norfk
89 J2 **Stowlangtoft** Suffk	80 B4 **Stretford** Herefs	267 G4 **Stynie** Moray	117 K4 **Sutton** Notts
90 B3 **Stowmarket** Suffk	80 C4 **Stretford** Herefs	134 C2 **Styrrup** Notts	66 B6 **Sutton** Oxon
40 F7 **Stowting** Kent	130 F1 **Stretford** Traffd	218 D6 **Succoth** Ag & B	54 E4 **Sutton** Pembks
40 F6 **Stowting Common** Kent	87 K7 **Strethall** Essex	81 G5 **Suckley** Worcs	112 E6 **Sutton** Shrops
90 C3 **Stowupland** Suffk	103 K8 **Stretham** Cambs	81 G4 **Suckley Green** Worcs	96 C1 **Sutton** Shrops
253 J8 **Straanruie** Moray	20 E5 **Strettington** W Susx	101 L7 **Sudborough** Nhants	113 L5 **Sutton** Shrops
244 F5 **Strachan** Abers	113 G1 **Stretton** Ches	91 J4 **Sudbourne** Suffk	97 G6 **Sutton** Shrops
217 H6 **Strachur** Ag & B	133 H7 **Stretton** Derbys	118 C3 **Sudbrook** Lincs	129 M1 **Sutton** St Hel
234 F2 **Strachro Hospital** Angus	118 B8 **Stretton** Rutlnd	45 G2 **Sudbrook** Mons	114 B7 **Sutton** Staffs
106 E8 **Stradbroke** Suffk	97 K1 **Stretton** Staffs	135 L4 **Sudbrooke** Lincs	
46 D8 **Stradbrook** Wilts			

91 G6 **Sutton** Suffk
21 G4 **Sutton** W Susx
52 C5 **Sutton at Hone** Kent
101 G5 **Sutton Bassett** Nhants
46 D3 **Sutton Benger** Wilts
31 J8 **Sutton Bingham** Somset
116 E6 **Sutton Bonington** Notts
120 B7 **Sutton Bridge** Lincs
99 L3 **Sutton Cheney** Leics
98 E4 **Sutton Coldfield** Birm
66 D8 **Sutton Courtenay** Oxon
119 M7 **Sutton Crosses** Lincs
134 D3 **Sutton cum Lound** Notts
116 E6 **Sutton Fields** Notts
160 D7 **Sutton Grange** N York
66 B5 **Sutton Green** Oxon
50 C8 **Sutton Green** Surrey
112 F2 **Sutton Green** Wrexhm
160 D6 **Sutton Howgrave** N York
133 K7 **Sutton in Ashfield** Notts
100 B4 **Sutton in the Elms** Leics
131 H5 **Sutton Lane Ends** Ches
97 G3 **Sutton Maddock** Shrops
30 E3 **Sutton Mallet** Somset
33 G5 **Sutton Mandeville** Wilts
129 L2 **Sutton Manor** St Hel
80 D6 **Sutton Marsh** Herefs
31 K6 **Sutton Montis** Somset
137 K3 **Sutton on Sea** Lincs
115 L5 **Sutton on the Hill** Derbys
134 F6 **Sutton on Trent** Notts
16 D5 **Sutton Poyntz** Dorset
34 F3 **Sutton Scotney** Hants
103 H1 **Sutton St Edmund** Lincs
119 L7 **Sutton St James** Lincs
80 C6 **Sutton St Nicholas** Herefs
39 K2 **Sutton Street** Kent
151 L6 **Sutton upon Derwent** E R Yk
39 K3 **Sutton Valence** Kent
32 E3 **Sutton Veny** Wilts
32 E7 **Sutton Waldron** Dorset
130 A4 **Sutton Weaver** Ches
45 H7 **Sutton Wick** BaNES
66 C8 **Sutton Wick** Oxon
149 H7 **Sutton-in-Craven** N York
144 E1 **Sutton-on-Hull** C KuH
151 J3 **Sutton-on-the-Forest** N York
83 G7 **Sutton-under-Brailes** Warwks
161 G6 **Sutton-under-Whitestonecliffe** N York
137 G4 **Swaby** Lincs
116 A7 **Swadlincote** Derbys
105 G2 **Swaffham** Norfk
87 L3 **Swaffham Bulbeck** Cambs
88 B2 **Swaffham Prior** Cambs
122 F5 **Swafield** Norfk
161 G2 **Swainby** N York
80 B7 **Swainshill** Herefs
106 E3 **Swainsthorpe** Norfk
45 M5 **Swainswick** BaNES
83 J7 **Swalcliffe** Oxon
40 F2 **Swalecliffe** Kent
144 F7 **Swallow** Lincs
135 J6 **Swallow Beck** Lincs
133 J3 **Swallow Nest** Rothm
33 G5 **Swallowcliffe** Wilts
49 H6 **Swallowfield** Wokham
70 F7 **Swallows Cross** Essex
34 E1 **Swampton** Hants
130 E5 **Swan Green** Ches
72 C2 **Swan Street** Essex
98 C5 **Swan Village** Sandw
17 K6 **Swanage** Dorset
67 K2 **Swanbourne** Bucks
43 J8 **Swanbridge** V Glam
97 G4 **Swancote** Shrops
144 C2 **Swanland** E R Yk
52 B5 **Swanley** Kent
52 B5 **Swanley Village** Kent
35 J7 **Swanmore** Hants
116 C8 **Swannington** Leics
122 C7 **Swannington** Norfk
135 J6 **Swanpool Garden Suburb** Lincs
52 D4 **Swanscombe** Kent
57 J6 **Swansea** Swans
122 F6 **Swanton Abbot** Norfk
121 M8 **Swanton Morley** Norfk
121 M5 **Swanton Novers** Norfk
53 J7 **Swanton Street** Kent
116 C1 **Swanwick** Derbys
19 H2 **Swanwick** Hants
118 D3 **Swarby** Lincs
106 D3 **Swardeston** Norfk
116 B6 **Swarkestone** Derbys

191 H6 **Swarland** Nthumb
191 H5 **Swarland Estate** Nthumb
35 H3 **Swarraton** Hants
149 J6 **Swartha** Brad
156 C7 **Swarthmoor** Cumb
118 F4 **Swaton** Lincs
87 G2 **Swavesey** Cambs
18 D4 **Sway** Hants
118 C7 **Swayfield** Lincs
34 F7 **Swaythling** C Sotn
80 F3 **Sweet Green** Worcs
13 K3 **Sweetham** Devon
38 D7 **Sweethaws** E Susx
39 K4 **Sweetlands Corner** Kent
11 G3 **Sweets** Cnwll
5 J3 **Sweetshouse** Cnwll
91 H3 **Swefling** Suffk
99 K1 **Swepstone** Leics
66 A1 **Swerford** Oxon
130 F6 **Swettenham** Ches
61 K7 **Swffryd** Blae G
39 L4 **Swift's Green** Kent
90 E4 **Swilland** Suffk
138 F1 **Swillbrook** Lancs
142 B2 **Swillington** Leeds
27 L5 **Swimbridge** Devon
27 L5 **Swimbridge Newland** Devon
65 L4 **Swinbrook** Oxon
141 K2 **Swincliffe** Kirk
150 C4 **Swincliffe** N York
28 B3 **Swincombe** Devon
148 E5 **Swinden** N York
135 H7 **Swinderby** Lincs
64 D2 **Swindon** Gloucs
190 D6 **Swindon** Nthumb
97 J5 **Swindon** Staffs
47 H2 **Swindon** Swindn
153 J8 **Swine** E R Yk
143 J3 **Swinefleet** E R Yk
45 K5 **Swineford** S Glos
85 L2 **Swineshead** Beds
119 H3 **Swineshead** Lincs
119 H3 **Swineshead Bridge** Lincs
275 H1 **Swiney** Highld
100 C7 **Swinford** Leics
66 C5 **Swinford** Oxon
41 G6 **Swingfield Minnis** Kent
41 H6 **Swingfield Street** Kent
89 K6 **Swingleton Green** Suffk
203 K7 **Swinhoe** Nthumb
145 G8 **Swinhope** Lincs
159 J5 **Swinithwaite** N York
80 F7 **Swinmore Common** Herefs
115 J2 **Swinscoe** Staffs
165 H6 **Swinside** Cumb
118 D7 **Swinstead** Lincs
135 L4 **Swinthorpe** Lincs
202 C4 **Swinton** Border
160 B6 **Swinton** N York
162 D8 **Swinton** N York
142 C7 **Swinton** Rothm
140 A7 **Swinton** Salfd
100 C1 **Swithland** Leics
263 G6 **Swordale** Highld
238 B5 **Swordland** Highld
278 C4 **Swordly** Highld
130 D3 **Sworton Heath** Ches
77 J2 **Swydd-ffynnon** Cerdgn
114 D4 **Swynnerton** Staffs
15 M5 **Swyre** Dorset
112 B6 **Sycharth** Powys
93 L7 **Sychnant** Powys
94 B2 **Sychtyn** Powys
129 G8 **Sydallt** Flints
64 D5 **Syde** Gloucs
51 K4 **Sydenham** Gt Lon
67 H6 **Sydenham** Oxon
12 A7 **Sydenham Damerel** Devon
36 E4 **Sydenhurst** Surrey
121 H5 **Syderstone** Norfk
16 C3 **Sydling St Nicholas** Dorset
48 C7 **Sydmonton** Hants
97 H2 **Sydnal Lane** Shrops
117 K2 **Syerston** Notts
140 D4 **Syke** Rochdl
143 G4 **Sykehouse** Donc
106 E7 **Syleham** Suffk
56 F3 **Sylen** Carmth
281 e5 **Symbister** Shet
196 D5 **Symington** S Ayrs
199 G6 **Symington** S Lans
63 H4 **Symonds Yat** Herefs
15 K4 **Symondsbury** Dorset
150 A8 **Sympson Green** Brad
15 J2 **Synderford** Dorset

76 D4 **Synod Inn** Cerdgn
278 B7 **Syre** Highld
64 F3 **Syreford** Gloucs
84 C7 **Syresham** Nhants
100 D1 **Syston** Leics
118 B3 **Syston** Lincs
81 J2 **Sytchampton** Worcs
84 F2 **Sywell** Nhants

T

130 E4 **Tabley Hill** Ches
66 C3 **Tackley** Oxon
106 C4 **Tacolneston** Norfk
151 G7 **Tadcaster** N York
132 C5 **Taddington** Derbys
65 G1 **Taddington** Gloucs
27 H7 **Taddiport** Devon
48 F6 **Tadley** Hants
86 F5 **Tadlow** Cambs
83 J7 **Tadmarton** Oxon
45 L5 **Tadwick** BaNES
51 G7 **Tadworth** Surrey
75 J5 **Tafarn-y-bwlch** Pembks
128 E7 **Tafarn-y-Gelyn** Denbgs
61 H5 **Tafarnaubach** Blae G
43 H5 **Taff's Well** Cardif
93 J3 **Tafolwern** Powys
60 F2 **Tai'r Bull** Powys
57 L7 **Taibach** Neath
280 B3 **Tain** Highld
263 L3 **Tain** Highld
282 e5 **Tairbeart** W Isls
70 E3 **Takeley** Essex
70 E3 **Takeley Street** Essex
92 E5 **Tal-y-bont** Cerdgn
126 F6 **Tal-y-Bont** Conwy
109 L7 **Tal-y-bont** Gwynd
126 C5 **Tal-y-bont** Gwynd
126 F5 **Tal-y-Cafn** Conwy
62 E4 **Tal-y-coed** Mons
42 F5 **Tal-y-garn** Rhondd
92 F2 **Tal-y-llyn** Gwynd
61 L6 **Tal-y-Waun** Torfn
78 F8 **Talachddu** Powys
128 D3 **Talacre** Flints
14 C3 **Talaton** Devon
54 D4 **Talbenny** Pembks
43 G5 **Talbot Green** Rhondd
17 L4 **Talbot Village** Bmouth
14 C3 **Taleford** Devon
93 K3 **Talerddig** Powys
76 D5 **Talgarreg** Cerdgn
79 G8 **Talgarth** Powys
246 D3 **Talisker** Highld
114 C1 **Talke** Staffs
114 C1 **Talke Pits** Staffs
178 D7 **Talkin** Cumb
187 H2 **Talla Linnfoots** Border
260 E6 **Talladale** Highld
183 K3 **Tallaminnock** S Ayrs
113 G3 **Tallarn Green** Wrexhm
164 F4 **Tallentire** Cumb
59 H2 **Talley** Carmth
102 B2 **Tallington** Lincs
112 D2 **Tallwrn** Wrexhm
277 K4 **Talmine** Highld
58 B4 **Talog** Carmth
77 G4 **Talsarn** Cerdgn
109 L4 **Talsarnau** Gwynd
4 E2 **Talskiddy** Cnwll
125 J4 **Talwrn** IOA
112 F2 **Talwrn** Wrexhm
61 H3 **Talybont-on-Usk** Powys
109 J1 **Talysarn** Gwynd
93 K3 **Talywern** Powys
139 J7 **Tamer Lane End** Wigan
6 F3 **Tamerton Foliot** C Plym
99 G3 **Tamworth** Staffs
119 L3 **Tamworth Green** Lincs
158 F1 **Tan Hill** N York
110 C3 **Tan-y-Bwlch** Gwynd
127 J6 **Tan-y-fron** Conwy
112 D1 **Tan-y-fron** Wrexhm
110 C3 **Tan-y-Grisiau** Gwynd
76 B5 **Tan-y-groes** Cerdgn
151 G4 **Tancred** N York
74 E7 **Tancredston** Pembks
38 B3 **Tandridge** Surrey
180 F7 **Tanfield** Dur
180 F8 **Tanfield Lea** Dur
54 E7 **Tangiers** Pembks
47 L8 **Tangley** Hants

20 E5 **Tangmere** W Susx
283 b13 **Tangusdale** W Isls
275 d4 **Tankerness** Ork
142 A7 **Tankersley** Barns
40 F2 **Tankerton** Kent
280 D6 **Tannach** Highld
245 H6 **Tannachie** Abers
234 D4 **Tannadice** Angus
98 E4 **Tanner's Green** Worcs
90 F2 **Tannington** Suffk
209 J6 **Tannochside** N Lans
132 F7 **Tansley** Derbys
102 B5 **Tansor** Nhants
180 E7 **Tantobie** Dur
170 C8 **Tanton** N York
97 K8 **Tanwood** Worcs
82 D1 **Tanworth in Arden** Warwks
282 d6 **Taobh Tuath** W Isls
49 M3 **Taplow** Bucks
205 L6 **Tarbert** Ag & B
206 D5 **Tarbert** Ag & B
282 e5 **Tarbert** W Isls
218 D6 **Tarbet** Ag & B
276 B6 **Tarbet** Highld
238 C5 **Tarbet** Highld
129 K2 **Tarbock Green** Knows
196 E5 **Tarbolton** S Ayrs
199 H2 **Tarbrax** S Lans
82 B2 **Tardebigge** Worcs
244 B7 **Tarfside** Angus
244 B3 **Tarland** Abers
138 F4 **Tarleton** Lancs
138 E5 **Tarlscough** Lancs
64 D7 **Tarlton** Gloucs
44 D8 **Tarnock** Somset
164 F1 **Tarns** Cumb
156 F4 **Tarnside** Cumb
130 A7 **Tarporley** Ches
28 F4 **Tarr** Somset
29 K5 **Tarr** Somset
17 H2 **Tarrant Crawford** Dorset
32 F8 **Tarrant Gunville** Dorset
32 F8 **Tarrant Hinton** Dorset
17 H2 **Tarrant Keyneston** Dorset
17 J1 **Tarrant Launceston** Dorset
17 J1 **Tarrant Monkton** Dorset
17 H1 **Tarrant Rawston** Dorset
17 H2 **Tarrant Rushton** Dorset
23 G6 **Tarring Neville** E Susx
80 E7 **Tarrington** Herefs
247 J6 **Tarskavaig** Highld
256 F5 **Tarves** Abers
232 F3 **Tarvie** P & K
129 L6 **Tarvin** Ches
129 L6 **Tarvin Sands** Ches
106 D4 **Tasburgh** Norfk
96 F4 **Tasley** Shrops
65 M3 **Taston** Oxon
115 K7 **Tatenhill** Staffs
84 F6 **Tathall End** M Keyn
147 M2 **Tatham** Lancs
136 F3 **Tathwell** Lincs
51 L7 **Tatsfield** Surrey
129 L7 **Tattenhall** Ches
121 J6 **Tatterford** Norfk
121 J5 **Tattersett** Norfk
136 D8 **Tattershall** Lincs
136 C8 **Tattershall Bridge** Lincs
136 D7 **Tattershall Thorpe** Lincs
90 D7 **Tattingstone** Suffk
90 D7 **Tattingstone White Horse** Suffk
15 H2 **Tatworth** Somset
267 H6 **Tauchers** Moray
30 C6 **Taunton** Somset
122 D8 **Taverham** Norfk
70 E3 **Taverners Green** Essex
55 L4 **Tavernspite** Pembks
12 C7 **Tavistock** Devon
12 F3 **Taw Green** Devon
27 K5 **Tawstock** Devon
131 K4 **Taxal** Derbys
217 G3 **Taychreggan Hotel** Ag & B
205 M7 **Tayinloan** Ag & B
63 L3 **Taynton** Gloucs
65 K4 **Taynton** Oxon
216 F1 **Taynuilt** Ag & B
223 H2 **Tayport** Fife
215 L7 **Tayvallich** Ag & B
136 C2 **Tealby** Lincs
181 G7 **Team Valley** Gatesd
247 K6 **Teangue** Highld
263 G7 **Teanord** Highld
157 K2 **Tebay** Cumb
68 C2 **Tebworth** Beds

13 J4	**Tedburn St Mary** Devon
81 M8	**Teddington** Gloucs
50 F5	**Teddington** Gt Lon
80 F3	**Tedstone Delamere** Herefs
80 F3	**Tedstone Wafer** Herefs
170 D6	**Teesport** R & Cl
170 B7	**Teesside Park** S on T
84 D1	**Teeton** Nhants
33 G4	**Teffont Evias** Wilts
33 G4	**Teffont Magna** Wilts
75 L5	**Tegryn** Pembks
117 M8	**Teigh** Rutlnd
12 F5	**Teigncombe** Devon
13 K7	**Teigngrace** Devon
13 L7	**Teignmouth** Devon
188 D4	**Teindside** Border
96 F2	**Telford** Wrekin
46 A7	**Tellisford** Somset
22 F6	**Telscombe** E Susx
22 F7	**Telscombe Cliffs** E Susx
231 J4	**Tempar** P & K
176 E2	**Templand** D & G
11 G7	**Temple** Cnwll
211 K7	**Temple** Mdloth
99 G8	**Temple Balsall** Solhll
76 F4	**Temple Bar** Cerdgn
45 J7	**Temple Cloud** BaNES
88 D5	**Temple End** Suffk
41 J6	**Temple Ewell** Kent
82 D4	**Temple Grafton** Warwks
65 G2	**Temple Guiting** Gloucs
142 F3	**Temple Hirst** N York
133 H6	**Temple Normanton** Derbys
245 H7	**Temple of Fiddes** Abers
250 F5	**Temple Pier** Highld
166 E5	**Temple Sowerby** Cumb
32 B6	**Templecombe** Somset
28 F8	**Templeton** Devon
55 J4	**Templeton** Pembks
168 E1	**Templetown** Dur
86 D4	**Tempsford** Beds
104 B4	**Ten Mile Bank** Norfk
80 E2	**Tenbury Wells** Worcs
55 K6	**Tenby** Pembks
73 H2	**Tendring** Essex
73 H2	**Tendring Green** Essex
73 H2	**Tendring Heath** Essex
73 G3	**Tenpenny Heath** Essex
39 M6	**Tenterden** Kent
71 J4	**Terling** Essex
113 K8	**Tern** Wrekin
113 L5	**Ternhill** Shrops
176 B3	**Terregles** D & G
151 L2	**Terrington** N York
120 C7	**Terrington St Clement** Norfk
103 L1	**Terrington St John** Norfk
98 E8	**Terry's Green** Warwks
39 H3	**Teston** Kent
34 D7	**Testwood** Hants
64 C8	**Tetbury** Gloucs
64 C8	**Tetbury Upton** Gloucs
112 F5	**Tetchill** Shrops
11 L3	**Tetcott** Devon
136 F5	**Tetford** Lincs
145 J7	**Tetney** Lincs
145 J7	**Tetney Lock** Lincs
67 G6	**Tetsworth** Oxon
97 K3	**Tettenhall** Wolves
97 K3	**Tettenhall Wood** Wolves
86 E4	**Tetworth** Cambs
133 J7	**Teversal** Notts
87 K3	**Teversham** Cambs
188 C5	**Teviothead** Border
69 H4	**Tewin** Herts
81 K8	**Tewkesbury** Gloucs
40 B3	**Teynham** Kent
149 M8	**Thackley** Brad
164 F6	**Thackthwaite** Cumb
166 A5	**Thackthwaite** Cumb
21 J3	**Thakeham** W Susx
67 H6	**Thame** Oxon
50 F5	**Thames Ditton** Surrey
52 A3	**Thamesmead** Gt Lon
40 F4	**Thanington** Kent
199 G5	**Thankerton** S Lans
106 D4	**Tharston** Norfk
48 D5	**Thatcham** W Berk
129 L1	**Thatto Heath** St Hel
70 F1	**Thaxted** Essex
131 G8	**The Bank** Ches
96 E3	**The Bank** Shrops
64 F6	**The Beeches** Gloucs.
115 G6	**The Blythe** Staffs
95 J4	**The Bog** Shrops
82 A4	**The Bourne** Worcs

247 H2	**The Braes** Highld
97 K4	**The Bratch** Staffs
80 C3	**The Broad** Herefs
212 F4	**The Brunt** E Loth
154 e5	**The Bungalow** IOM
64 C4	**The Butts** Gloucs
64 C5	**The Camp** Gloucs
113 H3	**The Chequer** Wrexhm
86 C3	**The City** Beds
67 J7	**The City** Bucks
65 L2	**The Common** Oxon
34 B4	**The Common** Wilts
46 F2	**The Common** Wilts
39 H5	**The Corner** Kent
95 K6	**The Corner** Shrops
154 d3	**The Cronk** IOM
196 C1	**The Den** N Ayrs
178 D3	**The Flatt** Cumb
79 L3	**The Forge** Herefs
38 E6	**The Forstal** E Susx
40 A6	**The Forstal** Kent
40 D7	**The Forstal** Kent
113 L5	**The Fouralls** Shrops
156 A5	**The Green** Cumb
71 J3	**The Green** Essex
162 D2	**The Green** N York
81 K7	**The Grove** Worcs
37 G5	**The Haven** W Susx
64 B2	**The Haw** Gloucs
170 C4	**The Headland** Hartpl
156 A6	**The Hill** Cumb
49 K3	**The Holt** Wokham
80 C2	**The Hundred** Herefs
40 C8	**The Leacon** Kent
67 L6	**The Lee** Bucks
154 e2	**The Lhen** IOM
266 F4	**The Lochs** Moray
95 H4	**The Marsh** Powys
180 F8	**The Middles** Dur
39 J7	**The Moor** Kent
57 H7	**The Mumbles** Swans
209 H8	**The Murray** S Lans
81 K8	**The Mythe** Gloucs
63 G6	**The Narth** Mons
245 G4	**The Neuk** Abers
63 L7	**The Quarry** Gloucs
39 M4	**The Quarter** Kent
64 C3	**The Reddings** Gloucs
131 G8	**The Rookery** Staffs
220 D3	**The Ross** P & K
36 C2	**The Sands** Surrey
46 A4	**The Shoe** Wilts
96 F4	**The Smithies** Shrops
87 K5	**The Spike** Cambs
83 G1	**The Spring** Warwks
62 B7	**The Square** Torfn
38 F4	**The Stair** Kent
25 G2	**The Stocks** Kent
36 A3	**The Straits** Hants
46 D7	**The Strand** Wilts
2 E3	**The Towans** Cnwll
80 C5	**The Vauld** Herefs
97 G3	**The Wyke** Shrops
160 D5	**Theakston** N York
143 M4	**Thealby** N Linc
31 G2	**Theale** Somset
48 F5	**Theale** W Berk
153 G8	**Thearne** E R Yk
91 K2	**Theberton** Suffk
35 L3	**Thedden Grange** Hants
100 E6	**Theddingworth** Leics
137 J2	**Theddlethorpe All Saints** Lincs
137 J2	**Theddlethorpe St Helen** Lincs
28 D8	**Thelbridge Cross** Devon
105 L7	**Thelnetham** Suffk
106 D7	**Thelveton** Norfk
130 C2	**Thelwall** Warrtn
122 B6	**Themelthorpe** Norfk
83 M7	**Thenford** Nhants
46 F5	**Theobald's Green** Wilts
87 G7	**Therfield** Herts
105 H6	**Thetford** Norfk
165 L2	**Thethwaite** Cumb
70 C7	**Theydon Bois** Essex
151 L7	**Thicket Priory** E R Yk
46 B4	**Thickwood** Wilts
136 D5	**Thimbleby** Lincs
161 G3	**Thimbleby** N York
129 G3	**Thingwall** Wirral
161 G6	**Thirkleby** N York
161 G6	**Thirlby** N York
201 H4	**Thirlestane** Border
165 K7	**Thirlspot** Cumb
160 B5	**Thirn** N York

160 F6	**Thirsk** N York
144 F1	**Thirtleby** E R Yk
147 H8	**Thistleton** Lancs
118 B7	**Thistleton** Rutlnd
104 D8	**Thistley Green** Suffk
152 C4	**Thixendale** N York
179 M3	**Thockrington** Nthumb
103 H2	**Tholomas Drove** Cambs
151 G2	**Tholthorpe** N York
55 J5	**Thomas Chapel** Pembks
166 B3	**Thomas Close** Cumb
82 C3	**Thomas Town** Warwks
255 M4	**Thomastown** Abers
105 J4	**Thompson** Norfk
52 E5	**Thong** Kent
159 H5	**Thoralby** N York
134 C5	**Thoresby** Notts
137 J4	**Thoresthorpe** Lincs
144 F8	**Thoresway** Lincs
145 G8	**Thorganby** Lincs
151 L7	**Thorganby** N York
162 C3	**Thorgill** N York
107 J8	**Thorington** Suffk
89 K8	**Thorington Street** Suffk
149 H5	**Thorlby** N York
70 C3	**Thorley** Herts
18 F6	**Thorley** IOW
70 C3	**Thorley Houses** Herts
18 F6	**Thorley Street** IOW
161 H7	**Thormanby** N York
170 B7	**Thornaby-on-Tees** S on T
122 B4	**Thornage** Norfk
84 E8	**Thornborough** Bucks
160 D6	**Thornborough** N York
141 J1	**Thornbury** Brad
12 A1	**Thornbury** Devon
80 E3	**Thornbury** Herefs
45 J1	**Thornbury** S Glos
177 J8	**Thornby** Cumb
100 E8	**Thornby** Nhants
131 K7	**Thorncliff** Staffs
15 J2	**Thorncombe** Dorset
36 F3	**Thorncombe Street** Surrey
86 C5	**Thorncott Green** Beds
19 G7	**Thorncross** IOW
90 D1	**Thorndon** Suffk
12 D4	**Thorndon Cross** Devon
143 H5	**Thorne** Donc
31 H7	**Thorne** Somset
29 K6	**Thorne St Margaret** Somset
7 M2	**Thornecroft** Devon
27 G7	**Thornehillhead** Devon
150 E7	**Thornes** Leeds
98 D3	**Thornes** Staffs
141 M4	**Thornes** Wakefd
50 D3	**Thorney** Bucks
102 F3	**Thorney** C Pete
135 G5	**Thorney** Notts
30 F6	**Thorney** Somset
18 B4	**Thorney Hill** Hants
103 G3	**Thorney Toll** Cambs
30 D6	**Thornfalcon** Somset
31 K8	**Thornford** Dorset
179 H6	**Thorngrafton** Nthumb
30 E4	**Thorngrove** Somset
145 G3	**Thorngumbald** E R Yk
121 G3	**Thornham** Norfk
90 C1	**Thornham Magna** Suffk
90 D1	**Thornham Parva** Suffk
102 B3	**Thornhaugh** C Pete
19 G1	**Thornhill** C Sotn
43 J5	**Thornhill** Caerph
186 C7	**Thornhill** D & G
132 D3	**Thornhill** Derbys
141 L4	**Thornhill** Kirk
219 L7	**Thornhill** Stirlg
141 K4	**Thornhill Lees** Kirk
141 J3	**Thornhills** Calder
153 H3	**Thornholme** E R Yk
17 G2	**Thornicombe** Dorset
202 D6	**Thornington** Nthumb
168 E3	**Thornley** Dur
169 K3	**Thornley** Dur
179 J7	**Thornley Gate** Cumb
208 F7	**Thornliebank** E Rens
88 E4	**Thorns** Suffk
130 F3	**Thorns Green** Ches
131 K2	**Thornsett** Derbys
165 H5	**Thornthwaite** Cumb
149 L4	**Thornthwaite** N York
234 B6	**Thornton** Angus
141 H1	**Thornton** Brad
84 E8	**Thornton** Bucks
152 A6	**Thornton** E R Yk
222 E7	**Thornton** Fife

146 F7	**Thornton** Lancs
100 A2	**Thornton** Leics
136 D6	**Thornton** Lincs
170 B7	**Thornton** Middsb
202 E4	**Thornton** Nthumb
54 E5	**Thornton** Pembks
138 D7	**Thornton** Sefton
144 D4	**Thornton Curtis** N Linc
129 K5	**Thornton Green** Ches
51 J5	**Thornton Heath** Gt Lon
129 G3	**Thornton Hough** Wirral
158 B8	**Thornton in Lonsdale** N York
162 E6	**Thornton le Dale** N York
144 D8	**Thornton le Moor** Lincs
159 G5	**Thornton Rust** N York
160 A5	**Thornton Steward** N York
160 C5	**Thornton Watlass** N York
148 F6	**Thornton-in-Craven** N York
160 F4	**Thornton-le-Beans** N York
151 L3	**Thornton-le-Clay** N York
160 F5	**Thornton-le-Moor** N York
129 K5	**Thornton-le-Moors** Ches
160 F5	**Thornton-le-Street** N York
209 G8	**Thorntonhall** S Lans
213 G4	**Thorntonloch** E Loth
70 C6	**Thornwood Common** Essex
201 J3	**Thornydykes** Border
165 L6	**Thornythwaite** Cumb
117 K3	**Thoroton** Notts
150 F6	**Thorp Arch** Leeds
115 J2	**Thorpe** Derbys
152 F6	**Thorpe** E R Yk
137 J3	**Thorpe** Lincs
149 H3	**Thorpe** N York
107 J4	**Thorpe** Norfk
117 K2	**Thorpe** Notts
50 C5	**Thorpe** Surrey
106 D7	**Thorpe Abbotts** Norfk
116 E7	**Thorpe Acre** Leics
117 K7	**Thorpe Arnold** Leics
142 D4	**Thorpe Audlin** Donc
162 F8	**Thorpe Bassett** N York
53 K2	**Thorpe Bay** Sthend
101 K4	**Thorpe by Water** Rutlnd
133 G1	**Thorpe Common** Rothm
99 H2	**Thorpe Constantine** Staffs
106 F1	**Thorpe End** Norfk
73 H3	**Thorpe Green** Essex
139 H3	**Thorpe Green** Lancs
89 J4	**Thorpe Green** Suffk
142 B8	**Thorpe Hesley** Rothm
142 F5	**Thorpe in Balne** Donc
135 H4	**Thorpe in the Fallows** Lincs
101 G5	**Thorpe Langton** Leics
169 K5	**Thorpe Larches** Dur
152 C7	**Thorpe le Street** E R Yk
50 C5	**Thorpe Lea** Surrey
101 H7	**Thorpe Malsor** Nhants
83 M6	**Thorpe Mandeville** Nhants
122 E4	**Thorpe Market** Norfk
89 J4	**Thorpe Morieux** Suffk
141 M2	**Thorpe on the Hill** Leeds
135 H6	**Thorpe on the Hill** Lincs
133 K3	**Thorpe Salvin** Rothm
100 F1	**Thorpe Satchville** Leics
106 F2	**Thorpe St Andrew** Norfk
137 J7	**Thorpe St Peter** Lincs
169 L6	**Thorpe Thewles** S on T
136 B8	**Thorpe Tilney** Lincs
151 G4	**Thorpe Underwood** N York
101 H7	**Thorpe Underwood** Nhants
102 A7	**Thorpe Waterville** Nhants
142 F2	**Thorpe Willoughby** N York
73 J3	**Thorpe-le-Soken** Essex
91 L3	**Thorpeness** Suffk
104 C2	**Thorpland** Norfk
73 G3	**Thorrington** Essex
13 L2	**Thorverton** Devon
68 E4	**Thrales End** Beds
106 C8	**Thrandeston** Suffk
101 M7	**Thrapston** Nhants
165 G3	**Threapland** Cumb
149 H4	**Threapland** N York
113 G3	**Threapwood** Ches
115 G3	**Threapwood** Staffs
115 G3	**Threapwood Head** Staffs
183 J2	**Threave** S Ayrs
63 G3	**Three Ashes** Herefs
37 L3	**Three Bridges** W Susx
4 B5	**Three Burrows** Cnwll
39 K5	**Three Chimneys** Kent
79 G7	**Three Cocks** Powys
57 G6	**Three Crosses** Swans
23 L3	**Three Cups Corner** E Susx
80 F3	**Three Gates** Worcs

11 J5 **Three Hammers** Cnwll
103 K3 **Three Holes** Norfk
140 C6 **Three Lane Ends** Rochdl
39 H7 **Three Leg Cross** E Susx
17 L2 **Three Legged Cross** Dorset
49 H5 **Three Mile Cross** Wokham
4 C6 **Three Mile Stone** Cnwll
210 E4 **Three Miletown** W Loth
24 F4 **Three Oaks** E Susx
123 G7 **Threehammer Common** Norfk
118 E4 **Threekingham** Lincs
201 G4 **Threepwood** Border
165 K5 **Threlkeld** Cumb
149 H3 **Threshfield** N York
107 J1 **Thrigby** Norfk
167 L6 **Thringarth** Dur
116 D8 **Thringstone** Leics
160 D4 **Thrintoft** N York
87 J6 **Thriplow** Cambs
133 K2 **Throapham** Rothm
103 G2 **Throckenhalt** Lincs
69 J1 **Throcking** Herts
180 E5 **Throckley** N u Ty
82 A5 **Throckmorton** Worcs
17 M3 **Throop** Bmouth
16 F4 **Throop** Dorset
180 D2 **Throphill** Nthumb
190 E5 **Thropton** Nthumb
209 M1 **Throsk** Stirlg
64 D5 **Througham** Gloucs
185 L6 **Throughgate** D & G
12 F4 **Throwleigh** Devon
40 C4 **Throwley** Kent
40 C4 **Throwley Forstal** Kent
116 E5 **Thrumpton** Notts
134 D4 **Thrumpton** Notts
280 D7 **Thrumster** Highld
145 J6 **Thrunscoe** NE Lin
190 F4 **Thrunton** Nthumb
65 L7 **Thrup** Oxon
64 B6 **Thrupp** Gloucs
66 C4 **Thrupp** Oxon
12 B5 **Thrushelton** Devon
70 D5 **Thrushesbush** Essex
117 H8 **Thrussington** Leics
34 C2 **Thruxton** Hants
80 B8 **Thruxton** Herefs
142 D8 **Thrybergh** Rothm
116 C5 **Thulston** Derbys
53 G1 **Thundersley** Essex
100 C1 **Thurcaston** Leics
133 K2 **Thurcroft** Rothm
26 E8 **Thurdon** Cnwll
122 D4 **Thurgarton** Norfk
117 J2 **Thurgarton** Notts
141 L7 **Thurgoland** Barns
100 B4 **Thurlaston** Leics
83 L1 **Thurlaston** Warwks
30 C6 **Thurlbear** Somset
135 H7 **Thurlby** Lincs
118 E8 **Thurlby** Lincs
137 J4 **Thurlby** Lincs
85 L3 **Thurleigh** Beds
7 K6 **Thurlestone** Devon
88 D5 **Thurlow** Suffk
30 C5 **Thurloxton** Somset
141 K7 **Thurlstone** Barns
107 J4 **Thurlton** Norfk
130 F8 **Thurlwood** Ches
100 D2 **Thurmaston** Leics
100 E3 **Thurnby** Leics
123 H8 **Thurne** Norfk
53 H7 **Thurnham** Kent
102 B6 **Thurning** Nhants
122 B5 **Thurning** Norfk
142 C6 **Thurnscoe** Barns
165 K1 **Thursby** Cumb
140 D1 **Thursden** Lancs
121 L5 **Thursford** Norfk
36 D3 **Thursley** Surrey
279 K3 **Thurso** Highld
128 F3 **Thurstaston** Wirral
89 J2 **Thurston** Suffk
140 E6 **Thurston Clough** Oldham
89 J2 **Thurston Planch** Suffk
177 K7 **Thurstonfield** Cumb
141 J5 **Thurstonland** Kirk
107 G3 **Thurton** Norfk
115 L4 **Thurvaston** Derbys
105 L2 **Thuxton** Norfk
158 F3 **Thwaite** N York
90 D2 **Thwaite** Suffk
156 E4 **Thwaite Head** Cumb
107 G4 **Thwaite St Mary** Norfk

149 K7 **Thwaites** Brad
149 K7 **Thwaites Brow** Brad
153 G2 **Thwing** E R Yk
221 J3 **Tibbermore** P & K
186 C6 **Tibbers** D & G
63 M3 **Tibberton** Gloucs
81 L4 **Tibberton** Worcs
113 L7 **Tibberton** Wrekin
187 K2 **Tibbie Shiels Inn** Border
106 C5 **Tibenham** Norfk
133 J7 **Tibshelf** Derbys
152 E5 **Tibthorpe** E R Yk
39 H7 **Ticehurst** E Susx
35 H5 **Tichborne** Hants
101 L2 **Tickencote** Rutlnd
44 F4 **Tickenham** N Som
85 H6 **Tickford End** M Keyn
134 B1 **Tickhill** Donc
96 B5 **Ticklerton** Shrops
116 B6 **Ticknall** Derbys
153 G7 **Tickton** E R Yk
98 E8 **Tidbury Green** Solhll
47 L7 **Tidcombe** Wilts
67 G6 **Tiddington** Oxon
82 F4 **Tiddington** Warwks
38 F7 **Tidebrook** E Susx
6 C3 **Tideford** Cnwll
6 C3 **Tideford Cross** Cnwll
63 H7 **Tidenham** Gloucs
132 C4 **Tideswell** Derbys
48 F4 **Tidmarsh** W Berk
83 G7 **Tidmington** Warwks
33 J7 **Tidpit** Hants
54 E5 **Tiers Cross** Pembks
84 D5 **Tiffield** Nhants
234 E3 **Tigerton** Angus
282 b7 **Tigh a Ghearraidh** W Isls
282 b7 **Tigharry** W Isls
206 F4 **Tighnabruaich** Ag & B
7 L3 **Tigley** Devon
86 B2 **Tilbrook** Cambs
52 D4 **Tilbury** Thurr
88 E7 **Tilbury Green** Essex
98 F6 **Tile Cross** Birm
99 H7 **Tile Hill** Covtry
98 F8 **Tilehouse Green** Solhll
49 G4 **Tilehurst** Readg
36 C2 **Tilford** Surrey
37 L4 **Tilgate** W Susx
37 L4 **Tilgate Forest Row** W Susx
31 J4 **Tilham Street** Somset
80 F8 **Tillers Green** Gloucs
221 G7 **Tillicoultry** Clacks
198 D4 **Tillietudlem** S Lans
72 E6 **Tillingham** Essex
80 B6 **Tillington** Herefs
36 E6 **Tillington** W Susx
80 B6 **Tillington Common** Herefs
244 F2 **Tillybirloch** Abers
244 A4 **Tillycairn** Abers
244 E1 **Tillyfourie** Abers
256 F7 **Tillygreig** Abers
221 K6 **Tillyrie** P & K
41 J5 **Tilmanstone** Kent
134 D3 **Tiln** Notts
120 C7 **Tilney All Saints** Norfk
120 C8 **Tilney High End** Norfk
120 C8 **Tilney St Lawrence** Norfk
33 H1 **Tilshead** Wilts
113 J4 **Tilstock** Shrops
113 G1 **Tilston** Ches
130 A7 **Tilstone Bank** Ches
130 A7 **Tilstone Fearnall** Ches
68 B2 **Tilsworth** Beds
101 G2 **Tilton on the Hill** Leics
64 B7 **Tiltups End** Gloucs
70 E2 **Tilty** Essex
136 B7 **Timberland** Lincs
131 H7 **Timbersbrook** Ches
29 G2 **Timberscombe** Somset
149 M5 **Timble** N York
29 H5 **Timewell** Devon
177 K4 **Timpanheck** D & G
130 F2 **Timperley** Traffd
45 K7 **Timsbury** BaNES
34 D6 **Timsbury** Hants
282 d3 **Timsgarry** W Isls
282 d3 **Timsgearraidh** W Isls
89 H2 **Timworth** Suffk
89 H2 **Timworth Green** Suffk
16 E4 **Tincleton** Dorset
178 E7 **Tindale** Cumb
169 G5 **Tindale Crescent** Dur
84 C8 **Tingewick** Bucks
141 L3 **Tingley** Leeds

68 C1 **Tingrith** Beds
12 A5 **Tinhay** Devon
34 E2 **Tinker's Hill** Hants
132 E6 **Tinkersley** Derbys
133 H2 **Tinsley** Sheff
37 L3 **Tinsley Green** W Susx
10 F5 **Tintagel** Cnwll
63 G7 **Tintern Parva** Mons
31 H7 **Tintinhull** Somset
140 F8 **Tintwistle** Derbys
176 D3 **Tinwald** D & G
101 M2 **Tinwell** Rutlnd
103 K4 **Tipp's End** Norfk
28 D2 **Tippacott** Devon
18 C4 **Tiptoe** Hants
97 L5 **Tipton** Sandw
98 B5 **Tipton Green** Sandw
14 C4 **Tipton St John** Devon
72 C4 **Tiptree** Essex
72 C4 **Tiptree Heath** Essex
129 G7 **Tir-y-fron** Flints
78 B7 **Tirabad** Powys
206 A6 **Tiretigan** Ag & B
64 B2 **Tirley** Gloucs
61 H6 **Tirphil** Caerph
166 C5 **Tirril** Cumb
32 F5 **Tisbury** Wilts
37 G4 **Tisman's Common** W Susx
115 K1 **Tissington** Derbys
26 D5 **Titchberry** Devon
19 J3 **Titchfield** Hants
19 J2 **Titchfield Common** Hants
102 A7 **Titchmarsh** Nhants
121 G3 **Titchwell** Norfk
117 J4 **Tithby** Notts
79 L3 **Titley** Herefs
69 G2 **Titmore Green** Herts
51 L7 **Titsey** Surrey
114 D4 **Tittensor** Staffs
121 K7 **Tittleshall** Norfk
81 J1 **Titton** Worcs
130 A7 **Tiverton** Ches
29 G8 **Tiverton** Devon
106 D6 **Tivetshall St Margaret** Norfk
106 D6 **Tivetshall St Mary** Norfk
29 G2 **Tivington** Somset
141 L6 **Tivy Dale** Barns
114 F7 **Tixall** Staffs
101 L3 **Tixover** Rutlnd
133 H8 **Toadhole** Derbys
116 B1 **Toadmoor** Derbys
226 F1 **Tobermory** Ag & B
215 L3 **Toberonochy** Ag & B
283 b10 **Tobha Mor** W Isls
256 C5 **Tocher** Abers
267 K3 **Tochieneal** Moray
46 F3 **Tockenham** Wilts
46 F3 **Tockenham Wick** Wilts
170 E7 **Tocketts** R & Cl
139 K3 **Tockholes** Bl w D
45 J2 **Tockington** S Glos
151 G5 **Tockwith** N York
32 D7 **Todber** Dorset
191 J7 **Todburn** Nthumb
68 C2 **Toddington** Beds
82 B8 **Toddington** Gloucs
69 G2 **Todds Green** Herts
82 F8 **Todenham** Gloucs
234 C7 **Todhills** Angus
177 L6 **Todhills** Cumb
169 G4 **Todhills** Dur
140 E3 **Todmorden** Calder
133 K3 **Todwick** Rothm
87 G4 **Toft** Cambs
130 E4 **Toft** Ches
118 E8 **Toft** Lincs
281 e4 **Toft** Shet
83 L1 **Toft** Warwks
168 F5 **Toft Hill** Dur
136 D7 **Toft Hill** Lincs
107 J4 **Toft Monks** Norfk
135 L2 **Toft next Newton** Lincs
121 K6 **Toftrees** Norfk
105 K1 **Toftwood** Norfk
191 K5 **Togston** Nthumb
247 J6 **Tokavaig** Highld
49 H3 **Tokers Green** Oxon
282 h2 **Tolastadh** W Isls
4 F3 **Toldish** Cnwll
142 E6 **Toll Bar** Donc
29 K4 **Tolland** Somset
32 F7 **Tollard Farnham** Dorset
32 F7 **Tollard Royal** Wilts
99 K8 **Tollbar End** Covtry
16 B3 **Toller Fratrum** Dorset

260 D8 **Torridon House** ...
247 ...
72 ...
72 D5 ...
72 D4 **To...**
72 C5 **Tolles...**
281 d9 **Tolob** Sh...
16 F4 **Tolpuddle** D...
282 h2 **Tolsta** W Isls
3 H5 **Tolvan** Cnwll
2 D4 **Tolver** Cnwll
51 G5 **Tolworth** Gt Lon
252 E6 **Tomatin** Highld
239 M1 **Tomchrasky** Highld
239 K3 **Tomdoun** Highld
272 F7 **Tomich** Highld
250 B6 **Tomich** Highld
250 F2 **Tomich** Highld
263 J5 **Tomich** Highld
254 D7 **Tomintoul** Moray
83 K3 **Tomlow** Warwks
250 F3 **Tomnacross** Highld
254 D6 **Tomnavoulin** Moray
114 E1 **Tompkin** Staffs
62 C6 **Ton** Mons
62 D7 **Ton** Mons
43 H4 **Ton-teg** Rhondd
38 F4 **Tonbridge** Kent
42 D5 **Tondu** Brdgnd
29 L6 **Tonedale** Somset
141 K2 **Tong** Brad
40 C4 **Tong** Kent
97 H2 **Tong** Shrops
40 C4 **Tong Green** Kent
97 H2 **Tong Norton** Shrops
141 J2 **Tong Street** Brad
116 C7 **Tonge** Leics
36 C1 **Tongham** Surrey
175 H4 **Tongland** D & G
277 K5 **Tongue** Highld
118 F7 **Tongue End** Lincs
43 H5 **Tongwynlais** Cardif
57 L5 **Tonna** Neath
69 J4 **Tonwell** Herts
42 F3 **Tonypandy** Rhondd
42 F4 **Tonyrefail** Rhondd
66 E7 **Toot Baldon** Oxon
70 D6 **Toot Hill** Essex
34 E7 **Toot Hill** Hants
47 G2 **Toothill** Swindn
51 H5 **Tooting** Gt Lon
51 H4 **Tooting Bec** Gt Lon
85 L3 **Top End** Beds
140 C6 **Top of Hebers** Rochdl
128 F2 **Top-y-rhos** Flints
160 F7 **Topcliffe** N York
106 F5 **Topcroft** Norfk
106 F5 **Topcroft Street** Norfk
143 G4 **Topham** Donc
88 E7 **Toppesfield** Essex
139 L5 **Toppings** Bolton
106 D4 **Toprow** Norfk
13 M5 **Topsham** Devon
194 D5 **Torbeg** N Ayrs
273 H8 **Torboll** Highld
251 H3 **Torbreck** Highld
8 B2 **Torbryan** Devon
239 J7 **Torcastle** Highld
8 B6 **Torcross** Devon
251 G1 **Tore** Highld
5 J4 **Torfrey** Cnwll
206 C6 **Torinturk** Ag & B
135 G4 **Torksey** Lincs
45 M3 **Tormarton** S Glos
194 D4 **Tormore** N Ayrs
252 E2 **Tornagrain** Highld
244 D2 **Tornaveen** Abers
251 G6 **Torness** Highld
8 B1 **Tornewton** Devon
169 G4 **Toronto** Dur
227 L5 **Torosay Castle** Ag & B
165 G3 **Torpenhow** Cumb
210 C4 **Torphichen** W Loth
244 E3 **Torphins** Abers
6 E4 **Torpoint** Cnwll
8 D2 **Torquay** Torbay
200 F3 **Torquhan** Border
7 H4 **Torr** Devon
259 K6 **Torran** Highld
209 G4 **Torrance** E Duns
196 D2 **Torranyard** N Ayrs
29 J3 **Torre** Somset
260 E8 **Torridon** Highld

	...don House	Highld
	Torrin	Highld
194 B4	Torrisdale	Ag & B
278 B4	Torrisdale	Highld
274 C4	Torrish	Highld
147 J3	Torrisholme	Lancs
272 E7	Torrobull	Highld
245 L3	Torry	C Aber
210 D2	Torryburn	Fife
81 J1	Tortan	Worcs
9 h4	Torteval	Guern
176 D3	Torthorwald	D & G
21 G6	Tortington	W Susx
63 L8	Tortworth	S Glos
259 H7	Torvaig	Highld
156 C4	Torver	Cumb
209 M2	Torwood	Falk
201 G5	Torwoodlee	Border
134 D2	Torworth	Notts
247 L1	Toscaig	Highld
86 E3	Toseland	Cambs
148 D4	Tosside	N York
89 J3	Tostock	Suffk
258 B6	Totaig	Highld
259 G6	Tote	Highld
259 J4	Tote	Highld
36 C6	Tote Hill	W Susx
137 H3	Tothill	Lincs
18 E6	Totland	IOW
132 F4	Totley	Sheff
132 F4	Totley Brook	Sheff
8 B3	Totnes	Devon
116 E4	Toton	Notts
224 F4	Totronald	Ag & B
258 F3	Totscore	Highld
51 J1	Tottenham	Gt Lon
104 C1	Tottenhill	Norfk
69 H8	Totteridge	Gt Lon
68 C3	Totternhoe	Beds
140 A5	Tottington	Bury
139 L2	Tottleworth	Lancs
34 D8	Totton	Hants
49 L4	Touchen End	W & M
151 G7	Toulston	N York
30 B4	Toulton	Somset
264 D4	Toulvaddie	Highld
39 J3	Tovil	Kent
168 E3	Tow Law	Dur
10 B7	Towan	Cnwll
5 G5	Towan	Cnwll
207 J5	Toward	Ag & B
207 J5	Toward Quay	Ag & B
84 D5	Towcester	Nhants
2 D3	Towednack	Cnwll
67 H6	Towersey	Oxon
244 A1	Towie	Abers
103 J4	Town End	Cambs
156 C4	Town End	Cumb
156 E1	Town End	Cumb
166 E5	Town End	Cumb
156 E5	Town End	Cumb
156 F6	Town End	Cumb
138 E6	Town Green	Lancs
107 G1	Town Green	Norfk
156 F2	Town Head	Cumb
148 E4	Town Head	N York
149 L6	Town Head	N York
169 K3	Town Kelloe	Dur
139 K7	Town Lane	Wigan
22 F4	Town Littleworth	E Susx
139 J8	Town of Lowton	Wigan
38 E7	Town Row	E Susx
104 F6	Town Street	Suffk
202 C7	Town Yetholm	Border
208 C4	Townend	W Duns
166 C1	Towngate	Cumb
102 C1	Towngate	Lincs
141 J7	Townhead	Barns
164 E3	Townhead	Cumb
166 E4	Townhead	Cumb
176 D1	Townhead	D & G
175 J2	Townhead of Greenlaw	D & G
210 F1	Townhill	Fife
12 A7	Townlake	Devon
48 E7	Towns End	Hants
30 E7	Townsend	Somset
2 F4	Townshend	Cnwll
45 K1	Townwell	S Glos
152 D3	Towthorpe	E R Yk
151 K4	Towthorpe	York
151 G7	Towton	N York
127 K4	Towyn	Conwy
129 H2	Toxteth	Lpool
38 D3	Toy's Hill	Kent
137 G7	Toynton All Saints	Lincs

137 G7	Toynton Fen Side	Lincs
137 G7	Toynton St Peter	Lincs
196 E6	Trabboch	E Ayrs
196 F6	Trabbochburn	E Ayrs
3 J6	Traboe	Cnwll
29 K6	Tracebridge	Somset
264 D8	Tradespark	Highld
76 A5	Traethsaith	Cerdgn
60 E1	Trallong	Powys
211 L4	Tranent	E Loth
129 H2	Tranmere	Wirral
2 F4	Trannack	Cnwll
278 F5	Trantelbeg	Highld
278 F5	Trantlemore	Highld
180 F2	Tranwell	Nthumb
82 D1	Trap's Green	Warwks
59 J5	Trapp	Carmth
212 D4	Traprain	E Loth
48 A6	Trapshill	W Berk
200 D6	Traquair	Border
49 G5	Trash Green	W Berk
27 L5	Traveller's Rest	Devon
148 F8	Trawden	Lancs
77 J1	Trawscoed	Cerdgn
110 D4	Trawsfynydd	Gwynd
43 G7	Tre Aubrey	V Glam
92 E5	Tre Taliesin	Cerdgn
92 E5	Tre'r-ddol	Cerdgn
63 G5	Tre-gagle	Mons
60 F6	Tre-Gibbon	Rhondd
76 D6	Tre-groes	Cerdgn
128 D4	Tre-Mostyn	Flints
58 D4	Tre-Vaughan	Carmth
62 C3	Tre-wyn	Mons
42 F3	Trealaw	Rhondd
138 F1	Treales	Lancs
4 C4	Treamble	Cnwll
124 D4	Trearddur Bay	IOA
258 F6	Treaslane	Highld
10 C7	Treator	Cnwll
42 F4	Trebanog	Rhondd
57 K4	Trebanos	Neath
11 K7	Trebartha	Cnwll
3 H5	Trebarvah	Cnwll
10 E5	Trebarwith	Cnwll
11 J5	Trebeath	Cnwll
2 B6	Trebehor	Cnwll
4 D2	Trebelzue	Cnwll
10 C7	Trebetherick	Cnwll
29 H4	Treborough	Somset
4 E3	Trebudannon	Cnwll
11 L6	Trebullett	Cnwll
10 E6	Treburgett	Cnwll
10 B8	Treburick	Cnwll
11 L7	Treburley	Cnwll
10 B8	Treburrick	Cnwll
5 J2	Trebyan	Cnwll
60 C1	Trecastle	Powys
11 K6	Trecogo	Cnwll
12 F3	Trecott	Devon
74 F5	Trecwn	Pembks
60 F6	Trecynon	Rhondd
11 J6	Tredaule	Cnwll
2 C5	Tredavoe	Cnwll
61 J5	Tredegar	Blae G
10 F8	Tredethy	Cnwll
64 C1	Tredington	Gloucs
83 G6	Tredington	Warwks
4 F1	Tredinnick	Cnwll
5 H3	Tredinnick	Cnwll
5 K2	Tredinnick	Cnwll
5 M3	Tredinnick	Cnwll
6 B3	Tredinnick	Cnwll
61 H1	Tredomen	Powys
75 J4	Tredrissi	Pembks
10 D7	Tredrizzick	Cnwll
62 D8	Tredunhock	Mons
61 H1	Tredustan	Powys
2 C3	Treen	Cnwll
2 B6	Treen	Cnwll
5 J4	Treesmill	Cnwll
133 J2	Treeton	Rothm
74 E4	Trefasser	Pembks
125 G5	Trefdraeth	IOA
61 J1	Trefecca	Powys
93 L5	Trefeglwys	Powys
77 H2	Trefenter	Cerdgn
54 F2	Treffgarne	Pembks
74 E7	Treffgarne Owen	Pembks
43 G4	Trefforest	Rhondd
74 D6	Treffynnon	Pembks
61 H4	Trefil	Blae G
77 G4	Trefilan	Cerdgn
74 D5	Trefin	Pembks
112 C6	Treflach Wood	Shrops

112 C8	Trefnannau	Powys
128 C5	Trefnant	Denbgs
112 C6	Trefonen	Shrops
108 F2	Trefor	Gwynd
124 F4	Trefor	IOA
10 F5	Treforda	Cnwll
10 F5	Trefrew	Cnwll
126 F7	Trefriw	Conwy
11 K6	Tregadillett	Cnwll
125 H4	Tregaian	IOA
62 E5	Tregare	Mons
3 K6	Tregarne	Cnwll
77 J3	Tregaron	Cerdgn
126 B6	Tregarth	Gwynd
4 E2	Tregaswith	Cnwll
10 F5	Tregatta	Cnwll
5 G2	Tregawne	Cnwll
4 E5	Tregear	Cnwll
11 J5	Tregeare	Cnwll
112 B5	Tregeiriog	Wrexhm
124 F1	Tregele	IOA
10 E7	Tregellist	Cnwll
4 E6	Tregenna	Cnwll
10 F7	Tregenna	Cnwll
2 B5	Tregeseal	Cnwll
3 K4	Tregew	Cnwll
3 J6	Tregidden	Cnwll
3 H6	Tregiddle	Cnwll
4 F5	Tregidgeo	Cnwll
5 G5	Tregiskey	Cnwll
74 D6	Treglemais	Pembks
11 H3	Tregole	Cnwll
3 J4	Tregolls	Cnwll
10 C7	Tregonce	Cnwll
4 F2	Tregonetha	Cnwll
4 F6	Tregony	Cnwll
11 G6	Tregoodwell	Cnwll
3 H6	Tregoose	Cnwll
4 F3	Tregoss	Cnwll
3 K6	Tregowris	Cnwll
79 H7	Tregoyd	Powys
5 H4	Tregrehan Mills	Cnwll
5 H2	Tregullon	Cnwll
10 D7	Tregunna	Cnwll
11 J6	Tregunnon	Cnwll
4 D2	Tregurrian	Cnwll
5 G2	Tregustick	Cnwll
94 D4	Tregynon	Powys
43 G3	Trehafod	Rhondd
6 D3	Trehan	Cnwll
43 H2	Treharris	Myr Td
10 E6	Treharrock	Cnwll
10 B7	Trehemborne	Cnwll
77 G6	Treherbert	Carmth
42 E2	Treherbert	Rhondd
4 C5	Treheveras	Cnwll
6 C2	Trehunist	Cnwll
11 L6	Trekelland	Cnwll
11 L6	Trekenner	Cnwll
10 E5	Treknow	Cnwll
3 J7	Trelan	Cnwll
11 H4	Trelash	Cnwll
4 E4	Trelassick	Cnwll
5 L4	Trelawne	Cnwll
128 C4	Trelawnyd	Flints
3 K6	Treleague	Cnwll
3 K7	Treleaver	Cnwll
58 A3	Trelech	Carmth
58 B3	Trelech a'r Betws	Carmth
74 B6	Treleddyd-fawr	Pembks
3 K4	Trelew	Cnwll
43 H2	Trelewis	Myr Td
10 E5	Treligga	Cnwll
10 D6	Trelights	Cnwll
10 E7	Trelill	Cnwll
11 K6	Trelinnoe	Cnwll
4 F4	Trelion	Cnwll
3 L3	Trelissick	Cnwll
63 G6	Trelleck	Mons
62 F6	Trelleck Grange	Mons
128 D4	Trelogan	Flints
4 E6	Trelonk	Cnwll
4 F1	Trelow	Cnwll
3 J6	Trelowarren	Cnwll
6 B3	Trelowia	Cnwll
4 F4	Treluggan	Cnwll
95 G3	Trelystan	Powys
109 K3	Tremadog	Gwynd
11 H5	Tremail	Cnwll
75 M3	Tremain	Cerdgn
11 J5	Tremaine	Cnwll
6 B1	Tremar	Cnwll
6 D3	Trematon	Cnwll
6 B2	Trembraze	Cnwll
128 C5	Tremeirchion	Denbgs

2 C5	Tremethick Cross	Cnwll
11 K7	Tremollett	Cnwll
5 G2	Tremore	Cnwll
3 K6	Trenance	Cnwll
4 D1	Trenance	Cnwll
10 C8	Trenance	Cnwll
3 H7	Trenance	Cnwll
5 H5	Trenarren	Cnwll
11 K6	Trenault	Cnwll
96 F1	Trench	Wrekin
49 G3	Trench Green	Oxon
4 D3	Trencreek	Cnwll
11 H3	Trencreek	Cnwll
4 E4	Trendeal	Cnwll
2 D3	Trendrine	Cnwll
10 D8	Treneague	Cnwll
3 H5	Trenear	Cnwll
11 H5	Treneglos	Cnwll
2 F4	Trenerth	Cnwll
5 K4	Trenewan	Cnwll
10 F6	Trenewth	Cnwll
11 H4	Trengune	Cnwll
4 D3	Treninnick	Cnwll
4 C3	Trenowah	Cnwll
3 J4	Trenoweth	Cnwll
31 K7	Trent	Dorset
135 G3	Trent Port	Lincs
114 D3	Trent Vale	C Stke
114 D3	Trentham	C Stke
28 A1	Trentishoe	Devon
116 E5	Trentlock	Derbys
42 E6	Treoes	V Glam
42 E2	Treorchy	Rhondd
10 E7	Trequite	Cnwll
42 F6	Trerhyngyll	V Glam
6 C3	Trerulefoot	Cnwll
3 J5	Tresahor	Cnwll
4 E5	Tresawle	Cnwll
97 J4	Trescott	Staffs
2 F5	Trescowe	Cnwll
4 C3	Tresean	Cnwll
46 A1	Tresham	Gloucs
4 E5	Tresillian	Cnwll
10 F6	Tresinney	Cnwll
11 H3	Treskinnick Cross	Cnwll
5 K1	Treslea	Cnwll
11 J5	Tresmeer	Cnwll
11 G4	Tresparrett	Cnwll
232 B3	Tressait	P & K
281 d6	Tresta	Shet
281 f3	Tresta	Shet
134 F4	Treswell	Notts
3 G3	Treswithian	Cnwll
6 B2	Trethawle	Cnwll
10 F5	Trethevey	Cnwll
2 B6	Trethewey	Cnwll
43 J4	Trethomas	Caerph
4 F4	Trethosa	Cnwll
5 H4	Trethurgy	Cnwll
74 C6	Tretio	Pembks
63 G2	Tretire	Herefs
61 J3	Tretower	Powys
128 F8	Treuddyn	Flints
11 K6	Trevadlock	Cnwll
11 J6	Trevague	Cnwll
10 F4	Trevalga	Cnwll
129 J8	Trevalyn	Wrexhm
10 D7	Trevanger	Cnwll
10 D7	Trevanson	Cnwll
2 D5	Trevarrack	Cnwll
4 E3	Trevarren	Cnwll
4 D2	Trevarrian	Cnwll
5 G6	Trevarrick	Cnwll
3 J3	Trevarth	Cnwll
55 L4	Trevaughan	Carmth
2 D3	Treveal	Cnwll
4 C3	Treveal	Cnwll
4 E4	Treveale	Cnwll
10 F6	Treveighan	Cnwll
4 B4	Trevellas Downs	Cnwll
5 L2	Trevelmond	Cnwll
4 D3	Trevemper	Cnwll
2 E4	Treveneague	Cnwll
5 G6	Treveor	Cnwll
4 E5	Treverbyn	Cnwll
5 G3	Treverbyn	Cnwll
3 J5	Treverva	Cnwll
2 B6	Trevescan	Cnwll
62 B6	Trevethin	Torfn
10 F6	Trevia	Cnwll
6 C1	Trevigro	Cnwll
3 L3	Trevilla	Cnwll
4 E1	Trevilledor	Cnwll
4 D4	Trevilson	Cnwll
4 F4	Treviscoe	Cnwll

4 F6 **Treviskey** Cnwll
5 H5 **Trevissick** Cnwll
2 D5 **Trevithal** Cnwll
4 E2 **Trevithick** Cnwll
4 F6 **Trevithick** Cnwll
11 H5 **Trevivian** Cnwll
4 D3 **Trevoll** Cnwll
10 B7 **Trevone** Cnwll
112 C3 **Trevor** Denbgs
2 B6 **Trevorgans** Cnwll
10 B8 **Trevorrick** Cnwll
10 C7 **Trevorrick** Cnwll
10 B7 **Trevose** Cnwll
3 G5 **Trew** Cnwll
10 F6 **Trewalder** Cnwll
61 J1 **Trewalkin** Powys
11 L6 **Trewarlett** Cnwll
10 F5 **Trewarmett** Cnwll
4 E6 **Trewarthenick** Cnwll
11 G5 **Trewassa** Cnwll
2 F5 **Trewavas** Cnwll
11 J6 **Treween** Cnwll
2 B4 **Trewellard** Cnwll
11 J6 **Trewen** Cnwll
10 E7 **Trewen** Cnwll
3 H5 **Trewennack** Cnwll
55 G7 **Trewent** Pembks
95 G1 **Trewern** Powys
10 E6 **Trewetha** Cnwll
10 E7 **Trewethern** Cnwll
6 B3 **Trewidland** Cnwll
3 K7 **Trewillis** Cnwll
3 L4 **Trewince** Cnwll
11 G8 **Trewint** Cnwll
11 J6 **Trewint** Cnwll
6 B2 **Trewint** Cnwll
4 E6 **Trewirgie** Cnwll
3 M4 **Trewithian** Cnwll
11 L8 **Trewoodloe** Cnwll
2 C6 **Trewoofe** Cnwll
3 H7 **Trewoon** Cnwll
5 G4 **Trewoon** Cnwll
4 D5 **Treworgan** Cnwll
4 E7 **Treworlas** Cnwll
11 G4 **Treworld** Cnwll
3 M3 **Treworthal** Cnwll
10 B7 **Treyarnon** Cnwll
20 D3 **Treyford** W Susx
141 G3 **Triangle** Calder
17 L2 **Trickett's Cross** Dorset
178 E5 **Triermain** Cumb
75 G7 **Triffleton** Pembks
11 K4 **Trillacott** Cnwll
169 K4 **Trimdon** Dur
169 K4 **Trimdon Colliery** Dur
169 K3 **Trimdon Grange** Dur
122 F4 **Trimingham** Norfk
91 G7 **Trimley** Suffk
91 G7 **Trimley Lower Street** Suffk
97 H7 **Trimpley** Worcs
70 C4 **Trims Green** Herts
56 E4 **Trimsaran** Carmth
27 J2 **Trimstone** Devon
231 K3 **Trinafour** P & K
61 K7 **Trinant** Caerph
68 A5 **Tring** Herts
68 A4 **Tring Wharf** Herts
67 M4 **Tringford** Herts
234 F3 **Trinity** Angus
9 d2 **Trinity** Jersey
221 G3 **Trinity Gask** P & K
29 G3 **Triscombe** Somset
29 L4 **Triscombe** Somset
239 H8 **Trislaig** Highld
4 D5 **Trispen** Cnwll
191 J7 **Tritlington** Nthumb
4 E3 **Troan** Cnwll
232 E7 **Trochry** P & K
61 H6 **Troedrhiwfuwch** Caerph
76 B6 **Troedyraur** Cerdgn
61 G6 **Troedyrhiw** Myr Td
127 G5 **Trofarth** Conwy
9 c2 **Trois Bois** Jersey
3 G3 **Troon** Cnwll
196 C5 **Troon** S Ayrs
89 H1 **Troston** Suffk
11 J4 **Troswell** Cnwll
81 K4 **Trotshill** Worcs
52 D7 **Trottiscliffe** Kent
36 B6 **Trotton** W Susx
140 D3 **Trough Gate** Lancs
190 B7 **Troughend** Nthumb
165 L5 **Troutbeck** Cumb
156 F2 **Troutbeck** Cumb
156 F3 **Troutbeck Bridge** Cumb

133 H4 **Troway** Derbys
46 B7 **Trowbridge** Wilts
116 E3 **Trowell** Notts
46 B7 **Trowle Common** Wilts
106 E2 **Trowse Newton** Norfk
150 C8 **Troy** Leeds
32 C2 **Trudoxhill** Somset
30 B6 **Trull** Somset
142 F5 **Trumfleet** Donc
258 C4 **Trumpan** Highld
80 F7 **Trumpet** Herefs
87 J4 **Trumpington** Cambs
50 C5 **Trumpsgreen** Surrey
122 F4 **Trunch** Norfk
147 G7 **Trunnah** Lancs
4 D6 **Truro** Cnwll
11 K5 **Truscott** Cnwll
13 K6 **Trusham** Devon
115 L4 **Trusley** Derbys
137 K3 **Trusthorpe** Lincs
97 J4 **Trysull** Staffs
66 B7 **Tubney** Oxon
8 B4 **Tuckenhay** Devon
97 H5 **Tuckhill** Shrops
3 G3 **Tuckingmill** Cnwll
32 F5 **Tuckingmill** Wilts
18 A5 **Tuckton** Bmouth
4 F5 **Tucoyse** Cnwll
88 E1 **Tuddenham** Suffk
90 E5 **Tuddenham** Suffk
38 F4 **Tudeley** Kent
169 H3 **Tudhoe** Dur
63 H3 **Tudorville** Herefs
108 D4 **Tudweiliog** Gwynd
36 E3 **Tuesley** Surrey
64 B4 **Tuffley** Gloucs
34 F2 **Tufton** Hants
75 H6 **Tufton** Pembks
101 G3 **Tugby** Leics
96 D6 **Tugford** Shrops
203 K7 **Tughall** Nthumb
220 E8 **Tullibody** Clacks
251 H6 **Tullich** Highld
264 D4 **Tullich** Highld
232 F5 **Tulliemet** P & K
256 E5 **Tulloch** Abers
219 H3 **Tulloch** Stirlg
240 B7 **Tulloch Station** Highld
216 F8 **Tullochgorm** Ag & B
232 F8 **Tullybeagles Lodge** P & K
255 L7 **Tullynessle** Abers
51 J4 **Tulse Hill** Gt Lon
58 F6 **Tumble** Carmth
71 K2 **Tumbler's Green** Essex
136 D7 **Tumby** Lincs
136 E8 **Tumby Woodside** Lincs
231 L4 **Tummel Bridge** P & K
38 F5 **Tunbridge Wells** Kent
177 G3 **Tundergarth** D & G
122 F5 **Tungate** Norfk
45 K7 **Tunley** BaNES
114 D1 **Tunstall** C Stke
145 J2 **Tunstall** E R Yk
40 A3 **Tunstall** Kent
157 K8 **Tunstall** Lancs
160 B3 **Tunstall** N York
107 J2 **Tunstall** Norfk
114 B6 **Tunstall** Staffs
91 H4 **Tunstall** Suffk
181 J8 **Tunstall** Sundld
132 B5 **Tunstead** Derbys
122 F7 **Tunstead** Norfk
131 K4 **Tunstead Milton** Derbys
35 K1 **Tunworth** Hants
80 C7 **Tupsley** Herefs
100 F4 **Tur Langton** Leics
49 G7 **Turgis Green** Hants
65 G4 **Turkdean** Gloucs
46 A6 **Turleigh** Wilts
97 H6 **Turleygreen** Shrops
140 B4 **Turn** Lancs
79 L7 **Turnastone** Herefs
182 F2 **Turnberry** S Ayrs
6 F4 **Turnchapel** C Plym
116 A2 **Turnditch** Derbys
139 J2 **Turner Green** Lancs
23 L3 **Turner's Green** E Susx
82 E2 **Turner's Green** Warwks
38 A6 **Turner's Hill** W Susx
16 F4 **Turners Puddle** Dorset
69 K6 **Turnford** Herts
211 G4 **Turnhouse** C Edin
16 F1 **Turnworth** Dorset
268 C6 **Turriff** Abers
139 L4 **Turton Bottoms** Bl w D

103 G4 **Turves** Cambs
85 J5 **Turvey** Beds
49 J1 **Turville** Bucks
49 H1 **Turville Heath** Bucks
84 B7 **Turweston** Bucks
187 L3 **Tushielaw Inn** Border
113 H2 **Tushingham cum Grindley** Ches
115 L6 **Tutbury** Staffs
82 A1 **Tutnall** Worcs
63 G8 **Tutshill** Gloucs
122 E6 **Tuttington** Norfk
11 M7 **Tutwell** Cnwll
134 E5 **Tuxford** Notts
275 b3 **Twatt** Ork
281 d6 **Twatt** Shet
209 J4 **Twechar** E Duns
202 F3 **Tweedmouth** Nthumb
187 G1 **Tweedsmuir** Border
24 C3 **Twelve Oaks** E Susx
4 B6 **Twelveheads** Cnwll
130 F6 **Twemlow Green** Ches
118 F7 **Twenty** Lincs
45 L6 **Twerton** BaNES
50 F4 **Twickenham** Gt Lon
64 B3 **Twigworth** Gloucs
22 C3 **Twineham** W Susx
22 C3 **Twineham Green** W Susx
45 L7 **Twinhoe** BaNES
89 H7 **Twinstead** Essex
28 D5 **Twitchen** Devon
95 J7 **Twitchen** Shrops
41 H4 **Twitham** Kent
12 E7 **Two Bridges** Devon
132 E7 **Two Dales** Derbys
99 G3 **Two Gates** Staffs
8 C1 **Two Mile Oak Cross** Devon
27 J2 **Two Pots** Devon
68 D6 **Two Waters** Herts
99 J2 **Twycross** Leics
67 G2 **Twyford** Bucks
35 G6 **Twyford** Hants
100 F2 **Twyford** Leics
118 B6 **Twyford** Lincs
121 M6 **Twyford** Norfk
49 J4 **Twyford** Wokham
80 C8 **Twyford Common** Herefs
61 H5 **Twyn-carno** Caerph
62 E6 **Twyn-y-Sheriff** Mons
43 H7 **Twyn-yr-Odyn** V Glam
175 G4 **Twynholm** D & G
81 K8 **Twyning** Gloucs
81 L7 **Twyning Green** Gloucs
59 L4 **Twynllanan** Carmth
101 L7 **Twywell** Nhants
112 C3 **Ty'n-dwr** Denbgs
42 F4 **Ty'n-y-bryn** Rhondd
43 K7 **Ty'n-y-coedcae** Caerph
126 F5 **Ty'n-y-Groes** Conwy
111 J3 **Ty-nant** Conwy
111 H6 **Ty-nant** Gwynd
79 M7 **Tyberton** Herefs
98 E5 **Tyburn** Birm
57 H3 **Tycroes** Carmth
111 L7 **Tycrwyn** Powys
120 A7 **Tydd Gote** Lincs
119 M8 **Tydd St Giles** Cambs
119 M7 **Tydd St Mary** Lincs
20 B6 **Tye** Hants
70 D2 **Tye Green** Essex
88 B8 **Tye Green** Essex
71 J3 **Tye Green** Essex
141 J1 **Tyersal** Brad
139 K7 **Tyldesley** Wigan
40 F3 **Tyler Hill** Kent
70 D6 **Tyler's Green** Essex
67 L8 **Tylers Green** Bucks
51 K8 **Tylers Green** Surrey
42 F3 **Tylorstown** Rhondd
93 L7 **Tylwch** Powys
43 G4 **Tyn-y-nant** Rhondd
218 E1 **Tyndrum** Stirlg
181 J5 **Tynemouth** N Tyne
60 E7 **Tynewydd** Rhondd
212 D3 **Tyninghame** E Loth
185 K4 **Tynron** D & G
125 J3 **Tynygongl** IOA
77 J1 **Tynygraig** Cerdgn
85 G6 **Tyringham** M Keyn
98 E6 **Tyseley** Birm
42 C6 **Tythegston** Brdgnd
131 H4 **Tytherington** Ches
45 K1 **Tytherington** S Glos
32 C2 **Tytherington** Somset
32 F3 **Tytherington** Wilts

15 H2 **Tytherleigh** Devon
46 D4 **Tytherton Lucas** Wilts
5 J4 **Tywardreath** Cnwll
5 J4 **Tywardreath Highway** Cnwll
126 F4 **Tywyn** Conwy
92 C3 **Tywyn** Gwynd

U

91 H1 **Ubbeston Green** Suffk
45 G7 **Ubley** BaNES
160 C2 **Uckerby** N York
23 H3 **Uckfield** E Susx
81 K7 **Uckinghall** Worcs
64 C2 **Uckington** Gloucs
96 D2 **Uckington** Shrops
209 J6 **Uddington** S Lans
198 E6 **Uddington** S Lans
24 F3 **Udimore** E Susx
256 F6 **Udny Green** Abers
257 G6 **Udny Station** Abers
47 H3 **Uffcott** Wilts
29 K8 **Uffculme** Devon
102 B2 **Uffington** Lincs
47 L1 **Uffington** Oxon
96 C1 **Uffington** Shrops
102 B3 **Ufford** C Pete
91 G5 **Ufford** Suffk
83 J3 **Ufton** Warwks
48 F5 **Ufton Nervet** W Berk
194 B5 **Ugadale** Ag & B
7 K4 **Ugborough** Devon
107 J7 **Uggeshall** Suffk
162 F1 **Ugglebarnby** N York
132 E2 **Ughill** Sheff
70 D2 **Ugley** Essex
70 D2 **Ugley Green** Essex
171 J8 **Ugthorpe** N York
224 F4 **Uig** Ag & B
258 B6 **Uig** Highld
258 F4 **Uig** Highld
282 d3 **Uig** W Isls
259 G7 **Uigshader** Highld
226 D8 **Uisken** Ag & B
280 D7 **Ulbster** Highld
165 L6 **Ulcat Row** Cumb
137 H5 **Ulceby** Lincs
144 E5 **Ulceby** N Linc
137 H5 **Ulceby Cross** Lincs
144 E5 **Ulceby Skitter** N Linc
39 L4 **Ulcombe** Kent
165 H3 **Uldale** Cumb
63 M7 **Uley** Gloucs
191 J7 **Ulgham** Nthumb
261 J1 **Ullapool** Highld
82 D2 **Ullenhall** Warwks
64 D4 **Ullenwood** Gloucs
151 H7 **Ulleskelf** N York
100 B6 **Ullesthorpe** Leics
133 J2 **Ulley** Rothm
80 E5 **Ullingswick** Herefs
246 D1 **Ullinish Lodge Hotel** Highld
164 E6 **Ullock** Cumb
156 B4 **Ulpha** Cumb
157 G6 **Ulpha** Cumb
153 J4 **Ulrome** E R Yk
281 e4 **Ulsta** Shet
71 K5 **Ulting Wick** Essex
98 E7 **Ulverley Green** Solhll
156 C7 **Ulverston** Cumb
17 K6 **Ulwell** Dorset
259 K6 **Umachan** Highld
27 L6 **Umberleigh** Devon
271 H2 **Unapool** Highld
178 B2 **Under Burnmouth** Border
38 E3 **Under River** Kent
157 G4 **Underbarrow** Cumb
141 J1 **Undercliffe** Brad
96 B1 **Underdale** Shrops
157 K6 **Underley Hall** Cumb
39 J4 **Underling Green** Kent
116 D2 **Underwood** Notts
104 D7 **Undley** Suffk
44 E2 **Undy** Mons
154 e6 **Union Mills** IOM
39 H7 **Union Street** E Susx
133 G4 **Unstone** Derbys
133 G4 **Unstone Green** Derbys
140 B6 **Unsworth** Bury
165 L1 **Unthank** Cumb
166 B3 **Unthank** Cumb
166 E3 **Unthank** Cumb

132 F4 **Unthank** Derbys
202 F3 **Unthank** Nthumb
166 B4 **Unthank End** Cumb
16 C2 **Up Cerne** Dorset
13 L2 **Up Exe** Devon
139 G6 **Up Holland** Lancs
20 C4 **Up Marden** W Susx
31 J7 **Up Mudford** Somset
49 G8 **Up Nately** Hants
34 E4 **Up Somborne** Hants
16 B2 **Up Sydling** Dorset
47 H7 **Upavon** Wilts
53 H5 **Upchurch** Kent
27 K3 **Upcott** Devon
28 D5 **Upcott** Devon
79 K5 **Upcott** Herefs
28 F6 **Upcott** Somset
50 B6 **Updown Hill** Surrey
88 D3 **Upend** Cambs
122 C7 **Upgate** Norfk
106 B5 **Upgate Street** Norfk
106 F5 **Upgate Street** Norfk
16 A2 **Uphall** Dorset
210 E4 **Uphall** W Loth
13 K1 **Upham** Devon
35 H6 **Upham** Hants
79 M3 **Uphampton** Herefs
81 J2 **Uphampton** Worcs
44 C7 **Uphill** N Som
208 D8 **Uplawmoor** E Rens
63 L2 **Upleadon** Gloucs
170 E6 **Upleatham** R & Cl
40 C2 **Uplees** Kent
15 L4 **Uploders** Dorset
29 J7 **Uplowman** Devon
15 H4 **Uplyme** Devon
52 C2 **Upminster** Gt Lon
14 E1 **Upottery** Devon
12 B6 **Uppaton** Devon
86 C8 **Upper & Lower Stondon** Beds
95 K6 **Upper Affcot** Shrops
263 G2 **Upper Ardchronie** Highld
97 H7 **Upper Arley** Worcs
66 F4 **Upper Arncott** Oxon
83 L7 **Upper Astrop** Nhants
48 F4 **Upper Basildon** W Berk
141 K3 **Upper Batley** Kirk
22 B5 **Upper Beeding** W Susx
101 L5 **Upper Benefield** Nhants
82 B2 **Upper Bentley** Worcs
278 F5 **Upper Bighouse** Highld
133 J8 **Upper Birchwood** Derbys
43 H4 **Upper Boat** Rhondd
83 L5 **Upper Boddington** Nhants
92 D5 **Upper Borth** Cerdgn
83 G7 **Upper Brailes** Warwks
247 L4 **Upper Breakish** Highld
80 B7 **Upper Breinton** Herefs
81 J4 **Upper Broadheath** Worcs
117 J6 **Upper Broughton** Notts
48 D5 **Upper Bucklebury** W Berk
33 K7 **Upper Burgate** Hants
52 E5 **Upper Bush** Medway
86 D6 **Upper Caldecote** Beds
44 D7 **Upper Canada** N Som
18 D1 **Upper Canterton** Hants
83 M3 **Upper Catesby** Nhants
98 B8 **Upper Catshill** Worcs
78 D7 **Upper Chapel** Powys
30 C5 **Upper Cheddon** Somset
33 G5 **Upper Chicksgrove** Wilts
47 L8 **Upper Chute** Wilts
51 K2 **Upper Clapton** Gt Lon
34 D2 **Upper Clatford** Hants
109 H2 **Upper Clynnog** Gwynd
64 E4 **Upper Coberley** Gloucs
21 K6 **Upper Cokeham** W Susx
115 G2 **Upper Cotton** Staffs
96 C2 **Upper Cound** Shrops
142 B5 **Upper Cudworth** Barns
141 K6 **Upper Cumberworth** Kirk
59 L6 **Upper Cwmtwrch** Powys
267 G4 **Upper Dallachy** Moray
41 K5 **Upper Deal** Kent
85 L2 **Upper Dean** Beds
141 K6 **Upper Denby** Kirk
178 E5 **Upper Denton** Cumb
23 J5 **Upper Dicker** E Susx
95 L6 **Upper Dinchope** Shrops
279 H3 **Upper Dounreay** Highld
73 K1 **Upper Dovercourt** Essex
219 L6 **Upper Drumbane** Stirlg
150 F3 **Upper Dunsforth** N York
36 E2 **Upper Eashing** Surrey

263 K7 **Upper Eathie** Highld
80 E6 **Upper Egleton** Herefs
131 L7 **Upper Elkstone** Staffs
115 J3 **Upper Ellastone** Staffs
132 B4 **Upper End** Derbys
34 E1 **Upper Enham** Hants
97 H5 **Upper Farmcote** Shrops
35 L4 **Upper Farringdon** Hants
63 L5 **Upper Framilode** Gloucs
35 M2 **Upper Froyle** Hants
31 H2 **Upper Godney** Somset
86 C8 **Upper Gravenhurst** Beds
88 B8 **Upper Green** Essex
62 D3 **Upper Green** Mons
88 E2 **Upper Green** Suffk
48 A6 **Upper Green** W Berk
63 H2 **Upper Grove Common** Herefs
132 F7 **Upper Hackney** Derbys
36 B1 **Upper Hale** Surrey
50 E5 **Upper Halliford** Surrey
52 E6 **Upper Halling** Medway
101 K2 **Upper Hambleton** Rutlnd
40 F4 **Upper Harbledown** Kent
40 F5 **Upper Hardres Court** Kent
79 M4 **Upper Hardwick** Herefs
38 C6 **Upper Hartfield** E Susx
116 C2 **Upper Hartshay** Derbys
64 D3 **Upper Hatherley** Gloucs
114 C4 **Upper Hatton** Staffs
142 C8 **Upper Haugh** Rothm
96 C7 **Upper Hayton** Shrops
141 J4 **Upper Heaton** Kirk
151 L4 **Upper Helmsley** N York
79 J4 **Upper Hergest** Herefs
84 C3 **Upper Heyford** Nhants
66 D2 **Upper Heyford** Oxon
80 B4 **Upper Hill** Herefs
52 B5 **Upper Hockenden** Kent
141 K4 **Upper Hopton** Kirk
81 H5 **Upper Howsell** Worcs
131 K7 **Upper Hulme** Staffs
36 F4 **Upper Ifold** Surrey
65 J7 **Upper Inglesham** Swindn
46 A1 **Upper Kilcott** Gloucs
57 G6 **Upper Killay** Swans
217 J2 **Upper Kinchrackine** Ag & B
47 L3 **Upper Lambourn** W Berk
98 C2 **Upper Landywood** Staffs
44 F7 **Upper Langford** N Som
133 K6 **Upper Langwith** Derbys
223 G6 **Upper Largo** Fife
115 G4 **Upper Leigh** Staffs
63 L4 **Upper Ley** Gloucs
45 H6 **Upper Littleton** N Som
115 H8 **Upper Longdon** Staffs
97 H4 **Upper Ludstone** Shrops
275 H1 **Upper Lybster** Highld
63 J4 **Upper Lydbrook** Gloucs
80 C6 **Upper Lyde** Herefs
79 M2 **Upper Lye** Herefs
79 L8 **Upper Maes-coed** Herefs
141 K7 **Upper Midhope** Sheff
81 J1 **Upper Milton** Worcs
46 E1 **Upper Minety** Wilts
82 A5 **Upper Moor** Worcs
141 K2 **Upper Moor Side** Leeds
267 G6 **Upper Mulben** Moray
96 E5 **Upper Netchwood** Shrops
115 G4 **Upper Nobut** Staffs
20 F3 **Upper Norwood** W Susx
132 E4 **Upper Padley** Derbys
18 D4 **Upper Pennington** Hants
67 H4 **Upper Pollicott** Bucks
151 J5 **Upper Poppleton** York
82 E6 **Upper Quinton** Warwks
34 D6 **Upper Ratley** Hants
80 E2 **Upper Rochford** Worcs
174 E3 **Upper Ruscoe** D & G
80 F3 **Upper Sapey** Herefs
46 D3 **Upper Seagry** Wilts
85 K6 **Upper Shelton** Beds
122 C3 **Upper Sheringham** Norfk
83 L3 **Upper Shuckburgh** Warwks
207 K5 **Upper Skelmorlie** N Ayrs
65 H3 **Upper Slaughter** Gloucs
63 K5 **Upper Soudley** Gloucs
79 K4 **Upper Spond** Herefs
41 H7 **Upper Standen** Kent
86 C3 **Upper Staploe** Beds
185 L6 **Upper Stepford** D & G
106 E3 **Upper Stoke** Norfk
84 C4 **Upper Stowe** Nhants
33 K7 **Upper Street** Hants
123 G7 **Upper Street** Norfk
123 G8 **Upper Street** Norfk

106 D7 **Upper Street** Norfk
88 F5 **Upper Street** Suffk
90 C5 **Upper Street** Suffk
90 D8 **Upper Street** Suffk
81 K7 **Upper Strensham** Worcs
68 D2 **Upper Sundon** Beds
65 H2 **Upper Swell** Gloucs
142 A7 **Upper Tankersley** Barns
106 E4 **Upper Tasburgh** Norfk
115 G4 **Upper Tean** Staffs
113 G3 **Upper Threapwood** Ches
115 L1 **Upper Town** Derbys
132 E7 **Upper Town** Derbys
168 D3 **Upper Town** Dur
80 D5 **Upper Town** Herefs
45 G6 **Upper Town** N Som
89 J2 **Upper Town** Suffk
59 G6 **Upper Tumble** Carmth
83 H6 **Upper Tysoe** Warwks
91 G4 **Upper Ufford** Suffk
47 J3 **Upper Upham** Wilts
53 G5 **Upper Upnor** Medway
234 E8 **Upper Victoria** Angus
32 B1 **Upper Vobster** Somset
83 L6 **Upper Wardington** Oxon
84 F7 **Upper Weald** M Keyn
84 B3 **Upper Weedon** Nhants
23 G4 **Upper Wellingham** E Susx
45 L5 **Upper Weston** BaNES
106 E7 **Upper Weybread** Suffk
81 J5 **Upper Wick** Worcs
35 K3 **Upper Wield** Hants
67 H4 **Upper Winchendon** Bucks
33 K3 **Upper Woodford** Wilts
48 E7 **Upper Wootton** Hants
46 A4 **Upper Wraxall** Wilts
81 H6 **Upper Wyche** Worcs
177 L8 **Upperby** Cumb
258 E6 **Upperglen** Highld
140 F6 **Uppermill** Oldham
141 H6 **Upperthong** Kirk
133 J4 **Upperthorpe** Derbys
143 J7 **Upperthorpe** N Linc
36 E6 **Upperton** W Susx
132 F6 **Uppertown** Derbys
280 D1 **Uppertown** Highld
64 F7 **Upperup** Gloucs
132 F8 **Upperwood** Derbys
13 L1 **Uppincott** Devon
101 J3 **Uppingham** Rutlnd
17 K1 **Uppington** Dorset
96 D2 **Uppington** Shrops
161 G5 **Upsall** N York
202 D4 **Upsettlington** Border
69 L7 **Upshire** Essex
41 H3 **Upstreet** Kent
89 K1 **Upthorpe** Suffk
67 J5 **Upton** Bucks
102 C3 **Upton** C Pete
102 D7 **Upton** Cambs
129 J6 **Upton** Ches
11 H2 **Upton** Cnwll
11 K8 **Upton** Cnwll
165 K3 **Upton** Cumb
14 C2 **Upton** Devon
7 K6 **Upton** Devon
16 E6 **Upton** Dorset
17 J4 **Upton** Dorset
153 J5 **Upton** E R Yk
129 L2 **Upton** Halton
47 M7 **Upton** Hants
34 E7 **Upton** Hants
99 K3 **Upton** Leics
135 H2 **Upton** Lincs
84 D3 **Upton** Nhants
107 H1 **Upton** Norfk
117 J1 **Upton** Notts
134 E4 **Upton** Notts
65 K4 **Upton** Oxon
48 D2 **Upton** Oxon
55 G6 **Upton** Pembks
50 B3 **Upton** Slough
29 H5 **Upton** Somset
31 G5 **Upton** Somset
142 D5 **Upton** Wakefd
82 D4 **Upton** Warwks
32 E4 **Upton** Wilts
129 G2 **Upton** Wirral
63 K2 **Upton Bishop** Herefs
45 K5 **Upton Cheyney** S Glos
96 E5 **Upton Cressett** Shrops
63 J2 **Upton Crews** Herefs
11 K8 **Upton Cross** Cnwll
86 C8 **Upton End** Beds
35 L1 **Upton Grey** Hants

129 K5 **Upton Heath** Ches
13 K2 **Upton Hellions** Devon
32 F3 **Upton Lovell** Wilts
96 C1 **Upton Magna** Shrops
32 B3 **Upton Noble** Somset
13 L3 **Upton Pyne** Devon
32 E1 **Upton Scudamore** Wilts
81 L4 **Upton Snodsbury** Worcs
64 B4 **Upton St Leonards** Gloucs
2 F3 **Upton Towans** Cnwll
81 K7 **Upton upon Severn** Worcs
81 L2 **Upton Warren** Worcs
20 F4 **Upwaltham** W Susx
87 L1 **Upware** Cambs
103 K3 **Upwell** Norfk
16 C5 **Upwey** Dorset
70 C2 **Upwick Green** Herts
102 E6 **Upwood** Cambs
46 F7 **Urchfont** Wilts
80 C5 **Urdimarsh** Herefs
150 D1 **Ure Bank** N York
169 L7 **Urlay Nook** S on T
130 E1 **Urmston** Traffd
266 F4 **Urquhart** Moray
161 J2 **Urra** N York
250 E1 **Urray** Highld
235 H4 **Usan** Angus
169 G2 **Ushaw Moor** Dur
62 D7 **Usk** Mons
136 A1 **Usselby** Lincs
181 H7 **Usworth** Sundld
130 A6 **Utkinton** Ches
149 J7 **Utley** Brad
13 J3 **Uton** Devon
136 F1 **Utterby** Lincs
115 H5 **Uttoxeter** Staffs
108 B6 **Uwchmynydd** Gwynd
50 D2 **Uxbridge** Gt Lon
281 F2 **Uyeasound** Shet
54 F4 **Uzmaston** Pembks

V

9 k2 **Vale** Guern
124 E4 **Valley** IOA
50 B6 **Valley End** Surrey
10 F6 **Valley Truckle** Cnwll
259 J4 **Valtos** Highld
282 e3 **Valtos** W Isls
43 J4 **Van** Caerph
52 F2 **Vange** Essex
61 L6 **Varteg** Torfn
281 e3 **Vatsetter** Shet
258 D7 **Vatten** Highld
61 G5 **Vaynor** Myr Td
9 i2 **Vazon Bay** Guern
79 H7 **Velindre** Powys
29 K3 **Vellow** Somset
26 E6 **Velly** Devon
11 K1 **Venn** Cnwll
8 C5 **Venn** Devon
14 C4 **Venn Ottery** Devon
26 F8 **Venngreen** Devon
95 H2 **Vennington** Shrops
13 J3 **Venny Tedburn** Devon
11 L7 **Venterdon** Cnwll
19 J8 **Ventnor** IOW
7 H3 **Venton** Devon
47 M7 **Vernham Dean** Hants
47 M7 **Vernham Street** Hants
95 L7 **Vernolds Common** Shrops
17 L1 **Verwood** Dorset
4 E7 **Veryan** Cnwll
4 F6 **Veryan Green** Cnwll
146 C2 **Vickerstown** Cumb
141 J6 **Victoria** Barns
61 J5 **Victoria** Blae G
5 G3 **Victoria** Cnwll
281 e5 **Vidlin** Shet
266 F3 **Viewfield** Moray
209 J6 **Viewpark** N Lans
52 D6 **Vigo** Kent
9 a1 **Ville la Bas** Jersey
9 i3 **Villiaze** Guern
24 D3 **Vinehall Street** E Susx
23 K4 **Vines Cross** E Susx
50 C5 **Virginia Water** Surrey
11 M4 **Virginstow** Devon
72 D4 **Virley** Essex
32 B1 **Vobster** Somset
281 d5 **Voe** Shet
79 L7 **Vowchurch** Herefs
130 B1 **Vulcan Village** St Hel

Wackerfield - Waterhouses 363

W

168 F6 **Wackerfield** Dur
106 D5 **Wacton** Norfk
81 K5 **Wadborough** Worcs
67 H4 **Waddesdon** Bucks
8 C3 **Waddeton** Devon
138 E7 **Waddicar** Sefton
144 B8 **Waddingham** Lincs
148 C7 **Waddington** Lancs
135 K6 **Waddington** Lincs
13 K6 **Waddon** Devon
16 B5 **Waddon** Dorset
10 D8 **Wadebridge** Cnwll
30 D8 **Wadeford** Somset
101 M6 **Wadenhoe** Nhants
69 K4 **Wadesmill** Herts
39 G7 **Wadhurst** E Susx
132 F5 **Wadshelf** Derbys
46 B5 **Wadswick** Wilts
142 F8 **Wadworth** Donc
127 K7 **Waen** Denbgs
128 D6 **Waen** Denbgs
112 C7 **Waen** Powys
112 B8 **Waen Fach** Powys
125 K6 **Waen-pentir** Gwynd
125 K6 **Waen-wen** Gwynd
95 J3 **Wagbeach** Shrops
44 E5 **Wain's Hill** N Som
62 B6 **Wainfelin** Torfn
137 J7 **Wainfleet All Saints** Lincs
137 J7 **Wainfleet Bank** Lincs
107 G5 **Wainford** Norfk
11 H3 **Wainhouse Corner** Cnwll
52 F5 **Wainscott** Medway
141 G2 **Wainstalls** Calder
158 C1 **Waitby** Cumb
145 H7 **Waithe** Lincs
98 E6 **Wake Green** Birm
142 A4 **Wakefield** Wakefd
101 L3 **Wakerley** Nhants
72 C2 **Wakes Colne** Essex
128 E4 **Wal-wen** Flints
107 K8 **Walberswick** Suffk
21 G5 **Walberton** W Susx
180 E5 **Walbottle** N u Ty
175 J1 **Walbutt** D & G
178 B6 **Walby** Cumb
31 J2 **Walcombe** Somset
118 E4 **Walcot** Lincs
143 M3 **Walcot** N Linc
96 D1 **Walcot** Shrops
95 J6 **Walcot** Shrops
47 H2 **Walcot** Swindn
82 D4 **Walcot** Warwks
106 C7 **Walcot Green** Norfk
100 C6 **Walcote** Leics
136 B8 **Walcott** Lincs
123 G5 **Walcott** Norfk
159 H6 **Walden** N York
159 H6 **Walden Head** N York
142 E4 **Walden Stubbs** N York
53 G6 **Walderslade** Medway
20 C5 **Walderton** W Susx
15 L4 **Walditch** Dorset
115 J4 **Waldley** Derbys
169 H1 **Waldridge** Dur
91 G6 **Waldringfield** Suffk
23 J3 **Waldron** E Susx
133 J3 **Wales** Rothm
31 K6 **Wales** Somset
136 B1 **Walesby** Lincs
134 D5 **Walesby** Notts
79 M1 **Walford** Herefs
63 H3 **Walford** Herefs
113 G7 **Walford** Shrops
114 C5 **Walford** Staffs
113 G7 **Walford Heath** Shrops
113 M2 **Walgherton** Ches
84 F1 **Walgrave** Nhants
18 E4 **Walhampton** Hants
140 C2 **Walk Mill** Lancs
139 L7 **Walkden** Salfd
181 H6 **Walker** N u Ty
148 B7 **Walker Fold** Lancs
80 C5 **Walker's Green** Herefs
98 D7 **Walker's Heath** Birm
200 D5 **Walkerburn** Border
134 F1 **Walkeringham** Notts
134 F1 **Walkerith** Lincs
69 H2 **Walkern** Herts
222 C7 **Walkerton** Fife
18 C5 **Walkford** Dorset
7 G1 **Walkhampton** Devon
152 F8 **Walkington** E R Yk
133 G2 **Walkley** Sheff
82 B2 **Walkwood** Worcs
2 F4 **Wall** Cnwll
179 L5 **Wall** Nthumb
98 E2 **Wall** Staffs
156 B6 **Wall End** Cumb
80 B4 **Wall End** Herefs
97 K5 **Wall Heath** Dudley
180 C5 **Wall Houses** Nthumb
96 C5 **Wall under Haywood** Shrops
183 H2 **Wallacetown** S Ayrs
196 C6 **Wallacetown** S Ayrs
22 F5 **Wallands Park** E Susx
129 G1 **Wallasey** Wirral
53 J4 **Wallend** Medway
80 F7 **Waller's Green** Herefs
178 B6 **Wallhead** Cumb
48 F1 **Wallingford** Oxon
51 H6 **Wallington** Gt Lon
19 K2 **Wallington** Hants
86 F8 **Wallington** Herts
98 C3 **Wallington Heath** Wsall
75 G7 **Wallis** Pembks
17 L4 **Wallisdown** Poole
37 H3 **Walliswood** W Susx
281 c6 **Walls** Shet
181 H5 **Wallsend** N Tyne
165 K5 **Wallthwaite** Cumb
211 L4 **Wallyford** E Loth
41 L5 **Walmer** Kent
138 F3 **Walmer Bridge** Lancs
140 B5 **Walmersley** Bury
41 H3 **Walmestone** Kent
98 F5 **Walmley** Birm
98 F5 **Walmley Ash** Birm
137 G4 **Walmsgate** Lincs
30 D3 **Walpole** Somset
107 H8 **Walpole** Suffk
120 B7 **Walpole Cross Keys** Norfk
120 B8 **Walpole Highway** Norfk
120 B8 **Walpole St Andrew** Norfk
120 B8 **Walpole St Peter** Norfk
30 E2 **Walrow** Somset
98 C4 **Walsall** Wsall
98 D3 **Walsall Wood** Wsall
140 D3 **Walsden** Calder
99 K7 **Walsgrave on Sowe** Covtry
89 K1 **Walsham le Willows** Suffk
140 A5 **Walshaw** Bury
140 E2 **Walshaw** Calder
150 F5 **Walshford** N York
103 K1 **Walsoken** Norfk
199 H4 **Walston** S Lans
69 G1 **Walsworth** Herts
67 K7 **Walter's Ash** Bucks
38 D5 **Walters Green** Kent
43 G7 **Walterston** V Glam
62 D2 **Walterstone** Herefs
40 E5 **Waltham** Kent
145 H7 **Waltham** NE Lin
69 K7 **Waltham Abbey** Essex
35 H7 **Waltham Chase** Hants
69 K7 **Waltham Cross** Herts
117 L6 **Waltham on the Wolds** Leics
49 K4 **Waltham St Lawrence** W & M
71 G1 **Waltham's Cross** Essex
102 D3 **Walton** C Pete
178 C6 **Walton** Cumb
133 G6 **Walton** Derbys
150 F6 **Walton** Leeds
100 D6 **Walton** Leics
85 H7 **Walton** M Keyn
79 J3 **Walton** Powys
95 L7 **Walton** Shrops
31 G4 **Walton** Somset
114 D6 **Walton** Staffs
114 D5 **Walton** Staffs
91 G8 **Walton** Suffk
20 D6 **Walton** W Susx
142 A4 **Walton** Wakefd
83 G4 **Walton** Warwks
113 K7 **Walton** Wrekin
64 C1 **Walton Cardiff** Gloucs
55 H2 **Walton East** Pembks
32 C7 **Walton Elm** Dorset
83 L8 **Walton Grounds** Nhants
51 G7 **Walton on the Hill** Surrey
73 K3 **Walton on the Naze** Essex
117 G7 **Walton on the Wolds** Leics
44 E4 **Walton Park** N Som
54 D4 **Walton West** Pembks
44 E4 **Walton-in-Gordano** N Som
139 H2 **Walton-le-Dale** Lancs
50 E5 **Walton-on-Thames** Surrey
114 F7 **Walton-on-the-Hill** Staffs
115 L7 **Walton-on-Trent** Derbys
128 D4 **Walwen** Flints
128 E5 **Walwen** Flints
179 L5 **Walwick** Nthumb
169 G7 **Walworth** Darltn
51 J3 **Walworth** Gt Lon
169 G6 **Walworth Gate** Darltn
54 E4 **Walwyn's Castle** Pembks
15 G1 **Wambrook** Somset
177 H7 **Wampool** Cumb
36 D1 **Wanborough** Surrey
47 J2 **Wanborough** Swindn
68 E3 **Wandon End** Herts
51 H4 **Wandsworth** Gt Lon
107 J7 **Wangford** Suffk
100 D1 **Wanlip** Leics
186 C4 **Wanlockhead** D & G
23 K6 **Wannock** E Susx
102 B4 **Wansford** C Pete
153 G4 **Wansford** E R Yk
39 J4 **Wanshurst Green** Kent
51 L1 **Wanstead** Gt Lon
32 B3 **Wanstrow** Somset
63 K6 **Wanswell** Gloucs
48 B1 **Wantage** Oxon
81 H4 **Wants Green** Worcs
45 L3 **Wapley** S Glos
83 J2 **Wappenbury** Warwks
84 C6 **Wappenham** Nhants
23 K4 **Warbleton** E Susx
66 F8 **Warborough** Oxon
102 F7 **Warboys** Cambs
146 F8 **Warbreck** Bpool
11 H4 **Warbstow** Cnwll
130 D2 **Warburton** Traffd
167 H7 **Warcop** Cumb
98 E5 **Ward End** Birm
90 B2 **Ward Green** Suffk
53 M5 **Warden** Kent
179 L5 **Warden** Nthumb
169 K1 **Warden Law** Sundld
86 C6 **Warden Street** Beds
85 L8 **Wardhedges** Beds
83 L6 **Wardington** Oxon
130 B8 **Wardle** Ches
140 D4 **Wardle** Rochdl
181 H6 **Wardley** Gatesd
101 H3 **Wardley** Rutlnd
140 A7 **Wardley** Salfd
132 D5 **Wardlow** Derbys
131 J3 **Wardsend** Ches
103 K7 **Wardy Hill** Cambs
69 K4 **Ware** Herts
39 K2 **Ware Street** Kent
17 H5 **Wareham** Dorset
25 J1 **Warehorne** Kent
203 J6 **Waren Mill** Nthumb
203 J7 **Warenford** Nthumb
203 H7 **Warenton** Nthumb
69 K4 **Wareside** Herts
86 E4 **Waresley** Cambs
81 J1 **Waresley** Worcs
49 L4 **Warfield** Br For
8 C5 **Warfleet** Devon
119 H5 **Wargate** Lincs
49 J3 **Wargrave** Wokham
80 B7 **Warham** Herefs
121 L3 **Warham All Saints** Norfk
121 L3 **Warham St Mary** Norfk
202 C5 **Wark** Nthumb
179 K3 **Wark** Nthumb
27 M6 **Warkleigh** Devon
101 K7 **Warkton** Nhants
83 L7 **Warkworth** Nhants
191 K5 **Warkworth** Nthumb
160 E4 **Warlaby** N York
140 E4 **Warland** Calder
5 K1 **Warleggan** Cnwll
46 A6 **Warleigh** BaNES
141 G3 **Warley Town** Calder
51 K7 **Warlingham** Surrey
177 G5 **Warmanbie** D & G
115 M1 **Warmbrook** Derbys
142 B4 **Warmfield** Wakefd
130 D7 **Warmingham** Ches
102 B5 **Warmington** Nhants
83 K5 **Warmington** Warwks
32 E2 **Warminster** Wilts
45 K4 **Warmley** S Glos
142 E7 **Warmsworth** Donc
16 E5 **Warmwell** Dorset
81 K4 **Warndon** Worcs
35 J6 **Warnford** Hants
37 J4 **Warnham** W Susx
37 J4 **Warnham Court** W Susx
21 H5 **Warningcamp** W Susx
37 K5 **Warninglid** W Susx
131 H5 **Warren** Ches
54 F7 **Warren** Pembks
49 K3 **Warren Row** W & M
40 B5 **Warren Street** Kent
69 H2 **Warren's Green** Herts
170 D5 **Warrenby** R & Cl
198 F5 **Warrenhill** S Lans
85 H4 **Warrington** M Keyn
130 B2 **Warrington** Warrtn
211 H4 **Warriston** C Edin
19 H2 **Warsash** Hants
132 B7 **Warslow** Staffs
133 L6 **Warsop** Notts
133 L6 **Warsop Vale** Notts
152 D5 **Warter** E R Yk
152 C6 **Warter Priory** E R Yk
160 B6 **Warthermaske** N York
151 L5 **Warthill** N York
24 B5 **Wartling** E Susx
117 J7 **Wartnaby** Leics
138 E2 **Warton** Lancs
147 K2 **Warton** Lancs
190 E5 **Warton** Nthumb
99 H3 **Warton** Warwks
178 B7 **Warwick** Cumb
83 G2 **Warwick** Warwks
178 B7 **Warwick Bridge** Cumb
178 B3 **Warwicksland** Cumb
275 c3 **Wasbister** Ork
156 B1 **Wasdale Head** Cumb
131 L3 **Wash** Derbys
7 M2 **Wash** Devon
70 C1 **Washall Green** Herts
5 H1 **Washaway** Cnwll
8 B4 **Washbourne** Devon
30 F1 **Washbrook** Somset
90 D6 **Washbrook** Suffk
29 G7 **Washfield** Devon
159 J2 **Washfold** N York
29 J3 **Washford** Somset
28 E8 **Washford Pyne** Devon
135 L5 **Washingborough** Lincs
181 H7 **Washington** Sundld
21 J4 **Washington** W Susx
98 E5 **Washwood Heath** Birm
48 E6 **Wasing** W Berk
168 D2 **Waskerley** Dur
83 G3 **Wasperton** Warwks
135 M6 **Wasps Nest** Lincs
161 J6 **Wass** N York
29 K2 **Watchet** Somset
47 K1 **Watchfield** Oxon
30 E2 **Watchfield** Somset
157 H3 **Watchgate** Cumb
165 G2 **Watchill** Cumb
8 D2 **Watcombe** Torbay
165 J7 **Watendlath** Cumb
13 H6 **Water** Devon
140 C3 **Water** Lancs
66 D5 **Water Eaton** Oxon
97 K1 **Water Eaton** Staffs
85 L7 **Water End** Beds
86 C5 **Water End** Beds
86 C5 **Water End** Beds
152 B8 **Water End** E R Yk
88 B7 **Water End** Essex
68 D5 **Water End** Herts
69 G6 **Water End** Herts
142 D2 **Water Fryston** Wakefd
102 C4 **Water Newton** Cambs
98 F5 **Water Orton** Warwks
84 C8 **Water Stratford** Bucks
42 B5 **Water Street** Neath
156 D5 **Water Yeat** Cumb
139 K6 **Water's Nook** Bolton
87 K2 **Waterbeach** Cambs
20 E5 **Waterbeach** W Susx
177 H3 **Waterbeck** D & G
16 E5 **Watercombe** Dorset
121 J4 **Waterden** Norfk
164 F6 **Waterend** Cumb
115 H1 **Waterfall** Staffs
140 C3 **Waterfoot** Lancs
208 F7 **Waterfoot** S Lans
69 J4 **Waterford** Herts
11 G6 **Watergate** Cnwll
156 E2 **Waterhead** Cumb
197 G8 **Waterhead** E Ayrs
200 B3 **Waterheads** Border
168 F3 **Waterhouses** Dur

115 H2 **Waterhouses** Staffs	46 F7 **Wedhampton** Wilts	135 K4 **Welton** Lincs	21 G4 **West Burton** W Susx
39 H3 **Wateringbury** Kent	31 G1 **Wedmore** Somset	84 B2 **Welton** Nhants	168 E2 **West Butsfield** Dur
64 D6 **Waterlane** Gloucs	98 C4 **Wednesbury** Sandw	137 J6 **Welton le Marsh** Lincs	143 L6 **West Butterwick** N Linc
10 F7 **Waterloo** Cnwll	97 L3 **Wednesfield** Wolves	136 E2 **Welton le Wold** Lincs	50 D6 **West Byfleet** Surrey
133 H7 **Waterloo** Derbys	135 G6 **Weecar** Notts	145 J3 **Welwick** E R Yk	172 E8 **West Cairngaan** D & G
79 L5 **Waterloo** Herefs	67 K3 **Weedon** Bucks	69 G4 **Welwyn** Herts	107 K1 **West Caister** Norfk
247 K4 **Waterloo** Highld	84 C3 **Weedon** Nhants	69 G4 **Welwyn Garden City** Herts	210 D6 **West Calder** W Loth
209 L8 **Waterloo** N Lans	84 B6 **Weedon Lois** Nhants	113 H5 **Wem** Shrops	31 J6 **West Camel** Somset
122 E7 **Waterloo** Norfk	98 F3 **Weeford** Staffs	30 D3 **Wembdon** Somset	16 E6 **West Chaldon** Dorset
233 G7 **Waterloo** P & K	27 K5 **Week** Devon	50 F2 **Wembley** Gt Lon	48 A1 **West Challow** Oxon
55 G6 **Waterloo** Pembks	28 C7 **Week** Devon	7 G5 **Wembury** Devon	7 L6 **West Charleton** Devon
17 K4 **Waterloo** Poole	8 A2 **Week** Devon	12 F1 **Wembworthy** Devon	15 M2 **West Chelborough** Dorset
138 C8 **Waterloo** Sefton	29 G4 **Week** Somset	207 K5 **Wemyss Bay** Inver	191 J6 **West Chevington** Nthumb
29 J8 **Waterloo Cross** Devon	11 J3 **Week St Mary** Cnwll	77 J1 **Wenallt** Cerdgn	21 J3 **West Chiltington** W Susx
125 J6 **Waterloo Port** Gwynd	13 H1 **Weeke** Devon	87 K8 **Wendens Ambo** Essex	31 G8 **West Chinnock** Somset
19 M2 **Waterlooville** Hants	34 F5 **Weeke** Hants	66 E3 **Wendlebury** Oxon	47 H8 **West Chisenbury** Wilts
166 B6 **Watermillock** Cumb	101 J7 **Weekley** Nhants	105 J1 **Wendling** Norfk	50 D8 **West Clandon** Surrey
66 F6 **Waterperry** Oxon	153 G7 **Weel** E R Yk	67 L5 **Wendover** Bucks	41 K6 **West Cliffe** Kent
29 J6 **Waterrow** Somset	73 H3 **Weeley** Essex	3 H5 **Wendron** Cnwll	31 H8 **West Coker** Somset
113 K7 **Waters Upton** Wrekin	73 H3 **Weeley Heath** Essex	87 G5 **Wendy** Cambs	7 L2 **West Combe** Devon
21 G4 **Watersfield** W Susx	232 B5 **Weem** P & K	10 F7 **Wenfordbridge** Cnwll	31 K2 **West Compton** Somset
139 L3 **Waterside** Bl w D	114 E7 **Weeping Cross** Staffs	107 J8 **Wenhaston** Suffk	16 A4 **West Compton Abbas** Dorset
68 B7 **Waterside** Bucks	82 C4 **Weethley** Warwks	102 E7 **Wennington** Cambs	151 L7 **West Cottingwith** N York
165 H2 **Waterside** Cumb	104 F5 **Weeting** Norfk	52 B3 **Wennington** Gt Lon	143 G3 **West Cowick** E R Yk
143 H5 **Waterside** Donc	145 K4 **Weeton** E R Yk	147 M2 **Wennington** Lancs	57 H7 **West Cross** Swans
184 C1 **Waterside** E Ayrs	138 D1 **Weeton** Lancs	132 E7 **Wensley** Derbys	11 K4 **West Curry** Cnwll
196 F2 **Waterside** E Ayrs	150 C6 **Weeton** N York	159 K5 **Wensley** N York	165 K1 **West Curthwaite** Cumb
209 H4 **Waterside** E Duns	150 C8 **Weetwood** Leeds	142 D4 **Wentbridge** Wakefd	20 E4 **West Dean** W Susx
258 A7 **Waterstein** Highld	140 C3 **Weir** Lancs	95 J5 **Wentnor** Shrops	34 B5 **West Dean** Wilts
66 F6 **Waterstock** Oxon	6 E2 **Weir Quay** Devon	103 K7 **Wentworth** Cambs	102 C2 **West Deeping** Lincs
54 F5 **Waterston** Pembks	112 E6 **Weirbrook** Shrops	142 B8 **Wentworth** Rothm	129 J1 **West Derby** Lpool
68 E7 **Watford** Herts	133 L5 **Welbeck Abbey** Notts	141 M7 **Wentworth Castle** Barns	104 D3 **West Dereham** Norfk
84 B2 **Watford** Nhants	106 B2 **Welborne** Norfk	43 H7 **Wenvoe** V Glam	27 J3 **West Down** Devon
149 L2 **Wath** N York	118 C1 **Welbourn** Lincs	79 M5 **Weobley** Herefs	50 D3 **West Drayton** Gt Lon
160 D7 **Wath** N York	151 M2 **Welburn** N York	80 A5 **Weobley Marsh** Herefs	134 D5 **West Drayton** Notts
142 C7 **Wath upon Dearne** Rothm	160 F2 **Welbury** N York	21 H5 **Wepham** W Susx	280 B2 **West Dunnet** Highld
104 C1 **Watlington** Norfk	118 C4 **Welby** Lincs	104 D3 **Wereham** Norfk	144 C2 **West Ella** E R Yk
67 G8 **Watlington** Oxon	103 K6 **Welches Dam** Cambs	97 K3 **Wergs** Wolves	85 J4 **West End** Beds
116 E2 **Watnall** Notts	26 D7 **Welcombe** Devon	109 K4 **Wern** Gwynd	49 L5 **West End** Br For
280 B5 **Watten** Highld	191 G6 **Weldon Bridge** Nthumb	93 L1 **Wern** Powys	43 K3 **West End** Caerph
105 K8 **Wattisfield** Suffk	100 E7 **Welford** Nhants	95 G1 **Wern** Powys	87 G2 **West End** Cambs
89 K5 **Wattisham** Suffk	48 B4 **Welford** W Berk	61 H3 **Wern** Powys	177 K7 **West End** Cumb
15 K4 **Watton** Dorset	82 D5 **Welford-on-Avon** Warwks	112 D4 **Wern** Shrops	144 A2 **West End** E R Yk
152 F6 **Watton** E R Yk	101 G5 **Welham** Leics	128 F6 **Wern-y-gaer** Flints	144 F2 **West End** E R Yk
105 J3 **Watton** Norfk	134 E3 **Welham** Notts	131 J1 **Werneth Low** Tamesd	145 H2 **West End** E R Yk
105 J3 **Watton Green** Norfk	69 G6 **Welham Green** Herts	56 F6 **Wernffrwd** Swans	34 F7 **West End** Hants
69 J3 **Watton-at-Stone** Herts	36 A2 **Well** Hants	102 D3 **Werrington** C Pete	35 K4 **West End** Hants
70 D8 **Wattons Green** Essex	137 H5 **Well** Lincs	11 L5 **Werrington** Cnwll	69 H5 **West End** Herts
209 K5 **Wattston** N Lans	160 C6 **Well** N York	114 E2 **Werrington** Staffs	69 J6 **West End** Herts
42 F3 **Wattstown** Rhondd	49 L1 **Well End** Bucks	129 K5 **Wervin** Ches	139 L2 **West End** Lancs
43 K3 **Wattsville** Caerph	69 G7 **Well End** Herts	138 E1 **Wesham** Lancs	150 B8 **West End** Leeds
144 B2 **Wauldby** E R Yk	68 F2 **Well Head** Herts	133 G8 **Wessington** Derbys	145 K8 **West End** Lincs
244 E5 **Waulkmill** Abers	52 B6 **Well Hill** Kent	42 F8 **West Aberthaw** V Glam	44 F5 **West End** N Som
57 H6 **Waunarlwydd** Swans	13 L1 **Well Town** Devon	121 G8 **West Acre** Norfk	149 L4 **West End** N York
92 D7 **Waunfawr** Cerdgn	81 H7 **Welland** Worcs	202 F4 **West Allerdean** Nthumb	151 H7 **West End** N York
125 J7 **Waunfawr** Gwynd	81 J7 **Welland Stone** Worcs	7 L6 **West Alvington** Devon	105 H2 **West End** Norfk
57 G4 **Waungron** Swans	234 D7 **Wellbank** Angus	33 K3 **West Amesbury** Wilts	107 K1 **West End** Norfk
61 J5 **Waunlwyd** Blae G	68 F1 **Wellbury** Herts	28 E5 **West Anstey** Devon	48 E2 **West End** Oxon
85 H7 **Wavendon** M Keyn	83 G4 **Wellesbourne** Warwks	160 B4 **West Appleton** N York	45 L1 **West End** S Glos
165 H1 **Waverbridge** Cumb	83 G4 **Wellesbourne Mountford** Warwks	136 E5 **West Ashby** Lincs	31 L4 **West End** Somset
129 K7 **Waverton** Ches	48 D4 **Wellhouse** W Berk	20 D5 **West Ashling** W Susx	50 B6 **West End** Surrey
165 H1 **Waverton** Cumb	51 M4 **Welling** Gt Lon	46 C7 **West Ashton** Wilts	50 E6 **West End** Surrey
153 H8 **Wawne** E R Yk	85 H2 **Wellingborough** Nhants	168 F5 **West Auckland** Dur	49 K4 **West End** W & M
123 J6 **Waxham** Norfk	121 J7 **Wellingham** Norfk	163 H5 **West Ayton** N York	22 B4 **West End** W Susx
145 J2 **Waxholme** E R Yk	135 K8 **Wellingore** Lincs	30 A4 **West Bagborough** Somset	32 F6 **West End** Wilts
41 K2 **Way** Kent	155 K4 **Wellington** Cumb	11 K3 **West Balsdon** Cnwll	46 E3 **West End** Wilts
13 L4 **Way Village** Devon	80 C5 **Wellington** Herefs	61 K6 **West Bank** Blae G	33 G6 **West End** Wilts
44 D6 **Way Wick** N Som	29 L6 **Wellington** Somset	129 L3 **West Bank** Halton	49 G6 **West End Green** Hants
13 H8 **Waye** Devon	96 E1 **Wellington** Wrekin	136 C4 **West Barkwith** Lincs	51 G6 **West Ewell** Surrey
15 J1 **Wayford** Somset	81 G7 **Wellington Heath** Herefs	171 J8 **West Barnby** N York	39 H3 **West Farleigh** Kent
15 L3 **Waytown** Dorset	80 C6 **Wellington Marsh** Herefs	212 E3 **West Barns** E Loth	83 M5 **West Farndon** Nhants
29 K3 **Weacombe** Somset	45 L7 **Wellow** BaNES	121 K5 **West Barsham** Norfk	112 E6 **West Felton** Shrops
65 L6 **Weald** Oxon	18 F6 **Wellow** IOW	15 K4 **West Bay** Dorset	23 G6 **West Firle** E Susx
50 F1 **Wealdstone** Gt Lon	134 D6 **Wellow** Notts	122 C4 **West Beckham** Norfk	135 K3 **West Firsby** Lincs
150 D7 **Weardley** Leeds	69 L3 **Wellpond Green** Herts	50 D4 **West Bedfont** Surrey	163 K6 **West Flotmanby** N York
44 E8 **Weare** Somset	31 J2 **Wells** Somset	72 D2 **West Bergholt** Essex	142 B1 **West Garforth** Leeds
27 H6 **Weare Giffard** Devon	113 M1 **Wells Green** Ches	15 M5 **West Bexington** Dorset	48 C2 **West Ginge** Oxon
167 K3 **Wearhead** Dur	141 G1 **Wells Head** Brad	120 F8 **West Bilney** Norfk	47 K7 **West Grafton** Wilts
30 F5 **Wearne** Somset	121 K3 **Wells-next-the-sea** Norfk	22 D6 **West Blatchington** Br & H	49 H7 **West Green** Hants
158 B2 **Weasdale** Cumb	99 K3 **Wellsborough** Leics	181 J6 **West Boldon** S Tyne	33 L5 **West Grimstead** Wilts
121 J7 **Weasenham All Saints** Norfk	70 F3 **Wellstye Green** Essex	32 C5 **West Bourton** Dorset	37 J6 **West Grinstead** W Susx
121 J7 **Weasenham St Peter** Norfk	221 G3 **Welltree** P & K	141 J2 **West Bowling** Brad	142 E2 **West Haddlesey** N York
140 B8 **Weaste** Salfd	210 E1 **Wellwood** Fife	40 E6 **West Brabourne** Kent	84 C1 **West Haddon** Nhants
98 D8 **Weatheroak Hill** Worcs	103 L4 **Welney** Norfk	105 J2 **West Bradenham** Norfk	48 D2 **West Hagbourne** Oxon
130 B5 **Weaverham** Ches	63 H4 **Welsh Bicknor** Herefs	148 C7 **West Bradford** Lancs	97 K7 **West Hagley** Worcs
115 J7 **Weaverslake** Staffs	113 H4 **Welsh End** Shrops	31 J3 **West Bradley** Somset	116 D3 **West Hallam** Derbys
152 E2 **Weaverthorpe** N York	112 E5 **Welsh Frankton** Shrops	141 L5 **West Bretton** Wakefd	116 C3 **West Hallam Common** Derbys
45 K4 **Webb's Heath** S Gloss	74 F6 **Welsh Hook** Pembks	117 G4 **West Bridgford** Notts	144 A4 **West Halton** N Linc
44 D7 **Webbington** Somset	63 G3 **Welsh Newton** Herefs	168 B6 **West Briscoe** Dur	51 K2 **West Ham** Gt Lon
82 B2 **Webheath** Worcs	42 F6 **Welsh St Donats** V Glam	98 C5 **West Bromwich** Sandw	133 H4 **West Handley** Derbys
80 A7 **Webton** Herefs	113 G4 **Welshampton** Shrops	188 B3 **West Buccleuch Hotel** Border	66 B8 **West Hanney** Oxon
256 E5 **Wedderlairs** Abers	94 F2 **Welshpool** Powys	28 B4 **West Buckland** Devon	71 H7 **West Hanningfield** Essex
149 G6 **Wedding Hall Fold** N York	165 K2 **Welton** Cumb	30 B6 **West Buckland** Somset	33 K5 **West Harnham** Wilts
41 J3 **Weddington** Kent	144 B2 **Welton** E R Yk	159 H5 **West Burton** N York	
99 K5 **Weddington** Warwks			

45 H7 West Harptree BaNES
20 C3 West Harting W Susx
30 D6 West Hatch Somset
32 F5 West Hatch Wilts
234 E8 West Haven Angus
104 B2 West Head Norfk
98 C7 West Heath Birm
48 E7 West Heath Hants
274 D5 West Helmsdale Highld
48 C1 West Hendred Oxon
163 G7 West Heslerton N York
44 D6 West Hewish N Som
14 C4 West Hill Devon
38 A6 West Hoathly W Susx
17 G5 West Holme Dorset
52 D1 West Horndon Essex
31 J2 West Horrington Somset
50 D8 West Horsley Surrey
203 G7 West Horton Nthumb
41 H7 West Hougham Kent
17 L3 West Howe Bmouth
29 G4 West Howetown Somset
221 K2 West Huntingtower P & K
30 D2 West Huntspill Somset
68 E4 West Hyde Beds
50 C1 West Hyde Herts
40 F8 West Hythe Kent
28 C2 West Ilkerton Devon
48 C3 West Ilsley W Berk
20 C6 West Itchenor W Susx
137 G7 West Keal Lincs
47 G5 West Kennett Wilts
195 K1 West Kilbride N Ayrs
52 C6 West Kingsdown Kent
46 A3 West Kington Wilts
128 F2 West Kirby Wirral
162 F7 West Knapton N York
16 D5 West Knighton Dorset
32 E4 West Knoyle Wilts
30 F7 West Lambrook Somset
41 K6 West Langdon Kent
229 H4 West Laroch Highld
20 E3 West Lavington W Susx
46 E8 West Lavington Wilts
168 F8 West Layton N York
116 E6 West Leake Notts
202 C5 West Learmouth Nthumb
161 G2 West Lees N York
13 G2 West Leigh Devon
7 L3 West Leigh Devon
29 L5 West Leigh Somset
121 J8 West Lexham Norfk
151 K3 West Lilling N York
199 K3 West Linton Border
45 M4 West Littleton S Glos
48 B2 West Lockinge Oxon
16 F6 West Lulworth Dorset
152 E2 West Lutton N York
31 J4 West Lydford Somset
28 C1 West Lyn Devon
30 D5 West Lyng Somset
120 D7 West Lynn Norfk
52 E7 West Malling Kent
81 H6 West Malvern Worcs
20 C4 West Marden W Susx
134 E5 West Markham Notts
145 H5 West Marsh NE Lin
148 F5 West Marton N York
32 E6 West Melbury Dorset
142 C7 West Melton Rothm
35 K6 West Meon Hants
35 K5 West Meon Hut Hants
35 K5 West Meon Woodlands Hants
72 E4 West Mersea Essex
180 C6 West Mickley Nthumb
15 L3 West Milton Dorset
53 K4 West Minster Kent
50 E5 West Molesey Surrey
30 C5 West Monkton Somset
17 L2 West Moors Dorset
17 H3 West Morden Dorset
201 J5 West Morriston Border
149 K7 West Morton Brad
31 J6 West Mudford Somset
162 B6 West Ness N York
169 K7 West Newbiggin Darltn
53 K8 West Newton E R Yk
120 F6 West Newton Norfk
30 D5 West Newton Somset
51 J4 West Norwood Gt Lon
8 B1 West Ogwell Devon
32 D7 West Orchard Dorset
47 H5 West Overton Wilts
11 L4 West Panson Devon

17 L3 West Parley Dorset
39 G3 West Peckham Kent
180 F8 West Pelton Dur
31 J3 West Pennard Somset
4 C3 West Pentire Cnwll
86 C2 West Perry Cambs
28 F2 West Porlock Somset
7 M7 West Prawle Devon
16 D1 West Pulham Dorset
26 F7 West Putford Devon
29 K3 West Quantoxhead Somset
13 L2 West Raddon Devon
169 J1 West Rainton Dur
135 L2 West Rasen Lincs
145 G7 West Ravendale NE Lin
121 J6 West Raynham Norfk
134 D3 West Retford Notts
160 F2 West Rounton N York
104 D8 West Row Suffk
121 H6 West Rudham Norfk
122 D3 West Runton Norfk
212 A5 West Saltoun E Loth
13 J2 West Sandford Devon
281 e3 West Sandwick Shet
159 K6 West Scrafton N York
181 G2 West Sleekburn Nthumb
123 K7 West Somerton Norfk
16 D4 West Stafford Dorset
134 F1 West Stockwith Notts
20 D5 West Stoke W Susx
158 F2 West Stonesdale N York
30 F1 West Stoughton Somset
32 C6 West Stour Dorset
41 H3 West Stourmouth Kent
89 G1 West Stow Suffk
47 H6 West Stowell Wilts
35 H3 West Stratton Hants
40 A4 West Street Kent
41 K4 West Street Kent
52 F4 West Street Medway
89 K1 West Street Suffk
160 C7 West Tanfield N York
5 K2 West Taphouse Cnwll
206 D5 West Tarbert Ag & B
21 J6 West Tarring W Susx
191 H6 West Thirston Nthumb
20 C6 West Thorney W Susx
117 G6 West Thorpe Notts
52 C3 West Thurrock Thurr
52 E3 West Tilbury Thurr
35 K5 West Tisted Hants
136 B3 West Torrington Lincs
45 G6 West Town BaNES
20 B7 West Town Hants
80 B3 West Town Herefs
44 F5 West Town N Som
31 J4 West Town Somset
32 B3 West Town Somset
34 C5 West Tytherley Hants
103 K1 West Walton Norfk
103 K1 West Walton Highway Norfk
34 C7 West Wellow Hants
7 G5 West Wembury Devon
222 E8 West Wemyss Fife
44 D6 West Wick N Som
88 C5 West Wickham Cambs
51 K6 West Wickham Gt Lon
55 H5 West Williamston Pembks
120 E8 West Winch Norfk
34 B4 West Winterslow Wilts
20 C7 West Wittering W Susx
159 J5 West Witton N York
179 K2 West Woodburn Nthumb
48 B6 West Woodhay W Berk
32 C2 West Woodlands Somset
165 J1 West Woodside Cumb
35 M3 West Worldham Hants
21 K6 West Worthing W Susx
88 C5 West Wratting Essex
67 K8 West Wycombe Bucks
180 D6 West Wylam Nthumb
46 B4 West Yatton Wilts
52 D5 West Yoke Kent
26 D7 West Youlstone Cnwll
41 G3 Westbere Kent
117 M3 Westborough Lincs
17 L4 Westbourne Bmouth
20 B5 Westbourne W Susx
41 K1 Westbrook Kent
48 B4 Westbrook W Berk
46 D5 Westbrook Wilts
84 B8 Westbury Bucks
95 J2 Westbury Shrops
46 C8 Westbury Wilts
32 E1 Westbury Leigh Wilts

63 L4 Westbury on Severn Gloucs
45 H3 Westbury-on-Trym Bristl
31 H1 Westbury-sub-Mendip Somset
138 D2 Westby Lancs
53 J2 Westcliff-on-Sea Sthend
31 L3 Westcombe Somset
65 J3 Westcote Gloucs
66 B2 Westcote Barton Oxon
67 H4 Westcott Bucks
14 B2 Westcott Devon
28 F6 Westcott Somset
37 H1 Westcott Surrey
47 J6 Westcourt Wilts
23 J7 Westdean E Susx
33 H2 Westdown Camp Wilts
10 F6 Westdowns Cnwll
52 B5 Wested Kent
64 A5 Westend Gloucs
179 H6 Westend Town Nthumb
40 F7 Westenhanger Kent
251 G5 Wester Drumashie Highld
210 D4 Wester Ochiltree W Loth
223 K6 Wester Pitkierie Fife
279 K6 Westerdale Highld
161 L2 Westerdale N York
90 E5 Westerfield Suffk
20 F6 Westergate W Susx
51 L8 Westerham Kent
180 F5 Westerhope N u Ty
8 C2 Westerland Devon
45 K3 Westerleigh S Glos
235 G4 Westerton Angus
20 E5 Westerton W Susx
45 K8 Westfield BaNES
164 C5 Westfield Cumb
24 E4 Westfield E Susx
279 J3 Westfield Highld
209 J4 Westfield N Lans
105 K2 Westfield Norfk
210 B4 Westfield W Loth
53 G6 Westfield Sole Kent
16 D1 Westfields Dorset
80 C7 Westfields Herefs
233 J6 Westfields of Rattray P & K
29 L6 Westford Somset
167 L3 Westgate Dur
143 K6 Westgate N Linc
121 L3 Westgate Norfk
141 K2 Westgate Hill Brad
41 K1 Westgate on Sea Kent
122 D7 Westgate Street Norfk
107 J7 Westhall Suffk
16 C6 Westham Dorset
23 L6 Westham E Susx
30 F2 Westham Somset
20 E5 Westhampnett W Susx
31 G2 Westhay Somset
138 F6 Westhead Lancs
80 D6 Westhide Herefs
245 J2 Westhill Abers
31 J3 Westholme Somset
80 B5 Westhope Herefs
95 L6 Westhope Shrops
83 L5 Westhorp Nhants
119 H5 Westhorpe Lincs
90 B2 Westhorpe Suffk
139 K6 Westhoughton Bolton
157 L7 Westhouse N York
133 H8 Westhouses Derbys
50 F8 Westhumble Surrey
7 J4 Westlake Devon
70 B3 Westland Green Herts
27 H5 Westleigh Devon
29 J7 Westleigh Devon
91 K2 Westleton Suffk
95 J2 Westley Shrops
89 G2 Westley Suffk
88 C4 Westley Waterless Cambs
67 J5 Westlington Bucks
177 L6 Westlinton Cumb
41 J3 Westmarsh Kent
22 E4 Westmeston E Susx
69 K2 Westmill Herts
69 J4 Westmill Herts
51 J3 Westminster Gt Lon
234 A5 Westmuir Angus
164 F2 Westnewton Cumb
181 J5 Westoe S Tyne
45 L5 Weston BaNES
114 A1 Weston Ches
14 D3 Weston Devon
14 E5 Weston Devon
16 D8 Weston Dorset
129 L3 Weston Halton

35 M6 Weston Hants
79 L4 Weston Herefs
69 H1 Weston Herts
119 J6 Weston Lincs
149 M6 Weston N York
84 B6 Weston Nhants
134 F6 Weston Notts
96 D5 Weston Shrops
112 D6 Weston Shrops
95 H8 Weston Shrops
114 F6 Weston Staffs
48 B4 Weston W Berk
80 D7 Weston Beggard Herefs
101 G5 Weston by Welland Nhants
35 G3 Weston Colley Hants
88 C4 Weston Colville Cambs
35 L2 Weston Corbett Hants
114 E3 Weston Coyney C Stke
84 F3 Weston Favell Nhants
88 C5 Weston Green Cambs
97 H1 Weston Heath Shrops
119 J7 Weston Hills Lincs
99 K6 Weston in Arden Warwks
114 B6 Weston Jones Staffs
122 C8 Weston Longville Norfk
112 F6 Weston Lullingfields Shrops
35 L2 Weston Patrick Hants
112 D4 Weston Rhyn Shrops
82 D7 Weston Subedge Gloucs
67 K5 Weston Turville Bucks
63 J3 Weston under Penyard Herefs
83 J1 Weston under Wetherley Warwks
115 M3 Weston Underwood Derbys
85 G5 Weston Underwood M Keyn
44 F4 Weston-in-Gordano N Som
66 D3 Weston-on-the-Green Oxon
44 C6 Weston-Super-Mare N Som
97 H1 Weston-under-Lizard Staffs
113 J5 Weston-under-Redcastle Shrops
116 C6 Weston-upon-Trent Derbys
46 B1 Westonbirt Gloucs
85 K8 Westoning Beds
68 C1 Westoning Woodend Beds
30 E4 Westonzoyland Somset
152 A3 Westow N York
11 L4 Westpeek Devon
30 F6 Westport Somset
210 B3 Westquarter Falk
43 J7 Westra V Glam
48 E3 Westridge Green W Berk
210 B5 Westrigg W Loth
65 J8 Westrop Swindn
201 K3 Westruther Border
103 H4 Westry Cambs
133 J4 Westthorpe Derbys
165 J2 Westward Cumb
27 G5 Westward Ho! Devon
40 C6 Westwell Kent
65 J5 Westwell Oxon
40 C5 Westwell Leacon Kent
87 J2 Westwick Cambs
168 D7 Westwick Dur
122 F6 Westwick Norfk
14 B3 Westwood Devon
52 D5 Westwood Kent
41 K2 Westwood Kent
116 D1 Westwood Notts
179 H6 Westwood Nthumb
46 A7 Westwood Wilts
99 H8 Westwood Heath Covtry
143 J7 Westwoodside N Linc
53 H5 Wetham Green Kent
178 B7 Wetheral Cumb
150 F6 Wetherby Leeds
89 K3 Wetherden Suffk
90 D2 Wetheringsett Suffk
71 H1 Wethersfield Essex
90 D2 Wetherup Street Suffk
114 F2 Wetley Rocks Staffs
130 C7 Wettenhall Ches
132 B8 Wetton Staffs
152 E4 Wetwang E R Yk
114 B5 Wetwood Staffs
47 K7 Wexcombe Wilts
50 C3 Wexham Slough
50 C2 Wexham Street Bucks
122 C3 Weybourne Norfk
106 E7 Weybread Suffk
106 E7 Weybread Street Suffk
50 D6 Weybridge Surrey
15 G3 Weycroft Devon
279 L3 Weydale Highld

34 D2 **Weyhill** Hants
16 C6 **Weymouth** Dorset
84 F8 **Whaddon** Bucks
87 G6 **Whaddon** Cambs
64 B4 **Whaddon** Gloucs
46 C6 **Whaddon** Wilts
33 L5 **Whaddon** Wilts
166 C6 **Whale** Cumb
133 K5 **Whaley** Derbys
131 K3 **Whaley Bridge** Derbys
133 K5 **Whaley Thorns** Derbys
280 D8 **Whaligoe** Highld
148 C8 **Whalley** Lancs
139 L1 **Whalley Banks** Lancs
180 D3 **Whalton** Nthumb
119 K6 **Whaplode** Lincs
103 G1 **Whaplode Drove** Lincs
83 K5 **Wharf** Warwks
148 D2 **Wharfe** N York
147 J8 **Wharles** Lancs
85 J6 **Wharley End** Beds
179 K5 **Wharmley** Nthumb
132 F1 **Wharncliffe Side** Sheff
152 C3 **Wharram-le-Street** N York
130 C6 **Wharton** Ches
80 C4 **Wharton** Herefs
159 L2 **Whashton** N York
159 L2 **Whashton Green** N York
157 H6 **Whasset** Cumb
83 G6 **Whatcote** Warwks
99 G3 **Whateley** Warwks
89 L6 **Whatfield** Suffk
15 H1 **Whatley** Somset
32 B2 **Whatley** Somset
45 K3 **Whatley's End** S Glos
24 D4 **Whatlington** E Susx
40 F6 **Whatsole Street** Kent
116 B1 **Whatstandwell** Derbys
117 K4 **Whatton** Notts
173 K5 **Whauphill** D & G
159 H2 **Whaw** N York
4 B6 **Wheal Rose** Cnwll
107 J4 **Wheatacre** Norfk
67 G7 **Wheatfield** Oxon
68 F4 **Wheathampstead** Herts
96 E7 **Wheathill** Shrops
31 J5 **Wheathill** Somset
141 G3 **Wheatley** Calder
36 A3 **Wheatley** Hants
66 E6 **Wheatley** Oxon
169 K3 **Wheatley Hill** Dur
142 F6 **Wheatley Hills** Donc
148 E8 **Wheatley Lane** Lancs
97 J1 **Wheaton Aston** Staffs
112 D1 **Wheatsheaf** Wrexhm
29 G3 **Wheddon Cross** Somset
3 H6 **Wheel Inn** Cnwll
40 F6 **Wheelbarrow Town** Kent
49 J4 **Wheeler's Green** Oxon
39 L4 **Wheeler's Street** Kent
67 K8 **Wheelerend Common** Bucks
36 E3 **Wheelerstreet** Surrey
130 E7 **Wheelock** Ches
130 E8 **Wheelock Heath** Ches
139 J3 **Wheelton** Lancs
142 C3 **Wheldale** Wakefd
151 L6 **Wheldrake** York
65 H7 **Whelford** Gloucs
68 C6 **Whelpley Hill** Bucks
165 J3 **Whelpo** Cumb
128 F4 **Whelston** Flints
69 J3 **Whempstead** Herts
151 K2 **Whenby** N York
89 G4 **Whepstead** Suffk
90 E7 **Wherstead** Suffk
34 E3 **Wherwell** Hants
132 C4 **Wheston** Derbys
39 G4 **Whetsted** Kent
69 H8 **Whetstone** Gt Lon
100 C4 **Whetstone** Leics
165 G1 **Wheyrigg** Cumb
155 L6 **Whicham** Cumb
83 H8 **Whichford** Warwks
180 F6 **Whickham** Gatesd
12 B3 **Whiddon** Devon
13 G4 **Whiddon Down** Devon
90 D6 **Whight's Corner** Suffk
234 D6 **Whigstreet** Angus
84 C2 **Whilton** Nhants
11 L2 **Whimble** Devon
14 B3 **Whimple** Devon
123 H5 **Whimpwell Green** Norfk
147 H7 **Whin Lane End** Lancs
105 K2 **Whinburgh** Norfk

175 H4 **Whinnie Liggate** D & G
177 J8 **Whinnow** Cumb
169 K6 **Whinny Hill** S on T
257 K5 **Whinnyfold** Abers
19 H5 **Whippingham** IOW
68 C3 **Whipsnade** Beds
13 M4 **Whipton** Devon
132 F3 **Whirlow** Sheff
135 H6 **Whisby** Lincs
117 L8 **Whissendine** Rutlnd
121 K7 **Whissonsett** Norfk
218 C8 **Whistlefield** Ag & B
217 J8 **Whistlefield Inn** Ag & B
49 J4 **Whistley Green** Wokham
129 L2 **Whiston** Knows
85 G3 **Whiston** Nhants
133 J2 **Whiston** Rothm
114 D8 **Whiston** Staffs
115 G2 **Whiston** Staffs
97 H3 **Whiston Cross** Shrops
115 G2 **Whiston Eaves** Staffs
129 L2 **Whiston Lane End** Knows
99 H5 **Whitacre Fields** Warwks
155 K5 **Whitbeck** Cumb
81 G4 **Whitbourne** Herefs
181 K6 **Whitburn** S Tyne
210 C6 **Whitburn** W Loth
129 J4 **Whitby** Ches
171 K8 **Whitby** N York
129 J5 **Whitbyheath** Ches
212 F7 **Whitchester** Border
45 J5 **Whitchurch** BaNES
67 J3 **Whitchurch** Bucks
43 J5 **Whitchurch** Cardif
12 C8 **Whitchurch** Devon
34 F1 **Whitchurch** Hants
63 H4 **Whitchurch** Herefs
48 F3 **Whitchurch** Oxon
74 C7 **Whitchurch** Pembks
113 J3 **Whitchurch** Shrops
15 J3 **Whitchurch Canonicorum** Dorset
48 F3 **Whitchurch Hill** Oxon
16 D5 **Whitcombe** Dorset
95 J5 **Whitcot** Shrops
95 G6 **Whitcott Keysett** Shrops
29 K7 **White Ball** Somset
147 L7 **White Chapel** Lancs
82 C7 **White Chapel** Worcs
72 C1 **White Colne** Essex
139 J4 **White Coppice** Lancs
3 H6 **White Cross** Cnwll
81 H8 **White End** Worcs
168 C3 **White Kirkley** Dur
16 D3 **White Lackington** Dorset
81 L4 **White Ladies Aston** Worcs
58 E4 **White Mill** Carmth
71 J3 **White Notley** Essex
45 L7 **White Ox Mead** BaNES
137 G4 **White Pit** Lincs
70 E4 **White Roding** Essex
139 G3 **White Stake** Lancs
80 D6 **White Stone** Herefs
49 K3 **White Waltham** W & M
180 E7 **White-le-Head** Dur
40 E5 **Whiteacre** Kent
99 G5 **Whiteacre Heath** Warwks
71 J1 **Whiteash Green** Essex
139 L2 **Whitebirk** Bl w D
250 E8 **Whitebridge** Highld
63 G6 **Whitebrook** Mons
257 G8 **Whitecairns** Abers
51 J3 **Whitechapel** Gt Lon
75 K5 **Whitechurch** Pembks
63 H5 **Whitecliffe** Gloucs
211 K5 **Whitecraig** E Loth
63 J6 **Whitecroft** Gloucs
172 F3 **Whitecrook** D & G
2 E4 **Whitecross** Cnwll
10 D8 **Whitecross** Cnwll
210 C4 **Whitecross** Falk
263 J2 **Whiteface** Highld
194 D3 **Whitefarland** N Ayrs
183 H1 **Whitefaulds** S Ayrs
140 B6 **Whitefield** Bury
28 C4 **Whitefield** Devon
29 K5 **Whitefield** Somset
129 K2 **Whitefield Lane End** Knows
256 C6 **Whiteford** Abers
130 C6 **Whitegate** Ches
49 H8 **Whitehall** Hants
275 e3 **Whitehall** Ork
37 H6 **Whitehall** W Susx
164 C7 **Whitehaven** Cumb
36 B4 **Whitehill** Hants

40 C3 **Whitehill** Kent
99 L1 **Whitehill** Leics
268 B3 **Whitehills** Abers
256 A8 **Whitehouse** Abers
206 C6 **Whitehouse** Ag & B
98 E4 **Whitehouse Common** Birm
212 D3 **Whitekirk** E Loth
30 F7 **Whitelackington** Somset
19 J2 **Whiteley** Hants
19 J7 **Whiteley Bank** IOW
131 H4 **Whiteley Green** Ches
50 E6 **Whiteley Village** Surrey
22 D2 **Whitemans Green** W Susx
253 J1 **Whitemire** Moray
116 F3 **Whitemoor** C Nott
5 G3 **Whitemoor** Cnwll
116 B2 **Whitemoor** Derbys
131 H7 **Whitemoor** Staffs
281 d6 **Whiteness** Shet
65 M4 **Whiteoak Green** Oxon
34 B6 **Whiteparish** Wilts
256 F7 **Whiterashes** Abers
280 E6 **Whiterow** Highld
265 G8 **Whiterow** Moray
64 B5 **Whiteshill** Gloucs
23 J4 **Whitesmith** E Susx
30 D8 **Whitestaunton** Somset
13 K4 **Whitestone** Devon
13 L4 **Whitestone Cross** Devon
89 K7 **Whitestreet Green** Suffk
152 B2 **Whitewall Corner** N York
45 L6 **Whiteway** BaNES
64 C5 **Whiteway** Gloucs
148 B6 **Whitewell** Lancs
12 E8 **Whiteworks** Devon
41 J6 **Whitfield** Kent
84 B7 **Whitfield** Nhants
179 H7 **Whitfield** Nthumb
63 K8 **Whitfield** S Glos
179 H7 **Whitfield Hall** Nthumb
14 F3 **Whitford** Devon
128 D4 **Whitford** Flints
143 K3 **Whitgift** E R Yk
114 D6 **Whitgreave** Staffs
174 C6 **Whithorn** D & G
195 G6 **Whiting Bay** N Ayrs
142 B1 **Whitkirk** Leeds
55 L3 **Whitland** Carmth
188 E4 **Whitlaw** Border
196 D6 **Whitletts** S Ayrs
142 E4 **Whitley** N York
49 H5 **Whitley** Readg
133 G1 **Whitley** Sheff
46 C5 **Whitley** Wilts
181 J4 **Whitley Bay** N Tyne
179 L7 **Whitley Chapel** Nthumb
114 C6 **Whitley Heath** Staffs
141 K4 **Whitley Lower** Kirk
38 D3 **Whitley Row** Kent
98 E8 **Whitlock's End** Solhll
63 M5 **Whitminster** Gloucs
17 L1 **Whitmore** Dorset
114 C3 **Whitmore** Staffs
29 J7 **Whitnage** Devon
83 H3 **Whitnash** Warwks
79 J5 **Whitney-on-Wye** Herefs
165 G3 **Whitrigg** Cumb
177 H7 **Whitrigg** Cumb
177 H7 **Whitrigglees** Cumb
33 K7 **Whitsbury** Hants
28 B4 **Whitsford** Devon
202 D3 **Whitsome** Border
44 D2 **Whitson** Newpt
40 E2 **Whitstable** Kent
11 K3 **Whitstone** Cnwll
190 F4 **Whittingham** Nthumb
95 K5 **Whittingslow** Shrops
133 H4 **Whittington** Derbys
64 E3 **Whittington** Gloucs
157 K7 **Whittington** Lancs
104 E3 **Whittington** Norfk
112 E5 **Whittington** Shrops
98 F2 **Whittington** Staffs
97 J6 **Whittington** Staffs
99 J4 **Whittington** Warwks
81 K4 **Whittington** Worcs
133 G5 **Whittington Moor** Derbys
139 H3 **Whittle-le-Woods** Lancs
84 D6 **Whittlebury** Nhants
102 F4 **Whittlesey** Cambs
87 K5 **Whittlesford** Cambs
139 L4 **Whittlestone Head** Bl w D
143 M3 **Whitton** N Linc
190 F6 **Whitton** Nthumb
79 J2 **Whitton** Powys

169 K6 **Whitton** S on T
80 D1 **Whitton** Shrops
90 D5 **Whitton** Suffk
47 L4 **Whittonditch** Wilts
180 C7 **Whittonstall** Nthumb
48 C7 **Whitway** Hants
133 K4 **Whitwell** Derbys
68 F3 **Whitwell** Herts
19 J8 **Whitwell** IOW
160 D3 **Whitwell** N York
101 K2 **Whitwell** Rutlnd
122 B7 **Whitwell Street** Norfk
151 M3 **Whitwell-on-the-Hill** N York
116 D8 **Whitwick** Leics
142 B3 **Whitwood** Wakefd
140 D4 **Whitworth** Lancs
113 H4 **Whixall** Shrops
150 F4 **Whixley** N York
168 E7 **Whorlton** Dur
161 G2 **Whorlton** N York
80 D3 **Whyle** Herefs
51 J7 **Whyteleafe** Surrey
63 H7 **Wibdon** Gloucs
141 J2 **Wibsey** Brad
100 B6 **Wibtoft** Warwks
81 H3 **Wichenford** Worcs
40 B4 **Wichling** Kent
18 B5 **Wick** Bmouth
14 E2 **Wick** Devon
280 E6 **Wick** Highld
45 K4 **Wick** S Glos
30 B2 **Wick** Somset
30 F5 **Wick** Somset
42 D7 **Wick** V Glam
21 H6 **Wick** W Susx
33 L6 **Wick** Wilts
81 M6 **Wick** Worcs
85 K5 **Wick End** Beds
44 D6 **Wick St Lawrence** N Som
88 B1 **Wicken** Cambs
84 E7 **Wicken** Nhants
87 K8 **Wicken Bonhunt** Essex
136 A3 **Wickenby** Lincs
89 K6 **Wicker Street Green** Suffk
133 J2 **Wickersley** Rothm
71 H8 **Wickford** Essex
19 K2 **Wickham** Hants
48 B5 **Wickham** W Berk
71 K5 **Wickham Bishops** Essex
90 C2 **Wickham Green** Suffk
48 B4 **Wickham Green** W Berk
48 B5 **Wickham Heath** W Berk
91 G4 **Wickham Market** Suffk
90 C2 **Wickham Skeith** Suffk
89 G7 **Wickham St Paul** Essex
88 F4 **Wickham Street** Suffk
90 C1 **Wickham Street** Suffk
41 H3 **Wickhambreaux** Kent
88 E4 **Wickhambrook** Suffk
82 C7 **Wickhamford** Worcs
107 J2 **Wickhampton** Norfk
106 B3 **Wicklewood** Norfk
122 D5 **Wickmere** Norfk
23 J5 **Wickstreet** E Susx
45 L1 **Wickwar** S Glos
70 D1 **Widdington** Essex
140 D1 **Widdop** Calder
191 K7 **Widdrington** Nthumb
191 J7 **Widdrington Station** Nthumb
181 G4 **Wide Open** N Tyne
13 G7 **Widecombe in the Moor** Devon
6 B3 **Widegates** Cnwll
11 H2 **Widemouth Bay** Cnwll
71 G6 **Widford** Essex
70 B4 **Widford** Herts
65 K5 **Widford** Oxon
47 G1 **Widham** Wilts
19 M2 **Widley** Hants
67 L7 **Widmer End** Bucks
117 G6 **Widmerpool** Notts
51 L5 **Widmore** Gt Lon
129 L3 **Widnes** Halton
14 F3 **Widworthy** Devon
139 H6 **Wigan** Wigan
31 G7 **Wigborough** Somset
14 C4 **Wiggaton** Devon
120 D8 **Wiggenhall St Germans** Norfk
104 B1 **Wiggenhall St Mary Magdalen** Norfk
104 B1 **Wiggenhall St Mary the Virgin** Norfk
88 D6 **Wiggens Green** Essex

132 B7 **Wiggenstall** Staffs
112 E4 **Wiggington** Shrops
68 B5 **Wigginton** Herts
83 J8 **Wigginton** Oxon
99 G2 **Wigginton** Staffs
151 J4 **Wigginton** York
68 B5 **Wigginton Bottom** Herts
148 E4 **Wigglesworth** N York
64 F6 **Wiggold** Gloucs
177 J8 **Wiggonby** Cumb
21 H3 **Wiggonholt** W Susx
151 G6 **Wighill** N York
121 L3 **Wighton** Norfk
97 K4 **Wightwick** Wolves
132 F5 **Wigley** Derbys
34 D7 **Wigley** Hants
80 A2 **Wigmore** Herefs
53 G6 **Wigmore** Medway
135 G5 **Wigsley** Notts
102 A6 **Wigsthorpe** Nhants
100 D4 **Wigston** Leics
100 D3 **Wigston Fields** Leics
100 A5 **Wigston Parva** Leics
134 B3 **Wigthorpe** Notts
119 J4 **Wigtoft** Lincs
165 H1 **Wigton** Cumb
174 C4 **Wigtown** D & G
141 L8 **Wigtwizzle** Sheff
150 D7 **Wike** Leeds
101 H5 **Wilbarston** Nhants
151 M5 **Wilberfoss** E R Yk
103 K8 **Wilburton** Cambs
85 G2 **Wilby** Nhants
105 L5 **Wilby** Norfk
90 F1 **Wilby** Suffk
47 H6 **Wilcot** Wilts
112 F7 **Wilcott** Shrops
44 E2 **Wilcrick** Newpt
132 F5 **Wilday Green** Derbys
131 K6 **Wildboarclough** Ches
86 B4 **Wilden** Beds
81 J1 **Wilden** Worcs
34 D1 **Wildhern** Hants
69 H5 **Wildhill** Herts
209 L8 **Wildmanbridge** S Lans
98 B8 **Wildmoor** Worcs
143 K8 **Wildsworth** Lincs
116 F4 **Wilford** C Nott
113 K3 **Wilkesley** Ches
264 E3 **Wilkhaven** Highld
210 F5 **Wilkieston** W Loth
69 G5 **Wilkin's Green** Herts
136 E7 **Wilksby** Lincs
29 J8 **Willand** Devon
24 C2 **Willards Hill** E Susx
129 H4 **Willaston** Ches
113 L1 **Willaston** Ches
85 G7 **Willen** M Keyn
99 K8 **Willenhall** Covtry
98 B4 **Willenhall** Wsall
144 C2 **Willerby** E R Yk
163 H6 **Willerby** N York
82 D7 **Willersey** Gloucs
79 K6 **Willersley** Herefs
40 D7 **Willesborough** Kent
40 D7 **Willesborough Lees** Kent
51 G2 **Willesden** Gt Lon
27 L4 **Willesleigh** Devon
46 B1 **Willesley** Wilts
29 K4 **Willett** Somset
96 F3 **Willey** Shrops
100 B6 **Willey** Warwks
50 B8 **Willey Green** Surrey
83 L6 **Williamscot** Oxon
42 F4 **Williamstown** Rhondd
69 G1 **Willian** Herts
82 E5 **Willicote** Warwks
70 E5 **Willingale** Essex
23 K6 **Willingdon** E Susx
87 H1 **Willingham** Cambs
35 H3 **Willingham by Stow** Lincs
88 C4 **Willingham Green** Cambs
86 C5 **Willington** Beds
116 A6 **Willington** Derbys
169 G4 **Willington** Dur
39 K3 **Willington** Kent
99 G7 **Willington** Warwks
99 M6 **Willington Corner** Ches
181 H5 **Willington Quay** N Tyne
143 J1 **Willitoft** E R Yk
29 K3 **Williton** Somset
37 J5 **Willoughby** Lincs
83 M2 **Willoughby** Warwks
119 K2 **Willoughby Hills** Lincs
100 C5 **Willoughby Waterleys** Leics

117 H6 **Willoughby-on-the-Wolds** Notts
135 J1 **Willoughton** Lincs
130 B4 **Willow Green** Ches
71 H3 **Willows Green** Essex
45 K5 **Willsbridge** S Glos
12 D6 **Willsworthy** Devon
30 F6 **Willtown** Somset
82 E4 **Wilmcote** Warwks
45 K6 **Wilmington** BaNES
14 F3 **Wilmington** Devon
23 J6 **Wilmington** E Susx
52 B4 **Wilmington** Kent
131 G3 **Wilmslow** Ches
99 G3 **Wilnecote** Staffs
139 K1 **Wilpshire** Lancs
149 K8 **Wilsden** Brad
118 D3 **Wilsford** Lincs
47 G7 **Wilsford** Wilts
33 K3 **Wilsford** Wilts
28 D1 **Wilsham** Devon
141 H6 **Wilshaw** Kirk
150 A3 **Wilsill** N York
39 K6 **Wilsley Green** Kent
39 K6 **Wilsley Pound** Kent
63 H2 **Wilson** Herefs
116 C6 **Wilson** Leics
198 F2 **Wilsontown** S Lans
85 L6 **Wilstead** Beds
102 B1 **Wilsthorpe** Lincs
67 L4 **Wilstone** Herts
67 M4 **Wilstone Green** Herts
164 D8 **Wilton** Cumb
63 H2 **Wilton** Herefs
162 F6 **Wilton** N York
170 D6 **Wilton** R & Cl
33 J4 **Wilton** Wilts
47 K6 **Wilton** Wilts
188 E3 **Wilton Dean** Border
88 B7 **Wimbish** Essex
88 C8 **Wimbish Green** Essex
51 G5 **Wimbledon** Gt Lon
103 J5 **Wimblington** Cambs
130 D7 **Wimboldsley** Ches
17 K3 **Wimborne Minster** Dorset
33 H8 **Wimborne St Giles** Dorset
104 C2 **Wimbotsham** Norfk
87 G5 **Wimpole** Cambs
82 F5 **Wimpstone** Warwks
32 B5 **Wincanton** Somset
136 F6 **Winceby** Lincs
130 C4 **Wincham** Ches
210 E4 **Winchburgh** W Loth
64 F2 **Winchcombe** Gloucs
25 G4 **Winchelsea** E Susx
25 G4 **Winchelsea Beach** E Susx
35 G5 **Winchester** Hants
39 J5 **Winchet Hill** Kent
49 J8 **Winchfield** Hants
68 B8 **Winchmore Hill** Bucks
69 J8 **Winchmore Hill** Gt Lon
131 J6 **Wincle** Ches
133 G1 **Wincobank** Sheff
164 D7 **Winder** Cumb
156 F3 **Windermere** Cumb
83 H7 **Winderton** Warwks
250 F2 **Windhill** Highld
131 J3 **Windlehurst** Stockp
50 A6 **Windlesham** Surrey
10 B7 **Windmill** Cnwll
132 C4 **Windmill** Derbys
23 L5 **Windmill Hill** E Susx
30 D7 **Windmill Hill** Somset
65 J4 **Windrush** Gloucs
267 L4 **Windsole** Abers
50 B4 **Windsor** W & M
89 H4 **Windsor Green** Suffk
64 B7 **Windsoredge** Gloucs
83 G1 **Windy Arbour** Warwks
129 G8 **Windy Hill** Wrexhm
222 F7 **Windygates** Fife
131 G5 **Windyharbour** Ches
22 C3 **Wineham** W Susx
145 J3 **Winestead** E R Yk
148 F7 **Winewall** Lancs
106 C6 **Winfarthing** Norfk
19 J6 **Winford** IOW
45 G6 **Winford** N Som
79 K6 **Winforton** Herefs
16 F5 **Winfrith Newburgh** Dorset
67 L3 **Wing** Bucks
101 K3 **Wing** Rutlnd
169 L3 **Wingate** Dur
139 K6 **Wingates** Bolton
191 G7 **Wingates** Nthumb

133 G6 **Wingerworth** Derbys
68 C2 **Wingfield** Beds
106 E7 **Wingfield** Suffk
46 B7 **Wingfield** Wilts
106 E7 **Wingfield Green** Suffk
41 H4 **Wingham** Kent
41 G6 **Wingmore** Kent
67 L3 **Wingrave** Bucks
134 E7 **Winkburn** Notts
49 L4 **Winkfield** Br For
49 L5 **Winkfield Row** Br For
49 L4 **Winkfield Street** Br For
115 H1 **Winkhill** Staffs
38 D3 **Winkhurst Green** Kent
12 F1 **Winkleigh** Devon
150 C2 **Winksley** N York
18 B4 **Winkton** Dorset
180 E6 **Winlaton** Gatesd
180 E6 **Winlaton Mill** Gatesd
280 D5 **Winless** Highld
112 C7 **Winllan** Powys
147 J6 **Winmarleigh** Lancs
35 G5 **Winnall** Hants
81 J2 **Winnall** Worcs
49 J5 **Winnersh** Wokham
130 C5 **Winnington** Ches
164 D5 **Winscales** Cumb
44 E7 **Winscombe** N Som
130 C6 **Winsford** Ches
28 F4 **Winsford** Somset
27 J3 **Winsham** Devon
15 J1 **Winsham** Somset
115 M7 **Winshill** Staffs
57 J5 **Winshwen** Swans
166 D4 **Winskill** Cumb
35 K1 **Winslade** Hants
46 A6 **Winsley** Wilts
67 J2 **Winslow** Bucks
65 G5 **Winson** Gloucs
34 D8 **Winsor** Hants
156 F4 **Winster** Cumb
132 E7 **Winster** Derbys
168 F7 **Winston** Dur
90 E3 **Winston** Suffk
90 E3 **Winston Green** Suffk
64 D5 **Winstone** Gloucs
27 J8 **Winswell** Devon
16 D5 **Winterborne Came** Dorset
17 G2 **Winterborne Clenston** Dorset
16 D5 **Winterborne Herringston** Dorset
16 F2 **Winterborne Houghton** Dorset
17 G3 **Winterborne Kingston** Dorset
16 C5 **Winterborne Monkton** Dorset
16 F2 **Winterborne Stickland** Dorset
17 G3 **Winterborne Tomson** Dorset
17 G2 **Winterborne Whitechurch** Dorset
17 H3 **Winterborne Zelston** Dorset
45 J3 **Winterbourne** S Glos
48 C4 **Winterbourne** W Berk
16 B4 **Winterbourne Abbas** Dorset
47 G4 **Winterbourne Bassett** Wilts
33 L4 **Winterbourne Dauntsey** Wilts
33 L4 **Winterbourne Earls** Wilts
33 L4 **Winterbourne Gunner** Wilts
47 G4 **Winterbourne Monkton** Wilts
16 B4 **Winterbourne Steepleton** Dorset
33 J3 **Winterbourne Stoke** Wilts
48 F1 **Winterbrook** Oxon
149 G4 **Winterburn** N York
144 A3 **Winteringham** N Linc
130 E8 **Winterley** Ches
142 B4 **Wintersett** Wakefd
34 B4 **Winterslow** Wilts
144 A4 **Winterton** N Linc
123 K7 **Winterton-on-Sea** Norfk
137 K6 **Winthorpe** Lincs
135 G8 **Winthorpe** Notts
17 L4 **Winton** Bmouth
167 H8 **Winton** Cumb
23 H6 **Winton** E Susx
160 F3 **Winton** N York
162 F8 **Wintringham** N York

102 B7 **Winwick** Cambs
100 D8 **Winwick** Nhants
130 B1 **Winwick** Warrtn
115 M1 **Wirksworth** Derbys
113 J3 **Wirswall** Ches
103 J2 **Wisbech** Cambs
103 J2 **Wisbech St Mary** Cambs
37 G5 **Wisborough Green** W Susx
55 K5 **Wiseman's Bridge** Pembks
134 E2 **Wiseton** Notts
64 D5 **Wishanger** Gloucs
209 L7 **Wishaw** N Lans
98 F4 **Wishaw** Warwks
50 D7 **Wisley** Surrey
136 D5 **Wispington** Lincs
40 B7 **Wissenden** Kent
107 H7 **Wissett** Suffk
104 D4 **Wissington** Norfk
89 J8 **Wissington** Suffk
95 K6 **Wistanstow** Shrops
113 L5 **Wistanswick** Shrops
113 L1 **Wistaston** Ches
130 D8 **Wistaston Green** Ches
131 G5 **Wisterfield** Ches
55 H3 **Wiston** Pembks
198 F6 **Wiston** S Lans
21 K4 **Wiston** W Susx
102 F7 **Wistow** Cambs
100 E4 **Wistow** Leics
142 F1 **Wistow** N York
148 C8 **Wiswell** Lancs
103 J7 **Witcham** Cambs
17 J1 **Witchampton** Dorset
103 K7 **Witchford** Cambs
31 G6 **Witcombe** Somset
71 K4 **Witham** Essex
32 B3 **Witham Friary** Somset
118 D8 **Witham on the Hill** Lincs
135 H7 **Witham St Hughs** Lincs
136 E3 **Withcall** Lincs
22 D5 **Withdean** Br & H
23 L2 **Witherenden Hill** E Susx
28 D8 **Witheridge** Devon
99 J4 **Witherley** Leics
137 H3 **Withern** Lincs
145 J2 **Withernsea** E R Yk
153 K7 **Withernwick** E R Yk
106 F7 **Withersdale Street** Suffk
88 D5 **Withersfield** Essex
156 F5 **Witherslack** Cumb
156 F5 **Witherslack Hall** Cumb
5 G2 **Withiel** Cnwll
29 H4 **Withiel Florey** Somset
5 G2 **Withielgoose** Cnwll
64 F4 **Withington** Gloucs
80 D6 **Withington** Herefs
131 G1 **Withington** Manch
96 D1 **Withington** Shrops
115 G4 **Withington** Staffs
130 F5 **Withington Green** Ches
80 D6 **Withington Marsh** Herefs
28 F8 **Withleigh** Devon
139 J3 **Withnell** Lancs
45 K7 **Withy Mills** BaNES
82 B1 **Withybed Green** Worcs
99 L6 **Withybrook** Warwks
29 J3 **Withycombe** Somset
38 D6 **Withyham** E Susx
28 E4 **Withypool** Somset
45 H5 **Withywood** Bristl
36 E3 **Witley** Surrey
90 E5 **Witnesham** Suffk
65 M5 **Witney** Oxon
102 B3 **Wittering** C Pete
25 G2 **Wittersham** Kent
98 D5 **Witton** Birm
107 G2 **Witton** Norfk
123 G5 **Witton** Norfk
169 G2 **Witton Gilbert** Dur
107 J3 **Witton Green** Norfk
168 F4 **Witton le Wear** Dur
168 F4 **Witton Park** Dur
29 K5 **Wiveliscombe** Somset
35 K3 **Wivelrod** Hants
22 E3 **Wivelsfield** E Susx
22 E3 **Wivelsfield Green** E Susx
22 E3 **Wivelsfield Station** W Susx
72 F3 **Wivenhoe** Essex
72 F2 **Wivenhoe Cross** Essex
122 A3 **Wiveton** Norfk
73 H2 **Wix** Essex
73 H2 **Wix Green** Essex
82 C4 **Wixford** Warwks
113 J6 **Wixhill** Shrops
88 E6 **Wixoe** Essex

85 J8 **Woburn** Beds	40 B8 **Woodchurch** Kent	81 L6 **Woodmancote** Worcs	130 C2 **Woolston** Warrtn
85 H8 **Woburn Sands** M Keyn	129 G2 **Woodchurch** Wirral	35 H2 **Woodmancott** Hants	8 A2 **Woolston Green** Devon
49 G6 **Wokefield Park** W Berk	29 G2 **Woodcombe** Somset	153 G8 **Woodmansey** E R Yk	64 D1 **Woolstone** Gloucs
50 C7 **Woking** Surrey	51 J6 **Woodcote** Gt Lon	36 C5 **Woodmansgreen** W Susx	85 G7 **Woolstone** M Keyn
49 K5 **Wokingham** Wokham	48 F3 **Woodcote** Oxon	51 H7 **Woodmansterne** Surrey	47 L2 **Woolstone** Oxon
8 C1 **Wolborough** Devon	114 B8 **Woodcote** Wrekin	14 B5 **Woodmanton** Devon	129 K2 **Woolton** Lpool
163 J8 **Wold Newton** E R Yk	81 L1 **Woodcote Green** Worcs	46 B7 **Woodmarsh** Wilts	48 B6 **Woolton Hill** Hants
145 G8 **Wold Newton** NE Lin	48 B7 **Woodcott** Hants	115 J7 **Woodmill** Staffs	90 E7 **Woolverstone** Suffk
51 K7 **Woldingham** Surrey	63 G7 **Woodcroft** Gloucs	33 H6 **Woodminton** Wilts	46 A8 **Woolverton** Somset
179 G7 **Wolf Hills** Nthumb	33 G7 **Woodcutts** Dorset	41 J4 **Woodnesborough** Kent	51 L3 **Woolwich** Gt Lon
74 F6 **Wolf's Castle** Pembks	88 D3 **Woodditton** Cambs	102 A4 **Woodnewton** Nhants	79 L5 **Woonton** Herefs
199 H6 **Wolfclyde** S Lans	66 D5 **Woodeaton** Oxon	116 D1 **Woodnook** Notts	80 D3 **Woonton** Herefs
80 F3 **Wolferlow** Herefs	55 J6 **Wooden** Pembks	139 G1 **Woodplumpton** Lancs	190 F2 **Wooperton** Nthumb
120 E6 **Wolferton** Norfk	228 B3 **Woodend** Highld	105 K3 **Woodrising** Norfk	114 A3 **Woore** Shrops
83 M2 **Wolfhampcote** Warwks	84 B5 **Woodend** Nhants	97 K8 **Woodrow** Worcs	90 F1 **Wootten Green** Suffk
233 H8 **Wolfhill** P & K	115 K6 **Woodend** Staffs	113 M5 **Woodseaves** Shrops	85 K6 **Wootton** Beds
54 F3 **Wolfsdale** Pembks	210 B5 **Woodend** W Loth	114 B6 **Woodseaves** Staffs	18 C4 **Wootton** Hants
97 K6 **Wollaston** Dudley	20 D5 **Woodend** W Susx	47 J4 **Woodsend** Wilts	79 L4 **Wootton** Herefs
85 H3 **Wollaston** Nhants	70 E2 **Woodend Green** Essex	133 L3 **Woodsetts** Rothm	19 J5 **Wootton** IOW
95 H1 **Wollaston** Shrops	33 L6 **Woodfalls** Wilts	16 E4 **Woodsford** Dorset	41 H6 **Wootton** Kent
116 E4 **Wollaton** C Nott	26 C8 **Woodford** Cnwll	50 B5 **Woodside** Br For	144 D4 **Wootton** N Linc
13 J6 **Wolleigh** Devon	8 B5 **Woodford** Devon	164 D4 **Woodside** Cumb	84 E4 **Wootton** Nhants
113 K5 **Wollerton** Shrops	63 K7 **Woodford** Gloucs	70 C6 **Woodside** Essex	66 B3 **Wootton** Oxon
97 L6 **Wollescote** Dudley	69 L8 **Woodford** Gt Lon	223 G5 **Woodside** Fife	66 C6 **Wootton** Oxon
115 G7 **Wolseley Bridge** Staffs	101 L8 **Woodford** Nhants	51 J5 **Woodside** Gt Lon	112 E6 **Wootton** Shrops
168 D3 **Wolsingham** Dur	131 H3 **Woodford** Stockp	18 E5 **Woodside** Hants	114 C6 **Wootton** Staffs
114 D2 **Wolstanton** Staffs	70 B8 **Woodford Bridge** Gt Lon	69 H5 **Woodside** Herts	115 H3 **Wootton** Staffs
140 C5 **Wolstenholme** Rochdl	84 A5 **Woodford Halse** Nhants	233 J7 **Woodside** P & K	46 F3 **Wootton Bassett** Wilts
99 L8 **Wolston** Warwks	69 L8 **Woodford Wells** Gt Lon	40 B4 **Woodside Green** Kent	19 J5 **Wootton Bridge** IOW
176 E8 **Wolsty** Cumb	98 C6 **Woodgate** Birm	66 C4 **Woodstock** Oxon	85 K6 **Wootton Broadmead** Beds
66 D5 **Wolvercote** Oxon	29 K7 **Woodgate** Devon	75 H7 **Woodstock** Pembks	19 J5 **Wootton Common** IOW
97 K4 **Wolverhampton** Wolves	121 K8 **Woodgate** Norfk	102 D4 **Woodston** C Pete	29 G2 **Wootton Courtenay** Somset
113 G5 **Wolverley** Shrops	121 M8 **Woodgate** Norfk	133 J5 **Woodthorpe** Derbys	15 J3 **Wootton Fitzpaine** Dorset
97 J7 **Wolverley** Worcs	20 F6 **Woodgate** W Susx	116 F8 **Woodthorpe** Leics	47 J6 **Wootton Rivers** Wilts
48 E7 **Wolverton** Hants	81 M2 **Woodgate** Worcs	137 H4 **Woodthorpe** Lincs	48 E8 **Wootton St Lawrence** Hants
41 H6 **Wolverton** Kent	33 L7 **Woodgreen** Hants	106 F4 **Woodton** Norfk	82 E3 **Wootton Wawen** Warwks
84 F7 **Wolverton** M Keyn	66 A5 **Woodgreen** Oxon	27 G6 **Woodtown** Devon	81 K4 **Worcester** Worcs
82 F3 **Wolverton** Warwks	136 D6 **Woodhall** Lincs	138 C5 **Woodvale** Sefton	51 G6 **Worcester Park** Gt Lon
32 C4 **Wolverton** Wilts	159 H4 **Woodhall** N York	116 A7 **Woodville** Derbys	97 K6 **Wordsley** Dudley
48 E7 **Wolverton Common** Hants	141 K1 **Woodhall Hill** Leeds	114 B5 **Woodwall Green** Staffs	97 G4 **Worfield** Shrops
62 F7 **Wolvesnewton** Mons	136 C7 **Woodhall Spa** Lincs	28 B1 **Woody Bay** Devon	17 H5 **Worgret** Dorset
99 L6 **Wolvey** Warwks	67 H3 **Woodham** Bucks	33 H7 **Woodyates** Dorset	86 B5 **Workhouse End** Beds
99 L5 **Wolvey Heath** Warwks	169 H5 **Woodham** Dur	80 C2 **Woofferton** Shrops	164 D5 **Workington** Cumb
170 B5 **Wolviston** S on T	50 D6 **Woodham** Surrey	31 H2 **Wookey** Somset	134 B4 **Worksop** Notts
161 L6 **Wombleton** N York	71 J7 **Woodham Ferrers** Essex	31 H2 **Wookey Hole** Somset	136 F4 **Worlaby** Lincs
97 K5 **Wombourne** Staffs	71 K6 **Woodham Mortimer** Essex	17 G5 **Wool** Dorset	144 C5 **Worlaby** N Linc
142 B7 **Wombwell** Barns	71 K5 **Woodham Walter** Essex	27 H2 **Woolacombe** Devon	48 C3 **World's End** W Berk
41 H5 **Womenswold** Kent	256 E4 **Woodhead** Abers	41 H5 **Woolage Green** Kent	67 L5 **Worlds End** Bucks
142 E4 **Womersley** N York	30 E5 **Woodhill** Somset	41 H5 **Woolage Village** Kent	19 L1 **Worlds End** Hants
62 F5 **Wonastow** Mons	181 H1 **Woodhorn** Nthumb	63 H7 **Woolaston** Gloucs	22 E3 **Worlds End** W Susx
36 F2 **Wonersh** Surrey	181 H1 **Woodhorn Demesne** Nthumb	63 H6 **Woolaston Common** Gloucs	44 D6 **Worle** N Som
13 L4 **Wonford** Devon	141 L1 **Woodhouse** Leeds	30 E3 **Woolavington** Somset	130 C8 **Worleston** Ches
12 F4 **Wonson** Devon	116 F8 **Woodhouse** Leics	36 C6 **Woolbeding** W Susx	107 J5 **Worlingham** Suffk
35 G3 **Wonston** Hants	133 H3 **Woodhouse** Sheff	14 D5 **Woolbrook** Devon	28 D8 **Worlington** Devon
49 M2 **Wooburn** Bucks	142 B3 **Woodhouse** Wakefd	29 H4 **Woolcotts** Somset	104 D8 **Worlington** Suffk
49 M1 **Wooburn Green** Bucks	116 F8 **Woodhouse Eaves** Leics	141 J6 **Wooldale** Kirk	90 F2 **Worlingworth** Suffk
49 M1 **Wooburn Moor** Bucks	131 H7 **Woodhouse Green** Staffs	202 F7 **Wooler** Nthumb	150 D3 **Wormald Green** N York
82 C4 **Wood Bevington** Warwks	133 H3 **Woodhouse Mill** Sheff	26 F6 **Woolfardisworthy** Devon	62 E1 **Wormbridge** Herefs
84 D6 **Wood Burcot** Nhants	211 H6 **Woodhouselee** Mdloth	13 J1 **Woolfardisworthy** Devon	104 D1 **Wormegay** Norfk
122 B6 **Wood Dalling** Norfk	177 L4 **Woodhouselees** D & G	140 B5 **Woolfold** Bury	62 F1 **Wormelow Tump** Herefs
114 C7 **Wood Eaton** Staffs	177 K8 **Woodhouses** Cumb	199 G2 **Woolfords** S Lans	132 C5 **Wormhill** Derbys
85 K6 **Wood End** Beds	140 D7 **Woodhouses** Oldham	48 E5 **Woolhampton** W Berk	80 A7 **Wormhill** Herefs
86 B2 **Wood End** Beds	98 D2 **Woodhouses** Staffs	28 B2 **Woolhanger** Devon	72 D1 **Wormingford** Essex
103 H8 **Wood End** Cambs	115 J7 **Woodhouses** Staffs	80 E8 **Woolhope** Herefs	66 F5 **Worminghall** Bucks
50 E3 **Wood End** Gt Lon	8 D4 **Woodhuish** Devon	16 E1 **Woolland** Dorset	82 B7 **Wormington** Gloucs
69 J2 **Wood End** Herts	103 G8 **Woodhurst** Cambs	45 J6 **Woollard** BaNES	31 J2 **Worminster** Somset
82 D1 **Wood End** Warwks	22 E6 **Woodingdean** Br & H	69 K5 **Woollensbrook** Herts	223 G2 **Wormit** Fife
99 H4 **Wood End** Warwks	141 L3 **Woodkirk** Leeds	45 L5 **Woolley** BaNES	83 K4 **Wormleighton** Warwks
99 J6 **Wood End** Warwks	256 F7 **Woodland** Abers	102 C8 **Woolley** Cambs	69 K6 **Wormley** Herts
97 L3 **Wood End** Wolves	8 B1 **Woodland** Devon	26 D7 **Woolley** Cnwll	36 E3 **Wormley** Surrey
136 E6 **Wood Enderby** Lincs	7 J4 **Woodland** Devon	133 G7 **Woolley** Derbys	143 G4 **Wormley Hill** Donc
51 J1 **Wood Green** Gt Lon	168 D5 **Woodland** Dur	141 M5 **Woolley** Wakefd	69 K6 **Wormleybury** Herts
97 L3 **Wood Hayes** Wolves	40 F7 **Woodland** Kent	131 K1 **Woolley Bridge** Derbys	39 M2 **Wormshill** Kent
112 F5 **Wood Lane** Shrops	182 F4 **Woodland** S Ayrs	49 K3 **Woolley Green** W & M	80 A5 **Wormsley** Herefs
114 C2 **Wood Lane** Staffs	13 H3 **Woodland Head** Devon	69 H3 **Woolmer Green** Herts	50 B8 **Worplesdon** Surrey
121 M6 **Wood Norton** Norfk	31 J3 **Woodland Street** Somset	81 M3 **Woolmere Green** Worcs	132 F1 **Worrall** Sheff
142 B2 **Wood Row** Leeds	132 F2 **Woodland View** Sheff	30 D4 **Woolmerston** Somset	63 J4 **Worrall Hill** Gloucs
123 H7 **Wood Street** Norfk	245 H4 **Woodlands** Abers	15 J1 **Woolminstone** Somset	142 A7 **Worsbrough** Barns
36 E1 **Wood Street** Surrey	142 E6 **Woodlands** Donc	39 L6 **Woolpack** Kent	142 A7 **Worsbrough Bridge** Barns
147 L7 **Wood Top** Lancs	17 L1 **Woodlands** Dorset	89 K3 **Woolpit** Suffk	142 B7 **Worsbrough Dale** Barns
102 E7 **Wood Walton** Cambs	18 E1 **Woodlands** Hants	89 K3 **Woolpit Green** Suffk	139 M7 **Worsley** Salfd
24 B3 **Wood's Corner** E Susx	52 C6 **Woodlands** Kent	83 L2 **Woolscott** Warwks	139 H7 **Worsley Mesnes** Wigan
39 G6 **Wood's Green** E Susx	150 D5 **Woodlands** N York	13 J2 **Woolsgrove** Devon	122 F6 **Worstead** Norfk
159 J6 **Woodale** N York	29 L3 **Woodlands** Somset	180 F5 **Woolsington** N u Ty	140 C1 **Worsthorne** Lancs
133 J3 **Woodall** Rothm	49 L3 **Woodlands Park** W & M	95 L4 **Woolstaston** Shrops	7 H4 **Worston** Devon
123 G8 **Woodbastwick** Norfk	47 M4 **Woodlands St Mary** W Berk	117 L5 **Woolsthorpe** Lincs	148 D7 **Worston** Lancs
134 F4 **Woodbeck** Notts	7 L5 **Woodleigh** Devon	118 B6 **Woolsthorpe-by-**	41 K4 **Worth** Kent
117 G2 **Woodborough** Notts	142 B2 **Woodlesford** Leeds	**Colsterworth** Lincs	31 H2 **Worth** Somset
47 G7 **Woodborough** Wilts	131 J1 **Woodley** Stockp	19 G2 **Woolston** C Sotn	37 L4 **Worth** W Susx
14 E3 **Woodbridge** Devon	49 J4 **Woodley** Wokham	7 L6 **Woolston** Devon	37 M4 **Worth Abbey** Surrey
32 E7 **Woodbridge** Dorset	64 E2 **Woodmancote** Gloucs	7 L5 **Woolston** Devon	17 J7 **Worth Matravers** Dorset
91 G5 **Woodbridge** Suffk	64 E5 **Woodmancote** Gloucs	112 E6 **Woolston** Shrops	106 B7 **Wortham** Suffk
14 B5 **Woodbury** Devon	63 M7 **Woodmancote** Gloucs	95 K6 **Woolston** Shrops	95 H2 **Worthen** Shrops
14 B5 **Woodbury Salterton** Devon	20 C5 **Woodmancote** W Susx	29 K3 **Woolston** Somset	112 F2 **Worthenbury** Wrexhm
64 B6 **Woodchester** Gloucs	22 C4 **Woodmancote** W Susx	31 L5 **Woolston** Somset	121 M7 **Worthing** Norfk

21 K6	**Worthing** W Susx	

21 K6 **Worthing** W Susx
116 C7 **Worthington** Leics
62 F5 **Worthybrook** Mons
48 F8 **Worting** Hants
141 M7 **Wortley** Barns
141 L1 **Wortley** Leeds
159 G5 **Worton** N York
46 E7 **Worton** Wilts
106 F6 **Wortwell** Norfk
95 G3 **Wotherton** Shrops
101 M2 **Wothorpe** C Pete
7 H3 **Wotter** Devon
37 H2 **Wotton** Surrey
67 G4 **Wotton Underwood** Bucks
63 M8 **Wotton-under-Edge** Gloucs
85 G7 **Woughton on the Green** M Keyn
52 F6 **Wouldham** Kent
97 H5 **Woundale** Shrops
73 J1 **Wrabness** Essex
27 J4 **Wrafton** Devon
136 B4 **Wragby** Lincs
142 C4 **Wragby** Wakefd
106 C2 **Wramplingham** Norfk
7 K3 **Wrangaton** Devon
142 D5 **Wrangbrook** Wakefd
119 M2 **Wrangle** Lincs
119 M1 **Wrangle Common** Lincs
119 M1 **Wrangle Lowgate** Lincs
29 L7 **Wrangway** Somset
30 D6 **Wrantage** Somset
144 C6 **Wrawby** N Linc
44 F4 **Wraxall** N Som
31 K4 **Wraxall** Somset
147 M2 **Wray** Lancs
156 E3 **Wray Castle** Cumb
50 C4 **Wraysbury** W & M
147 M2 **Wrayton** Lancs
138 E2 **Wrea Green** Lancs
156 B5 **Wreaks End** Cumb
166 B1 **Wreay** Cumb
166 B6 **Wreay** Cumb
36 B2 **Wrecclesham** Surrey
181 G7 **Wrekenton** Gatesd
162 D5 **Wrelton** N York
113 K2 **Wrenbury** Ches
163 H5 **Wrench Green** N York
106 D4 **Wreningham** Norfk
107 K6 **Wrentham** Suffk
141 M3 **Wrenthorpe** Wakefd
95 K3 **Wrentnall** Shrops
143 H2 **Wressle** E R Yk
144 B6 **Wressle** N Linc
86 E5 **Wrestlingworth** Beds
104 D3 **Wretton** Norfk
112 E2 **Wrexham** Wrexhm
97 H8 **Wribbenhall** Worcs
96 E6 **Wrickton** Shrops
70 D4 **Wright's Green** Essex
139 G5 **Wrightington Bar** Lancs
114 B2 **Wrinehill** Staffs
44 F6 **Wrington** N Som
6 B3 **Wringworthy** Cnwll
45 K8 **Writhlington** BaNES
71 G6 **Writtle** Essex
96 E1 **Wrockwardine** Wrekin
143 H7 **Wroot** N Linc
149 L8 **Wrose** Brad
52 D7 **Wrotham** Kent
52 D7 **Wrotham Heath** Kent
97 J3 **Wrottesley** Staffs
47 H3 **Wroughton** Swindn
19 J7 **Wroxall** IOW
82 F1 **Wroxall** Warwks
96 D2 **Wroxeter** Shrops
122 F8 **Wroxham** Norfk
83 K7 **Wroxton** Oxon
115 K3 **Wyaston** Derbys
70 F7 **Wyatt's Green** Essex
119 K3 **Wyberton East** Lincs
119 J3 **Wyberton West** Lincs
86 D4 **Wyboston** Beds
113 M2 **Wybunbury** Ches
15 L4 **Wych** Dorset
38 C7 **Wych Cross** E Susx
81 L2 **Wychbold** Worcs
115 K8 **Wychnor** Staffs
35 M3 **Wyck** Hants
65 J3 **Wyck Rissington** Gloucs
168 E7 **Wycliffe** Dur
149 G8 **Wycoller** Lancs
117 K6 **Wycomb** Leics
67 L8 **Wycombe Marsh** Bucks
69 K1 **Wyddial** Herts
40 D6 **Wye** Kent

63 G5 **Wyesham** Mons
117 L7 **Wyfordby** Leics
141 J2 **Wyke** Brad
13 K3 **Wyke** Devon
15 G3 **Wyke** Devon
32 D5 **Wyke** Dorset
96 E3 **Wyke** Shrops
50 A8 **Wyke** Surrey
31 L4 **Wyke Champflower** Somset
16 C7 **Wyke Regis** Dorset
162 E7 **Wykeham** N York
163 H6 **Wykeham** N York
99 K7 **Wyken** Covtry
97 H4 **Wyken** Shrops
112 F6 **Wykey** Shrops
99 L4 **Wykin** Leics
180 D6 **Wylam** Nthumb
98 E4 **Wylde Green** Birm
33 H3 **Wylye** Wilts
117 G6 **Wymeswold** Leics
85 J2 **Wymington** Beds
117 M7 **Wymondham** Leics
106 C3 **Wymondham** Norfk
42 E3 **Wyndham** Brdgnd
16 B3 **Wynford Eagle** Dorset
169 L5 **Wynyard Park** S on T
81 M5 **Wyre Piddle** Worcs
117 G6 **Wysall** Notts
80 C2 **Wyson** Herefs
98 D8 **Wythall** Worcs
66 C5 **Wytham** Oxon
165 K7 **Wythburn** Cumb
131 G2 **Wythenshawe** Manch
165 G5 **Wythop Mill** Cumb
86 F1 **Wyton** Cambs
144 F1 **Wyton** E R Yk
90 B2 **Wyverstone** Suffk
89 L2 **Wyverstone Street** Suffk
118 A5 **Wyville** Lincs

Y

125 J6 **Y Felinheli** Gwynd
75 L2 **Y Ferwig** Cerdgn
109 G4 **Y Ffor** Gwynd
128 C8 **Y Gyffylliog** Denbgs
111 K3 **Y Maerdy** Conwy
112 D2 **Y Nant** Wrexhm
108 D6 **Y Rhiw** Gwynd
143 M6 **Yaddlethorpe** N Linc
19 G7 **Yafford** IOW
160 E4 **Yafforth** N York
8 C3 **Yalberton** Torbay
39 H3 **Yalding** Kent
166 C5 **Yanwath** Cumb
65 G4 **Yanworth** Gloucs
152 B5 **Yapham** E R Yk
21 G6 **Yapton** W Susx
44 D7 **Yarborough** N Som
19 K6 **Yarbridge** IOW
136 F1 **Yarburgh** Lincs
14 F1 **Yarcombe** Devon
28 D6 **Yard** Devon
98 E6 **Yardley** Birm
84 E6 **Yardley Gobion** Nhants
85 G4 **Yardley Hastings** Nhants
98 E7 **Yardley Wood** Birm
79 J3 **Yardro** Powys
30 B5 **Yarford** Somset
80 E6 **Yarkhill** Herefs
31 H2 **Yarley** Somset
31 L5 **Yarlington** Somset
148 C2 **Yarlsber** N York
169 L8 **Yarm** S on T
18 E5 **Yarmouth** IOW
27 L5 **Yarnacott** Devon
46 C7 **Yarnbrook** Wilts
13 H7 **Yarner** Devon
114 D5 **Yarnfield** Staffs
27 K6 **Yarnscombe** Devon
66 C5 **Yarnton** Oxon
80 B2 **Yarpole** Herefs
200 D7 **Yarrow** Border
30 E2 **Yarrow** Somset
200 D7 **Yarrow Feus** Border
200 E7 **Yarrowford** Border
80 A6 **Yarsop** Herefs
102 B4 **Yarwell** Nhants
45 L3 **Yate** S Glos
49 K6 **Yateley** Hants
46 F4 **Yatesbury** Wilts
48 E4 **Yattendon** W Berk
80 A2 **Yatton** Herefs

63 J1 **Yatton** Herefs
44 E6 **Yatton** N Som
46 C4 **Yatton Keynell** Wilts
19 K6 **Yaverland** IOW
15 H4 **Yawl** Devon
135 H1 **Yawthorpe** Lincs
105 K1 **Yaxham** Norfk
102 D5 **Yaxley** Cambs
106 C8 **Yaxley** Suffk
79 M6 **Yazor** Herefs
50 E3 **Yeading** Gt Lon
150 B7 **Yeadon** Leeds
157 H7 **Yealand Conyers** Lancs
157 H7 **Yealand Redmayne** Lancs
157 H7 **Yealand Storrs** Lancs
7 H4 **Yealmbridge** Devon
7 H4 **Yealmpton** Devon
170 E6 **Yearby** R & Cl
164 F2 **Yearngill** Cumb
161 J7 **Yearsley** N York
113 G7 **Yeaton** Shrops
115 K3 **Yeaveley** Derbys
202 E7 **Yeavering** Nthumb
162 F6 **Yedingham** N York
66 A6 **Yelford** Oxon
27 J4 **Yelland** Devon
86 F3 **Yelling** Cambs
100 D8 **Yelvertoft** Nhants
7 G1 **Yelverton** Devon
106 F3 **Yelverton** Norfk
32 B6 **Yenston** Somset
28 E5 **Yeo Mill** Somset
27 G6 **Yeo Vale** Devon
13 H3 **Yeoford** Devon
11 L5 **Yeolmbridge** Cnwll
31 J7 **Yeovil** Somset
31 J7 **Yeovil Marsh** Somset
31 J6 **Yeovilton** Somset
55 H5 **Yerbeston** Pembks
275 b4 **Yesnaby** Ork
190 E4 **Yetlington** Nthumb
31 K8 **Yetminster** Dorset
8 B4 **Yetson** Devon
14 B5 **Yettington** Devon
221 H6 **Yetts o' Muckhart** Clacks
82 F2 **Yew Green** Warwks
98 C4 **Yew Tree** W Mids
141 H2 **Yews Green** Brad
85 K2 **Yielden** Beds
97 K7 **Yieldingtree** Worcs
198 E3 **Yieldshields** S Lans
50 D3 **Yiewsley** Gt Lon
43 G3 **Ynysboeth** Rhondd
43 J3 **Ynysddu** Caerph
57 J5 **Ynysforgan** Swans
42 F3 **Ynyshir** Rhondd
92 D5 **Ynyslas** Cerdgn
42 F5 **Ynysmaerdy** Rhondd
57 K4 **Ynysmeudwy** Neath
57 J5 **Ynystawe** Swans
60 C4 **Ynyswen** Powys
42 E2 **Ynyswen** Rhondd
43 G3 **Ynysybwl** Rhondd
92 D3 **Ynysymaengwyn** Gwynd
158 F6 **Yockenthwaite** N York
95 K2 **Yockleton** Shrops
143 K3 **Yokefleet** E R Yk
208 E5 **Yoker** C Glas
139 L1 **York** Lancs
151 J5 **York** York
49 L7 **York Town** Surrey
40 E3 **Yorkletts** Kent
63 J5 **Yorkley** Gloucs
113 H7 **Yorton Heath** Shrops
132 D6 **Youlgreave** Derbys
152 B5 **Youlthorpe** E R Yk
151 G3 **Youlton** N York
71 H3 **Young's End** Essex
69 K3 **Youngsbury** Herts
115 J7 **Yoxall** Staffs
91 J2 **Yoxford** Suffk
91 J1 **Yoxford Little Street** Suffk
93 G7 **Ysbyty Cynfyn** Cerdgn
110 F2 **Ysbyty Ifan** Conwy
77 K1 **Ysbyty Ystwyth** Cerdgn
128 D5 **Ysceifiog** Flints
92 E4 **Ysgubor-y-Coed** Cerdgn
57 L3 **Ystalyfera** Powys
42 F3 **Ystrad** Rhondd
76 F4 **Ystrad Aeron** Cerdgn
77 L6 **Ystrad Ffin** Carmth
77 K2 **Ystrad Meurig** Cerdgn
43 J3 **Ystrad Mynach** Caerph
60 D4 **Ystradfellte** Powys
60 B5 **Ystradgynlais** Powys

42 F6 **Ystradowen** V Glam
92 F7 **Ystumtuen** Cerdgn
257 G5 **Ythanbank** Abers
256 B4 **Ythanwells** Abers
256 F5 **Ythsie** Abers

Z

13 G2 **Zeal Monachorum** Devon
32 C4 **Zeals** Wilts
4 C4 **Zelah** Cnwll
2 C3 **Zennor** Cnwll
3 J7 **Zoar** Cnwll
116 E6 **Zouch** Notts